FOURTH EDITION

Psychology Applied to Modern Life

Adjustment in the 90s

Wayne Weiten is a graduate of Bradley University and earned his Ph.D. from the University of Illinois at Chicago in 1981. He is the author of *Psychology: Themes and Variations* (Brooks/Cole, 1992) and teaches psychology at Santa Clara University. He has received distinguished teaching awards from Division 2 of the American Psychological Association and the College of DuPage, where he taught until 1991. He has conducted research on a wide range of topics, including cerebral specialization, educational measurement, jury behavior, attribution theory, and pressure as a form of stress.

Margaret A. Lloyd is a graduate of the University of Denver and received her Ph.D. from the University of Arizona in 1973. She is the author of *Adolescence* (Harper & Row, 1985) and is currently President-Elect of Division 2 (Teaching of Psychology) of the American Psychological Association and Professor of Psychology at Georgia Southern University. Her research interests lie in the areas of identity and gender roles.

FOURTH EDITION

Psychology Applied to Modern Life

Adjustment in the 90s

Wayne Weiten
Santa Clara University

Margaret A. Lloyd
Georgia Southern University

BROOKS/COLE PUBLISHING COMPANY Pacific Grove, California

To two pillars of stability in this era of turmoil—my parents
W.W.

To my father and the memory of my mother—models of integrity and courage
M.A.L.

 The trademark ITP is used under license.

 A CLAIREMONT BOOK

Consulting Editor: *Lawrence S. Wrightsman,*
University of Kansas

Brooks/Cole Publishing Company
A Division of Wadsworth, Inc.

Printed in the United States of America

10 9 8 7 6 5 4 3 2 1

Library of Congress Cataloging-in-Publication Data

Weiten, Wayne, [date]
   Psychology applied to modern life : adjustment in the
90s / Wayne Weiten, Margaret A. Lloyd. — 4th ed.
      p.   cm.
   Includes bibliographical references and index.
   ISBN 0-534-19890-2 :
   1. Adjustment (Psychology) 2. Interpersonal relations.
3. Adulthood—Psychological aspects. 4. Self-help techniques
I. Lloyd, Margaret A. (Margaret Ann), [date]. II. Title.
BF335.W423 1993
158—dc20
                      93-19884
                        CIP

Sponsoring Editor: *Claire Verduin*
Editorial Associate: *Gay C. Bond*
Production Coordinator: *Fiorella Ljunggren*
Art Direction: *Vernon T. Boes*
Manuscript Editors: *John Bergez and Barbara Salazar*
Permissions Editor: *May Clark*
Interior and Cover Design: *Leesa Berman, Vernon T. Boes,*
   and Valerie Ostenak Taylor
Cover Illustration: *Leesa Berman*
Art Coordinator: *Susan Haberkorn*
Interior Illustration: *Susan Haberkorn and*
   John Odam Design Associates
Photo Coordinator: *Larry Molmud*
Photo Researcher: *Susan Friedman*
Digital Typography/Page Layout: *Valerie Ostenak Taylor*
Print Buyer: *Vena M. Dyer*
Color Separations: *GTS Graphics*
Cover Printing: *Lehigh Press Lithographers/Autoscreen*
Printing and Binding: *Arcata Graphics/Hawkins*
(Credits continue on page 604.)

Many students enter adjustment courses with great expectations. They've ambled through their local bookstores, and in the "Psychology" section they've seen numerous self-help books that offer highly touted recipes for achieving happiness for a mere $4.95. After paying far more money to enroll in a collegiate course that deals with the same issues as the self-help books, many students expect a revelatory experience. However, the majority of us with professional training in psychology or counseling take a rather dim view of self-help books and the pop psychology they represent. We tend to see this literature as oversimplified, intellectually dishonest, and opportunistic. Often we summarily dismiss the pop psychology that so many of our students have embraced. We then try to supplant it with our more sophisticated academic psychology, which is more complex and less accessible.

In this textbook, we have tried to come to grips with this problem of differing expectations between student and teacher. Our goal has been to produce a comprehensive, serious, research-oriented treatment of the topic of adjustment that also acknowledges the existence of popular psychology and looks critically at its contributions. Our approach involves the following:

• In Chapter 1 we confront the phenomenon of popular self-help books. We try to take the student beneath the seductive surface of such books and analyze some of their typical flaws. Our goal is to make the student a more critical consumer of this type of literature.

• While encouraging a more critical attitude toward self-help books, we do not suggest that they should all be dismissed. Instead, we acknowledge that some of them offer authentic insights. With this in mind, we highlight some of the better books in Recommended Reading boxes sprinkled throughout the text. These recommended readings tie in with the adjacent topical coverage and show the student the interface between academic and popular psychology.

• We try to provide the student with a better appreciation of the merit of the empirical approach. This effort to clarify the role of research, which is rare for an adjustment text, appears in the first chapter.

• Recognizing that adjustment students want to leave the course with concrete, personally useful information, we end each chapter with an application section. The Applications are "how to" discussions that address everyday problems. While they focus on issues that are relevant to the content of the particular chapter, they contain more explicit advice than the text proper.

In summary, we have tried to make this book both rigorous and applied. We hope that our approach will help students to better appreciate the value of scientific psychology.

Philosophy

A certain philosophy is inherent in any systematic treatment of the topic of adjustment. Our philosophy can be summarized as follows:

• *We believe that an adjustment text should be a resource book for students.* We have tried to design this book so that it encourages and facilitates the pursuit of additional information on adjustment-related topics. It should serve as a point of departure for more learning.

• *We believe in theoretical eclecticism.* This book will not indoctrinate your students along the lines of any single theoretical orientation. The psychodynamic, behavioral, and humanistic schools of thought are all treated with respect, as are cognitive, biological, and other perspectives.

• *We believe that effective adjustment requires "taking charge" of one's own life.* Throughout the book we try to promote the notion that active coping efforts are generally superior to passivity and complacency.

Changes in the Fourth Edition

One of the exciting things about psychology is that it is not a stagnant discipline. It continues to progress at what seems a faster and faster pace. A good textbook must evolve with the discipline. Although the professors and students who used the first three editions of this book did not clamor for change, there are some significant alterations.

Authorship

The authorship of *Psychology Applied to Modern Life* continues to evolve. The third edition saw the addition of two coauthors, Margaret (Marky) A. Lloyd and Robin L. Lashley, who took responsibility for four and three chapters, respectively. Because Robin subsequently decided to invest her energies in other projects, the fourth edition has just two authors, Wayne Weiten and Marky Lloyd, who each revised eight chapters. We are very grateful to Robin for her contributions to the previous edition, and we wish her well in all her professional endeavors.

Content

To improve the book and keep up with new developments in psychology, we have made a variety of content changes—adding and deleting some topics, condensing and reorganizing others. The major alterations from the third edition include the following.

Chapter 1: Adjusting to Modern Life. We have added a new section on the codependency movement as another example of the search for a sense of direction. A section summarizing research on the key ingredients of happiness, which was dropped in the third edition, has been brought back, with major revisions.

Chapter 2: Theories of Personality. The changes in this chapter are relatively minor, but we have expanded our discussion of self-efficacy, added a compelling new illustration of Adler's theory of overcompensation, and included a chart that provides a systematic comparison of the personality theories discussed in the chapter.

Chapter 3: Stress and Its Effects. New sections on environmental stress and on the role of autonomic reactivity in stress reactions have been added to this chapter.

Chapter 4: Coping Processes. Among the new features are expanded coverage of Epstein's constructive thinking, new evidence on the value of learning systematic problem-solving skills, coverage of Pennebaker's research on the value of talking and writing about stressful events, and an updated discussion of research on the benefits of meditation.

Chapter 5: Person Perception. This chapter has undergone significant reorganization and has been rewritten with a social cognition slant. It includes an expanded discussion of self-concept and a new section on self-enhancement strategies.

Chapter 6: Interpersonal Communication. The chapter has benefited from a major reorganization of content centering around a new section on maladaptive communication. Material on ways of dealing with interpersonal conflict has been moved from the Application section to the main body of the chapter to allow for the Application on assertiveness to be moved from Chapter 10 to this chapter.

Chapter 7: Social Influence and Group Membership. This chapter now includes coverage of deindividuation, social facilitation, and other examples of how the presence of others affects behavior, along with new discussions of the "darker side" of yielding to social pressure and of "fatal persuasion" in cults.

Chapter 8: Friendship and Love. Among the additions is new material on identity and intimacy and on sexual orientation and romantic love, as well as a more thorough discussion of the development of close relationships.

Chapter 9: Marriage and Intimate Relationships. This chapter's features include an expanded discussion of the effects of divorce on children and recent findings on cohabitation and subsequent marital stability. Also, the coverage of gay relationships has been increased.

Chapter 10: Gender and Behavior. The discussion of gender comparisons has been updated extensively, and new material has been added on gender role socialization in childhood, sexual harassment, rape, and battered women. This chapter also features a new Application on gender and communication style.

Chapter 11: Development in Adolescence and Adulthood. The coverage of major theories of development has been reorganized, and the material on adolescence has undergone significant revision.

Chapter 12: Work and Career Development. This chapter now includes a discussion of contemporary trends in the world of work, new coverage of occupational hazards in the workplace, and Ouchi's Theory (Z) of work motivation.

Chapter 13: Development and Expression of Sexuality. Our treatment of sexual adjustment features increased emphasis on the interpersonal context of sex and new material on gender differences in sexual socialization, the prevention of AIDS, and sex in gay relationships.

Chapter 14: Psychology and Physical Health. You will find extensive updating throughout this chapter, especially in the discussion of Type A personality and the health risks of smoking. Coverage of AIDS has been expanded considerably, and a new section on pain perception has been added.

Chapter 15: Psychological Disorders. Updated information on the prevalence of various disorders, an expanded discussion of biological factors in anxiety disorders, and new coverage of rumination as a factor contributing to depression are among this chapter's revisions.

Chapter 16: Psychotherapy. The chapter now includes material on how to evaluate insight therapies, coverage of new antipsychotic and antidepressant medications, and a revised discussion of the pros and cons of drug therapy.

Other Changes

As you look through this edition, you will see many other changes besides those in content. The Questionnaires and Personal Probes that in the third edition were found at the end of each chapter have been moved to a supplemental paperback, entitled the *Personal Explorations Workbook*. These experiential exercises, which took up a lot of space in the text, were heavily used by some professors but ignored by others. The new arrangement, which allows those professors who use the exercises to order them for their students, leaves more space in the text for basic content. You'll also notice that we have continued to upgrade our illustration program to enhance its instructional value.

Writing Style

This book has been written with the student reader in mind. We have tried to integrate the technical jargon of our discipline into a relatively informal and down-to-earth writing style. We use concrete examples extensively to clarify complex concepts and to help maintain student interest.

Features

This text contains a number of features intended to stimulate interest and enhance students' learning. These special features include Applications, Recommended Reading boxes, a didactic illustration program, and cartoons.

Applications

The Applications should be of special interest to most students. They are tied to chapter content in a way that should show students how practical applications emerge out of theory and research. Although some of the material covered in these sections shows up frequently in adjustment texts, much of it is unique. Some of the unusual Applications include the following:

- Monitoring Your Stress
- Seeing through Social Influence Tactics
- Getting Ahead in the Job Game
- Building Self-Esteem
- Understanding the Games Couples Play
- Enhancing Sexual Relationships
- Becoming an Effective Parent

Recommended Reading Boxes

Recognizing students' interest in self-help books, we have sifted through hundreds of them to identify some that may be especially useful. These are highlighted in boxes that briefly review the book and include a provocative excerpt or two. These Recommended Reading boxes are placed where they are germane to the material being covered in the text. Some of the recommended books are very well known, whereas others are obscure. Although we make it clear that we don't endorse every idea in every book, we think they all have something worthwhile to offer. This feature replaces the conventional suggested readings lists that usually appear at the end of chapters, where they are almost universally ignored by students.

We consider these boxes to be an important element of this book, and we invite your participation in suggesting self-help books to recommend in the next edition. If you have a self-help book that you and your students find exceptionally useful, please write to us about it in care of Brooks/Cole Publishing Company, Pacific Grove, CA 93950.

Didactic Illustration Program

The illustration program is once again in full color, and the number of photographs and figures has been increased in this edition. Although the illustrations are intended to make the book attractive and help maintain student interest, they are not merely decorative. They have been carefully selected for their didactic value to enhance the educational goals of the text.

Cartoons

Because a little comic relief usually helps keep a student interested, numerous cartoons are sprinkled throughout the book. Like the figures, most of these have been chosen to reinforce ideas in the text. Some of them do exceptional jobs of driving points home.

Learning Aids

Because this book is rigorous, substantive, and sizable, a number of learning aids have been incorporated into the text to help the reader digest the wealth of material:

- The *outline* at the beginning of each chapter provides the student with a preview and overview of what will be covered.

- *Headings* are employed very frequently to keep material well organized.
- *Key terms* are identified with ***italicized boldface*** type to alert students that these are important vocabulary items that are part of psychology's technical language.
- An *integrated running glossary* provides an on-the-spot definition of each key term as it is introduced in the text. These formal definitions are printed in **boldface** type.
- An *alphabetical glossary* is found in the back of the book, since key terms are usually defined in the integrated running glossary only when they are first introduced.
- *Italics* are used liberally throughout to emphasize important points.
- *Chapter summaries* are provided to give the student a quick review of the chapter's major points.
- A *Chapter Review* is found at the end of each chapter. Each review includes a list of learning objectives for the chapter, a list of the key terms that were introduced in the chapter, and a list of important theorists and researchers who were discussed in the chapter.

Supplementary Materials

A complete teaching/learning package has been developed to supplement *Psychology Applied to Modern Life*. These supplementary materials have been carefully coordinated to provide effective support for the text.

Instructor's Manual

An Instructor's Manual is available as a convenient aid for your educational endeavors. Written by Patrick Williams, it provides a brief overview of each chapter, along with a list of relevant films. It also includes lecture suggestions, as well as questions for class discussion and/or essay exams. Most important, it contains an extensive collection of multiple-choice questions for objective tests. We're confident that you will find this to be a dependable and usable test bank.

Study Guide

Written by Michael Sosulski, the Study Guide is designed to help students master the information contained in the text. For each chapter, it contains a brief overview, learning objectives, a programmed review, several other types of review exercises, and a self-test. We're confident that your students will find it very helpful in their study efforts.

Personal Explorations Workbook

The *Personal Explorations Workbook* is a small paperback that contains experiential exercises for each text chapter, designed to help your students achieve personal insights. The Questionnaires are psychological tests or scales that your students can administer and score for themselves. The Personal Probes consist of questions intended to help students think about themselves in relation to issues raised in the text. Most students find these exercises interesting. They can also be fruitful in stimulating class discussion.

Acknowledgments

This book has been an enormous undertaking, and we want to express our gratitude to the innumerable people who have influenced its evolution. To begin with, we must cite the contribution of our students who have taken the adjustment course. It is trite to say that they have been a continuing inspiration—but they have.

The quality of a textbook depends greatly on the quality of the prepublication reviews by psychology professors around the country. The reviewers listed on page x have contributed to the development of this book by providing constructive reviews of various portions of the manuscript in this or earlier editions. We are very grateful to all of them.

Perceptive professional review has also been provided by Larry Wrightsman, the consulting editor on this project. Superlatives are in order for Claire Verduin, who has served as project editor through all four editions of this book and has been a great source of encouragement and insight. Fiorella Ljunggren, whose long association with our books is much valued, has handled the production with efficiency and skill. Vernon Boes deserves great credit for rising to the challenge of art-directing the project and creating a very attractive design for the book. Others who have made significant contributions are Leesa Berman (interior and cover design), Valerie Ostenak Taylor (digital typography and page layout), May Clark (permissions), Susan Haberkorn (art program), Ruthanne Lowe (indexing), Tessa McGlasson (copyediting of the references), Larry Molmud and Susan Friedman (photo program).

In addition, Wayne Weiten would like to thank his wife, Beth Traylor, who has been a steady source of emotional support while enduring the grueling demands of her medical career. Marky Lloyd would like to thank her student assistants—Kelli Cobb, Lisa Forrer-Laskowski,

Heather Kennedy, Cheryl Peacock, Vann Scott, and Janice Weaver—and reference librarian Barbara Strickland for their help with library research. She would also like to thank her colleagues Russell A. Dewey, Janice N. Steirn, and Pamela S. Thomason and undergraduates Ellen Garrett and Todd McConnell for sharing their specific expertise. She is also grateful to Judith A. Holleman for her support, encouragement, and wise counsel. Finally, she wishes to acknowledge the psychology faculty at Georgia Southern and Marie Bailey, department secretary, for their support and patience while she juggled writing and administrative responsibilities over many months.

Wayne Weiten
Margaret A. Lloyd

REVIEWERS

Marsha K. Beauchamp
 Mt. San Antonio College
John R. Blakemore
 Monterey Peninsula College
Paul Bowers
 Grayson County College
Robert Cameron
 Fairmont State College
M. K. Clampit
 Bentley College
Meg Clark
 California State Polytechnic University
Stephen S. Cocia
 Orange County Community College
Dennis Coon
 Santa Barbara City College
Salvatore Cullari
 Lebanon Valley College
Kenneth S. Davidson
 Wayne State University
Richard Fuhrer
 University of Wisconsin–Eau Claire
Lee Gillis
 Georgia College
Lawrence Grebstein
 University of Rhode Island
Robert Helm
 Oklahoma State University
Robert Higgins
 Central Missouri State University
Clara E. Hill
 University of Maryland
Michael Hirt
 Kent State University
Fred J. Hitti
 Monroe Community College
Joseph Horvat
 Weber State University
Kathy Howard
 Harding University
Walter Jones
 College of DuPage
Wayne Joose
 Calvin College
Susan Kupisch
 Austin Peay State University
Barbara Hansen Lemme
 College of DuPage

Harold List
 Massachusetts Bay Community College
Louis A. Martone
 Miami–Dade Community College
Richard Maslow
 San Joaquin Delta College
William T. McReynolds
 University of Tampa
Fred Medway
 University of South Carolina–Columbia
Frederick Meeker
 California State Polytechnic University–Pomona
John Moritsugu
 Pacific Lutheran University
Gary Oliver
 College of DuPage
Joseph Philbrick
 California State Polytechnic University–Pomona
James Prochaska
 University of Rhode Island
Joan Royce
 Riverside Community College
Joan Rykiel
 Ocean County College
Thomas K. Saville
 Metropolitan State College of Denver
Norman R. Schultz
 Clemson University
Dale Simmons
 Oregon State University
Karl Swain
 Community College of South Nevada
Kenneth L. Thompson
 Central Missouri State University
David L. Watson
 University of Hawaii
Deborah S. Weber
 University of Akron
J. Oscar Williams
 Diablo Valley College
Raymond Wolf
 Moraine Park Technical College
Raymond Wolfe
 State University of New York at Geneseo
Michael Wolff
 Southwestern Oklahoma State University
Norbert Yager
 Henry Ford Community College

BRIEF CONTENTS

CONTENTS

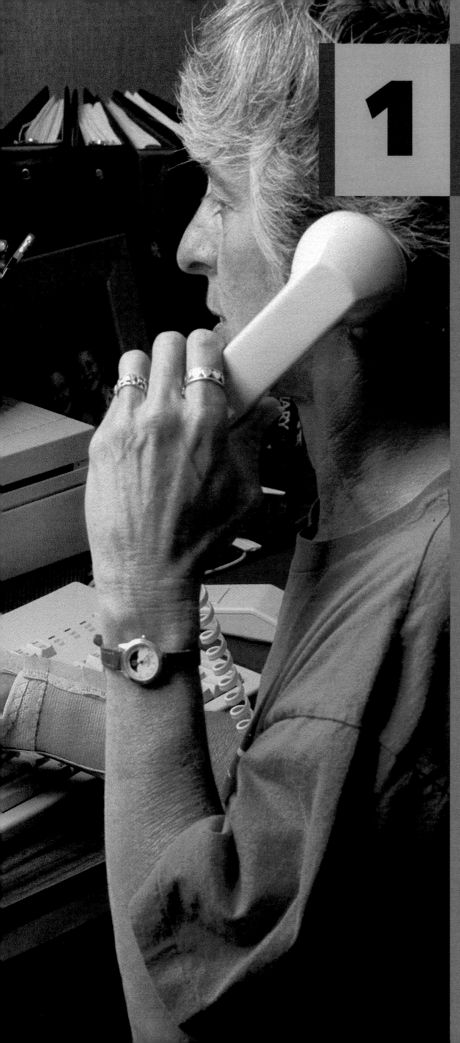

1 Adjusting to Modern Life 1

Theories of Personality 35

2

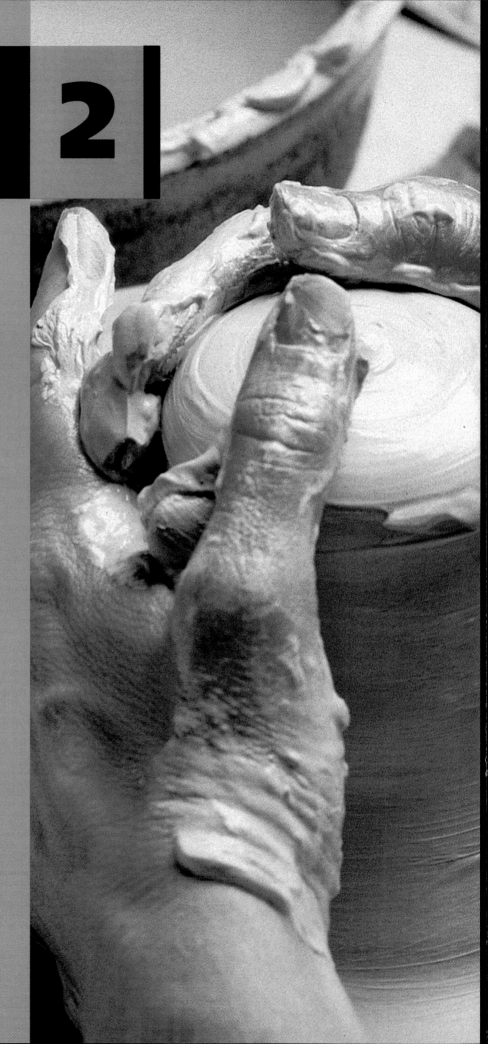

3 Stress and Its Effects 67

Coping
Processes 101

4

5 Person Perception 135

Interpersonal Communication 163

6

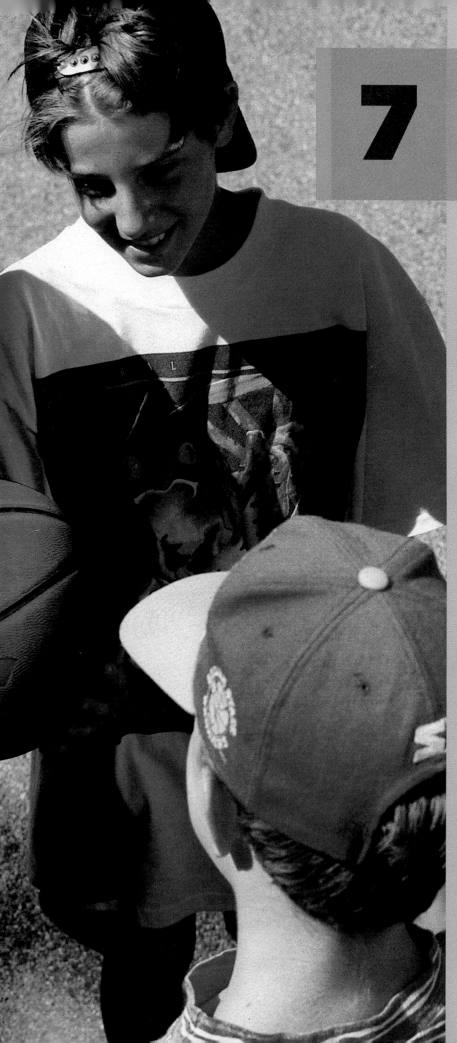

7 Social Influence and Group Membership 195

Friendship and Love 231

8

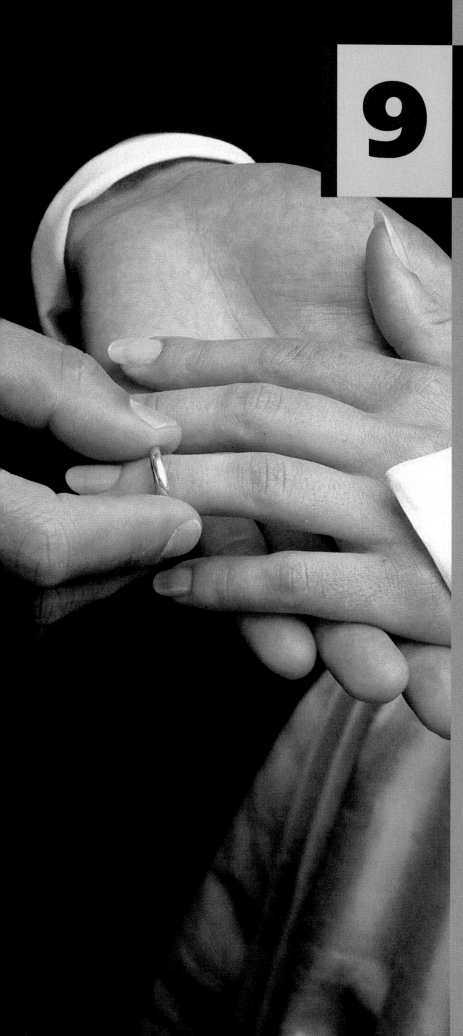

9 Marriage and Intimate Relationships 265

Gender and Behavior 297

10

Work and Career Development 365

12

Development and Expression of Sexuality 401

Psychology and Physical Health 437

14

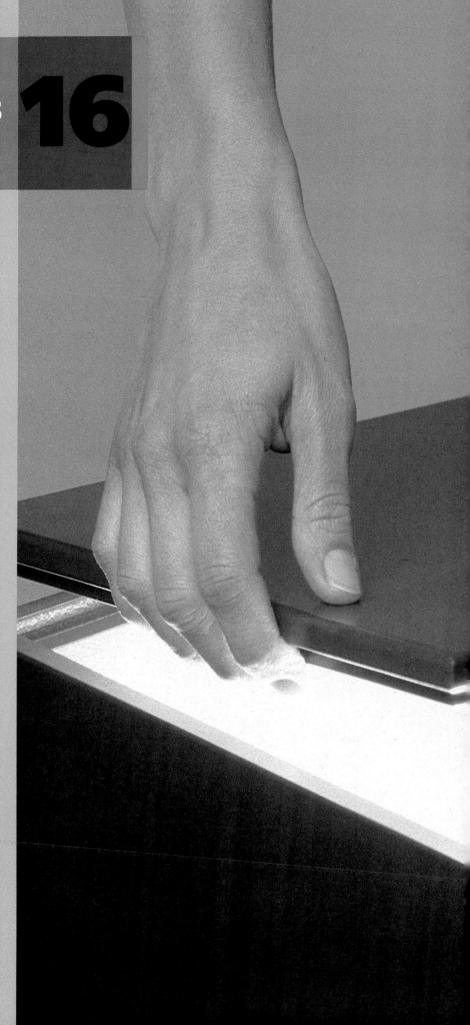

Psychotherapy 505

16

In most college courses students spend more time with their textbooks than with their professors. Given this reality, it helps if you like your textbook. Making textbooks likable, however, is a tricky proposition. By its very nature, a textbook must introduce a great many new concepts, ideas, and theories. If it doesn't, it isn't much of a textbook, and instructors won't choose to use it—so you'll never see it anyway. Consequently, we have tried to make this book as likable as possible without compromising the academic content that your instructor de-mands. Thus, we have tried to make the book lively, informal, engaging, well organized, easy to read, practical, and occasionally humorous. Before you plunge into Chapter 1, let us explain some of the key features that can help you get the most out of the book.

Learning Aids

Mastering the content of this text involves digesting a great deal of information. To facilitate this learning process, we've incorporated a number of instructional aids into the book.

- *Outlines* at the beginning of each chapter provide you with both a preview and an overview of what will be covered.
- *Headings* are employed very frequently to keep material well organized.
- *Key terms* are identified with **italicized boldface** type to alert you that these are important vocabulary items that are part of psychology's technical language.
- An *integrated running glossary* provides an on-the-spot definition of each key term as it's introduced in the text. These formal definitions are printed in **boldface** type. It is often difficult for students to adapt to the jargon used by scientific disciplines. However, learning this terminology is an essential part of your educational experience. The integrated running glossary is meant to make this learning process as painless as possible.
- An *alphabetical glossary* is provided in the back of the book, since key terms are usually defined in the running glossary only when they are first introduced. If you run into a technical term that was introduced in an earlier chapter and you can't remember its meaning, you can look it up in the alphabetical glossary instead of backtracking to find the place where it first appeared. You can also use the Subject Index to locate references to important terms and concepts.

- *Italics* are used liberally throughout the book to emphasize important points.
- *Chapter summaries* are provided near the end of each chapter (before the chapter's Application) to help you quickly review the chapter's major points.
- A *Chapter Review* is found at the end of each chapter. Each review includes lists of learning objectives, key terms, and important theorists and researchers. Reading over these review materials can help you ensure that you've digested the key points in the chapter.

Recommended Reading Boxes

This text should function as a resource book. To facilitate this goal, particularly interesting self-help books on various topics are highlighted in boxes within the chapters. Each box provides a brief description of the book and a provocative excerpt. We do not agree with everything in these recommended books, but all of them are potentially useful or intriguing. The main purpose of this feature is to introduce you to some of the better self-help books that are available.

Study Guide

The Study Guide that accompanies this text is an excellent resource designed to assist you in mastering the information contained in the book. It includes a wealth of review exercises to help you organize information and a self-test for assessing your mastery. The Study Guide itself contains a much more detailed description of its features. You should be able to purchase it at your college bookstore. If it is not available there, you can obtain a copy by contacting the publisher (phone: 1-800-354-9706).

A Concluding Note

We sincerely hope that you find this book enjoyable. If you have any comments or advice that might help us improve the next edition, please write to us in care of the publisher, Brooks/Cole Publishing Company, Pacific Grove, California 93950. There is a form in the back of the book that you can use to provide us with feedback. Finally, let us wish you good luck. We hope you enjoy your course and learn a great deal.

Wayne Weiten
Margaret A. Lloyd

1

Adjusting to Modern Life

THE IMMENSE BOEING 747 LUMbers into position to accept its human cargo. The eager passengers scurry on board. In a tower a few hundred yards away, air traffic controllers diligently monitor radar screens, radio transmissions, and digital readouts of weather information. At the reservation desks in the airport terminal, clerks punch up the appropriate ticket information on their computer terminals and quickly process the steady stream of passengers. Mounted on the wall are video terminals displaying up-to-the-minute information on flight arrivals, departures, and delays. Back in the cockpit of the plane, the flight crew calmly scan the complex array of dials, meters, and lights to assess the aircraft's readiness for flight. In a few minutes, the airplane will slice into the cloudy, snow-laden skies above Chicago. In a mere three hours its passengers will be transported from the piercing cold of a Chicago winter to the balmy beaches of the Bahamas. Another everyday triumph for technology will have taken place.

The Paradox of Progress

We are the children of technology. We take for granted such impressive feats as transporting 300 people over 1500 miles in a matter of hours. After all, we live in the space age—a time of unparalleled progress. Our modern Western society has made extraordinary strides in transportation, energy, communication, agriculture, and medicine. Yet in spite of our technological progress, social problems and personal difficulties seem more prevalent and more prominent than ever

before. This paradox is evident in many aspects of contemporary life, as the following examples demonstrate.

Point. Modern technology has provided us with countless time-saving devices—automobiles, telephones, vacuum cleaners, dishwashers, photocopiers, fax machines. Cellular phones allow people to talk to friends or colleagues and battle rush hour at the same time. In a matter of seconds a personal computer can perform calculations that would take months to do by hand.

Counterpoint. Nonetheless, most of us complain about not having enough time. Our schedule books are overflowing with appointments, commitments, and plans. Surveys indicate that most of us spend more and more time working and have less and less time for ourselves (see Figure 1.1). As the social critic Jeremy Rifkin (1987) notes, "It is ironic [that] in a culture so committed to saving time we feel increasingly deprived of the very thing we value. The modern world of streamlined transportation, instantaneous communication, and time-saving technologies was supposed to free us from the dictates of the clock and provide us with increased leisure. Instead there seems never to be enough time. . . . Despite our alleged efficiency, as compared to almost every other period in history, we seem to have less time for ourselves and far less time for each other" (p. 19).

Point. Thanks in large part to technological advances, we live in extraordinary affluence. Undeniably, there are pockets of genuine poverty, but Paul Wachtel (1989) argues convincingly that the middle and upper classes are larger and wealthier than ever before. Most of us take for granted things that were once con-

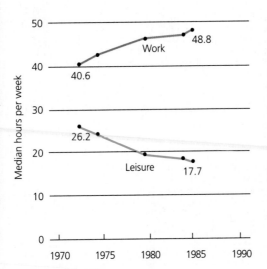

FIGURE 1.1
Trends in the time devoted to work and leisure
Harris Survey respondents were asked to estimate how many hours per week they devoted to their job, school, house cleaning, and chores (work) as opposed to relaxation, hobbies, and entertainment (leisure). Since the early 1970s, the amount of time devoted to leisure has been declining, while the time devoted to work has been increasing.

sidered luxuries, such as color television and air-conditioning. People spend vast amounts of money on expensive automobiles, stereo systems, video decks, clothing, and travel. Wachtel quotes a New York museum director who asserts that "shopping is the chief cultural activity in the United States" (p. 23).

Counterpoint. In spite of this economic abundance, Wachtel notes that a "sense of economic decline is widespread nowadays. . . . [We feel] that declining productivity has pinched our pocketbooks, that inflation has eaten up our buying power, that we can't catch up, much less get ahead" (p. 9). According to Wachtel, our economic system's commitment to growth, coupled with the effects of mass media advertising, has created an insatiable thirst for consumption. Although our standard of living has risen, most of us feel that we need still more goods and services. Rich by any previous standard, we are nevertheless subjectively distressed about our economic plight.

Point. Our ability to process, store, and communicate information has improved dramatically in recent years. Using satellites, we can beam live telecasts around the globe almost instantaneously. We can access on-line computerized data bases to track the stock market or to check airline schedules. Even more impressive, we can store the entire *Encyclopaedia Britannica* on a couple of compact disks.

Counterpoint. Yet Richard Saul Wurman (1989) asserts that nearly everyone suffers from *information anxiety*—concern about the ever-widening gap between what we understand and what we think we *should* understand. The crux of the problem is the explosive growth of available information, which now doubles in amount about every five years. Wurman points out that a single weekday edition of the *New York Times* "contains more information than the average person was likely to come across in a lifetime in seventeenth-century England" (p. 32). According to Wurman, people exhibit symptoms of information anxiety when they complain about stacks of unread periodicals, when they bemoan their inability to keep up with what's going on, when they pretend that they are familiar with a book or artist that they've never heard of, when they feel overwhelmed by the 50 or 60 channels

available on cable TV, and when they feel bewildered by the intricacies of their computers, VCRs, and digital watches.

Point. Agricultural productivity has moved forward by leaps and bounds, thanks to improvements in farm machinery, fertilizers, and pesticides. Since 1820, food output per farmer in the United States has increased eightfold. In 1983 the average farmworker produced enough food to feed 77 people (Miller, 1985).

Counterpoint. In spite of these improvements in agricultural output, hunger and malnutrition continue to be problems in the United States. According to Patrick Quillin (1987), "While 10 percent of Americans are underfed, many of the remaining 90 percent are overfed or improperly fed" (p. 43). Nutritional deficiencies are found in all social classes. One national survey discussed by Quillen revealed that only 3% of the respondents in the best-fed nation in history were free of the 48 most common symptoms of malnutrition.

Point. We have made stunning advances in medicine. Doctors can reattach severed limbs, use lasers to correct microscopic defects in the eye, and even replace the human heart. Contagious diseases (those caused by infectious agents), such as tuberculosis, typhoid fever, smallpox, and cholera, are largely under control. Since the turn of the century, life expectancy in the United States has increased from 47 to 75 years.

Counterpoint. Nonetheless, a *Time* magazine article has noted, "Never have doctors been able to do so much for their patients, and rarely have patients seemed so ungrateful" (Gibbs, 1989, p. 49). The number of malpractice lawsuits doubled in the 1980s, and patients' confidence in the medical profession has declined noticeably. Moreover, as we'll discuss in Chapter 14, the void left by contagious diseases has been filled all too quickly by chronic diseases that develop gradually, such as cancer, heart disease, hypertension, and ulcers. The

CATHY copyright Cathy Guisewite. Reprinted with permission of UNIVERSAL PRESS SYNDICATE. All rights reserved

increase in chronic diseases is attributable to stress and certain features of our modern lifestyle, such as our penchant for smoking and overeating, and our tendency to get little physical exercise.

All of these apparent contradictions reflect the same theme: *The technological advances of the 20th century, impressive though they may be, have not perceptibly improved our collective health and happiness.* Indeed, many social critics argue that the quality of our lives and our sense of personal fulfillment have declined rather than risen. This is the paradox of progress.

What is the cause of this paradox? There are many potential explanations. Let's turn now to the analyses of Erich Fromm, who offers some worthwhile insights into this perplexing situation.

Technology has enhanced our lives in uncountable ways; one of them is by making available to us a host of time-saving devices, from vacuum cleaners to cellular phones. But this same technology has also complicated our lives in innumerable ways; consider, for example, the hassles involved in dealing with large shopping malls or in deciding which computer or fax machine or VCR to buy.

It seems trite and self-centered to carry on about how we live in "troubled times." Certainly our ancestors had their share of problems, and it would be shortsighted to idealize the "good old days." However, in *Escape from Freedom*, Fromm (1963) has described how the character of personal problems has changed as we have evolved from a static, agricultural society into a modern, industrial world marked by instability.

Until a couple of centuries ago, Fromm points out, people's lives tended to be clearly laid out for them. Peasants in a feudal society, for instance, typically knew that they were going to adhere to the same religion their parents practiced, pledge allegiance to the same feudal lord who ruled their parents, and plow the same fields that their parents worked. According to Fromm's analysis, *people had relatively little personal freedom in a static society*. Our prototype peasants may even have had their marriage arranged for them. They had few major decisions to make about their lifestyle and virtually no alternative pathways to ponder.

With the advent of the Renaissance, the Reformation, and the Industrial Revolution, the static quality of society began to erode. The yoke of economic, political, and religious bondage was thrown off, and people gradually acquired more and more personal freedom. According to Fromm, this trend toward greater individual freedom has continued unabated, peaking in our present society.

Today we face a vast array of decisions about how to lead our lives. We must choose a career from a bewildering galaxy of options and hope to find it rewarding. We must decide where to live, whether to stay near our parents or move on to greener pastures. In the political arena, we must decide whether to be apathetic or concerned, liberal or conservative, Democrat, Republican, or Independent. In regard to religion and values, we must decide how we feel about changing gender roles, the new morality, and abortion. The list of decisions extends even to the details of everyday life. Every time we walk into a grocery store, we must choose from six brands of tuna fish, 20 brands of soda, and 40 brands of cereal. In all these ways we have more personal freedom than ever before.

Unfortunately, Fromm suggests, *while our personal freedom has been growing, our old sources of emotional sustenance and security have diminished in effectiveness*. Fromm notes that the church, the village, and the family used to provide people with a more solid base of security. In a static society people had a resolute faith in a single church, which told them exactly how to behave in order to gain eternal salvation. Today we have a multiplicity of churches that provide a clear value system for fewer people (see Figure 1.2). Likewise, the residential stability of the old villages permitted solid friendship networks to develop over generations. Today our tendency to pick up and move repeatedly leads us to live in ever-shifting communities where we may barely know our next-door neighbors. The family, too, is no longer the source of security it was. In most segments of our society, the closely knit extended family—encompassing aunts, uncles, grandparents, and cousins—has become a relic of the past. Today, with our penchant for divorce and mobility, even the nuclear family is a less dependable source of emotional support.

This analysis leads Fromm to a rather startling conclusion. He argues that as our old sources of security have declined, we have found it more difficult to cope with our newfound freedom. He suggests that, *rather than embrace our increased freedom, many of us find it scary and threatening*. In fact, many of us find our freedom so aversive that we try to escape from it. Escape often takes the form of submitting passively to authority figures, such as political leaders, charismatic cult figures, or self-styled "gurus," who tout simple solutions to complex problems.

To summarize, Fromm's analysis suggests that the progress we value so much has undermined our sense of security, scrambled our value systems, and confronted us with difficult new problems of adjustment. Hence *the basic challenge of life becomes the search for a sense of direction*. This search involves struggling with such problems as developing a solid sense of identity, a coherent philosophy of life, and a clear vision of a future that realistically promises fulfillment. Centuries ago, problems of this kind were probably much simpler. As we'll see in the next section, today it appears that many of us are floundering in a sea of confusion.

The Search for Direction

ur search for a sense of direction is manifested in many ways. Let's look at three striking expressions of this quest: the emergence of "self-realization" programs, the recent popularity of the codependency movement, and the spectacular success of best-selling "self-help" books. An examination of these phenomena can help us to understand the modern struggle for a sense of direction and some of the ways it can go awry.

Self-Realization Programs

Since the 1960s, many Americans have shown a willingness to invest large sums of money in "self-realization" programs. These various training programs are supposed to provide enlightenment and turn one's life around, usually very quickly. They vary greatly in orientation, format, and theme, but most promise participants spectacular benefits. Some of these training regimens have enjoyed enormous success, earning glowing testimonials from thousands of converts. We'll look at three programs (The Forum, Scientology, and Silva Mind Control) that have attained a fair amount of popularity and evaluate their worth.

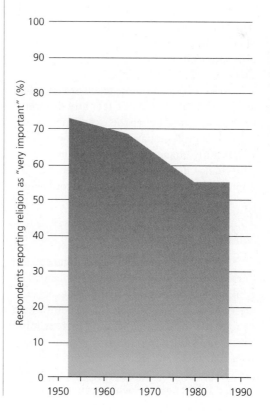

FIGURE 1.2
The importance of religion in people's lives
This graph shows the percentage of respondents to Gallup polls who report that religion is "very important" in their lives. Over 50% continue to view religion as very important, but this percentage has been declining since the 1950s.

The Forum

The Forum is an approach to personal growth developed by Werner Erhard; it used to be called *est* (Bry, 1976). The training consists of four intensive, day-long seminars conducted on two weekends and one week-night seminar, with 250 to 300 participants who pay $625 for their shot at enlightenment (Kaminer, 1992). The goal of The Forum is "getting it." The "it" is rather mysterious, and most Forum graduates have difficulty describing or explaining it. "It" allegedly involves some profound insight that revolutionizes the graduate's life.

It is hard to describe The Forum's training without making it sound bland. Forum proponents argue that this difficulty occurs because "The Forum experience cannot be described. It can only be experienced"; but others assert that the seminars are simply devoid of content (Efran, Lukens, & Lukens, 1986; Kaminer, 1992). In any case, the seminars are led by a trainer who is usually extremely articulate, with a commanding presence. The trainer lectures and leads the discussion. The basic strategy is to break down the trainees' self-esteem and then gradually rebuild it. The trainees are told that they are bungling their way through life. They are often intimidated and made to feel foolish. After their self-esteem is lowered, they are offered a variety of insights borrowed primarily from mainstream psychology. For example, much is made of Fritz Perls's (1969) idea that one should take responsibility for one's own life. The Forum emphasizes that it is useless to blame your problems on others; you can solve problems only if you accept responsibility for them.

Although many Forum graduates complain afterward that they don't feel any different, many others rave about the experience. Many prominent professionals claim that the training significantly changed their lives (Burg, 1974). The change most commonly reported includes improvement in self-image and self-confidence, accompanied by reduction in anxiety.

Scientology/Dianetics

Scientology is a quasi-religious organization founded in the 1950s by L. Ron Hubbard. The goal in Scientology is to become "clear." Getting "clear" involves reaching a point where you are free of all programming in your mind that is not under your control. What exactly does that mean? Well, according to Hubbard (1989), people acquire automatic behavior patterns, called "engrams," which can be problematic. These engrams often take the form of non-adaptive emotional responses to situations. Hubbard asserts that you can rid yourself of a troublesome engram by consciously and completely reliving the original experience that created it, under the guidance of an "auditor." Scientology training may take a couple of years and can cost thousands of dollars. Some wealthy converts have spent as much as $130,000 on their training (Behar, 1991).

Like The Forum, Scientology borrows liberally from the mainstream of psychological theory. An engram is very similar to the conditioned response described by the Russian physiologist Ivan Pavlov some 90 years ago. The idea that it might be useful to relive emotional experiences and thereby discharge the emotion was proposed by Sigmund Freud, the developer of psychoanalysis, over 100 years ago.

Silva Mind Control

Silva Mind Control courses have been available to the public since the mid-1960s. Developed by José Silva, the courses are supposed to train participants to control their brain activity (Silva & Miele, 1977). Silva maintains that it is optimal to operate at the lower rather than the higher brain-wave frequencies. Trainees are taught to use relaxation exercises and visual imagery in order to gain conscious control over brain activity.

As trainees acquire better mind control, behavioral self-control supposedly follows. Silva graduates purportedly can use their power of visualization to achieve great self-control. They can eat less, sleep less, work harder, or do whatever is necessary to achieve their goals in life. The mind-control training is also supposed to provide graduates with at least some extrasensory perception (ESP) capabilities.

The Silva Mind Control courses resemble The Forum in cost and time commitment. The sequence of courses costs a few hundred dollars and requires about a week's time. Generally the courses are conducted in small groups.

Critique

Although their teachings differ greatly, The Forum, Scientology, and Silva Mind Control have much in common. First, they are, above all else, moneymaking propositions for their developers. None of them offers self-realization free; it costs, and the fees aren't low. All three organizations seem to be more interested in making money than in spreading enlightenment.

Second, the inventors of all three systems

have little or no formal training in psychology. They all appear to have emerged from the ranks of hucksterism rather than science. Werner Erhard, for instance, was previously a door-to-door salesman named Jack Rosenberg. He has had a long history of involvement with questionable sales schemes (Brewer, 1975). The Church of Scientology has a sinister reputation for coaxing large sums of money out of naive members and for subjecting its critics to vicious harassment. A *Time* magazine exposé characterized Scientology as a multimillion-dollar racket and as "the most ruthless, the most classically terroristic, the most litigious and the most lucrative cult the country has ever seen" (Behar, 1991, p. 51).

Third, to be blunt, all three systems are intellectual mush. Each system offers a few worthwhile insights, but these either are borrowed from mainstream psychology or are simple common sense. Most of their principles, however, are hopelessly vague or easily refuted by available scientific data.

The Forum, Scientology, and Silva Mind Control have one other perplexing thing in common: all three have many disciples who claim that the training they received revolutionized their lives. If the systems have little real merit, how do we account for this puzzling reality? In all probability, it is primarily a matter of placebo effects.

Placebo effects occur when people experience some change after an empty, fake, or ineffectual treatment because of their positive expectations about the treatment. Numerous studies show that if people believe a treatment or program will affect them in certain ways, then they are prone to see the expected effects. For instance, many a patient has been "cured" of a physical illness by the administration of "drugs" that were really sugar pills. Placebo effects can occur even when people are likely to observe themselves very objectively—and such objectivity is not common when people are seeking self-realization. People who take Forum, Scientology, or Silva training are clearly searching for something. They want, sometimes desperately, to see improvement in themselves. After investing time, money, and hope to embark on some pathway to growth, they badly want to believe that it has paid off. Thus they are exceedingly biased observers who are predisposed to see the effects that they have been led to expect. With this strong bias, it is not surprising that many participants in self-realization programs offer glowing endorsements. Unfortunately, most of their gains appear to be illusory and short-lived.

The Codependency Movement

Another manifestation of our collective malaise and never-ending search for fulfillment is the codependency movement, which has grown like a firestorm on a dry, windy prairie. The fire was ignited in 1987 with the publication of *Codependent No More,* by Melody Beattie. Beattie's description of the codependency syndrome clearly struck a chord, as codependency has become "the chic neurosis of our time" (Lyon & Greenberg, 1991, p. 435). The movement has spawned a host of books, workshops, seminars, support groups, and treatment programs designed to help people overcome their codependency.

Description

What is codependency? It was an obscure concept in the field of alcoholism counseling before Beattie (1987, 1989) and others (Bradshaw, 1988; Schaef, 1986; Whitfield, 1987) borrowed, broadened, and popularized it. The term originally referred to the tendency of alcoholics' spouses—typically wives of alcoholic men—to get entangled in their partner's addiction in ways that inadvertently supported the addictive behavior (Cocores, 1987). For example, the wife of an alcoholic might protect him from the consequences of his addiction by not confronting him about his problem, by lying to people to cover up his drinking, and by taking on many of his parental, household, and financial responsibilities.

Beattie (1987) greatly expanded the codependency concept. Arguing that people can be addicted to love, sex, work, food, gambling, and shopping, as well as to drugs and alcohol, she described the codependent person as anyone who has let another person's addictive

Recovery groups intended to help people overcome their codependency have proliferated in recent years. Are recovery groups just another pop psych fad? Or do they offer valuable and helpful insights about human suffering? The answer appears to lie somewhere between these two extremes.

behavior affect him or her and is obsessed with controlling that behavior. By equating any kind of self-control problem with addiction, Beattie made the notion of codependency applicable to an enormous range of people. Indeed, she estimated that as many as 80 million Americans suffer from codependency. Other theorists have offered a variety of somewhat different definitions of codependency (Whitfield, 1991), and some are even broader than Beattie's. Most of the definitions center on the idea that codependency involves becoming enmeshed in a dysfunctional relationship marked by excessive preoccupation with another person's needs and problems to the virtual exclusion of one's own.

According to some codependency theorists, these dysfunctional relationships are not a matter of happenstance. They maintain that many people—especially women—unwittingly *seek out* relationships with troubled individuals to satisfy an excessive need to be needed (O'Brien & Gaborit, 1992; Wright & Wright, 1991). In these relationships, codependents become obsessed with trying to protect, control, and change their partners. Pouring their energy into these largely unsuccessful efforts, codependent people consistently subordinate their own needs to those of their partner. Hence they end up leading anguished, unfulfilling lives. The codependency literature provides lengthy recitations of the personal problems that may be attributable to codependency (Loughead, 1991). These symptoms of codependency range from common minor problems, such as boredom, indecision, and lack of spontaneity, to profound, debilitating problems, such as anorexia, depression, and attempts at suicide.

What are the origins of the codependency syndrome? Codependent people are thought to be motivated by an overly strong need for affection and approval, which they attempt to earn by rescuing their partners from their troubles. Their pathological need to be needed is usually blamed on their upbringing in a dysfunctional family. Women are assumed to be more vulnerable to codependency than men because females' socialization typically places more emphasis on the importance of selflessness, being emotionally supportive, and taking care of others (Haaken, 1990). As Kaminer (1992) notes, "In our culture, women have long been assigned primary responsibility for the family's emotional balance, and codependency is often described as a feminine disease" (p. 14).

What's the solution to the widespread affliction of codependency? Most codependency experts advocate recovery programs, such as Codependents Anonymous, which follow the model Alcoholics Anonymous developed in 1935 as a treatment for drinking problems. According to this model, codependency is an addictive disease and recovery can begin only when people admit that they have lost control over their disease. Victims must then commit themselves to the twelve-step path to recovery. The twelve-step program requires a spiritual conversion in which addicts turn their lives over to a "higher power." Recovery programs also depend heavily on peer self-help groups in which codependent people meet to discuss their problems, vent their emotions, exchange insights, and provide encouragement for one another.

Evaluation

Is the codependency movement just another pop psych fad? Or does it contribute genuine insights into human suffering and effective methods for alleviating it? The answer appears to lie somwhere between these two extremes.

On the one hand, there is much to be said for the family systems perspective adopted by the codependency movement. Clinical work with substance abusers provides evidence that addicts and their family members are often enmeshed in dysfunctional relationships that may contribute to the addicts' problems and undermine the morale and mental health of the family members (Cermak, 1986; Mendenhall, 1989). Spouses and other family members clearly have complex, reciprocal influences on one another (Robins, 1990), and the codependency movement has increased the public's appreciation of this reality. Furthermore, the popularity of the codependency movement suggests that it has uncovered a genuine malady that meshes with the subjective experience of many people in our society. As Haaken (1990) puts it, "The co-dependence literature expresses the pain, anguish and helplessness, combined with an overwhelming, wearisome responsibility for others, that dominates the lives of many women" (p. 397).

What about the recovery programs advocated by codependency theorists? Their efficacy hasn't been evaluated yet (Harper & Capdevila, 1990), but they include elements that appear to have some legitimate value. For example, recovery groups seek to provide participants with social support, which has well-documented value in helping people cope with stress (Leavy, 1983), as we'll see in Chapter 3. Recovery groups also encourage participants to talk about their problems and vent their emotions. Research suggests that these are healthy coping strategies (Pennebaker, Colder, & Sharp, 1990; Spielberger et al., 1985) (see Chapter 4). The personal stories shared in recovery groups obviously show participants that they are not alone in their misery. Research on group therapy suggests that this is a valuable insight (Yalom, 1985), as we'll discuss in Chapter 16. Thus it is plausible that many people benefit from their participation in the recovery programs promoted by the codependency movement.

On the other hand, critics argue that codependency theory is riddled with holes and that the commotion about codependency has far outstripped the substance of what is known (Gierymski & Williams, 1986; Gomberg, 1989). Specific concerns include the following:

1. Definitions of codependency vary considerably. Whitfield (1991) reviews 23 widely disparate definitions. The problems that various theorists discuss often have little in common, and the concept of codependency remains vaguely defined at best (Myer, Peterson, & Stoffel-Rosales, 1991). Researchers have only recently begun to develop reliable methods for determining who is codependent and who is not (Fischer, Spann, & Crawford, 1991). People who label themselves as codependent are making highly subjective self-diagnoses of dubious validity based on simplistic stereotypes.

2. Controlled, scientific studies of codependency are virtually nonexistent and there is little or no evidence to support many of the basic tenets of codependency theory (Wright & Wright, 1991). For example, researchers have only just begun to test the idea that codependency occurs because people seek out relationships with troubled individuals (Lyon & Greenberg, 1991), or to study the applicability of the codependency concept to such problems as compulsive eating, gambling, and shopping (O'Brien & Gaborit, 1992).

3. As Kaminer (1992) notes, in codependency theory "every conceivable form of arguably compulsive behavior is classified as an addiction. We are a nation of sexaholics, rageaholics, shopaholics, and rushaholics" (p. 10). Critics assert that this view trivializes the concept of addiction, making it virtually meaningless.

4. Codependency theorists tend to blame addiction and codependence for virtually every conceivable type of psychological problem. Beattie's (1987) first book listed 234 symptoms of codependency! This tendency to explain everything in terms of addiction and codependency clearly represents a vast oversimplifica-

I'm Dysfunctional, You're Dysfunctional

by Wendy Kaminer (Addison-Wesley, 1992)

This book takes a penetrating look at self-help books, self-realization programs, the codependency movement, New Age spiritualism, and the curious tendency of people to go on TV talk shows to share their innermost secrets and their most embarrassing frailties with millions of strangers. Kaminer, a social critic who writes about politics, culture, and law, maintains that most self-help books are riddled with psychobabble and sloppy thinking, which undermine our intellectual standards. She also argues that the self-help tradition discourages independent thinking by touting the idea that there are universally applicable solutions for everyone's problems. In an analysis that echoes the themes of Erich Fromm's Escape from Freedom, Kaminer explains how people who jump on the self-help bandwagon give up their freedom to think for themselves by passively submitting to "expert" authority figures who provide simplistic prescriptions for attaining happiness and contentment.

In her analysis of the codependency movement, Kaminer questions the value of encouraging people to view themselves as helpless victims of their families and the wisdom of characterizing traditional feminine traits as pathological. She also questions the claim that women who remain in relationships with troubled, abusive men have a masochistic streak. Kaminer's book is a wide-ranging, easy-to-read, thought-provoking analysis of contemporary pop psychology.

The self-help tradition has always been covertly authoritarian and conformist, relying as it does on a mystique of expertise, encouraging people to look outside themselves for standardized instructions on how to be, teaching us that different people with different problems can easily be saved by the same techniques. It is anathema to independent thought. [p. 6]

Meanwhile, on daytime TV, middle-class Americans are busy practicing their worry habits, swapping stories of disease and controversial eccentricities. Here is a sampling of "Oprah": Apart from the usual assortment of guests who eat, drink, shop, worry, or have sex too much, there are fathers who sleep with their sons' girlfriends (or try to), sisters who sleep with their sisters' boyfriends, women who sleep with their best friends' sons, women who sleep with their husbands' bosses (to help their husbands get ahead), men who only hire pretty women, and men and women who only date interracially. Estranged couples share their grievances while an expert provides on-air counseling. . . . Couples glare at each other, sometimes the women cry, and the expert keeps advising them to get in touch with their feelings and build up their self-esteem. The chance to sit in on someone else's therapy session is part of the appeal of daytime TV. [p. 35]

tion of the complex causes of psychological maladies (Haaken, 1990).

5. The codependency movement speaks primarily to women, with an apparently sincere intent to help them grapple with certain problems associated with the traditional female role in our society. Some critics argue, however, that *codependent* has become a derogatory label that is applied to women in a discriminatory fashion (Van Wormer, 1989). There's also concern that codependency theory implicitly blames women for their own suffering, their

dysfunctional relations with men, and their husbands' problems (Tavris, 1992).

6. Most codependency theorists tout twelve-step recovery programs as the only way to overcome codependency problems. As we have already noted, it is plausible that some people benefit from recovery programs, but the efficacy of such programs in the treatment of codependency hasn't been subjected to careful research yet. Furthermore, research on conventional forms of psychotherapy suggests that a variety of therapeutic approaches can be effective in the treatment of most psychological disorders (Smith, Glass, & Miller, 1980), so it seems unlikely that a twelve-step program will prove to be the only viable method for ameliorating codependency.

In sum, codependency started out as a specific, researchable, and potentially insightful idea about how family dynamics may sometimes contribute to addictive behavior. Unfortunately, in the rush to popularize codependency, the concept has become a catchall scapegoat that is blamed for nearly every form of human misery. Nonetheless, the codependency movement has tapped a fountain of discontent that provides another demonstration that many people are desperately searching for simple answers to complex questions about adjustment in contemporary society.

Self-Help Books

A third demonstration of our search for a sense of direction is the popularity of self-help books that offer do-it-yourself treatments for common personal problems. A glance at the best-seller lists of recent years reveals that our nation has displayed a voracious appetite for self-help books: *I'm OK—You're OK* (Harris, 1967),

Your Erroneous Zones (Dyer, 1976), *How to Be Awake and Alive* (Newman & Berkowitz, 1976), *Winning through Intimidation* (Ringer, 1978), *Living, Loving, & Learning* (Buscaglia, 1982), *The Art of Self-Fulfillment* (Litwack & Resnick, 1984), *Women Men Love—Women Men Leave* (Cowan & Kinder, 1987), *The Good News about Panic, Anxiety and Phobias* (Gold, 1989b), *Willpower's Not Enough* (Watson & Boundy, 1989), *Positive Solitude* (Andre, 1991), *Awakening the Giant Within* (Robbins, 1991)— all have had huge sales. With their simple recipes for achieving happiness, these books have generally not been timid about promising to change the quality of the reader's life. Consider the following excerpt from the back cover of a self-help book titled *Self Creation* (Weinberg, 1979):

> More than any book ever written, *Self Creation* shows you who you are and reveals the secret to controlling your own life. It contains an action blueprint built around a clear-cut principle as basic and revolutionary as the law of gravity. With it you will discover how to conquer bad habits, solve sexual problems, overcome depression and shyness, deal with infuriating people, be decisive, enhance your career, increase creativity. And it will show you how to love and be loved. You created you. Now you can start to reap the boundless benefits of self-confidence, self-reliance, self-determination with *Self Creation*.

If only it were that easy! If only someone could hand you a book that would solve all your problems! Unfortunately, it is not that simple. Merely reading a book is not likely to turn your life around. If the consumption of these literary narcotics were even remotely as helpful as their publishers claim, we would be a nation of serene, happy, well-adjusted people. It is clear, however, that serenity is not the dominant national mood. The multitude of self-help books that crowd bookstore shelves represent just one more symptom of our collective distress and our search for the elusive secret of happiness.

The Value of Self-Help Books

It is somewhat unfair to lump all self-help books together for a critique, because they vary widely in quality. Some are excellent books that offer authentic insights and sound advice. It would be foolish to dismiss all these books as shallow drivel (as many psychologists do). In fact, some of the better self-help books are highlighted in the Recommended Reading boxes that appear throughout this text. Unfortunately, however, the few gems are dwarfed by the mountains of rubbish. Most self-help books offer little of real value to the reader. In general, they have four fundamental shortcomings.

First, they are dominated by "psychobabble." The term *psychobabble*, coined by R. D. Rosen (1977), seems appropriate to describe the "hip" but hopelessly vague language used in many of these books. Statements such as "It's beautiful if you're unhappy," "You've got to get in touch with yourself," "You have to be up front," "You gotta be you 'cause you're you," and "You need a real high-energy experience" are typical examples of this new language. At best, such terminology is ill defined; at worst, it is meaningless. Consider the following example, taken from a question/answer booklet promoting The Forum (then called *est* training).

> The EST training doesn't change the content of anyone's life, nor does it change what anyone knows. It deals with the context or the way we hold the content. . . . Transformation occurs as a recontextualization. . . . "Getting it" means being able to discover when you have been maintaining (or are stuck with) a position which costs you more in aliveness than it is worth, realizing that you are the source of that position, and being able to choose to give up that position or hold it in a way that expands the quality of your life.

What exactly do those words say? Who knows? The statements are so ambiguous and enigmatic that you can read virtually any meaning into them. Therein lies the problem with psychobabble: it is often so obscure that it is unintelligible. Clarity is sacrificed in favor of a hip jargon that prevents rather than enhances effective communication.

A second problem is that self-help books tend to place more emphasis on sales than on scientific soundness. The advice offered in these books is far too rarely based on solid, scientific research (Rosen, 1987). Instead, the ideas are frequently based on the authors' intuitive analyses, which may be highly speculative. Thus Gerald Rosen (1987) concludes that "consumers increasingly risk the purchase of untested do-it-yourself programs" (p. 48). Moreover, even when responsible authors provide scientifically valid advice and are careful not to mislead their readers, sales-hungry publishers often slap outrageous, irresponsible promises on the books' covers (much to the dismay of some authors).

The third shortcoming is that self-help books usually don't provide explicit directions about how to change your behavior. These books tend to be smoothly written and "touchingly human" in tone. They often strike responsive chords in the reader by aptly describing a common problem that many of us experience. The reader says, "Yes, that's me!" Unfortunately, when the book focuses on how to deal with the problem, it usually provides only a vague distillation of simple common sense, which often could be covered in two rather than 200 pages. These books often fall back on inspirational cheerleading in the absence of sound, explicit advice.

Fourth, many of these books encourage a remarkably self-centered approach to life. Although there are plenty of exceptions, the basic message in many self-help books is "Do whatever you feel like doing, and don't worry about the consequences for other people." This "me first" philosophy emphasizes self-determined ethics and an exploitive approach to interpersonal relationships.

A glance at bookstore shelves verifies that the boom in self-help books continues unabated, fueled by people's ongoing need for guidance and direction in their personal lives.

What to Look For in Self-Help Books

Since self-help books vary so widely in quality, it seems a good idea to provide you with some guidelines about what to look for in seeking genuinely helpful books. The following thoughts give you some criteria for judging books of this type.

1. Clarity in communication is essential. Advice won't do you much good if you can't understand it. Try to avoid drowning in the murky depths of psychobabble.

2. This may sound backward, but look for books that do not promise too much in the way of immediate change. The truly useful books tend to be appropriately cautious in their promises and realistic about the challenge of altering one's behavior.

3. Try to select books that mention, at least briefly, the theoretical or research basis for the program they advocate. It is understandable that you may not be interested in a detailed summary of research that supports a particular piece of advice. However, you should be interested in whether the advice is based on published research, widely accepted theory, anecdotal evidence, clinical interactions with patients, or pure speculation by the author. Books that are based on more than personal anecdotes and speculation should have a list of references in the back (or at the end of each chapter).

4. Intellectually honest authors don't just talk about what we know—they also discuss what we do not know. There is much to be said for books that are candid about the limits of what the so-called experts really know.

5. Look for books that provide detailed, explicit directions about how to alter your behavior. Generally, these directions represent the crucial core of the book. If they are inadequate in detail, you have been shortchanged.

6. More often than not, books that focus on a particular kind of problem, such as overeating, loneliness, or marital difficulties, deliver more than those that promise to cure all of life's problems with a few simple ideas. Books that cover everything are usually superficial and disappointing. Books that devote a great deal of thought to a particular topic tend to be written by authors with genuine expertise on that topic. Such books are more likely to pay off for you. Figure 1.3 lists the ten self-help books that were recommended most frequently in a survey of therapists (Stark, 1989). As you can see, all of them focus on a specific topic.

The Approach of This Textbook

Clearly, in spite of our impressive technological progress, we are a people beset by a great variety of personal problems. Living in our complex, modern society is a formidable challenge. This book is about that challenge. It is about you. It is about life. Specifically, it summarizes for you the scientific research on human behavior that appears relevant to the challenge of living effectively in the 1990s. It draws primarily, but not exclusively, on the science we call psychology.

This text deals with the same kinds of problems addressed by self-help books and self-realization programs: anxiety, stress, interpersonal relationships, frustration, loneliness, depression, self-control. However, it makes no boldly seductive promises about solving your personal problems, turning your life around, or helping you to achieve tranquillity. Such promises simply aren't realistic. Psychologists have long recognized that changing one's behavior is a difficult challenge, fraught with frustration and failure. Psychologists sometimes do intensive therapy with a person for years without solving the client's problem.

All this does not mean that you should be pessimistic about your potential for personal growth. You most certainly can change your behavior. Moreover, you can often change it on

FIGURE 1.3
Therapists' top ten self-help books
Steven Sarker surveyed therapists about the self-help books they recommend to their patients. The ten most frequently recommended titles are listed here.

Therapists' Top Ten Self-Help Selections

1 *The Relaxation Response*
by Herbert Benson and Miriam Z. Klipper (Avon)

2 *On Death and Dying*
by Elisabeth Kübler-Ross (Macmillan)

3 *Parent Effectiveness Training*
by Thomas Gordon (McKay)

4 *Between Parent and Child*
by Haim G. Ginott (Avon)

5 *Your Perfect Right: A Guide to Assertive Living*
by Robert E. Alberti and Michael L. Emmons (Impact Publishers)

6 *What Color Is Your Parachute?*
by Richard N. Bolles (Ten Speed Press)

7 *When I Say No, I Feel Guilty*
by Manuel Smith (Bantam)

8 *The Boys and Girls Book about Divorce*
by Richard A. Gardner (Bantam)

9 *Feeling Good: The New Mood Therapy*
by David D. Burns (Morrow)

10 *How to Survive the Loss of a Love*
by Melba Colgrove, Harold Bloomfield, and Peter McWilliams (Bantam)

your own without consulting a professional psychologist. We would not be writing this text if we did not believe that some of our readers might experience some personal benefit from this literary encounter. But it is important that you have realistic expectations. Reading this book will not be a revelatory experience. There are no mysterious secrets about to be unveiled before you. All this book can do is give you some potentially useful information and point you in some potentially beneficial directions. The rest is up to you.

In view of our criticisms of many self-realization programs and self-help books, it seems essential that we lay out explicitly the philosophy that underlies this text. The following statements summarize the assumptions and goals of this book.

1. *This text is based on the premise that accurate knowledge about the principles of psychology is of value to you in everyday life.* It has been said that knowledge is power. Greater awareness of why people behave as they do should help you in your interactions with others as well as in your efforts to understand yourself.

2. *This text will attempt to foster a critical attitude toward psychological issues and to enhance your critical thinking skills.* Information is important, but people also need to develop effective strategies for evaluating information. To think

critically is to subject ideas to systematic, skeptical scrutiny. Critical thinkers ask tough questions, such as: What exactly is the assertion? What assumptions underlie this assertion? What evidence or reasoning supports this assertion? Are there alternative explanations? Some general guidelines for thinking critically are outlined in Figure 1.4. We have already attempted to illustrate the importance of a critical attitude in our evaluation of self-realization programs, the codependency movement, and self-help books, and we'll continue to model critical thinking strategies throughout the text.

3. *This text should open doors.* The coverage in this book is very broad; we will tackle many topics. Therefore, there may be places where it lacks the depth or detail that you would like. However, you should think of it as a resource book that can introduce you to other books or techniques or therapies, which you can then pursue on your own.

4. *This text assumes that the key to effective adjustment is to "take charge" of your own life.* If you are dissatisfied with some aspect of your life, it does no good to sit around and mope about it. You have to take an active role in attempting to improve the quality of your life. This may involve learning a new skill or pursuing a particular kind of help. In any case, it is generally best to meet problems head on rather than try to avoid them.

Guidelines for Thinking Critically

1 *Ask questions; be willing to wonder.* To think critically you must be willing to think creatively—that is, to be curious about the puzzles of human behavior, to wonder why people act the way they do, and to question received explanations and examine new ones.

2 *Define the problem.* Identify the issues involved in clear and concrete terms, rather than vague generalities such as "happiness," "potential," or "meaningfulness." What does meaningfulness mean, exactly?

3 *Examine the evidence.* Consider the nature of the evidence that supports all aspects of the problem under examination. Is it reliable? Valid? Is it someone's personal assertion or speculation? Does the evidence come from one or two narrow studies, or from repeated research?

4 *Analyze biases and assumptions*—your own and those of others. What prejudices, deeply held values, and other personal biases do you bring to your evaluation of a problem? Are you willing to consider evidence that contradicts your beliefs? Be sure you can identify the biases of others, in order to evaluate their arguments as well.

5 *Avoid emotional reasoning* ("If I feel this way, it must be true"). Remember that everyone holds convictions and ideas about how the world should operate—and that your opponents are as serious about their convictions as you are about yours. Feelings are important, but they should not substitute for careful appraisal of arguments and evidence.

6 *Don't oversimplify.* Look beyond the obvious. Reject simplistic, either-or thinking. Look for logical contradictions in arguments. Be wary of "arguments by anecdote."

7 *Consider other interpretations.* Before you leap to conclusions, think about other explanations. Be especially careful about assertions of cause and effect.

8 *Tolerate uncertainty.* This may be the hardest step in becoming a critical thinker, for it requires the ability to accept some guiding ideas and beliefs—yet the willingness to give them up when evidence and experience contradict them.

FIGURE 1.4
Guidelines for thinking critically
Critical thinking should not be equated with negative thinking; it's not a matter of learning how to tear down others' ideas. Rather, critical thinkers carefully subject others' ideas—and their own—to careful, systematic, objective evaluation. The guidelines shown here (from Wade & Tavris, 1990) provide a succinct overview of what it means to think critically.

The Psychology of Adjustment

N ow that we have spelled out our approach in writing this text, it is time to turn to the task of introducing you to some basic concepts. In this section we'll discuss the nature of psychology and the concept of adjustment.

What Is Psychology?

Psychology **is the science that studies behavior and the physiological and mental processes that underlie it and the profession that applies the accumulated knowledge of this science to practical problems.** Psychology leads a complex dual existence as both a *science* and a *profession*. Let's examine the science first.

Psychology is an area of scientific study, much like biology or physics. Whereas biology focuses on life processes, and physics on matter and energy, psychology focuses on *behavior and related processes*.

Behavior **is any overt (observable) response or activity by an organism.** Psychology does *not* confine itself to the study of human behavior. Many psychologists believe that the principles of behavior are much the same for animals and humans. These psychologists often prefer to study animals—mainly because they can exert more control over the factors that influence the animals' behavior.

Psychology is also interested in the mental processes—the thoughts, feelings, and wishes—that accompany behavior. Mental processes are more difficult to study than behavior because they are private and not directly observable. However, they exert critical influence over human behavior, so psychologists strive to improve their ability to "look inside the mind."

Finally, psychology includes the study of the physiological processes that underlie behavior. Thus some psychologists try to figure out how bodily processes such as neural impulses, hormonal secretions, and genetic coding regulate behavior. Practically speaking, all this means that psychologists study a great variety of phenomena. Psychologists are interested in the way rats run mazes, dogs salivate, and cats' brains function, as well as in the way children play and adults engage in social interaction.

As you probably know, psychology is not all pure science. It has a highly practical side, represented by the many psychologists who provide a variety of professional services to the public. Although the profession of psychology is very prominent today, this aspect of psychol-ogy was actually slow to develop. Psychology emerged as an independent science back in the 19th century, but until the 1950s psychologists were found almost exclusively in the halls of academia, teaching and doing research. However, the demands of World War II (1942–1945) stimulated rapid growth in psychology's first professional specialty—clinical psychology. *Clinical psychology* **is the branch of psychology concerned with the diagnosis and treatment of psychological problems and disorders.** During World War II a multitude of academic psychologists were pressed into service as clinicians to screen military recruits and treat soldiers suffering from trauma. Frequently they found their clinical work interesting, and many of them returned from the war to set up training programs to meet the continued high demand for clinical services. Soon about half of the new Ph.D.s in psychology were specializing in clinical work. Psychology had come of age as a profession.

Since then, the trend toward professionalization has continued. A variety of new professional specialties have emerged, including school psychology, industrial/organizational psychology, and counseling psychology. The growth of these professional arms of psychology, which concern themselves with practical problems, eventually led to increased interest in our topic—adjustment.

What Is Adjustment?

We have referred to the term *adjustment* several times without clarifying its exact meaning. The concept of adjustment was originally borrowed from biology. It was modeled after the biological term *adaptation*, which refers to efforts by a species to adjust to changes in its environment. Just as a field mouse has to adapt to an unusually brutal winter, a person has to adjust to changes in circumstances such as a new job, a financial setback, or the loss of a loved one. Thus *adjustment* **refers to the psychological processes through which people manage or cope with the demands and challenges of everyday life.**

The demands of everyday life are diverse, so in studying the process of adjustment we will examine a broad variety of topics. In the first section of this book, "The Dynamics of Adjustment," we discuss general issues, such as how personality affects our patterns of adjustment, how we are affected by stress, and how we use coping strategies to deal with stress. In the second section, "The Interpersonal Realm," we'll examine the adjustments that we make in our social relationships, exploring such topics as how we view others, communication, behavior in groups, friendship, and intimate relationships. In the third section, "Developmental Transitions," we'll look at how we adjust to changing demands as we grow older. We'll discuss such topics as the development of gender roles, the emergence of sexuality, phases of adult development, and transitions in the world of work. Finally, in the fourth section, "Mental and Physical Health," we'll discuss how the process of adjustment influences our psychological and physical wellness.

As you can see, the study of adjustment delves into nearly every corner of our lives, and we'll be discussing a diverse array of issues and topics. Before we begin considering these topics in earnest, however, we need to take a closer look at psychology's approach to investigating behavior—the scientific method.

The Scientific Approach to Behavior

e all expend a great deal of effort in trying to understand our own behavior as well as the behavior of others. We wonder about any number of behavioral questions: Why am I so anxious when I interact with new people? Why is Sam always trying to be the center of attention at the office? Why does Joanna cheat on her wonderful husband? Are extraverts happier than introverts? Is depression more common during the Christmas holidays? Given that psychologists' principal goal is to explain behavior, how are their efforts different from everyone else's? The key difference is that psychology is a *science*, committed to *empiricism*.

Empiricism

Empiricism is the premise that knowledge should be acquired through observation. When we say that scientific psychology is empirical, we mean that its conclusions are based on systematic observation rather than on reasoning, speculation, traditional beliefs, or common sense. Scientists are not content with having ideas that sound plausible; they conduct research to test their ideas. Whereas our everyday speculations are informal, unsystematic, and highly subjective, scientists' investigations are formal, systematic, and objective. To gain more understanding of the empirical approach, let's look at how scientific studies are conducted.

Steps in a Scientific Investigation

Your best friend has been raving for weeks about a meditation group he has joined. He says it has turned his life around! He claims to be happier, more energetic, and less anxious. You are skeptical. The only clear behavioral change you can see is that meditation is all he ever talks about. You wonder: Does meditation really have beneficial effects on one's mental health?

A question or problem like this one is the point of departure for any research endeavor. The question stimulates the scientist to seek information that may provide at least a partial answer. A scientist, however, seeks information in a particular way. Scientific investigations are systematic. They follow an orderly pattern that can be broken up into a number of separate steps. Let's use our question about meditation to look at three key steps in scientific studies.

1. *Formulate a testable hypothesis.* The first step in a scientific study is to translate a general idea into a testable hypothesis. **A *hypothesis* is a tentative statement about the relationship between two or more variables.** Variables in a study are any measurable conditions, events, characteristics, or behaviors that are controlled or observed. Thus, in our imaginary study, you might hypothesize that learning to meditate (the first variable) will lead to reduced anxiety (the second variable).

To be testable, hypotheses must be formulated precisely, with clear definitions of the variables under study. To achieve this goal, researchers depend on operational definitions. An operational definition describes the actions or operations that will be made to measure or control a variable. For example, you might hypothesize that people who meditate four hours a week should score lower on the Taylor Manifest Anxiety Scale than comparable people who do not meditate. Thus, in the context of our study, "learning to meditate" is defined as following a prescribed four-hour regimen of meditation, and "anxiety" is defined as a person's score on the Taylor Manifest Anxiety Scale (Taylor, 1953).

2. *Gather the appropriate data.* After you have clearly stated your hypothesis, the second step in a scientific investigation is to put it to a test. This step involves selecting a research method and conducting a study. The research method chosen depends on the nature of the question under study. The various methods—experiments, case studies, surveys, and naturalistic observation—all have their advantages and disadvantages, some of which we'll discuss later.

To conduct your study, you will need to procure a sample of subjects. **Subjects are the persons or animals whose behavior is systematically observed in a study.** To gather data to test our hypothesis about meditation, you would assemble two similar groups of subjects and require one of the groups to practice meditation four hours weekly for several months. You would then administer your measure of anxiety to see whether there was a substantial difference between the two groups, as our hypothesis predicts.

3. *Report the findings.* Progress in understanding the world around us requires that scientists share their findings with one another and with the general public. The final step in a scientific investigation is to write up a concise summary of the study and its findings. If our meditation study yielded interesting results, we would prepare a report that could be submitted to a technical journal for publication or presented at a scientific meeting (such as the annual convention of the American Psychological Association).

The process of publishing scientific studies allows other experts to evaluate and critique new research findings. Sometimes this process of critical evaluation discloses flaws in a study. If the flaws are serious enough, the results may be discounted or discarded. This evaluation process is intended to weed out erroneous findings.

Advantages of the Scientific Approach

Science is certainly not the only method that we can use to draw conclusions about behavior. We all use logic, casual observation, and good old-fashioned common sense. Since the scientific method often requires painstaking effort, it seems reasonable to ask what the advantages of the empirical approach are.

The scientific approach offers two major advantages. The first is its clarity and precision. Common-sense notions about behavior tend to be vague and ambiguous. Consider the old truism "Spare the rod and spoil the child." What exactly does this generalization about child rearing amount to? How severely should the rod be applied if we are not to spoil the child? How do we assess whether a child qualifies as "spoiled"? A fundamental problem is that such statements mean different things to different people. When people disagree about this assertion, it may be because they are talking about entirely different things. The scientific approach, in contrast, requires that we specify *exactly* what we are talking about when we formulate hypotheses. Clarity and precision enhance communication about important ideas.

The second advantage offered by the scientific approach is its relative intolerance of error. Scientists subject their ideas to empirical tests. They also scrutinize one another's findings with a critical eye. They demand objective data and thorough documentation before they accept ideas. When the findings of two studies conflict, they try to figure out why the studies reached different conclusions, usually by conducting additional research. Common sense and casual observation, in contrast, often tolerate contradictory generalizations, such as "Opposites attract" and "Birds of a feather flock together." Furthermore, common-sense analyses involve little effort to verify ideas or detect errors, so that many myths about behavior come to be widely believed.

All this is not to say that science has a copyright on truth. However, the scientific approach does tend to yield more accurate and dependable information than casual analyses and armchair speculation. Empirical data can thus provide a useful benchmark against which to judge claims and information from other kinds of sources.

Now that we have an overview of how the scientific enterprise works, we can look at some of the specific research methods that psychologists depend on most. The two main types of research methods in psychology are *experimental research methods* and *correlational research methods*. We will discuss them separately because there is an important distinction between them.

Experimental Research: Looking for Causes

Does misery love company? This question intrigued the social psychologist Stanley Schachter. How does anxiety affect our desire to be with others? When people feel anxious, do they want to be left alone, or do they prefer to have others around? Schachter's hypothesis was that increases in anxiety would cause increases in the desire to be with others, which psychologists call the *need for affiliation*. To test this hypothesis, Schachter (1959) designed a clever experiment. **The *experiment* is a research method in which the investigator manipulates an (independent) variable under carefully controlled conditions and observes whether there are changes in a second (dependent) variable as a result.** Psychologists depend on this method more than any other.

Independent and Dependent Variables

An experiment is designed to find out whether changes in one variable (let's call it *x*) cause changes in another variable (let's call it *y*). To put it more concisely, we want to know *how* x *affects* y. In this formulation, we refer to *x* as the independent variable, and we call y the dependent variable. **An *independent variable* is a condition or event that an experimenter varies in order to see its impact on another variable.** The independent variable is the variable that the experimenter controls or manipulates. It is hypothesized to have some effect on the dependent variable. The experiment is conducted to verify this effect. **The *dependent variable* is the variable that is thought to be affected by the manipulations of the independent variable.** In psychology studies, the dependent variable usually is a measurement of some aspect of the subjects' behavior.

In Schachter's experiment, the *independent variable was the subjects' anxiety level*, which he manipulated in the following way. Subjects assembled in his laboratory were told by a Dr. Zilstein that they would be participating in a study on the physiological effects of electric shock and that they would receive a series of electric shocks. Half of the subjects were warned that the shocks would be very painful. They made up the *high-anxiety* group. The other half of the subjects, assigned to the *low-anxiety* group, were told that the shocks would be mild and painless. These procedures were simply intended to evoke different levels of anxiety. In reality, no one was actually shocked at any time. Instead, the experimenter indicated that there would be a delay while he prepared the shock apparatus for use. The subjects were asked whether they would prefer to wait alone or in the company of others. *This measure of the subjects' desire to affiliate with others was the dependent variable.*

Experimental and Control Groups

To conduct an experiment, an investigator typically assembles two groups of subjects who are treated differently in regard to the independent variable. We call these groups the experimental and control groups. **The *experimental group* consists of the subjects who receive some special treatment in regard to the independent variable. The *control group* consists of similar subjects who do *not* receive the special treatment given to the experimental group.** In Schachter's study, the subjects in the high-anxiety condition were the experimental group.

They received a special treatment designed to create an unusually high level of anxiety. The subjects in the low-anxiety condition were the control group.

It is crucial that the experimental and control groups be very similar, except for the different treatment they receive in regard to the independent variable. This stipulation brings us to the logic that underlies the experimental method. If the two groups are alike in all respects *except for the variation created by the manipulation of the independent variable*, then any differences between the two groups on the dependent variable *must be due to this manipulation of the independent variable*. In this way researchers isolate the effect of the independent variable on the dependent variable. Thus Schachter isolated the impact of anxiety on need for affiliation. What did he find? As he had predicted, he found that increased anxiety led to increased desire for affiliation. The percentage of subjects who wanted to wait with others was nearly twice as high in the high-anxiety group as in the low-anxiety group (see Figure 1.5).

The logic of the experimental method rests heavily on the assumption that the experimental and control groups are alike—except for their different treatment in regard to the independent variable. Any other differences between the two groups cloud the situation and make it difficult to draw solid conclusions about the relationship between the independent variable and the dependent variable. To summarize our discussion of the experimental method, Figure 1.6 provides an overview of the various elements in an experiment, using Schachter's study as an example.

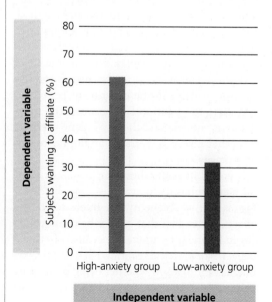

**FIGURE 1.5
Results of Schachter's study of affiliation**
The percentage of subjects who wanted to wait with others was higher in the high-anxiety (experimental) group than in the low-anxiety (control) group. These results supported Schachter's hypothesis that anxiety would increase the desire for affiliation.

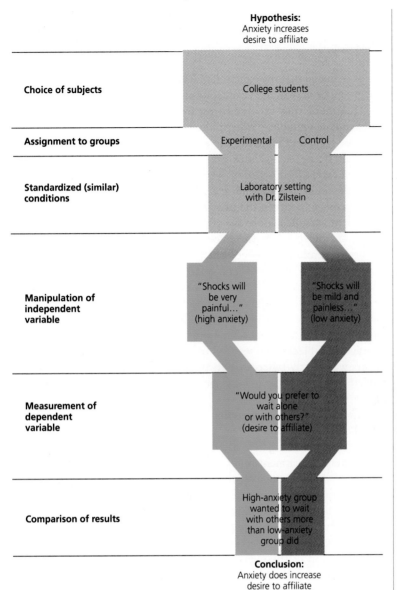

Hypothesis:
Anxiety increases
desire to affiliate

Choice of subjects	College students
Assignment to groups	Experimental Control
Standardized (similar) conditions	Laboratory setting with Dr. Zilstein
Manipulation of independent variable	"Shocks will be very painful..." (high anxiety) "Shocks will be mild and painless..." (low anxiety)
Measurement of dependent variable	"Would you prefer to wait alone or with others?" (desire to affiliate)
Comparison of results	High-anxiety group wanted to wait with others more than low-anxiety group did

Conclusion:
Anxiety does increase
desire to affiliate

FIGURE 1.6
The basic elements of an experiment
This diagram provides an overview of the key features of the experimental method, as illustrated by Schachter's study of anxiety and affiliation. The logic of the experiment rests on treating the experimental and control groups alike except for the manipulation of the independent variable.

Advantages and Disadvantages

The experiment is a powerful research method. Its principal advantage is that it allows us to draw conclusions about cause-and-effect relationships between variables. We can draw these conclusions about causation because the precise control available in the experiment permits us to isolate the relationship between the independent variable and the dependent variable. No other research method can duplicate this advantage.

For all its power, however, the experimental method has its limitations. One disadvantage is that we frequently are interested in the effects of variables that cannot be manipulated (as independent variables) because of ethical concerns or practical realities. For example, you might want to know whether being brought up in an urban area as opposed to a rural area

affects people's values. A true experiment would require you to assign similar families to live in urban and rural areas, and you can't do that. To explore this question, you would have to use a correlational research method.

Correlational Research: Looking for Links

When psychologists cannot exert experimental control over the variables they want to study, all they can do is make systematic observations to see whether there is a link or association between the variables of interest. Such an association is called a correlation. **A correlation exists when two variables are related to one another.** The definitive aspect of correlational studies is that the researchers cannot control the variables under study.

Measuring Correlation

The results of correlational research are often summarized with a statistic called the *correlation coefficient.* This widely used statistic will be mentioned frequently as we discuss studies throughout the remainder of this text. **A correlation coefficient is a numerical index of the degree of relationship that exists between two variables.** A correlation coefficient tells us (1) how strongly related two variables are and (2) the direction (positive or negative) of the relationship.

A correlation can describe two *kinds* of relationships. A *positive* correlation indicates a *direct* relationship between two variables. This means that high scores on variable *x* are associated with high scores on variable *y*, and that low scores on variable *x* are associated with low scores on variable *y*. For example, there is a positive correlation between high school grade-point average (GPA) and subsequent college GPA. That is, people who do well in high

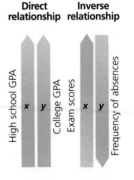

FIGURE 1.7
Positive and negative correlations
Variables are positively correlated if they tend to increase and decrease together and negatively correlated if one variable tends to increase when the other decreases. Hence the terms *positive correlation* and *negative correlation* refer to the *direction* of the relationship between two variables.

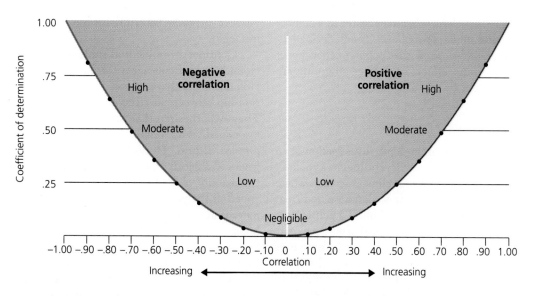

FIGURE 1.8
Interpreting correlation coefficients
The magnitude of a correlation coefficient indicates the strength of the relationship between two variables. The closer a correlation is to either +1.00 or −1.00, the stronger the relationship between the variables. The square of a correlation (called the coefficient of determination) is an index of the correlation's predictive power. The coefficient of determination tells us the percentage of variation in one variable that can be predicted on the basis of the other variable. The correlation between SAT scores and college GPA, for example, is roughly .50, which means that the abilities measured by SAT scores can account for about 25% of the variation among students in GPA.

school tend to do well in college, and those who perform poorly in high school tend to perform poorly in college (see Figure 1.7).

A *negative* correlation, in contrast, indicates that there is an *inverse* relationship between two variables. This means that people who score high on variable *x* tend to score low on variable *y*, whereas those who score low on *x* tend to score high on *y*. In most college courses, for example, there is a negative correlation between how frequently a student is absent and how well the student performs on exams. Students who have a large number of absences tend to earn low exam scores, while students who have a small number of absences tend to get higher exam scores (see Figure 1.7).

While the positive or negative sign indicates whether an association is direct or inverse, the *size* of the coefficient indicates the *strength* of the association between two variables. This coefficient can vary between 0 and +1.00 (if positive) or between 0 and −1.00 (if negative). A coefficient near zero tells us there is no relationship between the variables. The closer the correlation is to either −1.00 or +1.00, the stronger the relationship is (see Figure 1.8). Thus a correlation of +.90 represents a stronger tendency for variables to be associated than does a correlation of +.40. Likewise, a correlation of −.75 represents a stronger relationship than does a correlation of −.45. Keep in mind that the *strength* of a correlation depends only on the size of the coefficient. The positive or negative sign simply shows whether the correlation is direct or inverse. Therefore, a correlation of −.60 reflects a stronger relationship than a correlation of +.30.

There are a variety of correlational research methods, including naturalistic observation, case studies, and surveys. Let's examine each of these methods to see how researchers use them to detect associations between variables.

Naturalistic Observation

A researcher who engages in *naturalistic observation* carefully observes behavior without intervening directly with the subjects. This type of research is called *naturalistic* because behavior is allowed to unfold naturally (without interference) in its natural environment—that is, the setting in which it normally occurs.

As an example, consider a study by Stoffer, Davis, and Brown (1977), which sought to determine whether it is a good idea for students to reconsider and change some of their answers on multiple-choice tests. The conventional wisdom is that "your first hunch is your best hunch," and it is widely believed that students should not go back and change their answers. To put this idea to an empirical test, Stoffer and his colleagues studied the answer changes made by college students on their regular exams in a psychology course. They simply examined students' answer sheets for evidence of response changes, such as erasures or crossing out of responses. As Figure 1.9 shows, they found that changes that went from a wrong answer to a right answer outnumbered changes that went from a right answer to a wrong answer by a margin of nearly 3 to 1! The correlation between the number of changes students made and their net gain from answer changing was +.49, indicating that the more answers students changed, the more they improved their scores. These

FIGURE 1.9
The effects of answer changing on multiple-choice exams
In a study of answer changes, Stoffer and his colleagues (1977) found that wrong-to-right changes outnumbered right-to-wrong changes by a sizable margin. These results are very similar to those of other studies on this issue.

results, which have been replicated in a number of other studies (Benjamin, Cavell, & Shallenberger, 1984), show that popular beliefs about the harmful effects of answer changing are inaccurate.

Case Studies

A *case study* is an in-depth investigation of an individual subject. Psychologists typically assemble case studies in clinical settings where an effort is being made to diagnose and treat some psychological problem. To achieve an understanding of an individual, a clinician may use a variety of procedures, including interviews of the subject, interviews of others who know the subject, direct observation, examination of records, and psychological testing. Usually a single case study does not provide much basis on which to formulate general laws of behavior. If researchers have a number of case studies available, however, they can look for threads of consistency among them, and they may be able to draw some general conclusions.

This was the strategy employed by a research team (Farina, Burns, Austad, Bugglin, & Fischer, 1986) that studied psychiatric patients' readjustment to their community after their release from a mental hospital. The researchers wanted to know whether the patients' physical attractiveness was related to their success in readjustment. As we'll discuss in upcoming chapters, good-looking people tend to be treated more nicely by others than homely people, suggesting that attractive patients may have an easier time adjusting to life outside the hospital. To find out, the research team compiled case history data (and ratings of physical attractiveness) for patients just before their discharge from a mental hospital and six months later. A modest positive correlation (+.38) was found between patients' attractiveness and their postdischarge social adjustment. Thus the better-looking patients were better off, suggesting that physical attractiveness plays a role in psychiatric patients' readjustment to community living.

Surveys

***Surveys* are structured questionnaires designed to solicit information about specific aspects of subjects' behavior.** They are sometimes used to measure dependent variables in experiments, but they are used mainly in correlational research. Surveys are frequently employed to gather data on subjects' attitudes and on aspects of behavior that are difficult to observe directly (marital interactions, for instance).

Consider an influential study by Thomas Holmes and his colleagues (Wyler, Masuda, & Holmes, 1971) that explored the possible relationship between life stress and physical illness. They hypothesized that high stress would be associated with a relatively high frequency of physical illness. To test this hypothesis they gave 232 subjects a questionnaire that assessed the amount of stress the subjects had experienced in the past year and another questionnaire that assessed the amount of illness they had recently experienced. As predicted, they found a positive correlation (+.32) between the level of stress subjects had experienced and the amount of illness they had suffered. This ground-breaking investigation inspired hundreds of follow-up studies that have enhanced our understanding of how stress is related to physical health (see Chapter 3).

Advantages and Disadvantages

Correlational research methods give us a way to explore questions that we could not examine with experimental procedures. Consider the study we just discussed on the association between life stress and health. Obviously, Holmes could not manipulate the life stress experienced by his subjects. Their divorces, retirements, pregnancies, and mortgages were far beyond his control. But correlational methods allowed him to gather useful information on whether there is a link between life stress and illness. Thus *correlational research broadens the scope of phenomena that psychologists can study.*

Unfortunately, correlational methods have one major disadvantage. The investigator does not have the opportunity to control events so as to isolate cause and effect. Consequently, *correlational research cannot demonstrate conclusively that two variables are causally related.* The crux of the problem is that correlation is no assurance of causation.

When we find that variables x and y are correlated, we can safely conclude only that x and y are related. We do not know *how* x and y are related. We do not know whether x causes y, or y causes x, or whether both are caused by a third variable. Survey studies show, for example, that marital satisfaction is positively correlated with sexual satisfaction (Hunt, 1974; Tavris & Sadd, 1977). Although it's clear that good sex and a healthy marriage go hand in hand, it's hard to tell what's causing what. We don't know whether healthy marriages promote good sex, or whether good sex promotes healthy marriages. Moreover, we can't rule out the possibility that both are caused by a third variable. Perhaps sexual satisfaction and marital satisfaction are both caused by compatibility in values. The plausible causal relationships in this case are diagrammed for you in Figure 1.10 which illustrates the "third-variable problem" in interpreting correlations. This is a frequent problem in correlational research. Indeed, it will surface in the next section, where we review the empirical research on the determinants of happiness.

The Roots of Happiness: An Empirical Analysis

hat exactly makes a person happy? This question has been the subject of much speculation. Common-sense hypotheses about the roots of happiness abound. We have all heard, for example, that money cannot buy happiness. But do you believe it? A television commercial tells us, "If you've got your health, you've got just about everything." Is health indeed the key? What if you're healthy but poor, unemployed, and lonely? We often hear about the joys of parenthood, the joys of youth, and the joys of the simple rural life. Are these the factors that promote happiness?

In recent years social scientists have begun to subject these and other hypotheses to empirical tests. Quite a number of survey studies have been conducted to explore the determinants of happiness, or *subjective well-being*, as social scientists like to call it. The findings of these studies (which have been summarized effectively by Freedman, 1978; Diener, 1984; Argyle, 1987; and Myers, 1992) are quite interesting. We review this research because it illustrates the value of collecting data and putting ideas to an empirical test. As you will see, many common-sense notions about happiness appear to be inaccurate.

What Isn't Very Important?

Let us begin by discussing those things that turn out to be relatively unimportant. A number of factors widely believed to influence one's sense of well-being appear to bear little or no relation to general happiness.

Money. There is a positive correlation between income and subjective feelings of hap-

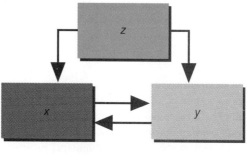

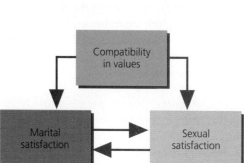

FIGURE 1.10
Possible causal relations between correlated variables
When two variables are correlated, there are several possible explanations. It could be that x causes y, or that y causes x, or that a third variable, z, causes changes in both x and y. As the correlation between marital satisfaction and sexual satisfaction illustrates, the correlation itself does not provide the answer.

piness, but the association is surprisingly weak (Argyle, 1987). According to Freedman (1978), money is important only when you don't have any. People at the very bottom of the economic ladder are relatively unhappy. Once people rise above the poverty level, however, there is little relation between income and happiness. On the average, wealthy people are only marginally happier than the middle classes. The problem with money is that in this era of voracious consumption, most of us find a way to spend all our money and come out short, no matter how much money we make. Complaints about not having enough money are routine even among affluent people who have six-figure incomes.

Age. Age and happiness are consistently found to be unrelated. Age accounts for less than 1% of the variation in people's happiness (Myers, 1992). The key factors influencing subjective well-being may shift some as people grow older—work becomes less important, health more so—but people's average level of happiness tends to remain remarkably stable over the life span.

Gender. Women are treated for depressive disorders about twice as often as men, so one might expect that women are less happy on the average. Like age, however, gender accounts for less than 1% of the variation in people's subjective well-being (Myers, 1992). How can we reconcile these seemingly contradictory data? Evidence suggests that gender differences in the prevalence of depression may be smaller than treatment statistics suggest. Men may actually experience depression nearly as often women, but they are less inclined to admit it and less willing to seek treatment for it.

Parenthood. Children can be a tremendous source of joy and fulfillment, but they can also be a tremendous source of headaches and hassles. Parents worry more than childless couples and experience more marital problems (Argyle, 1987). Apparently the good and bad aspects of parenthood balance each other out, because the evidence indicates that people who have children are neither more nor less happy than people without children.

Intelligence. Intelligence is a highly valued trait in modern society, but researchers have not found an association between IQ scores and happiness. Educational attainment also appears to be unrelated to subjective well-being (Diener, 1984).

Community. According to Freedman (1978), when asked where they would most like to live, people show a clear preference for the stereotype of the tranquil, pastoral life believed to exist in rural areas. However, when actual reported happiness is related to type of community, people living in urban, suburban, and rural areas are found to be equally happy.

Sex. Sex appears to be a lot like money: it has a significant effect on happiness only if you don't have any. Freedman (1978) reports that frequency of sexual encounters and number of sexual partners are unrelated to level of happiness, with the exception that people who have little or no sex life are relatively unhappy. Freedman also notes that homosexuals seem to be just as happy as heterosexuals.

What Is Somewhat Important?

Research has identified three facets of life that appear to have a moderate impact on subjective well-being: health, social activity, and religious belief.

Health. Good physical health would seem to be an essential requirement for happiness, but people adapt to health problems. Research reveals that individuals who develop serious, disabling health conditions aren't as unhappy as one might guess (Myers, 1992). Furthermore, Freedman (1978) argues that good health does not, by itself, produce happiness because people who are healthy tend to take good health for granted. Considerations such as these may help to explain why researchers find only a moderate positive correlation (average = .32) between health status and subjective well-being (Diener, 1984).

Social activity. Humans are social animals and our interpersonal relations do appear to contribute to our happiness. People who are satisfied with their friendship networks and

If wealth, fame, and success bring happiness, then rock star Bruce Springsteen should be as happy as they come. In recent interviews, however, Springsteen has revealed that his wealth and fame have not made him immune to personal doubts or depression. His story illustrates that the ingredients of happiness are more complex and subjective than many of us imagine.

people who are socially active report above-average levels of happiness (Diener, 1984). At the other end of the spectrum, people troubled by loneliness tend to be very unhappy (Argyle, 1987).

Religion. The link between religiosity and subjective well-being is modest, but a number of large-scale surveys suggest that people with heartfelt religious convictions are more likely to be happy than people who characterize themselves as nonreligious (Argyle, 1987; Myers, 1992). Researchers aren't sure how religious faith fosters happiness (Diener, 1984), but David Myers (1992) offers some interesting conjectures. Among other things, he discusses how religion can give people a sense of purpose and meaning in their lives, help them to accept their setbacks gracefully, connect them to a caring, supportive community, and comfort them by putting their ultimate mortality in perspective.

What Is Very Important?

The list of factors that turn out to be very important is surprisingly short. Only a few variables are strongly related to overall happiness.

Love and marriage. Romantic relationships can be stressful, but people consistently rate being in love as one of the most critical ingredients of happiness (Diener, 1984). More than any other single thing, unhappy people mention love as the one missing element in their lives that could make them happy (Freedman, 1978). Furthermore, although people complain a lot about their marriages, the evidence indicates that marital status is a key correlate of happiness. Among both men and women, married people are happier than people who are single or divorced. However, the causal relations underlying this correlation are unclear. It may be that people who are happy tend to have better intimate relationships and more stable marriages, while people who are unhappy have more difficulty finding and keeping mates.

Work. Given the frequency with which people complain about their jobs, one might not expect work to be a key source of happiness, but it is. Although less critical than love and marriage, job satisfaction is strongly related to general happiness (Argyle, 1987). Studies also show that unemployment has devastating effects on subjective well-being (Diener, 1984). Work is important for both sexes, but it appears to be somewhat less important for married peo-

ple than for singles (Freedman, 1978). It is difficult to sort out whether job satisfaction causes happiness or vice versa, but evidence suggests that causation flows both ways (Argyle, 1987).

Personality. The best predictor of individuals' future happiness is their past happiness (Myers, 1992). Some people seem destined to be happy and others unhappy, regardless of their triumphs or setbacks. The limited influence of life events was apparent in a study that found only marginal differences between lottery winners and quadriplegics in overall happiness (Argyle, 1987). Several lines of evidence suggest that happiness depends less on external circumstances—having a nice house, good friends, and an enjoyable job—than on internal factors, such as one's outlook on life. With this reality in mind, researchers have begun to look for links between personality and subjective well-being, and they have found some relatively strong correlations. Self-esteem, for example, is one of the best predictors of happiness. Not surprisingly, people who like themselves tend to be happier than those who do not. Other personality correlates of happiness include extraversion, optimism, and a sense of personal control over one's life.

Conclusions

We must be cautious in drawing inferences about the causes of happiness because most of the available data are correlational (see Figure 1.11). Nonetheless, the empirical evidence suggests that many popular beliefs about the sources of happiness are unfounded. The data also demonstrate that happiness is shaped by a complex constellation of variables. In spite of this complexity, however, some worthwhile insights about human adjustment can be gleaned from research on the correlates of subjective well-being.

First, it's important to understand that there is no simple recipe for happiness. As Freedman (1978) puts it, "I can suggest no religious beliefs, mystical practices (I suppose it helps to have a guardian angel or spirit, but I don't know how to find one), meditative exercises (the TM publicity to the contrary), strange diets, biofeedback procedures, or a system of philosophy that will produce happiness" (p. 9). In a similar vein, Myers (1992) discusses the futility of trying to attain happiness through simplistic "quick-fix" methods, such as firewalking, hypnosis, and subliminal tapes.

Second, research on happiness demonstrates that the determinants of subjective well-being are precisely that: subjective. Objective realities are not as important as subjective feelings. In other words, your health, your wealth, your job, and your age are not as influential as how you feel about your health, wealth, job, and age (Argyle, 1987).

Third, when we make the subjective assessments that shape our happiness, everything is relative (Freedman, 1978; Myers, 1992). In other words, you evaluate what you have in relation to what the people around you have and in relation to what you expected to have. Generally, we compare ourselves with others who are similar to us. Thus people who are wealthy assess what they have by comparing themselves with their wealthy friends and neighbors. This is one reason why there is little correlation between wealth and happiness. You

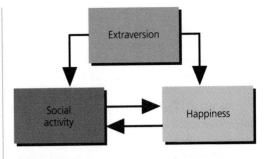

FIGURE 1.11
Possible causal relations among the correlates of happiness
Although we have considerable data on the correlates of happiness, it is difficult to untangle the possible causal relationships. We know, for example, that there is a moderate positive correlation between social activity and happiness, but we can't say for sure whether high social activity causes happiness or whether happiness causes people to be more socially active. Moreover, in light of the finding that a third variable—extraversion—correlates with both variables, we have to consider the possibility that extraversion causes both greater social activity and greater happiness.

may have a lovely home, but if it sits next door to a neighbor's palatial mansion, it may be a source of more dissatisfaction than happiness. In addition to comparing ourselves with other people, we compare what we have with what our expectations were. When we exceed our expectations, we are more likely to be happy. Thus people living in a lovely home next door to a much lovelier mansion could still be quite happy—if they never expected to live in such an affluent neighborhood. To a large degree, then, happiness is measured on a relative rather than an absolute scale.

Fourth, although happiness can be an elusive goal, research shows that the quest for happiness is never hopeless (Freedman, 1978). The evidence indicates that some people find happiness in spite of seemingly insurmountable problems. Nothing short of terminal illness—no setback, shortcoming, difficulty, or inadequacy—makes happiness impossible.

Summary

In spite of the great technological progress in our modern era, personal problems have not declined. In fact, theorists such as Fromm suggest that our progress brings new and possibly more difficult adjustment problems.

Self-help books, self-realization programs, and the codependency movement are three interesting manifestations of our struggle to find a sense of direction in our confusing world. Unfortunately, self-realization programs have little real value, and their alleged benefits are probably due to placebo effects. The codependency movement is motivated by good intentions, but it vastly oversimplifies the roots of human distress and has little empirical basis. Some self-help books offer worthwhile advice, but most are dominated by psychobabble and are not based on scientific research. Many also lack explicit advice on how to change behavior, and some encourage a self-centered approach to interpersonal relations. Although this text deals with many of the same issues as self-realization programs, the codependency movement, and self-help books, its philosophy and approach differ considerably from theirs.

Psychology is both a science and a profession that focuses on behavior and related mental and physiological processes. Adjustment is a broad area of study in psychology concerned with how people adapt effectively or ineffectively to the demands and pressures of everyday life.

The scientific approach to understanding behavior is empirical. Psychologists base their conclusions on formal, systematic, objective research rather than on reasoning, speculation, or common sense. Scientific studies include three key steps: (1) formulating a testable hypothesis, (2) gathering the appropriate data to assess its validity, and (3) reporting the findings. The scientific approach is advantageous in that it puts a premium on clarity and has little tolerance for error.

Experimental research involves manipulating an independent variable to discover its effects on a dependent variable. The experimenter usually does this by comparing experimental and control groups, which must be alike except for the variation created by the manipulation of the independent variable. Experiments allow us to draw conclusions about cause-effect relationships between variables, but many problems do not lend themselves to this approach.

Psychologists conduct correlational research when they are unable to exert control over the variables they want to study. The correlation coefficient is a numerical index of the degree of relationship between two variables. Correlational research methods include naturalistic observation, case studies, and surveys. Correlational research allows us to investigate issues that may not be open to experimental study, but it cannot demonstrate that two variables are causally related.

A scientific analysis of happiness reveals that many common-sense notions about the roots of happiness appear to be incorrect. The only factors that are clearly and strongly related to happiness are love and marriage, work satisfaction, and personality. There are no simple recipes for achieving happiness, but it helps to understand that happiness is a relative concept mediated by our highly subjective assessments of our lives.

We turn next to an example of how psychological research can be applied to everyday problems. In our first application section, we'll review evidence related to the challenge of being a successful student.

APPLICATION Improving Academic Performance

Answer the following true or false.

1.

It's a good idea to study in as many different locations (your bedroom or kitchen, the library, lounges around school, and so forth) as possible.

2.

If you have a professor who delivers chaotic, hard-to-follow lectures, there is little point in attending class.

3.

Cramming the night before an exam is an efficient way to study.

4.

In taking lecture notes, you should try to be a "human tape recorder" (that is, take down everything exactly as your professor says it).

5.

Outlining reading assignments is a waste of time.

As you will soon learn, all of the statements on the left are false. If you answered them all correctly, you may already have acquired the kinds of skills and habits that lead to academic success. If so, however, you are not typical. Today a huge number of students enter college with remarkably poor study skills and habits—and it's not entirely their fault. Our educational system generally does not provide much in the way of formal instruction on good study techniques. In this first Application we will try to remedy this oversight to some extent by sharing with you some insights that psychology can provide on how to improve your academic performance. We will discuss how to promote better study habits, how to enhance reading efforts, how to get more out of lectures, how to make your memory more effective, and how to improve your test-taking strategies.

Developing Sound Study Habits

Effective study is crucial to success in college. You may run into a few classmates who boast about getting good grades without studying. But you can be sure that if they perform well on exams, they study. Students who claim otherwise simply want to be viewed as extremely bright rather than studious.

Learning can be immensely gratifying, but studying is usually hard work. The first step toward effective study habits is to face this reality. You don't have to feel guilty if you don't look forward to studying. Most students don't. Once you accept the premise that studying doesn't come naturally, it should be clear that you need to set up an organized program to promote adequate study. Such a program should include the following steps.

1. *Set up a schedule for studying.* If you wait until the urge to study hits you, you may still be waiting when the exam rolls around. Thus it is important to allocate definite times to studying. Review your time obligations (work, housekeeping, and so on) and figure out in advance when you can study. In allotting certain times to studying, keep in mind that you need to be wide awake and alert. It won't do you much good to plan on studying when you're likely to be very tired. Be realistic, too, about how long you can study at one time before you wear down from fatigue. Allow time for study breaks; they can revive sagging concentration.

It's important to write down your study schedule. Writing it down serves as a reminder and increases your commitment to the schedule. You should begin by setting up a general schedule for the quarter or semester, like the one shown in Figure 1.12. Then, at the beginning of each week, plan the specific assignments that

you intend to work on during each study session. This approach should help you to avoid cramming for exams at the last minute.

In planning your weekly schedule, try to avoid the tendency to put off work on major tasks such as term papers and reports. Time management experts, such as Alan Lakein (1973), point out that many of us tend to tackle simple, routine tasks first and save larger tasks for later, when we supposedly will have more time. This common tendency leads many of us to delay work on major assignments until it's too late to do a good job. You can avoid this trap by breaking major assignments into smaller component tasks that you schedule individually.

2. *Find a place to study where you can concentrate.* Where you study is also important. The key is to find a place where distractions are likely to be minimal. Most people cannot study effectively while watching TV, listening to the stereo, or overhearing conversations. Don't depend on willpower to carry you through these distractions. It's much easier to plan ahead and avoid the distractions altogether.

There is evidence that it helps to set up one or two specific places for study. If possible, use these places for nothing else. These places may become strongly associated with studying, so that they serve as cues that evoke good study behavior (Beneke & Harris, 1972). In contrast, places

Although some students downplay the significance of effective study, sound study habits are crucial to academic success.

FIGURE 1.12
A typical activity schedule
One student's general activity schedule for a semester is shown here. Each week the student fills in the specific assignments to work on during the upcoming study sessions.

	Mon	Tues	Wed	Thurs	Fri	Sat	Sun
6 A.M.							
7 A.M.							
8 A.M.						Work	
9 A.M.	History	Study	History	Study	History	Work	
10 A.M.	Psych	French	Psych	French	Psych	Work	
11 A.M.	Study		Study		Study	Work	
NOON	Math	Study	Math	Study	Math	Work	Study
1 P.M.							Study
2 P.M.	Study	English	Study	English	Study		Study
3 P.M.	Study		Study		Study		Study
4 P.M.							
5 P.M.							
6 P.M.	Work	Study	Study	Work			Study
7 P.M.	Work	Study	Study	Work			Study
8 P.M.	Work	Study	Study	Work			Study
9 P.M.	Work	Study	Study	Work			Study
10 P.M.	Work			Work			
11 P.M.							

associated with other activities may serve as cues for these other activities. Studying in your kitchen, for example, may evoke more eating than reading.

3. *Reward your studying.* One of the reasons it is so difficult to motivate oneself to study regularly is that the payoffs for studying often lie in the distant future. The ultimate reward, a degree, may be years away. Even more short-term rewards, such as an A in the course, may be weeks or months away. To combat this problem, it helps to give yourself immediate rewards for studying. It is easier to motivate yourself to study if you reward yourself with a tangible payoff, such as a snack, TV show, or phone call to a friend, when you finish. Thus you should set realistic study goals for yourself and then reward yourself when you meet them. This systematic manipulation of rewards involves harnessing the principles of *behavior modification*, which are described in some detail in the Chapter 4 Application.

Improving Your Reading

Much of your study time is spent reading and absorbing information. *These efforts must be active.* If you engage in passive reading, the information will pass right through you. Many students deceive themselves into thinking that they are studying by running a marker through a few sentences here and there in their book. If this isn't done with thoughtful selectivity, the student is simply turning a textbook into a coloring book. Underlining in your text can be useful, but you have to distinguish between important ideas and mere supportive material.

There are several ways to attack your reading assignments actively. One of the more worthwhile strategies is Robinson's (1970) SQ3R method. *SQ3R is a study system that consists of five steps—survey, question, read, recite, and review—designed to promote effective reading.* Its name is an abbreviation for the five steps in the procedure:

Step 1: Survey. Before you plunge into the actual reading, glance over the topic headings in the chapter and try to get an overview of the material. Try to understand how the various chapter segments are related. If a chapter outline or summary is provided, consult it to get a feel for the chapter. If you know where the chapter is going, you can better appreciate and organize the information you are about to read.

Step 2: Question. Once you have an overview of your reading assignment, proceed through it one section at a time. Take a look at the heading of the first section and convert it into a question. This is usually quite a simple process. If the heading is "Prenatal Risk Factors," your question should be "What are sources of risk during prenatal development?" If the heading is "Stereotyping," your question should be "What is stereotyping?" Asking these questions gets you actively involved in your reading and helps you to identify the main ideas.

Step 3: Read. Only now, in the third step, are you ready to sink your teeth into the reading. Read only the specific section that you have decided to tackle. Read it with an eye toward answering the question that you just formulated. If necessary, reread the section until you can answer that question. Decide whether the segment addresses any other important questions and answer these as well.

Step 4: Recite. Now that you can answer the key question for the section, recite it out loud to yourself in your own words. Use your own words because that requires understanding instead of simple memorization. Don't move

Obviously, this procedure will require you to formulate some questions without the benefit of topic headings. However, the headings are not absolutely necessary for the use of this technique. If you don't have enough headings, you can simply reverse the order of steps 2 and 3. Read the paragraph first and then formulate a question that addresses the basic idea of the paragraph. The point is that you can be flexible in your use of the SQ3R technique. *What makes SQ3R effective is that it breaks a reading assignment down into manageable segments and requires understanding before you move on.* Any method that leads you toward these goals should enhance your reading.

It is easier to use the SQ3R method when your textbook has plenty of topic headings. This brings up another worthwhile point about improving your reading. It pays to take advantage of the various learning aids incorporated in many textbooks. If a book provides a chapter outline or chapter summary, don't ignore it. These elements can help you to recognize the important points in the chapter and to understand how the various parts of the chapter are interrelated. If your book furnishes learning objectives, use them. They tell you what you should get out of your reading.

Getting More out of Lectures

Although lectures are sometimes boring and tedious, it is a simple fact that poor class attendance is associated with poor grades. Lindgren (1969) found, for example, that absences from class were much more common among "unsuccessful" students (grade average: C– or below) than among "successful" students (grade average: B or above), as Figure 1.13 indicates. Even if your instructor delivers hard-to-follow lectures from which you learn virtually nothing, it is still important to go to class. If nothing else, you'll get a feel for the way the instructor thinks. This insight can help you to anticipate the content of exams and to respond in the manner your professor expects.

Fortunately, most lectures are

on to the next section until you understand the main idea(s) of the present section. You may want to write down these ideas for review later. When you have fully digested the first section, go on to the next. Repeat steps 2 through 4 with the next section. Once you have mastered the crucial points there, you can go on again. Keep repeating steps 2 through 4, section by section, until you finish the chapter.

Step 5: Review. When you have read the chapter, test and refresh your memory by going back over the key points. Repeat your questions and try to answer them without consulting your book or notes. This review should fortify your retention of the main ideas and should alert you to any key ideas that you haven't mastered. It should also help you to see the relationships between the main ideas.

The SQ3R method does not have to be applied rigidly. For example, it is often wise to break your reading assignment down into smaller segments than those separated by section headings. In fact, you should probably apply SQ3R to many texts on a paragraph-by-paragraph basis.

reasonably coherent. Research indicates that accurate note taking is related to better test performance (Palkovitz & Lore, 1980). Good note taking requires you actively to process lecture information in ways that should enhance both memory and understanding. Books on study skills (Pauk, 1984; Sotiriou, 1989) offer suggestions on how to take good lecture notes. Some of them are summarized here.

• Extracting information from lectures requires *active listening procedures,* which are described in more detail in Chapter 6. Focus full attention on the speaker. Try to anticipate what's coming and search for deeper meanings. Pay attention to nonverbal signals that may serve to clarify the lecturer's intent or meaning.

• When course material is especially complex and difficult, it is a good idea to prepare for the lecture by reading ahead on the scheduled subject in your text. Then you have less brand-new information to digest.

• You should not try to be a human tape recorder. Instead, try to write down the lecturer's thoughts in your own words. This practice forces you to organize the ideas in a way that makes sense to you. In taking notes, pay attention to clues about what is most important. Many instructors give subtle and not-so-subtle clues about what is important. These clues may range from simply repeating main points to saying such things as "You'll run into this again."

• Asking questions during lec-

RECOMMENDED READING

College Learning and Study Skills

by Debbie G. Longman and Rhonda H. Atkinson (West, 1988, 1991)

Twenty to 30 books are currently available on how to survive the trials and tribulations of college life. Most of them are sound, but this new entry stands out as one of the very best. The book covers the full range of topics relevant to success in college, including curriculum planning, choosing a major, time management, study techniques, how to improve memory, testwiseness, library research, and how to write papers. It is easy to read and includes an extensive collection of self-analysis exercises. Programs designed to improve various academic skills are laid out in a logical, step-by-step format. Each chapter ends with a succinct summary of its major ideas.

Winning the game of higher education is like winning any other game. It consists of the same basic process. First, you decide if you really want to play. If you do, then you gear your attitudes and habits to learning. Next, you learn the rules. To do this, you need a playbook, a college catalog. Third, you learn about the other players–administration, faculty, and other students. Finally, you learn specific plans to improve your playing skills. That's what the rest of this book is about. If you play the game well, you win. If you don't, you're on the bench. Your success or failure depends on you. [1988, p. 4]

Another book worth reading is *College Is Only the Beginning,* by John N. Gardner and A. Jerome Jewler (Wadsworth, 1989). It doesn't have the involving self-analysis exercises found in the book by Longman and Atkinson, but it is loaded with worthwhile advice. Each chapter is written by an expert on the topic. Many chapters are aimed at audiences ignored by other books, including community college students, minority students, disabled students, and returning (older) students.

tures can be very helpful. This practice keeps you actively involved in the lecture. It also allows you to clarify points you may have misunderstood. Many students are more bashful about asking questions than they should be. They don't realize that most professors welcome questions.

Applying the Principles of Memory

Scientific investigation of memory processes dates back to 1885, when Hermann Ebbinghaus published a series of insightful studies. During the 100-odd years

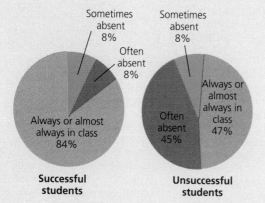

Successful students

Unsuccessful students

FIGURE 1.13
Class attendance of successful and unsuccessful students
Lindgren (1969) found that attendance was much better among successful students than among unsuccessful students.

since then, psychologists have formulated several principles that are relevant to effective study.

Engage in Adequate Practice

Practice makes perfect, or so you've heard. In reality, practice is not likely to guarantee perfection, but repeatedly reviewing information usually leads to improved retention. Studies show that retention improves with increased rehearsal. Continued rehearsal may also pay off by improving your *understanding* of assigned material (Bromage & Mayer, 1986). As you go over information again and again, your increased familiarity with the material may permit you to focus selectively on the most important points, thus enhancing your understanding.

There is evidence that it even pays to overlearn material. *Overlearning* is continued rehearsal of material after you first appear to master it. In one study, after subjects mastered a list of nouns (they recited the list without error), Krueger (1929) required them to continue rehearsing for 50% or 100% more trials. Measuring retention at intervals of up to 28 days, Krueger found that overlearning led to better recall of the list. The implication of this finding is simple: you should not quit rehearsing material as soon as you appear to have mastered it.

Use Distributed Practice

Let's assume that you are going to study nine hours for an exam. Is it better to cram all of your study into one nine-hour period (massed practice) or distribute it among, say, three three-hour periods on successive days (distributed practice)? The evidence indicates that retention tends to be greater after distributed practice than after massed practice, especially if the intervals between practice periods are fairly long, such as 24 hours (Zechmeister & Nyberg, 1982). The inefficiency of massed practice makes cramming an ill-advised study strategy for most students. Cramming will strain your memorization capabilities and tax your energy level. It may also stoke the fires of test anxiety.

Minimize Interference

Interference occurs when people forget information because of competition from other learned material. Research suggests that interference is a major cause of forgetting, so you'll probably want to think about how you can minimize it. This is an especially important point for students because memorizing information for one course can interfere with retention of information learned for another course. It may help to allocate study for specific courses to specific days. Thorndyke and Hayes-Roth (1979) found that similar material produced less interference when it was learned on different days. Thus the day before an exam in a course, it is probably best to study for that course only. If the demands of other courses make that impossible, study the test material last.

Of course, studying for other classes is not the only source of interference in a student's life. Other normal waking activities also produce interference. Therefore, it is a good idea to conduct one last, thorough review of material as close to exam time as possible (Anderson, 1980). This last-minute review helps you to avoid memory loss due to interference from intervening activities.

Organize Information

Retention tends to be greater when information is well organized. Gordon Bower (1970) has shown that hierarchical organization is particularly helpful. Hence one of the most potent weapons in your arsenal of study techniques is to outline reading assignments. Outlining is probably too time-consuming to do for every class. In particularly important or particularly difficult classes, however, it is worth the effort, as it can greatly improve retention.

Use Verbal Mnemonics

The more meaningful people can make information, the better they retain it (Raugh & Atkinson, 1975). A very useful strategy is to make material *personally* meaningful. When you read your textbooks, try to relate information to your own life and experience. If you're reading in your psychology text about the personality trait of assertiveness, for example, you can think of someone you know who is very assertive.

Of course, it's not always easy to make something personally meaningful. When you study chemistry, you may have a hard time relating to polymers at a personal level. This problem has led to the development of many *mnemonic devices,* or strategies for enhancing memory, which are designed to make abstract material more meaningful.

Acrostics and acronyms. Acrostics are phrases (or poems) in which the first letter of each word (or line) functions as a cue to help you recall the abstract words that begin with the same letters. You may remember the order of musical notes, for example, by reciting "**E**very **g**ood **b**oy **d**oes **f**ine" (or "**d**eserves **f**avor"). A variation on acrostics is the *acronym*—a word formed out of the first letters of a series of words. Students memorizing the order of colors in the light spectrum often store the name "Roy G. Biv" to remember **r**ed, **o**range, **y**ellow, **g**reen, **b**lue, **i**ndigo, and **v**iolet.

Narrative methods. Another useful way to remember a list of words is to create a story that includes all of the words in the right order. The narrative increases the meaningfulness of the words and links them in a specific order. Examples of this technique can be seen in Figure 1.14. Bower and Clark (1969) found that this procedure enhanced subjects' recall of lists of unrelated words.

Why—and how—would you use the narrative method? Let's assume that you always manage to forget to put one item in your gym bag on your way to the pool. Short of pasting a list on the inside of the bag, how can you remember everything you need? You could make up a story that includes the items you need.

The wind and rain in COMBINATION LOCKED out the rescue efforts—nearly. CAP, the flying ace, TOWELED the SOAP from his eyes, pulled his GOGGLES from his SUIT pocket, and COMBED the BRUSH for survivors.

Word Lists to Be Memorized and Stories Constructed from Them	
Word lists	Stories
Bird Costume Mailbox Head River Nurse Theater Wax Eyelid Furnace	A man dressed in a *Bird Costume* and wearing a *Mailbox* on his *Head* was seen leaping into the *River*. A *Nurse* ran out of a nearby *Theater* and applied *Wax* to his *Eyelids*, but her efforts were in vain. He died and was tossed into the *Furnace*.
Rustler Penthouse Mountain Sloth Tavern Fuzz Gland Antler Pencil Vitamin	A *Rustler* lived in a *Penthouse* on top of a *Mountain*. His specialty was the three-toed *Sloth*. He would take his captive animals to a *Tavern* where he would remove *Fuzz* from their *Glands*. Unfortunately, all this exposure to sloth fuzz caused him to grow *Antlers*. So he gave up his profession and went to work in a *Pencil* factory. As a precaution he also took a lot of *Vitamin* E.

FIGURE 1.14
The narrative method
Two examples of the narrative method for memorizing lists are shown here (Bower & Clark, 1969). The words to be memorized are listed on the left, and the stories constructed to remember them are shown on the right.

Rhymes. Another verbal mnemonic that we often rely on is rhyming. You've probably repeated "*I* before *e* except after *c*" thousands of times. Perhaps you also remember the number of days in each month with the old standby, "Thirty days hath September . . ." Rhyming something to remember it is an old and very useful trick.

Use Visual Imagery

Memory can be improved through the use of visual imagery. One influential theory (Paivio, 1986) proposes that visual images create a second memory code and that two codes are better than one. Many popular mnemonic devices depend on visual imagery.

Link method. The *link method* involves forming a mental image of items to be remembered in a way that links them together. Suppose you are going to stop at the drugstore on the way home and you need to remember to pick up a news magazine, shaving cream, film, and pens. To remember these items, you might visualize a public figure likely to be in the magazine shaving with a pen while being photographed. There is evidence that the more bizarre you make your image, the more helpful it will be (McDaniel & Einstein, 1986).

Method of loci. The *method of loci* involves taking an imaginary walk along a familiar path along which you have associated images of items you want to remember with certain locations. The first step is to commit to memory a series of loci, or places along a path. Usually these loci are specific locations in your home or neighborhood. Then envision each thing you want to remember in one of these locations. Try to form distinctive, vivid images. When you need to remember the items, imagine yourself walking along the path. The various loci on your path should serve as retrieval cues for the images that you formed (see Figure 1.15). The method of loci ensures that items are remembered in their correct order because the order is determined by the sequence of locations along the pathway. This method has demonstrated value for memorizing lists (Crovitz, 1971).

Improving Test-Taking Strategies

Let's face it: some students are better than others at taking tests. *Testwiseness* is the ability to use the characteristics and formats of an exam to maximize one's score. Students clearly vary in testwiseness, and these variations influence performance on exams (Fagley, 1987; Sarnacki, 1979). Testwiseness is not a substitute for knowledge of the subject matter; but, skill in taking tests can help you to show what you know when it is critical to do so.

General Tips

The principles of testwiseness were first described by Millman, Bishop, and Ebel (1965). Let's look at some of their general ideas.

• If efficient use of time appears crucial, set up a mental schedule for progress through the test. Make a mental note to check whether you're one-third finished when one third of your time is gone. You may want to check again at the two-thirds time mark.

• Do not waste time by excessive pondering over troublesome, difficult-to-answer items. If you have no idea at all what the answer is, just guess and go on. If you think you need to devote a good deal of time to the item, skip it and mark it so you can return to it later if time permits.

• If you complete all of the questions and still have some time remaining, review the test. Make sure that you have recorded your answers correctly. If you were unsure of some answers, go back and reconsider them.

FIGURE 1.15
The method of loci
In this example (from Bower, 1970), a person about to go shopping pairs items to be remembered with familiar places (loci) arranged in a natural sequence: (1) hot dogs/driveway; (2) cat food/garage; (3) tomatoes/front door; (4) bananas/coat closet; (5) whiskey/kitchen sink. As the last panel shows, the shopper recalls the items by mentally touring the loci associated with them.

• Adopt the appropriate level of sophistication for the test. Don't read things into questions. Sometimes students make things more complex than they were intended to be. Often simple-looking questions are just what they appear to be—simple.

• Unless it is explicitly forbidden to do so, don't hesitate to ask the examiner to clarify a question when necessary. Many examiners will graciously provide a great deal of useful information.

Tips for Multiple-Choice Exams

Sound test-taking strategies are especially important on multiple-choice (and true-false) exams. Questions of these types often include clues that may lead you to the correct answer (Mentzer, 1982; Weiten, 1984). You may be able to improve your performance on such tests by considering the following points.

• As you read the stem of each multiple-choice question, *anticipate* the answer if you can, before looking at the options. If the answer you anticipated is found among the options, there is a high probability that it is correct.

• Even if you find your anticipated answer among the options, you should always continue through and read all the options. Perhaps another option farther down the list encompasses the one you anticipated. You should always read each question completely.

• Learn to eliminate quickly options that are highly implausible. Many questions have only two plausible options, accompanied by "throwaway" options for filler. You should work at spotting these implausible options so you can quickly discard them and narrow your search.

• Be alert to the fact that examiners sometimes "give away" information relevant to one question in another test item.

• On items that have "all of the above" as an option, if you know that two of the options are correct, you should choose "all of the above." If you are confident that any one of the options is incorrect, you should eliminate both the incorrect option and "all of the above," and choose from the remaining options.

• Although there will always be exceptions, options that are more detailed than the others tend to be correct. Hence it's a good idea to pay special attention to options that are extra-long or highly specific.

• Options that create broad, sweeping generalizations tend to be incorrect. Be vigilant for words such as *always, never, necessarily, only, must, completely, totally,* and so forth, which create improbable assertions.

•Options that create carefully qualified statements tend to be correct. Words such as *often, sometimes, perhaps, may,* and *generally* tend to show up in these well-qualified statements.

In summary, sound study skills and habits are crucial to academic success. Intelligence alone won't do the job (although it certainly helps). Good academic skills do not develop overnight. They are acquired gradually, so be patient with yourself. Fortunately, tasks such as reading textbooks, writing papers, and taking tests get easier with practice. Ultimately, you'll find that the rewards—knowledge, a sense of accomplishment, and progress toward a degree—are worth the effort.

CHAPTER 1 REVIEW

Key Learning Objectives

1. Explain what is meant by the paradox of progress.
2. Summarize the theme of Fromm's book *Escape from Freedom*.
3. Summarize the text's critique of The Forum, Scientology, and Silva Mind Control.
4. Explain the key ideas of codependency theory and summarize the text's critique of these ideas.
5. List four problems that are common in popular self-help books.
6. Summarize advice about what to look for in quality self-help books.
7. Describe the two key facets of psychology and explain the concept of adjustment.
8. Describe three major steps in a scientific investigation.
9. Explain two advantages of the scientific approach to understanding behavior.
10. Describe the experimental method, distinguishing between independent and dependent variables and between experimental and control groups.
11. Distinguish between positive and negative correlation and explain what the size of a correlation coefficient indicates.
12. Describe the three correlational methods discussed in the text.
13. Compare the advantages and disadvantages of experimental and correlational research.
14. List the various factors that empirical research suggests are not crucial ingredients of happiness.
15. Discuss the three factors that do appear to be crucial ingredients of happiness and the conclusions drawn about the determinants of happiness.
16. List three steps in the development of sound study habits.
17. Describe the SQ3R method and what makes it effective.
18. Summarize advice on how to get more out of lectures.
19. Summarize how memory is influenced by practice, interference, and organization.
20. Describe several verbal and visual mnemonic devices.
21. Summarize advice on improving test-taking strategies.

Key Terms

adjustment
behavior
case study
clinical psychology
control group
correlation
correlation coefficient
dependent variable
empiricism
experiment
experimental group
hypothesis
independent variable

interference
mnemonic devices
naturalistic observation
operational definition
overlearning
placebo effects
psychology
SQ3R
subjects
surveys
testwiseness
variables

Key People

Erich Fromm

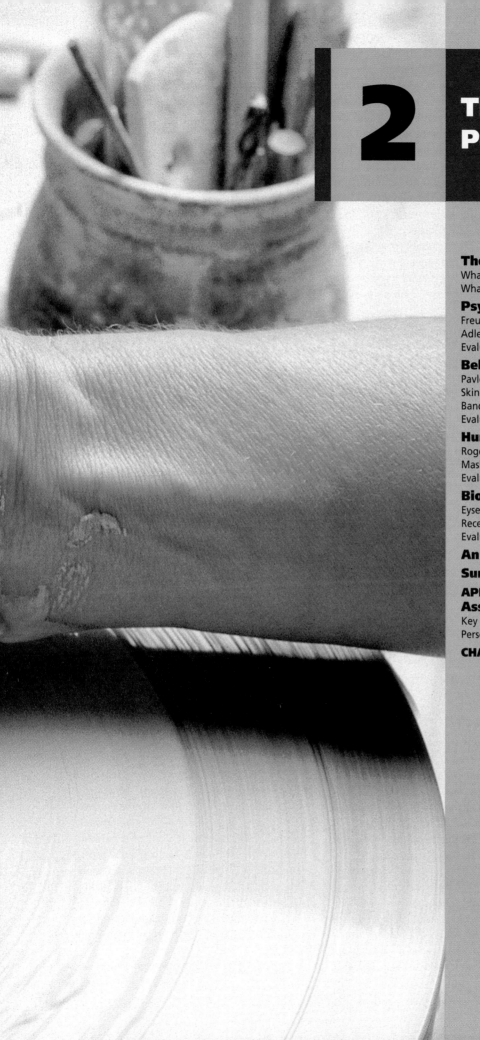

2 Theories of Personality

MAGINE THAT YOU ARE HURTLING upward in an elevator with three other people when suddenly the power goes out and the elevator grinds to a halt 45 stories above the ground. Your three companions may adjust to this predicament in different ways. One may crack jokes to relieve tension. Another may make ominous predictions that "we'll never get out of here." The third person may calmly think about how to escape from the elevator. These people respond to the same stressful situation in distinctive ways because each person has a distinct personality. Our personality significantly influences our pattern of adjustment. Thus theories intended to explain personality can contribute to our effort to understand adjustment processes.

In this chapter we will introduce you to various theories that attempt to explain the structure and development of personality. Our review of personality theory will also serve to acquaint you with four major theoretical perspectives in psychology: the psychodynamic, behavioral, humanistic, and biological perspectives. These theoretical approaches are conceptual models that help us explain behavior. Familiarity with them will help you understand many of the ideas that you will encounter in this book, as well as in other books about psychology.

The Nature of Personality

 o discuss theories of personality effectively, we need to digress for a moment to examine a definition of personality and to discuss the concept of personality traits.

What Is Personality?

What do you mean if you say that a friend has an optimistic personality? Your assertion indicates that the person has a fairly *consistent tendency* to behave in a cheerful, hopeful, enthusiastic way, looking at the bright side of things, across a wide variety of situations. In a similar vein, if you note that a friend has an "outgoing" personality, you mean that she or he consistently behaves in a friendly, open, and extraverted manner in a variety of circumstances. Although none of us are entirely consistent in our behavior, this quality of *consistency across situations* lies at the core of the concept of personality.

Distinctiveness is also central to the concept of personality. We all have traits seen in other people, but we each have our own, distinctive set of personality traits. Each of us is unique, and all of us, like those people in the stalled elevator, respond to situations in our own way. Thus we use the concept of personality to explain why we don't all act alike in the same situation.

In summary, we use personality to explain (1) the stability in a person's behavior over time and across situations (consistency) and (2) the behavioral differences among people in reaction to the same situation (distinctiveness). We can combine these ideas into the following definition: **personality refers to an individual's unique constellation of consistent behavioral traits.** Let's look more closely at the concept of traits.

What Are Personality Traits?

We all make such remarks as "Melanie is very *shrewd*" or "Doug is too *timid* to do well in that job" or "I wish I could be as *self-assured* as Marlene." When we attempt to describe an individual's personality, we usually do so in terms of specific aspects of personality, called *traits*. **A personality trait is a durable disposition to behave in a particular way in a variety of situations.** Adjectives such as honest, dependable, moody, impulsive, suspicious, anxious, excitable, domineering, and friendly describe dispositions that represent personality traits.

Most approaches to personality assume that some traits are more basic than others. According to this notion, a small number of fundamental traits determine other, more superficial traits. For example, a person's tendency to be impulsive, restless, irritable, boisterous, and impatient might all derive from a more basic tendency to be excitable.

Gordon Allport (1937, 1961) was one of the first theorists to make systematic distinctions among traits in accordance with their importance. After sifting through an unabridged dictionary, Allport identified over 4500 personality traits. To impose some order on this chaos, he distinguished between three levels of traits. **A cardinal trait is a dominant trait that permeates nearly all of a person's behavior.** The influence of a cardinal trait is overwhelming. Mother Teresa's altruism, Machiavelli's manipulativeness, and William F. Buckley's arrogance are typical of cardinal traits. According to Allport, cardinal traits are rare; only a small minority of people display them.

In Allport's model, **central traits are**

prominent, general dispositions found in anyone. They are the basic building blocks of personality. Central traits are very influential, but they do not rule our behavior in the way cardinal traits do. How many central traits do we usually have? Allport's research led him to conclude that most of us have only five to ten central traits.

At the bottom of Allport's hierarchy are secondary traits. **Secondary traits are less consistent dispositions that surface in some situations but not in others.** A person may be passive in most circumstances, for example, but highly aggressive in dealing with subordinates at work. Such occasional aggressiveness is a secondary trait.

Following Allport's lead, several psychologists have taken on the challenge of identifying the basic traits that form the core of personality. Raymond Cattell (1950, 1966) has used complex statistical analyses to reduce Allport's list of traits to just 16 basic dimensions of personality, which he calls *source traits*. Cattell believes that all our other traits are derived from our source traits. He asserts further that we can thoroughly describe an individual's personality by measuring these 16 traits. Indeed, they are the 16 dimensions of personality measured by Cattell's widely used Sixteen Personality Factor Questionnaire (see Figure 2.21 in the application section).

More recently Robert McCrae and Paul Costa (1985, 1987) have arrived at an even simpler *five-factor model of personality*. McCrae and Costa maintain that the vast majority of personality traits derive from just five critical traits: (1) neuroticism, (2) extraversion, (3) openness to experience, (4) agreeableness, and (5) conscientiousness. Widely dubbed the "big five," these dimensions of personality are described in Figure 2.1. Like Cattell, McCrae and Costa maintain that personality can be described adequately by measurement of the basic traits they have identified. Their bold proposal to reduce the complexity of personality to just five fundamental dimensions is currently generating considerable debate. Although Cattell (1990) still insists that at least 16 trait dimensions are needed to account for the variations in personality, the evidence in support of the "big five" model is impressive (John, 1990).

The debate about the number of dimensions that must be measured to describe personality is likely to continue for many years to come. As you'll see throughout the chapter, the study of personality is an area in psychology that has a long history of "dueling theories." We'll begin our tour of these theories by examining the influential work of Sigmund Freud and his followers.

McCrae and Costa's Five-Factor Model of Personality	
Basic factor	Subsidiary traits
Neuroticism	Anxious, insecure, guilt-prone, self-conscious
Extraversion	Talkative, sociable, fun-loving, affectionate
Openness to experience	Daring, nonconforming, showing unusually broad interests, imaginative
Agreeableness	Sympathetic, warm, trusting, cooperative
Conscientiousness	Ethical, dependable, productive, purposeful

FIGURE 2.1
The five-factor model of personality
According to McCrae and Costa (1987), all personality traits are derived from the five basic traits listed in the column at the left. These traits are viewed as "higher-order" dimensions of personality, which determine the "lower-order" traits seen in the right column.

Psychodynamic Perspectives

sychodynamic theories include all the diverse theories descended from the work of Sigmund Freud, which focus on unconscious mental forces. Freud inspired many brilliant scholars to follow in his intellectual footsteps. Some of these followers simply refined and updated Freud's theory. Others veered off in new directions and established independent, albeit related, schools of thought. Today the psychodynamic umbrella covers a large collection of related theories. In this section we'll examine the ideas of Sigmund Freud in some detail and then take a brief look at the work of one of his most significant followers, Alfred Adler. Another psychodynamic theorist, Erik Erikson, is discussed in Chapter 11, where we explore adolescent and adult development.

Freud's Psychoanalytic Theory

Born in 1856, Sigmund Freud grew up in a middle-class Jewish home in Vienna, Austria. He showed an early interest in intellectual pursuits and became an intense, hardworking young man. He dreamed of achieving fame by making an important discovery. His determination was such that in medical school he dissected 400 male eels to prove for the first time that they had testes. His work with eels did not make him famous. His later work with people, however, made him one of the most influential and controversial figures of modern times.

Freud specialized in neurology when he

began his medical practice in Vienna toward the end of the 19th century. Like other neurologists in his era, he often treated people troubled by nervous problems, such as irrational fears, obsessions, and anxieties. Eventually he devoted himself to the treatment of mental disorders by an innovative procedure he developed, called *psychoanalysis*.

Psychoanalysis required lengthy verbal interactions with patients in which Freud probed deep into their lives. Decades of experience with his patients provided much of the inspiration for Freud's theory of personality. He also gathered material by looking inward and examining his own anxieties and conflicts. For over 40 years Freud devoted the last half-hour of each workday to self-analysis.

Freud's theory attracted relatively little attention at first. It took his publisher eight years to sell the 600 copies of the first printing of his classic book, *The Interpretation of Dreams*—a humble beginning for a theorist who would greatly influence modern thought. After this slow beginning, Freud's ideas gradually gained prominence, but his success was not without its costs.

Most of Freud's contemporaries were uncomfortable with his theory for at least three reasons. First, he argued that unconscious forces govern our behavior. This idea was disturbing because it suggested that we are not masters of our own minds. Second, he claimed that childhood experiences strongly determine adult personality. This notion distressed people because it suggested that we are not masters of our own destinies. Third, he said that our personalities are shaped by the way we cope with our sexual urges. This assertion offended the conservative, Victorian values of his time. Thus Freud endured a great deal of criticism, condemnation, and outright ridicule, even after his work began to attract more favorable attention. Let's examine the ideas that generated so much controversy.

Structure of Personality

Freud (1901, 1924) divided personality structure into three components: the id, the ego, and the superego. He saw a person's behavior as the outcome of interactions among these three components.

The *id* is the primitive, instinctive component of personality that operates according to the pleasure principle. Freud referred to the id as the reservoir of psychic energy. He meant that the id housed the raw biological urges (to eat, sleep, defecate, copulate, and so

on) that energize our behavior. The id operates according to the *pleasure principle,* **which demands immediate gratification of its urges.** The id engages in *primary process thinking*, which is primitive, illogical, irrational, and fantasy-oriented.

The *ego* is the decision-making component of personality, which operates according to the reality principle. The ego mediates between the id, with its forceful desires for immediate satisfaction, and the external social world, with its expectations and norms regarding suitable behavior. The ego considers social realities—society's norms, etiquette, rules, and customs—in deciding how to behave. The ego is guided by the *reality principle,* **which seeks to delay gratification of the id's urges until appropriate outlets and situations can be found.** In short, to stay out of trouble, the ego often works to tame the unbridled desires of the id. As Freud put it, the ego is "like a man on horseback, who has to hold in check the superior strength of the horse" (Freud, 1923, p. 15).

In the long run, the ego wants to maximize gratification, just like the id. The ego, however, engages in *secondary process thinking*, which is relatively rational, realistic, and oriented toward problem solving. Thus the ego strives to avoid negative consequences from society and its representatives (for example, punishment by parents or teachers) by behaving "properly." It also attempts to achieve long-range goals that sometimes require it to put off gratification.

While the ego concerns itself with practical realities, the *superego* **is the moral component of personality that incorporates social standards about what represents right and wrong.** Throughout our lives, but especially during childhood, we receive training about what is good and bad behavior. Eventually we internalize many of these social norms. In other words, we truly *accept* certain moral principles, and then *we* put pressure on *ourselves* to live up to these standards. The superego emerges out of the ego around 3 to 5 years of age. In some people the superego can become irrationally demanding in its striving for moral perfection. Such people are plagued by excessive guilt. According to Freud, the id, ego, and superego are distributed across three levels of awareness.

Levels of Awareness

Perhaps Freud's most enduring insight was his recognition of how unconscious forces can influence behavior. He contrasted the unconscious with the conscious and preconscious, creating three levels of awareness. **The *conscious***

Sigmund Freud maintained that underlying forces within us begin interacting early in life to shape our personalities.

consists of whatever you are aware of at a particular point in time. At this moment, for example, your conscious may include the present train of thought in this text and a dim awareness in the back of your mind that your eyes are getting tired and you're beginning to get hungry. **The *preconscious* contains material just beneath the surface of awareness that can be easily retrieved**—your middle name, say, or what you had for supper last night, or an argument you had with a friend yesterday. **The *unconscious* contains thoughts, memories, and desires that are well below the surface of conscious awareness, but that nonetheless exert great influence on our behavior.** Material in your unconscious might include a forgotten trauma in your childhood or hidden feelings of hostility toward a parent.

Freud compared the mind to an iceberg: most of it is hidden beneath the surface (see Figure 2.2). He believed that our unconscious (the area below the surface) is much larger than our conscious or preconscious. In his model, the ego and superego operate at all three levels of awareness. The id, however, is entirely unconscious, expressing its urges at a conscious level through the ego. Of course, the id's desires for immediate satisfaction often trigger internal conflicts with the ego and superego. These conflicts play a key role in Freud's theory.

Conflict and Defense Mechanisms

Freud assumed that our behavior is the outcome of an ongoing series of internal conflicts. Internal battles between the id, ego, and superego are routine. Why? Because the id wants to gratify its urges immediately, but the norms of civilized society frequently dictate otherwise. For example, your id might feel an urge to clobber a co-worker who constantly irritates you. Society frowns on such behavior, however, so your ego would try to hold this urge in check, and you would find yourself in a conflict. You may be experiencing conflict at this very moment. In Freudian terms, your id may be secretly urging you to stop reading this chapter and watch television. Your ego may be weighing this appealing option against your society-induced need to excel in school.

Freud believed that conflicts dominate our lives. He asserted that we career from one conflict to another. The following scenario provides a fanciful illustration of how the three components of personality interact to create constant conflicts.

Imagine your alarm clock ringing obnoxiously as you lurch across the bed to shut it off. It's 7 A.M. and time to get up for your history class. However, your id (operating according to the pleasure principle) urges you to return to the immediate gratification of additional sleep. Your ego (operating according to the reality principle) points out that you really must go to class, since you haven't been able to decipher the stupid textbook on your own. Your id (in its typical unrealistic fashion) smugly assures you that you will get the A that you need. It suggests lying back to dream about how impressed your roommate will be. Just as you're relaxing, your superego jumps into the fray. It tries to make you feel guilty about the tuition your parents paid for the class that you're about to skip. You haven't even gotten out of bed yet—and already a pitched battle is under way in your psyche.

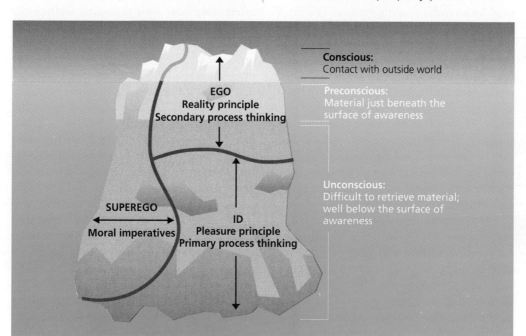

FIGURE 2.2
Freud's model of personality structure
Freud theorized that we have three levels of awareness: the conscious, preconscious, and unconscious. To dramatize the size of the unconscious, he compared it with the portion of an iceberg that lies beneath the water's surface. Freud also divided personality structure into three components—id, ego, and superego—which operate according to different principles and exhibit different modes of thinking. In Freud's model, the id is entirely unconscious, but the ego and superego operate at all three levels of awareness.

Let's say your ego wins the battle. You pull yourself out of bed and head for class. On the way, you pass a donut shop and your id clamors for cinnamon rolls. Your ego reminds you that you're getting overweight and that you're supposed to be on a diet. Your id wins this time. After you've attended your history lecture, your ego reminds you that you need to do some library research for a paper in philosophy. Your id, however, insists on returning to your apartment to watch some sitcom reruns. As you re-enter your apartment, you notice how messy it is. It's your roommates' mess and your id suggests that you tell them off. As you're about to lash out, however, your ego convinces you that diplomacy will be more effective. Three sitcoms later you find yourself in a debate about whether to go to the gym to work out or to the student union to watch MTV. It's only midafternoon—and already you've been through a series of internal conflicts.

Freud believed that conflicts centering on sexual and aggressive impulses were especially likely to have far-reaching consequences. Why did he emphasize sex and aggression? Two factors were prominent in his thinking. First, Freud thought that sex and aggression are subject to more complex and ambiguous social controls than other basic motives. The norms governing sexual and aggressive behavior are subtle, and we often get mixed messages about what is appropriate. Thus he believed that these two drives are the sources of much confusion.

Second, Freud noted that the sex and aggressive drives are thwarted more regularly than other basic biological urges. Think about it: If you get hungry or thirsty, you can simply head for a nearby vending machine or a drinking fountain. But if a department store clerk infuriates you, you aren't likely to slug the clerk, because that is socially unacceptable behavior. Likewise, when you see an attractive person who inspires lustful urges, you don't normally walk up and propose a tryst in a nearby broom closet. There is nothing comparable to vending machines or drinking fountains for the satisfaction of our sexual and aggressive urges. Thus Freud ascribed great importance to these needs because social norms dictate that they be routinely frustrated.

Most of our conflicts are trivial and quickly resolved one way or the other. Occasionally, however, a conflict will linger on for days, months, and even years, creating internal tension. Indeed, Freud believed that lingering conflicts rooted in childhood experiences cause most personality disturbances. More often than not, these prolonged and troublesome conflicts

involve sexual and aggressive impulses that society wants to tame. These conflicts are often played out entirely in the unconscious. Although you may not be aware of these unconscious battles, they can produce anxiety that slips to the surface of conscious awareness. This anxiety can be traced to your ego's worrying that the id will get out of control and do something terrible.

The arousal of anxiety is a crucial event in Freud's theory of personality functioning. Anxiety is distressing, so people try to rid themselves of this unpleasant emotion any way they can. This effort to ward off anxiety often involves the use of defense mechanisms. *Defense mechanisms* **are largely unconscious reactions that protect a person from painful emotions such as anxiety and guilt.** Typically, they are mental maneuvers that work through self-deception. Consider *rationalization,* **which involves the creation of false but plausible excuses to justify unacceptable behavior.** After cheating someone in a business transaction, for example, you might reduce your guilt by rationalizing that "everyone does it."

According to Freud, the most basic and widely used defense mechanism is repression. *Repression* **involves keeping distressing thoughts and feelings buried in the unconscious.** We tend to repress desires that make us feel guilty, conflicts that make us anxious, and memories that are painful. Repression is "motivated forgetting." If you forget a dental appointment or the name of someone you don't like, repression may be at work.

Self-deception can also be seen in projection and displacement. *Projection* **involves attributing your own thoughts, feelings, or motives to another person.** The thoughts we defend ourselves against by projecting them onto someone else are usually throughts that make us feel guilty. If your lust for a co-worker makes you feel guilty, for example, you may attribute any latent sexual tension between the two of you to the *other person's* desire to seduce you. *Displacement* **involves diverting emotional feelings (usually anger) from their original source to a substitute target.** If your boss gives you a hard time at work and you come home and slam the door, kick the dog, and scream at your spouse, you are displacing your anger onto irrelevant targets. Unfortunately, social constraints often force us to hold back our anger until we end up lashing out at the people we love the most.

Other prominent defense mechanisms include reaction formation, regression, and identification. *Reaction formation* **involves** behaving in a way that is exactly the opposite of one's true feelings. Guilt about sexual desires often leads to reaction formation. Freud theorized that many males who ridicule homosexuals are defending against their own latent homosexual impulses. The telltale sign of reaction formation is the exaggerated quality of the opposite behavior. *Regression* involves a **reversion to immature patterns of behavior.** Some adults who feel anxious about their self-worth respond with childish boasting and bragging (as opposed to subtle efforts to impress others). A fired executive who is having difficulty finding a new job might start making ridiculous statements about his incomparable talents and achievements. Such bragging is regressive when it is marked by massive exaggerations that anyone can see through. *Identification* involves **bolstering self-esteem by forming an imaginary or real alliance with some person or group.** Youngsters often shore up precarious feelings of self-worth by identifying with rock stars, movie stars, or famous athletes. Adults may join exclusive country clubs or civic organizations.

Additional examples of the defense mechanisms we've described can be found in Figure 2.3. If you see defensive maneuvers that you have employed, you shouldn't be surprised. According to Freud, we all use defense mechanisms to some extent. They become problematic only when we depend on them excessively. The seeds for psychological disorders are sown when our defenses lead to wholesale distortion of reality.

Various theorists have added to Freud's original list of defenses. We'll examine some of these additional defense mechanisms in Chapter 4, when we discuss the role of defenses in coping with stress. For now, however, let's turn our attention to Freud's ideas about the development of personality.

Development: Psychosexual Stages

Freud made the startling assertion that the foundation of an individual's personality is laid down by the tender age of 5! To shed light on these crucial early years, Freud formulated a stage theory of development. He emphasized how young children deal with their immature but powerful sexual urges (he used the term "sexual" in a general way to refer to many urges for physical pleasure, not just the urge to copulate). According to Freud, these sexual urges shift in focus as children progress from one stage to another. Indeed, the names for the stages (oral, anal, genital, and so on) are based on where children are focusing their erotic energy at the time. Thus *psychosexual stages* are **developmental periods with a characteristic sexual focus that leave their mark on adult personality.**

Freud theorized that each psychosexual stage has its own unique developmental challenges or tasks, as outlined in Figure 2.4. The way these challenges are handled supposedly shapes personality. The notion of *fixation* plays an important role in this process. *Fixation* **involves a failure to move forward from one stage to another as expected.** Essentially, the child's development stalls for a while. Fixation is caused by *excessive gratification* of needs at a particular stage or by *excessive frustration* of those needs. Either way, fixations left over from childhood affect adult personality. Generally, fixation leads to an overemphasis on the psychosexual needs that were prominent during

Defense Mechanisms, with Examples	
Definition	Example
Repression involves keeping distressing thoughts and feelings buried in the unconscious.	A traumatized soldier has no recollection of the details of a close brush with death.
Projection involves attributing one's own thoughts, feelings, or motives to another person.	A woman who dislikes her boss thinks she likes her boss but feels that the boss doesn't like her.
Displacement involves diverting emotional feelings (usually anger) from their original source to a substitute target.	After a parental scolding, a young girl takes her anger out on her little brother.
Reaction formation involves behaving in a way that is exactly the opposite of one's true feelings.	A parent who unconsciously resents a child spoils the child with outlandish gifts.
Regression involves a reversion to immature patterns of behavior.	An adult has a temper tantrum when he doesn't get his way.
Rationalization involves the creation of false but plausible excuses to justify unacceptable behavior.	A student watches TV instead of studying, saying that "additional study wouldn't do any good anyway."
Identification involves bolstering self-esteem by forming an imaginary or real alliance with some person or group.	An insecure young man joins a fraternity to boost his self-esteem.

FIGURE 2.3
Defense mechanisms
According to Freud, we use a variety of defense mechanisms to protect ourselves from painful emotions. Definitions of seven commonly used defense mechanisms are shown at the left; an example of each appears at the right. This list is not exhaustive; other defense mechanisms are discussed in Chapter 4.

FIGURE 2.4
Freud's stages of psychosexual development
Freud theorized that people develop through the series of stages summarized here. The manner in which certain key tasks and experiences are handled during each stage is thought to leave a lasting imprint on one's adult personality.

Freud's Stages of Psychosexual Development

Stage	Approximate ages	Erotic focus	Key tasks and experiences
Oral	0–1	Mouth (sucking, biting)	Weaning (from breast or bottle)
Anal	1–3	Anus (expelling or retaining feces)	Toilet training
Phallic	3–6	Genitals (masturbating)	Identifying with adult role models; coping with oedipal crisis
Latency	6–12	None (sexually repressed)	Expanding social contacts
Genital	Puberty onward	Genitals (being sexually intimate)	Establishing intimate relationships; contributing to society through working

the fixated stage. Freud described a series of five psychosexual stages. Let's examine some of the major features of this developmental sequence.

Oral stage. The oral stage usually encompasses the first year of life. During this stage the main source of erotic stimulation is the mouth (in biting, sucking, chewing, and so on). The way caretakers handle the child's feeding experiences is supposed to be crucial to subsequent development. Freud attributed considerable importance to the manner in which the child is weaned from the breast or the bottle. According to Freud, fixation at the oral stage could form the basis for obsessive eating or smoking later in life (among many other things).

Anal stage. In their second year, children supposedly get their erotic pleasure from their bowel movements, through either the expulsion or retention of the feces. The crucial event at this time is toilet training, society's first systematic effort to regulate the child's biological

urges. Severely punitive toilet training is thought to lead to a variety of possible outcomes. For example, excessive punishment might produce a latent feeling of hostility toward the "trainer," who usually is the mother. This hostility might generalize to women in general. Another possibility is that heavy reliance on punitive measures might lead to an association between genital concerns and the anxiety that the punishment arouses. This genital anxiety derived from severe toilet training could evolve into anxiety about sexual activities later in life.

Phallic stage. In the third through fifth years, the genitals become the focus for the child's erotic energy, largely through self-stimulation. During this pivotal stage the *Oedipus complex* emerges. Little boys develop an erotically tinged preference for their mother. They also feel hostility toward their father, whom they view as a competitor for mom's affection. Little girls develop a special attachment to their father. Around the same time, they learn that their genitals are very different from those of little boys, and they supposedly develop penis envy. According to Freud, the girls feel hostile toward their mother because they blame her for their anatomical "deficiency."

To summarize, **the *Oedipus complex* consists of the child's erotically tinged desires for the other-sex parent, accompanied by feelings of hostility toward the same-sex parent.** Freud named this syndrome after the tragic hero of an ancient Greek legend. According to the legend, Oedipus was separated from his parents at birth. Not knowing the identity of his real parents, he inadvertently killed his father and married his mother. (For many years the term *Oedipus complex* was applied to boys only, and the comparable syndrome in girls was called the *Electra complex*. However, use of a separate term for the female form of this syndrome has diminished in recent years.)

According to Freud, the way parents and

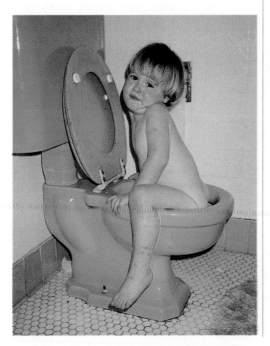

According to Freudian theory, toilet training is the first systematic social effort to control the child's biological urges.

children deal with the sexual and aggressive conflicts inherent in the Oedipus complex is of paramount importance. The child has to resolve the oedipal dilemma by giving up the sexual longings for the parent of the other sex and the hostility felt toward the parent of the same sex. Healthy psychosexual development is supposed to hinge on the resolution of the oedipal conflict. Why? Because continued hostile relations with the same-sex parent may prevent the child from identifying adequately with that parent. Freudian theory predicts that without such identification many aspects of the child's development won't progress as they should.

Latency and genital stages. Freud believed that from age 5 through puberty, the child's sexuality is suppressed—it becomes "latent." Important events during this *latency stage* center on expanding social contacts beyond the family. With the advent of puberty, the child enters into the *genital stage*. Sexual urges reappear and focus on the genitals once again. At this point the sexual energy is normally channeled toward peers of the other sex, rather than toward oneself, as in the phallic stage.

In arguing that the early years shape personality, Freud did not mean that personality development comes to an abrupt halt in middle childhood. He did believe, however, that the foundation for one's adult personality was solidly set by this time. He maintained that future developments would be rooted in early, formative experiences and that significant conflicts in later years would be replays of crises that arose in childhood. Some influential psychodynamic theorists, such as Erik Erikson (1963), have taken issue with this view, arguing that personality evolves across the entire life span. We'll discuss Erikson's theory of development in Chapter 11; for now, let's turn to a theorist who agreed with Freud on the importance of childhood while disagreeing with him on many other matters.

Adler's Individual Psychology

Like Freud, Alfred Adler grew up in Vienna in a middle-class Jewish home. He was a sickly child who struggled to overcome rickets and an almost fatal case of pneumonia. He earned his medical degree and practiced ophthalmology and general medicine before his interest turned to psychiatry. He was a charter member of Freud's inner circle—the Vienna Psychoanalytic Society. Soon, however, he began to develop his own theory of personality, which he called *individual psychology*.

According to Adler (1917, 1927), the foremost human drive is not sexuality but a *striving for superiority*. For Adler, this striving did not necessarily translate into pursuit of dominance or high status. Adler viewed striving for superiority as a universal drive to adapt, improve oneself, and master life's challenges. He noted that young children understandably feel weak and helpless in comparison with more competent older children and adults. These early inferiority feelings supposedly motivate us to acquire new skills and develop new talents.

Adler asserted that everyone has to work to overcome some feelings of inferiority. **Compensation involves efforts to overcome imagined or real inferiorities by developing one's abilities.** Adler believed that compensation was entirely normal. In some people, however, inferiority feelings can become excessive, resulting in what is widely known today as an *inferiority complex*—exaggerated feelings of weakness and inadequacy. Adler thought that either parental pampering or parental neglect (or an actual physical handicap) could cause an inferiority problem. Thus he agreed with Freud on the importance of early childhood, although he focused on different aspects of parent-child relations.

According to Adler, "All neurotic symptoms are safeguards of persons who do not feel adequately equipped or prepared for the problems of life" (Adler, 1964, p. 95). Thus he explained personality disturbances by noting that an inferiority complex can distort the normal process of striving for superiority (see Figure 2.5). He maintained that some people engage in *overcompensation* in order to conceal, even from themselves, their feelings of inferiority. Instead of working to master life's challenges, people with an inferiority complex work to achieve status, gain power over others, and acquire the trappings of success (fancy clothes, impressive cars, or whatever looks important to them). They tend to flaunt their success in an effort to cover up their underlying inferiority complex. The problem is that such people engage in unconscious self-deception, worrying more about *appearances* than about *reality*.

Adler's theory stressed the social context of personality development. It was Adler, for instance, who first focused attention on the possible importance of birth order as a factor in the shaping of personality. He noted that only children, first-borns, second-borns, and subsequent children enter very different social environments. Only children, he theorized, are often spoiled by excessive attention from their parents. He thought that first-borns often are

FIGURE 2.5
Adler's view of personality development
Like Freud, Adler believed that early childhood experiences exert momentous influence over adult personality. However, he focused on children's social interactions rather than on their grappling with their sexuality. According to Adler, the roots of personality disturbances typically lie in excessive parental neglect or pampering.

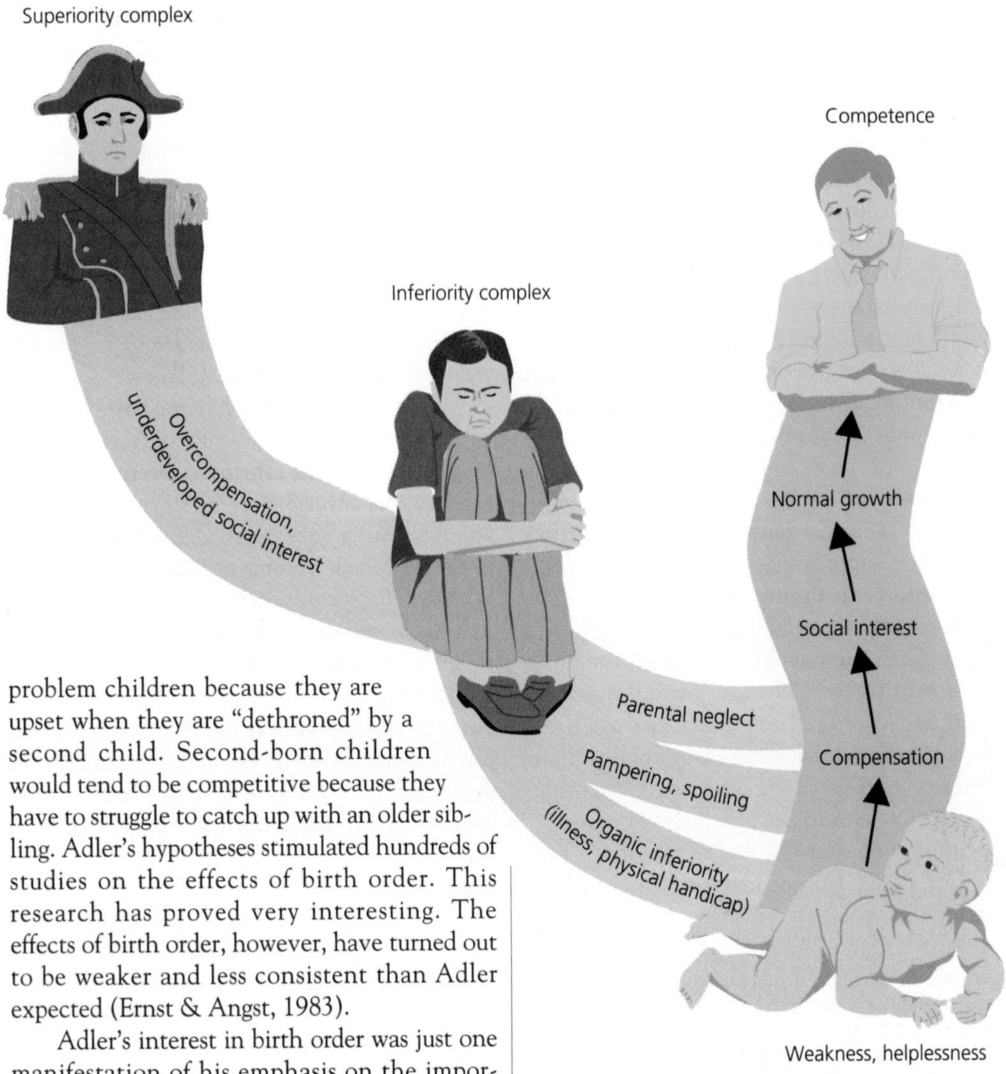

Superiority complex

Competence

Inferiority complex

Overcompensation, underdeveloped social interest

Normal growth

Social interest

Parental neglect

Compensation

Pampering, spoiling

Organic inferiority (illness, physical handicap)

Weakness, helplessness

problem children because they are upset when they are "dethroned" by a second child. Second-born children would tend to be competitive because they have to struggle to catch up with an older sibling. Adler's hypotheses stimulated hundreds of studies on the effects of birth order. This research has proved very interesting. The effects of birth order, however, have turned out to be weaker and less consistent than Adler expected (Ernst & Angst, 1983).

Adler's interest in birth order was just one manifestation of his emphasis on the importance of the social environment in the shaping of personality. The tragedies and heroism that he witnessed as a physician during World War I increased his appreciation of the social context in which we evolve. He concluded that human nature includes a unique *social interest*, an innate sense of kinship and belongingness with the human race. He saw this social interest as the source of humans' willingness to work together for the common good.

Evaluating Psychodynamic Perspectives

The psychodynamic approach has given us several far-reaching theories of personality. These theories have yielded some bold new insights (Westen, 1990). Psychodynamic theory and research have demonstrated (1) that unconscious forces can influence behavior, (2) that internal conflict often plays a key role in generating psychological distress, and (3) that early childhood experiences can exert considerable influence over adult personality. Psychodyna-

mic models have also been praised because they probe beneath the surface of personality and because they focus attention on how personality develops over time. Many widely used concepts in psychology emerged out of psychodynamic theories, including the unconscious, defense mechanisms, and the inferiority complex.

In a more negative vein, psychodynamic formulations have been criticized on several grounds, including the following.

1. *Poor testability*. Scientific investigations require testable hypotheses. Psychodynamic ideas have often been too vague to permit a clear scientific test. Concepts such as the superego, the preconscious, and social interest are difficult to measure.

2. *Inadequate evidence*. The empirical evidence on psychodynamic theories has often been characterized as inadequate. Clinicians rely too heavily on case studies, in which it is easy for them to see what their theory leads them to expect to see. Recent reexaminations of Freud's own clinical work suggest that he

sometimes distorted his patients' case histories to make them mesh with his theory (Sulloway, 1991). Furthermore, the subjects observed in clinical situations are not particularly representative of the population at large. Insofar as researchers have accumulated evidence on psychodynamic theories, it has provided only modest support for the central hypotheses.

3. *Sexism*. Many critics have argued that psychodynamic theories are biased against women. Freud believed that females experienced penis envy, which made them feel inferior to men. He also thought that females tended to develop weaker superegos and to be more prone to neurosis than men. He dismissed female patients' reports of sexual molestation during childhood as mere fantasies. Admittedly, sexism isn't unique to Freudian theories, and the sex bias in modern psychodynamic theories has been reduced to some degree. But the psychodynamic approach has generally provided a male-centered viewpoint.

It's easy to ridicule Freud for such concepts as penis envy and to point to ideas that have turned out to be wrong. Remember, though, that Freud and Adler began to fashion their theories about a century ago. It is not entirely fair to compare these theories with other models that are only a decade old. That's like asking the Wright brothers to race the Concorde. Freud and his psychodynamic colleagues deserve great credit for breaking new ground. Standing at a distance a century later, one has to be impressed by the extraordinary impact that psychodynamic theory has had on modern thought. No other theoretical perspective in psychology has been so influential, except for the one we turn to next—behaviorism.

Behavioral Perspectives

Behaviorism is a theoretical orientation based on the premise that scientific psychology should study observable behavior. Behaviorism has been a major school of thought in psychology since 1913, when John B. Watson published an influential article. Watson argued that psychology should abandon its earlier focus on the mind and mental processes and focus exclusively on overt behavior. He contended that psychology could not study mental processes in a scientific manner because those processes are private and not accessible to public observation.

In completely rejecting mental processes as a suitable subject for scientific study, Watson took an extreme position that is no longer dominant among modern behaviorists. Nonetheless, his influence was enormous, as psychology did shift its primary focus from the study of the mind to the study of behavior.

The behaviorists have shown little interest in internal personality structures similar to Freud's id, ego, and superego, because such structures can't be observed. They prefer to think in terms of response tendencies, which can be observed. Thus most behaviorists view an individual's personality as a *collection of response tendencies that are tied to various stimulus situations*. A specific situation may be associated with several response tendencies that vary in strength, depending on an individual's past experience (see Figure 2.6). Consider the stimulus situation of a large party where you know few people. Your response tendencies in this situation, in order of strength, might be (1) to circulate, speaking to others only if they approach you first, (2) to stick close to the few guests you already know, making no effort to meet anyone new, (3) to withdraw politely by getting wrapped up in your host's book, record, or compact disc collection (or whatever is available), and (4) to leave as soon as you can.

Although behaviorists have shown relatively little interest in personality structure, they have focused extensively on personality *development*. They explain development the same way they explain everything else—through learning. In their scheme, the term *learning* is used very broadly to refer to any durable changes in behavior that are due to experience. Some behaviorists (for example, Dollard & Miller, 1950) agree with Freud on the importance of early childhood experiences, but most see personality development as a life-

FIGURE 2.6
A behavioral view of personality
Behaviorists devote little attention to the structure of personality because it cannot be observed, but they implicitly view personality as a collection of response tendencies. A possible hierarchy of response tendencies associated with a specific stimulus situation is shown here.

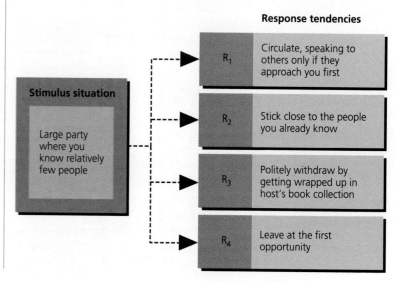

Response tendencies

Stimulus situation	
Large party where you know relatively few people	R₁ — Circulate, speaking to others only if they approach you first
	R₂ — Stick close to the people you already know
	R₃ — Politely withdraw by getting wrapped up in host's book collection
	R₄ — Leave at the first opportunity

long journey. They maintain that personality is shaped through a continual evolutionary process. Hence they see little value in proposing developmental stages. They focus, instead, on how our response tendencies are shaped through classical conditioning, operant conditioning, and observational learning. Let's look at these processes.

Pavlov's Classical Conditioning

Do you go weak in the knees when you get a note at work that tells you to go see your boss? Do you get anxious when you're around important people? When you're driving, does your heart skip a beat at the sight of a police car—even when you're driving under the speed limit? If so, you probably acquired these common responses through classical conditioning. **Classical conditioning is a type of learning in which a neutral stimulus acquires the capacity to evoke a response that was originally evoked by another stimulus.** This process, which is also called *respondent conditioning*, was first described back in 1903 by Ivan Pavlov.

Pavlov was a prominent Russian physiologist who did Nobel Prize–winning research on digestion. He was a dedicated scientist who was obsessed by his research. Legend has it that

Pavlov severely reprimanded an assistant who was late for an experiment because he was trying to avoid street fighting in the midst of the Russian Revolution. The assistant defended his tardiness, saying, "But Professor, there's a revolution going on, with shooting in the streets!" Pavlov supposedly replied, "Next time there's a revolution, get up earlier!" (Fancher, 1979; Gantt, 1975).

The Conditioned Reflex

Pavlov (1906) was studying digestive processes in dogs when he discovered that the dogs could be trained to salivate in response to the sound of a bell. What was so significant about a dog's salivating when a bell was rung? The key was that the bell started out as a *neutral* stimulus; that is, originally it did not produce the response of salivation (after all, why should it?). However, Pavlov managed to change that by pairing the bell with a stimulus (meat powder) that did produce the salivation response. Through this process, the bell acquired the capacity to trigger the response of salivation. What Pavlov had demonstrated was *how learned reflexes are acquired.*

A special vocabulary is associated with classical conditioning. In Pavlov's experiment the bond between the meat powder and salivation was a natural association that was not created through conditioning. In unconditioned bonds, **the *unconditioned stimulus* (UCS) is a stimulus that evokes an unconditioned response without previous conditioning. The *unconditioned response* (UCR) is an unlearned reaction to an unconditioned stimulus that occurs without previous conditioning.**

The link between the bell and salivation, in contrast, was established through conditioning. In conditioned bonds, **the *conditioned stimulus* (CS) is a previously neutral stimulus that has acquired the capacity to evoke a conditioned response through conditioning. The *conditioned response* (CR) is a learned reaction to a conditioned stimulus that occurs because of previous conditioning.** Note that the unconditioned response and conditioned response often involve the same behavior (although they may differ in subtle respects). In Pavlov's initial demonstration, salivation was an unconditioned response when it was evoked by the UCS (meat powder) and a conditioned response when it was evoked by the CS (the bell). The procedures involved in classical conditioning are outlined in Figure 2.7.

Pavlov's discovery came to be called the *conditioned reflex.* Classically conditioned

FIGURE 2.7
The process of classical conditioning
The sequence of events in classical conditioning is outlined here. As we encounter new examples of classical conditioning throughout the book, we will see diagrams like that shown in the fourth panel, which summarizes the process.

Before conditioning
The unconditioned stimulus elicits the unconditioned response, but the neutral stimulus does not

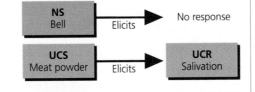

During conditioning
The neutral stimulus is paired with the unconditioned stimulus

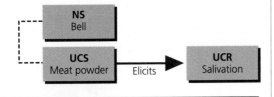

After conditioning
The neutral stimulus alone elicits the response; the neutral stimulus is now a conditioned stimulus, and the response to it is a conditioned response

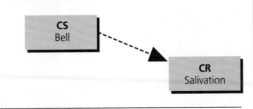

Summary
An originally neutral stimulus comes to elicit a response that it did not previously elicit

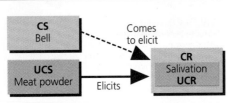

responses are viewed as reflexes because most of them are relatively involuntary. Responses that are products of classical conditioning are said to be *elicited*. This word is meant to convey the idea that these responses are triggered automatically.

Classical Conditioning in Everyday Life

What is the role of classical conditioning in shaping personality in everyday life? Classical conditioning contributes to the acquisition of emotional responses, such as fear and anxiety. This is a relatively small but very important class of responses, as maladaptive emotional reactions underlie many adjustment problems. For example, one middle-aged woman reported being so fearful of bridges that she couldn't drive on interstate highways because of all the viaducts she would have to cross. She was able to pinpoint the source of her phobia. Many years before, when her family would drive to visit her grandmother, they had to cross a little-used, rickety, dilapidated bridge out in the countryside. Her father, in a misguided attempt at humor, made a major production out of these crossings. He would stop short of the bridge and carry on about the enormous danger of the crossing. Obviously, he thought the bridge was safe, or he wouldn't have driven across it. The naive child, however, was terrified by her father's scare tactics, and the bridge became a conditioned stimulus that elicited great fear

(see Figure 2.8). Unfortunately, the fear spilled over to *all* bridges, and 40 years later she was still carrying the burden of this phobia. Although a variety of processes can cause phobias (Marks, 1977), it is clear that classical conditioning is responsible for many of our irrational fears.

Classical conditioning also appears to account for more realistic and moderate anxiety. For example, imagine a news reporter in a high-pressure job who consistently gets negative feedback about his work from his bosses. The negative comments from his supervisors function as a UCS to elicit anxiety. These reprimands are paired with the noise and sight of the newsroom, so that the newsroom becomes a CS that triggers anxiety, even when his supervisors are absent (see Figure 2.9). Our poor reporter may even reach a point at which the mere *thought* of the newsroom elicits anxiety when he is elsewhere.

Fortunately, not every frightening experience leaves a conditioned fear in its wake. Several factors influence whether a conditioned response is acquired in a particular situation. Furthermore, a newly formed stimulus-response bond does not necessarily last indefinitely. The right circumstances can lead to **extinction—the gradual weakening and disappearance of a conditioned response tendency.** What leads to extinction in classical conditioning? The consistent presentation of the CS *alone*, without

Ivan Pavlov

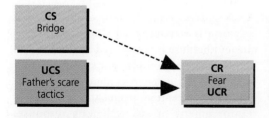

FIGURE 2.8
Classical conditioning of a phobia
Many emotional responses that would otherwise be puzzling can be explained as a result of classical conditioning. In the case of the woman's bridge phobia, the fear originally elicited by her father's scare tactics became a conditioned response to the stimulus of bridges.

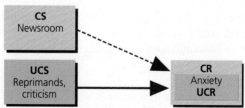

FIGURE 2.9
Classical conditioning of anxiety
A stimulus (in this case, a newsroom) that is frequently paired with anxiety-arousing events (reprimands and criticism) may come to elicit anxiety by itself, through classical conditioning.

the UCS. For example, when Pavlov consistently presented *only* the bell to a previously conditioned dog, the bell gradually stopped eliciting the response of salivation. How long it takes to extinguish a conditioned response depends on many factors. Foremost among them is the strength of the conditioned bond when extinction begins. Some conditioned responses extinguish very quickly, while others are very difficult to weaken.

Skinner's Operant Conditioning

Even Pavlov recognized that classical conditioning was not the only form of conditioning. Classical conditioning best explains reflexive responding controlled by stimuli that *precede* the response. Both animals and humans, however, make many responses that don't fit this description. Consider the response that you are engaging in right now—studying. It is definitely not a reflex (life might be easier if it were). The stimuli that govern it (exams and grades) do not precede it. Instead, your studying response is influenced mainly by events that follow it—specifically, its *consequences*.

This kind of learning is called *operant conditioning*. **Operant conditioning is a form of learning in which voluntary responses come to be controlled by their consequences.** Operant conditioning probably governs a larger share of human behavior than classical conditioning, since most of our responses are voluntary rather than reflexive. Because they are voluntary, operant responses are said to be *emitted* rather than *elicited*.

The study of operant conditioning was led by B. F. Skinner (1953, 1974, 1990), an American psychologist who spent most of his career at Harvard University. Skinner achieved renown for his research on learning in lower organisms, mostly rats and pigeons. Like Pavlov, Skinner never set out to develop a theory of personality. And again like Pavlov, he conducted deceptively simple research that became enormously influential, affecting thinking in all areas of psychology, including the explanation of personality.

The fundamental principle of operant conditioning is uncommonly simple. Skinner demonstrated that organisms tend to repeat those responses that are followed by favorable consequences, and that they tend not to repeat those responses that are followed by neutral or unfavorable consequences. In Skinner's scheme, favorable, neutral, and unfavorable consequences involve reinforcement, extinction, and punishment, respectively. We'll look

at each of these phenomena in turn, and then discuss stimulus control of operant behavior.

The Power of Reinforcement

According to Skinner, reinforcement can occur in two ways, which he called *positive reinforcement* and *negative reinforcement*. **Positive reinforcement occurs when a response is strengthened (increases in frequency) because it is followed by the arrival of a (presumably) pleasant stimulus.** Positive reinforcement is roughly synonymous with reward. Notice, however, that reinforcement is defined *after the fact*, in terms of its effect on behavior. Why? Because reinforcement is subjective. Something that serves as a reinforcer for one person may not function as a reinforcer for another person. Peer approval, for example, is a potent reinforcer for most people, but not for all.

Positive reinforcement motivates much of our everyday behavior. You study hard because good grades are likely to follow as a result. You go to work because this behavior produces paychecks. Perhaps you work extra hard in the hope of winning a promotion or a pay raise. In each of these instances, certain responses occur because they have led to positive outcomes in the past.

Positive reinforcement influences personality development in a straightforward way. Responses followed by pleasant outcomes are strengthened and tend to become habitual patterns of behavior. For example, a youngster may clown around in class and gain appreciative comments and smiles from schoolmates. This social approval will probably reinforce clowning-around behavior (see Figure 2.10). If such behavior is reinforced with some regularity, it will gradually become an integral element of the youth's personality. Similarly, whether or not a youngster develops a trait such as independence, assertiveness, or selfishness depends on whether such behaviors are reinforced by the child's parents and by other influential persons.

Negative reinforcement occurs when a response is strengthened (increases in frequency) because it is followed by the removal of a (presumably) unpleasant stimulus. Don't let the word *negative* here confuse you. Negative reinforcement is reinforcement. Like positive reinforcement, it strengthens a response. However, this strengthening occurs because the response gets rid of an aversive stimulus. Consider a few examples. You rush home in the winter to get out of the cold. You may clean your house to get rid of a mess. Parents often

B. F. Skinner

give in to their children's begging to halt the whining.

Negative reinforcement plays a major role in the development of avoidance tendencies. As you may have noticed, many people tend to avoid facing up to awkward situations and sticky personal problems. This personality trait typically develops because avoidance behavior gets rid of anxiety and is therefore negatively reinforced. Recall our imaginary newspaper reporter, whose work environment (the newsroom) elicits anxiety (as a result of classical conditioning). He may notice that on days when he calls in sick, his anxiety evaporates, so that this response is gradually strengthened—through negative reinforcement (see Figure 2.10). If his avoidance behavior continues to be successful in reducing his anxiety, it may carry over into other areas of his life and become a central aspect of his personality.

Extinction and Punishment

Like the effects of classical conditioning, the effects of operant conditioning may not last forever. Whether a response results from classical or operant conditioning, it may gradually weaken and disappear. Extinction of an operantly conditioned response begins when a previously reinforced response stops producing positive consequences. As extinction progresses, the response typically becomes less and less frequent and eventually disappears.

Thus the response tendencies that make up one's personality are not necessarily permanent. The youngster who found that his classmates reinforced clowning around in grade school, for example, may find that his attempts at comedy earn nothing but indifferent stares in high school. This termination of reinforcement will probably lead to the gradual extinction of the clowning-around behavior. How quickly an operant response extinguishes depends on many factors in the person's earlier reinforcement history.

Some responses may be weakened by punishment. In Skinner's scheme, **punishment occurs when a response is weakened (decreases in frequency) because it is followed by the arrival of a (presumably) unpleasant stimulus.** The concept of punishment in operant conditioning confuses many students on two counts. First, it is often mixed up with negative reinforcement because both involve aversive stimuli. Please note, however, that they are altogether different events with opposite outcomes! A negatively reinforced response leads to the removal of something aversive, so the response

Positive reinforcement

Pleasant stimulus presented

Clowning around → Attention, appreciation

Response **Reinforcer**

Negative reinforcement

Aversive stimulus removed

Calling in sick → Anxiety (⊘)

Response **Reinforcer**

FIGURE 2.10
Positive and negative reinforcement in operant conditioning
Positive reinforcement occurs when a response is followed by a favorable outcome, so that the response is strengthened. In negative reinforcement, the removal (symbolized here by the "No" sign) of an aversive stimulus serves as a reinforcer. Negative reinforcement produces the same result as positive reinforcement: the person's tendency to emit the reinforced response is strengthened (the response becomes more frequent).

is strengthened. A response that is punished leads to the arrival of something aversive, so the response tends to be weakened.

The second source of confusion is the common view of punishment as only a disciplinary procedure used by parents, teachers, and other authority figures. In the operant model, punishment occurs whenever a response leads to negative consequences. Defined in this way, punishment goes far beyond a spanking delivered by a parent or a detention slip handed out by a teacher. If you wear a new outfit and your friends make fun of it and hurt your feelings, for example, your behavior has been punished, and consequently your tendency to wear that clothing will decline. Similarly, if you go to a restaurant and have a horrible meal, in Skinner's ter-

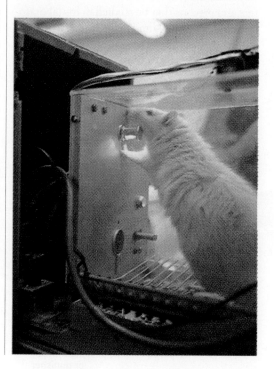

Skinner placed rats and other animal subjects in controlled environments where reinforcement could be regulated and responses accurately measured.

minology, your response has led to punishment.

The impact of punishment on personality development is just the opposite of reinforcement. Generally speaking, those patterns of behavior that lead to punishing (that is, negative) consequences tend to be weakened. If your impulsive decisions always backfire, for example, your tendency to be impulsive should decline.

Stimulus Control of Operant Behavior

Although operant behavior is ultimately controlled by its consequences, stimuli that *precede* a response can also influence operant behavior. If a response is consistently reinforced in the presence of a particular stimulus, that stimulus may come to serve as a signal indicating that the response is likely to lead to reinforcement. Once we pick up on these signals, we tend to respond accordingly. Thus *discriminative stimuli* are cues that influence operant behavior by indicating the probable consequences of a response.

Social behavior is regulated extensively by discriminative stimuli. Consider the behavior of asking someone out for a date. Many people emit this behavior only very cautiously, after receiving many signals (eye contact, smiles, encouraging conversational exchanges) that reinforcement (an affirmative answer) is fairly likely. Learning to read subtle discriminative stimuli in social interactions is a significant part of developing adequate social skills.

According to Skinner (1987), conditioning in humans operates much as it does in the rats and pigeons that he studied in his laboratory. Hence he assumed that conditioning strengthens and weakens our response tendencies "mechanically"—that is, without our conscious participation. Like John Watson (1913) before him, Skinner asserted that we can explain behavior without being concerned about individuals' mental processes.

Skinner's ideas continue to be very influential, but his mechanical view of conditioning

has not gone unchallenged. Such behavioral theorists as Albert Bandura have developed somewhat different behavioral models in which cognition plays a role. *Cognition* refers to the thought processes involved in acquiring knowledge. In other words, cognition is another name for the mental processes in which behaviorists have traditionally shown little interest.

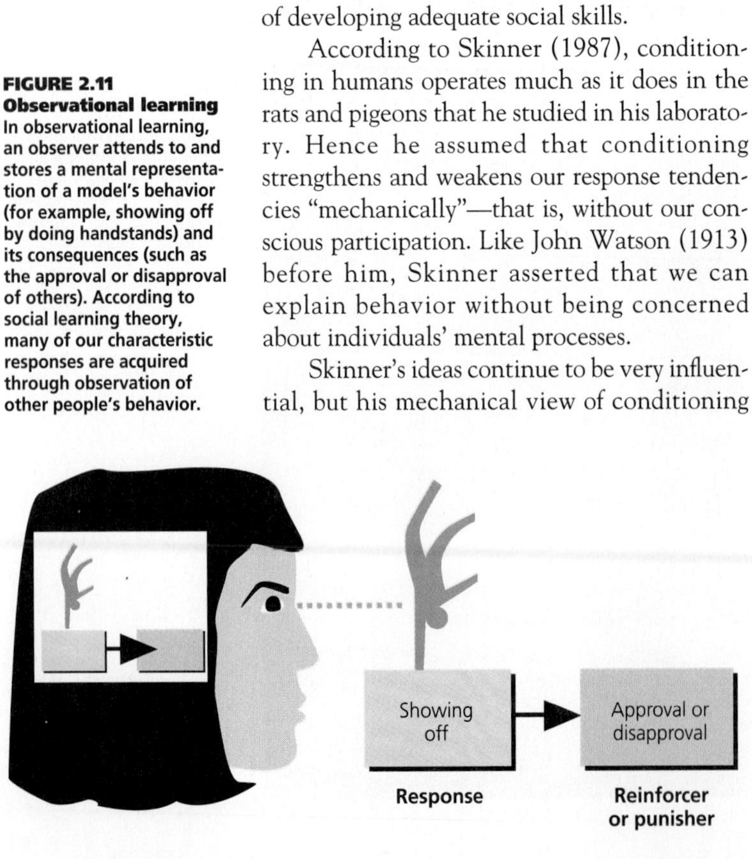

Bandura and Social Learning Theory

Albert Bandura is one of several behaviorists who have added a cognitive flavor to behaviorism since the 1960s. Bandura (1977), Walter Mischel (1973), and Julian Rotter (1982) take issue with Skinner's view. They point out that humans obviously are conscious, thinking, feeling beings. Moreover, they argue that in neglecting cognitive processes, Skinner ignored the most distinctive and important feature of human behavior. Bandura and like-minded theorists call their modified brand of behaviorism *social learning theory*.

Bandura (1977, 1986) agrees with the basic thrust of behaviorism in that he believes that personality is shaped largely through learning. However, he contends that conditioning is not a mechanical process in which we are passive participants. Instead, he maintains that we actively seek out and process information about our environment in order to maximize our favorable outcomes.

Observational Learning

Bandura's foremost theoretical contribution has been his description of observational learning. *Observational learning* occurs when an organism's responding is influenced by the observation of others, who are called models. Bandura does not view observational learning as entirely separate from classical and operant conditioning. Instead, he asserts that both classical and operant conditioning can take place indirectly when one person observes another's conditioning (see Figure 2.11).

To illustrate, suppose you observe a friend behaving assertively with a car salesman. Let's say that her assertiveness is reinforced by the exceptionally good buy she obtains on the car. Your own tendency to behave assertively with salespeople may well be strengthened as a result. Notice that the favorable consequence is experienced by your friend, not by you. Your friend's tendency to bargain assertively should be reinforced directly. But your tendency

FIGURE 2.11
Observational learning
In observational learning, an observer attends to and stores a mental representation of a model's behavior (for example, showing off by doing handstands) and its consequences (such as the approval or disapproval of others). According to social learning theory, many of our characteristic responses are acquired through observation of other people's behavior.

Showing off	Approval or disapproval
Response	**Reinforcer or punisher**

to bargain assertively may also be reinforced indirectly.

The theories of Skinner and Pavlov make no allowance for this type of indirect learning. After all, observational learning requires that you pay *attention* to your friend's behavior, that you *understand* its consequences, and that you store this *information* in your *memory*. Obviously, attention, understanding, information, and memory involve cognition, which behaviorists used to ignore.

In recent decades the potential influence of observational learning has been tragically demonstrated by the proliferation of "copycat crimes." One person hijacks an airliner, sticks a razor blade in Halloween candy, or slips cyanide into a few drug capsules, and before you know it a half-dozen wretches are demonstrating the power of observational learning. The power of models is often in evidence at rock concerts. Many fans try to emulate their favorite performers, leaving concert audiences choked with a surplus of Prince, Madonna, and David Byrne look-alikes.

Some models are more influential than others. Both children and adults tend to imitate people they like or respect more than people they don't. We also are especially prone to imitate the behavior of people we consider attractive or powerful (such as rock stars). In addition, imitation is more likely when we see similarity between the model and ourselves. Thus children imitate same-sex role models somewhat more often than other-sex models. Finally, as we noted before, we are more likely to copy a model if we see the model's behavior leading to positive outcomes.

According to social learning theory, models have a great impact on personality development. Children learn to be assertive, conscientious, self-sufficient, dependable, easygoing, and so forth by observing others behaving in these ways. Parents, teachers, relatives, siblings, and peers serve as models for young children. Bandura and his colleagues have done extensive research showing how models influence the development of aggressiveness, gender roles, and moral standards in children (Bandura, 1973; Bussey & Bandura, 1984; Mischel & Mischel, 1976). Their research on modeling and aggression has been particularly influential.

In a classic study, Bandura, Ross, and Ross (1963) showed how the observation of filmed models can influence the learning of aggressive behavior in children. They manipulated whether or not nursery school children saw an aggressive model on film and whether the aggressive models experienced positive or negative consequences. Soon after the manipulations, the children were taken to a toy room where their play was observed through a one-way mirror. Children who had seen the aggressive model rewarded engaged in more aggression than children in the other conditions. This landmark study was one of the earliest experimental demonstrations of a cause-effect relationship between media violence and aggressive behavior.

Self-Efficacy

Bandura believes that *self-efficacy* is a crucial element of personality. **Self-efficacy is our belief about our ability to perform behaviors that should lead to expected outcomes.** When self-efficacy is high, we feel confident that we can execute the responses necessary to earn reinforcers. When self-efficacy is low, we worry that the necessary responses may be beyond our abilities. Perceptions of self-efficacy are subjective and specific to various kinds of tasks. You may feel extremely confident about your ability to handle difficult social situations, for instance, but very doubtful about your ability to handle academic challenges. Although specific perceptions of self-efficacy predict behavior best, these perceptions are influenced by general feelings of self-efficacy, which can be measured by the scale shown in Figure 2.12 (Sherer et al., 1982). Perceptions of self-efficacy can influence which challenges we tackle and how well we perform. Studies have related perceptions of self-efficacy to feelings of anxiety in

FIGURE 2.12
Sample items from the Self-Efficacy Scale
Here are eight of the 23 items in the Self-Efficacy Scale, developed by Mark Sherer and his colleagues (1982), to measure general expectations of self-efficacy that are not tied to specific situations. The more items you agree with, the stronger your self-efficacy is. A high score on the complete scale is predictive of vocational and educational success.

The Self-Efficacy Scale

Instructions: This questionnaire is a series of statements about your personal attitudes and traits. Each statement represents a commonly held belief. Read each statement and decide to what extent it describes you. There are no right or wrong answers. You will probably agree with some of the statements and disagree with others. Please indicate your own personal feelings about each statement below by marking the letter that best describes your attitude or feeling. Please be very truthful and describe yourself as you really are, not as you would like to be.

A = Disagree strongly
B = Disagree moderately
C = Neither agree nor disagree
D = Agree moderately
E = Agree strongly

1 ____ When I make plans, I am certain I can make them work.

2 ____ If I can't do a job the first time, I keep trying until I can.

3 ____ If I see someone I would like to meet, I go to that person instead of waiting for him or her to come to me.

4 ____ When I have something unpleasant to do, I stick to it until I finish it.

5 ____ When I decide to do something, I go right to work on it.

6 ____ When I'm trying to become friends with someone who seems uninterested at first, I don't give up very easily.

7 ____ Failure just makes me try harder.

8 ____ I am a self-reliant person.

social encounters (Leary & Atherton, 1986), career choice (Betz & Hackett, 1986), and success in athletic performance (Wurtele, 1986), among many other things.

Evaluating Behavioral Perspectives

Behavioral theories are firmly rooted in empirical research rather than in clinical intuition. This commitment to research has kept the behavioral approach open to new findings and new ideas. Pavlov's model has shed light on how conditioning can account for our sometimes troublesome emotional responses. Skinner's work has demonstrated how our personalities are shaped by the consequences of our behavior. Bandura's social learning theory has shown how our observations mold our characteristic behavior. Behavioral theory has enhanced our understanding of psychological disorders by demonstrating that many disorders, such as phobias, are by-products of normal learning processes.

Behaviorists, in particular Walter Mischel (1973, 1990), have also provided the most thorough explanations for the fact that people are only moderately consistent in their behavior. A person who is shy in one context, for example, may be quite outgoing in another. Other models of personality largely ignore such inconsistency. The behaviorists have shown that our behavior is not always consistent because we behave in ways that we think will lead to reinforcement in the situation at hand. In other words, situational factors have a significant influence on our behavior.

Of course, each theoretical approach has its shortcomings, and the behavioral approach is no exception. Major lines of criticism include the following.

1. *Overdependence on animal research.* Many principles in behavioral theories were discovered through research on animals. Some critics argue that behaviorists depend too much on animal research and that they indiscriminately generalize from the behavior of animals to the behavior of humans.

2. *Dilution of the behavioral approach.* The behaviorists used to be criticized for their neglect of cognitive processes, which clearly are important factors in human behavior. The rise of social learning theory, which focuses heavily on cognitive factors, blunted this criticism. However, social learning theory undermines the foundation on which behaviorism was built—the idea that psychologists should study only observable behavior. Thus some critics complain that behavioral theories aren't very behavioral anymore.

3. *Fragmentation of personality.* Behaviorists have also been criticized for providing a fragmented view of personality. The behavioral approach carves personality into stimulus-response associations. It offers no unifying structural concepts (such as Freud's ego) to tie these pieces together. Humanistic theorists have been particularly vocal in criticizing this piecemeal analysis of personality.

Humanistic Perspectives

Humanistic theory emerged in the 1950s as something of a backlash against the behavioral and psychodynamic theories. The principal charge hurled at these two models was that they were dehumanizing. Freudian theory was criticized for its belief that primitive, animalistic drives dominate behavior. Behaviorism was criticized for its preoccupation with animal research and for its fragmented analysis of personality. Critics argued that both schools viewed people as helpless pawns controlled by their environment and their past, with little capacity for self-direction. Many of these critics blended into a loose alliance that came to be known as the "third force" in psychology because it surfaced as an alternative to the two dominant "forces" at the time (the psychodynamic and behavioral orientations).

This third force came to be called humanism because of its exclusive interest in human behavior. **Humanism is a theoretical orientation that emphasizes the unique qualities of humans, especially their free will and their potential for personal growth.** Humanistic psychologists are interested only in issues important to human existence, such as love, creativity, loneliness, and personal growth. They do not believe that we can learn anything of any significance about the human condition from animal research.

Humanistic theorists take an optimistic view of human nature. In contrast to most psychodynamic and behavioral theorists, humanistic theorists believe (1) that human nature includes an innate drive toward personal growth, (2) that we have the freedom to chart our own courses of action and are not pawns of our environment, and (3) that we are largely conscious and rational beings who are not dominated by unconscious, irrational needs and conflicts. Humanistic theorists also maintain that one's subjective view of the world is more important than objective reality. According to this notion, if you *think* you are homely, or bright, or sociable, then these beliefs will influence your behavior more than the actual realities of how homely, bright, or sociable you are.

The humanistic approach clearly provides a different perspective on personality than either the psychodynamic or behavioral approach. Two of the most influential humanistic theorists were Carl Rogers and Abraham Maslow.

Rogers's Person-Centered Theory

Carl Rogers (1951, 1961, 1980) was one of the founders of the human potential movement, which emphasizes personal growth through sensitivity training, encounter groups, and other exercises intended to help people get in touch with their true selves. Working at the University of Chicago in the 1940s, Rogers devised a major new approach to psychotherapy. Like Freud, Rogers based his personality theory on his extensive therapeutic interactions with many clients. Because of his emphasis on a person's subjective point of view, Rogers called his approach a *person-centered theory*.

The Self and Its Development

Rogers viewed personality structure in terms of just one construct. He called this construct the *self*, although it is more widely known today as the *self-concept*. **A self-concept is a collection of beliefs about one's own nature, unique qualities, and typical behavior.** Your self-concept is your mental picture of yourself. It is a collection of self-perceptions. A self-concept might include such beliefs as "I am easygoing" or "I am pretty" or "I am hardworking."

Rogers stressed the subjective nature of the self-concept. Your self-concept may not be entirely consistent with your actual experiences. To put it more bluntly, your self-concept may be inaccurate. Most of us are prone to distort our experiences to some extent to promote a relatively favorable self-concept. You may believe that you are quite bright academically, for example, but your grade transcript might suggest otherwise. Rogers used the term *incon-*

RECOMMENDED READING

Three Psychologies: Perspectives from Freud, Skinner, and Rogers
by Robert D. Nye (Brooks/Cole, 1992)

One would be hard pressed to identify anyone who has had more influence over the evolution of psychology in the 20th century than the three theorists profiled in this book. The ideas of Sigmund Freud, B. F. Skinner, and Carl Rogers provide the preeminent examples of the psychodynamic, behavioral, and humanistic approaches to understanding behavior. In this concise (160 pages), highly readable book, Robert Nye gives readers a simple—but not oversimplified—introduction to the theories of Freud, Rogers, and Skinner. After providing a brief overview of all three theories in the first chapter, Nye devotes a chapter to each theorist in which he attempts to present that theorist's ideas "as convincingly as possible, holding back judgments and criticisms until later" (p. vii). Each of these chapters includes a short biographical sketch of the theorist and discusses practical examples and real-world implications of his provocative ideas. In the fifth and final chapter, Nye systematically compares the three theorists, reviews criticism of each, and adds his own personal comments. All in all, this is a superb introduction to the three major perspectives that have shaped contemporary psychology.

> *Freud* makes me ask myself "Do I really know *why* I'm doing what I'm doing?" He causes me to question my motives and to try to reduce my possible blindness to characteristics, prejudices, and biases I might have. . . .
>
> With regard to *Skinner*, he made an extremely important contribution by pointing repeatedly to the environment's effects on behavior. . . . Skinner drew attention to an obviously important aspect of human life: reinforcement. It is significant for controlling our own behaviors, raising children, improving education, getting along with others, and most other activities. Reinforcement seems so simple that we often ignore it. . . .
>
> What about *Rogers*? Well, after I read his works, I generally come away feeling good. However, this is sometimes tempered by my impression that he was overly optimistic about the force toward growth and fulfillment that supposedly resides within us. [pp. 148–150]

gruence **to refer to the disparity between one's self-concept and one's actual experience.** If a person's self-concept is reasonably accurate, it is said to be *congruent* with reality. Everyone experiences *some* incongruence; the crucial issue is how much (see Figure 2.13). Rogers maintained that a great deal of incongruence undermines our psychological well-being.

Rogers was concerned with how childhood experiences promote congruence or incongruence. According to Rogers, we have a strong need for affection, love, and acceptance from others. Early in our lives, our parents provide most of the affection we receive. Some parents, Rogers pointed out, make their affection very *conditional*. That is, they make it depend on the child's ability to behave as they demand and to live up to their expectations. When parents'

FIGURE 2.13
Rogers's view of personality structure
In Rogers's model, the self-concept is the only important structural construct. Rogers acknowledged, however, that one's self-concept may not coincide with the realities of one's actual experience—a condition called incongruence. The amount of incongruence between one's self-concept and reality may be small or so great that it threatens one's psychological being.

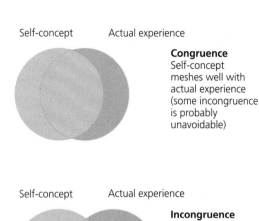

Congruence
Self-concept meshes well with actual experience (some incongruence is probably unavoidable)

Incongruence
Self-concept does not mesh well with actual experience

Carl Rogers

love seems conditional, children often distort and block out of their self-concept those experiences that make them feel unworthy of love. At the other end of the spectrum are parents who make their affection very *unconditional*. Their children have less need to block out unworthy experiences because they have been assured that they are worthy of affection no matter what they do.

Rogers believed that unconditional love from parents fosters congruence and that conditional love fosters incongruence. He further theorized that if we grow up believing that the affection of others (besides our parents) is very conditional, we go on to distort more and more of our experiences in order to feel worthy of acceptance by a wider and wider array of people, so that incongruence continues to grow.

A person's self-concept evolves throughout childhood and adolescence. As our self-concept gradually stabilizes, we begin to feel comfortable with it and we usually are loyal to it. This loyalty produces two effects. First, our self-concept becomes a self-fulfilling prophecy in that we tend to behave in ways that are consistent with it. If you see yourself as an even-tempered, reflective person, you'll consciously work at behaving in these ways. If you happen to behave impulsively, you'll probably feel some discomfort because you're acting "out of character." Second, we become resistant to information that contradicts our self-concept. Contradictory information threatens our comfortable equilibrium. If your experiences begin to suggest that you are not as even-tempered as you thought, you will probably find ways to dismiss this evidence.

Anxiety and Defense

According to Rogers, experiences that threaten our personal views of ourselves are the principal cause of troublesome anxiety. The more inaccurate your self-concept is, the more likely you are to have experiences that clash with your self-perceptions. Thus people with highly incongruent self-concepts are especially likely to be plagued by recurrent anxiety.

To ward off this anxiety, we often behave defensively. Thus we ignore, deny, and twist reality to protect our self-concept. Consider a young woman who, like most of us, considers herself a "nice person." Let us suppose that in reality she is rather conceited and selfish, and she gets feedback from both boyfriends and girlfriends that she is a "self-centered, snotty brat." How may she react in order to protect her self-concept? She may ignore or block out those occasions when she behaves selfishly and then deny her friends' accusations that she is self-centered. She may attribute her girlfriends' negative comments to their jealousy of her good looks and blame the boyfriends' negative remarks on their disappointment because she won't get more serious with them. Meanwhile, she may start doing some kind of charity work to show everyone (including herself) that she really is a nice person. As you can see, when our self-concept is threatened, we often go to great lengths to defend it.

Rogers's theory can explain defensive behavior and personality disturbances, but he believed that it is also important to focus attention on psychological health. Rogers asserted that psychological health is rooted in a congruent self-concept. Congruence in turn is rooted in a sense of personal worth, which stems from a childhood saturated with unconditional affection from parents and others. These themes are similar to those that were emphasized by the other major humanistic theorist, Abraham Maslow.

Maslow's Theory of Self-Actualization

Abraham Maslow grew up in Brooklyn and spent much of his career at Brandeis University, where he provided crucial leadership for the fledgling humanistic movement. Like Rogers, Maslow (1968, 1970) argued that psychology should take a greater interest in the nature of the healthy personality, instead of dwelling on the causes of disorders. "To over-simplify the matter somewhat," he said, "it is as

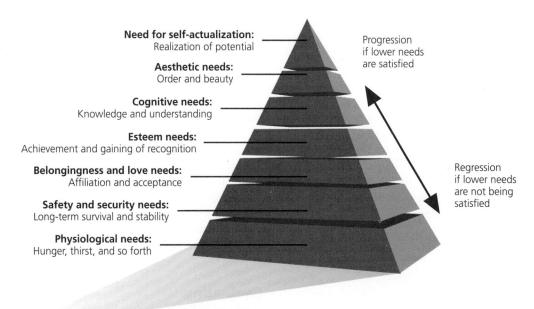

Need for self-actualization:
Realization of potential

Aesthetic needs:
Order and beauty

Cognitive needs:
Knowledge and understanding

Esteem needs:
Achievement and gaining of recognition

Belongingness and love needs:
Affiliation and acceptance

Safety and security needs:
Long-term survival and stability

Physiological needs:
Hunger, thirst, and so forth

Progression
if lower needs
are satisfied

Regression
if lower needs
are not being
satisfied

FIGURE 2.14.
Maslow's hierarchy of needs
According to Maslow, our needs are arranged in a hierarchy, and we must satisfy our basic needs first, before we progress to higher needs. Higher levels in the pyramid represent progressively less basic needs. We progress upward in the hierarchy when lower needs are satisfied reasonably well, but we may regress back to lower levels if basic needs cease to be satisfied.

if Freud supplied to us the sick half of psychology and we must now fill it out with the healthy half" (Maslow, 1968, p. 5). Maslow's key contributions are his analysis of how motives are organized and his description of the healthy personality.

The Hierarchy of Needs

Maslow proposed that human motives are organized into a *hierarchy of needs*—**a systematic arrangement of needs, according to priority, in which basic needs must be met before less basic needs are aroused.** This hierarchical arrangement is usually portrayed as a pyramid (see Figure 2.14). The needs at the bottom of the pyramid are the most basic. They are fundamental physiological needs that are essential to survival, such as the need for oxygen, food, and water. These needs must be satisfied fairly well before we become concerned about needs at higher levels in the hierarchy. When we manage to satisfy a level of needs reasonably well (complete satisfaction is not necessary), *this satisfaction activates needs at the next level.*

The second tier in Maslow's pyramid is made up of safety and security needs. These needs reflect concern about *long-term* survival.

People seek to live in a stable, safe world. Safety and security needs motivate adults to seek a secure job, buy insurance, and put money in their savings accounts. When safety and security needs are met adequately, needs for love and belongingness become more prominent. These needs lead people to seek affection—from family, from friends, and in intimate relationships. When these needs are gratified, esteem needs are activated. People then become more concerned about their achievements and the recognition, respect, and status they earn.

Like Rogers, Maslow argued that humans have an innate drive toward personal growth—that is, evolution toward a higher state of being. Thus he described the needs in the uppermost reaches of his hierarchy as *growth needs*. These include the need for knowledge, understanding, order, and aesthetic beauty.

Foremost among them is the ***need for self-actualization,* which is the need to fulfill one's potential; it is the highest need in Maslow's motivational hierarchy.** Maslow summarized this concept with a simple statement: "What a man *can* be, he *must* be." According to Maslow, people will be frustrated if they are unable to use their talents fully or pursue their true interests. For example, if you have great musical tal-

ent but must work as an accountant, or if you have scholarly interests but must work as a sales clerk, your need for self-actualization will be thwarted.

Maslow theorized that the various levels of needs are ordered in the same way for nearly everyone. He recognized, however, that hierarchy may become scrambled for some people because of unusual factors in their personal history. He speculated that the most common rearrangement of levels occurs when adults put higher priority on their esteem needs than on their love and belongingness needs. Such people often pour all their energy into their careers while their marriage or personal life deteriorates.

The Healthy Personality

Because of his interest in self-actualization, Maslow set out to discover the nature of the healthy personality. He tried to identify people of exceptional mental health, so that he could investigate their characteristics. In one case, he used psychological tests and interviews to sort out the healthiest 1% of a sizable population of college students. He also studied admired historical figures (such as Thomas Jefferson and the psychologist-philosopher William James) and personal acquaintances characterized by superior adjustment. Over a period of years he accumulated his case histories and gradually sketched, in broad strokes, a picture of ideal psychological health.

Maslow called people with exceptionally healthy personalities *self-actualizing persons* because of their commitment to continued personal growth. He identified various traits characteristic of self-actualizing people, which are listed in Figure 2.15. In brief, Maslow found that self-actualizers are accurately tuned in to reality and that they are at peace with them-

selves. He found that they are open and spontaneous and that they retain a fresh appreciation of the world around them. Socially, they are sensitive to others' needs and enjoy rewarding interpersonal relations. However, they are not dependent upon others for approval. Nor are they uncomfortable with solitude. They thrive on their work, and they enjoy their sense of humor. Maslow also noted that they enjoy "peak experiences" (profound emotional highs) more often than others. Finally, he found that they strike a nice balance between many polarities in personality, so that they can be both childlike and mature, rational and intuitive, conforming and rebellious.

Evaluating Humanistic Perspectives

The humanists added a refreshing perspective to the study of personality. Their argument that a person's subjective views may be more important than objective reality has proved compelling. Today even behavioral theorists have begun to consider subjective personal factors such as beliefs and expectations. The humanistic approach also deserves credit for making the self-concept an important construct in psychology. Finally, the humanists have often been applauded for focusing attention on the issue of what constitutes a healthy personality.

Of course, there is a negative side to the balance sheet as well. Critics have identified some weaknesses in the humanistic approach to personality, including the following.

1. *Poor testability.* Like psychodynamic theorists, the humanists have been criticized for proposing hypotheses that are very difficult to put to a scientific test. Such humanistic concepts as personal growth and self-actualization are difficult to define and measure.

2. *Unrealistic view of human nature.* Critics also charge that the humanists have been overly optimistic in their assumptions about human nature and unrealistic in their descriptions of the healthy personality. Maslow's self-actualizing people, for instance, sound perfect. In reality, Maslow had a very hard time finding self-actualizing persons. When he searched among the living, the results were so disappointing that he turned to the study of historical figures. Thus humanistic portraits of psychological health are perhaps a bit unrealistic.

3. *Inadequate evidence.* Humanistic theories are based primarily on discerning but uncontrolled observations in clinical settings. Case studies can be valuable in generating ideas, but

FIGURE 2.15
Characteristics of self-actualizing people
Humanistic theorists emphasize psychological health instead of maladjustment. Maslow's sketch of the self-actualizing person provides a provocative picture of the healthy personality.

Characteristics of Self-Actualizing People

• Clear, efficient perception of reality and comfortable relations with it	• Feelings of kinship and identification with the human race
• Spontaneity, simplicity, and naturalness	• Strong friendships, but limited in number
• Problem centering (having something outside themselves they "must" do as a mission)	• Democratic character structure
• Detachment and need for privacy	• Ethical discrimination between means and ends, between good and evil
• Autonomy, independence of culture and environment	• Philosophical, unhostile sense of humor
• Continued freshness of appreciation	• Balance between polarities in personality
• Mystical and peak experiences	

they are ill suited for building a solid data base. More experimental research is needed to catch up with the theorizing in the humanistic camp. This is precisely the opposite of the situation we'll encounter in the next section, on biological perspectives, where more theorizing is needed to catch up with the research.

Biological Perspectives

> Like many identical twins reared apart, Jim Lewis and Jim Springer found they had been leading eerily similar lives. Separated four weeks after birth in 1940, the Jim twins grew up 45 miles apart in Ohio and were reunited in 1979. Eventually, they discovered that both drove the same model blue Chevrolet, chain-smoked Salems, chewed their fingernails and owned dogs named Toy. Each had spent a good deal of time vacationing at the same three-block strip of beach in Florida. More important, when tested for such personality traits as flexibility, self-control and sociability, the twins responded almost exactly alike. [Leo, 1987, p. 63]

So began a *Time* magazine summary of a major twin study conducted at the University of Minnesota, where investigators have been exploring the hereditary roots of personality. The research team has managed to locate and complete testing on 44 rare pairs of identical twins separated early in life. Not all the twin pairs have been as similar as Jim Lewis and Jim Springer, but many of the parallels have been uncanny. The identical twins Oskar Stohr and Jack Yufe were separated soon after birth. Oskar was sent to a Nazi-run school in Czechoslovakia, while Jack was raised in a Jewish home on a Caribbean island. When they were reunited for the first time during middle age, they showed up wearing similar mustaches, haircuts, shirts, and wire-rimmed glasses. When a pair of previously separated female twins arrived at the Min-

neapolis airport, each was wearing seven rings on her fingers. One had a son named Richard Andrew, and the other had a son named Andrew Richard. Still another pair of separated twin sisters shared a phobia: both were afraid of water. They even dealt with it in the same peculiar way—by backing into the ocean.

Could personality be largely inherited? These anecdotal reports of striking resemblances between identical twins reared apart certainly raise this possibility. In this section we'll discuss Hans Eysenck's theory, which emphasizes the influence of heredity, and look at recent research on the biological bases of personality.

Eysenck's Theory

Hans Eysenck was born in Germany but fled to London during the era of Nazi rule. He went on to become one of Britain's most prominent psychologists. According to Eysenck (1967), "Personality is determined to a large extent by a person's genes" (p. 20). How is heredity linked to personality in Eysenck's model? In part, through conditioning concepts borrowed from behavioral theory. Eysenck (1967, 1982) theorizes that some people can be conditioned more readily than others because of inherited differences in their physiological functioning (specifically, their level of arousal). These variations in "conditionability" are assumed to influence the personality traits that people acquire through conditioning.

Like Gordon Allport and Raymond Cattell, Eysenck maintains that some traits are more important than others. Eysenck views personality structure as a hierarchy of traits. Numerous superficial traits are derived from a smaller number of more basic traits, which are derived from a handful of fundamental higher-order traits, as shown in Figure 2.16.

Eysenck has shown a special interest in ex-

Hans Eysenck

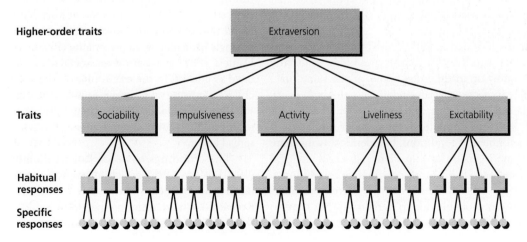

FIGURE 2.16
Eysenck's model of personality structure
Eysenck describes personality structure as a hierarchy of traits. In this scheme, a few higher-order traits (such as extraversion) determine a host of lower-order traits (such as sociability), which determine our habitual responses (such as going to lots of parties). Habitual responses in turn, determine our specific responses to situations.

Higher-order traits — Extraversion

Traits — Sociability · Impulsiveness · Activity · Liveliness · Excitability

Habitual responses

Specific responses

plaining variations in *extraversion-introversion*, which is one of the fundamental personality traits in his model. **Introverts tend to be preoccupied with the internal world of their own thoughts, feelings, and experiences.** They generally are inhibited, contemplative, and aloof. In contrast, **extraverts tend to be interested in the external world of things and people.** They're more likely to be sociable, talkative, and venturesome. Eysenck has proposed that people who become introverts tend to condition more easily than extraverts because they have inherited a relatively high level of physiological arousal. According to Eysenck, people who condition easily acquire more conditioned inhibitions than others. These inhibitions make them more bashful, tentative, and uneasy in social situations. This social discomfort leads them to turn inward. Hence they become introverted.

Is there any empirical evidence to support Eysenck's theory? Yes. Eysenck and Levey (1972) found that introverts developed a classically conditioned eye-blink response more easily than extraverts, and various studies have found that introverts tend to exhibit higher levels of arousal than extraverts (Gale, 1983; Wilson, 1990). Eysenck (1990) acknowledges, however, that the evidence on his theory is mixed and that the concept of physiological arousal has turned out to be much more complex and difficult to measure than he originally anticipated.

Recent Research

Recent twin studies have also provided impressive support for Eysenck's hypothesis that personality is largely inherited. In **twin studies researchers assess hereditary influence by comparing the resemblance of identical twins and fraternal twins on a trait.** The logic underlying such comparisons is as follows. Identical twins emerge from one egg that splits, so that their genetic makeup is exactly the same (100% overlap). Fraternal twins result when two eggs are fertilized simultaneously; their genetic overlap is only 50%. Both types of twins usually grow up in the same home, at the same time, exposed to the same relatives, neighbors, peers, teachers, events, and so forth. Thus both kinds of twins normally develop under similar environmental conditions, but identical twins share more genetic kinship. Hence, if sets of identical twins exhibit more personality resemblance than sets of fraternal twins, this greater similarity is probably due to heredity rather than to environment.

In one large study, 573 pairs of twins responded to five personality scales that measured altruism, empathy, nurturance, aggressiveness, and assertiveness (Rushton et al., 1986). Figure 2.17 shows the mean correlations observed on three of these traits. Higher correlations are indicative of greater similarity on a trait. On all five traits, identical twins were found to be much more similar to each other than fraternal twins. The investigators attribute the identical twins' greater personality resemblance to their greater genetic similarity. On the basis of the observed correlations, they *estimate* that genetic factors account for about 56% to 72% of the variation in the five traits studied.

Some skeptics still wonder whether identical twins may exhibit more personality resemblance than fraternal twins because they are raised more similarly. In other words, they wonder whether environmental factors (rather than heredity) could be responsible for identical twins' greater similarity. This nagging question can be answered only by studies of identical twins who have been reared apart. This is why the twin study at the University of Minnesota is so important.

The Minnesota study (Tellegen et al., 1988) is the first to administer the same personality test to identical and fraternal twins reared together as well as apart. Most of the twins reared apart were separated quite early in life (median age of 2.5 months) and remained separated for a long time (median period of almost 34 years). Nonetheless, on all three of the higher-order traits examined, the identical twins reared apart displayed more personality resemblance than fraternal twins reared together. On the basis of the pattern of correlations observed, the researchers estimate that genetic inheritance accounts for at least 50% of the variation among people in personality.

Research on the genetic bases of personality has inadvertently turned up an interesting finding that was apparent in the Minnesota twin study. A number of recent studies have found that shared family environment has surprisingly little impact on personality (Plomin & Daniels, 1987). For many years, social scientists have assumed that the environment shared by children growing up together leads to some personality resemblance among them. However, recent findings seriously undermine this widespread belief.

These findings have led Robert Plomin (1990) to ask, "Why are children in the same family so different from one another?" Researchers have only just begun to explore this perplexing question. Plomin speculates

Reprinted with special permission of King Features Syndicate.

that children in the same family experience home environments that are not nearly so homogeneous as most people had assumed. He notes that children in the same home may be treated quite differently, because gender and birth order can influence parents' approaches to child rearing. Temperamental differences between children may also evoke differences in styles of parenting. A focus on how environmental factors vary *within* families represents a promising new way to explore the determinants of personality.

Evaluating Biological Perspectives

Recent studies have provided convincing evidence that biological factors help to shape personality. Nonetheless, we must take note of some weaknesses in biological approaches to personality.

1. *Problems with estimates of hereditary influ-* *ence.* The statistics produced in efforts to carve personality into genetic and environmental components are ultimately artificial. The effects of heredity and environment are twisted together in complicated interactions that can't be separated cleanly. Although estimates of the genetic component in personality sound very precise, they are *estimates* based on a complicated chain of inferences that are subject to debate. Some theorists argue that twin studies inflate the apparent influence of heredity and that the genetic component of personality is closer to 20% than 50% (Plomin, Chipuer, & Loehlin, 1990).

2. *Lack of adequate theory.* At present there is no comprehensive biological theory of personality. Eysenck's model does not provide a systematic overview of how biological factors govern personality development (and was never intended to). Additional theoretical work is needed to catch up with recent empirical findings on the biological basis for personality.

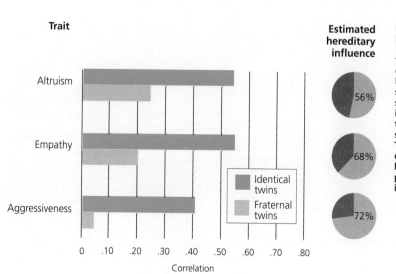

FIGURE 2.17
Heredity and personality
Selected results from the twin study of personality conducted by Rushton and his colleagues (1986) are shown here. Identical twins showed stronger correlations in personality than fraternal twins, suggesting that personality is partly inherited. The correlational data yielded rather high estimates of hereditary influence for the personality traits examined in the study.

An Epilogue on Theoretical Diversity

Figure 2.18 provides a comparative overview of the ideas of Freud, Skinner, Rogers, and Eysenck, as representatives of the pyschodynamic, behavioral, humanistic, and biological approaches to personality. Most of this information has been covered in the chapter, but the figure organizes it so that the similarities and differences between the theories become more apparent. As you can see, there are many fundamental points of disagreement. Our review of the various perspectives on personality should have made one thing abundantly clear: Psychology is marked by theoretical diversity.

Why do we have so many competing points of view? One reason is that no single theory can adequately explain everything that we know about personality. Some theories focus on aspects of behavior that others neglect. Sometimes there is simply more than one way to look at something. Is the glass half empty or half full? Obviously, it is both. To take an example from another science, physicists wrestled for years with the nature of light. Is it a wave or is it a particle? In the end, it proved useful to think of light sometimes as a wave, sometimes as a particle. Similarly, if a business executive lashes out at her employees with stinging criticism, is she releasing pent-up aggressive urges (a psychoanalytic view)? Is she making a habitual response to the stimulus of incompetent work (a behavioral view)? Is she trying to act like a tough boss because that's a key aspect of her self-concept (a humanistic view)? Or is she exhibiting an inherited tendency to be aggressive (a biological view)? In some cases, all four of these explanations may have some validity.

In short, to expect one view to be right while all others are wrong is to oversimplify the situation. Life is rarely that simple. In view of the complexity of personality, it would be surprising if there were *not* a variety of theories.

It's probably best to think of the various theoretical orientations in psychology as complementary viewpoints, each with its own advantages and limitations. Indeed, modern psychologists increasingly recognize that theoretical diversity is a strength rather than a weakness (Hilgard, 1987; Kleinginna & Kleinginna, 1988). As we proceed through this text, you will see how differing theoretical perspectives often inspire fruitful research and how they sometimes converge on a more complete understanding of behavior than could be achieved by any one perspective alone.

FIGURE 2.18
Four theoretical perspectives on personality
This overview of the theories of Freud, Skinner, Rogers, and Eysenck highlights the similarities and differences between the psychodynamic, behavioral, humanistic, and biological approaches to personality.

Overview of Four Approaches to Personality

	Sigmund Freud A psychodynamic view	B. F. Skinner A behavioral view	Carl Rogers A humanistic view	Hans Eysenck A biological view
Source of data and observations	Case studies from clinical practice of psychoanalysis	Laboratory experiments, primarily with animals	Case studies from clinical practice of client-centered therapy	Twin, family, and adoption studies of hereditary influence; factor analysis studies of personality structure
Key motivational forces	Sex and aggression; need to reduce tension produced by internal conflicts	Pursuit of primary (unlearned) and secondary (learned) reinforcers; priorities depend on personal history	Actualizing tendency (need for personal growth) and self-actualizing tendency (need to maintain self-concept)	No specific motivational forces singled out
Model of personality structure	Three interacting components (id, ego, superego) operating at three levels of consciousness	Collection of response tendencies tied to specific stimulus situations	Self-concept, which may or may not be congruent with actual experience	Hierarchy of traits, with specific traits derived from more fundamental, general traits
View of personality development	Emphasis on fixation or progress through psychosexual stages; experiences in early childhood leave lasting mark on adult personality	Personality evolves gradually over the life span (not in stages); responses followed by reinforcement become more frequent	Children who receive unconditional love have less need to be defensive; they develop more accurate, congruent self-concepts; conditional love fosters incongruence	Emphasis on unfolding of genetic blueprint with maturation; inherited predispositions interact with learning experiences
Roots of disorders	Unconscious fixations and unresolved conflicts from childhood, usually centered on sex and aggression	Maladaptive behavior due to faulty learning; the "symptom" is the problem, not a sign of underlying disease	Incongruence between self-concept and actual experience; overdependence on others for approval and sense of worth	Genetic vulnerability activated in part by environmental factors
Importance of nature (biology, heredity) vs. nurture (environment, experience)	Nature: emphasis on biological basis of instinctual drives	Nurture: strong emphasis on learning, conditioning, role of experience	Nurture: interested in innate potentials, but humanists believe we can rise above our biological heritage	Nature: strong emphasis on how hereditary predispositions shape our personalities
Importance of person factors vs. situation factors	Person: main interest is in internal factors (id, ego, conflicts, defenses, etc.)	Situation: strong emphasis on how we respond to specific stimulus situations	Person: Focus on self-concept, which is stable	Person: interested in stable traits molded by heredity

Summary

The concept of personality explains the consistency in our behavior over time and situations while also explaining individuals' distinctiveness. Personality traits are dispositions to behave in certain ways. As Allport first noted, some traits are more basic than others.

Freud's psychoanalytic theory emphasizes the importance of the unconscious. Freud described personality structure in terms of three components that are involved in internal conflicts, which generate anxiety. According to Freud, we often ward off anxiety and other unpleasant emotions with defense mechanisms, which work through self-deception. Freud believed that the first five years of life are extremely influential in shaping adult personality. Adler's individual psychology emphasizes how we strive for superiority in order to compensate for our feelings of inferiority. Adler also emphasized the social context in which personality develops.

Psychodynamic theories have produced many insights into the unconscious, the role of conflict, and the importance of early, formative childhood experiences. However, they have been criticized for their poor testability, their inadequate base of empirical evidence, and their male-centered views of the human condition.

Behavioral theories view personality as a collection of response tendencies shaped through learning. Pavlov's classical conditioning can explain how we acquire emotional responses. Skinner's model of operant conditioning shows how consequences such as reinforcement, extinction, and punishment shape our habitual patterns of behavior. Bandura's social learning theory adds a cognitive flavor to behaviorism. It shows how we can be conditioned indirectly, through observation.

Behavioral approaches to personality are based on rigorous research. They have provided ample insights about how situational factors and learning mold our personalities. However, behavioral theories aren't strictly behavioral anymore, and the behaviorists have been criticized for their overdependence on animal research and their fragmented analysis of personality.

Humanistic theories take an optimistic view of our conscious, rational ability to chart our own courses of action. Rogers focused on the self-concept as the critical aspect of personality. He maintained that incongruence between one's self-concept and reality creates anxiety and leads to defensive behavior. Maslow theorized that our needs are arranged hierarchically. He asserted that psychological health depends on fulfilling our need for self-actualization.

Humanistic theories deserve credit for highlighting the importance of subjective views of oneself and for confronting the question of what makes for a healthy personality. However, they lack a firm base of research, are difficult to put to an empirical test, and may be overly optimistic about human nature.

Eysenck believes that individual differences in physiological functioning affect our conditioning and thus influence personality. Recent twin studies have provided impressive evidence that genetic factors shape personality. The biological approach has been criticized because estimates of hereditary influence fail to reflect the difficulty of disentangling hereditary and environmental factors and because no comprehensive biological model of personality has been developed.

The study of personality illustrates how great the theoretical diversity in psychology is. This diversity is a strength in that it fuels research that helps us move toward a more complete understanding of behavior. The Application discusses how you can learn more about your personality (and abilities) through psychological testing. It describes the logic and limitations of such tests.

APPLICATION Assessing Your Personality

1.

Responses to personality tests are subject to unconscious distortion.

2.

The results of personality tests are often misunderstood.

3.

Personality test scores should be interpreted with caution.

4.

Personality tests may be quite useful in helping people to learn more about themselves.

If you identified all four statements as true, you earned a perfect score. Yes, personality tests are subject to distortion. Admittedly, test results are often misunderstood, and they should be interpreted cautiously. In spite of these problems, however, psychological tests can be very useful.

The value of psychological tests lies in their ability to help people form a realistic picture of their personal qualities. In light of this value, we have included a variety of personality tests in the *Personal Explorations Workbook* that is available to accompany this text and we have sprinkled a number of short tests throughout the text itself. Most of these questionnaires are widely used personality tests. We hope you may gain some insights by responding to these questions. But it's important to understand the logic and limitations of such tests. To facilitate your use of these and other tests, this Application discusses some of the basics of psychological testing.

Key Concepts in Psychological Testing

A *psychological test* is a standardized measure of a sample of a person's behavior. Psychological tests are measurement instruments. They are used to measure abilities, aptitudes, and personality traits.

Note that your responses to a psychological test represent a *sample* of your behavior. This reality should alert you to one of the key limitations of psychological tests. It's always possible that a particular behavior sample is not representative of your characteristic behavior. We all have our bad days. A stomachache, a fight with a friend, a problem with your car—all may affect your responses to a particular test on a particular day. The problem of getting a good sample is *not* unique to testing. It's a problem for any measurement technique. For example, someone taking your blood pressure might get an unrepresentative reading. Because of the limitations of the sampling process, test scores should always be interpreted *cautiously.* Most psychological tests are sound measurement

devices, but test results should *not* be viewed as the final word on one's personality and abilities because of the ever-present sampling problem.

Most psychological tests can be placed in one of two broad categories: (l) mental ability tests and (2) personality tests. *Mental ability* tests, such as intelligence tests, aptitude tests, and achievement tests, often serve as gateways to schooling, training programs, and jobs. *Personality tests* measure various aspects of personality, including motives, interests, values, and attitudes. Many psychologists prefer to call these tests personality *scales,* since the questions do not have right and wrong answers, as the questions that test mental abilities do.

Standardization and Norms

Both personality scales and tests of mental abilities are *standardized* measures of behavior. *Standardization* refers to the uniform procedures used to administer and score a test. All subjects get the same instructions, the same questions, the same time limits, and so on, so that their scores can be compared meaningfully.

The standardization of a test's scoring system includes the development of test norms. *Test norms* provide information about where a score on a psychological test ranks in relation to other scores on that test. Why do we need test norms? Because in psychological testing, everything is relative. Psychological tests tell you how you score *in relation to other people.* They tell you, for instance, that you are average in impulsiveness, or slightly above average in assertiveness, or far below average in anxiety. These interpretations are derived from the test norms.

The sample of people on whom the norms are based is called a test's *standardization group.* Ideally, test norms are based on a large sample of people who were carefully selected to be representative of the broader population. In reality, the representativeness of standardization groups varies considerably from one test to another.

Reliability and Validity

Any kind of measuring device, whether it's a tire gauge, a stopwatch, or a psychological test, should be reasonably consistent. That is, repeated measurements should yield reasonably similar results. To appreciate the importance of reliability, think about how you would react if a tire pressure gauge gave you several very different readings for the same tire. You would probably conclude that the gauge was broken and toss it into the garbage because you know that consistency in measurement is essential to accuracy.

Reliability refers to the consistency of a test's measurements. A reliable test is one that yields similar results each time it is repeated (see Figure 2.19). Like most other types of measuring devices, psychological tests are not perfectly reliable. They usually do not yield precisely the same score when they are repeated. A certain amount of inconsistency is unavoidable because human behavior is variable. Personality tests tend to have lower reliability than tests of mental ability because daily fluctuations in mood influence the way we respond to such tests.

Even if a test is quite reliable, we still need to be concerned about its validity. A test's *validity* is its ability to measure what it was designed to measure. If we develop a new test of assertiveness, we have to provide some evidence that it really measures assertiveness. Validity can be demonstrated in a variety of ways. Most of them involve correlating scores on a test with other measures of the same trait, or with related traits.

Personality Testing

We all engage in efforts to size up our own personality as well as the personalities of others. When you think to yourself that "this salesman is untrustworthy," or when you remark to a friend that "Howard is too timid and submissive," you are making a personality assessment. In a sense, then, personality assessment is part of daily life. However, psychological tests provide much more system-

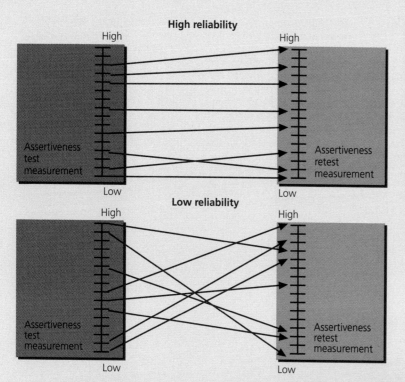

High reliability

High · Assertiveness test measurement · Low

High · Assertiveness retest measurement · Low

Low reliability

High · Assertiveness test measurement · Low

High · Assertiveness retest measurement · Low

FIGURE 2.19
Test reliability
Subjects' scores on the first administration of an assertiveness test are represented on the left, and their scores on a second administration (a few weeks later) are represented on the right. If subjects obtain similar scores on the two administrations, the test measures assertiveness consistently and is said to have high reliability. If subjects get very different scores when they take the assertiveness test a second time, the test is said to have low reliability.

atic assessments than our casual observations.

The vast majority of personality tests are self-report inventories. *Self-report inventories* ask individuals to answer a series of questions about their characteristic behavior. When you take a self-report personality scale, you endorse statements as true or false as they apply to you, or indicate how often you behave in a particular way, or rate yourself with respect to certain qualities. On the Minnesota Multiphasic Personality Inventory, for example, people respond "true," "false," or "cannot say" to 550 statements such as the following:

I get a fair deal from most people.
I have the time of my life at parties.
I am glad that I am alive.
Several people are following me everywhere.

The logic underlying this approach is very simple. Who knows you better than you do? Who has known you longer? Who has more access to your private feelings?

The entire range of personality traits can be measured with self-report inventories. Some scales measure just one trait dimension, such as the Self-Efficacy Scale (see Figure 2.12) and the measure of introversion-extraversion shown in Figure 2.20. Others assess a multitude of traits simultaneously . The Sixteen Personality Factor Questionnaire (16PF), developed by Raymond Cattell and his colleagues (Cattell, Eber, & Tatsuoka,

FIGURE 2.20
The Maudsley Personality Inventory, Short Form
The items shown here, taken from the Maudsley Personality Inventory, provide a very brief measure of one's extraversion-introversion. The items are worded so that a "yes" response is indicative of extraverted tendencies. If you answered "yes" to all six questions, you are probably more extraverted than introverted, although one should be cautious about basing any conclusions on such a short scale.

The Maudsley Personality Inventory, Short Form

Instructions: The following questions pertain to the way people behave, feel, and act. Decide whether the items represent your *usual* way of acting or feeling, and circle either a "Yes" or "No" for each. If you find it absolutely impossible to decide, circle the "? answer" but use this answer sparingly.

1 Do you prefer action to planning for action?

YES   ?   NO

2 Are you happiest when you get involved in some project that calls for rapid action?

YES   ?   NO

3 Do you usually take the initiative in making new friends?

YES   ?   NO

4 Are you inclined to be quick and sure in your actions?

YES   ?   NO

5 Would you rate yourself as a lively individual?

YES   ?   NO

6 Would you be very unhappy if you were prevented from making numerous social contacts?

YES   ?   NO

1970), is a representative multi-trait inventory. The 16PF is a 187-item scale that measures 16 basic dimensions of personality, called *source traits,* which are listed in Figure 2.21.

To appreciate the strengths of self-report inventories, consider how else you might assess your personality. For instance, how assertive are you? You probably have some vague idea, but can you accurately estimate how your assertiveness compares with others'? To do that, you need a great deal of information about others' usual behavior—information that all of us lack. A self-report inven-

tory inquires about your typical behavior in a wide variety of circumstances that require assertiveness and generates an exact comparison with the behavior typically reported by many other respondents for the same circumstances. Thus self-report inventories are much more thorough and precise than our casual observations.

However, they are only as accurate as the information we give them. In responding to self-

report inventories, some people are unconsciously influenced by the social desirability or acceptability of the statements. Without realizing it, they endorse only those statements that make them look good. The problem of unconscious distortion provides another reason why personality test results should always be regarded as suggestive rather than definitive.

FIGURE 2.21
The Sixteen Personality Factor Questionnaire (16PF)
Cattell's 16PF is designed to assess normal aspects of personality. The pairs of traits that appear opposite each other define the 16 factors measured by this self-report inventory. The profile shown is the average profile seen among a group of airline pilots who took the test.

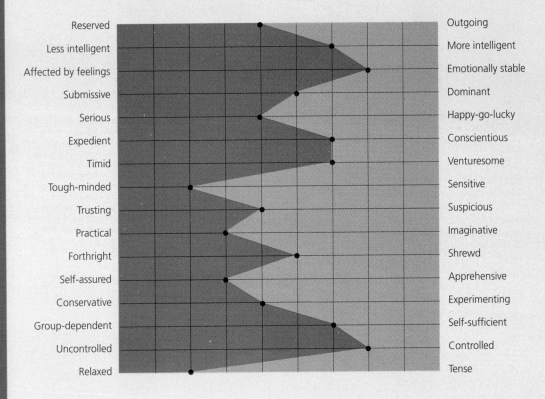

Reserved	Outgoing
Less intelligent	More intelligent
Affected by feelings	Emotionally stable
Submissive	Dominant
Serious	Happy-go-lucky
Expedient	Conscientious
Timid	Venturesome
Tough-minded	Sensitive
Trusting	Suspicious
Practical	Imaginative
Forthright	Shrewd
Self-assured	Apprehensive
Conservative	Experimenting
Group-dependent	Self-sufficient
Uncontrolled	Controlled
Relaxed	Tense

CHAPTER 2 REVIEW

Key Learning Objectives

1. Explain the concepts of personality and traits and describe Allport's system for organizing traits.
2. Describe Freud's three components of personality and how they are distributed across levels of awareness.
3. Explain the importance of sexual and aggressive conflicts in Freud's theory and describe seven defense mechanisms.
4. Outline Freud's stages of psychosexual development and their theorized relations to adult personality.
5. Describe Adler's views on striving for superiority, inferiority feelings, and compensation.
6. Summarize the strengths and weaknesses of psychodynamic theories.
7. Describe Pavlov's classical conditioning and its contribution to our understanding of personality.
8. Discuss how Skinner's principles of operant conditioning can be applied to personality development.
9. Describe Bandura's social learning theory and its relation to personality.
10. Summarize the strengths and weaknesses of behavioral theories.
11. Explain Rogers's views on self-concept, development, and defensive behavior.
12. Explain Maslow's hierarchy of needs and summarize his findings on self-actualizing persons.
13. Summarize the strengths and weaknesses of humanistic theories.
14. Describe Eysenck's biological theory of personality and recent twin studies that support it.
15. Summarize the strengths and weaknesses of biological theories of personality.
16. Discuss the value and the limitations of self-report inventories in personality assessment.

Key Terms

behaviorism
cardinal trait
central trait
classical conditioning
cognition
compensation
conditioned response (CR)
conditioned stimulus (CS)
conscious
defense mechanisms
discriminative stimuli
displacement
ego
extinction
extraverts
fixation
hierarchy of needs
humanism
id

identification
incongruence
introverts
need for self-actualization
negative reinforcement
observational learning
Oedipus complex
operant conditioning
personality
personality trait
pleasure principle
positive reinforcement
preconscious
projection
psychodynamic theories
psychological test
psychosexual stages
punishment
rationalization

reaction formation
reality principle
regression
reliability
repression
secondary trait
self-concept
self-efficacy
standardization
superego
test norms
twin studies
unconditioned response (UCR)
unconditioned stimulus (UCS)
unconscious
validity

Key People

Alfred Adler
Albert Bandura
Hans Eysenck

Sigmund Freud
Abraham Maslow
Ivan Pavlov

Carl Rogers
B. F. Skinner

3

Stress and Its Effects

YOU'RE IN YOUR CAR HEADED home from school with a classmate. Traffic is barely moving. A radio report indicates that the traffic jam is only going to get worse. You groan audibly as you fiddle impatiently with the radio dial. Another motorist nearly takes your fender off trying to cut into your lane. Your pulse quickens as you shout insults at the unknown driver, who cannot even hear you. You think about the term paper that you have to work on tonight. Your stomach knots up as you recall all the crumpled drafts you tossed into the wastebasket last night. If you don't finish the paper soon, you won't be able to find any time to study for your math test, not to mention your biology quiz. Suddenly you remember that you promised the person you're dating that the two of you would get together tonight. There's no way. Another fight looms on the horizon. Your classmate asks how you feel about the tuition increase the college announced yesterday. You've been trying not to think about it. You're already in debt up to your ears. Your parents are bugging you about changing schools, but you don't want to leave your friends. Your heartbeat quickens as you contemplate the debate you'll have to wage with your parents. You feel wired with tension as you realize that the stress in your life never seems to let up.

Many circumstances can create stress in our lives. Stress comes in all sorts of packages: large and small, pretty and ugly, simple and complex. All too often, the package is a surprise. In this chapter we'll try to sort out these packages. We'll analyze the nature of stress, outline the major types of stress, and discuss how people respond to stressful events at several levels.

In a sense, stress is what a course on adjustment is all about. Recall from Chapter 1 that adjustment is essentially the way people manage to cope with various demands and pressures. These demands or pressures that require adjustment represent the core of stressful experience. Thus the central theme in a course such as this is: How do people adjust to stress, and how might they adjust more effectively?

Interest in stress as a topic has intensified markedly in the last decade. The gradual realization that stress has a considerable impact on our physical and psychological health has led to explosive growth in scientific research on stress. This expansion of research has been accompanied by a corresponding increase in the public's thirst for information on the subject. We'll begin our discussion by examining the nature of stress.

The Nature of Stress

The term *stress* has been used in many ways by many theorists. Some, such as Thomas Holmes (1979), define stress as a *stimulus* event that presents difficult demands (for instance, a divorce). Others, such as Hans Selye (1976), define stress as the *response* of physiological arousal elicited by troublesome events. A point of view that lies between these extremes is gradually taking hold in psychology. This viewpoint is the *transactional model of stress* advocated by Richard Lazarus and his colleagues, among others (Lazarus, 1990; Lazarus & Folkman, 1984).

Lazarus argues that stress is neither a stimulus nor a response, but a special stimulus-response transaction in which one feels threatened. Lazarus points out that a single event may be stressful for one person but not for another. Getting up to talk in front of a speech class, for example, is a piece of cake for some people. For others, it can be a paralyzing experience. If specific events are stressful only for some people, then stress cannot lie entirely in the stimulus events. In a similar vein, Lazarus argues against equating stress with the response of physiological arousal, because we routinely experience such arousal in the absence of stress. For example, a beautiful sunset, lust, and a brisk walk can all cause physiological arousal.

Thus Lazarus concludes that "stress resides neither in the situation nor in the person; it depends on a transaction between the two. It arises from how the person appraises an event and adapts to it" (Goleman, 1979, p. 52). In keeping with this theoretical perspective, we will define **stress as any circumstances that threaten or are perceived to threaten our well-being and thereby tax our coping abilities.** The threat may be to our immediate physical safety, to our long-range security, to our self-esteem, to our reputation, or to our peace of mind. This is a complex concept, so let's dig a little deeper.

Richard Lazarus

Stress Is an Everyday Event

The term *stress* tends to spark images of overwhelming, traumatic crises. People think of hijackings, hurricanes, military combat, and nuclear accidents. Undeniably, these are extremely stressful events. Studies conducted in the aftermath of tornadoes, floods, earthquakes, and the like typically find elevated rates of anxiety, depression, and drug abuse in the communities affected by these disasters (Rubonis & Bickman, 1991). These unusual and infrequent events, however, represent the tip of the iceberg. Many everyday events such as waiting in line, having car trouble, shopping for Christmas presents, misplacing your checkbook, and staring at bills you can't pay are also stressful. Researchers have found that everyday problems and the minor nuisances of life are also important forms of stress (Burks & Martin, 1985).

You might guess that minor stresses would produce minor effects, but that isn't necessarily true. Research shows that routine hassles may have significant negative effects on our mental and physical health (DeLongis, Folkman, & Lazarus, 1988; Kanner, Coyne, Schaefer, & Lazarus, 1981). Richard Lazarus and his colleagues have devised a scale to measure stress in the form of daily hassles. Their scale lists 117 everyday problems—misplacing things, struggling with rising prices, dealing with delays, and so forth. When they compared their hassles scale against another scale that assessed stress in the form of major life events (Kanner et al., 1981), they found that scores on their hassles scale were more strongly related to subjects' mental health than scores on the scale that measured major stressful events. Other investigators, working with other types of samples and other measures of hassles, have also found that everyday hassles are predictive of mental and physical health (Kohn, Lafreniere, & Gurevich, 1991; Rowlison & Felner, 1988).

Why would minor hassles be more strongly related to mental health than major stressful events? The answer isn't entirely clear yet, but most theories of stress assume that stressful events have a *cumulative* impact (Seta, Seta, & Wang, 1991). In other words, stresses add up. Routine stresses at home, at school, and at work might be fairly benign individually, but collectively they could create great strain.

The everyday nature of stress need not alarm you. Discussions of stress usually emphasize its negative effects, but stress isn't all bad. Some types of stress can be enjoyable challenges, and stress can sometimes lead to a positive outcome. Although you might find a new

An infinite variety of circumstances, including many of the routine hassles of daily living such as traffic jams, can create stress in our lives.

job highly stressful, you might also find it interesting and exciting. Moreover, this stress might force you to develop new skills and acquire new strengths. Hans Selye (1974, 1982) coined the term *eustress* to refer to "good stress" that has beneficial effects. He pointed out that life would be very dull indeed if it were altogether free of stress.

Stress Lies in the Eye of the Beholder

The experience of feeling threatened depends on what events we notice and how we choose to appraise or interpret them. Events that are stressful for one person may be ho-hum routine for another. Many people find flying in an airplane somewhat stressful, for example, but frequent fliers may not even raise an eyebrow. Some people enjoy the excitement of going out on a date with someone new; others find the uncertainty terrifying.

In discussing appraisals of stress, Lazarus and Folkman (1984) distinguish between primary and secondary appraisal. **Primary appraisal is an initial evaluation of whether an event is (1) irrelevant to you, (2) relevant but not threatening, or (3) stressful.** When you view an event as stressful, you are likely to make a **secondary appraisal, which is an evaluation of your coping resources and options for dealing with the stress.** Thus your primary appraisal would determine whether you saw an upcoming job interview as stressful. Your secondary appraisal would determine how stressful

the interview appeared, in light of your assessment of your ability to deal with the event.

Often we are not very objective in our appraisals of potentially stressful events. A study of hospitalized patients awaiting surgery showed only a slight correlation between the objective seriousness of a person's upcoming surgery and the amount of fear the person experienced (Janis, 1958). Clearly, some people are more prone than others to feel threatened by life's difficulties. This reality was apparent in a study by Lundberg and Theorell (1976), who compared neurotic subjects against control subjects in regard to their perception of the stressfulness of various life events. As we saw in Chapter 2, *neuroticism is a broad personality trait associated with chronic anxiety, insecurity, and self-consciousness.* Lundberg and Theorell found that neurotic subjects' ratings of how "upsetting" various stressful events would be were consistently higher than the control subjects' ratings of the same events. A number of studies have shown that neurotic individuals report more stress than others (Brett et al., 1990). Thus stress lies in the eye (actually, the mind) of the beholder, and our appraisals of stressful events are highly subjective.

Stress May Be Embedded in the Environment

Although the perception of stress is a highly personal matter, many kinds of stress emanate from the environmental circumstances that we share with others. *Ambient stress consists of* chronic environmental conditions that, although not urgent, are negatively valued and place adaptive demands on people (Holahan, 1986). Features of the environment, such as excessive noise, heat, and pollution, can threaten our well-being and leave their mark on our mental and physical health. For example, investigators have found an association between exposure to high levels of noise and elevated blood pressure among children attending school near Los Angeles International Airport (Cohen, Evans, Krantz, & Stokols, 1980). Research has also revealed that people exposed to excessive noise at work experience more headaches, nausea, and moodiness than others (Cohen, Glass, & Phillips, 1977). Evidence suggests that excessive heat may impair task performance and increase the likelihood of aggressive behavior (Fisher, Bell, & Baum, 1984). In a study conducted in Dayton, Ohio, Rotton and Frey (1984) found that psychiatric emergencies increased when air pollution was high.

Crowding is another source of environmental stress. Temporary experiences of crowding, such as when you're packed together with thousands of other fans at a rock concert can be stressful, but most of the research on crowding has been concerned with the effects of residential density. In general, studies find an association between high density and aggression, poor task performance, and social withdrawal (Sundstrom, 1978). One does not have to live in an urban skyscraper or tenement to experience crowding. Even an overcrowded dormitory, with three students in a room built for two, can be stressful (Mullen & Felleman, 1990). Psychologists have also explored the repercussions of living in areas that are at risk for disaster. For instance, studies suggest that people who live near a nuclear power plant or in an area prone to earthquakes may experience increased stress (Baum, 1990; Nolen-Hoeksema & Morrow, 1991).

The experience of environmental stress, like that of other types of stress, is subjective. A specific level of noise, heat, or crowding that is aversive for one person may not be bothersome to another. Even in the aftermath of a major disaster, only some people will feel stressed out. For example, in a study of Stanford students' adjustment to the 1989 Loma Prieta earthquake, which crippled the San Francisco Bay area, Nolen-Hoeksema and Morrow (1991) found negative emotional effects primarily among students who tended to ruminate about their problems and students who had been depressed before the earthquake.

Stress May Be Self-Imposed

We tend to think of stress as something imposed on us from without by others and their demands. A recent study (Epstein & Katz, 1992) of college students' stress found that stress, however, is self-imposed surprisingly often. For example, you might sign up for extra classes to get through school quickly. Or you might actively seek additional responsibilities at work to impress your boss. People frequently put pressure on themselves to get good grades or to climb the corporate ladder rapidly. Many people create stress by embracing unrealistic expectations for themselves.

Meyer Friedman and Ray Rosenman (1974) have described a personality syndrome, the Type A personality, that involves a great deal of self-imposed stress. **The *Type A personality* is characterized by competitive, aggressive, impatient, hostile behavior.** Type A people are highly motivated, and they have to "win" at everything they do. They usually are workaholics who have a hard-driving involvement in their jobs. They tend to take on too many projects and to drive themselves with many deadlines. They are exceedingly time-conscious and fidget frantically over the briefest delays. These intense individuals clearly subject themselves to unnecessary and avoidable stress. That's apparently why they have an elevated vulnerability to heart disease (Friedman & Booth-Kewley, 1988). We'll discuss the link between Type A behavior and heart disease in more detail in Chapter 14.

Because stress is often self-imposed, we have more control over our stress than many people realize. To exert control, however, we need to be able to recognize the sources of stress in our lives. Hence, in the next section we'll discuss the major types of stress.

Major Types of Stress

An enormous variety of events can be stressful for one person or another. To achieve a better understanding of stress, theorists have tried to classify the principal types of stress. None of their organizational schemes has turned out to be altogether satisfactory. It's virtually impossible to classify stressful events into nonintersecting categories. Although this problem presents conceptual headaches for researchers, it need not prevent us from describing four major types of stress: frustration, conflict, change, and pressure. As you read about each of them, you'll surely recognize four very familiar adversaries.

Frustration

> "It has been very frustrating to watch the rapid deterioration of my parents' relationship. Over the last year or two they have argued constantly and have refused to seek any professional help. I have tried to talk to them, but they kind of shut me and my brother out of their problem. I feel very helpless and sometimes even very angry, not at them, but at the whole situation."

This scenario illustrates frustration. As psychologists use the term, *frustration* **occurs in any situation in which the pursuit of some goal is thwarted.** In essence, you experience frustration when you want something and you can't have it. We all have to deal with frustration virtually every day. Traffic jams, for instance, are a routine source of frustration that can affect mood and blood pressure (Novaco, Stokols, Campbell, & Stokols, 1979). Fortunately, most of our frustrations are brief and insignificant. You may be quite upset when you go to a repair shop to pick up your ailing stereo and find that it hasn't been fixed as promised. A week later, however, you'll probably have your precious stereo, and all will be forgotten.

Of course, some frustrations can be sources of significant stress. Failures and losses are two common kinds of frustration that are often very stressful. We all fail in at least some of our endeavors. Some of us make failure almost inevitable by setting unrealistic goals for ourselves. People tend to forget that for every newly appointed vice president in the business world there are dozens of middle-level executives who don't get promoted. Losses may be especially frustrating because we are deprived of something that we are accustomed to having. Few things are more frustrating than losing a dearly loved boyfriend, girlfriend, or spouse.

Frustration may be self-imposed in that we frequently erect barriers to our own success. For instance, if you choose not to study adequately for an exam and then experience frustration when you flunk it, you have created your own frustration. Similarly, if your absenteeism at work prevents you from getting the promotion you wanted, your frustration is your responsibility. Such self-defeating patterns of behavior are surprisingly common (Baumeister & Scher, 1988).

More often than not, frustration appears to be the culprit when we feel troubled by environmental stress. Insofar as excessive noise,

Neal Miller

heat, pollution, and crowding are stressful, it's probably because they frustrate our desire for quiet, a comfortable body temperature, clean air, and adequate privacy.

Conflict

"Should I or shouldn't I? I became engaged at Christmas. My fiancé surprised me with a ring. I knew if I refused the ring he would be terribly hurt and our relationship would suffer. However, I don't really know whether or not I want to marry him. On the other hand, I don't want to lose him either."

Like frustration, conflict is an unavoidable feature of everyday life. That perplexing question "Should I or shouldn't I?" comes up countless times in our lives. ***Conflict occurs when two or more incompatible motivations or behavioral impulses compete for expression.*** As we discussed in Chapter 2, Sigmund Freud proposed nearly a century ago that internal conflicts generate considerable psychological distress. This link between conflict and distress was measured with new precision in a recent study by Robert Emmons and Laura King (1988). They used an elaborate questionnaire to assess the overall amount of internal conflict experienced by 88 subjects in two studies. They found that higher levels of conflict were associated with higher levels of anxiety, depression, and physical symptoms.

Conflicts come in three types, which were originally described by Kurt Lewin (1935) and investigated extensively by Neal Miller (1944, 1959). The types of conflict are approach-approach, avoidance-avoidance, and approach-avoidance. They are diagrammed in Figure 3.1.

In an *approach-approach conflict* a choice must be made between two attractive goals. The problem, of course, is that you can choose just one of the two goals. You have a free afternoon, say; should you play tennis or racquetball? You're out for a meal; do you want to order the pizza or the spaghetti? You can't afford both the blue sweater and the gray jacket; which should you buy?

Among the three kinds of conflict, the approach-approach type tends to be the least stressful. People usually don't stagger out of restaurants, exhausted by the stress of choosing which of several appealing entrees to eat. In approach-approach conflicts you typically have a reasonably happy ending, whichever way you decide to go. Nonetheless, approach-approach conflicts centering on important issues may sometimes be troublesome. If you are torn between two appealing college majors or two attractive boyfriends, you may find the decision-making process quite stressful.

In an *avoidance-avoidance conflict* a **choice must be made between two unattractive goals.** Forced to choose between two repellent alternatives, you are, as they say, "caught between the devil and the deep blue sea." Let's say you have very painful backaches. Should you submit to surgery, which you dread, or should you continue to live with the pain?

Obviously, avoidance-avoidance conflicts are most unpleasant and very stressful. Typically, people keep delaying their decision as long as possible, hoping that they will somehow be able to escape the conflict situation. For example, you might delay the surgery to alleviate your backaches in the hope that the backaches would disappear on their own.

In an *approach-avoidance conflict* a **choice must be made about whether to pursue a single goal that has both attractive and unattractive aspects.** For instance, imagine that you're offered a career promotion that will mean a large increase in pay. The catch is that you will have to move to a city that you hate. Approach-avoidance conflicts are very common, and they can be very stressful. Any time you have to take a risk to pursue some desirable outcome, you are likely to find yourself in an approach-avoidance conflict. Should you risk rejection by asking out that attractive person in class? Should you risk your savings by investing in a new business that could fail?

Approach-avoidance conflicts often produce *vacillation*. That is, we go back and forth, beset by indecision. We decide to go ahead, then we decide not to, then we decide to go ahead again. Humans are not unique in this respect. Many years ago Neal Miller (1944)

FIGURE 3.1
Types of conflict
Psychologists have identified three basic types of conflict. In an approach-approach or avoidance-avoidance conflict, the person is torn between two goals. In an approach-avoidance conflict there is only one goal under consideration, but it has both positive and negative aspects.

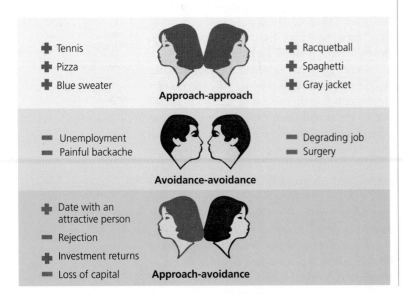

- Tennis
- Pizza
- Blue sweater

- Racquetball
- Spaghetti
- Gray jacket

Approach-approach

- Unemployment
- Painful backache

- Degrading job
- Surgery

Avoidance-avoidance

- Date with an attractive person
- Rejection
- Investment returns
- Loss of capital

Approach-avoidance

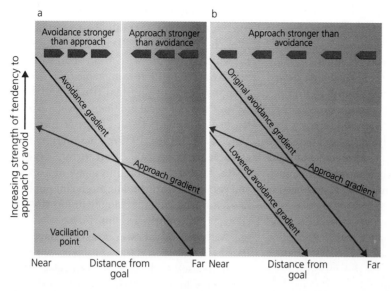

a

Avoidance stronger than approach | Approach stronger than avoidance

b

Approach stronger than avoidance

Increasing strength of tendency to approach or avoid

Avoidance gradient

Approach gradient

Vacillation point

Original avoidance gradient

Lowered avoidance gradient

Approach gradient

Near   Distance from goal   Far   Near   Distance from goal   Far

FIGURE 3.2
Approach-avoidance conflict
(a) According to Miller (1959), as you near a goal that has positive and negative features, avoidance motivation tends to rise faster than approach motivation (that's why the avoidance gradient has a steeper slope than the approach gradient), sending you into retreat. If you retreat far enough, however, you'll eventually reach a point where approach motivation is stronger than avoidance motivation, and you may decide to go ahead once again. The ebb and flow of this process leads to vacillation around the point where the two gradients intersect. (b) As the avoidance gradient is lowered, the person comes closer and closer to the goal. If the avoidance gradient can be lowered far enough, the person should be able to resolve the conflict and reach the goal.

observed the same vacillation in his groundbreaking research with rats. Miller created approach-avoidance conflicts in hungry rats by alternately feeding and shocking them at one end of a runway apparatus. Eventually these rats tended to hover near the center of the runway. They would alternately approach and retreat from the goal box at the end of the alley.

In a series of studies, Miller (1959) plotted out how an organism's tendency to approach a goal (the approach gradient in Figure 3.2a) and its tendency to retreat from the goal (the avoidance gradient in Figure 3.2a) increase as the organism nears the goal. He found that avoidance motivation increases more rapidly than approach motivation (as reflected by the avoidance gradient's steeper slope in Figure 3.2a). On the basis of this principle, Miller concluded that *in trying to resolve an approach-avoidance conflict, we should focus more on decreasing avoidance motivation than on increasing approach motivation.*

How would this insight apply to complex human dilemmas? Imagine that you are counseling a friend who is vacillating over whether to ask someone out on a date. Miller would assert that you should attempt to downplay the negative aspects of possible rejection (thus lowering the avoidance gradient) rather than dwell on how much fun the date could be (thus raising the approach gradient). Figure 3.2b shows the effects of lowering the avoidance gradient. If it is lowered far enough, the person should reach the goal (make a decision and take action).

More recent research has revealed that avoidance tendencies do not always increase more rapidly than approach tendencies (Epstein, 1982). In light of this new finding, the best advice for resolving an approach-avoidance conflict may be to work on both aspects of the conflict. In other words, you may want to attempt to lower the avoidance tendency and at the same time raise the approach tendency.

Change

"After my divorce, I lived alone for four years. Six months ago, I married a wonderful woman who has two children from her previous marriage. My biggest stress is suddenly having to adapt to living with three people instead of by myself. I was pretty set in my ways. I had certain routines. Now everything is chaos. I love my wife and I'm fond of the kids, and they're not really doing anything wrong, but my house and my life just aren't the same and I am having trouble dealing with it all."

There is evidence that life changes may represent a key type of stress. **Life changes are any noticeable alterations in one's living circumstances that require readjustment.**

Are major life changes inherently stressful? Empirical evidence suggests that they are not. Although many life changes can be very difficult, stress lies in the eye of the beholder. The transition to parenthood, for example, is stressful for some people but not for others.

Research on life change began when Thomas Holmes, Richard Rahe, and their colleagues set out to explore the relation between stressful life events and physical illness (Holmes & Rahe, 1967; Rahe & Arthur, 1978). They interviewed thousands of tuberculosis patients to find out what kinds of events preceded the onset of their disease. Surprisingly, the frequently cited events were not uniformly negative. There were plenty of aversive events, as expected, but there were also many seemingly positive events, such as getting married, having a baby, and getting promoted.

Why would positive events, such as moving to a nicer home, produce stress? According to Holmes and Rahe, it is because they produce *change*. Their thesis is that disruptions of our daily routines are stressful. According to their theory, changes in personal relationships, changes at work, changes in finances, and so forth can be stressful even when the changes are welcomed.

On the basis of this analysis, Holmes and Rahe (1967) developed the Social Readjustment Rating Scale (SRRS) to measure life change as a form of stress. The scale assigns numerical values to 43 major life events, each value supposedly reflecting the magnitude of the readjustment required by the indicated change (see Figure 3.3). In taking the scale, respondents are asked to indicate how often they experienced any of these 43 events during a certain time period (typically, the past year). The person then adds up the numbers associated with all the events checked. This sum is an index of the amount of change-related stress the person has recently experienced.

The SRRS and similar scales have been used in thousands of studies by researchers all over the world. Overall, these studies have shown that people with high scores on the SRRS tend to be more vulnerable than average to many kinds of physical illness and many types of psychological problems as well (Barrett, Rose, & Klerman, 1979; Elliott & Eisdorfer, 1982; T.W. Miller, 1989). These results have attracted a great deal of attention, and the SRRS has been reprinted in many newspapers and popular magazines. The attendant publicity has led to the widespread conclusion that life change is inherently stressful.

More recently, however, experts have criticized this research, citing problems with the methods used (Johnson & Bornstein, 1991; Raphael, Cloitre, & Dohrenwend, 1991) and problems in interpreting the findings (Brett et al., 1990; Watson & Pennebaker, 1989). At this point, it is a key interpretive issue that concerns us. Many critics have argued that the SRRS does not measure *change* exclusively. The main problem is that the list of life changes on the SRRS is dominated by events that are clearly negative or undesirable (death of a spouse, fired at work, and so on). These negative events probably generate great frustration. Although the scale includes some positive events, it is possible that frustration (generated by negative events) rather than change creates most of the stress assessed by the scale.

To investigate this possibility, researchers have begun to take into account the desirability and undesirability of subjects' life changes. Subjects are asked to indicate the desirability of the events that they check off on the SRRS and

FIGURE 3.3
Social Readjustment Rating Scale (SRRS)
Devised by Holmes and Rahe (1967), this scale measures the change-related stress in one's life. The numbers on the right are supposed to reflect the average amount of stress (readjustment) produced by each event. Respondents check off the events that have occurred to them recently and add up the associated numbers to arrive at their stress scores. The Application at the end of this chapter gives a detailed critique of the SRRS.

Social Readjustment Rating Scale

Life event	Mean value	Life event	Mean value
Death of a spouse	100	Son or daughter leaving home	29
Divorce	73	Trouble with in-laws	29
Marital separation	65	Outstanding personal achievement	28
Jail term	63	Wife begins or stops work	26
Death of close family member	63	Begin or end school	26
Personal injury or illness	53	Change in living conditions	25
Marriage	50	Revision of personal habits	24
Fired at work	47	Trouble with boss	23
Marital reconciliation	45	Change in work hours or conditions	20
Retirement	45	Change in residence	20
Change in health of family member	44	Change in school	20
Pregnancy	40	Change in recreation	19
Sex difficulties	39	Change in church activities	19
Gain of a new family member	39	Change in social activities	18
Business readjustment	39	Mortgage or loan for lesser purchase (car, TV, etc.)	17
Change in financial state	38	Change in sleeping habits	16
Death of a close friend	37	Change in number of family get-togethers	15
Change to a different line of work	36	Change in eating habits	15
Change in number of arguments with spouse	35	Vacation	13
Mortgage or loan for major purchase (home, etc.)	31	Christmas	12
Foreclosure of mortgage or loan	30	Minor violations of the law	11
Change in responsibilities at work	29		

similar scales. The findings in these studies clearly indicate that life change is not the crucial dimension measured by the SRRS. Undesirable or negative life events cause most of the stress tapped by the SRRS (Brown & McGill, 1989; Perkins, 1982; Zeiss, 1980).

Should we discard the notion that change is stressful? Not entirely. Other lines of research, independent of work with the SRRS, support the hypothesis that change is an important form of stress. Evidence links geographic mobility, for instance, to impaired mental and physical health (Brett, 1980). And research on becoming a parent, which is a highly positive life change for the vast majority of people, shows that the transition to parenthood can be extremely stressful (Miller & Sollie, 1986). A study by Brown and McGill (1989) suggests that desirable life changes may be stressful for some people but not for others. They found a link between positive life changes and increased illness only among subjects low in self-esteem. Positive events, in contrast, were correlated with improved health among their high self-esteem subjects. On the basis of these results, Brown and McGill suggest that positive events are stressful to the extent that they disrupt one's sense of identity.

More research is needed, but it is quite plausible that change constitutes a major type of stress in our lives. At present, however, we have little reason to believe that change is inherently or inevitably stressful. Some life changes may be quite challenging, while others may be quite benign.

Pressure

"My father questioned me at dinner about some things I did not want to talk about. I know he doesn't want to hear my answers, at least not the truth. My father told me when I was little that I was his favorite because I was 'pretty near perfect,' and I've spent my life trying to keep that up, even though it's obviously not true. Recently, he has begun to realize this, and it's made our relationship very strained and painful."

At one time or another, most of us have probably remarked that we were "under pressure." What does this mean? **Pressure involves expectations or demands that one behave in a certain way.** Pressure can be divided into two subtypes: the pressure to *perform* and the pressure to *conform*. You are under pressure to perform when you are expected to execute tasks and responsibilities quickly, efficiently, and successfully. Salespeople, for example, usually are

under pressure to move lots of merchandise. Professors at research institutions are often under pressure to publish papers in prestigious journals. Comedians are under pressure to be amusing. Secretaries are often under pressure to complete tremendous loads of work in very little time. Pressures to conform to others' expectations are also common in our lives. Businessmen are expected to wear suits and ties. Suburban homeowners are expected to keep their lawns manicured. Teenagers are expected to adhere to their parents' values and rules. Young adults are expected to get married by the time they're 30.

Although the concept of pressure has been widely discussed by the general public, it has received scant attention from researchers. Under development, however, is a scale to measure pressure as a form of life stress (Weiten, 1988; Weiten & Dixon, 1984). In the first two studies conducted with this 48-item self-report measure, called the Pressure Inventory, a strong relationship has been found between pressure and a variety of psychological symptoms and problems. In fact, pressure has turned out to be more strongly related to measures of mental health than the SRRS and other established measures of stress (see Figure 3.4). These findings suggest that pressure may be an important form of stress that merits more attention from researchers.

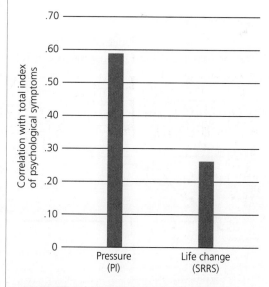

FIGURE 3.4
Pressure and psychological symptoms
A comparison of pressure and life change as sources of stress suggests that pressure may be more strongly related to mental health than change. In one study, Weiten (1988) found a correlation of .59 between scores on the Pressure Inventory (PI) and symptoms of psychological distress. In the same sample, correlation between SRRS scores and psychological symptoms was only .28.

Key Factors in Our Appraisal of Stress

e noted earlier that stress lies in the eye of the beholder. Quite a variety of factors influence our subjective appraisals of potentially stressful events. Four that stand out are (1) our familiarity with the challenge, (2) the controllability of the events, (3) the predictability of the events, and (4) the imminence of the threat.

Familiarity

An important consideration in your appraisal of stress is your familiarity with the stressful demands. Generally, the more unfamiliar you are with a potentially stressful event, the more threatened you are likely to feel (McGrath, 1977). The importance of familiarity was apparent in a study that compared the arousal of novice and experienced parachute jumpers as they prepared for a jump (Fenz & Epstein, 1967). As Figure 3.5 shows, the novices experienced considerably more arousal during the jump than the experienced parachutists. Given the influence of familiarity, a person's first major job interview or first appearance in a courtroom or first purchase of a home tends to be more stressful than subsequent similar events. Familiarity with a challenge can make yesterday's crisis today's routine.

Controllability

Another factor that influences your appraisal of stress is your perception of how much control you can exert over the event in question. If you are facing surgery and a lengthy rehabilitation period, for example, your feelings may range from a sense of powerlessness to a firm belief that you will be able to speed up the recovery process. Stern, McCants, and Pettine (1982) found that when events are viewed as controllable, they tend to be less stressful.

In another study (Breier et al., 1987) subjects were exposed to equal amounts of controllable and uncontrollable loud noise as a form of stress. In the controllable condition, subjects could learn a sequence of button pushes that would temporarily stop the noise. When the noise was controllable, subjects reported less stress and less tension. Furthermore, objective indicators of physiological arousal showed that the subjects in the study experienced less arousal when they could control the noise (see Figure 3.6).

The finding that controllability reduces stress is fairly typical in this line of research, although it is not universal (Folkman, 1984). Jerry Burger (1989) has identified some situations in which greater control is associated with *increased stress*. Burger points out that control has negative as well as positive aspects. On the negative side, when events are controllable, people have to accept greater responsibility for their outcomes. Hence, *people who are very concerned about how others will evaluate them often find being in control quite stressful*. Nonetheless, the general trend is for people to view events over which they have more control as less stressful.

Predictability

If you experience a stressful event—for instance, being fired at work—is it more traumatic when the event comes out of nowhere (unpredictable stress) or when you can see the event coming for some time (predictable stress)? In general, it appears that we prefer predictable stress over surprise packages. When researchers expose subjects to the stress of predictable and unpredictable noise, they usually find that subjects are bothered more by the unpredictable noise (Matthews, Scheier, Brunson, & Carducci, 1989). Major stressors, such as the progression of an illness or loss of a job, seem to be less devastating when they can be anticipated over a period of time. We may prefer predictability because it allows us to engage in anticipatory coping to prepare for the stress.

However, the effects of predictability are complex. In some situations people prefer not

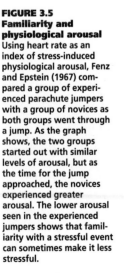

**FIGURE 3.5
Familiarity and physiological arousal**
Using heart rate as an index of stress-induced physiological arousal, Fenz and Epstein (1967) compared a group of experienced parachute jumpers with a group of novices as both groups went through a jump. As the graph shows, the two groups started out with similar levels of arousal, but as the time for the jump approached, the novices experienced greater arousal. The lower arousal seen in the experienced jumpers shows that familiarity with a stressful event can sometimes make it less stressful.

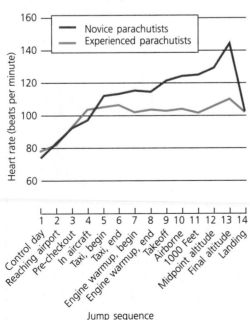

Jump sequence

to know about stress in advance (Burger, 1989). For instance, when understudy actors or rookie athletes are pressed into service as last-minute substitutes for more experienced performers, many comment, "It was better that way. I didn't have time to dwell on it and get nervous." The value of predictability probably depends on whether there's much that you can do to prepare for the stress. If preparation won't help (or if you already feel prepared), knowing about stress in advance may only allow you to dwell on the threatening event until the threat appears even greater.

Imminence

If you *do* know about a threatening event in advance, your stress usually increases as the event becomes more imminent (comes closer in time). When a threat lies in the distant future, its stressfulness may be minimal. As the challenge looms near, however, concern and distress typically escalate (Lazarus & Folkman, 1984). Thus, as you approach the day on which you have to take a critical exam, or submit to serious surgery, or speak at a convention, you generally find the stress increasing (Bolger, 1990). In fact, your stress may peak during the period of anticipation rather than with the event itself. After a big exam, for example, students often remark, "Taking it wasn't nearly as bad as anticipating it and worrying about it."

In summary, the appraisal of stress is a complicated process. The way such factors as controllability and predictability affect our appraisal of stress depends on the exact circumstances. Research on this process is important, however, because the way we appraise stress makes all the difference in the world to the way we respond to it.

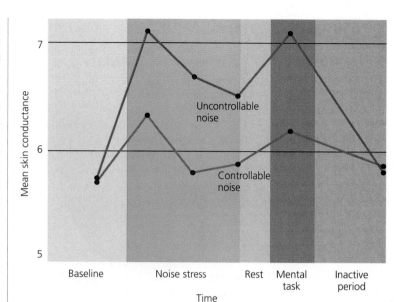

Responding to Stress

Our response to stress is complex and multidimensional. Stress affects us at several levels. Consider again the chapter's opening scenario, in which you're driving home in heavy traffic, thinking about an overdue paper, tuition increase, and parental pressures. Let's look at some of the reactions we mentioned. When you groan audibly in reaction to the traffic report, you're experiencing an *emotional response* to stress—in this case, annoyance and anger. When your pulse quickens and your stomach knots up, you're exhibiting *physiological responses* to stress. When you shout insults at another driver, your verbal aggression is a *behavioral response* to the stress at hand. Thus we can analyze our reactions to stress at three levels: (1) our emotional responses, (2) our physiological responses, and (3) our behavioral responses. Figure 3.7 depicts these three levels of response.

FIGURE 3.6
Controllability and physiological arousal
Skin conductance is an easily measured index of the physiological arousal that may be produced by stress. Subjects who were exposed to loud noise experienced considerably higher physiological arousal when the noise was uncontrollable than when they were able to exercise some control over it (Breier et al., 1987).

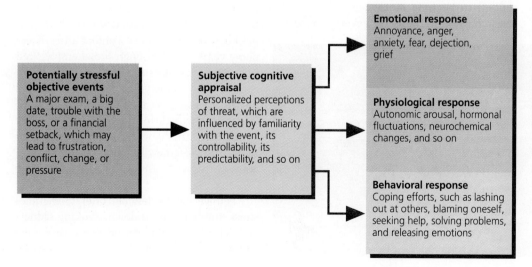

FIGURE 3.7
Our multidimensional response to stress
A potentially stressful event, such as a major exam, will elicit a subjective, cognitive appraisal of how threatening the event is. If the event is viewed with alarm, the stress may trigger emotional, physiological, and behavioral reactions. Our response to stress is multidimensional.

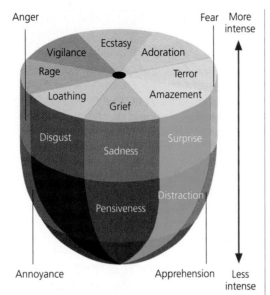

FIGURE 3.8
The dimensions of emotion
Plutchik's model of emotion provides a useful scheme for analyzing the emotional reactions evoked by stressful events. Plutchik identified eight primary emotions that vary in intensity. Stress can trigger a wide range of emotions, but reactions involving three of the eight primary emotions are especially common: anger, sadness, and fear.

The roots of stress are often interpersonal. Studies show, for example, that arguments with spouses and co-workers are a very common and significant source of stress.

Emotional Responses

Emotion is an elusive concept. How to define emotion is a subject of much debate, and many conflicting theories purport to explain emotion. Yet we all have extensive personal experience with emotions. We all know what it means to be anxious, elated, gloomy, jealous, disgusted, excited, guilty, or nervous. Rather than pursue the technical debates about emotion, we'll rely on your familiarity with the concept and simply note that **emotions are powerful, largely uncontrollable feelings, accompanied by physiological changes.** When we are under stress, we often react emotionally. More often than not, stress tends to elicit unpleasant emotions rather than pleasurable feelings.

The link between stress and emotion was apparent in a study of 96 women who filled out diaries about stresses and moods they experienced over 28 days (Caspi, Bolger, & Eckenrode, 1987). The investigators found that daily fluctuations in stress correlated with daily fluctuations in mood. As stress increased, mood tended to become more negative. As the researchers put it, "Some days everything seems

to go wrong, and by day's end, minor difficulties find their outlet in rotten moods" (p. 184). Other studies that have tracked daily mood fluctuations have found that arguments are particularly potent triggers of negative emotions (Bolger, DeLongis, Kessler, & Schilling, 1989; Clark & Watson, 1988).

Emotions Commonly Elicited

There are no simple one-to-one connections between certain types of stress and particular emotions. Stressful events may evoke a wide variety of emotions, although some are certainly more likely than others. We'll use Plutchik's (1980) model of primary emotions to highlight the types of emotions that are especially common in response to stress. Figure 3.8 shows the eight primary emotions that Plutchik identified and the varying levels of intensity of some of them. Although stress can elicit any of the emotions shown in Figure 3.8, Woolfolk and Richardson (1978) suggest that reactions along the following dimensions are particularly likely: (1) annoyance, anger, and rage; (2) apprehension, fear, and terror; and (3) pensiveness, sadness, and grief.

Annoyance, anger, and rage. Stress frequently produces feelings of anger, ranging in intensity from mild annoyance to uncontrollable rage. Frustration is particularly likely to generate anger. Some people become visibly angry in response to nearly every trivial setback. The pressure to conform also seems likely to elicit anger and resentment.

Apprehension, fear, and terror. The dimension of emotion ranging from apprehension to terror is probably evoked by stress more than any other. Anxiety falls along this dimension, somewhere between apprehension and fear. Psychologists have conducted thousands upon thousands of studies on anxiety since Freud pinpointed the link between conflict and anxiety many years ago. Although Freud emphasized how conflict causes anxiety, it is clear that apprehension, anxiety, and fear can be elicited by the pressure to perform, the threat of impending frustration, and the uncertainty associated with change. Thus all of the major types of stress can evoke emotions in this category.

Pensiveness, sadness, and grief. Sometimes stress simply brings us down, evoking sadness and dejection. We all get depressed from time to time, especially in response to frustration.

Sadness and depression are particularly likely when we feel powerless to do anything about the stress in our lives.

Effects of Emotional Arousal

Emotional responses are a natural and normal part of life. Even unpleasant emotions serve important purposes. Like physical pain, painful emotions can serve as warnings that we need to take action. It is important to note, however, that strong emotional arousal can sometimes interfere with efforts to cope with stress.

The well-known problem of *test anxiety* demonstrates how emotional arousal can hurt performance. Many students who score poorly on an exam nonetheless insist that they know the material. Many of them are probably telling the truth. Researchers have found test-related anxiety to be negatively correlated with exam performance. Students who display high test anxiety tend to score low on exams (Wine, 1982). Test anxiety can interfere with test taking in several ways, but the critical consideration appears to be the disruption of attention to the test (Sarason, 1984). Test-anxious students waste too much time worrying about how they are doing and wondering whether others are having similar problems. In other words, their minds wander too much from the task of taking the test.

Although emotional arousal may hurt coping efforts, this is not *necessarily* the case. Various theories of "optimal arousal" predict that performance on a task should improve as emotional arousal increases—up to the point where arousal becomes so high as to be disruptive (Anderson, 1990; Humphreys & Revelle, 1984). The level of arousal at which performance peaks is called the *optimal level of arousal.*

This optimal level of arousal varies from one task to another. It appears to depend (in part) on the complexity of the task at hand. The conventional wisdom is that *as a task becomes more complex, the optimal level of arousal (for peak performance) tends to decrease.* Figure 3.9 shows this relationship. As you can see, a fairly high level of arousal should be optimal on simple tasks (for example, driving eight hours to help a friend in a crisis). However, performance should peak at a lower level of arousal on complex tasks (for example, making a complicated decision that requires you to weigh many factors).

Most of the research evidence on optimal levels of arousal comes from rather simple animal learning studies. Hence it may be risky to generalize these principles to human coping efforts. Nonetheless, optimal-arousal theories provide a plausible model of how emotional arousal could have either beneficial or disruptive effects on coping.

FIGURE 3.9
Arousal and performance
The effect of emotional arousal on task performance depends on the complexity of the task. On complicated tasks, a relatively low level of arousal tends to be optimal (results in the best performance). On simpler tasks, however, performance may peak at much higher levels of arousal.

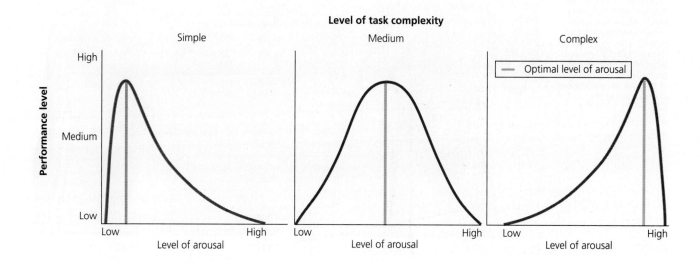

Physiological Responses

The emotional responses elicited by stress bring about important physiological changes. Even when stress is moderate, you may notice that your heart has started to beat faster, you have begun to breathe harder, and you are perspiring more than usual. How does all this (and much more) happen? Let's see.

The Fight-or-Flight Response

The *fight-or-flight response* **is a physiological reaction to threat that mobilizes an organism for attacking (fight) or fleeing (flight) an enemy.** First described by Walter Cannon (1932), the fight-or-flight response occurs in the body's autonomic nervous system. **The** *autonomic nervous system (ANS)* **is made up of the nerves that connect the heart, blood vessels, smooth muscles, and glands.** As its name suggests, the autonomic nervous system is somewhat *autonomous*. That is, it controls involuntary, visceral functions that we don't normally think about, such as heart rate, digestion, and perspiration.

The autonomic nervous system can be broken into two divisions (see Figure 3.10). The *parasympathetic division* of the ANS generally conserves bodily resources. For instance, it slows heart rate and promotes digestion to help the body save and store energy. The fight-or-flight response is mediated by the *sympathetic division* of the ANS, which mobilizes bodily resources for emergencies. In one experiment, Cannon studied the fight-or-flight response in cats by confronting them with dogs. Among other things, he noticed an immediate acceleration in breathing and heart rate and a reduction in digestive processes.

Elements of the fight-or-flight response are also seen in humans. Imagine your reaction if your car nearly spun out of control on the highway. Your heart would race and your blood pressure would surge. You might get "goose bumps" and experience a "knot in your stomach." These reflex responses are part of the fight-or-flight response.

In a sense, this automatic reaction is a leftover from our evolutionary past. It is clearly an adaptive response in the animal kingdom, where the threat of predators often requires a swift response: fight or flight. But among humans, the fight-or-flight response appears less adaptive. Most of our stresses cannot be handled simply through fight or flight. Work pressures, marital problems, and financial difficulties require far more complex responses. Moreover, our stresses often continue for lengthy periods of time, so that our fight-or-flight response leaves us in a state of enduring physiological arousal. Concern about the effects of prolonged physical arousal was first voiced by Hans Selye, a Canadian scientist who conducted extensive research on stress.

The General Adaptation Syndrome

The concept of stress was added to our language by Hans Selye (1936, 1956, 1982). Selye was born in Vienna but spent his entire profession-

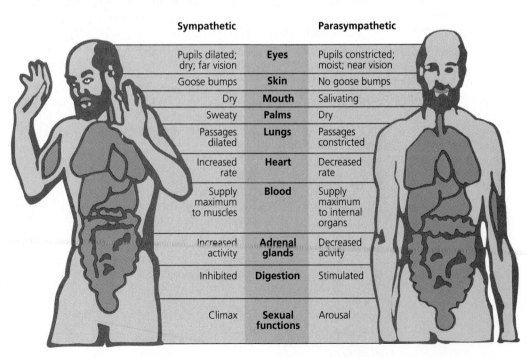

FIGURE 3.10
The autonomic nervous system (ANS) The ANS is composed of the nerves that connect the heart, blood vessels, smooth muscles, and glands. The ANS is subdivided into the sympathetic division, which mobilizes bodily resources in times of need, and the parasympathetic division, which conserves bodily resources. Some of the key functions controlled by each division of the ANS are summarized in the center of the diagram.

Sympathetic		Parasympathetic
Pupils dilated; dry; far vision	**Eyes**	Pupils constricted; moist; near vision
Goose bumps	**Skin**	No goose bumps
Dry	**Mouth**	Salivating
Sweaty	**Palms**	Dry
Passages dilated	**Lungs**	Passages constricted
Increased rate	**Heart**	Decreased rate
Supply maximum to muscles	**Blood**	Supply maximum to internal organs
Increased activity	**Adrenal glands**	Decreased acivity
Inhibited	**Digestion**	Stimulated
Climax	**Sexual functions**	Arousal

al career at McGill University in Montreal. Beginning in the 1930s, Selye exposed laboratory animals to a diverse array of both physical and psychological stressors (heat, cold, pain, mild shock, restraint, and so on). The patterns of physiological arousal seen in the animals were largely the same, regardless of the type of stress. Thus, Selye concluded that stress reactions are *nonspecific*. In other words, he maintained that they did not vary according to the specific type of stress encountered.

At first, Selye wasn't sure what to call this nonspecific response to a variety of noxious agents. In the 1940s he decided to call it stress, and the word has been part of our vocabulary ever since. In Selye's theory, *stress* referred to the body's *response* to threat. Ironically, late in his career, he admitted that it would have been better to use the word *strain* to refer to the body's response to noxious stimuli, and to reserve *stress* for the noxious stimulus events. But, as he explained, "My English was not yet good enough for me to distinguish between the words 'stress' and 'strain'" (Selye, 1976, p. 50). As the years passed, other theorists began to use the term *stress* to refer to troublesome stimulus events, creating some confusion. As we noted at the beginning of the chapter, most modern theorists sidestep this confusion by defining stress as neither a stimulus nor a response but a certain type of stimulus-response transaction.

In any case, Selye (1956, 1974) formulated an influential theory of stress reactions called the general adaptation syndrome. **The *general adaptation syndrome* is a model of the body's stress response, consisting of three stages: alarm, resistance, and exhaustion.** In the first stage of the general adaptation syndrome, an *alarm reaction* occurs when an organism recognizes the existence of a threat. Physiological arousal increases as the body musters its resources to combat the challenge. Selye's alarm reaction is essentially the fight-or-flight response originally described by Cannon.

However, Selye took his investigation of stress a couple of steps further by exposing laboratory animals to *prolonged* stress, similar to the chronic stress often endured by humans. If stress continues, the organism may progress to the second phase of the general adaptation syndrome, called the *stage of resistance*. During this phase, physiological changes stabilize as coping efforts get under way. Typically, physiological arousal continues to be higher than normal, although it may level off somewhat as the organism becomes accustomed to the threat.

If the stress continues over a substantial period of time, the organism may enter the third stage, called the *stage of exhaustion*. According to Selye, the body's resources for fighting stress are limited. If the stress cannot be overcome, the body's resources may be depleted, and physiological arousal will decrease. Eventually the organism may collapse from exhaustion. The decline in the organism's resistance during this phase is seen in Figure 3.11. This reduction in resistance may lead to what Selye called "diseases of adaptation," such as ulcers and high blood pressure.

Selye's theory and research forged a link between stress and physical illness. He showed how physiological arousal that originally was an adaptive response may, if prolonged, lead to disease. His theory has been criticized because it ignores individual differences in the appraisal of stress (Lazarus & Folkman, 1984), and his belief that stress reactions are nonspecific remains controversial (Baum, 1990; Hobfoll, 1989). Nonetheless his model provided guidance for a generation of researchers who worked out the details of how stress reverberates throughout the body. Let's look at some of those details.

Brain-Body Pathways

When we experience stress, the brain sends signals to the endocrine system along two major pathways (Asterita, 1985). **The *endocrine system* consists of glands that secrete chemicals called hormones into the bloodstream.** The

Hans Selye

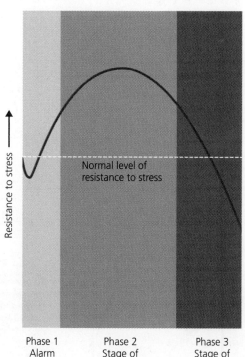

FIGURE 3.11
The general adaptation syndrome
According to Selye, our physiological response to stress can be broken into three phases. During the first phase, the body mobilizes its resources for resistance after a brief initial shock. In the second phase, resistance levels off and eventually begins to decline. If the third phase of the general adaptation syndrome is reached, resistance is depleted, leading to health problems and exhaustion.

FIGURE 3.12
The endocrine system
The endocrine glands secrete hormones into the bloodstream. The locations of the principal endocrine glands are shown here. The hormones released by these glands regulate a variety of physical functions and play a key role in our response to stress.

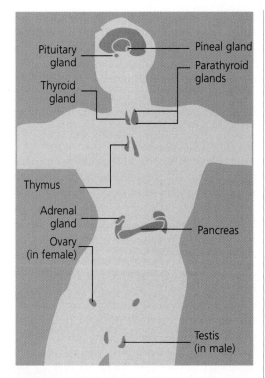

major endocrine glands, such as the pituitary, pineal, thyroid, and adrenal glands, are shown in Figure 3.12.

The hypothalamus, a small structure near the base of the brain, appears to initiate action along both pathways. The first

FIGURE 3.13
Brain-body pathways during stress
In times of stress, the brain sends signals along two pathways. The pathway through the autonomic nervous system controls the release of catecholamine hormones, which help mobilize the body for action. The pathway through the pituitary gland and the endocrine system controls the release of corticosteroid hormones, which increase energy and ward off inflammation of the tissues.

Stress

Pituitary ← Hypothalamus

Adrenocorticotropic hormone (ACTH)

Autonomic nervous system (sympathetic division)

Adrenal medulla

Adrenal cortex

Secretion of corticosteroids

Increased protein and fat mobilization
Increased access to energy storage
Decreased inflammation

Secretion of catecholamines

Increased cardiovascular response
Increased respiration
Increased perspiration
Increased blood flow to active muscles
Increased muscle strength
Increased mental activity

pathway (shown on the right in Figure 3.13) is routed through the autonomic nervous system. The hypothalamus activates the sympathetic division of the ANS. A key part of this activation involves stimulation of the central part of the adrenal glands (the adrenal medulla) to release large amounts of *catecholamines* into the bloodstream. These hormones radiate throughout your body, producing many important physiological changes. The net result of catecholamine elevation is that your body is mobilized for action. Heart rate and blood flow increase, pumping more blood to your brain and muscles. Respiration and oxygen consumption speed up, facilitating alertness. Digestive processes are inhibited to conserve your energy. The pupils of your eyes dilate, increasing visual sensitivity.

The second pathway (shown in Figure 3.13) involves more direct communication between the brain and the endocrine system. The hypothalamus sends signals to the so-called master gland of the endocrine system, the pituitary gland. The pituitary secretes a hormone (ACTH) that stimulates the outer part of the adrenal glands (the adrenal cortex) to release another important set of hormones—*corticosteroids*. These hormones stimulate the release of more fats and proteins into circulation, thus helping to increase your energy. They also mobilize chemicals that help to inhibit inflammation of tissues in case of injury.

Stress can also produce other physiological changes that we are just beginning to understand. The most critical changes occur in the immune system. Your immune system provides you with resistance to infections. Mounting evidence indicates, however, that stress can suppress the functioning of the immune system, making it less effective in repelling invasions by infectious agents (Solomon, Amkraut, & Rubin, 1985; Zautra et al., 1989). The exact mechanism by which the immune system is suppressed remains a mystery for the moment. It may be mediated by the release of endorphins, internally produced chemicals that resemble opiate drugs (such as morphine) in structure and effects (Meyerhoff, Oleshansky, & Mougey, 1988). In any case, it is becoming clear that our physiological responses to stress extend into every corner of our bodies. As you will see, these physiological reactions can have an impact on both our mental and our physical health.

Behavioral Responses

Although we respond to stress at several levels, our behavior is the crucial dimension of our reactions. Our emotional and physiological responses to stress—which are often undesirable—tend to be largely automatic. If we deal effectively with stress at the behavioral level, however, we may shut down these potentially harmful emotional and physiological responses.

Most behavioral responses to stress involve coping. *Coping* **refers to active efforts to master, reduce, or tolerate the demands created by stress.** Notice that this definition is neutral as to whether coping efforts are healthy or maladaptive. The popular use of the term often implies that coping is inherently healthy. When we say that someone "coped with her problems," we imply that she handled them effectively.

In reality, coping responses may be either healthy or unhealthy. If you were flunking a history course at midterm, for example, you might cope with this stress in the following ways. (1) You could increase your study efforts. (2) You could seek special help from a tutor. (3) You might blame your professor for your poor grade. (4) Or you might give up on the class without really trying. Clearly, the first two coping responses would be healthier than the latter two. Thus, coping efforts may range from healthy to unhealthy.

People cope with stress in an endless variety of ways. Because of the complexity and importance of coping processes, we'll devote all of the next chapter to ways of coping. At this point, it is sufficient to note that our coping strategies help to determine whether stress has any positive or negative effects on us. In the next section, we'll see what some of those effects can be as we discuss the possible outcomes of our struggles with stress.

The Potential Effects of Stress

e struggle with many stresses every day. Most of them come and go without leaving any enduring imprint. When stress is severe or when demands pile up, however, stress may have lasting effects. These effects are often called "adaptational outcomes." They are relatively durable (though not necessarily permanent) consequences of exposure to stress. Although stress can have

beneficial effects, research has focused mainly on possible negative outcomes, so you'll find our discussion slanted in that direction.

Impaired Task Performance

Frequently stress takes a toll on our ability to perform effectively on the task at hand. For instance, Roy Baumeister's work shows how pressure can interfere with performance. Baumeister's (1984) theory assumes that pressure to perform often makes us self-conscious and that this elevated self-consciousness disrupts our attention. He theorizes that attention may be distorted in two ways. First, elevated self-consciousness may divert attention from the demands of the task, creating distractions. Second, when the task is so well learned that it should be executed almost automatically, the self-conscious person may focus *too much* attention on it. Thus the person thinks too much about what he or she is doing.

Baumeister (1984) found support for his theory in a series of laboratory experiments in which he manipulated the pressure to perform well on a simple perceptual-motor task. Even

Olympic athletes like gymnast Kim Zmeskal are under intense pressure to succeed. High-pressure situations can produce heightened self-consciousness and impaired performance—what has been described as "choking under pressure."

onships in professional baseball and basketball. These sports settle their championships with a series of games. Thus the performance of the home teams in early games can be compared against their performance in the final game. As Baumeister and Steinhilber hypothesized, they found that the winning percentage for home teams was significantly lower in final games than in early games in both sports (see Figure 3.14). Furthermore, statistics showed that the home baseball team made more fielding errors in game 7 than in early games, and the home basketball team's free-throw shooting percentage went down in the last game.

The most obvious explanation for these findings is that the home team frequently "chokes under pressure," as Baumeister's theory predicts. Thus stress can impair one's ability to perform a task even if one is a gifted professional athlete.

Disruption of Cognitive Functioning

An interesting experimental study suggests that Baumeister is on the right track in looking to *attention* to explain how stress impairs task performance. In a study of stress and decision making, Keinan (1987) was able to measure three specific aspects of subjects' attention under stressful and nonstressful conditions. Keinan placed subjects under stress by telling them that they might receive painful but harmless electric shocks while working on a decision-making task at a computer. No one was actually shocked, and subjects were given the option of quitting the study when they were told about the shock. Keinan found that stress disrupted two out of the three aspects of attention measured in the study. Stress increased subjects' tendency (1) to jump to a conclusion too quickly without considering all their options and (2) to do an unsystematic, poorly organized review of their available options.

Stress may disrupt other aspects of our cognitive processes besides attention. In some people, a high level of emotional and physiological arousal leads to reduced flexibility in thinking, poor concentration, and less effective memory storage (Mandler, 1982).

Furthermore, *severe* stress can leave people dazed and confused, in a state of shock (Horowitz, 1979). In these states, people report feeling emotionally numb, and they respond in a flat, apathetic fashion to events around them. They often stare off into space and have difficulty maintaining a coherent train of thought.

more impressive, his theory was supported in a study of the past performance of professional sports teams in championship contests (Baumeister & Steinhilber, 1984). According to Baumeister, when a championship series such as baseball's World Series goes to the final, decisive game, the home team is under greater pressure than the visiting team. Why? Because players desperately want to succeed in front of their hometown fans. As a result, they experience elevated self-consciousness. Conventional wisdom suggests that home teams have the advantage in sports. But Baumeister argues that the performance of the home team declines when pressure mounts in the final game of a championship series.

To test this hypothesis, Baumeister and Steinhilber (1984) analyzed past champi-

FIGURE 3.14
Choking under pressure
In early World Series and NBA championship contests that involve less pressure, the home team enjoys an advantage. But when it comes to the last game, the home team frequently chokes under pressure, as evidenced by the decreased winning percentages shown here. (Data from Baumeister & Steinhilber, 1984.)

Home team wins (%)

.600					
.400					
.200					
0					

Games 1–2 | Last game (game 5 or 6) | Last game (game 7)
Baseball: World Series results, 1924–1982

Games 1–4 | Last game (game 5 or 6) | Last game (game 7)
Basketball: NBA semifinal series and championship results, 1967–1982

Their behavior frequently has an automatic, rigid, stereotyped quality. Fortunately, this disorientation usually occurs only in extreme situations involving overwhelming stress. For instance, you will sometimes see shock among people who have just been through a major disaster, such as a fire, a flood, or a tornado.

Burnout

Burnout is an overused buzzword that means different things to different people. Nonetheless, Ayala Pines and her colleagues have described burnout in a systematic way that has facilitated scientific study of the syndrome (Pines & Aronson, 1988; Pines, Aronson, & Kafry, 1981). **Burnout involves physical, mental, and emotional exhaustion that is attributable to work-related stress.** The physical exhaustion includes chronic fatigue, weakness, and low energy. The mental exhaustion is manifested in highly negative attitudes toward oneself, one's work, and life in general. The emotional exhaustion leaves one feeling hopeless, helpless, and trapped.

What causes burnout? According to Pines and her colleagues (1981), "it usually does not occur as the result of one or two traumatic events but sneaks up through a general erosion of the spirit" (p. 3). They view burnout as an emotional disturbance that is brought on gradually by heavy, chronic job-related stress.

Initially theorists thought that burnout was unique to the helping professions, such as social work, clinical psychology, and counseling. The high burnout rate in the helping professions was blamed on helpers' emotionally draining relations with their clients. It has gradually become clear, however, that burnout is a potential problem in all occupations (Maslach, 1982). Indeed, work stress may not be the only cause of burnout. It's possible that chronic stress created by other roles, such as parenting and being a student, may lead to burnout.

Delayed Effects: Post-Traumatic Stress Disorders

The effects of stress are not necessarily apparent right away. Some time may elapse between the occurrence of stress and the appearance of its effects. The *post-traumatic stress disorder* **involves disturbed behavior attributed to a major stressful event that emerges after the stress is over.** Post-traumatic stress disorders have mostly been seen in veterans of the Vietnam war. Among Vietnam veterans, post-traumatic disorders typically began to surface anywhere from 9 to 60 months after the soldier's discharge from military service (Shatan, 1978). Of course the soldiers exhibited immediate stress reactions as well but these were expected. The delayed reactions were something of a surprise.

While post-traumatic stress disorders are widely associated with the experiences of Vietnam veterans, they have also been seen in response to other cases of severe stress. A recent study of mental health by Helzer, Robins, and McEvoy (1987) suggests that post-traumatic stress disorders have been experienced by roughly 5 out of every 1000 men and 13 out of every 1000 women in the general population.

What types of stressful situation other than

Experiencing the horrors of natural disasters can sometimes lead to post-traumatic stress disorder.

combat are severe enough to produce post-traumatic disorders? Among females, the most common cause found by Helzer and his colleagues was a physical attack, such as a rape. Other causes among women included seeing someone die (or seeing someone seriously hurt), close brushes with death, serious accidents, and discovering a spouse's affair. Among men, all the post-traumatic disorders were due to combat experiences or to seeing someone die.

In the study by Helzer and his associates (1987), a long time lag between the severe stress and the onset of the post-traumatic disorder was seen only in cases caused by war experiences. There may be something unique about the way people cope with the stress of war. In all the other cases, the post-traumatic stress syndrome surfaced soon after the occurrence of the extremely stressful event.

What are the symptoms of post-traumatic stress disorders? Common symptoms seen in combat veterans have included nightmares, paranoia, emotional numbing, guilt about surviving, alienation, and problems in social relations (A. Blank, 1982). In the more diverse collection of cases identified by Helzer and his colleagues (1987), the most common symptoms were nightmares, difficulties in sleeping, and feelings of jumpiness.

Psychological Problems and Disorders

Post-traumatic stress disorders are caused by a single episode of extreme stress. Of greater relevance to most of us are the effects of chronic, prolonged, everyday stress. On the basis of clinical impressions, psychologists have long suspected that chronic stress may contribute to many types of psychological problems and mental disorders. Since the late 1960s, advances in the measurement of stress have allowed researchers to confirm these suspicions in empirical studies. In the domain of common psychological problems, studies indicate that stress may contribute to poor academic performance (Lloyd, Alexander, Rice, & Greenfield, 1980), insomnia (Hartmann, 1985), nightmares (Cernovsky, 1989), sexual difficulties (Malatesta & Adams, 1984), drug abuse (Krueger, 1981), and anxiety and dejection (Weiten, 1988).

Above and beyond these everyday problems, research reveals that stress often contributes to the onset of full-fledged psychological disorders, including depression (Hammen, Mayol, deMayo, & Marks, 1986), schizophrenia (Spring, 1989), neurotic disorders (McKeon, Roa, & Mann, 1989), and eating disorders (Strober, 1989). We'll discuss the relations between stress and mental disorders in detail in Chapter 15. Of course, stress is only one of many factors that may contribute to psychological disorders. Nonetheless, it is sobering to realize that stress can have a dramatic impact on our mental health.

Physical Illness

It is just as sobering to realize that stress can also have a dramatic impact on our physical health. The idea that stress can contribute to physical diseases is not entirely new. Evidence that stress can cause physical illness began to accumulate back in the 1930s. By the 1950s, the concept of psychosomatic disease was widely accepted. *Psychosomatic diseases* **are genuine physical ailments caused in part by psychological factors, especially emotional distress.** The underlying assumption is that stress-induced autonomic arousal contributes to most psychosomatic diseases. Please note, these diseases are not *imagined* physical ailments. The term *psychosomatic* is often misused to refer to ailments that are "all in the head." This is an entirely different syndrome, which we'll discuss in Chapter 15.

Common psychosomatic diseases include high blood pressure, ulcers, asthma, skin disorders such as eczema and hives, and migraine and tension headaches (Kaplan, 1985). These diseases do not *necessarily* have a strong psychological component in every affected individual. There is a genetic predisposition to most psychosomatic diseases, and in some people these diseases are largely physiological in origin (Weiner, 1977). More often than not, however, psychological factors contribute to psychosomatic diseases. When they do, stress is the culprit.

Before the 1970s, it was thought that stress contributed to the development of only a few physical diseases (the psychosomatic diseases). In the 1970s, however, researchers began to uncover new links between stress and a great variety of diseases previously believed to be purely physiological in origin. Although there is room for debate on some specific diseases, stress may influence the onset and course of heart disease, stroke, tuberculosis, multiple sclerosis, arthritis, diabetes, leukemia, cancer, various types of infectious disease, and the common cold (Elliott & Eisdorfer, 1982; Miller, 1983). We'll take a more detailed look at the evidence linking stress to some of these diseases in Chapter 14.

Beneficial Effects

The beneficial effects of stress are more difficult to pinpoint than the harmful effects because they tend to be more subtle. Although research data are sparse, they point to at least three ways in which stress can have positive effects.

First, stressful events help to satisfy our need for stimulation and challenge. Studies suggest that most people prefer an intermediate level of stimulation and challenge in their lives (Suedfeld, 1979). Although we think of stress in terms of stimulus overload, underload can be extremely unpleasant as well. Most of us would experience a suffocating level of boredom if we lived a stress-free existence. In a sense, then, stress fulfills a basic need of the human organism.

Second, stress frequently promotes personal growth or self-improvement (Holahan & Moos, 1990). Stressful events sometimes force us to develop new skills, acquire new insights, and develop new strengths. In other words, the adaptation process initiated by stress may lead to personal changes that are for the better. Confronting and conquering a stressful challenge may lead to improvements in specific coping abilities and to enhanced self-esteem. A breakup with a boyfriend or a girlfriend, for example, frequently leads individuals to change aspects of their behavior that they find unsatisfactory. Moreover, even if we do not conquer stressors, we may be able to learn from our mistakes.

Third, today's stress can inoculate us so that we are less affected by tomorrow's stress. Some studies suggest that exposure to stress can increase our tolerance of stress—as long as the stress isn't overwhelming (Epstein, 1983; Janis, 1983). Thus a woman who has previously endured business setbacks may be much better prepared than most people to deal with a bank foreclosure on her home.

In light of the negative effects that stress can have, an increase in tolerance of stress is a desirable goal. We'll look next at the factors that influence our ability to tolerate stress.

Factors Influencing Tolerance of Stress

The effects of stress vary from one person to another. Some people seem to be able to withstand the ravages of stress better than others (Holohan & Moos, 1990). Why? Because several variables moderate the impact of stress on our physical and mental health. To shed

light on differences in people's ability to tolerate stress, we'll look at five key *moderator variables*: social support, hardiness, optimism, sensation seeking, and autonomic reactivity. As you'll see, these factors influence our appraisals of potentially stressful events and our emotional, physical, and behavioral responses to stress. These complexities are diagrammed in Figure 3.15, which builds on Figure 3.7 to provide a more complete overview of all the factors involved in our reactions to stress.

Social Support

Friends may be good for your health! This startling conclusion emerges from studies on social support as a moderator of stress. **Social support involves various types of aid and succor provided by members of one's social networks.** In one study of social support, Gore (1978) looked at the moderating role of support in 100 stably employed married men who were facing a very powerful form of stress: the loss of their jobs after a plant shutdown. Social support from wives, friends, and relatives was assessed. Gore found that men who had relatively strong social support showed (1) less emotional response to the frustration and (2) fewer symptoms of physical illness.

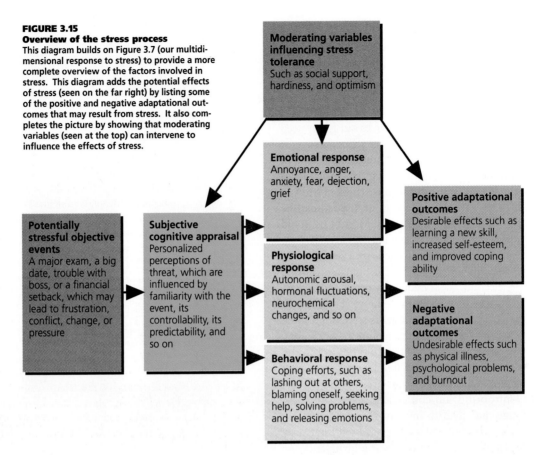

FIGURE 3.15
Overview of the stress process
This diagram builds on Figure 3.7 (our multidimensional response to stress) to provide a more complete overview of the factors involved in stress. This diagram adds the potential effects of stress (seen on the far right) by listing some of the positive and negative adaptational outcomes that may result from stress. It also completes the picture by showing that moderating variables (seen at the top) can intervene to influence the effects of stress.

Moderating variables influencing stress tolerance
Such as social support, hardiness, and optimism

Emotional response
Annoyance, anger, anxiety, fear, dejection, grief

Potentially stressful objective events
A major exam, a big date, trouble with boss, or a financial setback, which may lead to frustration, conflict, change, or pressure

Subjective cognitive appraisal
Personalized perceptions of threat, which are influenced by familiarity with the event, its controllability, its predictability, and so on

Physiological response
Autonomic arousal, hormonal fluctuations, neurochemical changes, and so on

Behavioral response
Coping efforts, such as lashing out at others, blaming oneself, seeking help, solving problems, and releasing emotions

Positive adaptational outcomes
Desirable effects such as learning a new skill, increased self-esteem, and improved coping ability

Negative adaptational outcomes
Undesirable effects such as physical illness, psychological problems, and burnout

In a more recent study, Jemmott and Magloire (1988) examined the effect of social support on the functioning of the immune system in a group of students going through the stress of final exams. They found that students who reported stronger social support had higher levels of an antibody that plays a key role in warding off respiratory infections. Positive correlations between high social support and effective functioning of the immune system were also seen in a study that focused on spouses of cancer patients (Baron et al., 1990).

Many other studies have found evidence that social support is favorably related to physical health (Cohen, 1988). Indeed, in a major review of the relevant research, House, Landis, and Umberson (1988) argue that the evidence linking social support to health is roughly as strong as the evidence linking smoking to cancer. Social support seems to be good medicine for the mind as well as the body, as most studies find an association between social support and mental health (Leavy, 1983). It appears that social support serves as a protective buffer for us during times of high stress, reducing the negative impact of stressful events. Furthermore, social support has its own positive effects on health, which may be apparent even when we aren't under great stress (Cohen & Syme, 1985).

Social support has such power that even the special bonds provided by pets may buffer the effects of stress! For instance, Siegel (1990) found that elderly pet owners required less medical care than comparable subjects who did not own pets. In another study, women exposed to brief stress showed less physiological reaction when their pets were with them (Allen, Blascovich, Tomaka, & Kelsey, 1991).

Interest in the effects of social support has led researchers to construct classification schemes that specify the types of support people may provide. House (1981) proposed that social support can serve four important functions.

- *Emotional support* involves expressions of affection, interest, and concern that tell us we are appreciated. It includes such behaviors as listening sympathetically to our problems. Presumably it bolsters our self-esteem.
- *Appraisal support* involves helping people to evaluate and make sense of their troubles and problems. It includes efforts to clarify the nature of the problem and provide feedback about its significance.
- *Informational support* involves advice about how to handle the problem, including discussions of possible solutions and the relative merits of alternative coping strategies.
- *Instrumental support* involves material aid and

services. Such activities cover a wide range, such as providing someone with a place to stay, lending money, accompanying the person to a social service agency, and helping to assume work or family responsibilities.

Given that people can provide various types of social support, Carolyn Cutrona (1990) argues that the benefits of social support may hinge on whether the nature of the support matches the nature of the person's problem. She points out, for instance, that it would be useless to offer financial assistance (instrumental support) to console a wealthy man whose wife has just died, when the man clearly needs emotional support. According to Cutrona, the *controllability* of a stressful event is a key consideration governing the type of support that is optimal. When an event is uncontrollable, there is nothing one can do to prevent it, so instrumental and informational support are largely irrelevant; but emotional support is critical. When people are grappling with controllable events, though, instrumental and informational support are likely to be especially valuable

It is important to note that social *relationships* are not equivalent to social *support*. Some friends and family members may be sources of more *strain* than *support* (Rook, 1990). People close to us can put us under pressure, criticize us, make us feel guilty, break promises, make excessive demands on us, provoke arguments, and otherwise compound our stress.

Pagel, Erdly, and Becker (1987) looked at both the good and the bad sides of social relations in measuring subjects' satisfaction with their social networks. They found that the *helpfulness* of friends and family was less important than whether friends and family *caused emotional distress*. Adapting a line from an old Beatles song, the investigators concluded that "we get by with *and in spite of* a little help from our friends." To some extent, then, people who report good social support may really mean that their friends and family aren't driving them crazy.

Hardiness

Suzanne Kobasa reasoned that if stress affects some people less than others, then some people must be *hardier* than others. To test this hypothesis, she set out to determine whether personality factors might be the key to these differences in hardiness.

Kobasa (1979) used a modified version of the Holmes and Rahe (1967) stress scale (SRRS) to measure the amount of stress experienced by a group of executives. As in most other studies, she found a modest correlation between stress and the incidence of physical illness. However, she carried her investigation one step further than previous studies. She compared the high-stress executives who exhibited the expected high incidence of illness against the high-stress executives who stayed healthy. She administered a battery of psychological tests, comparing the executives along 18 dimensions of personality. She found that the hardier executives "were more committed, felt more in control, and had bigger appetites for challenge" (Kobasa, 1984, p. 70). Thus the personality traits found to be associated with hardiness include the following (Kobasa, Maddi, & Kahn, 1982).

• *A sense of commitment.* The hardy executives typically displayed a clear sense of values. They had well-defined goals and a commitment to their importance. The less hardy executives were characterized as alienated (lacking direction and commitment to a value system).

• *An appetite for challenge.* The stress-resistant executives tended to seek out and actively confront challenges. They viewed change, rather than stability, as the norm in life. They welcomed change instead of clinging to the past. The less stress-resistant executives were more likely to view change as alarming.

• *An internal locus of control.* **Locus of control is a personality dimension centering on whether people believe that their outcomes are governed by their own actions,** which was first described by Julian Rotter (1966, 1990). Individuals with an *external locus of control* believe that their successes and failures are governed by external factors, such as fate, luck, and chance. In contrast, individuals with an *internal locus of control* believe that their successes and failures are determined by internal factors, such as their actions and abilities. Kobasa found that hardy executives tended to exhibit a more internal locus of control whereas the less stress-resistant executives were more likely to feel like powerless pawns of fate.

Thus **hardiness is a personality syndrome marked by commitment, challenge, and control that is purportedly associated with strong resistance to stress.** Hardiness appears to buffer the effects of stress by altering the way stress is appraised. Hardy subjects tend to appraise potentially stressful events as less threatening and less undesirable than others (Rhodewalt & Zone, 1989; Wiebe, 1991). Doubts have been voiced, however, about the relevance of the

Suzanne Ouelette (formerly Kobasa)

health in a sample of college students. In a pair of subsequent studies, they found that optimists and pessimists cope with stress differently (Scheier, Weintraub, & Carver, 1986). Optimists are more likely to engage in action-oriented, problem-focused coping. They are more willing than pessimists to seek social support, and they are more likely to emphasize the positive in their appraisals of stressful events. Pessimists are more likely to deal with stress by giving up or engaging in denial. In another study that focused on surgical patients, optimism was found to be associated with a faster recovery and a quicker return to normal activities after coronary artery bypass surgery (Scheier et al., 1989). According to Scheier and Carver (1992), optimism leads people to cope more adaptively with stress.

In a related line of research, Christopher Peterson and Martin Seligman have studied how people explain bad events (personal setbacks, mishaps, disappointments, and such). They identified a pessimistic explanatory style, whereby some people tend to blame setbacks on their personal shortcomings. In a retrospective study of men who graduated from Harvard back in the 1940s, they found an association between this pessimistic explanatory style and relatively poor health (Peterson, Seligman, & Vaillant, 1988). In their attempt to explain this association, they speculate that pessimism leads to passive coping efforts and poor health-care practices.

Only a few studies have been carried out to compare the effects of optimism and pessimism, but they all suggest that this aspect of personality influences the impact of stress. Future research on this dimension of personality should clarify its role in moderating the effects of stress.

hardiness syndrome to women (Wiebe, 1991), and the key elements of hardiness are being actively debated (Funk & Houston, 1987; Hull, Van Treuren, & Virnelli, 1987). Some researchers believe that it all boils down to having an internal locus of control (Cohen & Edwards, 1989). Nonetheless, Kobasa's work has stimulated research on the way personality affects our health and our tolerance of stress. Of particular interest is new work on optimism, a widely discussed trait that researchers have paid little attention to until recently.

Optimism

Defining *optimism* **as a general tendency to expect good outcomes,** Michael Scheier and Charles Carver (1985) found a correlation between optimism and relatively good physical

Sensation Seeking

Sensation seeking is yet another personality trait that affects our response to stress. First described by Marvin Zuckerman (1971, 1979,

Reprinted with special permission of King Features Syndicate.

1990), *sensation seeking* is a generalized preference for high or low levels of sensory stimulation (see Figure 3.16). People who are high in sensation seeking prefer, and perhaps even need, a high level of stimulation. They are easily bored, and they enjoy challenges. They like activities that may involve some physical risk, such as mountain climbing, white-water rafting, and surfing. They satisfy their appetite for stimulation by experimenting with drugs, numerous sexual partners, and novel experiences (such as travel to unusual places). They relish gambling, spicy foods, provocative art, wild parties, and unusual friends.

Obviously, high sensation seekers actively pursue experiences that many people would find very stressful. Now that you know how subjective stress is, though, it should come as no surprise that sensation seekers see these experiences as less threatening, risky, and anxiety-provoking than other people would (Franken, Gibson, & Rowland, 1992). Zuckerman (1990) believes that there is a biological predisposition to seek a high level of sensation.

Zuckerman makes a couple of intriguing points about sensation seeking in relation to adjustment processes. First, he suggests that people very high and very low in sensation seeking may have difficulty understanding each other, not to mention finding mutually enjoyable activities. Thus progress in a romantic relationship may be easier when the partners are compatible in sensation seeking. This hypothesis received support in a recent study by Marvin Schroth (1991). He found that the extent of disparity between partners in sensation seeking correlated negatively with couples' satisfaction with their relationship. In other words, the more dissimilar couples were in sensation seeking, the less satisfied with their relationship they tended to be. Second, Zuckerman suggests that it is important for high and low sensation seekers to select the "right" type of occupation. It seems likely that a high sensation seeker would be frustrated by routine, monotonous work, while a low sensation seeker might be overwhelmed easily by the stress of a high-pressure job.

Although sensation seeking may be associated with resistance to stress, we hasten to point out that high sensation seeking may often be more maladaptive than adaptive. High sensation seekers are more likely than other people to indulge in drug abuse, to have difficulty in school, to exhibit unhealthy habits (such as smoking and driving too fast), and to engage in impulsive behavior, including fighting (Zuckerman, 1979, 1990). Some studies have

Learned Optimism: How to Change Your Mind and Your Life

by Martin E. P. Seligman (Pocket Books, 1990)

Martin Seligman is an outstanding researcher who has done pioneering work on classical conditioning, learned helplessness, phobic disorders, depression, and most recently, optimism. In *Learned Optimism* Seligman touches on all these topics and more, although he focuses primarily on the implications of his work on explanatory style—that is, the way people explain their successes and failures. This is a highly personal book in which Seligman describes how his research on optimism grew out of his earlier work on learned helplessness and depression. It offers some interesting insights into how a scientist's thinking evolves as research progresses and new evidence emerges.

According to Seligman, people have characteristic ways of explaining and thinking about their successes, their failures, and their challenges in life. Pessimists expect the worst possible scenario from every setback and they blame themselves for their failures. Optimists are much the opposite. They see life's difficulties in the least threatening light and they tend to attribute setbacks to circumstances rather than to their personal flaws and inadequacies. Seligman reviews research on how these differences in explanatory style affect mental and physical health, as well as performance in school, sports, and work. In addition to highlighting the significance of optimism versus pessimism, Seligman offers extensive advice on how people can change their characteristic ways of thinking, borrowing liberally from the ideas of other influential theorists, such as Albert Ellis and Aaron Beck. *Learned Optimism* is a well-written, readable, practical book, loaded with fascinating anecdotes and firmly grounded in empirical research.

> There was a lot of hype in the press about Berkeley swimming star Matt Biondi's chances in the 1988 Seoul Olympics. . . . The first event Biondi swam was the two-hundred-meter freestyle. He finished a disappointing third. The second event was the one-hundred-meter butterfly, not his premier event. Overpowering the field, he led all the way. But in the last two meters, rather than taking one extra stroke and crashing into the finish wall, he appeared to relax and coast the final meter. You could hear the groan in Seoul, and imagine it across America, as he was inched (centimetered?) out by Anthony Nesty of Surinam, who took the extra stroke to win Surinam's first medal ever. The "agony of defeat" interviewers hammered Biondi on the disappointment of a bronze and a silver medal and speculated that he might not be able to rebound. Would Biondi carry home gold in his five remaining events after this embarrassing start?
>
> I sat in my living room confident that he would. I had reason to believe this, because we had tested Matt Biondi in Berkeley four months before to determine his capacity to do just what he had to do now—come back from defeat.
>
> Along with his teammates, he had taken the Attributional Style Questionnaire, and he had come out in the top quarter of optimism of an optimistic bunch. We had then simulated defeat under controlled conditions in the pool. Nort Thornton, Biondi's coach, had him swim the one-hundred-yard butterfly all out. Biondi swam it in 50.2 seconds, a very respectable time. But Thornton told him he had swum 51.7, a very slow time for Biondi. Biondi looked disappointed and surprised. Thornton told him to rest up for a few minutes and then swim it again—all out. Biondi did. His actual time got even faster, 50.0. Because his explanatory style was highly optimistic and he had shown us that he got faster—not slower—after defeat, I felt he would bring back gold from Seoul.
>
> In his last five events in Seoul, Biondi won five gold medals. [pp. 163–164]

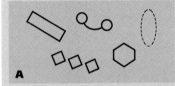 
FIGURE 3.16
A brief scale to assess sensation seeking as a trait
As the text explains, people high in sensation seeking tend to appraise potentially stressful events as less threatening than others do. Follow the instructions for this scale to obtain a rough estimate of your own sensation-seeking tendencies.

even found an association between high sensation seeking and criminal behavior (L. Ellis, 1987; Young, 1990). Thus the disadvantages of high sensation seeking may well outweigh the advantages.

Autonomic Reactivity

In light of the physiological response that we often make to stress, it makes sense that our physical makeup may influence our tolerance of stress. According to this line of thinking, those of us who have a relatively placid autonomic nervous system should be less affected by stress than those equipped with a highly reactive ANS. Thus far, most of the research on autonomic reactivity has focused on autonomically regulated cardiovascular (heart rate and blood pressure) reactivity in response to stress.

Subjects exposed to stressful tasks in laboratory settings show consistent personal differences in cardiovascular reactivity over a 1-year period (Manuck & Garland, 1980) and across types of stressful tasks (Lawler, 1980). A recent twin study suggests that there's a genetic basis

for these differences in cardiovascular reactivity (Smith et al., 1987). Other studies suggest that high cardiovascular reactivity contributes to heart disease, although more research is needed (Manuck & Krantz, 1986).

Summary

tress involves transactions with the environment that are perceived as threatening. Stress is a common, everyday event, and even routine hassles can be problematic. To a large degree, stress lies in the eye of the beholder. Whether we feel threatened by events depends on how we appraise them. Some of the stress that we experience emanates from our environment. Some environmental stimuli that can be stressful are excessive noise, heat, pollution, and crowding. Much of our everyday stress is self-imposed.

Major types of stress include frustration, conflict, change, and pressure. Frustration occurs when an obstacle prevents us from attaining some goal. There are three principal types of conflict: approach-approach, avoidance-avoidance, and approach-avoidance. The latter is especially stressful. Vacillation is a common response to approach-avoidance conflict. A large number of studies with the SRRS suggest that change is stressful. This may indeed be the case, but it is now clear that the SRRS is a measure of general stress rather than just change-related stress. Two kinds of pressure (to perform and to conform) also appear to be stressful.

Our appraisals of potentially threatening events are highly subjective. Stressful events are usually viewed as less threatening when they are familiar, controllable, and predictable, and when they lie in the distant future. However, the effects of controllability and predictability on the way we appraise stress vary with the circumstances.

Emotional reactions to stress typically involve anger, fear, or sadness. Emotional arousal may interfere with our coping. The optimal level of arousal on a task depends on the complexity of the task.

Our physiological arousal in response to stress was originally called the fight-or-flight response by Walter Cannon. Hans Selye's general adaptation syndrome describes three stages in our physiological reaction to stress: alarm, resistance, and exhaustion. Diseases of adaptation may appear during the stage of exhaustion.

In response to stress the brain sends signals to the endocrine system along two major pathways. These signals trigger the release of two sets of hormones into the bloodstream, catecholamines and corticosteroids. Stress can also affect our immune system.

Our efforts to cope with stress may be healthy or maladaptive. If we cope effectively with stress, we can short-circuit potentially harmful emotional and physical responses.

Stress can have positive effects, but research on the effects of stress has concentrated on negative outcomes. Common negative effects include impaired task performance, disruption of attention and other cognitive processes, pervasive exhaustion known as burnout, post-traumatic stress disorders, a host of everyday psychological problems, full-fledged psychological disorders, and varied types of damage to one's physical health. At the same time, stress fulfills a basic human need for challenge and can lead to personal growth and self-improvement.

People differ in the amount of stress they can tolerate without experiencing ill effects. A person's social support is a key consideration. The personality factors associated with hardiness—commitment, challenge, and an internal locus of control—increase one's tolerance of stress. People high in optimism and sensation seeking also have advantages in coping with stress. A relatively placid autonomic nervous system may also shield people from some of the detrimental health effects associated with stress.

In the Application we'll discuss how you can monitor the amount of stress in your life. You'll get to see how you score on a widely used measure of life stress.

APPLICATION Monitoring Your Stress

Rank the following five events in terms of how stressful they would be for you (1 = most stressful, 5 = least stressful).

1
Change in residence

2
Fired at work

3
Death of a close family member

4
Pregnancy

5
Personal injury or illness

All five events on the left appear on the Social Readjustment Rating Scale (SRRS), developed by Holmes and Rahe (1967), which we described earlier (see Figure 3.3). If you ranked them in the same order as Holmes and Rahe's subjects, the rankings would be 5, 3, 1, 4, and 2. If you didn't rank them in that order, don't worry about it. That merely shows that the perception of stress is very personal and subjective. Unfortunately, the SRRS fails to take this subjectivity into account. That is just one of the basic problems with the SRRS.

The SRRS and the research associated with it have received a great deal of publicity. The scale has been reprinted in many popular newspapers and magazines. These articles have encouraged readers to attribute great significance to their scores. Some have told readers that they should reduce or minimize change in their lives if their scores are high (Cohen, 1979). Such bold advice could be counterproductive and it needs to be qualified carefully. Therefore, we'll elaborate on some of the problems with the SRRS as a measurement scale, introduce you to an improved scale for measuring stress, and explain why you should exercise caution when you interpret your score on any stress scale.

Problems with the SRRS

As you learned earlier in this chapter, Holmes and Rahe designed the SRRS to measure the amount of change-related stress that people experience. The scale assigns normative values to 43 life

Thomas Holmes

events that supposedly indicate how stressful those events are. You respond to the scale by checking off those events that have happened to you in a recent time period. Then you add up the values of the checked events to arrive at your score. A host of studies have found these scores to be related to the likelihood of developing an intimidating array of physical illnesses and psychological problems (Barrett et al., 1979; Elliott & Eisdorfer, 1982; Miller, 1989).

Before we discuss the shortcomings of the SRRS, we should emphasize that Holmes and Rahe deserve enormous credit for having had the imagination to tackle the difficult task of measuring life stress over two decades ago. They had the insight to recognize the potential importance of stress and the ingenuity to develop a scale that would permit its measurement. They pioneered a new area of research that has turned out to be extremely productive. However, their ground-breaking foray into the assessment of stress was not without its flaws, and their scale has been improved on. So, borrowing from the analyses of several critics (notably Cleary, 1980; Derogatis, 1982; Monroe, 1982; Rabkin & Streuning, 1976; Schroeder & Costa, 1984), let's look at some (not all) of the major problems with the SRRS. The key problems are as follows.

First, as we have seen, the assumption that the SRRS measures change exclusively has been shown to be inaccurate. We now have ample evidence that the desirability of the events experienced affects adaptational outcomes more than the amount of change that they require (Brown & McGill, 1989; Perkins, 1982). Thus it seems prudent to view the SRRS as a measure of diverse forms of stress rather than as a measure of change-related stress.

Second, the SRRS fails to take into account differences among people in their subjective perceptions of how stressful an event is. Divorce may deserve a stress value of 73 for *most* people, for instance, but a particular person's divorce might generate much less stress and merit a value of only

25. Cohen, Karmarck, and Mermelstein (1983) have suggested that it might be better to have respondents rate how personally stressful events are rather than to use the standardized, average weights. Thus the normative weights assigned to events on the SRRS may not capture the true impact of an event on a particular person.

Third, many of the events listed on the SRRS and similar scales are highly ambiguous, leading to inconsistency in the reporting of events (Raphael et al., 1991). For instance, what qualifies as "trouble with boss"? Should you check that item because you're sick and tired of your supervisor? What constitutes a "change in living conditions"? Does your purchase of a great new stereo qualify? How should the "pregnancy" item be interpreted? Should a man who has a pregnant wife check that item? As you can see, the SRRS includes many "events" that are described inadequately, producing considerable ambiguity in the meaning of the responses. Problems in recalling events over a period of a year also lead to inconsistent responding on stress scales, thus lowering their reliability (Klein & Rubovits, 1987).

Fourth, the SRRS does not sample from the domain of stressful events very thoroughly. Could the 43 events listed on the SRRS exhaust all the major stresses that people typically experience? Studies designed to explore that question have found many significant omissions (Dohrenwend, Krasnoff, Askenasy, & Dohrenwend, 1978; Kanner et al., 1981; Weiten, 1988).

Fifth, the correlation between SRRS scores and health outcomes may be inflated because subjects' neuroticism affects both their responses to stress scales and their self-reports of health problems. Neurotic individuals have a tendency to recall more stress than others and to recall more symptoms of illness than others (Brett et al., 1990; Watson & Pennebaker, 1989). Some of the correlation between high stress and high incidence of illness, then, may simply reflect the effects of subjects' neuroticism. This is another case

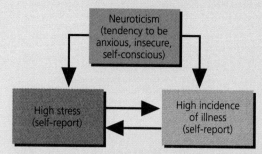

FIGURE 3.17
Neuroticism as a possible factor underlying the stress-illness correlation

FIGURE 3.17
Neuroticism as a possible factor underlying the stress-illness correlation
Many studies have found a correlation between subjects' scores on self-report stress scales, such as the SRRS, and their reports of how much illness they have experienced. However, neurotic subjects, who are anxious, insecure, and self-conscious, tend to recall more stress and more illness than others do. Although a great deal of evidence suggests that stress contributes to illness, some of the stress-illness correlation may be due to the effects of neuroticism as a cause of both high stress and a high incidence of illness.

of the third-variable problem that we introduced in Chapter 1 (see Figure 3.17). The possible contaminating effects of neuroticism obscure the meanings of scores on the SRRS and similar measures of stress.

The Life Experiences Survey

In light of the problems outlined above, researchers have attempted to develop improved versions of the SRRS (for instance, Dohrenwend et al., 1978; Paykel, 1974). The scale that seems to be gaining the most adherents is the Life Experiences Survey (LES), assembled by Irwin Sarason and his colleagues (Sarason, Johnson, & Siegel, 1978). The LES revises and builds on the SRRS in a variety of ways that correct, at least in part, most of the problems just discussed.

The LES recognizes that stress involves more than mere change and asks respondents to indicate whether events had a positive or negative impact on them. This strategy permits the computation of positive change, negative change, and total change scores, which helps researchers to gain much more insight into which facets of stress are most crucial.

By dropping the normative weights and replacing them with personally assigned weightings of the impacts of relevant events, the LES also takes into consideration differences among people in their appraisal of stress. It decreases ambiguity by providing more elaborate descriptions of many items to clarify their meaning. Ambiguity cannot be eliminated entirely, but this scale reduces it considerably.

The failure of the SRRS to sample the domain of stressful events fully is dealt with in several ways. First, the LES includes some significant items omitted from the SRRS. Second, the LES allows the respondent to write in personally important events that are not included on the scale. Third, the LES reprinted here has an extra section just for students. Sarason and his colleagues (1978) suggest that researchers add special sections of this sort tailored to specific populations whenever it is useful to do so.

We suggest that you respond to the LES, which is reprinted in Figure 3.18. Although we have been critical of the practice of overinterpreting SRRS scores, there is much to be said for making an estimate of how much stress you've been under recently. If you score high, you may want to think about ways to reduce some of the stress in your life.

Arriving at your scores on the LES is very simple. Just add up all the positive impact ratings on the right side. That sum is your positive change score. Your negative change score is the sum of all of the negative impact ratings that you noted on the left. Added together these two values yield your total change score. Approximate norms for all three of these scores are listed in Figure 3.19 (on p. 98), to give you some idea of what your score means.

Research to date suggests that

Stress results from a wide array of situations and events. Some of them—such as the loss of one's home to fire—are traumatic to anyone who experiences them. Others are stressful for some but not for others.

FIGURE 3.18
FIGURE 3.18
The Life Experiences Survey (LES)
Like the SRRS, the LES is designed to measure change-related stress. However, Sarason et al. (1978) corrected many of the problems apparent in the SRRS. Follow the instructions in the text to determine your positive, negative, and total change scores.

INSTRUCTIONS. Listed below are a number of events that sometimes bring about change in the lives of those who experience them and that necessitate social readjustment. Please check those events you have experienced in the recent past and indicate the time period during which you have experienced each event. Be sure that all checkmarks are directly across from the items that they correspond to. Also, for each item checked below, please indicate the extent to which you viewed the event as having either a positive or a negative impact on your life at the time the event occurred. That is, indicate the type and extent of impact that the event had. A rating of –3 would indicate an extremely negative impact. A rating of 0 suggests no impact, either positive or negative. A rating of +3 would indicate an extremely positive impact.

The Life Experiences Survey (LES)

	0 to 6 mo	7 mo to 1 yr	Extremely negative	Moderately negative	Somewhat negative	No impact	Slightly positive	Moderately positive	Extremely positive
Section 1									
1. Marriage			–3	–2	–1	0	+1	+2	+3
2. Detention in jail or comparable institution			–3	–2	–1	0	+1	+2	+3
3. Death of spouse			–3	–2	–1	0	+1	+2	+3
4. Major change in sleeping habits (much more or much less sleep)			–3	–2	–1	0	+1	+2	+3
5. Death of a close family member:									
a. Mother			–3	–2	–1	0	+1	+2	+3
b. Father			–3	–2	–1	0	+1	+2	+3
c. Brother			–3	–2	–1	0	+1	+2	+3
d. Sister			–3	–2	–1	0	+1	+2	+3
e. Grandmother			–3	–2	–1	0	+1	+2	+3
f. Grandfather			–3	–2	–1	0	+1	+2	+3
g. Other (specify)			–3	–2	–1	0	+1	+2	+3
6. Major change in eating habits (much more or much less food intake)			–3	–2	–1	0	+1	+2	+3
7. Foreclosure on mortgage or loan			–3	–2	–1	0	+1	+2	+3
8. Death of close friend			–3	–2	–1	0	+1	+2	+3
9. Outstanding personal achievement			–3	–2	–1	0	+1	+2	+3
10. Minor law violations (traffic tickets, disturbing the peace, etc.)			–3	–2	–1	0	+1	+2	+3
11. *Male*: Wife/girlfriend's pregnancy			–3	–2	–1	0	+1	+2	+3
12. *Female*: Pregnancy			–3	–2	–1	0	+1	+2	+3
13. Changed work situation (different work responsibility, major change in working conditions, working hours, etc.)			–3	–2	–1	0	+1	+2	+3
14. New job			–3	–2	–1	0	+1	+2	+3
15. Serious illness or injury of close family member									
a. Father			–3	–2	–1	0	+1	+2	+3
b. Mother			–3	–2	–1	0	+1	+2	+3
c. Sister			–3	–2	–1	0	+1	+2	+3
d. Brother			–3	–2	–1	0	+1	+2	+3
e. Grandfather			–3	–2	–1	0	+1	+2	+3
f. Grandmother			–3	–2	–1	0	+1	+2	+3
g. Spouse			–3	–2	–1	0	+1	+2	+3
h. Other (specify)			–3	–2	–1	0	+1	+2	+3
16. Sexual difficulties			–3	–2	–1	0	+1	+2	+3
17. Trouble with employer (in danger of losing job, being suspended, being demoted, etc.)			–3	–2	–1	0	+1	+2	+3
18. Trouble with in-laws			–3	–2	–1	0	+1	+2	+3
19. Major change in financial status (a lot better off or a lot worse off)			–3	–2	–1	0	+1	+2	+3
20. Major change in closeness of family members (increased or decreased closeness)			–3	–2	–1	0	+1	+2	+3
21. Gaining a new family member (through birth, adoption, family member moving in, etc.)			–3	–2	–1	0	+1	+2	+3
22. Change of residence			–3	–2	–1	0	+1	+2	+3
23. Marital separation from mate (due to conflict)			–3	–2	–1	0	+1	+2	+3
24. Major change in church activities (increased or decreased attendance)			–3	–2	–1	0	+1	+2	+3
25. Marital reconciliation with mate			–3	–2	–1	0	+1	+2	+3

	0 to 6 mo	7 mo to 1 yr	Extremely negative	Moderately negative	Somewhat negative	No impact	Slightly positive	Moderately positive	Extremely positive
26. Major change in number of arguments with spouse (a lot more or a lot fewer)			−3	−2	−1	0	+1	+2	+3
27. *Married male*: Change in wife's work outside the home (beginning work, ceasing work, changing to a new job, etc.)			−3	−2	−1	0	+1	+2	+3
28. *Married female*: Change in husband's work (loss of job, beginning new job, retirement, etc.)			−3	−2	−1	0	+1	+2	+3
29. Major change in usual type and/or amount of recreation			−3	−2	−1	0	+1	+2	+3
30. Borrowing for a major purchase (buying a home, business, etc.)			−3	−2	−1	0	+1	+2	+3
31. Borrowing for smaller purchase (buying a car or TV, getting school loan, etc.)			−3	−2	−1	0	+1	+2	+3
32. Being fired from job			−3	−2	−1	0	+1	+2	+3
33. *Male*: Wife/girlfriend having abortion			−3	−2	−1	0	+1	+2	+3
34. *Female*: Having abortion			−3	−2	−1	0	+1	+2	+3
35. Major personal illness or injury			−3	−2	−1	0	+1	+2	+3
36. Major change in social actiivities, e.g., parties, movies, visiting (increased or decreased participation)			−3	−2	−1	0	+1	+2	+3
37. Major change in living conditions of family (building new home, remodeling, deterioration of home or neighborhood, etc.)			−3	−2	−1	0	+1	+2	+3
38. Divorce			−3	−2	−1	0	+1	+2	+3
39. Serious injury or illness of close friend			−3	−2	−1	0	+1	+2	+3
40. Retirement from work			−3	−2	−1	0	+1	+2	+3
41. Son or daughter leaving home (due to marriage, college, etc.			−3	−2	−1	0	+1	+2	+3
42. End of formal schooling			−3	−2	−1	0	+1	+2	+3
43. Separation from spouse (due to work, travel, etc.)			−3	−2	−1	0	+1	+2	+3
44. Engagement			−3	−2	−1	0	+1	+2	+3
45. Breaking up with boyfriend/girlfriend			−3	−2	−1	0	+1	+2	+3
46. Leaving home for the first time			−3	−2	−1	0	+1	+2	+3
47. Reconciliation with boyfriend/girlfriend Other recent experiences that have had an impact on your life. List and rate.			−3	−2	−1	0	+1	+2	+3
48. _____			−3	−2	−1	0	+1	+2	+3
49. _____			−3	−2	−1	0	+1	+2	+3
50. _____			−3	−2	−1	0	+1	+2	+3

Section 2. Students only

	0 to 6 mo	7 mo to 1 yr	Extremely negative	Moderately negative	Somewhat negative	No impact	Slightly positive	Moderately positive	Extremely positive
51. Beginning a new school experience at a higher academic level (college, graduate school, professional school)			−3	−2	−1	0	+1	+2	+3
52. Changing to a new school at same academic level (undergraduate, graduate, etc.)			−3	−2	−1	0	+1	+2	+3
53. Academic probation			−3	−2	−1	0	+1	+2	+3
54. Being dismissed from dormitory or other residence			−3	−2	−1	0	+1	+2	+3
55. Failing an important exam			−3	−2	−1	0	+1	+2	+3
56. Changing a major			−3	−2	−1	0	+1	+2	+3
57. Failing a course			−3	−2	−1	0	+1	+2	+3
58. Dropping a course			−3	−2	−1	0	+1	+2	+3
59. Joining a fraternity/sorority			−3	−2	−1	0	+1	+2	+3
60. Financial problems concerning school (in danger of not having sufficient money to continue)			−3	−2	−1	0	+1	+2	+3

your negative change score is the crucial one. Positive change has not been found to be a very good predictor of adaptational outcomes. In direct comparisons with the SRRS, the negative change score has turned out to be a better predictor of mental and physical health than SRRS scores (Sarason et al., 1978). Thus far, research has shown that negative change scores are related to a variety of negative adaptational outcomes, including menstrual discomfort, nonconformity, job dissatisfaction, athletic injuries, vaginal infections, anxiety, psychological discomfort, depression, and coronary disease (Passer & Seese, 1983; Sarason, Levine & Sarason, 1982; Williams & Deffenbacher, 1983).

A Cautionary Note

There is merit in getting an estimate of how much stress you have experienced lately, but scores on the LES or any other measure of stress should be interpreted with caution. You need not panic if you add up your negative change score and find that it falls in the "high" category. Although it is clear that there is a connection between stress and a variety of undesirable adaptational outcomes, there are a couple of reasons why a high score is not necessarily a cause for concern.

First, the strength of the association between stress and adaptational problems is modest. Most of the correlations observed between stress scores and illness have been relatively low, often less than .30 (Dohrenwend & Dohrenwend, 1981; Kobasa, 1979). To researchers and theorists, it is very interesting to find any relationship at all. The link between stress and adaptational problems, however, is too weak to permit us to make confident predictions about individuals. Many

Norms for LES

Score category	Negative change	Positive change	Total change
High	14 and above	16 and above	28 and above
Medium	4–13	7–15	12–27
Low	0–3	0–6	0–11

FIGURE 3.19
Norms for the Life Experiences Survey (LES)
Approximate norms for college students taking the LES are shown for negative, positive, and total change scores. These norms are based on 345 undergraduates studied by Sarason et al., (1978). Data for males and females are combined, as sex differences are negligible. Negative change scores are the best predictors of adaptational outcomes.

people endure high levels of stress without developing significant problems.

Second, stress is only one of a multitude of variables that affect your susceptibility to various maladies. Stress interacts with many other factors, such as your lifestyle, coping skills, social support, hardiness, and genetic inheritance, in influencing your mental and physical health. It's important to remember that stress is only one actor on a crowded stage.

In light of these considerations, you should evaluate the potential meaning of SRRS or LES scores with caution. A high score is food for thought but not reason for alarm.

CHAPTER 3 REVIEW

Key Learning Objectives

1. Define stress in terms of Lazarus's transactional model.
2. Summarize four general points about the nature of stress.
3. List four principal types of stress.
4. Describe three types of conflict and discuss our reactions to conflicts.
5. Summarize evidence on life change as a form of stress.
6. Explain how familiarity, controllability, predictability, and imminence influence our appraisal of stress.
7. List three dimensions of emotion commonly elicited by stress.
8. Discuss the effects of emotional arousal on coping efforts.
9. Describe the fight-or-flight response.
10. Describe the three stages of the general adaptation syndrome.
11. Describe the two major pathways along which the brain sends signals to the endocrine system in response to stress.
12. Discuss the effects of stress on task performance.
13. Describe burnout and post-traumatic stress disorders.
14. Discuss the potential impact of stress on mental and physical health.
15. Discuss three ways in which stress may lead to beneficial effects.
16. Discuss how social support and hardiness affect tolerance of stress.
17. Discuss how optimism, sensation seeking, and autonomic reactivity influence resistance to stress.
18. List five problems with the SRRS.
19. Summarize how the LES corrects some of the problems that are characteristic of the SRRS.
20. Explain why one should be cautious in interpreting scores on stress scales.

Key Terms

ambient stress
approach-approach conflict
approach-avoidance conflict
autonomic nervous system (ANS)
avoidance-avoidance conflict
burnout
conflict
coping
emotions
endocrine system
fight-or-flight response
frustration
general adaptation syndrome
hardiness

life changes
locus of control
neuroticism
optimism
post-traumatic stress disorder
pressure
primary appraisal
psychosomatic diseases
secondary appraisal
sensation seeking
social support
stress
Type A personality

Key People

Thomas Holmes and Richard Rahe
Suzanne Kobasa
Richard Lazarus

Neal Miller
Hans Selye
Marvin Zuckerman

Coping Processes

HAVE BEGUN TO BELIEVE THAT I have intellectually and emotionally outgrown my husband. However, I'm not really sure what this means or what I should do. Maybe this feeling is normal and I should ignore it and continue my present relationship. This seems to be the safest route. Maybe I should seek a lover while continuing with my husband. Then again, maybe I should start anew and hope for a beautiful ending with or without a better mate."

The woman quoted above is in the throes of a thorny conflict. Although it is hard to tell just how much emotional turmoil she is experiencing, it's clear that she is under substantial stress. What should she do? Is it psychologically healthy to remain in an emotionally hollow marriage? Is seeking a secret lover a reasonable way to cope with this unfortunate situation? Should she just strike out on her own and let the chips fall where they may? There are no simple answers to these questions. As you'll soon see, decisions about how to cope with life's difficulties can be terribly complex.

This chapter focuses on how we cope with stress. In Chapter 3 we learned that stress can be a challenging, exciting stimulus to personal growth. We also saw, however, that stress can prove damaging to our psychological and physical health because it often triggers emotional and physiological responses that may be harmful. These emotional and physiological responses to stress tend to be largely automatic. Controlling them depends on the coping responses that we make to stressful situations. Thus our mental and physical health depend, in part, on our ability to cope effectively with stress.

Our plan of attack in this chapter is as follows. We'll begin with a general discussion of the concept of coping. Then we will review some common coping patterns that tend to have relatively little value. After discussing these ill-advised coping techniques, we'll sketch an overview of what it means to engage in healthier, "constructive" coping. The remainder of the chapter will expand on the specifics of constructive coping. We hope our discussion will provide some new ideas about how to deal with the inevitable stresses of modern life.

The Concept of Coping

In Chapter 3 we learned that **coping consists of efforts to master, reduce, or tolerate the demands created by stress.** Let's take a closer look at this concept and discuss some general points about coping.

1. *We cope with stress in many ways.* In recent years, a large number of researchers have attempted to identify and classify the various techniques people use in their efforts to cope with stress. Their work reveals that we use quite a variety of coping strategies. In a study of how 255 adult subjects dealt with stress, McCrae (1984) identified 28 coping techniques. In another study, Carver, Scheier, and Weintraub (1989) found that coping tactics could be sorted into 14 categories, which are listed in Figure 4.1. When we grapple with stress, then, we select our coping tactics from a large and varied menu of options.

2. *We exhibit consistent styles of coping.* Although we have a large menu of coping tactics to choose from, most of us come to rely on some strategies more than others (Folkman, Lazarus, Gruen, & DeLongis, 1986). We do, of course, adapt our coping techniques to situational demands. For instance, you might suppress a general tendency to lash out sarcastically at others when you deal with your boss. Nonetheless, our coping strategies show some stability across situations. We each have our personal style of coping with life's difficulties. As we progress through this chapter, it may be fruitful for you to analyze your style of coping.

3. *Coping strategies vary in their adaptive value.* In everyday terms, when we say that someone "coped with his problems," we imply that he handled them effectively. In reality, however, coping processes may range from healthy to downright pathological. For example, if you coped with the disappointment of not getting a promotion by plotting to sabotage your company's computer system, there would be little argument that this was an unhealthy way of coping. Differences in the value of various coping strategies were apparent in the study that identified the 14 coping techniques listed in Figure 4.1. Charles Carver and his colleagues correlated subjects' reliance on each coping strategy with various personality measures, such as their self-esteem and anxiety. They found that some coping patterns (active coping, planning, positive reinterpretation) were associated with relatively high self-esteem and low anxiety, whereas other coping patterns were associated with lower self-esteem and higher anxiety (see Figure 4.1).

In light of findings such as these, we will distinguish between coping patterns that tend to be healthy and those that tend to be maladaptive. Bear in mind, however, that our generalizations about the adaptive value of various coping strategies are based on trends or tendencies. No coping strategy can ensure a successful outcome. Furthermore, the adaptive value of a coping technique depends on the exact nature of the situation. As you'll see in the next section, even ill-advised coping strategies may have adaptive value in some instances.

Common Coping Patterns of Limited Value

"Recently, after an engagement of 22 months, my fiancée told me that she was in love with someone else, and that we were through. I've been a wreck ever since. I can't study because I keep thinking about her. I think constantly about what I did wrong in the relationship and why I wasn't good enough for her. Getting drunk is the only way I can get her off my mind. Lately I've been getting plastered about five or six nights a week. My grades are really hurting, but I'm not sure that I care."

This young man is going through a very hard time and does not appear to be handling it very well. He's blaming himself for the breakup with his fiancée. He's turning to alcohol to dull the pain that he feels, and it sounds as though he may be giving up on school. Given his situation, these coping responses aren't particularly unusual, but they're only going to make his problems worse.

In this section we'll examine some relatively common coping patterns that tend to be less than optimal. Specifically, we'll discuss giving up, aggression, blaming yourself, indulging yourself, and defense mechanisms. Some of these coping tactics may be helpful in certain circumstances, but more often than not, they are counterproductive.

Giving Up

When confronted with stress, sometimes we simply give up and withdraw from the battle. This response of apathy and inaction tends to be associated with the emotional reactions of sadness and dejection. Bruno Bettelheim (1943) observed this reaction among prisoners in the Nazi concentration camps of World War II. Some prisoners aggressed against their captors through acts of sabotage and worked valiantly to maintain their will to live. Many others, however, sank into apathy and abandoned all efforts to adapt and survive.

Martin Seligman (1974) has developed a model of this giving-up syndrome that appears to shed light on its causes. In Seligman's research, animals are subjected to electric shocks they cannot escape. The animals are then given an opportunity to learn a response that will allow them to escape the shock. However, many of the animals have become so apathetic and listless that they don't even try to learn the escape response. When researchers made similar manipulations with *human* sub-

FIGURE 4.1
Classifying coping strategies
Carver et al. (1989) sorted their subjects' coping responses into 14 categories. The categories are listed here (column 1) with a representative example from each category (column 2). Carver and his colleagues correlated subjects' reliance on each coping category with their self-esteem (column 3) and their anxiety (column 4). Many of the observed correlations (those with the asterisks) were statistically significant. Positive correlations with self-esteem and negative correlations with anxiety suggest that a coping strategy is relatively effective. As you can see, some coping strategies appear to be healthier than others.

Types of Coping Strategies

Coping strategy	Example	Correlation with self-esteem	Correlation with anxiety
Active coping	I take additional action to try to get rid of the problem.	.27*	−.25*
Planning	I try to come up with a strategy about what to do.	.22*	−.15
Suppression of competing activities	I put aside other activities in order to concentrate on this.	.07	−.10
Restraint coping	I force myself to wait for the right time to do something.	−.03	−.19*
Seeking social support for instrumental reasons	I ask people who have had similar experiences what they did.	.12	.01
Seeking social support for emotional reasons	I talk to someone about how I feel.	.06	.14
Positive reinterpretation and growth	I look for something good in what is happening.	.16*	−.25*
Acceptance	I learn to live with it.	.12	−.15
Turning to religion	I seek God's help.	−.06	.11
Focus on and venting of emotions	I get upset and let my emotions out.	−.01	.36*
Denial	I refuse to believe that it has happened.	−.28*	.35*
Behavioral disengagement	I give up the attempt to get what I want.	−.31*	.37*
Mental disengagement	I turn to work or other substitute activities to take my mind off things.	−.08	.21*
Alcohol-drug disengagement	I drink alcohol or take drugs in order to think about it less.	−.11	.11

jects using inescapable noise (rather than shock) as the stressor, they observed parallel results (Hiroto & Seligman, 1975). This syndrome is referred to as learned helplessness. *Learned helplessness* **involves passive behavior produced by exposure to unavoidable aversive events.** Unfortunately, this tendency to give up may be transferred to situations in which we are not really helpless. Some people routinely respond to stress with fatalism and resignation. They passively accept setbacks that might be dealt with effectively.

Seligman originally viewed learned helplessness as a product of conditioning. Research with human subjects, however, has led Seligman and his colleagues to revise their theory. The current model proposes that our *cognitive interpretation* of aversive events determines whether we develop learned helplessness. Specifically, helplessness seems to occur when we come to believe that events are beyond our control. This belief is particularly likely to emerge when we tend to attribute setbacks to personal inadequacies rather than situational factors (Abramson, Seligman, & Teasdale, 1978).

As you might guess, giving up is not a highly regarded method of coping. Carver and his colleagues (1989) found that the strategy of giving up (behavioral disengagement) showed some of the highest correlations with anxiety and poor self-esteem. Furthermore, many studies suggest that learned helplessness can contribute to depression (Peterson & Seligman, 1984).

However, giving up could be adaptive in some instances. If you were thrown into a job that you were not equipped to handle, for example, it might be better to quit rather than face constant pressure and diminishing self-esteem. There is something to be said for recognizing our limitations. There may also be occa-

Martin Seligman

As a coping tactic, verbal aggression is almost always counterproductive.

sions when we need to recognize that our goals are unrealistic. The highly competitive nature of American society leads many of us to push ourselves toward heights that are very difficult to achieve. A goal such as gaining admission to medical school, becoming a professional actress, or buying an expensive home may be better discarded if it is not realistic. The value of any coping response depends on the situation. Even a coping strategy such as giving up, which sounds terribly uninspiring, may sometimes be adaptive. As you will see again and again, there are no simple rules regarding the best ways to cope with life's challenges.

Striking Out at Others

A young man, aged 17, cautiously edged his car into traffic on the Corona Expressway in Los Angeles. His slow speed apparently annoyed the men in a pickup truck behind him. Unfortunately, he angered the wrong men—they shot him to death. During that same weekend in 1987 there were six other roadside shootings in the Los Angeles area. All of them were triggered by minor incidents or fender benders. Frustrated motorists are attacking each other more and more frequently, especially on the overburdened highways of Los Angeles.

These tragic incidents of highway violence vividly demonstrate that people often respond to stressful events by striking out at others with aggressive behavior. *Aggression* **is any behavior intended to hurt someone, either physically or verbally.** Snarls, curses, and insults are much more common than shootings or fistfights, but aggression of any kind can be problematic. Many years ago a team of psychologists (Dollard et al., 1939) proposed the *frustration-aggression hypothesis,* which held that aggression is always due to frustration. Decades of research have verified their proposal that there is a causal link between frustration and aggression.

However, this research has also shown that there isn't an inevitable, one-to-one correspondence between frustration and aggression. In a discussion of qualifications to the frustration-aggression hypothesis, Leonard Berkowitz (1969) concluded (1) that frustration does not *necessarily* lead to aggression, (2) that many factors in addition to frustration (such as one's personality) influence the likelihood of aggression, and (3) that frustration may produce responses other than aggression (such as apathy). Although these are important qualifications, it is clear that frustration often leads to aggression.

Frequently we lash out aggressively at others who have nothing to do with our frustration.

Often we cannot vent our anger at the real source of our frustration. You'll probably suppress your anger rather than lash out verbally at a police officer who gives you a speeding ticket. Twenty minutes later, however, you may be downright brutal in rebuking a gas station attendant who is slow in servicing your car. As we discussed in Chapter 2, this diversion of anger to a substitute target was noticed long ago by Sigmund Freud, who called it *displacement*.

Freud theorized that behaving aggressively could get pent-up emotion out of your system and thus be adaptive. He coined the term **catharsis to refer to this release of emotional tension.** There is some experimental evidence to support Freud's theory of catharsis. In a widely cited study, Hokanson and Burgess (1962) found that the opportunity to aggress physically or verbally after frustration led to a smaller increase in subjects' blood pressure (see Figure 4.2). Given the potential negative effects of emotional arousal, this study suggests that expressing aggression may have some adaptive value.

After reviewing additional research by Hokanson and others, however, Carol Tavris (1982, 1989) concludes that aggressive behavior does not reliably lead to catharsis. She asserts, "Aggressive catharses are almost impossible to find in continuing relationships because parents, children, spouses and bosses usually feel obliged to aggress back at you; and indirect, 'displaced' aggression does nothing but make you angrier and more upset" (1982, p. 131). Thus the adaptive value of aggressive behavior tends to be minimal. Hurting someone, especially an irrelevant someone, is not likely to alleviate frustration. Moreover, the interpersonal conflicts that often emerge from aggressive behavior may produce additional stress. If you pick a fight with your spouse after a terrible day at work, you may create new stress and lose valuable empathy and social support from your spouse.

Indulging Yourself

Stress sometimes leads to self-indulgence. When troubled by stress, many of us engage in excessive consummatory behavior. For instance, after an exceptionally stressful day, some people head for their refrigerator, a grocery store, or a restaurant in pursuit of something chocolate. Others cope with stress by making a beeline for the nearest shopping mall for a spending spree. An excess of consummatory behavior is any pattern of injudicious eating, drinking, smoking, using drugs, spending money, or the like.

In their classification of coping responses, Moos and Billings (1982) list *developing alternative rewards* as a common response to stress. It makes sense that when things are going poorly in one area of our lives, we may try to compensate by pursuing substitute forms of satisfaction. When this happens, consummatory responses probably rank high. They are relatively easy to execute, and they tend to be very pleasurable. Thus it is not surprising that there is evidence relating stress to increases in eating (Slochower, 1976), smoking (Tomkins, 1966), consumption

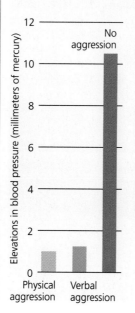

FIGURE 4.2
Aggression and blood pressure
After frustrating subjects, Hokanson and Burgess (1962) found that those who were allowed to engage in either physical or verbal aggression showed smaller increases in blood pressure than subjects who had no opportunity for aggression. These findings support the idea that aggressive behavior permits us to drain off emotional tension. As the text notes, however, many other studies have failed to support the catharsis value of aggression.

of alcohol (Marlatt & Rose, 1980), and some types of drug use (Krueger, 1981).

There is nothing inherently maladaptive about indulging oneself as a way of coping with life's stresses. The pursuit of alternative rewards is a readily available coping strategy that may have merit if it is kept under control. If a hot fudge sundae or some new clothes calm your nerves after a major setback, who can argue? However, if a person consistently responds to stress with chronic and excessive consummatory behavior, obvious problems are likely to develop. Excesses in eating may produce obesity. Excesses in drinking can lead to alcoholism, drunk driving, and a host of other problems. Excesses in drug use may endanger one's health and result in drug dependence. Excesses in spending may create havoc in one's personal finances. Given the risks associated with self-indulgence, it has rather marginal adaptive value.

Some people cope with stress by indulging themselves—with a shopping spree, for instance, or with some other type of enjoyable activity. There's nothing inherently wrong with a little self-indulgence, but this coping strategy sometimes leads to injudicious spending, eating, drinking, or drug use.

Blaming Yourself

In a postgame interview after a tough defeat, a prominent football coach was brutally critical of himself. He said that he was outcoached, that he had made poor decisions, and that his game plan was faulty. He almost eagerly assumed all the blame for the loss himself. In reality, he had taken some reasonable chances that didn't go his way and had suffered the effects of poor execution by his players. Looking at it objectively, we can see that the loss was attributable to the collective failures of 50 or so players and coaches. However, the coach's unrealistically negative self-evaluation was a fairly typical response to frustration. When we are confronted by stress (especially frustration and pressure), we often become highly self-critical.

Our tendency to engage in negative self-talk in response to stress has been noted by several influential theorists. Albert Ellis (1973, 1987) calls this phenomenon "catastrophic thinking" and focuses on its roots in irrational assumptions. Aaron Beck (1976, 1987) finds specific tendencies in negative self-talk. Among other things, he asserts that people often (1) unreasonably attribute their failures to personal shortcomings, (2) focus on negative feedback from others while ignoring favorable feedback, and (3) make unduly pessimistic projections about the future. Thus, if you performed poorly on an exam, you might blame it on your woeful stupidity, dismiss a classmate's comment that the test was unfair, and hysterically predict that you will flunk out of school.

Although there is some value in recognizing our weaknesses, Ellis and Beck agree that negative self-talk tends to be counterproductive. According to Ellis, catastrophic thinking causes, aggravates, and perpetuates emotional reactions to stress that are often problematic. Along even more serious lines, Beck marshals evidence that negative self-talk can contribute to the development of depressive disorders. The bottom line is that people who blame themselves for their difficulties tend to be less happy and less well adjusted than those who do not display this coping style (Revenson & Felton, 1989; Vitaliano, Katon, Maiuro, & Russo, 1989). In general, then, it appears that self-blame and self-criticism are not very healthy ways to cope with stress.

Defensive Coping

Defensive coping is very common in response to stress. We noted in Chapter 2 that the concept of defense mechanisms was originally developed by Sigmund Freud. Though rooted in the psychoanalytic tradition, this concept has gained widespread acceptance among psychologists of most persuasions. Building on Freud's initial insights, modern psychologists have broadened the scope of the concept and added to Freud's list of defense mechanisms.

Defense mechanisms **are largely unconscious reactions that protect a person from unpleasant emotions such as anxiety and guilt.** There are many specific mechanisms of defense. For example, Laughlin (1979) lists 49 defenses. In our discussion of Freud's theory in Chapter 2, we described rationalization, repression, projection, displacement, reaction formation, regression, and identification. Here we'll introduce some additional defense mechanisms and elaborate on the nature and value of defensive coping.

Additional Defense Mechanisms

Figure 4.3 lists five more defenses that people frequently employ in addition to the seven commonly used defense mechanisms discussed in Chapter 2. *Denial* **is the refusal to perceive or face unpleasant realities.** Unlike repression, which involves unconscious blocking of distressing material, denial involves a *conscious* effort to suppress unpleasant thoughts. The person who engages in denial is fully aware of threatening thoughts, but refuses to believe them. In spite of substantial evidence, for example, you might deny that your spouse appeared to be having an extramarital affair. In contrast, *intellectualization* **involves suppressing unpleasant emotions while engaging in detached analyses of threatening problems.** If your spouse were having an affair, for instance, you might endlessly analyze the sad state of modern marriage instead of expressing your anger—thus turning your problem into an impersonal, intellectual puzzle.

Fantasy, overcompensation, and undoing are three other ways of coping with problems defensively. *Fantasy* **involves gratifying frustrated desires by thinking about imaginary achievements and satisfactions.** In response to a string of financial setbacks, for example, you might daydream frequently about making a killing in the stock market. We often express our hostile feelings in fantasy. Thus you might daydream about gaining revenge on the people you hold responsible for your financial problems. *Overcompensation* **involves making up for frustration in one area by seeking overgratification in another area.** You might compensate for financial frustration, for instance, by recklessly pursuing many sex partners. If your sexual manipulations made you feel bad, you might engage in undoing, a defense that we use to cope with guilt. *Undoing* **involves rituals intended to atone for unacceptable desires or behaviors.** For example, you might atone for your sexual excesses by remaining abstinent for a certain number of days.

The Nature of Defense Mechanisms

Although widely discussed in the popular press,

Common Defense Mechanisms	
Mechanism	Example
Denial of reality. Protecting oneself from unpleasant reality by refusing to perceive or face it.	A smoker concludes that the evidence linking cigarette use to health problems is scientifically worthless.
Fantasy. Gratifying frustrated desires by imaginary achievements.	A socially inept and inhibited young man imagines himself chosen by a group of women to provide them with sexual satisfaction.
Intellectualization (isolation). Cutting off emotion from hurtful situations or separating incompatible attitudes in logic-tight compartments.	A prisoner on death row awaiting execution resists appeal on his behalf and coldly insists that the letter of the law be followed.
Undoing. Atoning for or trying to magically dispel unacceptable desires or acts.	A teenager who feels guilty about masturbation ritually touches door knobs a prescribed number of times after each occurrence of the act.
Overcompensation. Covering up felt weaknesses by emphasizing some desirable characteristic, or making up for frustration in one area by overgratification in another.	A dangerously overweight woman goes on eating binges when she feels neglected by her husband.

**FIGURE 4.3
Additional defense mechanisms**
Like the seven defense mechanisms described in our discussion of Freudian theory in Chapter 2 (see Figure 2.3), these five defenses are frequently used in our efforts to cope with stress.

defense mechanisms are often misunderstood. We will use a question-answer format to elaborate on the nature of defense mechanisms in the hope of clearing up any misconceptions.

What do defense mechanisms defend against? Above all else, defense mechanisms shield us from the *emotional discomfort* elicited by stress. Their main purpose is to ward off unwelcome emotions or to reduce their intensity. Foremost among the emotions guarded against is anxiety. We are especially protective when the anxiety is due to some threat to our self-esteem. We also use defenses to suppress dangerous feelings of anger so they do not explode into acts of aggression. Guilt and dejection are two other emotions that we often try to evade through defensive maneuvers.

How do they work? Defense mechanisms work through self-deception. They achieve their goals by distorting reality so it does not appear so threatening. Let's say you're doing very poorly in school and are in danger of flunking out. At first, you may use *denial* to block awareness of the possibility that you could flunk out. This strategy may temporarily fend off feelings of anxiety. If it becomes difficult to deny the obvious, you may resort to *fantasy*, daydreaming about how you will salvage adequate grades by getting spectacular scores on the upcoming final exams, when the objective fact is that you are hopelessly behind in your studies. Thus defense mechanisms work their magic by bending reality in self-serving ways.

Are they conscious or unconscious? Defense mechanisms are both conscious and unconscious. Freud originally assumed that our defenses operate entirely at an unconscious level. Other theorists, however, have broadened the concept of defense mechanisms to

include maneuvers that we may be aware of. Thus defense mechanisms operate at varying levels of awareness, although they are largely unconscious.

Are they normal? Defense mechanisms are entirely normal patterns of coping. We all use them fairly regularly. The notion that only neurotic people use defense mechanisms is inaccurate.

Can Illusions Be Healthy?

The most critical question concerning defense mechanisms is "Are they healthy?" This is a complicated question. More often than not, the answer is no. Generally, defense mechanisms are poor ways of coping, for several reasons. First, defensive coping is an avoidance strategy, and avoidance rarely provides a genuine solution to our problems. Holahan and Moos (1985, 1990) have found that people who exhibit relatively high resistance to stress use avoidance strategies less than people who are frequently troubled by stress. Second, defenses such as denial, fantasy, and projection represent wishful thinking, which is likely to accomplish little. In fact, in a study of how students coped with the stress of taking the Medical College Admissions Test (MCAT), Bolger (1990) found that students who engaged in a lot of wishful thinking experienced greater increases in anxiety than other students as the exam approached. Third, defensive tactics use up energy that could be spent more wisely by tackling the problem. In other words, defensive pseudosolutions may prevent us from employing more constructive coping strategies. Fourth, defensive coping often leads us to delay facing up to a problem. This delay may allow the problem to fester and grow. For example, if you blocked out obvious warning signs of cancer or diabetes and failed to obtain needed medical care, your defensive behavior could be fatal.

The shortcomings of defensive coping were highlighted in a long-term study of men graduated from Harvard. Periodic interviews and tests allowed George Vaillant (1977) to distinguish between men who depended on "immature" defense mechanisms that involved radical distortions of reality and those who depended on "mature" defenses that involved much less distortion of reality. As Figure 4.4 shows, the men who used immature defenses experienced much poorer outcomes than the men who relied on more mature defenses. They exhibited less happiness, poorer adjustment, fewer harmonious marriages, more barren friendship net-

FIGURE 4.4
A comparison of men who used mature and immature defenses
In a long-running study of Harvard graduates, Vaillant (1977) was able to compare the adjustments of men who depended on mature (reality-oriented) versus immature coping strategies. Only statistically significant differences are shown here. All of them favor the men who appeared to depend more on realistic coping mechanisms.

Defensive Coping and Adjustment

Adjustment	Predominant adaptive style (%)	
	Mature (N=25)	Immature (N=31)
Overall		
Top third in adult adjustment	60	0
Bottom third in adult adjustment	4	61
Top third rating for "happiness"	68	16
Career and social		
High income	88	48
Rich friendship pattern	64	6
Marriage at least harmonious	61	28
Barren friendship pattern	4	52
Psychological		
10+ psychiatric visits	0	45
Ever diagnosed mentally ill	0	55

works, and a higher incidence of mental illness. Thus, when defenses lead to wholesale distortions of reality, they clearly are not healthy.

Although defensive behavior tends to be relatively unhealthy, it can sometimes be adaptive. *Overcompensation* for failure in athletics, for example, could lead you to work extra-hard in the classroom. Creative use of *fantasy* is sometimes the key to dealing effectively with temporary periods of frustration, such as a stint in the military service or a period of recovery in the hospital.

Most theorists used to regard accurate contact with reality as the hallmark of sound mental health (Jahoda, 1958; Jourard & Landsman, 1980). After studying *denial* and other defenses, however, Richard Lazarus acknowledges that sometimes "illusion and self-deception can have positive value in a person's psychological economy" (Goleman, 1979, p. 47). In accord with this notion, Ward, Leventhal, and Love (1988) found that cancer patients who relied on repression experienced fewer side effects from treatment than patients who carefully monitored the course of their disease.

Shelley Taylor and Jonathon Brown (1988) have reviewed several lines of evidence suggesting that "certain illusions may be adaptive for mental health and well-being" (p. 193). First, they note that "normal" people tend to have overly favorable self-images. Depressed subjects exhibit less favorable—but more realistic—self concepts. Second, normal subjects overestimate the degree to which they control chance events. Depressed subjects are less prone to this illusion of control. Third, normal individuals are more likely than depressed subjects to display unrealistic optimism in making projections about the future.

Thus it is hard to make sweeping generalizations about the adaptive value of self-deception. Some of the personal illusions that we create through defensive coping may help us to deal with life's difficulties. Roy Baumeister (1989) theorizes that it's all a matter of degree and that there is an "optimal margin of illu-

sion." According to Baumeister, extreme distortions of reality are maladaptive, but small illusions are often beneficial.

In summary, defensive coping and self-deception can be healthy or unhealthy, depending on the circumstances. As a rule, the more your defenses prevent you from engaging in constructive coping, the more unhealthy they probably are. To appreciate this point fully, we need to consider what it is that makes coping constructive.

The Nature of Constructive Coping

Our discussion thus far has focused on coping strategies that usually are less than ideal. But we also exhibit many healthy strategies for dealing with stress. We will use the term **constructive coping to refer to efforts to deal with stressful events that are judged to be relatively healthy.** No strategy of coping can *guarantee* a successful outcome. Even the healthiest coping responses may turn out to be ineffective in some cases. Thus the concept of constructive coping is simply meant to convey a healthy, positive connotation, without promising success.

Constructive coping does not appear to depend particularly on one's intelligence—at least not the abstract, "academic" intelligence measured by conventional IQ tests. Seymour Epstein (1990), a professor at the University of Massachusetts, has shown an interest in "why smart people think dumb." His interest was stimulated in part by a course that he teaches in which students keep daily records of their most positive and negative emotional experiences for class discussion. Commenting on these discussions, Epstein says, "One cannot help but be impressed, when observing students in such a situation, with the degree to which some otherwise bright people lead their lives in a manifestly unintelligent and self-defeating manner" (Epstein & Meier, 1989, p. 333).

MOM! YOU ADJUST THE SCALE SO IT DOESN'T READ YOUR CORRECT WEIGHT!

YOU ROUND OFF THE AMOUNTS OF YOUR CHECKS SO YOU DON'T HAVE TO SEE YOUR REAL BANK BALANCE!

YOU TURN UP THE RADIO SO YOU WON'T HEAR THE RATTLE UNDER THE HOOD! AREN'T YOU RUNNING AWAY FROM YOUR PROBLEMS?

NO...

I'M PRESENTING A MOVING TARGET.

Reprinted with special permission of North America Syndicate.

To investigate this matter more systematically, Epstein and Petra Meier (1989) devised an elaborate scale to assess the degree to which people engage in constructive coping and thinking. They found that constructive thinking was favorably related to mental and physical health, and to measures of "success" in work, love, and social relationships. Subjects' IQ scores, however, were only very weakly related to their constructive coping scores and largely unrelated to the measures of success in work, love, and social relationships.

In a subsequent study, Katz and Epstein (1991) compared good and poor constructive thinkers as they worked on laboratory tasks that subjected them to modest stress. Under stress, the good constructive thinkers reported fewer negative thoughts and less negative emotion. They also exhibited lower physiological arousal as indexed by heart rate. In another follow-up study, Epstein and Katz (1992) uncovered a negative correlation between constructive thinking and a measure of self-produced stress, thus supporting the notion that "some people, because of their disorganized, provocative, or otherwise maladaptive behavior, instigate more stressors in their lives than do others" (p. 814). In other words, they found that good constructive thinkers not only cope more effectively with stress, they also create less stress for themselves than poor constructive thinkers.

What makes certain coping strategies constructive? Frankly, in labeling certain coping responses constructive or healthy, psychologists are making value judgments. It's a gray area in which opinions will vary to some extent. Nonetheless, some consensus is emerging from the burgeoning research on coping and stress management. Key themes in this literature include the following.

1. Constructive coping involves confronting problems directly. It is task-relevant and action-oriented. It involves a conscious effort to evaluate your options rationally in an effort to solve your problems.
2. Constructive coping is based on reasonably realistic appraisals of your stress and coping resources. A little self-deception may sometimes be adaptive, but excessive self-deception and highly unrealistic negative thinking are not.
3. Constructive coping involves learning to recognize, and in some cases inhibit, potentially disruptive emotional reactions to stress.
4. Constructive coping involves learning to exert some control over potentially harmful or destructive habitual behaviors. It requires the acquisition of some behavioral self-control.

These points should give you a general idea of what we mean by "constructive coping." These assumptions will guide our discourse in the remainder of this chapter as we discuss how to cope more effectively with stress.

To organize our discussion, we will use a classification scheme proposed by Rudolph Moos and Andrew Billings (1982) to divide constructive coping techniques into three broad groups. These three types of coping strategies are classified according to their focus or goal:

- *Appraisal-focused coping* involves efforts to reevaluate the apparent demands or redefine the apparent meaning of stressful events. Its goal is to alter your appraisal of the threat in the situation.
- *Problem-focused coping* involves efforts to circumvent, modify, remedy, or conquer the problem and its consequences. Its goal is to master the threat or problem directly.
- *Emotion-focused coping* involves efforts to control and usually reduce the emotional reactions aroused by stress. Its goal is to reestablish a healthy emotional equilibrium.

It should be kept in mind that, like most efforts to classify complex behavior, this scheme is not entirely satisfactory. Some coping tactics are difficult to categorize because they have more than one goal. Nonetheless, this scheme gives us a framework for analyzing healthy approaches to coping.

Appraisal-Focused Constructive Coping

People often underestimate the importance of the appraisal phase in the stress process. They fail to appreciate the highly subjective feelings that color the perception of threat to one's well-being. One very useful way to deal with stress is to alter your appraisal of threatening events. In this section we'll examine Albert Ellis's ideas about reappraisal and discuss the value of using humor and positive reinterpretation to cope with stress.

Ellis's Rational Thinking

Albert Ellis (1977, 1985) is a prominent theorist who believes that we can short-circuit our emotional reactions to stress by altering our appraisals of stressful events. Ellis's insights about stress appraisal are the foundation for a widely used system of therapy that he devised. ***Rational-emotive therapy* is an approach to**

Albert Ellis

therapy that focuses on altering clients' patterns of irrational thinking to reduce maladaptive emotions and behavior.

Ellis maintains that *you feel the way you think.* He argues that problematic emotional reactions are caused by negative self-talk, which he calls catastrophic thinking. **Catastrophic thinking consists of unrealistic appraisals of stress that exaggerate the magnitude of one's problems.** Ellis uses a simple ABC sequence to explain his ideas (see Figure 4.5).

A: Activating event. The A in Ellis's system stands for the activating event that produces the stress. The activating event may be any potentially stressful transaction—an automobile accident, the cancellation of a date, a delay while waiting in line at the bank, a failure to get a promotion you were expecting.

B: Belief system. B stands for your belief about the event, and thus your appraisal of the stress. According to Ellis, we often view minor setbacks as disasters. We engage in catastrophic thinking: "How awful this is. I can't stand it! Things never turn out fairly for me. I'll be in this line forever. I'll never get promoted."

C: Consequence. C stands for the consequence of your negative thinking. When your appraisals of stressful events are terribly negative, the consequence tends to be emotional distress. Thus we feel angry, or outraged, or anxious, or panic-stricken, or disgusted, or dejected.

Ellis asserts that most of us do not understand the importance of phase B in this three-stage sequence. We unwittingly believe that the activating event (A) *causes* the consequent emotional turmoil (C). Ellis maintains, however, that A does not cause C; it only appears to do so. The cause of C, Ellis asserts, is B. Our emotional distress is actually caused by our catastrophic thinking in our appraisal of stressful events.

According to Ellis, it is commonplace for people to turn inconvenience into disaster and make mountains out of molehills. Imagine that someone has stood you up on a date that you were eagerly looking forward to. You may think, "Oh, this is terrible. I'm going to have another rotten, boring weekend. People always mistreat me. I'll never find anyone to fall in love with. I must be a crummy, worthless person." Ellis would argue that such thoughts are terribly irrational. He would point out that it does not follow logically from being stood up that you (1) must have a lousy weekend,

(2) will never fall in love, or (3) are a worthless person.

The Roots of Catastrophic Thinking

Ellis theorizes that unrealistic appraisals of stress are derived from irrational assumptions that we hold. He maintains that if you scrutinize your catastrophic thinking, you will find that your reasoning is based on an indefensibly unreasonable premise, such as "I must have approval from everyone" or "I must perform well in all endeavors." These faulty assumptions, which we often hold unconsciously, generate our catastrophic thinking and our emotional turmoil. To facilitate emotional self-control, it is important to learn to spot irrational assumptions and the unhealthy patterns of thought that they generate. Let's look at five particularly common irrational assumptions. A lengthier list can be found in Figure 4.6.

1. *I must have love and affection from certain people.* We all want to be liked and loved. There is nothing wrong with that. Many of us, however, foolishly believe that we should be liked by everyone we come into contact with. If you stop to think about it, that's clearly unrealistic. Once we fall in love, we tend to believe that our future happiness depends absolutely on the continuation of that one special relationship. We believe that if our current love rela-

**FIGURE 4.5
Albert Ellis's
ABC model of
emotional reactions**
Most of us are prone to attribute our negative emotional reactions (C) directly to stressful events (A). Ellis argues, however, that our emotional reactions are really caused by the way we think about these events (B).

The commonsense view

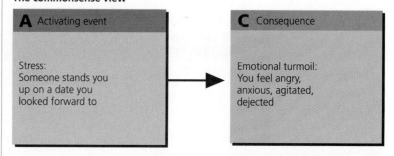

Ellis's view

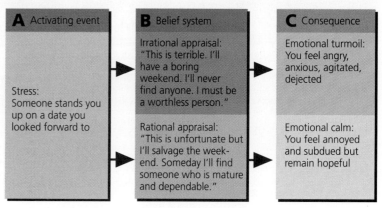

FIGURE 4.6
Irrational assumptions that can cause emotional disturbance
Irrational assumptions such as those listed here are often held unconsciously. According to Ellis, constructive coping depends on detecting these assumptions and replacing them with more rational views, such as the examples provided here. (Adapted by Basil Najjar from Ellis, 1977.)

tionship were to end, we would never again be able to achieve a comparable one. This is an unrealistic view of the future. Such views make us anxious during a relationship and severely depressed if it comes to an end.

2. I must perform well in all endeavors. We live in a highly competitive society. We are taught that victory brings happiness. Consequently, we feel that we must always win. Many sports enthusiasts, for example, are never satisfied unless they perform at their best level. By definition, however, their best level is not their typical level, and they set themselves up for inevitable frustration.

3. Other people should always behave competently and be considerate of me. We are often angered by others' stupidity and selfishness. You may become outraged when a mechanic fails to fix your car properly, for example, or when a salesperson treats you rudely. It would be nice if

people were always competent and considerate, but you know better—they are not! Yet many of us go through life unrealistically expecting efficiency and kindness.

4. Everyone I identify with should have pleasant experiences. Many of us extend our personal boundaries so that we become very upset when unfortunate events happen to others. When a friend's wife walks out on him, we become furious and depressed for him. The broader your personal boundaries are, the more you are likely to experience others' stress. Consider sports fans who go berserk when a referee or umpire makes a bad call that goes against their team. Such people are becoming stressed over events that have little direct bearing on their lives.

5. Events should always go the way I like. Some people simply won't tolerate any kind of setback. They assume that things should always go their way. Some commuters become very

Irrational Assumptions in Everyday Thinking

Irrational assumption	Rational alternative
1 I must be loved or approved of by everyone for everything I do.	It's best to concentrate on my own self-respect, on winning approval for practical purposes, and on loving rather than being loved.
2 I must be thoroughly competent, adequate, and achieving in order to be worthwhile.	I'm an imperfect creature who has limitations and fallibilities like anyone else—and that's okay.
3 It's horrible when things aren't the way I'd like them to be.	I can try to change or control the things that disturb me—or temporarily accept conditions I can't change.
4 There isn't much I can do about my sorrows and disturbances, because unhappiness comes from what happens to you.	I feel how I think. Unhappiness comes mostly from how I look at things.
5 If something is dangerous or fearsome, I'm right to be terribly upset about it and to dwell on the possibility of its occurring.	I can frankly face what I fear and either render it nondangerous or accept the inevitable.
6 It's easier to avoid facing difficulties and responsibilities than to face them.	The "easy way out" is invariably the much harder alternative in the long run.
7 I'm dependent on others and need someone stronger than I am to rely on.	It's better to take the risk of relying on myself and thinking and acting independently.
8 There's always a precise and perfect solution to human problems, and it's catastrophic not to find it.	The world is full of probability and chance, and I can enjoy life even though there isn't always an ideal solution to a problem.
9 The world—especially other people—should be fair, and justice (mercy) must triumph.	I can work toward seeking fair behavior, realizing that there are few absolutes in life.
10 I must not question the beliefs held by society or respected authorities.	It's better to evaluate beliefs for myself—on their own merits, not on who happens to hold them.

tense and angry each time they get stuck in a rush-hour traffic jam. They seem to believe that they are entitled to coast home easily every day, even though they know that rush hour rarely is a breeze. Such expectations are clearly unrealistic and doomed to be violated. Yet few people recognize the obvious irrationality of the assumption that underlies their anger unless it is pointed out to them.

Reducing Catastrophic Thinking

How can you reduce your unrealistic appraisals of stress? Ellis says that you must learn (1) how to detect catastrophic thinking and (2) how to dispute the irrational assumptions that cause it. Detection involves acquiring the ability to spot unrealistic pessimism and wild exaggeration in your thinking. Examine your self-talk closely. Ask yourself why you're getting upset. Force yourself to verbalize your concerns, covertly or out loud. Look for key words that often show up in catastrophic thinking, such as *should*, *ought*, *never*, and *must*.

Disputing your irrational assumptions requires you to subject your entire reasoning process to scrutiny. Try to root out the assumptions from which your conclusions are derived. We often are unaware of these assumptions. Once they are unearthed, their irrationality may be quite obvious. If your assumptions seem reasonable, ask yourself whether your conclusions follow logically. Try to replace your catastrophic thinking with more low-key, rational analyses. These strategies should help you to redefine stressful situations in ways that are less threatening. Strangely enough, another way to do this is to turn to humor.

Humor as a Stress Reducer

A few years ago the Chicago area experienced its worst flooding in about a century. Thousands of people saw their homes wrecked when two rivers spilled over their banks. As the waters receded, the flood victims returning to their homes were subjected to the inevitable TV interviews. A remarkable number of victims, surrounded by the ruins of their homes, *joked* about their misfortune. When the going gets tough, it may pay to laugh about it. In a study of coping styles, McCrae (1984) found that 40% of his subjects reported using humor to deal with stress.

In analyzing the stress-reducing effects of humor, Dixon (1980) emphasizes its impact on the appraisal of stress. Finding a humorous aspect in a stressful situation redefines the situ-

ation in a less threatening way. Dixon notes that laughter can also discharge pent-up emotions. These dual functions of humor may make joking about life's difficulties a particularly useful coping strategy.

Some psychologists have long suspected that humor may be a worthwhile coping response. But empirical evidence to that effect has emerged only in recent years (Martin & Lefcourt, 1983; Nezu, Nezu, & Blissett, 1988). For instance, Martin and Lefcourt (1983) found that a good sense of humor functioned as a buffer to lessen the negative impact of stress on mood. Some of their results are shown in Figure 4.7. It plots how mood disturbance increased as stress went up in two groups of subjects—those who were high in their use of humor and those who scored low on that dimension. Notice how an increase in stress leads to a smaller increase in mood disturbance in the high humor group.

Positive Reinterpretation

When you are feeling overwhelmed by life's difficulties, there is merit in the commonsense strategy of recognizing that "things could be

FIGURE 4.7
Humor and coping
Martin and Lefcourt (1983) related stress to mood disturbance in subjects who were either high or low in their use of humor. Increased stress led to smaller increases in mood disturbance in the high humor group, suggesting that humor has some value in efforts to cope with stress.

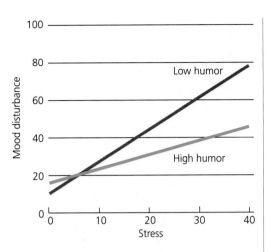

Steps in Systematic Problem Solving

In our efforts to deal with life's problems, the most obvious course of action is to tackle the problems head-on. In their study of coping, Carver et al. (1989) found that the two coping tactics that reflect this approach (active coping and planning) were favorably related to higher self-esteem and lower anxiety. D'Zurilla and Sheedy (1991) took a more focused look at the link between problem solving and stress. They used two scales to evaluate key aspects of subjects' social problem-solving ability. One scale gauged subjects' *problem orientation*—that is, whether they approached problems with a positive attitude, viewing them as challenges and opportunities. The other scale assessed a set of four *problem-solving* skills: (1) defining and formulating the problem, (2) generating alternative solutions, (3) making decisions, and (4) implementing and verifying solutions. Three months after the assessment of their problem-solving ability, subjects completed the Derogatis Stress Profile (Derogatis, 1987), which measures various symptoms of stress. D'Zurilla and Sheedy found that the level of subjects' symptoms of stress was correlated –.53 with their problem orientation and –.23 with their problem-solving skills. In other words, the better subjects' problem-solving abilities were, the fewer stress-related difficulties they experienced. In accord with this finding, research reveals that the acquisition of systematic problem-solving skills can help depressed patients to reduce their feelings of depression (Nezu, 1986).

Since the number of personal problems that may arise is infinite, we can only sketch a very general outline of how to engage in systematic problem solving. The problem-solving plan to be described here is a synthesis of observations by various experts, especially Mahoney (1979) and Miller (1978). The four steps closely parallel the four problem-solving skills measured by D'Zurilla and Sheedy (1991): (1) clarify the problem, (2) generate alternative courses of actions, (3) evaluate your alternatives and select a course of action, and (4) take action while maintaining flexibility.

worse." No matter how terrible our problems seem, most of us know people who have even bigger troubles. That is not to say that you should derive satisfaction from others' misfortune. However, comparing your own plight with others' even tougher struggles can help you put your problems in perspective. Research by McCrae (1984) suggests that this strategy of making positive comparisons with others is a widely used coping mechanism. It seems to be a relatively healthy one, in that it can facilitate calming reappraisals of stress without the necessity of distorting reality.

Another way to engage in positive reinterpretation is to search for something good in a bad experience. Distressing though they may be, many of our setbacks have positive elements. After experiencing divorces, illnesses, firings, financial losses, and such, many people remark that "I came out of the experience better than I went in," or "I grew as a person." The positive aspects of a personal setback may be easy to see after the stressful event is behind you. The challenge is to recognize these positive aspects while you are still struggling with the setback, so that it becomes less stressful. Research suggests that positive reinterpretation is an effective coping method (Folkman, Lazarus, Gruen, & DeLongis, 1986).

Problem-Focused Constructive Coping

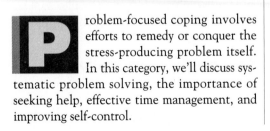

roblem-focused coping involves efforts to remedy or conquer the stress-producing problem itself. In this category, we'll discuss systematic problem solving, the importance of seeking help, effective time management, and improving self-control.

Clarify the Problem

You can't tackle a problem head-on if you're not sure what the problem is. Therefore, the first step in any systematic problem-solving effort is to clarify the nature of the problem. Sometimes the problem will be all too obvious. At other times it may be quite difficult to pin down the source of trouble. In any case, you need to arrive at a specific and concrete definition of your problem.

Two common tendencies typically hinder our efforts to get a clear picture of our problems. First, we often describe our problems in vague generalities (for example, "My life isn't going anywhere" or "I never have enough time"). Second, we tend to focus too much on negative feelings. This tendency confuses the consequences of problems ("I'm so depressed all the time" or "I'm so nervous I can't concentrate") with the problems themselves.

To overcome these tendencies and develop a clear specification of your problem, it may be helpful to think in terms of the four types of stress discussed in Chapter 3. Most problems can be analyzed in terms of frustration, conflict, pressure, and change. In the case of frustration, you need to identify the motive being thwarted and the barrier preventing you from attaining your goal. In the case of pressure, it helps to pinpoint the source of the pressure. Once you start thinking in these terms, you may be surprised how often your problem boils down to internal conflict. Whatever your troubles are, it is crucial that you dig beneath the superficial appearances to arrive at a specific and concrete definition of your problem.

Generate Alternative Courses of Action

The second step in systematic problem solving is to generate alternative courses of action. Notice that we did not call these alternative *solutions*. Many problems do not have a readily available solution that will completely resolve the problem. If you think in terms of searching for complete solutions, you may prevent yourself from considering many worthwhile courses of action. It is more realistic to search for alternatives that may produce some kind of improvement in your situation.

Besides avoiding the tendency to insist on solutions, you need to avoid the temptation to go with the first alternative that comes to mind. Many of us are a little trigger-happy. We thoughtlessly try to follow through on the first response that occurs to us. Various lines of evidence suggest that it is wiser to engage in brainstorming about a problem. **Brainstorming involves generating as many ideas as possible while withholding criticism and evaluation.** In other words, you generate alternatives without paying any attention to their apparent practicality. This approach facilitates creative expression of ideas.

Evaluate Your Alternatives and Select a Course of Action

Once you've generated as many alternatives as you can, you need to start evaluating the possibilities. There are no simple criteria for judging the relative merits of your alternatives, but you will probably want to address three general issues. First, ask yourself whether each alternative is a realistic plan. In other words, what is the probability that you can successfully execute the intended course of action? Try to think of any obstacles you may have failed to anticipate. As you make this assessment, it is important to try to avoid both foolish optimism and unnecessary pessimism.

Second, consider any costs or risks associated with each alternative. The "solution" to a problem is sometimes worse than the problem itself. Assuming you can successfully implement your intended course of action, what are the possible negative consequences? Finally, compare the desirability of the probable outcomes of all the alternatives. After eliminating the unrealistic possibilities, list the probable consequences (both good and bad) associated with each alternative. Then review and compare the desirability of these potential outcomes. In making your decision, you have to ask yourself, "What is important to me? Which outcomes do I value the most?"

Take Action while Maintaining Flexibility

Once you have chosen your course of action, you should follow through and try to implement your plan. In doing so, try to maintain flexibility. Do not get locked into a particular course of action. Few choices are truly irreversible. You need to monitor results closely and be willing to revise your strategy.

Being flexible does not mean that you should execute your plan halfheartedly. To be able to evaluate your plan accurately, you must enact it with vigor and confidence and give it time to succeed. In evaluating your course of action, try to avoid the simplistic success/failure dichotomy. You should simply look for any improvement of any kind. If your plan doesn't work out too well, consider whether it was undermined by any unforeseen circumstances that you could not have anticipated. Finally, remember that you can learn from your failures. Even if things did not work out, you may now have new information that will facilitate a new attack on the problem.

Seeking Help

In Chapter 3 we learned that social support can be a powerful force that helps to buffer the deleterious effects of stress. We discussed social support as if it were a stable, external resource to which some people had greater access than others. In reality, our social support fluctuates over time and evolves out of our interactions with others (Newcomb, 1990). Some people have more support than others in part because they have personal characteristics that attract more support or because they make more effort to seek support.

Hence, when you try to tackle problems directly, it pays to keep in mind the value of seeking aid from friends, family, co-workers, and neighbors. Because of potential embarrassment, many people are reluctant to acknowledge their problems and seek help from others. What makes this reality so lamentable is that others can provide a great deal of help in many ways.

Two of the four types of social support discussed in Chapter 3, *informational support* and *instrumental support,* may aid problem-focused coping. As you proceed through the first three steps of systematic problem solving, informational support in the form of advice can be of immense value. It helps to be able to bounce ideas off someone as you try to clarify your problem, generate alternative strategies, and evaluate those alternatives. Once you decide on a course of action, instrumental support in the form of material aid may make all the difference in the world.

Social support can have an impact in other coping domains besides problem-solving efforts. According to House's (1981) analysis of social

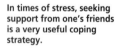

In times of stress, seeking support from one's friends is a very useful coping strategy.

support (see Chapter 3), others may often provide *emotional support* in the form of affection. This type of support may aid emotion-focused coping. Our friends may also provide *appraisal support* by helping us to make sense of life's difficulties. This type of social support may aid appraisal-focused coping. Thus seeking help from others is a strategy that has enormous potential in that social support can facilitate all three types of coping.

Using Time More Effectively

Do you constantly feel as though you had too much to do and too little time to do it? Do you feel overwhelmed by your responsibilities at work, at school, and at home? Does it seem as if you're always rushing around, trying to meet an impossible schedule? If you answered yes to some of these questions, you're struggling with time pressure. You can estimate how well you manage time by responding to the brief questionnaire in Figure 4.8. If the results suggest that your time is out of your control, you may be able to make your life less stressful by learning sound time-management strategies.

R. Alec Mackenzie (1972), a prominent time-management researcher, points out that time is a unique resource. It can't be stockpiled like money, food, or other precious resources. Time is a nonrenewable resource: you can't turn back the clock. Furthermore, everyone, whether rich or poor, gets an equal share of time—24 hours a day, 7 days a week. Whether it seems to fly by or to drag along, time actually flows at the same steady pace for everyone. Although time is the most equitably distributed resource we have, some of us spend it much more wisely than others. Let's look at some of the ways in which we let time slip through our fingers without accomplishing much.

The Causes of Wasted Time

When people complain about "wasted time," they're usually upset because they haven't accomplished what they really wanted to with their time. Wasted time is time devoted to unnecessary, unimportant, or unenjoyable activities. Why do we waste our time on such activities? There are many reasons. Prominent among them are the following.

Inability to set or stick to priorities. The time consultant Alan Lakein (1973) emphasizes that it's often tempting to deal with routine, trivial tasks ahead of larger and more difficult tasks. Thus students working on a major

term paper often read their mail, do the dishes, fold the laundry, reorganize their desk, or dust the furniture instead of concentrating on the paper. Routine tasks are easy, and working on them allows us to rationalize our avoidance of more important tasks. Unfortunately, we often use up too much time on trivial pursuits, so that our more important tasks are left undone.

Inability to say no. Other people are constantly seeking our time. They want us to exchange gossip in the hallway, go out to dinner on Friday night, cover their hours at work, help with a project, listen to their sales pitch on the phone, join a committee, or coach Little League. Clearly, we can't do everything that everyone wants us to. Some people, however, just can't say no to others' requests for their time. Such people end up fulfilling others' priorities instead of their own. Thus, McDougle

**FIGURE 4.8
Assessing your
time management**
This brief questionnaire (from Le Boeuf, 1987) is designed to evaluate the quality of one's time management. Although it is geared more to working adults than to college students, it should allow you to get a rough handle on how well you manage your time.

How Well Do You Manage Your Time?

Listed below are ten statements that reflect generally accepted principles of good time management. Answer these items by circling the response most characteristic of how you perform your job. Please be honest. No one will know your answers except you.

1 Each day I set aside a small amount of time for planning and thinking about my job.
0. Almost never 1. Sometimes 2. Often 3. Almost always

2 I set specific, written goals and put deadlines on them.
0. Almost never 1. Sometimes 2. Often 3. Almost always

3 I make a daily "to do list," arrange items in order of importance, and try to get the important items done as soon as possible.
0. Almost never 1. Sometimes 2. Often 3. Almost always

4 I am aware of the 80/20 rule and use it in doing my job. (The 80/20 rule states that 80 percent of your effectiveness will generally come from achieving only 20 percent of your goals.)
0. Almost never 1. Sometimes 2. Often 3. Almost always

5 I keep a loose schedule to allow for crises and the unexpected.
0. Almost never 1. Sometimes 2. Often 3. Almost always

6 I delegate everything I can to others.
0. Almost never 1. Sometimes 2. Often 3. Almost always

7 I try to handle each piece of paper only once.
0. Almost never 1. Sometimes 2. Often 3. Almost always

8 I eat a light lunch so I don't get sleepy in the afternoon.
0. Almost never 1. Sometimes 2. Often 3. Almost always

9 I make an active effort to keep common interruptions (visitors, meetings, telephone calls) from continually disrupting my work day.
0. Almost never 1. Sometimes 2. Often 3. Almost always

10 I am able to say no to others' requests for my time that would prevent my completing important tasks.
0. Almost never 1. Sometimes 2. Often 3. Almost always

To get your score, give yourself
   3 points for each "almost always"
   2 points for each "often"
   1 point for each "sometimes"
   0 points for each "almost never"
Add up your points to get your total score.

If you scored
  0–15   Better give some thought to managing your time.
  15–20   You're doing OK, but there's room for improvement.
  20–25   Very good.
  28–30   You cheated!

(1987) concludes, "Perhaps the most successful way to prevent yourself from wasting time is by saying *no*" (p. 112).

Inability to delegate responsibility. Some tasks should be delegated to others—secretaries, subordinates, fellow committee members, other coaches, spouses, children, and so on. However, many people have difficulty delegating work to others. Barriers to delegation include unwillingness to give up any control, lack of confidence in subordinates, fear of being disliked, the need to feel needed, and the attitude that "I can do it better myself" (Mitchell, 1987). The problem, of course, is that people who can't delegate waste a lot of time on trivial work or on others' work.

Inability to throw things away. Some people are "pack rats" who can't throw anything into the wastebasket. Their desks are cluttered with piles of mail, newspapers, magazines, reports, and books. Their filing cabinets overflow with old class notes or ancient memos. At home their kitchen drawers bulge with rarely used utensils, their closets bulge with old clothes that are never

FIGURE 4.9
A time log
Experts recommend keeping a detailed record of how you use your time to improve your time management. The example depicted here shows the kind of record keeping that should be done.

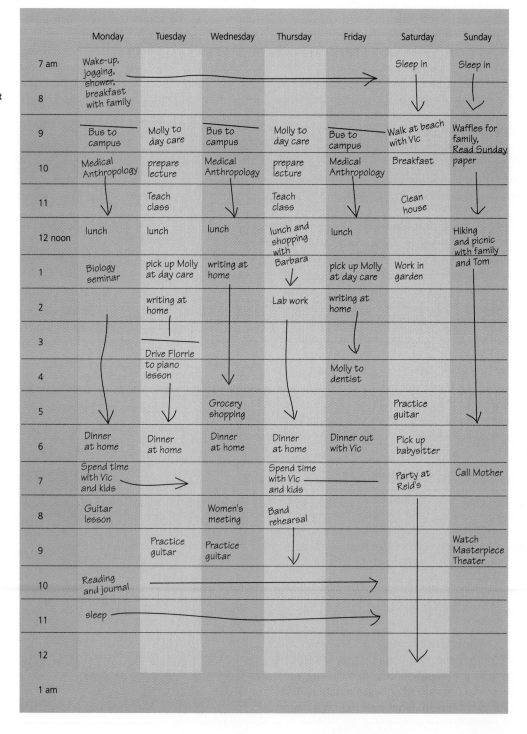

worn, and their attics bulge with junk. Pack rats waste time in at least two ways. First, they lose time looking for things that are lost among all the chaos. Second, they end up reshuffling the same paper, rereading the same mail, resorting the same reports, and so on. They would be better off if they made more use of their wastebaskets. Indeed, Mackenzie (1972) notes that "the art of wastebasketry has been designated by at least one management consultant as the most critical skill in managing one's work" (p. 69).

Inability to accept anything less than perfection. High standards are admirable, but some people have difficulty finishing projects because they expect them to be flawless. They can't let go. They dwell on minor problems and keep making microscopic changes in their papers, projects, and proposals. They are caught in what Emanuel (1987) calls the "paralysis of perfection." They end up spinning their wheels, redoing the same work over and over. There's nothing inherently wrong with trying to improve the quality of your work. But it pays to recognize when you have reached a point of diminishing returns, where further changes result in imperceptible improvements—if they're improvements at all.

Time-Management Techniques

What's the key to better time management? Most people assume that it's increased *efficiency*—that is, learning to perform tasks more quickly. Improved efficiency may help a little, but time-management experts maintain that efficiency is overrated. They emphasize that the key to better time management is increased *effectiveness*—that is, learning to allocate time to your most important tasks. This distinction is captured by a widely quoted slogan in the time-management literature: "Efficiency is doing the job right, while effectiveness is doing the right job." Let's look at the experts' suggestions about how to use time more effectively (based on Lakein, 1973; Lebov, 1980; Mackenzie, 1972).

1. *Monitor your use of time.* The first step toward better time management is to monitor your use of time to see where it all goes. Keep a written record of your activities, similar to that shown in Figure 4.9. At the end of each week, analyze how your time was allocated. Create categories of time use that accord with your personal roles and responsibilities such as studying, child care, housework, commuting, work at the office, work at home, eating, and sleeping. For each day, add up the hours allocated to each category. Record this information on a summary sheet like that in Figure 4.10. Two weeks of record keeping should allow you to draw some conclusions about where your time goes. Your records will help you to make informed decisions about reallocating your time. When you begin your time-management program, these records will also give you a baseline for comparison, so that you can see whether your program is working.

2. *Clarify your goals.* You can't wisely allocate your time unless you decide what you want to accomplish with your time. Lakein (1973) suggests that you ask yourself, "What are my lifetime goals?" Write down all the goals that you can think of, even relatively frivolous things like going deep-sea fishing or becoming a wine expert. Some of your goals will be in conflict. For instance, you can't become a vice president at your company in Wichita and move to

FIGURE 4.10
Time use summary
To analyze where your time goes, you need to review your time log and create a weekly time use summary, like the one shown here. The exact categories to be listed on the left depend on your circumstances and responsibilities.

Time Use Summary Form

	Activity	Mon.	Tues.	Wed.	Thurs.	Fri.	Sat.	Sun.	Total	%
1	Sleeping	8	6	8	6	8	7	9	52	31
2	Eating	2	2	3	2	3	2	3	17	10
3	Commuting	2	2	2	2	2	0	0	10	6
4	Housework	0	1	0	3	0	0	2	6	4
5	In class	4	2	4	2	4	0	0	16	9
6	Part-time job	0	5	0	5	0	3	0	13	8
7	Studying	3	2	4	2	0	4	5	20	12
8	Relaxing	5	4	3	2	7	8	5	34	20
9										
10										

The use of modern technology, such as cellular phones, can improve one's efficiency, but it doesn't guarantee effective use of one's time.

the West Coast. So the tough part comes next. You have to wrestle with your goal conflicts. Figure out which goals are most important to you, and list them in the order of their importance. The priorities thus established should guide you as you plan your activities on a daily, weekly, and monthly basis.

3. *Use a schedule to plan your activities.* People resist planning because it takes time, but in the long run it saves time. Thorough planning is essential to effective time management. At the beginning of each week, make up a list of short-term goals. This list should be translated into daily "to do" lists of planned activities. To avoid the tendency to put off larger projects, break them into smaller, manageable components, and set deadlines for completing the components.

Your planned activities should be allocated to various time slots on a written schedule. In making your plans, beware of the tendency to overschedule. Be realistic about what you can

accomplish. Since unexpected interruptions and problems are inevitable, don't schedule every minute of the day. Schedule your most important activities in the time periods when you tend to be most energetic and productive.

4. *Protect your prime time.* The best-laid plans can quickly go awry because of interruptions. There is no foolproof way to eliminate interruptions. But you may be able to shift most of them into certain time slots while protecting your most productive time. The trick is to announce to your family, friends, and co-workers that you're blocking off certain periods of "quiet time" when visitors and phone calls will be turned away. Of course, you also have to block off periods of "available time" when you're ready to deal with everyone's problems.

5. *Increase your efficiency.* Although efficiency is not the key to better time management, it's not irrelevant. Time-management experts do offer some suggestions for improving efficiency, including the following (Klassen, 1987; Schilit, 1987).

- *Handle paper once.* When memos, letters, reports, and such arrive on your desk, they should not be stashed away to be read again and again before you deal with them. Most paperwork can and should be dealt with immediately.

- *Tackle one task at a time.* Jumping from one problem to another is inefficient. Insofar as possible, stick with a task until it's done. In scheduling your activities, try to allow enough time to complete tasks.

- *Group similar tasks together.* It's a good idea to bunch up small tasks that are similar in nature. This strategy is useful when you're paying bills, replying to letters, returning phone calls, and so forth.

- *Make use of your downtime.* Most of us endure a lot of "downtime," waiting in doctors' offices, sitting in needless meetings, riding on buses and trains. In many of these situations, you may be able to get some of your easier work done—if you think ahead and bring it along.

Reprinted with special permission of North America Syndicate.

Improving Self-Control

Self-discipline and self-control are the key to handling many of life's problems effectively. All four forms of stress described in Chapter 3 can create challenges to your self-control. Whether you're struggling with the *frustration* of poor grades in school, constant *conflicts* about your overeating, *pressure* to do well in sports, or downhill *changes* in finances that require readjustment, you will need reasonable self-control if you expect to make much progress.

For many of us, however, satisfactory self-control is difficult to achieve. Fortunately, the last several decades have produced major advances in the technology of self-control. These advances have emerged from research on *behavior modification*, an approach to controlling behavior that relies on the principles of learning and conditioning. Because of its importance, we'll devote the entire Application at the end of this chapter to improving self-control through behavior modification.

Emotion-Focused Constructive Coping

Let's be realistic: There are going to be occasions when appraisal-focused coping and problem-focused coping are not successful in warding off emotional turmoil. Some problems are too serious to be whittled down much by reappraisal, and others simply can't be "solved." Moreover, even well-executed coping strategies may take time to work before emotional tensions begin to subside. Hence it is helpful to have some coping mechanisms that are useful in reducing emotional arousal. We'll discuss the merits of four such coping strategies in this section: releasing pent-up emotions, distracting yourself, meditation, and relaxation exercises.

Releasing Pent-Up Emotions

In view of the potential problematic physiological arousal that accompanies emotions, it's probably not a good idea to let strong emotions seethe within you for a long time. One study of high school students found that those who tended to hold their anger in were more likely to have higher blood pressure (Spielberger et al., 1985). So there may be some merit in Freud's notion that you should try to release emotions, or experience what he called *catharsis*. We noted earlier that aggressive behavior

doesn't consistently produce catharsis of anger, but Freud believed that catharsis could also occur in other ways.

When you're dejected, for example, it may be worthwhile to go ahead and "cry your heart out." We have a natural inclination to use this simple response. Unfortunately, many of us—especially men—are taught that crying is inappropriate behavior for an adult. However, there is nothing wrong with crying if the situation merits it. Admittedly, the evidence for catharsis effects from crying is rather weak, coming mostly from clinical reports and anecdotal accounts. A recent experimental study did not support the idea that crying is cathartic (Kraemer & Hastrup, 1988). However, crying doesn't create interpersonal complications the way aggressive behavior does. Thus it may be a reasonable, albeit unproven, coping strategy.

Recent studies suggest that verbalization may have considerable value in releasing anxiety and other problematic emotions. In other words, it could help to "talk it out." James Pennebaker and his colleagues have shown that

How to Get Control of Your Time and Your Life
by Alan Lakein (Peter H. Wyden, 1973)

Alan Lakein's book takes a more conventional approach to time management, although he too emphasizes the importance of evaluating one's priorities rather than cramming more activity into less time. Lakein is an expert on time management who has served as a consultant for numerous corporations. Although his book is slanted toward improving time use in the business world, its basic ideas can be useful to anyone. He emphasizes that he is not an "efficiency expert" who tries to reduce wasted motion. Instead, he sees himself as an "effectiveness expert" who has a system that can help you make the right decisions about how to allocate your time.

At the core of his system is the idea that you have to decide what is important to you. Lakein suggests that you closely examine your goals and make a list of both long-term and short-term priorities. Then, each day, review the tasks at hand and tackle those that will contribute the most to achievement of your life goals. Lakein points out that many of us tend to tackle simple, routine tasks first and save the important tasks for later, when we supposedly will have more time. He mercilessly flays the logic underlying this tendency, citing the "80/20 rule" as a reason to concentrate on important tasks:

> The 80/20 rule says, "If all items are arranged in order of value, 80 percent of the value would come from only 20 percent of the items, while the remaining 20 percent of the value would come from 80 percent of the items." Sometimes it's a little more, sometimes a little less, but 80 percent of the time I think you will find the 80/20 rule is correct.
>
> 80 percent of sales comes from 20 percent of customers
> 80 percent of production is in 20 percent of the product line
> 80 percent of sick leave is taken by 20 percent of employees
> 80 percent of dinners repeat 20 percent of recipes
> 80 percent of TV time is spent on 20 percent of programs most popular with the family
> 80 percent of telephone calls come from 20 percent of all callers.
> [p. 71]

talking or writing about traumatic events can have beneficial effects. According to Pennebaker (1990), a large proportion of people do not discuss their personal problems—even major traumas—with others. This reality is unfortunate in light of the finding that people who do not talk about traumatic events that they have experienced suffer more health problems than those who confide in others (Pennebaker & O'Heeron, 1984; Pennebaker & Susman, 1988). To test the value of talking it out, Pennebaker, Kiecolt-Glaser, and Glaser (1988) asked college students to write four brief essays about their difficulties in adjusting to college. Subjects in the control group wrote four essays about superficial topics. The subjects who wrote about their personal problems and traumas showed better immune function than the subjects who did not. In a subsequent, similar study, the students who wrote about their personal problems were found to enjoy better health in the following months than the other subjects (Pennebaker, Colder, & Sharp, 1990). Thus, if you can find a good listener, it may be wise to try to discharge problematic emotions by letting your secret fears, misgivings, and suspicions spill out in a candid conversation. Admittedly, talking about one's problems can be awkward and difficult. Pennebaker's research suggests that confiding in others does have short-term costs in that it may elicit anxiety and other negative emotions. In the long run, however, those who open up to others enjoy better mental and physical health than those who hold back.

Distracting Yourself

Distraction involves diverting your attention from a problem by thinking about other things or engaging in other activities. Substantial reliance on this strategy was observed in a study of the coping efforts of 60 married couples (Stone & Neale, 1984). If your stomach is churning over a snafu at work, it may be a good idea to go out to a movie, take up your knitting, or head for the bowling alley. Activities that require focused attention are probably best for distraction.

The adaptive merits of distraction are open to debate. On the one hand, distracting yourself is probably inferior to problem-focused coping that might yield a longer-lasting solution. On the other hand, distracting yourself clearly is a better idea than self-indulgence, lashing out at others, or getting bogged down in negative self-talk. Thus it appears to be a strategy that has modest short-term value when more direct tactics have failed to produce progress.

Meditation

Recent years have seen an explosion of interest in meditation as a method for relieving stress. *Meditation* **refers to a family of mental exercises in which a conscious attempt is made to focus attention in a nonanalytical way.** There are many approaches to meditation. In the United States, the most widely practiced approaches are those associated with yoga, Zen, and transcendental meditation (TM). Although all three of these approaches are rooted in Eastern religions (Hinduism, Buddhism, and Taoism), most Americans who practice meditation have only vague ideas regarding its religious significance. Of interest to us is the idea that meditation can calm inner emotional turmoil.

Most meditative techniques look deceptively simple. In TM, for example, a person is supposed to sit in a comfortable position with eyes closed and silently focus attention on a *mantra,* a specially assigned Sanskrit word that creates a resonant sound. This exercise in mental self-discipline is to be practiced twice daily for 20 minutes. The technique has been described as "diving from the active surface of the mind to its quiet depths" (Bloomfield & Kory, 1976, p. 49).

Advocates of TM claim that it can improve energy level, health, interpersonal relationships, and general happiness while reducing tension and anxiety caused by stress (Bloomfield & Kory, 1976; Schwartz, 1974). These are not exactly humble claims. Moreover, TM advocates assert that they can back up their claims with scientific evidence. Let's examine that evidence.

What are the *physical effects* of going into the meditative state? Some studies suggest that there are changes in the electrochemical activity of the brain. Most studies also find declines in subjects' heart rate, respiration rate, oxygen consumption, and carbon dioxide elimination (see Figure 4.11). Many researchers have also observed increases in skin resistance and decreases in blood lactate—physiological indicators associated with relaxation (Davidson, 1976; Fenwick, 1987; Woolfolk, 1975). Taken together, these bodily changes suggest that meditation can lead to a potentially beneficial physiological state characterized by relaxation and suppression of arousal.

These findings generated quite a bit of excitement in the 1970s. However, additional research employing better experimental controls soon dampened some of this enthusiasm. It turns out that these physical changes are not unique to meditation. A variety of systematic

One constructive means of coping with stress is daily meditation.

relaxation training procedures can produce similar results (Holmes, 1984; Shapiro, 1984).

The findings on the *psychological effects* of meditation are similar. There is some evidence that meditation can improve mood, lessen fatigue, and reduce anxiety (Carrington, 1987; Jangid, Vyas, & Shukla, 1988). However, some psychologists question whether meditation is any more likely to achieve these effects than other systematic relaxation or mental focusing procedures that are practiced regularly and effectively (Shapiro, 1984, 1987).

Hence, if you are troubled by chronic emotional tension, learning to meditate may be an effective way to reduce your troublesome arousal. However, the benefits of meditation are not as spectacular as some proponents have claimed. Furthermore, you may be able to attain the same benefits through less exotic relaxation techniques, such as the one we discuss next.

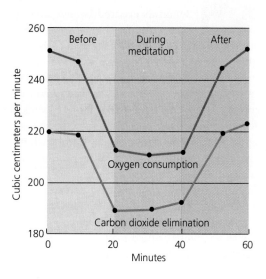

FIGURE 4.11
Transcendental meditation (TM) and physiological arousal
The physiological changes shown on this graph (based on Wallace & Benson, 1972) are evidence of physical relaxation during the meditative state. However, such changes can also be produced by other systematic relaxation procedures.

Relaxation Procedures

There is ample evidence that systematic relaxation procedures can soothe emotional turmoil and reduce problematic physiological arousal (Lehrer & Woolfolk, 1984). One study even suggests that relaxation training may improve the effectiveness of one's immune response (Kiecolt-Glaser et al., 1985). Beneficial relaxation can be achieved in a variety of ways. The most prominent systems are Jacobson's (1938, 1970) *progressive relaxation*, Luthe's (1962) *autogenic training*, and Benson's (1975; Benson & Klipper, 1988) *relaxation response*. We'll discuss Benson's approach because it is a simple one that virtually anyone can learn to use.

After studying various approaches to meditation, Herbert Benson, a Harvard Medical School cardiologist, came to the same conclusions as most other researchers. He decided that elaborate religious rituals and beliefs are not necessary to profit from meditation. He also concluded that what makes meditation beneficial is the relaxation it induces. After "demystifying" meditation, Benson (1975) set out to devise a simple, nonreligious procedure that could provide similar benefits. He calls his procedure the "relaxation response."

After studying meditation and a variety of relaxation techniques, Benson concluded that the following four factors are critical to effective relaxation.

Herbert Benson

1. A *quiet environment.* It is easiest to induce the relaxation response in a distraction-free environment. After you become skilled at the relaxation response, you may be able to achieve it in a crowded subway. Initially, however, you should practice it in a quiet, calm place.
2. A *mental device.* To shift attention inward and keep it there, you need to focus your attention on a constant stimulus, such as a sound or word that you recite over and over. You may also choose to gaze fixedly at a bland object, such as a vase. Whatever the case, you need to focus your attention on something.
3. A *passive attitude.* It is important not to get upset when your attention strays to distracting thoughts. You must realize that such distractions are inevitable. Whenever your mind wanders from your attentional focus, calmly redirect attention to your mental device.
4. A *comfortable position.* Reasonable body comfort is essential to avoid a major source of potential distraction. Simply sitting up straight works well for most people. Some people can practice the relaxation response lying down, but for most people such a position is too conducive to sleep.

Benson's (1975, pp. 114–115) actual procedure for inducing the relaxation response is deceptively simple. For full benefit, it should be practiced daily.

1. Sit quietly in a comfortable position.
2. Close your eyes.
3. Deeply relax all your muscles, beginning at your feet and progressing up to your face. Keep them relaxed.
4. Breathe through your nose. Become aware of your breathing. As you breathe out, say the word "ONE" silently to yourself. For example, breathe IN . . . OUT, "ONE"; IN . . . OUT, "ONE"; and so on. Breathe easily and naturally.
5. Continue for 10 to 20 minutes. You may open your eyes to check the time, but do not use an alarm clock. When you finish, sit quietly for several minutes, at first with your eyes closed and later with your eyes opened. Do not stand up for a few minutes.
6. Do not worry about whether you are successful in achieving a deep level of relaxation. Maintain a passive attitude and permit relaxation to come at its own pace. When distracting thoughts occur, try to ignore them by not dwelling on them and return to repeating "ONE." With practice, the response should come with little effort. Practice the technique once or twice daily, but not within two hours after any meal, since the digestive processes seem to interfere with the elicitation of the relaxation response.

Summary

Coping involves behavioral efforts to master, reduce, or tolerate the demands created by stress. We cope with stress in many ways, but most of us have certain styles of coping. Coping strategies vary in their adaptive value.

Giving up, possibly best understood in the context of learned helplessness, is a common coping pattern that tends to be of limited value. Another is striking out at others with acts of aggression. Frequently caused by frustration, aggression tends to be counterproductive because it often creates new sources of stress. Blaming yourself with negative self-talk and indulging yourself are other relatively nonadaptive coping patterns. Particularly common is defensive coping, which may involve any of a number of defense mechanisms. Although the adaptive value of defensive coping tends to be less than optimal, it depends on the situation. Some of our illusions may be healthy.

Constructive coping is rational, realistic, and action-oriented. It also involves inhibiting troublesome emotions and learning self-control. Appraisal-focused constructive coping is facilitated by Ellis's suggestions on how to reduce catastrophic thinking by digging out the irrational assumptions that cause it. Other valuable strategies include using humor to deal with stress and looking for the positive aspects of setbacks and problems.

Problem-focused constructive coping can be facilitated by a four-step process: (1) clarify the problem, (2) generate alternative courses of action, (3) evaluate your alternatives and select a course of action, and (4) take action while maintaining flexibility. Other coping tactics with potential value include seeking social support and acquiring strategies to improve self-control. Effective time management can also aid problem-focused coping. Better time management depends less on increased efficiency than on setting priorities and allocating time wisely.

Our discussion of emotion-focused coping noted the possible value of releasing pent-up emotions and the occasional efficacy of distracting yourself. Meditation can be helpful in reducing emotional turmoil, but its benefits have been exaggerated. Although such systematic relaxation procedures as Benson's "relaxation response" are less exotic, they can be very effective ways to cope with troublesome emotional arousal.

In our application section, we return to the issue of problem-focused coping and discuss how to improve self-control. We'll examine a step-by-step program for using behavioral techniques to enhance self-discipline.

APPLICATION Achieving Self-Control

If you answered yes to any of these questions, you have struggled with the challenge of self-control. This application discusses how you can use the techniques of behavior modification to improve your self-control. If you stop to think about it, self-control—or, actually, a lack of it—underlies many of the personal problems that we struggle with in everyday life.

Behavior modification is a systematic approach to changing behavior through the application of the principles of conditioning. Advocates of behavior modification assume that our behavior is a product of learning, conditioning, and environmental control. They further assume that what is learned can be unlearned. Thus they set out to "recondition" people to produce more desirable patterns of behavior.

Behavior modification can be a powerful tool. Beginning in the 1960s, advocates of behavior modification fanned out across the country, applying their technology with great success in schools, businesses, hospitals, factories, child-care facilities, prisons, mental health centers, and drug-abuse programs (Goodall, 1972; Kazdin, 1982). The technology of behavior modification can also be very useful in efforts to improve self-control.

Our discussion will borrow liberally from an excellent book on self-modification by David Watson and Roland Tharp (1993). There are five steps in the process of self-modification. These steps are listed below and outlined in a flowchart in Figure 4.12.

Step 1: Specify your target behavior.
Step 2: Gather baseline data.
Step 3: Design your program.
Step 4: Execute and evaluate your program.
Step 5: Bring your program to an end.

Specifying Your Target Behavior
The first step in any systematic effort at self-modification is to specify the "target" behaviors. These are the behaviors that you will try to change in some way. This crucial step can be more complicated than it sounds.

A behavior modification program can be applied only to a clearly defined, overt behavioral response. However, many of us tend to be vague in describing our problems and identifying the exact nature of the behavior we want to change.

The basic problem is that we usually think in terms of negative personality traits rather than undesirable behaviors. For example, asked what behaviors he would like to change, a man might say, "I'm too irritable." That may well be accurate as far as it goes, but it is of little help in designing a self-modification program. To use a behavioral approach, we need to translate vague statements about traits into clear descriptions of the specific behaviors that lead us to think of ourselves as having those traits.

The best way to do this is to ponder past behavior or closely observe future behavior in order to list specific examples of responses that lead to the trait description. For instance, the man who characterizes himself as "too irritable" might translate this description into two overly frequent responses, such as arguing with his wife and snapping at his children. These are specific responses for which a self-modification program could be designed.

Gathering Baseline Data
The second step in your behavior modification effort is to gather baseline data. The *baseline period* is a span of time before you begin your program, during which you systematically observe your target behavior. People are often tempted to skip this step and move ahead. It is imperative to resist this temptation because you need to know the original response level of your target behavior in order to evaluate your progress. You can't tell whether your program is working unless you have a baseline for comparison. In gathering your baseline data, you need to monitor three things: (1) the initial response level of the target behavior, (2) the typical antecedents of the target behavior, and (3) the typical consequences of the target behavior.

Initial Response Level
In most cases, you simply need to keep track of how often the target response occurs in a certain time interval. Thus, you might count the daily frequency of snapping at your children, smoking cigarettes, biting your fingernails, or what-

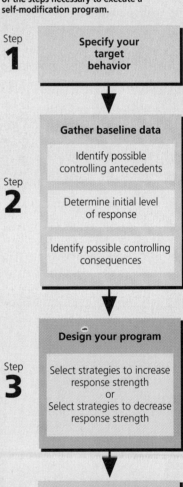

FIGURE 4.12
Steps in a self-modification program
This flowchart provides an overview of the steps necessary to execute a self-modification program.

Step **1** — Specify your target behavior

Step **2** — Gather baseline data
- Identify possible controlling antecedents
- Determine initial level of response
- Identify possible controlling consequences

Step **3** — Design your program
- Select strategies to increase response strength
or
- Select strategies to decrease response strength

Step **4** — Execute and evaluate your program

Step **5** — Bring your program to an end

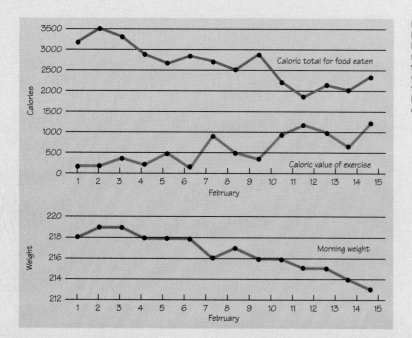

FIGURE 4.13
Example of record keeping in a self-modification program for losing weight
Graphic records are ideal for tracking progress in behavior modification efforts.

ever the target behavior happens to be.

The appropriate unit of measurement depends on the nature of the target response. If studying is your target behavior, you will probably monitor hours of study. If you want to modify your eating habits, you will probably want to keep track of how many calories you consume. Whatever the unit of measurement, it is crucial to gather accurate data. You may need to carry some sort of portable device for recording your behavior, such as a hand-held counter or an index card on which you make notes. Keep permanent written records. It is usually best to portray these records graphically (see Figure 4.13). There are no simple guidelines for how long you should gather baseline data. Generally, you need to gather data until you can identify a pattern of responding.

Antecedents

Antecedents are events that typically precede your target behavior. Often these events play a major role in governing your target response. If classical conditioning controls the behavior, antecedents may literally trigger your target response. If operant conditioning controls the behavior, antecedents may serve as signals (discriminative stimuli) that affect the probability that

you will emit the target response. In either case, recognizing links between antecedents and target behaviors can be very helpful as you design your program. For example, if your target is overeating, you might discover that the bulk of your overeating occurs late in the evening after you've had a couple of beers. Once you pinpoint this kind of antecedent-response connection, you can design your program to circumvent it or to break it down.

Consequences

Finally, you need to identify the reinforcement that is maintaining a target behavior or the punishment that is suppressing it. There are several things worth remembering as you try to identify reinforcers. First, sometimes the response itself is the reinforcement. Consummatory responses such as smoking and eating are intrinsically reinforcing. Second, remember that avoidance behavior is usually maintained by negative reinforcement. That is, the payoff for avoidance usually is the removal of something aversive, such as anxiety or a threat to self-esteem. Third, bear in mind that some responses receive only intermittent reinforcement. You can avoid unnecessary confusion in your search for reinforcers by being aware that a response may not be reinforced every time.

Designing Your Program

Once you have selected a target behavior and gathered adequate baseline data, it is time to assemble your program. Generally, your program will be designed either to increase or to decrease the frequency of a target response. These are somewhat different tasks, so we'll discuss each type of program separately.

Increasing Response Strength

Efforts to increase the frequency of a target response depend largely on the use of positive reinforcement. In other words, you reward yourself for behaving properly. Although the basic strategy is quite simple, a variety of factors have to be considered if it is to be carried out skillfully.

Selecting a reinforcer. If you intend to reward yourself for increasing a response, you need to find an effective reinforcer. Your choice will depend on your unique personality and situation. Reinforcement is subjective; something that is reinforcing for one person may not be reinforcing for another. Figure 4.14 lists questions that you can ask yourself in order to ascertain what your personal reinforcers are. Be sure to be realistic and choose a

What Are Your Reinforcers?

1 What will be the rewards of achieving your goal?

2 What kind of praise do you like to receive, from yourself and others?

3 What kinds of things do you like to have?

4 What are your major interests?

5 What are your hobbies?

6 What people do you like to be with?

7 What do you like to do with those people?

8 What do you do for fun?

9 What do you do to relax?

10 What do you do to get away from it all?

11 What makes you feel good?

12 What would be a nice present to receive?

13 What kinds of things are important to you?

14 What would you buy if you had an extra $20? $50? $100?

15 On what do you spend your money each week?

16 What behaviors do you perform every day? (Don't overlook the obvious or commonplace.)

17 Are there any behaviors you usually perform instead of the target behavior?

18 What would you hate to lose?

19 Of the things you do every day, which would you hate to give up?

20 What are your favorite daydreams and fantasies?

21 What are the most relaxing scenes you can imagine?

FIGURE 4.14
Selecting a reinforcer
The questions listed here (from Watson & Tharp, 1993, pp. 213–214) may help you to identify your personal reinforcers.

reinforcer that is available to you.

You don't have to come up with spectacular new reinforcers that you've never experienced before. You can use reinforcers that you are already getting. However, you have to restructure the contingencies so that you get them only if you behave appropriately. For example, let's assume that you usually buy a record or two each week. In designing a program to increase your studying, you could make your reinforcer the purchase of two compact discs each week. Of course, you would have to eliminate all other CD purchases except those that you earn through your self-modification program. Thus reinforcers that are already available to you can be made contingent upon your target behavior in order to strengthen that behavior.

Arranging the contingencies. Once you have chosen your reinforcer, you then have to set up reinforcement contingencies. Your reinforcement contingencies will describe the exact behavioral goals that must be met and the reinforcement that may then be awarded. For example, in a program to increase exercise, you might make spending $40 on clothes (the reinforcer) contingent upon jogging 15 miles during the week (the target behavior). In a program to increase study behavior, you might make listening to your stereo each night contingent upon studying three hours each day.

Try to set behavioral goals that are both challenging and realistic. You want your goals to be challenging so that they lead to improvement in your behavior.

However, setting unrealistically high goals—a common mistake in self-modification—often leads to unnecessary discouragement.

You also need to be concerned about doling out too much reinforcement. If reinforcers are too easy to get, you may become satiated, and the reinforcer may lose its motivational power. For example, if you designed a program in which the reinforcer was the purchase of two rock albums each week, it might work fine for a while—until all the albums you really wanted were salted away. Thus reinforcement contingencies have to be set up so they don't lose their effectiveness.

The token economy. One way to avoid the satiation problem is to put yourself on a token economy. A *token economy* is a system for doling out symbolic reinforcers that are exchanged later for a variety of genuine reinforcers. Thus, you might develop a "point system" for exercise behavior, accumulating points that can be spent on albums, movies, restaurant meals, and so forth (see Figure 4.15). You can also use a token economy to reinforce a variety of related target behaviors, as opposed to a single specific response. The token economy in Figure 4.15, for example, is set up to strengthen three different, though related, responses (jogging, tennis, and sit-ups).

Another advantage of the token economy is that it permits you symbolically to reinforce yourself immediately when you engage in appropriate behavior. Without the token economy you might have to wait until the end of the day or the week before you received any reinforcement. Such delays make a reinforcer less effective.

Generally, rapid reinforcement works better than delayed reinforcement. In fact, this is the heart of the problem when we struggle with self-discipline. For example, the reinforcement for overeating, your enjoyment of the food, is immediate. In contrast, the reinforcement for eating less (a slimmer, better-looking, healthier you) is typically several months away. It's not a fair contest. The more rapid reinforcement will win out most of the time. However, the rapid reinforcement provided in token economies can often neutralize this problem.

Shaping. In some cases, you may want to reinforce yourself for a response that you are not currently capable of making, such as speaking in front of a large group, smoking no cigarettes whatsoever, or jogging five miles a day. This task calls for the technique of shaping to build gradually toward your ultimate behavioral goal. ***Shaping* is modifying behavior by reinforcing closer and closer approximations of the desired response.** Thus you might initially reward yourself for jogging two miles a day and add a half-mile each week until you reached your goal of five miles a day. In shaping yourself, you should set up a schedule spelling out how and when your target behaviors and reinforcement contingencies should change. It's a good idea to move forward very gradually.

RECOMMENDED READING

Self-Directed Behavior: Self-Modification for Personal Adjustment

by David L. Watson & Roland G. Tharp (Brooks/Cole, 1989, 1993)

Behavior modification procedures are powerful tools that can help you gain greater control over your behavior. Numerous books purport to explain how the average person can use behavioral techniques. This is clearly the best of these books. It is solidly based on scientific research, admirably systematic, and yet very practical. It is written in an engaging, nonpatronizing style and makes ample use of anecdotal evidence. This application on behavior modification borrows liberally from this excellent book. If you have difficulty with self-control, behavior modification is your best bet for remedying the problem. Watson and Tharp provide a detailed, step-by-step analysis of how to achieve self-control through self-modification.

> Casual assessments of ourselves are often inaccurate. . . . [A] group of people who wanted to lose weight were asked by an experimenter how much they ate. Many assured themselves and the researcher that they "really didn't eat very much." Then they were asked to remember and write down everything they had eaten in the preceding two days. Their lists were checked, and it appeared that the people were not overeating. The researcher then put them all on a diet consisting of the foods they had reported eating. Every one of them began to lose weight. [1993, p. 65]

Decreasing Response Strength

Let's turn now to the challenge of reducing the frequency of an undesirable response. You can go

Responses Earning Tokens

Response	Amount	Number of tokens
Jogging	1/2 mile	4
Jogging	1 mile	8
Jogging	2 miles	16
Tennis	1 hour	4
Tennis	2 hours	8
Sit-ups	25	1
Sit-ups	50	2

Redemption Value of Tokens

Reinforcer	Tokens required
Purchase one record album of your choice	30
Go to movie	50
Go to nice restaurant	100
Take special weekend trip	500

FIGURE 4.15
Example of a token economy to reinforce exercise
This token economy was set up to strengthen three types of exercise behavior. The person can exchange tokens for any of four types of reinforcers.

Self-control problems, such as chronic overeating, can often be improved through the use of self-modification techniques.

about this task in a number of ways. You might guess that extinction (terminating reinforcement) would be the obvious strategy for decreasing the strength of a response. This is often the case when a program is to be designed to modify someone else's behavior. Self-modification programs, however, often center on unwanted responses that are inherently reinforcing (smoking and eating, for example), so that it is impossible to cut off reinforcement for the response. In such cases, your principal options include the use of reinforcement, control of antecedents, and punishment.

Reinforcement. Reinforcement can be used in an indirect way to decrease the frequency of a response. This may sound paradoxical, since by definition reinforcement strengthens a response. The trick lies in how you define the target behavior. In the case of overeating, for example, you might define your target behavior as eating more than 1600 calories a day (an excess response to be decreased) or eating fewer than 1600 calories a day (a deficit response to be increased). You can choose the latter definition and reinforce yourself whenever you eat less than 1600 calories in a day. Thus you can reinforce

yourself for not emitting a response, or for emitting it less, and thereby decrease a response through reinforcement.

Control of antecedents. There are antecedents that increase the likelihood of many unwanted responses. A worthwhile strategy for decreasing the occurrence of an undesirable response is to identify these antecedents and avoid exposure to them. This strategy is especially useful when you are trying to decrease the frequency of a consummatory response, such as smoking or eating. In the case of overeating, for instance, the easiest way to resist temptation is to avoid having to face it. A good behavioral program to reduce overeating often depends on controlling exposure to antecedents that promote extravagant eating. Figure 4.16 lists a variety of suggestions for controlling antecedents to reduce overeating.

Control of antecedents can also be helpful in a program to increase studying. Although the core of such a program should involve the reinforcement of good study behavior, control of antecedents may be needed to reduce loafing, daydreaming, and socializing when you are supposed to be studying. For example, the key to increasing study behavior

often lies in where you study. You can reduce excessive socializing by studying somewhere devoid of people. Similarly, you can reduce loafing by studying someplace where there is no TV, stereo, or phone to distract you.

Punishment. The strategy of decreasing unwanted behavior by punishing yourself for that behavior is an obvious option, and one that people overuse. The biggest problem with punishment in a self-modification effort is that it is difficult to follow through and punish yourself. Nonetheless, there may be situations in which your manipulations of reinforcers need to be bolstered by the threat of punishment.

If you're going to use punishment, keep two guidelines in mind. First, do not use punishment alone; use it in conjunction with positive reinforcement. If you set up a program in which you can earn nothing but negative consequences, you probably won't stick to the program. So make sure you can earn some positive outcomes. Second, use a relatively mild punishment so you will actually be able to administer it to yourself.

Nurnberger and Zimmerman (1970) have developed a creative method of self-punishment. They had subjects write out a check to an organization they hated (for

Controlling the Antecedents of Overeating

A. Shopping for food

1. Do not purchase problematic foods. These include
   a. very fattening, high-calorie foods
   b. your favorite foods, unless they have very low caloric values (you will be tempted to overconsume favorite foods)
   c. foods requiring little preparation (they make it too easy to eat)

2. To facilitate the above, you should
   a. use a shopping list from which you do not deviate
   b. shop just after eating (your willpower is reduced to jelly when you're hungry)
   c. carry only enough money to pay for items on your list

B. In your kitchen

1. Don't use your kitchen for anything other than food preparation and consumption. If you study or socialize there, you'll be tempted to eat.
2. Keep food stock stored out of sight.
3. If you have problematic foods in your kitchen (for other household members, of course), arrange cupboards and the refrigerator so that these foods are out of reach or in the rear.
4. Don't hover over cooking food. It will cook itself.
5. Prepare only enough food for immediate consumption.

C. While eating

1. Don't do anything besides eating. Watching TV or reading promotes mindless consumption.
2. Leave serving dishes on the kitchen counter or stove. Don't set them right in front of you.
3. Eat from a smaller dish. It will make a quantity of food appear greater.
4. Slow the pace of eating. Relax and enjoy your food.

D. After eating

1. Quickly put away or dispose of leftover foods.
2. Leave the kitchen as soon as you are through.

E. In regard to restaurants

1. Insofar as possible, do not patronize restaurants. Menus are written in a much too seductive style.
2. If social obligations require that you eat out, go to a restaurant that you don't particularly like.
3. When in restaurants, don't linger over the menu, and don't gawk at the food on other tables.
4. Avoid driving down streets and going to shopping centers that are loaded with alluring fast-food enterprises.

F. In general

1. Try to avoid boredom. Keep yourself busy.
2. Try to avoid excessive sleep loss and fatigue. Your self-control diminishes when you are tired.
3. Avoid excessive fasting. Skipping meals often leads to overeating later.

FIGURE 4.16
Control of antecedents
Controlling antecedents that trigger overeating is often a crucial part of behavioral programs for weight loss. The tips listed here have proved useful to many people.

instance, the campaign of a political candidate they despised). The check was held by a third party. If the subjects failed to meet their behavioral goals, the third party actually mailed the check. Such a punishment is relatively harmless but can serve as a strong source of motivation.

Executing and Evaluating Your Program

Once you have designed your program, the next step is to put it to work by enforcing the contingencies that you have carefully planned. During your intervention period, continue to record the frequency of your target behavior accurately so you can evaluate your progress. The success of your program depends on your not "cheating." The most common form of cheating is to give yourself a reward when you have not actually earned it.

You can increase the likelihood that you will comply with your program by writing up a *behavioral contract*—a written agreement outlining a promise to adhere to the contingencies of a behavior modification program (see Figure 4.17). The formality of signing such a contract in front of friends or family seems to make many people take their program more seriously. You can further reduce the likelihood of cheating by having someone other than yourself dole out the reinforcers and punishments. When a spouse, friend, or family member is monitoring your behavior, it is much harder to cheat.

When set into action, behavior modification programs often turn out to need some fine-tuning. So don't be surprised if you need to make a few adjustments. Several flaws are especially common in the design of self-modification programs. Among the things you should look out for are (1) depending on a weak reinforcer, (2) permitting lengthy delays between appropriate behavior and the actual reinforcement, and (3) trying to do too much too quickly by setting an unrealistic goal. Often a small revision or two can turn a failing program around and make it a success.

Ending Your Program

Generally, when you design your program you should spell out the conditions under which you will bring it to an end. Set a final goal such as reaching a certain weight, studying with a certain regularity, or going without ciga-

rettes for a certain length of time. Often it is a good idea to phase out your program by planning a gradual reduction in the frequency or potency of your reinforcement for appropriate behavior.

If your program is successful, it may fade away without a conscious decision on your part. New and improved patterns of behavior often become self-maintaining. A response such as eating right, exercising regularly, or studying

diligently may become habitual so that it no longer needs to be supported by an elaborate program. Whether your program fades out intentionally or spontaneously, you should always be prepared to reinstitute it if you find yourself slipping back to your old patterns of behavior.

FIGURE 4.17
A behavioral contract
Behavior modification experts recommend the use of a formal, written contract similar to the one shown here.

I, _____ , do hereby agree to initiate my self-change strategy as of (date) _____ and to continue it for a minimum period of _____ weeks—that is, until (date) _____ .

My specific self-change strategy is to _____

_____

_____

I will do my best to execute this strategy to my utmost ability and to evaluate its effectiveness only after it has been honestly tried for the specified period of time.

Optional Self-Reward Clause: For every _____ day(s) that I successfully comply with my self-change contract, I will reward myself with _____

_____

In addition, at the end of my minimum period of personal experimentation, I will reward myself for having persisted in my self-change efforts. My reward at that time will be _____

_____

I hereby request that the witnesses who have signed below support me in my self-change efforts and encourage my compliance with the specifics of this contract. Their cooperation and encouragement throughout the project will be appreciated.

Signed _____ Date_____

Witness_____

Witness_____

CHAPTER 4 REVIEW

Key Learning Objectives

1. Discuss three general points about coping.
2. Discuss the adaptive value of giving up as a response to stress.
3. Discuss the adaptive value of aggression.
4. Discuss the adaptive value of indulging yourself.
5. Discuss the adaptive value of negative self-talk.
6. Describe the five defense mechanisms introduced in this chapter and explain how defense mechanisms work.
7. Discuss the adaptive value of defense mechanisms, including healthy illusions.
8. Describe the nature of constructive coping and list the three categories of constructive coping tactics.
9. Describe Ellis's analysis of how catastrophic thinking causes maladaptive emotions.
10. Discuss the merits of positive reinterpretation and humor as coping strategies.
11. List and describe four steps in systematic problem solving.

12. Discuss the diverse benefits of seeking help as a coping strategy.
13. Explain five common causes of wasted time and summarize advice on managing time effectively.
14. Discuss the adaptive value of releasing pent-up emotions and distracting yourself.
15. Summarize the evidence on the effects of meditation.
16. Describe the requirements and procedure for Benson's relaxation response.
17. Explain why traits cannot be target behaviors in self-modification programs.
18. Discuss the three kinds of information you should pursue in gathering your baseline data.
19. Discuss how to use reinforcement to increase the strength of a response.
20. Discuss how to use reinforcement, control of antecedents, and punishment to decrease the strength of a response.
21. Discuss issues related to fine-tuning and ending a self-modification program.

Key Terms

aggression
antecedents
baseline period
behavioral contract
behavior modification
brainstorming
catastrophic thinking
catharsis
constructive coping
coping
defense mechanisms

denial
fantasy
intellectualization
learned helplessness
meditation
overcompensation
rational-emotive therapy
shaping
token economy
undoing

Key People

Albert Ellis
Seymour Epstein
Sigmund Freud

James Pennebaker
Martin Seligman

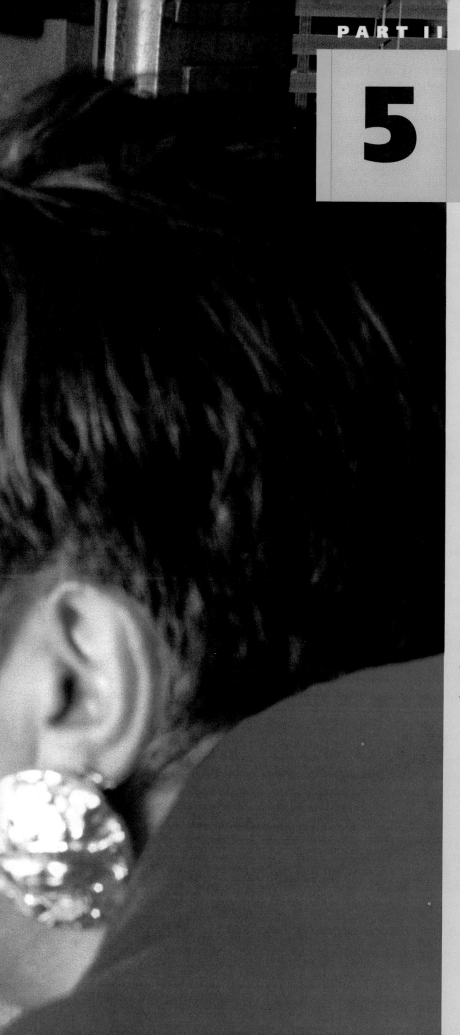

5

Person Perception

T'S FRIDAY NIGHT, AND YOU'RE bored. The thought of studying on a Friday night is a real turn off. The menu of TV shows for the evening looks pretty dull. You call a couple of friends to see whether they want to go to a movie. Both friends tell you they'd "love" to go, but they can't. One needs to study, and the other has to go grocery shopping. Their reasons for not going out with you seem rather flimsy to you. If they really wanted to go with you, they could have worked it in. To what do you attribute these rejections? Do the friends really have other demands on their time? Are they apathetic about going out? Are they being sincere when they say they would love to go out with you? Is it possible that they really don't enjoy spending time with you? Could it be that they find you boring? Are you boring?

These questions illustrate the process of social perception. We engage in this process constantly in order to understand both our own behavior and that of others. In our efforts to explain behavior, we create and rely on impressions and beliefs about ourselves and other people. This chapter discusses how we develop these explanations of behavior and how they influence our personal adjustment and social interactions. In the application section we provide some suggestions for building self-esteem.

Basic Principles of Social Perception

e'll begin our discussion by examining some basic principles of social perception. In this section we'll take a look at the attribution process, our preference for consistency among our beliefs, and our penchant for selective perception.

The Attribution Process

Attributions **are inferences that people draw about the causes of events, others' behavior, and their own behavior.** Let's say that someone compliments you on your clothing. To what should you *attribute* this compliment? Did this person *really* like your outfit? Or was the compliment merely part of everyday social routine? Could the compliment be part of an effort to butter you up? Or suppose your boss bawls you out for doing a sloppy job on an insignificant project. To what do you *attribute* this tongue-lashing? Was your work really that sloppy? Is your boss just feeling grouchy? Is your boss under too much pressure?

"I think you'll find my test results are a pretty good indication of your abilities as a teacher."

These two examples from everyday life illustrate the nature of the attribution process. We routinely make attributions in an effort to make sense of our experiences. These attributions involve inferences that ultimately represent guesswork on our part.

Key Dimensions of Attributions

Internal or external factors. Fritz Heider (1958) was the first to describe the crucial dimension along which we make attributions. Heider asserted that we tend to locate the cause of behavior either *within* a person, attributing it to personal factors, or *outside* of a person, attributing it to environmental factors.

Elaborating on Heider's insight, various theorists have agreed that our explanations of behavior and events can be categorized as internal or external attributions (Jones & Davis, 1965; Kelley, 1967; Weiner, 1974). *Internal* *attributions* **ascribe the causes of behavior to personal dispositions, traits, abilities, and feelings.** *External attributions* **ascribe the causes of behavior to situational demands and environmental constraints.** If a friend's business failed, for example, you might attribute the failure to your friend's lack of business acumen (an internal factor) or to negative trends in the economy (an external explanation). Parents who discover that their teenage son just banged up the family car may blame the accident on his carelessness (an internal attribution) or on slippery road conditions (an external attribution).

Whether our attributions are internal or external can have a tremendous impact on our everyday social interactions. Blaming a friend's business failure on poor business sense rather than on a poor economy obviously will affect the way you view your friend—not to mention whether you'll lend her money! Likewise, if parents attribute their son's automobile accident to slippery road conditions, they are likely to deal with him very differently than they would if they attributed it to his carelessness.

Furthermore, certain patterns of attribution can significantly affect our personal adjustment. As we'll see in Chapter 8, lonely people tend to attribute the cause of their loneliness to stable, internal causes ("I'm unlovable"). Similarly, studies suggest that people who attribute their setbacks to internal, personal causes while discounting external, situational explanations may be more prone to depression than people who display opposite tendencies (Alloy, Clements, & Kolden, 1985; Huesmann & Morikawa, 1985). In addition, there is evidence that the attributions spouses make to explain each other's behavior can affect their marital satisfaction (Bradbury & Fincham, 1988).

Stability or instability. A second dimension of causal attributions is the stability of the causes underlying behavior (Weiner, 1974; Weiner et al., 1972). A *stable* cause is one that is more or less permanent and unlikely to change over time. A sense of humor and intelligence, for example, are *stable internal* causes of behavior. *Stable external* causes of behavior include such things as laws and rules (speed limits, no smoking). An *unstable* cause of behavior is one that is variable or subject to change. *Unstable internal* causes of behavior include such things as mood (good or bad) and motivation (strong or weak). *Unstable external* causes could be the weather and the presence or absence of other people. According to Weiner, the stable-unstable dimension of attribution cuts across the internal-external dimension, creating four types of attributions for success and failure, as shown in Figure 5.1.

Let's apply Weiner's model to a concrete event. Imagine that you are wondering why you failed to get a job you wanted. You might attribute your setback to internal factors that are stable (lack of ability) or unstable (inadequate effort to put together an eye-catching résumé). Or you might attribute the outcome to external factors that are stable (too much competition in your field) or unstable (bad luck). If you got the job, the explanations you might offer for your success would fall in the same four categories: internal-stable (excellent ability), internal-unstable (hard work assembling your résumé), external-stable (lack of top-flight competition), and external-unstable (good luck).

Controllability or uncontrollability. A third dimension of the attribution process is the controllability of the causes underlying our actions (Weiner, 1986). The amount of effort we expend on a task, for example, is typically perceived as something under our control, but our aptitude for music is viewed as something we're born with (beyond our control). This dimension acknowledges the fact that sometimes our behavior is under our control and sometimes it isn't. Controllability can vary with each of the other two factors.

These three dimensions appear to be the central ones in the attribution process. Research has documented people's consistent use of them to explain a wide variety of behaviors and events, including achievement behavior, helping behavior (Schmidt & Weiner, 1988), loneliness (Michela, Peplau, & Weeks, 1983), and gender stereotyping (Deaux, 1976). They also operate in our explanations of the outcomes of sports events (Tenenbaum & Furst, 1986), as well as in our perceptions of people with social stigmas, such as AIDS (Weiner, 1988).

Actor-Observer Differences

Of course, attributions are only inferences. Our attributions may not correctly explain events. Paradoxical as it may seem, we often arrive at inaccurate explanations even when we contemplate the causes of our own behavior. Ultimately, attributions represent *guesswork* about the causes of events. Interestingly, these guesses tend to be slanted in certain directions.

In particular, our explanations of our own behavior can be quite different from those of someone else observing us. In other words, when an actor and an observer draw inferences about the causes of the actor's behavior, they often

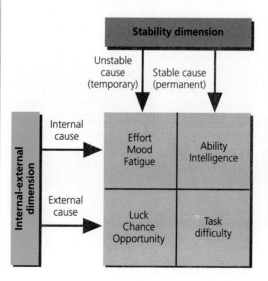

FIGURE 5.1
Key dimensions of attributional thinking
Weiner's model assumes that our explanations for success and failure emphasize internal versus external causes and stable versus unstable causes. If you attribute an outcome to great effort or to lack of effort, for example, you are citing internal factors that lie within the person. Since effort can vary over time, the causal factors at work are unstable. Other causal factors that fit into each of the four cells in Weiner's model are shown in the diagram.

Leon Festinger

make different attributions. Imagine that you've come to pick up your car at a garage where you left it to be serviced. When you're told that it isn't ready, you become angry and insulting. Observers who overhear your harsh, surly remarks are likely to make an internal attribution and infer that you are a rude and obnoxious person. Of course, they may be right, but if asked, *you* would probably attribute your behavior to the situation. Perhaps you called just before you came to the garage and were assured that your car was ready. Because observers often are unaware of such situational considerations, they understandably tend to make internal attributions for another's behavior.

Actors are more aware than observers of the situational factors that have influenced their behavior. Hence they are more likely than observers to locate the cause of their behavior in the situation. In general, then, actors favor external attributions for their behavior, while observers tend to explain the same behavior by internal attributions. This phenomenon is termed the *actor-observer effect* (Jones & Nisbett, 1971).

Actor-observer differences in attribution become a bit more complicated when people are explaining success and failure (Whitley & Frieze, 1983, 1985). When we explain *failure*, the usual actor-observer biases are apparent. Actors tend to make external attributions, blaming their failures on unfavorable situational factors. Observers tend to attribute the same failures to the actors' personal shortcomings. Thus, if you fail an exam, you may place the blame on the poorly constructed exam, lousy teaching, distractions in the hallway, or a bad week at work (all external attributions). An observer is more likely to attribute your failure to your lack of ability or to your lack of preparation (both of which are internal attributions).

When we explain *success*, however, the usual actor-observer differences are reversed to some degree. Thus, if you get a high grade on an exam, you'll probably make an internal attribution and point to your ability or your hard work (Forsyth & McMillan, 1981). An observer may be more likely to infer that the test was easy or that you were lucky (external attributions). In other words, actors like to take credit for their successes, while observers lean toward situational explanations for others' triumphs.

The Premium on Consistency

In developing our perceptions of ourselves and others, we strive for consistency. That is, we prefer that our attitudes and beliefs mesh together nicely. **Cognitive dissonance exists when related cognitions are inconsistent—that is, when they contradict each other.** First described by Leon Festinger (1957), cognitive dissonance is assumed to create an unpleasant state of tension. This tension is supposed to motivate people to reduce their dissonance, usually by altering one or both of the clashing cognitions.

Consider a simple example. Let's say that you see yourself as a hardworking, reliable person. At the moment, however, you are sitting in the bleachers taking in a baseball game after calling in sick at work. Obviously, the cognitions "I'm reliable" and "I'm skipping work" are inconsistent, so they create dissonance. Festinger's theory suggests that you will feel some need to modify one of the cognitions in order to reduce the disturbing feeling of dissonance. Thus you may admit to yourself that you're not all that reliable. Or you may look for some way to rationalize skipping work so that it doesn't appear that you're being unreliable ("Even the best of us play hooky once in a while"). The first alternative would require you to modify your self-concept, a threatening prospect for most people. Hence, you're more likely to choose the second, less drastic alternative. In any situation of this kind, we try to maintain consistency among our beliefs, even if we have to twist reality a little bit (or a lot).

Selectivity in Social Perception

There is an old saying that "people see what they expect to see." This commonsense notion that our expectations influence our perceptions has been confirmed repeatedly by social scientists. In a classic study, Harold Kelley (1950) showed how a person is preceded by his or her reputation. Students in a class at the Massachusetts Institute of Technology (MIT) were told that a new lecturer would be speaking to them that day. Before the instructor arrived,

FIGURE 5.2
Descriptions of the guest lecturer in Kelley's (1950) study
These two descriptions, provided to two groups of students before the lecturer spoke, differ by only a single word, but that one small difference caused the two groups to form altogether different perceptions of the lecturer.

Mr. Blank is a graduate student in the Department of Economics and Social Science here at M.I.T. He has had three semesters of teaching experience in psychology at another college. This is his first semester teaching Ec.70. He is 26 years old, a veteran, and married. People who know him consider him to be a rather cold person, industrious, critical, practical, and determined.

Mr. Blank is a graduate student in the Department of Economics and Social Science here at M.I.T. He has had three semesters of teaching experience in psychology at another college. This is his first semester teaching Ec. 70. He is 26 years old, a veteran, and married. People who know him consider him to be a very warm person, industrious, critical, practical, and determined.

the students were given a short description of him, with one important variation. Half of the students were led to expect a "warm" person, while the other half were led to expect a "cold" one (see Figure 5.2). All of the subjects were exposed to exactly the same 20 minutes of lecture and interaction with the new instructor. Yet those who had been led to expect a warm person rated the instructor as significantly more considerate, sociable, humorous, good-natured, informal, and humane than those who had been led to expect a cold person.

Especially if there's any ambiguity in someone's behavior, we're likely to interpret what we see in a way that is consistent with our expectations (Darley & Gross, 1983). Thus, after dealing with a forthright female customer, a salesman who thought in gender stereotypes might characterize the woman as "pushy," whereas he might describe a male customer who exhibited exactly the same behavior as "aggressive."

In summary, the process of social perception is highly subjective. Our attributions are ultimately guesses about the causes of events, and these hunches are influenced by a variety of biases. We prefer consistency among our cognitions, even if we have to distort reality to achieve it. And we have a strong tendency to see what we expect to see in our interpersonal interactions.

Because of the differences between the perspectives of actors and observers, we'll discuss self-perception and perception of others separately. Although the two topics have much in common, the crucial issues are somewhat different. We'll take up the topic of self-perception first.

Self-Perception

In a significant departure from the conventional wisdom that our attitudes determine our behavior, Daryl Bem (1972) suggested that sometimes the reasons for our behavior are not always readily apparent—even to ourselves. According to Bem's *self-perception theory*, **when we are unsure of our beliefs, we try to understand ourselves by inferring our attitudes from our behavior.** Typically, a person might explain his habits by saying, "I don't like plays; that's why I don't go to them." Bem suggests, however, that sometimes the reasoning proceeds in the opposite direction. Thus a person may say, "Gee, I don't go to any plays. I guess I don't like them." When we are certain

about how we feel, we're less likely to make inferences on the basis of our behavior (Chaiken & Baldwin, 1981). Nonetheless, we are frequently engaged in efforts to understand our own behavior.

Self-Concept

Through the processes of social perception, you develop a self-concept. A *self-concept* is a **collection of beliefs about one's basic nature, unique qualities, and typical behavior.** Your self-concept might include such beliefs as "I'm tall," "I'm blonde," "I play the clarinet," "I'm a good student," and "I'm friendly." As you can see, the self-concept includes many separate but interrelated dimensions. Although we usually talk about the self-concept as a single entity, it is probably more accurate to say that we have a variety of specific self-concepts that operate in different situations. Don Hamachek (1992) has suggested that we have separate concepts of our physical, social, emotional, and intellectual selves.

Our various self-concepts are characterized by relatively distinct thoughts and feelings. That is, we may have considerable information about our social skills and feel quite confident with regard to them but have limited information about our physical skills and feel less confident about this aspect of our self. When a particular self-concept is operating, its attendant thoughts and feelings will strongly influence the way we process self-relevant information (Fiske & Taylor, 1991). When you're in class, for example, the thoughts and feelings associated with your intellectual self-concept usually dominate the way you process class-relevant information and feelings. Similarly, when you're at a party (or thinking about a party when you're in class!), you tap into your social self-concept and its attendant thoughts and feelings.

The self-concept is not merely an abstract idea of interest to psychologists. Because it guides the processing of self-relevant information, the self-concept obviously plays a powerful role in the way we see ourselves and others, the way we feel, and the way we behave (Fiske & Taylor, 1991). If you have been eyeing an attractive classmate recently, for instance, your social self-concept may be the critical factor that determines whether you actually approach that person. Not only do our self-concepts affect our *present* behavior, they also influence our *future* behavior. The term *possible selves* has been used to describe the future-oriented components of the self system (Markus & Nurius, 1986). Possible selves are developed from past experiences, current behavior, and future expectations. If you have narrowed your career choices down to personnel manager and psychologist, say, these choices would represent two possible selves in the career realm. Possible selves function to make us more attentive to goal-related information and role models, as well as mindful of the need to practice goal-related skills. Thus, they help us not only to envision desired future goals but also to achieve them (Markus & Ruvolo, 1989). Sometimes possible selves are negative and represent what we *fear* we might become—an alcoholic like our uncle George or an adult without an intimate relationship. In this case, a possible self functions as an image to be avoided.

A person's self-concept is not set in concrete—but it is not easily changed, either. Once our self-concepts are established, we have a tendency to preserve and defend them, whether they are positive or negative. That's why our pictures of ourselves tend to be fairly stable. In the context of this stability, however, the self-concept has a certain dynamic quality. Although it rarely changes overnight, your self-concept may very well undergo gradual change over time.

Cutting across all these components of the self is the crucial dimension of *self-evaluation*. We generally look at ourselves in an approving or disapproving manner. These favorable or unfavorable self-evaluations determine our self-esteem. As we shall see, self-esteem is probably the most important aspect of our self-concept.

Factors That Shape Your Self-Concept

A variety of sources influence your self-concept. Chief among them are your own observations, feedback from others, and cultural values.

Your Own Observations

Your observations of your own behavior are obviously a major source of information about what you are like. Early in childhood we start observing our own behavior and drawing conclusions about ourselves. You remember how often children make statements about who is the tallest, who can run fastest, or who can swing the highest.

Obviously, our observations of ourselves do not take place in a social vacuum. Even in early childhood they involve comparisons with other children. **Social comparison theory proposes that people need to compare themselves with others in order to gain insight into their own behavior** (Festinger, 1954; Goethals & Darley, 1977; Wood, 1989). The potential impact of such social comparisons was dramatically demonstrated in an interesting study (Morse & Gergen, 1970). Subjects thought they were being interviewed for a job. Half of the subjects met another applicant who appeared to be extremely impressive. The other half were exposed to a competitor who appeared to be a clod. All subjects filled out measures of self-esteem both before and after the bogus job interviews. The results indicated that subjects who encountered the impressive competitor showed a decrease in self-esteem after the interview. Those who met the unimpressive competitor, in contrast, showed increases in self-esteem. Thus our comparisons with others can have immediate effects on our self-concept.

Of course, we don't choose just anyone for a point of comparison. **A reference group is a set of people against whom you compare yourself.** Our reference groups are usually made up of people who are similar to us in certain key ways. The specific dimensions of similarity depend on which aspects of our behavior we are trying to evaluate. If you want to judge the progress of your racquetball game, you will probably compare yourself with people who have been playing for a similar length of time. If you want to evaluate your career progress, you'll compare yourself with people of roughly the same age who are in the same general occupational area. In accord with this hypothesis, one study found that when subjects were led to believe that performance on a task was influenced by biological sex, men wanted to know how other men did, while women sought information about the performance of other women (Zanna, Goethals, & Hill, 1975).

Our observations of our own behavior are not entirely objective. As you may recall from our discussion of Carl Rogers's (1959) views on personality (see Chapter 2), we learn early in life about what is judged to be "good" and "bad" behavior. In order to feel worthy of others' affection, we tend to distort our perceptions of our behavior in ways that permit positive self-evaluations. Your self-concept, then, may not be a particularly accurate reflection of your behavior. We'll take a look at some common biases in self-perception later on.

The general tendency is to distort reality in a positive direction (see Figure 5.3). Research findings support the idea that most of us tend to evaluate ourselves in a more positive light than we really merit. The strength of this tendency was highlighted in a large survey conducted as part of the Scholastic Aptitude Test (SAT) (Myers, 1980). Of some 829,000 high school seniors, 70% rated themselves above average in "leadership ability." Only 2% rated themselves below average. Obviously, by definition, 50% must be "above average" and 50% below. Nonetheless, in regard to "ability to get along with others," 100% of the subjects saw themselves as above average. Furthermore, 25% of the respondents thought that they belonged in the top 1%. These findings call to mind Garrison Keillor's description of the inhabi-

As she sees herself: Unchanged since age 22. Sociable, scintillating, sexy.

As the husband sees her: Older than her years. Someone more suited to suburban domesticity and PTA.

As he sees himself: Stylish haircut, rakish moustache; benevolent, generous, powerful. A smooth operator.

As the wife sees him: Somewhat of a slob, moody, not very decisive or strong.

**FIGURE 5.3
Distortions in our self-images**
The way we see ourselves may not be at all the way other people see us. Here we see the subjective quality of self-concept and our perception of others. Generally our self-images tend to be distorted in a positive direction.

tants of Lake Woebegone, a mythical town where "all the women are strong, all the men are good-looking, and all the children are above average."

Although the general tendency is to distort reality in a positive direction, a minority of people tend to do just the opposite. They constantly evaluate themselves in an unrealistically negative way. Moreover, most of us tend to make both negative and positive distortions, although positive ones are more common. For example, you may overrate your social skill, emotional stability, and intellectual ability while underrating your physical attractiveness. Thus the tendency to see ourselves in an overly favorable light is strong but not universal.

Feedback from Others

Your self-concept is also shaped by the feedback you get about your behavior from other people. It should be readily apparent that not everyone has equal influence in our lives. Early in life, our parents and other family members play dominant roles in providing us with feedback. As we grow older, the number of significant others who give us feedback increases.

Parents give their children a great deal of direct feedback. They constantly express approval or disapproval, making such statements as "You're just the neatest kid" or "You're a lazy bum just like your uncle Patrick." Most of us, especially when we are young, take this sort of feedback to heart. Thus, it comes as no surprise that studies find that there is an association

between the parents' views of a child and the child's self-concept (Wylie, 1979). There is even stronger evidence for a relationship between children's *perceptions* of their parents' attitudes toward them and their own self-perceptions (Wylie, 1979).

Parents and other family members are not the only sources of feedback during childhood. Teachers, Little League coaches, Scout leaders, and others also provide significant feedback. In adolescence, as one's peer group becomes more influential, friends play an important role in the development of our self-concepts (Smollar & Youniss, 1985).

The feedback we receive from others is filtered through our social perception systems. As a consequence, it may be as distorted as our self-observations. As you would intuitively expect, most people tend to be more receptive to positive than to negative feedback (Eagly & Whitehead, 1972). Interestingly, people with low self-esteem react more positively to those who compliment them and respond more negatively to critics than do people with high self-esteem (Berscheid, 1985).

Cultural Guidelines

Your self-concept is also shaped, albeit indirectly, by cultural values. The society in which we are brought up defines what is "good" and "bad" in personality and behavior. American culture tends to put a premium on individuality, competitive success, strength, and skill. These cultural values influence the way we interpret our behavior. Understandably, we are more likely to make distortions in areas that our culture considers important.

Our cultural background is also responsible for various stereotypes that may mold our self-perceptions. Gender stereotypes, for instance, influence males' and females' self-perceptions and behavior. One study found that college students' gender stereotypes predicted which activities they tried and how much they enjoyed them (Carter & Myerowitz, 1984). In a similar manner, stereotypes of race, class, sexual orientation, and religion can influence our self-perceptions, an issue we'll discuss later in the chapter.

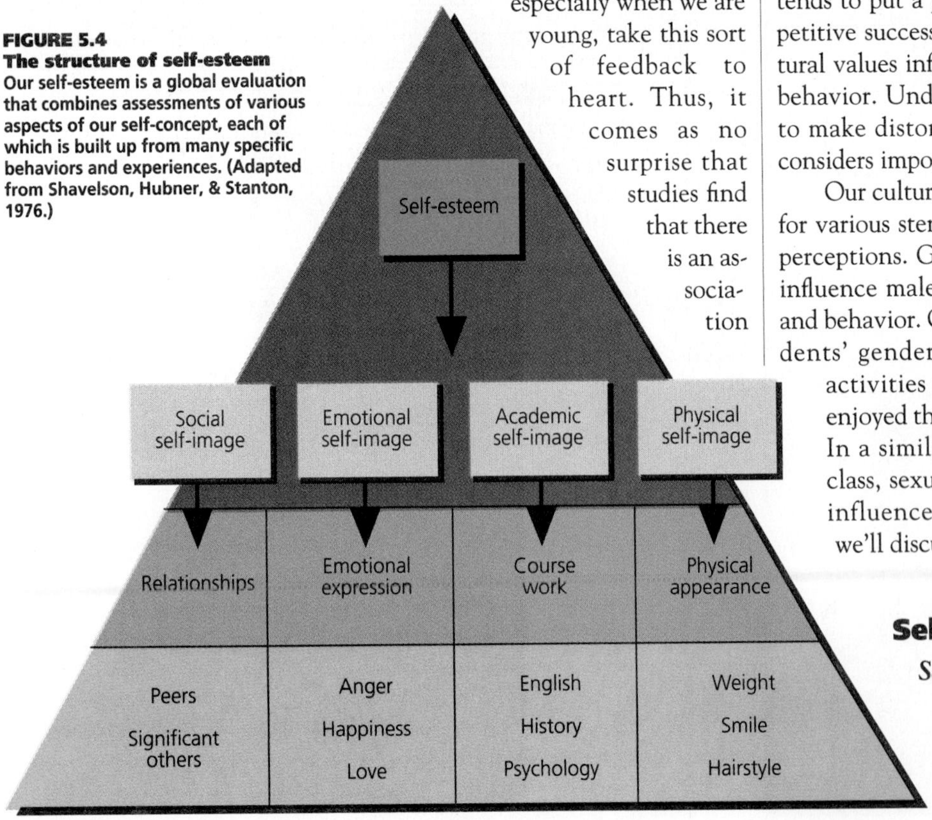

Self-Esteem

Self-esteem refers to your overall assessment of your worth as a person; it is the evaluative component of your self-concept. Self-esteem is a

FIGURE 5.4
The structure of self-esteem
Our self-esteem is a global evaluation that combines assessments of various aspects of our self-concept, each of which is built up from many specific behaviors and experiences. (Adapted from Shavelson, Hubner, & Stanton, 1976.)

global evaluation that blends many specific evaluations about your adequacy as a student, as an athlete, as a worker, as a spouse, as a parent, or whatever is relevant to you. Figure 5.4 shows how specific elements of self-concept may contribute to self-esteem. If you feel basically good about yourself, you can be said to have high self-esteem. Sometimes the term "positive self-concept" is used as a synonym for "self-esteem."

Self-esteem is a difficult concept to investigate, for two reasons. First, there is some doubt about the validity of many measures of self-esteem. The problem is that researchers tend to rely on subjects' self-reports, which obviously may be biased. The self-esteem many people really feel may differ considerably from the level of self-esteem that they report on a questionnaire (Wells & Marwell, 1976). Second, in probing self-esteem it is often quite difficult to separate cause from effect. A large volume of correlational data tells us that certain behavioral characteristics are associated with positive or negative self-esteem; but it is hard to tell whether these behavioral tendencies are the cause or the effect of a particular level of self-esteem. This problem in pinpointing causation should be kept in mind as we look at the determinants and effects of self-esteem.

The Importance of Self-Esteem

The importance of adequate self-esteem can hardly be overestimated. To illustrate the potential influence of self-esteem, we will review some of the many problematic characteristics that often accompany low self-esteem.

People with unfavorable self-concepts tend to develop more emotional problems than people with high self-esteem (Fitts, 1972; Rosenberg, 1985; Wylie, 1979). They are more likely to report that they are troubled by anxiety, depression, irritability, aggressiveness, feelings of resentment and alienation, unhappiness, insomnia, and psychosomatic symptoms, among other things.

Low self-esteem is also associated with shyness (Cheek & Buss, 1981). People low in self-esteem often feel socially awkward, self-conscious, and especially vulnerable to rejection (Rosenberg, 1985). They have a particularly great need for acceptance by others, but they are often unable to take the initiative to seek it out. Thus they rarely join formal groups and do not participate very actively in social encounters. As a result, they are often lonely (Jones, Freeman, & Goswick, 1981).

People who have a negative self-concept are also less likely than most people to feel an authentic liking for other people (Baron, 1974; Wylie, 1979). They tend to look for flaws. Disparaging others allows them to feel a little better about themselves when they make their inevitable social comparisons. However, it also gives them a tendency to dislike others. They therefore tend to relate to others in negative ways—thereby courting rejection and compounding their problems.

Determinants of Self-Esteem

The foundations for high or low self-esteem appear to be laid very early in life. There is evidence that some children already have an unfavorable self-image when they enter the first grade (Wattenberg & Clifford, 1964).

Such an unfortunate circumstance so early in life would almost have to be attributable to parental feedback. Indeed, there is ample evidence that parents have a marked influence on their children's self-esteem (Baumrind, 1978). Let's review the findings of a classic study of self-esteem in young boys conducted by Stanley Coopersmith (1967, 1975). When he compared the child-rearing styles of parents of boys with high self-esteem, he found that the parents of boys with high self-esteem (1) expressed more affection to their children, (2) were more interested in their children's activities, (3) were more accepting of their children, (4) used sound, consistent disciplinary procedures, and (5) had relatively high self-esteem themselves (see Figure 5.5). In particular, it was the parents' sincere interest in their children that seemed most strongly related to the development of a positive self-concept.

While parental feedback may be the crucial childhood determinant of self-esteem, it is

**FIGURE 5.5
Self-esteem and parents' child-rearing techniques**
Parents strongly influence youngsters' self-esteem. Coopersmith (1975) found interesting differences in child-rearing practices among the mothers of boys with high, medium, and low self-esteem.

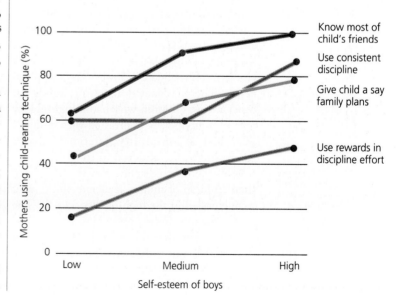

Popular TV evangelist Jimmy Swaggart was forced to resign his ministry in 1989 because of allegations of sexual misconduct. In his televised resignation speech (shown here), Swaggart said he begged for forgiveness. Do you think Swaggart was truly remorseful, or were his tears part of a skillful impression-management effort?

clear that children (and adults) make their own judgments about themselves as well. Of course, an important basis for our judgments of our own success and failure is how well we stack up in comparison with others. Hence schoolchildren whose academic performance is consistently and significantly lower than that of their peers are likely to have a negative self-image (Glasser, 1975). Yet seeing ourselves succeed in an endeavor as simple as learning to swim can enhance our self-esteem (Koocher, 1971). Thus our self-esteem may be augmented or diminished by our own observations of our successes and failures.

Of course, other people—especially parents and teachers—greatly influence our definitions of success and failure. Some overly demanding parents and teachers set unrealistically high standards and are virtually never satisfied with children's performance. Sometimes these unrealistic standards are an unfortunate by-product of good intentions. The parents and teachers simply want to push the children to high levels of achievement. This push for excellence can backfire, however, when it leads some children to set unrealistically high standards for themselves. These unrealistic standards may cause the children to make largely unfavorable appraisals of their performance, thus lowering their self-esteem.

Perceptions of success and failure are also influenced by the nature of one's reference group. One study found that preadolescents' self-esteem can be affected by the quality of competition they face in school (Marsh & Parker, 1984). These researchers compared children from schools in affluent neighborhoods, where they faced stiff competition with children from schools in lower-class neighborhoods, where competition was negligible. In other words, children who had a high-ability reference group were contrasted with children who had a low-ability reference group. Interestingly, the children in the low-quality schools tended to display greater self-esteem than children of similar academic ability who were enrolled in the high-quality schools. The reason for this finding appears to be that students compare themselves with others in their own schools, not with a hypothetical reference group of, say, all bright students in the country (Rosenberg, 1979). Thus it has been suggested

that it may be beneficial to one's self-esteem to be "a large fish in a small pond" (Davis, 1966; Marsh & Parker, 1984). This finding that the self-esteem of kids with similar talents varies with the reference group demonstrates the immense importance of social comparison in the development of our self-concepts.

Public Selves

Whereas your self-concept expresses the way you see yourself, your public self expresses the way you want others to see you. **A *public self* is an image or facade presented to others in social interactions.** We rarely behave totally spontaneously. Let's face it: Most people see only an edited version of our behavior, which is usually calculated to present a certain image. This presenting of a public self may sound deceitful, but it is perfectly normal, and all of us do it (Alexander & Knight, 1971; Goffman, 1959, 1971). Actually, most of us are not limited to a single public self. Typically, we have a number of public selves that are tied to certain situations and certain people with whom we interact. You may have one public self for your parents, for instance, and another for your siblings. You may have still others for your teachers, your same-sex friends, your other-sex friends, your spouse, your boss, your colleagues, your customers, and your neighbors.

Impression Management

Impression management **refers to usually conscious efforts to influence the way others think of us.** Why do we engage in impression management? Basically, it's a matter of necessity. Erving Goffman (1959) argues that social norms virtually require us to engage in careful self-presentation. In other words, we are expected to portray ourselves in certain ways when we interact with our parents, peers, coworkers, and so forth. Goffman further points out that social norms also support others' acceptance of these efforts at impression management. Although people may be skeptical, they rarely challenge our self-presentations. Unless your self-presentation is clearly and extremely out of line with reality, people will keep their suspicions to themselves.

Normally, we try to make a *positive* impression on others (Baumeister, Tice, & Hutton, 1989). Obviously a positive impression is important if we want people to like us, respect us, hire us, buy products from us, and so forth. Let's take a look at the operation of impression management by reviewing a study of behavior in job interviews (von Baeyer, Sherk, & Zanna, 1981). In this study, female job applicants were led to believe that the man who would interview them held either very traditional, chauvinistic views of women or just the opposite. Applicants who expected a chauvinist presented themselves in a more traditionally "feminine" manner than subjects in the other condition. Their self-presentation efforts affected both their appearance (they wore more makeup) and their communication style (they talked less and gave more traditional answers to a question about marriage and children). The bottom line is this: Impression management is a normal feature of everyday social interactions. Although we certainly don't engage in it all the time, we probably do so a lot more often than many of us realize.

Interestingly, our tendency to present ourselves in a favorable light is apparently not just an act we put on to make ourselves look good to others. Several studies support the idea that impression-management techniques are probably also used to impress *ourselves* (Breckler & Greenwald, 1986; Tetlock & Manstead, 1985)! We use a variety of strategies to make favorable impressions on others (Fiske & Taylor, 1991; Jones, 1964; Jones & Pittman, 1982). Here are some of the more common ones.

- *Conforming to situational norms.* Going along with others tends to promote liking, and non-conformity can have the opposite effect.
- *Giving compliments.* Good old-fashioned flattery is far from obsolete. But sincerity is important, and people can usually detect insincerity by mismatches in verbal and nonverbal messages.
- *Doing favors.* It doesn't hurt to do favors for people you want to like you. The favors, however, shouldn't be too spectacular, or they may leave the target person with an irritating feeling of social indebtedness.
- *Presenting a favorable self-image.* If you expect to win someone's liking, it certainly helps to portray yourself as likable. Depending on the situation, some false modesty may be useful.
- *Being consistent.* People trust and like those who behave in accordance with their professed beliefs.

In conclusion, we offer a word of caution in the use of impression-management techniques. Most people are sensitive to sincerity in another person. And research indicates that when we doubt the sincerity of someone's flattering statements, we may like that person less (Kauffman & Steiner, 1968; Lowe & Goldstein, 1970).

Self-Monitoring

According to Mark Snyder (1979, 1986), people vary in their awareness of the way other people perceive them. *Self-monitoring* **refers to the degree to which people attend to and control the impressions they make on others.** People who are high in self-monitoring are very sensitive to their impact on others. Those who are low in self-monitoring are less concerned about impression management and behave more spontaneously.

Mark Snyder

Compared with low self-monitors, high self-monitors display the following characteristics: They actively seek information about how they are expected to behave and try to tailor their actions accordingly (Snyder & Campbell, 1982). They are very sensitive to situational cues and relatively skilled at deciphering what others want to see. Moreover, they tend to act more in accordance with situational expectations than with their true feelings or attitudes (Zanna & Olson, 1982). Since high self-monitors control their emotions well and deliberately regulate nonverbal signals that are more spontaneous in others, they are relatively talented at self-presentation. In addition, they have been shown to be more accurate in judging other people's feelings (Geiser, Rarick, & Soldow, 1977). Low self-monitors, in contrast, are more likely to express their true beliefs, since they are more motivated to behave consistently with their internal feelings (McCann & Hancock, 1983).

Some people use vanity license plates to capture their identity in a word or phrase.

Identity

A widely discussed concept related to self-perception is "ego identity." According to Erik Erikson (1968), a very influential psychoanalytic theorist (see Chapter 11), **one's *identity* is a relatively clear and stable sense of who one is and what one stands for.** Although we have a multiplicity of thoughts and feelings and engage in many diverse activities, we remain "familiar" to ourselves in a fundamental way. In addition, our own sense of who we are must match pretty well with other people's views of us. This latter idea reflects Erikson's assertion that identity is rooted in both self and society.

According to James Marcia (1976), another authority on this subject, identity may be viewed from three perspectives. First, a sense of identity depends on your ability to integrate your own and your parents' expectations of you into a relatively congruent sense of self. Again we see the emphasis on self and society (society being mediated by our parents' expectations). Much of the process of identity formation is unconscious, but we do create our identity. We do not just unquestioningly assume the roles and beliefs designated for us by our parents and society. Second, developing a sense of identity gives individuals the ability to perceive themselves as ongoing entities—beings who have a past, present, and future, all of which feel connected. Finally, Marcia says that our unique identity will be reflected in our choices of careers, personal values, and beliefs.

FIGURE 5.6
Marcia's four identity statuses
According to Marcia, the occurrence of an identity crisis and the development of personal commitments can combine into four possible identity statuses, as shown in this diagram.

Development of Identity

Obviously, your identity has its roots in childhood. Ideally, it continues to develop throughout adulthood. However, Erikson views adolescence as the most significant period for identity development, and research has supported his view. Studies show that identity concerns are particularly prominent among young people of college age (Archer, 1982; Marcia, 1980; Meilman, 1979). The fact that identity achievement is a concern during late adolescence probably reflects the conjunction of several developmental milestones during this time (Lloyd, 1985). That is, the achievement of a stable and familiar sense of self depends on physical and sexual maturity, competence in abstract thought, and a degree of emotional stability. In addition, identity achievement requires a certain amount of freedom from the constraining influences of parents and peers. As it happens, late adolescence is the period during which such conditions are first likely to exist.

Identity Statuses

According to Erikson, identity emerges out of crisis. Erikson uses the term "identity crisis" to refer to a normal developmental process. That is, for most people, an identity crisis is not a sudden or personally agonizing experience, but rather the gradual evolution of a sense of who one is (Coleman, 1978; Dusek & Flaherty, 1981).

The experience of an identity crisis usually results in a commitment to a specific career and personal ideology. According to Marcia, these two factors of *crisis* and *commitment* combine in various ways to produce four distinct identity statuses (see Figure 5.6). These are not stages that people pass through, but rather statuses that characterize a person's identity orientation at any particular time. In other words, it is possible that a person may never experience some of the statuses, including that of identity achievement. Let's examine the identity statuses described by Marcia.

Identity foreclosure. Some people do not exhibit a struggle for a unique, personal identity. Individuals in the foreclosure status have unquestioningly adopted the values and expectations of their parents rather than going through the process of developing their own beliefs and career choices. Adolescents (or adults) who select a career because that is the career their parents want them to pursue are

Marcia's Four Identity Statuses		
	Crisis present	Crisis absent
Commitment present	Identity achievement (successful achievement of a sense of identity)	Identity foreclosure (unquestioning adoption of parental or societal values)
Commitment absent	Identity moratorium (active struggling for a sense of identity)	Identity diffusion (absence of struggle for identity, with no obvious concern about this)

classified in the foreclosure status. These individuals have made a commitment—or rather, adopted someone else's commitment—but because they haven't gone through an identity crisis, they don't qualify as having achieved an independent identity.

Moratorium. Individuals who are currently struggling with a sense of identity are classified as being in the moratorium status. As part of the process of evolving a personally satisfying identity, adolescents are likely to engage in a variety of identity experiments, trying on different roles, beliefs, and behaviors. Most move on to the identity achievement status, but some drift into the status of identity diffusion.

Identity diffusion. Identity diffusion is characterized by a failure to achieve a stable and integrated sense of self. Individuals in this category experience considerable self-doubt, but they don't appear to be concerned about doing anything to change their circumstances. Hence they are different from those in the moratorium status, who are still struggling to resolve identity conflicts. People in the diffusion status are not currently experiencing an identity crisis, nor are they able to make career or value commitments (see Figure 5.6). Identity diffusion is a serious problem for only a small number of adolescents, and then only when it is prolonged.

Identity achievement. The preferred identity status, of course, is that of identity achievement. In this case, a person has successfully passed through an identity crisis and is now able to make a commitment to a career objective and a set of personally meaningful beliefs.

To summarize, both identity achievement and identity foreclosure can be seen as resolutions of the identity crisis because a sense of commitment characterizes both statuses. Of course, in foreclosure, the commitment is not an independently developed one, as is desirable. Individuals in both the moratorium and diffusion statuses have only vague commitments, or sometimes none. While those in identity diffusion have given up the search for identity, those in the moratorium status are still pursuing it.

To tie together our wide-ranging exploration of various aspects of self-perception (self-concept, self-esteem, public selves, and identity), we turn now to the issue of the "authentic" self.

The Search for the Authentic Self

Although we may be aware of the dubious accuracy of our self-presentations, Erving Goffman (1959) has argued that we sometimes come to believe our fabrications. In other words, if you present yourself in a certain way often enough, you may begin actually to see yourself in that way. For example, if you are really quite conceited, but you incorporate false humility into many of your public selves, you may begin to view yourself as a humble person. There is empirical evidence to support Goffman's assertion that our self-presentations may affect our actual self-concepts (Jones, Rhodewalt, Berglas, & Skelton, 1981; Rhodewalt & Agustsdottir, 1986).

Although we all engage in some impression management, we vary greatly in how much we edit our behavior. As we have seen, some people are more concerned than others about portraying themselves appropriately for various audiences. Moreover, people differ in the degree of congruence or overlap among their various public selves (see Figure 5.7). Recall here Erikson's emphasis on the congruence between one's own sense of self and others' perceptions of us. In a similar fashion, Sidney Jourard (1971) maintained that constant misrepresentation for purposes of impression management may lead people to lose touch with their authentic selves. Jourard argued that this kind of confusion is very dangerous and may cause much psychological distress.

It is this identity-related confusion that leads many people to be concerned about "finding" themselves. This search for the real self became something of a fad in the 1970s, and many people used the concept to rationalize their rudderless lives. It has since become common to ridicule people who say they are "looking for the real me." However, this search for the authentic self may often be a genuine effort to come to grips with a self-concept and an identity that are in disarray.

Two practical points can be derived from this discussion. First, it is probably a good idea to avoid going overboard on self-presentation efforts. Taken to excess, impression management may be harmful to one's sense of identity. Second, there is some merit in seeking knowledge about oneself. Accurate self-knowledge may facilitate development of a well-defined self-concept.

Self-Enhancement

Earlier, we noted that self-perceptions are not always objective. Normally our self-perceptions are biased in a positive direction, because we seem to have a need to feel good about the way we see ourselves. We employ a variety of strategies to maintain these positive feelings. This **tendency to use various strategies to maintain positive views of ourselves is termed *self-enhancement*.** When we feel threatened, our need for self-enhancement increases. Maintaining good feelings about our self *may* require some distortion of reality. In this section we'll discuss several commonly used self-enhancement strategies, and we will also look at the issue of self-deception and mental health.

The Self-Serving Bias

Suppose that you and three other individuals apply for a part-time job in the psychology department and you are selected for the position. How do you explain your good fortune? Chances are you tell yourself that you were hired because you had the most outstanding qualifications for the job. And how do the other three people who weren't hired interpret the negative outcome? Do they tell themselves that you got the job because you were the most able? Unlikely! Instead, they probably attribute their loss to bad luck or to lack of time to prepare for the interview. These different explanations for success and failure reflect the ***self-serving bias,* or the tendency to take credit for our success and deny responsibility for our failures** (Miller & Ross, 1975).

Research indicates that the self-serving bias is quite potent, although it seems that people are more likely to take credit for their successes than they are to disavow their failures (Fiske & Taylor, 1991). There are *some* occasions when we don't rush to take credit for our successes. For instance, if our role in our success is quite obvious to others, we may opt for modesty—at least to others (Schlenker, Weigold, & Hallam, 1990). Ironically, this strategy also turns out to be self-serving, because we fear that blowing our horn too loudly could cause others to dislike us.

Interestingly, studies have shown that subjects who publicly take credit for their successes and disavow responsibility for their failures are expressing their real perceptions (Greenberg, Pyszczynski, & Solomon, 1982; Reiss, Rosenfeld, Melburg, & Tedeschi, 1981). Hence it is likely that we portray ourselves favorably not only for the purpose of impression management but also to maintain our self-esteem.

The Self-Centered Bias

Reflect for a minute on who does most of the cleaning of your apartment: you or your room-

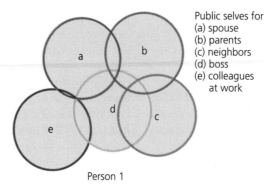

FIGURE 5.7
Public selves and identity confusion
Person 1 has very divergent public selves with relatively little overlap among them. Person 1 is more likely to develop identity confusion than person 2, whose public selves are more congruent with one another.

Person 1

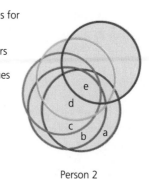

Public selves for
(a) spouse
(b) parents
(c) neighbors
(d) boss
(e) colleagues at work

Person 2

mate? You were probably quick to name yourself. If we asked your roommate the same question, though, she would probably tell us that *she* did most of the cleaning. Since both of you can't be right, what's going on here? This is the *self-centered bias,* **or the tendency to take more than one's share of responsibility for a joint venture** (Ross & Sicoly, 1979). There are some noteworthy differences between this bias and the self-serving bias. For one thing, the self-centered bias involves a joint outcome, whereas the self-serving bias concerns only one individual's performance. For another, the success or failure of the outcome is irrelevant in the self-centered bias, but it's central to the self-serving bias.

One of the first studies on this phenomenon asked husbands and wives to indicate who had responsibility for each of 20 household tasks (Ross & Sicoly, 1979). The results revealed a discrepancy in the perceptions of both members of each couple. That is, each member of a couple believed that he or she had done more than his or her spouse thought was the case. What seems to be behind the self-serving bias? An intuitively obvious explanation is that by claiming more than our share of responsibility for joint ventures, we can raise our self-esteem. Yet, the fact that we take more credit for joint outcomes *whether or not they result in success* seems to refute such an interpretation (Ross & Sikoly, 1979). Two other explanations do seem to be supported by research: (1) individuals are better at recalling instances of their own behavior than those of others and (2) when people perceive that they are the kind of person who would typically perform such a task, they are likely to believe that they have contributed more to it (Fiske & Taylor, 1991).

Downward Comparisons

Earlier, we mentioned that people compare themselves with others as a means of learning more about themselves (social comparison). We engage in the process both when we actively seek such information and when we feel threatened by it. Once threat enters the picture, however, it seems to change the type of person we choose to compare ourselves with (Fiske & Taylor, 1991). That is, when we feel threatened, we frequently choose to compare ourselves with someone who is worse off than we are (Wills, 1981). **The defensive tendency to compare ourselves with someone whose troubles are more serious than our own is termed** *downward social comparison.*

Suppose you get a C on an exam. Though you're not happy about it, you may tell yourself, "Well, at least I didn't get a D or an F." Or if you are in a serious car accident and your car is totaled, you may reassure yourself by thanking your stars that at least no one was seriously injured. Similarly, people with chronic illnesses may compare themselves with those who have life-threatening diseases. Talk shows that feature people with assorted life tragedies provide numerous opportunities for downward social comparison. No doubt this is one reason for their popularity.

Attributional Style

Imagine that you and a friend are college freshmen who have just received the results of your first psychology exam. Let's assume that both of you are reasonably bright and studied moderately hard for the test. Both of you are disappointed to get Cs on the exam. After class you talk to each other about the situation. You attribute your grade to not studying harder and vow to really be prepared for the next exam. Your friend, though, mumbles, "I guess I'm just not that smart. I'm probably going to flunk out of school." On the basis of these comments, who do you think is likely to do better on the next exam? If you guessed that *you* will, you are probably correct. Let's see why.

Attributional style **refers to the tendency to use similar causal explanations for a wide variety of events in one's life.** According to Martin Seligman (1990), people tend to exhibit, to varying degrees, one of two attributional styles—either a *pessimistic explanatory style* or an

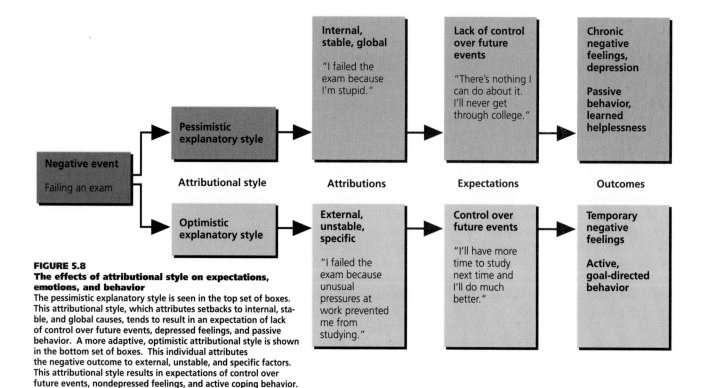

FIGURE 5.8
The effects of attributional style on expectations, emotions, and behavior
The pessimistic explanatory style is seen in the top set of boxes. This attributional style, which attributes setbacks to internal, stable, and global causes, tends to result in an expectation of lack of control over future events, depressed feelings, and passive behavior. A more adaptive, optimistic attributional style is shown in the bottom set of boxes. This individual attributes the negative outcome to external, unstable, and specific factors. This attributional style results in expectations of control over future events, nondepressed feelings, and active coping behavior.

optimistic explanatory style (see Figure 5.8). The person with an optimistic explanatory style has a tendency to attribute setbacks to external, unstable, and specific factors. A person who failed to get a desired job, for example, might attribute this misfortune to bad luck in the interview rather than to personal shortcomings. An optimistic attributional style can help people to discount their setbacks and thus maintain positive expectations for the future and a favorable self-image. In contrast, people with a pessimistic explanatory style tend to attribute their setbacks to internal, stable, and global (or pervasive) factors. These attributions make them feel bad about themselves and pessimistic about their ability to handle challenges in the future.

An optimistic attributional style, which promotes active goal-directed behavior even in the aftermath of failures and disappointments, is associated with students' academic success and salespersons' job success (Fiske & Taylor, 1991). Unfortunately, a pessimistic explanatory style appears to foster passive behavior and to make one more vulnerable to learned helplessness and depression (Peterson & Seligman, 1987; Sweeney, Anderson, & Bailey, 1986). This attributional style has also been tied to shyness and loneliness (see Chapter 8). Thus the self-enhancement facilitated by an optimistic attributional style generally leads to more favorable outcomes than the self-deprecation fostered by a pessimistic attributional style.

Perception of Others: Sources of Error

e are now ready to shift gears and move from the way we perceive ourselves to the way we perceive others. Here we are particularly interested in why we often see each other inaccurately. Mistakes in person perception appear to be quite common (Buckhout, 1980). We focus on this issue because accuracy in social perception can facilitate effective interpersonal relationships.

A multitude of factors contribute to inaccuracy in person perception. We have already mentioned the most obvious source of error—the pervasive tendency of people to create false impressions for one another. Some of our own perceptual tendencies, however, can also lead us to form inaccurate impressions of others.

Categorizing

People frequently categorize others on the basis of race, sex, age, sexual orientation, and so forth. We perceive people like ourselves to be members of our *in-group* ("us") and those who are dissimilar to be in the *out-group* ("them"). Three important things result from such categorizing. First, we usually have more favorable attitudes toward in-group members than out-group members (Tajfel, Billig, Bundy, & Flament,

The extremely hostile reactions of some of the white male senators on the Judiciary Committee to Anita Hill's allegations of sexual harassment were due in part to her surplus visibility.

1971). Second, we usually see out-group members as being much more similar to each other than they really are, whereas we see members of the in-group as unique individuals. In other words, we frequently explain the behavior of out-group members on the basis of their membership in the out-group ("Those Nerdians are all drunks"). In contrast, we often attribute the same behavior by an in-group member to unique personality traits ("Jack's a heavy drinker"). This phenomenon is termed the *out-group homogeneity effect*. This tendency is heightened if we view the behavior as negative.

A third result of categorizing is that it heightens the visibility of out-group members when there are only a few of them within a larger group. In other words, minority status in a group makes more salient the quality that distinguishes the person—race, sex, whatever. Under such conditions, minority individuals have *surplus visibility* (Patai, 1991), so that stereotypes are more likely to be invoked. It is surplus visibility that explains why many people notice nagging women (but not men), why many white people notice noisy blacks (but not whites), and why many Christians notice Jewish names among cheating stockbrokers (but not British or Italian names) (Patai, 1991).

Another phenomenon related to surplus visibility occurs when minority-group members voice opinions, especially if they vary from those of the majority. When minority-group members disagree with majority opinion, they are often derided as loud, offensive, pushy, and trying to take over. We have all noticed the strong aversion of some individuals to academic courses that deal with minority-group issues, the effort to lift the ban on homosexuals in the military, and the reporting of sexual harassment. What accounts for these intense negative reactions? In large part, they're responses to the violation of an unarticulated belief held by the majority group. That belief is that minorities should remain silent and invisible (so as to keep things the way they are) (Patai,

1991). But because members of minority groups have less than their fair share of political and economic resources in a society, it's understandable that they want things to change. This state of affairs places minority-group members struggling for increased power in a double bind. If they remain silent and invisible, they're ignored by the dominant majority; if they speak up, they often generate undue hostility.

Stereotypes

Stereotypes **are widely held beliefs that people have certain characteristics simply because of their membership in a particular group.** For example, many people assume that Jews are shrewd and ambitious, that blacks have special athletic and musical abilities, that Germans are methodical and efficient, that women are dependent and concerned about their appearance, and that men are unemotional and domineering.

The most prevalent kinds of stereotypes are those based on sex and race. Gender stereotypes, although in transition, remain pervasive. In a study of gender stereotypes in 30 countries, males were typically characterized as adventurous, powerful, and independent, while females were characterized as sentimental, submissive, and superstitious (Williams & Best, 1982). Because of their great significance, we will focus on gender stereotypes in detail in our chapter on gender roles (Chapter 10). Ethnic and racial stereotypes have also undergone some changes, but are still quite common (Dovidio & Gaertner, 1986; Jackman & Senter, 1981).

Although a kernel of truth may underlie some stereotypes, it should be readily apparent that not all Jews, Mexicans, lawyers, women, and so forth behave alike. There is enormous diversity in behavior within any group. Stereotyping involves a process of overgeneralizing that leads to a great deal of inaccuracy in social perception.

Why do stereotypes persist? One reason is

that they are functional. Because we are deluged with much more information than we can process, our tendency is to reduce complexity to simplicity. Unfortunately, there is a trade-off for such simplification, and that is inaccuracy, much of which we are unaware of.

A second reason that stereotypes persist is the selectivity in social perception discussed earlier. Because we tend to see what we expect to see, we twist and distort the behavior of others until it fits our stereotypes. In one study, male students were asked to have a brief telephone conversation with a female student (Snyder, Tanke, & Berscheid, 1977). Half of the men were led to believe that the woman was physically attractive, while the other half were told that she was unattractive. In reality, there was no difference in the attractiveness of the female telephone partners. Before the actual telephone conversations, the men were asked to rate their partners-to-be on a variety of dimensions. Those men who believed that their partners were attractive judged that they would be poised, humorous, outgoing, and socially adept. Men with "unattractive" partners judged them to be awkward, serious, unsociable, and socially inept.

Television, movies, and magazines constantly brainwash us into placing great emphasis on physical beauty. Our culture emphasizes physical appearance to such an extent that it is a central factor in our perception and judgments of others.

A third reason our stereotypes persist is that our beliefs about another person may actually elicit the expected behavior. In the study we were just describing (Snyder et al., 1977), after the men had completed their ratings of their partners, they spoke with the women for ten minutes on the telephone. Later, audio tapes of these conversations were analyzed by a judge who was "blind" to the nature of the study. Although there were no actual differences in attractiveness, independent judges rated the "attractive" women as more confident and animated than the "unattractive" women. In addition, the "attractive" women were judged to have displayed greater enjoyment of the conversations and greater liking for the men they spoke with than the "unattractive" women. These findings suggest that our expectations can actually alter others' behavior.

Thus we confirm and perpetuate our stereotypes in several ways. The unfortunate result of this process is that our stereotypes often lead to unfair treatment of others. In particular, women, African Americans, members of certain ethnic groups, and homosexuals are often victims of discrimination.

Excessive Focus on Physical Appearance

As we have seen, we often draw inferences about people's personality from their physical appearance. There is plenty of evidence that physically attractive people are believed to possess many desirable personality traits. In fact, this perception is so widespread that social psychologists have developed a term for it: the *"what-is-beautiful-is-good"* stereotype (Dion, Berscheid, & Walster, 1972). That is, beautiful people are usually viewed as more socially competent, more assertive, better adjusted, and more intellectually competent than those who are less attractive (Eagly, Ashmore, Makhijani, & Longo, 1991). Yet research findings indicate that most of these perceptions have little basis in fact. Attractive people *do* have an advantage in the social arena. They have better social skills, are more popular, are less socially anxious (especially about interactions with the other sex), are less lonely, and are more sexually experienced (Feingold, 1992). However, they do *not* rate more highly than others on intelligence, personality traits, mental health, or self-esteem (Feingold, 1992).

It is interesting that, despite all their social advantages, attractive people don't have higher self-esteem than others. To understand this apparent contradiction, we need to distinguish between physical attractiveness as perceived by others and as perceived by oneself. That is, individuals who believe that they are physically attractive *do* have high self-esteem and better mental health than do people who see themselves as less attractive (Feingold, 1992). But research shows only modest correlations between observers' and individuals' ratings of physical attractiveness. In other words, some people whom others judge to be beautiful honestly don't see themselves as attractive. For these individuals, physical attractiveness does not have much of a bearing on self-esteem and mental health.

It does seem that attractive people are perceived in a more favorable light than is actually justified (Dion, 1986; Eagly et al., 1991; Feingold, 1992). As you may have inferred, all of these biases can also be reversed. Thus we unjustifiably tend to see unattractive people as less well adjusted and less intellectually competent than others. This prejudice against the plain and homely is clearly unfair.

Our social perceptions are also affected by other aspects of physical appearance. Tall people have been perceived, at various times, to be delicate, introverted, and intelligent, while short people have been viewed as passionate, petty, and negative (Roberts & Herman, 1986). Greater virility, confidence, maturity, and courage are attributed to bearded men than to clean-shaven men (Verinis & Roll, 1970). For women, the "dumb blonde" stereotype is alive and well. One study found that blonde women were seen as more beautiful and feminine than other women but less intelligent and dependable (Lawson, 1971). We also judge people differently when they wear eyeglasses. People with glasses are perceived as being relatively intelligent, industrious, and reliable (Argyle & McHenry, 1971; Boshier, 1975; Harris, Harris, & Bochner, 1982). On the other hand, they are not judged to be as attractive, outgoing, or athletic as those who don't wear glasses (Harris et al., 1982; Terry & Kroger, 1976).

Clothing is also a powerful determinant of our perceptions of others. For instance, there is evidence that people may be treated more honestly when they are well dressed. In one clever study of this issue, a dime was left in an obvious place in a public phone booth (Bickman, 1971). When unsuspecting subjects pocketed the dime, an experimental confederate went into action. The confederate approached the subjects and asked whether they had found the dime that the confederate claimed to have forgotten in the booth. The confederate's mode of dress was varied to convey either high social status (suit and tie) or low status (work clothes, lunch pail). The confederates got the dime back about twice as often when they were well dressed as when they were more poorly dressed.

The Fundamental Attribution Error

As we saw in our earlier discussion of attribution, observers tend to attribute the behavior of others to dispositional tendencies and to discount the influence of situational factors. Although this tendency is not universal (Harvey, Town, & Yarkin, 1981), it is strong enough so that Lee Ross (1977) called it the "fundamental attribution error." The *fundamental attribution error* is the tendency of observers to attribute others' behavior to internal factors. We leap to conclusions about others' personal qualities.

The fundamental attribution error differs from stereotyping or focusing on physical appearance in that our inferences *are* based on actual behavior. Those inferences, however, may still be inaccurate. Because we underestimate the importance of situational factors, we often attribute to people motives and traits that they don't actually have. Imagine that you're at your bank and the person in line ahead of you flies into a rage over an error made in his account. You will probably infer that this person is temperamental or quarrelsome—and you may be right. However, this person may be an easygoing individual who is late for an appointment, has waited in line 30 minutes, and just straightened out a similar error by the same bank last week. Thus a person's behavior at a given time may or may not reflect his or her personality—but we tend to assume that it does.

Defensive Attribution

The observer's tendency to make internal attributions becomes even stronger than normal when we attempt to explain the calamities and setbacks that befall other people. Let's say that a friend is mugged and severely beaten. You may attribute the mugging to your friend's carelessness or stupidity ("He should have known better than to be in that neighborhood after dark") rather than to bad luck. Why? Because if you attribute your friend's misfortune to bad luck, you have to face the ugly reality that it could just as easily happen to you. To avoid

Defensive attribution is one aspect of social perception that contributes to prejudice. For example, some people blame the homeless for their plight to avoid the unpleasant thought that they themselves could one day suffer the same misfortune.

such disturbing thoughts, we often attribute mishaps to the victims' negligence (Thornton, 1984).

Defensive attribution is a tendency to blame victims for their misfortune, so that we feel less likely to be victimized in a similar way. Blaming victims for their calamities also helps us to maintain our belief that we live in a "just world," where people get what they deserve and deserve what they get (Lerner & Miller, 1976). If we acknowledged to ourselves that the world is not just—that bad things do happen to nice people—we would have to admit the frightening possibility that the catastrophes that befall others could also happen to us. By using defensive attribution, we can avoid such disturbing thoughts. Unfortunately, when we blame victims for their setbacks, we unfairly attribute undesirable traits to them, such as incompetence, foolishness, laziness, and greed. Thus defensive attribution often leads us to derogate victims of misfortune.

The tendency to blame the victim is particularly common when the victim is a woman. The rape victim, people say, "asked for it." When a woman is killed by an abusive boyfriend or husband, people shake their heads in disbelief at her stupidity: Why on earth did she stay with the man?

The Power of First Impressions

Although the evidence is not overwhelming, some studies suggest that first impressions have a powerful influence on our perceptions of others (Asch, 1946; Friedman, 1983; Hodges, 1974). A *primacy effect* occurs when initial information carries more weight than subse-

quent information. First impressions tend to be particularly potent for a couple of reasons. This tendency is caused in part by the fact that people see what they expect to see. Once the initial impression creates a particular expectation, we may be equipped with a somewhat distorted perceptual set. Thereafter, we tend to see the person in the light of our expectations. Moreover, our preference for consistency in social perception may lead us to discount later information that contradicts our initial impression. In either case, it is clear that primacy effects may undermine the accuracy of our impressions of other people.

Of course, it is possible to override a primacy effect. First impressions are not likely to last forever if most subsequent interactions contradict them. Interestingly, one study suggests that it may be easier to override positive first impressions than negative ones (Rothbart & Park, 1986). When the initial impression is negative, it may be especially difficult to change. Thus "getting off on the wrong foot" may be particularly damaging to a person.

False Consensus and False Uniqueness Effects

We often tend to assume that other people think and act just the way we do (Ross, Greene, & House, 1977; Marks & Miller, 1987; Mullen, et al., 1985). The *false consensus effect* involves our tendency to overestimate the degree to which others think and behave as we do. This bias provides yet another source of error in social perception. Let's say you know a man who cheats on his wife every chance he gets. When this person spots friends dining out with members of the other sex who are not their spouses, he is likely to assume that they, too, are engaging in marital infidelity, even though their socializing is probably entirely innocent. Essentially, he attributes his own behavioral tendencies to others.

Although this tendency is quite common, we do not falsely assume consensus in regard to all of our qualities. Though we tend to overestimate the extent to which others share our opinions, we underestimate the likelihood that others possess our talents (Marks, 1984). Thus the *false uniqueness effect* involves our tendency to underestimate the likelihood that others possess our admirable qualities.

In summary, our perceptions of others are very subjective. Many of the tendencies that we exhibit in person perception contribute to inaccurate views of the people around us. Much of the time these inaccurate perceptions are probably harmless. Clearly, however, there are occasions when these inaccuracies interfere with rewarding social interactions. This is certainly the case when we permit prejudice to distort our perceptions.

Social Perception and Prejudice

I n this section, we'll explore two major issues concerning social perception and the problem of prejudice. The first is how distortions in the process of person perception contribute to prejudice; the second is how being a member of a minority group can affect self-esteem. To illustrate these ideas, we'll draw on examples of prejudice based on race, sex, ethnicity, and sexual orientation.

Before we address these topics, we need to clarify a couple of terms that are often confused. *Prejudice* is a negative attitude toward members of a group; *discrimination* involves behaving differently, usually unfairly, toward members of a group. Whereas prejudice is a negative cognitive set, discrimination is negative behavior (unfair treatment). Prejudice and discrimination do tend to go together, but there is no necessary correspondence between the two (see Figure 5.9). A restaurant owner might be prejudiced against Chicanos, for example, yet treat them like anyone else because she needs their business. This is an instance of prejudice without discrimination. Although it is probably less common, discrimination without prejudice may also occur. A manager who has favorable attitudes toward blacks, for example, may not hire them because his boss would be upset.

Social Perception Errors and Prejudice

Inaccuracy in social perception is both a cause and an effect of prejudice. Below we'll see how five sources of inaccuracy that we discussed earlier contribute to prejudice in important ways.

• *Categorizing.* When people categorize others on the basis of race, sex, age, or sexual orientation, the out-group homogeneity effect kicks in. In other words, we will perceive members of that category to be much more homogeneous than they really are, and we will probably try to explain their behavior on the basis of stereotypes we associate with the characteristic that distinguishes them. We'll probably view them as tokens of their group rather than as individuals in their own right. Thus the only woman in an otherwise all-male organization is

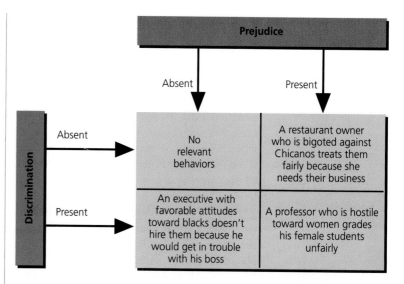

more likely to be stereotyped than a woman in an organization in which the numbers of men and women are in balance (Kanter, 1977; Pettigrew & Martin, 1987).

• *Stereotypes.* Perhaps no factor plays a larger role in prejudice than stereotyping. Many people subscribe to derogatory stereotypes of various ethnic groups. Studies suggest that racial stereotypes have declined over the last 50 years, but they're not a thing of the past (Dovidio & Gaertner, 1986). Unfortunately, the *selectivity* of person perception makes it likely that people will see what they expect to see when they actually come in contact with minorities they view with prejudice. For example, Duncan (1976) had white subjects watch and evaluate an interaction on a TV monitor that was supposedly live (actually it was a videotape). Subjects saw two people get into an argument, during which one of them gave the other a slight shove. The race of the person who did the shoving was varied across groups of subjects. The shove was coded as "violent behavior" by 73% of the white subjects when the actor was black, but by only 13% of the subjects when the actor was white. As we have noted before, our perceptions are highly subjective. Because of stereotypes, even violence may lie in the eye of the beholder.

• *First impressions.* There is another problem related to the power of first impressions. The problem is that many people's first impressions of minorities come not from actual interactions but from disparaging remarks made by parents, neighbors, and others. Thus many impressionable children develop unfavorable views of African Americans, Hispanics, and homosexuals before they have any opportunity for rewarding interactions with members of these groups. Although these negative first impressions may eventually be overridden by

FIGURE 5.9
Prejudice and discrimination
Prejudice and discrimination are highly correlated, but they don't necessarily go hand in hand. As the examples in the yellow cells show, there can be prejudice without discrimination and discrimination without prejudice.

contradictory experiences, the primacy effects probably contribute to prejudice.

•*Fundamental attribution error.* Recall that the fundamental attribution error is a bias toward explaining events by pointing to the personal characteristics of the actors as causes (internal attributions). Pettigrew (1979) maintains that we are particularly prone to this error when we evaluate targets of prejudice. Thus when people take note of ethnic neighborhoods where crime and poverty are prevalent, they tend to blame these problems on the personal qualities of the residents. Other explanations emphasizing situational factors (job discrimination, poor police service, and so on) are downplayed or ignored. The common complaint that "they should be able to pull themselves up the same way my ancestors did" is a blanket dismissal of the unique situational factors that may make it especially difficult for some minorities to achieve upward mobility.

•*Defensive attribution.* We have already seen that people sometimes unfairly blame victims of adversity to reassure themselves that they are unlikely to experience a similar fate. There is evidence that many of us make such defensive attributions when we encounter people who have been victimized by prejudice and discrimination. Many Germans who lived through the Nazi persecutions of Jews, for example, have managed to convince themselves that the people sent to concentration camps must have done something to deserve their fate (Hallie, 1971). Individuals who say that people who contract AIDS are responsible for their own misfortune may be "blaming the victim" to reassure themselves that they are safe from the disease.

Role models from one's in-group are critical to the development of self-esteem.

Minority-Group Membership: Effects on Self-Esteem

We have seen that perceptions of the self develop in a social context. Thus minority-group membership is a factor in the development of self-esteem. Morris Rosenberg (1979), a well-known researcher in this area, has asserted that a key factor in the development of self-esteem is the extent to which people perceive themselves to be similar to others in their social environment. If individuals live in an environment that makes them feel different and deficient, they can suffer from lowered self-esteem.

Because of the existence of prejudice and discrimination in the United States, it has generally been assumed (and sometimes demonstrated) that members of minority groups have lower self-esteem than members of the dominant majority group. In fact, there is a good deal of evidence to the contrary (Garnets & Kimmel, 1991; Rosenberg, 1979; Soares & Soares, 1971).

How does it happen that minority-group members often have high self-esteem when it seems they shouldn't? Rosenberg explains the paradox as follows. Rather than using the majority group as their dominant reference group, minority-group members compare themselves with members of their own group. This in-group comparison ensures that minority-group members are similar to others, and therefore that they compare positively with them. This experience leads them to feel good about themselves.

An important implication here is that minority-group role models play a critical part in the development of self-esteem. Because of recognizable markers (skin color, sex), many minority groups are visible. The high visibility of minority-group role models makes them easy to identify. Of course, this isn't always the case with respect to homosexuals because sexual orientation isn't obvious unless individuals choose to make it so. Because of the social stigma still attached to homosexuality, many homosexuals prefer not to declare their sexual orientation openly. Their reticence is understandable, but it makes gay and lesbian role models more difficult to identify. Obviously, role models are important for the development of anyone's self-esteem. Members of the dominant majority, however, typically have lots of role models to choose from, whereas minority-group members do not. Hence it's the *relative availability* of role models that distinguishes members of minority and majority groups, not their need for them.

Summary

Social perception involves the creation of images of ourselves and of others. Patterns of attribution contribute to these images, and these patterns can be slanted in a variety of ways. Generally we tend to attribute behavior to internal or external factors and to stable or unstable factors. Controllability/uncontrollability is another key dimension of attributions. Observers tend to favor internal attributions in explaining an actor's behavior, whereas the actor is more likely to make an external attribution. These tendencies depend to some extent on whether attributions are being made about success or about failure. We usually try to maintain consistency among our beliefs because cognitive dissonance is unpleasant. Also, social perception is highly selective. Many lines of evidence demonstrate that we tend to see what we expect to see in our interpersonal interactions.

Your self-concept is a set of ideas about what you are like, and it is not easily changed. It governs both present and future behavior. It is shaped by your own observations, which often involve social comparisons with others—usually similar others who make up your reference group. Of course, your observations may be distorted. Feedback from others also shapes your self-concept, but you may distort it as well. Finally, cultural guidelines can affect the way we see ourselves.

Self-esteem is your global evaluation of your worth. Low self-esteem tends to be associated with emotional problems, difficulties in social interactions, and negative feelings toward others. Parents are especially important in determining our self-esteem. They provide direct feedback and influence the standards against which we evaluate ourselves.

Public selves are the various images that we project to others. Generally we try to create positive impressions for others, and we do so by employing a variety of impression-management strategies. A certain amount of impression management is expected, but some people edit their behavior more than others. People who are high in self-monitoring are especially sensitive to the impressions they make on others.

Identity is a relatively clear and stable sense of who you are and what you stand for. According to Erik Erikson, developing a sense of identity is a key challenge of adolescence. James Marcia has proposed that identity outcomes include foreclosure, moratorium, diffusion, and achievement. A number of theorists emphasize the importance of congruence between one's public selves and one's self-concept and sense of identity.

Our self-perceptions are often biased in a positive direction. Common self-enhancement strategies include the self-serving bias, the self-centered bias, downward social comparison, and an optimistic attributional style.

Many aspects of person perception lead us to see others inaccurately. We may be swayed by categorizing, stereotypes, or excessive attention to physical attractiveness or other features of appearance. Misperceptions are also fostered by the fundamental attribution error and defensive attribution. Inaccuracy in our perceptions tends to persist because first impressions can be difficult to overcome. Finally, the false consensus and false uniqueness effects can promote erroneous beliefs about others.

Prejudice is a particularly unfortunate outcome of our tendency to view others inaccurately. Most of the usual sources of error in person perception contribute to prejudicial beliefs about minority groups. Minority-group members frequently use in-group members as their dominant reference group, and this strategy contributes to self-esteem.

Because of the enormous importance of self-esteem, the Application will discuss ways to build a more positive self-concept.

Indicate whether the following statements are true or false.

1.

❚ *am very sensitive to criticism.*

2.

❚ *tend to have a hard time accepting praise or flattery.*

3.

❚ *have very little confidence in my abilities.*

4.

❚ *often feel awkward in social situations and just don't know how to take charge.*

5.

❚ *tend to be highly critical of other people.*

If you indicated that most of these statements are true, you may be suffering from what Alfred Adler called an *inferiority complex* (see Chapter 2). This syndrome, which is dominated by low self-esteem, is fairly common. It is also quite unfortunate. People with very low self-esteem tend to develop more emotional problems than others, set low goals for themselves, become socially invisible, conform against their better judgment, and court rejection by putting down others.

Self-esteem is obviously a very important component of your self-concept. It appears that an overly negative self-image can contribute to many kinds of behavioral problems. An overly positive image can also cause problems, but people characterized by excessive conceit do not suffer in the same way that self-critical people do.

In this Application we will describe seven guidelines for building higher self-esteem. These guidelines are based on our own distillation of the advice of many theorists, including Rogers (1977), Ellis (1984), Jourard (Jourard & Landsman, 1980), Hamachek (1992), Mahoney (1979), and Zimbardo (1977).

Recognize that you control your self-image. The first thing you must do is recognize that *you* ultimately control the way you see yourself. You *do* have the power to change your self-image. True, we have discussed at length how

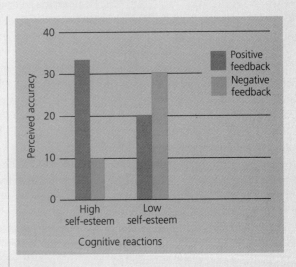

FIGURE 5.10
Self-esteem and acceptance of positive and negative feedback
In a study by Swann and his associates (1987), students received either positive or negative feedback after giving a speech. The high self-esteem students tended to view positive feedback as more accurate, but low self-esteem students tended to see negative feedback as more accurate. Thus people often have a bias in favor of verifying their self-concept. Unfortunately, this bias can help to strengthen a negative self-concept and perpetuate low self-esteem.

feedback from others influences your self-concept. Yes, social comparison theory suggests that we need such feedback and that it would be unwise to ignore it completely. However, the final choice to accept or reject such feedback rests with you. Your self-image resides in your mind and is a product of your thinking. Although others may influence your self-concept, you are the final authority. The key in this regard is to avoid the trap that people with unfavorable self-images tend to

fall into. Research shows that people with low self-esteem tend to be more accepting of negative feedback about themselves than of positive feedback (Swann, Griffin, Predmore, & Gaines, 1987; see Figure 5.10).

Don't let others set your goals. A common trap that many of us fall into is to let others set the standards by which we evaluate ourselves. People around us are constantly telling us that we should do this or we ought to do that. We hear that we "should study computer science" or "ought to lose weight" or "must move to a better neighborhood." Most of these people mean well, and many of them may have good ideas. Still, as you will recall from our discussion of identity, it is important that you make your own decisions about what you will do and what you will believe in. Consider a business executive in his early 40's who sees himself in a negative light because he has not climbed very high in the corporate hierarchy. The crucial question is: Did he ever *really* want to make that arduous climb? Maybe he has misgivings about the value of such an effort. Perhaps he has

©Punch/Rothco

I don't suppose it's much compared with other inferiority complexes

gone through life thinking he should pursue that kind of success only because that standard was imposed on him by society. You should think about the source of and basis for your personal goals and standards. Do they really represent ideals that *you* value? Or are they beliefs that you have passively accepted from others without thinking?

Recognize unrealistic goals. Even if you truly value certain ideals and sincerely want to achieve certain goals, another question remains. Are your goals realistic? Many people get in the habit of demanding too much of themselves. They always expect themselves to perform at their best, and obviously we are none of us at our best all the time. Do you have a burning desire to achieve international acclaim in films? The odds against such an achievement are enormous. It is important to recognize this reality so that you will not condemn yourself if you fail. Some overly demanding people pervert the social comparison process by always comparing themselves with the *best* rather than with similar others. They assess their looks by comparing themselves with famous models, and they judge their finances by comparing themselves with the wealthiest people they know. Such comparisons are unrealistic and almost inevitably undermine self-esteem.

Modify negative self-talk. The way you analyze your life influences the way you see yourself (and vice versa). People who are low in self-esteem tend to engage in various counterproductive modes of thinking. When they succeed, they may attribute their success to good luck, and when they fail, they may blame themselves. Quite to the contrary, you should take credit for your successes and consider the possibility that your failures may not be your fault. As we saw in Chapter 4, Albert Ellis has pointed out that we often think irrationally and draw unwarranted negative conclusions about ourselves. If you apply for a job and are rejected,

you may think, "They didn't hire me. I must be a worthless, inept person." The conclusion that you are a worthless person does *not* follow logically from the fact that you were not hired. Such irrational thinking and negative self-talk breed poor self-esteem. It is important to recognize the destructive potential of negative self-talk and bring it to a halt.

Emphasize your strengths. This advice may seem trite, but it has merit. People with low self-esteem often derive little satisfaction from their accomplishments and virtues. They dismiss compliments as foolish, unwarranted, or insincere. They pay little heed to their good qualities while talking constantly about their defeats and frailties. The fact is that we all have our strengths and weaknesses. You should accept those personal shortcomings that you are powerless to change and work on those that are changeable, without becoming obsessed by them.

At the same time, you should take stock of your strengths and learn to appreciate them.

Work to improve yourself. As we just mentioned, some personal shortcomings *can* be overcome. Although it is important to reassess your goals and discard those that are unrealistic, this advice is not intended to provide a convenient rationalization for complacency. There is much to be said for setting out to conquer personal problems. In a sense, this entire text is based on a firm belief in the value of self-control and self-improvement. There is ample evidence that efforts at self-improvement can pay off by boosting self-esteem.

Approach others with a positive outlook. People who are low in self-esteem often try to cut others down to their (subjective) size through constant criticism. As you can readily imagine, this faultfinding and generally negative approach to interpersonal transactions does not go over well with other people. Instead, it leads to tension, antagonism, and rejection. Rejection lowers self-esteem still further (see Figure 5.11). You can enhance your self-esteem by recognizing and reversing this self-defeating tendency. Approaching people with a positive, supportive outlook will promote rewarding interactions and help you earn their acceptance. Probably nothing enhances self-esteem more than the acceptance and genuine affection of others.

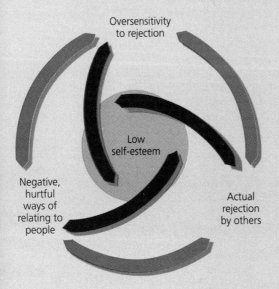

FIGURE 5.11
The vicious circle of low self-esteem and rejection
A negative self-image can make expectations of rejection a self-fulfilling prophecy, because people with low self-esteem tend to approach others in negative, hurtful ways. Real or imagined rejections lower self-esteem still further, creating a vicious circle.

CHAPTER 5 REVIEW

Key Learning Objectives

1. Describe the attribution process, including the key dimensions of attributions.
2. Describe how actors and observers differ in their attributional biases.
3. Explain why cognitive dissonance leads us to strive for consistency in our beliefs.
4. Explain what is involved in selectivity in social perception.
5. Define self-concept and explain how it guides present and future behavior.
6. Summarize how various factors influence one's self-concept.
7. Define self-esteem and summarize evidence on the correlates of self-esteem.
8. Discuss the determinants of self-esteem.
9. Explain public selves and why we engage in impression management.
10. Summarize how people who are high in self-monitoring tend to behave.
11. Define identity and explain why it becomes a concern during late adolescence.
12. Describe Marcia's four identity statuses.
13. Explain why some people are involved in a search for their authentic self.
14. Explain how the self-serving bias and the self-centered bias foster self-enhancement.
15. Explain how downward social comparisons and an optimistic attributional style can contribute to self-enhancement.
16. Explain how surplus visibility puts those minority-group members who advocate social change in a double-bind.
17. Explain how stereotypes contribute to inaccuracy in person perception.
18. Discuss how aspects of physical appearance influence our perceptions of others.
19. Describe the fundamental attribution error and defensive attribution.
20. Explain primacy, false consensus, and false uniqueness effects.
21. List five sources of error in person perception that commonly contribute to prejudice.
22. Discuss the relationship between minority-group status and self-esteem.
23. Briefly describe seven principles for building higher self-esteem.

Key Terms

attributional style
attributions
cognitive dissonance
defensive attribution
discrimination
downward social comparison
external attributions
false consensus effect
false uniqueness effect
fundamental attribution error
identity
impression management
internal attributions

prejudice
primacy effect
public self
reference group
self-centered bias
self-concept
self-enhancement
self-esteem
self-monitoring
self-perception theory
self-serving bias
social comparison theory
stereotypes

Key People

Daryl Bem
Erik Erikson
Leon Festinger

Erving Goffman
James Marcia
Mark Snyder

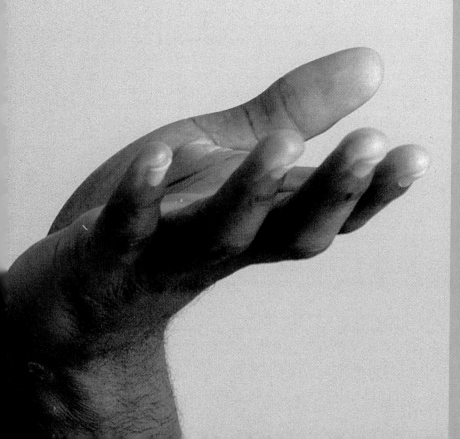

 Interpersonal Communication

HAVE YOU EVER RACED HOME, eager to tell someone about something that happened that day, only to find no one at home to listen to your story? It may not have been a spectacular or earthshaking tale; maybe you simply picked up an intriguing bit of gossip or met someone who was a little unusual. Still, it was something you wanted to share with others. Chances are you rehearsed your fascinating account all the way home. Do you remember how frustrated you felt when you found no receptive ears for your story? As this common experience makes clear, people have a powerful need to share information about interesting or important events with others and to hear their reactions.

Interpersonal communication is an integral part of human experience. Moreover, our interpersonal skills are highly relevant to adjustment, because they can be critical to our happiness and success in life. In this chapter we'll look at the process of interpersonal communication and discuss both nonverbal and verbal communication. Then we'll turn our attention to some ways in which poor communication can cause interpersonal conflict and offer some suggestions for communicating more effectively. In the Application we'll consider ways to develop an assertive communication style.

The Process of Interpersonal Communication

Communication can be defined as the process of sending and receiving messages that have meaning. Our personal thoughts have meaning, of course, but when we talk to ourselves, we are engaging in *intra*personal communication. In this chapter we will focus on *inter*personal communication—the face-to-face transmission of meaning between two or more people. For the most part, we'll concentrate on two-person interactions, and save communication in groups for Chapter 7. We define **interpersonal communication as an interactional process whereby one person sends a message to another.**

It is important to note several points about this definition. First, for communication to qualify as *interpersonal*, at least two people must be involved. Second, interpersonal communication is a *process*. By this we simply mean that it is usually composed of a series of actions:

Mary talks/John listens, John responds/Mary listens, and so on. Third, this process is *interactional*. Communication is generally not a one-way street: both participants send as well as receive information when they're interacting. An important implication of this fact is that we need to pay attention to both our *speaking* and our *listening* skills if we want to improve the effectiveness of our communication.

Components of the Communication Process

Let's take a look at the essential components of the interpersonal communication process. David Berlo (1960) has divided the interpersonal communication process into four basic components: (1) the source of the message, (2) the message itself, (3) the channel in which the message is sent, and (4) the receiver of the message (see Figure 6.1).

The *source* is the person who initiates, or sends, the message. In a typical two-way conversation, both people serve as sources (as well as receivers) of messages. Keep in mind that each source person brings a unique set of expectations and understandings to each communication situation. We will return to this important point shortly.

The *message* is the information or meaning that is transmitted from one person to another. The message is the content of the communication—that is, the ideas and feelings we convey to another person. Language is our primary means of sending messages, but we also communicate to others nonverbally. Nonverbal communication includes the facial expressions, gestures, and vocal inflections we use to supplement (and sometimes entirely change) the meaning of our verbal messages. When you say "Thanks a lot," for example, your nonverbal communication can convey either sincere gratitude or heavy sarcasm.

The *channel* is the medium through which the message reaches the receiver. Unless our hearing is impaired, we receive verbal messages by hearing them. We hear both the literal content of messages and the vocal inflections people use to communicate. Sometimes sound is the only channel available for receiving information—when you talk on the telephone for example. More often, however, we receive information from multiple channels simultaneously. We not only hear what people tell us, we also see the expressions on their faces, observe their gestures, experience eye contact with them, and sometimes feel their physical touch. Note that the messages in the various channels may be consistent or inconsistent, making our interpretation of them more or less difficult.

The *receiver* is the person to whom the message is targeted. As we noted before, in a two-person interaction, each participant serves as both a source and a receiver. Each source/receiver has a unique history and a unique set of beliefs and expectations that influence the communication process (Chelune, 1987). Communication is more effective (and less problematic) when people have similar frames of reference (Clark, 1985).

Importance of Communication

Before we get into the details of interpersonal communication, let's take a moment to emphasize its significance. Communication with others—friends, lovers, parents, spouses, children, employers, co-workers—is such an essential and commonplace aspect of our lives that it's hard to overstate the importance of being able to communicate effectively. Moreover, many of life's satisfactions (and frustrations and heartaches as well) hinge on our ability to communicate effectively with others. Research has shown that good communication can enhance satisfaction in marriage and that poor communication can be a factor in marital dissatisfaction (Cleek & Pearson, 1985; Dindia & Fitzpatrick, 1985; Fitzpatrick, 1987). Most of our coverage in this chapter will be organized around two basic categories of communication: verbal (linguistic) and nonverbal. We'll tackle nonverbal communication first.

Nonverbal Communication

You're standing at the bar in your favorite lounge, gazing across a dark, smoky room filled with people drinking, dancing, and talking. You motion to the bartender that you'd like another drink. Your companion comments on the loudness of the music, and you nod in agreement. You spot an attractive stranger across the bar; your eyes meet for a moment and you smile. In a matter of seconds, you have sent three messages without uttering a syllable. To put it another way, you have just sent three nonverbal messages. **Nonverbal communication is the transmission of meaning from one person to another through means or symbols other than words.** Communication at the nonverbal level takes place through a variety of

behaviors: interpersonal distance, facial expression, eye contact, body posture and movement, gestures, physical touch, and tone of voice.

Some experts maintain that most of the message transmissions in face-to-face interactions actually occur at the nonverbal level (Mehrabian, 1971; Philpott, 1983). Clearly, a great deal of information is exchanged through nonverbal channels—perhaps more than most people realize. Thus, to enhance our effectiveness in communication, it's helpful to become more knowledgeable about the nature of nonverbal cues. Let's begin by examining some general principles of nonverbal communication.

General Principles

1. *Nonverbal communication is multichanneled.* Nonverbal communication typically involves simultaneous messages sent through several channels. For instance, information may be transmitted through gestures, facial expressions, eye contact, and vocal tone at the same time. In contrast, verbal communication is limited to a single channel: speech. If you have ever tried to follow two people speaking at once, you are aware of how difficult it is to process multiple inputs of information. The multichanneled nature of nonverbal communication is one of the reasons that many nonverbal transmissions sail by the receiver unnoticed.

2. *Nonverbal communication frequently conveys emotions.* Sometimes we can communicate our feelings without saying a word (we've all heard of "a look that kills"). Nonverbal demonstrations of positive feelings include sitting or standing close to people we care for, touching them often, and looking at them frequently (Fletcher & Fitness, 1990; Patterson, 1988).

3. *Nonverbal communication is relatively spontaneous.* Nonverbal transmissions tend to be more spontaneous than verbal communication (Verderber & Verderber, 1989). In other words, we often send nonverbal messages with-

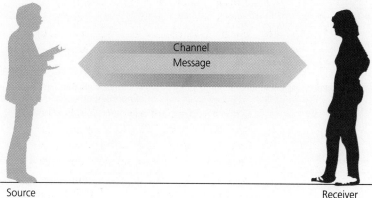

FIGURE 6.1
A model of interpersonal communication
According to David Berlo (1960), interpersonal communication involves four elements: the source, the receiver, the message, and the channel through which the message is transmitted. In conversations, both participants function as source and receiver.

165
CHAPTER 6
Interpersonal
Communication

out thinking about them. Although it is certainly not unheard of for people to speak thoughtlessly, speech is usually under more conscious control than most nonverbal communications. It is this less guarded quality of nonverbal communication that often makes it a more accurate index of a person's true feelings.

4. *Nonverbal communication may contradict verbal messages.* We have all seen people who proclaim "I'm not angry" while their bodies clearly convey that they are positively furious. It is well known that verbal and nonverbal messages may be quite inconsistent. When you confront such inconsistency, which message should you believe? There are no absolute rules, but you're probably better off betting on the nonverbal signs because of their greater spontaneity. Indeed, there is evidence that deception by someone instructed to tell a lie is most readily detected in the nonverbal channels of communication (DePaulo, LeMay, & Epstein, 1991; DePaulo, Lanier, & Davis, 1983).

5. *Nonverbal communication is relatively ambiguous.* Nonverbal messages tend to be less clear than spoken words. Although there is room for considerable ambiguity in speech, there usually is more consensus about the meanings of words than about the meaning of nonverbal signs. A shrug or a raised eyebrow can mean different things to different people. Moreover, it is always difficult to know whether nonverbal messages are being sent intentionally. Although some popular books on body language imply otherwise, very few nonverbal signals carry universally accepted meanings (Swenson, 1973), so they should be interpreted with caution.

6. *Nonverbal communication is very culture-bound.* Like language, nonverbal signals vary from culture to culture (Hall, 1973). People of northern European heritage, for instance, tend to engage in less physical contact and keep a greater distance between themselves than people of Latin or Middle Eastern heritage. Thus an Englishman may be quite upset when a well-meaning Brazilian "trespasses" on his personal space. Sometimes cultural differences can be quite dramatic.

Nonverbal signals can provide information about many things in interpersonal interactions. As we discuss specific forms of nonverbal communication, we will place special emphasis on information regarding social affiliation (or liking for another) and information about the status of the people with whom we are interacting.

Personal Space

Proxemics is the study of people's use of interpersonal space. *Personal space* is a zone of space surrounding a person that is felt to "belong" to that person. This personal space that we consider "ours" is like an invisible bubble we carry around with us. As we will see, although the boundaries of our personal space are imaginary, this space may be marked off in tangible ways under some conditions. The size of this mobile zone is related to our cultural background, social status, personality, age, and sex. Interestingly, animals show a similar tendency, called **territoriality—the marking off and defending of certain areas as their own.**

As you might guess, the amount of distance people feel comfortable with between themselves and others depends on the nature of the social interaction. On the basis of his observations and analysis of social interactions in the United States, the anthropologist Edward Hall (1990) has described four interpersonal distance zones that are appropriate for particular

**FIGURE 6.2
Interpersonal
distance zones**
According to Edward Hall (1990), we like to keep a certain amount of distance between ourselves and others. The distance that makes us feel comfortable depends on whom we are interacting with and the nature of the situation. The zones depicted on the left are generally appropriate for the people and situations listed on the right.

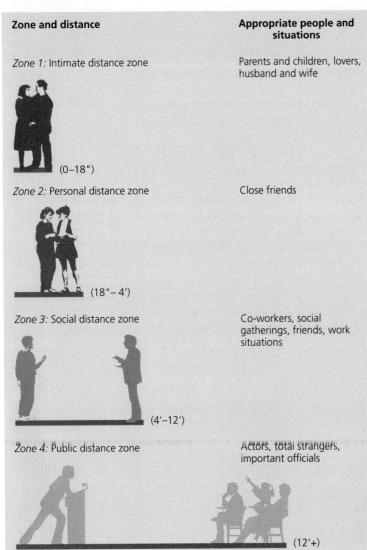

Zone and distance	Appropriate people and situations
Zone 1: Intimate distance zone (0–18")	Parents and children, lovers, husband and wife
Zone 2: Personal distance zone (18"–4')	Close friends
Zone 3: Social distance zone (4'–12')	Co-workers, social gatherings, friends, work situations
Zone 4: Public distance zone (12'+)	Actors, total strangers, important officials

kinds of encounters in American culture (see Figure 6.2).

- *Public distance (12 feet and beyond)*: People often prefer to maintain this distance because it gives them the option of choosing to ignore someone without appearing rude. Though interpersonal interactions can take place at distances beyond 12 feet, they tend to be quite impersonal.
- *Social distance (4–12 feet)*: Most social interactions in the United States take place within this zone. It is a nice intermediate distance that makes most of us feel comfortable.
- *Personal distance (18 inches–4 feet)*: This is the minimum distance maintained in most encounters between friends. In some situations, such as a cocktail party, strangers may venture into this zone.
- *Intimate distance (0–18 inches)*: This distance obviously represents tight quarters and is appropriate only for very intimate relationships, such as those between parents and children or between lovers. Of course, there are obvious exceptions, as in crowded subways and elevators, but these situations are often experienced as stressful.

Hall's analysis indicates that the appropriate distance between people is regulated by social norms and that these norms are determined in large part by the nature of the relationship and the situation. A large body of research supports his basic ideas (Darley & Gilbert, 1985). Like other aspects of nonverbal communication, personal distance can convey information about status. People of similar status tend to stand closer together than do people whose status is unequal (J. A. Hall, 1990). Moreover, it is the prerogative of the more powerful person in an interaction to set the "proper" interpersonal distance (Henley, 1977).

What happens when someone approaches us more closely than we feel is appropriate? Such invasions of personal space invariably result in feelings of discomfort, and we attempt to bring the interpersonal distance more in line with our expectations. Let's say that you have staked out some territory for yourself at a table in the library. Although there is space at other tables, a stranger sits down at "your" table and forces you to share it. How might you react? First, you will probably experience some tension, which may be betrayed by nonverbal signals such as body rigidity, a shuffling of position, or a lack of eye contact. Then you may express your disapproval nonverbally through a hostile stare or frown. You may decide to move to another table to reestablish a distance that feels comfortable to you. If moving away is not practical, you will probably reorient your body away from the intruder. Another common response to invasions of personal space is to place some barrier (such as a stack of books) between you and the invader. Invasions of personal space rarely go unnoticed and they usually elicit a variety of reactions.

Facial Expression

Facial expressions convey emotions. In an extensive research program, Paul Ekman, Wallace Friesen, and their colleagues have identified six primary emotions that have distinctive facial expressions. These six emotions are anger, disgust, fear, happiness, sadness, and surprise (Ekman, 1992; Ekman & Friesen, 1984). The facial expressions that convey these six emotions appear to be universal. That is, individuals from a variety of cultures are able to identify them correctly (Ekman & Friesen, 1984, 1986; Ekman et al., 1987). The typical strategy in such research is to show subjects from a variety of Western and non-Western cultures photographs depicting various emotions and ask them to match the photographs with the appropriate emotions. Some representative results of this research are depicted in Figure 6.3.

Although a small number of basic facial

CATHY copyright Cathy Guisewite. Reprinted with permission of UNIVERSAL PRESS SYNDICATE. All rights reserved.

Emotion displayed

	Fear	Disgust	Happiness	Anger

Country	Agreement in judging photos (%)			
United States	85	92	97	67
Brazil	67	97	95	90
Chile	68	92	95	94
Argentina	54	92	98	90
Japan	66	90	100	90
New Guinea	54	44	82	50

FIGURE 6.3
Facial expressions and emotions
Ekman and Friesen (1984) found that people in highly disparate cultures showed fair agreement on the emotions portrayed in these photos. This consensus across cultures suggests that the facial expressions associated with certain emotions may have a biological basis.

expressions are universally recognizable, people in all cultures do not necessarily display the same emotions in the same ways. Further, sometimes we consider it inappropriate to express our feelings, so we try to hide them. The facial expression of emotion is regulated by a given society's norms. *Display rules* **are norms that govern the appropriate display of emotions.**

Sometimes we may not want to communicate everything we feel to someone else. Is it possible to deceive others deliberately through facial expression? Yes indeed. In fact, it appears that we are better at sending deceptive messages with our faces than with other areas of our bodies (Ekman, Friesen, & Ellsworth, 1982). Recall the term "poker face," an allusion to the cultivated ability of poker players to control their excitement about a good hand of cards (or their dismay about a bad one).

Eye Contact

Eye contact (also called mutual gaze) is another major channel of nonverbal communication.

Above all else, it is the duration of eye contact between people that is most meaningful. A great deal of research has been done on communication through the eyes, and we will briefly summarize some of the more interesting findings (Kleinke, 1986).

People who engage in high levels of eye contact are likely to be judged as more attentive than those who maintain less eye contact. Speakers, interviewers, and experimenters receive higher ratings of competence when they maintain high rather than low eye contact with their audience. Similarly, those who engage in high levels of mutual gaze are likely to be perceived as having effective social skills and credibility. Gaze is also a means of communicating the *intensity* (but not the positivity or negativity) of feelings.

The *positivity and negativity* of feelings are communicated by the context of the communication, timing, and accompanying nonverbal behaviors (position of the mouth, for example) (J. A. Hall, 1990). On the positive side, eye contact is strongly related to feelings of interperson-

Sustained eye contact can convey either intense positive emotions or strong negative feelings.

al attraction (Kleinke, 1986). For example, couples who say they are in love spend more time gazing at each other than other couples do (Goldstein, Kilroy, & Van de Voort, 1976; Patterson, 1988; Rubin, 1970). Also, people who engage in high mutual gaze are judged by observers to like each other more than those who engage in relatively little eye contact. Finally, maintaining eye contact with others generally causes them to like us, although people prefer a moderate amount of eye contact rather than constant (or no) mutual gaze.

In a negative interpersonal context, a steady gaze becomes a stare. A stare causes most people to feel uncomfortable and to flee the situation (Ellsworth, Carlsmith, & Henson, 1972; Kleinke, 1986). Moreover, like threat displays among nonhuman primates such as baboons and rhesus monkeys, a stare can convey aggressive intent (Henley, 1986).

We can also communicate by reducing our eye contact with others. Mutual gaze is usually reduced when an interaction is unpleasant or embarrassing (Edelman & Hampson, 1981) or when people feel that their personal space is being invaded (Argyle & Dean, 1965; Kleinke, 1986). It is widely believed that a speaker trying to deceive a listener engages in relatively little eye contact (Hemsley & Doob, 1978), but studies suggest that liars are actually fairly skilled at maintaining normal eye contact (DePaulo, Stone, & Lassiter, 1985). Thus eye contact is *not* a very reliable index of deceptive intent.

Some sex and racial differences have been found in patterns of eye contact. Women tend to gaze more at others in interactions than men do, as the research results shown in Figure 6.4 demonstrate (Giles & Street, 1985), and white listeners tend to gaze more when someone else is speaking than black listeners do (LaFrance & Mayo, 1976). Perhaps eye contact is more likely to be considered rude or confrontational in black culture (Scheflen & Scheflen, 1972). Obviously, such differences in nonverbal communication can lead to misunderstandings if eye-gaze behaviors intended to convey interest and respect are interpreted as evidence of disrespect or dishonesty.

Body Language

Body movements—those of the head, trunk, hands, legs, and feet—also provide nonverbal avenues of communication. **Kinesics is the study of communication through body movements.** What can body posture convey? For one thing, it provides information about the level of

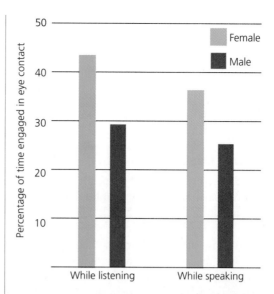

FIGURE 6.4
Gender differences in eye contact
In social interactions, women gaze at others more than men do. Exline (1963) found this difference whether subjects were speaking or listening.

tension or relaxation that a person is experiencing. Leaning back with arms or legs arranged in an asymmetrical ("open") position, for example, conveys a feeling of relaxation.

Body posture can also indicate a person's attitude toward you (Mehrabian, 1972). If someone leans toward you, the posture typically indicates interest and a positive attitude. When people angle their bodies away from you or cross their arms, their posture may indicate a negative attitude or defensiveness.

In addition, body posture can convey status differences. The higher-status person generally looks more relaxed. The lower-status person tends to exhibit a more rigid body posture, often sitting up straight with feet together, flat on the floor, and arms close to the body (a "closed" position) (Mehrabian, 1972). Erving Goffman (1956) noticed this disparity long ago in hospital staff meetings. The relatively high-status doctors tended to assume careless and comfortable positions, while lower-status personnel, such as nurses and social workers (who presum-

People in higher-status positions tend to adopt an "open" body posture, and those in lower-status roles usually adopt a "closed" position.

ably would be more tense), tended to display less casual posture. Again, as we saw with eye contact, status and sex differences are frequently parallel. That is, men are more likely to exhibit the high-status "open" posture and women the lower-status "closed" posture (J. A. Hall, 1990).

Hand Gestures

Hand gestures are used primarily to regulate conversations and to supplement speech (Scheflen & Scheflen, 1972). The *referencing gesture* is used to refer to an object or person who is the subject of conversation. For example, you might point at a car that you're commenting on. The *gesture of emphasis* is used to stress a point that is being made verbally. Thus you might slam your fist onto a desk to emphasize the importance of your statement. *Demonstrative gestures* mimic what is being said. In discussing a cutoff of someone's financial support, for instance, you might make chopping motions with your hand.

Touch

Touch takes many forms and can convey a variety of meanings. Most people are aware that touch can express intimacy, but many are unaware that it can convey messages of status and power as well. The person who initiates a touch, for example, is generally assumed to have higher status than the person who receives the touch. How we interpret the possible messages communicated by touch depends on the age and sex of the two individuals involved, the setting in which the touching takes place, and the

In recreational settings, men touch each other more than women do.

relationship between the toucher and recipient, among other things (Major, Schmidlin, & Williams, 1990).

Studies on touching are difficult to conduct and interpret, so generalizations are risky. Nonetheless, research to date supports the following conclusions. First, men touch women more often than vice versa when touching is intentional (vs. accidental) (Major et al., 1990). Second, touching is more frequent between cross-sex adult pairs than between same-sex pairs. In other words, research does not support the popular belief that women always touch each other more often than men touch other men. In public, nonintimate settings, women touch each other more than men touch each other; in recreational settings, men touch each other more than women touch each other; and in hello-and-goodbye settings (airports, for example), no differences between the sexes have been found (Major et al., 1990). A third conclusion we can draw from research findings is that there are strong norms as to *where* people are allowed to touch friends. The norms for same-sex interactions are quite different from those for cross-sex interactions, as Figure 6.5 indicates.

Regarding people's *responses* to touching, it has been found that women generally respond more favorably than men to touching (Henley & Freeman, 1981). This sex difference may depend on status differences. Support for this interpretation comes from the finding that both women and men react favorably to touching when the person who initiates the touch is higher in status than the recipient (Major, 1981). Of course, whenever touching is unwelcome (as in the case of sexual harassment), these findings do not hold.

Paralanguage

The term *paralanguage* refers to *how* something is said rather than *what* is said. Thus **paralanguage includes all vocal cues other than the content of the verbal message itself.** These cues may include the loudness or softness with which people speak, the speed with which they talk, and the rhythm and quality of their speech (Burgoon, 1987). Each of these aspects of vocalization can affect the message being transmitted.

Variations in vocal emphasis can give the same set of words very different meanings. Consider the sentence "I really enjoyed myself!" If you vary the word that is accented, you can speak this sentence in three ways, each resulting in a different meaning.

- I really enjoyed myself! (Even though others may not have had a good time, I did.)
- I *really* enjoyed myself! (My enjoyment was exceptional or greater than expected.)
- I really *enjoyed* myself! (Much to my surprise, I had a great time.)

As you can see, the way we say something can make a considerable difference in the meaning we convey. In fact, we can actually reverse the literal meaning of a verbal message by the way we say it. For example, "That's just great!" can convey a feeling of genuine excitement or a sarcastic putdown. Thus variations in vocal emphasis constitute a language within a language.

Aspects of vocalization can also communicate emotions. For example, rapid speech may mean that a person is happy, frightened, or nervous. Slower speech may be used when we are uncertain or when we want to emphasize a point. Loud vocalization often indicates anger. A relatively high pitch may indicate anxiety (Verderber & Verderber, 1989). Slow speech, low volume, and low pitch are often associated with sadness. Thus vocal quality is another clue that you can use to discern someone's true feelings.

Keep in mind, however, that it is easy to assign meanings to voice quality that aren't valid. It is quite common for people to stereotype certain vocal characteristics as indicative of specific personality traits even though research doesn't support such associations (Heun & Heun, 1978). A deep voice is often stereotyped as indicating masculinity and maturity, for instance, and a high breathy voice is often associated with femininity and youth.

Detecting Deception

As we have noted, the spontaneous nature of nonverbal communication often makes it a better index of a person's true feelings than what the person actually says. This reality raises an obvious question. Is it possible to detect deceit by monitoring nonverbal signals? Yes, but it isn't easy. The clues that suggest dishonesty don't necessarily correspond to popular notions about how liars give themselves away.

Evidence on the nonverbal behaviors associated with deception is summarized in Figure 6.6. The vocal and visual cues that have been studied are listed in the first column. The second column indicates whether these cues are really associated with deception. The third column indicates whether the same cues are widely believed to be associated with deception. As

you can see, research does not support many stereotypical notions about lying. Contrary to popular belief, lying is *not* associated with slow talking, long pauses before speaking, excessive shifting of posture, reduced smiling, or lack of eye contact.

Nonetheless, some cues do seem to be associated with dishonesty. Vocal cues include excessive hesitations and stammering, speaking with a higher pitch, and giving relatively short answers. Visual cues include excessive blinking and dilation of the pupils. Also, liars nervously touch themselves more than normal. Too, it's helpful to look for inconsistencies between messages expressed through the face and those from the lower part of the body. A friendly smile accompanied by a nervous shuffling of feet, for example, may be cause for concern. Another clue is whether the facial message seems less spontaneous than the verbal message. People tend to take more time to muster and send deceptive nonverbal signals than authentic ones. Because of this tendency, liars' verbal and facial expressions may be out of sync.

Deception is potentially detectable, then, but detecting it is not a simple matter. The nonverbal behaviors that tend to accompany lying are subtle and can be difficult to spot.

Significance of Nonverbal Communication

Although we often are unaware of nonverbal communication, it clearly plays an important role in our lives. Various studies demonstrate the significance of nonverbal communication,

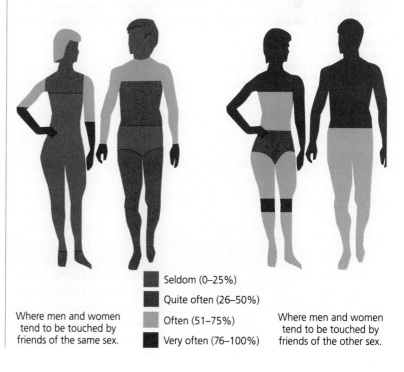

Where men and women tend to be touched by friends of the same sex.

Seldom (0–25%)
Quite often (26–50%)
Often (51–75%)
Very often (76–100%)

Where men and women tend to be touched by friends of the other sex.

**FIGURE 6.5
Where friends touch each other**
Social norms govern where friends tend to touch each other. As these figures show, the patterns of touching in same-sex interactions differ considerably from those in cross-sex interactions. (Adapted from Marsh, 1988.)

Nonverbal Cues and Deception

Kind of cue	Are cues associated with actual deception?	Are cues believed to be a sign of deception?
Vocal cues		
Speech hesitations	YES: Liars hesitate more.	YES
Voice pitch	YES: Liars speak with higher pitch.	YES
Speech errors (stutters, stammers)	YES: Liars make more errors.	YES
Speech latency (pause before starting to speak or answer)	NO	YES: People think liars pause more.
Speech rate	NO	YES: People think liars talk slower.
Response length	YES: Liars give shorter answers.	NO
Visual cues		
Pupil dilation	YES: Liars show more dilation.	(No research data)
Adaptors (self-directed gestures)	YES: Liars touch themselves more.	NO
Blinking	YES: Liars blink more.	(No research data)
Postural shifts	NO	YES: People think liars shift more.
Smiling	NO	YES: People think liars smile less.
Gaze (eye contact)	NO	YES: People think liars engage in less eye contact.

FIGURE 6.6
Detecting deception from nonverbal behaviors
This chart, based on a research review by DePaulo et al. (1985), summarizes evidence on nonverbal cues that are *actually* associated with deception and those that are *believed* to be signs of deception.

and many of them have examined its importance in marital relationships. For example, it has been shown that husbands and wives in unhappy marriages send more negative nonverbal messages and fewer positive nonverbal messages than do couples who are happily married (Noller, 1982, 1985). Research has also been done on other aspects of nonverbal communication. One such study looked at differences between people in nonverbal expressive talent (Friedman, Prince, Riggio, & Di Matteo, 1980). Specifically, this study focused on individual differences in the ability to use facial expressions, gestures, body movements, and so forth to enhance the impact of verbal statements. The main conclusion was that high expressiveness may be the key element in what we often vaguely label "charisma." *Charisma* usually refers to a special ability to lead, inspire, or captivate others. Thus there is some reason to believe that nonverbal talent may be a crucial factor that helps make some people charismatic leaders. Of course, leaders also depend heavily on verbal communication.

Verbal Communication

 erbal communication involves sending and receiving messages through written or spoken words. Although much of what we say will be relevant to written communication, we will focus on speaking and listening because of their role in face-to-face interactions. In this section, we'll discuss some general principles and the complex topic of self-disclosure.

General Principles

Let's examine some general ideas that can be helpful in efforts to understand the dynamics of verbal communication.

1. *Both speaking and listening are essential components of verbal communication.* Recall that, in interpersonal communication, individuals typically take the roles of *both* source (speaker) and receiver (listener). Obviously, verbal communication is enhanced when speakers can clearly articulate what they mean and when listeners can understand and interpret accurately what they hear. Unfortunately, we don't always manage to do so.

2. *We are often careless and sloppy speakers.* The fact that we are not always careful to say what we mean can result in misunderstanding. Sometimes such miscommunication stems from simple carelessness. Virtually all of us can recall an instance in which we hurt someone's feelings unintentionally because we said the first thing that came to mind. At other times, miscommunication occurs because we aren't clear about what we are trying to express. Taking the time to think carefully about what we want to say and how we can best express it is especially important when we are communicating about important issues.

3. *We are often inattentive and preoccupied listeners.* Although we can process speech at up to about 600 words per minute, most people speak at a rate of only 100 to 140 words per minute (Adler & Towne, 1987). Thus it is understandable that receivers can become bored, distracted, and inattentive. This is likely to be the case when we know the speaker well (and therefore expect that we know what he or she will say) and when we are tired and lack the energy to pay careful attention. Preoccupation with our own thoughts is also a common tendency. Sometimes we focus our attention on how we will respond instead of on what the speaker is saying, especially when we are discussing issues that are important to us.

Self-Disclosure: The Key to Intimacy

In our discussion of public selves in Chapter 5, we noted that people don't always behave spontaneously and naturally. We all engage in *impression management*. That is, we carefully edit our behavior and consciously monitor what we reveal about ourselves to others. When we choose to reveal things about ourselves, we are engaging in self-disclosure.

Self-disclosure is the voluntary act of verbally communicating private information about yourself to another person. By "private" we mean information that would not otherwise be available to the other party. It doesn't have to be a deeply hidden secret, but it may be. In general terms, self-disclosure involves opening up about yourself to others. Conversations that include self-disclosure are experienced as deeper and more personally meaningful than our more routine, superficial interactions.

Self-disclosure is a critical issue in our lives. Why? Because self-disclosure is a key vehicle through which emotional intimacy develops (Taylor & Altman, 1987). And intimacy is the element that distinguishes those relationships we experience as meaningful and sustaining from those we experience as superficial and unsupportive. Intimate relationships in this sense may be platonic or sexual. Indeed, as you may have discovered, a sexually intimate relationship is not necessarily an emotionally intimate relationship. When we speak of intimacy, the important factor is not the presence of a sexual relationship but rather the degree to which people are open and honest with each other.

One way of looking more closely at self-disclosure is to characterize it in terms of breadth and depth (Altman & Haythorn, 1965). *Breadth* refers to the variety of topics we discuss with another person. *Depth* refers to the degree to which we disclose personal information. For example, you would probably feel quite comfortable chatting about your feelings about the weather and today's sports scores with strangers (not much breadth or depth). In contrast, your best friend probably knows a wide variety of information about you (greater breadth) as well as how you feel about more private concerns, such as your jealousy toward your sister or your self-consciousness about your weight (greater depth). Figure 6.7 is a visual representation of breadth and depth in self-disclosure.

Self-disclosure can be risky. When we reveal important and private things about ourselves to others, we become more vulnerable to

them. We often worry about self-disclosure. What if others don't respond to what we say, or what if they laugh at us? Because of our fears of being rejected or humiliated, we are often unsure about whether we should open up to others. How can you know whether it's safe to share personal information with someone else? In the discussion that follows, we'll try to respond to this and related questions about self-disclosure.

Why Do We Engage in Self-Disclosure?

If self-disclosure is so scary—since it leaves us open to possible rejection—why do we take the gamble? Because the potential payoffs are so great. Self-disclosure serves many important functions in our personal and social lives (Derlega & Grezlak, 1979).

First, self-disclosure helps us clarify our thoughts and feelings. We all get confused from time to time and feel overwhelmed by our problems. Talking about these things can help us sort them out. Even thinking about talking to someone can help us to analyze the problem and clarify our feelings.

Second, self-disclosure helps us express our feelings. As we saw in our discussion of coping in Chapter 4, expressing feelings to someone else can help to reduce stress. For the most part, it's not a good idea to keep frustration and tension bottled up inside.

Third, self-disclosure aids in social comparison and self-understanding. As we saw in Chapter 5, social comparison theory suggests that we need to compare ourselves with others to gain a better understanding of ourselves (Festinger, 1954). To obtain the comparative information we seek, we often need to engage in self-disclosure. If you wanted to know

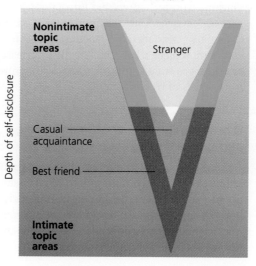

FIGURE 6.7
Breadth and depth of self-disclosure
The breadth of self-disclosure encompasses the variety of things you open up about; depth encompasses the amount of private information you reveal. Both the breadth and the depth of our disclosures are greater with best friends than with casual acquaintances or strangers. (Adapted from Altman & Taylor, 1973.)

whether your anxieties about a particular class were realistic, for instance, you would probably have to divulge those anxieties to your fellow students to obtain the kind of feedback you needed.

Fourth, self-disclosure is crucial in developing interpersonal relationships. If you would like to turn an acquaintanceship into a friendship, or if you want a friendship to be closer, self-disclosure may be the key. To get to know others better, you usually have to let them get to know you better. Your willingness to disclose yourself to others is an important signal that you trust them. This is an important message to send to someone with whom you want to develop or deepen a relationship. We hasten to add, however, that simply spilling your guts indiscriminately is likely to have a negative effect.

Inappropriate Self-Disclosure

If you engage in little or no self-disclosure, your personal and social satisfactions are likely to be limited. On the other hand, telling everyone everything about you will land you in trouble fast. Self-disclosure, then, can be appropriate or inappropriate. If you are to reap its benefits, you have to know the difference.

When is self-disclosure inappropriate? One instance is divulging personal information to almost anyone, regardless of the nature of your relationship. Perhaps you have been on the receiving end of this mistake. If so, you probably recall how awkward you felt when someone you barely knew revealed his or her innermost secrets. Although we find our own personal business of great significance, it's important to remember that not everyone else is always interested in it.

Self-disclosure is also inappropriate when we share private information with the wrong person. Here the mistake lies in opening up to someone who isn't interested in your concerns or who betrays your confidence. And it is always inappropriate to talk about private information in a place where you can be overheard by others you would rather *didn't* know the intimate details of your life.

Who Reveals What to Whom, When, and under What Circumstances?

As we have seen, it is important to engage in self-disclosure in ways that work to your benefit, not to your detriment. Before considering guidelines for appropriate self-disclosure, let's look at research findings on who tends to reveal what to whom, when, and under what circumstances.

Who? Some people are more open and willing to engage in self-disclosure than others. However, this inclination to be open to others does not appear to be closely related to other personality traits. Research that has attempted to relate self-disclosure tendencies to personality factors has generally yielded weak and inconsistent results. These findings suggest that situational factors must also be taken into account (Archer, 1979; Miller, 1990).

There are some gender differences in self-disclosure, but they, too, depend on the situation. In general, it has been found that females tend to be more openly self-disclosing than males (Cohn & Strassberg, 1983; Cozby, 1973; Gerdes, Gehling, & Rapp, 1981). This disparity is typically attributed to differences in gender-role socialization. In our culture, most men are taught to be unexpressive, particularly about tender emotions and feelings of vulnerability. Hence, it comes as no surprise that females disclose more about personal information and feelings, whereas males disclose more impersonal information (Rubin, Peplau, & Hill, 1981). When disclosing emotions, females talk more often about negative feelings, while males more often disclose feelings that are positive or neutral in tone (Rubin, et al., 1981). Here, we might point out that there is an inverse relationship between disclosure and power. To the extent that men have more power in a relationship, they need not disclose as much personal information (Henley & Freeman, 1981).

Both males and females are more likely to share personal information with females than with males (Derlega, Winstead, Wong, & Hunter, 1985). Because females have been socialized to share personal information with one another, they are likely to do so. Males, however, are not encouraged to have close relationships with other men. Particularly men who hold traditional gender-role attitudes often interpret disclosure of personal information as a sign of weakness and effeminacy. Therefore, males often withhold personal self-disclosures from one another for fear of appearing effeminate (Lombardo & Lavine, 1981).

In *some* situations, however, men may be more prone to self-disclosure than women. For example, in dealing with strangers (as opposed to friends), men tend to be more self-disclosing than women (Rosenfeld, Civikly, & Herron, 1979; Rubin, 1974). Also, in the beginning stages of an other-sex relationship, men may disclose more than women (Derlega et al., 1985; Stokes, Childs, & Fuehrer, 1981). This finding is consistent with the traditional gender-role expectation that men should initiate relationships and women should encourage males to talk (Hill & Stull, 1987). Thus it appears to be an oversimplification to say that women are more open than men.

What? Obviously it is easier for us to be open about some topics than about others. We quickly give biographical information (where we live, our age, our education) but are understandably reluctant to divulge inner fears, such as insecurities about our work. Also, we are generally willing to reveal socially desirable things about ourselves, such as our membership in the Jaycees. In contrast, we tend to be reticent about socially undesirable things, such as our conviction for tax evasion (Altman & Taylor, 1983).

When? *Social penetration theory* focuses on how relationships develop and sometimes dissolve (Altman & Taylor, 1983; Taylor & Altman, 1987). This theory, developed by Irwin Altman and Dalmas Taylor, has contributed significantly to our understanding of the role of self-disclosure in relationship development. Among other things, it predicts that there are gradual changes in the breadth and depth of self-disclosure as relationships develop. That is, early in a relationship, disclosures are restricted to a narrow range of impersonal topics; as the relationship grows, however, the number of topics increases, as does our willingness to discuss more personal concerns. Research generally supports these predictions of social penetration theory, and also shows that we expand the range of topics we discuss with others before we increase the depth of our personal revelations (Altman, Vinsel, & Brown, 1981). Once we begin to share personal information with another person, the depth of our disclosures increases without much change in their breadth.

Not all relationships develop according to the principle of gradual self-disclosure. Many individuals seem to be capable quite early of distinguishing between those relationships they wish to remain relatively superficial and those they would like to become more intimate (Berg & Clark, 1986). And at least one study on friendship development has reported that the progression of relationships to more intimate levels is not so gradual as social penetration theory predicts (Hays, 1985). Obviously, then, there is variability in the timing of self-disclosure in relationship development. Nonetheless, because it entails less risk and stress, we suggest that gradual self-disclosure may be the optimal route to close relationships.

Two apparent exceptions to social penetration theory's prediction that self-disclosure proceeds gradually are what have been called the "stranger-on-the-train phenomenon" and "boom-and-bust encounters."

Many people report the experience of sitting next to a stranger while traveling, and pouring out the intimate details of their lives. This *stranger-on-the-train phenomenon* obviously contradicts the principle of gradual self-disclosure, so how does social penetration theory explain it? According to Altman and Taylor, we behave in this unusual manner only because we believe that we'll never see this person again, and therefore won't suffer the negative consequences that would usually result from intimate self-disclosure to a stranger. Because these circumstances are not typical of most relationships, Altman and Taylor feel that the phenomenon does not really contradict their theory.

Sometimes two people meet, feel very compatible, and proceed immediately to tell each other "everything" about themselves. The experience of love at first sight and some college roommate situations are two instances of what Altman and Taylor term *boom-and-bust encounters*. In these relationships, things are wonderful for awhile, but shortly they turn sour. The reason such a relationship inevitably fails is that too much has been disclosed too soon. That is, when people reveal intimate details about themselves, they usually discover that they have important differences that cause con-

Irwin Altman

Reprinted with special permission of North America Syndicate.

The Transparent Self

by Sidney M. Jourard (Van Nostrand Reinhold, 1971)

This is a classic humanistic manifesto extolling the importance and value of self-disclosure. Jourard argues convincingly that many of us are troubled by an inability to open up to others. He explains the roots of this problem and discusses how self-disclosure can promote psychological health.

Jourard was a rare animal—an authentic humanist who backed up his ideas with hard-nosed research. Although he was research-oriented, the book is skillfully written in everyday language. Jourard discourses eloquently on the key role played by self-disclosure in love, marriage, family, education, health care, and therapy.

Jourard was a pioneer researcher who worked in previously unexplored territory. Consequently, some of his ideas have turned out to be a bit oversimplified. Nonetheless, the book has some timeless advice about relationships and interpersonal communication.

> Now I think unhealthy personality has a similar root cause, one which is related to Selye's concept of stress. Every maladjusted person is a person who has not made himself known to another human being and in consequence does not know himself. Nor can he be himself. More than that, he struggles actively to avoid becoming known by another human being. He works at it ceaselessly, twenty-four hours daily, and it is work! In the effort to avoid becoming known, a person provides for himself a cancerous kind of stress which is subtle and unrecognized, but nonetheless effective in producing not only the assorted patterns of unhealthy personality which psychiatry talks about, but also the wide array of physical ills that have come to be recognized as the province of psychosomatic medicine. [pp. 32–33]

flicts. Because they haven't had time to develop trust, they're unable to deal constructively with their differences, and so the relationship ends.

To whom? A critical factor in self-disclosure is the target person who will receive the information. As we mentioned earlier, people usually are more likely to disclose personal information to women than to men. However, this trend is moderated by situational variables (Hill & Stull, 1987) such as the exact nature of the topic (Cunningham, 1981). As you might expect, we tend to disclose more to people we like and to people we know relatively well (Derlega, Winstead, Wong, & Greenspan, 1987). The social status of the target person is also important (Slobin, Miller, & Porter, 1968). Self-disclosure is most common when people are of similar status. When there is a status discrepancy, we are more likely to reveal ourselves to people of higher status than to people of subordinate status.

As individuals move from adolescence toward adulthood, they tend to disclose less to their parents and same-sex friends and more to their other-sex friends. Sidney Jourard (1971) has found that we usually disclose more to a spouse or partner than to anyone else. In accord with the predictions of social penetration theory, partners who engage in a good deal of self-disclosure report relatively high levels of satisfaction in their relationships (Hansen & Schuldt, 1984; Hendrick, 1981; Rubin, Hill, Peplau, & Dunkel-Schetter, 1980). On the other hand, it has also been suggested that *equity* in self-disclosure, rather than high self-disclosure, may be the critical factor that helps couples avoid stress (Bowers, Metts, & Duncanson, 1985).

Some people are particularly skilled at getting others to open up and engage in self-disclosure. Sociability, self-esteem, empathy, and lack of shyness are associated with this ability to elicit self-disclosure from others (Miller, Berg, & Archer, 1983).

Under what circumstances? If you want to tell someone that you want to discontinue a relationship, you will normally wait for the appropriate time and place. You don't reveal this kind of information at the ballpark, as you wait in line to register for classes, or as you're casually walking out the door. Thus there are appropriate situations for certain kinds of self-disclosure. Generally we value privacy when we want to engage in significant self-disclosure.

Though it is clear that the setting or circumstance has an enormous impact on self-disclosure, this issue has not been addressed adequately in self-disclosure research (Chelune, 1979). However, there is one situational variable that we know figures prominently in self-disclosure: *reciprocity*. Several studies have shown that *we disclose more when people reciprocate by making disclosures to us*. Typically, we return a disclosure of approximately the same intimacy as the one revealed to us (Archer, 1980; Cunningham, Strassberg, & Haan, 1986). Thus, in a cyclical manner, self-disclosure breeds more self-disclosure.

The reciprocity norm governing self-disclosure appears to be most influential in the early stages of a relationship (Cunningham et al., 1986; Taylor & Altman, 1987). Hence, unless special circumstances are operating, you can usually assume that if you engage in appropriate self-disclosure with a person to whom you'd like to feel closer, your listener will reciprocate. Awareness of this tendency may alleviate some of your anxiety about opening up to others you do not know well.

Once a relationship is well established, reciprocity in self-disclosure seems to taper off (Derlega, Wilson, & Chaikin, 1976; Taylor & Altman, 1987). Instead of reciprocating to a personal revelation by a close friend or lover, we frequently respond with statements of sympathy and understanding. This movement away from equal exchanges of self-disclosure appears to be based on needs that emerge as intimate relationships develop: (1) the need for support from those we feel close to and (2) the need to maintain privacy in close relationships (Altman et al., 1981). Reciprocating support with friends and lovers, then, enables us to strengthen our relationships at the same time that it allows us to maintain a sense of privacy. In fact, the ability to balance the needs for self-disclosure and privacy seems to be an important factor in maintaining satisfying close relationships (Baxter, 1988).

Altman and Taylor use the term "*depenetration*" to describe the dynamics of relationships that are moving toward dissolution. Although little research has been done on the topic, self-disclosure seems to change when relationships are in distress. One or both individuals may decrease the breadth and depth of their self-disclosures, indicating that they are emotionally withdrawing (Baxter, 1988). Another study of troubled relationships found that the breadth of self-disclosure decreased but the depth increased because of the rise in the number of *negative* personal statements expressed (Tolstedt & Stokes, 1984).

When Is Self-Disclosure Appropriate?

To disclose or not to disclose—that is the question. By now you should be able to appreciate the complexity of this question. The crucial issue concerning self-disclosure is: When is it appropriate?

The answer is both simple and complex. We'll give you the simple part first. *Self-disclosure is appropriate when your listener is sincerely interested and willing to hear what you have to say.* But how do you know whether your target person is interested? This is where the answer gets complex. When you are trying to avoid inappropriate self-disclosure, it helps to go slowly and pay close attention to the other person's reaction. It's something like testing the water to see whether it's warm enough. Instead of jumping in all at once, you tentatively stick in a toe.

In assessing the other person's reaction, you need to pay close attention to both verbal and nonverbal cues. The positive verbal signs to listen for are empathy and reciprocity. If the

other person reciprocates with self-disclosure, this generally indicates a willingness to proceed to a more intimate level of communication. Of course, some people who aren't very comfortable engaging in self-disclosure themselves are sincerely willing to listen to you anyway. Hence you cannot depend on reciprocity alone as an indicator of the other person's interest.

This is why tuning in to nonverbal signals is of crucial importance. When people are uncomfortable with your self-disclosure, they usually try to send you a nonverbal message to that effect, to avoid embarrassing you with a more obvious verbal warning. Often they will deliver this "stop" message by reducing eye contact and by displaying a puzzled, apprehensive, or pained facial expression. If seated, the other person may angle his or her body away from you; if the person is standing, he or she may increase the distance between you or shuffle his or her feet impatiently. In contrast, if your target person faces you squarely, leans forward, appears relaxed, and maintains good eye contact, you can be fairly certain that he or she is willing to listen to your self-disclosure.

Interestingly, it has been suggested that there is a curvilinear relationship between self-disclosure and psychological adjustment (Archer, 1980; Derlega & Chaikin, 1975; Jourard, 1971). As Figure 6.8 shows, either too little or too much self-disclosure may be associated with relatively poor adjustment. That is, an inability to be open is unhealthy, but so is overdisclosure. According to this theory, a well-adjusted person engages in discriminating self-disclosure, revealing the appropriate thing to the appropriate person at the appropriate time. Of course, while self-disclosure and mental health are probably related, it would be a mistake to conclude that too much or too little self-disclosure causes poor adjustment or vice versa. More studies are needed to clarify the relationship between the two factors and to identify specific factors that mediate the relationship between self-disclosure and mental health—social skills, social anxiety, and the like.

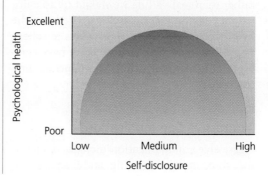

**FIGURE 6.8
Self-disclosure and psychological health**
According to Derlega and Chaikin (1975), both too much and too little self-disclosure are unhealthy. A moderate amount of disclosure appears to be optimal.

Maladaptive Communication and Interpersonal Conflict

Up to now, we've considered verbal and nonverbal communication separately. From now on, we'll use the term communication to mean both types of messages. In this section we'll discuss some common communication habits that can contribute to interpersonal conflict.

Barriers to Effective Communication

A *communication barrier* is anything in the communication process that inhibits or blocks the accurate transmission and reception of messages. Barriers to effective communication can reside in the source, in the receiver, and sometimes in both. Common barriers to effective communication include defensiveness, aggressive communication, submissive communication, motivational distortion, self-preoccupation, game playing, and collusion.

Defensiveness

Perhaps the most basic barrier to effective communication is *defensiveness*—an excessive concern with protecting oneself from being hurt. We're prone to react defensively when we feel threatened. We tend to get defensive when we feel that others are going to evaluate us or when we believe that they are trying to control or manipulate us. Defensiveness is also easily elicited when others attempt to communicate their superiority over us. Thus people who overemphasize their status, wealth, brilliance, or power often put us on the defensive. Dogmatic people who convey "I'm always right" also tend to breed defensiveness.

It's important to note that a threat will elicit defensive behavior even if it is imagined rather than real. While we should try to cultivate a communication style that reduces the likelihood of arousing defensiveness in others, we need to remember that we don't have complete control over others' perceptions and reactions.

Aggressive Communication

Aggressive communication includes dominating, threatening, ridiculing, and blaming others. Criticizing another person can also be aggressive when it's done without thought for the target person's feelings. Other forms of aggressive communication include deliberately annoying and provoking others to get a rise out of them and constantly competing with others.

Sharon Anthony Bower and Gordon Bower (1991) have found that people whose behavior is aggressive often get their way, but they usually pay a high price for it. That is, such behavior typically produces feelings of fear, hurt, and anger in others and promotes mistrust, resentment, and attempts to get back at the instigator. Aggressive communication also often produces defensiveness in others, as we have seen.

Many people resort to aggressive communication because they are afraid they won't get what they want any other way; others do so because they haven't learned more effective ways to communicate.

Submissive Communication

The opposite of aggressive communication is submissive or passive communication—habitual giving in to others on points of possible disagreement. When the issue under discussion really doesn't matter much to us, there isn't any harm in going along with someone else. Also, from time to time, many people step back from difficult interactions to keep conflict from escalating. Passive communication typically becomes a problem only when we engage in it frequently—when we often find ourselves unable to say no. People whose communication is habitually submissive find that others often take advantage of them. The college student who can't tell her roommate not to borrow her clothes is in this predicament.

Many people who use this style do so because they fear others won't like them if they don't always do what others want. Ironically, such behavior often generates contempt. Moreover, individuals who use a submissive communication style often feel bad about themselves (for being pushovers) and resentful of those whom they allow to take advantage of them. These feelings often lead the submissive individual to try to punish the other person by withdrawing, sulking, or crying (Bower & Bower, 1991). These manipulative attempts to get one's own way are sometimes referred to as "passive aggression" or "indirect aggression."

Motivational Distortion

In Chapter 5, we discussed at length how wishes, needs, and expectations can distort person perception. The same process commonly takes place in communication. That is, we often hear what we want to hear instead of what is actually being said.

Each of us has a unique frame of reference—certain attitudes, values, and expectations—that can influence what we hear. We also tend to experience emotional discomfort when we hear information that contradicts our views. One way of avoiding these unpleasant feelings is to engage in *selective attention*. That is, we actively choose to attend to information that supports our beliefs and to ignore information that contradicts them. Similarly, we may read meanings into statements that are not intended, and we may jump to erroneous conclusions. This tendency to distort information occurs most often in discussions of issues that we feel strongly about. Certain issues (politics, racism, sexism, abortion) are often highly charged for both the source and the receiver. Misperceptions are especially likely to occur in these situations and to interfere with effective communication.

Self-Preoccupation

We have all had the experience of trying to communicate with someone who is so self-focused as to make enjoyable two-way conversation impossible. Such people seem to talk for the sake of hearing themselves talk. Further, they rarely listen attentively. When another person is talking, they're wrapped up in rehearsing what they're going to say when they get a chance. These self-preoccupied people show little awareness of the negative effects they have on their listeners.

People who are self-preoccupied can cause negative reactions in others for several reasons. First, the content of their remarks is usually so self-serving (seeking to impress, to gain unwarranted sympathy, and so on) that others find it offensive. Another problem is that these people consistently take up more than their fair share of conversation time. Some individuals do

both—that is, they talk only about themselves *and* they do so at great length. After a "conversation" with someone like this, we typically feel that our need to communicate has been ignored. Usually we try to avoid these people if we can. If we cannot avoid them, we tend to respond only minimally in an effort to end the conversation as quickly as possible. Needless to say, people who fail to respect the social norm that conversations entail a mutual sharing of information risk alienating others.

Game Playing

Game playing is another barrier to effective communication. Game playing was first described by Eric Berne (1964), who originated transactional analysis. **Transactional analysis is a broad theory of personality and interpersonal relations that emphasizes patterns of communication.** In Berne's scheme, *games* are **manipulative interactions that progress toward a predictable outcome, in which people conceal their real motivations.** In the broadest sense, game playing can include the deliberate (or sometimes unintentional) use of ambiguous, indirect, or deceptive statements. Some game playing involves verbal fencing to avoid having to make one's meaning or intent clear. Particularly problematic are repetitive games that result in bad feelings and erode the trust and respect that are essential to good relationships. Games interfere with effective communication and are a destructive element in relationships. (A more detailed discussion of games in intimate relationships is found in the Chapter 9 Application.)

Collusion

In contrast to the other barriers to effective communication, collusion requires at least two willing partners. These partners are usually involved in an intimate relationship. **Two people who engage in *collusion* have an unspoken agreement to deny some problematic aspect of**

reality in order to sustain their relationship. To accomplish this mutual denial, both suppress all discussion of the problem area. The classic colluders are the partners in an alcoholic relationship. The alcoholic requires the partner to join him or her in denying the existence of a drinking problem. To maintain the relationship, the partner goes along with the tacit agreement. The two people go to great lengths to avoid any comment about alcohol-related difficulties. Over time, the drinking usually gets worse and the relationship often deteriorates, thereby making it more difficult for the partner to continue the collusion. Since it is based on a mutual agreement to deny a specific aspect of reality, collusion obviously prevents effective communication.

Miscommunication and Date Rape

Although date rape involves more than just communication gone awry, poor communication is a key factor in it surprisingly often. We have chosen to discuss this subject here rather than in our chapter on sexuality, because the evidence indicates that rape is *not* really a sexual act but rather an expression of power and aggression. Sex is the means by which the rapist expresses power and hostility, not attraction and passion. Because the vast majority of rapes are committed by men, our discussion will center on women as the victims of rape. While rape is typically discussed in a heterosexual context, it also occurs among homosexuals, although little if any research exists on the topic (Lobel, 1986; Rozee, Bateman, & Gilmore, 1991).

Mary Koss

Types of Rape

Acquaintance rape occurs when a woman is forced to have unwanted intercourse with someone she knows. Acquaintance rape includes not only rapes committed on dates but also those committed by nonromantic acquaintances ("friends," co-workers, neighbors, relatives). *Date rape is a more restrictive term that refers to forced and unwanted intercourse with someone in the context of dating.* Date rape has been receiving increased attention recently, both by researchers and by the media.

Date rape can occur on a first date, with someone you've dated for awhile, or with someone to whom you're engaged. Many people confuse date rape with seduction. A woman is seduced when she is persuaded *and agrees* to have sex. Date rape often follows an attempt at seduction that has failed.

The force involved in date rape typically takes the form of verbal or physical coercion, but it may sometimes involve the use of a weapon. One study of 190 male undergraduates at a southern university found that the following tactics were used: verbal persuasion (70%), ignoring a woman's protests (35%), physical restraint (11%), threats of physical aggression (3%), and physical aggression (3%) (Rapaport & Burkhart, 1982).

One form of rape specific to college campuses is *campus gang rape*. The following scenario played out at a small eastern liberal arts college, is one of about 50 that have been documented by the Project on the Status and Education of Women of the Association of American Colleges (Ehrhart & Sandler, 1985):

> It was her first fraternity party. The beer flowed freely and she had much more to drink than she had planned. It was hot and crowded and the party spread out all over the house, so that when three men asked her to go upstairs, she went with them. They took her into a bedroom, locked the door and began to undress her. Groggy with alcohol, her feeble protests were ignored as the three men raped her. When they finished, they put her in the hallway, naked, locking her clothes in the bedroom. [p.1]

Of the campus gang rapes studied by these authors, about 70% occurred at fraternity parties and an additional 20% included athletes. Some occurred in residence halls. One factor that distinguishes gang rape from other forms of rape is peer pressure. That is, one man may initiate the rape, and others go along with it for fear of being seen as sexually inadequate. Because male peers play an important role in confirming each other's sexual competence (Gagnon & Simon, 1973; Miller & Simon, 1974), sex is often a vehicle by which males confirm their social status with other males—with tragic consequences for females.

Incidence of Rape

It is difficult to obtain accurate information about the prevalence of any form of rape (it is estimated that 90% of all rapes are never reported). Experts estimate that approximately 25% of women in the United States will be victims of rape or attempted rape by the time they are in their mid 20s (Parrot & Bechhofer, 1991) and that as many as 50% of American women have been or will be raped or will experience an attempted rape in their lifetime (Mahoney, Shively, & Traw, 1986; Muehlenhard & Linton, 1987). It does appear that the problem of rape is growing (U.S. Bureau of the

Census, 1991), although it is unclear whether the increase is in the number of rapes committed or in the number reported. Contrary to popular belief, only a minority of reported rapes are committed by strangers: 20%, or 1 out of 5. The majority of rape victims are between the ages of 15 and 25.

How common is rape among college students? In a widely cited study, Mary Koss and her colleagues surveyed approximately 7,000 students at 32 colleges about their sexual experiences since age 14 (Koss, Gidycz, & Wisniewski, 1987). They found that 15% of the women had been victims of actual rape and that another 12% had experienced attempted rape. Moreover, 8% of the men admitted either to having forced a woman to have intercourse or to having tried to do so. Yet *none* of these men identified himself as a rapist. Similarly, among the women who reported experiencing sexual aggression that met the legal definition of rape, only 27% actually labeled their own experience "rape."

These findings suggest that there is a lot of confusion and self-deception about what constitutes rape. It seems that many people believe that if a stranger leaps out of the bushes and sexually attacks you, it's rape, but if someone you know coerces you into having sex, it isn't. In fact, of the women in the college survey who reported experiences that met the legal definition of rape, only 11% had been raped by strangers. The vast majority had been raped by someone they knew: 30% by steady dates, 25% by nonromantic acquaintances, and 9% by husbands or other family members. Because of the widespread reluctance to see acquaintance rape for what it is, Koss (1985) has called it a "hidden crime." Its hidden nature allows men to deny their responsibility and causes women who have been raped to question and doubt themselves. These patterns of thinking also encourage "blaming the victim."

Consequences of Rape

All rape is traumatic, but it is particularly shattering when a woman is raped by someone she has liked and trusted. In addition, because most women are not used to the idea that they can be raped by someone they know, it is particularly difficult for a victim of date or acquaintance rape to deal with her feelings of betrayal, rage, and shame (Katz, 1991). (A helpful book for survivors of date and acquaintance rape, *Coping with Date Rape and Acquaintance Rape,* is described in the recommended reading on this page.) Though not all women are affected by

rape in precisely the same way, most rape survivors go through three stages: trauma, denial, and resolution.

• *Trauma.* Many women experience a variety of emotional reactions to rape. Chief among them are fear of being alone, fear of men, fear of retaliation (especially if charges are filed), and fear of trusting subsequent dating partners. Feelings of depression, anger, helplessness, guilt, pain, shame, and anxiety are also common. Many rape victims show signs of stress-related physical problems. Emotional reactions can be exacerbated if the woman's family and friends are not supportive—particularly if they blame her for the attack. As we saw in Chapter 5, it is common for people to blame victims of calamities (defensive attribution).

- *Denial.* In this stage—which may last for months or years—rape victims try to put the trauma behind them and get on with life. During this period, women avoid talking about their rape as they try to deny that it took place. This strategy generally fails as a long-term solution because the powerful and painful emotions don't just go away.

- *Resolution.* In order to move beyond the experience, a woman needs to deal with her feelings by talking with someone who is supportive and understanding: a friend, a counselor, or a member of the clergy. Once she has worked through her feelings and fears, she may be able to put the trauma in the past and begin to feel in control of her life again. Still, it is likely that she will always be haunted by the experience.

There are other consequences of rape, some affecting both the man and the woman. It is not uncommon, for example, for women to drop out of school because of the trauma and lack of social support. Also, the grades of the man and woman may suffer because of emotional distress and inability to concentrate on their studies. Moreover, if the rape survivor prosecutes her attacker, the man faces criminal proceedings. If he is a student, he may be suspended from school whether or not the woman takes the case to court. And both may have to deal with negative publicity and social stigma.

Factors That Contribute to Date Rape

The phenomenon of date rape can be traced to a variety of underlying factors. Communication problems are often critical, but before we focus on them, let's briefly examine other contributing factors.

- *The double standard.* Traditional norms of courtship suggest that men should initiate dates and sex, while women either consent or decline their advances. Society still encourages a double standard for men and women when it comes to sexual behavior. Men are encouraged to have sexual feelings, to act on them, and to "score," whereas women are made to feel that sexual activity is never justified unless they are "carried away" by passion. The double standard promotes hidden norms that condone sexual aggression by men in dating relationships.

- *Changing sexual values.* A variety of social trends have made sexual activity in the context of dating more common than it once was (see Chapter 13). Because sexual values are still in transition, however, we lack widely accepted standards about how people should behave. Until the mid-1960s, campus curfews and other restrictions functioned to control and structure college students' social and sexual behavior. For better or for worse, those controls no longer exist. Today's students are left to make their own rules without much guidance.

- *Alcohol and drugs.* Drinking heavily or taking drugs on dates makes it likely that a person's judgment will be impaired. In these circumstances, both men and women are likely to lose their inhibitions. Unfortunately, alcohol and drugs make some men more willing to use force and women more vulnerable to the use of force. A woman who passes out, for example, is easy prey for anyone who is willing to take advantage of her.

- *Sexual violence in the media.* Laboratory research on the effects of aggressive pornography (depicting rape and other sexual violence against women) suggests that such material elevates some men's tendency to behave aggressively toward women (Malamuth & Donnerstein, 1982). Related research has shown that exposure to such material can increase male viewers' willingness to say that they would commit a rape, while decreasing their sensitivity to rape and the plight of its victims (Donnerstein & Linz, 1984). Furthermore, men who have viewed sexually violent films report greater acceptance of rape myths as well as greater acceptance of interpersonal violence against women (Malamuth & Check, 1981). In Figure 6.9 we show selected items from two scales often used to measure sexual aggression. Because aggressive pornography is being displayed more frequently in films and on television, it is rea-

FIGURE 6.9
Assessing attitudes toward sex and aggression
Researchers use carefully constructed scales to assess individuals' attitudes toward sex and aggression. Sample items from two such scales are shown here. (Adapted from Burt, 1980.)

Measuring Attitudes toward Sexual Aggression

Rape Myth Acceptance Scale	Acceptance of Interpersonal Violence Scale
1 When women go around braless or wearing short skirts and tight tops, they are just asking for trouble.	**1** Being roughed up sexually is stimulating to many women.
2 If a girl engages in necking or petting and she lets things get out of hand, it is her own fault if her partner forces sex on her.	**2** Sometimes the only way a man can get a cold woman turned on is to use force.
3 Many women have an unconscious wish to be raped, and may then unconsciously set up a situation in which they are likely to be attacked.	**3** A man is never justified in hitting his wife.
SCORING: People who score high on this scale agree with all of the above items	SCORING: People who score high on this scale agree with items 1 and 2 and disagree with item 3.

sonable to speculate that media depictions are contributing to an increase in rape.

The Role of Communication in Date Rape

Miscommunication between dating partners often is a key factor in date rape. Among dating couples, frank conversations about whether to engage in sexual activities, which behaviors are permissible, and what to do about birth control are, regrettably, the exception rather than the rule (Knox & Wilson, 1981). For one thing, most people (and young people especially) are embarrassed to talk about sex. For another, many feel that talking about sex takes the mystery out of it. Also, many women apparently tell themselves that they'll wait until the occasion arises and then "decide" what to do. Such an approach places women in a position in which they are easily influenced by men and by situational forces.

Another problem is that dating partners often misunderstand what the other means. Research shows that men are more likely than women to perceive friendly behavior as having sexual intent (Muehlenhard, 1988; Shotland, 1989). Thus a man can think a woman has communicated sexual interest (and act accordingly) when in fact she has not. If a man makes no effort to clarify a woman's intentions, he can easily let himself feel that he has been led on. He may then use his anger as an excuse to force himself on the woman. And some men still think that if they spend money on a woman, she owes them sex.

Misunderstandings also occur in dating relationships because social norms encourage game playing—manipulative interactions in which people conceal their true feelings. Thus dating partners may not say what they mean or mean what they say. It is true that some women say no (in words or in nonverbal behavior) to sexual activity when they actually mean maybe or yes, but such behavior is much less common than men think it is. Studies that have surveyed the extent of token resistance among college women report that only about a third of them have ever engaged in this behavior and most of them have done so infrequently (Muehlenhard & Hollabaugh, 1988). Nonetheless, television programs and films (mainstream and pornographic) frequently portray women as engaging in token resistance. Hence men sometimes are genuinely confused about what a woman really means. A majority of men who responded to a survey on sexual coercion and aggression believed that when their dating partners said

no to sex, they really meant yes (Sandberg, Jackson, & Petretic-Jackson, 1987).

The double standard presents women with an avoidance-avoidance conflict. That is, if they openly acknowledge their interest in sex (don't use token resistance), they risk being perceived as "easy" by men who believe in the double standard. But if women use token resistance as a tactic for coping with their dates' standards, they also put themselves at risk because token resistance sets the stage for miscommunication—and sometimes for tragedy (Muehlenhard & McCoy, 1991).

Reducing the Incidence of Date Rape

What can be done to reduce the incidence of date rape? We offer the following suggestions to people in dating relationships. (1) Recognize date rape for what it is: an act of aggression. (2) Think through your feelings, values, and intentions about sexual relations *before* the question of having sex arises. (3) Work on communicating your feelings and expectations about sex by engaging in appropriate self-disclosure. (4) Listen carefully to each other and respect each other's wishes. (5) Beware of excessive alcohol and drug use, which may deprive you of control. (6) Exercise control over your environment: agree to go only to *public* places (not apartments) until you know someone very well, and always carry enough money for transportation back home. (7) Know the warning signs that are associated with pre-rape behavior (see Figure 6.10) and be cautious in dating those who exhibit more than one of them. (8) Be prepared to act *aggressively* if assertive refusals don't stop unwanted advances.

Many of these suggestions involve efforts to improve interpersonal communication. Obviously, improved communication will not eliminate date rape, but it can go a long way toward reducing the problem.

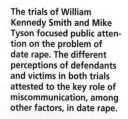

The trials of William Kennedy Smith and Mike Tyson focused public attention on the problem of date rape. The different perceptions of defendants and victims in both trials attested to the key role of miscommunication, among other factors, in date rape.

FIGURE 6.10
Date and acquaintance rape: Warning signs
According to Rozee et al. (1991), four factors appear to distinguish date rapists: feelings of sexual entitlement, a penchant for exerting power and control, high hostility and anger, and acceptance of interpersonal violence. The presence of more than one of these characteristics is an important warning sign (Malamuth, 1986). When sexual entitlement is coupled with any other factor, special heed should be taken.

Typical Characteristics of Date Rapists

Sexual entitlement	Power and control	Hostility and anger	Acceptance of interpersonal violence
Touching women with no regard for their wishes	Interrupting people, especially women	Showing quick temper	Using threats in displays of anger
Sexualizing relationships that are appropriately not sexual	Being a bad loser	Blaming others when things go wrong	Using violence in borderline situations
Engaging in conversation that is inappropriately intimate	Exhibiting inappropriate competitiveness	Tending to transform other emotions into anger	Approving observed violence
Telling sexual jokes at inappropriate times or places	Using intimidating body language		Justifying violence
Making inappropriate comments about women's bodies, sexuality, and so on	Game playing		

Toward More Effective Communication

Communication is effective when the message we intend to convey is the message that is actually received. Therefore, it entails both the accurate transmission of a message and the accurate reception of a message. To communicate effectively, we must be good at both functions. We can also enhance communication by creating a positive interpersonal climate.

Creating a Positive Interpersonal Climate

An interpersonal climate is positive when people feel that they can be open rather than guarded or defensive in their communication. You can go a long way toward creating such a climate by putting the following suggestions into practice.

• *Learn to feel and communicate empathy.* **Empathy involves adopting another's frame of reference so you can understand his or her point of view.** When you empathize with others, you genuinely appreciate their feelings and understand their problems. Empathy includes sensitivity to others' needs and acceptance of their feelings. To clarify the meaning of empathy, it may be helpful to make a distinction between a person and his or her behavior. Being accepting and understanding toward a person does *not* necessarily mean that you must also condone or endorse the individual's behavior. What if your roommate confides in you that he is worried about his drinking? In discussing the issue with him, you can come to understand the reasons for his excessive drinking without condoning this behavior. You can communicate your support for him by continuing to be his friend—without encouraging him to continue drinking.

• *Practice withholding judgment.* You can promote an open climate for communication by trying to be nonjudgmental. This doesn't mean that you give up your right to have opinions and make judgments. It merely means that you should strive to interact with people in ways that don't put them on the spot (forced to offer an opinion when they would rather not) or make them feel put down (or inadequate).

• *Strive for honesty.* Mutual trust and respect thrive on authenticity and honesty. So-called hidden agendas often don't stay hidden very long. Even if others don't know exactly what your underlying motives are, they often can sense that you're not being entirely honest. Of course, striving for honesty does not mean that we are bound to communicate everything we feel at any time to any person. Though it is true that some interactions necessarily involve pain—for example, breaking up with a girlfriend or boyfriend—we can avoid many unpleasant interactions by being truthful without being needlessly hurtful.

• *Approach others as equals.* You may know from personal experience that most of us don't like to be reminded of another's higher status or greater ability. You can improve the effectiveness of your communication if you try to disregard status differences in your conversations. Especially when you have the higher status, it is better to approach people on equal terms.

• *Express your opinions tentatively.* Rather than give the impression that you know all the answers, strive to communicate that your beliefs and attitudes are flexible and subject to revision. You can convey this message by using qualifying words or phrases. For instance, instead of saying, "This is how we should do it," you might say, "There seem to be several possible approaches; the one that seems the best to me is . . . What do you think?"

Guidelines for Effective Speaking

Speaking effectively requires skills that are developed over a lifetime. We are realistic enough to know that a few paragraphs of advice won't produce dramatic changes in your speaking skills. Nonetheless, observing a few general guidelines can enhance the effectiveness of your communication. If you want more detailed information on this topic, we suggest that you consult Verderber and Verderber (1989), an excellent communications text.

• *Consider the frame of reference of your listener or listeners.* In most situations, you are likely to have some knowledge about your listeners. It is a good idea to consider their background, intelligence, attitudes, and so forth, so that you can put your message in terms that they can understand. In particular, try to avoid talking over the heads of your audience, and avoid jargon or special terminology that is foreign to them. Also, try to illustrate your ideas with examples that your listeners can relate to from their own experience.

• *Use an assertive communication style.* In our earlier discussion of barriers to effective communication, we mentioned assertive communication as an effective alternative to aggressive and submissive communication. When you communicate assertively, you express your thoughts and feelings directly and honestly (Alberti & Emmons, 1990). Essentially, to be assertive is to stand up for your rights when someone else is about to infringe on them. Aggressive communication sends the message "I count; you don't"; submissive communication conveys the idea "You count; I don't"; assertiveness communicates "We both count." For a more detailed discussion of assertive communication, see the Application at the end of this chapter.

• *Be specific and concrete.* Effective communication is hampered when you speak in vague generalities. If you don't communicate your ideas clearly, you usually leave listeners confused and frustrated. And don't confuse lengthy talk with clear communication. You can speak for a long time without saying anything. Unless you're a politician, this is not something you want to do.

• *Avoid loaded words.* Certain words are loaded in the sense that they tend to trigger

negative emotional reactions in listeners. In the interests of effective speech, it is usually best to avoid using words that are unnecessarily derogatory. You can discuss politics, for example, without using such terms as "rock-ribbed reactionary" and "knee-jerk liberal." Similarly, such labels as "male chauvinist pig" and "women's libber" need not come up in discussions of gender roles. You can remind children of chores left undone without calling them lazy. You can ask a sales clerk to correct an error without referring to it as a stupid mistake. And you can disagree with people who are older or younger than you without calling them senile or immature.

• *Make your verbal and nonverbal messages congruent.* Now that you are aware of the great amount of information that is transmitted at the nonverbal level, you can appreciate the importance of consistency in your verbal and nonverbal messages. Inconsistency between the verbal and nonverbal channels can generate confusion and mistrust in your listeners. The relative spontaneity of nonverbal communica-

Messages: The Communication Book

by Matthew McKay, Martha Davis, and Patrick Fanning (New Harbinger Publications, 1983)

In this short book, you will find a wealth of useful information that will help you improve your communication skills in a wide variety of situations. It is organized according to six types of communication skills: basic, advanced, conflict, social, family, and public. Within each of these sections, chapters address important issues. The section on family skills, for example, includes chapters on sexual communication, parent effectiveness, and family communications; the section on public skills addresses communication in small groups and public speaking. As you can tell from the excerpt below, the authors have a breezy style and offer many examples to illustrate their points. Here they address one of several hidden agendas that are commonly encountered in conversations:

I'm Helpless, I Suffer

This is the agenda of the victim. The stories focus on misfortune, injustice, abuse. The stories are about someone who's stuck, who tries but can't escape, who endures without hope of remedy. The person is implicitly saying, "Don't ask me to do anything about all this pain, I'm not responsible."

A classic *I'm Helpless, I Suffer* game is *Why Does This Always Happen to Me?* One man, who'd gotten a little break from his ulcer symptoms, complained of a reoccurrence after he got stuck in traffic without his antacids. "This always happens. I feel a little better and then some crazy thing comes up to set me back. Somebody puts pepper on my salad or sales take a plunge at work. It never fails." The *I'm Helpless, I Suffer* agenda is ideal for avoiding scary new solutions, or for accepting pain that otherwise suggests the need for a major life decision. "I'm ugly, ill, too nervous" will often help put off the change indefinitely. [pp. 79–80]

tion does make it somewhat difficult to control. Nonetheless, you can work at becoming more aware of your nonverbal signals. Furthermore, if you strive for honesty in your verbal communications, you will lessen the likelihood of incongruence in the nonverbal channel.

Guidelines for Effective Listening

As we have stressed, effective listening is a vital component of effective communication. What do we mean by "effective listening"? We are simply referring to the ability to receive the message that the sender intends. Listening is a vastly underappreciated skill. This is unfortunate, because we spend far more time listening than we do speaking. To paraphrase an old saying, we have two ears and only one mouth, so we should listen twice as much as we speak.

Although you are not likely to experience a dramatic change in your speaking skills overnight, you *may* be able to improve your lis-

tening substantially in very little time. For one thing, most people probably are ineffective listeners because they are unaware of the elements of effective listening. Also, effective listening hinges largely on your attitude. If you're willing to work at it, you can become a good listener.

The key to effective listening is to devote active effort to the task. We tend to think of listening as something we do with our ears, but to do it right, you have to use what lies between your ears. As you'll see in the guidelines that follow, successful listening requires that you actively attend to and process incoming information.

• *Attend physically to the speaker.* The first step in active listening is to position yourself so that you can see and hear the speaker. Face the person squarely and maintain good eye contact. When you do so you are signaling your attentiveness to the speaker. In addition, if you adopt an "open" posture and lean forward, you will send a clear nonverbal message that you are interested in what the other person has to say (Egan, 1990).

• *Actively attend to and process the verbal message.* As we noted earlier, although we can process speech at up to about 600 words per minute, most people speak at a rate of only 100 to 140 words per minute (Adler & Towne, 1987). This rate of speech leaves extra time for the listener's attention to wander. The key to effective listening is to devote this extra time to the incoming stream of information rather than to irrelevant lines of thought. For example, you can review points already made, try to anticipate what the speaker will say next, and search for deeper meanings that may underlie the surface message (Huseman, Lahiff, & Hatfield, 1976).

• *Pay attention to nonverbal signals.* You already know that much of information transmission takes place in the nonverbal channel. As we have noted, when verbal and nonverbal messages conflict, people are more likely to rely on nonverbal cues. Furthermore, while we use verbal cues to get the objective meaning of a message, we depend on nonverbal cues for information about the emotional and interpersonal meanings of the message (Burgoon, 1987). Obviously, then, it is very important that you focus on nonverbal signals to achieve a full understanding of the message.

• *Check your understanding of the message.* One of the most useful listening habits you can develop is to check with the speaker from time to time to be sure that you have understood the message properly. The simplest way to do so is to ask a direct question to clarify a point: "Do you mean that . . . ?" Another way is to summarize briefly what has just been said and see whether the speaker offers any objections or clarifications: "Let's see, I believe I heard you say that . . . " If you think there was a deeper meaning underlying the words, a simple summary may not be sufficient. Instead, you may want to translate the ideas (including the underlying ones) into your own words to see whether the speaker agrees with your interpretation.

Sending clear messages and listening attentively are essential components of effective communication. Another important factor in this process is the ability to resolve interpersonal conflicts.

Dealing Constructively with Conflict

Conflict is an unavoidable feature of interpersonal interaction. Therefore, learning to deal constructively with it is an important aspect of effective communication. People do not have to be enemies to be in conflict, and being in conflict does not make people enemies. *Interpersonal conflict exists whenever two or more people disagree.* By this definition, conflict will occur between friends and lovers as well as between competitors and enemies. The discord may be caused by a simple misunderstanding or may be a product of incompatible goals, values, attitudes, or beliefs.

Many people have the impression that conflict is inherently bad and that it should be suppressed if at all possible. In reality, conflict is neither inherently bad nor inherently good. Conflict is a natural phenomenon that may lead to either good or bad outcomes, depending on how people deal with it. Avoidance tends to be one of the worst ways of coping with conflict. Interpersonal discord that is suppressed usually affects a relationship in spite of efforts to conceal it, and the effects of suppressing it tend to be negative (Baxter & Wilmot, 1985). When dealt with openly and constructively, interpersonal conflict can lead to a variety of valuable outcomes (Johnson & Johnson, 1991). Among other things, constructive confrontation may (1) bring problems out into the open where they can be solved, (2) put an end to chronic sources of discontent in a relationship, and (3) lead to new insights through the clashing of divergent views.

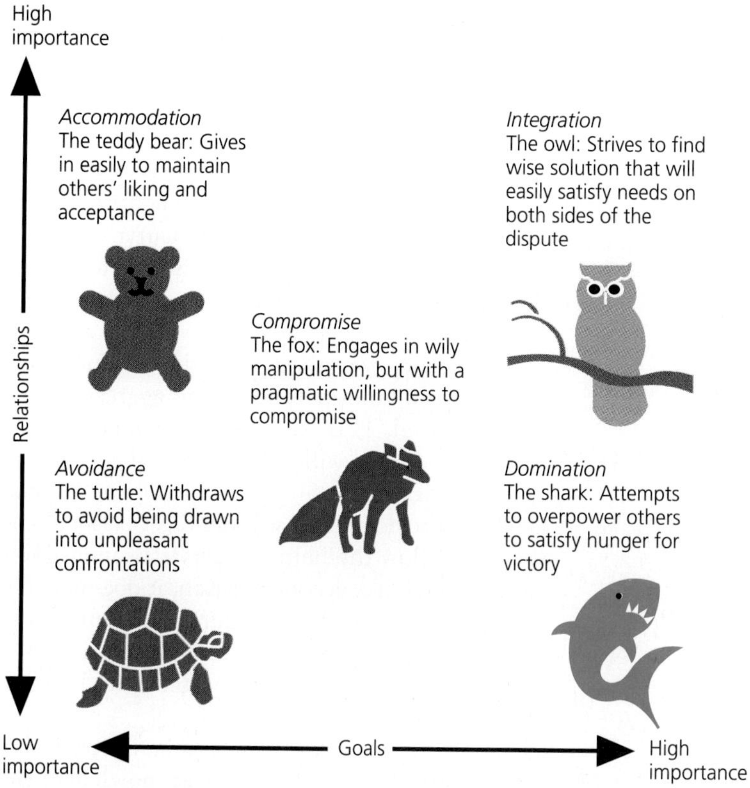

High importance

Relationships

Accommodation
The teddy bear: Gives in easily to maintain others' liking and acceptance

Integration
The owl: Strives to find wise solution that will easily satisfy needs on both sides of the dispute

Compromise
The fox: Engages in wily manipulation, but with a pragmatic willingness to compromise

Avoidance
The turtle: Withdraws to avoid being drawn into unpleasant confrontations

Domination
The shark: Attempts to overpower others to satisfy hunger for victory

Low importance — Goals — High importance

FIGURE 6.11
Johnson's (1981) characterization of the five styles of dealing with interpersonal conflict David Johnson has playfully used the stereotypic characteristics of five animals to capture the essence of the five basic styles of dealing with conflict.

Personal Styles of Dealing with Conflict

How do you react to conflict? Most people have a certain personal style in dealing with conflict (Sternberg & Soriano, 1984). The five modes of dealing with conflict illustrated in Figure 6.11—avoidance, accommodation, domination, compromise, and integration—are based on theoretical models pioneered by Blake and Mouton (1964) and Thomas (1976).

• *Avoidance.* Some people simply don't like to face up to the existence of conflict. They operate under the unrealistic hope that if they ignore the problem, it will go away. When a conflict emerges, the avoider will change the subject, make a hasty exit, or pretend to be preoccupied with something else. This person finds conflict extremely unpleasant and distasteful and will go to great lengths to avoid being drawn into a confrontation. Of course, most problems will not go away while you pretend they don't exist. This style generally just delays the inevitable clash. Avoidance is not an adequate means of dealing with conflict.

• *Accommodation.* Like the avoider, the accommodating person feels uncomfortable with conflict. Instead of ignoring the disagreement, however, this person brings the conflict to a quick end by giving in easily. This style grows out of basic feelings of insecurity. People who are overly worried about acceptance and approval are likely to use this strategy of surrender. Accommodation is a poor way of dealing with conflict because it does not generate creative thinking and genuine solutions. Moreover, feelings of resentment may develop (on both sides) because the accommodating person often likes to play the role of martyr.

• *Domination.* The dominator turns every conflict into a black-and-white, win-or-lose situation. This person will do virtually anything to emerge victorious from the confrontation. The dominator tends to be aggressive and deceitful. This person rigidly adheres to one position and will use threats and coercion to force the other party to submit. Giving no quarter, the dominator will often get personal and hit below the belt. This style is undesirable because, like accommodation, it does not generate creative thinking aimed at mutual problem solving. Moreover, this approach is particularly likely to lead to postconflict tension, resentment, and hostility.

• *Compromise.* Compromise is a pragmatic approach to conflict that acknowledges the divergent needs of both parties. A compromise approach involves negotiation and a willingness to meet the other person halfway. While trying to be reasonable, the compromiser nonetheless works hard to maximize the satisfaction of his or her own needs. Thus the compromise approach may involve some manipulation and misrepresentation. Compromise is a fairly constructive approach to conflict, but its manipulative aspects make it somewhat inferior to the final approach, that of integration.

• *Integration.* While compromise simply entails splitting the difference between positions, integration involves a sincere effort to find a solution that will maximize the satisfaction of both parties. When this approach is used, the conflict is viewed as a mutual problem to be solved as effectively as possible. Integration thus encourages openness and honesty. Also, integration stresses the importance of criticizing the other person's ideas in a disagreement rather than the other person. Integration requires putting a lot of effort into clarifying differences and similarities in positions, so that you can build on the similarities. Generally this is the most productive approach for dealing with conflict. Instead of resulting in a postconflict residue of tension and resentment, integration tends to produce a climate of trust.

Guidelines for Constructive Conflict Resolution

We have seen the desirability of integration as an approach to conflict resolution. Here now are explicit guidelines on how to achieve an integrative style of dealing with interpersonal conflict (Alberti & Emmons, 1990; Johnson & Johnson, 1991).

• To begin with, acknowledge the existence of a conflict and the legitimacy of the other person's needs and goals.
• Define the conflict as a mutual problem to be solved cooperatively, rather than as a win-lose proposition.
• Choose a mutually acceptable time to sit down and work on resolving the conflict. It is not always best to tackle the conflict when and where it first arises.
• Show respect for the other person's position. Try to empathize with and fully understand the other person's frame of reference.
• Make communication honest and open. Don't withhold information or misrepresent your position. Avoid deceit and manipulation.
• Phrase your statements about another person's annoying habits in terms of specific behaviors rather than global personality traits. (Remarks of the latter sort are more likely to be taken personally.) Similarly, avoid saying "You always . . ."
• Approach the conflict as equals, with a balance of power between the two of you. If you have a higher status or more power (parent, supervisor), try to set this difference aside.
• Put a great deal of effort into clarifying your respective positions. It is imperative that each of you understands the exact nature of your disagreement.
• Communicate your flexibility and willingness to modify your position.
• Emphasize the similarities in your positions rather than the differences. Try to use those similarities to build toward a mutually satisfactory solution.

Summary

Interpersonal communication is the interactional process whereby one person sends a message to another. Communication takes place when a source sends a message to a receiver either verbally or nonverbally. Although we often take it for granted, communication plays an exceptionally important role in our lives.

Nonverbal communication tends to be more spontaneous than verbal communication, but it is also more ambiguous. Sometimes it contradicts what is communicated verbally. It is often multichanneled, and like language, it is culturally bound. Nonverbal communication frequently conveys emotions and provides information about social affiliation and about status. Elements of nonverbal communication include personal space, facial expression, eye contact, body language, hand gestures, touch, and paralanguage.

Proxemics deals with the use of personal space. Hall has described how specific distances are maintained in certain kinds of social relationships. When these norms are violated and personal space is invaded, people tend to react negatively.

Facial expressions often convey emotional states. However, it is relatively easy to send deceptive signals by the face. The duration of eye contact is an important cue and is influenced by a variety of factors. Body posture may indicate degree of tension and attitude. Hand gestures are used primarily to regulate and supplement speech. Touching can convey a variety of meanings. Paralanguage is concerned with the use of vocal emphasis in speaking. Slight variations in vocal emphasis can reverse the literal meaning of a message.

Some nonverbal cues are associated with deception, but many of these cues do not correspond to popular beliefs about how liars give themselves away. Discrepancies between facial expressions and other nonverbal signals may suggest dishonesty. The vocal and visual cues associated with lying are so subtle, however, that the detection of deception is difficult.

Verbal communication consists of both speaking and listening. We are often careless and sloppy speakers as well as inattentive and preoccupied listeners. Self-disclosure—revealing ourselves to others—is a significant aspect of verbal communication. We take the risk of opening up to others because self-disclosure serves many important functions, and chief among them is developing emotional intimacy. Inappropriate self-disclosure, however, can cause interpersonal difficulties. Women tend to engage in more self-disclosure than men, but this disparity is not so consistent as it was once believed to be. The reciprocity norm is a key situational factor that influences self-disclosure. It appears that learning to engage in appropriate self-disclosure—revealing the appropriate thing to the appropriate person at the appropriate time—may be important to psychological health.

Sometimes communication can produce negative interpersonal outcomes. Barriers to effective communication include defensiveness, aggressive communication, submissive communication, motivational distortion, self-preoccupation, game playing, and collusion. Sometimes miscommunication figures in tragic situations such as date rape, or forced intercourse in the context of dating. Date rape appears to be increasingly common, especially on college campuses, where most rape victims are raped by someone they know. Misunderstandings about sexual intentions are common in dating relationships because partners often fail to engage in adequate self-disclosure, misinterpret ambiguous nonverbal signals, and engage in game playing.

Communication is effective when the message the sender intends to convey is the message that is actually received. To promote a positive interpersonal climate, it helps to show empathy, treat people as equals, withhold judgment, strive for honesty, and express opinions tentatively. In speaking, it helps to consider your listener's frame of reference, use an assertive communication style, be specific and concrete, avoid loaded words, and keep your verbal and nonverbal messages consistent. Effective listening depends on physically attending to the speaker, paying careful attention to both verbal and nonverbal signals, and checking your perceptions.

Dealing constructively with interpersonal conflict is an important aspect of effective communication. Five common styles of dealing with conflict, ranging from less to more effective, are avoidance, accommodation, domination, compromise, and integration.

In our Application we will discuss assertive communication, a communication style that has proved extremely effective across a wide variety of interpersonal communication situations—for example, making acquaintances, developing relationships, and resolving interpersonal conflicts.

If you answered yes to several of these questions, you may have difficulty being assertive. Many people of both sexes have a hard time being assertive, but this problem is more common among females because they are socialized to be more submissive than males—to be "nice" and not to make waves. Consequently, assertiveness training has become especially popular among women. Men, too, find assertiveness training helpful, both because some males have been socialized to be passive and because some need to learn to be less aggressive and more assertive. It is important, then, to understand the differences between assertive, submissive, and aggressive behavior.

The Nature of Assertiveness

As we noted earlier, *assertiveness* involves acting in your own best interests by expressing your thoughts and feelings directly and honestly (Alberti & Emmons, 1990; Bower & Bower, 1991). Essentially, to be assertive is to stand up for your rights when someone else is about to infringe on them. It is to speak out openly rather than pull your punches.

We can best clarify the nature of assertive behavior by contrasting it with submissive behavior and aggressive behavior. *Submissive behavior* involves consistently giving in to others on points of possible contention. Submissive people tend to let others take advantage of them. Typically, their biggest problem is that they cannot say no to unreasonable requests. They also have difficulty voicing disagreement with others and making requests.

Although the roots of submissiveness have not been investigated fully, they appear to lie in excessive concern about gaining social approval. However, the strategy of not making waves is more likely to garner others' contempt than to win their approval.

It is sometimes difficult to differentiate between assertive behavior and aggressive behavior. In principle, the distinction is fairly simple. *Aggressive behavior* is intended to hurt or harm someone. Assertive behavior has no such motivation, but it is intended to defend your rights. The problem is that assertive and aggressive behavior *may* overlap. When someone is about to infringe on their rights, people often lash out at the other party (aggression) while defending their rights (assertion). The challenge, then, is to learn to be firm and assertive without going a step too far and becoming aggressive.

Advocates of assertive behavior argue that it is much more adaptive than either submissive or aggressive behavior (Alberti & Emmons, 1990; Bower & Bower, 1991). They maintain that submissive behavior leads to poor self-esteem, self-denial, suppression of emotion, and strained interpersonal relationships. They assert that aggressive behavior tends to promote guilt, alienation, and disharmony. Assertive behavior, in contrast, is said to foster high self-esteem and satisfactory interpersonal relationships.

Of course, behaving assertively does *not* ensure that you will always get what you want. The essential advantage of assertiveness is that it enables you to state what you want clearly and directly. Your ability to do so makes you

feel good about yourself and will usually make others feel good about you too. But while being assertive probably improves your chances of getting what you want, it certainly doesn't guarantee that you will.

Steps in Assertiveness Training

Numerous assertiveness training programs are available in book form or through seminars. Some recommendations about books appear in the Recommended Readings box in this section. Most of the programs are behavioral in orientation and emphasize gradual improvement and reinforcement of appropriate behavior. Here we will summarize the key steps in assertiveness training.

Clarify the Nature of Assertive Behavior

Most programs begin, as we have done, by clarifying the nature of assertive behavior. In order to produce assertive behavior, you need to understand what it looks and sounds like. One way to do so is to imagine situations that call for assertiveness and compare hypothetical submissive (or passive), assertive, and aggressive responses. Let's consider one such comparison. In this example, a woman in assertiveness training is asking her roommate to cooperate in cleaning the apartment once a week. The roommate, who has no interest in the problem, is listening to music when the conversation begins. The roommate is playing the role of the antagonist—the "downer" in the scripts below (excerpted from Bower & Bower, 1991, pp. 8, 9, 11).

KUDZU by Doug Marlette. By permission of Doug Marlette and Creators Syndicate.

The Passive Scene

SHE: Uh, I was wondering if you would be willing to take time to decide about the house-cleaning.

DOWNER: (listening to the music) Not now, I'm busy.

SHE: Oh, okay.

The Aggressive Scene

SHE: Listen, I've had it with you not even talking about cleaning this damn apartment. Are you going to help me?

DOWNER (listening to the music) Not now, I'm busy.

SHE: Why can't you look at me when you turn me down? You don't give a damn about the housework or me! You only care about yourself!

DOWNER: That's not true.

SHE: You never pay any attention to the apartment or to me. I have to do everything around here!

DOWNER: Oh, shut up! You're just neurotic about cleaning all the time. Who are you, my mother? Can't I relax with my stereo for a few minutes without you pestering me? This was my apartment first, you know!

The Assertive Scene

SHE: I know housework isn't the most fascinating subject, but it needs to be done. Let's plan when we'll do it.

DOWNER: (listening to music) Oh, c'mon—not now! I'm busy.

SHE: This won't take long. I feel that if we have a schedule, it will be easier to keep up with the chores.

DOWNER: I'm not sure I'll have time for all of them.

SHE: I've already drawn up a couple of rotating schedules for housework, so that each week we have an equal division of tasks. Will you look at them? I'd like to hear your decisions about them, say, tonight after supper?

DOWNER: [indignantly] I have to look at these now?

SHE: Is there some other time that's better for you?

DOWNER: Oh, I don't know.

SHE: Well, then let's discuss plans after supper for fifteen minutes. Is that agreed?

DOWNER: I guess so.

SHE: Good! It won't take long, and I'll feel relieved when we have a schedule in place.

For people to whom assertive behavior is unfamiliar, this process of clarifying the nature of assertiveness can be critical. In such cases, it may be a good idea to read two or three books on assertiveness to get a good picture of assertive behavior. The differences between the three types of behavior may best be conceptualized in terms of how people deal with their own rights and the rights of others. Submissive people sacrifice their own rights. Aggressive people tend to ignore the rights of others. Assertive people consider both their own rights *and* the rights of others.

To ensure that your assertive words have impact, back them up with congruent nonverbal messages. You'll come across as more assertive if you face the person you're talking with, look directly at him or her, and maintain eye contact, rather than look-ing away from the other person, fidgeting, slouching, and shuffling your feet (Bower & Bower, 1991).

Monitor Your Assertive Behavior

Most people vary in assertiveness from one situation to another. In other words, they may be assertive in some social contexts and timid in others. Consequently, once you understand the nature of assertive behavior, you should monitor yourself and figure out *who* intimidates you, on *what topics*, and in *which situations*.

Observe a Model's Assertive Behavior

Once you have identified the situations in which you are nonassertive, think of someone who behaves assertively in those situations and observe that person's behavior closely. In other words, find someone to model yourself after. Observation of that person should help you to learn how to behave assertively in situa-

Asserting Yourself: A Practical Guide for Positive Change

by Sharon Anthony Bower and Gordon H. Bower (Addison-Wesley, 1991)

More than 20 books on assertiveness training are currently available, and many of them are fairly good. The Bowers' book is especially strong because it is specific, detailed, and concrete. Bower and Bower put the problem of nonassertiveness into perspective, relating it to self-esteem and anxiety. They then lay out a systematic program for increasing assertive behavior. They make extensive use of probing questions so that you can work out a plan of action that is relevant to you. They also provide sample verbal scripts for numerous common situations that typically call for assertive behavior. Among the situations they cover are requesting a raise, saying no to unreasonable demands, protesting unjust criticism, dealing with a substance abuser, protesting annoying habits, and dealing with the silent treatment. They devote a whole chapter to the role of assertive behavior in developing friendships—initiating and ending conversations, keeping conversations going, making dates, self-disclosure, listening, and coping with social anxieties. The book is smoothly written in a nonpatronizing tone. (An excerpt is quoted in this Application.)

Other books on assertiveness can also be recommended highly. Especially worthy of note is one of the very first entries in this area, *Your Perfect Right*, by Robert E. Alberti and Michael L. Emmons (1990), which is now in its sixth edition. Many of these books are written with women in mind and focus on the unique problems women encounter. *The Assertive Woman*, by Stanlee Phelps and Nancy Austin (1987), appears to be particularly useful.

tions crucial to you. Your observations should also allow you to see how rewarding assertive behavior can be, and the promise of those rewards should strengthen your assertive tendencies.

If an assertive model isn't available, another option is to rely on the relevant scenarios depicted in most self-help books on assertiveness. The passive, aggressive, and assertive dialogues we presented earlier are representative of the scenes that most books use. Typically, the authors describe a variety of problematic interactions along with some standard assertive responses that you can adapt to your own specific situation (see Figure 6.12).

Practice
Assertive Behavior

Ultimately the key to achieving assertive behavior is to practice it and work toward gradual improvement. Your practice can take several forms. In *covert rehearsal*, you can imagine a situation that calls for assertion and the dialogue that you would engage in. In *role playing*, you might get a therapist or friend to play the role of an antagonist. Then you act out your new assertive behaviors in this artificial situation.

Eventually, of course, you want to transfer your assertiveness skills to real-life situations. Most experts recommend that you use *shaping* to increase your assertive behavior gradually. As we discussed in the Chapter 4 Application, shaping involves rewarding yourself for making closer and closer approximations of a desired behavior. In the early stages of your behavior-change program, for example, your goal might be to make at least one assertive comment every day, while toward the end you might be striving to make at least eight such comments every day. Obviously, when you design a shaping program, it is important to set realistic goals for yourself.

Adopt an
Assertive Attitude

Most assertiveness training programs have a behavioral orientation and focus on specific responses for specific situations. Obviously, however, real-life situa-

tions are rarely just like those portrayed in books. Some experts maintain that acquiring a repertoire of verbal responses for certain situations is less important than developing a new attitude: you're not going to let people push you around (or let yourself push others around, if you're the aggressive type) (Alberti & Emmons, 1990). Although most programs don't talk explicitly about attitudes, they do appear to instill a new attitude indirectly. A change in attitude is probably crucial to the achievement of flexible, assertive behavior.

Assertive Responses to Some Common Put-Downs

Nature of remark	Put-down sentence	Suggested assertive reply
Nagging about details	"Haven't you done this yet?"	"No, when did you want it done?" (Answer without hedging, and follow-up with a question.)
Prying	"I know I maybe shouldn't ask, but . . ."	"If I don't want to answer, I'll let you know." (Indicate that you won't make yourself uncomfortable just to please this person.)
Putting you on the spot socially	"Are you busy Tuesday?"	"What do you have in mind?" (Answer the question with a question.)
Pigeonholing you	"That's a woman for you!"	"That's one woman, not *all* women." (Disagree—assert your individuality.)
Using insulting labels for your behavior	"That's a dumb way to . . ."	"I'll decide what to call my behavior." (Refuse to accept the label.)
Basing predictions on an amateur personality analysis	"You'll have a hard time. You're too shy."	"In what ways do you think I'm 'too shy'?" (Ask for clarification of the analysis.)

FIGURE 6.12
Assertive responses to common put-downs
Having some assertive replies at the ready can increase your confidence in difficult social interactions. (Adapted from Bower & Bower, 1991.)

Key Learning Objectives

1. List and describe the four components of the communication process.
2. List and discuss six general principles of nonverbal communication.
3. Describe Hall's four interpersonal distance zones and how people respond to invasions of personal space.
4. Discuss what can be discerned from facial cues.
5. Discuss characteristics associated with high levels of eye contact, including racial and gender differences.
6. Discuss how eye contact is related to social status and interpersonal attraction.
7. Discuss what can be discerned from body postures and hand gestures.
8. Discuss some of the research findings with regard to the communication meaning of touching.
9. Describe the role of paralanguage in communication.
10. Summarize evidence on detecting deception from nonverbal cues.
11. Discuss the significance of nonverbal messages in interpersonal relations.
12. Discuss three general principles of verbal communication.
13. Explain why we engage in self-disclosure and when it may be inappropriate.
14. Summarize evidence on who tends to disclose what to whom and under what circumstances.
15. Discuss when self-disclosure is appropriate and its relation to adjustment.
16. List and discuss seven barriers to effective communication.
17. Explain how poor communication and other factors contribute to date rape.
18. Describe five communication behaviors that tend to produce a positive interpersonal climate.
19. List four guidelines for effective speaking.
20. List four guidelines for effective listening.
21. List and describe five personal styles of dealing with interpersonal conflict.
22. List ten guidelines for constructive conflict resolution.
23. Differentiate assertive behavior from submissive and aggressive behavior and discuss the adaptiveness of each style.
24. Describe five steps in increasing assertive behavior.

Key Terms

acquaintance rape
channel
collusion
communication barrier
date rape
display rules
empathy
games
interpersonal communication
interpersonal conflict
kinesics
message

nonverbal communication
paralanguage
personal space
proxemics
receiver
self-disclosure
social penetration theory
source
territoriality
transactional analysis
verbal communication

Key People

Irwin Altman and Dalmas Taylor
Sharon Anthony Bower and Gordon Bower
Paul Ekman and Wallace Friesen

Edward Hall
Sidney Jourard
Mary Koss

7

Social Influence and Group Membership

WHEN AN AUTHORITY FIGURE says, "Jump!" a surprising number of us simply ask, "How high?" Consider the experience of several suburbs just west of Chicago, which in 1987 experienced a severe flood that required the mobilization of the National Guard and various emergency services. At the height of the crisis, a young man arrived on the scene, announced that he was from an obscure state agency in charge of emergency services, and proceeded to take control of the situation. City work crews, the fire department, local police, municipal officials, and the National Guard followed his orders with dispatch for several days, evacuating entire neighborhoods—until an official thought to check, and found out that the man was just someone who had walked in off the street. The impostor, who had small armies at his beck and call, had no training in flood control or emergency services, just a history of unemployment and psychological problems.

After news of the hoax spread, people criticized red-faced local officials for their unthinking compliance with the impostor's orders. Many of the critics, however, would probably have cooperated in much the same way if they had been in the officials' shoes. For most people, obedience to an authority figure is the rule, not the exception. And when we work together in groups, we often conform to the example of other group members without asking questions.

In this chapter we will examine some ways in which social influence, the presence of other people, and membership in groups can affect behavior. Among other things, we'll address such questions as the following:

- If we expect someone to try to persuade us, does our expectation reduce the impact of the message?
- Is conformity more likely in a small group or a large group?
- Why do we sometimes choke under pressure?
- Why is it hard to talk in front of a group?
- Are individuals more productive when they work alone or when they work together in groups?
- Are leaders born or made?
- What tactics do advertisers, salespeople, charlatans, and other influence artists employ to gain their ends?

Persuasion: The Power of Rhetoric

Every day we are bombarded by efforts to alter our attitudes through persuasion. You may not even be out of bed before you hear radio commercials designed to persuade you to buy specific mouthwashes, computers, and tennis shoes. When you unfurl your newspaper, you find many quotes from government officials, all of which have been carefully crafted to shape your opinions. On your way to school, you see billboards showing attractive models draped over automobiles and bottles of Scotch in the hopes that they'll affect your feelings about these products. When you arrive on campus, you find a group passing out leaflets that urge you to repent your sins and join the group in worship. In class your economics professor champions the wisdom of the free market in international trade. At lunch the person you've been dating argues about the merits of an "open relationship." Your argument is interrupted by someone who wants both of you to sign a petition for nuclear disarmament. Doesn't it ever let up? you wonder.

When it comes to persuasion, the answer is no. As the survey data in Figure 7.1 show, a host of people are involved in efforts to persuade us. Indeed, the people closest to us (our immediate family and close friends) are the ones who exert the most effort to mold our behavior through persuasion (Rule, Bisanz, & Kohn, 1985).

Persuasion involves the communication of arguments and information intended to change another person's attitudes. What are

"Who Tries to Persuade You?"	
Source	Percent
Immediate family	27
Extended family	7
Close friends	18
Circumstantial friends	7
Instructors	13
Salespeople	11
Other professionals	10
Trait-defined people (e.g., religious people)	5
Goal-defined people (e.g., people who are trying to impress me)	2

FIGURE 7.1
Sources of persuasion
When Rule et al. (1985) asked subjects, "Who tries to persuade you?" they found that family and friends are our major sources of persuasive efforts.

attitudes? For the purposes of our discussion, we'll define **attitudes** as beliefs and feelings about people, objects, and ideas. Let's look more closely at two of the terms in this definition. We use the term *beliefs* to mean thoughts and judgments about people, objects, and ideas. For example, we may *believe* that equal pay for equal work is a fair policy or that capital punishment is not an effective deterrent to crime. The "feeling" component of attitudes encompasses the positivity and negativity of our feelings about an issue as well as the strength of our feelings about it. For example, you may *strongly favor* equal pay for equal work, but only *mildly disagree* with the idea that capital punishment reduces the crime rate.

Like other forms of communication, the process of persuasion includes four basic elements, which were introduced in Chapter 6. The *source* is the person who sends a communication, and the *receiver* is the person to whom the message is sent. Thus, if you watched a presidential address on TV, the president would be the source. You and millions of other listeners would be the receivers in this persuasive effort. The *message* is the information transmitted by the source. The *channel* is the medium through which the message is sent. In examining communication channels, investigators have often compared face-to-face interaction against appeals sent via mass media (mass publications, television, radio). Although the research on communication channels is interesting, we'll confine our discussion to source, message, and receiver variables. Let's examine some of the factors that determine whether persuasion works.

Source Factors

Persuasion tends to be more successful when the source has high *credibility*. What gives a person credibility? Either expertise or trustworthiness. People try to convey their *expertise* by mentioning their degrees, their training, and their experience, or by showing an impressive grasp of the issue at hand (Hass, 1981; Wood & Kallgren, 1988).

Expertise is a plus, but *trustworthiness* is even more important (McGinnies & Ward, 1980). Whom would you believe if you were told that your state needs to reduce corporate taxes to stimulate its economy—the president of a huge corporation in your state or an economics professor from out of state? Probably the latter. Trustworthiness is undermined when a source, such as the corporation president, appears to have something to gain. In contrast,

trustworthiness is enhanced when people appear to argue against their own interests (Eagly, Wood, & Chaiken, 1978). This effect explains why salespeople often make such remarks as "No, this snowblower isn't the top of the line. We don't carry the deluxe model because it costs nearly twice as much and the difference in performance isn't all that great. But if that's the one you want, you can get it at Scrimshaw's."

Likability also increases the effectiveness of a persuasive source. Likability depends on a host of factors (see Chapter 8). A key consideration is a person's physical attractiveness. The favorable effect of physical attractiveness on persuasion was apparent in a study by Chaiken (1979), who asked students to obtain signatures for a petition. Chaiken found that the more attractive students were more successful. Other studies have also shown the effect of physical attractiveness on persuasion (Kahle & Homer, 1985; Pallak, 1983). We also respond better to sources who are *similar* to us in ways that are relevant to the issue at hand (Berscheid, 1966).

The importance of source variables can be seen in advertising. Many companies spend a fortune to obtain an ideal spokesperson, such as Bill Cosby, who combines trustworthiness, expertise (a doctorate in education), likability, and a knack for connecting with the average person. Companies quickly abandon spokespersons whose likability is in decline. Pepsi, for example, immediately canceled an advertising campaign centered on the rock star Madonna when one of her videos offended many people's religious values. Thus source variables are extremely important factors in persuasion.

Message Factors

Imagine that you are going to give a speech to a local community group advocating a reduction in state taxes on corporations. In preparing your speech, you will probably wrestle with questions about how to structure your message. Should you look at both sides of the issue or just present your own side? Should you deliver a low-key, logical speech, or should you try to strike fear in the hearts of your listeners? Should you spell out your conclusions for your listeners or use rhetorical questions to stimulate their thinking? Let's look at these message factors.

We'll assume that you're aware that there are two sides to the taxation issue. On the one hand, you are convinced that lower corporate taxes will bring new companies and factories to your state, stimulate economic growth, and create jobs. On the other hand, you realize that reduced tax revenues may gradually hurt the quality of education and roads in your state. Nevertheless, you believe that the benefits of a lower rate will outweigh the costs. Should you present a *one-sided argument* that ignores the possible problems for education and road quality? Or should you present a *two-sided argument* that acknowledges concern about education and road quality, and then downplays the magnitude of these problems?

In general, two-sided arguments seem to be more effective. Just mentioning that there are two sides to an issue can increase your credibility with an audience (Jones & Brehm, 1970). One-sided messages work only when your audience is uneducated about the issue or when they are already very favorably disposed to your point of view (Lumsdaine & Janis, 1953).

Persuasive messages frequently attempt to arouse fear. Opponents of nuclear power scare us with visions of meltdowns. Antismoking campaigns emphasize the threat of cancer. Deodorant ads highlight the risk of embarrassment. You could follow their lead and argue that if corporate taxes aren't reduced, your state will be headed toward massive unemployment and economic ruin. Does *fear arousal* work? Yes, studies involving a wide range of issues (nuclear policy, auto safety, and dental hygiene, among others) have shown that the arousal of fear often increases persuasion. However, there are limiting conditions (Leventhal, 1970; Rogers, 1975).

Fear arousal is likely to work if your listeners view the dire consequences that you describe as exceedingly unpleasant, fairly probable if they don't take your advice, and avoidable if they do. In our hypothetical case, your listeners will surely agree that economic ruin is terrible. But you may have trouble convincing them that your state is headed toward ruin or that reduced taxes are the way to avoid it. If you aren't confident about the weight of evidence on these points, you shouldn't attempt to arouse fear in your audience. A *high* level of fear may make them defensive, so that they tune you out (Jepson & Chaiken, 1986).

Generating *positive feelings* is also an effective way to persuade people. Commercial firms are employing such tactics when they include music in TV commercials, wine and dine prospective customers, and give away small gifts (key chains, pencils, etc.). Recent research has shown that arousing positive feelings in an effort to win us over *can* be effective—provided we don't care too much about the issue. If we do care about the topic, it takes more than good feelings to move us. One study showed that the use of music in TV commercials was effective in persuading viewers, but only when the message concerned a trivial topic (Park & Young, 1986).

Receiver Factors

What about the receiver of the persuasive message? Are some people easier to persuade than others? Undoubtedly, but the personality traits that account for these differences interact with other considerations in complicated ways. Transient factors, such as forewarning of a persuasive effort and a receiver's initial position on an issue, seem to be more influential than a receiver's personality.

An old saying suggests that "forewarned is forearmed." The value of *forewarning* applies to targets of persuasive efforts (McGuire, 1964; Petty & Cacioppo, 1979). When you shop for a new TV, you *expect* salespeople to work at persuading you. To some extent this forewarning reduces the impact of their arguments.

The effect of a persuasive effort also depends on the discrepancy between a *receiver's initial position* on an issue and the position advocated by the source. Persuasion tends to work best when the discrepancy between the two is moderate. Why? According to *social judgment theory*, people usually are willing to consider alternative views on an issue if the views aren't too different from their own (Sherif & Hovland, 1961; Upshaw, 1969). This range of potentially acceptable positions on an issue is referred to as the *latitude of acceptance*. Persuasive messages that fall outside a receiver's latitude of acceptance usually fall on deaf ears. When a message falls within a receiver's latitude of acceptance, persuasion is much more likely to be successful (Atkins, Deaux, & Bieri, 1967).

Within the latitude of acceptance, however, a *larger* discrepancy between the receiver's initial position and the position advocated should produce greater attitude change than a smaller discrepancy. The reason is that people often "meet part way" to resolve disagreement. Figure 7.2 shows how this theory could apply to a person who heard your presentation advocating a reduction in corporate taxes.

Our review of source, message, and receiver variables has shown that persuasion involves a complex interplay of factors. We can see these factors operating as we examine a real-life, tragic example of the power of persuasion.

A Case of Fatal Persuasion: The Jonestown Massacre

The impressive power of persuasion was made vividly apparent in the infamous Jonestown massacre in Guyana, South America, in 1978. As you may know, Jim Jones was the charismatic leader of an American religious cult called the People's Temple, which had set up a large encampment in the isolated wilderness of Guyana. Feeling pressured by a U.S. congressional investigation, Jones persuaded his followers to commit suicide by drinking cyanide-laced Kool-Aid. Although a small minority of Jones's followers refused to cooperate (a few escaped, a few were shot), most went along with him and took their own lives. In all, 913 Americans died at Jonestown, including more than 200 children who were poisoned by their parents. How can we explain such extraordinary behavior?

Social psychologists who have studied this event tell us that this unusual behavior was due to Jim Jones's highly skilled use of persuasion and social influence tactics (Galanter, 1989; Zimbardo & Leippe, 1991). To begin with, Jonestown members were already heavily dependent on Jones and trusted him, as they made clear when they abandoned their homes in the United States and followed him to Guyana. These individuals were persuaded to join Jonestown in the first place because they felt alienated from American society and therefore were particularly vulnerable to Jones's promise of a better life in a better place (*receiver* factors). But the fact that Jones could persuade people to move to an isolated place in an undeveloped foreign country gives us an idea of his impressive rhetorical skills. As a *source*, Jones was perceived by his followers as an expert who was credible and trustworthy (Zimbardo & Leippe, 1991).

Jones also had an unusual amount of control over the content of the information his followers received and how it was presented to them (*message* factors). Specifically, he could prevent his people from coming into contact with ideas or values that differed from those he espoused and permit them to receive only the information he wanted them to have. Of course this degree of control over people is quite unusual, and it is one of the key factors that explains how Jones was able to persuade hundreds of people to kill themselves.

Jones's ability to control the information his followers received is apparent in the way he presented to them the scenario that set the stage for the mass suicide. What happened was this: Some concerned relatives back home had charged Jones with abuse of their family members, and a congressman and some reporters had come to Jonestown to investigate the charges. Jones managed to persuade them that his followers were free to leave at any time, but he panicked when some cult members said they

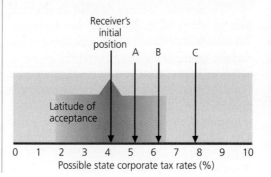

FIGURE 7.2
Latitude of acceptance and attitude change
A, B, and C are positions on the tax rate that one might advocate. A and B both fall within the receiver's latitude of acceptance, but position B should produce a larger attitude shift. Position C is outside the receiver's latitude of acceptance and should fall on deaf ears.

wanted to return to the United States on the plane with the congressman. Under the influence of drugs and suffering from paranoid delusions, Jones believed word of his coercive activities would get out and that the U.S. military would invade Jonestown and kill his people—and that he would lose control of the Temple (Galanter, 1989; Zimbardo & Leippe, 1991).

Panic-stricken, Jones ordered the murder of the congressman and the small group from the People's Temple as they were getting ready to board the plane. Realizing that this turn of events made it even more likely that the U.S. military would invade Jonestown, he gathered the faithful together and told them that the visiting congressman was going to be killed by an angered cult member acting on his own, and that the murder would prompt intervention by the U.S. military. They would probably all be killed, he told them. The only way to prevent this fate was to commit mass "revolutionary suicide." Jones's intuitive ability to invoke the tactics of persuasion is vividly portrayed in the following description based on the videotape that Jones made of the last hour of Jonestown:

> Masterfully, Jones destroyed dissent by first inviting it. When a vocal young woman made reasonable arguments for alternative solutions short of suicide, Jones conveyed an air of support and fair-mindedness. "I like you Christina: I've always liked you," he told her. But he refuted her arguments with platitudes that stirred the crowd and ultimately compelled his most committed followers to come forth and publicly question her faith and allegiance. In the end, she was shouted down—and with her defeat, Jones won and the people lost.
>
> As the universal approval for this prophet's visionary "final solution" began carrying people up to the Kool-Aid crucible, Jones began to express displeasure with those who still hesitated. He alternated between a soothing tone ("Go with your child—I think it's humane . . . it is painless") and the impatient tone of a disappointed parent ("Lay down your life with dignity . . . stop these hysterics"). [Zimbardo & Leippe, 1991, p. 20]

Tactics that did not depend on rhetoric were also at work in the Jonestown massacre. Very much in evidence were the power of social pressure (going along with others), the power of authority (doing what you are told), the power of group dynamics (violating personal standards in order to be liked by other members of a cohesive group), modeling, and playing on guilt. The persuasion and social influence tactics used by Jim Jones are normal and familiar to all of us. What was unusual was the degree of control he had over his members' psychological environment, and this fact allowed him to employ a large number of techniques that combined to produce uncommonly powerful—and tragic—results. We'll examine social influence and group dynamics in detail in the rest of the chapter and in the Application.

Conformity and Compliance: The Power of Social Pressure

If you keep a well-manicured lawn or extol the talents of Bruce Springsteen, are you exhibiting conformity? According to social psychologists, it depends on whether your behavior is the result of group pressure. **Conformity occurs when people yield to real or imagined social pressure.** If you maintain a well-groomed lawn only to avoid complaints from your neighbors, you are yielding to social pressure. If you like Springsteen because you genuinely enjoy his records, that's *not* conformity. But if you like Springsteen because it's cool to be a fan of his and your friends would question your taste if you weren't, then you're conforming.

Asch's Studies

In the 1950s Solomon Asch (1951, 1955, 1956) devised a clever procedure that minimized ambiguity about whether subjects were conforming, allowing him to investigate the variables that govern conformity. Let's recreate one of Asch's (1955) classic experiments. The subjects are male undergraduates recruited for a study of visual perception. A group of seven subjects are shown a large card with a vertical line on it. Then they are asked to indicate which of three lines on a second card matches the original "standard line" in length (see Figure 7.3). All seven subjects are given a turn at the task, and each announces his choice to the group. The subject in the sixth chair doesn't know it, but everyone else in the group is an accomplice of the experimenter. They're about to make him wonder whether he has taken leave of his senses.

The accomplices give accurate responses on the first two trials. On the third trial, line 2 clearly is the correct response, but the first five "subjects" all say that line 3 matches the standard line. The genuine subject can't believe his ears. Over the course of the experiment, the

FIGURE 7.3
Stimuli used in Asch's conformity studies
Subjects were asked to match a standard line (top) with one of three other lines displayed on another card (bottom). The task was easy—until Asch's accomplices started to respond with obviously incorrect answers, creating a situation in which Asch could evaluate subjects' conformity.

accomplices all give the same incorrect response on 12 out of 18 trials. Asch wants to see how the subject responds in these situations. The line judgments are easy and unambiguous. Working alone, people achieve better than 95% accuracy in matching the lines. So if the subject consistently agrees with the accomplices, he isn't making honest mistakes—he is conforming. Will the subject stick to his guns and defy the group? Or will he go along with the group?

Averaging across 50 subjects, Asch (1955) found that the young men conformed on 37% of the trials. The subjects varied considerably in their tendency to conform, however. Of the 50 subjects, 13 never caved in to the group, while 14 conformed on more than half the trials.

In subsequent studies, *group size* and *group unanimity* turned out to be key determinants of conformity (Asch, 1956). To examine group size, Asch repeated his procedure with groups that included one to 15 accomplices. Little conformity was seen when a subject was pitted against just one accomplice. Conformity increased rapidly as group size went from two to four, peaked at a group size of seven, and then leveled off (see Figure 7.4). Thus, Asch concluded that as groups grow larger, conformity increases—up to a point.

Interestingly, group size made little difference if just one accomplice broke with the others, wrecking their unanimous agreement. The presence of another dissenter lowered conformity to about one-quarter of its peak, even when the dissenter made *inaccurate* judgments that happened to conflict with the majority view. Apparently the subjects just needed to hear someone else question the accuracy of the group's perplexing responses.

Conformity vs. Compliance

At first Asch wasn't sure whether conforming subjects were really changing their beliefs in response to social pressure or just pretending to change them. When subjects were interviewed later, many reported that they had begun to doubt their eyesight and that they thought "the majority must be right." These interviews suggested that the subjects had actually changed their beliefs. Critics suggested, however, that the subjects might have been trying to rationalize their conformity after the fact.

A study that included a condition in which subjects made their responses anonymously rather than publicly settled the question. Conformity declined dramatically when sub-

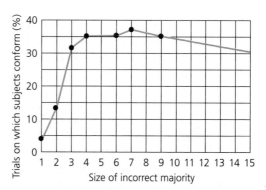

FIGURE 7.4
Conformity and group size
This graph shows the percentage of trials on which subjects conformed as a function of group size in Asch's research. Asch found that conformity became more frequent as group size increased, up to about seven persons, and then leveled off. (Data from Asch, 1955.)

jects recorded their responses privately. This finding suggests that subjects in the Asch studies were not really changing their beliefs (Deutsch & Gerard, 1955). On the basis of this evidence, theorists concluded that Asch's experiments evoked a particular type of conformity, called compliance. **Compliance occurs when people yield to social pressure in their public behavior, even though their private beliefs have not changed.** In the Asch studies, compliance resulted from subtle, implied pressure. However, compliance usually occurs in response to explicit rules, requests, and commands. For example, if you agree to wear formal clothes to a fancy restaurant that requires formal attire, even though you despise such rules, you're displaying compliance.

The Darker Side of Yielding to Social Pressure

Research confirms what every teenager knows—that conformity to peer-group norms is an important key to popularity (Sebald, 1981). In other words, peer pressure is a particularly powerful source of influence among adolescents and young adults. Often when we yield to social influence, the issue at hand is a relatively trivial matter—such as dressing up to go to a nice restaurant. In these cases, conformity and compliance with social norms help to minimize the confusion and anxiety we experience when we find ourselves in unfamiliar situations. When individuals are pressured to conform to antisocial group norms, however, the consequences can be tragic—recall the role of peer pressure in campus gang rape (Chapter 6). Other familiar examples of the negative effects of "going along with the crowd" include drinking more than we know we should because others tell us to "have just one more"; driving when we're under the influence of alcohol or drugs at someone's urging; refusing to socialize with someone we like because that person isn't liked

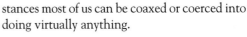

stances most of us can be coaxed or coerced into doing virtually anything.

Milgram's Studies

Stanley Milgram was a brilliantly creative social psychologist who set out to study the tendency to obey authority figures. Like many other people after World War II, he was troubled by how readily the citizens of Germany had followed the orders of Adolf Hitler, even when the orders required morally repugnant actions, such as the slaughter of millions of Jews. Milgram, who had worked with Solomon Asch, set out to design a standard laboratory procedure for the study of obedience, much like Asch's procedure for studying conformity. The clever experiment that Milgram devised became one of the most famous and controversial studies in the annals of psychology. Some people have hailed it as a "monumental contribution" to science and others have condemned it as "dangerous, dehumanizing and unethical research" (Ross, 1988).

Milgram's (1963) subjects were a diverse collection of 40 men from the local community. They were told that the study was concerned with the effects of punishment on learning. When they arrived at the lab, they drew slips of paper from a hat to get their assignments. The drawing was rigged so that the subject always became the "teacher" and an accomplice of Milgram's (a likable 47-year-old accountant) became the "learner."

The teacher watched while the learner was strapped into a chair and as electrodes were attached to his arms. Shocks were to be delivered through the electrodes whenever he made a mistake on the task. The subject was then taken to an adjoining room that housed the shock generator, which he would control in his role as the teacher. Although the apparatus looked and sounded realistic, it was a fake and the learner was never shocked. The experimenter played the role of the authority figure who told the teacher what to do and answered any questions that arose.

The experiment was designed in such a way that the learner would make many mistakes, and the teacher was instructed to increase the shock level after each wrong answer. At 300 volts, the learner began to pound on the wall between the two rooms in protest and soon stopped responding to the teacher's questions. From this point forward, subjects frequently turned to the experimenter for guidance. Whenever they did so, the experimenter

---

Peer pressure to "have one more" can result in tragedy.

by our social group; and failing to come to someone's defense or refusing to take a stand when it might make us unpopular to do so. We hope our discussion of social influence in this chapter will make you more aware of the operation of such tactics and better able to resist social pressure when negative consequences to you or others are a likely result. Next we'll consider another type of social influence, obedience to authority.

Obedience: The Power of Authority

bedience **is a form of compliance that occurs when people follow direct commands, usually from someone in a position of author-ity.** If you reluctantly follow a supervisor's suggestions at work, for example, even though you think they're lousy ideas, you're complying with a superior's wishes. In itself, obedience isn't good or bad. To get at that important issue, we need to consider what we are being asked to do. If the fire alarm goes off in your classroom and your instructor orders you to leave, it is good to be obedient. But if you're asked to engage in an illegal act by an authority figure or to do something that goes against your conscience, *disobedience* is probably in order. It is important to understand how the phenomenon of obedience operates because both anecdotal and empirical evidence suggests that in the right circum-

Stanley Milgram

(authority figure) firmly stated that the teacher should continue to give stronger and stronger shocks to the now-silent learner. The dependent variable was the maximum shock the subject was willing to administer before refusing to cooperate.

As Figure 7.5 shows, 26 of the 40 subjects (65%) administered all 30 levels of shock. Although they tended to obey the experimenter, many subjects voiced and displayed considerable distress about harming the learner. They groaned, bit their lips, stuttered, trembled, and broke into a sweat—but they continued to administer the shocks. On the basis of these findings, Milgram concluded that obedience to authority was even more common than he or others had anticipated.

Milgram found that obedience increased (1) when the authority figure was physically near the subjects rather than distant, (2) when the victim was less visible and less audible to the subjects, and (3) when the experiment was conducted at a prestigious university rather than at an unimpressive-looking office building. These findings suggest that our actions are determined less by the *kind of person* we are than by the *kind of situation* we are in. According to Milgram, the situational factors mentioned above combine to produce a shift in perspective that leads to obedience to the authority figure. That is, people in obedience situations don't suddenly lose their sense of morality. Rather, we begin focusing on how well we're living up to the expectations of the authority figure instead of evaluating our actions according to their harmful effects on the victim. In other words, we align ourselves with the authority figure instead of with the victim.

Applying this insight to Nazi war crimes and other atrocities, Milgram made a chilling assertion: Inhuman and evil visions may originate in the disturbed mind of an authority figure such as Hitler, but it is only through the obedient actions of normal people that such ideas can be turned into frightening reality. Given the right circumstances, he concluded, any of us might obey orders to inflict harm on innocent strangers.

After his initial demonstration, Milgram (1974) tried about 20 variations on his experimental procedure, looking for factors that influenced subjects' obedience. Milgram was surprised at how stable subjects' obedience remained as he changed various aspects of his experiment. In one of the later experiments, Milgram studied female subjects to see if there were gender differences in obedience to authority. He found no significant differences between men and women in obedience behavior. (Women *did* report higher levels of tension than male subjects did, but this difference may have been due to women's willingness to report high tension levels rather than to the actual experience of greater tension.)

If you're like most people, you're confident that you wouldn't follow an experimenter's

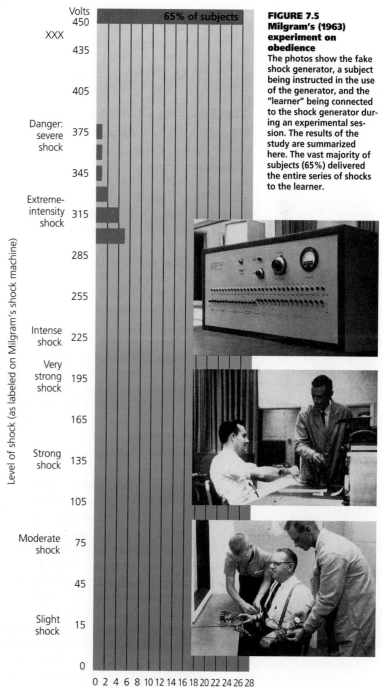

FIGURE 7.5
Milgram's (1963) experiment on obedience
The photos show the fake shock generator, a subject being instructed in the use of the generator, and the "learner" being connected to the shock generator during an experimental session. The results of the study are summarized here. The vast majority of subjects (65%) delivered the entire series of shocks to the learner.

demands to inflict harm on a helpless victim. But the empirical findings indicate that you're probably wrong. After many replications, the data are clear, and their implications are frightening and deplorable. Most of us can be coerced into engaging in actions that violate our morals and values. Perhaps we would all do well to heed the warning of Pastor Martin Niemoeller, a member of the clergy during the Nazi regime in Germany:

> "First the Nazis went after the Jews, but I wasn't a Jew, so I didn't react. Then they went after the Catholics, but I wasn't a Catholic, so I didn't object. Then they went after the workers, but I wasn't a worker, so I didn't stand up. Then they went after the Protestant clergy, and by then it was too late for anybody to stand up."

The Ensuing Controversy

Milgram's study evoked a controversy that continues today. Some critics argued that Milgram's results wouldn't generalize to the real world (Baumrind, 1964; Orne & Holland, 1968). They maintained that subjects who agree to participate in a scientific study *expect to obey* orders from an experimenter. Milgram (1964, 1968) replied by pointing out that so do soldiers and bureaucrats in the real world who are accused of villainous acts performed in obedience to authority. "I reject Baumrind's argument that the observed obedience doesn't count because it occurred where it is appropriate," said Milgram (1964). "That is precisely why it *does* count." Overall, the weight of evidence supports the generalizability of Milgram's findings. The results were consistently replicated for many years, in diverse settings, with a variety of subjects and procedural variations (A. G. Miller, 1986).

Critics also questioned the ethics of Milgram's procedure (Baumrind, 1964). They noted that, without prior consent, subjects were exposed to extensive deception that could undermine their trust in people and to severe stress that could leave emotional scars. Milgram's defenders argued that the brief distress experienced by his subjects was a small price to pay for the insights that emerged from his obedience studies. Looking back, however, many psychologists share the critics' concerns about the ethical implications of Milgram's work. His procedure is questionable by contemporary standards of research ethics. At most universities it would be difficult to obtain permission to replicate Milgram's study today—a bizarre epitaph for what may be psychology's best-known experiment.

How the Presence of Others Can Influence Our Behavior

 o far, we've discussed how attitudes and behaviors can be influenced by the *deliberate* attempts of others to influence us—by the use of rhetoric, social pressure, and the power of authority. Research suggests that others can also influence our behavior even when they are *not* attempting to do so. For example, what causes an outstanding athlete to choke under pressure in front of the hometown crowd? Why do some normally articulate people stutter and stammer when they have to talk in front of a group? It seems that the *mere presence* of others can sometimes cause us to behave in atypical ways.

Social Facilitation

The fact that the presence of other people can affect our behavior has been well documented in numerous psychology experiments. Interestingly, some research has shown that the presence of others *enhances* performance while other studies have demonstrated that the presence of others *impairs* performance. For many years social psychologists were puzzled by these inconsistent effects. Then Robert Zajonc (1965) provided a neat explanation for the confusion, which is diagrammed in Figure 7.6a. He showed that the presence of other people produces physiological arousal, which facilitates responses that are dominant in a given situation (dominant responses are simple, well-learned responses that are easy to perform in a particular situation). Sometimes, the facilitation of dominant responses improves performance, whereas at other times it hurts performance. When a task is simple or well known to us, the dominant response is usually the correct one, so arousal boosts performance. If you're instructed to add a few single-digit numbers in the presence of others, for example, you will probably do better with an audience than alone. But when tasks are complex or unfamiliar, our dominant response is often incorrect, and in these situations arousal tends to interfere with performance (Zajonc, 1965, 1980). If you're asked to solve a number of elaborate algebraic equations, for example, you'll probably do worse with an audience than on your own. The phenomenon described by Zajonc is called *social facilitation*—**the tendency to perform dominant responses when others are present.**

Zajonc's explanation for the confusing pattern of research findings was an important breakthrough, but debate continues about the exact conditions under which social facilitation is likely to occur. Zajonc believes that the mere presence of others is sufficient to produce arousal and social facilitation, while other theorists maintain that factors in addition to mere presence are needed. According to Nickolas Cottrell (1972), one of these additional factors is *evaluation apprehension, or the concern that others may evaluate us negatively.* To separate the effects of mere presence and evaluation apprehension, Cottrell and his colleagues looked at subjects working on a complex task in one of three conditions: no audience, a blindfolded audience of two other people (who were supposedly waiting to participate in a perception experiment), or a nonblindfolded audience of two (Cottrell, Wack, Sekerak, & Rittle, 1968). They found that the subjects with the nonblindfolded audience made more dominant responses than did the subjects who had no audience. However, subjects with the blindfolded audience made about the same number of dominant responses as subjects without an audience. Hence this study demonstrated that the mere presence of others does not always produce social facilitation. Cottrell's alternative model of social facilitation, which emphasizes the role of evaluation apprehension, is outlined in Figure 7.6b.

Still, it is important to note that numerous experiments support Zajonc's mere-presence explanation of the social facilitation effect (Markus, 1981). Therefore, it seems that mere presence may produce enough arousal to affect performance under certain conditions, but not enough to affect performance in others. In the latter case, the presence of additional factors such as evaluation apprehension seems to be necessary to produce the social facilitation effect.

Choking under Pressure

Just before the 1992 Summer Olympic Games in Barcelona, the gymnast Kim Zmeskal appeared on the cover of *Time* magazine as one of America's sure bets for a gold medal. On the basis of her performance in previous high-level competitions, her coach, Bela Karolyi, described her as having "an outstanding capability to pull herself together and perform consistently under pressure" (Smolowe, 1992, p. 58). Expecting easy victories for Zmeskal, television viewers watched in disbelief as, in event after event, the 16-year-old gymnast made critical mistakes in her programs. These errors cost her only fractions of points, but any deductions can be fatal in Olympic-level competition. Though she did win a gold medal in the team competition, she failed to win a medal of any kind in any of the individual events. Undoubtedly

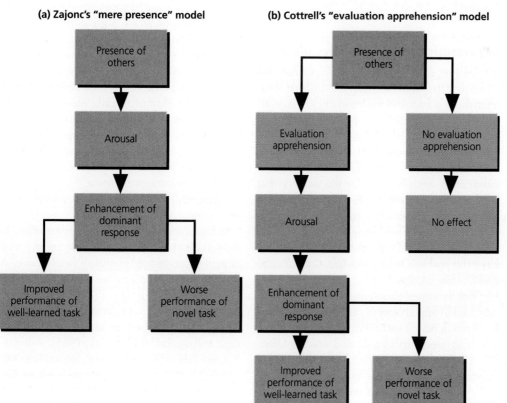

(a) Zajonc's "mere presence" model

Presence of others → Arousal → Enhancement of dominant response → Improved performance of well-learned task / Worse performance of novel task

(b) Cottrell's "evaluation apprehension" model

Presence of others → Evaluation apprehension → Arousal → Enhancement of dominant response → Improved performance of well-learned task / Worse performance of novel task

Presence of others → No evaluation apprehension → No effect

**FIGURE 7.6
Two models of social facilitation**
Several competing models have been proposed to explain the dynamics of social facilitation effects. The two most influential models are diagrammed here. Panel (a) shows the original model of social facilitation developed by Zajonc (1965), which assumes that the mere presence of others is sufficient to produce the arousal that leads to social facilitation. Panel (b) shows an alternative model developed by Cottrell (1972), which proposes that evaluation apprehension fosters the arousal that is the impetus for social facilitation. (Adapted from Sabini, 1992.)

there were many reasons for Zmeskal's disappointing performance at the Olympics, but an interesting hypothesis—which we have no way of proving—is that one of the causes of her poor performance was the intense pre-Olympics publicity she received. Similarly, consider the case of Dave O'Brien, the world-class American decathlete viewed as a serious contender for a gold medal: O'Brien, a seasoned competitor, shocked the sports world by not even making it past the Olympic qualifying trials. He, too, received considerable media attention. In fact, after O'Brien failed to make the American Olympic team, Reebok had to pull the television commercials that featured him and Dan Johnson as friendly competitors in the decathlon and reshoot them.

We recount these instances of unexpectedly disappointing performances not to disparage the impressive achievements of the athletes but to illustrate the phenomenon of choking under pressure, or failing to perform at an expected, high level when it is important to do so. Although choking under pressure isn't limited to situations in which individuals perform in front of others, it often occurs in this situation (Baumeister, 1984). As you'll recall from our earlier discussion of this issue as it relates to stress (Chapter 3), pressure to perform can produce *elevated self-consciousness*. When increased self-focus causes us to pay *too much* attention to almost automatic tasks, our performance can be impaired.

Communication Apprehension

It's the first day of child psychology class and you have just learned that 30-minute oral reports are a course requirement. Do you welcome this opportunity to polish your public speaking skills, or do you race in panic to the registrar's office to drop the class? If you opted for the latter choice, you may suffer from **communication apprehension, or the anxiety that is caused when we have to talk with others.** Some people experience communication apprehension in all speaking situations (even one-on-one encounters), but most people who have the problem notice it when they have to speak before groups.

Bodily experiences associated with communication apprehension can range from small increases in heart rate to butterflies in the stomach, cold hands, dry mouth, and a racing heartbeat (McKay, Davis, & Fanning, 1983). These physiological effects are stress-induced fight-or-flight responses of the autonomic nervous system (see Chapter 3). Interestingly, it isn't the

physiological responses themselves that are the root of communication apprehension, but rather our *interpretation* of our bodily responses (McCroskey & Beatty, 1986). That is, individuals who score high on measures of communication apprehension frequently interpret the bodily changes they experience in public speaking situations as indications of fear. In contrast, those who score low on these measures are likely to interpret such physiological reactions as excitement and as normal in such a situation (McCroskey & Beatty, 1986).

Four types of responses to high communication apprehension have been identified. The most common response is *communication avoidance*, a reaction that occurs when people are confronted with a communication situation and can choose whether or not they want to participate in it. If they believe that speaking will make them uncomfortable, these individuals will typically avoid participating. *Communication withdrawal* occurs when people unexpectedly find themselves in a communication situation that they can't get out of. In this case, people may clam up entirely or say as little as possible. *Communication disruption* refers to the inability to make fluent oral presentations or to the use of inappropriate verbal or nonverbal behavior. Of course, inadequate communication skills can produce the same behavioral effect, and it isn't always possible for the average person to identify the actual cause of the problem. *Excessive communication* is a relatively unusual response to high communication apprehension, but it does occur. Consider the person who attempts to dominate social situations. Although individuals who exhibit this response are perceived as poor communicators, most people do not usually identify them as having communication apprehension, because we expect to see it only in people who don't talk very much. Of course, excessive communication may be caused by factors other than communication apprehension.

James McCroskey, an expert who has written extensively on this topic, suggests that avoidance and withdrawal tactics are effective only as *short*-term strategies for coping with communication apprehension (McCroskey & Beatty, 1986). Because it is unlikely that we can go through life without ever having to speak in front of a group, it is important to learn to cope with this stressful event rather than avoid it time and again (McKay et al., 1983). Allowing the problem to get out of hand can result in self-limiting behavior such as refusing a job promotion that would entail public speaking. Not unexpectedly, research indicates that people with high levels of communication apprehension are likely to have difficulties in interpersonal relationships and in work and educational settings (McCroskey & Beatty, 1986). Both cognitive restructuring (Chapter 4) and systematic desensitization (Chapter 16) have proved to be very effective methods for dealing with this problem (McCroskey & Beatty, 1986).

The Bystander Effect

Imagine that you have a precarious medical condition, and you have to go through life worrying whether someone will leap forward to provide help if the need arises. Wouldn't you feel more secure when a lot of people were around? After all, there is safety in numbers. Logically, as the number of people increases, the probability that one of them will be a good Samaritan increases. Or does it? Apparently not. Many studies have uncovered a paradox called the *bystander effect*: **individuals are less likely to provide needed help when others are present than when they are alone.**

The existence of the bystander effect was first documented by John Darley and Bibb Latané (1968). In their groundbreaking study, students in individual cubicles connected by an intercom participated in discussion groups of three sizes. The separate cubicles allowed the researchers to examine each individual's behavior in the presence of others, thus minimizing the problem of confounded variables in individual-group comparisons. Early in the discussion, a student who was an accomplice of the experimenter hesitantly mentioned that he was prone to seizures. Later in the discussion, the accomplice feigned a severe seizure and called out for help. Figure 7.7 shows that although a majority of subjects sought assistance for the accomplice, the tendency to seek help *declined* as the number of bystanders increased.

Similar trends have been found in many other experiments. More than 6,000 subjects have had opportunities to respond to apparent emergencies—fires, asthma attacks, faintings, crashes, flat tires—as well as less pressing situations, as when a stranger drops a scattering of objects on the ground (Latané & Nida, 1981). Many of the experiments have been highly realistic studies conducted in subways, stores, and shopping malls. Many have compared individuals against groups in face-to-face interaction. Pooling the results of this research, Latané and Nida (1981) estimated that subjects who were alone provided help 75% of the time. In contrast, subjects in the presence of others provided help only 53% of the time. The only significant limiting condition on the bystander effect is that it is less likely to occur when the need for help is very clear.

What accounts for the bystander effect? Several factors appear to be at work. The bystander effect is most likely to occur in *ambiguous situations* because people look around to see if others think there's an emergency. If everyone hesitates, the general inaction suggests that there's no real need for help. ***Diffusion of responsibility,* or the expectation that others who are present will take responsibility for action,** is also an important factor. If you're by yourself when you encounter someone in need of help, the responsibility to provide help rests squarely on your shoulders. If other people are present, however, the responsibility is divided among you, and everyone may think: Someone else will help. We also see *evaluation apprehension* at work again—people worry that others will evaluate them negatively if they do something foolish, such as respond to an emergency when there really isn't one (Baumeister, 1982). The four topics we've discussed so far are produced by the presence of others and our awareness that they are observing us. Now let us look at what can happen when we believe that others are *not* able to identify us.

Deindividuation: Hiding in the Crowd

Americans watched their television sets in horror and disbelief in May 1992 as nightmarish scenes from Los Angeles flashed before their eyes: a truck driver hauled from his cab and beaten and kicked senseless; storefront windows being smashed; people running out of stores with as many stolen items as they could carry. Other chilling scenes also come to mind: lynch mobs that burned, whipped, and dismembered black men in the United States in the late 19th and early 20th centuries; violence erupting at soccer games in England; rock concerts and political marches that turn ugly.

How is it that normal, law-abiding citizens can turn into a dangerous mob? Social psychologists use the term ***deindividuation* to refer to the loss of self-awareness and evaluation apprehension that can occur when individuals believe they are anonymous.** Philip Zimbardo (1970) designed the experiment that first demonstrated this phenomenon in the laboratory. In this study, college women were led to believe that they would be participating in a study of empathic responses to strangers.

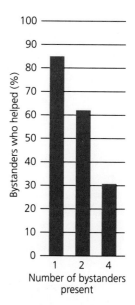

FIGURE 7.7
The bystander effect
As the number of apparent bystanders increased, the percentage of subjects who sought help for a victim of a (feigned) seizure declined. (Data from Darley & Latané, 1968.)

A group of anonymous subjects in the Zimbardo (1970) deindividuation study.

Subjects were assigned to one of four conditions that varied in degree of anonymity. In the "easily identifiable" condition, subjects were greeted by name and wore name tags. In the "anonymous" condition, subjects wore oversized lab coats and hoods and were never called by name (see the adjacent photo). Subjects in all of the conditions were given an opportunity to give electric shocks to a person who was not a member of the group. (As in Milgram's obedience experiments, all of the shocks were fake and the "victim" never received any shocks.) Zimbardo found that the anonymous group gave almost twice as many shocks as did the other groups whose members were more or less easily identified. Hence Zimbardo concluded that *anonymity* is the key factor that produces deindividuation.

Other factors that contribute to deindividuation have also been identified, among them *diffusion of responsibility* and a *shift in perspective*. The latter refers to the tendency, when we're in a deindividuated state, to evaluate our behavior as it relates to the crowd's actions, whereas we normally evaluate our actions in the context of our personal values (Diener, 1980).

Groups consist of individuals who interact and who depend on one another to achieve shared goals. At one time or another, people find themselves in many types of groups, such as sports teams, unions, civic organizations, and juries. Groups vary in size, purpose, formality, activities, and other characteristics, but all have important effects on their members.

Obviously, being a member of a large gathering allows individuals to hide in the crowd. Of course, people acting on their own can make themselves anonymous by wearing disguises or masks, for example. So is it being in a crowd or the anonymity that a crowd often provides that is the critical factor? Research indicates that it is anonymity and lowered self-awareness—whether or not others are present—that is the important factor (Diener, 1980). Hence it seems that a crowd can produce deindividuation, but *only when* those in it feel anonymous.

The Nature of Groups

e may not think about it much, but most of us belong to a diverse array of groups that play a large role in our lives. We are members of clubs, classes, work crews, unions, sports teams, churches, fraternities, sororities, cliques, and committees. But what makes a collection of people a group?

What Is a Group?

Are all the divorced fathers living in Baltimore a group? Are three strangers moving skyward in an elevator a group? What if the elevator gets stuck? How about four students from your psychology class who study together regularly? A jury deciding a court case? The Boston Celtics? The United States Congress? Some of these collections of people are groups and others aren't. Let's examine the concept of a group and find out which ones qualify.

In social psychologists' eyes, **a *group* consists of two or more individuals who interact and are interdependent.** The divorced fathers in Baltimore aren't likely to qualify on either count—they don't know one another and don't depend on one another to accomplish joint

goals. Strangers sharing an elevator might interact briefly, but they're not interdependent. If the elevator got stuck and they had to deal with an emergency together, however, they could suddenly become a group. Your psychology classmates who study together are a group because they interact and depend on one another to achieve shared goals. And so do the members of a jury, a sports team such as the Celtics, and a large organization such as the U.S. Congress.

Why Do We Join Groups?

We have little control over some of the groups we belong to. You were born into your family, and you were assigned to classes in grade school and high school. If you take a certain job, you may be required to join a union. However, we voluntarily join most of the groups that we belong to. Why do we seek membership in these groups? There are many reasons. Edgar Schein (1980), a prominent organizational theorist, suggests that we join groups to achieve five goals.

1. To fulfill our need for affiliation. Some animals (bears and bald eagles, for example) don't mind going it alone. Humans, however, react very badly to prolonged isolation. We need to spend time with others. Abraham Maslow referred to this need to associate with others as the need for belongingness. He saw it as a very basic human need and placed it at the third level in his hierarchy (see Chapter 2). Thus we belong to groups to fulfill our needs for companionship, friendship, social support, and affection.

2. To enhance our sense of identity and self-esteem. When we belong to groups such as fraternities, sororities, country clubs, and cliques, the acceptance we receive from others can enhance our feelings of self-worth. Our memberships in some groups also help us to define who we are. For instance, a young boy might join a neighborhood gang to fortify his view of himself as a tough guy. Similarly, a college professor might join the American Civil Liberties Union (ACLU) to enhance her vision of herself as a liberal intellectual.

3. To gain social comparison information. According to *social comparison theory* (Chapter 5), we need to compare ourselves with others to gain insight into our own feelings and behavior. In group interactions we can exchange information with others to check our perceptions of reality. Schein notes that when a group of workers agree that their boss is a slave driver, they are validating one another's feelings.

4. To increase mutual security and power. People often band together in groups to pursue common goals because there is power in numbers. One worker who complains about a slave-driver boss probably won't get very far. If all six of the workers under this boss unite in their complaint, however, they may have some impact. The power of numbers is the key principle underlying the formation of labor unions, consumers' rights groups, and grass-roots community organizations.

5. To get something accomplished. Obviously, an individual working alone cannot build a superhighway or a skyscraper. Many jobs of much smaller magnitude also require a team effort. Thus we join groups to accomplish an infinite variety of tasks.

Key Properties of Groups

When we join together in groups, we create social organisms with unique characteristics and dynamics that can take on a life of their own. Groups vary in many ways. Obviously, a study group, the Celtics, and the U.S. Congress differ considerably in purpose, formality, the similarity of their members, and the diversity of

their activities. Can anything meaningful be said about groups if they're so diverse? Yes. Despite their immense variability, groups share certain properties that affect their functioning. Knowing something about the key characteristics of groups and how they work can help you function more effectively as a group member.

Among other things, most groups have *roles* that allocate special responsibilities to some members, *norms* about suitable behavior, a *communication structure* that reflects who talks to whom, and a *power structure* that determines which members wield the most influence (Forsyth, 1983). A study group and the Celtics may appear to have little in common, but both may have a "harmonizer" whose role is to smooth over conflicts among members, a norm that "we all pull our own weight," and an unequal distribution of power among members. Other key properties of groups include their *size* and their *cohesiveness*. Let's examine each of these aspects of groups.

Roles and Norms

The members of a group are not necessarily interchangeable. In a small corporation, for instance, you wouldn't expect a computer programmer and a janitor to exchange responsibilities. In most groups, members develop specialized roles. This term is borrowed from the world of theater, where it refers to an actor's part in a play. **A *role* is a pattern of behavior expected of a person who has a certain position in a group.** There are role expectations associated with your status as a student, for example. You are expected to show up for classes, participate in discussions, ask questions, read assigned material, write papers, and take tests. The roles associated with being a student, a professor, a company president, a salesperson, and a secretary are *institutionalized roles*. These are formal roles defined by institutions, such as businesses and schools. The expectations that go along with institutionalized roles usually are fairly explicit.

As groups evolve, informal roles that are less explicit may also emerge. These informal roles fall into two categories: task-related roles and socioemotional roles (Bales, 1958). **_Task-related roles_ focus on moving the group toward completion of its mission.** Group members who fill task-related roles seek information, coordinate members' activities, refocus group discussion when necessary, and so forth. Their top priority is getting the job done. **_Socioemotional roles_ focus on keeping interactions in the group friendly and supportive.** Members of

the group who take on socioemotional roles offer praise and encouragement, make jokes to relieve tension, highlight areas of agreement, and so forth. Their top priority is maintaining group harmony.

In accord with traditional gender-role expectations, research on mixed-sex groups suggests that men are more likely to take task-oriented roles whereas women fill socioemotional roles (Eagly & Wood, 1991; Wood, 1987; Wood, Polek, & Aiken, 1985). When problems require task-oriented behavior (finding a single correct answer), all-male groups perform better than all-female groups, but when problems require complex social interactions (finding a solution through social interaction), all-female groups outperform their male counterparts (Wood, 1987).

Some common task-related and socioemotional roles are listed in Figure 7.8. Although some group members may fill both roles, most people specialize in one or the other.

Our behavior in groups is influenced by norms as well as roles. **_Group norms_ are rules regarding appropriate behavior.** Fraternities and sororities, for example, have norms about deference to senior members, adequate grades, and acceptable drinking. In the world of business, companies have norms about suitable attire, about going through appropriate channels to lodge complaints, and about how hard employees should work. Group norms usually are informal unwritten laws, and they may vary dramatically from one group to another. One company's employees may be under intense pressure to work long hours. At another firm down the street, employees may feel pressure not to show up others by working hard. Thus norms vary from one group to another, but all ongoing groups have normative expectations that can exert powerful effects on members' behavior.

Communication Structure

Perhaps the most important thing that we do in groups is to communicate with one another. As you may have noticed, some group members talk more than others. Interestingly, researchers who studied groups ranging in size from four to 12 members discovered that the pattern of talking follows a curve that can be represented mathematically (Stephan & Mishler, 1952). In eight-person groups, for example, the two most talkative members accounted for 60% of the group's discussion. In some groups, every member may be able to talk to every other member. However, many groups—for example, military units, corporations, and governmental bureaucracies—have prescriptions about appropriate channels of communication.

Communication in groups is generally described as being *centralized* (only one or a few people can talk to the group at large) or *decentralized* (communication is shared equally among members). Do centralized or decentralized networks solve problems more effectively? Which works faster? Which produces higher satisfaction among its members? Research on these issues has uncovered the following trends (McGrath, 1984). When problems are simple, people in centralized networks solve them faster and make fewer errors. When the problems are complex, however, decentralized networks are speedier and more effective. Group satisfaction is consistently higher in decentralized groups. We don't particularly like having our communication options heavily restricted.

Power Structure

Even more than communication opportunities, power tends to be unevenly distributed in most groups. Power is a murky concept, but most theorists define **power as the potential to influence the group's decisions and individual members' behavior.** Power is often confused with high status because they are associated, but they are *not* equivalent. At colleges around the country, for example, department chairpersons share a similar (high) status. The amount of power they wield over their faculties, however, varies enormously.

If status doesn't ensure power, what are the sources of social power? In a classic analysis, John R. P. French and Bertram Raven (1959) identified five key bases of power in groups, which are described in Figure 7.9. *Reward power* stems from a person's ability to control group members' reinforcers or payoffs. For example, a department chairperson who can control faculty members' promotions and pay raises (not all chairpersons can) has reward power. *Coercive power* is based on a person's ability or willingness to threaten and punish group members. In academia, a chairperson's coercive power is usually very limited because it is nearly impossible to fire a tenured faculty member, and there are no demotions. Coercive power tends to be greater in the business world, where many managers can easily demote or fire employees.

Expert power is derived from a person's spe-

Task and Socioemotional Roles in Groups

Role	Function
Task roles	
1 Information seeker	Emphasizes "getting the facts" by calling for background information from others
2 Opinion seeker	Asks for more qualitative types of data, such as attitudes, values, and feelings
3 Elaborator	Gives additional information—examples, rephrasing, implications—about points made by others
4 Coordinator	Shows the relevance of each idea and its relationship to the overall problem
5 Orienter	Refocuses discussion on the topic whenever necessary
6 Evaluator-critic	Appraises the quality of the group's efforts in terms of logic, practicality, or method
7 Energizer	Stimulates the group to continue working when discussion lags
Socioemotional roles	
1 Encourager	Rewards others through agreement, warmth, and praise
2 Harmonizer	Mediates conflicts among group members
3 Compromiser	Shifts his or her own position on an issue in order to reduce conflict in the group
4 Gatekeeper and expediter	Smooths communication by setting up procedures and ensuring equal participation from members
5 Standard setter	Expresses, or calls for discussion of, standards for evaluating the quality of the group process
6 Group observer and commentator	Informally points out the positive and negative aspects of the group's dynamics and calls for change if necessary
7 Follower	Accepts the ideas offered by others and serves as an audience for the group

FIGURE 7.8
Representative roles in groups
The roles we play in groups generally fall into two categories: task-related roles and socioemotional roles. Seven roles in each category are described here.

Five Bases of Power

Base	Definition
Reward power	Influence based on positive or negative reinforcers given or offered to the target
Coercive power	Influence based on punishment or threats directed toward the target
Expert power	Influence based on the target's belief that the power holder possesses superior skills and abilities
Referent power	Influence based on the target's identification with, attraction to, or respect for the power holder
Legitimate power	Influence based on the target's belief that the power holder has a justifiable right to demand the performance of certain behaviors

FIGURE 7.9
Sources of power
French and Raven (1959) identified five bases for power in groups.

cial skills, abilities, or knowledge. In designing a placement test, for example, the members of an academic department may defer to a chairperson who has great expertise in testing theory. *Referent power* depends on how much a person is liked and respected by group members. Other things being equal, people who are well liked can exert more influence over a group than those who inspire disdain. Department chairpersons who have minimal reward, coercive, or expert power often carefully cultivate referent power. Finally, *legitimate power* stems from a person's recognized right to make certain demands. When group members defer out of a sense of duty or obligation, they are being swayed by legitimate power. Department chairs who are freely elected by their departments probably can rely on more legitimate power than chairpersons who are appointed by higher-level administrators.

Group Cohesiveness

The term *group cohesiveness* refers to the strength of the bonds that link group members to one another and to the group itself. Members of cohesive groups are close-knit, have team spirit, and are very loyal to the group.

What makes a group cohesive? According to Ridgeway (1983), factors that foster cohesiveness include similar attitudes among group members, personal liking for one another, and warm, pleasant group interactions. Groups also tend to become more cohesive when they are successful in attaining their goals. A threat from outside the group may also serve to unify its members and bolster cohesiveness.

The consequences of high cohesiveness are a mixed bag of positive and negative effects (Cartwright, 1968). On the positive side of the ledger, people in cohesive groups communicate with one another more and participate more in

group activities. On the negative side, high cohesiveness increases the pressure on members to conform to the group's norms. Conformity is not inherently bad, but it can backfire if it suppresses critical thinking in a group. When members don't feel free to criticize their group's direction, poor decision making can result. We'll come back to the issue of poor decision making in groups later in the chapter when we discuss *groupthink*.

Group Size

Unlike cohesiveness, which is difficult to measure, size is a relatively unambiguous feature of groups. It is also an important feature. Variations in group size (the number of people in the group) can affect many aspects of the group experience. As groups increase in size, for instance, members' participation rates and the group's cohesiveness tend to decline (Shaw, 1981).

Productivity in Groups

opular wisdom has it that a group of people working on a task can accomplish more than a person working alone. While this is often the case, sometimes it is not. In this section we'll discuss two phenomena that interfere with group productivity and offer some suggestions for improving group productivity. Your awareness of this information can make you a more effective group member and leader.

Social Loafing

Have you ever driven through a road construction project—at a snail's pace, of course—and become irritated by the sight of many workers who seem to be just standing around? Maybe the irony of the posted sign "Your tax dollars at work" made you imagine that they were all dawdling. And then again, perhaps not. Individuals' productivity often *does* decline in larger groups (Latané, Williams, & Harkins, 1979).

Two factors appear to contribute to reduced individual productivity in larger groups. One factor is reduced *efficiency* due to the *loss of coordination* among workers' efforts. As you put more people on a yearbook staff, for instance, you'll probably create more and more duplication of effort. You may also increase the number of times group members end up working at cross-purposes.

Reduced coordination among workers can show up on the simplest of tasks, as an agricultural engineer named Max Ringelmann demonstrated years ago. He measured the amount of pressure exerted by individuals and groups who pulled on a rope as if they were playing tug-of-war. Ringelmann found that the amount of pressure produced per person declined steadily as the size of the group increased (Kravitz & Martin, 1986). He pointed out that even on this simple task, some group members pulled when others paused, so that lack of coordination undermined their efficiency.

The second factor contributing to low productivity in groups is *effort* rather than efficiency. **Social loafing is a reduction in effort by individuals when they work in groups.** To investigate social loafing, Latané and his colleagues (1979) measured the sound output produced by subjects who were asked to cheer or clap as loudly as they could. So they couldn't see or hear other group members, subjects were told that the study concerned the importance of sensory feedback and were asked to don blindfolds and put on headphones through which loud noise was played. This maneuver permitted a simple deception. Subjects were *led to believe* that they were working alone or in a group of two or six, when *individual* output was actually measured.

When subjects *thought* that they were working in larger groups (the pseudogroup condition), their individual output declined. Since lack of coordination could not affect individual output, the subjects' decreased sound production had to be due to reduced effort. Latané and his colleagues also had the same subjects clap and shout in genuine groups of two and six and found an additional decrease in production, which they attributed to loss of coordination. Figure 7.10 shows how social loafing and loss of coordination combined to reduce productivity as group size increased.

According to Latané (1981), social loafing is caused by *diffusion of responsibility*. Obviously, this phenomenon will be much more likely to operate in *large* groups. That is, as group size increases, the responsibility for getting a job done is divided among more people, and many group members ease up because their individual contributions are less recognizable. Social loafing is reduced when specific responsibilities are given to individuals in a group, so that their personal contributions remain recognizable (Weldon & Gargano, 1988). Motivating a group to evaluate its collective performance carefully may also reduce social loafing (Harkins & Szymanski, 1989).

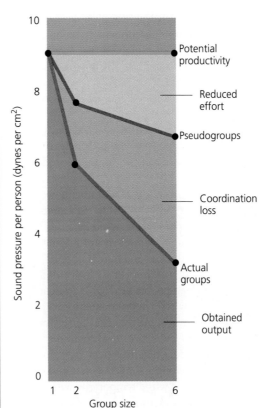

FIGURE 7.10
The effect of loss of coordination and social loafing on group productivity
The amount of sound that each person produced declined noticeably when people worked in pairs or in a group of six (red line). This decrease in productivity reflects both loss of coordination and social loafing. Sound per person also declined when subjects merely thought they were working in pairs or a group of six ("pseudogroups"; green line). This smaller decline in productivity is due to social loafing. (Data from Latané et al., 1979.)

In fairness to groups, although individual productivity usually declines, there may still be strength in numbers. The net productivity of 20 construction workers should dwarf that of one construction worker, barring inconceivable slacking off by the group. Obviously, there are many circumstances in which group performance is likely to exceed individual performance.

The nature of the task is a key determinant of whether groups or individuals tend to perform better (Steiner, 1976). Groups normally have an advantage on *additive tasks*, when the group's production is the sum of its members' efforts (for example, sandbagging the banks of a river in a flood or stuffing envelopes). However, groups are less likely to excel on *conjunctive tasks*, when the group's production cannot exceed that of its weakest member (for example, climbing a mountain or running a relay).

Improving Group Productivity

When we work together in groups, productivity often is a crucial concern. Is there anything that we can do to increase the likelihood of productive interactions in groups? Research on group performance yields the following suggestions.

1. *Increase members' commitment to group goals.* Group members tend to work harder and are less prone to social loafing when they iden-

tify strongly with the group's goals (Zaccaro, 1984). A strong commitment to group goals is more likely when members feel that they've had reasonable input into the group's objectives (Latham & Yukl, 1975). Thus it is wise to discuss and attempt to reach agreement on group goals to maximize motivation.

2. *Encourage open communication*. Groups that welcome open, candid interchanges among members tend to be more productive (Harper & Askling, 1980). A decentralized communication structure will usually work out best unless a group's tasks are very simple. It's especially important to avoid *defensiveness*—that is, excessive concern among members about being attacked and hurt (Gibb, 1973). As we discussed in Chapter 6, individuals get defensive when people are highly evaluative or controlling, when they act superior to others, and when they assume that they're always right. According to Osborn (1963), *brainstorming* is one way to reduce defensiveness. In brainstorming sessions, group members generate as many ideas as possible while temporarily withholding criticism and evaluation (see Chapter 4).

3. *Make use of process planning*. Process planning involves working out some ground rules about how the group will operate as it tackles a task. Process planning includes discussing matters such as the responsibilities of the chairperson, how frequently the group should meet, and the criteria that should be used in making decisions. Forsyth (1983) points out that most groups plunge right into tasks and devote little or no thought to process planning. Studies suggest, however, that attention to process planning can increase a group's productivity and members' satisfaction with leadership (Hackman, Brousseau, & Weiss, 1976; Hirokawa, 1980).

4. *Try to keep cohesiveness high*. Groups high in cohesiveness tend to be more effective in achieving their goals (Shaw, 1981). Hence it's usually a good idea to encourage members who assume socioemotional roles that promote harmonious relations in a group. Bear in mind, however, that high cohesiveness may create excessive pressure for conformity. Marvin Shaw (1981) notes that high cohesiveness can backfire when a group's goals are handed down from higher authorities. A group is more likely to rebel against leadership from outside the group (and thus undermine productivity) when its cohesiveness is high.

5. *Beware of overly large groups*. People organizing a group are often tempted to assemble as many people as they can, under the assumption that the larger the group, the more it can accomplish. As we have seen, however, larger groups may yield diminishing returns because of social loafing and poor coordination of effort (Latané et al., 1979). The group size that will maximize productivity will vary widely with the nature of the task, but try to avoid assembling overly large, unwieldy groups.

Decision Making in Groups

 roductivity is not the only issue of frequent concern to groups. When people join together in groups, they often have to make decisions about what the group will do and how it will use its resources. Whether it's your study group deciding what type of pizza to order, a jury deciding on a verdict, or Congress deciding whether to pass a bill, groups make decisions.

Evaluating decision making is often more complicated than evaluating productivity. In many cases, the "right" decision may not be readily apparent. Who can say whether your study group ordered the right pizza or whether Congress passed the right bill? Nonetheless, social psychologists have discovered some interesting tendencies in group decision making.

Group Polarization

Who leans toward more cautious decisions: individuals or groups? Common sense suggests that groups will work out compromises that cancel out members' extreme views, so the collective wisdom of the group should yield relatively conservative choices. Is common sense correct? Stoner (1961) investigated this question by asking individuals and groups to make decisions under conditions of uncertainty, such as those seen in the following dilemma.

> Mr. A., an electrical engineer who is married and has one child, has been working for a large electronics corporation since graduating from college five years ago. He is assured of a lifetime job with a modest, though adequate, salary and liberal pension benefits upon retirement. On the other hand, it is very unlikely that his salary will increase much before he retires. While attending a convention, Mr. A. is offered a job with a small, newly founded company which has a highly uncertain future. The new job would pay more to start and would offer the possibility of a share in the ownership if the company survived the competition of the larger firms.

Imagine that you are advising Mr. A. Listed below are several probabilities or odds of the new company proving financially sound. Please check the lowest probability that you would consider acceptable to make it worthwhile for Mr. A. to take the new job.

____The chances are 1 in 10 that the company will prove financially sound.

____The chances are 3 in 10 that the company will prove financially sound.

____The chances are 5 in 10 that the company will prove financially sound.

____The chances are 7 in 10 that the company will prove financially sound.

____The chances are 9 in 10 that the company will prove financially sound.

____Place a check here if you think Mr. A. should not take the new job no matter what the probabilities. [Kogan & Wallach, 1964]

Stoner had individual subjects give their recommendations and then asked the same subjects to engage in group discussion to arrive at a joint recommendation. Stoner then compared the average recommendation of a group's members against their group decision generated through discussion. He found that groups arrived at *riskier* decisions than individuals. Stoner's finding was replicated in other studies (Pruitt, 1971), and the phenomenon acquired the name *risky shift.*

Investigators eventually determined, however, that groups can shift either way, toward risk or toward caution, depending on which way the group leans to begin with (Myers & Lamm, 1976). A shift toward a more extreme position, an effect called polarization, is the frequent result of group discussion. Thus **group polarization occurs when discussion strengthens a group's dominant point of view and produces a shift toward a more extreme decision in that direction** (see Figure 7.11). Group polarization has nothing to do with widening the gap between factions in a group, as its name might suggest. In fact, group polarization can contribute to consensus in a group, as we'll see in our discussion of groupthink.

Groupthink

In contrast to group polarization, which is a normal process in group dynamics, groupthink is more like a disease that can infect decision making in groups. **Groupthink occurs when members of a cohesive group emphasize concurrence at the expense of critical thinking in arriving at a decision.** As you might imagine, groupthink does not produce very effective decision making. Indeed, groupthink often leads to major blunders that may look incomprehensible after the fact.

Irving Janis (1972, 1982) first described groupthink in an effort to explain how President John Kennedy and his advisers could miscalculate so badly in deciding to invade Cuba at the Bay of Pigs in 1961. The attempted invasion failed miserably, and in retrospect it seemed remarkably ill conceived. As Janis put it, "I was puzzled: How could bright men like John F. Kennedy and his advisers be taken in by such a stupid, patchwork plan as the one presented to them by the C.I.A. representatives?" (1973, p. 16). Applying his many years of research and theory on group dynamics to the Bay of Pigs

Irving Janis

FIGURE 7.12
A model of groupthink
The antecedent conditions and symptoms of groupthink are outlined here, along with the effects on a group's decision making.

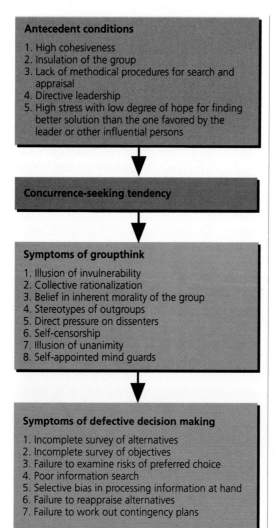

Antecedent conditions

1. High cohesiveness
2. Insulation of the group
3. Lack of methodical procedures for search and appraisal
4. Directive leadership
5. High stress with low degree of hope for finding better solution than the one favored by the leader or other influential persons

Concurrence-seeking tendency

Symptoms of groupthink

1. Illusion of invulnerability
2. Collective rationalization
3. Belief in inherent morality of the group
4. Stereotypes of outgroups
5. Direct pressure on dissenters
6. Self-censorship
7. Illusion of unanimity
8. Self-appointed mind guards

Symptoms of defective decision making

1. Incomplete survey of alternatives
2. Incomplete survey of objectives
3. Failure to examine risks of preferred choice
4. Poor information search
5. Selective bias in processing information at hand
6. Failure to reappraise alternatives
7. Failure to work out contingency plans

fiasco, Janis developed a model of groupthink, which is summarized in Figure 7.12.

Symptoms of Groupthink

According to Janis, when groups get caught up in groupthink, members suspend their critical judgment. The group starts censoring dissent as the pressure to conform increases. Soon everyone begins to think alike. Moreover, "mind guards" try to shield the group from information that contradicts the group's view. At a critical meeting, for instance, President Kennedy did not give a key adviser who opposed the Cuban invasion an opportunity to speak.

If the group's view *is* challenged from outside, victims of groupthink tend to think in simplistic terms. They divide the world into the *in-group*, the group they belong to and identify with, and the *out-group*, people who are not part of the in-group. When groups shift into this "us versus them" thinking, members begin to overestimate the in-group's unanimity and to view the out-group as the enemy. Groupthink also promotes incomplete gathering of information. The group's search for information is biased in favor of facts and opinions that support their decision.

After his description of groupthink, Janis and others reviewed other presidential blunders and found clear signs of groupthink underlying President Franklin Delano Roosevelt's lack of preparation for Japan's attack on Pearl Harbor. Janis also found evidence of groupthink in President Lyndon Johnson's continued escalation of the Vietnam War and in President Richard Nixon's cover-up of the Watergate break-in. Of course, groupthink is not limited to the highest levels of government. It can also occur in less public groups that make decisions every day in boardrooms, committee rooms, courtrooms, and back rooms all over the world.

Sources of Groupthink

What causes groupthink? According to Janis, the probability of groupthink depends on three factors: (1) cohesiveness, (2) certain characteristics of the leader and of the group's structure that encourage premature agreement on a particular solution, and (3) stressful situations.

It makes intuitive sense that groupthink would be greater in groups that exhibit *high cohesiveness*. The pressure to go along with others can be very intense in cohesive groups. Members of cohesive groups are also more likely to adhere to group norms, such as "Don't rock the boat." Under these conditions, group discussions can easily lead to group polarization, strengthening the group's dominant view. Research indicates that high cohesiveness leads to groupthink under some conditions but not others (Longley & Pruitt, 1980; Tetlock et al., 1992). That is, if group members feel insecure

© 1993 by Sidney Harris

and it appears that there is consensus on a particular solution, high cohesiveness can lead to groupthink. If the group's norms encourage the generation and evaluation of possible solutions, however, high cohesiveness leads away from groupthink (Longley & Pruitt, 1980).

Janis describes three other conditions that make groupthink likely: (1) relative *isolation* of the group (little or no input from people outside the group), (2) *directive leadership* (a strong leader who wants to push a particular decision through), and (3) *unsystematic procedures* for generating and evaluating possible decisions. Research findings indicate that structural and procedural factors are associated with the development of groupthink, and that the behavior of the group leader is especially important (Longley & Pruitt, 1980; Tetlock et al., 1992).

Finally, Janis's model predicts that the likelihood of groupthink increases in stressful situations, as when members feel pressured to make a very important decision. As we saw in Chapter 3, stress can impair cognitive functioning. People under stress often do a poor job of reviewing their options and jump to conclusions too quickly (Keinan, 1987). Although this idea is certainly plausible, the role of situational stressors in producing groupthink has not been supported by research (Longley & Pruitt, 1980; Tetlock et al., 1992).

Since research has supported some but not all of Janis's ideas regarding the causes of groupthink, we conclude that groupthink *can* occur (sometimes with disastrous consequences) but that it is not inevitable. Let's consider some things group leaders and members can do to minimize the occurrence of groupthink and improve decision making in groups.

Improving Group Decision Making

Research suggests that one way group members can improve decision making in groups is to support group norms that encourage the generation and evaluation of a variety of possible solutions to a problem. Another suggestion is to reduce the isolation of the group. Groups should be directed to seek input from nonmembers, and outsiders should occasionally be invited to meetings to provide fresh perspectives.

Another very important strategy for improving group decision making concerns the leader of the group. Leaders should strive to be impartial and to encourage open discussion. They should encourage group members to speak up if it looks as though the leader is stacking the deck in favor of a particular decision. The link between the leader's behavior and the group's functioning underscores the importance of leadership.

Leadership in Groups

Groups often need direction. Leadership is terribly important because the actions of leaders can have far-reaching consequences. Would World War II have occurred without the demented leadership of Adolf Hitler? Would the civil rights movement have progressed as it did in the 1960s without the inspirational leadership of Martin Luther King? It's hard to say for sure, but many scholars believe that these momentous events would not have occurred without the leadership of Hitler and King. In a similar vein, when people analyze the success or failure of corporations, colleges, unions, football squads, military units, work teams, clubs, and committees, they usually zero in on the issue of leadership.

What Is Leadership?

"A leader is a man who has the ability to get other people to do what they don't want to do, and like it." This tongue-in-cheek definition came from Harry S. Truman, the 32nd president of the United States. Does it capture the essence of leadership? In some ways, yes. It recognizes that a leader tries to influence and motivate others. It also highlights the reciprocal, interactive nature of leadership. You can't have leaders without followers—people who are willing to be led. One misleading aspect of Truman's definition of leadership is that it suggests that only men can be leaders. As we know, leadership behavior is not restricted to men. Incorporating these ideas into a formal definition, we find that **leadership is a reciprocal process in which certain people are permitted to motivate and influence others to facilitate the pursuit of group goals.** Does leadership always occur when people join together in groups? No. Let's look at some of the variables that influence the emergence of leadership.

When Do Leaders Emerge?

Leadership is not an inevitable outgrowth of group formation. In many simple situations, leadership may be unnecessary. Three friends ordering a pizza may not need a leader. But some situations call for leadership. A key factor affecting the emergence of leadership is the *size of the group* (Hemphill, 1961). Small groups can get by without leaders, but as groups become larger, the need for leadership grows. If a group ordering pizza contains 18 people rather than three, some member will have to take charge and get things organized. It is obvious that to function effectively, large organizations must have leaders. Recognizing this reality, such organizations don't wait for leadership to emerge spontaneously. They appoint presidents, department heads, managers, and so forth.

The nature of a group's tasks or activities also influences the need for leadership (Argyle, 1969). A leader is more likely to emerge when a group tackles complex tasks, because it helps to have someone coordinating the group's efforts. Groups also show more willingness to follow leaders when they engage in more important activities. Available decision time is another key consideration. Leadership is more likely when a group has to reach a decision quickly. Thus a variety of factors determine whether leaders emerge in group interactions.

Who Will Lead? Trait vs. Situational Theories

If leadership is needed, who is likely to come to the forefront to provide it? Are certain types of people born to be leaders? Early investigations of leadership were guided by the "great person" or *trait theory*. The *trait theory* assumes that leaders share certain personality traits that set them apart from followers. Hundreds of studies compared leaders and followers to identify these special leadership traits. These studies uncovered a handful of modest associations between personality traits and the emergence of leadership. Compared with nonleaders and ineffective leaders, effective leaders tend to possess the following traits: high energy level, enthusiasm, assertiveness, dominance, emotional balance,

tolerance of stress, self-control, self-efficacy, and extraversion (Bass, 1990). However, the results of these studies were generally regarded as disappointing. The findings were very inconsistent from one study to another, and the correlations between personality and leadership were very weak. Investigators finally concluded that there are no personality traits that reliably distinguish leaders from followers.

When it looked as if trait theory was not going to provide useful predictors of leadership, researchers turned their attention to identifying aspects of the situation (the group's task, for example) that might predict the emergence of leadership. *Situational theories* propose that the leader who emerges from a group depends on the fit between group members' abilities and the task at hand. When the members of a school board discuss building proposals, for example, someone with construction expertise may lead. When they discuss next year's budget, someone with accounting knowledge may lead. When they discuss educational innovations, someone with teaching experience may lead.

Like the early researchers of the trait theory of leadership, researchers of situational theories found their approach to be too simplistic. They failed to find a strong link between task demands and the selection of leaders. When groups work on a diverse array of tasks, the same people tend to assume leadership roles on task after task, even though situational demands have changed (Kenny & Zaccaro, 1983). Although they don't share highly similar personalities, some people apparently are cut out to be leaders.

Today theorists recognize that who will emerge as a leader of a group depends on a variety of factors (Bass, 1990). Among them are (1) the personality traits exhibited by potential leaders, (2) situational and task demands, and (3) the fit between prospective leaders' traits and followers' preferences (Hollander, 1985, 1992). Intricate interactions among these variables influence the selection of leaders. Thus

Reprinted with special permission of King Features Syndicate.

theories about the development of leadership have evolved from rather simple to very complex models.

What Do Leaders Do? Styles of Leadership

If you were the head of a department in a large corporation, how would you lead? Would you delegate authority readily, or would you closely supervise your workers? Would you welcome input from subordinates, or would you be a dictator? Would you motivate your staff with fear or with rewards? These are just a few of the questions that leaders face when they attempt to develop a personal leadership style.

Investigations of leadership style require assessments of what leaders do. In the decade after World War II, a team of psychologists at Ohio State University set out to develop a questionnaire to measure various aspects of leadership behavior (Halpin & Winer, 1952; Stogdill, 1963). They discovered that the activities of leaders sorted into two categories, representing two dimensions of leadership: initiating structure and consideration (see Figure 7.13). **Initiating structure is a dimension of leadership that reflects the degree to which a leader organizes, directs, and regulates the group's activities.** Leaders who are strong in initiating structure let members know what is expected of them. They emphasize deadlines, criticize poor work, enforce rules strictly, and push people to work hard. **Consideration is a dimension of leadership that reflects the degree to which a leader is warm, trusting, and supportive in interactions with group members.** Leaders who are high in consideration are friendly, approachable, and willing to listen. They explain their decisions, bend rules when necessary, and treat others as equals.

The Ohio State researchers who described initiating structure and consideration viewed them as independent, unrelated aspects of leadership. Thus they believed that a leader could be strong on one dimension and weak on the other, strong on both dimensions, or weak on both dimensions. Subsequent researchers have argued, however, that most leaders tend to be strong on one dimension or the other (Weissenberg & Kavanagh, 1972). Of course, some individuals are strong on both, and research indicates that these leaders are especially effective (Baron & Greenberg, 1990). Many theorists believe, then, that leaders can be differentiated into two basic types: task-oriented leaders and relationship-oriented leaders. *Task-*

Basic Dimensions of Leadership Style

Dimensions	Alternative labels	Conceptual meaning	Sample behaviors
Initiating structure	Task orientation Goal oriented Work facilitative	Extent to which leader organizes, directs, and defines the group's structure and goals; regulates group behavior, monitors communication, and reduces goal ambiguity	Assigns tasks to members Makes attitudes clear to the group Is critical of poor work Sees to it that the group is working to capacity Coordinates activity
Consideration	Relationship orientation Socioemotional Supportive	Degree to which the leader responds to group members in a warm and friendly fashion; openness, and willingness to explain decisions	Listens to group members Easy to understand Is friendly and approachable Treats group members as equals Is willing to make changes

oriented leaders score high in initiating structure. They focus on moving the group toward its goals and they emphasize performance and productivity. *Social-oriented leaders* score high in consideration. They try to keep everyone happy and they emphasize the group's cohesiveness and morale.

Which Leaders Will Be Most Effective?

Given their emphasis on productivity, you might expect that task-oriented leaders would be more effective than social-oriented leaders. This is not necessarily the case. In some situations, the domineering style of task-oriented leaders can undermine a group's morale and hurt productivity. Thus the question of leadership effectiveness is more complex than it may first appear.

Fiedler's Contingency Theory

Fred Fiedler (1967, 1978) has developed a prominent theory of leadership effectiveness. His model is called a *contingency theory* because it proposes that the most effective style of leadership is contingent upon (depends on) various situational factors. Fiedler measures leadership style in an unusual way. He asks a leader to identify the most difficult person to work with in the group. The leader is then asked to rate this *least-preferred co-worker* on 18 bipolar scales (cold/warm, sincere/insincere, and so forth). Leaders who return relatively *high ratings* of their least-preferred co-worker are assumed to be warm, supportive *relationship-oriented leaders*. Leaders who give relatively *low ratings* to their least-preferred co-worker are assumed to be hard-nosed *task-oriented leaders*.

FIGURE 7.13
Contrasting leadership styles
Since investigators at Ohio State University (Halpin & Winer, 1952; Stogdill, 1963) originally categorized leaders as being high in either initiating structure or consideration, many other researchers have also found that there are two basic approaches to leadership. Some of the other names for these two dimensions or styles of leadership are shown in the second column. Some characteristic behaviors associated with each style of leadership are listed in the fourth column.

Improving Leadership Effectiveness: The Leader Match Concept

by *Fred E. Fiedler* and *Martin M. Chemers* (Wiley, 1984)

Most books on enhancing leaders' effectiveness assume that the same general advice will apply equally well to all leaders and to all the situations in which they find themselves. Fred Fiedler's research suggests that this assumption is naive. The evidence indicates that different styles of leadership are optimal in different situations. Hence Fiedler and Chemers maintain that leadership effectiveness depends on the match between the leader and the situation. They therefore devised their Leader Match training program, which has been used with considerable success in many organizational settings since 1976.

This book summarizes their training program. It begins by using Fiedler's least-preferred co-worker measure and other exercises to help readers determine their leadership style. The next five chapters help leaders evaluate the situational factors that exist in their organizations. Elaborate questionnaires allow readers to assess the factors that are critical according to contingency theory: leader-member relations, position power, and task structure. The following chapters provide advice on how to create a better match between one's leadership style and the situation. Fiedler and Chemers point out that it isn't easy to change individuals' leadership styles because their styles are deeply embedded in their personalities. Hence they focus on how to modify leader-member relations, position power, and task structure in efforts to reengineer situations to fit better with one's style of leadership.

It is . . . difficult to change your basic leadership style. Practically speaking, it would be as difficult as suddenly trying to become a completely different person. If it were possible, everyone would be popular, lovable and effective. . . .

It is much easier to change your leadership situation than your personality. Although you may find this hard to believe at first, your ability to control your immediate leadership environment is considerably greater than most people realize. This is true even of jobs that seem highly circumscribed and specific. Job engineering provides an important method for improving your own leadership performance and the effectiveness of your organization. [pp. 177–178]

Fiedler's model also takes into account three group variables that are thought to influence the overall favorability of the leader's situation. Because his model is somewhat complex, we'll simply summarize its essential predictions. Task-oriented leaders are more effective in increasing productivity in group members when the situation is either highly favorable for them (group members like them, they have legitimate authority and a structured task) or highly unfavorable for them (group members dislike them, they have little authority and a poorly defined task). Relationship-oriented leaders, in contrast, are most effective when conditions are moderately favorable for them, as when they are moderately liked by the group, have moderate authority, and are faced with a moderately structured task.

Many studies of leadership have yielded findings consistent with Fiedler's model (House & Singh, 1987; Strube & Garcia, 1981). The predictions of his theory, however, are borne out more frequently in controlled laboratory settings than in the field (House & Singh, 1987). Some researchers complain that Fiedler has failed to explain *why* relationship-oriented and task-oriented leaders excel in different situations (Ashour, 1973). In recent years Fiedler has expanded his theory, looking at additional variables in an effort to understand why different types of leaders are effective in different situations (Fiedler & Garcia, 1987).

Transactional Models of Leadership

Until recently the dominant models of leadership have typically taken a top-down view of the relationship between leaders and their subordinates. In the 1980s a different perspective on leadership began to emerge—a perspective that sees leadership as "a process, not a person" (Hollander, 1992, p. 71). The *transactional model of leadership* focuses on the social interactions that take place between leaders and followers. In other words, to be effective, leaders must be able to satisfy the needs of group members. Leaders who are perceived as unfair or unethical, for example, will have a hard time gaining the support of subordinates.

Predictably, the transactional model has fostered research on followership and the interdependence between leaders and followers. Research by Hollander and his colleagues has shown that four interpersonal qualities can distinguish between effective and ineffective leadership: perceptiveness, involvement, trustworthiness, and rewardingness (Hollander, 1992). This broader view of leadership allows a leader to be seen and to function as a facilitator and coach of a mutual team effort rather than as the traditional "boss."

Another new development in the study of leadership is actually a variation on transactional leadership. *Transformational or charismatic leadership* is characterized by greater intensity of the leader and greater arousal of the follower than transactional leadership (Bass, 1985). Transformational leaders differ from other leaders in that they are able to *inspire* others to work toward a common vision. Examples of charismatic leaders come readily to mind—Adolph Hitler, Martin Luther King, Jr., Jim Jones, Mother Teresa. Notice that charismatic leaders may mobilize followers for constructive or destructive purposes. That is, when charismatic leadership is combined with a strong need for personal power and/or approval, the "dark side of charisma" may show its face (Hogan, Raskin, & Fazzini, 1990; Hollander, 1992).

Though the most familiar charismatic leaders are found in the political arena, this type of leadership can also be found in everyday work settings. In comparison with followers of effective traditional leaders, followers of charismatic leaders experienced more meaningfulness in their work, received more support from their leaders, felt more self-assured, worked for longer hours, and viewed their leaders as more dynamic (Smith, 1982). In a recent study that looked at this issue, actors were trained to portray three leadership styles: (1) structuring, (2) considerate, and (3) charismatic (Howell & Frost, 1989). As you will surmise, *structuring leaders* focused the attention of their group on the assigned task and acted in a neutral fashion with their workers (neither warm nor cold). *Considerate leaders* projected a friendly attitude toward their group and emphasized the comfort and satisfaction of the participants. *Charismatic leaders* communicated a broad vision of the nature of the task to workers, told them that high-quality work was expected, and expressed a high degree of confidence in their ability to complete the assigned task. Charismatic leaders also projected a high level of energy. When the three leadership styles were compared, the workers led by charismatic leaders were found to have the highest levels of both productivity and general satisfaction.

Because transformational theories are a recent development in the area of leadership, additional research is needed before we can draw any solid conclusions about them. At this point we can say that they raise interesting questions that deserve to be studied further.

Gender and Leadership

The notion that leadership is a male domain is still prevalent (Bass, 1990). But though women remain underrepresented in middle- and high-level leadership positions in almost all spheres, they are not so rare as they used to be. By the late 1980s women held 25% of the supervisory positions in U.S. business and industry (Bass, 1990). Also of note is the record number of women who ran and won in the 1992 state and national elections. In fact, this surge of women candidates prompted the designation of 1992 as the "year of the woman" in politics. (Even in "the year of the woman," however, many more men than women ran for and won political office.)

Research suggests that female leaders, such as Senators Barbara Boxer (CA) and Carol Mosley Braun (IL), use a participative leadership style and that male leaders, such as Senators Russ Feingold (WI) and Daniel Inouye (HI), use an autocratic leadership style. Of course, gender differences are group differences that may not apply to specific individuals.

Do women leaders behave any differently from men in leadership roles? To provide a definitive answer to this question, Alice Eagly and Blair Johnson (1990) used a complicated statistical technique (meta-analysis) to analyze more than 150 studies on leadership style and gender. One of their analyses looked at the two most heavily researched dimensions of leadership style: task orientation and interpersonal orientation. It is interesting to note that no significant differences were found between the leadership styles of men and women in studies conducted *in actual work settings*. In studies conducted *in laboratory settings*, however, women displayed more concern for interpersonal issues in groups, whereas men were more concerned with task issues.

According to Eagly and Johnson, the absence of gender differences in research conducted in the real world and the presence of such differences in laboratory studies can be explained by important differences in the settings. That is, in work settings, gender differences don't appear because the expectations for leaders are the same regardless of gender. In the laboratory, however, there are no powerful occupational expectations. The absence of (gender-neutral) occupational expectations in the lab setting allows traditional gender-role expectations to become salient, and these expectations cue the gender differences in behavior.

Eagly and Johnson also investigated the relationship between gender and the use of a democratic versus autocratic leadership style. This analysis showed a tendency for female leaders to adopt a participative style and men, to adopt an autocratic style. Eagly and Johnson offer several possible explanations of this difference. It may be a function of women's stronger interpersonal skills. That is, women leaders may invite group members to share in decision making because they know they are capable of handling the interpersonal dynamics inherent in a democratic style of leadership. Or perhaps a participatory style is more functional for women because it prevents challenges to their authority by subordinates who might object to their use of an autocratic style.

Eagly and Johnson note that management consultants have recently been recommending that organizations adopt a more democratic style of leadership to reduce worker alienation (a move also advocated by many feminist theorists). Though no research has been conducted on the actual effects of such a change, the results of studies on leadership styles suggest that it is unlikely that any single style will prove to be effective in all situations. We look to future research to inform us on this issue.

Alice Eagly

Summary

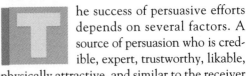

he success of persuasive efforts depends on several factors. A source of persuasion who is credible, expert, trustworthy, likable, physically attractive, and similar to the receiver tends to be relatively effective. Although there are some limitations, two-sided arguments, arousal of fear, and generation of positive feelings are effective elements in persuasive messages. Persuasion is undermined when a receiver is forewarned or when a receiver's initial position is very discrepant from the position advocated. Extremely effective communicators who have almost complete control over their audiences' psychological environment have been able to produce powerful, and sometimes tragic, results, as exemplified by the Jonestown massacre.

Asch found that subjects often conform to the group, even when the group reports inaccurate judgments. He found that conformity becomes more likely as group size increases, up to a membership of seven. Asch's experiments may have produced public compliance while subjects' private beliefs remained unchanged.

In Milgram's landmark study of obedience to authority, subjects showed a remarkable tendency to follow orders to shock an innocent stranger. Milgram concluded that situational pressures can make decent people do indecent things.

The presence of other people sometimes causes us to behave in atypical ways. Depending on the nature of the task and our skill at it, social facilitation can sometimes cause us to perform better in front of others than if we were alone, but the presence of other people can also cause us to perform more poorly than if we were alone. It can also cause us to choke under pressure and to have difficulty speaking in front of others.

The bystander effect is the curious tendency of people who would help someone in need if they were alone to be less likely to provide help when others are present. Deindividuation can cause normal, law-abiding citizens to become a dangerous, lawless mob.

Groups consist of two or more individuals who interact and are interdependent. We join groups to fulfill our affiliation needs, to enhance our sense of identity, to engage in social comparison, to increase our mutual security, and to get jobs done efficiently. People in groups fill a wide variety of roles. Most people specialize in either task-related roles or socioemotional roles. Group norms, which are rules about appropriate behavior, also influence the way we act in groups.

Centralized communication networks tend to work better when groups face simple problems, but decentralized networks are advantageous for more complex problems. There are five sources of power in groups: reward power, coercive power, expert power, referent power, and legitimate power. Cohesive groups are close-knit ones in which members like each other. Cohesiveness facilitates communication, but it can increase conformity. Cohesiveness tends to decline as groups increase in size.

Individuals' productivity often declines in larger groups because of loss of coordination and because of social loafing. Group productivity is enhanced by open communication, process planning, small size, cohesiveness, and agreement on group goals.

Decision making in groups can be affected by group polarization, a phenomenon that occurs when discussion leads groups to shift toward a more extreme decision in the direction in which they were already leaning. A cohesive group engages in groupthink when it suspends critical judgment in a misguided effort to promote agreement in decision making. Unfortunately, poor decisions often result. Groupthink is promoted by high cohesiveness, working in isolation, and biased leadership.

The need for leadership is greater when groups are large, when their problems are complex, and when time is precious. Who will lead depends on situational demands, the personality traits of potential leaders, and the fit between these traits and group members' preferences. Leaders can be differentiated into two basic types: task-oriented leaders and social-oriented leaders. According to Fiedler's contingency theory, the most effective leadership style depends on a variety of situational factors.

Transactional models of leadership view leadership as a process, not a person. They stress the interdependence between leaders and followers. Transformational leadership, a variation of transactional leadership, involves the ability to inspire followers to work to realize a common vision. Transformational leaders are sometimes also called charismatic leaders, and research has shown them to be somewhat more effective than the more traditional structuring and considerate leaders.

No gender differences in leadership styles have been found in actual work settings. In studies of leadership conducted in laboratory settings, women display more concern for interpersonal issues in groups and men more concern for task issues. These discrepancies have been attributed to differences in the settings that cue either gender-neutral or gendered behavior.

In the Application we'll look at some social influence strategies at work in everyday situations.

APPLICATION Seeing through Social Influence Tactics

Which of the following statements is true?

1.

It's a good idea to ask for a small favor first before soliciting the larger favor you really want.

2.

It's a good idea to ask for a large favor first before soliciting the smaller favor you really want.

**FIGURE 7.14
The foot-in-the-door and the door-in-the-face techniques**
These two influence techniques are essentially the reverse of each other, but both can work. In the foot-in-the-door technique, you begin with a small request and work up to a larger one. In the door-in-the-face technique, you begin with a large request and work down to a smaller one.

Would you believe that *both* of these statements are true? Although the two approaches involve opposite strategies, both can be very effective ways to get people to do what you want. This paradox illustrates the complexity of social influence processes. It pays to understand these strategies because advertisers, salespeople, and fund raisers (not to mention friends and neighbors) use them frequently in efforts to influence our behavior.

The Foot-in-the-Door Technique

Door-to-door salespeople have long recognized the importance of gaining a *little* cooperation from sales targets (getting a "foot in the door") before hitting them with the real sales pitch. The *foot-in-the-door technique* involves getting people to agree to a small request to increase the chances that they will agree to a larger request later (see Figure 7.14). This technique is widely used in all walks of life. Groups seeking donations often ask people to simply sign a petition first. Salespeople routinely ask individuals to try a product with "no obligation" before they launch their hard sell. In a similar vein, a wife might ask her husband to get her a cup of coffee, and when he gets up to fetch it say, "While you're up, why don't you make me a grilled cheese?"

The foot-in-the-door technique was first investigated by Jonathon Freedman and his colleagues. In one study (Freedman & Fraser, 1966) the large request involved telephoning homemakers to ask whether a team of six men doing consumer research could come into their home to classify all their household products. Imagine six strangers tramping through your home, pulling everything out of your closets, cupboards, and drawers, and you can understand why only 22% of the subjects in the control group agreed to this outlandish request. Subjects in the experimental group were contacted three days before the unreasonable request was made and asked to answer a few questions about the soaps used in their home. When the large request was made three days later, 53% of the experimental group complied with that request.

Many other studies have also shown that the foot-in-the-door technique is an effective strategy. Researchers aren't entirely sure why the technique is effective. One explanation is that when people grant the initial favor, they then feel more favorable about

whatever is requested next (DeJong, 1979; Dillard, 1991). This change in attitude, then, makes them more willing to go along with a subsequent request. Of course, no strategy works all the time. The foot-in-the-door technique may be ineffective if the initial request is too small to create a sense of commitment or if the second request is so large it's unreasonable (Foss & Dempsey, 1979; Zuckerman, Lazzaro, & Waldgeir, 1979).

The Door-in-the-Face Technique

The door-in-the-face technique reverses the sequence of requests employed with the foot-in-the-door technique. The *door-in-the-face technique* involves making a very large request that is likely to be turned down to increase the chance that people will agree to a smaller request later (see Figure 7.14). The name for this strategy is derived from the expectation that the initial request will be quickly rejected. A husband who wants to coax his frugal wife into agreeing to buy a $20,000 sports car, for example, might begin by proposing that they purchase a $30,000 sports car. By the time she has talked her husband out of the $30,000 car,

Goal: Obtain $50 contribution for youth group
Foot-in-the-Door Technique

Small request first · "Would you donate some old clothes for one of our charity programs?" · If yes, then... · Larger request (the one desired in the first place) · "Would you donate $50 to our organization?"

Door-in-the-Face Technique

Large request first · "Would you volunteer to run a weekly program for our youth group?" · If no, then... · Smaller request (the one desired in the first place) · "Would you donate $50 to our organization?"

the $20,000 price tag may look quite reasonable to her.

The potential effectiveness of the door-in-the-face technique was demonstrated in a study by Robert Cialdini and his colleagues (1975). Posing as representatives of a youth counseling program, they asked college students whether they would volunteer to spend two hours a week counseling juvenile delinquents for *two years*. All the subjects rejected this very large request. When the students later were asked to chaperon a group of juvenile delinquents on a one-day trip to the zoo, however, 50% agreed to this much smaller request. Subjects in a control group received only the latter of the two requests, and only 17% of them agreed to it.

The door-in-the-face technique works for two reasons (Cialdini, 1993). First, everything is relative, and we are easily swayed by *contrast effects*. A 6'3'' basketball player can look downright small when surrounded by teammates who are all over 6'8.'' Similarly, a $20,000 car may seem cheap in comparison with a $30,000 car. Second, when people make concessions by reducing the size of their requests, most of us feel obliged to reciprocate by making concessions of our own. Hence we agree to the smaller request. The belief that we should reciprocate others' kindness is a powerful norm. Let's examine some of the other ways in which it is used in efforts to exert social influence.

Using the Reciprocity Norm

Perhaps you have walked through a large airport and been approached by a member of the

RECOMMENDED READING

Influence: Science and Practice

by Robert B. Cialdini (HarperCollins, 1993)

This is a brilliant book about the dynamics of social influence. Cialdini, a social psychologist, has conducted extensive empirical research on influence tactics, such as the door-in-the-face technique and lowballing. Cialdini's book is based on his studies and his review of other scientific research on the topic. What makes his book unique is that he has gone far beyond laboratory research in his effort to understand the ins and outs of social influence. For three years he immersed himself in the real world of influence artists, becoming a "spy of sorts." As he puts it in his preface, "When I wanted to learn about the compliance tactics of encyclopedia (or vacuum cleaner, or portrait photography, or dance lessons) sales organizations, I would answer a newspaper ad for sales trainees and have them teach me their methods. Using similar but not identical approaches, I was able to penetrate advertising, public relations, and fund-raising agencies to examine their techniques." The result is an insightful book that bolsters scientific data with anecdotal accounts of how influence artists ply their trade. Familiarity with their strategies can help you to avoid being an easy mark.

A few years ago, a university professor tried a little experiment. He sent Christmas cards to a sample of perfect strangers. Although he expected some reaction, the response he received was amazing—holiday cards addressed to him came pouring back from people who had never met nor heard of him. The great majority of those who returned cards never inquired into the identity of the unknown professor. . . . While small in scope, this study nicely shows the action of one of the most potent of the weapons of influence around us—the rule of reciprocation. The rule says that we should try to repay, in kind, what another person has provided us. [p. 19]

Hare Krishna, an unconventional religious sect. If so, you may have been surprised when the Krishna member insisted on giving you a gift—usually a flower or a small book. What motivated this unexpected kindness? Calculated, cunning insight about how to manipulate people. The Krishnas are hoping that you'll feel obligated to repay their kindness when they ask you for a donation a moment later. Some people—especially those who have been approached before—aren't fooled by this strategem. But contributions *are* coaxed out of many people; indeed, the Krishnas have raised millions upon millions of dollars this way.

Most of us have been socialized to believe in the *reciprocity norm*—the rule that we should pay back in kind what we receive from others. Robert Cialdini (1993) has written exten-

sively about the use of the reciprocity norm. The Krishnas are hardly unique. Conventional charities also make use of the reciprocity principle. Groups seeking donations for the disabled, the homeless, and so forth routinely send address labels, key rings, and other small gifts with their pleas for donations.

Salespeople are using the reciprocity principle when they distribute free samples to prospective customers. Cialdini (1993) describes the procedures used by the Amway Corporation, which sells such household products as detergent, floor wax, and insect spray. Amway's door-to-door salespeople give homemakers many bottles of their products for a "free trial." When they return a few days later, most of the homemakers feel obligated to buy some of the products.

The reciprocity rule is meant to promote fair exchanges in social interactions. When people manipulate the reciprocity rule, however, they usually give something of minimal value in the hope of getting far more in return. A person selling large computer systems may treat a potential customer at a nice restaurant in an effort to close a deal worth hundreds of thousands of dollars. According to Cialdini, the reciprocity norm is so powerful that it often works even when (1) the gift is uninvited, (2) the gift comes from someone you dislike, or (3) the gift results in an uneven exchange.

The Lowball Technique

Manipulations of the reciprocity rule can involve some trickery, but the lowball technique is even more deceptive. The name for this technique derives from a common practice in automobile sales, in which customers are offered a terrific bargain on a car. The bargain price gets the customers to commit themselves to buy the car. Soon after the commitment is made, the dealer starts revealing some hidden costs. Typically the customers learn that options apparently included in the original price are actually going to cost

extra. Once they have committed themselves to buy a car, most customers are unlikely to cancel the deal. Thus the *lowball technique* involves getting people to commit themselves to an attractive proposition before its hidden costs are revealed.

Car dealers aren't the only ones who use this technique. A friend may ask if you want to spend a week with him at his charming backwoods cabin. After you accept this seemingly generous proposition, he may add, "Of course there's some work for us to do. We need to repair the pier, paint the exterior, and . . ." Lowballing is very dishonest. You might guess that people would become angry and back out of a deal once its hidden costs were revealed. Although some people do respond this way, lowballing is still a surprisingly effective strategy (Burger & Petty, 1981).

Reactance and Feigned Scarcity

Some years ago, Jack Brehm demonstrated that telling people they can't have something only makes them want it more. This finding emerged in his research on reactance. *Reactance* occurs when a person's freedom to behave in a certain way is impeded, and the person then attempts to restore the threatened freedom.

In one study of reactance (Brehm, 1966), subjects listened to four records and then were asked to indicate how much they liked each one. As a reward for participating in the study, some subjects were told that they could have the record of their choice when they returned to make additional ratings on a second occasion. When subjects returned for the second session, they were told that one of the four records was not available. The excluded record varied from subject to subject. It was always the record ranked third best by that individual in the first set of ratings. The subjects listened to the four records again and made their second set of ratings. Brehm found that the ratings of the excluded records increased signifi-

cantly. In other words, the record that a subject could not have became more desirable.

The reactance effect helps to explain why companies often try to create the impression that their products are in scarce supply. Scarcity threatens your freedom to choose a product, thus creating reactance and an increased desire for the scarce product. Advertisers frequently feign scarcity to drive up the demand for products. We constantly see ads that scream "Limited supply available!" "For a limited time only!" "While they last!" and "Time is running out!"

The effect of scarcity was demonstrated dramatically in 1989 when Mazda introduced a new convertible called the Miata. Mazda chose to make a limited number of the new cars available for sale in the United States. The scarcity of the car sent consumers into a buying frenzy. The cars were snapped up so rapidly that dealers started charging up to $5,000 over the list price!

The Severe-Initiation Effect

Creating the illusion of scarcity is not the only way to increase people's attraction to something. Putting people through a severe initiation is another way to make something seem more desirable. In a classic study of this effect, Aronson and Mills (1959) put college women through a severe initiation before they could qualify to participate in what promised to be an interesting discussion of sexuality. In the screening test that represented the severe initiation, the women had to read obscene passages out loud to a male experimenter. After all that, the highly touted discussion of sexuality turned out to be a boring, taped lecture on reproduction in lower animals. Subjects in the two control groups did not have to undergo this painful initiation. As a result of the severe initiation, subjects in this group experienced a great deal of cognitive dissonance. As you'll recall from Chapter 5, *cognitive dissonance* is an unpleasant state that is produced by experiencing contradictory thoughts, feelings, or behaviors. In this case, the women had gone through a highly stressful experience only to be "rewarded" with an incredibly boring lecture. Subjects in the two control groups didn't pay such a high price for the "reward" so they didn't experience the dissonance.

Because dissonance is a negative state, people are motivated to reduce it. How did subjects in the severe initiation condition reduce their negative feelings? Amazingly, subjects in this group rated the boring discussion as *significantly more interesting* than did subjects in the two control conditions (see Figure 7.15). By convincing themselves that the boring lecture was actually interesting, they could better accept it as a suitable reward for the severe initiation they had experienced, and thus reduce their dissonance.

The severe-initiation ruse is used in many facets of everyday life. A prominent example is the nightclubs that screen potential patrons and make them wait in lengthy lines. In many cases, these clubs have ample room inside, but they make it hard to get in so that entry to the club seems like a precious opportunity. Restaurants that require reservations weeks in advance and country clubs that make it difficult for one to join are also taking advantage of the severe-initiation effect. So are fraternities and sororities that put

potential members through elaborate screenings—not to mention "hell week."

The Power of Modeling

As we noted in Chapter 2, *observational learning* occurs when our behavior is swayed by our observations of others, who in this context are called *models*. According to Albert Bandura (1986), much of our behavior is the product of imitation or modeling effects. These modeling effects are sometimes used in efforts to exert social influence.

The power of modeling was demonstrated in an experiment designed to increase the contributions tossed into a Salvation Army kettle during the Christmas holiday (Bryan & Test, 1967). In this study, experimental accomplices posing as shoppers tossed money into a Salvation Army kettle as they walked by it. Thus they modeled generous behavior for real shoppers who witnessed their contributions. As predicted, the shoppers exposed to these generous models made more contributions than did the shoppers who passed by when the models were absent.

Potent modeling effects were also seen in a study in which the dependent variable was signing a petition (Helson, Blake, &

Mouton, 1958). The subjects were students at the University of Texas, and the petition was not one that you would expect them to sign readily. It advocated the removal of all soft-drink machines from university buildings. Arrangements were made so that the subject was always walking with an experimental accomplice when the two of them were approached to sign the petition. When the accomplice refused to sign the petition, all the subjects also refused. When the accomplice agreed to sign the petition, however, the proportion of subjects who signed jumped from zero to one-third.

Advertisers are well aware of our tendency to be influenced by what others do. That's why they run television commercials in which both celebrities and ordinary people testify about how they use a particular detergent, deodorant, or gasoline. Modeling effects also explain why television producers use laugh tracks in their comedy shows. Research reveals that canned laughter leads audiences to laugh at jokes more frequently and longer (Fuller & Sheehy-Skeffington, 1974; Smyth & Fuller, 1972). People try to take advantage of modeling effects in a wide variety of situations. Bartenders, for instance, often slip a few dollar bills into their tip jars to fraudulently "model" healthy tipping by previous customers.

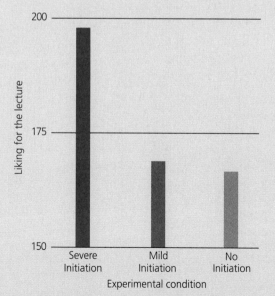

FIGURE 7.15
The severe-initiation effect
After going through a severe initiation, a mild initiation, or no initiation, subjects listened to a boring lecture and then rated their liking of it. Subjects who had endured the severe initiation reported liking the lecture more—because they were trying to reduce their cognitive dissonance. (Data from Aronson & Mills, 1959.)

Playing on Guilt

Another widely used influence technique is to make people feel guilty about something before advocating a response that should relieve some of their guilt. Charitable organizations seeking donations use this technique frequently, and studies suggest that it can be an effective strategy. In one study (Steele, 1975), some subjects contacted as part of a telephone poll were told that people in their area were generally unhelpful and unconcerned about the welfare of others. Control-group subjects received a neutral phone call from the same poller. Two days later, the subjects were called by a local food cooperative seeking their assistance. The subjects who had previously been made to feel guilty about their lack of concern showed more willingness to help than the subjects in the control group.

In summary, people use a host of methods to coax compliance from one another. Despite the fact that many of these influence techniques are more or less dishonest, they're widely used. There is no way to completely avoid being hoodwinked by influence strategies. Understanding these various strategies, however, can reduce the likelihood that you'll be a victim of influence artists. As we noted in our discussion of persuasion, forewarned is forearmed.

CHAPTER 7 REVIEW

Key Learning Objectives

1. Summarize findings on source, message, and receiver factors in persuasion and discuss how these factors played a role in the Jonestown massacre.
2. Describe Asch's work on conformity.
3. Describe Milgram's classic study of obedience and the controversy it caused.
4. Describe social facilitation and its effects.
5. Discuss choking under pressure and communication apprehension.
6. Explain the bystander effect and its causes.
7. Describe deindividuation and the factors that have been shown to produce it.
8. Explain the nature of groups and why we join them.
9. Describe the following properties of groups: roles, norms, communication structure, and power structure.
10. Describe group cohesiveness and summarize how it influences group dynamics and individual behavior.
11. Describe social loafing and its effects.
12. Discuss how group productivity can be improved.
13. Explain group polarization.
14. Describe the sources and symptoms of groupthink.
15. Discuss how group decision making can be improved.
16. Describe trait and situational theories of leadership.
17. Describe Fiedler's contingency theory of leadership effectiveness.
18. Describe transactional and transformational leadership.
19. Summarize findings on gender differences in leadership styles.
20. Describe the paradoxical foot-in-the-door and door-in-the-face strategies.
21. Explain how the reciprocity norm and lowballing are used in social influence.
22. Discuss how feigned scarcity and severe initiation can increase people's attraction to something.
23. Explain how modeling effects and guilt can be used in social influence.

Key Terms

attitudes
bystander effect
communication apprehension
compliance
conformity
consideration
deindividuation
diffusion of responsibility
door-in-the-face technique
evaluation apprehension
foot-in-the-door technique
group
group cohesiveness
group norms
group polarization

groupthink
initiating structure
leadership
lowball technique
obedience
persuasion
power
reactance
reciprocity norm
role
social facilitation
social loafing
socioemotional roles
task-related roles

Key People

Solomon Asch
Alice Eagly
Irving Janis

Stanley Milgram
Robert Zajonc
Philip Zimbardo

8 Friendship and Love

BILL WAS SO KEYED UP THAT HE tossed and turned all night. When morning finally arrived, he was elated. In less than two hours he would see Susan for coffee! When he got to his first class, he found it practically impossible to keep his mind on the lecture. He was constantly distracted by thoughts and images of Susan. When class was finally over, he had to force himself not to walk too fast to the Student Union, where they had agreed to meet. Sound familiar? Chances are that you recognize Bill's behavior as that of someone falling in love.

Love and friendship play vital roles in our lives. They also play a large role in our psychological adjustment. Given their importance, it's ironic that psychologists didn't start studying these phenomena scientifically until the 1970s (Rubin, 1973). Research on romantic love got off to an especially late start. Why? In part because many people don't believe that love is an appropriate topic for scientific study. In 1975, for example, Senator William Proxmire bestowed his infamous Golden Fleece Award (for waste of taxpayers' money) on two social psychologists who had had the audacity to study love. Ellen Berscheid and Elaine Hatfield (then Walster) had conducted pioneering research on love that was funded in part by a grant from the National Science Foundation. Their research was widely lauded in scientific circles, but Senator Proxmire was not impressed. "Americans want to leave some things in life a mystery," he asserted, "and right at the top of things we don't want to know is why a man falls in love with a woman and vice versa." Because many people shared Proxmire's view, psychological research on love and friendship got off to a late start. Interpersonal relationships are a very active area of research now, though, and we have a wealth of interesting findings to explore. First, we will look at some general theories about how close relationships develop and evolve. Next, we'll review some of the factors that are important in determining who is initially attracted to whom. Following that, we'll discuss what psychologists are discovering about friendships and romantic relationships, and we'll consider the problem of loneliness. In the application section, we'll focus on shyness.

The Nature and Development of Close Relationships

Social psychologists define **close relationships** as relatively long-lasting relationships in which there are frequent interactions in a variety of settings and in which the impact of these interactions is strong. In other words, we spend a lot of time and energy maintaining close relationships, and what the other person says or does matters to us a lot. It matters so much that close relationships have the capacity to arouse intense feelings—both positive (passion, concern, caring) and negative (rage, jealousy, despair).

There are several kinds of close relationships—friendships and relationships with family members and co-workers as well as romantic relationships. While many close relationships are based on mutual, intimate self-disclosure, many are not. When college students were asked to identify the person to whom they felt closest, 47% named a romantic partner, 36% listed a friend, 14% mentioned a family member, and 3% listed another individual, such as a co-worker (Berscheid, Snyder, & Omoto, 1989). Hence not all close relationships are characterized by emotional intimacy.

Identity and Intimate Relationships

As you'll recall from Chapter 5, Erikson posited that identity is a central issue in personality that typically develops during late adolescence (ages 17–22). In addition, he theorized that individuals need to be in the status of identity achievement in order to establish committed, intimate relationships, which typically develop in early adulthood (see Chapter 11). Elaborating on Erik Erikson's concept of intimacy, Jacob Orlofsky and his colleagues (1973) constructed interview questions to measure intimacy development based on the criteria of depth and mutuality of interpersonal relationships with same- and other-sex peers. They established five statuses of intimacy: intimate, preintimate, stereotyped, pseudointimate, and isolate. Note that with the exception of the isolate status,

Ellen Berscheid

"My preference is for someone who's afraid of closeness, like me."

one's intimacy status is determined not by whether or not one is *in* a relationship but rather by the *quality* of the relationship one has. That is, the distinctions among the statuses hinge on your ability to engage in self-disclosure, to feel emotionally close to another person, and to make a commitment to a relationship (Orlofsky, Marcia, & Lesser, 1973).

Individuals in the *intimate* status form close and open relationships with male and female friends and are involved in committed relationships. *Preintimate* individuals are also capable of mature, reciprocal relationships, but because of ambivalence about commitment, they have not yet had a relationship to which they are strongly committed. Individuals in the *stereotyped* status have relationships that are superficial. That is, there isn't much openness or closeness, and others are often seen as objects to manipulate rather than persons to share with. Those in the *pseudointimate* status are typically involved in a relatively permanent relationship, but it is one that resembles the stereotyped relationship in quality. *Isolates* avoid social situations and appear to be loners whose social interactions consist of casual conversations after class with a few acquaintances.

In line with Erikson's theory, research provides some evidence that emotional and sexual intimacy and identity are related. That is, several studies have found that college men and women in the more advanced identity statuses (achievement and moratorium) are most likely to be in the more advanced intimacy statuses (intimate and preintimate) (Fitch & Adams, 1983; Kacerguis & Adams, 1980; Marcia, 1976).

Likewise, foreclosures and diffusions are predominant in the less advanced statuses of intimacy (stereotyped, pseudointimate, and isolate).

While these studies demonstrate that intimacy is a correlate of identity status, more research is needed in order to determine whether the achievement of identity actually precedes intimacy and how the development of intimacy and identity may vary with sex or gender-role orientation (Adams, 1992). Some theorists (and some research) suggest that intimacy precedes identity development in females (Chodorow, 1978; Gilligan, 1982; Josselson, 1987). Nonetheless, Erikson offers a thought-provoking explanation for why some people are motivated to develop committed, intimate relationships and are capable of doing so while others are not.

Development of Close Relationships

Close relationships usually take time and nurturing to develop. George Levinger (1980) has proposed a five-stage model that describes how close relationships evolve. Let's look at these five stages.

1. *Attraction.* All close relationships start with some degree of initial attraction. The determinants of initial attraction include such things as the opportunity to interact, physical attractiveness, and similar attitudes. (We'll discuss these factors in detail shortly.) The mere fact that we're attracted to someone, however, doesn't necessarily mean that we'll pursue a relationship with that person. According to Levinger, we'll do so only if we want to increase the number of our close relationships and if we anticipate that the other person will respond favorably to our attempts to establish a relationship.

2. *Building the relationship.* Once two individuals in a friendship or romantic relationship get to stage 2, they have essentially agreed to explore the possibilities of a relationship. In

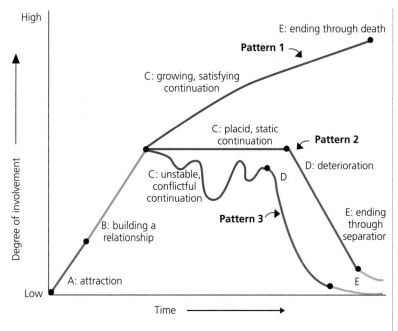

High

Degree of involvement

E: ending through death

Pattern 1 ↘

C: growing, satisfying
continuation

C: placid, static
continuation

← **Pattern 2**

C: unstable,
conflictful
continuation

D: deterioration

D

Pattern 3 ↗

E: ending
through
separation

B: building a
relationship

A: attraction

E

Low

Time →

FIGURE 8.1
**The long-term course
of close relationships**
Levinger (1980) has pro-
posed that close relationships typically evolve
through five stages:
A, attraction; B, building
the relationship;
C, continuation;
D, deterioration; and
E, ending. Three contrasting examples of how close
relationships might
progress through these
stages are shown here. In
pattern 1, the relationship
grows over time and ends
only with the death of one
of the partners. In pattern
2, the relationship under-
goes chronic deterioration
and terminates "prema-
turely." In pattern 3, the
relationship also termi-
nates, but for a different
reason—ongoing, severe
conflicts that cannot be
overcome.

this stage, they use their interactions to test out their initial attributions about the other's atti-tudes, personality characteristics, and so forth. As we saw in Chapter 6, self-disclosure is the key to building a relationship. Longitudinal studies of steadily dating couples indicate that couples who express strong love for each other are likely to have longer-lasting relationships than those whose feelings are less strong (Berscheid et al., 1989; Hill, Rubin, & Peplau, 1976). Levinger suggests that before relation-ships progress to stage 3, they pass through a transition labeled "commitment," a mutual agreement to try to maintain the relationship over time.

3. *Continuation.* Once two people have made a commitment to maintain a relation-ship, their ability to manage the inevitable con-flicts that arise is a crucial factor in its continu-ation. Effective conflict resolution also plays a key role in their perception of the relationship as happy and harmonious. External factors such as adequate income, family support, and joint property also contribute to long-lasting rela-tionships. Levinger speculates that individual partner characteristics such as tolerance, opti-mism, and a sense of humor, also probably help maintain a stable relationship. Many deep friendships and love relationships evolve to stage 3 and continue until death (see pattern 1 in Figure 8.1). Other relationships come to a "premature" end by way of a different path: stage 4.

4. *Deterioration.* The fourth stage is typical-ly marked by a couple's perception that the pre-viously satisfying relationship has become unsatisfying. They used to enjoy being together but now often they do not. Sometimes relation-ships deteriorate as a result of specific circum-stances, such as the serious illness of a child or a partner. Most of the time, however, the deteri-oration is the result of chronic unhappiness that erodes the relationship over time (pattern 2 in Figure 8.1) or the couple's inability to resolve numerous strong interpersonal conflicts (pat-tern 3 in Figure 8.1).

5. *Ending.* We all know that many relation-ships that outsiders judge to be "empty shell" liaisons continue indefinitely. Levinger specu-lates that whether a deteriorating relationship actually ends depends in great part on the avail-ability of a more attractive alternative relation-ship. Relationship endings can also be triggered by a partner's "going public" to another person about difficulties in the relationship or by important life turning points, such as a major job change or relocation to a different area of the country.

Social Exchange in Close Relationships

Using Levinger's model as a framework, let's look at some important principles by which relationships operate. *Social exchange theory postulates that interpersonal relationships are governed by perceptions of the rewards and costs of interactions.* Basically, this model pre-dicts that interactions between acquaintances, friends, and lovers are likely to continue as long as the participants feel that the benefits they derive from the relationship are reasonable in comparison with the costs (Kelley & Thibaut, 1978; Thibaut & Kelley, 1959). Harold Kelley and John Thibaut based their social exchange theory on B. F. Skinner's principle of reinforce-ment, which assumes that we try to maximize our rewards in life and minimize our costs (see Chapter 2). Of course, it is important to note that what is considered a reward or a cost in a relationship is a very subjective matter.

According to social exchange theory, we assess a relationship by its *outcome*—our subjec-tive perception of the rewards of the relation-ship minus its costs (see Figure 8.2). Rewards include such things as emotional support, sta-tus, and sexual gratification (in romantic rela-tionships); costs are such things as the time and energy that a relationship requires, emotional conflicts, and the inability to engage in other rewarding activities because of obligations entailed by the relationship.

We gauge our *satisfaction* in a relationship by comparing the relationship outcomes (rewards minus costs) with our subjective expectations (see Figure 8.2). **This standard of what constitutes an acceptable balance of rewards and costs in a relationship is referred to as your** *comparison level.* It is based on the outcomes you have experienced in previous relationships and the outcomes you have seen others experience in their relationships. Your comparison level may also be influenced by your exposure to fictional relationships, such as those you have read about or seen on television. In accord with the predictions of exchange theory, research indicates that satisfaction in a relationship is high when rewards are perceived to be high and costs low.

To understand the role of *commitment* in relationships, we need to look at two additional factors (see Figure 8.2). The first is our *comparison level for alternatives,* or our estimation of the outcomes available to us in alternative relationships. In using this standard, we compare relationship outcomes with the potential outcomes of other relationships that are actually available to us. As we noted in our discussion of Levinger's model, many unsatisfying relationships are not terminated until another love interest actually appears.

The second factor that figures in relationship commitment is *investments,* or things that we have contributed to a relationship (including time and money) that we can't get back if the relationship ends. Understandably, putting investments into a relationship strengthens our commitment to it.

But what happens if we feel that we have invested a lot in a relationship that starts to feel bad? Because they're unwilling to forfeit their investments, some people put even more into

Friends for Life: The Psychology of Close Relationships
by Steve Duck (St. Martin's Press, 1983)

This book, written for nonprofessionals, offers a review of current views and findings on close relationships: friendships, romantic relationships, and marriages. The book does a fine job of presenting information that has not been covered in similar books, especially in regard to the development and management of relationships over time. Another strength is its discussion of practical implications of research findings, such as the specific skills needed to maintain successful relationships and how the lack of these skills causes problems. While the book could be improved by the addition of case studies and a livelier writing style, it is worth your attention if you would like to explore further what contemporary psychology has to say about close and long-term relationships.

It is thus very important for couples to spend time negotiating and setting up patterns of activity and complementary roles of behaving that could help them to feel that they are close. For men, at least, the rewards of doing so are very significant, even vital in the literal sense. Happily married men have superior mental health, lower suicide rates, greater career prospects and longer lives. . . . Small wonder that the most farsighted business organizations are keenly interested in the stability of their executives' marriages. Happily married executives stay healthier and actually do a better job! For women, the picture is not quite so rosy as indicated by the fact that women are responsible for the legal initiation of about 75% of all divorces. . . . Equally, most recent research shows that the part of the population most depressed is composed of non-working married women with pre-school-age children—just those people most often represented by the media as most fulfilled. [pp. 101–102]

such a relationship. Others decide that they will probably have to forfeit their investments sooner or later so they choose not to wait— especially if an attractive alternative comes into the picture.

We'll use a hypothetical example to illustrate how the theory works. If both people in a romantic relationship feel that they are getting

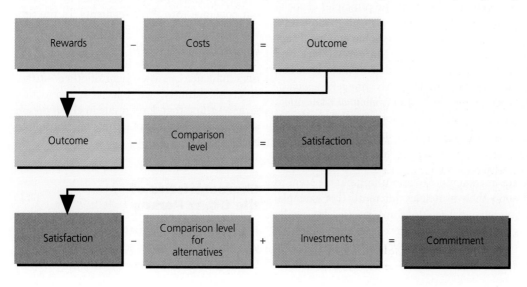

FIGURE 8.2
The key elements of social exchange theory and their effects on a relationship
According to social exchange theory, the outcome of a relationship is determined by its rewards minus its costs. Satisfaction in a relationship is based on the outcome matched against our comparison level (expectations). Commitment to a relationship is determined by our satisfaction minus our comparison level for alternatives plus our investments in the relationship. (Based on Brehm & Kassin, 1993.)

a lot out of the relationship (lots of strokes, high status) and that its costs are low (a few arguments, occasionally giving up preferred activities), the relationship will probably be perceived as satisfactory and will be maintained. However, if either person begins to feel that the ratio of rewards to costs is falling below his or her comparison level, then that person is likely to feel dissatisfied. The dissatisfied person may attempt to alter the balance of costs and rewards or try to ease out of the relationship. The likelihood of ending the relationship depends on the number of important investments a person has in the relationship and whether the person believes that an alternative relationship is available that could yield greater satisfaction.

Exchange theory principles seem to operate in this way regardless of a couple's sexual orientation (Peplau, 1991). Moreover, heterosexual and homosexual couples seem quite similar with regard to important aspects of relationships. Studies of heterosexual men and women, gay men, and lesbians found that all groups reported high satisfaction with their relationships (Duffy & Rusbult, 1986; Margolin & Wampold, 1981; Kurdek & Schmitt, 1986b; Peplau & Gordon, 1983), as well as moderately high investments in their relationships, moderately poor alternatives, and strong commitment (Duffy & Rusbult, 1986).

This theory of an "interpersonal marketplace" provides a useful model for analyzing many types of relationships. Nonetheless, many people resist the idea that close relationships operate according to an economic model. Much of this resistance probably stems from discomfort with the idea that self-interest plays such an important role in the maintenance of relationships. Some of this resistance may also be due to a feeling that the principles of social exchange theory don't apply well to close relationships. In fact, there is some empirical support for this position. Margaret Clark and Judson Mills (1979) distinguish between *exchange relationships* (with strangers, acquaintances, co-workers) and *communal relationships* (with close friends, lovers, family members). Research suggests that in exchange relationships, the usual principles of social exchange dominate. Social exchange principles also operate in communal relationships, but we seem to apply these principles differently. For example, in communal relationships, rewards are usually given freely, without any expectation of prompt reciprocation (Clark, 1984). Also, we pay more attention to the needs of a partner in a commu-

nal relationship than in an exchange relationship (Clark, Mills, & Powell, 1986). In other words, when people close to us need us, we help them without stopping to calculate whether and when they will reward us in turn.

Factors That Influence Interpersonal Attraction

"I just don't know what she sees in him. She could do so much better for herself." "Sure, she's an OK person, but he's too good for her." How many times have you heard remarks like these? Such comments demonstrate the great interest we have in analyzing the dynamics of attraction. **Interpersonal attraction refers to positive feelings toward another person.** Who is attracted to whom is an exceedingly complex matter. A multitude of factors influence your assessment of another person's attractiveness. Furthermore, attraction is a two-way street, so there are intricate interactions between factors.

Our review of research in this area pertains to initial attraction in friendships as well as in heterosexual and homosexual romantic relationships. Although liking and loving represent two different types of relationships, we believe that the dynamics of *initial attraction* in each case are sufficiently similar to justify a unified discussion. In some cases, a particular factor, such as physical attractiveness, may play a more influential role in love than in friendship, or vice versa. However, all the factors to be discussed in this section appear to enter into both types of attraction.

To simplify this complex issue, we'll divide our coverage into three segments. In the first part, we'll review the *characteristics of other people* that tend to make them attractive to us. In the second, we'll discuss how *our own characteristics* influence our assessment of others' attractiveness. Finally, we'll look at *interaction factors*—those that don't reside in either person alone, but emerge out of a pair's relationship to each other.

Characteristics of the Other Person

Have you ever had a friend attempt to set you up with a blind date? If so, what kinds of questions did you ask about the person? Did you inquire about your prospective date's manners, attitudes, and moral character? Probably not. Chances are, you wanted to know about your prospective date's looks, personality, and intelligence. Research suggests that these are the main characteristics that influence our attraction to other people. Let's look at the evidence.

Physical Attractiveness

Familiar sayings warn us about putting too much emphasis on physical attractiveness. Statements such as "Beauty is only skin deep" and "You can't judge a book by its cover" imply that we should be cautious about being seduced by physical beauty. Research evidence suggests, however, that we don't pay much attention to this advice!

Emphasis on physical attractiveness. The importance of physical attractiveness was clearly demonstrated in a classic study by Walster, Aronson, Abrahams, and Rottman (1966). They invited male and female freshmen to a dance for which their dates had supposedly been selected by a computer. In reality, the couples had been paired randomly. However, the computer cover story provided a good rationale for asking participants to rate the degree to which they would like to go out with their dates again. These ratings were then correlated with other data collected on the participants, including their physical attractiveness (as assessed by impartial judges), their intelligence, their social skills, and various personality characteristics.

Out of all these variables, only one was predictive of subjects' desire to see their dates again. That single variable of significance was physical attractiveness. For both sexes, more attractive partners were rated as more desirable for future dates. Obviously, the linkage of good looks to attraction is hardly an exciting discovery. However, the finding that physical appearance was the *only* significant determinant of attraction in this study certainly underscores the prominence of this factor.

"Hold on," you might say. "Maybe physical attractiveness is a powerful factor only in people's *initial* encounters." After all, what else is there to go on besides appearance when you've just met someone? Little research has been done on this question, but at least one study failed to support this explanation. In this study, college men and women agreed to complete five dates during the course of the experiment. Physical attractiveness increased in importance from the first to subsequent dates (Mathes, 1975).

"Well," you might respond, "maybe physical attractiveness is important only with *younger* subjects, such as college students." Once again, research is sparse, but it doesn't support this explanation. One relevant study recruited subjects in their 30s who were enrolled in a commercial dating service. Subjects were asked to screen prospective partners on the basis of a photo and background information about the person's interests, ideals, hobbies, and relationship goals (Green, Buchanan, & Heuer, 1984). They were asked to select five people they would like to date and five people they definitely would not date. The results indicated that physical attractiveness was a major factor in date selection for both sexes. Age was also found to be an important factor. Interestingly, most women preferred men who were older, while most men preferred women who were younger. These findings about physical attractiveness and age in the initial screening of prospective dates have been replicated with clients of a video dating service (Woll, 1986).

Is the physical attractiveness of a prospective dating partner as important for homosexuals as for heterosexuals? One study looked at similarities and differences in the way gay and straight individuals worded personal advertisements in newspapers (Deaux & Hanna, 1984). Some 800 ads were analyzed—200 each from heterosexual men, heterosexual women, homosexual men, and homosexual women. Interestingly, sex (male or female) turned out to be a more important factor than sexual orientation (heterosexual or homosexual). That is, both heterosexual and homosexual men placed more emphasis on physical attractiveness when they described themselves and their preferences in partners than did either heterosexual or homosexual women. Regardless of sexual orientation, women placed more importance on psychological characteristics when they described themselves and their preferences in partners.

Most of the studies of physical beauty and attraction have focused on dating relationships; only a few have looked at friendship formation. However, the studies of friendship suggest that people, especially men, prefer attractiveness in their same- and other-sex friends as well as in their dates (Berscheid, Dion, Walster, & Walster, 1971; Buss & Barnes, 1986; Feingold, 1988, 1990; Lyman, Hatlelid, & Macurdy, 1981).

The premium that many people appear to place on physical attractiveness presents some-

FIGURE 8.3
Characteristics com-
monly sought in a mate
Buss (1985) surveyed individuals in 37 countries on
the characteristics they
sought in a mate. Both
sexes ranked kindness-
understanding and intelligence higher than physical
attractiveness. Statistically
significant gender differences in rankings were
found for a variety of characteristics, which are
shown in italics. For example, men ranked physical
attractiveness higher than
women did.

Characteristics Commonly Sought in a Mate

Rank	Characteristics preferred by men	Characteristics preferred by women
1	Kindness and understanding	Kindness and understanding
2	Intelligence	Intelligence
3	*Physical attractiveness*	Exciting personality
4	Exciting personality	Good health
5	Good health	Adaptability
6	Adaptability	*Physical attractiveness*
7	Creativity	Creativity
8	Desire for children	*Good earning capacity*
9	College graduate	College graduate
10	Good heredity	Desire for children
11	*Good earning capacity*	Good heredity
12	Good housekeeper	Good housekeeper
13	Religious orientation	Religious orientation

thing of a problem. Obviously, we cannot all be beautiful. However, the emphasis on beauty may not be quite so great as the evidence reviewed thus far suggests. Figure 8.3 summarizes the results of a cross-cultural study conducted in 37 countries on the characteristics commonly sought in a mate (Buss, 1985). As you can see, personal qualities, such as kindness-understanding and intelligence, are

ranked higher than physical attractiveness by both sexes. These results are somewhat reassuring. Still, we have seen in earlier chapters that verbal reports are not necessarily accurate reflections of people's actual behavior.

What makes someone attractive? The advertising industry has fostered a rather narrow conception of physical attractiveness. In fact, research suggests that people differ in regard to what they actually find attractive. In one study subjects were asked, "When you first meet someone, which one or two things about physical appearance do you tend to notice first?" As Figure 8.4 indicates, responses varied widely. You can also see that what we notice in another person often depends on whether that person is a member of the other sex. Other research suggests that both facial and bodily appearance are important factors in perceived attractiveness, but an unattractive body is perceived as being a greater liability than an unattractive face (Alicke, Smith, & Klotz, 1986). Men especially place emphasis on body build.

Men are rated as highly attractive if they have broad shoulders, slim waists and legs, and small buttocks (Lavrakas, 1975), and are not obese (Harris, Harris, & Bochner, 1982). Women who are rated high in attractiveness are not overweight (Franzoi & Herzog, 1987) and have medium-sized breasts (Kleinke & Staneski, 1980). A study of preferences for body types among white college students found that men exaggerated the extent to which same- and other-sex peers perceived large physiques as most desirable for men. Similarly, women believed that their male and female peers preferred a much thinner female silhouette than was actually the case (Cohn & Adler, 1992). Incidentally, the modern emphasis on thinness as the ideal female body shape has been suggested as a major cause of the high incidence of eating disorders among adolescent Caucasian girls (Boskind-Lodahl, 1976; Garner, Garfinkel, Schwartz, & Thompson, 1980). We'll discuss this issue in more detail in Chapter 10.

Because our culture values attractiveness in females, physical attractiveness appears to be more important for females than for males (Feingold, 1990). This gender gap was apparent in a recent study of the tactics heterosexual individuals used in pursuing romantic relationships. David Buss (1988) asked 208 newlyweds to describe the things they did when they first met their spouse and during the remainder of their courtship to make themselves more appealing to their partner. Buss found that men were more likely than women to emphasize

According to the matching hypothesis, we tend to wind up with someone similar to ourselves in attractiveness.

their material resources by doing such things as flashing lots of money, buying nice gifts, showing off expensive possessions, and bragging about their importance at work (see Figure 8.5). Women were more likely than men to work at enhancing their appearance by dieting, wearing stylish clothes, trying new hairstyles, and getting a tan. Although there were differences between the sexes in emphasis on physical attractiveness, the data in Figure 8.5 show that *both* sexes relied on tactics intended to enhance or maintain good looks.

Some theorists have argued that analyzing attractiveness into specific components is hopeless because it's the *total* picture that's important (Murstein, 1971). The key point, however, is that one does not have to match up perfectly with Hollywood stereotypes of good looks. The range of what we consider attractive is probably wider than most people think.

The matching hypothesis. Most of us will be reassured to know that a person does not have to be spectacularly good-looking in order to enjoy a rewarding social life. People apparently take into consideration their own level of attractiveness in the process of dating and mating. **The *matching hypothesis* proposes that people of similar levels of physical attractiveness gravitate toward each other.** The matching hypothesis is supported by evidence that both heterosexual dating pairs and married couples tend to be similar in physical attractiveness (Feingold, 1988, 1990). (We are unaware of research on this question regarding homosexual couples.) There is some debate, however, about whether we match up by our own choice (Aron, 1988; Kalick & Hamilton, 1986). Some theorists believe that we mostly pursue high attractiveness in partners and that our matching is the result of social forces beyond our control, such as rejection by more attractive others.

Researchers have also found evidence for matching effects in same-sex friendships (McKillip & Riedel, 1983). As we mentioned earlier, matching effects appear stronger among men than among women, regardless of sexual orientation (Berscheid et al., 1971; Buss & Barnes, 1986; Feingold, 1988, 1990). The reasons for this gender difference are not readily apparent. Overall, additional research is needed on the matching hypothesis as it relates to friendship formation.

The pervasiveness of matching on physical attractiveness is reflected in our reactions to couples who are obviously mismatched as far as this factor is concerned. That is, we usually remark on these exceptions and feel the need to explain them by attributing unusual or special qualities to the less attractive partner, such as wealth, high status, or fame.

Desirable Personality Characteristics

Personality characteristics are another factor that obviously influences interpersonal attraction. Subjects rate a hypothetical person's likability much higher when the person is described as sincere, honest, and dependable rather than

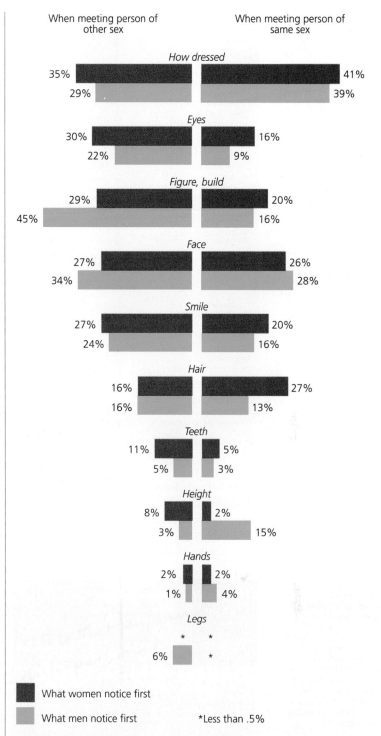

FIGURE 8.4
What men and women first notice about physical appearance
A Roper poll asked, "When you first meet someone, which one or two things about physical appearance do you tend to notice first?" The subjects' responses depended to some extent on the subjects' sex and on whether they were meeting someone of the same sex or the other sex. Overall, the subjects' responses were highly varied.

FIGURE 8.5
Similarities and differences between the sexes in the tactics of attraction
Buss (1988) asked newlyweds to rate how often they had used 23 tactics of attraction to make themselves more appealing to their partner. The tactics used by one sex significantly more often than the other are listed in the top two sections of the figure. Although there were significant differences between the sexes, there were also many similarities. The 11 tactics used most frequently by each sex (those above the median) are highlighted in boldface, showing considerable overlap between men and women in the tactics they used most. (Note: Higher means in the data reflect higher frequency of use, but the numbers do not indicate frequency per day or week.)

Tactics of Attraction	Mean frequency (N = 102)	Mean frequency (N = 106)
Tactics used significantly more by males	Men	Women
Display resources	0.67	0.44
Brag about resources	0.73	0.60
Display sophistication	**1.18**	0.88
Display strength	0.96	0.44
Display athleticism	**1.18**	0.94
Show off	0.70	0.47
Tactics used significantly more by females		
Wear makeup	0.02	**1.63**
Keep clean and groomed	**2.27**	**2.44**
Alter appearance—general	0.39	**1.27**
Wear stylish clothes	**1.22**	**2.00**
Act coy	0.54	0.73
Wear jewelry	0.25	**2.21**
Wear sexy clothes	0.68	0.91
Tactics for which no significant sex differences were found		
Act provocative	0.77	0.90
Flirt	**2.13**	**2.09**
Keep hair groomed	**2.20**	**2.31**
Increase social pressure	0.89	0.90
Act nice	**1.77**	**1.86**
Display humor	**2.42**	**2.28**
Act promiscuous	0.30	0.21
Act submissive	**1.24**	**1.11**
Dissemble (feign agreement)	**1.26**	1.09
Touch	**2.26**	**2.16**

FIGURE 8.6
Likableness of personality traits
Norman Anderson (1968) asked subjects to rate the likableness of 555 personality-trait descriptors. These data were collected to facilitate research on impression formation, but they provide us with some insight into the personality traits that we like and dislike in others.

Personality Traits People Like and Dislike		
Highly likable	Slightly positive to slightly negative	Highly unlikable
Sincere	Persistent	Ill-mannered
Honest	Conventional	Unfriendly
Understanding	Bold	Hostile
Loyal	Cautious	Loudmouthed
Truthful	Perfectionistic	Selfish
Trustworthy	Excitable	Narrow-minded
Intelligent	Quiet	Rude
Dependable	Impulsive	Conceited
Thoughtful	Aggressive	Greedy
Considerate	Shy	Insincere
Reliable	Unpredictable	Unkind
Warm	Emotional	Untrustworthy
Kind	Bashful	Malicious
Friendly	Naive	Obnoxious
Happy	Restless	Untruthful
Unselfish	Daydreamer	Dishonest
Humorous	Materialistic	Cruel
Responsible	Rebellious	Mean
Cheerful	Lonely	Phony
Trustful	Dependent	Liar

loudmouthed, deceitful, and obnoxious. Figure 8.6 displays some of the findings from a study that Anderson (1968) conducted to determine the likableness of 555 personality-trait descriptions. These ratings give us some insight into what personal qualities we value in other people.

A large-scale survey on people's perceptions of the ideal man and woman revealed that we look for qualities such as confidence, integrity, warmth, gentleness, and the ability to love (Tavris, 1977). Similar results were reported in a more recent study of British college students and clients of dating agencies regarding the personality characteristics they preferred in romantic partners (Goodwin, 1990). The most preferred qualities were kindness-consideration, honesty, and humor. Other studies indicate that we like pleasant, agreeable people who express positive attitudes about things more than unpleasant, disagreeable people who express negative attitudes (Folkes & Sears, 1977; Kaplan & Anderson, 1973).

Intelligence and Competence

Generally we prefer people who are bright and competent over those who are not. The data in Figure 8.3 support this idea. Most subjects sought mates who were intelligent college graduates with good earning capacity.

Sometimes, however, extremely competent people may make us feel so threatened that we dislike them. Interestingly, highly competent people may be able to enhance their attractiveness by showing themselves to be fallible and thus more "human." In a study that tested this idea, male students listened to a tape recording of another male student who was supposedly being interviewed for an important position on campus. The interviewee was portrayed in four conditions: (1) unusually competent, (2) unusually competent and makes an embarrassing blunder (he spills coffee on himself), (3) somewhat inept, and (4) somewhat inept and makes the same embarrassing blunder (Aronson, Willerman, & Floyd, 1966). Which interviewee did the subjects like best? They preferred the highly competent student who committed the blunder. But before you start making frequent blunders to enhance your likability, please note that the person the subjects liked least was the inept student who committed the blunder.

This preference for competent people who make humanizing mistakes may be limited to individuals of the same sex. Kay Deaux (1972) conducted an experiment that was basically the same as the one conducted by Aronson and his colleagues except that she added female subjects and had both men and women play the role of the stimulus person. As before, male subjects liked the competent man more when he made a blunder. Female subjects, however, preferred the competent man who did *not* blunder. Similarly, male subjects rated the competent woman who did not commit a blunder higher than the one who did. In explaining these perplexing findings, Deaux suggests that we may empathize more with people of our own sex and hence be more tolerant of their blunders. She also suggests that our idealized images of people of the other sex may make it more difficult for us to accept their mistakes.

Social Status

Social status is another important determinant of a person's appeal. Several studies have shown that heterosexual men "trade" occupational status for physical attractiveness in the women they date, and vice versa (Deaux & Hanna, 1984; Green et al., 1984). This finding appears to hold true in many other cultures as well. As we saw in the cross-cultural study summarized in Figure 8.3, men in most countries rate physical attractiveness in a prospective mate as more important than women do, whereas women rate "good financial prospects" and "ambitious and industrious" as more important characteristics than men do (Buss, 1989). Moreover, several studies have shown that more attractive women are more likely than less attractive ones to demand high status in their prospective dates (Harrison & Saeed, 1977). Of course, as women gain greater economic independence, men's social and financial status may have less impact on women's dating preferences.

Your Own Characteristics

Thus far we have discussed how others' characteristics influence your attraction to them. Now we are ready to turn the spotlight on you, examining the role that social motives, self-esteem, and self-perception processes play in attraction.

Social Motives

Social motives impel us to engage in social interaction and relationships. Obviously there are individual differences in the strengths of these motives. Some people thrive on many acquaintances and friends, while others are perfectly content with only a few close relationships. Dan McAdams (1982) has found some interesting differences between two important social motives. If you have a strong *need for affiliation*, you probably enjoy establishing and maintaining many rewarding interpersonal relationships as well as joining and participating in groups (see Chapter 7). Individuals who are low on this need feel less drawn to interact with others. If you prefer a few intimate relationships, you probably have a strong *need for intimacy*. Research has shown that individuals with high intimacy needs engage in deeper self-disclosure and experience a greater sense of well-being than do those with low intimacy needs (McAdams & Bryant, 1987; McAdams, Healy, & Krause, 1984).

Self-Esteem

As we noted in Chapter 5, our self-esteem influences the way we relate to others. For example, low self-esteem subjects select less attractive dates than high self-esteem subjects (Kiesler & Baral, 1970). Thus people with a favorable self-concept may see themselves as having a wider range of dating choices than those with an unfavorable self-concept.

Self-esteem also affects our reactions to others' evaluations of us (Berscheid, 1985; Jones, 1973). Individuals with low self-esteem tend to take negative feedback to heart more than do people with high self-esteem (Swan et al., 1987). Thus people may be more vulnerable to others' views of them if their self-esteem is low.

Self-Perception

Daryl Bem (1972) has theorized that we sometimes infer our attitudes from our overt responses and behavior (see Chapter 5). Various studies suggest that self-perception plays a key role in attraction. In one such study, male subjects were asked to view pictures of seminude women (Valins, 1966). A microphone was attached to the chest of each subject so that he could hear his heartbeat amplified. In reality, the experimenter controlled the auditory feedback of the heart rate. In this way, the men were led to believe that slides of certain women triggered a dramatic change in their heartbeat. Later the subjects were asked to rate their attraction to the women seen in the slides. The men were most attracted to the women who had apparently affected their heartbeat.

The Valins study illustrates our need to interpret our emotional states. In his theory of emotion, Stanley Schachter (1964) proposed that when we experience the physiological arousal that is usually associated with emotion (which the experimenter faked in this study by providing false feedback on heart rate), we try to explain our arousal by looking at the situation we are in. In the Valins study, the most plausible explanation the men had for their

speeded-up heartbeat was that they were really turned on by the women they were viewing at the time.

Similar evidence has been found in a study in a naturalistic setting. These experimenters arranged for young men crossing a footbridge to encounter a good-looking young woman who was actually a confederate of the experimenters (Dutton & Aron, 1974). The woman stopped the men on the bridge to ask them to complete a questionnaire for a class project she was doing. When the men returned the questionnaire, she offered to explain the research at some future time and gave them her phone number. The key to the experiment was that this procedure was carried out on two very different bridges. One was a long suspension bridge that swayed with seeming precariousness over a 230-foot gorge. The other bridge was a solidly anchored structure a mere 10 feet above a small stream. The experimenters reasoned that men crossing the high suspension bridge would experience emotional arousal and that some of them might misinterpret their arousal as being caused by the woman rather than the bridge. If these men attributed their arousal to the woman, they would probably infer that they found her very attractive. The dependent variable in the study was the percentage of men who later called the woman to pursue a date. In accord with the experimenters' hypothesis, those men who met the woman in an aroused state (on the seemingly precarious bridge) were more likely to ask her out than those who met her in a normal emotional state (on the steady bridge).

What does all this mean? These findings suggest that the self-perception processes described by Bem and Schachter may be quite relevant to our efforts to understand the emotional turmoil triggered by romantic attraction. Many of us spend long hours musing about whether someone is "right" for us. Much of this thought involves self-perception efforts: "Wow, I just glow when I'm around Bill. I can't stop smiling. He must be the one." Or "Gee, I don't get very excited when Mary Ann calls. I guess maybe I'm not all that crazy about her." Thus it appears that interpersonal attraction may be influenced by the way we interpret our behavior and our feelings.

It's worth noting that our propensity to misinterpret emotional arousal may be the basis for the tendency to mistake lust for love. If artificial manipulations of physical arousal in experiments can be misinterpreted, it is easy to imagine how arousal genuinely elicited by another person might be misunderstood. Thus the emotional arousal evoked by sexual attraction may often be mislabeled "love." Although sexual arousal is an important aspect of romantic love, love is more than mere lust. Nonetheless, research on self-perception shows just how easy it may be for people to mix up sexual arousal and more profound feelings of love.

Interaction Factors

Some factors in the dynamics of attraction lie neither in you nor in the other person. Instead, they emerge out of your unique relationship with each other. Hence they are called interaction factors. They include proximity, similarity, and reciprocity.

Proximity

It would be difficult for you to develop a friendship with someone you never met. Although it happens occasionally (between pen pals, for instance), attraction usually depends on proximity: people have to be in the same place at the same time. **Proximity refers to geographic, residential, and other forms of spatial close-**

ness. Generally we become acquainted with and attracted to people who live, work, shop, and play nearby.

The importance of proximity was apparent in a classic study of friendship patterns among married graduate students living in a university housing project (Festinger, Schachter, & Back, 1950). People whose doors were close together were most likely to become friends. Moreover, those whose homes faced the central court area had more than twice as many friends in the complex as those whose homes faced outward. Use of the central court area apparently increased the likelihood that people would meet and befriend others.

Proximity effects were also found in a study of Maryland State Police trainees (Segal, 1974). At the training academy, both dormitory rooms and classroom seats were assigned in alphabetical order. Six months after their arrival, subjects were asked to name their three closest friends among the group of trainees. The trainees whose last names were close together in the alphabet were much more likely to be friends than trainees whose names were widely separated in the alphabet.

Proximity effects may seem self-evident, but it is sobering to realize that our friendships and love interests are shaped by seating charts, desk arrangements in offices, and floor assignments in residence halls. In spite of our increasing geographic mobility, we still tend to marry someone who grew up nearby (Ineichen, 1979).

Similarity

Is it true that "birds of a feather flock together," or do "opposites attract"? Research provides far more support for the first adage than for the second. Heterosexual married and dating couples tend to be similar in age, race, religion, social class, education, intelligence, physical attractiveness, and attitudes (Brehm, 1992; Hendrick & Hendrick, 1983). We are unaware of research on similarity effects among homosexual couples; however, one study that compared heterosexual, homosexual, and bisexual individuals reported that members of all three groups agreed that it was important that lovers have similar interests, share the same religious beliefs, and have similar values (Engel & Saracino, 1986). The factor on which the groups differed was similarity in ethnic background. That is, heterosexuals were significantly more likely than homosexuals or bisexuals to say that having a partner of the same ethnic background was important.

Also, people with similar *personalities* are more likely to be attracted to each other than to people with dissimilar personalities. For example, it has been found that men and women who identify strongly with traditional gender-role characteristics are more likely to be attracted to each other than to people who identify less strongly with stereotypic gender roles (Pursell & Banikiotes, 1978). Similarly, Type A individuals are attracted to each other (Morell, Twillman, & Sullaway, 1989).

Similarity is also important among friends (Newcomb, 1961). Among adolescents, for instance, best friends are similar in age, sex, race, educational goals and performance, political and religious activities, and illicit drug use (Kandel, 1978).

The most obvious explanation for these correlations is that similarity causes attraction. Laboratory experiments on *attitude similarity* conducted by Donn Byrne and his colleagues suggest that similarity does cause liking (Byrne, 1971; Byrne, Clore, & Smeaton, 1986). In these studies, subjects who have previously provided information on their own attitudes are led to believe that they will be meeting a stranger. They are given information about the stranger's views that has been manipulated to show various degrees of similarity to their own views. As attitude similarity increases, subjects' ratings of the likability of the stranger increase (see Figure 8.7). This evidence supports the notion that similarity promotes attraction. However, it's also consistent with a somewhat different explanation proposed by Rosenbaum (1986).

Rosenbaum has marshaled evidence suggesting that similarity effects occur in attrac-

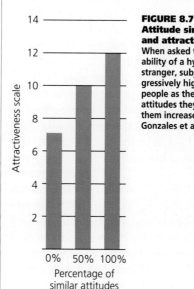

**FIGURE 8.7
Attitude similarity and attraction**
When asked to rate the likability of a hypothetical stranger, subjects give progressively higher ratings to people as the number of attitudes they share with them increases. (Data from Gonzales et al., 1983.)

tion not because similarity fosters liking but because *dissimilarity* leads us to *dislike* others (he termed this phenomenon the *repulsion hypothesis*). In one study of this hypothesis, Rosenbaum (1986) found that Democrats did not rate other Democrats (similar others) higher than controls as much as they rated Republicans (dissimilar others) lower than controls. Thus Rosenbaum downplays the importance of attitude similarity, arguing instead that *dissimilarity causes disdain.* More recent evidence suggests that liking is influenced by *both* similarity and dissimilarity in attitudes (Smeaton, Byrne, & Murnen, 1989).

Reciprocity

In his best-selling book *How to Win Friends and Influence People*, Dale Carnegie (1936) suggested that people can gain others' liking by showering them with praise and flattery. Yet we all have heard that "flattery will get you nowhere." Which advice is right?

The evidence suggests that flattery will get you somewhere, with some people, some of the time. So far as interpersonal attraction is concerned, **reciprocity involves liking those who show that they like us.** In general, it does appear that liking breeds liking and loving promotes loving (Byrne & Murnen, 1988).

But what if other people say nice things about us that are inconsistent with our self-perceptions? Do we still like them? Studies suggest that we like people more when they give us positive evaluations that match our self-concepts as opposed to positive evaluations that contradict our self-concepts (Berscheid, 1985; Shrauger, 1975). Why? Because when we have doubts about the sincerity of another's positive evaluation, we tend to like that person less (Kauffman & Steiner, 1968; Lowe & Goldstein, 1970). Thus flattery can sometimes have the opposite effect of the one Carnegie predicted.

You might expect that another qualification to the reciprocity principle would involve the widely discussed strategy of playing hard to get. According to this strategy, showing relatively little interest in the social overtures of a person of the other sex (nonreciprocity) may make the other person even more eager to pursue the relationship. The empirical evidence suggests, however, that playing hard to get may not be advisable. Research indicates that we prefer members of the other sex who appear hard for *others* to get, but who eagerly accept us (Walster, Walster, Piliavin, & Schmidt, 1973).

Our review of the dynamics of attraction has shown that many factors influence the emergence of close relationships. In the next two sections we'll probe more deeply into the nature of friendship and romantic love.

Friendship

riends play a very significant role in our lives. They may provide help in times of need, advice in times of confusion, consolation in times of failure, and praise in times of achievement. The importance of friends was underscored in a survey of 40,000 readers of *Psychology Today* magazine. In the survey, 51% of the respondents indicated that in a crisis they were more likely to turn to friends than to family for help (Parlee et al., 1979). Let's explore what makes a good friend and how gender and marital status affect patterns of friendship.

What Makes a Good Friend?

The most intriguing aspect of the *Psychology Today* survey was its investigation of what makes a "good friend." Figure 8.8 lists the most frequently endorsed qualities. The results suggest that loyalty is the heart and soul of friendship. As you can see, the top two qualities in Figure 8.8 are keeping confidences (an aspect of loyalty) and loyalty itself. As one might guess, the next most important ingredients of friendship are warmth/affection and supportiveness. The high ratings of candor (frankness) and a sense of humor are interesting and well worth keeping in mind.

These results generally coincide with those of another survey on friendship, although one other important factor emerged in this second survey (Block, 1980). That additional factor was a willingness to let friends be themselves. Block points out that we often put people under pressure to behave in ways that are consistent with our expectations. Such "conditional" expectations appear to resemble those held by many parents for their children. As we discussed in Chapter 2, Carl Rogers believes that conditional affection contributes to distortions in our self-concepts, and for this reason he advocates unconditional acceptance in child rearing. In accord with Rogers's theory, Block's respondents emphasized the importance of relatively unconditional acceptance by their friends.

A slightly different way of looking at what is important in friendship comes from a cross-cultural study. The investigators (Argyle & Henderson, 1984) interviewed students in four

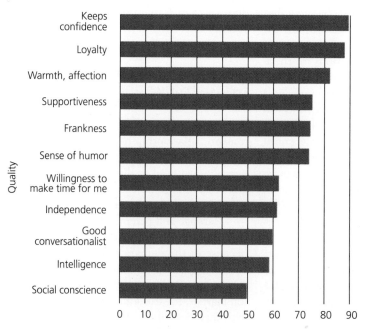

FIGURE 8.8
Important qualities in a friend
The traits listed here are those that subjects cited most often when asked what makes a good friend. (Based on Parlee et al., 1979.)

countries (England, Italy, Japan, and Hong Kong) to see whether they could find enough agreement on how friends should conduct themselves to permit the formulation of some informal rules governing friendships. For a behavior to qualify as a rule, subjects had to agree that the behavior was important in a friendship, that failure to behave in this way could destroy the friendship, and that the behavior could differentiate between current and former friends and between intimate and nonintimate friends. On the basis of students' responses, the authors identified six informal rules. As Figure 8.9 indicates, the common thread running through these rules seems to be the provision of emotional and social support to friends. Hence we can conclude that loyalty, emotional support, and letting us be ourselves appear to be the most important expectations that we have of our friends.

Gender Differences in Friendship

Men's and women's same-sex friendships have a lot in common, but there are some interesting differences that appear rooted in traditional gender roles and socialization. For one thing, men's friendships tend to be based on shared interests and things they do together (Hays, 1985; Sherrod, 1989). Women's friendships are more likely to focus on talking and emotional intimacy. Men seem to view their friends as serving specific functions (one may be a fishing partner, another a traveling companion). Women seem to react to their friends in a more

"global" way (Wright, 1982). Also, many men seem willing to tolerate and work around sources of tension in friendships, whereas women are more likely to confront friends about conflicts in an effort to resolve them (Wright, 1982).

Men's and women's friendships can also be differentiated by topics of their conversation. Women are far more likely than men to discuss personal problems, feelings, and people (Caldwell & Peplau, 1982; Davidson & Duberman, 1982). Men who don't adhere to traditional gender roles are exceptions to this rule. That is, these men appear to divulge as much to their best male friend as most women do to their best female friend (Lavine & Lombardo, 1984).

Friendships between men tend to be regulated by social roles. That is, men tend to relate to each other as business partners, as tennis rivals, or as baseball fans. Moreover, men generally rate their same-sex friendships as less intimate than women rate theirs. Men also per-

The Rules of Friendship

Share news of success with a friend

Show emotional support

Volunteer help in time of need

Strive to make a friend happy when in each other's company

Trust and confide in each other

Stand up for a friend in his or her absence

FIGURE 8.9
Vital behaviors in friendship
A cross-cultural inquiry (Argyle & Henderson, 1984) into the behaviors that are vital to friendship identified the six rules of friendship listed here.

245

ceive less emotional support to be available from their friends than most women do (Sherrod, 1989).

There are several likely reasons for these gender differences in friendships (Reis, Senchak, & Solomon, 1985). First, men and women appear to have different pathways to intimacy (shared activities and self-disclosure, respectively). Second, men may have less need for intimacy than women do. Third, traditional gender-role expectations encourage men to be "strong and silent." As we saw in Chapter 6, when self-disclosure is socially acceptable for men, they sometimes engage in it more than women do.

We noted in Chapter 3 that social support from friends (and others) reduces the impact of stress and is associated with mental health. This finding raises an interesting question. Do women's same-sex friendships yield greater mental health benefits than men's because of their greater intimacy? There is evidence on both sides of this question. On one hand, evidence suggests that same-sex friendships buffer stress and reduce depression in both men and women (Cohen, Sherrod, & Clark, 1986; Cohen & Wills, 1985). On the other, the relative lack of emotional support from same-sex friends often means that men are heavily dependent on their wives for such support. Should this be the case, a man whose marriage ends in divorce will have less emotional support from friends than his former wife (Gerstel, 1988). This may be one of the reasons that men typically have a harder time adjusting to

divorce than women do (Price & McKenry, 1988).

Committed Romantic Relationships and Friendship Patterns

What effect, if any, does being in a committed romantic relationship have on the number and quality of one's friendships? To answer this question, we need to distinguish between heterosexual and homosexual couples. We'll look at heterosexual couples first.

Marriage and parenthood appear to reduce the development of friendships, primarily because of the demands on time and energy these changes in status bring with them (Dickens & Perlman, 1981). Also, when a person marries, the freedom to develop friendships with members of the other sex is curtailed by social norms (Bell, 1981). For one thing, cross-sex friendships may be seen as a threat by the spouse. There is also a tendency for some people to assume that something must be missing in a marital relationship if either spouse is involved in a close cross-sex friendship. Because of these norms, married people tend to form their friendships with other *couples*. Some studies suggest that these friendships between couples tend to involve less intimacy than friendships between individuals (Bell, 1981).

In spite of these constraints, wives are more likely than husbands to depend on a close friend rather than on their spouse as their principal confidant (Blau, 1971; Gerstel, 1988).

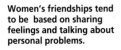
Women's friendships tend to be based on sharing feelings and talking about personal problems.

This finding suggests, among other things, that while most wives are expected to listen to their husbands' personal concerns, many husbands may be unwilling or unable to do the same for their wives. If so, this problem may be a major cause of strain in many marriages.

A somewhat different picture emerges for homosexual couples. Like heterosexuals, homosexuals in committed relationships form friendships with other couples. The difference is that "coupled" (and "noncoupled") gay people rely more than married couples on "noncoupled" friends (Garnets & Kimmel, 1991). This difference in friendship patterns seems to be due in part to the fact that gays and lesbians receive less support than heterosexuals from their families of origin. Families of gay males and lesbians often have negative attitudes toward a homosexual orientation (homophobia).

The social norms that limit the freedom of married people to pursue new friendships seem unfortunate. As we have noted, friends are a valuable resource in times of stress. Moreover, with close-knit kinship networks becoming less common, it seems even more important for people to be free to develop worthwhile friendships outside of marriage. The increasing rate of divorce provides yet another reason for encouraging people to seek nonmarital companionships. In times of marital distress, it is especially important for a person to have friends to depend on for emotional support.

Romantic Love

ander through a bookstore and you'll see an overwhelming array of titles such as *How to Be Loved*; *Love Can Be Found*; *Men Who Can't Love*, *Women Who Love Too Much*; and *How to Survive the Loss of a Love*. Turn up your radio and you'll hear the refrains of "I Will Always Love You," "Love Will Find a Way," "Prove Your Love," "Endless Love," and "Love Will Keep Us Together." Although there are other forms of love, such as parental love and platonic love, these books and songs are all about *romantic love*, a subject of consuming interest to most of us.

People have always been interested in love and romance, yet the scientific study of love dates back only to the 1970s. Love has proved to be an elusive subject of study. It is difficult to define, difficult to measure, and frequently difficult to understand. Nonetheless, psychologists

have begun to make some progress in their study of love. Given all the confusion about love, we'll first attempt to debunk some myths about it.

Myths about Love

Romantic love is a highly idealized concept in our culture. Some interesting as well as troublesome myths have been nurtured by this idealism—as well as by American television and movies. Accordingly, our first task is to take a realistic look at love and dispel some of these problematic notions. Most of our discussion will be based on the writings of Elaine Hatfield (formerly Walster) and Ellen Berscheid (Berscheid, 1988; Berscheid & Walster, 1978; Hatfield, 1988; Walster & Berscheid, 1974), who probably have conducted more research on love than anyone else. Although they're rigorous researchers who have made major contributions to the scientific study of love, Berscheid and Hatfield have also been willing to offer down-to-earth, practical insights into the nature of love.

A New Look at Love
by Elaine Hatfield and G. William Walster (University Press of America, 1985)

This book represents a fine effort at combining empirical research with practical advice. Hatfield and Walster have conducted a great deal of research on the mysteries of love. Moreover, they have been among the more innovative and down-to-earth investigators in this area. Although their own work is highlighted in this book, their review of research is broad in scope. The book is smoothly written, with minimal dependence on technical jargon.

Unlike many psychologists with backgrounds in research, Hatfield and Walster are not timid about giving practical advice on ordinary questions. Drawing upon scientific research, casual observation, and their own extensive thinking about the subject, they offer astute advice on how to deal with the intricacies of romantic relationships. The book is filled with fascinating case histories and intriguing questionnaires. Unfortunately, the second edition has not been revised or updated. Since the first edition was printed in 1978, some of the findings may be out of date. Even so, we think the book has a lot to offer.

Critics of Hatfield and Walster appear to have derived some amusement from the fact that this former husband-and-wife team was broken up by divorce soon after the publication of the first edition of this book. Although admittedly ironic, the parting of their ways in no way undermines the quality of their contribution to the understanding of love. As they have pointed out themselves, love is a beautiful but *fragile* flower.

> Passionate love is characterized by fragility. Every lover always hopes that this love will last forever. But the rest of us, looking on, know that that's unlikely. [p. 108]

Elaine Hatfield

Myth 1: When you fall in love, you'll know it. People often spend a great deal of time agonizing over whether they are experiencing true love or mere infatuation. When these people consult others, they are often told, "If it's true love, you'll know it." This statement, which is tantamount to telling the person that he or she is not really in love, is simply not accurate. A few people may recognize love clearly and quickly. For most of us, however, no "bolt out of the blue" marks the beginning of love. On the contrary, love usually grows gradually, and doubts are quite normal.

Myth 2: When love strikes, you have no control over it. This myth suggests that love is so powerful that we are incapable of behaving wisely once we are under its spell. While it may be comforting to tell ourselves that we have no control in matters of the heart, this rationalization can lead to big mistakes. This myth encourages people to act irresponsibly in matters of the heart. But irresponsible behavior can result in tragic outcomes—sexually transmitted diseases (including AIDS), unwanted pregnancy, and unhappy marriages, to name a few. In the early stages of romantic relationships it's

especially hard to sort out our many intense feelings. For that very reason, however, we need to proceed cautiously in making important decisions about sexual involvements and long-term commitments.

Myth 3: Love is a purely positive experience. Our idealization of love sometimes creates unrealistic expectations that love should be an exclusively enjoyable experience. In reality, love may bring intense negative emotions and great pain. Ambivalent feelings in love are quite common. We tend to expect and demand a lot from someone we love. Research indicates that we tend to be more critical and less tolerant of lovers and spouses than we are of friends (K. E. Davis, 1985). People often ask, "Can you love and hate someone at the same time?" This common question shows that many people find that love brings with it feelings of intense anger as well as sublime joy. The passions that accompany love can take us to the emotional depths as well as the heights.

Myth 4: True love lasts forever. Love *may* last forever, but unfortunately, you can't count on it. People perpetuate this myth in an interesting way. If they have a romantic relationship that eventually disintegrates, they conclude that it was never really love. Hence they relegate the dissolved relationship to the inferior status of infatuation. This rationalization allows people to continue their search for the one great ideal lover who will supposedly bring complete happiness. It's more realistic to view love as a sometimes wonderful, sometimes frustrating experience that may be encountered a number of times in one's life.

Myth 5: Love can conquer all problems. This myth is the basis for many unsuccessful marriages. Numerous couples, fully aware of problems in their relationship (for example, poor communication, disagreement about gender roles) forge ahead into marriage anyway. Well intentioned but naive, they say to themselves, "As long as we love each other, we'll be able to work it out." While authentic love certainly helps in tackling marital problems, it is no guarantee of success. In fact, there is some provocative evidence that how much you *like* your lover may be more important than how much you *love* your lover. When researchers correlated a host of variables with a measure of the "successfulness" of romantic relationships, liking for one's partner was more highly correlated (.62) with relationship success than was love (.50) of one's partner (Sternberg & Grajek, 1984). Such a small difference in just one study is hardly definitive, but it raises the possibility that liking may conquer problems more effectively than love.

Sexual Orientation and Romantic Love

Sexual orientation refers to a person's preference for emotional and sexual relationships with individuals of the same sex, the other sex, or either sex. *Heterosexuals* seek emotional-sexual relationships with members of the other sex. *Homosexuals* seek emotional-sexual relationships with members of the same sex. *Bisexuals* seek emotional-sexual relationships with members of both sexes. In recent years the terms *gay* and *straight* have become widely used to refer to homosexuals and heterosexuals, respectively. *Gay* can refer to homosexuals of either sex, but most homosexual women prefer to call themselves *lesbians*.

Most studies of romantic love and relationships suffer from **heterosexism, or the assumption that *all* individuals and relationships are heterosexual.** Most questionnaires on romantic love and romantic relationships, for example, fail to ask subjects about their sexual orientation. When data are analyzed, there is no way to know whether subjects are referring to same- or other-sex romantic partners. Assuming that their subjects are all heterosexuals, researchers proceed to describe their findings without any mention of homosexuals. Of course, because many more people identify themselves as heterosexual, heterosexism in research probably doesn't distort the conclusions about heterosexuals very much. A more important problem of heterosexism is that it renders homosexual relationships invisible. Consequently, psychologists don't know as much about the role of sexual orientation as they would like to. Currently more research attention is being devoted to the experience of being homosexual. Where evidence is available, we'll attempt to mention it.

In the experience of love relationships, biological sex (male or female) and identification with traditional or nontraditional gender roles seem to be more critical factors than sexual orientation (Garnets & Kimmel, 1991; Peplau, 1981). According to Linda Garnets and Greg Kimmel (1991), two psychologists well known for their research and writing on gay and lesbian issues, "Many similarities are found between heterosexual and homosexual couples, indicating commonality in dynamics within the relationship and a similar range of diversity among relationships" (p. 170). Both heterosexual and homosexual couples say they want their

The experience of romantic love seems to be the same regardless of a person's sexual orientation.

partners to have characteristics similar to theirs, hold similar values in respect to relationships, report similar levels of satisfaction in their relationships, and perceive their relationships to be loving and satisfying.

For these reasons, our discussion of love will presume that *experiences of love* are similar regardless of sexual orientation. Research has shown some differences between homosexual and heterosexual *relationships*—for example, in the division of labor and balance of power—but we'll hold our discussion of these issues for Chapter 9, which is concerned with marriage and other intimate relationships.

Gender Differences in Regard to Love

The differences in how males and females are socialized in our society appear to affect their attitudes toward love. The traditional stereotype suggests that women are more romantic than men. Interestingly, much of the research evidence suggests just the opposite—men are the more romantic sex. One study reported that men score higher than women on romanticism scales and that men recognize love earlier than women do (Kanin, Davidson, & Scheck, 1970). The same study also found that women are more cautious and rational than men in selecting their mates. Other researchers report that men tend to fall in love more easily than women, whereas women fall out of love more easily than men (Hill et al., 1976; Rubin, Peplau, & Hill, 1981). Furthermore, these researchers found that women seem to experience less emotional turmoil than men when romantic relationships break up.

As a whole, the evidence suggests that men are more romantic than women. However, we should note that women do seem to be more romantic with regard to *expressions* of love. That is, women are more willing to verbalize and display their affection (Balswick & Avertt, 1977). There is also evidence that women may be more sensitive than men to problems that occur in relationships (Hill et al., 1976).

What might account for the surprising finding that men are more romantic than women? It may be a reflection of economic realities. Heterosexual women are still more economically dependent on their partners than the partners are on them. Hence they may assume that the decision about whom they will marry is a decision about the kind of lifestyle (status and income) they will have. According to this view, being romantic in the choice of a potential partner may be a luxury that men (gay or straight) can afford more readily than heterosexual women can. We are unaware of research on this question with homosexual subjects. Hence we don't know if this principle holds for all women and, if it does, whether the reasons for it are similar.

Theories of Love

How do romantic love relationships differ from other types of close relationships? Can the experience of love be broken down into certain key components? Are some of these elements more important than others? These are the

kinds of questions addressed by new theories of love that have emerged from the recent explosion of research on romantic relationships. In this section we'll look at two particularly prominent theories of love.

Triangular Theory of Love

Robert Sternberg's (1986, 1988) *triangular theory of love* posits that all love experiences have three components: intimacy, passion, and commitment. Each of these components is represented as a point of a triangle, from which the theory derives its name (see Figure 8.10).

Intimacy refers to warmth, closeness, and sharing in a relationship. Signs of intimacy include giving and receiving emotional support, wanting to promote the welfare of the loved one, and sharing oneself and one's possessions with another. As we've already discussed, self-disclosure is necessary to achieve and maintain feelings of intimacy in a relationship.

Passion refers to the intense feelings (both positive and negative) experienced in love relationships, including sexual desire. Sternberg suggests that while sexual needs may be dominant in many close relationships, other needs also figure in the experience of passion. Among them are our needs for affiliation, self-esteem, dominance, submission, and self-actualization. For example, our self-esteem is threatened when we experience jealousy.

Commitment involves the decision and intent to maintain a relationship in spite of the difficulties and costs it may entail. According to Sternberg, commitment has a short-term and a long-term aspect. The short-term one concerns our conscious decision that we love someone. The long-term aspect reflects our determination to make a relationship endure. Although the decision that we love someone usually comes before commitment, some people make a commitment without consciously deciding that they love the other person.

Sternberg has described eight types of relationships that can result from the presence or absence of each of the three components of love (see Figure 8.10). One of these relationship types, *nonlove*, is not pictured in the diagram because it is defined as the absence of any of the three components. According to Sternberg, most of our interpersonal relationships—casual interactions—fall into this category.

Liking is found at the top of Sternberg's triangle. Liking involves the experience of only one component of love—intimacy. In liking relationships we feel warm and close to other people, but we don't experience passionate feel-

FIGURE 8.10
Sternberg's triangular theory of love
According to Robert Sternberg (1986), love has three components: intimacy, passion, and commitment. These components are portrayed here as points on a triangle. The absence of all three components, or nonlove, is not shown in the diagram. The other possible combinations of these three components yield the seven types of relationships mapped out here.

ings for them or make long-term commitments to them.

Infatuation represents a second point on the triangle that involves only one component of love—in this case, passion. When people talk about "falling in love at first sight," they're experiencing infatuation. Sternberg mentions three problems typically associated with infatuation. First, the partner is loved only as an idealized object—a projection of the lover's needs—rather than as the person he or she really is. Second, infatuation tends to be obsessive, consuming time and energy needed for other activities. Third, since infatuations are usually one-sided, they often cause feelings of distress. Because of the nature of infatuated relationships, they are likely to be troublesome.

Empty love, the third point on the triangle, is a relationship in which only commitment is currently present. In our culture, this type of relationship is most commonly found in the last stages of a long-term relationship. In other cultures where marriages are arranged by parents, this type of love typically exists in the initial stages of a marital relationship.

In Sternberg's model, four types of love can result from various combinations of the three components. The first is *fatuous love*, which is a combination of passion and commitment. This type of love often occurs in "whirlwind courtships." People meet, fall in love, and get married so quickly that the intimacy component has no time to develop. This kind of relationships is quite likely to break up when the passion fades, because the usually shallow commitment has little intimacy to sustain it.

In Sternberg's scheme, the combination of intimacy and passion is called *romantic love*. Two people involved in romantic love feel strongly drawn to each other and share highly personal information with each other. Still they have made no long-term commitment to maintain the relationship. The commitment component may be added to the relationship later or it may never develop, as in a summer love affair. Romantic love can begin as infatua-

tion (passion only) or liking (intimacy only). Each of these states can develop into romantic love with the addition of the other necessary component.

Companionate love combines intimacy and commitment. This type of love is seen in marriages in which passion has faded, or in lifelong intimate friendships. According to Sternberg, most romantic love relationships eventually become companionate love relationships as passion subsides. For some couples, the relative lack of passion in their relationship is acceptable. Other couples (or one of the partners) may be motivated to seek passion in extramarital affairs. Or they may dissolve the companionate love relationship for the opportunity to develop a new romantic love—which will very likely change into companionate love eventually.

Last, *consummate love* results when all three components of love—intimacy, passion, and commitment—are present. Although many of us wish and strive for consummate love, attaining it is difficult. As you might speculate, maintaining consummate love is even harder.

Intimacy, commitment, and passion combine to produce consummate love.

Romantic Love as Attachment

In a second ground-breaking theory of love, Cindy Hazan and Phillip Shaver (1987) have looked not at the components of love but at similarities between adult romantic love and attachment relationships in infancy. **Infant attachment refers to the strong emotional bond that infants usually develop with their caregivers during the first year of their lives.** Hazan and Shaver suggest that infant attachments and romantic attachments share a number of features: intense fascination with the other person, distress at separation, and efforts to stay close and spend time together. They also make the provocative suggestion that our romantic relationships in adulthood follow the same form as our attachments in infancy (see Figure 8.11).

What forms do attachments in infancy take? Research indicates that these early attachments vary in quality and that infants tend to fall into three groups (Ainsworth, Blehar, Waters, & Wall, 1978). Most infants develop a *secure attachment*. Some, however, are very anxious when they are separated from their caretaker, a syndrome called *anxious-ambivalent attachment*. A third group of infants, characterized by *avoidant attachment*, never connect very well with their caretaker.

How do attachments in infancy develop? Research indicates that these early attachments are related to parent-child interactions. (While earlier research focused mainly on mother-child interactions, more recent research looks at father-child interactions as well.) In the domain of attachment research, three parenting styles have been identified as possible determinants of attachment quality. A *warm/responsive* approach to caregiving is thought to promote secure attachments. A *cold/rejecting* style is thought to be associated with avoidant attachments, and an *ambivalent/inconsistent* style, with anxious-ambivalent attachments.

According to Hazan and Shaver, our early bonding experiences produce relatively enduring relationship styles, which we carry over into romantic partnerships. They theorize, for example, that an adult who had an anxious-ambivalent attachment in infancy will tend to have romantic relations marked by anxiety and ambivalence. Hazan and Shaver's (1987) initial survey study provided some support for their theory. They found that adults' love relationships could be sorted into groups that paralleled the patterns of attachment seen in infants. Specifically, they found that their subjects fell into the following three categories.

• *Secure adults* (56% of subjects). People in this category found it easy to get close to others, trusted other people, and were comfortable with mutual dependence. Further, they rarely worried about being abandoned by their partner. Of the three groups of adults, these subjects were found to have the longest-lasting relation-

Cindy Hazan

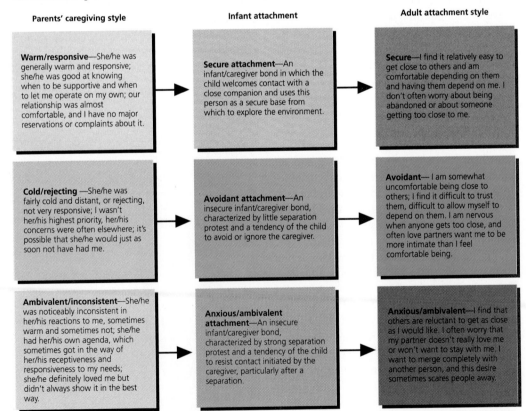

FIGURE 8.11
Infant attachment and romantic relationships
According to Hazan and Shaver (1987), our romantic relationships are similar in form to the attachment patterns we developed in infancy, which are determined in part by our parents' caregiving styles. The theorized relations between parental styles, attachment patterns, and intimate relations are outlined here. Hazan and Shaver's (1987) study sparked a flurry of follow-up research, which has largely supported the basic premises of their ground-breaking theory, although the linkages between infant experiences and close relationships in adulthood appear to be somewhat more complex than those portrayed here (Shaver & Hazan, 1992). (Sources: Parental caregiving styles and adult attachment styles are based on Hazan & Shaver, 1986, 1987; infant attachment patterns are adapted from Shaffer, 1989.)

ships and the fewest divorces. They described their parents as behaving warmly to them and to each other.

• *Avoidant adults* (24% of subjects). These individuals felt somewhat uncomfortable getting close to others and had difficulty trusting their partners completely. They reported experiencing jealousy, emotional highs and lows, and a fear of intimacy in their relationships. They described their parents as less warm than did secure adults and saw their mothers as cold and rejecting.

• *Anxious-ambivalent adults* (20% of subjects). Subjects in this category found their partners unwilling to get as close as they would like and they worried about their lovers' leaving them. They also reported feelings of extreme sexual attraction and jealousy in their relationships. They described their relationships with their parents as less warm than did secure adults and felt that their parents' marriages were unhappy.

Hazan and Shaver (1987) found that the percentage of adults in each category was roughly the same as the percentage of infants in each comparable category. Also, subjects' recollections of their childhood relations with their parents were consistent with the idea that we relive our infant attachment experiences in adulthood. Of course, longitudinal studies are needed to demonstrate conclusively a causal link between infant and adult attachment styles.

Understandably, Hazan and Shaver's theory has attracted considerable interest and has generated other studies within a relatively short time. Research has shown that securely attached individuals have more committed, satisfying, interdependent, and well-adjusted relationships than people with either anxious-ambivalent or avoidant attachment styles (Collins & Read, 1990; Hendrick & Hendrick, 1989; Kobak & Sceery, 1988; Levy & Davis, 1988; Simpson, 1990). Studies have also found that an anxious-ambivalent style is associated with not being in a relationship and with being in relationships of shorter duration, and that an avoidant style is associated with shorter relationships (Collins & Read, 1990; Feeney & Noller, 1990; Shaver & Brennan, 1992).

Research on adult attachment styles and self-disclosure with Israeli undergraduates indicates that both secure and anxious-ambivalent individuals disclose more than avoidant people in the early stages of social interaction (Mikulincer & Nachshon, 1991). Secure people showed more flexibility in self-disclosure

and were more responsive to their conversation partners than those who were ambivalent and anxious-avoidant. These findings generally support Hazan and Shaver's theory of adult attachment styles and romantic love. Nonetheless, much more research is needed on this thought-provoking theory.

The Course of Romantic Love

Must passion fade? Regrettably, the answer to this question appears to be yes. Several theorists suggest that the intense attraction and arousal we feel for a lover seems destined to subside. Sternberg (1986) hypothesizes that passion reaches its peak early and then declines in intensity. In contrast, both intimacy and commitment appear to increase as time progresses, though they develop at different rates (see Figure 8.12).

Berscheid and Hatfield's research also leads them to conclude that passionate love tends to peak early and then fights a difficult battle against the erosion of time. At first love is "blind," so we usually develop a very idealized picture of our lover. As time passes, however, the intrusion of reality often undermines this idealized view.

Must the decline of passion lead to the demise of a relationship? Not necessarily. Some relationships do dissolve when passion fades. However, many others evolve into different but still satisfying phases. Let's examine the research on why some romantic relationships endure while others end.

Why Relationships Fail

Most people find being in love exhilarating and wish it could last forever. Indeed, when we're consumed by passionate love, it's hard to believe our feelings for the other person won't

Phillip Shaver

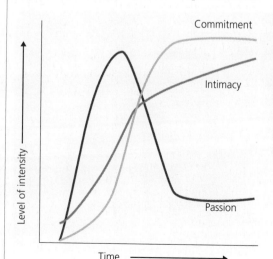

**FIGURE 8.12
The course of love over time**
According to Sternberg (1986), the three components of love typically follow different courses over time. He theorizes that passion peaks early in a relationship and then declines. Intimacy and commitment, in contrast, are thought to build gradually.

last forever. Unfortunately, while many relationships do withstand the test of time, many others do not.

A recent longitudinal study of undergraduate dating couples revealed that 42% of couples who had designated their relationship as their closest interpersonal relationship had split up within nine months (Berscheid et al., 1989). Similarly, the Boston Study, a longitudinal study of couples in the Boston area we've discussed before, reported that almost half (45%) of the relationships had dissolved at the end of two years (Hill et al., 1976). The Boston Study provides some interesting insights about what causes couples to break up. In this study, 200 couples (predominantly college students) were followed over a period of two years. To participate in the study, couples had to be going steady and believe that they were in love. The reasons these couples gave for going their separate ways are shown in Figure 8.13. The results of this and other studies suggest that three prominent factors contribute to the breakup of romantic relationships.

• *Premature commitment.* Virtually all of the reasons for breakups involved things that could be known only after some sharing of personal information over time. Hence it seems that many couples make romantic commitments without taking the time to really get to know each other. These individuals may find out later that they don't really like each other or that they have very little in common.

• *Ineffective conflict-resolution skills.* The vast majority of couples report having disagreements. One study of 1,000 engaged couples reported that 80% of them had arguments (Burgess & Wallin, 1953). Research indicates that the likelihood of disagreements increases as couples learn more about each other and

become more interdependent. One study reported that disagreements were significantly lower among casually dating couples than among couples who were dating seriously (Braiker & Kelley, 1979). Unfortunately, as we discussed in Chapter 6, many people do not know how to deal with conflict constructively. This inability to resolve conflicts effectively appears to be a key factor in the breakup of romantic relationships.

• *Availability of a more attractive relationship.* Whether a deteriorating relationship actually ends depends in great part on the availability of a more attractive alternative. We all know of individuals who bided their time in unsatisfying relationships only until they met someone new.

Helping Relationships Last

Are there things we can do to increase the chances that our love relationships will last? Amazingly, it has been only very recently that researchers have addressed this critical question. Fortunately, enough research has been done to permit us to offer some tentative advice.

1. *Engage in extensive self-disclosure and take plenty of time to get to know the other person before you make a long-term commitment.* Some recent research based on Sternberg's theory found that the best predictors of whether dating couples' relationships would continue were their levels of commitment and intimacy (Hendrick, Hendrick, & Adler, 1988). Hence it appears that early attention to the intimacy foundations of a relationship and ongoing mutual efforts to build a commitment can help foster more enduring love. These factors are evident in the responses of long-married couples to the question why they thought that their relationship had lasted (Lauer & Lauer, 1985). The most frequently given responses of 351 couples who had been married for 15 years or more were: (1) friendship ("I like my spouse as a person"); commitment to the relationship ("I want the relationship to succeed"); (3) similarity in values and relationship issues ("We agree on how and how often to show affection"); and (4) positive feelings about each other ("My spouse has grown more interesting").

2. *Emphasize the positive qualities in your partner and in your relationship.* It is crucial to communicate more positive feelings than negative ones to your partner (Byrne & Murnen, 1988). We find this easy to do early in a relationship, but harder as relationships continue.

FIGURE 8.13
Factors contributing to the breakup of romantic relationships
Couples who broke up after dating steadily were asked why by Hill et al. (1976). The factors commonly cited are listed here. The researchers distinguished between *interactive factors*, which consisted of problems that emerged out of the partners' ways of relating to each other, and *noninteractive factors*.

What Causes Couples to Break Up?		
Factors	Women's reports (%)	Men's reports (%)
Interactive factors		
Becoming bored with relationship	77	77
Differences in interests	73	61
Differences in backgrounds	44	47
Differences in intelligence	20	10
Conflicting sexual attitudes	48	43
Conflicting marriage ideas	43	29
Noninteractive factors		
Woman's desire to be independent	74	50
Man's desire to be independent	47	61
Woman's interest in someone else	40	31
Man's interest in someone else	18	29
Living too far apart	28	41
Pressure from woman's parents	18	13
Pressure from man's parents	10	9

For one thing, once the initial glow of the relationship wears off, we revert to the common tendency to attribute our own negative behaviors to external causes and the negative behaviors of our partner to internal causes (see Chapter 5). This tendency can set up the destructive habit of chronically blaming the other person for problems and not taking responsibility when we should. Ironically, married couples generally make more negative and fewer positive statements to their spouse than to strangers (we presume this finding holds for people in other types of committed relationships as well) (Billings, 1979; Birchler, Weiss, & Vincent, 1975; Koren, Carlton, & Shaw, 1980). This tendency is more prevalent among distressed than among nondistressed couples. Unfortunately, when one partner engages in this behavior, the other often responds in kind. This development can set in motion a pattern of reciprocal negativity that makes things worse. Hence there's a lot of good sense in the old song that advises us to "accentuate the positive, eliminate the negative."

3. *Develop effective conflict-resolution skills.* Because conflicts arise in all relationships, it's important to be able to deal successfully with them. For one thing, it's useful to distinguish between minor annoyances and important relationship issues. We often need to learn to see minor irritations in perspective and recognize how little they matter. When problems are really important, however, it's usually best to avoid the temptation to sweep them under the rug in the hope that they'll disappear. Important issues rarely disappear on their own, and if you postpone the inevitable discussion, sweepings will have accumulated, thus making it more difficult to sort out the various issues and feelings. For more specific suggestions, refer to our earlier discussion of this issue in Chapter 6.

Loneliness

A lthough individuals vary in their need for affiliation, friendship and love play important roles in people's lives. Let's see what happens when this fundamental need for these social relations is thwarted. **Loneliness occurs when a person has fewer interpersonal relationships than desired or when these relationships are not as satisfying as desired.** *Loneliness is not the same as spending time alone.* People can feel lonely even when they are surrounded by others (at a party or concert, for instance). Conversely, some people cherish solitude and are content with less social interaction than most of us prefer. Thus loneliness is a highly subjective and personal feeling.

Jeffrey Young (1982) has identified three kinds of loneliness. *Chronic loneliness* is a condition that affects people who have been unable to develop a satisfactory interpersonal network over a period of years. *Transitional loneliness* occurs when people who have had satisfying social relationships in the past become lonely because of a specific disruption of their social network (the death of a loved one, say, or divorce, or moving to a new locale). One study reported that 75% of new college students reported experiencing loneliness in their first few weeks on campus (Cutrona, 1982). *Transient loneliness* involves brief and sporadic feelings of loneliness, which many people may experience even when their social lives are reasonably adequate.

Loneliness may not occur in all areas of a person's life. For instance, you may be highly satisfied with your friendship network but feel very dissatisfied about not having a suitable romantic relationship. Psychologists have been interested in identifying specific types of relationship deficits that produce feelings of loneliness. Research suggests that loneliness can be attributed to perceived deficits in four areas: (1) romantic/sexual relationships, (2) friendship relationships, (3) family relationships, and (4) community relationships (Schmidt & Sermat, 1983). Because it is likely that each problem will have its own solution, it's important to pinpoint the exact nature of your social deficits to understand how to cope with loneliness.

Prevalence and Consequences of Loneliness

How many people are chronically tormented by severe loneliness? Although we don't have sound data for a precise answer to this question, anecdotal evidence suggests that the number of people plagued by severe loneliness is substantial. Telephone hotlines for troubled people report that complaints of loneliness dominate their calls. Survey studies designed to gain some insight into the prevalence of loneliness in our society have yielded notably disparate figures, depending on the nature of the sample interviewed and the shaping of the questions. For example, in a survey of some 400 Los Angeles workers, the statement "I often feel lonely" was endorsed by 10% of the respondents (Seeman, 1971). In contrast, in the previously mentioned *Psychology Today* survey on friendship, 67% of the respondents indicated that they felt lonely either "sometimes" or "often" (Parlee et al., 1979).

Research on the prevalence of loneliness in specific age groups reveals some findings that many people will find surprising because it contradicts stereotypes: (1) adolescents and young adults are the loneliest age group and (2) loneliness decreases with age, at least until the much later years of adulthood when one's friends begin to die (Peplau, Bikson, Rook, & Goodchilds, 1982; Rubenstein & Shaver, 1982).

The *personal* consequences of loneliness can be overwhelming. Painful thoughts of one's plight may come to dominate one's consciousness. As might be expected, studies have found a strong correlation between feelings of loneliness and feelings of depression (Anderson & Harvey, 1988; Rook, 1984; Young, 1982). Similarly, researchers have reported a relationship between loneliness and poor physical and psychological health (Rubenstein & Shaver, 1982).

Unfortunately, loneliness seems to have some *social* consequences, too. A recent study by Lau and Gruen (1992) found that when a hypothetical target person was characterized as socially isolated and lonely, subjects rated that person as less well adjusted, less achieving and intellectually competent, and less socially competent than a nonlonely target person. In addition, the lonely target person was less preferred as a friend and rated as weaker, more passive, less attractive, and less sincere than a nonlonely target person. Lonely men were evaluated more negatively than lonely women. Of course, we need to be careful about generalizing too much from a single study, but it does seem that poor social skills are evaluated negatively by others. The good news is that effective social skills can be learned—recall our discussion of assertive communication in Chapter 6.

The Roots of Loneliness

A number of factors can contribute to feelings of loneliness. Since any event that ruptures the social fabric of a person's life may lead to lone-

liness, no one is immune. Social trends as well as personal qualities are among the more prominent causes of loneliness.

Contributing Social Trends

Theorists have commented on various social trends that have undermined the sharing of intimacy in our culture (Flanders, 1982; Keyes, 1980; Packard, 1972). Because of people's busy schedules, social interactions at home are reduced as family members eat on the run, on their own, or in front of the TV. And the fact that people watch television so much tends to diminish meaningful family conversation. While technology makes life easier in some respects, it can also have negative effects on our personal lives. For example, superficial social interactions become prevalent as we order our meals at drive-up windows, do our banking at drive-through facilities, and so forth. Finally, with the advent of personal computers, more and more people spend time at terminals in their offices and homes, alone.

As might be expected, individuals whose parents have been divorced report feeling more lonely than those whose families are intact (Rubenstein & Shaver, 1982; Shaver & Rubenstein, 1980). Moreover, the earlier in their lives the divorce occurred, the stronger the feelings of loneliness they experience in adulthood. In contrast, no differences in loneliness were found between individuals who had lost a parent through death and those from intact families. Interestingly, research does not support two intuitive expectations in regard to loneliness. That is, loneliness is not correlated with the nature of the residential setting (urban or rural) or with the frequency of changes in location (Rubenstein & Shaver, 1982).

Negative Attitudes toward Others

Lonely individuals seem to hold more negative attitudes toward others than people who aren't lonely. That is, research has found that those who describe themselves as lonely don't like others very much (Rubenstein & Shaver,

1980); don't trust others very much (Vaux, 1988); often evaluate others negatively (Jones, Sansome, & Helm, 1983; Wittenberg & Reis, 1986); and have hostile attitudes toward others (Check, Perlman, & Malamuth, 1985).

Poor Social Skills

Interpersonal skills, although not particularly difficult to develop, do have to be acquired. Poor social skills probably prevent many people from experiencing rewarding social interactions. One study found that lonely people tend to pay inadequate attention to their conversation partners (Jones, Hobbs, & Hockenbury, 1982). Another study of conversational style concluded that lonely people are relatively inhibited, speaking less than nonlonely people (Sloan & Solano, 1984). Anxiety about social skills is also correlated with loneliness (Anderson & Harvey, 1988; Solano & Koester, 1989) and shyness (Anderson & Harvey, 1988), a topic we'll consider in the Application.

Fear of Intimacy

Some people with positive self-concepts and sound social skills seem overly wary of intimate interactions. For one thing, the level of self-disclosure is lower for lonely people than for those who are not lonely (Davis & Franzoi, 1986; Sloan & Solano, 1984; Solano, Batten, & Parish, 1982; Williams & Solano, 1983). This (often unconscious) tendency has the effect of keeping people at an emotional distance and limits interactions to a relatively superficial level. Fear of intimacy is also seen in the fact that lonely people are relatively reluctant to take social risks (Schultz & Moore, 1984; Vaux, 1988).

Low Self-Esteem

A key personal factor that seems to promote loneliness is low self-esteem (Cutrona, 1982; Hanson, Jones, & Carpenter, 1984; Rubenstein & Shaver, 1982). People who have unfavorable opinions of themselves often do not feel worthy of others' affection. They may make little effort to pursue close relationships. This lack of confidence probably has a spiraling effect, as low self-esteem begets loneliness and loneliness begets still lower self-esteem.

Negative Self-Talk

Ultimately, what underlies many of the factors just discussed is negative self-talk. Lonely people are prone to irrational thinking about their social skills, the probability of achieving intimacy, the likelihood of rejection, and so forth. For example, there is evidence that lonely people tend to attribute their loneliness to *stable, internal causes* (Anderson, Horowitz, & French, 1983; Michela, Peplau, & Weeks, 1982). That is, lonely people may tell themselves that they're lonely because they're basically unlovable individuals. Not only is that a devastating belief, it also provides no way to change the situation. From our discussion on attribution in Chapter 5, recall that there are *other* attributions a lonely person could make *and* that these explanations point to solutions. If a person says, "My conversational skills are weak" (unstable, internal cause), the solution is at hand: "I'll try to find out how to improve them." Or if a person tells herself, "It's always hard to meet people when you move to a new situation" (unstable, external cause), the obvious solution is to try harder to develop new relationships and give them time to work. The attribution "I've really looked hard, but there just don't seem to be very many people in the organization who share my interests and attitudes" (stable, external cause) may lead to the decision "I guess it's time to look for a new job." As you can see, the last three attributions lead to active modes of coping.

Young (1982) points out that lonely people engage in negative self-talk that prevents them from pursuing intimacy in an active and positive manner. He has identified some clusters of ideas that foster loneliness. Figure 8.14 shows typical thoughts in six of these clusters of cognitions and the overt behaviors that result.

Coping with Loneliness

It is disheartening to report that there are no simple solutions for those who suffer from loneliness. A major reason that people have difficulty overcoming loneliness is that many of them tend to withdraw socially. One study that asked people what they did when they felt lonely reported that the top responses were read and listen to music (Rubenstein & Shaver, 1982). These activities can be constructive ways of dealing with loneliness occasionally, but as long-term strategies they do nothing to help a lonely person acquire new friends.

Keys to overcoming loneliness include engaging in positive self-talk, avoiding the temptation to withdraw from social situations, and working on your conversational skills. The importance of staying active socially cannot be overemphasized. As we learned earlier in this

FIGURE 8.14
Patterns of thinking underlying loneliness
According to Young (1982), negative self-talk contributes to loneliness. Six clusters of irrational thoughts are illustrated here. Each cluster of cognitions leads to certain patterns of behavior (shown on the right) that promote loneliness.

Clusters of Cognitions Typical of Lonely Clients

Clusters	Cognitions	Behaviors
A	1. I'm undesirable. 2. I'm dull and boring.	Avoidance of friendship
B	1. I can't communicate with other people. 2. My thoughts and feelings are bottled up inside.	Low self-disclosure
C	1. I'm not a good lover in bed. 2. I can't relax, be spontaneous, and enjoy sex.	Avoidance of sexual relationships
D	1. I can't seem to get what I want from this relationship. 2. I can't say how I feel, or he/she might leave me.	Lack of assertiveness in relationships
E	1. I won't risk being hurt again. 2. I'd screw up any relationship.	Avoidance of potentially intimate relationships
F	1. I don't know how to act in this situation. 2. I'll make a fool of myself.	Avoidance of other people

chapter, proximity is a powerful factor in the development of close relationships. You have to be around people in order to expand your network of friends.

It is difficult to offer more specific suggestions for overcoming loneliness because the remedy depends on the precise causes of the loneliness. Each of the loneliness-inducing clusters of cognitions and behaviors summarized in Figure 8.14 is discussed at some point in this text. Clusters A (poor self-concept, Chapter 5), B (low self-disclosure, Chapter 6) and D (lack of assertiveness, Chapter 6) have already been covered. Clusters E and F represent the core of shyness and are addressed in the Application at the end of this chapter. Cluster C (sexual anxiety) is discussed in Chapter 13. The fact that the problems relevant to loneliness are distributed across so many chapters should serve to demonstrate the complexity of this painful condition.

Summary

Close relationships are characterized as long-lasting ones in which two people interact frequently in a variety of settings and in which the impact of these interactions is strong. Close relationships include friendships as well as work, family, and romantic relationships. The ability to establish and maintain committed, intimate relationships appears to be related to identity development.

Levinger proposed a five-stage model that describes how relationships can evolve over time. Social exchange theory provides some useful principles that determine a person's satisfaction with and commitment to a close relationship.

The dynamics of attraction are similar for friendship and love. Physical attractiveness seems to play a larger role in initial attraction for males (heterosexual and homosexual) than for females (heterosexual and homosexual). This sex difference holds true for both friendships and romantic relationships. There is some support for the what-is beautiful-is-good stereotype in the social arena. Generally, people seem to match up according to attractiveness in romantic relationships. This matching effect also operates in same-sex friendships, but more strongly among men than among women.

In addition to people who are physically attractive, we are drawn to those who are pleasant to be with, and who are intelligent, competent, and high in status. Our own needs for affiliation and intimacy, as well as our self-esteem and self-perception processes, also figure importantly in our attraction to others. Also, research indicates that proximity, similarity, and reciprocity promote attraction.

The key ingredients of friendship are loyalty, emotional support, and letting friends be themselves. Women's same-sex friendships tend to be characterized by intimacy and self-disclosure, whereas men's same-sex friendships typically involve doing things together. Sex differences are also found in willingness to confront friends about conflicts and in topics of conversation. Friendship involvement is reduced for those who are married, but not for those in committed homosexual relationships.

A number of myths have developed around the concept of romantic love, including the idea that when you fall in love you'll know it, and the notion that you have no control over yourself when love strikes. Other myths include the beliefs that love is purely positive, that it lasts forever, and that it can conquer all problems. Heterosexism has rendered homosexual relationships relatively invisible. Research indicates that the experience of romantic love is the same for heterosexual and homosexual individuals. Gender differences found in regard to love are interesting in that these findings do not support the traditional stereotype that women are more romantic than men.

Sternberg's triangular theory of love proposes that passion, intimacy, and commitment combine in different types of love. Hazan and Shaver theorize that our love relationships follow the forms of our attachments in infancy. Initially, romantic love is usually characterized by passion, but strong passion appears to fade over time. In relationships that continue, passionate love evolves into a less intense, more mature form of love. Romantic relationships fail for many reasons. Chief among them are the tendency to make premature commitments, ineffective conflict-resolution skills, and the availability of a more attractive relationship. To help ensure that relationships last, couples should engage in extensive self-disclosure, take plenty of time to get to know each other, emphasize the positive qualities in their partner and relationship, and develop effective conflict-resolution skills.

Loneliness involves discontent with the extent and quality of one's interpersonal network. Evidence suggests that a surprisingly large number of people in our society are troubled by loneliness. Although loneliness is promoted by a number of social trends, it appears to be due mainly to personal factors, such as negative attitudes toward others, poor social skills, fear of intimacy, low self-esteem, and negative self-talk. Coping with loneliness is difficult. The keys seem to be engaging in positive self-talk, avoiding the temptation to withdraw from social situations, and working on your communication skills.

Shyness intersects with loneliness to some degree. In the Application that follows, we will discuss the prevalence and consequences of shyness and how to cope with this problem.

APPLICATION Understanding Shyness

Indicate whether the following statements are true or false.

1.

When I am the focus of attention, I often become anxious.

2.

In interacting with people, I tend to be very self-conscious.

3.

I get embarrassed in social situations quite easily.

4.

I wish that I could be more assertive about pursuing social relationships.

5.

I am often concerned about being rejected by others.

If you indicated that several of these statements are true as they apply to you, you may be hampered in your social life by a very common problem—shyness. Loneliness and shyness are intersecting problems. Although many lonely people are not shy and many shy people are not lonely, it is nonetheless true that loneliness is a common consequence of shyness (Cheek & Busch, 1981). In that case, it isn't surprising that shy and lonely people have some characteristics in common. Two of them are poor social skills and negative attitudes toward others (Jones & Carpenter, 1986).

Shyness refers to discomfort, inhibition, and excessive caution in interpersonal relations. Specifically, shy people tend (1) to be timid about expressing themselves, (2) to be overly self-conscious about how others are reacting to them, (3) to get embarrassed easily, and (4) to experience physiological symtoms of their anxiety, such as a racing pulse, blushing, or an upset stomach.

Prevalence and Consequences of Shyness

Philip Zimbardo (1977, 1987) and his associates have done pioneering research on shyness. Their survey data indicate that shyness may be more common than was previously realized. Over 80% of the respondents to their survey reported being shy during some stage of their lives. Moreover, 40% indicated that they were currently troubled by shyness. The personal implications of shyness are generally quite negative. Most shy people report that they do not like being shy. This is understandable in view of the common consequences of shyness. Shy people tend to have difficulty making friends, and they tend to be sexually inhibited. They also are lonely and depressed more often than others.

Situational Nature of Shyness

The traditional stereotype of the shy person as one who is timid all the time appears to be somewhat inaccurate. In Zimbardo's study, 60% of the shy people reported that their shyness was *situationally specific*. That is, they experienced shyness only in certain social contexts, such as asking someone for help or interacting with a large group of people. Figure 8.15 lists the situations that most commonly elicited shyness in Zimbardo's subjects.

FIGURE 8.15
The situational determinants of shyness
Zimbardo (1977) asked subjects about the people and circumstances that made them feel shy. The results of his survey showed that shyness depends to a great degree on situational factors.

The situational nature of shyness has led researchers to distinguish between state shyness and trait shyness (Asendorpf, 1989). *State shyness* involves a temporary elevation in anxiety in reaction to certain social situations. According to Asendorpf (1986), the crux of the problem is that people experience an approach-avoidance conflict (see Figure 8.16). They are

"What Makes You Shy?"

Other people	Percentage of shy students
Strangers	70
Opposite sex	64
Authorities by virtue of their knowledge	55
Authorities by virtue of their role	40
Relatives	21
Elderly people	12
Friends	11
Children	10
Parents	8

Situations	Percentage of shy students
Where I am focus of attention—large group (as when giving a speech)	73
Large groups	68
Of lower status	56
Social situations in general	55
New situations in general	55
Requiring assertiveness	54
Where I am being evaluated	53
Where I am focus of attention—small group	52
Small social groups	48
One-to-one different-sex interactions	48
Of vulnerability (need help)	48
Small task-oriented groups	28
One-to-one same-sex interactions	14

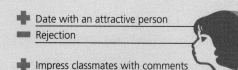

FIGURE 8.16
Shyness as an approach-avoidance conflict
State shyness involves an approach-avoidance conflict in which a person both desires and fears social interaction. As we noted in Chapter 3, approach-avoidance conflicts can be highly stressful.

➕ Date with an attractive person
➖ Rejection

➕ Impress classmates with comments
➖ Embarrass self in class

Approach-avoidance

torn between their desire to interact with someone (approach motivation) and their fear of making a social blunder (avoidance motivation). What types of situations tend to elicit state shyness? According to Asendorpf, the most common triggers appear to be the presence of strangers and the expectation of being evaluated by others.

Trait shyness is a consistent tendency to feel anxious and inhibited in a wide variety of social situations. People who are chronically tormented by discomfort in social interactions exhibit shyness as a stable personality trait (Jones, Briggs, & Smith, 1986). Some studies suggest that there is a genetic predisposition toward trait shyness (Daniels & Plomin, 1985).

Coping with Shyness

It would be naive to pretend that shyness can be overcome easily—but it *can* be overcome. Think about it. In Zimbardo's survey, 40% of the respondents reported that they were *currently* shy, while 80% indicated that they *had been* shy at some previous time. Obviously, half of the once-shy subjects felt that they had conquered their shyness.

Much of Zimbardo's (1977, 1990) book is devoted to how to deal with the problem of shyness. Basically, the three key steps in this process are: (1) analyzing your shyness, (2) building your self-esteem, and (3) improving your social skills.

Analyzing Your Shyness

The first step is the easiest. You should analyze your shyness and try to pinpoint exactly what social

situations tend to make you feel shy. You should further try to ascertain what causes your shyness in the specific situations. To help identify the situations that trigger your shyness, you may want to use some of the techniques for gathering baseline data that we discussed in our coverage of behavior modification (see the Chapter 4 Application). You might also benefit from scanning Figure 8.15, which summarizes findings on the situations that tend to generate shy behavior in others.

A number of reasons or combinations of reasons may account for trait shyness. Zimbardo enumerated eight common reasons: (1) concern about negative evaluation, (2) fear of rejection, (3) lack of self-confidence, (4) lack of specific social skills, (5) fear of intimacy, (6) preference for being alone, (7) emphasis on and enjoyment of nonsocial activities, and (8) personal inadequacy or handicap.

Building Your Self-Esteem

Poor self-esteem appears to be a key factor underlying trait shyness (Crozier, 1981). Hence it is important for shy people to work on improving their self-confidence. In his book Zimbardo spells out "fifteen steps to a more confident you." Many of these steps coincide with the suggestions made in the Chapter 5 Application, on building self-esteem.

Improving Your Social Skills

The third step is the most difficult. As we have said repeatedly, it is not easy to change deeply ingrained habits. Zimbardo suggests using many of the behavior modification techniques that we discussed in Chapter 4. Specifi-

cally, he recommends specifying certain target social responses to be increased and then setting up a reward system for engaging in those responses. He further emphasizes that one has to be realistic and work toward *gradual* improvement. For example, he suggests that people start with relatively simple and nonthreatening social behaviors, such as anonymous conversations. These are conversations with strangers in public places such as a theater line, a bank, or a stadium. Other simple social responses that one might start with include saying hello to strangers or giving compliments to others.

Zimbardo's other suggestions for improving social skills are too numerous to detail here. However, we can mention a few ideas to consider if you are troubled by shyness. First, it's a good idea to select a nonshy role model to watch closely. Identify someone in your personal sphere who is extraverted. It's probably a good idea to use a same-sex model. Observe how your role model handles various kinds of social situations. In particular, pay atten-

Philip Zimbardo

RECOMMENDED READING

Shyness

by Philip G. Zimbardo (Jove, 1987; Addison-Wesley, 1990)

Zimbardo, an outstanding social psychologist, focuses his keen insight on the frustrations of being shy. A lack of jargon and ample use of actual case histories make this book very readable. Zimbardo explores the roots of shyness in Part I of the book and then addresses what to do about it in Part II. The second part of the book is full of exercises and sound advice for tackling this problem head on.

Theories are like enormous vacuum cleaners, sucking up everything in their paths. Each of the theories outlined here has vigorous backers, hawkers of the best vacuum cleaner on the market. We shall borrow freely from any and all of them when we come to design programs for coping with shyness. [1987, p. 55]

tion to how he or she acts in the situations that trigger your shyness. Second, develop expertise in some area so that you have something to contribute to conversations. In other words, become a movie buff or a sports buff or an amateur political analyst. Third, listen actively and attentively. People love to talk about themselves. Encourage them to do so. After going on and on about themselves, they'll probably compliment you on what an interesting and enjoyable "conversation" the two of you just had!

As you work on developing your social skills, bear in mind that your progress will probably be gradual. Social skills are honed over a lifetime. Although they *can* be improved with practice, it normally takes a good bit of time, and your progress may seem barely perceptible. If you stick with it, though, you *can* conquer shyness.

CHAPTER 8 REVIEW

Key Learning Objectives

1. Describe Levinger's model of relationship development.
2. Describe the principles of social exchange theory.
3. Describe the what-is-beautiful-is-good stereotype and what the actual research shows.
4. Summarize research on physical appearance as a factor in attraction.
5. Discuss how personality, intelligence, competence, and social status influence interpersonal attraction.
6. Explain how self-esteem and self-perception may play a role in attraction.
7. Describe proximity, similarity, and reciprocity effects in attraction.
8. Summarize evidence on what makes a good friend.
9. Summarize gender differences in friendships.
10. Describe the effects of being in a committed romantic relationship on friendships.
11. List five myths about love.
12. Summarize the research findings on the experience of love in homosexual and heterosexual individuals.
13. Discuss evidence on gender differences in romanticism.
14. Summarize Sternberg's triangular theory of love.
15. Explain Hazan and Shaver's view of romantic love as an attachment process.
16. Discuss why love relationships fail and what can be done to help ensure that they last.
17. Describe three kinds of loneliness identified by Young.
18. Summarize evidence on the prevalence and consequences of loneliness.
19. List some social trends and personal factors that contribute to loneliness.
20. Summarize evidence on the prevalence and situational nature of shyness.
21. Discuss the steps suggested by Zimbardo for coping with shyness.

Key Terms

bisexuals
close relationship
commitment
comparison level
heterosexism
heterosexuals
homosexuals
infant attachment
interpersonal attraction

intimacy
loneliness
matching hypothesis
passion
proximity
reciprocity
sexual orientation
shyness
social exchange theory

Key People

Ellen Berscheid and Elaine Hatfield (Walster)
Cindy Hazan and Phillip Shaver
Harold Kelley and John Thibaut

George Levinger
Robert Sternberg
Philip Zimbardo

"Y HANDS ARE SHAKY. I want to call her again but I know it is no good. She'll only yell and scream. It makes me feel lousy. I have work to do but I can't do it. I can't concentrate. I want to call people up, go see them, but I'm afraid they'll see that I'm shaky. I just want to talk. I can't think about anything besides this trouble with Nina. I think I want to cry."

—A recently separated man quoted in *Marital Separation* (Weiss, 1975, p. 48)

The man quoted above is an emotional wreck. He is describing his feelings a few days after he and his wife have broken up. He is still hoping for a reconciliation with his wife. In the meantime he feels overwhelmed by anxiety, remorse, and depression. He feels very alone and very scared by the prospect of remaining alone. His emotional distress is so great that he can't think straight or work effectively.

This man's reaction to the loss of an intimate relationship is not at all unusual. Marital breakups are devastating for most people—a reality that confirms the enormous importance of intimate relationships in our lives.

In this chapter we will take a look at marriage and other intimate relationships. We will discuss why people marry and how they progress toward the selection of a mate. To shed light on marital adjustment, we will describe the life cycle of the family, highlighting key vulnerable spots in marital relations. We will also address issues related to divorce, cohabitation, remaining single, and being gay. In the Application we will examine the "games" that intimate couples play in their relationships. Let's begin by discussing recent challenges to our traditional concept of marriage.

Challenges to the Traditional Model of Marriage

arriage is the legally and socially sanctioned union of sexually intimate adults. Traditionally the marital relationship includes economic interdependence, common residence, sexual fidelity, and shared responsibility for children. Although the institution of marriage remains popular, it sometimes seems to be under assault from shifting social trends. Many experts have asked whether the institution of marriage is in serious trouble (Rodman & Sidden, 1992). It appears that marriage will weather the storm. But it's worth looking at some of the social trends that are shaking our traditional model of marriage.

• *Increased acceptance of singlehood.* An increasing proportion of the adult population under age 35 is remaining single (Stein, 1989). In part this trend reflects longer postponement of marriage than before. The median age at which people marry has been increasing gradually since the mid-1960s, as Figure 9.1 shows. Thus remaining single is becoming a more viable option. Furthermore, the negative stereotype of people who remain single, which pictures them as lonely, frustrated, and unchosen, is gradually evaporating.

• *Increased acceptance of cohabitation.* **Cohabitation** refers to living together in a sexually intimate relationship without the legal bonds of marriage. Negative attitudes toward "living together" appear to be declining, though many people continue to disapprove of the practice. It is difficult to get accurate informa-

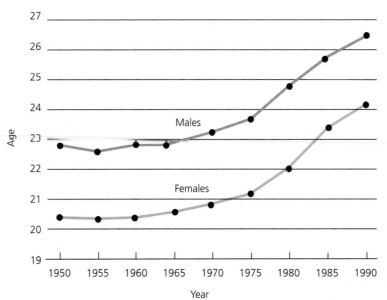

FIGURE 9.1
Median age at first marriage
The median age at which people marry for the first time has been creeping up for both men and women since the mid-1960s. This trend indicates that more people are postponing marriage.

tion on the number of couples who cohabit. However, various sources of data suggest that cohabitation has increased dramatically (Bumpass, Sweet, & Cherlin, 1991). Census data, for instance, indicate that the number of couples living together increased more than fivefold between 1970 and 1990, as Figure 9.2 shows.

• *Reduced premium on permanence.* Most people still view marriage as a permanent commitment, but many people are also strongly committed to their own personal growth (Morgan & Scanzoni, 1987). Marriage is often seen as just one context in which such growth can occur. Thus an increasing number of people regard divorce as justifiable if their marriage fails to foster their interests as individuals. Accordingly, the social stigma associated with divorce has lessened and divorce rates have risen. Some experts estimate that roughly two of every three marriages will ultimately result in separation or divorce (Wisensale, 1992).

• *Transitions in gender roles.* The women's movement and economic pressures have led to substantial changes in the expectations of many people entering marriage today. Many couples are discarding the traditional breadwinner and homemaker roles for the husband and wife as more and more married women enter the work force (see Figure 9.3). Role expectations for husbands and wives are becoming more varied, more flexible, and more ambiguous (Fine, 1992). Many people regard this trend as a step in the right direction (see Chapter 10). However, changing gender roles create new potential for conflict between marital partners.

• *Increased voluntary childlessness.* In the past two decades the percentage of women without children has climbed in all age groups (see Figure 9.4) as an increasing number of married couples have chosen not to have children (Seccombe, 1991). This trend is probably due to new career opportunities for women and the tendency to marry at a later age. Traditionally, many people have viewed married women who voluntarily remain childless as less well adjusted than those with children (Calhoun & Selby, 1980). However, this belief is not supported by the empirical evidence (Burman & de Anda, 1986).

• *The decline of the traditional nuclear family.* In the eyes of most people, the traditional American family consists of a husband and wife who have never been married to anyone else, rearing two or more children, with the man serving as the sole breadwinner and the woman filling the homemaker role. As Demo (1992) notes, "This ideal continues to serve as the ref-

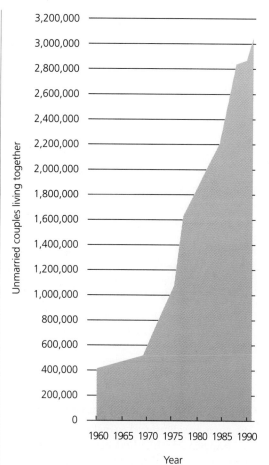

FIGURE 9.2
Cohabitation in the United States
The number of unmarried couples living together has been increasing rapidly since 1970 (according to U.S. Census data). This increase shows no signs of leveling off.

erence point against which contemporary families are judged, despite the fact that many families did not conform to these ideals even during the nostalgic 1950s and early 1960s" (p. 105). It is estimated that only 7% of American families match this idealized image of the "normal" family today (Otto, 1988). The increasing prevalence of single-parent homes, stepfamilies,

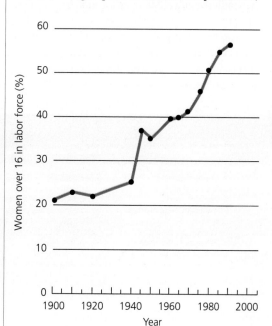

FIGURE 9.3
Women in the work force
The percentage of women over age 16 who work outside the home has been rising steadily throughout this century. Even among women with children under 6 years of age, about 57% are employed.
(Source: U.S. Bureau of Labor Statistics, 1991.)

FIGURE 9.4
Percentage of women without children, by age group
The proportion of adult women in the United States who have never had a child has been increasing gradually over the last two decades. (Source: U.S. Bureau of the Census, 1991.)

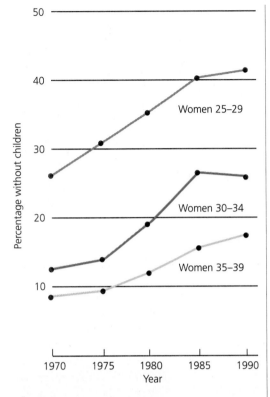

Women 25–29
Women 30–34
Women 35–39

Percentage without children

1970 1975 1980 1985 1990
Year

FIGURE 9.5
The decision to marry
Stein (1975) interviewed single people between 22 and 45 to ascertain the motivational factors that influence the decision to marry. *Pushes toward marriage* involve deficits supposedly felt by single persons. *Pushes toward singlehood* involve deficits felt by married people. *Pulls* are positive factors associated with marriage or singlehood. The first two boxes identify the factors favoring marriage, and the last two boxes identify those favoring singlehood. Not everyone weighs all these factors, but these lists make clear the complexity of the decision to marry.

Moving toward Marriage

"When you've been in love a few times, you start thinking of yourself as a used car. I started seeing a new man and I called him 'honey.' It was too soon and I saw him cringe when I did it. It made me feel so cheap. . . .

"I'm ashamed of being single, I have to admit it. I have grown to hate the word. The worst thing someone can say is, 'How come you're still not married?' It's like saying, 'What's wrong with you.' I look at women who are frumpy and physically undesirable and they're monochromatic and uninteresting and they don't seem unselfish and giving and I wonder, 'How did they become such an integral part of a man's life that he wanted to marry them and spend his life with them?' I'm envious. They're married and I date."

—A woman quoted in *Tales from the Front* (Kavesh & Lavin, 1988, p. 91)

The woman quoted above desperately wants to be married. Like most of us, she has been socialized to believe that our lives aren't complete until we find a mate.

Although alternatives to marriage are more viable than ever, experts project that over 90% of us will marry at least once. Some of us will do so several times. But why? What motivates us to marry? And how do we choose our partners?

The Motivation to Marry

A great variety of motivational factors propel people into marriage. Foremost among them is the desire to participate in a socially sanctioned, mutually rewarding, intimate relationship. Another key factor is the social pressure exerted on people to marry. Getting married is still the norm in our society. Our parents, relatives, and friends expect us to marry eventually,

childless marriages, unwed parents, and working wives has conspired to make the traditional nuclear family a highly deceptive mirage that does not reflect the diversity of family structures in America.

In summary, the norms that mold marital and intimate relationships have been restructured in fundamental ways in recent decades. Traditional values have eroded as people have increasingly embraced more individualistic values (Thornton, 1989). Thus the institution of marriage is in a period of transition, creating new adjustment challenges for modern couples. Support for the concept of monogamy remains strong, but changes in our society are altering our traditional model of marriage. The impact of these changes will be seen throughout this chapter as we discuss various facets of married life.

The Decision to Marry			
Pushes toward marriage	Pulls toward marriage	Pushes toward singlehood	Pulls toward singlehood
Economic security	Influence of parents	Restrictions	Career opportunities
Influence from mass media	Desire for family	Suffocating one-to-one relationships, feeling trapped	Variety of experiences
Pressure from parents	Example of peers	Obstacles to self-development	Self-sufficiency
Need to leave home	Romanticization of marriage	Boredom, unhappiness, anger	Sexual availability
Interpersonal and personal reasons	Love	Role playing and conformity to expectations	Exciting lifestyle
Fear of independence	Physical attraction	Poor communication with mate	Freedom to change and
Loneliness	Emotional attachment	Sexual frustration	experiment
Alternatives did not seem feasible	Security, social status, prestige	Lack of friends, isolation, loneliness	Mobility
Cultural expectations, socialization		Limitations on mobility and available experience	Sustaining friendships
Regular sex		Influence of and participation in women's movement	Supportive groups
Guilt over singlehood			Men's and women's groups
			Group living arrangements
			Specialized groups

and they often make this expectation abundantly clear by their comments and inquiries.

The popular view in our culture is that people marry because they have fallen in love. Although partially accurate, this view is terribly oversimplified. A multitude of motivational factors are involved in the decision to marry. Peter Stein (1975, 1976) interviewed single men and women aged 22 to 45 who were judged to be neither unattractive nor socially inept. As you can see in Figure 9.5, he learned that many forces push and pull us toward marriage or singlehood.

Although there are many good reasons for getting married, Stein's research reveals that people often marry for reasons that are less than ideal. Marriages motivated purely by physical attraction or the desire for a regular sexual outlet, for example, are likely to be fragile. Similarly, marriages motivated by the belief that one "should" be married by a particular age, or by a desire to escape an unsatisfactory home situation, have a weak base on which to build.

People vary greatly in the *strength* of their motivation to marry. Some people are eager to marry, while others are reluctant to assume the responsibility. Reiss (1980) has pointed out that marriage is a risky proposition. In deciding to get married, people make a long-range projection about the future of their relationship. Obviously, it is difficult to predict 50 years of commitment on the basis of one or two years of premarital interaction. There is no way to make this projection with absolute assurance of accuracy. Marriage requires a leap of faith. Variability in the threshold for this leap of faith is probably a major determinant of when and why people marry. Yet we know very little about how this threshold is shaped or how it is related to personality.

Selecting a Mate

Modern Western cultures are somewhat unusual in permitting free choice of one's marital partner. Most societies rely on parental arrangements and severely restrict the range of acceptable partners along religious and class lines (Bumiller, 1989). Mate selection in American culture is a gradual process that begins with dating and moves on to sometimes lengthy periods of courtship. In this section we will look at the impact of endogamy, homogamy, and personal ideals on marital choice. We'll also discuss Bernard Murstein's S-V-R theory, which provides a good overview of the process of mate selection.

People cling to an idealized image of the traditional nuclear family despite the fact that only 7% of American families match this stereotype.

Endogamy

Endogamy **refers to the tendency of people to marry within their own social group.** Buss (1985) reviews extensive evidence indicating that we tend to marry people of the same race, religion, ethnic background, and social class. Endogamy is promoted by cultural norms and by the way proximity and similarity influence interpersonal attraction (see Chapter 8). Although endogamy appears to be gradually declining, it's likely to remain influential for the foreseeable future (Surra, 1990).

Homogamy

Homogamy **refers to the tendency of people to marry others who have personal characteristics similar to their own.** Marital partners tend to be similar in age and education (Schoen & Wooldredge, 1989), physical attractiveness (Folkes, 1982), and attitudes and values (Honeycutt, 1986). Deviations from homogamy in age and education do not tend to be symmetric, as husbands are usually older and better educated than their wives. This pattern probably occurs because men place more emphasis than women do on physical attractiveness and youth, whereas women are less inclined than men to marry someone younger or someone with comparatively low educational attainment and earnings potential (South, 1991). Cultural norms that discourage women from dating younger men may contribute to a "marriage squeeze" for women. Without the freedom to date younger men, women are likely to find their pool of potential partners dwindling more rapidly than men of similar age (Oppenheimer, 1988).

Idealized Images

If you are not married, you can probably describe the kind of person you would like eventually to marry. Most of us develop a fairly clear picture of

People tend to marry others who are similar in age and physical attractiveness.

the man or woman we would like to have sweep us off our feet (Stiles, Gibbons, Hardardottir, & Schnellmann, 1987). Our idealized pictures influence our evaluation of potential mates. If a person does not compare favorably with our ideal, the discrepancy may undermine our attraction to the person. Some people create problems for themselves by holding highly unrealistic ideals of perfection that exclude virtually all potential partners.

Courtship progress may also be influenced by whether a potential mate measures up to the ideals and standards of our family and friends. Conventional wisdom suggests that parental disapproval of a dating partner often sparks greater interest in the partner, but empirical evidence suggests that this phenomenon, known as the "Romeo and Juliet effect," is relatively infrequent (Surra, 1990). In general, studies find that negative reactions from our social networks tend to hamper the progress of our relationships and positive reactions tend to promote it. Insofar as negative reactions are influential, our perceptions of whether family and friends disapprove of a potential mate appear to be more important than active interference from our social networks (Surra, 1990).

Stimulus-Value-Role Theory

Competing theories have attempted to shed light on the process of mate selection and the development of premarital relationships (see Berg & McQuinn, 1986; Cate, Huston, & Nesselroade, 1986; Stephen, 1985). A particularly prominent model is Bernard Murstein's (1976, 1986) *stimulus-value-role* (S-V-R) *theory*. According to Murstein, couples generally proceed through three stages—the stimulus, value, and role stages—as they move toward marriage.

During the first stage, our attraction to members of the other sex depends mainly on their *stimulus value*. At this point we focus on relatively superficial and easily identifiable characteristics of the other person—physical attractiveness, social status, occupational success, and reputation. Murstein borrows from *social exchange theory* (see Chapter 8) to argue that progress to the next stage depends on the

pair's having relatively similar stimulus value, so as to produce an "even" exchange. The two persons may derive their stimulus value from different characteristics—one from wealth, say, and the other from beauty. However, progress to stage 2 is thought to depend on the couple's subjective perception that they have similar stimulus value.

If a couple make it to the second stage, *value comparison*, the significance of stimulus variables may be reduced. Further progress now depends on compatibility in values. Typically the pair begin to explore each other's attitudes in regard to religion, politics, sex, gender roles, leisure activities, and so forth. If fundamental incompatibilities are uncovered, the relationship may stall at stage 2, or it may come to an end. However, if the two persons discover similarity in values as they open up to each other, they are more likely to progress to stage 3.

In the *role stage*, people begin to think about marrying each other. Hence they start to evaluate whether the other person does a satisfactory job in the role of intimate companion. At this point people focus on the distribution of power in their relationship, the reliability of emotional support, and the quality of their sexual liaison (if they have formed one). Although some people may marry after progressing through only the first two stages, Murstein maintains that marriage is generally delayed until couples are comfortable with role enactments in stage 3.

Murstein's theory has been questioned on the grounds that courtship relationships do not really evolve through distinct stages. Critics argue that individuals in romantic relationships acquire information about each other's stimulus characteristics, values, and roles continuously rather than in discrete stages (Leigh, Holman, & Burr, 1984, 1987). Although this criticism has some merit, S-V-R theory provides a useful overview of the factors that influence whether romantic relationships progress toward marriage.

Predictors of Marital Success

Are there any factors that predict marital success? A great deal of research has been devoted to this question. This research has been plagued by one obvious problem: How do you measure "marital success"? Some researchers have simply compared divorced and intact couples in regard to premarital characteristics. The problem with this strategy is that many intact couples obviously do not have happy or successful marriages. Other researchers have used elaborate questionnaires to measure couples' marital satisfaction. Unfortunately, these scales are plagued by problems. For one thing, they appear to measure complacency and lack of conflict more than satisfaction. Although our measures of marital quality are rather crude, some predictors of marital success have been found. These relations are all statistically weak, but they are intriguing nonetheless.

• *Family background.* The marital adjustment of parents is correlated with the marital satisfaction of their children. People whose parents were divorced are more likely than others to experience divorce themselves (White, 1990). For a variety of reasons, marital instability appears to run in families (Teachman, Polonko, & Scanzoni, 1987).

• *Age.* The ages of the bride and groom are also relevant. Couples who marry young have higher divorce rates (London & Wilson, 1988; White, 1990), as Figure 9.6 shows. Surprisingly, couples who marry late also have a greater propensity to divorce. Because they must select from a smaller pool of potential mates, older newlyweds are more likely to differ in age, religion, social status, and education (Bitter, 1986). Such differences may make marriage more challenging regardless of age.

• *Length of courtship.* Longer periods of courtship are associated with a greater probability of marital success (Grover, Russell, Schumm, & Paff-Bergen, 1985). The critical factor is probably not the duration of courtship itself but the probability that people who are cautious about marriage have attitudes and values that promote marital stability.

• *Socioeconomic class.* Divorce is more frequent in the working and lower classes than in the upper and middle classes. There are probably many reasons, but a key one appears to be the greater financial stress in lower socioeconomic strata (Conger et al., 1990).

• *Personality.* Studies have generally found that partners' personality traits are *not* very predictive of marital success. However, the presence of serious psychological and emotional disorders in one or both partners is associated with marital problems (Raschke, 1987). One recent study (Long & Andrews, 1990) found an interesting association between a trait called *perspective taking* and marital adjustment. **Perspective taking is a component of empathy that involves the tendency to put oneself in another person's place.** For both husbands and wives, high scores in perspective taking were found to be positively correlated with marital adjustment. Thus individuals who work to understand their partner's viewpoint appear to have a better chance of marital success.

In summary, there are some thought-pro-

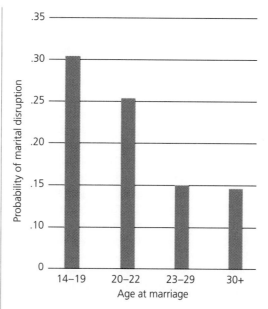

FIGURE 9.6
Age at marriage and probability of marital disruption in the first five years
Martin and Bumpass (1989) estimated the likelihood of marital disruption (either divorce or separation) within five years for various groups. The data summarized here, based on people who married between 1980 and 1985, show that the probability of marital disruption is substantially higher among couples who marry young.

voking correlations between couples' premarital characteristics and their marital adjustment. There are no reliable predictors of marital success, however, as all these correlations are quite small. Researchers have found some stronger correlations when they have investigated the relationship between marital adjustment and the family life cycle.

Marital Adjustment across the Family Life Cycle

"Jennifer has taken a lot of time away from us, the time that we normally spend doing things together or talking. It seems like maybe on a weekend when we would normally like to sleep in, or just have lazy sex, Jennifer wakes up and needs to be fed. . . . But I'm sure that will pass as soon as Jennifer gets a little older. We're just going through a phase."

—A new mother quoted in *American Couples* (Blumstein & Schwartz, 1983, p. 205)

e're just going through a phase." That statement highlights an important point: Predictable patterns of development can be seen in families, just as they can in individuals. These patterns make up the *family life cycle,* **an orderly sequence of developmental stages that families tend to progress through.** The institutions of marriage and family are inevitably intertwined. With the advent of marriage, two persons add a new member to their existing families and create an entirely new family. Typically this new family forms the core of one's life as an adult.

The study of the family life cycle has fallen primarily within the province of *sociology, the scientific study of human society and its institutions.* Sociologists have proposed several models to describe family development (Mattessich & Hill, 1987). These models are basically similar. Our discussion will be organized around a six-stage model of family development outlined by Carter and McGoldrick (1988; McGoldrick & Carter, 1989). Figure 9.7 provides an overview of their model. It spells out the developmental tasks during each stage of the life cycle for families that eventually have children and remain intact. Carter and McGoldrick have described variations on this basic pattern that are associated with remaining childless or going through a divorce, but we will focus mostly on the basic pattern here.

Research suggests that the family life cycle is an important determinant of marital satisfaction. Numerous studies have measured spouses' overall satisfaction in different stages of the family life cycle and found a U-shaped relationship like the one shown in Figure 9.8 (Belsky, 1990; Glenn, 1990). This U-shaped relationship reflects the fact that satisfaction tends to be greatest at the beginning and at the end of the family life cycle, with a noticeable decline in the middle. The conventional explanation for this pattern is that the burdens of child rearing undermine couples' satisfaction, but that

their satisfaction gradually begins to climb back up again as children grow up and these burdens ease. This explanation is plausible, but alternative analyses also might account for the U-shaped pattern. For example, the decline in satisfaction after the first few years of marriage could simply reflect the normal erosion of passionate love that is frequently seen in couples whether or not they are married or have children (see Chapter 8). The increase in satisfaction in the later stages of the family life cycle could be due to diminishing demands and stresses from spouses' work roles, which often have a deleterious effect on marital interactions. Although the exact reasons for the U-shaped pattern in marital satisfaction are not clear yet, virtually all of the potential explanations are based on the assumption that marital adjustment is influenced by the nature of the challenges that couples confront at various points in the family life cycle. Let's look at these challenges.

Between Families: The Unattached Young Adult

As young adults become independent of their parents, they go through a transitional period during which they are "between families" until they form a new family through marriage. What is interesting about this stage is that it is being

**FIGURE 9.7
Stages of the family life cycle**
The family life cycle can be divided into six stages, as shown here (based on Carter & McGoldrick, 1988). The family's key developmental task during each stage is identified in the second column. The third column lists additional developmental tasks at each stage.

The Family Life Cycle

Family life cycle stage	Emotional process of transition: Key developmental task	Additional changes in family status required to proceed developmentally
1 Between families: The unattached young adult	Accepting parent/offspring separation	a. Differentiation of self in relation to family of origin b. Development of intimate peer relationships c. Establishment of self in work
2 The joining of families through marriage: The newly married couple	Commitment to new system	a. Formation of marital system b. Realignment of relationships with extended families and friends to include spouse
3 The family with young children	Accepting new members into the system	a. Adjusting marital system to make space for child(ren) b. Taking on parenting roles c. Realignment of relationships with extended family to include parenting and grandparenting roles
4 The family with adolescents	Increasing flexibility of family boundaries to include children's independence	a. Shifting of parent-child relationships to permit adolescent to move in and out of system b. Refocus on midlife marital and career issues c. Beginning shift toward concerns for older generation
5 Launching children and moving on	Accepting a multitude of exits from and entries into the family system	a. Renegotiation of marital system as a dyad b. Development of adult-to-adult relationships between grown children and their parents c. Realignment of relationships to include in-laws and grandchildren d. Dealing with disabilities and death of parents (grandparents)
6 The family in later life	Accepting the shifting of generational roles	a. Maintaining own and/or couple functioning and interests in face of physiological decline; exploration of new familial and social role options b. Support for a more central role for middle generation c. Making room in the system for the wisdom and experience of the elderly; supporting the older generation without overfunctioning for them d. Dealing with loss of spouse, siblings, and other peers and preparation for own death; life review and integration

prolonged by more and more people. The percentage of young adults who are postponing marriage until their late 20s or early 30s has risen dramatically (Sporakowski, 1988). The frequent extension of this stage is probably due to a variety of factors. Chief among them are the availability of new career options for women, increased educational requirements in the world of work, and increased emphasis on personal autonomy.

Joining Together: The Newly Married Couple

The newly married couple settle gradually into their roles as husband and wife. This phase *can* be quite troublesome, as the early years of marriage are often marred by numerous problems and disagreements (Johnson, White, Edwards, & Booth, 1986). Difficulties are especially likely if the spouses enter the marriage with different expectations about marital roles. In general, however, this stage tends to be characterized by great happiness—the proverbial "marital bliss." Spouses' satisfaction with their relationship tends to be relatively high early in marriage, before the arrival of the first child (Glenn & McLanahan, 1982).

This prechildren phase used to be rather short for most newly married couples, as they quickly went about the business of having their first child. Traditionally, couples simply *assumed* that they would proceed to have children. Remaining childless by choice used to be virtually unthinkable. Although attitudes toward voluntary childlessness are still largely negative, the normative prescription against this choice has declined dramatically. In recent years more couples have found themselves struggling to *decide* whether to have children. Often they arrive at this decision after numerous postponements, when they finally acknowledge that the "right time" is never going to come (Crane, 1985).

A recent survey (Seccombe, 1991) of thousands of childfree married couples in their childbearing years found that the men rated the importance of having children higher than the women did and that the husbands were more inclined to want children than their wives. Couples who choose to remain childless cite the great costs incurred in raising children. In addition to the financial burdens, they mention such costs as giving up educational or career opportunities, loss of time for leisure activities and each other, loss of privacy and autonomy, and worry about the responsibility associated with child rearing (Bram, 1985; Seccombe,

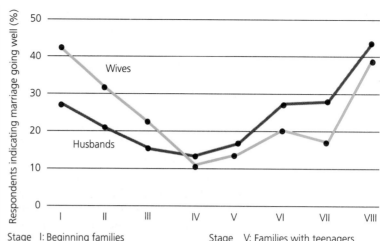

Stage I: Beginning families
Stage II: Child-bearing families
Stage III: Families with preschool children
Stage IV: Families with school-aged children
Stage V: Families with teenagers
Stage VI: Families as launching centers
Stage VII: Families in the middle years
Stage VIII: Aging families

1991). These considerable costs probably explain why couples with children tend to report lower levels of marital satisfaction than voluntarily childless couples (Burman & de Anda, 1986).

Nonetheless, the vast majority of married couples continue to plan on having children, although many expect to delay having their first child until their late 20s (Roosa, 1988). In explaining their decision to have children, couples cite many factors, including the responsibility to procreate, the joy of watching youngsters mature, the sense of purpose that children create, and the satisfaction associated with emotional nurturance and the challenge of child rearing (Goetting, 1986). In spite of the costs involved in raising children, most parents report no regret about their choice. The vast majority of parents rate parenthood as a very positive and satisfying experience (Demo, 1992).

The Family with Young Children

Although most parents are happy with their decision to have children, the arrival of the first child represents a major transition, and the disruption of old routines can be extremely stressful. The new mother, already physically exhausted by the birth process, is prone to postpartum distress (Harriman, 1986). The transition to parenthood tends to be more difficult for older women and for working wives. Women who have to shoulder the major burden of infant care and those whose babies have difficult temperaments are also especially vulnerable to distress (Kalmuss, Davidson, & Cushman, 1992).

Crisis during the transition to first parenthood is far from universal, however (Ruble,

FIGURE 9.8
Marital satisfaction across the family life cycle
This graph depicts the percentage of husbands and wives studied by Rollins and Feldman (1970) who said their marriage was going well "all the time" at various stages of the family life cycle. Rollins and Feldman (1970) broke the family life cycle into eight stages instead of six. The U-shaped relationship shown here has been found in many other studies as well.

Fleming, Hackel, & Stangor, 1988). Couples who have high levels of intimacy, closeness, and commitment before the first child's birth are likely to maintain a high level of satisfaction afterward (Lewis, 1988). They also tend to experience a smoother transition to parenthood, demonstrating greater warmth in their interactions with their infant (Lewis, Owen, & Cox, 1988).

The key to making this transition less stressful may be to have *realistic expectations* about parental responsibilities (Belsky, 1985; Kalmuss et al., 1992). Studies find that stress tends to be greatest in new parents—especially mothers—who have overestimated the benefits and underestimated the costs of their new role. Typically it is the new mother who experiences the greatest lifestyle change after the birth of the first child. Therefore, she tends to suffer more when her overly optimistic expectations are violated. Prospective parents need to realize that although children can be unparalleled sources of joy and satisfaction, they also can be a gigantic headache.

Although children bring their share of trials and tribulations to a marriage, evidence suggests that they should not have to shoulder all the blame for their parents' sagging marital satisfaction. Studies that have compared young married couples with children to similar couples without children have found that the early years of marriage typically bring a decline in marital satisfaction for both groups (Glenn, 1990). This decline may be somewhat steeper for parents because of the stress associated with raising children (Belsky, 1990), but it appears that some of the negative effects attributed to parenthood may be due to other processes that unfold as marriages evolve over the years.

In any case, parenting is a very complex topic to which many books have been devoted. Diverse styles of parenting tend to yield differ-

ent results (Baumrind, 1991). We will consider this topic in earnest in the application section of Chapter 11.

The Family with Adolescent Children

Although the adolescent years have long been viewed as a period of great stress and turmoil, research over the past decade has led to the conclusion that adolescence is not as turbulent or difficult for youngsters as it was once believed to be (Offer, Ostrov, Howard, & Atkinson, 1988; see Chapter 11). Ironically, though, studies indicate that it is an especially stressful period for adolescents' parents. Parents overwhelmingly rate adolescence as the most difficult stage of parenting (Gecas & Seff, 1990).

As children move into adolescence, parents are often making a major transition themselves—into middle age. Parents tend to experience more intense midlife identity concerns if they have same-sex adolescent children (Steinberg & Silverberg, 1987). These parents are often prompted to reexamine their own values, accomplishments, and commitments as they watch their same-sex children struggle with similar issues.

As adolescent children seek to establish their own identities, their parents' influence over them tends to decline while the influence of their peer groups tends to increase. Parents tend to retain more influence than peers over important matters, such as educational goals and career plans, but peers gradually gain more influence over less critical matters, such as style of dress and recreational plans (Gecas & Seff, 1990). The shifting sands of influence set the stage for more conflicts between adolescent children and their parents (Montemayor, 1986). Emotionally charged clashes over values are common, and power struggles frequently ensue. Conflict is particularly likely to surface between adolescents (of both sexes) and their mothers. Moreover, when conflict does occur, mothers are more adversely affected by it than fathers (Steinberg & Silverberg, 1987). The reason may be that women's self-esteem has tended to be more closely tied than men's to the quality of their family relationships.

In addition to worrying about their adolescent children, middle-aged couples often must worry about the care of their parents. Thanks to increased longevity and decreased family size, today's average married couple has more parents than children (Wisensale, 1992). Women tend to assume most of the responsibility for elderly relatives, and it is estimated that in the future they can expect to spend more years car-

Parental responsibilities are one of the sources of stress in relationships.

ing for their aging parents than for their dependent children (Brubaker, 1990).

Launching Children into the Adult World

When a couple's children begin to reach their 20s, the family has to adapt to a multitude of exits and entries as children leave and return, sometimes with their own spouses. During this period, children have to progress from dependence to independence. Their progress is sometimes complicated when parents have difficulty letting go. Young adults can benefit from assistance and support, but some parents insist on continuing to take care of everything for them. Generally it is counterproductive for parents to discourage young adults' movement toward independence.

One might argue that launching children into the adult world tends to be a lengthier and more difficult process today than it once was. The percentage of 18-to-29-year-olds who live with their parents has climbed in recent years (Aquilino, 1990; Glick & Lin, 1986). The rapidly rising cost of a college education and the shrinking job market have probably led many young adults to linger in their parents' homes. Moreover, crises such as separation, divorce, job loss, and pregnancy out of wedlock are increasingly forcing children who have ventured out on their own to return to their parents. The repercussions of these new trends are sure to be a subject of future research.

When parents do manage to get all their children launched into the adult world, they find themselves faced with an "empty nest." This was formerly thought to be a difficult transition for many parents, especially for mothers who were familiar only with the maternal role. Today, however, more women have experience with other roles outside the home, and most look forward to their "liberation" from child-rearing responsibilities (Reinke, Ellicott, Harris, & Hancock, 1985).

The Family in Later Life

Marital satisfaction tends to climb in the postparental period as couples find that they have more time to devote attention to each other (Brubaker, 1990). Whether this trend is due to reduced parental responsibilities, reduced work responsibilities, or other considerations remains unclear (Lee, 1988). In any case, many couples take advantage of their newfound freedom, traveling or developing new leisure interests. For many people this can be a period of increased intimacy. Spouses do have to adapt to

Couples have more time to enjoy leisure activities once their work and parental responsibilities decrease.

spending more time with each other, but most seem to make the adjustment without major problems (Treas, 1983). Of course, age-related considerations that are independent of the relationship, such as the increased likelihood of physical illness, can make the later years stressful. In general, however, the trend is for couples to report fairly high satisfaction until one of the spouses (usually the husband) dies.

Vulnerable Areas in Marital Adjustment

"When we first got married, the first six months of conflicts were all about getting him to take account of what I had planned for him at home. . . . He would come waltzing in an hour and a half late for dinner, or cancel an evening with friends, because he had to close a deal. . . . We would argue and argue . . . not because I didn't want him to make a living . . . but because I thought he had to be more considerate."

—A wife quoted in *American Couples* (Blumstein & Schwartz, 1983, p. 174)

 n unavoidable reality of marriage is that couples must confront a legion of problems together. During courtship, couples focus mostly on pleasurable activities. But when people marry, they must face many problems, such as arriving at acceptable role compromises, paying bills, and raising a family. There is no such thing as a problem-free marriage. Successful marriages depend on couples' ability to handle their problems. In this section

275

we will analyze the major kinds of difficulties that are likely to emerge. We can't offer simple solutions for these problems, but as you navigate your way through life, it helps to know where the most perilous reefs are.

Unrealistic Expectations

Sabatelli (1988) notes that many people enter marriage with unrealistic expectations about how wonderful it's going to be. When expectations are too high, disappointment is likely. Part of the problem is the degree to which media portrayals romanticize love and marriage. Films and TV shows tend to focus on the excitement of falling in love rather than on the sacrifice of caring for a sick spouse. Further, people who marry quickly may not know each other very well and tend to have an idealized picture of their new mate. This idealized picture often turns out to be inaccurate when they see their new mate in a wider variety of less pleasant situations. This kind of letdown can best be avoided by efforts to be realistic about a prospective mate's qualities. Such realism is more likely if lovers are open with each other during the courtship period and disclose their frailties instead of hiding them.

Gaps in Role Expectations

When a couple marry, they assume new roles—those of husband and wife. With each role go certain expectations that the partners hold about how wives and husbands should behave. These expectations may vary greatly from one person to another. Gaps between partners in their role expectations can cause serious problems. Kitson and Sussman (1982) note that agreement about marital roles is a major determinant of marital stability. However, substantial differences in role expectations seem particularly likely in this era of transition in gender roles.

Our marital role expectations are shaped significantly by our exposure to our parents' relationship. The role expectations passed on by parents used to be fairly clear. A husband was supposed to act as the principal breadwinner, make the important decisions, and take care of certain household chores, such as car and yard maintenance. A wife was supposed to raise the children, cook, clean, and follow her husband's lead. Because each sex viewed the other as fundamentally different, couples didn't expect to "understand" each other, or to share many interests and activities. Spouses had different spheres of influence. The working world was the domain of the husband, the home the domain of the wife.

In recent years, however, the women's movement and other forces of social change have led to new expectations about marital roles. Young adults no longer blindly follow the model of their elders. Today they have *options* from which to choose, so prospective mates can't assume that they share the same views on the appropriate responsibilities of spouses. Many people have changed their role conceptions, others cling to traditional views, and some are ambivalent. Still others claim to believe in equality in marriage but revert to traditional norms in their behavior. Thus we live in a time of transition and consequent confusion.

Women may be especially vulnerable to ambivalence and confusion about marital roles. Surveys of college women (Baber & Monaghan, 1988; Machung, 1989) show that more women than ever are aspiring to demanding professional careers. At the same time, virtually all these women plan to marry, and most expect to become mothers. The majority say they would like two or three children. The typical college woman plans to complete her education first, then get married and establish herself in her career. Finally, she anticipates starting a family in her late 20s. She expects to marry a man who will assume equal responsibility for child rearing and domestic chores. Clearly, these women want to "have it all." Yet some remnants of traditional thinking remain. When queried, the majority of women say their husband's career should take priority over their own (Machung, 1989). Most also say they should be the one to interrupt their career to raise young children, stay home when a child is sick, and arrange for child care.

And what about college men? Fewer men (49%) than women (69%) express a preference for an egalitarian marriage (Lewis, 1986). Men also tend to have more specific and better-informed career plans than their female counterparts (Machung, 1989). The vast majority of college men say their career should take priority over their wives' and that their wives should assume the major responsibility for child care. They are willing to "help out" with certain household chores (such as washing the dishes) but not others (such as cooking). In fact, men differ from women in their view of what equality in marriage means. When the subjects in one survey (Machung, 1989) were asked to define an egalitarian marriage, half the men could not. The other half defined it in purely psychological terms, saying a marriage is "equal" if it is based on mutual understanding and trust. The

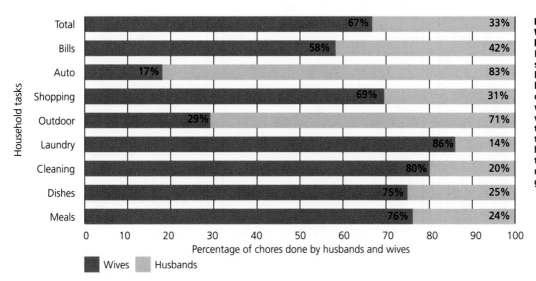

FIGURE 9.9
Who does the housework? Blair and Johnson (1992) studied the proportion of housework done by husbands and wives. This chart, based on employed wives, shows that even working women continue to do a highly disproportionate share of most household tasks and that the division of labor still meshes with traditional gender roles.

women were considerably more concrete and task-oriented. They defined marital equality in terms of an equal sharing of chores and responsibilities.

In the realm of housework, however, equality clearly is the exception rather than the norm. Recent studies indicate that wives are still doing the bulk of the housework in America, even when they are employed outside the home. Blair and Johnson (1992) found, for example, that working wives devoted an average of 31 hours per week to housework (not including child care) while their husbands contributed only 15 hours on the average. The gap was even greater for nonemployed wives, who averaged 42 hours per week of housework in comparison with 12 hours per week for their husbands. Moreover, Blair and Johnson found that wives still do the vast majority of "women's work," such as cooking, cleaning, and laundry, while men continue to do mostly traditional "male chores," such as auto maintenance and outdoor tasks (see Figure 9.9). The continued sex segregation in housework is important because wives' chores tend to be more aversive than husbands' chores, which tend to have clearer end points and more of a leisure component, and to permit more discretion as to when they must be completed. Of course, housework patterns vary and some husbands do more than others. Men tend to do more housework when they have lighter job demands, when their wives earn a larger portion of the family income, and when they or their wives hold less traditional beliefs about gender roles (Coltrane & Ishii-Kuntz, 1992). A recent study by McHale and Crouter (1992) suggests that housework arrangements are most likely to be a source of discontent when spouses' expectations and preferences clash with reality. They

found lower marital satisfaction when wives with nontraditional attitudes toward gender roles had to live with a traditional division of household labor and when husbands with traditional attitudes had to adapt to a more equal division of labor. Obviously, women's and men's varied expectations in regard to housework roles create considerable potential for conflict.

Another way to analyze the marital role expectations of today's youth is to assess how realistic these expectations are, given current social policies and trends. Recall that the majority of college women plan to have several children, to interrupt their careers to care for them, and then to resume their careers where they left off (Baber & Monaghan, 1988). They apparently assume that they can leave their employment for a long period without loss of momentum or seniority and that they can live adequately for some time on their husband's income alone. These expectations seem somewhat naive given the increasing necessity for two incomes, as well as organizational policies that make it difficult for wives *or* husbands to take more than a few months' parental leave. As Hochschild (1989) points out, changes in social institutions and policies have not kept pace with people's changing aspirations (although recent legislation mandating the availability of parental leave for many categories of employees is a step in the right direction).

In light of these realities, it is imperative that couples discuss role expectations in depth before marriage. If they discover that their views are very different, they need to take seriously the potential for problems. Many people casually dismiss gender-role disagreements, thinking they can "straighten out" their partner later on. But assumptions about marital roles,

whether traditional or not, may be strongly held and not easily changed.

Work and Career Issues

The possible interactions between one's occupation and one's marriage are numerous and complex. Individuals' job satisfaction and involvement can affect their own marital satisfaction, their partners' marital satisfaction, and their children's development.

Husbands' Work and Marital Adjustment

Work has traditionally played a central role in men's lives. Hence a host of studies have investigated the relationship between husbands' job satisfaction and their marital adjustment. One could speculate that these two variables might be either positively *or* negatively related. On the one hand, a husband who is highly committed to a satisfying career may have less time and energy to devote to his marriage and family. On the other hand, the frustration and stress of an unsatisfying job might spill over to contaminate one's marriage.

The research on this question suggests that both scenarios are realistic possibilities. Male executives and managers typically report high job satisfaction, but also a great deal of work/family conflict and low involvement with their wives and children (Piotrkowski, Rapoport, & Rapoport, 1987). Moreover, studies find that husbands' stress at work can have a substantial negative effect on their wives' emotional health and marital satisfaction (Rook,

Dooley, & Catalano, 1991; Small & Riley, 1990).

When husbands in a wide range of occupations are studied, however, most researchers find modest *positive* associations between the husbands' job satisfaction and marital satisfaction (Piotrkowski et al., 1987). That is, men who enjoy their work typically enjoy more satisfying marriages as well. How their wives feel about all this is less clear; little research has been conducted on the connection between husbands' job satisfaction and their wives' marital satisfaction.

Wives' Work and Marital Adjustment

There is also a dearth of research on the relationship between *wives'* job satisfaction and their marital satisfaction. One study (Greenhaus, Bedeian, & Mossholder, 1987) found that high job performance by female (but not male) accountants was associated with *decreased* marital satisfaction. The authors speculated that these successful career women may have been experiencing role conflict and guilt over their strong work commitment. These findings are interesting, but we need more research before we can draw conclusions about the effects of wives' work on their marital satisfaction.

Although few studies have looked at the impact of wives' work on their own marital satisfaction, many have examined the effect of wives' work on their husband's well-being or the couple's marital adjustment. This slant arises from traditional views that regard men's *lack* of employment and women's *employment* as departures from the norm (Bronfenbrenner &

Crouter, 1982). Typically, these studies simply categorize women as "working" or "nonworking" and compare the husbands' (or couples') marital satisfaction.

Most of these studies find no consistent differences in the marital adjustment of male-breadwinner versus dual-career couples (Piotrkowski et al., 1987; Spitze, 1988). Some investigators have begun to study the mediating influence of spouses' *attitudes* toward married women's employment, with enlightening results. It appears that marital satisfaction tends to be highest when partners share gender-role expectations and when the wife's employment status matches her own (and her husband's) preference (Menaghan & Parcel, 1990). In summary, although dual-earner couples do face special problems in negotiating career priorities, child-care arrangements, and other practical matters, these problems need not have a negative effect on their marriage.

Parents' Work and Children's Development

Another issue of concern has been the potential impact of parents' employment on their children. Virtually all of the research in this area has focused on the effects of mothers' employment outside the home. This research has been guided by two implicit assumptions. The first assumption is that the more time mothers spend with their children, the better off the children are. The second assumption is that the full-time housewives of previous generations devoted more time to their children than today's employed wives. Both assumptions have been questioned (Hoffman, 1987). Extremely high levels of mother-child interaction can backfire, contributing to excessive dependency in children. Furthermore, yesterday's full-time mothers did not have modern time-saving household conveniences, and they had more children. Thus they may not have devoted any more time to each individual child than today's working mothers do.

What does the research on maternal employment show? Although most Americans believe that mothers' employment is detrimental to children's development (Greenberger, Goldberg, Crawford, & Granger, 1988), a host of empirical studies have found that maternal employment is *not* harmful to children (Demo, 1992; Spitze, 1988). For instance, studies have found no link between mothers' employment status and the quality of infant-mother (or toddler-mother) emotional attachment (Chase-Lansdale, 1981; Easterbrooks & Goldberg, 1985). Clearly, a child *can* form a strong attachment to a working mother. Furthermore, the *attitudes* of both parents are important. Families in which both the wife and her husband are satisfied with the wife's role (whether she is employed or not) tend to have the most well-adjusted offspring (Easterbrooks & Goldberg, 1985). Not surprisingly, both spouses' degree of commitment to being effective parents is also critical. Fortunately, mothers' work generally does *not* interfere with commitment to children (Greenberger & Goldberg, 1989).

In fact, there is evidence that maternal employment can have *positive* effects on children (Demo, 1992). Some studies have found that children of working mothers tend to be especially self-reliant and responsible. This advantage appears to be particularly pronounced for girls. Daughters of working mothers also tend to exhibit higher than average academic competence and career aspirations (Hoffman, 1987).

The sparse research on fathers' work and their children's development has typically focused on the effects of fathers' *un*employment. This research suggests that fathers' unemployment can have negative effects on children. Fathers who lose their jobs tend to be more irritable, hostile, punitive, and arbitrary with their children than employed fathers (McLoyd, 1989). Another line of research has explored how fathers' interaction with their children has changed as more and more mothers have entered the work force. Furstenberg (1988) concludes that the changes have been rather modest. Today's fathers do interact with their children more, but in most homes the mother remains in charge of child rearing. As Furstenberg (1988) puts it, "fathers are still pinch hitters or part-time players rather than regulars" (p. 209).

Financial Difficulties

How do couples' financial resources affect their marital adjustment? Neither financial stability nor wealth can ensure marital satisfaction. However, poverty can produce serious problems (Conger et al., 1990; Voydanoff, 1990). Without money, families live in constant dread of financial drains such as illness, layoffs, or broken appliances. Husbands tend to view themselves as poor providers and become hostile and irritable. Their hostility can undermine the warm, supportive exchanges that help to sustain relationships. This problem is sometimes aggravated when disappointed wives criticize their husbands. Spontaneity in communication may be impaired by an understandable reluctance to talk about financial concerns. Thus it is clear that poverty produces significant stress for married couples. Given this reality, it is important that prospective partners be realistic about their ability to finance a viable future.

Even when financial resources are plentiful, money can be a source of marital strain. Quarrels about how to spend money are common and potentially damaging at all income levels. Pittman and Lloyd (1988), for instance, found that perceived financial stress (regardless of a family's actual income) was associated with decreased marital satisfaction. Another study examined how happily married couples handled their money in comparison with couples that eventually divorced (Schaninger & Buss, 1986). The happy couples were found to engage in more joint decision making on finances. Thus the best way to avoid troublesome battles over money is probably to engage in extensive planning of expenditures together.

Inadequate Communication

Effective communication is crucial to the success of a marriage. The damaging role that poor communication can play was clearly demonstrated in a study by Fowers and Olson (1989). They identified areas of marital functioning that differentiated satisfied and dissatisfied couples. Of the three most important areas of functioning, two involved communication. These were spouses' comfort in sharing information with each other and their willingness to recognize and resolve conflicts between them. (The third area was the quality of their sexual relationship.) Another study found that nearly

87% of couples who sought family counseling reported communication difficulties (Beck & Jones, 1973). As Figure 9.10 shows, poor communication was the leading problem among these distressed couples.

A number of studies have compared communication patterns in happy and unhappy marriages. This research indicates that unhappily married spouses (1) find it difficult to convey positive messages, (2) misunderstand each other more often, (3) are less likely to recognize that they have been misunderstood, (4) use more frequent and more intense negative messages, and (5) often differ in the amount of self-disclosure they prefer in the relationship (Noller & Fitzpatrick, 1990; Noller & Gallois, 1988). Moreover, gender differences in approaches to communication (see the application section of Chapter 10) are frequently exaggerated in unhappily married couples (Gottman & Levenson, 1988).

The importance of marital communication was underscored in a recent study that attempted to predict the likelihood of divorce in a sample of 52 married couples (Buehlman, Gottman, & Katz, 1992). Each couple provided an oral history of their relationship and a 15-minute sample of their interaction style, during which they discussed two problem areas in their marriage. The investigators rated the spouses on a variety of factors that mostly reflected the subjects' ways of relating to each other. On the basis of these ratings, they were able to predict which couples would divorce within three years with 94% accuracy!

In recent years investigators have increasingly turned to attribution theory to gain a better understanding of marital miscommunication (Fincham & Bradbury, 1992). As we saw in Chapter 5, *attributions* are inferences that we

FIGURE 9.10
Problems reported by couples seeking family counseling
Beck and Jones (1973) found that communication was the problem most frequently identified by troubled couples. Rounding out the top five problems were disagreements about child rearing, sex, finances, and the use of leisure time.

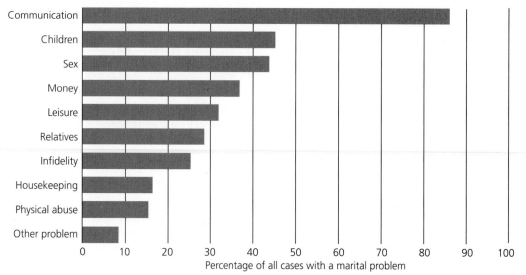

Percentage of all cases with a marital problem

draw about the causes of events, others' behavior, and even our own behavior. Attributing events to internal versus external factors, or stable versus unstable factors, can make all the difference in the world in how we relate to other people. Married people routinely make attributions to explain each other's behavior. If a wife forgets her husband's birthday, for example, he may conclude that she's self-centered and inconsiderate (an internal, stable attribution). Or he may conclude that she's drained by work overload at the office (an external, unstable attribution). Obviously, these attributions don't have the same implications for their relationship.

Research by Frank Fincham and his colleagues indicates that distressed spouses (usually defined as those seeking marital therapy) tend to explain their partners' negative behavior with internal, stable attributions that have global implications for their marriage ("She doesn't love me"). In contrast, they tend to explain their partners' positive behaviors with external, unstable attributions that have specific implications ("She was nice because she made a big sale today"). Patterns of attribution in happily married couples tend to be just the opposite (Bradbury & Fincham, 1988; Fincham, Beach, & Baucom, 1987). Thus, in contrast to happy couples, distressed spouses blame their problems on each other and view good behavior as a temporary aberration. Unhappy spouses' biases in attribution can be either a cause or an effect of marital distress, but their biases clearly aren't a promising foundation for marital bliss.

Communication can be improved in a variety of ways, many of which we discussed in Chapter 6. Most of the advice offered in that chapter can be applied to marital communication. In particular, it is important to avoid defensiveness and to attempt to create a positive climate for communication. Developing constructive approaches to conflict resolution is also critical.

Problems with In-Laws

Research on in-law conflict has diminished in recent years. This neglect may indicate that in-law trouble is less of a problem in our more mobile society. When intergenerational conflict does occur, it typically involves the wife and her mother-in-law. In fact, in-law trouble has been characterized as a "female problem," perhaps because women have traditionally shouldered the responsibility for maintaining kinship ties (Marotz-Baden & Cowan, 1987).

Innumerable books attempt to tell couples how to make it all work. Aaron Beck's entry in this market appears to be superior to most of the others. Beck is the founder of cognitive therapy (see Chapter 16) and a renowned expert on the distorted thought patterns that promote anxiety and depression. He makes a compelling case for the proposition that many married couples (especially those in distress) engage in the same errors of thinking as depressed and anxious people: namely, negativity, rigidity, and selectivity. If each spouse thinks about the other in such a distorted manner, then disillusionment, miscommunication, and frustration are inevitable.

Most of the chapters include one or more questionnaires that readers can use to probe their own relationships. In addition, Beck provides a great deal of practical advice about how to identify and change the distorted thought patterns that undermine the marital satisfaction of so many couples. A unique feature of Beck's book is its inclusion of many actual conversations of troubled couples, along with the unspoken thoughts that lie behind each line of dialogue.

The following interchange occurred when Marjorie wanted to hang a picture but had difficulty driving the nail into the wall:

KEN: [She's having a problem. I'd better help her.] Let me do it for you.

MARJORIE: [He has no confidence in my ability.] That's all right. I can do it myself [angrily].

KEN: What's the matter with you? I was only trying to help.

MARJORIE: That's all you ever do. You don't think I can do anything.

KEN: Well, you can't even drive a nail straight [laughs].

MARJORIE: There you go again—always putting me down.

KEN: I was just trying to help.

The spouses had completely different versions of Ken's intervention. Marjorie's goal of hanging the picture was to assure herself that she could handle manual tasks; in fact, she was looking forward to Ken's praise for her demonstration of competence and independence. His intrusion, though, brought her sense of incompetence to the surface. While each was correct in the belief that Ken lacked confidence in Marjorie's manual ability, Ken perceived himself as kind and considerate, while Marjorie viewed him as intrusive and patronizing. What started as an innocent gesture of helpfulness on his part led to hurt feelings and antagonism. [p. 59]

Fischer (1983) found that wives tend to turn to their own mothers for help after giving birth. Yet they may regard their mother-in-law's concern over her new grandchild as "interference." In general, in-law strife tends to be greatest for couples who have not yet attained emotional or financial independence from their parents.

Sexual Problems

There is a strong link between couples' marital satisfaction and their perception of the quality of their sexual relationship (Fowers & Olson,

Despite the impression you may get from this scene in the movie *The War of the Roses,* a couple's willingness to recognize and resolve conflict is a key factor in marital satisfaction.

1989). Although this association is quite strong, it is difficult to discern which is the cause and which is the effect. The assertion that sexual problems cause marital distress, though true, is an oversimplification, because marital distress also causes sexual problems (LoPiccolo & Daiss, 1987).

Sexual problems are often intertwined with other marital problems. Disagreement about the appropriate frequency of sex, for instance, may be due to differing role expectations. Communication problems may also be linked to sexual difficulties. Open sexual communication is associated with marital satisfaction, and inhibited sexual communication is associated with marital distress (Banmen & Vogel, 1985). In addition, some couples depend too much on sexual intimacy to resolve nonsexual conflicts. This tendency may mask underlying relationship problems and interfere with more direct conflict-resolution strategies (Maddock, 1989).

Jealousy

Romantic jealousy has been defined as a complex of thoughts, emotions, and behaviors that result from the perception of a threat to one's intimate relationship. To simplify, the green-eyed monster is aroused when you fear the loss of your romantic partner's affection. Although jealousy is a common and sometimes legitimate reaction, it is also a potentially destructive emotion in intimate relationships (Buunk & Bringle, 1987).

Some people are more prone to get jealous than others. It appears that this jealousy-prone disposition is primarily a function of poor self-esteem. Highly jealous persons tend to have a negative self-concept, to be relatively unhappy, and to feel insecure, inadequate, and dependent in their intimate relationships (Pines &

Aronson, 1983; White, 1981). Furthermore, after experiencing a jealousy-provoking situation, people feel even more insecure, unattractive, and dependent, making future jealous reactions even more likely (Radecki-Bush, Bush, & Jennings, 1988).

Jealousy typically is triggered by a specific event. This event usually involves either being left out of some activity involving one's partner or something that suggests, even remotely, that the partner's affection could be lost. Salovey and Rodin (1986) studied more than 50 jealousy-provoking circumstances. Here are the situations they found to elicit the greatest romantic jealousy: (1) You find out that your lover is having an affair. (2) Someone else goes out with the person you like. (3) Someone else gets closer to a person to whom you are attracted. (4) Your lover tells you how sexy an old boyfriend/girlfriend was. (5) Your lover visits a person he or she used to go out with.

Some jealousy-prone persons may *imagine* a threat to their relationship when there is none. Such tendencies are likely to create unnecessary problems in marital relations. Pfeiffer and Wong (1989) point out that attempts to gain control over a partner through jealousy tend to be resented. Correcting this problem is not easy, since it is usually rooted in a deep-seated negative self-concept. Efforts to remedy the problem should focus on improving one's self-esteem and learning to think more rationally about one's relationship. People who are secure in a relationship are less likely to overreact when a spouse pays some attention to someone else. They are more likely to regard the event as normal and to see the third person's interest in their spouse as an affirmation of their own good taste.

Growing in Different Directions

We have already mentioned the tendency for people to marry others similar to themselves (homogamy). It is always possible, however, for partners to diverge in their values and activity preferences. In the early years of a marriage, for instance, both members of a couple may enjoy a moderate amount of social entertaining with their friends. As the years wear on, one partner may find that activity tedious, while the other comes to enjoy it even more. Neither partner is wrong. They are simply evolving in different directions. This divergence, however, can lead to bitter disagreements about how the couple should spend their time.

It is important for spouses to allow each other room for personal growth, difficult though it may be to do so. They should recognize that it is unrealistic to expect anyone to remain exactly the same forever. In this era, with recreation playing an increasingly large role in our lives, more spouses may have to learn to engage in individual activities. At the same time, it is important to strive to maintain joint activities as well. Studies have uncovered a positive correlation between the amount of spouses' joint leisure time and their marital satisfaction, especially when their leisure activities involve high levels of communication (Holman & Jacquart, 1988; Smith, Snyder, Trull, & Monsma, 1988).

Divorce

"In the ten years that we were married I went from twenty-four to thirty-four and they were a very significant ten years. I started a career, started to succeed, bought my first house, had a child, you know, very significant years. And then all of a sudden, every goddamn thing, I'm back to zero. I have no house. I don't have a child. I don't have a wife. I don't have the same family. My economic position has been shattered. And nothing recoverable. All these goals which I had struggled for, every goddamn one of them, is gone."

—A recently divorced man quoted in *Marital Separation* (Weiss, 1975, p. 75)

 he dissolution of a marriage tends to be a bone-jarring event for most people, as the bitter words quoted above make clear. Any of the problems discussed in the preceding section may lead a couple to consider divorce. However, people appear to vary in their threshold for divorce just as they do in their threshold for marriage. Some couples will tolerate a great deal of disappointment and bickering without seriously considering divorce. Other couples are ready to call their attorney as soon as it becomes apparent that their expectations for marital bliss were somewhat unrealistic. Typically, however, divorce is the culmination of a gradual disintegration of the relationship brought about by an accumulation of many interrelated problems.

Increasing Rate of Divorce

Although relatively accurate statistics are available on divorce rates, it is still difficult to estimate the percentage of marriages that end in divorce. The usually cited ratio of marriages in a year to divorces in the same year is highly misleading. It would be more instructive to fol-

low people married in a particular year over a period of time, but little research of this nature has been done. In any case, it is clear that divorce rates have increased substantially in recent decades, as Figure 9.11 shows. The most widely cited recent estimates of future divorce risk are well over 50%. Martin and Bumpass (1989) project that *two-thirds* of today's marriages in the United States will result in separation or divorce.

A wide variety of social trends have probably contributed to the increase in the divorce rate (Raschke, 1987; White, 1990). The stigma attached to divorce has gradually eroded. Many religious denominations are becoming more tolerant of divorce, and marriage has thus lost some of its association with the sacred. The declining fertility rate and the consequent smaller families probably make divorce a more viable option. The entry of more women into the work force has made many wives less financially dependent on the continuation of their marriage. New attitudes emphasizing individual fulfillment seem to have counterbalanced older attitudes that encouraged dissatisfied spouses to suffer in silence. Reflecting all these trends, the legal barriers to divorce have also diminished.

Deciding on a Divorce

Divorces are often postponed repeatedly, and they are rarely executed without much forethought. Indecision is common, as roughly two out of five divorce petitions are eventually withdrawn (Donovan & Jackson, 1990). The

**FIGURE 9.11
Increasing divorce rates**
The percentage of marriages that end in divorce has been going up steadily for over a century. Today experts estimate that over 50% of marriages will end in divorce. (Source: Cherlin, 1981; Martin & Bumpass, 1989.)

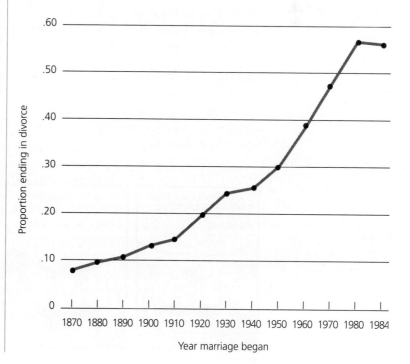

The high divorce rate has led to some novel ways of dealing with its worrisome legal aspects. Attorney Robert Nordyke discovered that the drive-up window at his new office—a former savings and loan branch in Salem, Oregon—was perfect for serving legal papers on his client's spouses.

decision to divorce usually is not a singular event, but rather the outcome of a long series of smaller decisions that may take years to unfold.

It is difficult to generalize about the relative merit of divorce as opposed to remaining in an unsatisfactory marriage. There is evidence that people who are currently divorced suffer a higher incidence of both physical and psychological maladies and are less happy than those who are currently married (Kitson & Morgan, 1990; Frank, 1985). Furthermore, divorce is often associated with great psychological distress in both spouses. Divorced men suffer primarily from a loss of emotional support and disrupted ties to friends and relatives (traditionally the wife's responsibility). Divorced women suffer more from reduced income (traditionally the husband's responsibility) (Gerstel, Reissman, & Rosenfield, 1985). Thus the distress of each spouse reflects the need to take over responsibilities that had been the traditional province of the other spouse. This observation suggests the intriguing possibility that a divorce may tend to be less upsetting for both partners in an egalitarian marriage that fails.

As painful as marital dissolution may be, remaining in an unhappy marriage is also distressing. A recent longitudinal study of wives (Schaefer & Burnett, 1987) found that marital quality was an even better predictor of a woman's psychological health three years later than her psychological health at the initial measurement. In particular, poor marital adjustment at time 1 was predictive of significant depression and anxiety at time 2. Other studies have found an association between marital distress and elevated rates of anxiety, depression, and drug disorders in both men and women, although it's hard to tell what's causing what in many of these studies (Gotlib & McCabe, 1990). These findings suggest that sticking it out in an unhappy marriage may be counterproductive.

Decisions about divorce must take into account the impact on a couple's children. Weighing this consideration is difficult, however, because divorces have highly varied effects on children, which depend on a complex constellation of interacting factors (Santrock & Sitterle, 1985). Whether children benefit if parents persevere and keep an unhappy marriage intact has been widely debated. Children of divorce and children from homes characterized by persistent marital discord are *both* more prone to adjustment problems than children of happily married parents. But several studies (e.g., Slater & Haber, 1984) have shown that children's adjustment is affected more by the amount of conflict between their parents than by family structure (divorced or intact) as such. All in all, the weight of evidence suggests that in the long run it is less damaging to the children if unhappy parents divorce than if the children grow up in an intact but dissension-ridden home (Demo & Acock, 1988). However, this assertion is based on the assumption that the parents' divorce brings their bickering to an end. Unfortunately, the conflicts between divorcing spouses often continue unabated for many years after they part. Goldberg (1985), for instance, describes a case history in which a man's ex-wife was still calling him 10 to 15 times a day to disturb and berate him three years after their divorce.

KUDZU by Doug Marlette. By permission of Doug Marlette and Creators Syndicate.

In any case, one should not underestimate the trauma that most children go through when their parents divorce. After a divorce, children may exhibit depression, anxiety, nightmares, dependency, aggression, withdrawal, distractibility, lowered academic performance, and reduced physical health (Guidubaldi, Perry, & Nastasi, 1987). Although these effects begin to dissipate in many children after a couple of years (Hetherington, 1991), divorce can have a lasting impact that may extend into adulthood. When Amato and Keith (1991) studied *adults* whose parents divorced when they were children, they found elevated rates of maladjustment, antisocial behavior, and marital instability and lower educational and occupational attainments than among adults whose parents stayed married.

Children have more adjustment problems when their parents go through a particularly bitter, acrimonious, and conflict-dominated divorce (Tschann, Johnston, Kline, & Wallerstein, 1989, 1990). Divorce also tends to be especially tough on boys whose mothers have sole custody and who therefore are denied a stable male role model (Hetherington, 1991). The children's recovery and subsequent adjustment seem to depend primarily on the quality of their relationship with the custodial parent and on how well the custodial parent is adjusting to the divorce (Stolberg, Camplair, Currier, & Wells, 1987).

Adjusting to Divorce

It is clear that divorce is an exceedingly stressful life event (Buehler & Langenbrunner, 1987). It often combines all four major sources of stress described in Chapter 3: frustration, conflict, pressure, and change. In most respects, divorce appears to be more difficult and disruptive for women than for men (Clarke-Stewart & Bailey, 1989). Women are more likely to assume the responsibility of raising the children, while they are less likely to have adequate income or a satisfying job. According to Weitzman (1989), divorced women experience greater stress and feel more financially strapped than divorced men. Paradoxically, though, women tend to experience serious mental health problems less often and have more positive feelings about their divorce than men (Diedrick, 1991; Kitson & Morgan, 1990). The reasons for these perplexing sex differences are not clear.

Obviously, newly divorced persons of either sex have numerous problems to confront. These problems include those in the following list (Raschke, 1987).

Second Chances: Men, Women, and Children a Decade after Divorce
by Judith S. Wallerstein and Sandra Blakeslee (Ticknor & Fields, 1990)

This book reports the findings of a large-scale longitudinal study of divorced couples and their children. Conventional wisdom holds that marital dissolution and its immediate aftermath constitutes a "crisis," after which each spouse has a "second chance" to find happiness. The children of divorce, too, are presumed to weather a time-limited trauma and ultimately to adjust positively to their parents' newly stabilized lives. Wallerstein and Blakeslee present surprising evidence that calls both assumptions into question. Many of the couples they studied were still grappling with negative emotions from their failed marriage *ten years* after it ended. Their children appeared to be even more vulnerable, often harboring intense fears of betrayal and rejection that carried into their own intimate relationships in adolescence and early adulthood.

Despite the sometimes disturbing nature of their findings, however, Wallerstein and Blakeslee maintain an upbeat attitude throughout. By deftly interweaving empirical findings with relevant case material, they educate the reader about potential pitfalls faced by members of dissolving families. Further, they convey hope that such awareness will enable everyone involved to cope with these challenges successfully.

Divorce is a different experience for children and adults because the children lose something that is fundamental to their development—the family structure. The family comprises the scaffolding upon which children mount successive developmental stages, from infancy into adolescence. It supports their psychological, physical, and emotional ascent into maturity. When that structure collapses, the children's world is temporarily without supports. And children, with a vastly compressed sense of time, do not know that the chaos is temporary. [p. 11]

• *The crisis of change.* It is hard to think of events that produce more far-reaching change than divorce. The divorced person's lifestyle is usually altered radically. Furthermore, because people tend to define themselves as somebody's spouse, the divorced person must revise his or her very sense of identity. The emotional crisis may peak long before the actual divorce. Nonetheless, the difficulties of postdivorce transitions in socializing, child rearing, and so forth may seem overwhelming.

• *Emotional problems.* A divorce may be preceded by much quarreling and reciprocal derogation by the partners. The hurtful remarks, although they may have been flung thoughtlessly in anger, are often difficult to dismiss. One or both of the former spouses may experience feelings of failure and shame. Divorced people may also be plagued by feelings of ambivalence toward their former partner. Feelings of continued attachment may be jumbled with feelings of bitterness and anger. Recently divorced people often experience separation distress marked by feelings of loneliness and longing for the presence of the former spouse.

• *Practical problems.* The emotional difficulties of divorce are usually accompanied by a variety of practical problems. If children are involved, arrangements for custody and support must be made. Both parents must adjust to a drastically different child-rearing situation. Patterns of socializing must be revamped. Old friendships with other couples are likely to decay, and new friendships must be forged. Although negative stereotypes of divorced people are less prevalent than before, they still exist. In particular, divorced women often are stereotyped as desperate for love and readily available for sex.

• *Rebuilding.* Although divorce is difficult, the difficulties are *not* insurmountable. People do successfully retrench and rebuild. One should not feel reluctant about seeking professional therapy or soliciting support from relatives or friends. In view of the enormous stress associated with divorce, a need for professional assistance should not be seen as an indication of personal inadequacy. Four common syndromes during the rebuilding period should be avoided (Cox, 1979).

1. *Retreat.* Some people retreat into a shell of self-pity. It is important to edge gradually back into interpersonal relationships.
2. *Rebound.* Some people jump back into the interpersonal marketplace too quickly and too eagerly. Obsessive pursuit of a new love may fog one's judgment and lead to another poor relationship.
3. *Return.* Some people are paralyzed by foolish and unrealistic yearning for the return of their former spouse. It is better to face up to reality and get on with life.
4. *Resentment.* Some people get bogged down by excessive resentment of their former spouse. This anger can have a very negative effect on children. It can also spill over and contaminate social relationships in general.

Remarriage

Evidence that courtship opportunities for the divorced are adequate is provided by the statistics on remarriage. Roughly three-quarters of divorced women and five-sixths of divorced men eventually remarry (Glick, 1984). About half of these remarriages occur within three years of the divorce. Among women, lesser education and lower income are associated with more rapid remarriage. In contrast, men who are better educated and financially well off tend to remarry more quickly. The greater one's age at the time of divorce, the lower the likelihood of remarriage, especially among women (Bumpass, Sweet, & Martin, 1990).

How successful are second marriages? The answer depends on your standard of comparison. Divorce rates *are* higher for second than for first marriages (White & Booth, 1985). However, this finding may simply indicate that this group of people see divorce as a reasonable alternative to an unsatisfactory marriage. Nonetheless, studies of marital adjustment suggest that second marriages are slightly less successful than first marriages and that marital satisfaction in remarriages is somewhat lower for women than men (Vemer, Coleman, Ganong, & Cooper, 1989). Of course, if you consider that in this pool of people *all* the first marriages ran into serious trouble, then the second marriages look rather good by comparison. In fact, in one study (Furstenberg & Spanier, 1984) the majority of remarried individuals reported that they had selected a spouse far more wisely the second time around.

It is more appropriate to evaluate remarriage by comparing divorced people who remarry against divorced people who do not. When Spanier and Furstenberg (1982) made this comparison, they found that those who remarried were *not* any healthier or happier, on the average, than those who did not. However, they did find that the quality of subjects' second marriage *was* related to their well-being. Thus many divorced people do eventually find happiness in a subsequent marriage.

Alternatives to Marriage

e noted at the beginning of the chapter that the traditional model of marriage has been undermined by a variety of social trends. More and more people are choosing alternatives to marriage. Let us examine some of these alternatives.

Remaining Single

There is substantial pressure to marry in our society. We are socialized to believe that we are not complete until we have found our "other half" and have entered into a partnership for life (Shostak, 1987). We also refer to people's "failure" to marry. In spite of this pressure, an increasing proportion of young adults are remaining single, as Figure 9.12 shows.

Does the increased number of single adults mean that people are turning away from the institution of marriage? Perhaps a little, but for the most part, no. A variety of factors have contributed to the growth of the single population. Much of this growth is due to the increase in the median age at which people marry and the increased rate of divorce. More important, the vast majority of single, never-married people *do* expect to marry eventually (Cargan & Melko, 1982). Furthermore, there has been no rush to embrace singlehood among young people, as the percentage of high school seniors expecting to marry (95% for girls and 90% for boys) has remained very high and very stable since the 1960s (Thornton, 1989).

Singlehood has been plagued by two very disparate stereotypes of the single life (Keith, 1986). On the one hand, single people are sometimes portrayed as carefree swingers who are too busy enjoying the fruits of promiscuity to shoulder marital responsibilities. On the other hand, they are seen as losers who did not succeed in snaring a mate. They may be portrayed as socially inept, maladjusted, frustrated, lonely, and bitter. These stereotypes do a great injustice to the diversity that exists among single people.

The swinging-single stereotype appears to be a media-manufactured illusion designed to lure singles and their money into nightclubs and bars. In reality, the singles-bar circuit is frequently described as an experience in alienation and disappointment. In comparison with married people, single people do have sex with more partners. They have sex less frequently, however, and they rate their sexual relations as less satisfying than their married counterparts (Cargan & Melko, 1982).

As for the "maladjusted, bitter" stereotype, it is true that single people have an elevated incidence of mental and physical health problems (Gotlib & McCabe, 1991; Trovato & Lauris, 1989) and they do rate themselves as less happy than married people (Lee, Seccombe, & Shehan, 1991). The differences are modest, however, and the happiness gap has shrunk in recent years, especially among women (Glenn & Weaver, 1988). Although popular stereotypes suggest that being single is more difficult for women than for men, the empirical data suggest just the opposite. Most studies find that single women are healthier and more satisfied with their lives than single men, and various lines of evidence suggest that women get along without men better than men get along without women (Cargan & Melko, 1982; Glenn & Weaver, 1988).

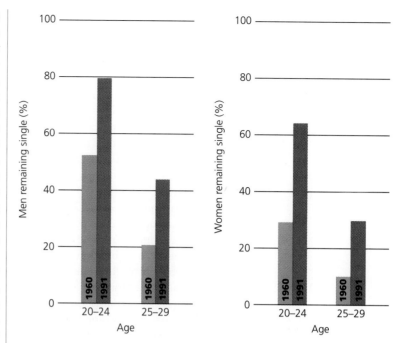

Many singles must cope with some special challenges in addition to the problems confronted by most adults. Since adult social interaction tends to revolve around couples, single people may experience some extra difficulty in developing a satisfactory friendship network. The absence of a spouse to lean on makes an independent personality a virtual necessity. Single people who try to climb the corporate ladder have some bias working against them, as they are seen as less stable than their married counterparts. In addition, singles generally have lower lifetime earnings and may face discrimination in credit, insurance, and housing (Keith, 1986).

Although the increase in the single population does not reflect a widespread rejection of marriage, it is leading to more favorable attitudes toward singles. People used to assume that there was something wrong with an adult who remained single. Today more people view singlehood as a reasonable option rather than a deviant lifestyle.

Cohabitation

As we saw earlier, *cohabitation* refers to living together in a sexually intimate relationship outside of marriage. Recent years have witnessed a tremendous increase in the number of cohabiting couples. In 1991 slightly over 3 million unmarried couples were living together in the United States. They represented about 5% of all couples (married and unmarried) sharing living quarters at that time. However, the percentage of couples living together at any one time does not accurately convey how wide-

FIGURE 9.12
The proportion of young people who remain single
This graph shows the percentage of single men and women, aged 20–24 and 25–29, in 1991 and in 1960 (based on U.S. Census data). The proportion of people remaining single has increased substantially for both sexes, in both age brackets. Single men continue to outnumber single women in these age groups.

spread this phenomenon has become because cohabiting unions tend to be short—about half of cohabiting couples either get married or break up within 18 months (Bumpass & Sweet, 1989). It is more instructive to study people getting married for the first time and determine what percentage of them have cohabited before their marriage (either with their spouse-to-be or with someone else). Studies indicate that this percentage has increased dramatically, from around 11% in 1970 to nearly 50% today (Bumpass et al., 1991).

Cohabitation tends to conjure up images of college students and other well-educated young couples without children, but these images are misleading. In reality, cohabitation rates have always been higher in the less educated segments of the population. Moreover, almost half of cohabitants have been married previously and one study found that 40% of cohabitating couples had children, mostly from previous marriages (Bumpass et al., 1991).

The principal motivations for cohabitation (as opposed to marriage) include more individualism, more freedom, no need to divorce, the advantage of sharing living expenses, and the opportunity to check compatibility before marriage (Bumpass et al., 1991; Kotkin, 1985). Those who choose cohabitation tend to be liberal in values, nonreligious, and pragmatic about intimate relationships (Macklin, 1983; Newcomb, 1983; Tanfer, 1987).

Although many people see cohabitation as a threat to the institution of marriage, most theorists see it as a new stage in the courtship process—a sort of trial marriage. In accord with the latter view, about three-quarters of cohabitants expect to marry their current partner

(Bumpass et al., 1991). Thus it appears that cohabitation does not represent a repudiation of marriage.

In discussing the pros and cons of cohabitation, White (1987) points out that it may provide an opportunity for young people to experiment with marital-like responsibilities. As a prelude to marriage, it should reduce the likelihood of entering marriage with unrealistic expectations. Living together may also permit people to identify incompatible mates more effectively than a traditional courtship. These considerations suggest that couples who cohabit before they marry should go on to more successful marriages than those who do not.

Although White's analyses seem plausible, researchers have *not* found that premarital cohabitation increases the likelihood of subsequent marital success. In fact, studies have found an association between premarital cohabitation and *higher* divorce rates in Canada, Sweden, and the United States (Schoen, 1992). Why is cohabitation associated with marital instability? Most theorists argue that it's because this nontraditional lifestyle has historically attracted a liberal and unconventional segment of the population with a weak commitment to the institution of marriage and relatively few qualms about getting divorced. There is considerable logical and empirical support for this explanation (Glenn, 1990; Thomson & Colella, 1992), which attributes the elevated divorce rates among cohabitants to their personal characteristics rather than to the experience of cohabitation itself. If this explanation is accurate, the elevated divorce rate among cohabitants should gradually shrink to normal as cohabitation becomes more common because the population of cohabitants will increasingly resemble the general population. A trend in this direction is already apparent (Schoen, 1992), as you can see in Figure 9.13.

Gay Relationships

Up to this point, for the sake of simplicity, we have focused our attention on *heterosexuals*, people who seek emotional-sexual relationships with members of the other sex. We have been ignoring a significant minority group: *homosexual* men and women, who seek emotional-sexual relationships with members of the same sex. How large is this minority group? It's difficult to say because negative attitudes toward homosexuality in our society continue to prevent many gays from "coming out of the closet." The best empirical data on the issue (which aren't very good) suggest that roughly 2% of women and 4

FIGURE 9.13
Cohabitation and marital instability
Comparisons of people who cohabit before marriage and those who do not have generally found higher rates of marital dissolution among the cohabiters. The data summarized here compare rates of marital disruption (either divorce or separation) in the first four years of marriage for cohorts of women born in various periods. These data, based on research by Schoen (1992), suggest that the differences between cohabiters and noncohabiters in marital instability are shrinking.

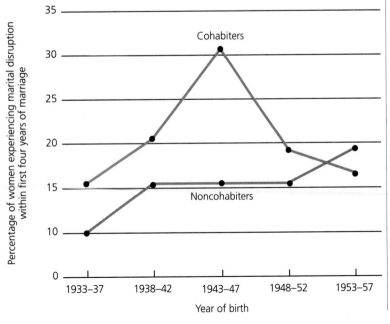

to 5% of men are *exclusively* homosexual (Van Wyk & Geist, 1984). These figures probably are on the low side, however, given the widespread wariness among gays about openly acknowledging their sexual orientation (Gonsiorek & Weinrich, 1991). Estimates by some gay-rights groups range as high as 10% for both sexes. Although these estimates are very speculative, they may not be unreasonable if one's definition of homosexuality does not require an exclusive commitment to same-sex relationships (Paul & Weinrich, 1982). Thus there may be as many as 25 million gay people in the United States.

A separate section devoted to gay couples may seem to imply that the dynamics of their close relationships are different from those of heterosexual couples. Actually, this assumption appears to be much less well founded than it is widely assumed to be, even though gays' close relationships unfold in a radically different social context than heterosexuals' marital relationships. As Garnets and Kimmel (1991) point out, gay relationships "develop within a social context of societal disapproval with an absence of social legitimization and support; families and other social institutions often stigmatize such relationships and there are no prescribed roles and behaviors to structure such relationships" (p. 170). About two-thirds of Americans still condemn homosexual relations as morally wrong, and gays continue to be frequent victims of discrimination in employment and housing, not to mention verbal and physical abuse (Herek, 1991). Gay couples cannot legally formalize their unions by getting married, and in fact laws prohibiting same-gender sexual relations are still on the books in 24 states in the United States. Gay couples are also denied various economic benefits available to married couples (Rivera, 1991). They can't file joint tax returns, for example, and they generally can't obtain employer-provided health insurance for their partner.

Given the lack of moral, social, legal, and economic supports for gay relationships, are gay unions less stable than marital unions? Researchers have not been able to collect adequate data on this question yet, but the very limited data available suggest that gay couples' relationships *are* somewhat briefer and more prone to breakups than heterosexual marriages (Peplau, 1991). Insofar as this may be true, Letitia Anne Peplau suggests that it's probably because gay relationships face fewer barriers to dissolution—that is, fewer practical problems that make breakups difficult or costly (Peplau, 1988; Peplau & Cochran, 1990). Married cou-

ples considering divorce often face a variety of such barriers—attorneys' fees, concerns about children, wrangling over joint investments, and the disapproval of their families—which may motivate them to salvage their deteriorating relationship. Gay couples do not have to wrestle with the legal formalities of divorce and they are less likely to have children, joint investments, or family opposition to worry about.

Although the social context in which gay relationships evolve differs greatly from that of marital relationships, recent studies have documented striking commonalities between heterosexual and homosexual couples. They report similar levels of love and commitment in their relationships, similar levels of overall satisfaction with their relationships, and similar levels of sexual satisfaction (Peplau, 1991). They are similar in the factors that predict satisfaction with a relationship (Kurdek & Schmitt, 1988) and in the problems that contribute to breakups (Blumstein & Schwartz, 1983). Resemblance is also apparent when researchers study what gays and heterosexuals want out of their relationships (Peplau, 1988; see Figure 9.14) and what they look for in a prospective partner (Laner, 1988).

Although research indicates that there is considerable continuity between homosexual and heterosexual relationships, basic misconceptions about the nature of gay relationships remain widespread. Let's look at some of these inaccurate stereotypes.

First, many people assume that most gay couples adopt traditional masculine and feminine roles in their relationships, with one part-

Despite the common stereotype that homosexuals rarely form long-term relationships, the fact is that they are similar to heterosexual couples in their attitudes and behaviors, and many enjoy long-term commitments in marriage-like arrangements.

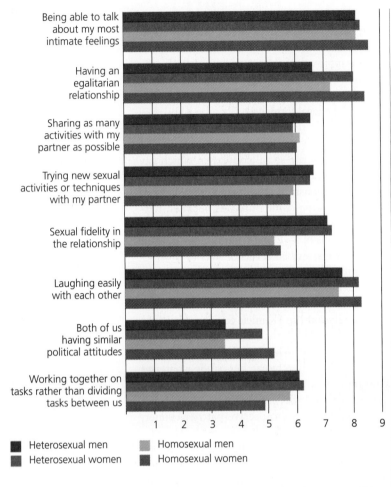

Being able to talk about my most intimate feelings

Having an egalitarian relationship

Sharing as many activities with my partner as possible

Trying new sexual activities or techniques with my partner

Sexual fidelity in the relationship

Laughing easily with each other

Both of us having similar political attitudes

Working together on tasks rather than dividing tasks between us

■ Heterosexual men   ▨ Homosexual men
▨ Heterosexual women   ▨ Homosexual women

FIGURE 9.14
Comparing priorities in intimate relationships Peplau (1981) asked heterosexual men and women and homosexual men and women to rate the significance (9 = high importance) of various aspects of their intimate relationships. As you can see, all four groups returned fairly similar ratings. Peplau concludes that gays and heterosexuals largely want the same things out of their relationships.

ner behaving in a cross-sexed manner. This appears to be the case in only a small minority of couples. In fact, on the whole, gay couples appear to be more flexible about role expectations than heterosexuals (Marecek, Finn, & Cardell, 1988; Zacks, Green, & Marrow, 1988). Gay couples display a more equitable balance of power in their relationships than married couples and are less likely to adhere to traditional gender roles.

Second, it is widely believed that gays are characterized by exceptionally high levels of sexual activity, and that they engage in casual sex with a spectacular number of partners. In reality, very high levels of sexual activity are characteristic only of certain segments of the gay male population, and are virtually nonexistent among lesbians (Tripp, 1987). In fact, within the context of committed relationships, lesbians exhibit strikingly low rates of sexual activity (Blumstein & Schwartz, 1990; Nichols, 1990). Regardless of their sexual orientation (gay or straight), males tend to have somewhat different motivations than females for engaging in sex. Women are more likely to regard sexual activity as an expression of affection and commitment. Men tend to attach more importance to sexual pleasure and conquest (Leigh, 1989).

Their socialization is more likely than women's to stress the desirability of varied and frequent sexual activity. The gay man, being free of the strictures of marriage and having his choice of like-minded partners, has simply been in a better position than his heterosexual counterpart to act on this masculine socialization (Blasband & Peplau, 1985). Since the advent of AIDS, however, homosexual men have faced unprecedented pressure, even within the gay community, to limit the number of their sexual partners (Kyle, 1989).

Third, popular stereotypes suggest that gays only rarely get involved in long-term intimate relationships. In reality, most homosexual men and nearly all homosexual women prefer stable, long-term relationships and at any one time roughly half of gay men and three-quarters of lesbians are involved in committed relationships (Macklin, 1987; Peplau, 1991). Lesbian relationships are generally sexually exclusive. About half of committed male couples have "open" relationships, allowing for the possibility of sexual activity (but not affection) with outsiders. While intimate relationships among gays appear to be less stable than marriages among straights, they may compare favorably with the relationships of heterosexual cohabitating couples, who offer a more appropriate baseline for comparison. Both gay and heterosexual cohabitants may face opposition to their relationship from their families and from society in general, and neither enjoys the legal and social sanctions of marriage.

Finally, an inevitable fate for any stereotyped group is that its members are lumped together and simplistically assumed to be identical. In reality, diversity is as great among gays as among straights, dooming to failure any attempt to classify gays into "types" (Tripp, 1987). To identify an individual as homosexual is to say nothing more about that person's unique lifestyle, personality, or values than to describe someone as heterosexual.

Summary

The traditional model of marriage is being challenged by the increasing acceptability of singlehood, the increasing popularity of cohabitation, the reduced premium on permanence, changes in gender roles, the increasing prevalence of voluntary childlessness, and the decline of the traditional nuclear family. Nonetheless, marriage remains quite popular.

People vary in the strength of their motivation to marry. Many people's reasons for marrying are less than ideal. Mate selection is influenced by endogamy, homogamy, and one's ideals. According to Murstein, the process of mate selection goes through three stages, in which the individual emphasizes the stimulus value of the potential partner, value compatibility, and the adequacy of role enactments.

When marital satisfaction is mapped across the family life cycle, researchers find a U-shaped curve reflecting lower satisfaction in the middle stages. Newly married couples tend to be very happy before the arrival of children. Today more couples are struggling with the decision whether to have children. The arrival of children is a major transition that is handled best by parents who have realistic expectations about the difficulties inherent in raising children. As children reach adolescence, parents should expect more conflict as their influence declines. They must learn to relate to their children as adults and help launch them into the adult world. Once the children have struck out on their own, marital satisfaction tends to rise once again.

Gaps in expectations about marital roles, or unrealistic expectations in general, may create marital stress. Disparities in expectations in regard to gender roles and the distribution of housework may be especially common and problematic. Work concerns clearly can spill over to influence marital functioning, but the links between parents' employment and marital adjustment are complex. Wealth does not ensure marital happiness, but a lack of money can produce marital problems. Inadequate communication is a commonly reported marital problem, which is increasingly analyzed from an attributional perspective. In-law problems appear to be declining. Sexual difficulties, jealousy, and growing in different directions are other problems that are common in marital relationships.

Divorce is becoming increasingly common for a variety of reasons. Unpleasant as divorce may be, the evidence suggests that toughing it out in an unhappy marriage is often worse. Divorce can create problems for children, but so does a strife-ridden intact home. Divorce is quite stressful and may lead to a variety of emotional and practical problems associated with the crisis of change. In rebuilding their lives, people should try to avoid four syndromes: retreat, rebound, return, and resentment. A substantial majority of divorced people remarry. These second marriages have a somewhat lower probability of success than first marriages.

An increasing portion of the young population is remaining single, but this does not mean that people are turning away from the institution of marriage. Single people are often stereotyped as unhappy losers or carefree swingers. Both pictures are largely inaccurate. Although singles generally have the same adjustment problems as married couples, evidence suggests that singles tend to be slightly less happy. The prevalence of cohabitation has increased dramatically. Nonetheless, it appears to be more of a prelude than an alternative to marriage. Logically, one might expect cohabitation to facilitate marital success, but research has consistently found an association between cohabitation and marital instability.

Gay relationships develop in a starkly different social context than marital relationships. Nonetheless, studies have found that heterosexual and homosexual couples are very similar in many ways. Gay relationships are characterized by great diversity. It is not true that gays usually assume traditional masculine and feminine roles. Nor is it true that they rarely get involved in long-term intimate relationships. Popular beliefs about extremely high levels of sexual activity among gays appear to be inaccurate for lesbians, though somewhat less so for gay men.

The Application focuses on the manipulative games that couples tend to play. We hope that your awareness of these game-playing tendencies may reduce your propensity to get locked into such counterproductive patterns.

APPLICATION Understanding the Games Couples Play

Indicate whether the following statements are true or false

1.

I sometimes catch myself being manipulative in intimate relationships.

2.

In interacting with my partner, I sometimes notice that we get into subtle little battles to demonstrate our superiority.

3.

It often seems that people are operating with a hidden agenda.

4.

Many people seem to derive some sort of perverse satisfaction from laying guilt trips on others.

5.

I sometimes think that life would be simpler if couples would tell each other what they are really thinking.

If you indicated that several of the items on the left are true, you have noticed that people often tend to play games with each other. We all play games at least occasionally. This reality has been most insightfully analyzed by Eric Berne (1961, 1964, 1972). He developed *transactional analysis,* a broad theory of personality and interpersonal relations that emphasizes patterns of communication.

What are games in interpersonal relationships? In Berne's scheme, *games* are manipulative interactions that progress toward a predictable outcome, in which people conceal their true motives. Games are not limited to intimate relationships. We may play games with co-workers, neighbors, and even strangers. However, games become particularly problematic in intimate relationships, where authentic communication is critical. Intimate couples are also vulnerable to games because their relationships offer opportunities for *repetition* of destructive patterns. In this Application we will introduce you to the basics of transactional analysis so that you can try to spot some of this game playing in your own intimate interactions.

Ego States in Transactional Analysis

In transactional analysis an *ego state* is a personality structure consisting of a coherent system of internal feelings. Berne postulated the existence of three ego states: the Child, the Parent, and the Adult. (When these terms are capitalized, they refer to the ego state; otherwise they refer to the actual statuses of child, parent, and adult.) The theory states that we directly experience these ego states and that we shift in and out of them in response to the demands of the situation and our personal history. It is important to understand that there is no one-to-one correspondence between these ego states and a person's actual status. In other words, one does not have to be a child to experience the Child ego state or a parent to experience the Parent ego state.

Child

The Child ego state consists of "recordings" of childhood experiences that we retain throughout adulthood. In some situations we fall back into our childlike patterns of spontaneity and irresponsibility. When faced with frustration, for instance, a person who used to throw temper tantrums in childhood may revert to this strategy as an adult. In doing so, the person is operating from the Child ego state. Although this particular example is somewhat negative, operating from the Child ego state should not be equated with behaving immaturely. On the positive side, it is entry into the Child ego state that facilitates fresh and spontaneous enjoyment of recreational activities.

Parent

The Parent ego state also consists of recordings from childhood. These recordings, however, largely involve assertions about right and wrong. They represent values and norms adopted from one's parents and other authority figures. Suppose you suddenly realized that you were reading this text too lackadaisically, without really digesting the information. If you scolded yourself for your lethargic attitude, you would be operating from the Parent ego state. The Parent in us jumps in with criticism when we violate the rules instilled by our parents. The Parent is like a solemn judge, handing down decisions about the acceptability of our own behavior and the behavior of others.

Adult

The Adult is more rational and less emotional than the Child or the Parent. We shift into the Adult ego state when we dispassionately weigh alternative courses of action, when we systematically endeavor to solve a problem, and so forth. The Adult is tuned to reality and attempts to maximize efficiency. Like the ego described by Freud, the Adult has "executive" responsibilities for making important decisions, which often involve mediating between the Child and the Parent.

Types of Transactions

The fundamental unit of social interaction in transactional analysis is the transaction. A *transaction* consists of an initial statement by a communicating source and a response by the receiver. There are several classes of transactions, depending on which ego states are communicating with each other.

In a *complementary transaction,* the receiver responds from the same ego state that the source has addressed. Thus the two persons communicate from *compatible* ego states. Two kinds of complementary transactions are possible. In Type I transactions the two persons are sending and receiving from the same ego state (see Figure 9.15). In other words, they communicate Adult-to-Adult, Child-to-Child, or Parent-to-Parent. In Type II transactions the two persons do not address each other as equals (see Figure 9.16). For example, the transaction might go Parent-to-Child and Child-to-Parent or Child-to-Adult and Adult-to-Child. In either kind of complementary transaction, people are cooperating in the communication effort.

In a *crossed transaction,* the receiver does not respond from the ego state addressed by the source. In a sense, the receiver refuses to cooperate with the source. Hence the two persons communicate from *incompatible* ego states. An Adult-to-Adult transmission, for example, might be answered with a Parent-to-Child response. A variety of combinations are possible for crossed transactions, as you can see in Figure 9.17. Crossed transactions tend to undermine effective communication and may create tension between the persons involved.

An *ulterior transaction* is a special type of complementary transaction that includes hidden messages intended to serve ulterior motives. These transactions are characterized by duplicity and pretense. They lie at the core of most games. In ulterior transactions *two* messages are sent and received. At the surface level is the readily manifest message. Beneath the surface is a latent but more meaningful exchange. Often the manifest transmission is Adult-to-Adult for the sake of appearances. Beneath the surface, however, an altogether different sort of communication may be taking place.

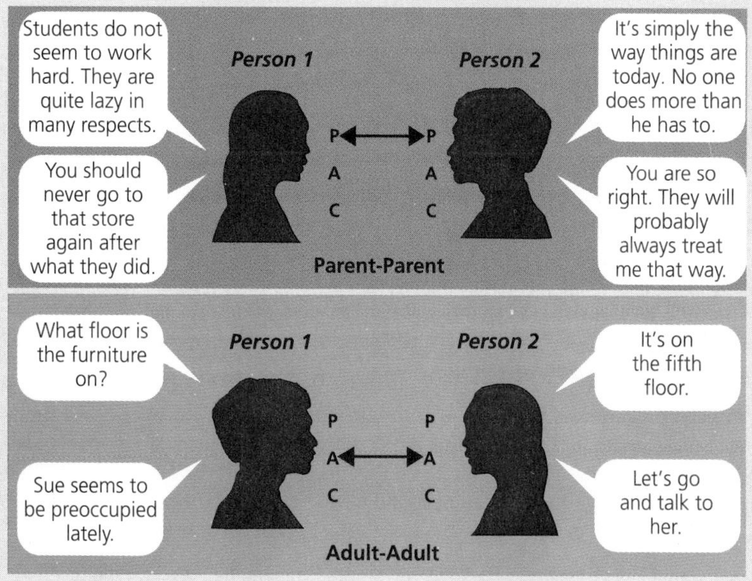

Games in Intimate Relationships

There are many kinds of games, including what Berne calls life games, party games, marital games, and sexual games. Our parents start shaping our preferences for certain games during our childhood. As adults, we may carry these game-playing tendencies into our intimate relationships. A common problem for couples is that they tend to play the same destructive games over and over, often without recognizing it.

If It Weren't for You

This game is commonly played by marital partners and other couples who have been together for awhile. One spouse charges the other with restricting her or his behavior. A wife, for example, may casually bring up the fact that a friend will be receiving a graduate degree soon. Her husband may innocently respond, "That's great." His response sets the stage for the wife to assert, "If it weren't for you, I could have gone to graduate school." Thus an old source of disharmony may be resurrected. There are a number of potential payoffs for the initiator of this game. Perhaps the wife didn't go to graduate school because she was afraid of the challenge. The self-deception in this game, however, permits her to deny her hidden insecurities and thereby maintain greater self-esteem. The guilt laid on her husband also provides a bargain-

ing advantage in subsequent transactions.

Courtroom

"Courtroom" requires the availability of a third party who gets thrust (often with much discomfort) into the center of the game. In the presence of one's partner, a person says to the third party, "Let me tell you what this clown [turkey, ogre, etc.] did yesterday." The "plaintiff" then launches into a distorted account of the other partner's allegedly terrible behavior. The aim in this game is to make the "defendant" partner feel guilty so as to gain an advantage in future transactions. Part of

the appeal of this game is that it's hard for the defendant not to play. Given the situation, the defendant has little choice but to mount a rebuttal.

Corner

In this game one partner corners the other in a no-win situation. For example, the initiator, who normally handles a particular household chore—buying the groceries, say—asks the other partner to assume the responsibility today. If the second partner says no, he or she is condemned for failing to take on an adequate share of household duties. If the second partner agrees and does the gro-

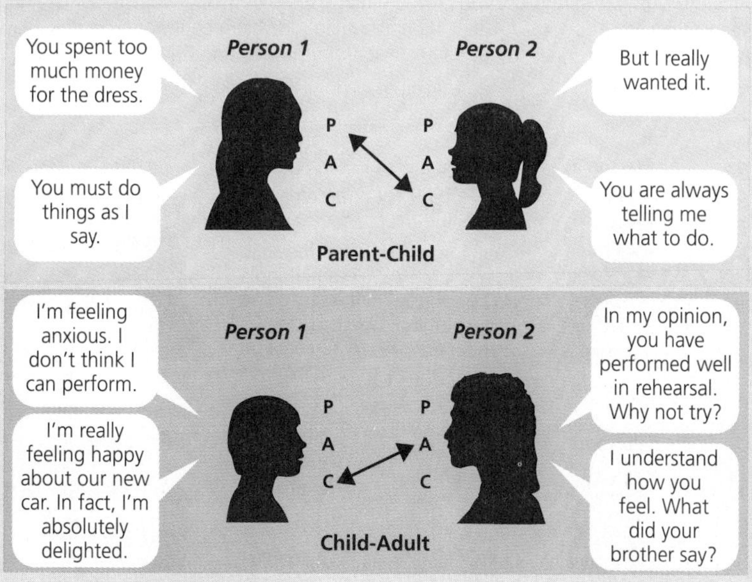

FIGURE 9.15
Type I complementary transactions
In Type I complementary transactions, two people address each other as equals.

Parent-Parent

Person 1: Students do not seem to work hard. They are quite lazy in many respects. / You should never go to that store again after what they did.

Person 2: It's simply the way things are today. No one does more than he has to. / You are so right. They will probably always treat me that way.

Adult-Adult

Person 1: What floor is the furniture on? / Sue seems to be preoccupied lately.

Person 2: It's on the fifth floor. / Let's go and talk to her.

FIGURE 9.16
Type II complementary transactions
In Type II complementary transactions, the receiver responds from the ego state addressed by the source, but the persons do not address each other as equals.

Parent-Child

Person 1: You spent too much money for the dress. / You must do things as I say.

Person 2: But I really wanted it. / You are always telling me what to do.

Child-Adult

Person 1: I'm feeling anxious. I don't think I can perform. / I'm really feeling happy about our new car. In fact, I'm absolutely delighted.

Person 2: In my opinion, you have performed well in rehearsal. Why not try? / I understand how you feel. What did your brother say?

Games People Play
by Eric Berne (Grove Press, 1964)

It's hard to believe that this classic best-seller is over 25 years old. Reviewers have called it "disturbing" and "chilling" because of the way it cuts through our social facades to lay bare the guile, sham, and fraud that characterize so much of our interpersonal behavior. The book has one shortcoming, in that some of Berne's analyses assume traditional gender roles, which are fading today. With the exception of this minor problem, Berne's descriptions of 120 games remain shrewd and discerning.

Fortunately, the rewards of game-free intimacy, which is or should be the most perfect form of human living, are so great that even precariously balanced personalities can safely and joyfully relinquish their games if an appropriate partner can be found for the better relationship. [p. 62]

cery shopping, the initiator finds fault with the job, asserting that "the asparagus looks terrible, you got the wrong kind of paper towels," and so forth. Thus the second partner can't win either way. Regardless of which way the second partner goes, the initiator garners more appreciation for the chore that he or she normally handles.

Threadbare

Spouses play "Threadbare" to gain more control over family finances. A spouse makes an apparent sacrifice, going without something that would require some expenditure. The hidden agenda is to make it difficult for the other spouse to spend money without guilt. Let's say a husband continues to drive a shabby old beat-up car that he really could afford to replace. Driving the car *appears* to be a sacrifice and allows him to harp constantly on any money his wife spends. Often the sacrifice only appears to be significant. The husband may not really care what kind of car he drives, but he pretends that he does. If the car were important to him, he would probably find some other sacrifice to make.

Why Don't You—Yes, But

This is a game of one-upmanship. One partner mentions a problem to the other, who innocently offers possible solutions—only to have them all rejected. Let's say a wife mentions some difficulty in correcting a child's problem behavior. The husband responds sincerely with a series of ideas: "Why don't you . . . ?" However, the issue was brought up not to solicit suggestions but to *reject* them. The wife has already thought of all the obvious possibilities and rattles off a putdown for each one: "Yes, but . . ." This game allows the initiator to demonstrate his or her superiority while making the other party feel inadequate.

Sweetheart

"Sweetheart" is a simple little gambit in which one partner tells a subtly derogatory story about the other partner, ending with "Isn't that right, sweetheart?" The pseudo-affectionate ending makes it more difficult for the second spouse to issue a denial.

Beyond Games

We have discussed only a small sampling of the games Berne described. This sampling, however, should clarify the problem with games: they are hollow, deceitful, manipulative patterns of interaction. Game playing sabotages genuine intimacy and promotes animosity and alienation.

Can couples get away from game playing? According to Berne, the answer is yes. The key is to become aware of your counterproductive patterns of interaction. Berne felt that once couples gained insight into their games, they could choose not to play. Thus, by promoting this kind of insight, transactional analysis may help people to achieve greater intimacy.

FIGURE 9.17
Crossed transactions
In crossed transactions, people communicate from incompatible ego states, as the receiver does not respond from the ego state addressed by the source. In the exchanges in the upper left portion of the figure, for example, the sender sends an Adult-to-Adult message, but the other person responds Parent-to-Child.

Key Learning Objectives

1. List six social trends that are undermining the traditional model of marriage.
2. Discuss several factors that influence the motivation to marry and the selection of a mate.
3. Summarize evidence on predictors of marital success.
4. Describe the family life cycle and its relation to marital satisfaction.
5. Discuss changing attitudes toward couples who choose not to have children.
6. Identify common problems that surface as a family's children reach adolescence and adulthood.
7. Discuss how unrealistic expectations and gaps in role expectations may affect marital adjustment.
8. Summarize how spouses' work affects their marital satisfaction and their children.
9. Discuss how financial issues and poor communication are related to marital adjustment.
10. Discuss how in-law problems and sexual problems are related to marital adjustment.
11. Discuss how the problems of jealousy and growing in different directions are related to marital adjustment.
12. Summarize evidence on divorce rates and the pros and cons of divorce.
13. List four sets of problems associated with divorce and four postdivorce syndromes to be avoided.
14. Summarize data on the frequency and success of remarriage.
15. Describe stereotypes of single life and summarize evidence on the adjustment of single people.
16. Discuss the prevalence of cohabitation and whether it improves the probability of marital success.
17. Summarize research on intimate relationships among homosexual couples.
18. Explain the games and ego states posited by Eric Berne's theory of transactional analysis.
19. Describe three types of transactions outlined by Berne.
20. Summarize the essence of the games described in the Application.

Key Terms

cohabitation
complementary transaction
crossed transaction
ego state
endogamy
family life cycle
games
homogamy

marriage
perspective taking
romantic jealousy
sociology
transaction
transactional analysis
ulterior transaction

Key People

Eric Berne
Bernard Murstein
Letitia Anne Peplau

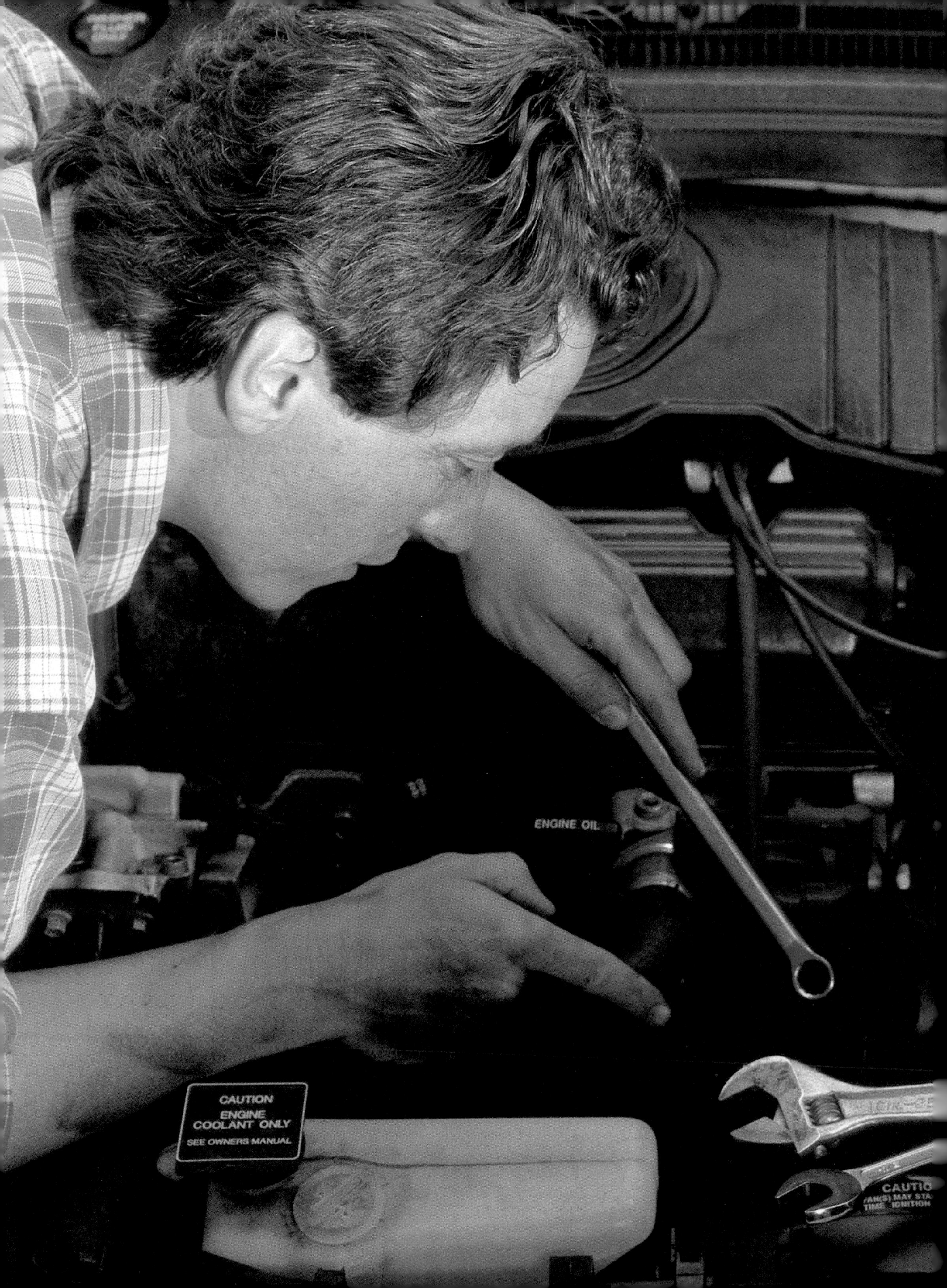
ENGINE OIL
CAUTION
ENGINE
COOLANT ONLY
SEE OWNERS MANUAL

10

Gender and Behavior

"N CLASSES, I EXPERIENCED MYSELF as a person to be taken lightly. In one seminar, I was never allowed to finish a sentence. There seemed to be a tacit understanding that I never had anything to say."

–A woman quoted in *The Classroom Climate: A Chilly One for Women* (Hall & Sandler, 1982, p. 7)

"I could have made her feel better," said the young man, "if I'd told her that I had trouble speaking in class because I was very self-conscious. But instead of telling her (which would have helped me too), I didn't say anything. Trivial as it was, I couldn't bring myself to say that I, at twenty-one, a man who hoped to be a great writer, couldn't raise my hand in class."

—A man quoted in *Dilemmas of Masculinity* (Komarovsky, 1976, p. 165)

The woman and man quoted above feel boxed in by gender roles. They're struggling with the limitations placed on their behavior by virtue of their sex. They aren't unique or unusual. Think about the times you have changed your behavior to bring it into line with society's concepts of masculinity and femininity.

Before proceeding further, we need to define some terms. In the context of this discussion, *sex refers to the biologically based categories of male and female.* In contrast, *gender refers to culturally constructed distinctions between masculinity and femininity* that don't necessarily correspond with one's biological sex (see Figure 10.1). For example, it is possible for males to be "feminine" and for females to be "masculine," although the opposite is more likely. Another way of making this distinction is this: We are *born* male or female (sex), but we gradually *become* masculine or feminine (gender) through complex developmental processes that take years to unfold.

In this chapter we'll examine the role of gender in our lives. We'll address a number of complex and controversial questions. Are there genuine behavioral differences between the sexes? If so, how do they develop? What are traditional gender-role expectations? Are they healthy or unhealthy? Why are gender roles in our society changing, and what does the future hold? In the Application we'll explore gender and communication styles.

Gender Stereotypes

bviously women and men differ biologically, both with regard to genitalia and other aspects of their anatomy and with regard to their physiological functioning. The readily apparent physical disparities between males and females lead us to expect other differences as well. You recall from Chapter 5 that *stereotypes* are widely held beliefs that people have certain characteristics simply because of their membership in a particular group. **Gender stereotypes are widely shared beliefs about males' and females' abilities, personality traits, and social behavior.** Stereotypes based on sex are very prevalent throughout the world. Research indicates that there is a great deal of consensus in our society on *supposed* behavioral differences between men and women (Broverman et al., 1972; Smith & Midlarsky, 1985). People seem to subscribe to this consensus regardless of their age, sex, marital status, or educational background.

These gender stereotypes are too numerous to summarize here. Instead, you can examine Figure 10.2, which lists some behavioral characteristics thought to be associated with femininity and masculinity. This list is based on a

Gender-Related Concepts	
Sex	Biologically based categories of male and female, determined at birth
Gender	Culturally determined distinctions between masculinity and femininity
Gender identity	An individual's perception of himself or herself as male or female
Gender stereotypes	Widely held and often inaccurate beliefs about males' and females' abilities, personality traits, and social behavior
Gender differences	Actual disparities in behavior between the sexes, based on research observations
Gender roles	Culturally defined expectations about appropriate behavior for males and females
Gender-role identity	A person's identification with the traits regarded as masculine or feminine (one's sense of being masculine or feminine)
Sexual orientation	A person's preference for sexual partners of the other sex (heterosexual), the same sex (homosexual), or both sexes (bisexual)

FIGURE 10.1
Terminology related to gender
The topic of gender involves many closely related ideas that are easy to confuse. The gender-related concepts introduced in this chapter are summarized here for easy comparison.

study in which subjects were asked to indicate the extent to which various traits were characteristic of each sex (Broverman et al., 1972). Although this particular study was conducted in 1972, its findings are still relevant to us today, for, in general, gender stereotypes have remained remarkably stable (Martin, 1987; Ruble, 1983). The list may contain a few surprises, but you have probably encountered most of these stereotypes before. After all, we all know that women are more dependent, emotional, irrational, submissive, persuadable, and talkative than men. Or do we? We'll examine the reality of the situation in a moment.

Before we review the actual evidence on gender differences in behavior, we want to emphasize one other point. In gender stereotypes, women definitely get the short end of the stick. The traditional male stereotype is far more complimentary than the conventional female stereotype. Figure 10.2 clearly suggests that men have cornered the market on competence and rationality. In contrast, the female stereotype is frequently negative and sometimes demeaning.

The fact that gender stereotypes favor males reflects an *androcentric bias*. That is, our society is organized in a way that favors "masculine" characteristics and modes of behavior (*andro-* is from the Greek word for "man"). One area in which androcentric bias has been shown to operate is mental health. In one widely cited study, mental health professionals were assigned to three groups and asked to evaluate the same list of personality characteristics (Broverman et al., 1972). Subjects in one group were asked to select the characteristics that best described the "mature, healthy adult male." Subjects in the other groups were asked to do the same for the "mature, healthy adult female" or the "mature, healthy adult" (sex unspecified). The characteristics these mental health professionals selected to describe the healthy *adult* (independent, self-confident, logical) were basically the same as those they used to describe the healthy adult *male*. In contrast, the

qualities they chose to describe the "healthy" adult *female* (submissive, emotional, less objective) were quite different from those used to describe the healthy adult. In other words, while many masculine characteristics were associated with good psychological adjustment, not many feminine traits were.

Such findings suggest that women face a dilemma that men do not. To oversimplify a bit, women must choose to be mentally healthy and masculine *or* mentally unhealthy and feminine. Furthermore, because many people regard masculine behavior in a female as unhealthy, women who struggle with this dilemma are like-

**FIGURE 10.2
Traditional gender stereotypes**
Broverman et al. (1972) identified a host of traits that are widely associated with masculinity and femininity. A partial list of these traits is shown here.

Elements of Traditional Gender Stereotypes	
Feminine	Masculine
Not at all aggressive	Very aggressive
Not at all independent	Very independent
Very emotional	Not at all emotional
Very easily influenced	Not at all easily influenced
Very submissive	Very dominant
Very excitable in a minor crisis	Not at all excitable in a minor crisis
Very passive	Very active
Very illogical	Very logical
Very home-oriented	Very worldly
Easily hurt emotionally	Not easily hurt emotionally
Generally indecisive	Decisive
Very easily moved to tears	Never moved to tears
Very dependent	Not at all dependent
Very conceited about appearance	Never conceited about appearance
Very talkative	Not at all talkative
Very tactful	Very blunt
Very gentle	Very tough
Very aware of feelings of others	Not at all aware of feelings of others
Very interested in own appearance	Not at all interested in own appearance
Very desirous of security	Not very desirous of security

ly to be in a no-win situation. For the most part, our androcentric bias seems to favor masculine behavior only in males (see Figure 10.3).

Of course, male gender-role stereotypes also have some negative aspects. "Real men," for instance, must be heavily into achievement and should not show a "softer" side. Such biased, narrowly defined norms make life hard for men who choose not to get on the fast track or who want to spend more time with their families. As we shall see, the stereotypes associated with traditional masculine and feminine roles often result in serious problems for both men and women.

Now that we've examined gender stereotypes, let's see what research shows about the *actual* behavior of males and females. Keep in mind that we'll be looking at gender comparisons in modern Western societies. The story can be quite different in other cultures.

Research on Gender Comparisons

Research on gender comparisons seeks to discover the actual similarities and differences between the sexes in their typical (average) behavior. The research on gender comparisons is not easy to summarize. A vast number of studies have been conducted, and many of their findings conflict. Moreover, new evidence is pouring in constantly. Needless to say, it has been an almost overwhelming task to keep up with trends in the field. Fortunately, a new research technique has come to the rescue. *Meta-analysis* **is a statistical technique that evaluates the results of many studies on the**

same question. Application of this technique to the research on gender comparisons yields two critical pieces of information: (1) how large the gender difference is (if indeed a difference is found to exist) and (2) whether males or females score higher on various measures. We've reviewed a variety of meta-analytic studies to give you an up-to-date picture of the research evidence on gender comparisons. We'll look at four areas: cognitive abilities, personality traits, social behavior, and psychological health.

Cognitive Abilities

Perhaps we should first point out that gender differences have *not* been found in *overall* intelligence. Of course, this shouldn't be surprising, because intelligence tests are intentionally designed to minimize differences between the scores of males and females.

What about gender differences in *specific* cognitive skills? Until very recently, it was generally agreed that females scored higher than males on measures of *verbal ability* and that this gap opened up during early adolescence (Hyde, 1981; Petersen, Crockett, & Tobin-Richards, 1982). However, a meta-analysis in this area conducted by Janet Shibley Hyde and Marcia Linn (1988) has altered the thinking on this issue. The current view is that gender differences in verbal ability don't exist (or that they are so small as to be unimportant). In addition, it seems that gender similarity in verbal ability is the rule from childhood through adulthood (Hyde & Linn, 1988). Is this change in perspective due entirely to the improvements in data analysis afforded by meta-analysis? Probably not. That is, Hyde and Linn did find evidence of gender differences (favoring females) in verbal ability in those studies that had been conducted before 1974. Hence it seems that there has been an actual change in gender differences in verbal ability, perhaps traceable to changes in gender-role socialization.

Hyde and her colleagues have performed another recent meta-analysis on tests of *mathematical ability*. This conclusion, too, represents a change from earlier thinking on the question: gender differences in mathematical ability in the general population no longer exist (Hyde, Fennema, & Lamon, 1990). (Once again, gender differences—this time favoring males— were found in the studies published before 1974.) Interestingly, when specific domains of mathematics are analyzed, some age trends emerge. On mathematical *problem solving*, boys and girls essentially perform the same until high

FIGURE 10.3
Androcentric bias in the workplace
In the world of work, women who exhibit traditional "masculine" characteristics are often perceived negatively. Thus a man and a woman who display essentially the same behavior may elicit very different reactions.

Androcentric Bias in the Workplace	
He's good on details.	She's picky.
He follows through.	She doesn't know when to quit.
He's assertive.	She's pushy.
He stands firm.	She's rigid.
He's a man of the world.	She's been around.
He's not afraid to say what he thinks.	She's outspoken.
He's close-mouthed.	She's secretive.
He exercises authority.	She's power-mad.
He climbed the ladder of success.	She slept her way to the top.
He's a stern taskmaster.	She's difficult to work for.

school, when boys begin to outperform girls. The authors note that in high school, boys are more likely than girls to elect math courses, and that is probably one reason for the observed gender difference in mathematical problem solving. Nonetheless, Hyde and her colleagues are concerned about this finding because problem-solving ability is essential for success in scientific courses and careers, arenas currently underpopulated by women.

A third important meta-analysis conducted by Hyde and her colleagues is in the area of *spatial ability*. Gender differences favoring males were found in one type of spatial ability: the ability to rotate a three-dimensional figure mentally (Linn & Petersen, 1986). This skill is important in such occupations as engineering. Apparently spatial ability can be improved by training (Baenninger & Newcombe, 1989).

To summarize, males and females seem to be basically similar in mental abilities. The differences that do exist are *quite limited*. We'll examine the possible causes of these differences after we have examined gender comparisons in some other areas.

Personality Traits

Investigators of gender differences have examined a variety of personality traits. We will discuss those that have attracted the most attention.

Self-Confidence

Many studies support the conclusion that, on the average, males are more self-confident than females (Block, 1976; McMahan, 1982). A common procedure used to study self-confidence is to ask people to estimate their scores on an exam or some other task they have just completed and to compare their estimates with their actual test scores. Those who estimate that they will perform better than they actually do are categorized as high in self-confidence, while those whose initial estimates are lower than their actual scores are categorized as low in self-confidence.

It's interesting to note, however, that women's self-confidence seems to fluctuate with the situation. That is, when women perform tasks that they view as gender-appropriate, when they get clear and direct feedback on their task performance, and when they work alone, their performance estimates are similar to men's (Lenney, 1977, 1981). It's easy to see the connection between self-confidence and expectations of success. And individuals with low expectations of success tend to avoid chal-

lenging situations and tend to achieve at lower levels than those who have high expectations of success. The fact that women tend to score lower than men in these areas has obvious implications for achievement among women.

Emotionality

For the purposes of our discussion, we will define *emotionality* as overreacting to a stressful situation. Popular stereotypes suggest that women are typically more upset by stressful events than men are. Men are supposedly more likely to remain cool and calm. The empirical evidence on this issue is sparse, but the available data do *not* support the stereotype. In fact, there is evidence that in reacting to frustration, males are more emotionally volatile than females (Haviland & Malatesta, 1982; Maccoby & Jacklin, 1974). The belief in females' emotional reactivity may be traceable to their greater willingness to acknowledge certain emotions openly. Many men consider it unmanly to express such emotions as hurt and fear. This difference in behavior, however, does not mean that women are more emotional than men. It merely means that most men are trained to hide some emotions that women typically are not reluctant to express.

Conventional wisdom also suggests that men vent their anger directly and often, whereas women either suppress their anger or express it indirectly, through sulking or nagging. Once again the empirical evidence undermines the popular stereotypes. Research suggests that there are more similarities than differences between men and women in their expression of anger. The two sexes seem to experience anger equally often and for the same reasons—insults, condescending treatment, and so forth (Averill, 1982; Tavris, 1982). Also, both men and women report that they have trouble expressing their angry feelings to those who have more power or status, such as parents, teachers, and employers. Both sexes tend to take their anger home and vent it at "safe" targets.

Nurturance

Nurturance is the provision of help, physical care, and emotional support to others. This term often is used in reference to caring for children. Because only women can bear children, it is widely assumed that women are predisposed to be more nurturant than men.

When self-reports are used or when individuals are openly observed, women *are* found to be more nurturing than men (Berman, 1976,

Janet Shibley Hyde

1980; Nash & Feldman, 1981). These gender differences disappear, however, when subjects are observed indirectly (without their knowledge). Hence it is likely that differences in nurturance reflect subjects' conformity with role expectations rather than actual gender differences. Moreover, the fact that some women opt not to have children rules out the existence of a maternal *instinct*. Women are assigned more responsibility for nurturance in our society, but current research doesn't support the idea that women are by nature more nurturant than men.

Social Behavior

Although gender differences in cognitive abilities and personality appear to be minimal, researchers have found some interesting disparities in social behavior.

Aggression

Aggression **involves behavior that is intended to hurt someone, either physically or verbally** (see Chapter 4). Research reveals that males are more aggressive than females, although the size of this difference is moderate (Eagly, 1987; Hyde, 1984; Maccoby & Jacklin, 1974). Furthermore, when distinctions are made among types of aggression, some researchers

have found that girls tend to engage in more verbal and disobedient aggressive acts, whereas boys engage in more physical and destructive aggression (Barfield, 1976; Hyde, 1984). Recent research also suggests that the sexes may *think* differently about aggression (Eagly, 1987). For example, women report more guilt and anxiety after they have engaged in aggressive behavior and more awareness of the potential harmfulness of their aggression. These patterns of thinking probably help inhibit women's expression of aggression.

The disparity between the sexes in aggressive behavior shows up early in childhood. That it continues through adulthood is supported by the fact that men account for a grossly disproportionate share of violent crime (Kenrick, 1987). When we look at aggression outside the laboratory, we find wide differences between women and men in such aggressive crimes as assault, armed robbery, rape, and homicide (see Figure 10.4).

Conformity

Conformity **involves yielding to real or imagined social pressure.** Traditional beliefs hold that females are more conforming than males, who are viewed as more independent-minded. Research has demonstrated that females *don't* conform to peer standards more than males unless they are subjected to group pressure to do so (Cooper, 1979; Eagly, 1978). When group pressure is applied, however, females *are* more likely to conform than males—frequently because of their lower status within the group or because of their efforts to preserve social harmony (Eagly, 1983; Eagly & Carli, 1981; Eagly & Wood, 1982, 1985).

Verbal Communication

Women are popularly presumed to talk a lot more than men. In fact, the opposite is the case: men talk more than women (Swacker, 1975). In addition, men interrupt more—but only when they're with women (McMillan, Clifton,

**FIGURE 10.4
Gender differences in violent crimes**
Men are arrested for violent crimes far more often than women, as these statistics show. These data support the findings of laboratory studies indicating that males tend to be more physically aggressive.

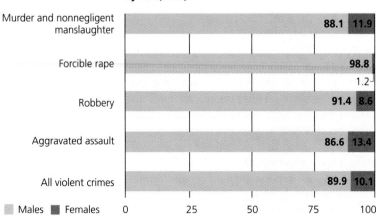

Type of offense	Percentage of arrests by sex (1989)
Murder and nonnegligent manslaughter	88.1 / 11.9
Forcible rape	98.8 / 1.2
Robbery	91.4 / 8.6
Aggravated assault	86.6 / 13.4
All violent crimes	89.9 / 10.1

Males ▪ Females   0   25   50   75   100

McGrath, & Gale, 1977). That is, men and women interrupt same-sex individuals at about the same rate, but men interrupt women much more than women interrupt men (see Figure 10.5). As we saw in Chapter 6, this difference seems to follow from the differences in the status and power of men and women.

Another gender difference in verbal communication is that females are about twice as likely as males to use "tag questions" at the end of sentences (Lakoff, 1973; McMillan et al., 1977). For example, a woman might say, "Let's go to a movie, *OK?*" or "This is a terrific concert, *isn't it?*" The reasons for this gender difference have been attributed both to women's greater insecurity and their greater interpersonal sensitivity.

Nonverbal Communication

Researchers have also studied how the sexes compare in the realm of nonverbal communication. With regard to the *display* of nonverbal cues, the typical finding is that females display more submission and warmth cues, while males display more dominance and high-status cues (Frieze & Ramsey, 1976). It is quite likely that status differences are responsible for these findings (Henley, 1977; Mayo & Henley, 1981). There also is a gender difference in *sensitivity* to nonverbal cues favoring women (Hall, 1984).

Psychological Health

The two sexes are both similar and different with respect to mental health. They are similar in that the overall incidence of mental disorders is roughly the same for both sexes. They differ in the kinds of disorders they tend to develop.

Before the 1980s, research suggested that about one of every five people developed a mental disorder at some point in life and that mental disorders were more common in women than in men (Neugebauer, Dohrenwend, & Dohrenwend, 1980). However, drug-related disorders and antisocial disorders, which are more common in men, were not adequately assessed, because they used to be defined vaguely. More recent studies, which have counted these disorders more effectively, yield a different picture. It now seems that about one of every *three* people will develop a psychological disorder at one time or another, whether they are males or females (Robins et al., 1984).

When researchers assess the prevalence of *specific* disorders, they do find differences between the sexes. As we just noted, antisocial

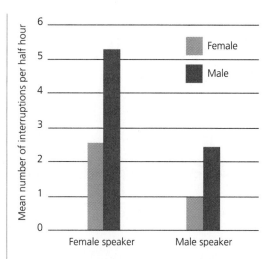

FIGURE 10.5
Gender differences in interruptions in mixed-sex groups
In a 30-minute period, men interrupted women about five times as often as women interrupted men. Men interrupted other men and women interrupted other women with about equal frequency. (Data from McMillan et al., 1977.)

behavior, alcoholism, and other drug-related disorders are more prevalent among men. Women, on the other hand, are more likely than men to suffer from depression and anxiety disorders (phobias, for example). They also show higher rates of eating disorders (Rodin, Silberstein, & Striegel-Moore, 1985). In addition, women *attempt* suicide more often than men, but men *complete* suicide (actually kill themselves) more frequently than women (Cross & Hirschfeld, 1986).

What accounts for these sex differences in types of mental illnesses? For one thing, there is a fairly obvious connection between the symptoms of "male" and "female" disorders and traditional gender roles. That is, women's disorders seem to reflect a turning *inward*—in other words, negative, hostile, or anxious feelings and conflicts are directed against the self. Men typically direct the same feelings and conflicts *outward*—against either other individuals or society. (Suicide is one obvious exception.)

Although the overall prevalence of psychological disorders is about the same for both sexes, substantially more women than men receive psychotherapy (Al-Issa, 1982; Russo & Sobel, 1981). Why might this be? For one thing, women are more willing than men to acknowledge their emotional problems and seek professional help. Many men are reluctant to admit that they are struggling with anxiety or depression for fear of seeming unmanly. For another, people who exhibit antisocial or drug-related disorders often don't see themselves as having a problem. Thus people are less likely to seek treatment for the disorders that are more common in men.

Gender bias in the *diagnosis* of mental disorders may also contribute to the disproportionate number of women in psychotherapy. Marci Kaplan (1983) has suggested that the way a behavior is evaluated depends on whether a

FIGURE 10.6
The nature of group differences
Gender differences are group differences that tell us little about individuals because the groups overlap to a great extent. One sex may have a higher average score than the other on a given trait, but the variation within each sex is far greater than the variation between the sexes.

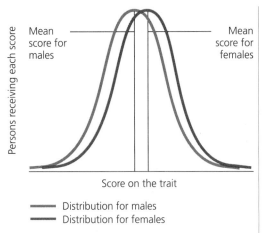

Persons receiving each score

Mean score for males

Mean score for females

Score on the trait

— Distribution for males
— Distribution for females

man or a woman exhibits it, and the evaluation seldom favors women. When men express little concern about others' feelings or put their career ahead of their family, for example, not much notice is taken. But when a woman behaves in the same way, her behavior may be interpreted as "disturbed." Of course, gender bias alone wouldn't account for the greater number of female patients, but it probably contributes to this inequality.

Putting Gender Differences in Perspective

Although there are some genuine gender differences in behavior, bear in mind that these are *group* differences. That is, they tell us nothing about individuals. Essentially, we are comparing the "average man" with the "average woman." However, every individual is unique. The average female and male are ultimately figments of our imagination. Furthermore, even these group differences are relatively small. Figure 10.6 shows how men's and women's scores on a trait might be distributed. Although the group averages are detectably different, you can see that there is great variability within

FIGURE 10.7
Meta-analyses of gender differences
Meta-analysis allows researchers to combine the results of many studies and estimate the amount of variation in a trait accounted for by a particular factor (in this case, sex). The influential meta-analyses of gender differences summarized here suggest that sex accounts for only a tiny portion of the variation among people in cognitive abilities and social behavior.

each group (sex) and huge overlap between the two group distributions. Thus a gender difference that shows up on the average does not by itself tell us anything about you or any other individual of either sex.

Another way to gauge the influence of gender on behavior is to estimate how much of the variation among people on a trait is accounted for by a person's sex. Estimates of these proportions can be made through meta-analysis. Figure 10.7 summarizes the findings of meta-analyses on gender effects by Janet Shibley Hyde and others. These meta-analyses suggest that sex accounts for 1% or less of the variation among people in verbal ability, mathematical ability, and conformity (susceptibility to social influence). Furthermore, on the traits with the largest gender differences, sex accounts for only about 4 to 6% of the variation among individuals. Factors other than sex, therefore, account for far more of the differences between individuals.

To summarize, the behavioral differences between males and females are fewer and smaller than popular stereotypes suggest. Moreover, gender-relevant behavior often seems to appear and disappear as gender-role expectations become more or less salient (Unger, 1981). *Ultimately, the similarities of females and males greatly outweigh the differences between them.* If gender differences in personality and behavior are relatively modest, why does it seem otherwise? One explanation is provided by Alice Eagly's *social role theory* (1987), which suggests that minor gender differences are exaggerated by the social roles that men and women play. Because women are assigned the role of caregiver, for example, they learn to behave in nurturing ways. Moreover, people come to associate such role-related behaviors with individuals of a given sex, not the actual roles they play. In other words, we come to see nurturing as a female trait rather than a characteristic that anyone in a nurturing role would demonstrate. This is one way in which stereotypes develop and persist.

Another explanation for the discrepancy between beliefs and reality is that the differences actually reside in the eye of the beholder, not in the beholdee. This *social constructionist* view asserts that individuals construct their own reality on the basis of societal expectations, conditioning, and self-socialization. According to social constructionists, the tendency to look for gender differences as well as our specific beliefs about gender are rooted in the "gendered" messages and conditioning that permeate our socialization experiences. To

Summary of Research on Gender Differences			
Characteristic	Researcher	Number of studies analyzed	Variance accounted for by sex (%)
Verbal abilities	Hyde & Linn (1988)	165	<1
Mathematical abilities	Hyde, Fennema, & Lamon (1990)	254	<1
Visual-spatial abilities	Hyde (1981)	10	4.5
Aggression	Hyde (1984)	143	6
Decoding of nonverbal cues	Hall (1978)	75	4
Susceptibility to social influence	Eagly & Carli (1981)	148	1

understand these issues better, we need to explore the role of biological and environmental factors as likely sources of gender differences.

Biological Origins of Gender Differences

Are the gender differences that do exist acquired through learning, or are they biologically built in? This is the age-old issue of nature versus nurture. This issue pits heredity and biological factors against the environment as the prime determinants of behavior. The "nature" theorists concentrate on biological disparities between the sexes to explain gender differences in behavior. "Nurture" theorists, on the other hand, emphasize the role of learning and the environment.

Freud's idea that "anatomy is destiny" was widely accepted during the first half of the 20th century. Indeed, during the early part of the century, researchers simply assumed that gender differences were due largely to biological factors (Shields, 1975). The bias of the male-dominated scientific community was so strong that scholars managed to find "proof" that the frontal lobes of the brain, thought to be the seat of reason, were larger in men than in women. When evidence later surfaced to suggest that the parietal lobes (rather than the frontal lobes) were crucial to complex cognition, scientists suddenly found that males had a size advantage in the parietal area instead (Shields, 1975). It is now clear that there are no meaningful size differences between male and female brains. This story simply demonstrates how our culture's androcentric bias can contaminate research. In recent decades biological explanations of gender differences have focused not on the brain's size but on its organization and on the possible role of hormonal influences. We'll examine the evidence on brain organization first.

Brain Organization

Some theorists believe that male and female brains may be organized differently. As you may know, the human brain is divided into two halves. **The *cerebral hemispheres* are the right and left halves of the cerebrum, which is the convoluted outer layer of the brain.** The largest and most complicated part of the human brain, the cerebrum is responsible for most complex mental activities.

There is evidence that the right and left cerebral hemispheres are specialized to handle different cognitive tasks (Sperry, 1982; Springer & Deutsch, 1984). It appears that the *left hemisphere* is more actively involved in *verbal and mathematical processing*, whereas the *right hemisphere* is specialized to handle *visual-spatial and other nonverbal processing*. This pattern is generally seen in both right-handed and left-handed people, though hemispheric specialization tends to be less consistent among the left-handed.

After these findings on hemispheric specialization surfaced, various theorists began to wonder whether there might be a connection between this division of labor in the brain and observed gender differences in verbal and spatial skills. Consequently, they began to look for disparities between males and females in brain organization.

They found some evidence that males exhibit more cerebral specialization than females (McGlone, 1980). In other words, men tend to depend more heavily than women on the left hemisphere in verbal processing and on the right hemisphere in spatial processing. Some theorists have argued that this difference in brain organization is responsible for gender differences in verbal and spatial ability (Goleman, 1978). As a result of the interest aroused by these findings, the popular press has often touted the idea that there are "male brains" and "female brains," which differ fundamentally (Bleier, 1984).

This idea is intriguing, but we have a long way to go before we can explain gender differences in terms of right brain/left brain specialization. For one thing, studies have not been consistent in finding that brain organization is more specialized in males than in females (Fausto-Sterling, 1985; Harris, 1980; Kinsbourne, 1980). Moreover, even if men did show stronger cerebral specialization than women, no one is really sure just how that would account for gender differences in cognitive abilities. It seems peculiar that strong specialization would produce an advantage for men in one kind of activity (spatial tasks) and a disadvantage in another (verbal tasks). In any case, as we noted earlier, recent studies indicate that there are no real gender differences in verbal ability to be explained. Thus the theory link-

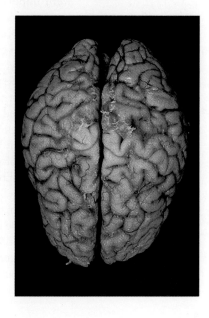

Studies have shown that the brain's cerebral hemispheres, shown here, are somewhat specialized in the kinds of cognitive tasks they handle and that such specialization is more pronounced in males than in females. Whether this difference bears any relation to gender differences in behavior is yet to be determined.

ing cerebral specialization to gender differences in mental abilities remains highly speculative.

Hormonal Influences

Biological explanations of gender differences have also focused on the possible role of hormones. **Hormones are chemical substances released into the bloodstream by the endocrine glands.** We know that hormones play a key role in sexual differentiation during prenatal development. Our biological sex is determined by our sex chromosomes. An XX pairing produces a female and an XY pairing produces a male. However, both male and female embryos are essentially the same until about 8 to 12 weeks after conception. Around this time, male and female gonads (sex glands) begin to secrete different hormones. The high level of *androgens* (the principal class of male hormones) in male fetuses and the low level of androgens in female fetuses leads to the differentiation of male and female genital organs.

The influence of prenatal hormones on sexual differentiation becomes apparent when something interferes with normal prenatal hormonal secretions. John Money and his colleagues have tracked the development of a small number of females who were exposed to high levels of androgens during their prenatal development. The girls were born to mothers who either had a hormonal malfunction during pregnancy or were given an androgen-like drug to prevent miscarriage. These *androgenized females* were born with genitalia that were partially male. The degree of masculinization of their genitals varied, depending on the extent of their prenatal hormonal imbalance. In some cases the masculinization was so subtle that it went unnoticed for months and even years. Once the anomaly was noticed, most cases were treated with a combination of hormone therapy and surgical correction of the genitals.

Money and his colleagues wondered whether the prenatal dose of male hormones would affect the behavioral tendencies of these androgenized females. Sure enough, they found that these girls showed "tomboyish" interests in vigorous outdoor activities. They also showed preferences for male playmates and "male" toys (Money & Ehrhardt, 1972).

The findings on androgenized females suggested to many theorists that prenatal hormones shape gender differences in humans. But there are—naturally—a few problems. First, it's always dangerous to base conclusions about the general population on a handful of subjects who have an abnormal condition. Second, most of the androgenized girls received drug treatments (cortisone) for their condition. These treatments could have influenced their activity levels. Third, the girls were born with male-looking genitals that often were not surgically corrected until age 2 or 3. Hence their families may not have reared them in quite the same way as they would have raised "normal" girls. In light of these problems, research on androgenized females cannot conclusively demonstrate that prenatal hormones cause gender differences in behavior.

Researchers have also tried to link hormone levels in adults to gender differences. Once again the findings are inconsistent and inconclusive. Even the seemingly plausible association between hormonal fluctuations and the premenstrual syndrome in women has been seriously questioned. **The *premenstrual syndrome* involves a negative shift in mood, thought to occur in the days preceding a female's menstrual period.** Although *some* women experience specific mood changes that are correlated with their menstrual cycle, there is little evidence to support the existence of a premenstrual syndrome defined as a specific *cluster of feelings* (Parlee, 1973). Some studies find no mood changes in female subjects as a function of their menstrual cycle (Golub & Harrington, 1981). In one study (Dan, 1976), husbands and wives kept daily records of their moods over a period of months. No significant mood differences between spouses were found, even though the wives were experiencing hormonal changes related to their menstrual cycles.

The purported link between hormones and the premenstrual syndrome has been further undermined by evidence that the syndrome is influenced by cultural expectations (Paige, 1973; Parlee, 1982). In one study, subjects filled out daily reports of physical and emotional symptoms. Women who were told that the study concerned *menstrual distress* reported more symptoms than their male counterparts. However, women who were led to believe that the study concerned their *general health* did not. Thus the "menstrual blues" may be due more to social training than to hormonal fluctuations. As a whole, the evidence indicates that environmental events and social variables account for more of the variability in mood than do hormone levels (Good & Smith, 1980; Landers, 1977).

In summary, researchers have made relatively little progress in their efforts to document the biological roots of gender differences in behavior. Many theorists remain convinced that biological factors contribute to gender differences. The overall evidence, however, or rather the lack of it, suggests that biology must play a relatively minor role. In contrast, efforts to link gender differences to disparities in the way males and females are socialized have proved to be more fruitful.

Environmental Origins of Gender Differences

Let's begin this section with a riddle.

A boy and his father are in an automobile accident. The father is killed and the boy is seriously injured. The boy is rushed to the hospital and taken into the operating room. A few minutes later the surgeon comes out of the operating room and says, "I cannot operate on this boy; he is my son." Explain how this could be.

In view of the topic at hand (gender roles), you probably had little difficulty with our riddle. The answer is quite simple: The surgeon is the boy's mother. A surprisingly large number of people fail to think of this explanation when the riddle isn't placed in the middle of a discussion of gender roles. Many people have a hard time envisioning a woman in the role of surgeon.

As we noted in Chapter 7, a *role* is a pattern of behavior expected on the basis of a person's social position. Student, professor, parent, salesperson, bartender, lawyer, neighbor—all of these roles are accompanied by expected patterns of behavior. **Gender roles are cultural expectations about what is appropriate behavior for each sex.** In our culture, for example, women have been expected to rear children, cook meals, do laundry, and sew. On the other hand, men have been expected to be the family breadwinner, watch football, and tinker with cars. In dating relationships, males have been expected to ask females out, open doors for them, drive the car, pick up the check, and so on.

Are gender roles in other cultures similar to those familiar in our society? Generally, yes—but not necessarily. Despite a fair amount of cross-cultural consistency in gender roles, some dramatic variability has been found (Munroe & Munroe, 1975). When the anthropologist Margaret Mead (1950) conducted her now-classic study of three tribes in New Guinea, for instance, she found that in one

tribe (the Mundugumor) both sexes followed our masculine role expectations. In another tribe (the Arapesh) both sexes approximated our feminine role. And in still another tribe (the Tchambuli) the male and female roles were roughly the reverse of our own. Such remarkable disparities among societies located within 100 miles of one another demonstrate that gender roles are not a matter of biological destiny. Like other roles, gender roles are acquired through socialization. **Socialization is the process by which individuals acquire the norms and roles expected of people in a particular society.** This process includes all the efforts made by a society to put its unique imprint on its members.

Processes in Gender-Role Socialization

How do we acquire our gender roles? Gender-role socialization operates through the learning processes of reinforcement and punishment, observation, and self-socialization.

Reinforcement and Punishment

One important way that children learn gender roles is by being reinforced for "gender-appropriate" behaviors and punished for "gender-

307

inappropriate" ones (recall our discussion of operant conditioning in Chapter 2). Our parents, siblings, teachers, and peers all reinforce and punish us to promote gender-appropriate behavior (Bandura, 1977; Mischel, 1970). A young boy who has just hurt himself may be told by his dad that "big boys don't cry." If the child succeeds in inhibiting his crying, he may get a pat on the back, a warm smile, or even an ice cream cone—all potent reinforcers.

To see the power of reinforcement to modify behavior, let's look at a representative experiment (Serbin, Connor, & Citron, 1978). For 20 minutes once a week, nursery school children were praised by their teachers whenever they engaged in two types of independent behavior (exploration and persisting on a task alone). During the same 20-minute period, teachers ignored two dependent behaviors (soliciting a teacher's attention and seeking to be near her). A second group of children were praised regardless of their behavior. After five weeks the behavior of the two groups of children was compared. Both girls and boys in the first group showed more independent and less dependent behavior than the children in the second group—thanks to just 20 minutes of reinforcement a week.

The evidence suggests that parents use punishment more than reward in socializing gender roles (O'Leary, 1977). Many parents probably take gender-appropriate behavior for granted and don't go out of their way to reward it. But they may react very negatively to gender-inappropriate behavior. A 10-year-old boy who enjoys playing with a dollhouse may elicit strong disapproval. Parents pay more attention to discouraging gender-inappropriate behavior in boys than in girls. Fathers are especially likely to punish gender-inappropriate behavior in their sons (Fagot, 1981; Langlois & Downs, 1980), usually by verbal reprimands or ridicule.

Observational Learning

As we explained in Chapter 2, *observational learning* occurs when a person's behavior is influenced by observations of *models*. Parents serve as models for children, as do siblings, teachers, relatives, and other people who are important in children's lives. Note, too, that models are not limited to real people. Characters on television and in films also function as role models.

According to *social learning theory* (see Chapter 2), young children are more likely to imitate people who are nurturant, powerful, and similar to them (Mischel, 1970). Children imitate both sexes, but most children tend to imitate same-sex models more often than other-sex models (Perry & Bussey, 1979). Thus observational learning often leads young girls to play with dolls, toy stoves, and so forth, whereas boys are more likely to tinker with toy trucks, miniature gas stations, and such. It's also likely that boys get more exposure to male models than girls and that girls get more exposure to female models than boys. Dad may take Johnny with him to the auto parts store while Mary goes grocery shopping with Mom. Similarly, girls and boys spend more time with same-sex peers, who serve as models for each other.

Self-Socialization

Children are not merely passive recipients of gender-role socialization. There is evidence that children themselves are active agents in their own gender-role socialization. Several influential *cognitive theories* of gender-role development (S. Bem, 1981; Kohlberg, 1966; Martin & Halverson, 1981) emphasize such *self-socialization*.

Self-socialization entails three steps. First, children develop **gender identity—the ability to correctly classify themselves as male or**

Children learn behaviors appropriate to their gender roles very early in life. According to social learning theory, girls do the sort of things their mothers do, while boys follow in dad's footsteps.

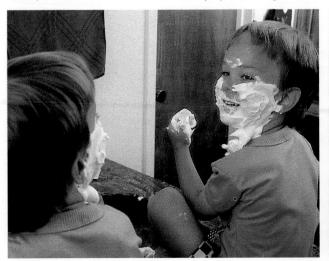

female. (Technically, this concept should be called *sex* identity; however, we will stick with standard terminology.) Most children develop gender identity by the time they are 3 years old. Second, gender identity motivates children to value those characteristics and behaviors that are associated with their sex. Third, they strive to bring their behavior in line with what is considered gender appropriate in their culture. In other words, children get involved in their own socialization, working diligently to discover the rules that are supposed to govern their behavior.

Sandra Bem (1981) has theorized that children gradually learn to see the world through "gender-colored" glasses, which she calls *gender schemas* (*schemas* are cognitive structures that guide our information processing). To investigate this idea, she devised a questionnaire to assess **gender-role identity—a person's identification with the traits regarded as masculine or feminine.** Males who describe themselves in accordance with society's definition of masculinity and females who describe themselves in accordance with society's definition of femininity are said to have a *sex-typed* gender identity. Individuals who don't describe themselves in these ways—people who see themselves as possessing both masculine and feminine characteristics—are said to have a *non-sex-typed* gender identity. (This second group includes several subgroups that we will describe later.)

According to Bem, sex-typed people spontaneously classify information on the basis of gender, even when other dimensions could serve equally well. Non-sex-typed individuals, on the other hand, are less likely to use gender to organize their perceptions. An interesting study appears to bear out this idea (S. Bem, 1981). Male and female undergraduates were classified as either sex-typed or non-sex-typed. Then each subject looked at 60 personality attributes (20 "masculine," 20 "feminine," and 20 gender-neutral). As the 60 attributes were flashed on a projection screen, subjects pushed a "me" button or a "not me" button to indicate whether the attributes were descriptive of them.

Bem predicted that sex-typed subjects would tend to push the buttons more quickly because their gender schema would allow them to process gender-relevant information without much thought. Non-sex-typed people were expected to take longer to respond, because they would need time to think about whether an attribute was characteristic of them. As Bem predicted, sex-typed individuals took less time than non-sex-typed individuals to push the but-

tons. She concluded that these results demonstrated the greater influence of gender schemas in sex-typed subjects.

Sources of Gender-Role Socialization

There are four major sources of gender-role socialization: parents, the media, schools, and peers. Because gender roles are changing, the generalizations that follow may say more about how you were socialized than about how your children will be.

Parents

Most parents dress baby girls and boys in different colors and treat them differently from the very beginning. One study asked adult subjects to observe a videotape of an infant's response to the opening of a jack-in-the box (Condry & Condry, 1976). Half of the subjects were told that the baby was a boy and half were told it was a girl. On the videotape the observers saw a baby who stared at the toy and then cried. The baby's presumed sex colored the subjects' perception of the baby's response: those who believed that the infant was a boy described the baby's emotions as "anger," but those who thought that the infant was a girl labeled its feelings as "fear." An implication of this finding is that parents' stereotyped interpretations of their children's behavior can cause them to shape their children's self-perceptions. The subjects of that study would teach the "boy" that his response was anger and the "girl" that what she was feeling was fear.

A British study also demonstrates the important role that a child's sex plays on parents' explanations of their children's behavior. Here it was found that parents of 2-year-olds used feminine attributions for girls and masculine attributions for boys (McGuire, 1988). Feminine attributions included references to physical attractiveness or appearance (mothers) or nurturing play with dolls, gentleness, and doing housework (fathers). Masculine attributions included references to physical ability or athletic skill. The author of this study reported another common finding—that fathers seem to take a more active role in gender-role socialization of their children, especially their sons.

Although many parents treat their children in gender-stereotypic ways, it is interesting that a lot of them seem to be unaware of this behavior and in fact deny it (Culp, Cook, & Housley, 1983; Fagot, 1978). Similarly, parents fail to notice that they choose gender-stereo-

Sandra Bem

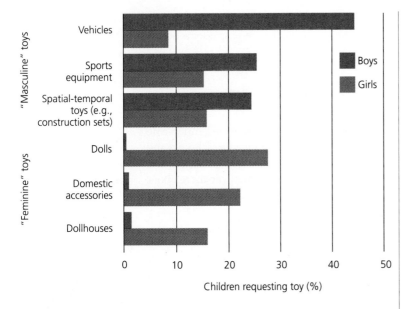

FIGURE 10.8
Toy preferences and gender
This graph depicts the percentage of boys and girls who asked for various types of toys in letters to Santa Claus (adapted from Richardson & Simpson, 1982). As you can see, boys and girls differ substantially in their toy preferences. These differences show the effects of gender-role socialization.

typed toys for their children in early childhood. Children's own toy preferences also reflect the influence of gender-role expectations (see Figure 10.8).

When kids are old enough to help with household chores, their assignments often depend on their sex. Girls may do laundry and dishes while boys mow the lawn and sweep the garage. Likewise, the leisure activities that children are encouraged to engage in often vary by sex. For instance, Johnny may be shipped off to baseball practice while Mary gets ballet lessons.

To summarize, parents' attitudes toward gender roles influence many aspects of their children's lives. Hence it isn't surprising that parents' attitudes toward gender roles have been shown to influence the gender roles their children acquire (Repetti, 1984). One study found that only mothers with nontraditional views seemed to encourage their daughters to be independent (Brooks-Gunn, 1986).

The Media

Television is yet another source of gender-role socialization (Morgan, 1982). Youngsters in the United States spend a lot of time watching TV (see Figure 10.9). Children between the ages of 3 and 11 watch an average of two to four hours of TV per day (Huston et al., 1990; Liebert & Sprafkin, 1988). Television shows have traditionally depicted men and women in highly stereotypic ways (Basow, 1986). Women have typically been portrayed as loving mothers and dedicated homemakers; men have been given dynamic, exciting roles as cool, competent leaders. When scriptwriters finally give a heroic role to a woman, they often have men come to her aid at the last minute. Even the commercials on TV contribute to gender-role socialization. Women are shown worrying about the ring around their husbands' collars, how shiny "their" dishes are, how white "their" laundry is, and how to use expensive cosmetics to "snare" a man. Although the stereotypic portrayals of women don't seem to have changed much over the past 20 years, at least one study of gender bias in television commercials reported that men are increasingly being shown in the roles of spouse and parent (Bretl & Cantor, 1988).

Given these facts, it should come as no surprise that children who watch TV frequently have been found to hold more stereotyped beliefs about gender than children who watch less TV (McGhee & Frueh, 1980). Children who watch a great deal of educational TV, in contrast, tend to be less traditional about gender roles than other children (Repetti, 1984). This difference probably is formed because many children's shows on educational TV systematically try to promote nontraditional gender roles. Thus there appears to be a clear link between media content and the acquisition of gender roles and stereotypes. As we saw in Chapter 5, once stereotypes are learned, they are difficult to change. Moreover, as long as TV continues to present gender-stereotyped programs and commercials, it perpetuates these beliefs—not only in children but also in adults.

Another form of gender bias in television is its inordinate emphasis on physical attractiveness in women. Although TV probably places undue emphasis on attractiveness in both sexes, the problem is more pronounced for women. Men on television may or may not be good-looking, but women almost have to be. Consider for a moment: How many old, overweight, unattractive female news anchors and reporters have you seen on TV? This bias is apparent in entertainment shows as well. One study analyzed the age and weight of 221 characters from the top 40 TV programs (Silverstein, Perdue, Peterson, & Kelly, 1986). Approximately 69% of the female characters but only 18% of the male characters were rated "thin." And whereas 26% of the male characters were rated "heavy," only 5% of the female characters were. Such role models exert much more pressure to be youthful, thin, and physically attractive on females than on males (Feingold, 1990). These cultural expectations have been frequently cited as a cause of the disproportionately high incidence of eating disorders in young women (Levenkron, 1982; Polivy & Thomsen, 1988).

Schools

Schools also make a major contribution to the socialization of gender roles (Busch-Rossnagel & Vance, 1982; Etaugh & Harlow, 1975). Traditionally, illustrations in readers for the early grades show stereotypic characteristics of males and females. One survey of 134 grade-school readers found that boy-centered stories outnumbered girl-centered stories 5 to 2 (Women on Words and Images, 1972). Moreover, the boys in these stories got to display cleverness 131 times, while girls were clever only 33 times. Girls were shown doing domestic chores more than three times as often as boys. Later studies still find numerous examples of gender bias in children's books (Bordelon, 1985).

Many high school and college textbooks also contain gender bias. A study of high school history texts, for instance, reported that on most issues they made no mention of women's contributions or their concerns (Kirby & Julian, 1981). Only when books discussed a specific woman or a topic obviously related to women (woman suffrage, for example) was the coverage judged to be balanced and objective. Complaints about gender bias in textbooks have led many publishers to reduce or eliminate their stereotypic portrayals of females and males and to increase the visibility of women. You might review your textbooks to see if such changes have been made.

Gender bias in schools also shows up in teachers' behaviors. Most studies have shown that boys tend to get more attention from teachers than girls (Good, Sikes, & Brophy, 1973; Sadker & Sadker, 1985). Also, teachers seem to respond differently to specific behaviors of boys and girls. Researchers who studied fourth- and fifth-graders observed that teachers gave boys more positive feedback than girls for the intellectual quality of their work (Dweck, Davidson, Nelson, & Enna, 1978). They also found that teachers tended to attribute girls' failures to lack of ability, whereas they attributed boys' failures to lack of motivation. Finally, it seems that teachers give more frequent and more negative attention to boys for misbehavior (Fagot & Hagan, 1985; Huston, 1983; Stake & Katz, 1982), thus reinforcing their aggressiveness. On balance, then, these findings show that girls are relatively invisible in the classroom and that they receive little encouragement for academic achievement from teachers.

Similar conclusions were stated in the recently published comprehensive report on gender bias in schools commissioned by the American Association of University Women (AAUW). It suggested that girls' self-esteem is gradually undermined in school through such experiences as (1) receiving less of the teachers' attention, (2) sexual harassment by male peers, (3) the stereotyping and invisibility of women and girls in textbooks, and (4) test bias that restricts their chances of being admitted to the college of their choice and awarded scholarships (Wellesley College Center for Research on Women, 1992).

Despite these obstacles, females still manage to obtain higher grades than males in all subjects from elementary school through college (Eccles, 1989; Kimball, 1989). Yet in high school and college, females continue to be underrepresented in math, physics, and chemistry courses (Linn & Hyde, 1989), and relatively few women opt for careers in mathematics and science. Hence it seems that many counselors are still encouraging male students to be physicians and engineers while they guide female students in the direction of nursing, teaching, and homemaking.

Peers

Peers form an important network for learning about gender-role stereotypes, as well as gender-appropriate and gender-inappropriate behavior. Between the ages of 4 and 6, children seem to separate into same-sex groups. A longitudinal study showed that the ratio of time spent with same-sex playmates versus other-sex playmates rose from 3:1 to 11:1 between these ages (Maccoby & Jacklin, 1987). Therefore, it seems that same-sex peers are the most powerful instruments of such learning during these years (Fagot, 1985).

Play among same-sex peers takes different forms for boys than for girls. Boys play in larger groups and roam farther from home, whereas girls prefer smaller groups and stay near the

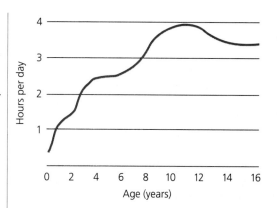

**FIGURE 10.9
Average number of hours per day children and adolescents watch television**
As children grow up, they spend more and more time watching TV until about age 12, when viewing time begins to decline slightly. Research shows that children's conceptions of gender roles are influenced to a considerable degree by what they watch on television. (Data from Liebert & Sprafkin, 1988.)

house (Feiring & Lewis, 1987). Boys achieve high status in their groups by engaging in dominant behavior (telling others what to do and enforcing orders), whereas girls usually express their wishes as suggestions rather than demands (Maltz & Borker, 1983). Also, boys engage in rough-and-tumble play much more frequently than girls do (Maccoby, 1988).

Children's behavior varies with the sex of the children they play with. Particularly noteworthy is a finding that somewhere between the ages of 4 and 6, boys seem to stop responding to the influence strategies of girls (Maccoby, 1988). When a boy and girl both want the same toy, for example, the boy will take it—unless a teacher is in the room. It has often been observed that girls stay closer to teachers than boys do. The reason offered to explain this observation has been that girls have greater dependency needs. More recently it has been found that this behavior occurs only in mixed-sex groups (Maccoby, 1990)—which suggests that girls stay near the teacher in mixed-sex groups as a way of having some influence over boys' behavior, not because of dependency needs.

In the Application we'll see that these differences in childhood play may lie behind the communication difficulties that some women and men experience.

Gender-Role Socialization in Childhood and Adolescence

Now let's trace the operation of these processes and sources of gender-role socialization through childhood and adolescence.

Little boys who show interest in dolls are likely to lose status among their male peers.

Infancy

Learning how to be a boy or a girl begins at birth with the announcement "It's a boy!" or "It's a girl!" Usually this exclamation is quickly followed by assigning the newborn a "sex-appropriate" name and by dressing him or her in blue or pink. Such actions imply that we believe that a child's sex is a critical factor in his or her life. In infancy few sex differences have been found besides the obvious biological differences.

Childhood

The way "gendered" behavior is shaped varies according to sex. Boys are subjected to a great deal of rigidity regarding gender-appropriate behavior and strong pressure to conform to these standards early in life (Archer, 1984). Girls have greater freedom to engage in cross-sex behavior (Hartley, 1959; Lloyd, 1985; Lynn, 1959; Pleck, 1981a). Little boys are usually severely punished for trying on a skirt, playing with lipstick, and sometimes even for playing with dolls. Yet no one raises an eyebrow when little girls wear baseball jackets and jeans or join soccer or softball teams. In other words, "tomboys" don't suffer from the same prejudice as "sissies."

Why do boys experience greater pressure to conform to gender stereotypes than girls? For one thing, males are more valued in our society than females, so more attention is paid to their socialization—that is, their actions receive more scrutiny. Second, because "masculine" activities have high status, girls are interested in them as a way of gaining status—provided they don't go "too far" (Unger & Crawford, 1992). Conversely, boys who show interest in lower-status "female" activities lose status. Peers serve as watchful guardians of cross-sex behavior and use teasing to maintain gender-appropriate behavior and contacts (Thorne & Luria, 1986). Male peers seem to be especially vigilant in this regard.

In childhood, consistent behavioral differences between the sexes are surprisingly few. Boys and girls do like different toys and different types of games (Maccoby & Jacklin, 1974). For instance, boys like to play with guns and toy trucks and do carpentry, while girls prefer sewing, stringing beads, and playing at housekeeping. Boys prefer more competitive games and are more resistant to parental influence than girls. Boys are more aggressive than girls (Hyde, 1984; Maccoby & Jacklin, 1974). In contrast to infants, children are subjected to gender typing from a variety of sources: parents, television, teachers, and peers. Because their cognitive abilities are better developed than are those of infants, children are more likely to attend to and comprehend these messages. For these reasons, it is interesting not to find more obvious differences between boys and girls at this age.

Adolescence

Some theorists suggest that gender-related role expectations intensify around the time of puberty (Hill & Lynch, 1983). That is, the changes in appearance that signal the onset of physical and sexual maturation are directly tied to gender-role issues. More specifically, these external changes produce alterations in self-perceptions and intensify other people's expectations that one will conform closely to gender-role expectations. Research findings support this idea (Simmons & Blyth, 1987).

If males are to function successfully in designated adult roles, they must achieve a sense of identity, become independent of their family, and decide upon an occupation (Lloyd, 1985). These developmental tasks are usually achieved during adolescence and young adulthood. In their classic study of adolescents, Elizabeth Douvan and Joseph Adelson (1966) found that vocational choice was the central identity issue for adolescent boys: "For most boys, the question of 'what to be' begins with work and the job, and he is likely to define himself and to be identified by occupation" (p. 17). Numerous recent studies support this finding (Marcia, 1980).

Adolescent girls are pressured to give up so-called masculine characteristics and behavior that were acceptable in childhood, especially those involving autonomy and achievement in "masculine" areas (Morgan & Farber, 1982). They are encouraged to focus on dating and social skills instead. Much of this energy is focused on learning skills that will ensure *heterosexual success*—learning how to attract and interest boys as prospective mates. This focus on attracting a mate typically results in excessive concern about body image and ambivalence about a career (Holland & Eisenhart, 1990).

It can also delay the development of an independent sense of identity. Traditional female norms dictate that a woman should build her identity around her roles as wife and mother rather than around a career, as men are expected to do (Lloyd, 1985). The girl cannot take the initiative in realizing these roles (she must be chosen as a mate, not do the choosing).

Hence gender-role expectations may delay the development of an independent sense of self (identity achievement) until adult roles are assumed. As you can see, the culturally created incompatibilities between femininity and achievement create psychological conflicts for adolescent girls and adult women (Hyde, 1991; Lloyd, 1985).

Traditional Gender Roles

he social norms that characterize traditional gender roles are based on the assumptions that all men have basically the same traits, that the traits of one sex differ from the traits of the other sex, and that masculine traits are more highly valued. Because traditional gender roles are based on the assumption that everyone is heterosexual (heterosexism), they say nothing about homosexual individuals. This fact and the relative invisibility of gay men and lesbians deprive young homosexuals of positive role models. This state of affairs obviously makes it more difficult for them to sort through the interrelated issues of identity, gender-role identity, and sexual orientation. Let's look at traditional gender-role expectations.

Role Expectations for Males

A number of psychologists have characterized the traditional male role (Brannon, 1976; Doyle, 1989; Keen, 1991; Pleck, 1981a). According to James Doyle and Michele Paludi (1991), it contains five key elements.

- *The antifeminine element.* As we have seen, "real men" shouldn't act in any way that might be perceived as feminine. As Robert Brannon (1976) puts it, "No sissy stuff."
- *The success element.* To prove their masculinity, men need to beat out other men at sports and at work. Having a high-status job, driving an expensive car, and making lots of money are aspects of this element.
- *The aggressive element.* Men are expected to fight for what they believe is right and to defend themselves aggressively against threats. Aggression may take the form of verbal or physical force, even violence.
- *The sexual element.* "Real men" should be the initiators and controllers of sexual activity.
- *The self-reliant element.* Being "in control" and remaining cool and calm under pressure are aspects of this element.

Males in a society that favors "masculine" modes of behavior grow up with the expectation that they'll have control over their lives in ways that females still do not. A man will "decide" what kind of work he wants to do. If he is a heterosexual, he will seek out a woman who meets his expectations of what he wants in a partner and ask her to share her life with him, and if they have children, he'll assume that she will have the major responsibility for caring for them. But the male role also has problems.

Problems with the Male Role

It is a common misconception that only women suffer from a narrow gender role. There are probably two reasons for this misconception. First, the negative aspects of the traditional role for women are more obvious than those associated with the man's role. Second, as we noted earlier, the women's movement stimulated concern about the costs of the female role during the 1950s and 1960s. Only more recently have similar concerns been raised about the costs of the male role (Emerson, 1985; Doyle, 1989; Fasteau, 1974; Goldberg, 1976, 1979; Keen, 1991; Pleck, 1981a).

Pressure to Succeed

Whereas many women are trained to be inhibited about pursuing success outside the home, most men are socialized to believe that job success is everything. They are encouraged to be highly competitive and are taught that a man's masculinity is measured by the size of his paycheck (Doyle, 1989; Gould, 1978; Keen, 1991). Small wonder, then, that so many men pursue success with a fervor that is sometimes dangerous to their health. The extent of this danger is demonstrated by males' life expectancy, which

is about eight years shorter than females' (of course, factors other than gender roles contribute to this difference).

The majority of men who have internalized this success ethic are unable to realize their dreams. How does this "failure" affect them? Though many are able to adjust to it, many are not. The latter group is likely to suffer from poor self-esteem and a diminished sense of virility (Doyle, 1989). Men's obsession with success also creates problems for women. For instance, it contributes to economic discrimination against women. Many men want to "keep women in their place" because their self-esteem is threatened when a woman earns more than they do (Blumstein & Schwartz, 1983; Rubin, 1983). Men's emphasis on success also makes it more likely that they will spend long hours on the job and thus will have fewer hours to spend at home. This situation decreases the amount of time families can spend together and increases the amount of time wives spend on housework and child care.

The Inexpressive Male

Most boys are trained to believe that men should be strong, tough, cool, and detached. Males are socialized in a way that leads many of them to work overtime at hiding their feelings. Public displays of tender emotions are especially taboo. Some years ago a presidential candidate, Edmund Muskie, made the mistake of shedding a few tears on the campaign trail. That incident, so antagonistic to the American male ideal, destroyed his campaign with an abruptness that was startling. The fact that President Clinton has been observed to shed a tear in public is a welcome signal that some of these restrictions may be starting to ease. Constraints still exist, however, in regard to the appropriate settings for such displays.

As we noted earlier, there is little evidence that men are truly less emotional than women. The difference is that many men cover up their emotions. Their reticence is unfortunate on two counts. First, it makes it difficult for men to express feelings of affection for their loved ones. Many men can barely bring themselves to stammer through "I love you." Second, as we saw in Chapter 3, there are some risks inherent in bottling up emotions. Suppressed emotions contribute to many stress-related disorders.

Sexual Problems

Like women, men may experience sexual problems that derive partly from their gender-role

Homophobia is more prevalent among males than among females.

socialization. The problem for men is that they have a macho sexual image to live up to. Thus there are few things that most men fear more than a sexual encounter in which they are unable to achieve an erection (Doyle, 1989). Unfortunately, these very fears often *cause* the impotence that men dread (as we shall see in Chapter 13). The upshot is that men's obsession with sexual performance often produces anxiety that may interfere with their sexual responsiveness.

A related problem is the phenomenon of homophobia. **Homophobia is intense fear and intolerance of homosexuality.** Because homosexuality is still so widely unaccepted, fear of being labeled homosexual keeps many people who might otherwise be more flexible, especially men, adhering to traditional gender roles. As we noted earlier, many people fall prey to such social pressure because they mistakenly believe that cross-sex behavior is an indication of homosexuality.

One reason that homophobia is more prevalent among males is that the male role is rooted in the fear of appearing feminine—and feminine characteristics are mistakenly associated with gay males (Herek, 1986; Pleck, 1981a; Thompson & Pleck, 1986). Second, homophobia is much more common in men than in women because men experience more pressure to avoid any behavior characteristic of the other sex (Herek, 1988; Kite, 1984). Although they will tolerate tomboyishness in girls, parents (especially fathers) are highly intolerant of any "sissy" behavior exhibited by their sons. This intense pressure against appearing feminine contributes to the greater prevalence of homophobic attitudes among heterosexual males (Herek, 1988; Kite, 1984) and to negative attitudes toward females, as well (Friedman, 1989).

Gender-role expectations for boys have remained relatively stable over the years. However, it appears that aspects of the male role may be undergoing some changes. According to Joseph Pleck (1981a), who has written extensively on this issue, in the *traditional male role*, masculinity is validated by individual physical strength, aggressiveness, and emotional inexpressiveness. In the *modern male role*, masculinity is validated by economic achievement, organizational power, emotional control (even over anger), and emotional sensitivity and self-expression, but only with women.

The traditional role persists along with the new expectations, so some men may experience role inconsistencies. Pleck (1976) explains:

"Where childhood socialization valued physical strength and athletic ability and taught boys to shun girls, adulthood confronts males with expectations for intellectual and social skills and for the capacity to relate to females as work peers and emotional intimates" (p. 16). The recent rise in popularity of various men's groups suggests that many men are feeling uncomfortably constrained by their traditional gender role.

Role Expectations for Females

The traditional female role consists of two major expectations (Doyle & Paludi, 1991):

- *The marriage mandate.* The ultimate goal of the focus on heterosexual success is to find a suitable mate. "Real women" attain adult status when they get married. In marriage, women are expected to be responsible for housework and cooking. The fact that large numbers of lesbians have previously been married indicates the power of the marriage mandate (Bell & Weinberg, 1978; Chapman & Brannock, 1987).

- *The motherhood mandate.* The imperative of the female role is to have children. Nancy Felipe Russo (1979) has called this expectation the "motherhood mandate." A woman should have at least two children, and at least one of them should be a son. Moreover, it is important that she be a "good mother."

Although women are increasingly opting for jobs and careers, the expectation of a career is still not widespread enough to be called a "mandate." In fact, as we mentioned earlier, the traditional female role is incompatible with achievement in traditionally masculine areas (Huston-Stein & Bailey, 1973; Hyde, 1991; Lloyd, 1985). Both the marriage and motherhood mandates fuel the intense focus on heterosexual success among women. The resulting emphasis on dating and marriage causes most women to feel ambivalent about a career, lest they drive away a prospective mate who might be threatened by a high-achieving woman. Research on women's "fear of success" (Horner, 1972) suggests that women associate high-level career achievement with social rejection (Cherry & Deaux, 1978; Tresemer, 1974).

If gender-role expectations continue to change so that women have a wider variety of lifestyle options and career opportunities, more heterosexual women will be faced with the inherent conflict between family responsibilities and career (a conflict most heterosexual men don't currently face). It is unlikely, however, that large numbers of women will invest much identity in occupational success unless and until the burden of role overload is lightened by subsidized child-care programs or the willingness of fathers to take equal responsibility for child-rearing and household tasks (Pleck, 1981b).

Problems with the Female Role

Concerns about the limitations of the woman's role have received the lion's share of attention. These concerns first became prominent with the advent of the feminist movement, which generated some compelling analyses of the problems associated with the traditional female role (especially Friedan, 1964; Millett, 1970). Since then research has shown that many of these concerns are justified.

Diminished Aspirations

Despite recent efforts to increase women's opportunities for achievement, young women continue to have lower aspirations than young men with comparable backgrounds and abilities. Higher intelligence and grades are generally associated with higher career aspirations, but this association is less likely to hold for girls than for boys (Danziger, 1983; Marini, 1978). This discrepancy between women's abilities and their level of achievement has been termed the *ability-achievement gap* (Hyde, 1991). Its roots seem to lie in traditional gender roles. For one thing, we have seen that conflict between achievement and femininity is built into the traditional female role. Some women worry that they will be seen as unfeminine if they boldly strive for success (Horner, 1972).

Another reason that women experience more conflict about achievement than men do is that gender-role expectations and societal institutions have not kept pace with the reality of women's lives. Traditional gender roles dictate that husbands go to work and wives stay home and take care of the house and children. Today, however, roughly 60% of married women with children under the age of 6 work outside the home (Ries & Stone, 1992). This gap between roles and reality ensures that women who want to "have it all" experience burdens and conflicts that can weaken a strong investment in a career. Men experience relatively little competition among the roles of worker, spouse, and parent. They typically have major day-to-day responsibilities in only one role (worker), which is also a high-status role. Women, on the other hand, traditionally have day-to-day responsibilities as both spouse and parent; and when they decide to take a job, they have major responsibilities in all three

areas. These facts of life require women to make choices among lifestyles that men need not make.

Women typically select one of three lifestyle choices: marriage/family only, career only, or a combination of the two. Each of these choices provides certain rewards, and each brings its own problems. Heterosexual women who choose the traditional pattern may later regret not having been successful in a job (Luria, 1974). Women who opt for a career over marriage may suffer from negative stereotypes associated with this choice (Simon, 1987). Women who try to have it all will experience considerable conflict in meeting the often incompatible demands of multiple roles (Hodgson & Fischer, 1981). If a woman is in an egalitarian marriage (one in which the husband assumes equal responsibility for child care and housework), combining a career and family becomes more feasible. Still, if a woman has a serious investment in her career, finding a supportive mate may be difficult. In trying to juggle these role incompatibilities, many women lower their aspirations or make unhappy compromises that men can avoid.

The Housewife Syndrome

Women who don't work outside the home may experience a problem that Carol Tavris and Carole Wade (1984) have called the "housewife syndrome." The *housewife syndrome* encompasses the frustrations experienced by many (certainly not all) women whose sole identity is that of housewife. There is evidence that full-time homemakers are less happy, more discouraged, and more self-doubting than single or married employed women (Nickerson & Pitochelli, 1978). Housewives tend to feel less in control of their environment than married career women do (Erdwins & Mellinger, 1984). Furthermore, several studies have shown that full-time homemakers have poorer psychological adjustment than either employed husbands (who have the best) or employed wives (who are intermediate) (Steil & Turetsky, 1987).

Why is staying at home hazardous to many women's health? Why isn't it beneficial to be out of the rat race? Two key aspects of the housewife role stand out as major contributors to the problem (Ferree, 1976). The first is the housewife's relative isolation from supportive adults. Years ago housewives were more likely to be part of a supportive social network consisting of other housewives and relatives living nearby. Today, in our more mobile society,

RECOMMENDED READING

The Mismeasure of Woman

by Carol Tavris (Simon & Schuster, 1992)

The title and thesis of this book refer to Protagoras' statement that "man is the measure of all things." Tavris, a social psychologist, has written this book for the nonprofessional audience, and uses her natural wit and humor to excellent advantage. She points out the fallacy of using a male-centered standard for evaluating what is "normal" for both men and women. Using research findings, she exposes numerous myths that are the sources of misunderstanding and frustration for many men and women.

Tavris is interested not in replacing a male-centered view with a female-dominant view but in expanding our view of what it means to be human. She urges us to move away from the tendency to think in "us/them" terms about gender issues. She suggests that men and women need to work together and rethink how we need to be in order to have the relationships and work that are life-enhancing. In the following excerpt she explains how gender-based attributions of behavior can be triggered by situational factors:

> Men and women do not have a set of fixed masculine or feminine traits; the qualities and behaviors expected of women and men vary, depending on the situation the person is in. A token woman in a group of men will feel highly aware of her femaleness and so will the group. Almost everything she does will be attributed to her gender, which is why she is likely to be accused of being too feminine (thus not "one of the boys") or too masculine ("trying to be something she's not")—but what's really at issue is her visible difference from the majority. A token man in a group of women will have the comparable experience. [p. 292]

fewer people live near their relatives or in close-knit neighborhoods. Also, housewives have fewer opportunities for companionship during the day because the majority of wives work outside the home. Thus many housewives spend their days in a social desert, yearning for adult conversation.

The second problem is the lack of status and recognition for child care and housework. "Women's work," especially that in the home, simply isn't highly valued (Porter, 1985). Because their work is taken for granted, housewives get relatively little overt appreciation. Moreover, child care and housework are tasks that are never really finished, so it is difficult to experience a sense of accomplishment.

Ambivalence about Sexuality

Both women and men may have sexual problems that stem in part from their gender-role socialization. For many women the problem is that they have difficulty enjoying sex. Why? Well, for one thing, rather than being encouraged to focus directly on getting sexual experience, as boys are, girls are encouraged to focus on romance (Simon & Gagnon, 1977). Also, more girls than boys are brought up in ways that generate guilt, shame, and fears about sex. These negative emotions stem in part from the experience of menstruation (and its association with blood and pain) and fear of pregnancy. Females' concerns about sexual exploitation, rape, and incest can also contribute to the development of negative feelings about sex. Hence many women approach sex with emotional baggage that men are less likely to carry—they are likely to have ambivalent feelings about sex instead of the largely positive feelings that most men have (Hyde, 1991; Lott, 1987). (We'll explore gender differences in sexual socialization in greater depth in Chapter 13.)

Sexism: A Special Problem for Females

Intimately intertwined with gender roles is the issue of sexism. *Sexism is discrimination against people on the basis of their sex.* Generally the term is used to describe discrimination by men against women. We should point out, however, that sometimes *women* discriminate against other women, and men are occasionally the victims of sex-based discrimination. In the broadest sense of the term, we have been discussing sexism throughout this chapter, in that we have talked about the many ways in which women are treated differently from men on the basis of their sex. In this section we'll focus on three specific issues: (1) the relegation of child care and housework to women even when they work full-time outside the home, (2) economic discrimination against women, and (3) aggression toward girls and women.

Child Care and Housework

One consequence of sexism is that women still do most of the child care and housework even when they work outside the home. You might expect that women in the work force would be relieved of part of their responsibilities on the home front, but as we discussed in Chapter 9, this doesn't seem to be the case. Although men *are* spending more time on child care and household chores (Model, 1982; Robinson, 1980), this change seems to be occurring very slowly. Even recent studies report that married women spend two to three times as much time on household tasks as their husbands (Antill & Cotton, 1988; Berardo, Shehan, & Leslie, 1987; Douthitt, 1989; Gunter & Gunter, 1990). This pattern holds regardless of the kind

of work the wife does. One study of married, full-time, practicing physicians found that female physicians spent more than twice as much time on domestic tasks as male physicians (Pyke & Kahill, 1983).

Economic Discrimination

A second consequence of sexism is economic discrimination. Statistics show that more and more women are entering the work force, yet they continue to be the victims of discrimination. There are two aspects to this problem: (1) differential access to jobs and (2) differential treatment once they are on the job (Levitin, Quinn, & Staines, 1971).

With regard to *job access*, the problem is that women still don't have the same employment opportunities as men. In 1990, for example, 46% of all women workers were employed in relatively low-paying and low-status jobs, such as secretary, waitress, and health aide (Ries & Stone, 1992). And black women were even more likely than white women to work in these occupations. Other "pink ghetto" occupations include preschool and kindergarten teaching and nursing (see Figure 10.10).

In one study of sex and job access, heads of psychology departments across the United States were asked to assess the quality of job applicants on the basis of what were really fake résumés (Fidell, 1970). The only thing that varied on the résumés was the sex of the applicant, as indicated by the name. Yet, female applicants received lower ratings than the male applicants. A more recent study (Glick, Zion, & Nelson, 1988) confirms that sex bias in access to jobs is still a problem. Women *are* gradually breaking into higher-status, male-dominated fields, but only very slowly.

Men, too, suffer from discrimination when they apply for jobs that are not consistent with gender stereotypes (Larwood & Gutek, 1984; Ruble, Cohen, & Ruble, 1984). But, because "male" jobs typically have higher status and pay more than "female" jobs, the burden of such discrimination falls more heavily on women.

The second aspect of economic discrimination is the *differential treatment* accorded women and men at work. Men benefit from favoritism in many areas, including performance evaluations (Dobbins, Cardy, & Truxillo, 1986, 1988). One study asked school-district superintendents to make decisions about hypothetical personnel issues (Frasher, Frasher, & Wims, 1982). The authors identified a number of instances of discriminatory decisions, including viewing a man's request for a leave of absence for child care as more appropriate than the same request made by a woman. Also, men who put family concerns above job responsibilities were more likely to be promoted than were women who had the same priorities. Supervisors are more likely to discriminate against women if they hold traditional gender stereotypes and if a job candidate's qualifications are ambiguous rather than clear-cut (Dobbins et al., 1986, 1988).

Another example of differential treatment of the sexes is salary. Women are usually paid less than men for the same work (see Figure 10.11). In 1990 the average woman earned 72 cents for every dollar earned by the average man in a comparable occupation (Ries & Stone, 1992). The size of the pay gap varies from one occupational area to another, but it does not disappear even when women break into higher-status occupations. Female attorneys, for instance, earn only 75 cents for every dollar earned by male attorneys (National Commission on Working Women, 1983). Indeed, the average woman with four years of college education earns slightly *less* than the average man with a high school diploma (U.S. Department of Labor Statistics, 1990). A third example of differential treatment at work is sexual harassment, but since it is also a form of aggression toward females, we'll discuss it in the next section.

Aggression toward Females

Aggression toward girls and women results from a complex web of factors: (1) sexist norms that devalue females, (2) aggression as an element of the male gender role, and (3) males' having more power than females. We'll consider three of the many forms of aggression toward women: sexual harassment, rape, and the battering of women by the men in their lives.

Sexual harassment occurs when individuals are subjected to unwelcome sexually oriented behavior. This broad definition includes behavior ranging from suggestive comments or looks to unwanted touching, pressure for sexual favors, and sexual assault. Although males are occasionally subjected to sexual harassment, the vast majority of incidents involve harassment of females by males (Fitzgerald, Weitzman, Gold, & Ormerod, 1988).

Many people see sexual harassment as a problem that is limited to the workplace (which we'll discuss in Chapter 12). Increasingly, however, sexual harassment is being recognized as a problem that occurs not only on the job but also at home (obscene telephone calls), on the street (catcalls and whistles), in medical and psychotherapy settings, and in schools and colleges. With regard to the latter, recall the finding of the AAUW study on gender bias in schools that girls were subjected to sexual

**FIGURE 10.10
Women in the
world of work**
The percentage of women who work outside the home has been increasing steadily over the past century. Nonetheless, women are still underrepresented in traditionally masculine occupations and overrepresented in traditionally feminine occupations. (Data from U.S. Bureau of the Census, 1991.)

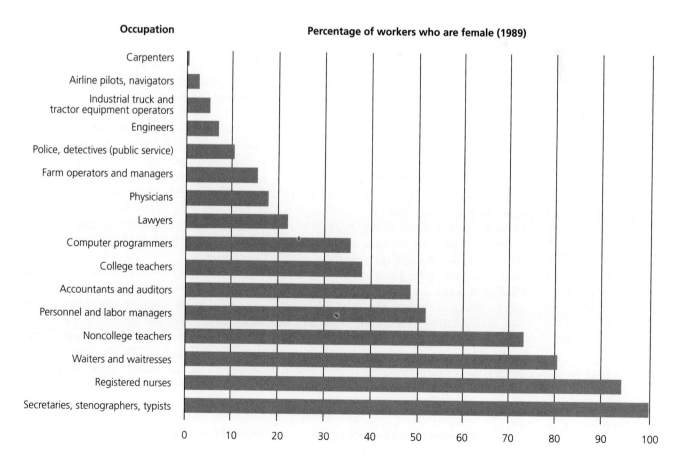

Occupation — Percentage of workers who are female (1989)

Carpenters
Airline pilots, navigators
Industrial truck and tractor equipment operators
Engineers
Police, detectives (public service)
Farm operators and managers
Physicians
Lawyers
Computer programmers
College teachers
Accountants and auditors
Personnel and labor managers
Noncollege teachers
Waiters and waitresses
Registered nurses
Secretaries, stenographers, typists

0 10 20 30 40 50 60 70 80 90 100

FIGURE 10.11
The gender gap in weekly wages
Women continue to earn less than men in all occupational categories, as these 1990 data for selected occupations make clear. (Data from U.S. Bureau of Labor Statistics, 1991.)

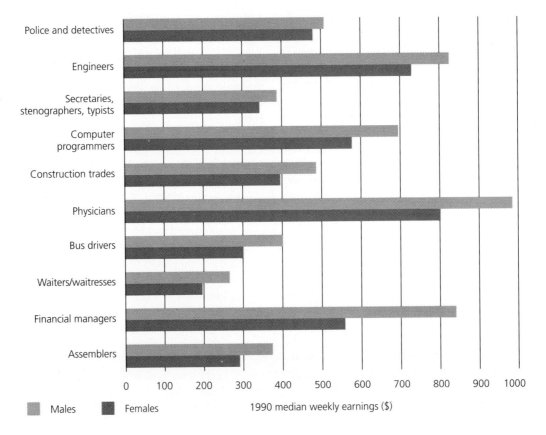

harassment by their male peers. Also, teachers and professors who pressure students for sexual favors in exchange for grades have been singled out for strong criticism (Dziech & Weiner, 1990; Quina & Carlson, 1989).

Because many women hesitate to report incidents of sexual harassment, it is difficult to obtain accurate estimates of the extent of this problem. Experts' estimates of the number of women who have experienced sexual harassment on the job range from 50% to 75% (Fain & Anderton, 1987; Lafontaine & Tredeau, 1986). On college campuses, estimates range from 17% to 38% (Dziech & Weiner, 1990).

Rape is forced sexual intercourse without consent. As we saw in our discussion of miscommunication and date rape in Chapter 6, experts estimate that as many as 50% of American women will be raped or subjected to attempted rape in their lifetime (Mahoney, Shively, & Traw, 1986; Muehlenhard & Linton, 1987). Women are raped by strangers, by acquaintances, by dates and lovers, and by partners in committed relationships. Contrary to popular belief, only about 20% of rapes are committed by strangers, and as many as 25% of rapes occur in the woman's own home (Katz & Mazur, 1979). The majority of rape victims are between the ages of 15 and 25, but infants and women in their 90s are also victimized in this way.

The experience of rape is so traumatic that it typically results in flashbacks, fear, suspiciousness, and depression (Martin, Warfield, & Braen, 1983). These feelings can last for months and even years after the attack (Nadelson, Notman, Jackson, & Gornick, 1982). Unfortunately, many people still blame the victim as a means of reassuring themselves that they could never be victims of rape. People with traditional gender-role attitudes are more tolerant of rape and more likely to blame the victim (Hall, Howard, & Boezio, 1986).

A *battered woman* is one who is subjected to serious psychological or physical abuse by her partner. Psychological abuse can include humiliation, name-calling, and refusal to speak. Physical abuse can include hitting, kicking, burning, use of a weapon, and rape. Unreasonable restriction of a woman's access to money is also a form of abuse (Schechter & Gary, 1988).

As in other taboo areas, accurate figures are difficult to come by. One estimate is that about 28% of all heterosexual couples experience some form of physical aggression (slapping, beating) over the life of their marriage (Straus, Gelles, & Steinmetz, 1980). Of course, this figure doesn't include the battering that goes on among couples who live together, and some researchers estimate that violence is even more common in these relationships (Stets & Straus, 1989). Moreover, this estimate excludes the physical abuse that goes on in some dating relationships and says nothing at all about psychological abuse. And we know that domestic violence is underreported because of the stigma attached to it.

According to a former surgeon general, domestic violence is the single largest cause of injury among women (Jones, 1990). Two-thirds of people who die as a result of domestic violence are women. Every day four women are killed by men who batter. Moreover, over one-half of all female murder victims are killed by their current or former partners (Walker, 1989). In contrast, only 6% of male murder victims are killed by their wives or girlfriends (Federal Bureau of Investigation, 1985). Hence, the belief that men are "protectors" can be a dangerous myth for the women who believe it.

Men who batter women typically have low self-esteem (Sigler, 1989; Walker, 1984), are often overly jealous and possessive, and were themselves beaten as children or witnessed their mothers being beaten (Okun, 1986). They often tend to deny the seriousness of their behavior and deny responsibility for it. Abuse is more likely among men in the military (where hyperaggressivity is encouraged), among men subjected to unemployment (a serious threat to masculinity), and among men who have problems with alcohol or drugs (which impairs judgment) (Okun, 1986).

Although some characteristics of battered women have been identified, it isn't clear whether these traits trigger the abuse or whether they are the result of the abuse. That is, it is easy to understand why an abused woman might begin to feel that she was worthless. Battered women typically have low self-esteem, blame themselves, change their own behavior to minimize the abuse rather than try to change that of their partner, and often deny what is really going on (Sigler, 1989; Walker, 1984).

Why do some women remain in an abusive relationship? One reason is that a woman may love her husband and truly believe that his behavior will change (Roy, 1977; Walker, 1980). Even if she is convinced that he won't change, she may remain in the relationship to avoid the social stigma of being divorced (remember the "marriage mandate") or to avoid the disapproval of her family and friends (who are likely to blame the victim). The economic factor is an extremely important roadblock to escape, and one that is often overlooked (Bograd, 1988; Roy, 1977). An abused woman probably has children and will need to support both them and herself. If they are young, she may not want to leave them to go to work. Even if she does want to work, she will probably have difficulty obtaining a job that will pay for child care on top of other living expenses. Because of attitudes toward domestic violence, the propensity to blame the victim, and the inadequacy of social services for abused women, they frequently have nowhere to go.

In summary, although costs are associated with traditional gender roles for both sexes, the heaviest costs of sexism are borne by women. When prejudice and discrimination prevent talented individuals from making contributions from which all could benefit, society as a whole suffers.

Gender in the Past and Future

Until now we have focused largely on traditional gender roles and some of the difficulties they tend to generate. In Western society, however, gender roles are in a state of transition (Dambrot, Papp, & Whitmore, 1984; Weeks & Gage, 1984). Sweeping changes have already occurred. Less than 100 years ago women were not allowed to vote or to manage their own finances. Only a few decades ago it was virtually unheard of for a woman to initiate a date, head a corporation, or run for public office. Let us consider *why* gender roles are changing and what the future may hold.

Why Are Gender Roles Changing?

Many people are baffled by the changes in gender roles. They can't understand why age-old traditions are being flouted and discarded. A number of theories have been proposed to explain why gender roles are in transition. Basically, they look to the past in order to explain the present and the future. A key consideration is that gender roles have always constituted a division of labor. In earlier societies the division of labor according to sex was a natural outgrowth of some simple realities. In most hunting-and-gathering societies, as well as most herding societies, an economic premium was put on physical strength. Men tend to be stronger physically than women, so men were better equipped to handle such jobs as hunting and farming. In most societies they got those assignments, whereas the women were responsible for gathering, home maintenance, and child rearing (Nielsen, 1978). Another consideration was that women had to assume responsibility for nursing young children. In summary, although people might have worked out other ways of doing things (and some cultures did), there were some basic reasons for dividing labor according to sex in premodern societies.

Essentially, our traditional gender roles today are a carryover from our past. Once traditions are established, they have a way of perpetuating themselves. Moreover, men have had a vested interest in maintaining these traditions, since the arrangements made them a privileged class. During the last century or so in Western society, these divisions of labor have become increasingly antiquated. Therein lies the prime reason for changes in gender roles, according to many theorists (Holter, 1975). *Traditional gender roles no longer make economic sense.* In our mechanized, industrial economy, physical strength has become important in fewer and fewer jobs. Moreover, as we move toward a service economy, physical strength will become even less relevant. Thus the principal cause of shifts in gender roles appears to be economic change that has rendered the distinctions between these roles obsolete.

The future is likely to bring even more dramatic changes in gender roles. We can see the beginnings of some of these changes now. Nursing of children, for example, is now optional. Moreover, as women become more economically independent, they will have less need to get married solely for economic reasons. As artificial insemination becomes more common, more women may choose to be single par-

ents. The possibility of developing a fetus outside the uterus may seem farfetched now, but some experts predict that it is only a matter of time. If so, both men and women could choose to be "mothers"!

Traditional gender roles used to be taken for granted. They were considered a "God-given" fact of life. As we have seen, however, what appear to be obvious behavioral differences between the sexes are often found to be stereotypes instead. Furthermore, the gender differences that do exist are most easily explained as differences in socialization. In recent decades we have become more aware of the social and political bases for gender roles (Tavris, 1992). This awareness has focused attention and public debate on the prejudices that underlie unequal treatment of females (and sometimes males). This attention seems likely to add momentum to the movement toward nontraditional gender roles. It is safe to predict that gender roles will remain in flux for some time to come.

Alternatives to Traditional Gender Roles

Gender-role identity was once conceptualized as either masculine or feminine. All males were expected to develop masculine gender-role identities and females, feminine gender-role identities. Individuals who did not identify with the gender-role expectations for their sex or who identified with the characteristics assigned to the other sex were judged to be few and to have psychological problems.

Recently the ways psychologists look at gender-role identity have changed significantly. One assumption that has been called into question is that males are and should be "masculine" and females, "feminine." For one thing, it appears that the number of people who don't conform to gender-role norms is relatively high, as is the amount of strain that accompanies attempts to conform to gender-role stereotypes (Pleck, 1981a). For another, research suggests that strong identification with traditional gender-role expectations may produce negative psychological outcomes in men and women. One summary of research findings has reported that highly feminine women are likely to show high anxiety, low self-esteem, and low self-acceptance (S. Bem, 1975). Although highly masculine males are often better adjusted during adolescence, in adulthood they often have high anxiety, high neuroticism, and low self-acceptance. Greater intellectual development

A division of labor based on gender no longer makes economic sense in our society. Relatively few jobs require great physical strength; the rest call for skills possessed by both men and women.

has been consistently related to masculinity in girls and femininity in boys. Highly masculine boys and highly feminine girls tend to have lower overall intelligence, low spatial ability, and less curiosity (S. Bem, 1975).

As we have seen, gender-role expectations can have some negative effects on the quality of life. It has been found that, on the average, males are more aggressive, less empathic, and less likely to express tender emotions, and their expressions of intimacy seem to be limited to women. They commit a disproportionate number of violent crimes, are more subject to substance-abuse disorders, and die younger than females. Women, on the average, have lower educational and occupational aspirations, are employed in low-prestige and low-salaried jobs, are less likely to run for and win political office, have less self-confidence, and have a high incidence of depression and anxiety disorders.

As people have become aware of the costs of traditional gender roles, there has been a lot of debate about moving beyond them. A big question in these discussions has been: What should we move toward? So far, two ideas have received the most attention: androgyny and gender-role transcendence. Let's examine these concepts.

Androgyny

Like masculinity and femininity, androgyny is a type of gender-role identity. **Androgyny is the coexistence of both masculine and feminine personality traits in an individual.** In other words, an androgynous person is one who scores above average on measures of *both* masculinity and femininity.

To appreciate the nature of androgyny we need to review briefly other kinds of gender-role identity (see Figure 10.12). As we noted earlier, males who score high on masculinity and low on femininity and females who score high on femininity and low on masculinity are said to be *sex-typed*. Males who score high on femininity but low on masculinity and females who score high on masculinity but low on femininity are said to be *cross-sex-typed*. Males and females who score low on both masculinity and femininity are characterized as *sex-role undifferentiated*.

Keep in mind that we are referring to individuals' descriptions of themselves in terms of personality traits traditionally associated with the two sexes (dominance, nurturance, etc.). People sometimes confuse gender-role identity with sexual orientation. They are not the same thing. One can be homosexual, heterosexual,

Femininity Score

	High	Low
Masculinity Score High	Androgynous	Masculine sex-typed (if male) or cross-sex-typed (if female)
Masculinity Score Low	Feminine sex-typed (if female) or cross-sex-typed (if male)	Undifferentiated

FIGURE 10.12
Possible gender-role identities
This diagram summarizes the relations between subjects' scores on measures of masculinity and femininity and four possible gender identities.

or bisexual (sexual orientations) and be androgynous, sex-typed, cross-sex-typed, or sex-role undifferentiated (gender-role identities).

As we have mentioned, it used to be assumed that males who scored high on masculinity and females who scored high on femininity were better adjusted than "masculine" women and "feminine" men. Sandra Bem (1975) challenged this prevailing view. She advanced the idea that androgynous people tend to be psychologically healthier than those who exhibit conventional sex typing. She argued that traditionally masculine men and feminine women feel compelled to adhere to rigid and narrow gender roles that unnecessarily restrict their behavior. In contrast, androgynous individuals ought to be able to function more flexibly, and such flexibility should be adaptive. Finally, she suggested that parents should rear their children to be androgynous instead of sex-typed.

What about Bem's ideas? Are androgynous individuals psychologically healthier than people who are sex-typed? Since 1976 more than 100 studies have been conducted to answer this question (S. Bem, 1985; Cook, 1985). Some early studies did find a positive correlation between androgyny and mental health. Ultimately, however, the weight of the evidence did not support Bem's hypothesis that androgyny is especially healthy (Locksley & Colten, 1979; Pedhazur & Tetenbaum, 1979; Taylor & Hall, 1982). In fact, a comprehensive survey of the research reported that *masculine* traits (in either sex) were more strongly associated with psychological health than androgyny (Taylor & Hall, 1982). These findings, as well as some problems with the concept of androgyny, have led Bem and other psychologists to take a different view of gender roles, as we shall see.

Gender-Role Transcendence

Some conceptual problems with androgyny caused theorists in this area to rethink their views. One of these problems is that androgyny requires people to develop both masculine and feminine characteristics rather than one or the other. While it can be argued that androgyny is less restrictive than traditional gender roles, it may also lead people to feel that they have two sources of inadequacy to contend with rather than only one (S. Bem, 1983).

Furthermore, the idea that people should have both masculine and feminine traits reinforces the assumption that gender is an integral part of human behavior (S. Bem, 1983; Lott, 1981). In other words, the androgyny perspective presupposes that masculine and feminine traits actually exist within us. Another way of saying this is that our current system is one that sets up self-fulfilling prophecies. That is, if we use gender-based labels ("masculine" and "feminine") to identify certain human characteristics and behavior, then we'll always, but wrongly, associate these traits with one sex or the other. Many theorists maintain, however, that masculinity and femininity are really only arbitrary labels that we have learned to impose on certain traits through societal conditioning.

This assertion is the foundation for the *gender-role transcendence* perspective (S. Bem, 1983; Lott, 1981; Spence, 1983). This perspective suggests that to be fully human, we need to transcend, or move beyond, gender roles as a way of organizing the world and of perceiving ourselves and others. This goal requires that we *not* simply divide human characteristics into masculine and feminine categories (and then combine them, as the androgyny perspective suggests). Rather, we should dispense with the artificially constructed gender categories and labels. Instead of the labels "masculine" and "feminine," we should use gender-neutral terms such as "instrumental" and "expressive" to describe personality traits and behaviors. This decoupling of traits and gender would eliminate the self-fulfilling-prophecy problem.

The advocates of gender-role transcendence argue that this practice would help us break our current habits of "projecting gender into situations irrelevant to genitalia" (S. Bem, 1985, p. 222) and hasten the advent of a gender-free society. They believe that if gender were eliminated (or even reduced) as a means of categorizing traits, each individual's unique capabilities and interests would assume greater importance. Individuals would then be more free to develop their own unique potentials.

Although many social scientists find the concept of a gender-free society appealing, some are concerned about the decline of traditional gender roles. Judith Bardwick (1973), for instance, has pointed out that the period of transition is apt to be quite stressful and that an egalitarian society might present some new problems. In a more polemical analysis, G. F. Gilder (1986) has argued that the demise of traditional gender roles could have disastrous consequences. Gilder maintains that conventional gender roles provide a fundamental underpinning for our economic and social order. Changes in gender roles, he asserts, will damage intimate relationships between women and men and have a devastating impact on family life. Gilder argues that women are needed in the home in their traditional homemaker role to provide for the socialization of the next generation. Without this traditional socialization, Gilder predicts, our moral fabric will decay, leading to an increase in crime, violence, and drug abuse. Given these very different projections, it will prove most interesting to see what unfolds during the next few decades.

Summary

Many stereotypes have developed around behavioral differences between the sexes. These stereotypes favor males, as our society is characterized by an androcentric bias. Research generally does not support our stereotypes. There are no gender differences in general intelligence, and if males have any advantage in visual-spatial ability, it is slight. Research shows that females are typically less self-confident than males but does not support the stereotypes of gender differences in emotionality or nurturance. More differences appear in the area of social behavior. For example, males do appear to be more aggressive and to talk more than females. Women seem to conform to group pressure a little more than men and use tag questions more often. Women appear to have the advantage in sensitivity to nonverbal communication. The sexes are similar in overall mental health, but they differ in prevalence rates for specific psychological disorders. For a variety of reasons, more women than men receive psychotherapy.

All in all, the gender differences that do exist are quite small. Moreover, they are group differences that tell us little about individuals. Nonetheless, the belief persists that there are dramatic psychological differences between males and females. Social role theory and social constructionism provide two explanations for this phenomenon.

Biological explanations of gender differences have focused on brain organization and hormonal influences. Some studies suggest that males exhibit more cerebral specialization than females. However, efforts to link this finding to gender differences in cognitive abilities are highly speculative, especially because cognitive differences appear to be disappearing. Efforts to link hormone levels to gender differences have also been troubled by interpretive problems. Thus most experts still believe that socialization is more important than biology in producing behavioral disparities between the sexes.

The socialization of gender roles appears to take place through the processes of (1) reinforcement and punishment, (2) observational learning, and (3) self-socialization. These processes operate through many social institutions, but parents, the media, schools, and peers are the four primary sources of gender-role socialization.

During infancy few gender differences are found. In childhood, boys experience much greater pressure to behave in gender-appropriate ways than do girls, and this pressure begins early in life. Even so, relatively few gender differences appear in childhood. Those differences that have been identified are in the areas of aggression and preferences in toys and games. At adolescence, physical and psychological maturation interacts with changes in gender-role expectations to make gender differences more obvious.

The five elements of the traditional male role include the antifeminine element, the success element, the aggressive element, the sexual element, and the self-reliant element. Problems associated with the traditional male role include (1) excessive pressure to succeed, (2) inability to express emotions, and (3) sexual difficulties. Homophobia is a particular problem for men.

The traditional role expectations for women include the motherhood mandate and the marriage mandate. Among the main costs of the traditional female role are (1) diminished aspirations, (2) frustration associated with the housewife role, and (3) ambivalence about sexuality. In addition to these psychological problems, women face sexist hurdles in the economic domain and on the home front. They are also victims of aggression in the form of sexual harassment, rape, and battering.

Gender roles have always represented a division of labor. They are changing today, and they seem likely to continue to change because they no longer mesh with economic reality. Consequently, an important question is how we may move beyond traditional gender roles. The perspectives of androgyny and gender-role transcendence provide two possible answers to this question. In the Application we'll explore gender and communication styles.

Indicate whether the following statements are true or false.

1

Men talk much more than women in mixed-sex groups.

2

Women are more likely to ask for help than men.

3

Women are more willing to initiate confrontations in relationships than men.

4

Men talk more about nonpersonal issues with their friends than do women.

If you indicated that all of the statements on the left are true, you were correct. These are just some of the observed differences in communication styles between men and women. These style differences appear to be the source of many misunderstandings. Though they do not apply to all men and women or to all mixed-sex conversations, gender differences in communication style can cause conflict and frustration.

When we are subjected to one of these distressing encounters in our personal or work relationships, we often see it as due to the other person's individual quirks or failings. Instead, it seems that some of these disheartening experiences may be due to gender differences in style. That is, sometimes men and women speak different "languages" in social interactions but don't realize that they do. In this Application we'll explore the nature of these gender-based style differences, how they develop, and how they can contribute to interpersonal conflicts. We'll also offer some suggestions for dealing more effectively with these style differences.

The Clash of Two Cultures

According to the sociolinguist Deborah Tannen (1990), males and females are typically socialized in different "cultures." That is, males are likely to learn a language of "status and independence" while females learn a language of "connection and intimacy" (p. 42). Tannen likens male-female communications to other cross-cultural communications—full of opportunities for misunderstandings to develop.

These differences in communication styles develop in childhood, fostered by traditional gender-role stereotypes and the socializing influences of parents, teachers, the media, and childhood social interactions—usually with same-sex peers. As we noted earlier, boys play in larger groups, usually outdoors, and farther away from home than girls (Feiring & Lewis, 1987). Boys, then, are under less scrutiny by adults and therefore

are more likely to engage in activities that encourage exploration and independence (Feiring & Lewis, 1987). Also, boys' groups are typically hierarchically organized (structured in terms of high- and low-status roles). Boys achieve high status in their groups by engaging in dominant behavior (telling others what to do and enforcing compliance). The games that boys play often result in winners and losers, and boys frequently bid for dominance by interrupting one another, calling one another names, boasting about their abilities, and refusing to cooperate with one another (Maltz & Borker, 1983).

Girls, in contrast, typically play in small groups or in pairs, often indoors, and gain high status through popularity—the key to which is intimacy with their peers. Many of the games girls play do not have winners or losers. And while it is true that girls vary in abilities and skills, to call attention to oneself as better than others is frowned upon. Girls are likely to express their wishes as suggestions rather than demands or orders (Maltz & Borker, 1983). Similarly, dominance is gained by verbal persuasion rather than the direct bids for power characteristic of boys' social interactions (Charlesworth & Dzur, 1987). These two cultures shape the functions of speech in different ways. Among boys, according to Eleanor Maccoby (1990), "Speech serves largely egoistic functions and is used to establish and protect an individual's turf. Among girls, conversation is a more socially binding process" (p. 516).

These different styles carry over into adult social interactions. According to Tannen, males' socialization experiences teach them to see the social world as hierarchical. If they are to maintain independence and avoid failure (in their own eyes and in the eyes of other men), they have to jockey for high status. Hence, she says, men tend to approach conversations as "negotiations in which people try to achieve and maintain the upper hand if they can and protect themselves from others' attempts to put them down and

push them around" (p. 25). Females, on the other hand, learn to see the social order as a community in which individuals are connected to others and the task is to preserve these connections. Consequently, women tend to approach conversations as "negotiations for closeness in which people try to seek and give confirmation and support, and to reach consensus. They try to protect themselves from others' attempts to push them away" (p. 25). These different views of the social order are at the root of the oft-heard complaint "You just don't understand"—the title of Tannen's book (see the Recommended Reading in this section).

Instrumental and Expressive Styles

Although not true of all men and women, there is evidence that men are more likely to use an "instrumental" style of communication and women an "expressive" one (Block, 1973; Tannen, 1990). Interestingly, this gender difference has been found across a number of cultures (D'Andrade, 1966). An *instrumental style* focuses on reaching practical goals and finding solutions to problems; an *expressive style* is characterized by the ability to express tender emotions easily and to be sensitive to the feelings of others. (Obviously, many individuals use both styles, depending on the situation.)

As we noted earlier, men tend to use instrumental communication styles more often than women. Research has shown, for example, that in conflict situations, husbands are more likely to stay calm and problem-oriented (Gottman, 1979) and to make more efforts to find compromise solutions to problems (Raush, Barry, Hertel, & Swain, 1974). However, an instrumental style, too, can have a darker side. When calmness changes to coldness and unresponsiveness, it becomes negative. Research has shown that lack of emotional responsiveness is characteristic of many men and that it seems to figure importantly in marital dissatisfaction (Christensen & Heavey, 1990; Dosser, Balswick, & Halverson, 1986; Roberts & Krokoff, 1990).

A large number of studies indicate that women, on the average, are more skilled than men in *nonverbal* communication—a key component of the expressive style. For example, they are better at reading and sending nonverbal messages (J. A. Hall, 1990). As for *verbal* communication, women are better listeners (Miller, Berg, & Archer, 1983) and better at consoling people in emotional distress (Burleson, 1982). But women have been found to engage in some negative expressive behaviors as well (Brehm, 1992). Research has shown, for example, that during relationship conflicts, women are more likely to (1) display strong negative emotions (Noller, 1985, 1987); (2) use psychologically coercive tactics (guilt, verbal attack, power plays) (Barnes & Buss, 1985); (3) reject attempts at reconciliation (Barnes & Buss, 1985); and (4) send double messages (make a negative verbal statement while smiling) (Noller, 1985, 1987). Women's greater use of such tactics may be attributable to their greater interest in changing relationships (Christensen & Heavey, 1990).

The idea that there are two cultures and gender-based communication styles has intuitive appeal because it confirms our stereotypes and simplifies complex issues. But there's an important caveat here. As we have often noted, research shows that status and power differences sometimes hide behind what seem to be gender differences. That is, because power and biological sex are often linked (males typically have more status than females) and because biological sex is a more visible factor than status, we often attribute differences in behavior to sex rather than power. Also, there are individual differences in preferred styles: some women prefer the "male style" and some men the "female style"; many will use either style, depending on the situation. Therefore, we caution you not to reduce *all* communica-

You Just Don't Understand: Women and Men in Conversation

by Deborah Tannen (Ballantine, 1990)

This bestseller addresses the communication gap between men and women. According to Tannen, a sociolinguist, boys and girls learn different styles of communication through same-sex social interactions in childhood. When used in other-sex interactions, these different styles can result in miscommunication and frustration because men and women often approach social interactions from different (and sometimes conflict-producing) perspectives. Tannen describes a wide variety of problematic interactions that result from style differences and gives numerous examples. In addition, she "translates" many conversations between men and women as a way of illustrating how the different styles operate—showing the reader the difference between what individuals think they are saying and how their messages may actually be interpreted. Tannen believes that many frustrations caused by gender differences in styles of communication could be alleviated if men and women learned to understand each other's perspective.

One of the many interesting issues Tannen discusses is the role and importance of metamessages—the attitudes, feelings, and status information behind the actual words people speak. According to the her, "metamessages frame a conversation much as a picture frame provides a context for the images in the picture" (p. 33)—they help us interpret what is going on in a conversation. To help readers understand how they operate in communication, she provides helpful examples of metamessages. Consider the following:

> The chivalrous man who holds a door open or signals a woman to go ahead of him when he's driving is negotiating both status and connection. The status difference is implied by a metamessage of control. The woman gets to proceed not because it is her right but because he has granted her permission, so she is being framed as subordinate. Furthermore, those in a position to grant privileges are also in a position to change their minds and take them away. This is the dimension to which some women respond when they protest gallant gestures as "chauvinist." Those who appreciate such gestures as "polite" see only the connection: He's being nice. And it is also the dimension the man performing the generous gesture is likely to see, and the reason he may be understandably incensed if his polite gesture sparks protest rather than thanks. [p. 34]

tion problems between males and females to differences in gender-based style.

Common Mixed-Sex Communication Problems

In this section we'll briefly review some common mixed-sex communication problems noted by Tannen. To keep things simple, we'll refer to "she" and "he" to illustrate various scenarios, but you should interpret these labels loosely for the reasons we have mentioned.

Mismatches

We expect our friends and partners to support and reassure us. When our expectations and reality fail to match, we can be confused and frustrated. Sometimes we are hurt or angry as well. Consider a woman who describes a recurring problem she is having at work to her partner because she wants some sympathy.

Thinking that she is seeking a solution to the problem, he gives her advice. Not receiving the consolation she seeks, she believes that he doesn't care. He, for his part, is frustrated by her repeated complaining because he has offered her the same advice in the past. Instead of taking his advice, she persists in complaining about the problem. In this scenario, neither wants to frustrate the other, but that's exactly what they are doing because they are talking at cross-purposes. She wants him to commiserate with her, but he thinks she wants him to help her solve a problem. Both assume the other knows what they want and neither does. These mismatches crop up quite frequently between couples.

Rapport Talk and Report Talk

Tannen suggests that most women engage in *rapport talk* (displaying similarities and matching experiences with others). Many men, on the other hand, seem to be more comfortable with *report talk* (exhibiting knowledge and skill to get and keep the attention of others). Also, men and women often have different ideas about what is important to talk about. She wants to talk about the personal details of her life and her feelings. He wants to talk about activities—things they do together or politics or sports. His failure to talk about personal things confirms her worst expectations (the relationship is falling apart). He fears that if he says

anything about emotions that might be fleeting—especially negative ones—they'll get blown up out of proportion and create a problem where one doesn't exist. Again, these differences are rooted in childhood experiences.

Talking about People vs. Things

Women's conversations frequently involve sharing the details of their personal lives, or "talking about people." It's important to understand that talking *about* people isn't necessarily destructive (although it can be if it turns into talk *against* people). As they did in childhood, women share secrets with one another as a way of being close. Men are interested in details, too, but of a different kind: politics, news, sports. Women fear being left out if they don't know what is going on in their friends' lives; men fear being left out if they don't know what is going on in the world. Interestingly, Tannen notes that exchanging information about public events (men's style) has an advantage over sharing private information (women's style): it doesn't make men personally vulnerable.

Tannen suggests that frustrations can be reduced if men and women understand how their style differences operate here. That is, men need to understand why many women like to talk about the details of their personal lives, and women need to understand that most men don't have this need. In addition, she says that both women and men need to

extend their communication strategies by adding aspects of the other style to their own. Some men may need to learn to feel more comfortable talking about their personal lives, while some women could benefit by talking more about impersonal topics and talking in a more assertive manner.

Lecturing and Listening

In mixed-sex conversations, particularly those in public settings, women frequently end up playing the listener to the man's "lecture." While this fact illustrates that women often don't get the same attention as men, Tannen suggests that we look more closely here. How does this situation come about? Are men self-centered loud-mouths? Are women meek and passive creatures? Instead of accepting these interpretations, Tannen suggests that men and women are playing different games that are rooted in childhood experiences. Men are playing "Do you respect me?" and women "Do you like me?"

As we noted, boys and men use words to jockey for status and challenge the authority of others—both men and women. Women who lack experience in defending themselves against these challenges can easily misinterpret an assertive man's style as an attack on her credibility. Similarly, women have been taught to "hand off" the conversational ball and expect that others will do the same. While most women reciprocate, many men don't. When this happens, some women may feel awkward drawing the focus of the conversation back to themselves because this style was frowned upon during childhood play with other girls.

Tannen suggests that women who tire of listening need to be more assertive and take some control of the conversation. Also, some men may be relieved to learn that they don't always have to talk. As we noted in Chapter 6, effective listening is a much-underrated communication skill.

The Woman's Double Bind

According to Tannen, mixed-sex communication situations often place women at a disadvantage. This is because the male style of communication is likely to predominate in these situations. If this were the only consideration, it wouldn't present much of a difficulty for women—they would just need to be proficient in the male style. The problem comes in because the male style is used as the norm against which both women's and men's speech is evaluated (recall the androcentric bias). So a woman is evaluated negatively regardless of which style (male or female) she adopts. The female style is devalued, and a woman's use of the male style is also evaluated negatively. Women in positions of authority experience a special version of this double bind. According to Tannen, "If they speak in ways expected of women, they are seen as inadequate leaders. If they speak in ways expected of leaders, they are seen as inadequate women" (p. 244).

Research supports this contention. When women failed to offer support for their arguments or used tag questions, subjects judged them to be less intelligent and less knowledgeable than men who behaved in an identical manner (Bradley, 1981). Similarly, students judged female professors as incompetent when they generated classroom discussion, but did not negatively evaluate male professors who did so (Macke, Richardson, & Cook, 1980).

Toward a Shared Language

According to Tannen, many frustrations in personal and work relationships could be avoided if men and women were more aware of gender-based differences in communication styles. Many people misperceive a style difference as the other person's personal failing. If we could see style differences for what they are, then a lot of blaming and negative feelings could be eliminated. As Tannen says, "Nothing hurts more than being told your intentions are bad when you know they are good, or being told that you are doing something wrong when you know you're just doing it your way" (pp.

Bridging the Communication Gap: Hints for Men

1 Notice whether or not you have a tendency to interrupt women. If you do, work on breaking this habit. When you catch yourself interrupting, say, "I'm sorry, I interrupted you. Go ahead with what you were saying."

2 Avoid responding to a woman's questions in monosyllables ("Yep," "Nope," "Uh-huh"). Give her more details about what you did and explain why.

3 Learn the art of conversational give and take. Ask women questions about themselves. And listen carefully when they respond.

4 Don't order women around. For example, don't say, "Get me the newspaper." First, notice whether it might be an inconvenience for her to do something for you. If it isn't, say, "Would you mind giving me the newspaper?" or "Would you please give me the newspaper?" If she's busy, get it yourself!

5 Don't be a space hog. Be more aware of the space you take up when you sit with others (especially women). Watch that you don't make women feel crowded out.

6 Learn to open up about personal issues. Talk about your feelings, interests, hopes, and relationships. Talking about personal things helps others know who you are (and probably helps you clarify your self-perceptions, too).

7 Learn to convey enthusiasm about things in addition to the victories of your favorite sports teams.

8 Don't be afraid to ask for help if you need it.

FIGURE 10.13
Overcoming gender-based communication difficulties: Hints for men
If we are to have productive personal and work relationships in today's world, we must be knowledgeable about gender and communication styles. Males may be able to benefit from the suggestions compiled here, which were taken from Deborah Tannen's (1990) book, *You Just Don't Understand: Women and Men in Conversation*. Among other things, men need to learn to listen more effectively when conversing with women.

297–298). We need to understand that there are different ways of listening, talking, and having conversations, not just our own way. Some advice on how to improve communication between the sexes can be found in Figure 10.13, which lists specific pointers for men, and in Figure 10.14, which lists specific suggestions for women.

Bridging the Communication Gap: Hints for Women

1 When others interrupt you, politely but firmly redirect the conversation back to you. You can say, for example, "Excuse me, I haven't finished my point."

2 Look the person you're talking with directly in the eye.

3 A lower-pitched voice gets more attention and respect than a higher-pitched one, which is associated with little girls. Keeping your abdominal muscles firm as you speak will help keep your voice low.

4 Learn to be comfortable claiming more space (without becoming a space hog). If you want your presence to be noted, don't fold yourself up into an unobtrusive object.

5 Talk more about yourself and your accomplishments. This isn't offensive as long as others are doing the same and the circumstances are appropriate. If the conversation turns to photography and you know alot about the topic, it's perfectly OK to share your expertise.

6 Make a point of being aware of current events so you'll be knowledgeable about what others are discussing and have an opinion to contribute.

7 Resist the impulse to be overly apologetic. Although many women say "I'm sorry" to convey sympathy or concern (not apology), these words are likely to be interpreted as an apology. Because apologizing puts one in a lower-power position, women who use apologetic words inappropriately put themselves at a disadvantage.

FIGURE 10.14
Overcoming gender-based communication difficulties: Hints for women
Women, too, can help to bridge the gender gap in communication. Tannen's (1990) suggestions for women emphasize the need to be more assertive in interacting with men.

CHAPTER 10 REVIEW

Key Learning Objectives

1. Explain androcentric bias in gender stereotypes.
2. Compare the cognitive abilities of males and females.
3. Discuss gender comparisons in personality.
4. Summarize the evidence on gender differences in social behavior.
5. Discuss gender comparisons and psychological health.
6. Discuss the size of gender differences and the nature of group differences.
7. Give two explanations for the discrepancy between beliefs and reality regarding gender differences.
8. Review the evidence relating gender differences in cognitive abilities to brain organization.
9. Review the evidence relating hormones to gender differences.
10. List and describe three processes in gender-role socialization.
11. Describe four sources of gender-role socialization.
12. Discuss the main points of gender-role socialization in childhood and adolescence.
13. List the five elements of the traditional male role.
14. Describe three common problems associated with the traditional gender role for men.
15. List the two major expectations of the traditional female role.
16. Describe three common problems associated with the traditional gender role for women.
17. Explain three ways in which women are victimized by sexism.
18. Explain why gender roles are currently in transition.
19. Describe the concepts of androgyny and gender-role transcendence.
20. Describe how the different socialization experiences of males and females contribute to communication problems between the sexes.
21. Define expressive and instrumental styles.
22. List five common mixed-sex communication problems.

Key Terms

aggression
androgyny
battered women
cerebral hemispheres
conformity
expressive style
gender
gender identity
gender-role identity
gender roles
gender stereotypes

homophobia
hormones
instrumental style
meta-analysis
nurturance
premenstrual syndrome
rape
sex
sexism
sexual harassment
socialization

Key People

Sandra Bem
Alice Eagly
Janet Shibley Hyde

John Money
Joseph Pleck
Deborah Tannen

11 Development in Adolescence and Adulthood

**"M**Y MOTHER ALWAYS COMplains that I spend too much time on the telephone. She thinks that I'm just gossiping with my friends and feels that my time would be better spent studying. She can't seem to understand that my friends and I help each other through some pretty rough situations. She thinks that way because she doesn't believe that anything a teenager does besides homework is important. My Mom tells me to learn in school, but she doesn't realize that I'm actually trying to learn to survive school. Attending school is like a tryout for life. I know that it sounds silly to adults, but at times getting a date, being invited to a certain party, or being chosen to work on the school's newspaper can mean more than getting an A on a test."

—"Tracy," quoted in *Teenagers Talk about School* (Landau, 1988, p. 31)

Do Tracy's—or her mother's—complaints sound familiar? Have you ever been frustrated by your parents' or your child's inability to understand your point of view? Psychologists attribute these contrasting perspectives to differences in development. Tracy and her mother are at different levels of development in a variety of areas: physical, cognitive, personality, and social. Thus they have different perspectives on themselves and the world.

Although the period of adolescence has been studied since the early 1900s, it is only since the 1970s that psychologists have given serious attention to development after adolescence. Until that time, it was widely assumed that developmental processes slowed to a crawl as people moved into adulthood. Now, however, social scientists realize that important developmental changes continue throughout adult life. As a result, they are probing into these changes to identify crucial patterns and trends. In this chapter we'll review some key concepts in human development and two important theories that have influenced our views in this area. Then we'll look at the major changes that take place during the developmental stages of adolescence and adulthood. We'll also examine

the topics of dying and death. In the Application we'll offer some suggestions for becoming an effective parent.

Key Developmental Concepts

ocial scientists who study human development employ special concepts in their work. We need to examine some of these concepts before we begin to trace the patterns of development in adolescence and adulthood.

Development and Aging

Development **refers to the sequence of age-related changes that occur as a person progresses from conception to death.** Development is a reasonably orderly, cumulative process. It includes both the biological and the psychological changes that take place as we grow older. An infant's newfound ability to grasp objects, a child's gradual mastery of grammar, and an adolescent's spurt in physical growth are all aspects of development. So are a young adult's increasing commitment to a vocation and a middle-aged person's struggle with a midlife crisis. All these transitions are predictable changes that are related to age.

Psychologists typically focus on changes in three key aspects of human functioning: physical development, cognitive abilities, and personality. The pacing of development in these areas may be highly variable. Periods of rapid development may alternate with periods of stability, or "plateaus." At any particular time, development in one area (say, physical growth) may be very rapid while development in another area (say, cognitive abilities) may be very slow. In other words, development does not proceed at a constant pace or at the same rate in all areas.

Changes in physical appearance are one aspect of aging.

People of the same age cohort often relate better to one another than to those who are younger or older.

Although there are many commonalities in the ways individuals experience development, there are also differences across groups and individuals. Some developmental trends are universal. Physical maturation, for example, occurs one to two years earlier in girls than in boys. Other trends may be unique to a particular culture or age cohort. **An *age cohort* is a group of people born in the same time period who develop in the same historical context.** People who belong to different age cohorts may be exposed to very different cultural experiences and expectations. The world in which teenagers are growing up in the 1990s, for example, is very different from the one teenagers experienced in the 1960s.

Although development is related to age, it is not the same as aging. **Aging is the biological process of growing older.** Aging is an inevitable, inexorable aspect of development. It takes place every minute of every day. It may or may not be accompanied by other developmental changes during a particular period. An individual's personality development, for instance, may be negligible during a particular time, even though aging continues. Aging in the later years is the focus of *gerontology*, a multidisciplinary field concerned with the study of the elderly.

Development: Stages or Processes?

Many theories of development propose that people evolve through a series of stages in a predictable, orderly sequence. For this reason, they are called stage theories. **A *stage* is a developmental period during which a person exhibits certain characteristic patterns of behavior and acquires specific capacities.** Stage theories focus on the *universals* in the developmental process, the *discontinuities* between the stages, and the *transitions* that facilitate movement from one stage to another. We encountered a stage theory in Chapter 2 when we discussed Sigmund Freud's notions about psychosexual development.

Stage theories are built on certain assumptions. First, they assume that people must progress through stages in a particular order because each stage builds on the previous stage. Second, they assume that progress through this orderly sequence is strongly related to age. In other words, they assume that we all go through the same stages at the same ages. Third, they assume that the transition from one stage to another involves a fundamental change or discontinuity in development.

Historically, theories of development have been stage-oriented (Petersen, 1988). Evidence is increasing, however, that human developmental patterns often do *not* coincide with these assumptions (T. O. Blank, 1982; Troll, 1985). Many changes are better described as continuous and quantitative rather than as dramatic, qualitative shifts from one distinct stage to another. Also, development often temporarily regresses to a less sophisticated level before it continues in a forward direction. These characteristics of development violate the assumption of stage theories that there are fundamental discontinuities between stages. Another problem with stage theories is that they don't account adequately for *individual differences* among people. Not everyone develops in the same way or at the same pace as everyone else. A variety of factors—gender, social class, race, ethnic background, personal experience—promote variability in development (Troll, 1982, 1985). Thus chronological age is only modestly related to developmental events in adolescence and adulthood.

The fact that age distinctions are blurring also calls the validity of stage theories into question. In present-day society, traditional barriers between childhood, adolescence, and adulthood may be breaking down. Today's children may be more knowledgeable than adults about such topics as drugs and computers. Some 16-year-olds are economically self-supporting, while some 30-year-olds are still financially dependent on their parents. Age ranges for specific life events are becoming increasingly wide (Neugarten & Neugarten, 1986). For instance, increasing numbers of first-time mothers may be found among 16-year-olds and also among 40-year-olds. College freshmen may be 16 or 60. Adults of all ages may be experiencing first marriage, remarriage, new parenthood, or career changes. In short, developmental patterns are becoming more variable.

For these reasons, current explanations of development seem to be shifting away from stage-oriented approaches (Petersen, 1988). Instead, interest is increasing in **process-oriented approaches, or the view that human development unfolds in a continuous fashion, often even regressing temporarily to earlier levels of functioning.** This approach has proved very useful in characterizing identity development. Recall Marcia's four identity statuses: foreclosure, achievement, diffusion, and moratorium. These categories are not stages that adolescents pass through in a particular order, but statuses that characterize an adolescent's identity orientation at a particular time. Process-oriented theories attempt to explain how various aspects of development unfold without being constrained by some of the questionable assumptions of stage theories.

Most of the early influential theories of human development are based on stages. Although they have their problems, stage theories do provide worthwhile descriptions of certain consistencies in human development. These descriptions can help us to achieve a better understanding of the challenges we confront throughout life. When we describe various stage theories later on, however, bear in mind that *development is probably not so orderly, uni-form, and predictable as these theories imply.* They are a bit too tidy to reflect the immense complexities of reality.

Age Roles and Social Clocks

You may recall that a *role* involves a pattern of behavior expected of a person in a particular social position. **Age roles are expectations about appropriate behavior that are based on one's chronological age.** The oft-heard lament "Why don't they act their age?" captures the essence of age roles. Our society has widely accepted norms that prescribe how people of a particular age should act, think, dress, and so forth. For example, age roles permit people in their 20s to live with their parents without attracting negative comment, but the same behavior in 30-year-olds is likely to raise some eyebrows.

Like the gender roles discussed in Chapter 10, age roles often place *constraints* on people that prevent them from behaving in certain ways. Thus some people decide they are too old to go back to school, too young to start a business, or too old to take care of themselves. Often these limitations are *self-imposed* simply because a person accepts traditional age roles. Constraints may also be *imposed by others* who discriminate against people because of their age. **Ageism is discrimination against people on the basis of their age.** Such discrimination usually occurs when people are perceived as being too old, but occasionally people are treated unfairly because they are seen as too young. Like other forms of discrimination (such as sexism and racism), ageism often leads to economic subjugation.

Closely related to age roles is the concept of a social clock. A **social clock is a person's notion of a developmental schedule that specifies what the person should have accomplished by certain points in life.** If you feel that you should be married by the time you're 30, for example, that belief creates a marker on your social clock. While we all have our own individual social clocks, they are very much the products of our socialization. The members of a given age cohort tend to have similar social clocks (Helson, Mitchell, & Moane, 1984).

Social clocks can exert considerable influence over decisions concerning education, career moves, marriage, parenting, and other life choices. Social clocks also provide a basis for self-assessment. As people progress through adolescence and adulthood, they periodically ask themselves, "How am I doing for my age?" Adherence to a social clock based on prevalent age norms brings social approval and thus is a way to evaluate one's own development. Social clocks can also increase the stressfulness of various life changes. Important events or transitions that come too early or too late according to one's social clock produce more stress than transitions that occur "on time" (Hogan, 1978). Indeed, it is easy to imagine how an early marriage, delayed career promotion, or premature retirement might be especially stressful. In particular, it appears that lagging behind one's personal schedule in regard to certain achievements produces chronic frustration and reduced self-esteem (Helson et al., 1984). Thus many of us listen carefully to our social clocks ticking in the background as we proceed through adolescence and adulthood.

Major Theories of Development

Before we turn our attention to the significant issues in adolescence and adulthood, we want to review two theories that have shaped much of the thinking about human development. We'll start with Piaget's theory of cognitive development and then turn to Erikson's theory of personality development.

Piaget's View of Cognitive Development

Cognitive development refers to age-related transitions in patterns of thinking, including reasoning, remembering, and problem solving. The study of cognitive development has been dominated in recent decades by the theory of Jean Piaget (1929, 1952, 1983), a Swiss biologist who devoted most of his life to the study of children's thinking.

Overview of Piaget's Theory

Piaget became interested in studying cognitive development while he was working with Theodore Simon, who had collaborated with Alfred Binet in devising the first useful intelligence test (Binet & Simon, 1905). In the process of administering IQ tests to many children, Piaget was intrigued to discover that children of the same age often gave similar wrong answers. This observation led him to hypothesize that children of the same age think alike. According to Piaget, older children do not simply know more than younger ones. Rather, they use different reasoning processes as they actively attempt to make sense of the world around them. Eventually Piaget proposed that children progress through four major stages, characterized by distinctive ways of thinking, which are shown in Figure 11.1.

Sensorimotor Period

Between birth and about age 2, children are unable to engage in symbolic thought or to use language. In other words, they are limited to immediate physical sensations, perceptions, and motor activity to make sense of the world and to control their environment. For example, a child may spy a red ball across the room (sensory perception) and crawl over to get it (motor response). Piaget aptly labeled this first stage of cognitive development the *sensorimotor period*. During this stage, infants progress from purely reflexive action to the beginnings of symbolic thought. The key to this transition is the young child's acquisition of the concept of object permanence. **Object permanence refers to the child's recognition that objects continue to exist even when they are no longer visible.** To an infant, out of sight is literally out of mind. If you show an eye-catching toy to a 4-month-old child and then cover it with a pillow, the child will not attempt to search for the toy. The child

Jean Piaget

Piaget's Stages of Cognitive Development

Approximate age range	Stage	Major characteristics
Birth to 2 years	Sensorimotor period	Coordination of sensory input and motor responses Development of object permanence Little or no capacity for symbolic representation
2 to 7 years	Preoperational period	Development of symbolic thought Heavy reliance on intuition No understanding of conservation or reversibility
7 to 11 years	Concrete operations period	Mental operations applied to concrete objects and events Development of conservation, mastery of concept of reversibility
11 through adulthood	Formal operations period	Mental operations applied to abstractions Development of logical and systematic thinking

FIGURE 11.1
Overview of Piaget's stages
Piaget's theory of cognitive development identifies four stages through which youngsters evolve. The age norms and key characteristics of thought at each stage are summarized here.

does not realize that the toy continues to exist under the pillow. Between the ages of 8 and 18 months, however, most babies gradually master object permanence as they become capable of picturing objects mentally. These mental images form the basis for symbolic thought.

Preoperational Period

During the *preoperational period*, which extends roughly from age 2 to age 7, children gradually improve in their use of mental images. In addition, they begin to use *words* as mental symbols, a feat that greatly expands their problem-solving capacity. Nonetheless, their thinking is still limited in important ways. Preoperational children are highly intuitive, for example, relying on evidence from their senses to solve problems rather than using logical operations. They tend to focus on a single dimension of a problem while ignoring other relevant aspects of it.

Piaget asserted that these flaws in preoperational thinking account for the child's inability to grasp the concept of conservation. **Conservation refers to the awareness that physical quantities remain constant despite changes in their shape or appearance.** For instance, after seeing one of two identical balls of clay flattened into a pancake, most preoperational children will insist that the pancake now has more clay. They are unable to grasp the idea that the amount of clay is conserved (remains the same) despite the change in shape.

Concrete Operations

Many of the weaknesses of preoperational thought are overcome during the *concrete operations period*. This stage usually lasts from about age 7 to age 11. During this stage, children gradually acquire the ability to solve problems logically rather than intuitively. They also learn to focus on more than one feature of a problem simultaneously and to reverse an action mentally, or "undo" it. For example, they can add and subtract. However, the child's new logical skills are typically restricted to *concrete* concepts. That is, the child can perform operations only on actual objects, or on mental images of actual objects. The ability to manipulate *abstract* concepts awaits the fourth and final stage, the stage of formal operations.

Formal Operations Period

As children move into adolescence, they gradually begin to apply the logical operations of the previous stage to a wider range of situations. In the *formal operations period*, youngsters' think-

ing is no longer constrained by physical reality or their personal experiences. Children under 12, for example, often have difficulty accepting contrary-to-fact assumptions ("Assume that cats fly") in order to solve hypothetical problems. They are likely to declare firmly that cats can't fly, so the problem can't be solved. Older children can accept the hypothetical assumption and proceed to solve the problem.

This ability to go beyond physical reality into the realm of hypothetical possibility is a hallmark of formal operational thought. Freed from the bounds of concrete reality, adolescents can now apply their logical skills to such abstract concepts as love, justice, and truth. They may spend hours contemplating heady social and political issues that would never occur to a younger child.

Children in the concrete operations stage are action-oriented. They attack problems by trial and error as they attempt to discover the underlying logic. In contrast, Piaget viewed adolescents as "amateur scientists." They conceive of the underlying logic first and then set about systematically testing their conceptions through experimentation. Piaget calls this kind of thinking **hypothetico-deductive reasoning— the ability to formulate specific hypotheses and test them systematically.**

Consider one of the problems devised by Piaget and his associate Barbel Inhelder (Inhelder & Piaget, 1958). Children between the ages of 8 and 15 were given materials to construct a pendulum. Their task was to figure out which of four factors determine how fast the pendulum swings. They were told to consider the *weight* of the pendulum, the *height* from which it was released, the *length* of the string from which it dangled, and the *force* with which it was pushed. Most of the younger children simply tried various random combinations of the four factors. Those who had achieved formal operations, however, used a better approach. They began by generating all of the possible solutions. Then they systematically varied each factor while holding the others constant. Thus they were able to eliminate hypothesized solutions one by one until only the correct one remained. In summary, formal operational thought is logical, abstract, reflective, and systematic.

Evaluating Piaget's Theory

In challenging the long-held assumption that children simply acquire increased knowledge with age, Piaget forced researchers to look at children's thinking in new ways. Piaget's theory has generated volumes of research, much of which supports his central propositions (Siegler, 1986). Such a far-reaching theory, though, is bound to have a few weak spots.

Piaget's description of the formal operations period has been criticized on several grounds. For one thing, there is some question about the universality of this stage. Many adults show little evidence of formal operational reasoning. For another, those who do reach formal operations generally do so later than Piaget thought (Neimark, 1982). Piaget (1972) himself acknowledged this problem. While continuing to maintain that everyone achieves formal operations, he proposed that these reasoning skills may be demonstrated only in content areas for which an individual has particular aptitude or special training. An auto mechanic, for instance, may evidence formal thought when diagnosing a car problem, but not when confronted with an unfamiliar physics problem. For many psychologists, however, this lack of generality of formal reasoning across content areas is damaging to the concept of formal operations as a distinct stage of development.

Other theorists have taken issue with Piaget's assertion that formal operational thought is the most mature form of reasoning (Basseches, 1984; Commons, Richards, & Kuhn, 1982; Datan, Rodeheaver, & Hughes, 1987). Patricia Arlin (1975) views formal operations as a problem-solving stage that describes how individuals answer questions presented to them by others. She believes, however, that there are higher-level thinkers (such as Piaget himself) who have the ability to *ask* new questions. Arlin calls these exceptional thinkers "problem finders."

In spite of these criticisms, Piaget's work is a landmark achievement. Without his theory to stimulate and guide research, crucial questions about cognitive development might not have been confronted for decades.

Erikson's View of Personality Development

Building on earlier work by Freud, Erik Erikson (1963) partitioned the life span into eight stages. Each stage is assumed to bring a *psychosocial crisis* involving transitions in social relationships. According to Erikson, our personality is shaped by the way we deal with these psychosocial crises. We have depicted all of Erikson's stages in Figure 11.2, but we will discuss only the last four, in keeping with our focus on adolescence and adulthood.

Stage 5: Identity vs. Diffusion

For Erikson (1963) adolescence is a period of pivotal importance. The outcome of the psychosocial crisis during this stage is either identity achievement or identity diffusion. According to Erikson (1968), adolescents must successfully pass through an "identity crisis" in order to develop a sense of identity. As we noted in Chapter 5, the identity crisis is not typically a traumatic event. Rather, it is a period during which adolescents wrestle with the important issues in their lives: who they are, what they stand for, and how they fit into society. They commit themselves to a vocational direction and an ideology, or system of values, that they can embrace as their own. Sexual orientation is also an important aspect of identity development. As adolescents formulate their identity, they slowly achieve some psychological distance from their parents, becoming auton-

**FIGURE 11.2
Overview of
Erikson's stages**
Erikson (1963) divides the life span into eight stages. Each stage involves a psychosocial crisis (column 2) that is played out in certain social relationships (column 3). If a crisis is handled effectively, a favorable outcome results (column 4).

Erikson's Stages of Psychosocial Development

	Stage	Psychosocial crisis	Significant social relationships	Favorable outcome
1	First year of life	Trust vs. mistrust	Mother or mother substitute	Trust and optimism
2	Second and third years	Autonomy vs. doubt	Parents	A sense of self-control and adequacy
3	Fourth through sixth years	Initiative vs. guilt	Basic family	Purpose and direction; ability to initiate one's own activities
4	Age 6 through puberty	Industry vs. inferiority	Neighborhood; school	Competence in intellectual, social, and physical skills
5	Adolescence	Identity vs. diffusion	Peer groups and outgroups; models of leadership	An integrated image of oneself as a unique person
6	Early adulthood	Intimacy vs. isolation	Partners in friendship and sex; competition, cooperation	An ability to form close and lasting relationships, to make career commitments
7	Middle adulthood	Generativity vs. stagnation	Divided labor and shared household	Concern for family, society, and future generations
8	The aging years	Integrity vs. despair	"Humankind," "my kind"	A sense of fulfillment and satisfaction with one's life; willingness to face death

omous individuals with their own consciously chosen values and goals.

Although the struggle for a sense of identity neither begins nor ends in adolescence, it does tend to be especially intense during this period, for many reasons. First, the physical changes of puberty force adolescents to revise their self-image and confront their sexuality. Second, the advent of formal operations promotes self-reflection. Third, faced with the end of mandatory schooling, adolescents must contemplate occupational choices and make decisions about their future.

Erikson and many other theorists believe that identity achievement is a cornerstone of sound psychological health. Identity diffusion can interfere with important developmental transitions that should unfold during the adult years.

Stage 6: Intimacy vs. Isolation

During the sixth stage, encompassing young adulthood, the psychosocial crisis centers on whether a person can develop the capacity to share intimacy with others. Erikson is not concerned simply with the young adult's need to find a marriage partner. He is concerned with more subtle issues, such as whether one can learn to open up to others, truly commit oneself to others, and give of oneself unselfishly. The person who can experience genuine intimacy is thought to be more likely to develop a mature and successful long-term relationship. Failure to resolve this psychosocial crisis favorably leads to difficulties in relating to others. The resulting sense of isolation often fosters manipulative interactions with friends and troublesome relationships.

As we noted in Chapter 8, Jacob Orlofsky and his colleagues found support for five intimacy statuses, based on the quality of a person's relationships (Orlofsky, Marcia, & Lesser, 1973).

- *Intimate.* Individuals in this status are capable of forming open and close relationships with both male and female friends and are involved in a committed relationship.
- *Preintimate.* Although people in this category are capable of mature, reciprocal relationships, they haven't yet experienced a committed relationship because they are ambivalent about making commitments.
- *Stereotyped.* Men and women in this status have relationships that are superficial and not very close. They often see others as objects to manipulate rather than as people to share with.

Erik Erikson

- *Pseudointimate.* These individuals are typically involved in a relatively permanent relationship, but it resembles the stereotyped relationship in quality.
- *Isolate.* Isolates avoid social situations and appear to be loners whose social interactions consist of casual conversations with a few acquaintances.

According to Erikson, the ability to establish and maintain intimate relationships depends on having successfully weathered the identity crisis of adolescence. In line with these predictions, several studies have found that college men and women in the more advanced identity statuses (achievement and moratorium) are most likely to be in the more advanced intimacy statuses (intimate and preintimate) (Fitch & Adams, 1983; Kacerguis & Adams, 1980; Marcia, 1976). Similarly, foreclosures and diffusions are predominantly in the less advanced intimacy statuses (stereotyped, pseudointimate, and isolate).

A recent study found support for Erikson's hypotheses, with an interesting gender difference (Kahn, Zimmerman, Csikszentmihalyi, & Getzels, 1985). This study found that men who had achieved a stable sense of identity were more likely to be married earlier than those who had not done so. Those men who had not achieved a stable sense of identity tended to remain single. In contrast, women's likelihood of marrying was not affected by their identity status. This finding can no doubt be attributed to the fact that women experience stronger pressure to marry (recall the marriage mandate). Women who lacked a strong sense of identity, however, were more likely to experience marital breakups. Thus this study showed that a stable sense of identity is related to men's *entering* committed relationships and to women's *remaining* in them.

Stage 7: Generativity vs. Stagnation

According to Erikson, developmental crises continue throughout adulthood. Next up, in middle adulthood, is the challenge of acquiring generativity, or a concern for the welfare of future generations. Adults demonstrate generativity when they provide unselfish guidance to younger people. The recipients of their guidance are often their own children, but not necessarily. A middle-aged college professor, for example, may gain great satisfaction from working with undergraduate and graduate students. Or a 50-year-old attorney may take on the role of mentor for a younger woman in her law firm. Thus generativity and its opposite, stagnation, do not hinge on whether we have children. Stagnation is characterized by self-absorption and self-indulgent preoccupation with our own needs.

Stage 8: Integrity vs. Despair

In Erikson's last stage, during the retirement years, the challenge is to achieve (ego) integrity. People who achieve integrity are able to look back on their lives with a sense of satisfaction and to find meaning and purpose there. Its opposite, despair, is the tendency to dwell on the mistakes of the past, bemoan paths not chosen, and contemplate with bitterness the approach of death. Erikson suggests that it is better to face the future in a spirit of acceptance than to wallow in regret and resentment.

Erikson's theory paved the way for a flurry of research on a number of important issues: identity development, adult personality development, and the validity of his proposed sequence of stages. A recent study tested some aspects of Erikson's theory with male and female subjects over a 20-year span of adulthood (Whitbourne, Zuschlag, Elliot, & Waterman, 1992). By using a complicated research design, the authors were able to demonstrate support for several of Erikson's propositions. For example, they found that psychosocial development proceeds in an orderly sequence of stages and that favorable resolutions of earlier stages lead to favorable resolutions of later stages. In sum, Erikson's ideas have greatly enriched our understanding of personality development over the lifespan.

Now, we turn our attention to the major developmental changes that take place in adolescence and adulthood.

The Transition of Adolescence

dolescence is a transitional period between childhood and adulthood. Its age boundaries are not exact, but in our society adolescence begins around age 13 and ends about age 22. In some ways, adolescents resemble the children they were, yet the many changes they undergo during this stage ensure that they will be different from children in many respects. Similarly, we see glimpses of the adults that adolescents will become, but we more often observe that they don't behave at all like adults. As adolescents mature, we see fewer resemblances to children and more similarities to adults.

Interestingly, a period of adolescence is *not*

universal. In many cultures, young people move directly from childhood to adulthood. The period of adolescence is seen primarily in industrialized nations, where technological progress has made lengthy education, and therefore prolonged economic dependence, the norm. Thus in our own culture, junior high school, high school, and college students often have a marginal status. They are capable of reproduction and so are physiologically mature, yet they have not achieved the emotional and economic independence from their parents that are the hallmarks of adulthood. Let's begin our discussion of adolescent development with its most visible aspect: the physical changes that transform the body of a child into that of an adult.

Physical Changes

Recall for a moment your junior high school days. Didn't it seem that your body grew so fast about this time that your clothes just couldn't keep up? Experts term this phase of rapid growth in height and weight the *adolescent growth spurt*—"spurt" because of the relatively sudden increases in body height and weight. It typically starts about 11 years of age in girls and about two years later in boys (Brooks-Gunn & Petersen, 1983). (Technically, this spurt should be called the *pre*adolescent growth spurt, because it actually occurs before puberty, which is generally recognized as the beginning of adolescence.)

Psychologists use the term **pubescence** to describe **the two-year span preceding puberty during which the changes leading to physical and sexual maturity take place.** In addition to growing taller and heavier during pubescence, children begin to take on the physical features that characterize adults of their respective sexes. These bodily changes are termed *secondary sex characteristics*—**physical features that distinguish one sex from the other but are not essential for reproduction.** These developments include voice changes, distribution of body hair, growth of breasts in girls, and body shape (see Figure 11.3). Boys experience greater skeletal and muscle growth in the upper torso, leading to broader shoulders and enhanced upper body strength. Girls experience a widening of the pelvic bones plus increased fat deposits in this area, which broaden their hips (Chumlea, 1982).

These various physical changes are triggered by the pituitary gland. This "master gland" sends signals to the adrenal glands (on top of the kidneys) and gonads (ovaries and testes). These glands in turn secrete the hormones that are responsible for the changes in

physical characteristics that differentiate males and females.

Note, however, that the capacity to reproduce is not attained in pubescence. That comes later. *Puberty is the stage during which sexual functions reach maturity and marks the beginning of adolescence.* It is during puberty that the *primary sex characteristics—the structures necessary for reproduction—*develop. In the male, these include the testes, penis, and related internal structures; primary sex characteristics in the female include the ovaries, vagina, uterus, and other internal structures (see Figure 11.3).

The onset of puberty in girls is typically signaled by *menarche—the first occurrence of menstruation.* American girls typically reach menarche about age 13, and further sexual mat-

uration continues until approximately 16. Most girls are sterile for 12 to 18 months after menarche. In the absence of visible external genitals, breast development and the presence of pubic hair serve as important social criteria of adolescence for girls.

There is no comparable clear-cut marker of the onset of sexual maturity in boys. The capacity to ejaculate sperm is used as a popular index of puberty (the onset of sperm production not being a visible event). The first ejaculation usually occurs through masturbation rather than nocturnal emission (Hyde, 1990). (Nocturnal emissions, or "wet dreams," occur during sleep and are sometimes accompanied by erotic dreams.) Ejaculation may not be a valid index of actual maturity, because early ejaculations may contain seminal fluid but not active sperm.

FIGURE 11.3
Physical development during pubescence and puberty
Hormonal changes during pubescence lead not only to a growth spurt but also to the development of secondary sex characteristics. During puberty the primary sex characteristics mature. These various physical changes are caused by the secretion of hormones.

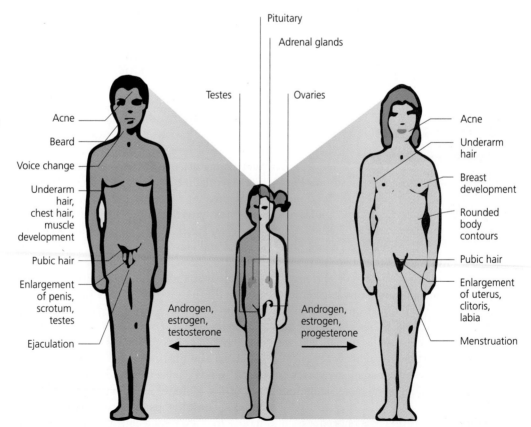

American boys begin to produce sperm and ejaculate at the average age of 14½, and complete sexual maturation occurs about age 18 (Tanner, 1978).

As we have noted, puberty arrives about two years earlier in girls than in boys. Indeed, the major reason that men are taller than women is that men typically have had two additional years of development before the onset of the growth spurt (Chumlea, 1982). Interestingly, there have been *generational* changes in the timing of puberty. Today's adolescents begin puberty earlier and complete it more rapidly than did their counterparts in earlier generations (Tanner, 1971). This trend apparently reflects improvements in nutrition and medical care.

After sexual maturation has been attained, adolescents continue to mature physically until the secondary sex characteristics are fully developed and the body has reached adult height and proportions. In girls, such growth continues until about 17 years of age; in boys, it goes on until about age 21 (Roche, 1979).

Although variation in the onset of pubescence and puberty is normal, adolescents who mature unusually early or unusually late often feel uneasy about it. Puberty is a major transition requiring significant psychological adjustment. Those who perceive their development as too early or too late may be particularly troubled. Girls who mature early and boys who mature late seem to feel especially awkward about their looks (Siegel, 1982). The early-maturing girl is taller and heavier than most of the girls and nearly all of the boys her age. The late-maturing boy is shorter and slighter than most of the boys and nearly all of the girls his age. To make matters worse, both groups have body types that are at odds with our cultural ideals of extreme slenderness for females and a muscular physique for males. Therefore, early-maturing girls and late-maturing boys may feel particularly anxious and self-conscious about their changing bodies.

The consequences of maturing early or late may extend into adulthood. In one influential study, Mary Cover Jones (1965) found that males who matured late tended to display less leadership and have more feelings of inferiority—even after they reached their 30s—than males who matured early. On a more positive note, the late-maturing males also tended to be more flexible, more perceptive about people, and more tolerant of ambiguity. In short, they were better able to cope with the complexities of adult life, perhaps because of the difficult adjustments they had to make in adolescence.

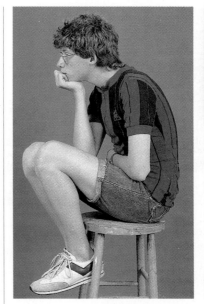

Gangly and awkward adolescents develop greater self-confidence and social skills as they mature.

Cognitive Changes

As we noted earlier, the thinking of adolescents is qualitatively different from that of younger children. Whereas youngsters go about solving problems by trial and error, adolescents approach problems by generating possible hypotheses and systematically testing them. Adolescents are freed from the cognitive limitations of the present; they are now able to conceive of possibilities they couldn't imagine before. The ability to conceive of future events is one of the reasons they spend so much time fantasizing, planning, and worrying about their lives to be.

A particularly interesting aspect of cognitive development is egocentrism. Piaget used the term **egocentrism to refer to the tendency to let idiosyncratic perceptions color our view of reality.** According to David Elkind (1967, 1988), egocentrism in adolescence appears to account for much of the experience and behavior typical of young people of this age. Elkind aptly labels one form of adolescent egocentrism the *imaginary audience*. Because adolescents are so focused on themselves, they wrongly assume that they are the center of others' attention as well. Hence adolescents often act as if they were performing for an audience. The imaginary audience is at work in adolescents' self-consciousness (both unwarranted self-criticism and self-admiration) and in their fantasies about how others will react to the news of their death (others realize—too late, of course—what a good person they really were).

A second form of adolescent egocentrism is the *personal fable*: Adolescents believe that they are unique and therefore that others (especially their parents) can't comprehend their special

experiences. Familiar personal fables come readily to mind: the ecstasy of one's first romantic love experience (no one else has ever loved so deeply) and the utter devastation of one's first break-up (no one else has ever suffered so much).

Elkind suggests that much of the high-risk behavior of some adolescents is due to the personal fable. The high incidence of injury and death by accident in this group is most likely based on adolescents' belief that they are immune to disaster (even though others are not). The high incidence of pregnancy attributed to the failure to use birth control probably reflects the personal fable that "other girls can get pregnant, but not me."

Egocentrism seems to disappear as we learn more about others through social interactions and intimate relationships in which there is mutual self-disclosure. That is, when we learn that others often have views that differ from our own, we replace the imaginary audience with a more realistic sense of the beliefs of others. Similarly, the personal fable is eventually abandoned as we come to see that our own experiences are not so different from those of others (Enright, Shukla, & Lapsley, 1980).

The Search for Identity

The key challenge to adolescents, according to Erikson, is to develop a sense of identity. To accomplish this goal, young people must go through a period of soul-searching (identity crisis) and emerge with commitments to an occupation and an ideology that are truly their own.

As we saw in Chapter 5, the psychosocial crisis of adolescence actually has four possible outcomes rather than just the two shown in Figure 11.2 (Marcia, 1980). Each of these identity statuses represents a distinctive way of dealing with the identity crisis. Young people in *foreclosure* make premature commitments to visions, values, and roles prescribed by their parents (identity crisis bypassed). Those in

moratorium delay commitment for awhile to experiment with alternative ideologies (identity crisis in progress). Those in *identity diffusion* are unable to make commitments (identity crisis unresolved). Those who succeed in *identity achievement* arrive at a sense of self and direction after some consideration of alternative possibilities (identity crisis resolved).

A sense of identity usually evolves gradually as a result of innumerable daily decisions: whether to date a particular person, take a particular course, use drugs, become sexually active, become politically involved, go to college, and so forth (Marcia, 1980).

Time of Turmoil?

Is adolescence a period of emotional turmoil? G. Stanley Hall (1904), one of the first psychologists to study adolescence, thought so. In fact, he specifically characterized adolescence as a period of "storm and stress." Hall attributed this turmoil to the conflicts between the physical changes of puberty and society's demands for social and emotional maturity.

Does the evidence support the idea that adolescence is a period of emotional turbulence? Overall, the consensus of the experts appears to be no. Research suggests that a majority of teenagers make it through adolescence without any more turmoil than one is likely to encounter in other periods of life. In one widely cited study of adolescent boys, a distinct minority (22%) went through a turbulent, crisis-dominated adolescence (Offer & Offer, 1975). After extensive studies of adolescents, Anne Petersen (1987) concludes, "The adolescent's journey toward adulthood is inherently marked by change and upheaval, but need not be fraught with chaos or deep pain" (p. 34).

No doubt because of popular expectations that the adolescent period will be filled with storm and stress, many parents, teachers, and counselors view the onset of the teen years with anxiety and dread. Young people, caught up in their own experiences and lacking a broader perspective, may perceive their conflicts and frustrations as indications of serious psychological disturbance rather than normal responses to adolescent development.

In the course of development, the differences between those who can cope with the transition to adulthood and those who cannot become increasingly obvious. Symptoms of those in the latter group include depression, suicidal behavior, drug and alcohol abuse, and chronic delinquency (Petersen, 1988; Takanishi, 1993). Because the incidence of such problems is relatively low, attention should be paid to such behavior when it does appear (Petersen, 1988; Weiner, 1980). Well-intentioned adults make a serious mistake by passing off such problems as "normal adolescent turmoil" that the young person will "outgrow." Early professional attention in such cases can often prevent more major problems from developing.

Although the number of adolescents with serious problems remains relatively small, in recent years there have been alarming increases in the incidence of some of these psychological and social problems. Deaths by homicide among 15-to-19-year-old African American males increased 115% between 1985 and 1990 (Children's Safety Network, 1991). The suicide rates in the same segment of the general population doubled between 1968 and 1985 (Children's Safety Network, 1991).

Adolescent Suicide

The upsurge in adolescent suicide is apparent in Figure 11.4a, which shows that suicide among 15- to 19-year-olds increased by more than 180% between 1968 and 1986, while it remained relatively stable in the general popula-

tion during that time. Despite these increases, fewer than 1% of adolescents attempt suicide. Figure 11.4b plots suicide rates as a function of age. Here you can see that even with this steep increase, the suicide rate for adolescents is lower than that of any other age group.

Actually, the suicide crisis among teenagers involves more *attempted* suicides than *completed* suicides. Experts estimate that when all age groups are lumped together, suicide attempts outnumber actual suicides by a ratio of about 8 to 1 (Cross & Hirschfeld, 1986). However, the ratio of attempted to completed suicides among adolescents may be 100 to 1 and possibly even higher—much higher than for any other age group (Sheras, 1983). According to David Curran (1987), a suicide attempt by an adolescent tends to be a "communicative gesture designed to elicit caring" (p. 12). To put it another way, it is a desperate cry for attention, help, and support.

What drives an adolescent to such a dramatic but dangerous gesture? Research by Jacobs (1971) suggests that the typical suicidal adolescent has a long history of stress and personal problems extending back into childhood. Unfortunately, for some people these problems—conflicts with parents, difficulties in school, loneliness—escalate during adolescence. As their efforts to cope with these problems fail, many teenagers rebel against parental authority, withdraw from social relations, and make dramatic gestures such as running away from home. These actions often lead to social isolation.

When an adolescent feels socially isolated, a pressing problem with great emotional impact may precipitate an attempt at suicide. The precipitating problem—a bad grade in school, not being allowed to go somewhere or buy something special—may appear trivial to an objec-

**FIGURE 11.4
Adolescent suicide**
(a) In recent decades the suicide rate has increased far more for adolescents (ages 15–19) than for the population as a whole. (b) Nonetheless, the suicide rate for the 15–19 age group is still lower than the suicide rates for older adults. (Data from the *Statistical Abstract of the United States*, 1991.)

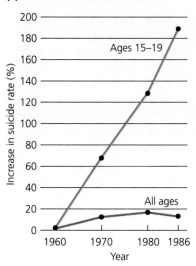

(a) Increase in adolescent suicide

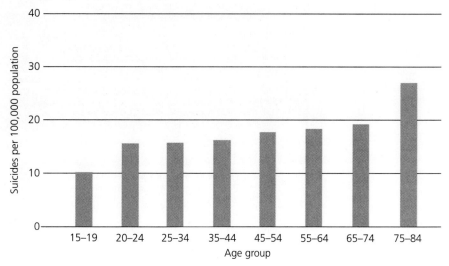

(b) U.S. suicide rates by age (1986)

tive observer. But the seemingly trivial problem may serve as the final thread in an adolescent's tapestry of frustration and distress.

The increase in adolescent suicide is a social tragedy that requires attention by parents, schools, and the helping professions (the Application in Chapter 15 discusses suicide prevention).

Phases of Adult Development: Gould and Levinson

Two independent studies of adult development attracted an enormous amount of attention during the 1970s. These two studies were summarized in a pair of widely read books: *Transformations*, by Roger Gould (1978), and *The Seasons of a Man's Life*, by Daniel Levinson and his colleagues (1978). Both focused on the central years of adulthood, from the 20s through the 50s.

Gould (1972, 1978) based his model on case histories and questionnaire data from two samples that included both men and women.

Gould identified seven phases in adult development, which are summarized in Figure 11.5. *In each phase, the crucial issue is how the person wrestles with certain false assumptions about life that are left over from childhood.*

Levinson's theory was originally based on interviews with a small sample of male subjects (Levinson et al., 1974, 1978). More recently Levinson and others have begun to apply his model to female subjects (Levinson, 1985, 1986; Roberts & Newton, 1987). Levinson has mapped out eight developmental phases in early and middle adulthood (Figure 11.5). He believes that *phases of relative stability alternate with phases characterized by turmoil and transition.* In describing these phases, he traces changes in what he calls one's "life structure." A **life structure encompasses the basic pattern or design of a person's life at a particular time** and is revealed through the choices the individual makes in regard to marriage, career, child rearing, and so forth. Although changes in a life structure do not take place in an orderly fashion, the age-related seasons in which they come are universal and predictable.

We will attempt to integrate Gould's and Levinson's observations to provide an overview of adult development. Although their findings

FIGURE 11.5
Overview of Gould's and Levinson's stages
Research led Gould and Levinson to propose different models of adult development, yet their ages and stages are remarkably similar.

Two Stage Theories of Adult Development	
Gould's seven stages	**Levinson's eight stages**
1 Ages 16 to 18 People feel a strong desire to get away from parents, but autonomy is precarious	**1** Ages 17 to 22 Leave adolescence, make preliminary choices for adult life
2 Ages 18 to 22 Feel halfway out of family and worry about being reclaimed; peer group important ally in cutting family ties	**2** Ages 22 to 28 Initial choices in love, occupation, friendship, values, lifestyle
3 Ages 22 to 28 Feel established, autonomous, and separate from family; feel "now" is the time for living, growing, and building; peers still important, but self-reliance paramount	**3** Ages 28 to 33 Change in life structure; either a moderate change or, more often, a severe and stressful crisis
4 Ages 29 to 34 Begin to question what they are doing; feel weary of being what they are supposed to be, but continue	**4** Ages 33 to 40 Establish a niche in society, progress on a timetable, both in family and in career accomplishments
5 Ages 35 to 43 Feel that time seems to constrict for shaping the behavior of their adolescent children or "making it"; their own parents turn to them with muffled renewal of old conflicts	**5** Ages 40 to 45 Life structure comes into question; usually a time of crisis in the meaning, direction, and value of each person's life; neglected parts of the self (talents, desires, aspirations) seek expression
6 Ages 43 to 53 Feel "die is cast" and view life with bitterness; blame parents and find fault with children but seek sympathy from spouse	**6** Ages 45 to 50 Choices must be made, a new life structure formed; person must commit to new tasks
7 Ages 53 to 60 Feel less negative feelings than in the 40s; relationships with selves, parents, children, and friends become warmer and more mellow; marital happiness and contentment increase	**7** Ages 50 to 55 Further questioning and modification of the life structure; men who did not have a crisis at age 40 are likely to have one now
	8 Ages 55 to 60 Build a new life structure; can be time of great fulfillment

are not identical, their models are compatible. As you can see in Figure 11.5, the age ranges for their stages are often similar, and many congruent themes are apparent. Occasionally, we will mention the findings of other recent studies on adult development.

Leaving the Family and Becoming Independent (Early 20s)

Both Gould and Levinson emphasize that the key transition in the early 20s is the movement away from the safe shelter of the family. This transition requires young adults to confront insecurity about the future as they attempt to establish independence. According to Gould, the false assumption that needs to be discarded is the idea that "I'll always belong to my parents and believe in their world." Levinson discusses how the young adult must scramble to achieve some financial independence while adapting to new roles, responsibilities, and living arrangements. Both theorists believe that this is a period characterized by considerable agitation and change.

According to Levinson, during this phase a young adult begins to shape a *Dream*—a vision of what she or he would like to become and accomplish as an adult. At first the Dream may be vague and unrealistic. Simplistic visions of becoming a baseball star, rising to the presidency, or finding a cure for cancer are common. Men's Dreams tend to center on occupational goals. Women are more likely to have "split Dreams" that include both career and family goals (Roberts & Newton, 1987). As young adults move through their 20s, they typically add definition, detail, and some realism to their vision of the future.

Entering the Adult World (Mid- to Late 20s)

The remainder of the 20s is typically devoted to completing the transition into the adult world. This tends to be a relatively stable phase in comparison with the early 20s. Tentative decisions from the preceding stage regarding marriage, family, and career are converted into deeper commitments that represent one's life structure.

The key conflict at this time centers on the contradictory urges to continue exploring various options and to make firm commitments to a vocation, an intimate relationship, and so forth. Thus people in this phase find themselves struggling with doubts about whether they have

committed themselves too quickly to an occupation or relationship, or delayed too long in making a decision. Gould emphasizes that the struggle to become fully independent of one's parents continues during this phase. Thus young adults must work free of the false assumption that "doing things my parents' way, with willpower and perseverance, will bring results."

Levinson believes that a very special and important relationship is often formed during this phase. This is the relationship with a *mentor*—an older, more experienced person who serves as a teacher, adviser, role model, and sponsor for the younger person. Usually (but not always) the mentoring relationship emerges in a work setting with a senior colleague. Typically the mentor is about a half-generation (8–15 years) older than the individual. The mentor's key function is to help define, support, and facilitate the younger person's Dream. The mentoring relationship is a transitional one, usually lasting from two to ten years.

Although Levinson found a great deal of mentoring among his male subjects, current

Finding a mentor is harder for women than for men.

evidence indicates that career women are less likely to enjoy the benefits of professional mentoring (Noe, 1988; Reinke, Ellicott, Harris, & Hancock, 1985). Presumably fewer older women are available in work settings to serve as mentors for younger women. The mentoring relationship tends to be emotionally intense. Consequently, it can be awkward for men to serve as mentors for younger women, since colleagues may misunderstand their relationship (Bowen, 1985). Interestingly, Reinke and her associates (1985) found that many of their female subjects had older friends or relatives whom they regarded as important role models. As more women move into higher-level positions in organizations, they will be able to serve as mentors for younger women.

Age 30 Transition: Doubts and Reevaluation

Around the age of 30, give or take a few years, both Gould and Levinson found signs of increased inner turmoil. Levinson found that the majority of his subjects experienced a crisis around this time. These crises centered on doubts about the commitments made in the preceding stage. These doubts surface just as the person is feeling that choices are getting locked in to an extent that will make it difficult to alter her or his life path. Among married women, the age 30 transition often stimulates a reevaluation of how they have balanced career and family goals (Roberts & Newton, 1987). Many of these women seek to renegotiate their marital roles with their husbands. Gould likewise sees this as a period of questioning decisions in regard to marriage, family, and career. Thus people struggle with the false assumption that "life is simple and controllable; there are no significant contradictory forces within me."

Settling Down and Becoming One's Own Person (30s)

According to Levinson, the vacillation found around age 30 is followed by a period of relative tranquility—for men, anyway. During this phase, men make a solid commitment to the life structure that they reformulated around age 30. They attempt to establish their niche in society and concentrate on climbing up the career ladder. Their pursuit of career advancement may require them to challenge their mentors in order to advance more rapidly.

Studies that have applied Levinson's model to women have not found a distinct period of settling down in the 30s. Continued questioning and instability in life structure are more likely among women (Roberts & Newton, 1987). Gould has observed similar instability in both sexes. He concluded that the period of questioning around age 30 lasts until the mid-30s, at which time people begin to enter the midlife transition.

The Midlife Transition (around Age 40)

A major landmark of adult development is the midlife transitional period, which Gould found to occur between ages 35 and 45. Levinson found the modal age for this transition to be 40 to 45. Both theorists view this period as a potentially turbulent time of reappraisal and restructuring.

Levinson found that people subjected their life structure to tough scrutiny and reevaluation. Most found that they had not fulfilled their Dream. Dismayed by this reality, they worked to revise their expectations or increased their efforts to achieve their goals. Even those who *had* reached or exceeded their Dream experienced a crisis. Many found their success less satisfying than they had expected. All of them had to confront the fact that success and acclaim do not arrest the inexorable process of aging. In addition, Levinson found many of his subjects struggling to acknowledge previously suppressed aspects of their personalities.

Both men and women sought to break down the rigid gender stereotypes by which they had structured their early adult lives. Women, freed from the responsibility of nurturing young children, began to express more independence, assertiveness, and competitiveness. Men, divesting themselves of their earlier assumption that career success would provide satisfaction, became more expressive and emotional. Gould, too, emphasizes the confrontation with the aging process during the midlife transition. He notes that many people are forced to acknowledge their mortality as they witness the deaths of parents, colleagues, and friends. Thus they wrestle with the false assumption that "there is no evil or death in the world." Women also tend to struggle with the assumption that their husbands can serve effectively as protectors. Those who succeed in outgrowing this assumption often become less dependent on their husbands. They tend to work harder toward their own goals, concentrating less on helping their husbands to realize theirs. Gould also emphasizes that during this period people feel pressured by time. They hear their social clocks ticking loudly as they frantically attempt to achieve their goals.

Since the landmark studies of Levinson and Gould, many other researchers have questioned whether the midlife crisis is a normal developmental transition. A host of studies have failed to detect an increase in emotional turbulence at midlife (Baruch, 1984; Farrell & Rosenberg, 1981; Roberts & Newton, 1987). How can we explain this discrepancy? Levinson and Gould both depended primarily on interviews and case studies to gather their data. Since the midlife crisis has long been a part of our developmental folklore, Levinson and Gould may have been prompted to interpret their case study data in this light (McCrae & Costa, 1984). In any case, investigators who have relied on more objective measures of emotional stability have found signs of midlife crises in only a minority of subjects (McCrae & Costa, 1990). Thus it's clear that the fabled midlife crisis is not universal, and it may not even be typical.

Restabilization (Mid- and Late 40s)

Both Gould and Levinson observed a period of relative calm after the instability frequently seen during the midlife transition. Although most people probably are not entirely satisfied with their lives, Gould notes that they feel that "the die is cast." Hence they begin to accept their fate with less resistance. Among his male subjects, Levinson found a tendency to shift some attention and energy away from career concerns in favor of family concerns. Levinson's female subjects showed a tendency to shift in the opposite direction, from family concerns to career concerns. Many of them entered or reentered the work force as their children left home. Although the "emptying of the nest" is

widely believed to be a traumatic event for women, few women seem to experience it as such (Datan & Thomas, 1984; Levinson, 1985; Reinke et al., 1985).

Culmination of Middle Adulthood (50s)

Information on developmental patterns after age 50 tapers off abruptly. Neither Gould nor Levinson has finished following his subjects through this decade. Although they lack concrete empirical data, both have made some theory-based projections. Gould suggests that the 50s are a period of "mellowing" as people continue to become more tolerant and accepting of their past. The limited data available seem to support this idea (Lowenthal, 1975; Reinke et al., 1985). Levinson speculates that those people who do not have much of a midlife crisis around age 40 may experience a delayed transitional crisis near age 50. Otherwise, Levinson projects that the mid- to late 50s may resemble the mid- to late 30s, with people settling into the life structures that they have recently rearranged for themselves.

Late Adulthood (after Age 60)

A prominent theory about late adulthood suggests that a process of disengagement should ensue (Cumming, 1963, 1975). According to *disengagement theory*, older people and society gradually withdraw from each other. Society withdraws from the elderly because it needs to replace older citizens with younger ones to remain vigorous and fully functioning. Older people gradually reduce their emotional investment in current events and reduce their interactions with others to protect themselves from the pain of personal failure and social rejection. According to Cumming, this process of mutual disengagement is both inevitable and mutually satisfying. That is, disengagement should foster high morale among older adults because it frees them from the necessity to behave in accordance with social norms. And society benefits from disengagement by being able to turn its attention and resources to younger people to maintain vital social institutions.

Some evidence supports the idea that there is a trend toward disengagement during late adulthood (Havighurst, Neugarten, & Tobin, 1968; Mindel & Vaughan, 1978). The percentage of people who report having extensive social interactions declines significantly between the ages 50 and 75, as Figure 11.6 indi-

FIGURE 11.6
Age trends in
social interaction
In a test of disengagement
theory, Cumming and
Henry (1961) interviewed
subjects of various ages
about their social roles and
networks. They found that
the percentage of inter-
viewees who reported
"high daily interaction"
with others declined
steadily after age 50.

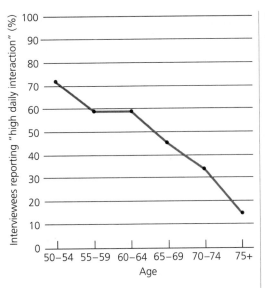

cates. Disengagement theory is very controversial, however, and available evidence suggests that this process is not inevitable (Palmore, 1975). Indeed, some critics suggest that when disengagement does occur, it is imposed on older people by society rather than being a matter of choice. In other words, society disengages from the elderly, but not the other way around.

Activity theory takes a different perspective on this issue and asserts that the social activity of older people is positively correlated with their satisfaction in life (Lemon, Bengston, & Peterson, 1972). There is some research support for this view (Lemon, Bengston, & Peterson, 1972; Palmore, 1975). That is, those individuals who minimize disengagement tend to be the most satisfied and contented during late adulthood.

How can we reconcile these contradictory findings? Perhaps the developmental stream flows in the direction of disengagement, but a portion of older people with certain values and personality characteristics manage to resist this undercurrent (Lemon et al., 1972).

Evaluating Gould and Levinson

The theories of Gould and Levinson have been highly influential in stimulating research on adult development, and they have achieved enormous popularity among the general public. Even so, these theories have been criticized on several grounds. Here are three of the principal criticisms:

First, there appear to be some errors in their conclusions. The lack of objective research support for a universal midlife crisis is a case in point. As we noted earlier, because Gould and Levinson relied only on interviews and case studies, their interpretations were open to subjective bias (McCrae & Costa, 1984).

Second, Gould and Levinson have mapped out the sequence of typical development but have said little about atypical development. Like most stage theorists, they ignore the great individual differences among people. Given the variability in both the timing and the sequence of events in adulthood, some theorists have questioned whether adult development should be viewed as an invariant, universal sequence of stages (Brim & Kagan, 1980).

Third, both theories describe the development of mainly middle- and upper-class people born in a particular historical period—just before or during the Great Depression of the 1930s. What these people went through is unlikely to be what their grandchildren and great-grandchildren will go through. Today's children are evolving in a very different world. Developmental patterns for women in particular seem likely to change in view of recent shifts in gender roles.

As an alternative to the ages-and-stages approach to adult development, many psychologists have simply set out to identify developmental trends across the expanse of adulthood. We'll summarize key trends in physical, cognitive, and personality functioning in the next section.

Aging: A Gradual Process

It is readily apparent that aging is accompanied by changes in a number of areas. While some of these age-related developments are quite obvious, others are very subtle. In either case, the changes take place gradually. We begin our discussion of the aging process by reviewing the changes in physical functioning.

Physical Changes

The changes that take place in the physical realm in adulthood affect one's appearance, nervous system, vision and hearing, hormone functioning, and health. (Unless we indicate otherwise, the following summary of trends in physical development is based on Whitbourne, 1985.)

Changes in Appearance

Height is rather stable in adulthood, although it

Many people, such as AARP president Lovola West Burgess and comic Bob Hope, remain active and productive in their 70s, 80s, and even 90s.

does tend to decline by an inch or so after age 55, as the spinal column "settles." Weight is more variable and tends to increase in most adults up through the mid-50s, when a very gradual decline typically begins. Although weight often goes down late in life, the percentage of body weight that is fat tends to increase throughout adulthood, much to the chagrin of many people. The skin of the face and body tends to wrinkle and sag. The appearance of the face may change, as the nose and ears tend to become longer and wider, and the jaw appears to shrink. Hair tends to thin and become gray, and many men have to confront receding hairlines and baldness.

The net effect of these changes is a general perception that one is no longer so attractive as one used to be. This unfortunate reality is probably aggravated by our society's obsession with youthful attractiveness. Older women suffer more than older men as a result of the decline in physical attractiveness. A recent study found that attractiveness ratings declined with age when the subject was a woman, but not when the subject was a man (Mathes, Brennan, Haugen, & Rice, 1985). Some people refer to this phenomenon as the double standard of aging (Sontag, 1972). That is, because much of a woman's worth is determined by her physical attractiveness to men, her social status declines along with her attractiveness (Bell, 1989). In contrast, older men don't have to rely on their looks for social status. Their occupational achievements and money serve this purpose.

Neurological Changes

The nervous system is composed of **neurons, individual cells that receive, integrate, and transmit information.** The number of active neurons in the brain declines steadily during adulthood. As neurons die, the brain decreases in both weight and volume, especially after age 50. Although this progressive neuronal loss sounds alarming, it is a normal part of aging that may not have much functional significance. Our brains have billions of neurons, so these losses may be mere drops in a very large bucket. At present there is little reason to suspect that this normal process contributes to the onset of *senile dementia,* **an abnormal and progressive decline in general cognitive functioning that is observed in people over 65.** It is estimated that about 12% of individuals in this age group have mild dementia and about 6% suffer from moderate to severe dementia (Mortimer, 1988).

Alzheimer's disease is a specific form of senile dementia. Although the precise causes of this disease are not yet known, it is associated with changes in brain chemistry (Coyle, Price, & DeLong, 1983) and structure (Hyman, Van Hoesen, Damasio, & Barnes, 1984). Alzheimer's disease is a vicious affliction that can strike during middle age (40–65) or later. The disease is one of progressive deterioration ending in death and may take from one to ten years to run its course. Tragically, no cure for the disease is known, nor can its course be slowed or reversed (Biegel, Sales, & Schulz, 1991).

The beginnings of Alzheimer's disease are so subtle that they are difficult to detect (Biegel et al., 1991). Individuals often forget common words, may report reduced energy, and may lose their temper. Later, obvious problems begin to emerge—difficulties in speaking and comprehending as well as in performing complicated tasks. Individuals don't seem to have trouble with familiar activities. Sometimes victims are insensitive to the feelings of others.

From this point, profound memory loss develops, especially for recent events. Patients may forget the time, date, current season of the year, and where they are. They may also fail to recognize familiar people, an occurrence that is particularly devastating to family and friends. Sometimes they experience hallucinations, delusions, and paranoid thoughts. Later, individuals become completely disoriented and lose control of bladder and bowel functions (Biegel et al., 1991). At this point they are unable to care for themselves at all. Finally death releases them.

Sensory Changes

The most important changes in sensory reception occur in the visual and auditory senses. Visual acuity is strongly related to age. The proportion of people with 20/20 vision declines steadily as age increases. From about age 30 to the mid-60s, the usual trend is toward increasing farsightedness. After the mid-60s, the trend is toward greater nearsightedness. Difficulty adapting to darkness, sensitivity to glare, reduced peripheral vision, and a yellowing of color perception are common among older people. Depth perception begins to decline in the mid-40s. This loss may impair the older adult's ability to negotiate obstacles and barriers successfully.

Noticeable hearing loss usually does not show up until people reach their 50s. Whereas the vast majority of the elderly require corrective treatment for visual loss, only about one-third of older adults suffer hearing loss that requires corrective treatment. In addition, small losses in touch, taste, and smell have been detected, usually after age 50. These losses generally have little effect on day-to-day functioning, although older people often complain that their food is somewhat tasteless. Visual and hearing losses, in contrast, often make interpersonal interaction awkward and difficult, thus promoting social withdrawal in some older people.

Endocrine Changes

There are age-related changes in hormonal functioning, but their significance is not well understood. They do *not* appear to be the chief cause of declining sexual activity during the later years. Any decline in this area seems to be due to acceptance of social norms that tell us that older people don't have sexual desires and that sexual activity is "inappropriate" in the elderly. For women, decreased sexual activity may simply reflect lack of opportunity, since the proportion of widows increases dramatically with age (Turner & Adams, 1988). The vast majority of older adults remain physically capable of engaging in rewarding sexual encounters right on through their 70s, although arousal tends to be somewhat slower and less intense.

Among women, **menopause, or the cessation of menstruation,** typically occurs in the early 50s. Not so long ago it was thought that menopause was almost universally accompanied by severe emotional strain. It is now clear that women are highly variable in their reactions to menopause and that the majority suffer little psychological distress (McKinlay, McKinlay, & Brambilla, 1987). Episodes of moderate physical discomfort during the transitional phase are fairly common. However, many women find this discomfort no more troublesome than that associated with menstruation itself, and some experience no discomfort at all. The loss of fertility that accompanies menopause is seldom traumatic, since it comes at an age when few women want to have more children. When emotional distress does occur, it is more often occasioned by the forced recognition that one is growing old than to a loss of reproductive capacity.

There has been much discussion of "male menopause" in recent years, but men really have no equivalent experience. Significant endocrine changes do occur in men in their later years, but these changes are very gradual and are largely unrelated to physical or psychological distress.

Changes in Health Status

Unfortunately, the quality of one's health does tend to diminish with age (Siegler, Nowlin, & Blumenthal, 1980). There are many reasons for this trend. Vital organ systems lose some of their functional capacity. Vulnerability to some diseases (such as heart disease) increases with age. Vulnerability to other diseases (such as pneumonia) may remain unchanged, but if one contracts them, their effects may be more serious. In any case, there is a clear trend in the direction of declining health, as you can see in Figure 11.7. The proportion of people with a chronic health problem climbs steadily with age. Older people who are poor are more likely to report that they are in ill health than those who are not (Birren, 1983).

Cognitive Changes

Notions about intellectual decline during adulthood are widely held. It is commonly believed that intelligence drops during middle age and that memory lapses become more frequent in the later years. Are these common conceptions correct? Let's review the evidence.

Intelligence

Researchers have long been interested in whether general intelligence, as measured by IQ tests, remains stable throughout the adult years. The early evidence on the stability of intelligence was rather disconcerting. Wechsler (1958) reported that intelligence peaked in the 20s and then declined across the remainder of the life span. We now understand that this finding was largely the product of methodological shortcomings associated with Wechsler's approach to data collection. More recent and better-designed studies have yielded a different picture (Hertzog & Schaie, 1988; Schaie, 1983). They suggest that IQ is fairly stable until about age 60, when a relatively small decline often begins (Hertzog & Schaie, 1988; Schaie, 1990). This post-60 decline appears to be associated with failing health (Field, Schaie, & Leino, 1988) and with problems in focusing attention (Stankov, 1988). These studies also indicate that there are large individual differences among people in IQ fluctuations. Although some people experience a modest decline during middle age, many others actually show an *increase* in IQ as late as their 50s. Overall, general intelligence seems to be stable throughout most of adulthood.

It does appear, though, that people's IQ scores drop precipitously within the last several years before death (Berg, 1987). This phenomenon is referred to as "terminal drop." It probably reflects the effects of declining health in those who are approaching death.

Memory

Many elderly people complain that their memory isn't what it used to be. In support of this perception, numerous studies report declines in the proficiency of long-term memory in older adults (Howe & Hunter, 1986; Hultsch & Dixon, 1990). Most of these studies, however, have asked subjects to memorize simple lists of words or paired associations. Older subjects may find such tasks meaningless and uninteresting. These artificial laboratory tasks bear little resemblance to the memory challenges that we encounter in everyday life. Thus it's hard to say whether the memory losses seen in these studies have much practical significance.

Investigators have only recently begun to study age-related changes in memory for more

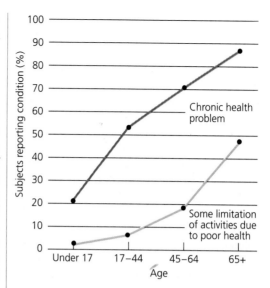

FIGURE 11.7
Age trends in health status
The data plotted here (from Wilder, 1971) show that the percentage of people with a chronic health problem increases with age, as does the percentage of people whose activities are limited by poor health.

meaningful, realistic content. There do seem to be some modest declines with age in memory for prose, television shows, conversations, past activities, and personal plans (Kausler, 1985). Such memory impairments could conceivably interfere with older adults' daily activities. However, the memory losses associated with aging are moderate and are *not* universal. Some older people, especially those who remain mentally active, suffer little memory impairment.

A popular misconception is that older people have very vivid recollections of events in the distant past but tend to forget recent events. In actuality, there is no evidence that the elderly have more numerous or more vivid early memories (Rabbitt & McGinnis, 1988). Their memories of events long ago may be loose reconstructions that are less accurate than people assume.

Learning and Problem Solving

Although intelligence and memory may be more stable during adulthood than many people believe, there *are* some significant cognitive changes during the adult years. These changes show up most clearly when researchers look at specific aspects of learning and problem solving.

There is ample evidence that the ability to narrow one's focus of attention diminishes somewhat with increasing age, as does the ability to handle simultaneous multiple inputs (Plude & Hoyer, 1985; Stankov, 1988). These changes may be due to decreased efficiency in filtering out irrelevant stimuli. Most of the studies have simply compared extreme age groups (very young subjects against very old subjects), so we're not sure about the age at which these changes tend to emerge.

In the cognitive domain, age seems to take its toll on *speed* first. Many studies indicate that speed in learning, solving problems, retrieving memories, and processing information tends to decline with age (Drachman, 1986). Although additional data are needed, some evidence suggests that this trend may be a gradual, lengthy one commencing in middle adulthood. The general nature of this trend (across differing tasks) suggests that it may be due to age-related changes in neurological functioning (Birren, Woods, & Williams, 1980). Alternatively, the slowing of cognitive processing with age could reflect increased cautiousness among older adults (Reese & Rodeheaver, 1985).

Overall *success* on laboratory problem-solving tasks also appears to decrease as people grow older (Charness, 1985). This decline is not so clear or strong as that observed for speed of processing (Reese & Rodeheaver, 1985). For the most part, problem-solving ability is unimpaired if older people are given adequate time to compensate for their reduced speed in cognitive processing. Furthermore, many of the age-related decrements in cognitive functioning can be partly compensated for by increases in older adults' knowledge.

It should be emphasized that many people remain capable of great intellectual accomplishment well into their later years. This reality was verified in a study of scholarly, scientific, and artistic productivity that examined lifelong patterns of work among 738 men who lived at least through the age of 79 (Dennis, 1966). Figure 11.8 plots the percentage of professional works completed by these men during each decade from their 20s through their 70s. As you can see, in most professions the 40s was the most productive decade. In many areas, however, productivity was remarkably stable through the 60s and even the 70s. Where researchers have focused on the quality rather than the quantity of output, they have typically found that masterpieces are produced with the same relative frequency by creators of all ages (Simonton, 1988).

Personality Changes

An article in the August 1989 issue of *Life* magazine featured then-and-now photographs and interviews of people who had attended the Woodstock Music Festival in 1969, an event that symbolized a youthful generation's rejection of the values of the majority culture. The interviews revealed that some of these music fans held on to the counterculture lifestyle of their youth. The vast majority, however, had

gone on to embrace the traditional values they had openly rejected two decades earlier. Is the Woodstock generation somehow unique in the extent of personality change? How stable is personality over the life span? Are there discernible trends in the personality development of adults?

Psychologists have engaged in lively debate about whether personality remains stable in adulthood, and both sides have been able to cite supportive research. On the one hand, large-scale longitudinal studies provide evidence for long-term stability in personality (Finn, 1986; Stevens & Truss, 1985). Costa and McCrae (1986) note that the available evidence "points clearly to the conclusion that personality is generally stable in adulthood" (p. 407). On the other hand, some studies suggest that substantial personality changes continue throughout the life span (Haan, Millsap, & Hartka, 1986; Helson & Moane, 1987; Whitbourne et al., 1992). Susan Whitbourne and her colleagues (1992) cite "a growing body of evidence indicating the existence of adult personality changes on a variety of . . . variables" (p. 268).

How can these seemingly incompatible conclusions be reconciled? Discrepant results from one study to the next may sometimes be due to dissimilar subject samples or to different data-collection techniques. For instance, many of the studies rely on self-report measures, in which subjects rate their own personality characteristics. As Finn (1986) has pointed out, stability in self-report ratings may mean only that people's *views* of themselves remain stable over time, not that their actual personalities do.

Furthermore, certain aspects of personality seem to be more consistent than others. For instance, Conley (1985) found several traits that remain highly stable throughout adulthood. They include emotional stability, sociability, extraversion, assertiveness, responsibility, and dependability.

Other traits are less stable over time. To demonstrate this phenomenon, let's briefly explore the personality dimension of **locus of control, a generalized expectancy about the degree to which individuals control their outcomes.** According to Julian Rotter (1966, 1975, 1990), individuals with an *external locus of control* believe that their successes and failures are governed by external factors such as fate, luck, and chance. Individuals with an *internal locus of control* believe that their successes and failures are determined by their own actions (internal factors). Although Rotter initially viewed locus

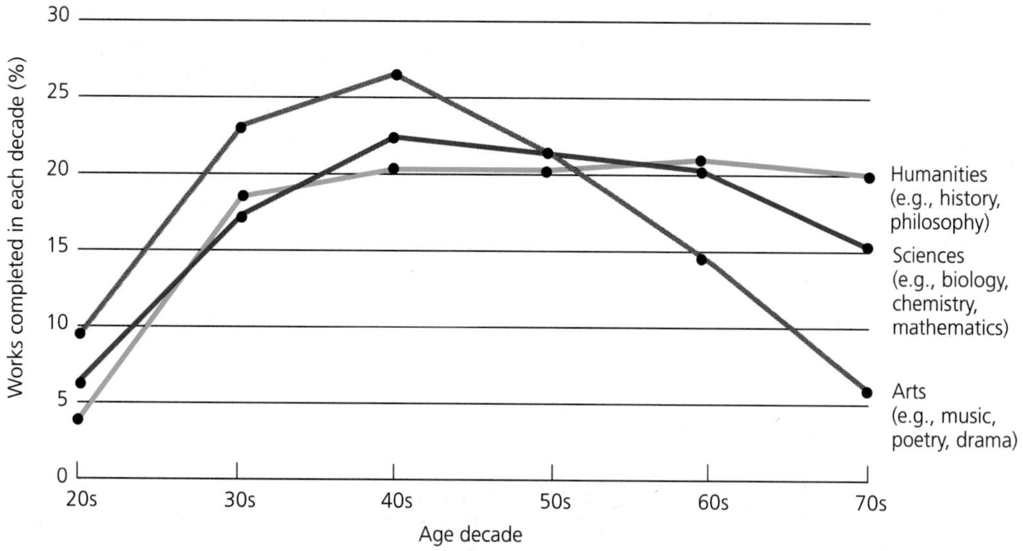

30
25
20
15
10
5
0
Works completed in each decade (%)
20s
30s
40s
50s
60s
70s
Age decade
Humanities (e.g., history, philosophy)
Sciences (e.g., biology, chemistry, mathematics)
Arts (e.g., music, poetry, drama)

FIGURE 11.8
Age trends in professional productivity
Dennis (1966) calculated the percentage of professional works completed in each decade of life by 738 men who lived to at least age 79. Productivity peaked when the men were in their 40s, but their professional output remained strong through the 60s, and even through the 70s for men in the humanities and sciences.

of control as a general tendency, research suggests that this aspect of personality might better be viewed as operating in specific contexts (Lachman, 1986). That is, a person might be "internal" about his intelligence and work but "external" about his health.

Does locus of control change with age? When the general dimension of locus of control is considered, the evidence on this question is conflicting (Lachman, 1983; Lachman, 1985; Siegler & Gatz, 1985). When researchers look at locus of control in specific areas of life, however, age-related changes do appear. On the dimensions of intelligence and health, for example, locus of control appears to decline with age (Lachman, 1986; Lachman & Leff, 1989; Siegler & Gatz, 1985).

In sum, adult personality is characterized by both stability and change. Although many aspects of personality are relatively stable over time, some others are likely to change.

Death and Dying

Dealing with the deaths of close friends and loved ones is an increasingly frequent adjustment problem as people move through adulthood. But the final challenge of life is to confront one's own death gracefully. In this section we discuss research on death and dying.

Attitudes toward Death

Research on death was relatively scarce until recently because death is a taboo topic in modern Western society. The most common strategy for dealing with death in our culture is *avoidance*. Evidence of our inability to confront death comfortably is plentiful. It is apparent in the way we talk about death, using such euphemisms as "passed away" to avoid the very word. Our discomfort often leads us to quarantine unnecessarily the dying in hospitals and nursing homes to minimize our exposure to the specter of death. These are all manifestations of what Kastenbaum (1986) calls a ***death system*****—the collection of rituals and procedures a society devises to handle death.** Death systems vary from one culture to another. Ours happens to be rather negative and evasive.

Negativism and avoidance are *not* features of all death systems. The Amish, for example, view death in a more calm and accepting fashion. They see death as a natural transition rather than as a dreaded adversary (Bryer, 1979). Thus some cultures and subcultures display less fear of death than our majority culture.

Within our culture, attitudes toward death vary greatly. Evidence as to whether *preoccupation* with thoughts about death peaks in middle or old age is conflicting. It is fairly clear that *fear* of death tends to decline after middle age (Kastenbaum, 1986). Perhaps older people begin to feel they have lived a full life, and they gradually work through the meaning of death as they confront others' deaths more frequently. One's particular religious affiliation isn't especially influential in determining feelings about death, but a strong, deeply felt religious commitment (regardless of denomination) is associated with lower anxiety about death. Ultimately, fear of death is an individual matter and is greatly influenced by personality and family background (Rosenheim & Muchnik, 1984–1985).

The Process of Dying

Pioneering research on the experience of dying was conducted by Elisabeth Kübler-Ross (1969, 1970) during the 1960s. At first her project met with immense resistance. Fellow physicians at the hospital where she worked were not inclined to cooperate with her requests to interview dying patients. Gradually, however, it became apparent that many such patients were enthusiastic about the discussions. They were frustrated by the conspiracy of silence that surrounds death and relieved to get things out in the open.

Eventually Kübler-Ross interviewed more than 200 terminally ill patients and developed a model of the process of dying. According to her model, people evolve through a series of five stages as they confront their own death. These stages often overlap, so it may be more accurate to characterize them as typical *reactions* that may or may not unfold sequentially. Huyck and Hoyer (1982, pp. 506–507) provide a succinct description of these reactions.

Stage 1: Denial. Denial, shock, and disbelief are the first reactions when one is informed of a terminal illness. According to Kübler-Ross, few patients maintain this stance to the end.

Stage 2: Anger. After denial, the patient often becomes demanding, difficult, and hostile. Asking and resolving the question "Why me?" can help the patient reduce resentment.

Stage 3: Bargaining. The patient wants more time and asks for favors to postpone death. The bargaining may be carried out with the physician or, more frequently, with God. One of Kübler-Ross's patients asked to be relieved of her severe pain just for one day so that she could attend her son's wedding. She promised that if she could just see her son married, she would then be able to die in peace. She was taught self-hypnosis to control the pain and was permitted to leave the hospital for one day. She did not want to return. "Dr. Ross," she said, "don't forget, I have another son."

Stage 4: Depression. Depression is a signal that the acceptance process has really begun. Kübler-Ross has referred to this stage as *preparatory grief*—the sadness of anticipating an impending loss.

Stage 5: Acceptance. The person who achieves acceptance has taken care of unfinished business. The patient has relinquished the unattainable and is now ready to die. He or she will want to be with close family members, usually a wife or husband and children; dying children want to be with their parents. Though patients desire the presence of someone warm, caring, and accepting, at this time verbal communication may be totally unnecessary.

Some doubts about the generality of Kübler-Ross's findings have been expressed (Kastenbaum, 1985). There is no question, however, that she greatly improved our understanding of the process of dying and stimulated research that continues to add to our knowledge.

Elisabeth Kübler-Ross

Summary

evelopment refers to age-related changes that occur as a person progresses from conception to death. Most models of development are stage theories, but interest in process-oriented approaches is increasing. Two important theories that have shaped thinking about human development are Piaget's theory of cognitive development and Erikson's theory of personality development. Piaget's theory describes age-related transitions in thinking that take place over the sensorimotor, preoperational, concrete operational, and formal operational stages. Erikson's psychoanalytic theory of development focuses on psychosocial crises in eight successive stages. These crises center on transitions in social relations.

During pubescence the adolescent growth spurt takes place and secondary sex characteristics develop. During puberty, which begins several years later, the primary sex characteristics mature. The onset of puberty marks the beginning of adolescence. Girls typically mature two years earlier than boys. Boys who mature late and girls who mature early may find puberty particularly stressful. According to Piaget, adolescent thought is characterized by formal operations, or the ability to apply logical operations to hypothetical possibilities and abstract concepts. The imaginary audience and personal fable are two forms of egocentrism in adolescence.

According to Erikson, the key challenge of adolescence is to progress toward a clear sense of identity. Some theorists have asserted that adolescence is a period of turmoil, but research does not support this view. For this reason, careful attention should be paid to young people who display symptoms of serious problems such as depression, suicidal behavior, drug and alcohol abuse, and chronic delinquency. Suicide among adolescents has been increasing, but fewer than 1% of young people actually take their lives. Social isolation seems to increase the emotional impact of personal problems and often precipitates suicide attempts.

In recent years social scientists have extended the study of development to the adult years. Research by Gould and Levinson led to the emergence of two new theories of adult development. Gould's theory emphasizes false assumptions that must be discarded. Levinson's theory focuses on age-related changes in one's life structure. Although the models are far from identical, they share many congruent themes. Both postulate a major life transition around age 20, another around age 40, and probably another around age 60.

Physical development during adulthood leads to many obvious changes in physical appearance and sensory acuity. After age 30 the number of active brain cells declines steadily, but this loss has not been clearly related to reductions in cognitive functioning. Similarly, hormonal changes appear to be only modestly related to midlife distress or declining sexual activity. Unfortunately, health does tend to decline with increasing age for a variety of reasons.

Intelligence seems to remain fairly stable during most of adulthood. Memory processes probably deteriorate less than most people believe. Attention span, speed of learning, and success in problem solving all tend to decline slightly during old age. Most people, however, remain capable of sound intellectual functioning in their later years. The adult personality seems to be characterized by both stability and change.

Attitudes toward death vary from one culture to another. Our culture fosters negativism, avoidance, and fear. Research by Kübler-Ross suggests that dying people experience a variety of reactions ranging from denial to anger, bargaining, depression, and finally acceptance. In the Application we'll look at some of the ways parents can facilitate the development of their children by providing optimal combinations of affection and discipline.

APPLICATION Becoming an Effective Parent

Are the following statements true or false?

1.

Historically, parents have always been deeply concerned about their children's development.

2.

Infant-mother emotional attachments are natural and are formed readily.

3.

Extensive use of punishment is the key to effective discipline.

4.

Parents shouldn't have to explain their reasons for punishing their children.

All of the statements on the left are false. All represent popular myths about child rearing that we will encounter in our discussion of effective parenting.

We live in a child-centered society. Many of today's parents have an abiding interest in learning all they can about children's development. They search to find new and better ways to ensure optimal physical, emotional, and cognitive development in their children. Things haven't always been this way, however. Let's take a brief look (based on LeVine & White, 1987) at how the nature of parenting has changed.

Historical Changes in Parent-Child Relationships

In preindustrial North America and Europe, young children worked along with their families in agriculture or craft production. Most families lived in rural areas, so formal schooling was available to few. Families typically had numerous children, some of whom were likely to die in infancy or childhood. Given this stark reality, parents used to be cautious about becoming deeply attached to any individual child.

Industrialization brought by many changes to the structure of families. Many people migrated to urban areas to find jobs. Formal education thus became more accessible. It also became more necessary. For the first time children were likely to grow up to make their living by work that could not be taught to them by their parents. By the late nineteenth century, legislation mandated formal schooling for all children and limited their participation in the labor force. Collectively, these changes had the effect of setting aside childhood and (eventually) adolescence as developmental stages distinct from adulthood. No longer were children regarded as miniature adults. Now they were seen as unique individuals with their own personalities and needs. Moreover, families had fewer children, and more of them survived to adulthood. Hence parents became more willing to allocate attention and affection to their children, a trend that has continued to the present.

Maternal Behavior and Infant-Mother Attachment

For the first few months of life, infants rely on built-in behaviors such as crying, cooing, and smiling to initiate and maintain contact with adult caregivers. Before long infants start to recognize their most frequent caregiver (typically the mother) and are more easily soothed by that person. By the age of 7 months or so, most babies develop a strong emotional attachment to a single, familiar caregiver (hereafter assumed to be the mother, to simplify our discussion). They often react with distress at separation from this attachment figure (Schaffer & Emerson, 1964).

Contrary to popular belief, however, infants' attachment to their mothers is *not* automatic. Indeed, as we mentioned in Chapter 8, not all infants develop a secure attachment to their mothers. After extensive study of infant-mother attachments, Mary Ainsworth and her colleagues concluded that infants could be grouped into three attachment styles (Ainsworth, Blehar, Waters, & Wall, 1978). Babies who develop *avoidant* attachment style tend to ignore their mothers. *Anxious-ambivalent* infants seem to desire contact with the mother, yet they actively resist her when she comes near. Fortunately, the majority of infants are *securely attached* and welcome contact with their mothers. A secure attachment to a caregiver during infancy is important because it seems to provide a basis for successful social relationships later in life (Bretherton, 1985). In Erikson's terms, the securely attached baby has developed a sense of trust in the mother and toward the world at large.

Recent research in this area suggests that there is a fourth attachment style—*disorganized/disoriented* (Main & Solomon, 1990). These infants are both drawn to their caregivers and fear them because of negative experiences with them. The disor-ganized/disoriented attachment style appears to be common among abused children (Carlson, Cicchetti, Barnett, & Braunwald, 1989).

Can a mother promote secure attachment in her baby? Ainsworth and her associates reported that the mothers of securely attached infants enjoyed physical contact with the baby, were perceptive about the baby's needs, and had a good sense of timing (for instance, they knew when the baby wanted to be picked up or put down). The implication is that these are among the key attributes of effective parenting of infants.

Dimensions of Child Rearing

As children move from infancy into toddlerhood, parents become more than mere caregivers. The manner in which parents react to a child's actions communicates their standards of appropriate and inappropriate behavior. Parents fulfill this role with varying degrees of conscious awareness.

Parenting behavior has two major dimensions (Maccoby & Martin, 1983). The more important is *parental acceptance.* Although most parents are at least moderately accepting of their children, some are indifferent or even hostile and rejecting. The parents' acceptance and warmth appear to influence the degree to which children internalize the behavioral standards of their parents (Greenberger & Goldberg, 1989). Children whose parents hold them in high regard are likely to incorporate their parents' values into their own personalities. This development should enable them to exercise self-control and to behave appropriately even when the parents are not present. Children whose parents show less acceptance may fail to internalize their parents' values and tend to be less self-controlled. They may comply with their parents' demands *in the parents' presence* (perhaps out of fear of punishment) but misbehave otherwise.

The second dimension is *parental control,* or the degree of strictness of the parents' stan-

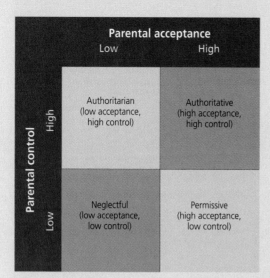

FIGURE 11.9
Baumrind's parenting styles
Four parenting styles result from the interactions of parental acceptance and parental control. (Adapted from Baumrind, 1971.)

dards. A parent who is moderately controlling sets high performance standards and expects increasingly mature behavior. A parent who is uncontrolling expects little of the child. The absence of control is related to high levels of aggression and maladjustment. Too strict and punitive control is associated negatively with moral development and also leads to rebellion in adolescents (Lloyd, 1985).

Diana Baumrind (1967, 1971, 1978) has looked at specific parenting styles as interactions between the two dimensions of acceptance and control. Baumrind was also interested in the effects of these parenting styles on children's social and intellectual competence. In her initial study, Baumrind observed a sample of preschool children in a nursery school and at home. Each child was rated on several social and cognitive dimensions. During the home observations, the parents' behavior was also observed and rated. Additional data were obtained through interviews with the parents. Baumrind was able to identify four distinct parenting styles: authoritarian, permissive, authoritative, and neglectful (see Figure 11.9), although she reported findings on only the first three of these styles.

Authoritarian parents (low acceptance, high control) are highly demanding and controlling, and use physical punishment or the threat of it with their children. By virtue of their higher status, they issue commands that are to be obeyed without question ("Do it because I say so"). Such parents rigidly maintain tight control even as their children mature. They tend to be somewhat emotionally distant and may be rejecting.

Permissive parents (high acceptance, low control) make few or no demands of their children. They allow children free expression of impulses and set few limits on appropriate behavior. Permissive parents are responsive and warmly accepting, and indulge their children's desires.

Authoritative parents (high acceptance, high control) set high goals for their children. But authoritative parents are also very accepting of their children and responsive to their needs. They encourage verbal give and take, and allow their children to question their requests. They also provide age-appropriate explanations that emphasize the consequences of "good" and "bad" behavior. Authoritative parents maintain firm control but take into account each child's unique and changing needs. They are willing to negotiate with their children, setting new and less restrictive limits when appropriate, particularly as children mature.

Effects of Parenting Styles

Baumrind found that these parenting styles were associated with distinctive clusters of traits in children, summarized in Figure 11.10. The children of authoritarian parents tended to be moody, fearful, resentful, irritable, and unfriendly. Permissive parents tended to have children who were rebellious, undisciplined, impulsive, aggressive, and domineering. Authoritative parenting, in contrast, was associated with more positive outcomes. The children of authoritative parents tended to be self-reliant, self-disciplined, cooperative, friendly, and intellectually curious.

Of course, these data are correlational and they do *not* establish the parenting style as a *cause* of the children's traits. The direction of influence probably goes both ways. For instance, parents may become increasingly authoritarian in response to their child's increasing resentment and irritability. Even so, Baumrind's findings imply that authoritative parenting is most likely to foster social and cognitive competence in children.

What happened when these children got older? Baumrind made follow-up observations of her subjects when they were 8 to 9 years old. She found that the children of authoritative parents—especially their daughters—were still the highest in both social and cognitive competence.

Baumrind (1978) points out that authoritative parents make adjustments to accommodate a child's increasing age and maturity. As their children get older, authoritative parents set increasingly high standards of behavior—high enough to encourage the

Parenting Styles and Children's Traits

Parenting style	Children's behavioral profile
Authoritative	**Energetic-friendly** Self-reliant Self-controlled Cheerful and friendly Copes well with stress Cooperative with adults Curious Purposive Achievement-oriented
Authoritarian	**Conflicted-irritable** Fearful, apprehensive Moody, unhappy Easily annoyed Passively hostile Vulnerable to stress Aimless Sulky, unfriendly
Permissive	**Impulsive-aggressive** Rebellious Low in self-reliance and self-control Impulsive Aggressive Domineering Aimless Low in achievement

FIGURE 11.10
Baumrind's findings on parenting styles and children's traits
Diana Baumrind has studied three styles of parenting and their relations to children's social and intellectual competence. As you can see, authoritative parenting is associated with the most desirable outcomes. (Summary adapted from Shaffer, 1989.)

child to try, but not so high that the child is doomed to fail. These parents also take into account the child's age when they explain and enforce these standards.

Issues in Rearing Adolescents

A widely held belief in our society is that adolescence is a time of rebellion and chronic conflict between parents and their teenage children. Fortunately, however, most families with adolescents manage to escape serious conflict and disorganization (Hill, 1987). Nevertheless, the rapid physical and cognitive development of adolescents does necessitate some parental adjustment. Adolescents' emerging cognitive abilities enable them to question their parents' values and to formulate a personal philosophy to guide their own behavior. Mundane conflicts between teens and their parents over such issues as curfews and choice of friends reflect adolescents' deeper concerns over issues of values, responsibilities, and roles (Powers, Hauser, & Kilner, 1989). One of the undercurrents in parent-adolescent relationships is the fact that the balance of power between parent and child is shifting. Younger children accept their parents' power as a legitimate source of authority, especially if they have a warm relationship. The increasing autonomy of adolescents, however, requires a more equal parent-child relationship. While this is a necessary step on the road to autonomous adulthood, negotiating these shifts in power can sometimes be difficult.

Authoritarian parents who are unwilling to relinquish their control promote hostility and rebellion

CALVIN AND HOBBES copyright Watterson. Reprinted with permission of UNIVERSAL PRESS SYNDICATE. All rights reserved.

in their adolescent children. Permissive parents, who never exercised control over their children, may find themselves faced with adolescents whose behavior is completely out of hand. Authoritative parents who are willing to respond to their teenagers' input are most likely to avoid such turmoil (Baumrind, 1978). As Baumrind continues to follow her subjects, she expects to find that effective parenting of adolescents involves increasing responsiveness and decreasing demandingness (Baumrind, 1989).

Toward Effective Parenting

Are there some basic rules for effective parenting? We offer five key principles. Of course, it's essential to tailor these suggestions to the age and developmental level of a specific child.

1. *Set high but reasonable standards.* Children should be expected to behave in a manner appropriate for their age and to do as well as they can in school and in other activities. Parents who don't expect much of their children are teaching them not to expect much of themselves.

2. *Stay alert for "good" behavior and reward it.* Most of us pay attention to children when they are misbehaving and ignore them when they're being good. This approach is backward. Develop the habit of praising good behavior so a child knows what you want.

3. *Explain your reasons when you ask a child to do something.* Don't assume that a child can read your mind. Explaining the purpose of a request can transform what might appear to be an arbitrary request into a reasonable one. It also encourages self-control in a child.

4. *Encourage children to take the perspective of others.* Talk to children about the effects of their behavior on others ("How would you feel if Mary did that to *you*?"). This role-playing approach fosters moral development and empathy in children.

5. *Enforce rules consistently.* Children need to have a clear idea of what is expected of them and

to know that there will be consequences when they fail to meet your standards. This practice also fosters self-control in children.

Parents often wonder how punishment can be used more effectively in disciplinary efforts. In the next section we'll elaborate on the principles of effective punishment.

Using Punishment Effectively

To use punishment effectively, parents should use if infrequently. This is because punishment often has unintended negative side

effects (Newsom, Favell, & Rincover, 1983; Van Houten, 1983). One of these side effects is that punishment often triggers strong *negative emotional responses*, including fear, anxiety, anger, and resentment. These emotional reactions can create a variety of problems, including hostility toward parents. A second side effect is that heavy punishment can result in the general suppression of behavioral activity. In other words, children who are strongly and frequently punished can become withdrawn, inhibited, and less active than other children. Finally, studies show that *physical* punishment often leads

RECOMMENDED READING

The Hurried Child: Growing Up Too Fast, Too Soon

by David Elkind (Addison-Wesley, 1988)

In this fascinating book David Elkind shows how recent changes in the structure of family life have altered our views of children and their needs. Earlier generations saw children as needing adult protection and guidance, a view consistent with the "traditional" family structure, in which at least one parent was available to the children at all times. Today parents in many step-, single-parent, and dual-earner families find such nurturing impossible to provide. Many of these parents have alleviated their anxiety about parenthood by adopting a new conception of children as "superkids" who can take care of themselves.

This new view of children as miniature adults is mirrored in every facet of children's culture: education, television, movies, and music. Thus society as a whole conspires with the parents to hurry children to outgrow their need for nurturance as quickly as possible.

According to Elkind, pressuring children to grow up fast can have negative outcomes, from academic failure to psychosomatic illness to teenage suicide. Nevertheless, he maintains an attitude of optimism and hope that, with awareness of the pressures today's children face, parents can and will seek to alleviate their children's stress. Reading this book can help a concerned parent to do just that.

> The conception of children as competent to deal with, and indeed as benefitting from, everything and anything that life has to offer was an effective rationalization for parents who continue to love their children but who have neither the time, nor the energy, for childhood. [p. xiii]

> If child-rearing necessarily involves stress, then by hurrying children to grow up, or by treating them as adults, we hope to remove a portion of our burden of worry and anxiety and to enlist our children's aid in carrying life's load. We do not mean our children harm in acting thus—on the contrary, as a society we have come to imagine that it is good for young people to mature rapidly. Yet we do our children harm when we hurry them through childhood. [p. 3]

Discipline is more effective when the parent explains why the child is being punished.

to an increase in aggressive behavior. Children who are subjected to a lot of physical punishment tend to become more aggressive than the average youngster. All of these unintended side effects of punishment make it less than ideal as a disciplinary procedure.

Although parents probably overuse punishment as a means of behavioral control, it does have a role to play in disciplinary efforts. The following guidelines summarize research evidence on how to make punishment effective while minimizing its unintended effects (Axelrod & Apsche, 1983; Parke, 1977; Walters & Grusec, 1977).

1. *Punishment should be swift.* A delay in delivering punishment undermines its impact. When mothers say, "Wait until your father gets home . . ." they are making a fundamental mistake in the use of punishment. (They are also unfairly setting up the father as the heavy.) Quick punishment highlights the connection between the prohibited behavior and its negative outcome.

2. *Punishment should be just severe enough to be effective.* The intensity of punishment is a two-edged sword. Although more severe punishments tend to be more effective in suppressing unwanted behavior, they also increase the likelihood of undesirable side effects. Thus it's best to use the least severe punishment

that seems likely to have some impact.

3. *Punishment should be consistent.* If you want to eliminate an undesirable behavior, punish it every time it occurs. When parents are inconsistent about punishing a particular behavior, they only create confusion in the child.

4. *Punishment should be explained.* When children are punished, the reason for their punishment should be explained as fully as possible, given the constraints of their age. The more children understand the reason why they are punished, the more effective the punishment tends to be. These explanations, characteristic of the authoritative style, also foster the development of self-control.

5. *Minimize the use of physical punishment.* Modest physical punishment may be necessary when children are too young to understand a verbal reprimand or the withdrawal of privileges. A light slap on the hand or bottom should suffice. Otherwise, physical punishment should be avoided because it tends to increase aggressive behavior in children.

6. *Withdraw privileges instead of using physical punishment.* If

you must punish your child, try the approach of withdrawing valued privileges. A vigorous spanking isn't felt by a child an hour later, but the experience of having to forego something desirable can give children hours to contemplate the wisdom of changing their ways.

7. *Point out alternative, positive ways for your child to behave and reinforce these actions.* One shortcoming of punishment is that it only tells a child what *not* to do. A better strategy is to punish an undesirable response *and* reward a positive alternative behavior. Most undesirable behaviors have a purpose. Suggest another response that serves the same purpose and reward a child for following the suggestion. Many of children's troublesome behaviors are primarily attention-seeking devices. Punishment of these responses will be more effective if you can provide a child with more acceptable ways to gain attention.

Key Learning Objectives

1. Explain the difference between stage-oriented and process-oriented approaches to development.
2. Summarize criticism of the ages-and-stages approach to development.
3. Explain the meaning of age roles and social clocks.
4. Provide an overview of Piaget's theory, including the major accomplishments of the four stages.
5. Describe stages 5 through 8 of Erikson's model of personality development.
6. Describe the changes that take place during pubescence.
7. Describe the events of puberty and the effects of late and early maturation.
8. Describe Piaget's formal operations period and two forms of adolescent egocentrism.
9. Describe Erikson's psychosocial crisis of adolescence and Marcia's four identity statuses.
10. Discuss the idea that adolescence is a period of emotional turmoil.
11. Discuss recent trends in adolescent suicide.
12. Describe the key concepts and assumptions of Gould's and Levinson's theories of adult development.
13. Describe the phases of adult development identified by Levinson and Gould.
14. Describe disengagement theory and activity theory and the evidence that supports them.
15. Summarize adult developmental trends in appearance, neurological functioning, and sensory acuity.
16. Discuss the significance of menopause and adult developmental trends in health status.
17. Summarize evidence on changes in cognitive functioning during the adult years.
18. Summarize evidence on personality change and stability in adulthood.
19. Discuss cultural and individual attitudes toward death.
20. Describe the five stages in the process of dying that were identified by Kübler-Ross.
21. Discuss the implications of Ainsworth's research on attachment.
22. Describe three parenting styles identified by Baumrind and their effects on children's development.
23. Discuss issues related to effective parenting of adolescents.
24. List five suggestions for more effective parenting.
25. List seven suggestions for the effective use of punishment.

Key Terms

age cohort
ageism
age roles
aging
cognitive development
conservation
death system
development
egocentrism
gerontology
hypothetico-deductive reasoning
life structure
locus of control

menarche
menopause
neurons
object permanence
primary sex characteristics
process-oriented approaches
puberty
pubescence
secondary sex characteristics
senile dementia
social clock
stage

Key People

Diana Baumrind
David Elkind
Erik Erikson
Roger Gould

Elisabeth Kübler-Ross
Daniel Levinson
Jean Piaget

12 Work and Career Development

"T HE [TELEPHONE] DICTATES. This crummy little machine with buttons on it—you've just got to answer it. . . . Your job doesn't mean anything. Because *you're* just a little machine. A monkey could do what I do. . . .

"Until recently, I'd cry in the morning. I didn't want to get up. I'd dread Fridays because Monday was always looming over me. Another five days ahead of me. . . .

"I'll be at home and the telephone will ring and I get nervous. It reminds me of the telephone at work. . . ."

—A receptionist quoted in *Working* (Terkel, 1974)

"Piano tuning is not really business. It's a dedication. There's such a thing as piano tuning, piano rebuilding, and antique restoration. There's such a thing as scale designing and engineering, to produce the highest sound quality possible. I'm in all of this and I enjoy every second of it. . . . I don't see any possibility of separating my life from my work. . . . There seems something mystic about music, about piano tuning. There's so much beauty comes out of music. There's so much beauty comes out of piano tuning."

—A piano tuner quoted in *Working* (Terkel, 1974)

These quotations attest to the crucial role of work in adult life. They speak poignantly of the tremendous impact, either positive or negative, that our jobs can have on the quality of our lives. The significance of work shouldn't be surprising, since many people's sense of identity is determined by the work they do. When adults meet for the first time, their initial "How do you do?" is often followed by the more crucial question "What do you do for a living?" The answer may convey information not only about one's occupation but also about one's social status, lifestyle, personality, interests, and aptitudes.

Because work plays such an important role in life, psychologists take a great interest in it. Those who study human behavior in work settings are *industrial/organizational psychologists*. They study, among other things, the workplace and its effects on workers' productivity and psychological adjustment, as well as job stress and its effects. They are also becoming increasingly interested in how individuals balance work, family life, and leisure activities. In this chapter we'll begin with a brief survey of contemporary trends in the world of work and the composition of today's labor force. We'll also look at the role of women in the workplace, as well as ways

of balancing work and other spheres of life. Then we'll discuss work motivation, job satisfaction, and hazards in the work setting. Finally, we'll explore several models of career development and some important considerations in choosing a career. In the Application we'll offer some concrete suggestions for enhancing one's chances of landing a desirable job.

Perspectives on Work

B efore we plunge into the world of work, let's take a look at several important background issues: what we mean by "work" and related terms, some contemporary trends in the workplace, and the composition of today's labor force.

The Nature of Work

Since work means different things to different people, it's important to clarify some potentially confusing issues before we get too far into this topic.

Jobs and Careers

For our purposes, we'll define **work as an activity that produces something of value for others.** For some people, work is just a way to earn a living. For others, work is a way of life. Technically, the first group would be said to have "jobs," while the second group have "careers." In other words, a *job* is of relatively little psychological importance to the person who holds it, aside from the fact that it puts food on the table. As long as one is paid a reasonable wage, it doesn't really matter what kind of work one does. Hence this person has little personal investment in or commitment to a particular type of work for its own sake.

A *career*, in contrast, typically implies that one views work as a central aspect of one's life (Almquist & Angrist, 1971). That is, a person with a career orientation wants to work, regardless of financial necessity. Indeed, some people feel so strongly drawn to their work that they describe it as a "calling." A career is consciously chosen and may require some years of education and preparation.

Sometimes it is useful to maintain the technical distinction between a job and a career. For example, because careers typically involve work that is more meaningful, pays better, and confers higher status, they often have positive psychological consequences for those who work in them (Betz & Fitzgerald, 1987). Jobs, on the other hand, are often repetitive, boring, and poorly paid. As you might expect, jobs do not provide the same psychological benefits as careers. Although this distinction is a useful one, often it is unimportant and artificial. For the most part, we'll use the two terms interchangeably.

Paid and Unpaid Work

Recall for a moment our definition of *work* (an activity that produces something of value for others). Note that this definition does not make a distinction between paid and unpaid work. Still, if you're like many people, you probably assumed that we were talking only about *paid* work. What about *unpaid* work? In our society, if work is unpaid, it isn't perceived as "real" work and is undervalued. Feminists have called people's attention to the fact that much of "women's work" falls into this category. The implied apology in the statement "I'm just a housewife" indicates that many homemakers acknowledge that their work is devalued by others.

Housework and child care are familiar kinds of unpaid work. Recently interest has turned to another type of "women's work"—relational work (Baruch, Barnett, & Rivers, 1983; Di Leonardo, 1987). Many women spend considerable time and energy attending to the needs of the immediate family, as well as maintaining ties to and harmony within the extended family by doing such things as planning and preparing family dinners, keeping up with numerous anniversaries and birthdays, and visiting and tending sick relatives. Yet another type of women's unpaid work consists of the many responsibilities of the "corporate wife." Wives of high-level executives are expected to promote their husbands' careers by arranging dinner parties and other social activities for their husbands' co-workers and their spouses. Husbands of female executives, in contrast, are not expected to perform the same type or amount of unpaid work on behalf of their wives' careers (Kanter, 1977).

As we saw in Chapters 9 and 10, wives spend many more hours per week on housework and child care than husbands do (relational work hasn't typically been factored in as a type of work in such studies). When wives work outside the home, they spend less time on "inside work." In this case, husbands don't perform more inside work to make up the difference; some work just doesn't get done (Berardo, Shehan, & Leslie, 1987).

This imbalance in the division of unpaid work is due in part to the fact that men and women have different areas of expertise because of differences in gender-role socialization. Many men aren't very competent cooks and plenty of women don't know how to fix a leaking faucet. Still, if we accept the fact that intelligent adults can and do learn new skills, it is curious that most heterosexual couples remain stuck in their gender-based areas of expertise and that men haven't taken on more of their share of unpaid work. Hilary Lips (1993) has nicely summarized the major reasons underlying this phenomenon.

First, not too many people would argue that unpaid work is particularly exciting. In truth, most men and women would be happy to pass off such work to someone else if they could get away with it. Traditional gender roles give men the advantage here. A man can fall back on the familiarity of these roles by telling his wife, "That's women's work" or "You know how to do it better than I do." Another reason women continue to do more unpaid work than men is that if a man does what he might perceive as "too much" unpaid work, he may feel that his status as head of the family is threatened. A third reason is related to the fact that employed wives usually contribute less money to the household income and therefore have less power in the relationship. This means that they are economically dependent on their husbands and so are more easily influenced. Finally, Lips points out that the domestic sphere represents an important area of control to some women. Thus a woman may view giving up some aspects of unpaid work as relinquishing some control in her marriage, even if the only alternative is to take on more work herself.

Contemporary Trends

The nature of work is undergoing numerous changes and will continue to do so. For obvious reasons, it behooves both current and prospective workers to be aware of trends in the workplace. Five trends are particularly evident.

1. *Temporary employment is increasing.* In 1988 temporary workers represented about 25% of the labor force; by the year 2000, some experts predict that the number of temporary workers will grow to 50% (Morrow, 1993). Corporations are downsizing and restructuring to cope with the changing economy and to be globally competitive. In doing so, they are elim-

26 King-Size Occupations

Retail salespeople	Registered nurses
Cashiers	General office clerks
Truck drivers	General managers
Janitors	Nursing aides
Food workers	High school teachers
Receptionists	Computer systems analysts
Child-care workers	Gardeners
Accountants	Computer programmers
Elementary teachers	Guards
Teacher aides	Licensed practical nurses
Clerical supervisors	Home health aides
Restaurant cooks	Maintenance repairers
Secretaries	Lawyers

FIGURE 12.1
High-growth occupations for the 21st century
According to Kennedy and Laramore (1993), these 26 occupations are expected to grow the most in the *number of job openings* between now and the year 2005. Although some other occupations may grow at a more rapid rate, more opportunities will be available in the listed occupations because they already employ very large numbers of people.

Advances in computer technology allow some employees to work at home.

inating large numbers of permanent jobs and doling out the work to temporary or contingent employees—clerical workers as well as professionals. By reducing the number of core (regular) workers, companies are able to cut dramatically their expenditures on payroll, health benefits, and pension plans, since temporary employees don't typically receive such benefits as health insurance, paid vacations, and pension plans. A leaner work force also enables organizations to respond more quickly to fast-changing markets. Many professionals thrive on temporary work; they have freedom, flexibility, and high incomes. Those who want only part-time work like the increased opportunities for contingent employment. The majority of temporary workers, however, are struggling to survive—with multiple jobs, low wages, wacky schedules, no benefits, and high anxiety (Morrow, 1993). If this trend continues, it will mean an almost unimaginable transformation of the relationship between Americans and their jobs (Kennedy & Laramore, 1993; Morrow, 1993).

2. *More and more jobs are in the service sector.* The United States, like many other industrialized nations, is shifting away from a manufacturing, or "goods-producing," economy to a service-producing one (Kennedy & Laramore, 1993). Whereas the bulk of yesterday's jobs were in manufacturing, mining, construction, and agriculture, the jobs of tomorrow will be in service, government, finance, trade, and trans-

portation. Figure 12.1 depicts 26 specific occupations expected to grow most rapidly between now and 2005.

3. *Dual-earner couples are becoming the norm.* As we have seen, increasing numbers of women are entering the work force, even among those women with children under the age of 6. In 1960 only 19% of women with young children were employed outside the home. In 1990 this number was close to 60% (Ries & Stone, 1992). These changes have implications not only for work and family life but also for men's and women's roles.

4. *Technological advances are changing the nature of work.* Computers have dramatically transformed the workplace. Because computers can automate many jobs that people once performed, fewer workers are needed. Workers can communicate electronically with others in distant offices and while traveling. Because work-related technology changes rapidly, lifelong learning and training will become essential for employees. Those who have "learned how to learn" will be able to keep pace with the rapidly changing workplace and will be highly valued. Those who cannot will be left behind.

5. *The boundaries between work and home are becoming blurred.* Computer technology is one force driving this change, because people can work at home yet still be in touch with the office. At the same time, a traditional home function has moved to the office as increasing numbers of companies are providing on-site day care. This development has arisen largely in response to the fact that the number of employed mothers of small children is increasing. The availability of quality on-site day care is obviously a big draw to these women.

Today's Workers

The *labor force* consists of all people who are employed plus those who are currently unemployed but are looking for work. Demographics forecast that the composition and skill level of the labor force will change in the years ahead.

Changing Demographics

In 1989 the labor force included 85% of men between the ages of 20 and 24 and about 93% of men between 24 and 54 years of age (U.S. Bureau of the Census, 1991). Comparable rates for women were 72% (20–24 years) and 75% (24–54 years). Participation rates decline after age 55 for both sexes and show an even sharper drop-off after age 65. In the last several decades the labor force participation rates for men have remained largely stable, while the participation rates for women have risen steadily.

Experts predict that a third of the new entrants to the work force between now and the year 2000 will be members of minority groups (Johnston & Packer, 1987). More than half of these workers will have been reared in families at or below the poverty level (Horowitz & O'Brien, 1989). Because personal income typically determines the quality of the schools one attends, many of these new workers will not have had the benefit of an adequate education. Consequently, they'll be at a disadvantage when they compete for the better jobs.

Education and Earnings

Although a college education is certainly not a requirement for everyone, the ability to read, write, and do basic mathematical computations is essential if one is to be competitive in the workplace. Ironically, as the years of education completed by the average American have increased, so have the problems of illiteracy and innumeracy. In a national survey of 3600 young people aged 21 to 25, the Educational Testing Service found that only 34% of whites, 20% of Hispanics, and 8% of African Americans could calculate the tip and change for a two-item restaurant meal (Hamilton, 1988). Hence it is not surprising that companies are having difficulty recruiting qualified entry-level workers. Consider two chilling examples of what can happen when workers can't do basic math or read (Kennedy & Laramore, 1993): (1) an insurance clerk issued a check for $2,200.00 to cover a dental bill that should have been only $22.00 (she didn't understand decimals); (2) a plant worker nearly killed several co-workers by fitting the wrong piece of heavy machinery onto a machine (he couldn't read). To prevent such costly errors, many organizations are investing in expensive programs to educate new workers in the basic skills they should have learned in school (Hamilton, 1988).

As new jobs develop, they will require higher educational and skill levels than the jobs that technology has rendered obsolete (K. Miller, 1989). Clearly, then, a good basic education will enhance a person's prospects for existing and future jobs. Moreover, the more education people have, the higher their income (see Figure 12.2). This relationship between level of education and income holds for both men and women. However, this figure also shows that men are paid from $5,000 to $14,000 more than women and that the gender gap increases as education increases. In the next section, we will examine more closely women's participation in the work force.

Women in the Workplace

For many years popular wisdom held that "a woman's place is in the home." Today, however, well over half of all American women either have jobs or are actively seeking employment (Rukeyser, Cooney, & Winslow, 1988). This dramatic change reflects the striking economic and social changes that have occurred in recent decades. Accordingly, let's begin our discussion with a brief historical overview. Much of the material in the following section is drawn from an excellent history of American women in the labor force by Alice Kessler-Harris (1982).

Historical Overview

The influx of women into the ranks of wage earners is often attributed to economic conditions that developed during World War II. The United States entered a period of rapid industrial expansion at the same time that the armed forces were depleting the supply of male workers. As a result, women were offered opportunities to enter fields that had previously been closed to them. Some companies hastily set up on-site child-care facilities, and a few even made available hot meals that women could take home to their families at the end of the workday. With such inducements, women entered the labor force in record numbers.

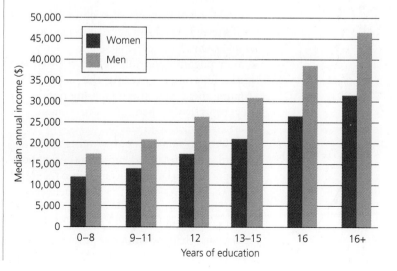

FIGURE 12.2
Education and income
The median incomes of year-round full-time workers in 1989, by sex and years of education, are shown here. As you can see, the more education people have, the higher their income tends to be; but women in each educational group earn less than men who have the same education. (Data from Ries & Stone, 1992.)

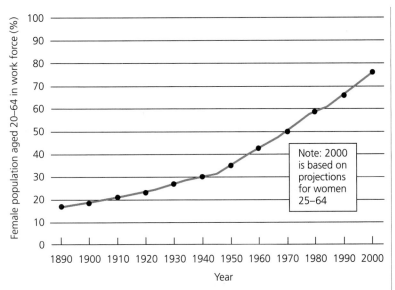

100
90
80
70
60
50
40
30
20
10
0

Female population aged 20–64 in work force (%)

1890 1900 1910 1920 1930 1940 1950 1960 1970 1980 1990 2000
Year

Note: 2000 is based on projections for women 25–64

FIGURE 12.3
Women in the work force
The percentage of women aged 20–64 who work outside the home has been increasing throughout the century. The rate of increase began to escalate in the 1950s. Experts estimate that 80% of women will be in the work force by the year 2000. (From Matthews & Rodin, 1989.)

For the most part, however, the gains made by women during the war did not last. When the soldiers came home, many women who had worked in low-paying industries quit their jobs. Women in higher-paying industries were more reluctant to quit, but most of them were discharged to make openings available for returning servicemen. Nor did any permanent change take place in people's attitudes toward women. In a 1946 survey by *Fortune* magazine, only a third of the men and two-fifths of the women queried believed that a childless woman whose husband could support her should be allowed to work if she wanted to (Kessler-Harris, 1982).

A more enduring trend began in the 1950s. The postwar migration to the suburbs was accompanied by demands for a higher standard of living. The "good life" required not only a house and a car but many expensive appliances as well. These lifestyle changes necessitated higher family incomes, and wives were the logical providers. Hence about 40% of women were employed by 1960 (see Figure 12.3).

The inflationary pressures of the 1960s and 1970s forced even more married women to seek employment. During the same time period, several demographic trends helped to swell the ranks of women entering the work force. Among them were the increasing number of never-married women, divorced women, and married women who elected to remain childless. At the same time, changing attitudes toward gender roles and improving occupational opportunities led more women into the world of work. By 1990 about 70% of women were in the labor force and roughly 60% of all married women with children under 6 were working at least part-time outside the home (Ries & Stone, 1992).

Today's Workplace for Women

Is today's workplace essentially the same for women as it is for men? In most respects, the answer appears to be no. Although job discrimination on the basis of sex has been illegal for more than 25 years, women continue to face subtle obstacles to occupational success. Foremost among them is *job segregation on the basis of gender.* Certain jobs have historically been regarded as men's and women's, and the stereotypes persist today (White, Kruczek, Brown, & White, 1989). Thus, as we noted in Chapter 10, a disproportionate number of women are employed in relatively low-paid "pink ghetto" occupations such as nurse, secretary, librarian, cashier, receptionist, domestic, bank teller, and waitress. Employees in female-dominated fields typically earn less than employees in male-dominated fields even when the jobs require similar levels of training, skill, and responsibility (Rukeyser et al., 1988). As a general rule, the greater the percentage of female workers within a field, the lower the average pay in that field (Folbre, 1987).

Nonetheless, more women are entering higher-status occupations, even if at a low rate. Unfortunately, they still face discrimination because they are frequently *passed over for promotion* in favor of men (Morrison & Von Glinow, 1990). This seems to be a problem especially at the higher levels of management. Less than 2% of the corporate officers of *Fortune* 500 companies are women (Morrison & Von Glinow, 1990). There appears to be a "glass ceiling" that prevents most women from advancing beyond middle-management positions.

When a woman is the only female in an office, she becomes a **token, or a symbol of all the members of her group.** As we discussed in Chapter 5, tokens have "surplus visibility" (Patai, 1991). Because they stand out, their actions are subject to intense scrutiny, stereotyping, and negative judgments. If a man makes a mistake, it is explained as an *individual* problem. When a token woman makes a mistake, it is seen as evidence that *all* women are incompetent. Hence tokens experience a lot of *performance pressure.* Interestingly, if a woman is perceived as being "too successful," she may be labeled a "workaholic" or accused of trying to "show up" men. These unfavorable perceptions may be reflected in performance appraisals. The performance of successful men is less likely to be interpreted in these negative ways.

Another way the world of work is different for men and women is that women have *fewer opportunities to observe and emulate same-sex role models* who occupy professional positions (Fitzgerald & Crites, 1980). As we noted in Chapter 11, women have a *harder time finding a mentor* in the workplace than men do (Yoder, Adams, Grove, & Priest, 1985). *Sexual harassment*, a topic we'll take up later, is yet another experience that makes the workplace different for women and men.

In sum, women must contend with discrimination on the job in a variety of forms. One consequence is that many women are leaving organizations to start their own businesses as a way of escaping their negative experiences in the workplace (Morrison & Von Glinow, 1990).

Balancing Work and Other Spheres of Life

 major challenge for workers today is balancing work, family, and leisure activities in ways that are personally satisfying. We noted earlier that dual-earner families are becoming increasingly common and that the traditional boundaries between family and paid work life are breaking down. These two developments are related. The earlier division of labor that assigned women's work to the home and men's work outside the home created boundaries between family life and paid work life. As more women enter the work force, these boundaries are becoming blurred. The technology-based changes in the workplace are also eroding these distinctions between family and paid work life.

Workaholism

Most of us cherish our leisure activities and our relationships with our families and friends. A small minority of people, however, devote nearly all their time and energy to their jobs.

These people tend to avoid nonwork activities. They put in considerable overtime, take few vacations, regularly bring work home from the office, and think about work most of the time. They are energetic, intense, and overly ambitious. In short, they are workaholics.

Psychologists are divided on whether workaholism is problematic. Should workaholics be praised for their dedication and encouraged in their single-minded pursuit of fulfillment through work? Or is workaholism a form of addiction, a sign that an individual is driven by a compulsion he or she cannot control?

In support of the former view, Machlowitz (1980) found that workaholics tend to be highly satisfied with their jobs and with their lives. They work hard simply because work is the most meaningful activity they know. Yet other evidence suggests that workaholics may have a pathological need to exercise rigid control over themselves and their environments (Schwartz, 1982).

Reprinted by permission: Tribune Media Services.

How can these conflicting findings be reconciled? Naughton (1987) has suggested that there may be two types of workaholics. One type, the job-involved workaholic, works for the pure joy of it. These people derive immense satisfaction from work and generally perform well in highly demanding jobs. The other type, the compulsive workaholic, is neither well adjusted nor an asset to an employer. Compulsive workaholics are addicted to work. Their devotion to work reflects a rigid, overcontrolling personality. They approach their jobs in a ritualized manner and cannot deviate from their set routines. They often alienate their supervisors and co-workers with their rigidity. Interestingly, compulsive workaholics are not necessarily satisfied with their jobs, and they may be prone to develop *burnout*, which we described in Chapter 3. Thus it appears that workaholism may be either constructive or problematic, depending on the motivation underlying a person's dedication to work.

Multiple Roles

The biggest recent change in the labor force has been the emergence of the dual-earner family, which currently makes up 40% of the work force (Zedeck & Mosier, 1990). Dual-earner couples are struggling to develop new ways of balancing family life and the demands of work. These changes in work and family life have sparked the interest of researchers in many disciplines, including psychology.

Key Concepts

New terms are needed to accommodate the new realities of work and family life. Some experts distinguish between the "dual-career family" and the "dual-worker family" (Zedeck & Mosier, 1990). A *dual-career family* is a family in which both members of the couple pursue work that is personally meaningful. In the *dual-worker family*, both are less personally involved in their work. A third type of family has also been identified: the *two-worker, one-career family* (Zedeck & Mosier, 1990). Here both people work, but only one partner's career is judged to be important. Both members of the couple view the second job merely as a source of additional income.

The distinctions among these three terms parallel the technical distinctions we noted earlier between jobs and careers. These distinctions are important, but one problem with these terms is that they assume that all work is paid work. As we noted earlier, many experts believe that it is important to differentiate between paid and unpaid work. The term *dual-earner family* is useful because it makes explicit reference to the fact that only paid work is being discussed (although it doesn't distinguish between types of work).

An important fact of life for dual-earner families is that two workers juggle three jobs: two paid jobs and one unpaid job at home. (In truth, if a couple have children, it is probably more realistic to describe them as having *four* jobs: two paid jobs and two unpaid jobs—housework and child care). It doesn't take too much thought to realize that what goes on at work can spill over to affect family life and vice versa. These *spillover effects* can be either positive or negative. If you have a great day at the office, you probably will come home in a good mood. But if your children are ill, your worry about them may interfere with your concentration at work.

Joseph Pleck (1977), a psychologist who has done considerable research on family and gender roles, suggests that spillover works differently for husbands and wives. For husbands, work most often intrudes into the family environment—time and energy devoted to work are not available for the family. For wives, the process works in reverse—time and energy devoted to the family can intrude on work time. As we saw in our discussion of paid and unpaid work, most of the burdens associated with dual-earner households are borne by wives (Alpert & Culbertson, 1987). Women's unpaid work at home after her paid workday ends has been termed "the second shift" (Hochschild, 1989).

Effects of Juggling Multiple Roles

Sometimes multiple roles are incompatible and cause *role conflict*. Because the division of labor in many homes is still based on traditional gender roles, women are more likely to experience role conflict. Let's say that a woman is scheduled to make a major presentation at work on Tuesday morning and her 2-year-old son wakes up with a fever and can't go to day care. If her husband can stay home with the baby, all is well. If he can't, then she either has to find someone else to care for him or stay home. Either way, she feels guilt, conflict, and stress. Because juggling multiple roles is still more of a problem for women than for men, almost all of the research on this topic has used women as subjects.

What are the effects on women of juggling multiple roles? There are two competing perspectives on this question (Baruch, Biener, & Barnett, 1987). The *scarcity hypothesis* assumes that everyone has a finite amount of energy. The more roles a person has, the more energy will be used. The more energy expended, the greater the stress and other negative consequences. The *enhancement hypothesis*, in contrast, asserts that people's energy resources are not limited. Psychologists who espouse this view point to the people who exercise (expend energy) yet say they actually feel less tired and more energetic. The more roles one has, these psychologists say, the more opportunities one has for stimulation, social status, and self-esteem. Also, multiple roles serve as a buffer against the assaults of painful experiences because negative events in one role can be balanced by the positive aspects of other roles.

Both hypotheses are supported by research. In support of the scarcity hypothesis, employed women report that the competing demands of work and family life are a major source of stress (Duxbury & Higgins, 1991). A study of 232 professional women (attorneys, physicians, and professors) reported that the majority of women often experienced conflicts between career and family (Gray, 1983). For obvious reasons, the presence of young children reduces women's satisfaction with their professional work (Amaro, Russo, & Johnson, 1987). A high income can ease the strains and increase work satisfaction, but as we know, most women do not have high-paying jobs.

In support of the enhancement hypothesis, it has been found that employed women are happier and healthier than full-time homemakers, except when their children are infants (Walker & Best, 1991). Other studies have reported similar findings (Amatea & Fong, 1991; Coleman & Antonucci, 1983). Still, because this research is correlational, we can't tell whether paid work itself makes women happier and healthier or whether they would be happier and healthier than the homemakers with whom they were compared even if they didn't work. Also, these studies haven't looked at whether the positive effects of employment are attributable to some other factor, such as salary, rather than to work per se. When researchers looked at possible correlates of self-esteem (employment, income, education, marital status, and developmental status), however, they found that employment was the *only* significant predictor of self-esteem in midlife women (Coleman & Antonucci, 1983). Thus, though we have no definitive proof of the positive benefits of paid work for women, the evidence points strongly to this conclusion.

Most of the research on multiple roles has focused on women with high-paying jobs. Additional research is needed on women in lower-paying jobs and on the effects of multiple roles on men. It is possible, for example, that if men spent less time and energy on work and more on their families, many of them would find closer relationships with their children more rewarding.

Leisure and Recreation

Computers and other machines are doing more of our work these days, and this trend is likely to continue. Is the 40-hour workweek on its way out then? It seems not. The number of hours one works typically affects the amount of money one makes. Hence it isn't too surprising to learn that most American workers would rather work more hours and make more money (Kennedy & Laramore, 1993). In fact, in one survey of American workers, a preference for a shorter workweek was expressed by only 6% of men and 9% of women (Kennedy & Laramore, 1993). Even among those workers who are highly paid, only about 10% of men and 20% of women were willing to trade hours of work—and money—for additional leisure. Still, given the high level of stress in modern life, Americans may need to learn to take more time for leisure activities.

What Is Leisure?

We'll define **leisure** as **unpaid activities people choose to engage in because they are personally meaningful.** Let's look more carefully at the two components of our definition. *Unpaid activ-*

ities include those that take place in a nonwork setting or that are unrelated to one's job. Hence we wouldn't classify a business lunch as a leisure activity. Neither would we so classify *paid* participation in sports by professional athletes. Some experts argue that paid work activities can sometimes qualify as leisure, provided that we experience them as highly meaningful. Though we wouldn't disagree, we feel that it is helpful, in most instances, to maintain the distinction between unpaid work and leisure.

Now let's consider the second component of our definition: *meaningfulness*. Relatively few people would classify grocery shopping, changing diapers, mowing the grass, and washing clothes as having deep personal significance. Although we don't perform these activities during our work hours, do they qualify as leisure activities? Usually not, because they don't meet the second condition of being personally meaningful. Instead, experts classify such functions as *maintenance activities* (Kabanoff, 1980). Of course, some so-called maintenance activities can qualify as leisure. Baking a birthday cake for your 4-year-old granddaughter or preparing a special meal for close friends could be classified as leisure activities because they contain the element of meaningfulness.

As we have noted, wives typically devote more time to maintenance activities than husbands do. In fact, some experts argue that the notion of "leisure" really applies only to men because it is usually defined in opposition to work outside the home. When men leave the workplace, their leisure time begins. But when women leave their jobs, they typically face a second shift of cooking, cleaning, and child-care responsibilities that most men do not.

Consider this example:

> If we say that "camping" is a leisure activity, we may be thinking from only the male's perspective. Suppose the female has had to do all the packing for the camping trip, prepare the children, plan the meals, cook the meals at the campsite, watch the children, wash up after each meal, get the children into their sleeping bags each night and get up with them if they are afraid in the middle of the night. Camping may simply be a round of labor for the female—housekeeping under inferior conditions. [Godbey, 1990, p. 9]

Finding time for true leisure pursuits is difficult for many men, but it is an even bigger challenge for most women.

What are true leisure activities? Does *any* nonmaintenance activity qualify as leisure? Not according to our definition. The determining factor is meaningfulness. How might we differentiate between activities that are meaningful and those that aren't? We may sometimes choose to veg out in front of the TV set for three hours, but most of us would acknowledge that there is an important difference between using our time in this manner and spending those same three hours, say, taking photographs of dazzling spring flowers. What distinguishes these two uses of our time? While one activity merely provides respite from a boring or exhausting day (which we sometimes need), the other genuinely revitalizes us. Being a couch potato will probably contribute nothing to our state of mind and may even result in feelings of physical apathy and depression (Csikszentmihalyi & Kubey, 1981; Kubey & Csikszentmihalyi, 1990). Participating in activities that are truly meaningful to us can produce

Participation in leisure activities can help reduce stress.

highly positive emotional states (Csikszent-mihalyi & Kleiber, 1991).

Types of Leisure Activities

The types of leisure activities that people prefer are quite diverse.

- *Hobbies*. Common hobbies include photography; acting; music (playing and listening); gardening; knitting; drawing; collecting stamps, autographs, and so forth; hiking; camping; fishing; and birdwatching.
- *Travel*. Many choose their destinations spontaneously, but others are more systematic in their travel plans. Some individuals want to travel to all of the U. S. national parks or all of the major Civil War battlefields. Those who can afford it may travel to other countries—to get a taste of real French cooking or a firsthand look at what remains of ancient Egyptian civilization.
- *Games*. Some people enjoy playing bridge for relaxation; others like to play board games, such as Scrabble and chess. Computerized games attract others.
- *Sports*. Many people like to play team sports, such as bowling and softball. Such sports give them the benefits of both physical exercise and social interaction. Others enjoy individual sports, such as jogging, swimming, surfing, ice skating, and skiing. Figure 12.4 depicts the ten most popular sports activities among Americans.
- *Volunteer activities*. Helping others appeals to individuals in almost all age groups. Moreover, we can use our skills to help others in an incredibly diverse array of settings: homeless shelters, hospitals, schools, battered women's shelters, boys' and girls' clubs, and sports teams, to name only a few.

Awareness of the broad range of recreational activities heightens our chances of selecting those that are most meaningful to us.

Benefits of Leisure Activities

The idea that a satisfying balance of work, relationships, and leisure activities will lead to a more rewarding and healthy life has intuitive appeal. But is there any evidence to support this assumption? Amazingly, not much well-designed research has been carried out on this important question. One study found that people who were dissatisfied at work compensated for their negative feelings by engaging in leisure pursuits (Mansfield & Evans, 1975). An interview-based study found that higher "overall

quality of life" was associated with satisfaction with one's job as well as with one's leisure activities (London, Crandall, & Seals, 1977). Some people include physical exercise in their leisure time. As you'll see in Chapter 14, regular exercise can reduce the effects of stress and improve one's mood and self-concept.

To summarize, meaningful work, rewarding family interactions and friendships, and revitalizing leisure pursuits are three components of a rewarding life. Maintaining a personally satisfying balance among these life components is a major challenge. In the next section, we'll turn our attention to the needs that motivate people to become and remain members of the work force.

Motivation to Work

Historically, workers have been motivated by two overriding considerations. The first is, of course, economic necessity. The income earned through employment is necessary to provide food, clothing, shelter, health care, and so on. Almost as important has been the so-called work ethic—the belief that a nonproductive life is morally unacceptable.

Today's workers, however, grew up in relative affluence, and many are inclined to take financial security almost for granted. Although

FIGURE 12.4
Participation in the ten most popular sports activities
Both males and females enjoy participating in sports, although there are some differences in the type of sport they prefer. (U.S. Bureau of the Census, 1991.)

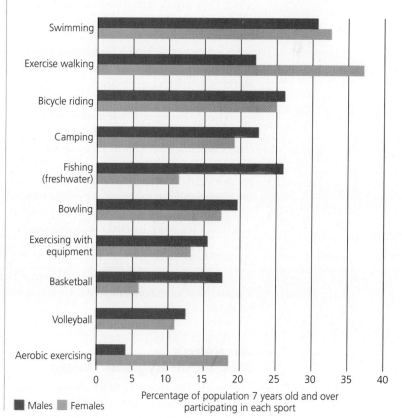

Percentage of population 7 years old and over participating in each sport

■ Males ■ Females

most people still have to earn money, money alone is no longer enough to guarantee job satisfaction. Nor do today's workers unhesitatingly endorse the work ethic. The emphasis on personal fulfillment that emerged in the 1970s and 1980s has extended to the workplace. Contemporary workers have high expectations for their jobs. They want opportunities to learn, to use and expand their talents, and to accomplish something worthwhile (Hall, 1986). With these historical trends in mind, let's examine three theories of work motivation—two classic theories, as well as a more recent one.

McGregor's Theory X and Theory Y

Douglas McGregor (1960) postulates that managers base decisions about their employees on implicit assumptions about human nature. In other words, managerial policy reflects management's "theory" about what motivates workers. McGregor describes two basic theories of work motivation. *Theory X* assumes that people inherently dislike work and that they have little ambition. According to Theory X, workers need and prefer to be coerced, directed, and threatened to be productive.

Theory Y, in contrast, assumes that people find work as natural and as satisfying as play or rest. According to Theory Y, workers can and will exercise self-direction and self-control when they are committed to achieving the organization's objectives. McGregor's view is that workers will be committed to attaining the organization's goals to the extent that they can simultaneously meet their personal needs for autonomy, achievement, status, recognition, and self-fulfillment.

Theory X suggests that managers need to direct and control employees through the exercise of authority in order to enhance their productivity. Theory Y suggests a profoundly different management style. It implies that managers are responsible for creating the conditions in which workers can best fulfill their personal needs as they work toward the organization's goals. According to McGregor, if workers are unproductive, apathetic, or irresponsible, this is *not* a reflection of "human nature." Rather, it is a signal that management needs to revise its methods and policies.

Herzberg's Motivation-Hygiene Theory

Frederick Herzberg (1968) proposes that humans have two basic needs. The first is one we share with animals. It is the need to avoid unpleasant situations that lead to physical or psychological pain. In the context of work, these avoidance needs are met when working conditions are pleasant: a comfortable physical environment, good relationships with supervisors and co-workers, a fair salary, and job security. These factors are not part of the job itself; they form the context in which the job must be performed. Herzberg refers to these things as *hygiene factors*. Their main effect is to *prevent* unhappiness and unproductivity on the job. Working conditions that fail to satisfy employees' need to avoid unpleasantness can produce dissatisfaction and poor job performance.

According to Herzberg, our second and more important need is uniquely human. It is our need for self-actualization, which was first described by Abraham Maslow (see Chapter 2). This motive reflects our need to fulfill our potential as creative, unique individuals. Workers meet this need through successful performance of job tasks, recognition and appreciation of this success, and opportunities for professional growth. These factors are associated with the job itself and are referred to as *motivators*, since they spur workers to greater effort. Opportunities for self-actualization on the job lead to higher satisfaction and enhance performance. Thus if workers are to be truly happy and productive, a pleasant working environment is not enough. Herzberg argues that jobs must also afford workers the opportunity for personal and professional growth.

Ouchi's Theory Z

William G. Ouchi (1981) has developed a theory of work motivation that is an extension of McGregor's Theory Y. Ouchi's *Theory Z* is based on the organizational structure and management style used in many highly successful Japanese corporations. The most important feature of a Theory Z approach is a corporate culture in which workers are made to feel that they are part of a family. These feelings are cultivated through a variety of company efforts. For one thing, workers at all levels are included in decisions regarding the items they produce. Their opinions are sought on ways to improve the work environment. Important decisions are often made by consensus rather than being dictated to workers by managers. Executives, managers, and production-line workers frequently get together for corporate social events. Such a corporate climate typically results in high productivity and positive feelings about the workplace. Workers feel that they are valued members of the organization and take pride in their contributions.

Of course, there are significant differences between the Japanese and American cultures, and these differences affect the way Theory Z works. For example, Japanese employees have typically worked for only one company during their lifetime (though this tradition is weakening today), whereas American workers are notorious job hoppers. Consensus-building around decisions is consistent with a group-based culture such as Japan's, and it is not so easily transferable to America's highly individualistic culture. Finally, Japanese workers expect to wait many years for promotions, whereas American workers are accustomed to relatively rapid advancement. Obviously, these cultural differences must be taken into consideration when Theory Z is used in American companies.

Have any American businesses tried to implement the principles of Theory Z? In fact, several major corporations have done so (Hewlett-Packard, for example). A more common practice, however, is to adopt selected aspects of the approach. These experiments have generally produced positive results, but there is some evidence that the effects may be short-lived. It's simply too early to offer a definitive evaluation of the benefits of Theory Z to American companies.

Although McGregor, Herzberg, and Ouchi differ somewhat in their views of work motivation, they agree that work can fill a variety of human needs. And all three theorists emphasize that the extent to which a job meets an individual's needs is closely related to the individual's satisfaction with that job. Job satisfaction, however, depends on other factors as well.

Understanding Job Satisfaction

In making a career choice, in a sense we make a prediction. We predict that the occupation we choose will lead to success and provide us with satisfaction. That is, we hope not only to do well in our chosen field but to enjoy it as well. *Job satisfaction* refers to the favorability or unfavorability of people's attitudes toward their jobs. When you make career decisions, it is important to be aware of some of the determinants of job satisfaction.

Importance of Job Satisfaction

Job satisfaction is a significant issue because it has important implications not only for the employee but also for the employer and even for

society at large. The employee has a variety of reasons to be concerned about job satisfaction. As we'll see shortly, work-related problems are a significant source of stress, so job dissatisfaction can have an adverse effect on an employee's physical health (Holt, 1982). The connection between job stress and disease may explain the dramatic finding that people who are satisfied with their work tend to live longer (Palmore, 1969). Other research suggests that job satisfaction is related to employees' overall adjustment and mental health (Warr, 1987).

The issue of job satisfaction is also important for employers. Although job satisfaction does not necessarily lead to increased productivity, job dissatisfaction can contribute to increased turnover, which is an expensive problem for most firms (Mobley, Horner, & Hollingsworth, 1978). Taking a broader perspective, we can see that job satisfaction can even have an impact on society at large. Given the link between job stress and disease, excessive numbers of dissatisfied workers may tax our already overburdened health-care system. Furthermore, consumers may find themselves paying higher prices for goods and services if companies pass on the cost of high turnover rates. Thus job satisfaction is an issue that concerns everyone.

Measuring Job Satisfaction

Before we explore the factors associated with job satisfaction, we need to emphasize the complexity of this issue. First, job satisfaction is a multidimensional concept that is not easily measured. A job has many aspects. A person may be satisfied with one aspect, such as promotion opportunities, and dissatisfied with another, such as job security.

Second, job satisfaction is a highly personal matter that depends on more than just the nature of one's work. Two people working at the same job may exhibit very different levels of satisfaction. Your job satisfaction depends on your subjective *perception* of your working conditions. Imagine that your company institutes a new policy whereby each worker will now perform a greater variety of tasks. If you view this change as an opportunity to broaden your skills and alleviate boredom, your job satisfaction will increase. But if you attribute this change to the company's desire to increase your duties without increasing your pay, your job satisfaction will probably decline.

To some extent, the tendency to feel satisfied with work may be a personality trait that transcends specific job characteristics. In one study, the job satisfaction of 5000 men was measured over a period of five years (Staw and Ross, 1985). Surprisingly, individuals' job satisfaction tended to remain very stable over this span of time, despite changes in their assignments, responsibilities, employers, and occupations.

As you can see, the assessment of job satisfaction is a complicated matter. Small wonder, then, that researchers have conducted well over 3000 studies on this issue (Locke, 1983). Although their findings are complex, they have isolated some factors that are related to job satisfaction for most people.

Ingredients of Job Satisfaction

Contrary to conventional wisdom, job satisfaction is not strongly related to job *level*. Many people assume that higher-status jobs bring greater satisfaction. There may be a trend in that direction, but Seashore and Barnowe (1972) found that it's not only blue-collar workers that get the blues. Perhaps people in high-status positions use different standards to judge their satisfaction. Or perhaps those in low-status fields simply expect less from their jobs. In any case, job level is *not* the crucial factor in job satisfaction.

What are the main ingredients of happiness at work? We will highlight some of the more important factors, basing our discussion primarily on three research reviews (Gruneberg, 1979; Hopkins, 1983; Locke, 1983).

Meaningfulness

Meaningfulness as it relates to work is rather difficult to define. When people say that their work is meaningful, they generally seem to be saying that it gives them a sense of real accomplishment (London & Strumpf, 1986). "Accomplishment" often translates into making a difference in the lives of others. The results of two large-scale surveys suggest that meaningfulness is one of the most important aspects of work. A Louis Harris (1987) poll reported that 48% of the respondents rated "gives feeling of real accomplishment" as the "most important" aspect of work. In an earlier survey of 23,000 *Psychology Today* readers, Patricia Renwick and Edward Lawler (1978) found that respondents ranked "chances to accomplish something worthwhile" second in importance of the 18 job characteristics studied (see Figure 12.5).

Challenge and Variety

In their analysis of the "blue-collar blues," Seashore and Barnowe (1972) found that people need challenge in their jobs. This makes sense in view of our earlier observation that people want to use their full potential in their work. This point was underscored in the *Psychology Today* survey (Renwick & Lawler, 1978). When asked to rate the importance of various aspects of their jobs, the respondents ranked "chances to learn new things" and "opportunity to develop your skills and abilities" third and fourth, respectively (see Figure 12.5).

A closely related consideration is the variety of work that a job provides. People tend to find repetitive, assembly-line work boring and dissatisfying. One way companies can increase their employees' satisfaction is by restructuring jobs so that each worker is allowed to perform a variety of what would otherwise be routine tasks.

The issue of challenging work has taken on new significance since the early 1970s. As we mentioned earlier, there has been an oversupply of professional talent since the baby-boom cohort began to enter the work force. The absorption of new workers into the labor force has been somewhat slower and more selective than it used to be. Many people have found that their college diplomas haven't won them the jobs they were trained for (Freeman, 1976), and many have found themselves underemployed. **Underemployment involves settling for a job that does not make full use of one's skills, abilities, and training.** This problem declined during the 1980s because of economic expansion, but it has risen again with the economic recession of the 1990s. Hence lack of challenge may contribute to job dissatisfaction for many people.

Autonomy

Most people prefer to have a sense of freedom on the job (London & Strumpf, 1986). Respondents in the *Psychology Today* survey ranked "the amount of freedom you have on your job" as fifth in importance (see Figure 12.5). They also want to have some control over the decisions that will affect them and their work. Employees want to have a say about how they perform their work, how to improve a product or the manufacture of it, and how to improve the work environment. One way organizations can increase employees' sense of autonomy is to involve them in decision making by developing Quality of Work Life programs (Offermann & Gowing, 1990). These programs are based on the principles of Theory Z, which works so well in Japanese industry. In these programs, workers at all levels are given maximum responsibility for the way they do their jobs (Levering, 1988).

The *quality circle*, an organizational mechanism commonly used in Japanese corporations, is one type of Quality of Work Life program (Offermann & Gowing, 1990). Each quality circle consists of a small group of employees who do similar work. They meet regularly to discuss how to improve their product, its production, and their work environment. Initial research on quality circles indicates that they can make a positive difference in the workplace. One study that compared participants and nonparticipants in quality circles found group differences on a variety of factors (Marks, 1986). Productivity was higher among members of quality circles and their absenteeism was lower. Also, participants' attitudes toward their accomplishments, opportunities for advancement, and the company were more positive than were those of nonparticipants. A second study found similar improvements in job performance and attitudes, although these changes diminished over time (Griffin, 1988).

Friendship and Recognition

In Chapter 8 we discussed the prominent role that friendships play in our lives. For many people, friendship circles emerge largely out of interactions at work. Consequently, it is logical that the social aspects of a job are a prime determinant of job satisfaction. When interpersonal relationships at work are pleasant, people are more likely to be content with their jobs.

Whether it is provided through pay raises, promotions, or praise, people crave recognition of their work. Most of us need to have the value of our work validated by others, especially supervisors and co-workers. Many of us are quite willing to go beyond the minimum requirements of our jobs as long as our extra efforts are recognized and appreciated. In the absence of such feedback, we tend to feel undervalued and dissatisfied.

Good Pay

When workers are asked to rate the importance of various job features, they generally rank pay surprisingly low. In the Renwick and Lawler (1978) survey, for instance, pay was ranked only 12th among the 18 items (see Figure 12.5). Their sample, however, was somewhat biased in that it contained a disproportionate number of affluent, well-educated professional subjects. Good pay is typically ranked higher in importance by people in nonprofessional positions. Nonetheless, in a poll that used a more representative sample of American workers, only 18% of the respondents rated good pay as "most

What Is Most Important in People's Jobs?

1 Chances to do something that makes you feel good about yourself

2 Chances to accomplish something worthwhile

3 Chances to learn new things

4 Opportunity to develop your skills and abilities

5 The amount of freedom you have on your job

6 Chances to do things you do best

7 The resources you have to do your job

8 The respect you receive from people you work with

9 Amount of information you get about your job performance

10 Your chances for taking part in making decisions

11 The amount of job security you have

12 Amount of pay you get

13 The way you are treated by the people you work with

14 The friendliness of the people you work with

15 Amount of praise you get for job well done

16 The amount of fringe benefits you get

17 Chances for getting a promotion

18 Physical surroundings of your job

FIGURE 12.5
Workers' evaluation of job characteristics
Renwick and Lawler (1978) asked subjects how important 18 aspects of their jobs were to them. These 18 job characteristics are ranked here from most to least important, on the basis of the averages of subjects' responses.

important" (Harris, 1987). These relatively low ratings may be misleading, though, because pay tends to be a major source of complaints. This paradoxical finding suggests that people may be more concerned about pay than they would like to believe.

Pay, by the way, is one of those things that tend to be evaluated on a relative basis. People are very sensitive to what *others* earn. Workers tend to be satisfied with their pay to the extent that they perceive it as *fair*. For most of us, a fair salary is one that (1) compares favorably with that of other employees with similar training and seniority who work in the same field and (2) is commensurate with the company's ability to pay (Levering, 1988). No matter how much we make, we may feel undercompensated if others like us are earning more or if our employers are making large profits that do not filter down to employees.

Security

"I used to joke at lunch. I'd say, 'If anybody hears that layoffs are comin', do me a favor. Send in my name.' Then a funny thing happened. I got laid off. I couldn't believe it. . . . I felt like a kid who wet his pants. I was afraid to go home and tell my wife. The rest of the day, nobody talked to me. They looked at me like I had cancer. I tried to smile, but I wanted to puke. The end of the day, I didn't want to leave. I even thought about just working through the next shift."

—A man quoted in *Psychology of Work Behavior* (Landy, 1989)

Being unemployed can have a devastating effect on one's psychological health. Job loss is related to the likelihood of psychological disorders (Banks & Jackson, 1982), substance abuse (Windshuttle, 1980), and marital separation (Liem & Rayman, 1982). Indeed, unemployment rates are a very significant predictor of suicide rates (Boor, 1980). Rankings of job security vary with the strength of the economy. When economic times are good, security is sometimes ranked low in importance because employees begin to take it for granted. But job security becomes very important as soon as it is threatened.

Other Considerations

According to Peter Warr (1987), some of the job attributes that we value may be desirable only up to a certain point. He draws an analogy between the ingredients of job satisfaction and the vitamins our bodies need. Although we need our minimum requirements of various vitamins, high doses of some vitamins can be toxic. Similarly, although we may desire challenge in our jobs, for instance, too much challenge may be harmful to our adjustment. Warr maintains that some desirable job attributes—such as good pay, job security, and recognition—have a consistent positive relation to mental health (see Figure 12.6). However, many other desirable job attributes—such as challenge, variety, autonomy, and decision-making input—have a curvilinear relation to mental health. That is, these job characteristics

have positive effects up to a point, but negative effects if they continue to increase (see Figure 12.6). Why should some valued attributes of work have negative effects on our job satisfaction and adjustment? Because too much challenge or autonomy may produce a high level of stress. We'll explore job stress as well as some other workplace hazards in the next section.

Occupational Hazards

Work can bring us deep satisfaction, but it can also be a source of frustration and conflict. Work in an unsafe environment can cause injuries and disease, even death. In this section, we'll explore three hazards in today's workplace: unsafe working conditions, job stress, and sexual harassment.

Unsafe Working Conditions

Many people work in unsafe conditions. Jobs that come easily to mind are firefighting, police work, mining, and construction. Every year one in ten workers in private industry suffers an occupational injury (Hatfield, 1990). Moreover, 16,000 workers lose their lives every year in work-related accidents, and thousands more are disabled (Boston Women's Health Book Collective, 1992). Work environments can also cause a variety of diseases. The five leading work-related diseases or injuries (evaluated on the basis of their frequency of occurrence, severity to the individual, and amenability to prevention) are (1) lung diseases, (2) musculoskeletal injuries, (3) cancers, (4) severe traumatic injuries, and (5) cardiovascular diseases. Psychological disorders, including alcohol and drug dependency, rank tenth on this list (National Institute for Occupational Safety and Health, 1988).

Work settings have typically been designed to maximize productivity and minimize costs (Levi, 1990). Although the short-run benefits of these developments have been greater productivity, lower costs, and increased profits, the long-run disadvantages have been the ill health, dissatisfaction, and alienation of many workers (Levi, 1990). In 1970, recognizing the problem of unsafe work environments, the U.S. Congress passed the Occupational Safety and Health Act, which requires employers to make their workplaces safe and free of health hazards "as far as possible." Among other things, this law established the Occupational Safety and Health Administration (OSHA) to set stan-

FIGURE 12.6
Warr's theory relating job characteristics to mental health
According to Peter Warr (1987), desirable job characteristics that are related to mental health (and job satisfaction) fall into two categories. Some job attributes—such as good pay and job security—have a consistent positive relation to mental health. Other job attributes—such as variety and autonomy—have a curvilinear relation to mental health. In other words, too much of a good thing (such as challenge) can have negative effects.

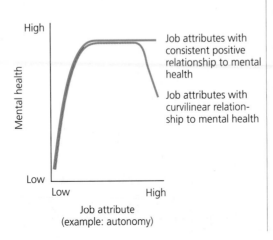

Job attributes with consistent positive relationship to mental health

Job attributes with curvilinear relationship to mental health

dards for workplace conditions and inspect places of employment to see if those standards are being met. OSHA can impose fines on employers who violate standards and order them to improve working conditions. Workers can file complaints with OSHA calling for inspections and evaluations of health hazards.

Many work-related injuries and diseases are preventable, either by the employer or by the employee. Today more companies appear to be recognizing this fact, as well as the relationship between worker satisfaction and productivity. Consequently, organizations are taking a more active role in improving and maintaining the health and safety of their workers. Many companies have instituted policies that relegate smoking to certain areas or ban it entirely. Some companies provide on-site health clubs for their employees.

Job Stress

We saw in Chapter 3 that stress can emerge from every corner of our lives, but many theorists suspect that the workplace is the primary source of stress in modern society. Job pressures may lie behind many stress-related illnesses (Hall & Savery, 1986). One study found that the principal difference between patients suffering from heart disease and matched control subjects was that the heart patients had experienced more occupational stress (Russek & Russek, 1976).

Sources of Stress on the Job

Even when working conditions are not bad enough to produce injury and disease, they can still be sources of stress. As such, they can have negative effects on employees' productivity and attitudes toward work. And as we have seen, *prolonged* stress can result in physical and psychological problems. Environmental stressors include extreme heat or cold, poor illumination, excessive noise, and air pollution. The effects of such stressors are more complex than we might

expect. Consider the effects of noise (Landy, 1989). Intense noise often impairs job performance, especially if it is intermittent, whereas low noise has little effect. Interestingly, *changes* in noise level often produce more distress and impaired performance than constant noise. Some individuals are more sensitive than others to noise and suffer more from exposure to it.

Of course, the characteristics of jobs may themselves be sources of stress. Some jobs require workers to do two or more things at once. Secretaries must attend to the boss's needs, office visitors, and telephone calls, while also working on reports that require them to pay careful attention as they move material from spreadsheets to word-processing programs on the computer. Other jobs demand virtually perfect performance because errors can have disastrous consequences. Consider the pressure under which surgeons and air traffic controllers must work. Still other jobs, such as coal mining and firefighting, require workers to face frequent threats to their physical safety. The list of potentially stressful job conditions is almost endless. Some of the more commonly experienced job stressors are prolonged physical labor, tedious work, work overload, long hours, unusual hours (such as rotating shifts), and the pressure of deadlines (Marshall & Cooper, 1981; Shostak, 1980). Another problem is "technostress" (Brod, 1988), experienced by the increasing number of people who are having difficulty adapting to the new technology in the workplace.

Additional sources of stress can come from human relations problems within organizations. Workers may be frustrated because they are denied input into decisions that will affect them. They may be underpromoted and underused. Conversely, they may find themselves promoted to positions for which they feel unprepared. Ultimately, many sources of occupational stress come from organizational factors, such as office politics, poor relations with supervisors, restrictions on communication, and the like (Blau, 1981).

CATHY copyright Cathy Guisewite. Reprinted with permission of UNIVERSAL PRESS SYNDICATE. All rights reserved.

FIGURE 12.7
Karasek's model of occupational stress as related to specific jobs
Robert Karasek theorizes that occupational stress is greatest in jobs characterized by high psychological demands and low decision control. This chart, based on survey data, shows where various familiar jobs fall on these two dimensions. The jobs that Karasek characterizes as the most stressful are those shown in the shaded area on the lower right.

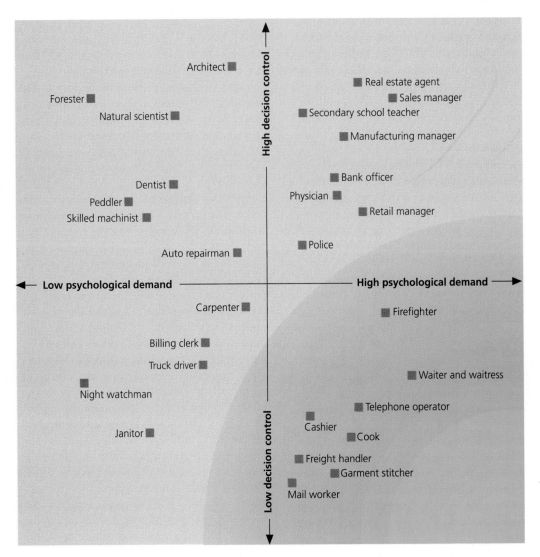

A document published by the Swedish government reported that the working conditions of employees in blue-collar jobs, nurses, and transportation workers have the most negative effects on their health (Levi, 1990). Because the nature of these jobs isn't significantly different in the United States, we presume that these findings apply to American workers as well. All of these jobs entail high psychosocial stress and physical work load, along with a low level of control over the decisions that affect the individual's work (Levi, 1990). As we have noted, there is evidence that having "decision control" is an important ingredient of job satisfaction.

According to Lennart Levi (1990), a well-known researcher in the area of job-related stress, four factors seem to play critical roles in the development of stress reactions. The first is the degree of *match between worker and job*. When the worker and the job environment are compatible, stress tends to be low. The greater the mismatch between the characteristics of the worker and the demands of the job, the greater the worker's stress is likely to be (French, Caplan, & Van Harrison, 1982). A good match occurs when the person has the abilities needed to be successful at the job and the job adequately meets the employee's needs.

A second very important factor is the degree to which workers have (or perceive that they have) *control over their working conditions*. Robert Karasek has proposed an intriguing model of occupational stress that supports this idea (Karasek, 1979; Karasek & Theorell, 1990). Karasek suggests that the *psychological demands* made upon a worker and the *decision control* a worker has are the two key factors in occupational stress. Psychological demands are measured by employees' answers to such questions as "Is there excessive work?" and "Must you work fast (or hard)?" Decision control is measured by their answers to such questions as "Do you have a lot of say in your job?" and "Do you have freedom to make decisions?" According to Karasek, *stress is greatest in jobs characterized by high psychological demands and low decision control.* On the basis of survey data

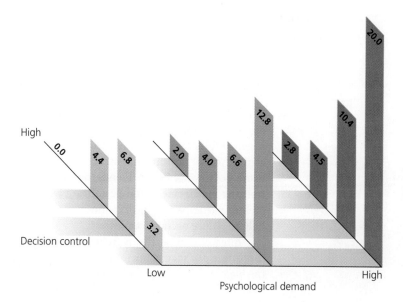

FIGURE 12.8
Job characteristics in Karasek's model and the prevalence of heart disease
Karasek and his colleagues (1981) interviewed 1,621 Swedish men about their work and assessed their cardiovascular health. The vertical bars show the percentage of the men with symptoms of heart disease as a function of the characteristics of their jobs. The highest incidence of heart disease was found among men who had jobs high in psychological demands and low in decision control, just as Karasek's model of occupational stress predicts.

obtained from workers, he has tentatively charted where various jobs fall on these two key dimensions of job stress. The jobs thought to be most stressful are those in the lower right area of Figure 12.7.

A worker's *coping skills* are a third critical factor. As we said earlier, stress lies in the eye of the beholder, and people vary widely in their ability to handle stress. Some of the personal qualities that may moderate the effects of job stress include physical stamina, tolerance for ambiguity, excellent job-related skills, and the ability to cope with change (French, Caplan, & Van Harrison, 1982; Matteson & Ivancevich, 1987). The impact of work stress may also be reduced by other factors that moderate the effects of stress in general, such as hardiness, optimism, sensation seeking, and autonomic reactivity (see Chapter 3). The fourth factor that determines whether or not job-related stress reactions develop is *social support*. As we noted in Chapter 3, supportive friends and family play an important role in both physical and psychological health.

Effects of Job Stress

Like other forms of stress, occupational stress is associated with a host of negative effects. In the work arena itself, job stress has been linked to increases in industrial accidents (Levenson, Hirschfeld, Hirschfeld, & Dzubay, 1983), poor job performance (Jackson & Schuler, 1985), high turnover rates (Powell, 1973), and high absenteeism (Rosch & Pelletier, 1987). Experts estimate that stress-related reductions in workers' productivity may cost American industry about $300 billion a year (Karasek & Theorell, 1990).

Of course, the negative effects of occupational stress extend beyond the workplace. Foremost among them are adverse effects on employees' physical health (Wolf, 1986). Work stress has been related to a variety of physical maladies, including heart disease, high blood pressure, stroke, ulcers, and arthritis (Holt, 1982). In a test of Karasek's model of work stress, more symptoms of heart disease were found among Swedish men whose jobs were high in psychological demands and low in decision control (Karasek et al., 1981; see Figure 12.8). Job-related stress can also have a negative impact on workers' psychological health. Occupational stress has been related to decreased self-esteem, frequent anxiety, bouts of depression, and abuse of alcohol or drugs (Fleming, 1986; Matteson & Ivancevich, 1987). Experts estimate that the health-care costs arising from occupational stress in the United States may run around $150 billion a year (Karasek & Theorell, 1990).

Dealing with Job Stress

The three avenues by which occupational stress can be attacked (Ivancevich, Matteson, Freedman, & Phillips, 1990) are summarized in Figure 12.9. One can intervene at the individual level by modifying workers' ways of coping with job stress. Or one can intervene at the organizational level by redesigning the work environment itself. The third method is to intervene at the individual-organizational interface by improving the fit between workers and their companies.

Intervention at the *individual* level is the most widely used strategy for managing work stress (Ivancevich et al., 1990). Many compa-

Work that some people find satisfying may be boring or stressful to others.

**FIGURE 12.9
Stress-management
interventions in
the workplace**
Ivancevich and his colleagues (1990) distinguish
three types of programs to
alleviate the effects of
occupational stress.
Interventions can occur at
the level of the individual
employee, at the organizational level, and at the individual-organizational
interface.

nies have instituted programs designed to improve their employees' coping skills. These programs usually focus on relaxation training, time management, cognitive approaches to reappraising stressful events, and other constructive coping strategies that we discussed in Chapter 4. Also popular are *workplace wellness programs*, which seek to improve employees' physical health (Gebhardt & Crump, 1990; Offermann & Gowing, 1990). These programs usually focus on exercise and fitness training, health screening, nutritional education, and the reduction of health-impairing habits, such as smoking and overeating.

Interventions at the *organizational* level are intended to make work environments less stressful. Some companies have attempted to reduce occupational stress by improving working conditions (making the surroundings more comfortable and attractive, for example). Many companies are also redesigning the require-

ments of jobs themselves (for instance, giving workers different tools or responsibilities). According to Karasek and Theorell (1990), the key here is to give adequate decision control to people in jobs that have high psychological demands. Job redesign may be especially critical in future years to accommodate the rapid influx of new technology into the workplace (Turnage, 1990). Many companies are also reevaluating their organizational structures (Offermann & Gowing, 1990). Trends toward decentralizing management and permitting workers greater participation in decision making may help to reduce occupational stress.

Interventions at the *individual-organizational interface* can take many forms. In future years the biggest challenge probably will be to accommodate the changing nature of the work force. The work force used to be dominated by married men who were the sole wage earners in their families. Now, however, dual-earner couples represent 40% of the work force. Another 6% of workers are single parents (Friedman, 1987). As we've seen, these trends indicate that more people will be struggling with conflicts between their work and family responsibilities. What kinds of accommodations are companies making in response to the changing needs of their workers? Quite a few interesting innovations are under way (Zedeck & Mosier, 1990). The more common options include flexible leave time, flextime, voluntary part-time work, and job sharing (see Figure 12.10). Less frequently offered benefits include counseling services, child-care information or referral services, work at home, employer-sponsored day care, and assistance with child care expenses (see Figure 12.10). The recently approved Family and Medical Leave Act will require larger organizations to provide workers with time off (unpaid) for the birth of a child or the serious illness of a family member. The availability of such benefits should help ease the stress on workers.

In another interesting development, companies are revising the way they handle the relocation of their employees. Because one partner is not necessarily free to follow the other, many organizations are moving to a policy of "joint career management" (Schein, 1981). Here attention is given to the employment opportunities for the partner in relocation planning.

Sexual Harassment

Sexual harassment burst upon the American consciousness in the fall of 1991 during the televised Senate hearings on the nomination of

Strategies for Managing Stress in the Workplace		
Individual	**Organizational**	**Individual-organizational interface**
Meditation	Organizational structure	Job demands/person's style fit
Exercise	Job design	Participation preferences/practices
Relaxation techniques	Selection and placement programs	Autonomy preferences/practices
Cognitive approaches	Working conditions	Co-worker relationships
Goal setting	Training and development	
Time management		

Clarence Thomas as a justice of the U. S. Supreme Court. For several days that October, Americans listened as law professor Anita Hill described incidents of alleged sexual harassment by (now Justice) Thomas when he was her supervisor at the U.S. Equal Employment Opportunity Commission.

Anita Hill's testimony set off shock waves that reverberated throughout the nation. Seeing the nomination of a prospective Supreme Court justice imperiled brought home the serious consequences of such behavior. The furor was fueled by several factors. First, individuals (and companies) woke up to the fact that they could be sued for such behavior (regulations were instituted in 1980). Second, as people came to see that they needed to take the problem more seriously, they also realized that they were relatively ignorant about what constituted sexual harassment. Because of the importance of this issue for men and women in the workplace today, we'll discuss it in some detail.

As we noted in Chapter 10, **sexual harassment is unwelcome sexually oriented behavior.** According to law, there are two types of sexual harassment. The first is *quid pro quo* (the Latin expression that translates as something given or received in exchange for something else). In this form of sexual harassment, a person in a position of power subjects a person of lower status to unwanted sexual advances and makes submission to them a condition of hiring, advancement, or firing. In other words, the worker's survival on the job depends on agreeing to have unwanted sex. *Environmental harassment* is any type of unwelcome sexual behavior that creates a hostile work environment.

Sexual harassment can take a variety of forms: unsolicited and unwelcome flirting, sexual advances, or propositions; insulting comments about an employee's appearance, dress, or anatomy; unappreciated dirty jokes and sexual gestures; intrusive or sexual questions about an employee's personal life; explicit descriptions of the harasser's own sexual experiences; abuse of familiarities such as "honey" and "dear"; unnecessary and unwanted physical contact such as touching, hugging, pinching, or kissing; catcalls; exposure of one's genitals; physical or sexual assault; and rape. As experts have pointed out, sexual harassment is an abuse of power by a person in authority.

Prevalence

Since public awareness of sexual harassment has been raised, so many instances of sexual

Worker-Responsive Innovations in the Workplace

Benefit	Percent of employers providing benefit	
	Private sector	**Government**
Flexible leave time	42.9	43.7
Flextime	43.6	37.5
Voluntary part-time work	35.3	26.7
Job sharing	15.0	23.5
Counseling services	4.2	18.2
Child-care information or referral services	4.3	15.8
Work at home	8.5	4.0
Employer-sponsored day care	1.6	9.4
Assistance with child-care expenses	3.1	2.9

**FIGURE 12.10
Worker-responsive innovations in the workplace**
Increasing numbers of employers are recognizing that they have to address the needs of the changing labor force by providing new benefits that help employees to meet family and leisure needs as well as work demands. Among innovative benefits, flexible leave time and flextime were the most widely offered in 1987.

harassment have received attention that we now know the problem is widespread. The serious consequences suffered by public figures also underscore the fact that sexual harassment is an issue to be taken seriously. At least one U. S. senator decided not to run for reelection in 1992 when accusations of sexual harassment against him surfaced. Also in the public eye was the Tailhook scandal, in which at least 26 women, more than half of whom were Navy officers, were groped and fondled by some 70 Navy and Marine aviators at a convention in a Las Vegas hotel in 1991. The Tailhook scandal has resulted in the resignation of the secretary of the Navy, and three admirals have lost their jobs. A separate investigation by the inspector general is expected to result in numerous courts-martial of career officers. Interestingly, some people have seen the ban against homosexuals in the military as encouraging sexual harassment (Gibbs, 1991): as long as the ban is in place, a military man can threaten to spread rumors that a woman colleague is a lesbian if she refuses to have sex with him. Because his rumors will result in her separation from military service if they are believed, she may feel compelled to engage in sex.

Sexual harassment in the workplace is more widespread than most people realize. Recent surveys estimate that 50 to 75% of female workers in the United States have experienced at least one instance of sexual harassment (Fain & Anderton, 1987; Lafontaine & Tredeau, 1986). The typical victim is young

Step Forward: Sexual Harassment in the Workplace—What You Need to Know
by Susan L. Webb (Mastermedia, 1991)

After the Clarence Thomas–Anita Hill sexual harassment controversy, both employers and workers were eager to learn what constituted sexual harassment and what did not. Although Susan Webb wrote this book to address employers' questions, workers will also find it quite informative. Chapters are devoted to the history of sexual harassment and to defining and clarifying the complexities of the issue. Webb also offers concrete steps to stop sexual harassment, specific suggestions for handling sexual harassment complaints, and information about training and education. In addition, she lists and responds to the questions most frequently asked and details things that all employees can do to stop and prevent sexual harassment. Some case studies and exercises are also included in the book.

How Can I Be Sure It's Sexual Harassment?

To recognize sexual harassment, first decide if the behavior in question is job-related. Does it go toward getting the work done? If the answer is "yes," the behavior is appropriate and will probably not cause a problem. If the answer is "no," and the behavior is social, then consider the following:

- Is the behavior directed toward employees of one gender only—only men or only women?
- Is it courting, flirting, or sexual behavior?
- Has the employee receiving the attention objected in any way, said or indicated "no," "stop," or "I don't like it"?
- Has the employee been asked if the attention is objected to or unwanted?
- Is the behavior or similar behavior repeated? Has it happened before?
- Does the offending employee behave this way deliberately, on purpose?
- Does the behavior interfere with the receiving employee's work performance?
- Does it create an environment that is hostile, intimidating, or offensive for an employee?
- Does the employee feel demeaned, degraded, or embarrassed by the behavior?

If the answer to several of the questions is "yes," the behavior may well be considered sexual harassment. [pp. 91–92]

and unmarried, has several years of technical training or college, and works in a male-dominated field. Still, if we believe Anita Hill's testimony, even a Yale Law School graduate can experience the problem. Victims of sexual harassment often develop physical and psychological symptoms of stress that can lead to decreased work motivation and productivity (Crull, 1979).

Stopping Sexual Harassment

In recognition of the prevalence and negative impact of sexual harassment, many organizations have taken steps to educate and protect their workers. Managers are publicly speaking out against sexual harassment, supporting programs designed to increase employees' awareness of the problem, instituting policies expressly forbidding harassment, and implementing formal grievance procedures for handling allegations of harassment. The Recommended Reading on this page describes a book that we believe both employers and employees will find helpful in this regard.

In the two remaining sections of the chapter, our focus will shift to the issues of career development and some important considerations in making career choices.

Models of Career Development

Psychologists have long been interested in understanding how individuals make decisions about career choices. Some theorists approach the issue from a developmental (stage) perspective. Others take a nondevelopmental view.

Trait Measurement and Matching Models

The nondevelopmental view asserts that career choice is related to an individual's personality traits. These traits, which are assumed to be relatively stable over time, are measured by psychological tests. In turn, the test results are used to match individuals to the jobs for which their personalities are best suited. The most influential model of this type has been developed by John Holland (1973, 1985). According to Holland, we have stereotypic views of the work environments associated with various occupations, and we search for a work environment that will fit our personality. Holland has identified six broad personality types, called *personal orientations*, and six matching *work environments*. For obvious reasons, Holland's approach is often called the *hexagonal model*. Here are the six orientations and their optimal work environments:

- *Realistic* people describe themselves as good at mechanical tasks and weak in social skills. They prefer jobs with tasks that are physical or mechanical and clearly defined, such as farming, auto mechanics, and engineering. They tend to avoid tasks that involve social

Holland's Personal Orientations and Related Work Environments

Themes	Personal orientations	Work environments
Realistic	Values concrete and physical tasks. Perceives self as having mechanical skills and lacking social skills.	*Settings:* concrete, physical tasks requiring mechanical skills, persistence, and physical movement. *Careers:* machine operator, truck driver, draftsperson, barber.
Investigative	Wants to solve intellectual, scientific, and mathematical problems. Sees self as analytical, critical, curious, introspective, and methodical.	*Settings:* research laboratory, diagnostic medical case conference, work group of scientists. *Careers:* marine biologist, computer programmer, clinical psychologist, architect, dentist.
Artistic	Prefers unsystematic tasks or artistic projects: painting, writing, or drama. Perceives self as imaginative, expressive, and independent.	*Settings:* theater, concert hall, library, radio or TV studio. *Careers:* sculptor, actor, designer, musician, author, editor.
Social	Prefers educational, helping, and religious careers. Enjoys social involvement, church, music, reading, and dramatics. Is cooperative, friendly, helpful, insightful, persuasive, and responsible.	*Settings:* school and college classrooms, psychiatrist's office, religious meetings, mental institutions, recreational centers. *Careers:* counselor, nurse, teacher, social worker, judge, minister, sociologist.
Enterprising	Values political and economic achievements, supervision, and leadership. Enjoys leadership control, verbal expression, recognition, and power. Perceives self as extraverted, sociable, happy, assertive, popular, and self-confident.	*Settings:* courtroom, political rally, car sales room, real estate firm, advertising company. *Careers:* realtor, politician, attorney, salesperson, manager.
Conventional	Prefers orderly, systematic, concrete tasks with verbal and mathematical data. Sees self as conformist and having clerical and numerical skills.	*Settings:* bank, post office, file room, business office, Internal Revenue office. *Careers:* banker, accountant, timekeeper, financial counselor, typist, receptionist.

FIGURE 12.11
Overview of Holland's theory of vocational choice
John Holland has identified six personality types (personal orientations), each of which prefers a different work environment. These connections between personality and vocational preferences are summarized here.

skills, abstract thinking, subjectivity, or verbal skill.

- *Investigative* people enjoy abstract thinking and logical analysis, preferring understanding to acting. They like working with ideas rather than with things or people. Investigative individuals can often be found working in research laboratories or libraries.
- *Artistic* people see themselves as imaginative and independent. They tend to be impulsive and creative and are socially aloof. These individuals dislike structured tasks, preferring to rely on their subjective impressions in dealing with the environment. They have a high need for emotional expression and often seek careers in art, music, or drama.
- *Social* people describe themselves as being understanding and wanting to help others. They prefer to interact with people, and they have the necessary social skills to do so comfortably. They typically have greater verbal ability than mathematical ability. Social types are often found in the helping professions, such as teaching, nursing, and social work.
- *Enterprising* people perceive themselves as happy, self-confident, sociable, and popular. They like to use their social skills to lead or persuade others. They prefer sales or supervisory positions, in which they can express these characteristics.

- *Conventional* people are conforming, systematic, and orderly. They typically have greater clerical and mathematical ability than verbal ability. They prefer work environments that are structured and predictable, and may be well suited to occupations in the business world.

Holland has developed several tests to measure the six basic personal orientations. One of them, the Self-Directed Search, or SDS, is a self-scoring test. Once individuals identify their personality type on the SDS, they can match it with various relevant occupations. Studies have shown that the SDS has helped students reduce career indecision and select occupations consistent with their personality traits (McGowan, 1977; Zener & Schnuelle, 1976). You can take a rough stab at categorizing your own personal orientation by studying Figure 12.11. Look at the matching work environments to get some ideas for possible career options.

Holland's hexagonal model has prompted considerable research, and much of it supports his theory. Holland reports that people in occupations that are well matched to their personalities are more satisfied with their jobs and are likely to remain in those jobs longer than individuals who are not so well matched to their jobs (Holland, 1985). Another study found that personal orientation was a much better predictor than other personal characteristics (age, sex, length of time on the job) of teachers' job satisfaction (Wiggins, Lederer, Salkowe, & Rys, 1983).

As you'll recall, one of the assumptions of trait measurement and matching models is that vocational interests remain stable during adulthood. On this question the research evidence is mixed. On the positive side, one study found that the interests underlying career choices remain stable after about age 17 (Hansen & Campbell, 1985). It has also been found that when people change occupations, they frequently choose new jobs that correspond to the same personal orientation in Holland's model (Gottfredson, 1977). On the negative side, at least one study has found that accountants differed significantly in their needs and work attitudes at different life stages and also in the extent to which they fitted Holland's conventional orientation (Adler & Aranya, 1984).

Hence, while the trait approach is useful, it fails to take into account the fact that people's interests, skills, motivations, aspirations, and situations change over time. Stage theories, in contrast, view occupational choice as a developmental process rather than a specific event (Crites, 1980; Osipow, 1987).

Developmental Models

The most influential stage theory of career choice is the one outlined by Donald Super (1957, 1985, 1988). He views vocational development as a process that unfolds gradually across most of the life span. This process begins in childhood and ends with retirement. Super asserts that one's self-concept is the critical factor that governs this developmental process. According to him, decisions about work and career commitments reflect people's attempts to express their changing views of themselves. To map these changes, Super breaks the vocational life cycle into five major stages and a variety of substages (see Figure 12.12).

Growth Stage

The growth stage encompasses childhood, a time when youngsters fantasize about exotic jobs they would enjoy. Generally they imagine themselves as detectives, airplane pilots, and brain surgeons rather than plumbers, grocers, and bookkeepers. Until the very end of this period, youngsters are largely oblivious of such realistic considerations as the abilities or education required for specific jobs. They base their fantasies purely on their likes and dislikes.

Exploration Stage

Pressures from parents, teachers, and peers to develop a general career direction begin to intensify during high school. By the end of high school, individuals are expected to have narrowed a general career direction to a specific one. Whether through studying about it or through part-time work, a person tries to get a real taste of the projected occupation. During the latter part of this stage, people typically attempt to enter the world of work on a full-time basis. Many individuals in this phase are still only tentatively committed to their chosen occupation. If their initial work experiences are gratifying, their commitment will be strengthened. If their first experiences are not rewarding, they may shift to another occupation, where they will continue the process of exploration.

Establishment Stage

Vacillation continues to be moderately common during the first part of the establishment stage. For some people, doubts begin to surface

**FIGURE 12.12
Overview of Super's theory of vocational development**
According to Donald Super, people go through five major stages (and a variety of substages) of vocational development over their life span. The approximate ages and key events associated with each stage are summarized here.

Stages of Vocational Development		
Stage	Approximate ages	Key events and transitions
Growth stage	*0–14*	*A period of general physical and mental growth*
Prevocational substage	0–3	No interest or concern with vocations
Fantasy substage	4–10	Fantasy is basis for vocational thinking
Interest substage	11–12	Vocational thought is based on individual's likes and dislikes
Capacity substage	13–14	Ability becomes the basis for vocational thought
Exploration stage	*15–24*	*General exploration of work*
Tentative substage	15–17	Needs, interests, capacities, values, and opportunities become bases for tentative occupational decisions
Transition substage	18–21	Reality increasingly becomes a basis for vocational thought and action
Trial substage	22–24	First trial job is entered after the individual has made an initial vocational commitment
Establishment stage	*25–44*	*The individual seeks to enter a permanent occupation*
Trial substage	25–30	A period of some occupational change due to unsatisfactory choices
Stabilization substage	31–44	A period of stable work in a given occupational field
Maintenance stage	*45–65*	*Continuation in one's chosen occupation*
Decline stage	*65+*	*Adaptation to leaving work force*
Deceleration substage	65–70	Period of declining vocational activity
Retirement substage	71+	A cessation of vocational activity

for the first time as they reappraise the match between their personal attributes and their current position. Others simply carry earlier doubts into this stage. If a person's career choice turns out to be gratifying, however, the individual becomes firmly committed to an occupation. With few exceptions, future job moves will take place *within* this occupational area. Having made a commitment, the person now has to demonstrate the ability to function effectively in the chosen occupation. To succeed, he or she must use previously acquired skills, learn new skills as they become necessary, and display flexibility in adapting to organizational changes.

Maintenance Stage

As the years go by, opportunities for further career advancement and occupational mobility decline (see Figure 12.13). Around their mid-40s, many people cross into the maintenance stage, during which they worry more about retaining their achieved status than about improving it. Rapidly changing technology may compel middle-aged employees to enhance and update their skills as they face competition from younger, more recently educated workers. The primary goal at this stage, however, is simply to protect the security, power, advantages, and perks that one has attained. With decreased emphasis on career advancement, many people shift energy and attention away from work toward family concerns or leisure activities.

Decline Stage

Deceleration involves a decline in vocational activity during one's later years as retirement looms near. People redirect their energy and attention toward planning for this major transition. In his original formulation, which was based on research in the 1950s, Super projected that deceleration ought to begin around age 65. Since the 1970s, however, slowed economic growth and the entry of the large baby-boom cohort into the work force have combined to create an oversupply of skilled labor and professional talent. This social change has created pressures that promote early retirement. For this reason, deceleration often begins earlier than Super initially indicated.

Retirement brings vocational activity to a halt. People approach this transition with highly varied attitudes. Many individuals look forward to it eagerly. Other people approach it with apprehension, unsure how they will occupy themselves and worried about their financial viability. Still others approach retirement with a combination of hopeful enthusiasm and anx-

ious concern. Although concern about what lies ahead is understandable, many studies have shown that retirement has no adverse effect on overall life satisfaction (Palmore, Fillenbaum, & George, 1984). Although retirement may lower one's income, it also brings more time to spend on hobbies, travel, and friends (George, Fillenbaum, & Palmore, 1984).

Alternate Patterns of Career Development

As we mentioned in Chapter 11, stage theories tend to highlight general trends while ignoring the variability in developmental patterns. Super, however, acknowledged that people follow different patterns in their vocational development. In fact, he identified several atypical patterns that do not coincide with the *conventional pattern* we have described.

Super described three atypical patterns for men. Men who follow the *stable pattern* enter a career immediately upon leaving school and remain in that career for their entire working lives. Men in the *unstable pattern* alternate between trial jobs (exploratory, entry-level positions) and stable jobs throughout life. These men get beyond entry-level jobs and earn positions with potential but then forsake their progress and move on to another occupational area. Finally, men who follow the *multiple-trial pattern* move quickly through an endless series of briefly held trial jobs. These men are occupational vagabonds who wander aimlessly from one career to another.

In addition to the four patterns seen in men, Super describes three career patterns unique to women. Women who follow the *stable homemaking pattern* never work outside the home. Those who follow the *double-track pattern* attempt to combine homemaking and out-

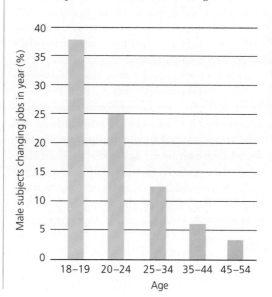

FIGURE 12.13
Occupational mobility as related to age
Occupational mobility declines dramatically with increasing age, as these data from a study by Byrne (1975) clearly show. (From Arbeiter, 1979.)

side work throughout adulthood. The *interrupted pattern* is seen in women who temporarily leave the work force one or more times because of family responsibilities.

In support of Super's model, it has been found that self-esteem and career maturity are positively correlated (Crook, Healy, & O'Shay, 1984). Also, recall the earlier-mentioned study reporting changes in accountants' personal orientations at different life stages (Adler & Aranya, 1984).

Women's Career Development

Until fairly recently, most of the theories and research on career development have focused on *men's* careers. One reason is that relatively few women worked. Today, however, women can expect to spend about 30 years in the labor force (men will spend about 40 years in the workplace) (U.S. Department of Labor, 1990). Once women began to enter the work force in large numbers, it was simply taken for granted that the theories and concepts used to explain men's vocational development would apply equally well to women. Evidence suggests, however, that men and women have different patterns of career development (Fitzgerald & Betz, 1983; Betz & Fitzgerald, 1987). For one thing, most women still subordinate their career goals to their husbands' goals (Unger & Crawford, 1992). If a married man wants or needs to move to another job, his wife typically follows him and takes the best job she can find in the new location. Thus married women usually have less control over their careers than married men do.

Another reason that women's career paths differ from men's is that women are more likely than men to interrupt their careers to concentrate on child rearing or family crises. Historically, women's participation in the labor force has typically shown a sharp rise as women take their first jobs, then a sharp dip as they leave the labor force to concentrate on rearing children, and finally a second sharp rise when they return to work, usually after the children are grown. Interestingly, this pattern has been labeled the *M-curve*—both for its shape on the graph and for "mother" (Farley, 1980). As we've mentioned, however, more and more mothers are returning to work when their children are small. In fact, over 70% of mothers who have held jobs return to the labor force within two years of their children's birth (Hofferth & Phillips, 1987). As women's participation in the labor force increasingly resembles that of men, the M-curve is disappearing.

Still, many women do leave the labor force, if for increasingly brief periods of time. This hiatus in employment is termed *labor force discontinuity*. Does labor force discontinuity pose any problems for women? Definitely. In fact, dropping out of the work force is an important, but not the only, cause of the gender gap in salaries and employment status. Moreover, when women want to return to the workplace, they are unlikely to find the welcome mat out for any but entry-level positions (Treiman, 1985). Studies show that women who do not have children remain in the labor force and have a pattern of career advancement, whereas women who have children typically drop out of the work force and show downward mobility in their career paths (Sewell, Hauser, & Wolf, 1980). An implication of this finding is that economic hardship is likely for mothers who become single parents. As we have mentioned, changes in the family and the work setting are needed to accommodate the changing roles of women and men.

Important Considerations in Career Choice

One of your biggest decisions in life is your choice of a career. The importance of this decision is enormous. It may determine whether you are employed or unemployed, financially secure or insecure, happy or unhappy. Given our rapidly advancing technology and the increased training and education required to break into most fields, it is more important than ever to choose thoughtfully. We have already described some of the factors that tend to promote job satisfaction, and you should take these factors into account when you choose an occupation. Additional information must be considered as well. To make an informed vocational choice, it is critical that you evaluate your personality, talents, and interests. It is also necessary to research the characteristics of the various job options available to you. The more accurate information you possess about your personal characteristics and your job options, the better prepared you will be to choose a career that is suitable for you.

General Principles

As you explore your personal characteristics and investigate career opportunities, keep the following generalizations in mind.

1. *Your career options have limits.* Entry into a particular occupation is not simply a matter of choosing what you want to do. It's a two-way street. You get to make choices, but you also have to persuade schools and employers to choose you. Your career options will be limited to some extent by factors beyond your control, including fluctuations in the economy and the job market (Lock, 1988).

2. *You have the potential for success in a variety of occupations.* Vocational counselors stress that people have multiple potentials (Gilmer, 1975). There are more than 20,000 occupations to choose from! In light of the huge variety in occupational opportunities, it's foolish to believe that only one career would be right for you. If you expect to find one job that fits you perfectly, you may spend your entire lifetime searching for it.

3. *Chance may play a role in your career development.* Unplanned, accidental events can influence one's occupational evolution (Hart, Rayner, & Christensen, 1971). For example, your career plans might be changed by a particular college course that you took only because the class you really wanted was full. This reality does not mean that you should leave career development to fate. Rather, your challenge is to minimize the role of chance in your vocational development through thoughtful planning.

4. *Career choice is a developmental process that extends throughout life.* Occupational choice involves not a single decision but a series of decisions. This process was once believed to extend only from prepuberty to one's early 20s, but it is now recognized that the process often continues throughout life (Ginzberg, 1972). In fact, a major survey of adults in the United States (Arbeiter, Aslanian, Schmerbeck, & Brickell, 1978) found that 36%—over a third—were in a career transition, either actively seeking or considering a new career. Many middle-aged people tend to underestimate the options available to them, however, and therefore miss opportunities to make constructive changes. It is important to realize that vocational choices are not limited to one's youth.

5. *Some career decisions are not easily undone.* Although it's never too late to strike out in new vocational directions, it is important to recognize that many decisions are not readily reversed. One influential theory of occupational choice in the 1950s (Ginzberg, 1952) went so far as to propose that vocational decisions are characterized by *irreversibility.* That assertion has since been retracted as an over-statement (Ginzberg, 1972). But it is clear that once you invest time, money, and effort in moving along a particular career path, it may not be easy to change paths. This reality was made clear by the Renwick and Lawler (1978) survey, in which nearly half (44%) of the respondents indicated that they felt locked into their current jobs. This potential problem highlights why it is important to devote systematic thought to your vocational choice.

6. *Career choice is an expression of one's personality.* As we have seen, various influential theories of vocational choice focus on how this process is related to personal orientation (Holland, 1985), self-concept (Super, 1988), ego functioning (Ginzberg, 1972), and psychological needs (Roe, 1977). Although these theories differ in their emphasis, they clearly agree that the choice of a career is an expression of one's personality.

Examining Your Personal Characteristics

Our discussion of career choice and job satisfaction points to the importance of self-knowledge when a career decision is to be made. To select an occupation that you will find rewarding, you need to have a clear picture of yourself. In piecing together this picture, you will want to consider your personality, your abilities, and your interests (Shertzer, 1985).

Personality

As we saw in our discussion of the career development models of Holland and Super, most vocational theorists agree that it is very important to choose an occupation that is compatible with your personality. In assessing your personality, you should try to identify your dominant traits, needs, and values. Holland's Self-Directed Search (SDS) can be useful in this regard. A particularly crucial characteristic to evaluate is how socially skilled you are. Some jobs require much more social dexterity than others.

Aptitudes and Abilities

It is important to evaluate your aptitudes and abilities realistically. Although intelligence does not necessarily predict occupational success, it does predict the likelihood of entering particular occupations, because intelligence is related to the academic success that is necessary to enter many fields. Certain professions, such as law and medicine, are open only to people who can meet increasingly selective criteria as they move from high school to college to graduate education and professional training.

Other aptitudes and abilities are important as well. In many occupations, special talents are more important than general intelligence. Specific aptitudes that might make a person well suited for certain occupations include perceptual-motor coordination, creativity, artistic or musical talent, mechanical ability, clerical skill, mathematical ability, and persuasive talents.

Interests

As you meander through life, you acquire interests in various kinds of activities. Are you intrigued by the business world? The academic world? International affairs? Agriculture? The outdoors? Physical sciences? Arts and crafts? Music? Travel? Athletics? Human services? The list of potential interests is virtually infinite. Although interests may change, they tend to be relatively stable, and they definitely should be considered in the development of career plans.

Using Tests to Aid Career Planning

Numerous psychological tests are available that can help you arrive at a good picture of your personality, abilities, and interests. There are standardized tests of intellectual abilities, tests of spatial and mechanical skills, of perceptual accuracy, and of motor abilities, as well as of personality and interests. If you are undecided about what kind of occupation might intrigue you, you might want to begin by taking a special kind of test. **Occupational interest inventories measure your interests as they relate to various jobs or careers.** The most widely used of the many tests in this category are the Strong Interest Inventory (SII) and the Kuder Occupational Interest Survey (KOIS), both of which can be taken at most college counseling centers.

Occupational interest inventories do not attempt to predict whether you would be successful in various occupations. They relate more to the likelihood of job *satisfaction* than job *success*. The tests are based on the assumption that if your interests are similar to the typical interests of people already in a particular occupation, then you might enjoy working in that occupational area.

The developers of most occupational interest inventories use the following general strategy. They begin by measuring the interests of people who are already established in various

occupations and who report that they enjoy their work. Typical interest profiles are compiled for many occupational groups. When you take an occupational interest inventory, your interests are compared with these occupational profiles. You receive many scores indicating how similar your interests are to the typical interests of people in various occupations. If you receive a high score on the accountant scale of a test, for example, your interests are similar to those of the average accountant. This correspondence in interests does not ensure that you would enjoy a career in accounting, but it is a moderately good predictor of job satisfaction (Swaney & Prediger, 1985).

The most recent revision of the Strong Interest Inventory groups occupations into six broad categories that correspond to the six types of work environments identified by John Holland (1985). Holland's six prototype work environments are called *general occupational themes*. Scores on these general themes indicate whether you have a realistic, investigative, artistic, social, enterprising, or conventional personality, as described by Holland. As you can see in Figure 12.14, the SII divides each theme into a few basic interest scales and then breaks basic interests down into specific occupational scores—162 in all.

Interest inventories such as the SII can provide food for thought about possible careers. The results may confirm your subjective guesses about your interests and strengthen already existing vocational preferences. The test results may also inspire you to investigate career possibilities that you had never thought of before. Unexpected results may stimulate you to rethink your career plans.

Although interest inventories can be helpful as you work through career decisions, several cautions are worth noting. First, you may score high on some occupations that you're sure you would hate. Given the sheer number of occupational scales on the tests, this can easily happen by chance. Don't dismiss the remainder of the test results just because you're sure that a few specific scores are "wrong." Second, don't let the test make career decisions for you. Some students naively believe that they should pursue whatever occupation yields their highest score. This is not how the tests are meant to be used. They merely provide information for you to consider. Ultimately, you have to think things out for yourself.

Third, you should be aware that there is a lingering gender bias on most occupational interest inventories. Many of these scales were originally developed 30 to 40 years ago, when outright discrimination or more subtle discouragement prevented women from entering many occupations. Critics assert that interest inventories have helped to channel women into sex-typed careers, such as nursing and secretarial work, while guiding them away from more prestigious "male" occupations, such as medicine and engineering (Diamond, 1979). Recently progress has been made toward reducing gender bias in occupational tests, but it has not been eliminated yet. So be wary of letting gender stereotypes limit your career options. A good career counselor should be able to help women—as well as men—sort through the effects of gender bias on their test results.

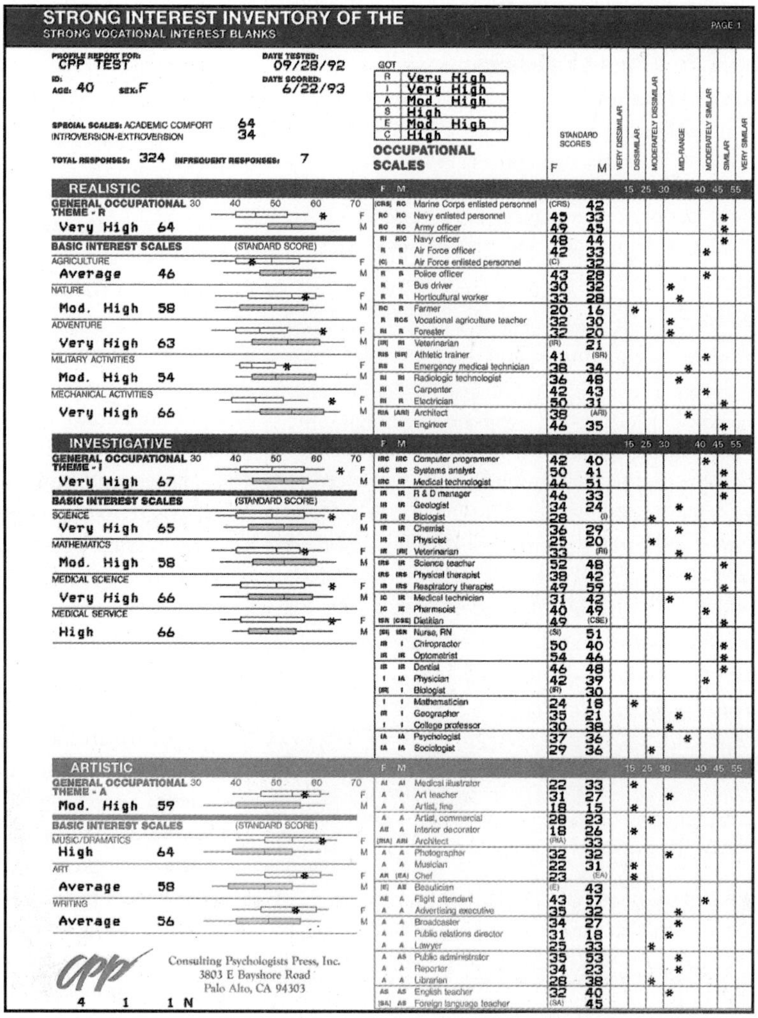

Two useful manuals have been developed to help people clarify personality-related questions as they relate to career choice. *Discover the Career within You*, by Clarke G. Carney and Cinda Field Wells (1991), and *What Color Is Your Parachute?* (see the Recommended Reading in the Application).

Researching Job Characteristics

In order to match yourself up with an occupation, you have to seek out information about jobs. As we have noted, there are over 20,000 occupations (Michelozzi, 1988). Their sheer number is overwhelming. Obviously, you have to narrow the scope of your search before you can start gathering information.

Once you have selected some jobs that might interest you, the next question is: Where do you get information on them? This is not a simple matter. The first step is usually to read some occupational literature. A very general reference is the *Occupational Outlook Handbook*, available in most libraries. This compre-hensive guide to occupations, published every two years by the Bureau of Labor Statistics, includes job descriptions, education and training requirements, advancement possibilities, salaries, and employment outlooks for 250 occupations. In addition, it describes other sources of career education, training, and financial aid information, as well as resources for such groups as youth, the handicapped, veterans, women, and minorities. Other helpful books are *Joyce Lain Kennedy's Career Book* (see the Recommended Reading on p. 394) and *Jobs! What They Are . . . Where They Are . . . What They Pay!* by Robert Snelling and Anne Snelling (1985). You can get more detailed information on many particular occupations from government agencies, trade unions, and professional organizations. If you're interested in a career in psychology, for example, you can obtain a variety of pamphlets and books from the American Psychological Association.

After reading the available literature about an occupation, it's often a good idea to talk to some people who work in that area. People in the field can provide you with more down-to-

FIGURE 12.14
The Strong Interest Inventory (SII)
The SII estimates the similarity of the respondent's interests to the interests of people working in various occupations. The occupations are grouped into six categories that are based on the six types of work environments described by Holland. The first page of a two-page score report for a female respondent is shown. It is normal to get high scores on many specific *occupational scales* (shown on the right side), and the test results should not be discounted if some of them seem farfetched (for example, this woman may be sure that she doesn't want to be a dietician or military officer). Broad patterns of interests captured by scores on the *general occupational themes* and *basic interest scales* (shown on the left side) often are more informative. For instance, this woman's high scores on the realistic and investigative themes may stimulate her to think about occupations that could satisfy these interests.

Joyce Lain Kennedy's Career Book
by Joyce Lain Kennedy and Darryl Laramore
(VGM Career Horizons, 1993)

Most career guidance books focus either on occupational choice or on job search skills. Kennedy and Laramore, however, manage to cover an extremely wide range of topics without sacrificing depth. They present a vast amount of information in a concise format. Although targeted at the 15-to-25 age bracket, this book is useful for first-time job seekers and career changers of all ages, because it focuses on occupational strategies and processes relevant to all stages of career development.

The various sections of the book cover topics as diverse as decision making, goal setting, information gathering, self-awareness, demographic trends, jobs of the future, educational options, and lifelong career management. The sections can be read consecutively or buffet style. Embedded in each section are numerous exercises and questionnaires designed to motivate the reader to apply the new information. The authors frequently direct the reader to additional sources of information as well. All in all, this is an extremely comprehensive and thorough work, and an invaluable reference.

We can't be sure what lies beyond the calendar horizon of January 1, 2000, but it is customary for authors and commencement speakers to solemnly inform each new crop of graduates that the challenges they face are greater than any since the Ice Age. In your case, it's true. That's because of the technological speedup that is occurring as you read this page.

You are going where no generation has gone before. But isn't that the same for everyone? Yes, but what's different for you, and why your challenge is greater than that of, say, your parents, is that your crystal ball is almost fogged over as a result of the rate of change: It's happening in fast-forward motion. [p. 408]

earth information than you can get by reading. Keep in mind, though, that the people you talk to may not be a representative sample of those who work in that occupation. Don't make the mistake of rejecting a potentially satisfying career just because one person hates it.

When you examine occupational literature and interview people, what kinds of information should you seek? To some extent, the answer depends on your unique values and needs. Some general information, however, should be of concern to virtually anyone (Shertzer, 1985; Weinrach, 1979). The questions you can ask include the following:

- *The nature of the work.* What would your day-to-day duties and responsibilities be?
- *Working conditions.* Is the work environment pleasant or unpleasant, low-key or high-pressure?
- *Entry requirements.* What education and training are required to break into this occupational area?
- *Potential earnings.* What are entry-level salaries, and how much can you hope to earn if you're exceptionally successful? What does the average person earn? What are the fringe benefits?
- *Potential status.* What is the social status associated with this occupation? Is it personally satisfactory for you?
- *Opportunities for advancement.* How do you move up in this field? Are there adequate opportunities for promotion and advancement?
- *Intrinsic job satisfaction.* Outside of money and formal fringe benefits, what can you derive in the way of personal satisfaction from this job? Will it allow you to have fun, to help people, to be creative, or to shoulder responsibility?
- *Future outlook.* How are supply and demand projected to shape up in the future for this occupational area?

By the way, if you're wondering whether your college education will be worth the effort in dollars and cents, the answer generally is yes. The jobs that you can obtain with a college degree do tend to yield higher pay than those available to people with less education (Murphy & Welch, 1989). Indeed, college

FIGURE 12.15
Trends in the wage gap between college and high school graduates
The graph shows the percentage by which the weekly earnings of college graduates exceeded the earnings of high school graduates for workers with varying levels of experience on the job. Back in 1965, college graduates were earning 40 to 55% more than high school graduates. This wage advantage grew some and then dipped during the 1970s. During the 1980s, however, the wage gap widened dramatically to nearly 70%. (Data from Murphy & Welch, 1989.)

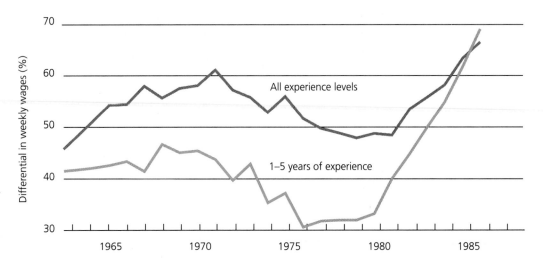

graduates' earnings advantage over high school graduates increased during the 1980s, especially in entry-level jobs, as Figure 12.15 shows.

Summary

ork is an activity that produces something of value for others. Individuals may or may not be paid for their work. Contemporary trends are changing the world of work. Between now and the year 2000, more women and minorities will join the labor force. Since the 1950s, the participation of women in the work force has increased at all occupational levels. Even so, most women continue to be concentrated in "pink ghetto" jobs. Discrimination makes today's workplace a different place for women than it is for men.

A major challenge for workers today is to balance work, family, and leisure activities in ways that are personally satisfying. Workaholism, the need to juggle multiple roles, and the effective use of leisure time are important issues in this regard. People work for a variety of reasons. Although financial necessity is a compelling factor for most people, work may satisfy many other needs as well. Theorists such as McGregor, Herzberg, and Ouchi agree that we all have needs for achievement, recognition, and self-fulfillment. Job satisfaction appears to be related to mental and physical health and even longevity. Meaningfulness, challenge and variety, autonomy, friendship and recognition, good pay, and security are important determinants of job satisfaction.

Major hazards in the workplace include unsafe work conditions, job stress, and sexual harassment. Many work-related injuries and diseases are preventable, either by the employer or by the employee. Although stress is subjective, people who work in jobs that have high psychological demands and low decision control are especially vulnerable to it. The negative effects of stress are felt by both employers and employees. Interventions to manage stress in the workplace can be made at the individual level, the organizational level, and the individual-organizational interface.

Sexual harassment is a widespread and long-standing problem that has just recently gained public exposure. Victims of sexual harassment often develop physical and psychological symptoms of stress that can decrease work motivation and productivity. Many organizations are taking steps to educate their workers about this problem.

Two major theories of career development are those of John Holland and Donald Super. Holland's hexagonal model asserts that we select careers on the basis of our personality characteristics. Holland has identified six personal orientations and matching work environments. Super's stage theory holds that self-concept development is the basis for career choice. According to this model, there are five stages in the occupational life cycle: growth, exploration, establishment, maintenance, and decline. Models of women's career development are still being developed. Women's career paths are often less orderly and predictable than men's because of the need to juggle multiple roles and because many women interrupt their careers to devote time to their children.

In making vocational decisions, individuals should consider how compatible their personality, abilities, and interests are with the demands of various jobs. Career-related interests can be assessed through interest inventories. To accurately evaluate their suitability for various jobs, people should seek information about the nature of the work, working conditions, entry requirements, potential earnings, potential status, opportunities for advancement, intrinsic satisfactions, and the future outlook for each occupational area they consider.

Armed with accurate information about oneself and about various job options, prospective workers are better equipped to narrow the list of possible careers to a select few. It is then time to obtain some actual work experience by securing the all-important first job. In our Application we'll describe how to conduct an effective job search.

**True or false?
Choose one.**

1.

The most common and most effective job search method is to answer classified ads.

2.

Your technical qualifications are the most important determinant of the success of your job search.

3.

Employment agencies are good sources of leads to high-level professional jobs.

4.

You should make sure that your résumé is very thorough and includes everything you have ever done.

5.

It's a good idea to inject some humor into your job interviews. It will help both you and your interviewer relax.

Most career counselors would agree that all of the statements on the left are false. Although there is no single tried-and-true method for obtaining a desirable job, a few considerations can increase your chances of success.

Above all else, your job search should be well organized, thorough, and systematic. Sending out a hastily written résumé to a few randomly selected companies is a waste of effort. An effective job search requires lots of time and careful planning. People who are desperate for a job tend to behave in ways that cause prospective employers to see them as bad risks. So it is crucial that you begin your search well in advance of the time you will need a job. The best time to look for a job is when you don't need one. Then you can select an employer rather than seeking an employer who will select *you*.

Of course, no amount of planning and effort can guarantee favorable results in a job search. Luck is definitely a part of the picture. Success may hinge on being in the right place or meeting the right person at the right time. Moreover, becoming a top candidate for a position will depend on factors other than your technical competence. This is not to say that technical competence isn't necessary; it is. But given the realities of today's job market, employers are often inundated with applicants who possess all of the required training and experience. The one who is ultimately selected often is *not* the one with the best technical qualifications. Rather, hiring decisions are made on the basis of subjective impressions gleaned from résumés, letters, telephone conversations, and face-to-face interviews (Lareau, 1985). These impressions will be based on perceptions of your personality, your appearance, your social skills, and your body language. You can practice certain strategies that may increase the odds in your favor.

No matter what type of job you are looking for, successful searches have certain elements in common. First, you must target specific companies or organizations you would like to work for. Then you must inform those com-

panies of your interest in such a way as to get them interested in you.

Finding Companies You Want to Work For

Your first task is to determine what general type of organization will best suit your needs. Do you want to work in a factory? A school? A hospital? A small business? A large corporation? A government agency? A human services agency? As we have seen, to select an appropriate work environment, you need an accurate picture of your personal qualities and knowledge of various job categories and their characteristics.

Once you've decided on a setting, you need to target specific companies. That's easy; you simply look for companies that have advertised openings in your field, right? Not necessarily. If you restrict yourself to this approach, you may miss many valuable opportunities. Up to 80% of all vacancies, especially those above entry level, are never advertised at all (Bolles, 1987).

How should you proceed? Certainly you should check the classified ads in newspapers to identify the many positions that *are* advertised. If you are willing to relocate anywhere, a good source for business and professional jobs is the *National Business Employment Weekly*. You should also consult any trade or professional newspapers, magazines, or journals in your field.

There are two additional options to consider. You could go to an employment agency. Keep in mind, however, that these agencies generally handle only entry-level, hourly-wage jobs. In addition, they may charge up to 15% of the first year's gross earnings (Lareau, 1985). If you're interested in professional jobs, you might consider contacting executive recruiters, widely known as "headhunters." Executive recruiters work on commission for organizations that have vacancies to fill. They earn their living by actively looking for people who have the qualifications being sought by the hiring organization. You can locate headhunters

nationwide by consulting *The Directory of Executive Recruiters*.

What about the 80% of openings that are not advertised? Actually, this statistic is somewhat misleading. It includes a large number of vacancies that are filled by promotions within organizations (Lareau, 1985). Nonetheless, many organizations do have openings that are not accessible through traditional channels. If you have targeted companies that haven't advertised any vacancies, you may want to initiate the contact yourself. In support of this approach, a survey by the Bureau of the Census indicated that "direct application to an employer" was both the most commonly used and the most effective job-search method (Bolles, 1987). Richard Bolles, author of *What Color Is Your Parachute?* suggests that you first identify a specific problem that the organization has and develop a strategy to solve it. Then find out who has the power to hire and fire (through either library research or a network of personal contacts). Finally, approach this person directly to convince him or her of your unique ability to help.

Landing an Interview

No one is going to hire you without checking you out first. The inspection process typically involves one or more formal interviews. How do you go about getting yourself invited for an interview? If you are applying for an advertised vacancy, the traditional approach is to mail a résumé with a cover letter to the hiring organization. If your letter and résumé stand out from the crowd, you may be invited for an interview. One way to increase your chances is to persuade the prospective employer that you are interested enough in the company to have done some research on the organization. If you take the time to learn something about a company, you should be in a better position to make a convincing case about the ways in which your expertise will be particularly useful to the organization. If you are approaching an organization in the absence of a known opening, your strategy may be somewhat different. You may still opt to send a résumé, along with a more detailed cover letter explaining why you have selected this particular company. Another option that Bolles (1987) suggests is to introduce yourself (by phone or in person) directly to the person in charge of hiring and request an interview. You can increase your chances of success by using your network of personal contacts to identify some acquaintance that you and the person in charge both know. Then you can use this person's name to facilitate your approach. Once you do get in to see a potential employer, you should follow up with a thank-you note and a résumé that will jog the employer's memory about your training and talents.

Putting Together a Résumé

No matter what your job-search strategy, an excellent résumé is a critical ingredient. The purpose of a résumé is not to get you a job; it is to get you an interview. To do so, it must communicate to the reader that you possess the minimum technical qualifications for the position, know the standard conventions of the business world, and are a person who is on the fast track to success. Furthermore, it must achieve these goals without being flashy or gimmicky.

Your résumé will project the desired positive yet conservative image if you follow these guidelines (Lareau, 1985; Lipman, 1983):

1. Use white, ivory, or beige (*never* any other color) paper high in rag content.
2. Make sure it contains not a single typographical error.
3. Use the best professional printing service available.
4. Keep it short. The normal maximum is two sides of an 8.5" x 11" sheet of paper.
5. Don't write in full sentences, and avoid using the word *I*. Instead, begin each statement with an "action" word that describes a specific achievement, as in: "Supervised a staff of 15"

or "Handled all customer complaints."
6. Avoid giving any personal information that is extraneous to the job. It is an unnecessary distraction and may give the reader cause to dislike you and therefore reject your application.

An effective résumé will generally contain the following information, laid out in an easy-to-read format (Figure 12.16 shows an attractively prepared résumé).

• *Heading*. At the top of the page give your name, address, and phone number. This is the only section of the résumé that is *not* given a label.
• *Objective*. State a precise career goal, remembering to use action words and to avoid the use of *I*. An example might be "Challenging, creative position in

the communication field requiring extensive background in newspaper, radio, and television."
• *Education*. List any degrees you possess, giving major field of study, date, and granting institution for each. (List the highest degree you received first. If you have a college degree, you don't need to mention your high school diploma.) If you received any *academic* honors or awards, mention them in this section.
• *Experience*. This section should be organized chronologically, beginning with your most recent job and working backward. Describe your responsibilities and your achievements in each position you've held. Be specific, and make sure your most recent position is the one with the greatest achievements. Never pad your résumé with trivial accomplishments. Readers find this prac-

TERESA M. MORGAN

Campus Address
1252 River St., Apt 808
East Lansing, MI 48823
(517) 332-6086

Permanent Address
1111 W. Franklin
Jackson, MI 49203
(517) 782-0819

OBJECTIVE
To pursue a career in interior design, or a related field, in which I can utilize my design training. Willing to relocate after June 19___.

EDUCATION
Sept. 19___
June 19___

Michigan State University, East Lansing, MI 48825.
Bachelor of Arts–Interior Design, with emphasis in Design Communication and Human Shelter. Courses include Lighting, Computers, Public Relations and History of Art. (F.I.D.E.R. accredited) 3.0 GPA (4.0 = A).

July 19___
Aug. 19___

Michigan State University overseas study, England and France, Decorative Arts and Architecture. 4.0 GPA (4.0 = A).

Sept. 19___
June 19___

Jackson Community College, Jackson, MI 49201.
Associate's Degree. 3.5 GPA (4.0 = A).

EMPLOYMENT
Sept. 19___
Present

Food Service and Maintenance, Owen Graduate Center, Michigan State University.
• Prepared and served food
• Managed upkeep of adjacent Van Hoosen Residence Hall.

Dec. 19___
June 19___

Food Service and Maintenance, McDonel Residence Hall.
• Served food and cleaned facility.
• General building maintenance.

June 19___
Dec. 19___

Waitress, Charlie Wong's Restaurant, Jackson, MI.
• Served food, dealt with a variety of people on a personal level.
• Additional responsibilities: cashier, hostess, bartender, and employee trainer.

HONORS
AND
ACTIVITIES

• Community College Transfer scholarship from MSU.
• American Society of Interior Design Publicity Chairman; Executive board, MSU Chapter.
• Wharton Center of the Performing Arts (MSU), usher.
• MSU Student Foundation member.
• Sigma Chi Little Sisters.
• Independent European travel, summer 19___.
• Stage manager and performer in plays and musicals.
• Jackson High School Senior Class Treasurer.
• Jackson High School Yearbook Assistant Editor.

REFERENCES and PORTFOLIO available upon request.

FIGURE 12.16
An attractively
formatted résumé
The physical appearance of a résumé is very important. This is what a well-prepared résumé looks like.

tice annoying. Moreover, it just calls attention to the fact that you don't have more important items to list.

If you are currently a student or if you're a recent graduate, your schooling will provide the basis for both your experience and your qualifications.

Polishing Your Interview Technique

The final and most crucial step in the process of securing a job is the face-to-face interview. If you've gotten this far, the employer already knows that you possess the requisite training and experience to do the job. Now your challenge is to convince the employer that you are the kind of person who would fit well in the organization. Your interviewer will attempt to verify that you have the intangible qualities that will make you a good team player. Even more important, the interviewer will attempt to identify any red-flag behaviors, attitudes, or traits that mark you as an unacceptable risk.

To create the right impression, you must appear to be confident, enthusiastic, and ambitious. Your demeanor should be somewhat

formal and reserved, and you should avoid any attempts at humor—you never know what might offend your interviewer (Lareau, 1985). Above all, never give more information than the interviewer requests, especially negative information. If asked directly what your weaknesses are—a common ploy respond with a "flaw" that is really an asset, as in "I tend to work too hard at times" (Lareau, 1985). Don't interrupt or contradict your interviewer. And don't ever blame or criticize anyone, especially previous employers, even if you feel that the criticism is justified (Lipman, 1983).

Developing an effective interview technique requires practice. Many experts suggest that you never turn down an interview. Even if you know you don't want the job, you can always benefit from the practice. Advance preparation is crucial. Never go into an interview cold. Find out all you can about the company before you go. Try to anticipate the questions that will be asked and have some answers ready. In general, you will not be asked simply to reiterate information on your résumé. Remember, it is your personal qualities that are being assessed now. A final word of advice: If possible, avoid any discussion of salary in an initial interview. The appropriate time for salary negotiation is *after* a firm offer of employment has been extended.

Careful preparation before a job interview will help you to be more confident and to put your best foot forward.

Key Learning Objectives

1. Define work and explain the technical distinctions between a job and a career and between paid work and unpaid work.

2. List four contemporary trends related to work.

3. Define labor force and describe how the composition of the labor force is expected to change between now and 2000.

4. Briefly discuss the problem of workplace illiteracy and describe the relationship between education and salary.

5. Summarize the history of women's participation in the work force.

6. Describe some problems women face in the workplace today.

7. Summarize current perspectives on workaholism.

8. Explain the scarcity hypothesis and the enhancement hypothesis and summarize the hypothesized effects of multiple roles.

9. Summarize current perspectives on leisure.

10. Compare and contrast McGregor's, Herzberg's, and Ouchi's views on work motivation.

11. Explain how and why job satisfaction can be important to one's adjustment.

12. List the ingredients that tend to contribute to job satisfaction.

13. Describe some of the sources of job stress.

14. Summarize the effects of job stress on physical and mental health.

15. Describe some things that organizations can do to reduce job stress.

16. Define sexual harassment and distinguish between its two forms.

17. Summarize Holland's hexagonal model of career development.

18. Summarize Super's five-stage model of career development.

19. Discuss women's career development.

20. List six general principles to keep in mind in choosing a vocation.

21. Discuss the personal characteristics that one should consider in making vocational decisions.

22. Discuss the value of occupational interest inventories as they relate to career planning.

23. List some job characteristics that one should be concerned about in making vocational decisions.

24. Discuss strategies for targeting companies you would like to work for and landing job interviews.

25. Summarize guidelines for putting together an effective résumé.

26. List the dos and don'ts of interviewing for jobs.

Key Terms

job satisfaction
labor force
leisure
occupational interest inventories

sexual harassment
token
underemployment
work

Key People

Frederick Herzberg
John Holland
Douglas McGregor

William Ouchi
Donald Super

13 Development and Expression of Sexuality

SEX. TO SOME PEOPLE IT'S A SPORT, to others an oppressive duty. For some it's recreation, for others it's business. Some people find it a source of great intimacy and pleasure. Others find it a source of extraordinary anxiety and frustration. Whatever the case, sexuality plays a central role in our lives. It sometimes seems that our culture is obsessed with sex. We joke and gossip about it constantly. Our magazines and novels are saturated with sex. The advertising business uses sex to sell us everything from automobiles to toothpaste. We have become voracious consumers of books purporting to tell us how to improve our sex lives. Yet many lovers find it excruciatingly difficult to talk to each other about sex, and misconceptions about sexual functioning abound.

In this chapter we'll consider how we express our sexuality and how this affects our adjustment. Specifically, we'll look at the development of sexuality, the interpersonal dynamics of sexual relationships, the psychology and physiology of sexual arousal, and patterns of sexual behavior. We'll also discuss contraception and sexually transmitted diseases. In the Application we'll turn our attention to some things that people can do to enhance their sexual relationships.

Let's begin with a cautionary note. Research on sexual behavior must be interpreted very carefully. Several problems are especially troublesome in this area of inquiry. It is particularly difficult, for example, to get representative samples of subjects in sex research. Many people are understandably reluctant to discuss their sex lives. The crucial problem is that people who *are* willing to volunteer information about their sexual behavior appear to be more liberal and more sexually experienced than the general population (Wolchik, Braver, & Jensen, 1985).

Furthermore, given the difficulties of observing sexual behavior directly, sex researchers have depended mostly on interviews and questionnaires. Unfortunately, when questioned about their sexual behavior, people are likely to let shame, embarrassment, boastfulness, or wishful thinking guide their responses (Bradburn & Sudman, 1979; Catania, McDermott, & Pollack, 1986). For these reasons, the results of sex research need to be evaluated with more than the usual caution.

Becoming a Sexual Person

There is immense variety in the ways people express their sexuality. Some people barely express it at all. Rather, they work to suppress their sexual feelings and desires. At the other extreme are individuals who express their sexual urges with abandon, engaging in casual sex with great ease. Some people need to turn the lights out before they can have sex, while others would like to be on camera with spotlights glaring. Some cannot even bring themselves to use sexual words without embarrassment, while others are eager to reveal the intimate details of their sex lives. To understand this diversity, we need to examine developmental influences on human sexual behavior.

FIGURE 13.1
Heterosexuality and homosexuality as end points on a continuum
Kinsey and other sex researchers view heterosexuality and homosexuality as a continuum rather than an all-or-none distinction. Kinsey created this seven-point scale (from 0 to 6) to describe one's sexual orientation. He used the term *ambisexual* to describe people who fall in the middle of the scale, but those people are commonly called *bisexual* today.

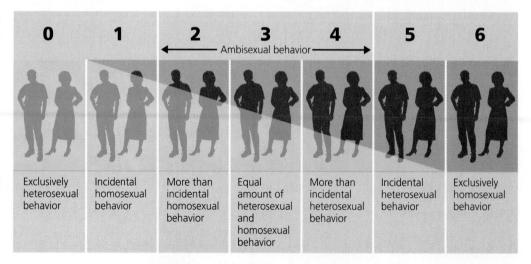

0	1	2	3	4	5	6
		←	Ambisexual behavior	→		
Exclusively heterosexual behavior	Incidental homosexual behavior	More than incidental homosexual behavior	Equal amount of heterosexual and homosexual behavior	More than incidental heterosexual behavior	Incidental heterosexual behavior	Exclusively homosexual behavior

Key Features of Sexual Identity

As we noted in Chapter 5, *identity* refers to a stable sense of who one is and what one stands for. We'll use the term *sexual identity* to refer to the complex of personal qualities, self-perceptions, attitudes, values, and preferences that guide one's sexual behavior. In other words, your sexual identity consists of your sense of yourself as a sexual person. This conception of sexual identity includes four key features: your sexual orientation, body image, sexual values and ethics, and erotic preferences.

Sexual Orientation

Earlier we noted that sexual orientation is a person's preference for emotional and sexual relationships with individuals of one sex or the other. *Heterosexuals* seek emotional-sexual relationships with members of the other sex. *Bisexuals* seek emotional-sexual relationships with members of both sexes. *Homosexuals* seek emotional-sexual relationships with members of the same sex.

People tend to view heterosexuality and homosexuality as an all-or-none distinction: you're one thing or the other. In large-scale surveys of sexual behavior, however, Alfred Kinsey and his colleagues (1948, 1953) discovered that many people who define themselves as heterosexuals have had homosexual experiences, and vice versa. Thus Kinsey and others have concluded that it is more accurate to view heterosexuality and homosexuality as end points of a continuum. Indeed, Kinsey devised a seven-point scale, shown in Figure 13.1, that can be used to characterize the sexual orientation of individuals.

How are people distributed on this scale? No one knows for sure. It's hard to get accurate data. Furthermore, there's some debate about where to draw the lines between heterosexuality, bisexuality, and homosexuality on the Kinsey scale. Estimates of the incidence of homosexuality range from 4% to 17% (Gonsiorek & Weinrich, 1991). A frequently cited estimate of the proportion of people who are predominantly homosexual is 10%. The author of a respected textbook on human sexuality suggests that the actual figure is probably a little higher for men and a little lower for women (Hyde, 1990).

Body Image

Your body image is your perception of your physical appearance. Like other aspects of your self-concept, it may or may not be a very accurate reflection of reality. It definitely affects the way you feel about yourself in the sexual domain. A positive body image is correlated with greater sexual activity and higher sexual satisfaction (Berscheid, Walster, & Bohrnstedt, 1973). The increasing resort to plastic surgery for breast enhancements, face lifts, and nose jobs testifies to the importance of body image (Hamburger, 1988).

Sexual Values and Ethics

All cultures impose morality-based constraints on expected sexual behavior (Davenport, 1977). We are trained to believe that certain expressions of sexuality are "right" while others are "wrong." Information about sex comes to us from a variety of sources: parents, peers, schools, religion, and the media. As with other aspects of socialization, the nature of the sexual messages we receive from these sources often varies with our sex, race, ethnicity, and socioeconomic status. For example, the double standard encourages sexual experimentation in males but not in females. Individuals are faced with the daunting task of sorting through these varied messages to develop their own sexual values and ethics. These standards of appropriate sexual conduct greatly influence our sexual behavior.

Erotic Preferences

Within the limits imposed by sexual orientation and values, people differ in what they find enjoyable (Blumstein & Schwartz, 1983). One's erotic preferences are one's personal tastes in sexual activities. Your erotic preferences encompass your attitudes toward self-stimulation, oral sex, styles of foreplay and intercourse, and other sexual activities. The years of childhood and adolescence are especially important in the development of sexual identity (Miller & Simon, 1980). This shaping process encompasses a complex interplay of physiological and psychosocial influences.

Physiological Influences

Among the various physiological factors involved in sexual behavior, hormones have been of particular interest to researchers.

Hormones and Sexual Differentiation

Biological changes during prenatal development result in a fetus that is a male or a female.

Hormones play an important role in this process, which is termed *sexual differentiation* (Money & Ehrhardt, 1972). Around the third month of prenatal development, different hormonal secretions begin to be produced by male and female **gonads—the sex glands.** In males, the testes produce **androgens, the principal class of male sex hormones.** *Testosterone* is the most important of the androgens. In females, the ovaries produce *estrogens,* **the principal class of female sex hormones.** Actually, both classes of hormones are present in both sexes, but in different proportions. During prenatal development, the differentiation of the genitals depends primarily on the level of testosterone produced—high in males, low in females.

With the arrival of adolescence, hormones once again play a key role in sexual development (Dreyer, 1982). As we saw in Chapter 11, adolescents attain reproductive capacity as hormonal changes stimulate the maturation of the sex organs. Hormonal changes also regulate the development of *secondary sex characteristics* (physical features that distinguish the sexes but are not directly involved in reproduction). Increased secretion of estrogens in girls leads to breast development, widened hips, and more rounded body contours; increased secretion of androgens in boys leads to the development of facial hair, a deeper voice, and more angular body contours.

Hormones and Sexual Behavior

Hormonal fluctuations clearly regulate sex *drive* in many species of animals (Feder, 1984). Their influence on sexual desire in humans, however, is much more modest. *Androgen* levels seem related to sexual motivation in both sexes. High levels of testosterone in female and male subjects are correlated with higher rates of sexual activity (Knussman, Christiansen, & Couwenbergs, 1986; Persky et al., 1978). Curiously, *estrogen* levels among women are *not* well correlated with sexual interest. There does appear to be an association between women's sex drive and their ovulation/menstruation cycles, but its hormonal basis is yet to be determined (Harvey, 1987; Stanislaw & Rice, 1988).

The correlations between hormone levels and human sexual activity are interesting, but they do *not* prove that hormonal surges *cause* sexual desire under normal circumstances. The correlations are relatively weak, and the *direction* of any causal relationship is ambiguous. Some evidence suggests that sexual arousal may cause hormonal surges rather than vice versa. Thus whether normal hormonal swings have much impact on sexual desire is doubtful (Persky, 1983).

Hormones unquestionably govern sexual anatomy and maturation, but their influence on *sexual orientation* is less clear. Some theorists believe that some people are biologically predisposed toward homosexuality (Doerr, Pirke, Kockott, & Dittmor, 1976; Dorner, 1988). These theorists maintain that hormonal differences between heterosexuals and homosexuals underlie a person's sexual orientation. This view is indirectly supported by evidence that many gay men and women can trace their homosexual leanings back to their childhood years (Bell, Weinberg, & Hammersmith, 1981; Garnets & Kimmel, 1991). However, studies comparing hormone levels in homosexuals and heterosexuals have found only very small, inconsistent differences (Ricketts, 1984; Tourney, 1980). At present we have no convincing evidence linking hormone patterns to sexual orientation, although this possibility can't be ruled out. If hormones shape sexual orientation, their effects must be complex and subtle (Garnets & Kimmel, 1991; Gladue, 1987).

In summary, physiological factors have important effects on sexual development. Their influence on *anatomy*, however, is much greater than their influence on sexual *activity*. To understand the determinants of sexual behavior, we must look to psychosocial factors.

Psychosocial Influences

The principal psychosocial influences on sexual identity are essentially the same as the main sources of gender-role socialization discussed in Chapter 10. Sexual identity is shaped by families, peers and schools, and the media.

Families

Parents and the home environment can affect the development of sexual identity throughout life, but they are especially influential in the early years. Children usually engage in some sex play and exploration before they reach school age (Martinson, 1980). Many experiment with self-stimulation of the genitals. Children also exhibit curiosity about sexual matters, asking such questions as "Where do babies come from?" Parental reactions to sexual exploration and curiosity can have a telling impact on a child's feelings about sex. Some parents respond to youngsters' sexual exploration with horror and dismay. Parents frequently punish innocent, exploratory sex play and squirm miserably when kids ask sexual questions. These sorts of reactions tend to convey the message that sex is "dirty." Children may begin to feel guilty about their sexual urges and curiosity. Thus parents who are uncomfortable with their sexuality can pass on that discomfort to their children at a very early age (Calderone & Ramey, 1982).

When it comes time for more systematic sex instruction, many parents have difficulty talking with their children. A poll has found that 31% of American teenagers have never talked to their parents about sex and 42% are were anxious about bringing up the topic with their parents (Louis Harris & Associates, 1986). As you might expect, open communication about sexual topics in the home is correlated with better sexual adjustment among college students (Lewis & Janda, 1988). Furthermore, adolescents' attitudes toward sexual conduct are more similar to their parents' attitudes when they are raised in families that encourage open sexual communication (Fisher, 1988).

Ultimately, parents who make sex a taboo topic end up reducing their influence on their kids' evolving sexual identity. Their children turn elsewhere to seek information about sexuality. Thus the conspiracy of silence about sex in the home often backfires by increasing the influence of peers, schools, and the media.

Peers and Schools

As you can see in Figure 13.2, friends are by far the principal source of sex information for both males and females (Reinisch, 1990). Of course, friends may be ill informed themselves, so one's peer group can be a source of highly misleading information. Furthermore, peers are unlikely to instill the same kinds of sexual ethics that parents tend to champion. Spanier (1977) found that girls who learned the facts of life from their mothers were less sexually active than girls who got their information from peers and other sources.

Schools may influence sexual identity through sex education programs. The majority of these programs attempt to promote the more conservative sexual values that most parents espouse (Spanier, 1977). Nonetheless, many parents try to extend the conspiracy of silence regarding sex into the classroom and campaign against such programs. Figure 13.2 shows that only about 14% of adult Americans had participated in sex education programs as children. Most parents who oppose sex education in the schools are worried that such programs will lead to increased sexual experimentation. To allay such fears, sex education programs usually focus

on anatomy and health-related issues and don't provide much useful practical information (Fine, 1988). Research suggests that sex education programs lead to neither the experimentation that parents worry about nor the restraint that the programs advocate (Eisen & Zellman, 1987).

Media

As Figure 13.2 indicates, books and magazines are another major source of information on sex. Unfortunately, many of these publications perpetuate myths about sex and miseducate their young readers. Although youngsters may pick up the facts of life from reading materials, music and television may have more impact on their sexual ethics. Sexual relationships are portrayed extensively on TV. These portrayals are likely to influence young people's emerging sexual values (Strouse & Fabes, 1985). Lowry and Towles (1989) found that sexual content on television soap operas increased during the 1980s and that soap operas portray sex "as a spur-of-the-moment activity pursued primarily by unmarried partners with little concern about either birth control or disease prevention" (p. 82).

The lyrics of rock music also contain extensive references to sexual behavior and norms of sexual conduct (Ray, Soares, & Tolchinsky, 1988). Some rap music has come under fire because it portrays women as sex objects and advocates sexual violence against

Main Sources of Sexual Information in Childhood

Sources of information	Percentage using source*
Friend	42
Mother	29
Books	22
Boyfriend or girlfriend	17
Sex education	14
Magazines	13
Father	12
Sister	8
Movies	6
Brother	6
Other relative	6
Television	5
Teacher	5

*Respondents could choose up to three sources.

FIGURE 13.2
Main sources of sexual information in childhood
When questioned about where they got their information about sex during childhood, adult respondents cited friends as their most important source of information. (Adapted from Reinisch, 1990.)

Sex-charged music videos such as those starring Madonna appear to affect viewers' attitudes about sexual behavior.

women (Cocks, 1991). Rock videos, which have become extremely popular, may have even more sexual content. One study of music videos found that over 75% contained provocative depictions of sexuality (Sherman & Dominick, 1986). Rock videos routinely portray women as sex objects, and these portrayals appear to influence viewers' attitudes toward sexual conduct (Hansen & Hansen, 1988).

The effects of erotic reading material, photographs, and films are the subject of considerable debate. Most people—not all—find depictions of sexual activity arousing (Miller, Byrne, & Fisher, 1980). When physiological responses to erotic materials are measured in laboratory studies, men and women usually appear equally aroused (Heiman, 1977). But how much impact does sexually explicit material have on actual sexual behavior? Research suggests that exposure to erotic material elevates the likelihood of overt sexual activity for only a few hours (Cattell, Kawash, & DeYoung, 1972).

Although erotic materials do not appear to incite overpowering sexual urges, they may alter *attitudes* in ways that eventually influence sexual behavior. Zillmann and Bryant (1984) found that subjects exposed to a large dose of pornography developed more liberal attitudes in regard to acceptable sexual practices. Furthermore, studies of *aggressive pornography* have raised concerns. Aggressive pornography typically depicts violence against women. As

we mentioned in our discussion of date rape in Chapter 6, some studies indicate that this type of material increases male subjects' aggressive behavior toward women (Malamuth & Donnerstein, 1982). Exposure to aggressive pornography may also change men's attitudes toward sexual aggression by perpetuating the myth that women enjoy being raped (Malamuth, 1984).

In summary, our sexual identities are shaped by a host of intersecting influences. Given the multiplicity of factors at work, it is not surprising that people bring highly diverse expectations to their sexual relationships. This diversity can make sexual interactions exceedingly complicated.

Gender and Sexual Orientation Differences in Sexual Socialization

Since males and females are socialized differently in respect to sex, sexuality typically has different meanings for males and females. This fact has important consequences for sexual relationships. We'll begin our discussion at adolescence because this is a critical time for sexual socialization (Lloyd, 1985).

The uncontrolled frequent erections caused by the increase in male hormones at puberty focus the boy's attention on his genitals. Boys are likely to begin masturbating at an earlier age than girls and to do so more frequently (Hunt, 1974), and these facts have been suggested as key factors in the development of gender differences in sexuality (Gagnon & Simon, 1973).

At the same time, powerful societal expectations encourage boys to be aggressive and conquest-oriented with regard to sex. Male adolescent peers play an important role in encouraging sexual experimentation and confirming each other's sexual competence (Gagnon & Simon, 1973; Garnets & Kimmel, 1991; Miller & Simon, 1974). As a result, sex becomes a vehicle by which adolescent boys validate their social status with other boys. Homophobia pushes some boys to initiate sex with girls to "prove" to their male peers that they are not gay (Friedman, 1989).

Adolescent boys are encouraged to experiment sexually, to take the initiative in sexual activities, to strive for immediate sexual gratification, to separate love and sex, and to enjoy sex without emotional involvement (Fracher & Kimmel, 1987; Gagnon & Simon, 1973). These experiences make it less likely that boys will experience sex solely, if at all, in the context of love and other tender emotions. As a result, sex has a greater variety of meanings for men. That is, they may emphasize "sex for fun" in casual relationships and reserve "sex with love" for committed relationships (Safilios-Rothschild, 1977).

Rather than learning about sex and orgasms, adolescent girls are usually taught that love "provides both the justification and meaning for sex" (Peplau, Rubin, & Hill, 1977). They learn about romance and the importance of physical attractiveness and catching a mate (Gagnon & Simon, 1973). It is not until women actually begin to have sexual experiences that they see themselves as sexual persons. Hence for girls it is the partner, not the peer group, who facilitates sexual activity; the female peer group functions to foster positive feelings about romantic love (Miller & Simon, 1974).

The process of sexual socialization appears to take longer in females than in males. One reason is *sexual guilt* (Lott, 1987). That is, while social norms encourage males to be sexually active, they typically discourage this behavior in females—sexually active women may be looked on as "sluts" or "easy lays." Thus women learn to feel guilty about having sexual feelings and wanting to act on them. Another reason that sexual socialization takes longer in females is that women typically have some *negative associations with their genitals and sex* that males don't experience. Among these associations are the blood and pain of menstruation, fears of pregnancy, and fears of penetration. Most girls hear some negative messages about sex and men from their mothers, siblings, and female peers ("Men only want one thing"; "Once they have sex with you, men will drop you cold"). Too, girls typically learn at an early age of instances of rape and incest. These negative associations with sex are combined with the positive rewards of dating and emotional intimacy. It is not surprising, then, that the sexuality of adolescent girls and many women is characterized by ambivalence (Hyde, 1991). These feelings can tilt in the negative direction if early sexual partners are impatient, unskillful, or selfish.

Because of these gender differences in sexual socialization, males and females are likely to enter relationships with different expectations, especially during adolescence and early adulthood (Lloyd, 1985). Many males tend to be interested in relationships because they provide opportunities for varying degrees of sexual intimacy without binding commitments. Females see a relationship as a means to gain social status

and as an opportunity to develop an emotional intimacy, which may or may not include sex.

Because of these different views of sexuality, males and females are likely to be out of sync regarding relationships and sexuality, particularly in adolescence and early adulthood (DeLamater, 1987; Whitley, 1988b). One study of college students found that 85% of the women indicated that emotional involvement was a prerequisite for sex all or almost all of the time, but only 40% of the men agreed (Carroll, Volk, & Hyde, 1985). Only 42% of the women reported having had sexual relationships without any emotional involvement, but 84% of the men had done so. Because of the effects of earlier socialization, apparently it is not until adulthood that men become comfortable with emotional intimacy and commitment and that women become comfortable with themselves as sexual persons. These gender differences in sexual socialization highlight the importance of communication in developing and maintaining sexual relationships that are mutually satisfying.

What implications do these differences in sexual socialization have for individuals in *homosexual* relationships? For one thing, the incompatible expectations of heterosexual couples are less likely to arise in homosexual relationships. Both members of the couple are the same sex and therefore have been socialized in the same general way. Like heterosexual women, lesbians typically experience emotional attraction to their partners before they experience sexual feelings (Blumstein & Schwartz, 1989; Garnets & Kimmel, 1991). In other words, sexual feelings are experienced in the context of romantic love and emotional attachment. Gay men (like heterosexual men) place much more importance on physical appearance and sexual compatibility in partners (Blumstein & Schwartz, 1983) and develop emotional relationships out of sexual ones (Harry, 1983).

As might be expected, research indicates that homosexuals seem to take longer to recognize their sexual orientation than heterosexuals do (Garnets & Kimmel, 1991; McDonald, 1982; Vance & Green, 1984). One reason for this time lag is the *assumption that heterosexuality is universal.* Because this belief is so widespread, some individuals never even consider the possibility that they might be homosexual until they have pretty strong evidence that they are. Another factor has to do with the *stigma* still associated with homosexuality—even if individuals believe they are homosexual, they may try to deny the fact (to themselves as well

as to others) to avoid social rejection. A third reason is that homosexuals report both same- and other-sex erotic arousal and sexual behavior during adolescence and early adulthood. Some experts speculate that *sexual experiences with the other sex* may cause gay men and lesbians to misclassify themselves as heterosexuals and thus delay their awareness of their true sexual orientation (Hencken, 1984).

As among heterosexuals, clarity about sexual orientation seems to take longer in lesbians than in gay men. It is suggested that this is so because lesbians are more likely than gay men to engage in sexual activity with the other sex, less likely to be involved in same-sex erotic activity, more likely to continue other-gender sexual activities after questioning their sexual identity, and more likely to get married than gay men (Garnets & Kimmel, 1991; Bell & Weinberg, 1978; Chapman & Brannock, 1987).

Linda Garnets and Greg Kimmel (1991) have summarized the research on identity development in gay men and lesbians. Developmental milestones in this process include the following:

1. *Initial awareness of same-sex erotic desires.* Individuals become aware of strong emotional and sexual attraction to members of the same sex. This recognition in turn triggers a "developmental transition in which individuals report feeling different and being off course" (Garnets & Kimmel, 1991, p. 154).

2. *Reconciliation of sexual orientation with negative societal attitudes.* The individual transforms "gay" or "lesbian" from a negative category to a positive one and gradually accepts the fact that the label applies to him- or herself. Individuals use a variety of cognitive strategies to reconcile negative societal attitudes with their own sexual orientation.

3. *Exploration of gay and lesbian subcultures.* Contact with these subcultures is available in most cities, by newspaper subscription, and by toll-free information services. Among other things, such contacts provide a range of role models and diminish feelings of isolation.

4. *Disclosure of sexual orientation to others.* Over time, homosexuals are usually motivated to disclose their identity to other people. According to Garnets and Kimmel (1991), "Data strongly suggest that a prerequisite for the emergence of a positive gay male or lesbian identity is the communication of one's sexual orientation to others" (p. 162). They add, however, that individuals need to balance the psychological and social benefits of doing so

against the costs. Because so much prejudice and discrimination still exist, openly gay individuals risk being fired from their jobs, losing custody of their children, and falling victim to hate crimes. *Rational outness* is endorsed as a pragmatic solution to the conflict—"to be as open as possible, because it feels healthy to be honest, and as closed as necessary to protect against discrimination" (Bradford & Ryan, 1987, p. 77). Homosexual individuals tend to disclose their sexual orientation to close heterosexual friends and siblings rather than to parents, co-workers, or employers.

Interaction in Sexual Relationships

Because of their importance to us, sexual relationships stir intense emotions. When things are going well, we feel on top of the world; when they're not, we feel in the grip of despair. In this section, we'll discuss the interpersonal dynamics of sexual relationships.

Motives Underlying Sexual Interactions

Many motives may lead people to enter into sexual relationships or to engage in sexual activities in an ongoing relationship. Two partners may be motivated by different desires or intentions. Not much research has been done on whether mismatched motives increase the likelihood of trouble in sexual interactions, but that's certainly a logical possibility.

What motivates us to engage in sexual encounters? Building on work by Neubeck (1972), Nass, Libby, and Fisher (1981, pp. 102–103) list a diverse array of motives underlying sexual interactions:

* *Affection:* A longing for love, closeness, and physical and emotional union.
* *Lust:* A passion for intensifying and gratifying sexual desires with a focus on sensual arousal, fantasies, and delight in touching and being touched.
* *Duty:* A feeling that it's our responsibility to have sex on schedule or to keep our partner from being frustrated. Typically a woman feels that she can't leave a man unsatisfied. The idea that he could masturbate or that she might feel equally uncomfortable if she were highly aroused but not satisfied is missing from the traditional script.

Some recent, groundbreaking studies suggest that there may be a genetic predisposition to homosexuality. For example, Bailey and Benishay (1993) found that lesbianism runs in families; Hamer and associates (1993) linked male homosexuality to genetic material on the X chromosome; and LeVay (1991) found anatomical differences between gay and straight men in a region of the brain (the anterior hypothalamus) thought to regulate sex drive. Although these widely publicized studies point to a biological basis for homosexuality, the evidence isn't nearly as conclusive as the popular press has often implied. The researchers themselves are quick to acknowledge that their studies have a variety of methodological weaknesses. Hence, the developmental roots of homosexuality remain obscure.

* *Boredom:* The use of sex to enhance a dull environment or routine activities.
* *Mending wounds:* The use of sex as a way to make up after an argument or even to avoid dealing with a conflict.
* *Accomplishment:* The wish to have sex as often as we think everyone else does, in every conceivable position, and perhaps to break records with our "scores."
* *Recreation:* Having sex for fun and games or for the sake of creating pleasant sensations for each other.
* *Self-affirmation:* The acting out of our perceived sexual identity so that the other will notice and approve of it.

Studies suggest that the motives underlying sexual activity vary by gender. Men appear to be motivated more by lust and the desire for physical gratification, whereas women are more likely to be motivated by their desire to express love and emotional commitment (Carroll et al., 1985; DeLamater, 1987; Whitley, 1988a). In one study, college students were asked, "What was your most important reason for having sexual intercourse on the most recent occasion?" (Whitley, 1988a). Lust and pleasure motives were cited by 51% of the men but by only 9% of the women. Love and emotional reasons were cited by 51% of the women but by only 24% of the men. Similar gender differences have been found in a community survey that looked at a broad sample of subjects (Leigh, 1989). These gender differences appear to transcend sexual orientation, as they were observed in homosexuals as well as heterosexuals. The basis for these differences between men and women remains to be investigated. Some theorists speculate that they can be traced to gender-role socialization (Carroll et al., 1985). Other theorists believe that they are products of biological influences (Knoth, Boyd, & Singer, 1988).

Sexual Scripts

When two people enter a sexual relationship they may be guided by very different scripts. *Scripts* are sets of expectations about the way certain common activities should unfold. People have scripts for many activities, such as going grocery shopping and doing the laundry. Many of our scripts are **social scripts—culturally programmed sets of expectations about the way various social transactions should evolve.** We have social scripts for such events as going to a restaurant and visiting a doctor. A social script is similar to a script for a movie or a play. It spells out a sequence of events and the interactions of the players. Real-life scripts tend to be sketchier, however, allowing for more spontaneity, or ad-libbing.

John Gagnon and William Simon have pointed out that we have social scripts for romantic relationships and sexual interactions (Gagnon & Simon, 1973; Simon & Gagnon, 1986). Our *sexual scripts* are products of lifelong learning and socialization. They vary with social class, ethnic background, and religious upbringing. Although sexual scripts can be individualized, a handful of scripts guide the sexual conduct of most of us. Nass and his colleagues (1981, pp. 23–24) describe five common sexual scripts in modern Western culture.

In the *traditional religious script*, sex is acceptable only within marriage. All other sexual activities are taboo, especially for women. Sex means reproduction, though it may also have something to do with affection.

In the *romantic script*, now the predominant one in our society, sex means love. According to this script, if we grow in love with someone, it's OK to "make love," either in or out of marriage. Without love, sex is a meaningless animal function. The eligible actors are two people who are in love, the ideal emotional state is uncontrollable loving passion, the words exchanged are assurances of affection, and all activities should appear to be spontaneous expressions of love.

In the *sexual friendship script*, people who are friends can also have an intimate sexual relationship. Although the association of the

actors in this script is usually ongoing, typically it's not sexually exclusive.

In the *casual/mutual horniness script*, increasingly publicized by the mass media, sex is defined as recreational fun. The actors are casual acquaintances who are mutually sexually aroused. The qualities looked for in sexmaking may include joy, playfulness, abandon, variety, and, increasingly, good technique.

In the *utilitarian-predatory script*, people have sex for some reason other than pleasure, reproduction, or love. The reason might be economic gain (as in prostitution), career advancement, or power. For example, to achieve power, some men see sex as "scoring" and believe they enhance their status in their male group by boasting of their sexual exploits. Some feminists also characterize some heterosexual activity as a power play rather than as a quest for love or pleasure.

The sexual scripts just described focus broadly on the *formation* of sexual liaisons. However, the day-to-day details of sexual interactions in established relationships are also guided by sexual scripts. People have expectations about which partner should initiate sexual encounters, where and when sex should take place, and the sequencing of sexual activities (Gagnon & Simon, 1987). One person's sexual script might dictate that sex should take place only in the evening, progressing quickly from hugging and kissing to intercourse in a single position. Another person's sexual script might dictate that sex should occur whenever the urge strikes, progressing slowly from mutual fondling to oral contact to intercourse in a variety of positions. Obviously, if these two people became involved with each other, their differing sexual scripts could be a source of considerable conflict.

Only recently have researchers begun to study the sexual scripts that govern day-to-day interactions in ongoing relationships. When Byers and Heinlein (1989) examined patterns of initiating and refusing sexual overtures among married and cohabiting heterosexual college students, they found that men initiated sexual encounters more often than women, though both sexes responded favorably to initiations equally often. Only about one-quarter of sexual initiations were turned away. Perhaps people learn to recognize when their partners will respond favorably to sexual overtures. Indirect support for that hypothesis comes from the finding that nonverbal signals—smiles, touches, eye contact—played a key role in both sexual initiations and partners' responses (Byers

& Heinlein, 1989). Alternatively, many people may feel duty-bound not to refuse their partners, so they have sex even when they are not really interested.

Influence of Personality and Attitudes

Differences among people in sexual interest and erotic preferences are influenced to a great degree by personality and attitudes. Research on *personality* suggests that *extraverts* are more sexually active than introverts (Eysenck, 1976). *Sensation seekers*—people who prefer a high level of stimulation (see Chapter 3)—also engage in a wider range of sexual activities with a greater variety of partners (Zuckerman, 1979). Correlations have also been found between sexuality and self-monitoring—the degree to which people are aware of the impressions they make on others (see Chapter 5). *High self-monitors* are more willing than low self-monitors to have sexual relations in the absence of emotional closeness (Snyder, Simpson, & Gangestad, 1986).

Studies on *attitudes* have focused on people who experience a lot of guilt about their sexual urges. People high in sex guilt have fewer sex partners, engage in sex less frequently, and employ a more limited range of sexual practices than others (Mosher, 1973). Sexually active women who score high on sex guilt are less likely to use effective contraceptive methods than those who score low (Gerrard, 1987).

Some researchers have drawn a distinction between erotophobes and erotophiles. **Erotophobes are people who have very negative attitudes toward sex. Erotophiles are people who have very favorable attitudes toward sex.** Erotophobes tend to feel embarrassed when discussing sex and tend to condemn premarital sex. They dislike erotic materials and view sex as unimportant in their lives (Fisher, Byrne, White, & Kelley, 1988). Erotophiles are more comfortable discussing sex and more liberal about premarital sex. They are more responsive than erotophobes to erotic materials and more likely to view sex as important in their lives. As you might anticipate, erotophiles are more sexually active than erotophobes.

Communicating about Sex

We bring differing motives, scripts, personality traits, and attitudes to our sexual liaisons, so it is not surprising that sexual interactions are a source of frequent conflict. Disagreements

The Kinsey Institute New Report on Sex: What You Must Know to Be Sexually Literate
by June M. Reinisch (St. Martin's Press, 1990)

June Machover Reinisch, a psychologist and current director of The Kinsey Institute for Research in Sex, Gender, and Reproduction, provides the latest factual information about a wide variety of sexual topics. The book starts off with a test of basic sex information and provides the reader with national norms by which to evaluate one's expertise. The book's 19 chapters range across a variety of topics: the anatomy and physical functioning of the male and female reproductive systems; sexual socialization; puberty; sex and the disabled; and sex and disease, surgery, and drugs, to name a few. Most of the book is written in a question-and-answer format (the questions are among those sent to the Institute). Reinisch also includes the names and addresses of helpful organizations and support groups for many kinds of sex-related issues. The book's informal style makes for not only informative but enjoyable reading. At the end of each chapter are recommended readings, and an appendix tells how to locate, select, and evaluate health-care specialists.

In the fall of 1989, The Kinsey Institute tested the basic sexual knowledge of a statistically representative group of 1,974 American adults. Unfortunately, Americans failed the test.... Of Americans taking our eighteen-question test, 55% failed.... Another 27% of respondents received Ds.... Fourteen percent obtained Cs. There were only five A students (less than .5%) and only sixty-eight people (4%) received Bs.

Who passed the test? These people tended to be 30–44 years old; with at least some college education; from higher income groups; with no religious affiliation; from the Midwest or West; politically liberal; single, married, divorced or separated but not widowed; and from more densely populated urban areas.

Who failed? They were more likely to be 60 years or older; to have no high school diploma; to come from lower income groups; to have a religious affiliation; to live in the South or Northeast; to be politically conservative or moderate; widowed; and to come from less densely populated or more rural areas. [p. 1]

about sex are commonplace (Blumstein & Schwartz, 1983; Levinger, 1970). Consider the following example:

> "When we first married, my wife wanted intercourse morning, noon, and night.... I was so sore I couldn't walk. Even now, she would prefer making love at least twice a day seven days a week. She knows I can't that often, but I know she would like to." [Quoted in Rice, 1989, p. 336]

Variations between partners in sexual appetite are normal. The disagreements produced by these variations do not necessarily reflect lack of affection or declining sexual interest. Nonetheless, they are likely to be a source of ongoing frustration in a relationship if they cannot be resolved to the couple's mutual satisfaction. Obviously, such resolution requires effective communication.

Unfortunately, many people find it very difficult to talk to their partner about sex. Let's look at four common barriers to communication about sex.

1. Fear of appearing ignorant. According to a recent Kinsey Institute/Roper poll, most Americans are woefully ignorant about sex (Reinisch, 1990). On an 18-item test of basic sexual knowledge, 55% of a statistically representative sample of American adults failed (could answer correctly only 50% or fewer of the questions). Another 27% received Ds (could answer correctly only between 56 and 66% of the questions). (You can test your own knowledge about some aspects of sex by responding to the questions in Figure 13.3.) Because most of us feel that we should be experts about sex and many of us know that we are not, we feel ashamed. To hide our ignorance, we often avoid talk about sex.

2. Concern about the partner's response. Sometimes the problem is that we worry that our partner may not continue to respect and love us if we express our authentic wishes in regard to sex. So we keep our preferences to ourselves. Unfortunately, the usual result is that one or both partners are unsatisfied and frustrated, as one woman's predicament demonstrates:

"I know what I need in a sexual relationship, but how do I get this message across to my part-

ner? I'm afraid that if I were to come right out and state my requests he would feel inadequate—like why didn't he think of it without me needing to tell him? But the truth of the matter is he usually doesn't come up with it on his own. So what do I do—keep my mouth shut and hope he will eventually figure it out or do I state specifically what I would like with the possibility of turning him off by being too demanding? At this point in my life I generally opt for the former. Obviously, it is easier and less risky to say nothing." [Quoted in Crooks & Baur, 1983, pp. 237–238]

3. Conflicting attitudes toward sex. Many of us, particularly women, carry into adulthood the negative sexual messages we learned as children. Too, most of us have contradictory beliefs about sex ("Sex is beautiful" and "Sex is dirty"), and they produce psychological conflicts. These contradictory beliefs may also cause us to feel uncomfortable with ourselves as sexual persons and to have difficulty talking about sex.

4. Early negative sexual experiences. Some people's enjoyment of sex is inhibited by their previous sexual experiences that have not been positive. If earlier negative experiences are due to ignorant or inconsiderate partners, subsequent positive sexual interactions will usually resolve the problem over time. If earlier sexual experiences have been traumatic, as in the case of rape or incest, counseling may be required to help the individual view sex positively and enjoy it. Such individuals may also benefit from reading *The Courage to Heal* (Bass & Davis, 1988), which is a very helpful book written for survivors of childhood sexual abuse (see the Recommended Reading on p. 413).

To prevent these differences in sexual appetite from becoming a source of frustration, couples need to learn how to negotiate about them. The bartering connotations associated with the word *negotiation* conflict with the religious and romantic sexual scripts that most of us follow. Guided by these scripts, we often keep the negotiation process veiled in ambiguity and subtlety. Nonetheless, intimate couples have to negotiate whether, how often, and when they will have sex, whether or not they acknowledge that they are negotiating. They also have to decide what kinds of erotic activities will take place and what it all means to their relationship. This negotiation process may not be explicit, but it's there.

The difficulty couples have in talking about sex is unfortunate. Studies show that open communication is associated with greater satisfaction in the relationship and greater sexual satisfaction (Markman, 1981; Zimmer, 1983). Most of the advice in Chapter 6 on how

**FIGURE 13.3
How knowledgeable about sex are you?**
Check your basic sexual knowledge by answering 5 of the 18 questions on the Kinsey Institute National Sex Knowledge Test. Information about each of the questions is discussed in this chapter. (Based on Reinisch, 1990.)

How Knowledgeable about Sex Are You?

1 Petroleum jelly, Vaseline Intensive Care, baby oil, and Nivea are *not* good lubricants to use with a condom or diaphragm.

_____True _____False _____Don't know

2 More than one out of four (25%) American men have had a sexual experience with another male during their teens or adult years.

_____True _____False _____Don't know

3 It is usually difficult to tell whether people are or are not homosexual just by their appearance or gestures.

_____True _____False _____Don't know

4 A woman or teenage girl can get pregnant during her menstrual flow (her "period").

_____True _____False _____Don't know

5 A woman or teenage girl can get pregnant even if the man withdraws his penis before he ejaculates (before he "comes").

_____True _____False _____Don't know

SCORING: 1. True. (Oil-based creams, lotions, and jellies can produce microscopic holes in rubber products within 60 seconds of their application.) 2. True. (A Kinsey Institute review of research estimated that at least 25% of American males have had at least one same-sex experience.) 3. True. (Gay males can be extremely masculine, average, or effeminate in their appearance and gestures. Lesbians can be extremely feminine, average, or masculine in their appearance and gestures). 4. True. (While the chance of a woman's becoming pregnant during her menstrual period is lower than at other times, pregnancy *can* occur if she has unprotected sex during her period. Sperm can live for up to 8 days in a woman's reproductive tract, and if the menstrual cycle is irregular, as it is likely to be in adolescence, sperm may still be present in the reproductive tract a week later to fertilize a new egg.) 5. True. (The pre-ejaculatory fluid secreted from the tip of the penis during arousal may contain enough sperm to fertilize an egg.)

to improve verbal and nonverbal communication can be applied to sexual relationships. You may want to think about how you can employ assertive communication and constructive conflict-resolution strategies to keep the process of sexual negotiation healthy. With these thoughts about interpersonal aspects of sex in mind, let's turn our attention to physiological aspects of sexuality.

The Human Sexual Response

hat exactly happens physically when partners are motivated to engage in sexual activity? This may sound like a very simple question, yet very little was known about the physiology of the human sexual response before William Masters and Virginia Johnson conducted their groundbreaking research in the 1960s. Although our society seems to be obsessed with sex, until relatively recently we did *not* encourage scientists to study sex. At first Masters and Johnson even had difficulty finding journals that were willing to publish their studies.

Masters and Johnson used physiological recording devices to monitor the bodily changes of volunteers as they engaged in sex. Their observations and interviews with their subjects yielded a detailed description of the human sexual response that has won them widespread acclaim.

The Sexual Response Cycle

Masters and Johnson (1966, 1970) divide the sexual response cycle into four stages: excitement, plateau, orgasm, and resolution. With the exception of orgasm, the transition from one stage to another is not clearly marked. Masters and Johnson's description of the sexual response cycle is a generalized one, outlining typical rather than inevitable patterns. Keep in mind that there is considerable variability among people. Figure 13.4 shows how the intensity of sexual arousal changes as women and men progress through the phases of the sexual response cycle.

Excitement Phase

During the initial phase of excitement, the level of arousal usually escalates rapidly. In both sexes, muscle tension, respiration rate, heart rate, and blood pressure increase quickly. *Vasocongestion*—engorgement of blood ves-

sels—produces erection of the man's penis, swelling of the testes, and movement of the scrotum (the sac containing the testes) closer to the body. In the woman, vasocongestion leads to a swelling of the clitoris and vaginal lips, vaginal lubrication, and enlargement of the uterus. Most women also experience nipple erection and a swelling of the breasts.

Plateau Phase

The name given the "plateau" stage is misleading, as physiological arousal does not level off. It usually continues to build, but at a much slower pace. In women, further vasocongestion produces a tightening of the lower one-third of the vagina, and a ballooning of the upper two-thirds of the vagina lifts the uterus and cervix away from the end of the vagina. The head of the man's penis may swell, and the testicles typically enlarge and move closer to the body. Many men secrete a bit of pre-ejaculatory fluid from the tip of the penis that may contain sperm.

Unsatisfying sex can be a source of frustration in relationships if couples are not able to talk about their needs and preferences.

Distractions during the plateau phase can delay or stop movement to the next stage. These include ill-timed interruptions like a telephone call, the doorbell ringing, or a child's knocking—or not!—on the bedroom door. Equally distracting can be such things as pain, physical discomfort, guilt, frightening thoughts, feelings of insecurity or anger toward one's partner, and anxiety about one's ability to have an orgasm. When the time between initial arousal and orgasm is lengthy, it is normal for arousal to fluctuate in both sexes. Fluctuation is more apparent in men; erections may increase and decrease noticeably. In women it may be reflected in changes in vaginal lubrication.

Orgasm Phase

Orgasm occurs when sexual arousal reaches its peak intensity and is discharged in a series of muscular contractions that pulsate through the pelvic area. Heart rate, respiration rate, and blood pressure increase sharply as one experiences this exceedingly pleasant spasmodic response. The male orgasm is usually accompanied by ejaculation of seminal fluid. Some women report that they ejaculate some kind of fluid at orgasm. The extent of this phenomenon as well as the source and nature of the fluid are matters still under debate (Reinisch, 1990).

The subjective experience of orgasm appears to be very similar for men and women. Some investigators (Vance & Wagner, 1976; Wiest, 1977) have had subjects write descriptions of what their orgasms feel like without using specific words for genitals. Even psychologists and physicians could not tell which descriptions were provided by women and which by men.

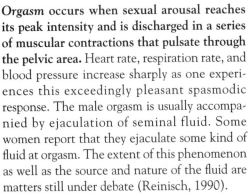

June Machover Reinisch

Resolution Phase

During the resolution phase the physiological changes produced by sexual arousal subside. If one has not had an orgasm, the reduction in sexual tension may be relatively slow and sometimes unpleasant. After orgasm, men generally experience a **refractory period, a time after male orgasm during which males are largely unresponsive to further stimulation.** The refractory period varies from a few minutes to a few hours and increases with age.

Gender Differences in Patterns of Orgasm

As a whole, the sexual responses of women and men parallel each other fairly closely. The similarities clearly outweigh the differences. Nonetheless, there are some interesting differences between females and males in their patterns of experiencing orgasms. In the context of *intercourse*, women are somewhat less likely than men to reach orgasm (that is, they are more likely to follow pattern B in Figure 13.4). Kinsey estimated that married women reached orgasm about 75% of the time during intercourse with their husbands and that about 30% of all married women never reached orgasm or did so only occasionally during intercourse (Kinsey, Pomeroy, Martin, & Gebhard, 1953). The latest data from the Kinsey Institute indicate that about 10% of women have never had an orgasm by any means (Reinisch, 1990). Hence the gap between the sexes appears to have shrunk somewhat since Kinsey's data were collected.

Masters and Johnson found that the men they studied took about 4 minutes to reach a climax with their partners in the laboratory. Women took about 10 to 20 minutes to reach orgasm with their partners but only about 4 minutes when they masturbated. This information tells us, among other things, that women are capable of reaching orgasm more quickly than they typically do. In mentioning this, we don't mean to suggest that men and women should race each other to the finish line. Rather, we are only pointing out that the observed differences in the timing of and difficulty in reaching orgasm are not likely to be due to physiological factors.

What, then, might account for these disparities? First, although most women report that they enjoy intercourse, it may not be the optimal mode of stimulation for women. In fact, June Machover Reinisch, a psychologist and current director of The Kinsey Institute for

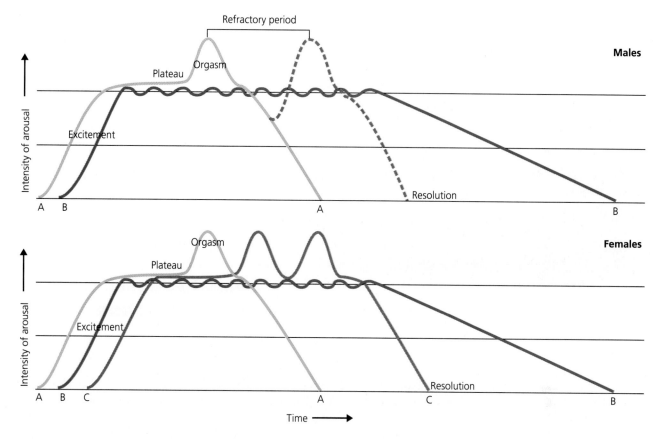

FIGURE 13.4
The human sexual response cycle Similarities and differences are found in the patterns of sexual arousal in men and women. Pattern A, which culminates in orgasm and resolution, is the most typical sequence for both sexes. Pattern B, sexual arousal without orgasm followed by a slow resolution, is also seen in both sexes but is more common among women. Pattern C, arousal culminating in multiple orgasms, is seen almost exclusively in women, as men go through a refractory period before they are capable of another orgasm. (Based on Masters & Johnson, 1966.)

Research in Sex, Gender, and Reproduction, estimates that between 50 and 75% of women who have orgasms by other means of stimulation do not have orgasms when the *only* form of stimulation is penile thrusting during intercourse (Reinisch, 1990). The reason is that intercourse provides rather indirect stimulation to the clitoris, which appears to be the most sexually sensitive genital area in most women. Thus approaches to arousal other than intercourse, such as manual or oral stimulation, may be more beneficial for many women. More lengthy foreplay is usually advised, too. Ignorance or fear of being "abnormal," however, locks many couples into a sexual script that prescribes that orgasms should be achieved through intercourse. (Even the word *foreplay* suggests that any other form of sexual stimulation is merely preparation for the main event.) Also, a man may have the mistaken idea that if his partner needs clitoral stimulation, he is a poor lover or his penis is too small.

A second factor that contributes to gender differences in orgasmic inconsistency is tied to gender differences in sexual socialization. Guilt and ambivalence about sex are more likely to undermine sexual arousal and expression in women than in men.

A third factor that can contribute to women's orgasmic inconsistency is excessively brief or mechanical intercourse. Women typically require lengthier intercourse to achieve orgasm (Gebhard, 1966; Wolfe, 1981). And since women's sexual scripts usually call for affection, most women want to hear some tender words and expressions of love during a sexual encounter. If a man is ignorant of this fact, discounts its importance, or is uncomfortable expressing his affection verbally, his partner may be inhibited in her sexual response. Consider one woman's experience:

"Sex for me is dull, boring, and uninspiring routine. My husband likes to 'make love' on Saturday night (he is too tired during the week). It's always the same way—a few kisses, some mechanical manipulation of my breasts, and presto, he is in and out and finished. I rarely am satisfied, but I don't even give a damn anymore. Actually I'm glad he finishes quickly. It's never fun to prolong boring things." [Quoted in Crooks & Baur, 1983, p. 218]

Is there any mystery about why this woman doesn't experience orgasm regularly? Obviously not. Intercourse with her husband is too brief, they have differing sexual scripts, and he is an inconsiderate sexual partner.

Since women reach orgasm through intercourse less consistently than men, they are more likely than men to fake it (Petersen et al.,

415

"I think you're being silly. Would you like it better if I was thinking of you and sleeping with Robert Redford?"

1983). Surveys reveal that both sexes fake orgasms—women just do it more often. People appear to fake orgasms to make their partners feel better or to bring sexual activity to an end when they're fatigued. In general, faking orgasm is probably not a good idea, as the practice undermines open communication about sex.

Data on the incidence of orgasm among lesbians also supports a socialization-based explanation of gender differences in orgasmic consistency. Kinsey et al. (1953) found that lesbians who had been sexually active for five years reached orgasm more consistently than heterosexual women who had been married for the same length of time. These differences are most likely attributable to the gender differences in sexual socialization we have discussed. Most male partners know less than female (lesbian) partners about women's sexuality and techniques for optimizing women's sexual satisfaction (Kinsey et al., 1953). Also, a lesbian partner is likely to put more emphasis than a man on the emotional aspects of lovemaking (Blumstein & Schwartz, 1983).

Although orgasmic consistency is lower in women than in men, women are more likely than men to be *multiorgasmic*. A woman is said to be multiorgasmic if she experiences more than one climax in a very brief time (pattern C in Figure 13.4) with some regularity. Just how brief the time limitation should be is the source of some debate. Masters and Johnson originally thought that multiorgasmic women typically experienced a series of moderately intense orgasms, culminating in a very intense climax.

A more recent study suggests, however, that multiorgasmic women are more likely to experience two or more orgasms of roughly equal and full intensity (Amberson & Hoon, 1985).

Only about 10 to 15% of female respondents to surveys report reaching multiple orgasms with some regularity (Athanasiou, Shaver, & Tavris, 1970; Wolfe, 1981). Thus women should certainly not feel inadequate if they are not multiorgasmic. Masters and Johnson's research led them to believe that the capacity for multiple orgasms is very rare in men, but more recent research suggests that more men may experience multiple orgasms than they thought (Dunn & Trost, 1989).

Sexual Arousal and Satisfaction

eople engage in a wide variety of activities to elicit sexual arousal and satisfaction. *Erogenous zones are areas of the body that are sexually sensitive or responsive.* Such areas as the genitals and breasts usually come to mind when people think of erogenous zones. These *are* particularly sensitive areas for most people. But it's worth noting that many individuals fail to appreciate the potential that lies in other areas of the body. Virtually any area of the body can function as an erogenous zone.

Indeed, one's mental set is so important to sexual arousal that the ultimate erogenous zone may be the mind. Vigorous and skillful genital stimulation by a partner may have absolutely no effect if a person is not in the mood for sex. Yet fantasy in the absence of any other stimulation can produce great arousal. In this section we'll discuss techniques for achieving sexual arousal and satisfaction, starting with the use of fantasy.

Fantasy

Sexual fantasies are common and normal. Some of the more common themes in sexual fantasies are listed in Figure 13.5, based on research by Sue (1979). It should be emphasized that if people fantasize about a particular kind of encounter, such as being forced to have sex, that does not necessarily mean that they would actually like to have such an encounter. Further, it has been suggested that having fantasies involving force may be a way to absolve oneself of any guilt that may come from enjoying sexual pleasure or from initiating sex (Reinisch, 1990).

Fantasy often occurs in conjunction with

other modes of sexual stimulation. Many people fantasize while they masturbate or engage in sexual activities with another person. Both men and women acknowledge that they fantasize during intercourse to increase their sexual arousal. Moreover, research suggests that fantasies *can* help people of both sexes to enhance their sexual excitement and achieve orgasm (Davidson, 1985).

Kissing and Touching

Most sexual activities begin with kissing. Usually kissing starts with the lips, but it may be extended to almost any area of the partner's body. Mutual caressing is also an integral element of sexual stimulation for most couples. Like kissing, tactile stimulation may be applied to any area of the body. Hand and oral stimulation of the other partner's genitals are related sexual practices. As with any type of sexual activity, specific techniques are not as important as good communication about one's preferences.

Some people can get so wrapped up in their anticipation of intercourse that they fail to appreciate the pleasure inherent in a variety of sexual activities. As we'll see in the Application, focusing solely on orgasm can foster an achievement ethic that can contribute to sexual problems (Masters & Johnson, 1970). That's why we have avoided referring to sexual activities as "foreplay."

Sex partners often have differing expectations about the significance and appropriate length of various sexual activities. Because of differences in sexual socialization, men often underestimate the importance of kissing and touching (including clitoral stimulation). It is not surprising, therefore, that heterosexual women commonly complain that their partners are in too big a hurry (Denny, Field, & Quadagno, 1984). These disparities should be brought out in the open and discussed. Partners who seek to learn about each other's preferences and try to accommodate them are much more likely to have mutually satisfying sexual experiences than those who ignore these issues.

Self-Stimulation

Stimulation of one's own genitals is commonly called *masturbation*. Because this term carries a decidedly negative connotation, many writers on sexuality prefer to use such terms as *self-stimulation* and *autoeroticism*. Because of its nonreproductive nature, autoeroticism has traditionally been condemned as immoral. In the 19th and early 20th centuries it was widely

Fantasies during Intercourse		
Theme	Subjects reporting fantasy (%)	
	Males	*Females*
A former lover	42.9	41.0
An imaginary lover	44.3	24.3
Oral-genital sex	61.2	51.4
Group sex	19.3	14.1
Being forced or overpowered into a sexual relationship	21.0	36.4
Others observing you engage in sexual intercourse	15.4	20.0
Others finding you sexually irresistible	55.2	52.8
Being rejected or sexually abused	10.5	13.2
Forcing others to have sexual relations with you	23.5	15.8
Others giving in to you after resisting you at first	36.8	24.3
Observing others engaging in sex	17.9	13.2
A member of the same sex	2.8	9.4
Animals	0.9	3.7

NOTE: For comparison, the responses of "frequently" and "sometimes" were combined for both males and females to obtain the percentages above. The number of respondents answering for a specific fantasy ranged from 103 to 106 for males and from 105 to 107 for females.

assumed that self-stimulation was also harmful to one's physical and mental health. During this period, disapproval and suppression of masturbation were truly intense. Many antimasturbation devices were marketed to concerned parents. Children were forced to sleep in manacles, and some were fitted with genital cages (Karlen, 1971).

Given this heritage, it is not surprising that disapproval of masturbation continues to be widespread in our culture (Gagnon, 1985). Although Kinsey discovered nearly 50 years ago that most people masturbate with no ill effects, guilt about self-stimulation is still prevalent.

Despite these negative attitudes, self-stimulation is very common. By adulthood, nine out of ten males and eight out of ten females report having masturbated at least once (Atwood & Gagnon, 1987). Masturbation by males almost always consists of stimulating the penis by hand (Kinsey, Pomeroy, & Martin, 1948). The technique that most females perfer is manipulation of the clitoris and inner lips (Hite, 1976; Kinsey et al., 1953). Self-stimulation remains common even after marriage. Among younger married couples, 72% of the husbands and 68% of the wives reported engaging in self-stimulation (Hunt, 1974). Marital partners generally do not

FIGURE 13.5
Common sexual fantasies
The percentages of men and women who reported various sexual fantasies during intercourse are shown here. Sue (1979) concludes that people often fantasize about experiences they wouldn't seek out in real life.

talk to each other about their masturbation. Most of them probably assume that their partner would view it as a sign of sexual discontent. However, the fact that self-stimulation is so widespread among married persons suggests that it probably is not a sign of dissatisfaction in most cases.

Experts on sexuality are gradually recognizing that self-stimulation is a normal, healthy, and sometimes important component of one's sexual behavior (Gadpaille, 1975). This route to sexual pleasure has obvious value when a sexual partner is unavailable. Moreover, many people are beginning to view self-stimulation as more than a poor substitute for "the real thing." Some people report that they derive more pleasure from self-stimulation than from intercourse (Hite, 1976).

Oral and Anal Sex

Oral sex is oral stimulation of the genitals. *Cunnilingus* **is oral stimulation of the female genitals.** *Fellatio* **is oral stimulation of the penis.** Partners may stimulate each other simultaneously, or one partner may stimulate the other without immediate reciprocation. Oral-genital sex may be one of several activities in a sexual encounter, or it may constitute the main event. Oral sex is a major source of orgasm for many heterosexual couples, and it plays a particularly central role in homosexual relationships. A positive aspect of oral sex is that it does not result in pregnancy. However, it is possible to contract AIDS through mouth-genital stimulation, especially if semen is swallowed (in fellatio).

As with masturbation, there is a residue of negative attitudes toward oral sex. However, the prevalence of oral sex appears to have increased dramatically since the Kinsey studies of the late 1940s and early 1950s (Gagnon & Simon, 1987). Indeed, one study found that high school students today are slightly more likely to have had oral sex than intercourse (Newcomer & Udry, 1985), and about 90% of adults report oral-genital contact (Blumstein & Schwartz, 1983; Wyatt, Peters, & Guthrie, 1988). Thus it appears that oral sex is now a conventional component of most couples' sexual relationships.

Anal intercourse **involves insertion of the penis into a partner's anus and rectum.** Legally, it is "sodomy" (and is still illegal in some states). When asked if they had ever had anal intercourse, 43% of the female respondents in a recent study replied yes, although only 2% indicated that they practiced it "often" (Wyatt et al., 1988). Anal intercourse is more popular among homosexual male couples than among heterosexual couples (Bell & Weinberg, 1978). Even among gay men, however, it ranks behind oral sex and mutual masturbation in prevalence. The low incidence of anal sex is probably a good thing because it is a major way by which AIDS can be contracted if either partner is infected with the disease.

Intercourse

Heterosexual intercourse, known technically as *coitus,* **involves insertion of the penis into the vagina and (typically) pelvic thrusting.** It is the most widely endorsed and widely practiced sexual act in our society. Kinsey and his associates (1948, 1953) found that it accounted for 80 to 85% of the total sexual outlets for married couples. Insertion of the penis generally requires adequate vaginal lubrication, or it may be difficult and painful for the woman—as will intercourse itself. This is another good reason for couples to spend plenty of time on mutual kissing and touching. In the absence of adequate lubrication, partners may choose to use artificial lubricants such as K-Y jelly. The actual insertion is typically a cooperative act.

Partners may use any of a variety of positions in their intercourse. Many couples use more than one position in a single encounter. The man-above, or "missionary," position is the most common. When Kinsey conducted his research 40-odd years ago, many couples limited themselves to this position exclusively. Studies indicate that there is more variation today, as Figure 13.6 indicates. Hunt (1974) found that 75% of married couples reported using the female-above position, the one often suggested for women who have difficulty expe-

**FIGURE 13.6
Changes in the use of coital positions**
About 20 to 25 years apart, Kinsey et al. (1948, 1953) and Hunt (1974) asked their subjects about coital positions they used besides the man-above position. As you can see, Hunt's data indicate that by the 1970s couples were using a greater variety of positions for intercourse.

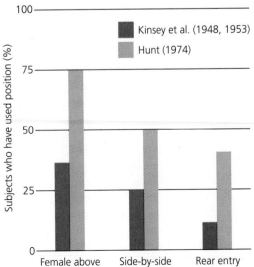

riencing orgasm during intercourse. Furthermore, 50% of couples in his study reported using the side-by-side position and 40% the rear-entry position.

According to Masters and Johnson (1970), each position has its advantages and disadvantages. Although people tend to be fascinated by the relative merits of various positions, specific positions may not be as important as the tempo, depth, and angle of movements in intercourse. Most people appreciate variations in tempo, depth, and angle. As with other aspects of sexual relations, the crucial consideration is that partners talk to each other about their preferences.

What kinds of sexual activities do homosexuals prefer in the absence of coitus (which is, by definition, a heterosexual act)? Gay men tend to engage in mutual masturbation, fellatio, and, less frequently, anal intercourse. Lesbians engage in mutual masturbation, cunnilingus, and *tribadism*, in which one partner lies on top of the other and makes thrusting movements so that both receive genital stimulation at the same time. Contrary to the stereotype, a dildo (an artificial penis) is rarely used by lesbian couples (Jay & Young, 1979).

William Masters and Virginia Johnson

Patterns of Sexual Behavior

hen we focused on the sexual response itself, our principal interests were physiology and technique. Here we'll discuss how such variables as age, sex, and type of relationship are related to patterns of sexual behavior. Let's begin by examining the so-called sexual revolution.

Has There Been a Sexual Revolution?

The popular media commonly suggest that we have undergone a sexual revolution. Just what would constitute a *revolution* in sexual behavior is unclear. Presumably a revolution would involve sudden, radical, and widespread changes in the expression of our sexuality. But what would qualify as sudden, radical, or widespread is a matter of opinion.

Most sex researchers seem to feel that it would be more accurate to characterize the changes in our sexual behavior as *evolutionary* rather than revolutionary. To some extent, the sexual revolution has been more evident in our popular media than in our bedrooms. There *has*

been radical change in the openness with which sex is discussed and portrayed in magazines, movies, and TV shows. A comparison of survey data across recent decades suggests, however, that our actual behavior has changed gradually rather than suddenly.

The amount of change has probably been magnified by our tendency to talk more openly about sex. The extent of change may also be exaggerated because most people have difficulty envisioning their parents as sexual beings (Pocs & Godow, 1977), so they tend to underestimate the sexual activity of the preceding generation. This is probably why a sexual revolution has been heralded in *every* decade of the 20th century. Undoubtedly there has been substantial change in our sexual behavior, but it appears to have been less abrupt and less spectacular than many people believe.

"Premarital" Sex

The term *premarital sex* conjures up images of furtive sex among teenagers. Of course, with more people delaying marriage, premarital sex increasingly involves relationships between mature adults. Obviously, the emotional implications of sex between a pair of 15-year-olds who live with their parents are likely to be quite different from those of sex between a pair of independent 30-year-olds. Another problem with the term *premarital* is that it doesn't apply to homosexuals, who aren't permitted to marry under the law. Although the term *premarital sex* is becoming dated, many contemporary researchers continue to use the term to refer to youthful sexual encounters.

Prevalence

It is clear that the prevalence of premarital sex has increased since the 1960s (Robinson &

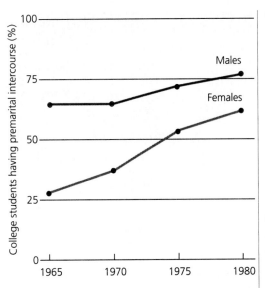

**FIGURE 13.7
Increase in premarital sex among college students**
The percentage of college students who report engaging in premarital intercourse has increased in recent decades. Men are still more likely to engage in premarital sex than women, but the gap has been closing. (Data from Robinson & Jedlicka, 1982.)

Jedlicka, 1982), as Figure 13.7 shows. By age 25, 97% of the men in our society and 67% of the women have engaged in premarital coitus (Hunt, 1974). Thus people entering marriage as virgins have become a rather small minority. Although the gap is shrinking, males are still more likely than females to engage in premarital sex. Some of the increase in premarital sex is attributable to later marriages, but premarital sex among teenagers has become more frequent as well (Dreyer, 1982). Interestingly, when adult homosexuals are questioned about their youthful sexual experiences, they report rates of *heterosexual* premarital intercourse that are nearly identical to those reported by heterosexuals (Saghir & Robins, 1973). Among other things, these findings support the view that adolescence is an important time for exploration and working out answers to questions about sexual orientation.

Males and females have different reactions to their first experience with sexual intercourse (Sorenson, 1973). Males typically report positive feelings such as joy and a sense of being more mature, while females report such emotions as guilt, sorrow, and disappointment. Also, it seems that the girl's partner is not usually aware of her unpleasant feelings. One study asked college women to rate their first coital experience on a scale ranging from 1 (no pleasure at all) to 7 (strongly experienced pleasure). Their average pleasure rating was 3.9 (Weis, 1983). These findings support the view that female sexuality involves more negative elements than does male sexuality.

Attitudes

People regard premarital sex from a variety of viewpoints. Ira Reiss (1967) has identified the following standards:

- *Traditional:* Both males and females should abstain from sexual intercourse before marriage.
- *Double standard:* Sex before marriage is acceptable for males but not for females.
- *Permissiveness with affection:* Sex before marriage is acceptable *if* it takes place in the context of a stable, loving relationship.
- *Permissiveness without affection:* Sex before marriage is acceptable whether or not two people care for each other.

Most parents and institutions (churches, schools, and so forth) in our society endorse abstinence, and many of them have voiced considerable dismay at their perception that permissiveness without affection has become the norm. What does the actual evidence indicate? Sprecher (1989) found no evidence of a double standard today. The data from several surveys suggest that permissiveness with affection is the dominant standard in our society (Dreyer, 1982; Earle & Perricone, 1986; Hunt, 1974; Zelnick & Kantner, 1977). The casual one-night stands that get so much attention in the media appear to be less frequent than they are commonly believed to be. In a study of college students, only 33% of the men and 3% of the women endorsed premarital sex with a "casual acquaintance" (Earle & Perricone, 1986). Thus concern that premarital promiscuity is rampant in our society may be exaggerated.

Sex in Committed Relationships

Sex is a very important element in most committed romantic relationships. Let us examine patterns of sexual activity in dating couples, married couples, and gay couples.

Sex between Dating Couples

Sooner or later couples who are dating and in love discuss whether or when they should have sexual intercourse. For some the decision is easy, but for others it isn't. Some worry that sex may adversely affect the relationship; others fear that *not* having sex will cause trouble. The Boston Couples Study we discussed in Chapter 8 provides answers to some of these questions (Peplau et al., 1977). Among other things, the authors looked at when sexually active unmarried heterosexual couples began to have sexual intercourse. Those who had sex within a month after their first date were classified as "early-sex" couples; those who didn't initiate sexual intercourse until after that (the average interval was 6 months) were classified as "later-sex" couples. Later-sex couples expressed significantly more emotional closeness than early-sex couples, had greater knowledge of their partners, thought it more likely that they would marry, but also felt more guilt about their sexual involvement. Women in couples who had delayed sexual intercourse reported less sexual satisfaction than women in early-sex couples. Two years later, however, there was no difference in the number of intact relationships between the two types of couples. Thus, despite its importance to the individuals involved, the timing of first intercourse doesn't appear to have a direct effect on the endurance of a relationship.

Marital Sex

There is ample evidence that couples' overall marital satisfaction is highly related to their satisfaction with their sexual interaction (Birchler & Webb, 1977; Hunt, 1974; Tavris & Sadd, 1977). Hunt found that spouses who characterized their marital relationship as "very close" were much more likely to rate their sex life as "very pleasurable" than those who characterized their marriage as "fairly close" or "not too close" (see Figure 13.8). Thus good sex and a good marriage tend to go hand in hand. Of course, it is difficult to tell whether good sex promotes good marriages or good marriages promote good sex. In all probability, it's a two-way street. It seems likely that marital closeness is conducive to sexual pleasure *and* that sexual satisfaction increases marital satisfaction.

Married couples vary greatly in how often they have sex. *On the average*, couples in their 20s and 30s engage in sex about two or three times a week (Reinisch, 1990; Westoff, 1974). It appears that marital sex has increased in frequency since the early Kinsey studies, but only slightly. As you can see in Figure 13.9, the frequency of sex among married couples tends to decrease as the years wear on (Trussell & Westoff, 1980). Couples report that this decline is due to increasing fatigue from work and child rearing and to growing familiarity with their sexual routine (Greenblat, 1983). As one man put it:

> "In the beginning it was five times a week, three times in one day. But it changed because the early adrenaline wore off. Karin took a trip for a month and when she came back we were both too busy because we were working sixteen-hour days. So we sort of settled down to your typical boring existence." [Quoted in Blumstein & Schwartz, 1983, p. 199]

Although married couples' intercourse tends to become less frequent as time goes on, marital sex certainly does not have to be bor-

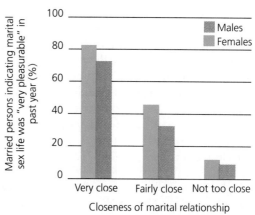

ing. A comparison of more recent surveys (Blumstein & Schwartz, 1983; Hunt, 1974; Tavris & Sadd, 1977) with the early Kinsey data suggests that the sexual practices of married couples have become more diversified. The evidence suggests that couples today engage in lengthier coitus after a longer period of sexual activities. Married couples also use oral-genital techniques of arousal more often and use a greater variety of coital positions. Recent studies also suggest that husbands have become more concerned about their wives' sexual pleasure. This may be why wives are reaching orgasm with greater regularity than the wives of a couple of generations ago.

Married couples' level of sexual activity tends to decline during middle and late adulthood (Weizman & Hart, 1987; Wilson, 1975). In some people, this decline is due to decreased sexual desire and sexual capability (Kaplan, 1974). In many couples, however, the decline in sexual activity may be due to changing attitudes more than to physiological factors. Our youth-oriented culture tends to discourage sexual expression in old age. People are led to believe that sexual activity among the elderly is inappropriate and even repugnant.

FIGURE 13.8
Sexual satisfaction and marital satisfaction
Hunt (1974) found that the better the subjects' marital relationship, the more likely they were to rate their sex life as very pleasurable. Thus good marriages are correlated with good sex.

FIGURE 13.9
Age trends in the frequency of marital coitus
Data from three studies conducted at different times are summarized in this graph, based on responses from white married women. All three studies indicate a gradual decline in the frequency of intercourse among married couples as the years go by. (From Trussell & Westoff, 1980.)

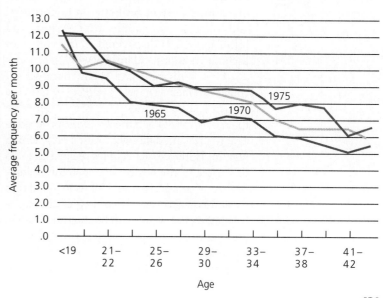

It *is* true that a person's sexual response changes with age (Diamond & Karlen, 1981). Arousal tends to build more slowly in both sexes, and orgasms tend to diminish in frequency and intensity. Men's refractory periods lengthen and women's vaginal lubrication and elasticity decrease. In spite of these changes, however, people over 60 remain capable of rewarding sexual encounters. In a study of healthy 80- to 102-year-olds, 62% of the men and 30% of the women reported that they still engaged in sexual intercourse (Bretschneider & McCoy, 1988). About 80% of couples over the age of 60 continue to engage in intercourse every week or two (Brecher, 1984). The married couples who remain sexually active in old age generally are those who had a relatively high level of sexual activity when they were younger (George & Weiler, 1981).

Sex in Homosexual Relationships

On the average, homosexual couples have sex about as often as heterosexual couples of similar ages—two or three times a week (Blumstein & Schwartz, 1983). Similarly, homosexual individuals vary widely in their desire for sex. One well-known survey reported that about 45% of lesbians wished that they had sex with their partners more often than they actually did, whereas only 5% preferred a lower frequency. Some 37% of gay men expressed a desire for sex more often and 21% preferred a lower frequency (Blumstein & Schwartz, 1983).

Traditional gender roles are less common in lesbian and gay couples than in heterosexual couples. Most gay and lesbian couples value power equality and shared decision making as a goal for their relationships (Blumstein & Schwartz, 1983; Kurdek & Schmitt, 1986b; Peplau, 1983). This fact may account for some interesting differences between homosexual and heterosexual couples that Masters and Johnson (1979) discovered in the course of their observations and interviews.

First, both male and female homosexual couples seemed to have a *non-goal-oriented view* of their sexual activities. That is, they were able to enjoy a variety of mutually pleasurable sexual activities and didn't get focused on reaching orgasm. Heterosexual couples seemed to focus on orgasm to the neglect of important preliminary activities. Masters and Johnson found that preliminary activities of both types of couples began the same way—with holding and kissing. Among heterosexual couples, this behavior lasted only about 30 seconds before they shifted to genital stimulation. Lesbian couples spent more time on the initial activities and also communicated more with each other than the heterosexual couples did. Gay male couples also took more time before moving to orgasm and engaged in a variety of techniques to prolong sexual pleasure before orgasm.

A second major finding by Masters and Johnson concerned the *subjective quality* of the couples' sexual experiences—that is, total body contact, enjoyment of each aspect of the sexual experience, psychological involvement, and responsiveness to the needs and desires of the partner. To the surprise of some readers, the researchers concluded that the subjective quality of the sexual experience was greater for the homosexual couples. Masters and Johnson offered three possible explanations for this finding. First, because homosexual partners are the same sex, they may have a better sense of what is pleasurable to each other than heterosexual couples do. Second, mutually satisfying heterosexual intercourse requires a degree of coordination not required by many of the noncoital techniques used by homosexual couples. Finally, Masters and Johnson noted that homosexual couples seem to communicate better about their sexual feelings than heterosexual couples do. In fact, Masters and Johnson were rather critical of the "persistent neglect" of sexual communication they observed in heterosexual couples. Their observations and comments underscore the importance of effective communication in maintaining satisfying sexual interactions.

Infidelity in Committed Relationships

Sexual infidelity occurs when a person who is in a committed relationship engages in erotic activity with someone other than his or her partner. Among married couples, this behavior is also called "adultery" or "extramarital sex." Clanton (1973) has differentiated among three types of extramarital liaisons. In *clandestine extramarital sex,* the nonmarital sexual activity is successfully kept secret from one's spouse. In *consensual extramarital sex,* the spouse is aware of the nonmarital activity. He or she accepts it and may even approve of it (as in "mate swapping" or "open marriage"). Finally, in *ambiguous extramarital sex,* a spouse becomes aware of secretive nonmarital sexual activity but chooses not to confront the participating spouse. Typically the spouse tolerates the activity without approving it for the sake of avoiding marital strife or a clash that might lead to divorce. Surveys suggest that consensual extramarital sex is relatively infrequent in our society (Davidson, 1988; Levin & Levin, 1975).

The attitudes of homosexual couples, especially gay men, are more favorable than those of heterosexual couples toward "open" relationships that permit sexual activity with other individuals (Blumstein & Schwartz, 1989; Garnets & Kimmel, 1991). Such relationships usually begin as sexually exclusive but over time shift toward sexual openness (Blasband & Peplau, 1985).

Because most conflicts over affairs outside of committed relationships are likely to develop with regard to clandestine or ambiguous "extramarital" sex, we'll limit our further discussion to these two types of liaisons.

Prevalence

The vast majority of people (about 75%) in our society express strong disapproval of extramarital sex (Reiss, Anderson, & Sponaugle, 1980), yet a substantial number of people get involved in it. Because of the stigma and secrecy associated with this behavior, accurate estimates of infidelity are difficult to come by. The data available suggest that extramarital involvement is increasing. One review of research on the topic suggests that about 40 to 50% of husbands and about 25 to 35% of wives engage in extramarital activity at least once (Thompson, 1983). Writing more recently, other experts speculate that some 50 to 65% of husbands and 45 to 55% of wives are unfaithful by the age of 40 (Scarf, 1987).

These figures *may* not mean that men are more likely than women to have an affair. Much of the higher incidence of extramarital sex among men is probably accounted for by visits to prostitutes and one-time-only encounters. These kinds of activities are less frequent among women (Bell, Turner, & Rosen, 1975). Thus, if we define an affair as repeated encounters with someone other than a prostitute, the incidence of affairs may be much the same for both sexes.

Motivations

Why do people pursue extramarital sexual encounters? There are many reasons. First, dissatisfaction with one's marriage is related to the likelihood of extramarital sex (Bell et al., 1975). People who are unhappy with their marriage may be seeking affection and emotional support that their marriage is not providing (Thompson, 1983). Some may also be expressing anger toward their spouse. Second, dissatis-

faction with just the *sexual* aspect of one's marriage may trigger interest in extramarital sex (Bell et al., 1975; Thompson, 1983).

Third, even when the sexual component of a marriage is satisfactory, some people desire new and different sexual experiences (Buunk, 1980). Interestingly, the evidence suggests that pursuit of variety and excitement may frequently lead to disappointment. Hunt (1974) found that extramarital sex involves less variety in arousal techniques and is less frequently viewed as "very pleasurable" than marital sex. Fourth, sometimes extramarital sexual activity occurs simply because two persons are attracted to each other. Erotic reactions to people other than one's spouse do not cease when one marries. Most people suppress these sexual desires because they disapprove of adultery, but some people have a relatively tolerant attitude toward extramarital sex (Atwater, 1982).

The gender differences in motivations for engaging in extramarital affairs parallel gender differences in sexual socialization. That is, men's motivations are tied to sex and women's to emotions. Research indicates that a husband's extramarital affair does not necessarily indicate unhappiness with his marriage, but a wife's affair probably does signal that she is not happy with her marriage (Glass & Wright, 1985; Thompson, 1984).

Impact

The impact of extramarital sexual activity on marriages has not been investigated extensively. The effects are likely to vary with the nature of the activity and with that of the marriage (Reiss & Furstenberg, 1981). Generally speaking, the deception and hypocrisy inherent in clandestine or ambiguous extramarital sex seem likely to undermine the trust and affection that are so important to a marriage. Of course, if one is motivated by marital dissatisfaction, there may be little trust or affection to undermine. Experts speculate that approximately 20% of all divorces are caused by infidelity (Reinisch, 1990). Occasionally an extramarital affair may have a positive effect on a marriage. Some participants inadvertently develop a new appreciation for the quality and importance of their marital union (Tavris & Sadd, 1977). Perhaps people who investigate the grass that looks so much greener on the other side of the fence discover that their own lawn is actually quite lush. One study found no reported differences in the perceived quality of "open" versus "closed" relationships among gay men (Kurdek, 1988), yet another found that male couples in closed relationships reported greater feelings of closeness, more favorable attitudes toward their relationship, and lower tension than couples in open relationships (Kurdek & Schmitt, 1986a). More research is needed on the repercussions of infidelity in gay and lesbian relationships.

Practical Issues in Sexual Activity

egardless of the context of sexual activity, two practical issues are often matters of concern: contraception and sexually transmitted diseases. These topics are more properly the concern of medicine than of psychology, but birth control and sex-related diseases certainly do have their behavioral aspects.

Contraception

Most people want to control whether and when they will conceive a child, and so they need reliable contraception. Despite the availability of effective contraceptive methods, however, many people fail to exercise much control.

Barriers to Effective Contraception

Effective contraception requires that intimate couples negotiate their way through a complex sequence of steps. First, they must define themselves as sexually active. Second, they must have accurate knowledge about fertility and conception. Third, their chosen method of contraception must be readily accessible. Finally, they must possess the motivation and

skill to use the method correctly and consistently. Failure to meet even one of these conditions can result in an unintended pregnancy.

Ineffective contraception is particularly prevalent among adolescents (Tanfer & Horn, 1985). Teens who are just beginning to experiment sexually often feel ambivalent about their behavior, so they are especially prone to deny their need for contraception. Raised in a society in which intentional wrongdoing is regarded as more culpable than unintentional acts, many adolescents feel that sex is justifiable only if "we got carried away" (Cvetkovich, Grote, Bjorseth, & Sarkissian, 1975). Furthermore, misinformation about both fertility and contraception is rampant among adolescents. Many teens underestimate their own fertility ("I'm too young to get pregnant"; "I don't have sex often enough"). Many also overestimate the "costs" of birth control ("You can die from the pill"; "It takes away all the romance") (Luker, 1975). Further, effective family planning requires a level of abstract thinking that many adolescents have not yet attained. They need the ability to anticipate future consequences (possible pregnancy) that they have never experienced and can't even imagine experiencing, and the ability to plan ahead to make sure these consequences *don't* happen (Spain, 1985). Finally, ready access to contraceptive devices is often a problem for adolescents. All these factors in combination make the incidence of contraceptive failure among teens very high.

Like their younger peers, college students engage in risky sexual practices for a variety of reasons. One factor that leads to unprotected sex is the consumption of alcohol, which doesn't increase sexual desire but does typically impair judgment. It is likely that many college students drink as a socially acceptable way of avoiding serious and potentially embarrassing discussions about sex.

Another problem is related to conflicting norms about gender and sexual behavior. As we have seen, men are socialized to be sexually active and to be the initiators of sexual activity, whereas women are socialized to feel guilty about having sexual feelings and to take a passive role in sexual activity. When it comes to birth control, however, men frequently rely on women to take charge (Geis & Gerrard, 1984). These contradictory expectations pose a problem for women and increase the likelihood that a couple will engage in unprotected sex. It is difficult to maintain an image of sexual naiveté and also be responsible for contraception. If a woman tells her partner that she is "on the pill" or whips out a condom at the appropriate time,

she is likely to convey quite a different message! Studies have shown that when college women feel that their sex partners are not supportive of contraception, couples are less likely to practice protected sex (Whitley & Hern, 1991). Research has also found that women who are likely to engage in unprotected sex are lower in self-esteem than those who practice contraception (Whitley & Schofield, 1986), suggesting that such women feel less able to resist pressures by their partners to engage in unprotected sex.

Even adults in stable relationships sometimes fail to practice birth control consistently. If the couple rely on a condom, its use has no immediately experienced positive effects, but the interruption of sexual activity to put it on can be seen as negative. Many people therefore find it difficult to sustain their contraceptive efforts over the long haul.

As we noted earlier, contraceptive failure is especially likely among people who experience guilt or anxiety about their sexuality. Gerrard (1987) has shown that women high in sex guilt tend to be less knowledgeable about contraception than others. They also select less reliable contraceptive methods, and they use their chosen method inconsistently. They're more prone to defer to their male partner's wishes about sexual activities and may leave birth control up to him as well. Unfortunately, this approach can backfire if the partner believes (as many men do) that contraception is the woman's responsibility.

Selecting a Contraceptive Method

If partners are motivated to control their fertility, how should they go about selecting a technique? A rational choice requires accurate knowledge of the effectiveness, benefits, costs, and risks of the various methods. Figure 13.10 summarizes information on most of the methods currently available. The *ideal failure rate* is the estimated probability of conception when the technique is used correctly and consistently. The *actual failure rate* is what occurs in the real world, when users' negligence is factored in.

Information about the various types of contraceptive methods will do you little good unless you put it to use. Contraception is a joint

FIGURE 13.10
Advantages and disadvantages of widely used contraceptive techniques
Couples can choose from a variety of contraceptive methods. Note that the typical failure rate is much higher than the ideal failure rate for all methods, because couples do not use contraceptive techniques consistently and correctly. (Based on Hatcher et al., 1990; Masters, Johnson, & Kolodny, 1988.)

Contraceptive Methods

Method	Ideal failure rate (%)	Actual failure rate (%)	Advantages	Disadvantages
Birth control pills (combination)	0.1	3	Highly reliable; coitus-independent; has some health benefits	Side effects; daily use; continual cost; health risks for some women; no protection against STDs*
Minipill (progestin only)	0.5	3	Thought to have low risk of side effects; coitus-independent; has some health benefits	Breakthrough bleeding; daily use; continual cost; health risks for some women; no protection against STDs*
IUD	1–2	3	No memory or motivation required for use; very reliable	Cramping, bleeding, expulsion; risk of pelvic inflammatory disease; no protection against STDs*
Diaphragm with cream or jelly	6	18	No major health risks; inexpensive	Aesthetic objections
Condom	2	12	Protects against STDs;* simple to use; male responsibility; no health risks; no prescriptions required	Unaesthetic to some; requires interruption of sexual activity; continual cost
Sponge	6–9	18–28	24-hour protection; simple to use; no taste or odor; inexpensive; effective with several acts of intercourse	Aesthetic objections; continual cost; no protection against STDs*
Cervical cap with cream or jelly	6	18	Can wear for weeks at a time; coitus-independent; no major health risks	May be difficult to insert; may irritate cervix
Spermicides	3	21	No major health risks; no prescription required; some protect against AIDS	Unaesthetic to some; must be properly inserted; continual cost
Rhythm	1–9	20	No cost; acceptable to Catholic church	Requires high motivation and periods of abstinence; unreliable; no protection against STDs*
Withdrawal	4	18	No cost or health risks	Reduces sexual pleasure; unreliable; requires high motivation
Implants	0.3–0.4	0.3–0.4	Highly reliable; continuous protection for up to 5 years; easily reversible; low risk of side effects; some health benefits	Slightly visible; costly; minor surgery required for insertion and removal; possible side effects; no protection against STDs*
No contraception	85	85	No immediate monetary cost	High risk of pregnancy and STDs*

* Sexually transmitted diseases

responsibility. It's essential to discuss your preferences for contraception with your partner, to decide together what method(s) you are going to use, and to *act* on your decision. Let's look in more detail at the two most widely used birth control methods in the Western world: oral contraceptives and condoms (Calderone & Johnson, 1989).

Oral contraceptives are pills taken daily by mouth. They contain synthetic forms of two hormones—estrogen or progesterone or both. "The pill" actually consists of more than 50 oral contraceptive products that inhibit ovulation in women. Oral contraception is preferred by many couples because it is the only widely available method that is separated in time from the sex act. With the exception of the intrauterine device, which is rarely prescribed today, no other method permits a similar degree of sexual spontaneity.

Despite much worrisome publicity, use of oral contraceptives does not appear to increase one's overall risk of cancer (Eichhorst, 1988). In fact, the likelihood of certain forms of cancer (such as uterine cancer) is reduced in women who use low-dosage oral contraceptives. The pill *does* slightly increase the risk of certain cardiovascular disorders, such as heart disease and stroke. Thus alternative methods of contraception should be considered by smokers over age 35 and by women with any suspicion of cardiovascular disease (Eichhorst, 1988).

A *condom* is a sheath worn over the penis during intercourse to collect ejaculated semen. The condom is the only widely available contraceptive device for use by males. It can be purchased in any drugstore without a prescription. If used correctly, the condom is highly effective in preventing pregnancy (Mishell, 1986). It must be placed over the penis after erection but before any contact with the vagina. Space must be left at the tip of the condom to collect the ejaculate. The man should withdraw before completely losing his erection, and hold the rim of the condom during withdrawal to prevent any semen from spilling into the vagina.

Condoms are generally made of latex rubber but are occasionally made from animal membranes ("skin"). The use of rubber condoms can reduce the chances of contracting or passing on various sexually transmitted diseases. *Oil*-based creams and lotions (petroleum jelly, hand creams, and baby oil, for example) should not be used as lubricants with rubber condoms (or diaphragms). Within 60 seconds these products can make microscopic holes in the rubber membrane that are large enough to allow passage of the AIDS virus and organisms

that cause other sexually transmitted diseases (Reinisch, 1990). *Water*-based lubricants such as K-Y jelly don't cause this problem. Skin condoms do *not* offer protection against sexually transmitted diseases.

Sexually Transmitted Diseases

A *sexually transmitted disease* (STD) is an illness that is transmitted primarily through sexual contact. When people think of STDs, they typically think of syphilis and gonorrhea, but these are only the tip of the iceberg. There are actually about 20 sexually transmitted diseases. Some of them, such as pubic lice, are minor nuisances that can readily be treated. But some STDs are severe, difficult-to-treat afflictions. Syphilis, for instance, can cause heart failure, blindness, and brain damage if it isn't detected early. The acquired immune deficiency syndrome (AIDS) is eventually fatal. We'll discuss AIDS in more detail in Chapter 14.

Prevalence and Transmission

No one is immune to sexually transmitted diseases. Even monogamous partners can develop some STDs (yeast infections, for instance). Sexually transmitted diseases occur more frequently than most people realize, and most STDs are increasing in prevalence. Health authorities estimate that there are about 10 million new cases in the United States each year. If you are between the ages of 15 and 55, you have about a one-in-four chance of developing a sexually transmitted disease other than AIDS during your lifetime (Gordon & Snyder, 1989). The highest incidence of STDs is found among adolescents (Krilov, 1988).

The principal types of sexually transmitted diseases are listed in Figure 13.11, along with their symptoms and modes of transmission. As you can see, most of these diseases are spread from one person to another through intercourse, oral-genital contact, or anal-genital contact. Six points are worth emphasizing.

1. You should consider *any* activity that exposes you to blood, semen, vaginal secretions, menstrual blood, urine, feces, or saliva as high-risk behavior *unless* you and your partner are in a sexually exclusive relationship and neither of you is infected (Reinisch, 1990).

2. The risk of contracting STDs is clearly related to the number of sex partners one has. The more numerous your sex partners, the greater your chances of exposure to a sexually transmitted disease.

3. Don't assume that the labels people attach to themselves (heterosexual or homosexual) accurately describe their actual sexual behavior (Reinisch, 1990). According to the director of the Kinsey Institute:

Studies of men from the general population show that more than 30% (1 out of 3) have had at least one sexual experience with another male since puberty. Three studies of homosexual men reported that between 62 and 79 percent had engaged in heterosexual intercourse. Four other studies found that 15 to 26 percent of homosexual men had been married. A recent Kinsey Institute study of lesbian women found that 74 percent had engaged in heterosexual intercourse at least once since age 18. [Reinisch, 1990, pp. 965–966]

4. People can often be carriers of sexually transmitted diseases without being aware of it. For instance, in its early stages gonorrhea may cause no readily apparent symptoms in women, and they may unknowingly transmit the disease to their partners.

5. Even when people know they have a sexually transmitted disease, they may not remain abstinent or inform their partners. Guilt and embarrassment cause many people to ignore symptoms of sexually transmitted diseases and continue their normal sexual activities (Kramer, Aral, & Curran, 1980). Close to half of the subjects in one study admitted that they had told dates that they had had fewer sex partners than was actually the case (Reinisch, 1990). People are probably even more likely to

FIGURE 13.11
Overview of common sexually transmitted diseases (STDs)
This table summarizes the symptoms and modes of transmission of 11 STDs. Note that intercourse is not required for transmission of all STDs. Many STDs can be contracted through oral-genital contact or other forms of physical intimacy. (Adapted from Crooks & Baur, 1990; Hyde, 1990.)

Sexually Transmitted Diseases (STDs)

STD	Transmission	Symptoms
Acquired immune deficiency syndrome (AIDS)	The AIDS virus is spread by coitus or anal intercourse. There is a chance the virus may also be spread by oral-genital sex, particularly if semen is swallowed. (AIDS can also be spread by nonsexual means: contaminated blood, contaminated hypodermic needles, and transmission from an infected woman to her baby during pregnancy or childbirth.)	Most people infected with the virus show no immediate symptoms; antibodies usually develop in the blood 2–8 weeks after infection. People with the virus may remain symptom-free for 5 years or more. No cure for the disease has yet been found, so once AIDS symptoms appear, death occurs within a few months to a few years.
Bacterial vaginosis	The most common causative agent, the *Gardnerella vaginalis* bacterium, is transmitted primarily by coitus.	In women, a fishy or musty-smelling thin discharge, like flour paste in consistency and usually gray. Most men are asymptomatic.
Candidiasis (yeast infection)	The *Candida albicans* fungus may accelerate growth when the chemical balance of the vagina is disturbed; it may also be transmitted through sexual interaction.	White, "cheesy" discharge; irritation of vaginal and vulvar tissue.
Trichomoniasis	The protozoan parasite *Trichomonas vaginalis* is passed through genital sexual contact or less frequently by towels, toilet seats, or bathtubs used by an infected person.	White or yellow vaginal discharge with an unpleasant odor; vulva is sore and irritated.
Chlamydial infection	The *Chlamydia trichomatis* bacterium is transmitted primarily through sexual contact. It may also be spread by fingers from one body site to another.	In men, chlamydial infection of the urethra may cause a discharge and burning during urination. Chlamydia-caused epidydimitis may produce a sense of heaviness in the affected testicle(s), inflammation of the scrotal skin, and painful swelling at the bottom of the testicle. In women, pelvic inflammatory disease caused by clamydia may disrupt menstrual periods, elevate temperature, and cause abdominal pain, nausea, vomiting, and headache.
Gonorrhea ("clap")	The *Neisseria gonorrhoeae* bacterium (gonococcus) is spread through genital, oral-genital, or genital-anal contact.	Most common symptoms in men are a cloudy discharge from the penis and burning sensations during urination. If the disease is untreated, complications may include inflammation of the scrotal skin and swelling at the base of the testicle. In women, some green or yellowish discharge is produced, but the disease commonly remains undetected. At a later stage, pelvic inflammatory disease may develop.
Syphilis	The *Treponema pallidum* bacterium (spirochete) is transmitted from open lesions during genital, oral-genital, or genital-anal contact.	*Primary stage:* A painless chancre appears at the site where the spirochetes entered the body. *Secondary stage:* The chancre disappears and a generalized skin rash develops. *Latent stage:* There may be no observable symptoms. *Tertiary stage:* Heart failure, blindness, mental disturbance, and many other symptoms may occur. Death may result.
Pubic lice ("crabs")	*Phthirus pubis*, the pubic louse, is spread easily through body contact or through shared clothing or bedding.	Persistent itching. Lice are visible and may often be located in pubic hair or other body hair.
Herpes	The genital herpes virus (HSV-2) appears to be transmitted primarily by vaginal, oral-genital, or anal-sexual intercourse. The oral herpes virus (HSV-1) is transmitted primarily by kissing.	Small red, painful bumps (papules) appear in the region of the genitals (genital herpes) or mouth (oral herpes). The papules become painful blisters that eventually rupture to form wet, open sores.
Viral hepatitis	The hepatitis B virus may be transmitted by blood, semen, vaginal secretions, and saliva. Manual, oral, or penile stimulation of the anus is strongly associated with the spread of this virus. Hepatitis A seems to be spread primarily via the fecal-oral route. Oral-anal sexual contact is a common mode of sexual transmission for hepatitis A.	Vary from nonexistent to mild, flulike symptoms to an incapacitating illness characterized by high fever, vomiting, and severe abdominal pain.
Genital warts (venereal warts)	The virus is spread primarily through genital, anal, or oral-genital interaction.	Warts are hard and yellow-gray on dry skin areas; soft pinkish red and cauliflowerlike on moist areas.

lie about homosexual activity, sex with prostitutes, and drug use (Reinisch, 1990). So don't assume that sex partners will warn you that they may be contagious.

6. Engaging in anal intercourse (especially being the receiving partner) puts one at very high risk for AIDS. Rectal tissues are very delicate and can easily be torn, so that the virus can pass through the membrane. Oral-genital sex may also transmit AIDS, particularly if semen is swallowed.

Prevention

Abstinence is the best way to minimize the risk of acquiring sexually transmitted diseases. Most people, however, consider this an unappealing and unrealistic option. Short of abstinence, the best strategy is to engage in sexual activity only in the context of a long-term relationship, so that you have an opportunity to know your partner reasonably well. Sexual interactions with casual acquaintances greatly increase your risk for STDs, including AIDS.

Talk openly about safer sexual practices with your partner. And if you don't carry the process one step further and practice what you preach, you're still at risk. Unfortunately, many people are still engaging in risky sexual behavior—a practice that no one can afford while we are in the grip of the deadly AIDS epidemic. A study of mostly heterosexual college students found little evidence that sexually active subjects had adopted "safer sex" practices, despite the fact that more than 40% of them *said* they had done so (Carroll, 1988). A slightly later study reported that condom use had increased among college women from 1975 to 1989, but found no evidence of a reduction in risky sex practices during that time (DeBuono, Zinner, Daamen, & McCormack, 1990). A recent government-sponsored nationwide survey of 10,630 heterosexuals between the ages of 18 and 75 suggests that the majority of heterosexuals are engaging in risky sex practices (Catania et al., 1992). Condoms were always used by only 17% of respondents with multiple partners, by only 13% of those with risky sex partners (partners who were HIV positive, injected drugs, were not monogamous, or had received blood transfusions), and by only 11% of untested transfusion recipients.

Safer sex practices have increased dramatically among older gay and bisexual men (Stall, Coates, & Hoff, 1988), but younger gay men may still be taking sexual risks (Griggs, 1990). Lesbians have the lowest rates of syphilis and gonorrhea among sexually active individuals, as well as extremely low rates of AIDS (Reinisch, 1990). Lesbian sexual behaviors don't typically involve penetration, so the risk of exposure to infectious organisms through breaks in oral, vaginal, or anal tissues is low. Lesbians also tend to have fewer sex partners than do other sexually active women or men. All the same, for reasons we have already mentioned, lesbians should still follow "safer sex" guidelines.

We offer the following seven suggestions for safer sex (Francoeur, 1982; Hyde, 1990; Reinisch, 1990):

- Because the AIDS virus is easily transmitted through anal intercourse, it's probably a good idea to avoid this type of sex.
- If you are not involved in a sexually exclusive relationship, always use rubber condoms. They have a good track record of preventing many STDs and offer effective protection against the AIDS virus. (Never use oil-based lubricants with rubber condoms; use water-based lubricants instead.)
- The spermicide *nonoxynol 9* has been found to be relatively effective in killing the AIDS virus (Peterman & Curran, 1986; Reinisch, 1990). Use it with a condom to make sex safer. Read the labels on spermicides or ask a pharmacist to help you find those with nonoxynol. (LifeStyles condoms are lubricated on the inside and outside with nonoxynol 9.)
- Wash your genitals with soap and warm water before and after sexual contact.
- Urinate soon after intercourse.
- Don't have sex with someone who has had many previous partners. People don't always tell the truth, so it's important to know whether a prospective partner's word can be trusted.
- Watch for sores, rashes, or discharge around the vulva or penis, or elsewhere on your body, especially the mouth. If you have cold sores, avoid kissing or oral sex.

If you have several sex partners in a year, it is important to have regular STD checkups. You will have to ask for these checkups, as most doctors and health clinics perform STD tests only when they're asked to. If you have any reason to suspect that you have an STD, find a good health clinic and get tested *as soon as possible*. It's normal to be embarrassed or afraid of getting bad news, but don't delay. Health professionals are in the business of helping people, not judging them.

Remember that the symptoms of some STDs disappear as the disease progresses. Don't make the mistake of thinking that you really don't have an STD when you might. To make really sure, have yourself tested twice. If both your tests are negative, you can stop worrying. If your test results are positive, it's essential to get the proper treatment *right away*. Notify your sex partner(s) so they can be tested immediately, too. In addition, it's important to avoid sexual intercourse and oral sex until you and your partner(s) are fully treated and a physician or clinic says you are no longer infectious.

Summary

Research on sexual behavior is particularly difficult to do because of problems in getting a representative sample and the dubious accuracy of self-report data. People vary greatly in sexual expression. One's sexual identity is made up of sexual orientation, body image, sexual values and ethics, and erotic preferences. Physiological factors such as hormones influence sexual differentiation, maturation, and anatomy more than sexual activity. Psycho-social factors appear to have more impact on sexual behavior. Sources of socialization that shape sexual identity include families, peers and schools, and the media. Because of differences in sexual socialization, sexuality usually has different meanings for males and females.

People frequently enter into sexual interactions for different reasons. Men tend to be motivated more by physical gratification, whereas emotional motives tend to be more important for women. Sexual scripts regulate the formation and evolution of sexual relationships. Variations among people in erotic preferences are also shaped by their personality traits and their attitudes. Disparities between partners in sexual interest and erotic preferences understandably lead to conflicts that necessitate negotiation. Effective communication plays an important role in satisfaction with one's sex life and with the relationship in general.

The physiology of the human sexual response was elucidated by Masters and Johnson. They analyzed the sexual response cycle into four phases: excitement, plateau, orgasm, and resolution. Women reach orgasm less consistently than men in intercourse, usually because sexual contact is too brief and because of gender differences in sexual socialization.

Sexual fantasies are normal and can play an important part in sexual arousal. Despite the traditionally negative attitudes toward masturbation in our society, self-stimulation is quite common, even among married people. A sexual episode may involve a wide range of erotic activities other than intercourse, and their importance is often underestimated, particularly by heterosexual men. Oral-genital sex has become a common element in most couples' sexual repertoire. Coitus is the most widely practiced sexual act in our society. Four coital positions are commonly used, each with its advantages and disadvantages. Sexual activities between gay men include mutual masturbation, fellatio, and, less often, anal intercourse. Lesbians engage in mutual masturbation, cunnilingus, and tribadism.

Though the prevalence and acceptability of "premarital" sex have increased, the widespread accounts of a sexual revolution appear to be exaggerated. Satisfaction with the sexual aspect of a relationship is correlated with the overall satisfaction with the relationship. Younger married couples tend to have sex about two or three times a week; frequency declines with age. Homosexual couples appear to spend more time on mutual sexual activities before moving to orgasm and communicate more with each other than heterosexual couples do. Consensual infidelity is uncommon among married couples and lesbians, and more common among gay male couples. Clandestine and ambiguous infidelity are much more prevalent forms of "extramarital" sex. Dissatisfaction, sexual discontent, curiosity, and chance attraction motivate people to get involved in sex outside of committed relationships.

Contraception and sexually transmitted diseases are two practical issues that concern many couples. For a variety of reasons, many people (especially adolescents) who do not want to conceive a child fail to use contraceptive procedures effectively, if at all. Contraceptive methods vary in effectiveness; all have advantages and disadvantages. STDs are increasing in prevalence, especially among teenagers. STDs can be transmitted unknowingly, but some people continue to have sexual relations even when they realize they are contagious. The danger of contracting STDs is higher among people who have had many sex partners. The use of condoms with spermicides containing nonoxynol 9 also decreases the risk of contracting STDs. Early treatment of STDs is important. In our Application we focus on issues that relate to enhancing sexual satisfaction and discuss advances in the understanding and treatment of sexual problems.

APPLICATION Enhancing Sexual Relationships

Are the following statements true or false?

1.

Sexual problems are very resistant to treatment.

2.

Sexual problems belong to couples rather than individuals.

3.

Most sexual problems have an organic basis.

4.

Sex therapists sometimes recommend masturbation treatment for certain types of problems.

The answers are (1) false, (2) true, (3) false, and (4) true. If you answered any of the questions incorrectly, you have misconceptions about sexual difficulties that may at some point affect your sexual relations; but you are by no means unusual. As we saw in our discussion of the results of the recent Kinsey Institute poll, misconceptions about sexuality are the norm rather than the exception. Fortunately, recent advances in our understanding of sexual functioning have yielded many useful ideas on how to improve sexual relationships.

In this Application we take a practical look at sexual problems and their possible solutions. Obviously, many readers may not be involved in a sexual relationship at present. If you're not, we'll assume that someday you will be. In the interest of simplicity, our advice is directed to heterosexual couples, but much of what we have to say is relevant to homosexual couples as well. For gay and lesbian students who want advice directed specifically to homosexual couples, we recommend Masters and Johnson's (1979) book *Homosexuality in Perspective*.

General Suggestions

Let's begin with some general ideas about how to enhance sexual relationships, drawn from several outstanding books on sexuality (Barbach, 1982; Crooks & Baur, 1990; Hyde, 1990; Reinisch, 1990). Even if you are satisfied with your sexual relations, these ideas may be useful as preventive medicine.

1. *Pursue adequate sex education.* A surprising number of people are ignorant about the realities of sexual functioning. In a book titled *Sexual Myths and Fallacies*, James McCary (1971) discusses more than 80 common miscon-

ceptions about sexuality. So the first step in promoting sexual satisfaction is to acquire accurate information about sex. The shelves of most bookstores are bulging with popular books on sex, but many of them are loaded with inaccuracies. The Recommended Readings in this chapter describe books on this topic that we think are excellent. Another good bet is to pick up a college textbook on human sexuality. Enrolling in a course on sexuality is also a good idea. More and more colleges are offering such courses today.

2. *Review your sexual value system.* Many sexual problems are derived from a negative sexual value system that encourages people to associate sex with immorality. The guilt feelings caused by such an orientation can interfere with sexual functioning. Experts on sexuality often encourage adults to examine the sources and implications of their sexual values.

3. *Communicate about sex.* Children often learn that they shouldn't talk about sex. Many people carry this feeling into adulthood and have great difficulty discussing sex even with their

partner. Good communication is extremely important in a sexual relationship. Figure 13.12 lists common problems in sexual relations reported by a sample of 100 couples (Frank, Anderson, & Rubinstein, 1978). Many of the problems reported by the couples—such as choosing an inconvenient time, too little erotic activity before intercourse, and too little tenderness afterward—are traceable largely to poor communication. Your partner is not a mind reader. You have to share your thoughts and feelings to promote mutual satisfaction. Ask questions if you have doubts about your partner's preferences. Provide candid (but diplomatic) feedback when your partner asks about your reactions. Learn to make specific requests that effectively convey your erotic preferences.

4. *Avoid goal setting.* Sexual encounters are not tests or races. Sexual relations usually work out best when people relax and enjoy themselves. Some people get overly concerned about orgasms. A grim determination to climax typically makes it harder to do so. This mental set can lead to *specta-*

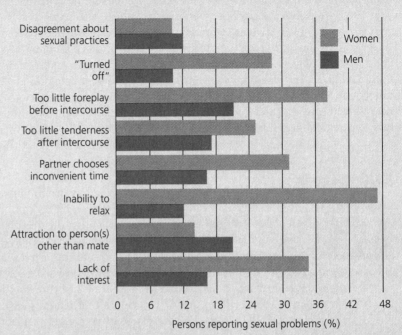

FIGURE 13.12
Common problems in sexual relations
The percentages of men and women (100 couples) who reported various types of problems in their sexual relationships are shown here. (Data from Frank et al., 1978.)

toring—a stance in which a person is too busy monitoring what is going on to enjoy it. It's better to recognize that getting there is at least half the fun.

5. *Enjoy your sexual fantasies.* As we noted earlier, the mind is the ultimate erogenous zone. Fantasizing during a sexual encounter is normal, and both sexes report that their sexual fantasies increase their excitement. Don't be afraid to use fantasy to enhance your sexual arousal. One woman's experience illustrates the potential value of both fantasy and open communication:

> "I had this sexual fantasy that kept going through my mind. I would imagine coming home after a long, hard day of classes and being met by my partner, who would proceed to take me into the bedroom and remove all my clothes. He would then pick me up and carry me into the bathroom where a tub full of hot water and bubbles awaited. The fantasy would end with us making passionate love in the bathtub with bubbles popping off around us. Finally, I shared my fantasy with him. Guess what happened when I came home after the next long day? It was even better than I had imagined!" [Quoted in Crooks & Baur, 1983, p. 234]

6. *Be selective about sex.* Sexual encounters generally work out better when you have privacy and a relaxed atmosphere, when you are well rested, and when you are enthusiastic. If you consistently have sex in bad situations, your sexual relations may not be very rewarding. Realistically, you can't count on (or insist upon) having ideal situations all the time, but you should be aware of the value of being selective. If your heart isn't in it, it may be wise to wait. It also helps to remember that it is quite common for partners to disagree about when, where, and how often they should have sex. This sort of disagreement is normal, so it should not be a source of resentment. Couples simply need to work toward reasonable compromises through open communication.

Understanding Sexual Dysfunction

Many people struggle with **sexual dysfunctions—impairments in sexual functioning that cause subjective distress.** One study of patients coming to a family practice center for medical treatment found that 75% had sexual problems of some kind (Schein, Zyzanski, Levine, & Medalie, 1988). This estimate may be a little high for the population as a whole, since some of the sexual problems may have been spin-offs from the patients' medical problems. Nonetheless, it is clear that sexual problems are more common than many people appreciate. Figure 13.13 shows the percentage of subjects in another study who reported the dysfunctions that we will discuss (Frank et al., 1978). These data—which are consistent with other estimates—suggest that roughly half of all couples are troubled by sexual problems to some degree.

Traditionally people have assumed that a sexual problem lies in one partner. Although it is convenient to refer to a man's erectile difficulties or a woman's orgasmic difficulties, research indicates that most sexual problems emerge out of partners' unique ways of relating to each other. In other words, sexual problems belong to couples rather than to individuals.

Masters and Johnson's research led them to conclude that a relatively small proportion of sexual dysfunctions have an organic basis. Most sexual problems, they maintain, are psychological in origin. Let's examine the symptoms and causes of three common sexual dysfunctions: erectile difficulties, premature ejaculation, and orgasmic difficulties (based on Levay, Weissberg, & Woods, 1981; Masters & Johnson, 1980).

Erectile difficulties occur **when a man is persistently unable to achieve or maintain an erection adequate for intercourse.** *Impotence* is the traditional name for this problem, but sex therapists have discarded this term because of its demeaning connotation. A man who has never had an erection sufficient for intercourse is said to have primary erectile difficulties. A man who has had intercourse in the past but is currently having problems achieving erections is said to have secondary erectile difficulties. The latter problem is more common and easier to overcome.

The most common cause of erectile difficulties is anxiety about sexual performance, which can undermine sexual arousal. What

FIGURE 13.13
Sexual dysfunctions in normal couples
This graph shows the prevalence of various sexual dysfunctions in a sample of 100 "normal" couples, 80% of whom reported having happy or satisfying marriages. These data indicate that the most common dysfunctions are premature ejaculation in men and secondary orgasmic difficulties in women. (Data based on Frank et al., 1978.)

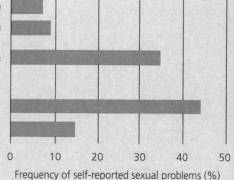

Erectile difficulties in men
Difficulty getting an erection
Difficulty maintaining an erection

Premature ejaculation in men

Orgasmic difficulties in women
Difficulty in reaching orgasm
Inability to have an orgasm

0   10   20   30   40   50
Frequency of self-reported sexual problems (%)

Understanding Human Sexuality
by Janet Shibley Hyde (McGraw-Hill, 1990)

College courses on sexuality are gradually appearing all over the country, and a host of new books to serve these courses are now available. If you can't enroll in a course on sexuality, you may want to read one of the better textbooks. Janet Shibley Hyde's *Understanding Human Sexuality* is an outstanding candidate. Hyde's text is accurate, thorough, up-to-date, well organized, and written in an engaging, highly readable style. What sets it apart from other texts is its clarity and sensitivity to readers' personal needs. It discusses the interpersonal aspects of sex without getting bogged down in physiology. Other excellent sexuality texts of similar quality include *Our Sexuality*, by Robert Crooks and Karla Baur (Benjamin/Cummings, 1990), and *Understanding Sexuality*, by Adelaide Haas and Kurt Haas (Times Mirror/Mosby, 1990). Any of these three books provides an excellent introduction to the realities of human sexual expression.

> Throughout most of recorded history, at least until about 100 years ago, religion (and rumor) provided most of the information that people had about sexuality. . . . It was against this background of religious understandings of sexuality that the scientific study of sex began in the late nineteenth century, although, of course, religious notions continue to influence our ideas about sexuality to the present day. . . . The scientific study of sex has still not emerged as a separate, unified academic discipline like biology or psychology or sociology. Rather, it tends to be interdisciplinary—a joint effort by biologists, psychologists, sociologists, anthropologists, and physicians. In a way, this is a major virtue in our current approach to understanding sexuality, since it gives us a better view of humans in all their sexual complexity. [pp. 3, 7]

leads to this troublesome anxiety? Its cause can range from a man's doubts about his virility to conflict about the morality of his sexual desires. Anxiety about sexual performance can also be caused by an overreaction to a specific incident in which a man cannot achieve sexual arousal. Many temporary conditions, such as fatigue, worry about work, an argument with his partner, a depressed mood, or too much alcohol can cause such incidents. If either partner turns the incident into a major catastrophe, the man may begin to get unduly concerned about his sexual response, and the seeds of anxiety may be sown.

Recent research suggests that physiological factors may contribute to erectile difficulties more often than Masters and Johnson's data suggested. A host of common diseases (such as diabetes) can produce erectile problems (Melman & Leiter, 1983). So can many of the medications used to treat physical illnesses (Buffum et al., 1981). Experts now estimate that organic factors may contribute to as many as one-quarter of all cases of erectile dysfunction.

Premature ejaculation **occurs when sexual relations are impaired because a man consistently reaches orgasm too quickly.** What is "too quickly"? Obviously, any time estimate is hopelessly arbitrary. The critical consideration is the subjective feelings of the partners. If either partner feels that the ejaculation is persistently too fast for sexual gratification, they have a problem.

What causes premature ejaculation? Some men simply don't exert much effort to prolong intercourse. Most of these men do not view their ejaculations as premature, even if their partners do. Among men who are concerned about their partners' satisfaction, problems may occur because their early sexual experiences emphasized the desirability of a rapid climax. Furtive sex in the back seat of a car, quick efforts at masturbation, and experiences with prostitutes are situations in which men typically attempt to achieve orgasm very quickly. A pattern of rapid ejaculation established by these formative experiences may become entrenched.

Orgasmic difficulties **occur when people experience sexual arousal but have persistent problems in achieving orgasm.** When this problem occurs in men, it is often called retarded ejaculation. The traditional name for this problem in women, *frigidity*, is no longer used because of its derogatory implications. Since this problem is much more common among women, we'll limit our discussion to them. As with erectile difficulties, it is useful to distinguish between primary and secondary difficulties. A woman who has never experienced an orgasm through any kind of stimulation is said to have primary orgasmic difficulties. Women who formerly experienced orgasms but are unable to do so now are said to have secondary orgasmic difficulties. Women who seek treatment because they experience orgasm only through noncoital techniques (oral, manual, and self-stimulation) are in the latter category. Although primary orgasmic difficulties may seem to be the more severe problem, they are actually more responsive to treatment than secondary orgasmic difficulties.

A negative attitude toward sex is one of the leading causes of orgasmic difficulties in women. Women who have been taught that sex is dirty are likely to approach it with shame and guilt. This negative attitude can inhibit sexual expression, undermine arousal, and impair orgasmic responsiveness.

A lack of authentic affection for one's partner seems to undermine sexual arousal in women more than in men. Thus women sometimes have orgasmic difficulties when the emotional closeness in their relationship deteriorates. Arousal may also be inhibited by

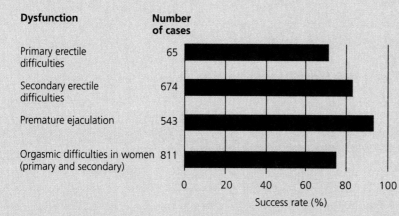

Dysfunction	Number of cases
Primary erectile difficulties	65
Secondary erectile difficulties	674
Premature ejaculation	543
Orgasmic difficulties in women (primary and secondary)	811

Success rate (%)

FIGURE 13.14
Success rates reported by Masters and Johnson in their treatment of sexual dysfunctions
This figure shows the success rates for cases treated between 1959 and 1985. Treatment was categorized as successful only if the change in sexual function was clear and enduring. The minimum follow-up period was two years, and in many cases it was five years. (Data from Masters et al., 1988.)

fear of pregnancy or excessive concern about achieving orgasm. Some women have orgasmic difficulties because intercourse tends to be too brief or because their partners are unconcerned about their needs and preferences. Another consideration is that intercourse provides less direct genital stimulation for women than it does for men. Thus some women do not experience orgasm simply because they and their partners haven't explored sexual activities that they might find more rewarding than intercourse.

Coping with Specific Problems

With the advent of modern sex therapy, sexual problems no longer have to be chronic sources of frustration and shame. *Sex therapy involves the professional treatment of sexual dysfunctions.* With professional assistance, most sexual difficulties can be resolved (Arentewicz & Schmidt, 1983). Masters and Johnson have reported very high success rates for their treatments of specific problems, as Figure 13.14 shows. Some critics argue that the cure rates reported by Masters and Johnson are overly optimistic in comparison with those reported by other investigators (Zilbergeld & Evans, 1980). Nonetheless, there is a consensus that sexual dysfunctions can be conquered with encouraging regularity.

Of course, sex therapy isn't for everyone. It can be expensive and time-consuming, and in some places, it is difficult to find.

However, many people can benefit from ideas drawn from the professional practice of sex therapy (Hartman & Fithian, 1974; Kaplan, 1979, 1983; Masters & Johnson, 1980).

Erectile Difficulties

The key to overcoming psychologically based erectile difficulties is to decrease the man's performance anxiety. It is a good idea for a couple to discuss the problem openly. The woman should be reassured that the difficulty does not indicate the man's lack of affection. Obviously, it is crucial for her to be emotionally supportive rather than hostile and demanding.

Masters and Johnson use a procedure called sensate focus in the treatment of erectile difficulties and other dysfunctions. *Sensate focus is an exercise in which partners take turns pleasuring each other with guided verbal feedback while certain kinds of stimulation are temporarily forbidden.* One partner stimulates the other, who simply lies back and enjoys it while giving instructions and feedback about what feels good. At first the partners are not allowed to touch each other's genitals or to attempt intercourse. This prohibition should free the man from feelings of pressure to "perform." Over a number of sessions the couple gradually include genital stimulation in their sensate focus, but intercourse is still banned. With the pressure to perform removed, many men spontaneously get erections. Repeated arousals should begin to restore

the man's confidence in his sexual response. As his confidence returns, the couple move on gradually to attempts at intercourse.

Premature Ejaculation

Men troubled by premature ejaculation range from those who climax almost instantly to those who cannot last the time that their partner requires. In the latter case, simply slowing down the tempo of intercourse may help. Sometimes the problem can be solved indirectly by abandonment of the traditional assumption that orgasm should come through intercourse. If the female partner enjoys oral or manual stimulation, it can be used to provide her with an orgasm either before or after intercourse. This strategy can reduce the performance pressure on the male partner, and couples may find that intercourse starts to last longer.

The problem of instant ejaculation is more challenging to remedy. Sex therapists rely primarily on certain sensate focus exercises in which the man is repeatedly brought to the verge of orgasm. These exercises can gradually help a man to recognize preorgasmic sensations and improve his control over his ejaculation response.

Orgasmic Difficulties

Since orgasmic difficulties among women are often due to negative attitudes toward sex, a restructuring of values frequently is the key to conquering the problem. Therapeutic discussions may be geared toward helping nonorgasmic women reduce their ambivalence about sexual expression. Sex

RECOMMENDED READING

Making Love: How to Be Your Own Sex Therapist

by Patricia Raley (Dial, 1976; Avon, 1980)

With the contemporary emphasis on achieving sexual satisfaction, more and more people are interested in reading books designed to help them cope with sexual problems or spice up their sex life. Many of the available books are of poor quality, but some are worthwhile. This is a very personal book that begins by having you take a look at your sexual history and attitudes. It is loaded with probing personal questions. The book devotes a good deal of attention to confronting sexual problems. It is nicely illustrated with many explicit and erotic photos. Furthermore, it does not assume that you are heterosexual.

> Poets, doctors and lexicographers have all taken a turn at describing orgasm, but there is no universally accepted definition. That's probably because it depends on individual expectations and experience. . . . Take the description of an orgasm being like a sneeze, for instance. There is a tricky premonition that it is coming, a muscular spasm when it does come, and a sense of relief afterward. . . . Although you might use this description for someone who has never had an orgasm, you'd have to add that orgasms are not the same as sneezes. People just don't look forward to sneezing the way they do to having an orgasm. They don't count sneezes and they usually aren't very concerned about the sneezes of others. [1976, p. 125]

therapists often suggest that women who have never had an orgasm try to have one through masturbation. Many women achieve orgasm in intercourse after an initial breakthrough with self-stimulation (LoPiccolo & Lobitz, 1972).

Treatment for orgasmic difficulties sometimes focuses on a couple's relationship problems more than on sexual functioning as such. Efforts are often made to improve partners' communication skills. Couples may discuss the complexities of initiating sexual overtures and the need to communicate openly about sexual turn-offs and turn-ons.

For reasons we have discussed earlier, it is not uncommon for women, especially sexually inexperienced ones, to be troubled by orgasmic difficulties only in the context of intercourse. If partners don't assume that orgasm must come through coitus, this need not be seen as a problem. However, many couples feel that it is important for the woman to experience orgasm during intercourse. Sensate focus exercises can help them to realize this goal. The guided verbal feedback from the woman can greatly improve her partner's appreciation of her unique erotic preferences.

CHAPTER 13 REVIEW

Key Learning Objectives

1. Describe four key aspects of sexual identity.
2. Discuss how hormones influence sexual differentiation and sexual behavior.
3. Discuss how families, peers, schools, and the media shape sexual behavior.
4. Discuss gender differences in sexual socialization and how they affect individuals in heterosexual and homosexual relationships.
5. Describe five common sexual scripts in our culture and research on initiating and refusing sex.
6. Discuss how personality and attitudes influence sexuality.
7. Describe four common barriers to communication about sex.
8. Describe the four phases of the human sexual response cycle.
9. Discuss gender differences in patterns of orgasm and some reasons for them.
10. Discuss fantasy, touching, and kissing as techniques of sexual arousal.
11. Discuss masturbation, coitus, and sex between homosexual couples.
12. Discuss the so-called sexual revolution.
13. Summarize the discussion of "premarital" sex and reactions to initial coitus.
14. Summarize the discussion on sex in dating couples.
15. Compare and contrast sexual behavior in married couples and committed homosexual couples.
16. Summarize evidence on infidelity in committed relationships.
17. Describe common barriers to effective contraception and discuss the merits of condoms and the pill.
18. Describe various types of STDs and discuss their prevalence and means of transmission.
19. List seven suggestions for safer sexual practices.
20. List six general suggestions for enhancing sexual relationships.
21. Discuss the nature, prevalence, and causes of sexual dysfunctions.
22. Describe the strategies for coping with three common sexual problems.

Key Terms

anal intercourse
androgens
bisexuals
coitus
cunnilingus
erectile difficulties
erogenous zones
erotophiles
erotophobes
estrogens
fellatio
gonads
heterosexuals

homosexuals
orgasm
orgasmic difficulties
premature ejaculation
refractory period
sensate focus
sex therapy
sexual dysfunctions
sexual identity
sexually transmitted disease (STD)
social scripts
vasocongestion

Key People

Alfred Kinsey
William Masters and Virginia Johnson
June Machover Reinisch

14 Psychology and Physical Health

HE PATTERNS OF ILLNESS FOUND in a society tend to fluctuate over time, and there have been some interesting trends in our society during the last century or so. Before the 20th century, the principal threats to health were *contagious diseases*, caused by invasions of the body by specific infectious agents. Because such diseases can be transmitted readily from one person to another, people used to live in fear of epidemics. The leading causes of death were such diseases as the plague, smallpox, typhoid fever, influenza, diphtheria, yellow fever, malaria, cholera, tuberculosis, polio, and scarlet fever. Today the incidences of these diseases have so far declined that none of them is among the leading killers in the United States (see Figure 14.1).

What neutralized these dreaded diseases? The general public tends to attribute the conquest of contagious diseases to advances in medical treatment. Although progress in medicine certainly played a role, Grob (1983) marshals evidence that the significance of such progress has been overrated. Of greater significance, according to Grob, are such trends as (1) improvements in nutrition, (2) improvements in public hygiene and sanitation (water filtration, treatment of sewage, and so forth), and (3) evolutionary changes in our resistance to the diseases. Whatever the causes, infectious diseases are no longer the major threats to physical health in the industrialized nations of the world (many remain quite prevalent in Third World countries).

Unfortunately, the void left by contagious diseases has been filled all too quickly by various *chronic diseases*—illnesses that develop gradually over years (refer to Figure 14.1). Psychosocial factors, such as lifestyle and stress, play much larger roles in the development of chronic diseases than they do in contagious diseases. Today the three leading chronic diseases (heart disease, cancer, and stroke) account for nearly two-thirds of the deaths in the United States. Moreover, these mortality statistics reveal only the tip of the iceberg. Many less serious illnesses (such as headaches, backaches, skin disorders, asthma, and ulcers) are also influenced by psychosocial factors.

FIGURE 14.1
Changing patterns of illness
Trends in the death rates for various diseases during the 20th century reveal that contagious diseases (shown in green) have declined as threats to our lives. However, the death rates for stress-related chronic diseases (shown in red) have remained quite high. The pie chart (inset), which depicts the percentages of deaths caused by the leading killers today, shows the results of these trends: three chronic diseases (heart disease, cancer, and stroke) account for 64% of all deaths.

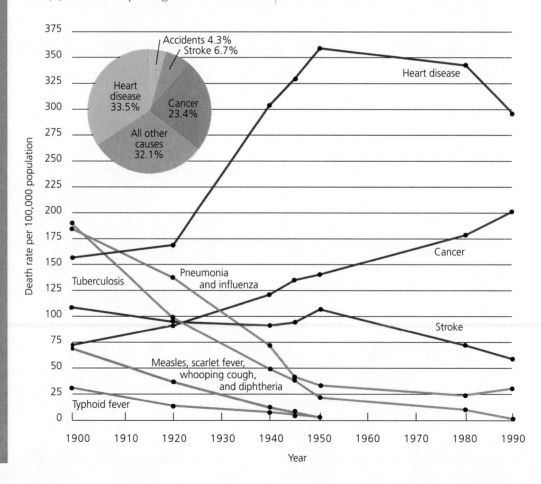

In light of these dramatic trends, it is not surprising that the way we think about illness is changing. Illness has traditionally been thought of as a purely biological phenomenon produced by an infectious agent or some internal physical breakdown. The shifting patterns of disease and new findings relating stress to physical illness have rocked the foundation of this biological model. In its place a new model is gradually emerging. **The *biopsychosocial model* holds that physical illness is caused by a complex interaction of biological, psychological, and sociocultural factors.** This model does not suggest that biological factors are unimportant; it simply asserts that they operate in a psychosocial context that can also be very influential.

The growing recognition that psychological factors influence our physical health has led to the emergence of a new specialty within psychology. ***Health psychology* is concerned with how psychosocial factors relate to the promotion and maintenance of health, and with the causation, prevention, and treatment of illness.** The Health Psychology division of the American Psychological Association was founded only in 1978. Our focus in this chapter will be on this exciting new domain of health psychology.

Psychological factors can influence our physical health in three general ways (Krantz, Glass, Contrada, & Miller, 1981):

1. *Direct effects of stress on physiological processes.* As we discussed in Chapter 3, stress tends to elicit wide-ranging physiological arousal, which can lead to bodily changes that may be damaging in the long run.

2. *Health-impairing habits.* Many habitual patterns of behavior can increase our vulnerability to various kinds of illnesses. There is ample evidence that the likelihood of developing heart disease, for instance, is influenced by cigarette smoking, physical inactivity, poor diet, and other aspects of lifestyle.

3. *Reactions to illness.* Our behavioral response to symptoms of illness can have a decided impact on our health. Many people delay seeking needed medical treatment and so increase their risk of serious illness. Furthermore, a surprisingly large number of people ignore their doctors' advice or are unable to comply successfully with their doctors' instructions.

The three ways in which behavior can influence physical health will serve as our organizing scheme in this chapter. The chapter's first section analyzes the link between stress and illness. The second section examines common health-impairing habits, such as smoking and overeating. The third section discusses how our reactions to illness can affect our health. In the Application we will expand on a particular type of health-impairing habit—the use of "recreational drugs."

Stress, Personality, and Illness

 s we noted in Chapter 3, during the 1970s researchers began to uncover new links between stress and a variety of diseases previously believed to be purely physiological in origin. Let's look at the evidence on the apparent link between stress and physical illness and discuss how personality factors contribute to this relationship.

Type A Behavior, Hostility, and Heart Disease

Heart disease accounts for nearly 40% of the deaths in the United States every year. ***Coronary heart disease* involves a reduction in blood flow from the coronary arteries, which supply the heart with blood.** This type of heart disease causes about 90% of heart-related deaths.

Atherosclerosis is the principal cause of coronary disease. ***Atherosclerosis* involves a gradual narrowing of the coronary arteries.** A buildup of fatty deposits and other debris on the inner walls of the arteries is the usual cause of this narrowing (see Figure 14.2). Atherosclerosis progresses slowly over periods of years. Narrowed coronary arteries may eventually cause the heart to be deprived temporarily of adequate blood flow, causing brief chest pain. This condition is known as *angina pectoris*. If a coronary artery is blocked completely (by a blood clot, for instance), the abrupt interruption of blood flow can produce a full-fledged heart attack, known as a *myocardial infarction*.

In the 1960s and 1970s a pair of cardiologists, Meyer Friedman and Ray Rosenman (1974), were investigating the causes of coronary disease. Originally they were interested in the usual factors that were thought to produce a high risk of heart attack: smoking, obesity, physical inactivity, and so forth. Although they found that these factors were important, they eventually recognized that a piece of the puzzle was missing. Many people smoked constantly, got little exercise, and were seriously overweight, yet avoided the ravages of heart disease.

FIGURE 14.2
Atherosclerosis
(a) Blood flows through a normal artery. (b) Fatty deposits on the walls of the artery have narrowed the path for blood flow. (c) Advanced atherosclerosis. In this situation, a blood clot may suddenly block the flow of blood through the artery.

(a)

(b)
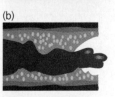

(c)
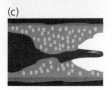

Chicago Bears coach Mike Ditka suffered a heart attack that was probably due in part to his competitive, easy-to-anger, hard-driving Type A personality.

At the same time, other people who seemed to be in much better shape in regard to these risk factors experienced the misfortune of a heart attack.

Gradually Friedman and Rosenman unraveled the riddle. What was their explanation for these perplexing findings? Stress. They found a connection between coronary risk and a pattern of behavior they called the *Type A personality*, which involves self-imposed stress and intense reactions to stress.

Elements of Type A Behavior

According to Friedman and Rosenman (1974) people can be divided into two basic types: Type A and Type B. **The *Type A* personality includes three elements: (1) a strong competitive orientation, (2) impatience and time urgency, and (3) anger and hostility.** Type A's are ambitious, hard-driving perfectionists who

are exceedingly time-conscious. They routinely try to do several things at once. A Type A person may watch TV, talk on the phone, work on a report, and eat dinner all at the same time. Type A's are so impatient that they frequently finish others' sentences for them. They fidget frantically over the briefest delays. Often they are highly competitive, achievement-oriented workaholics who drive themselves with many deadlines. They speak rapidly and emphatically. They are cynical about life and hostile toward others. They are easily irritated and get angry quickly. In contrast, **the *Type B personality* is marked by relatively relaxed, patient, easygoing, amicable behavior.** Type B's are less hurried, less competitive, and less easily angered than Type A's.

The strength of one's Type A tendencies can be measured by either structured interviews or questionnaires. There is quite a bit of debate about the best method for assessing Type A behavior (Matthews, 1982). The checklist in Figure 14.3 lists some questions that are representative of those used in measurements of Type A behavior. The Type A personality is seen less frequently in women than in men, but women who display it appear to be as much at risk for coronary disease as Type A men (Haynes, Feinleib, & Eaker, 1983).

Which aspects of Type A behavior are most strongly related to increased coronary risk? Are competitiveness, time urgency, and hostility equally important? Many researchers believe that hostility may be more important here than other elements of the Type A pattern (Booth-Kewley & Friedman, 1987; Smith & Pope, 1990; Williams & Barefoot, 1988). Investigators have been particularly impressed by the apparent relationship between *cynical hostility* and coronary disease, hypertension, and early mortality. People high in cynical hostility are moody, suspicious, resentful, and distrusting. They are quick to anger and to criticize others. When they get upset they tend to show relatively strong physiological reactions. They exhibit elevated heart rate and blood pressure reactivity (Smith & Brown, 1991) and elevated secretions of stress hormones (Pope & Smith, 1991). More research is needed and the evidence is far from conclusive (Rosenman, 1991), but cynical hostility may prove to be the most toxic element of the Type A syndrome.

FIGURE 14.3
The Type A personality
The ten questions shown here highlight some of the behavioral traits associated with the Type A personality.

Measuring the Type A Personality

You can use the checklist below to *estimate* the likelihood that you might be a Type A personality. However, the checklist should be regarded as providing only a rough estimate, because Friedman and Rosenman (1974) emphasize that *how* you answer certain questions in their interview is often more significant than the answers themselves. Nonetheless, if you answer "yes" to a majority of the items below, you may want to consider reading their book *Type A Behavior and Your Heart*.

_____ 1. Do you find it difficult to restrain yourself from hurrying others' speech (finishing their sentences for them)?

_____ 2. Do you often try to do more than one thing at a time (such as eat and read simultaneously)?

_____ 3. Do you often feel guilty if you use extra time to relax?

_____ 4. Do you tend to get involved in a great number of projects at once?

_____ 5. Do you find yourself racing through yellow lights when you drive?

_____ 6. Do you need to win in order to derive enjoyment from games and sports?

_____ 7. Do you generally move, walk, and eat rapidly?

_____ 8. Do you agree to take on too many responsibilities?

_____ 9. Do you detest waiting in lines?

_____ 10. Do you have an intense desire to better your position in life and impress others?

Evaluating the Risk

How strong is the link between Type A personality and coronary risk? Friedman and his associates originally estimated that Type A's were six times as prone to heart attack as Type B's. At the other extreme, some studies have failed to find an association between Type A behavior and coronary risk (Ragland & Brand, 1988; Shekelle et al., 1985). What can we make of these inconsistent findings? Miller and his associates (1991) have demonstrated convincingly that most of the studies that have found no link between Type A behavior and coronary disease have suffered from one or more of several methodological limitations (chief among them is poor sample selection). Nonetheless, the mixed findings suggest that the relationship between Type A behavior and coronary risk is more modest than it was thought to be. As a whole, the data suggest that the increased coronary risk for Type A's is perhaps double that for Type B's (Weaver & Rodnick, 1986). The modest size of this relationship probably means that Type A behavior increases coronary risk for only a portion of the population. Perhaps it makes a difference only among those who exhibit certain other risk factors (a genetic predisposition to heart disease, for example).

The health risks associated with Type A behavior may not be confined to heart disease. Recent studies have found a positive correlation between Type A behavior and the incidence of various minor illnesses (Suls & Marco, 1990). There is reason to believe that the Type A syndrome may be part of a *generic* disease-prone personality that predisposes people to a diverse array of health problems (Friedman & Booth-Kewley, 1987).

Explaining the Connection

Why is Type A behavior associated with coronary risk and perhaps other health problems? Research on the Type A syndrome has uncovered several possible explanations.

First, Type A individuals appear to exhibit greater physiological reactivity than Type B's (Krantz & Manuck, 1984; Smith & Brown, 1991). The frequent ups and downs in heart rate and blood pressure may cause wear and tear on their cardiovascular systems.

Second, Type A's probably create more stress for themselves than for others (Byrne & Rosenman, 1986). Their competitiveness may lead them to put themselves under a lot of pressure and their hostility may provoke many arguments and conflicts. In accord with this line of thinking, Smith, Pope, et al. (1988) found that subjects high in hostility reported more hassles, more negative life events, more marital conflict, and more work-related stress than subjects who were lower in hostility.

Third, we learned in Chapter 3 that social support promotes health and buffers the effects of stress, but people high in hostility and Type A behavior tend to have less social support than others (Hardy & Smith, 1988; Houston & Kelly, 1989). Their quick tempers and antagonistic ways of relating to people probably undermine the support that might otherwise be available from family, friends, and colleagues.

Fourth, perhaps because of their cynicism and their tendency to push themselves to work hard, Type A's tend to exhibit health habits that are less than ideal. In comparison with others they drink more alcohol, get less exercise, and ignore symptoms of fatigue more often (Carver, Diamond, & Humphries, 1985; Leiker & Hailey, 1988). Each of these considerations could contribute to an increased risk for coronary disease, as well as a variety of other health problems.

In sum, there are a variety of plausible explanations for the connection between the

"While you've been learning to relax, Tom, I'm afraid a less enlightened 'Type A' personality got your job."

Type A syndrome and heart disease. With all these mechanisms at work, it's not surprising that Type A behavior is associated with increased coronary risk. What's surprising is that the association isn't even stronger.

Modifying Type A Behavior

Can Type A's be trained to mend their ways and reduce their risk for heart disease? Yes, there is some evidence that coronary risk can be reduced by therapeutic programs that decrease subjects' Type A behavior (Powell et al., 1984). Such programs train Type A persons to talk and move more slowly, to do only one thing at a time, to take life less seriously, to allow themselves to lose in competitive endeavors, to wait in lines patiently, to control their anger, and so forth. Unfortunately, however, the Type A pattern of behavior turns out to be quite resistant to modification (Rosenman & Chesney, 1982). Our competitive Western culture tends to value and reward Type A behavior. Type A habits that are developed over a lifetime are deeply entrenched and are given up only very reluctantly, despite their dire consequences.

Cancer

If there is a single word that can strike terror into most of our hearts, it is probably *cancer*. We generally view cancer as the most sinister, tragic, loathsome, and unbearable of diseases. In reality, cancer is actually a *collection* of more than 100 closely related diseases that vary in their characteristics and amenability to treatment.

Cancer refers to malignant cell growth, which may occur in many organ systems in the body. The core problem in cancer is that cells begin to reproduce in a rapid, disorganized fashion. As this reproduction process lurches out of control, the teeming new cells clump together to form tumors. If this wild growth continues unabated, the spreading tumors create tissue damage and begin to interfere with normal functioning in the affected organ systems.

The causes of cancer are not well understood, in part because different factors appear to contribute to different types of cancer. Exposure to carcinogens—cancer-promoting agents, such as tobacco and radiation—clearly plays a very important role (Greenwald & Sondik, 1986). Most experts believe that a modest genetic predisposition is involved. Deficiencies in immune functioning are also thought to contribute to its occurrence. However, the evidence supporting these hypotheses is far from clear (Barofsky, 1981).

The research linking stress to cancer is thought-provoking but hardly definitive. Some studies *have* found a connection between high stress, as measured by the Social Readjustment Rating Scale (SRRS), and the onset of cancer (for example, Jacobs & Charles, 1980). Generally, however, the results of these kinds of investigation have been very inconsistent (Cooper, 1984). There is ample evidence that experimentally induced stress can affect the development of cancer in laboratory animals, but the relevance of such research to humans is difficult to judge (Sklar & Anisman, 1981).

Many studies have attempted to ascertain whether there is a *cancer-prone personality*, which might reflect unsuccessful patterns of coping with stress. These studies have yielded some intriguing threads of consistency, suggesting that lonely, depressed people who have difficulty expressing anger and hostility may have an elevated risk for cancer (Cox & Mackay, 1982; Dattore, Shontz, & Coyne, 1980; Eysenck, 1988; LeShan, 1966; Temoshok, 1987). These studies must be viewed with caution, however, given the possibility that one's personality may change after the discovery that one has cancer (Scherg, 1987). Furthermore, the personality traits tentatively linked to cancer vulnerability may not be specific to cancer. The same traits have been linked to an elevated risk for a variety of diseases, including coronary disease, asthma, and arthritis (Friedman & Booth-Kewley, 1987)

Thus the evidence linking stress, coping, and personality to cancer is weak and ambiguous. This weakness may simply reflect our general inability to pin down the causes of this very complicated and mysterious ailment. Or it may mean that the contribution of psychological factors to the development of cancer is small and marginal. Future research should shed more light on this important question.

Other Diseases

The development of questionnaires to measure life stress has allowed researchers to look for correlations between stress and a variety of diseases. These researchers have uncovered many connections between stress and illness. Baker (1982) found an association between life stress and the onset of rheumatoid arthritis, for example, in a sample of female patients. Williams and Deffenbacher (1983) found that life stress was correlated with the number of vaginal (yeast) infections that female students reported in the past year. Other investigators exposed quarantined volunteers to respiratory viruses that cause the common cold and found that those under high stress were more likely to be infected by the viruses (Cohen, Tyrrell, & Smith, 1991). Researchers have also found an association between high stress and hypertension (high blood pressure) in cultures as disparate as India (Lal, Ahuja, & Madhukar, 1982) and the United States (Egan, Kogan, Garber, & Jarrett, 1983).

These are just a handful of representative studies relating stress to physical diseases. Figure 14.4 provides a longer list of health problems that have been linked to stress. Many of these stress/illness connections are based on very tentative or inconsistent findings, but the sheer length and diversity of the list is remarkable.

The studies described thus far have looked at relations between stress and *specific* diseases. Many studies have also looked at the relationship between stress and the occurrence of illness of any kind. Typically these studies have found significant correlations between high stress and a high incidence of physical illness in general (Holmes & Masuda, 1974). Why should stress increase our risk for many kinds of illness? A partial answer may lie in our immune functioning.

Effects on Immune Functioning

The apparent link between stress and illness raises the possibility that stress may undermine the functioning of our immune systems. **The *immune response* involves the body's defensive reaction to invasion by bacteria, viral agents, or other foreign substances.** Our immune response works to protect us from many forms of disease. Immune reactions are multifaceted, but they depend heavily on actions initiated by specialized white blood cells, called *lymphocytes*.

A wealth of studies indicate that experimentally induced stress can impair immune functioning *in animals* (Ader & Cohen, 1984). Stressors such as crowding, shock, and restraint reduce various aspects of lymphocyte reactivity in laboratory animals.

Studies by Janice Kiecolt-Glaser and her

FIGURE 14.4
Stress and health problems
The onset or progress of the health problems listed here may be affected by stress. The evidence is fragmentary in many instances, but the number and diversity of problems on this list are alarming.

Health Problems That May Be Linked to Stress	
Health problem	Representative evidence
Common cold	Totman, Kiff, Reed, & Craig (1980)
Peptic ulcers	Cobb & Rose (1973)
Asthma	Plutchik, Williams, Jerrett, Karasu, & Kane (1978)
Headaches	Featherstone & Beitman (1984)
Menstrual discomfort	Siegel, Johnson, & Sarason (1979)
Vaginal infections	Williams & Deffenbacher (1983)
Genital herpes	VanderPlate, Aral, & Magder (1988)
Skin disorders	Brown (1972)
Rheumatoid arthritis	Baker (1982)
Chronic back pain	Holmes (1979)
Female reproductive problems	Fries, Nillius, & Petersson (1974)
Diabetes	Bradley (1979)
Complications of pregnancy	Georgas, Giakoumaki, Georgoulias, Koumandakis, & Kaskarelis (1984)
Hernias	Rahe & Holmes (1965)
Glaucoma	Cohen & Hajioff (1972)
Hyperthyroidism	Weiner (1978)
Hemophilia	Buxton, Arkel, Lagos, Deposito, Lowenthal, & Simring (1981)
Tuberculosis	Wolf & Goodell (1968)
Leukemia	Greene & Swisher (1969)
Stroke	Stevens, Turner, Rhodewalt, & Talbot (1984)
Appendicitis	Creed (1989)
Multiple sclerosis	Grant, McDonald, Patterson, & Trimble (1989)
Periodontal disease	Green, Tryon, Marks, & Huryn (1986)
Hypertension	Egan, Kogan, Garber, & Jarrett (1983)

FIGURE 14.5
The stress/illness correlation
The association between stress and illness that has been found in thousands of studies suggests that stress causes illness. The evidence as a whole would probably lead most health psychologists to accept the assertion that stress often contributes to the causation of illness. Some critics argue, however, that the stress-illness correlation could reflect other causal processes. One or more aspects of personality, physiology, or memory may contribute to the correlation between stress and illness. (This complex issue is discussed further in Chapter 3.)

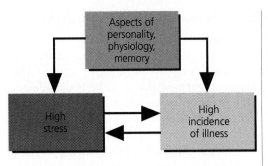

colleagues (1984) have also related stress to suppressed immunal activity *in humans*. In one study, medical students provided researchers with blood samples so that their immune responses could be assessed. The students provided the baseline sample a month before final exams and contributed the "high-stress" sample on the first day of their finals. The subjects also responded to the SRRS as a measure of recent stress. Reduced levels of immune activity were found during the extremely stressful finals week. Reduced immune activity was also correlated with higher scores on the SRRS.

Other studies have found evidence of reduced immune activity among people who scored relatively high on a stress scale measuring daily hassles (Levy et al., 1989), among recently bereaved women (Irwin et al., 1987), among recently divorced or separated men (Kiecolt-Glaser et al., 1988), and among people struggling with the stress of loneliness (Glaser, Kiecolt-Glaser, Speicher, & Holliday 1985). Thus scientists are beginning to assemble some impressive evidence that stress can temporarily impair our immune functioning. Suppression of our immune response may be the key to many of the links between stress and illness.

Accidents and Injuries

The role of stress in accidents has not attracted much publicity, but research on this issue is remarkably consistent. Nearly all the studies find that high stress is associated with an increased incidence of personal accidents. Among other things, stress has been shown to be related to the likelihood of industrial accidents (Levenson, Hirschfeld, Hirschfeld, & Dzubay, 1983), automobile accidents (Isherwood, Adam, & Hornblow, 1982), and sports injuries among high school athletes (Smith, Smoll, & Ptacek, 1990).

The associations between stress and accidents have been modest, but the consistency of the evidence suggests that stress elevates the probability of an accident for at least a portion

of the population. Our analysis of the effects of stress in Chapter 3 suggests some possible explanations for this relationship. The emotional arousal generated by stress may lead people to drive their cars aggressively (and dangerously), work too fast on the job, become reckless on the football field, and so forth. Emotional arousal can also impair cognitive functioning, with resultant narrowed attention, distractibility, or poor judgment. Any of these effects could increase accident-proneness in a variety of settings. And when stress elicits either anger or dejection, people may simply become more careless.

Conclusions

In summary, a wealth of evidence suggests that stress influences our physical health. Virtually all of the relevant research is correlational, however, so it cannot demonstrate conclusively that stress *causes* illness (Brett et al., 1990; Watson & Pennebaker, 1989). The association between stress and illness could be due to a third variable. Perhaps some aspect of personality or some type of physiological predisposition makes people overly prone to interpret events as stressful *and* overly prone to interpret unpleasant physical sensations as symptoms of illness (see Figure 14.5).

Critics of this research note that many of the studies employed research designs that may have inflated the apparent link between stress and illness (Schroeder & Costa, 1984). For example, researchers often have subjects make after-the-fact reports of how much stress and illness they endured during the last year or two. If some subjects have a tendency to recall more stress than others *and* to recall more illness than others, their better memories would artificially increase the correlation between stress and illness.

In spite of methodological problems favoring inflated correlations, the research in this area consistently indicates that the *strength* of the relationship between stress and health is modest. The correlations typically fall in the .20s and .30s. Clearly, stress is not an irresistible force that produces inevitable effects on our health. As we saw in Chapter 3, some people handle stress better than others, and stress is only one actor on a crowded stage. A complex network of biopsychosocial factors influence our health, including genetic endowment, exposure to infectious agents and environmental toxins, nutrition, exercise, alcohol and drug use, smoking, use of medical care, cooperation with medical advice, and current health status. In the next section we'll discuss some of these factors as we examine health-impairing habits and lifestyles.

Habits, Lifestyles, and Health

Some people seem determined to dig an early grave for themselves. They do precisely those things they have been warned are particularly bad for their health. Some people drink heavily even though they know they're corroding their liver. Others eat all the wrong foods even though they know they're increasing their risk for a heart attack. Such downright self-destructive behavior is much more common than most people realize. In fact, research reveals that *chronic self-destructiveness* is a measurable personality trait that is related to a variety of potentially harmful behaviors, from driving recklessly (as reflected by traffic tickets) to postponing important medical tests (Kelley et al., 1985).

It may seem puzzling that people behave in self-destructive ways. Why do they do it? Several considerations are involved. First, many health-impairing habits creep up on people slowly. Drug use may grow imperceptibly over years, or exercise habits may decline ever so gradually. Second, many health-impairing habits involve activities that are quite pleasant at the time. Actions such as eating favorite foods, smoking cigarettes, and getting high are potent reinforcing events. Third, the risks associated with most health-impairing habits are chronic diseases that usually lie 10, 20, or 30 years down the road. It is relatively easy to ignore risks that lie in the distant future. Fourth, it appears that *people have a tendency to underestimate the risks associated with their own health-impairing habits*, while viewing the risks associated with others' self-destructive behaviors much more accurately (Weinstein, 1984). In other words, most people are aware of the dangers associated with certain habits, but they often engage in *denial* when it is time to apply this information to themselves.

In this section we'll discuss how health is affected by smoking, overeating and obesity, poor nutrition, and lack of exercise. We'll also look at lifestyle factors that relate to AIDS. The health risks of alcohol and drug use are covered in the Application.

Smoking

The smoking of tobacco is widespread in our culture, with current consumption running around 2800 cigarettes a year per adult in the United States (Fiore, 1992). The percentage of people who smoke has declined noticeably since the mid-1960s, but about 32% of adult men and 27% of adult women in the United States continue to smoke regularly. Moreover, among those who continue to smoke, the proportion who smoke "heavily" has increased (McGinnis, Shopland, & Brown, 1987).

Health Effects

Suspicions about the health risks associated with tobacco use were voiced in some quarters throughout the 20th century, but the risks of smoking were not widely appreciated until the mid-1960s. Since then, accumulating evidence has clearly shown that smokers face a much greater risk of premature death than nonsmokers (Hammond & Horn, 1984; USDHHS, 1989, 1990). The estimated life expectancy of a 30-year-old man who smokes two packs a day is *eight years shorter* than that of a similar nonsmoker. The overall risk is positively related to the number of cigarettes smoked and their tar and nicotine content. Cigar and pipe smoking are also associated with elevated health risks, although they are less hazardous than cigarette smoking. Jarvik and Schneider (1992) put the health costs of smoking in perspective by noting that smoking accounts for roughly 60 times as many deaths per year as cocaine and heroin use combined.

Why are mortality rates higher for smokers? Smoking increases the likelihood of a surprisingly large range of diseases, as Figure 14.6 shows. Many of these diseases are highly lethal, including 7 of the 14 leading causes of death among people over age 65 (Rimer et al., 1990). Lung cancer and heart disease are the two types of illness that kill the largest number of smokers (Fielding, 1985). Smokers also have an elevated risk for oral, bladder, and kidney cancer, as well as cancer of the larynx, esophagus, and pancreas (Newcomb & Carbone, 1992); arteriosclerosis, hypertension, stroke, and other cardiovascular diseases (McBride, 1992); and bronchitis, emphysema, and other pulmonary diseases (Sherman, 1992).

The increased prevalence of diseases among smokers may not be due to their smoking alone. Some studies suggest that smokers are more likely than nonsmokers to exhibit a variety of health-impairing habits (Castro,

FIGURE 14.6
Smoking and health
Smoking is associated with
increased risk for a diverse
array of diseases. The magnitude of the elevated risk
varies with the condition,
ranging as high as 11 times
normal in the case of lung
cancer.

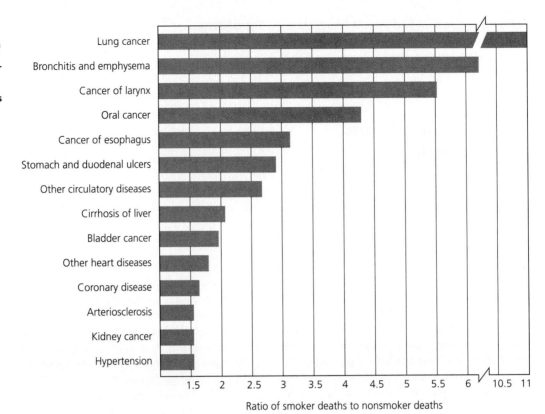

Ratio of smoker deaths to nonsmoker deaths

Newcomb, McCreary, & Baezconde-Garbanati, 1989). For example, they may tend to consume more alcohol, more coffee, and more unhealthy foods than nonsmokers, while exercising less as well.

The dangers of smoking are not limited to smokers themselves. Family members and co-workers who spend a lot of time around smokers are exposed to secondhand smoke, which can increase their risk for a variety of illnesses, especially lung cancer (Byrd, 1992). One report estimates that passive smoking is the third leading cause of preventable deaths in the United States (Glantz & Parmley, 1991). Children with asthma are particularly vulnerable to the effects of passive smoking (Shephard, 1989).

Why Do People Smoke?

People typically begin to smoke during their teen years. Adolescents who smoke are 16 times more likely to smoke as adults than their non-smoking counterparts (Chassin, Presson, Sherman, & Edwards, 1990). The vast majority of youngsters try a cigarette or two at one time or another, but most find them unappealing and do not continue. Those who get around to try-ing a fourth time usually go on to become regu-lar smokers (Leventhal & Cleary, 1980). Ado-lescents are more likely to take up smoking if their parents smoke or if they experience peer pressure to smoke (Hansen et al., 1987). Al-

though todays's teens are aware of the dangers of smoking, they discount the risks because they tend to assume they will smoke for only a few years. Once people begin to smoke regularly, however, they find it very difficult to stop.

A variety of models have been proposed to explain why people acquire the habit of smok-ing. These models are not incompatible and it is possible that each accurately highlights some of the factors that support smoking.

Social learning models emphasize the impor-tance of advertising and role models. Tobacco companies spend about $1.5 billion annually on sophisticated advertisements designed to con-vince us that smoking is glamorous and gratify-ing. Parents, friends, and co-workers provide an abundance of role models who smoke.

Affect regulation models emphasize that smoking can function as a coping device that helps to regulate emotional states. In some peo-ple, smoking can reduce feelings of tension, anger, and anxiety. Furthermore, many people find the pharmacological effects of nicotine to be quite pleasant. Thus the act of smoking is reinforced on a very regular basis.

Addiction models assert that tobacco use can lead to physical dependence. The addiction model is supported by the finding that the relapse patterns for programs designed to help people quit smoking are very similar to the relapse patterns seen in the treatment of alco-hol and heroin addiction (Hunt & Matarazzo,

1982). These striking parallels are apparent in Figure 14.7.

Giving Up Smoking

Studies show that if people can give up smoking, their health risks decline reasonably quickly (Samet, 1992). Five years after people stop smoking, their health risks are already noticeably lower than those of people who continue to smoke, and those risks continue to decline until they reach a normal level after about 15 years. Evidence suggests that most smokers would like to quit, but they are reluctant to give up a major source of pleasure and they worry about craving cigarettes, gaining weight, and becoming tense and irritable (Grunberg, Bowen, & Winders, 1986; Orleans et al., 1991).

There are nearly 40 million ex-smokers in the United States. Collectively, they clearly demonstrate that it is possible to give up smoking successfully. But many didn't succeed until their third, fourth, or fifth attempt, and most would testify that quitting isn't easy. Research shows that long-term success rates are in the vicinity of only 25% (Cohen et al., 1989). Light smokers (fewer than 20 cigarettes per day) are somewhat more successful at quitting than heavy smokers. The probability of a relapse after quitting is much greater among people who experience high levels of stress (Cohen & Lichtenstein, 1990). People who enroll in formal smoking-cessation programs are no more successful than people who try to quit on their own (Cohen et al., 1989). In fact, it is estimated that 80 to 90% of the people who give up smoking quit on their own, without professional help.

No single approach to quitting smoking is most effective for everyone, but if you want to give up smoking, the following advice may be helpful.

1. *Educate yourself thoroughly about the dangers of smoking.* Giving up smoking requires strong motivation. You can increase your motivation by becoming very familiar with the health problems caused by smoking. Programs that concentrate on education alone can be effective for some people (Windsor et al., 1985).

2. *Quit cold turkey.* Success rates for giving up smoking appear to be somewhat higher for people who quit cold turkey than for those who reduce tobacco consumption gradually (Glasgow, Klesges, Mizes, & Pechacek, 1985).

3. *Use self-modification techniques.* The self-modification techniques described in Chapter 4 can be invaluable in efforts to quit smoking. A

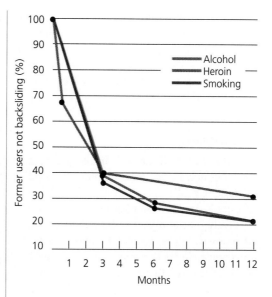

FIGURE 14.7
Relapse in efforts to quit smoking
It is quite difficult to give up smoking. As the graph shows, the relapse rates for returning to smoking within a year are similar to those for returning to alcohol and heroin use. This finding supports the notion that nicotine is an addictive drug. (From Hunt & Matarazzo, 1982.)

good program should include careful monitoring of smoking habits, ample rewards for going without cigarettes, and control of antecedents to avoid situations that trigger smoking.

4. *If you don't succeed, try again.* People who attempt to give up smoking often fail several times before they eventually succeed. Evidence suggests that the readiness to quit builds gradually as people cycle through periods of abstinence and relapse (Biener & Abrams, 1991; Prochaska, Velicer, Di Clemento, & Fava, 1988). So if your effort to quit smoking ends in failure, don't give up—try again in a few weeks or few months.

In recent years *nicotine substitutes*—nicotine gum and the newer nicotine skin patch, which releases a steady dose of nicotine into the wearer—have received considerable publicity. The rationale for nicotine substitutes is that insofar as nicotine is addictive, it may be helpful to employ a substitute during the transition period, as one tries to give up cigarettes. Do nicotine substitutes work? The evidence is ambiguous. On the positive side of the ledger, controlled studies have demonstrated that long-term rates of quitting are higher with nicotine substitutes than with placebos (Oster, Huse, Delea, & Colditz, 1986; Tonnesen, Norregaard, Simonsen, & Sawe, 1991). The increases are small, however, and the success rates are still discouragingly low. In one study (Tonneson et al., 1991) the "increased" abstinence rates for subjects who used the nicotine patch were only 24% after 6 months and 17% after 12 months. Clearly nicotine substitutes are not a panacea and they are not a substitute for a firm determination to quit. Furthermore, some people experience side effects, such as nausea and headaches, from nicotine replacements. Finally, some experts question the wisdom of giving people nicotine in a new form, inasmuch as people attempt to quit smoking because nicotine is bad for their health (Pomerleau & Pomerleau, 1988).

Overeating

Obesity, **the condition of being overweight,** is a very common health problem, affecting as many as 70 million people in the United States. Obesity is similar to smoking in that it exerts a relatively subtle impact on health that is easy for many people to ignore. Though subtle, the long-range effects of obesity can be quite dangerous. Overweight people have an increased risk of coronary disease, hypertension, stroke, respiratory problems, arthritis, diabetes, gall bladder disease, back problems, infertility, and at least four types of cancer (Jeffrey & Lemnitzer, 1981; Kannel & Cupples, 1989; Kissebah, Freedman, & Peiris, 1989). Figure 14.8 shows estimates of just how much obesity elevates the risk for some of these diseases.

Determinants of Obesity

A few decades ago it was widely believed that obesity was a function of personality. Obesity was thought to occur mostly in depressed, anxious, compulsive people who overate to deal with their negative emotions. However, research eventually showed that there is no such thing as an "obese personality" (Rodin, Schank, & Striegel-Moore, 1989), and that a complex network of interacting factors determine whether people develop weight problems.

Chief among these factors is *genetic predisposition.* In one influential study, adults raised by foster parents were compared with their biological and foster parents in regard to *body mass index*—a measure of weight that controls for variations in height (Stunkard et al., 1986). The investigators found that the adoptees resembled their biological parents more than their adoptive parents. In a subsequent twin study, Stunkard, Harris, Pederson, and McClearn (1990) found that identical twins reared apart were far more similar in body mass index than fraternal twins reared together (Chapter 2 discusses the logic underlying twin studies). On the basis of their correlational data, these researchers estimate that genetic factors account for roughly 70% of the variation among people in weight. These genetic factors probably explain why some people can eat constantly without gaining weight while less fortunate people eat far less and grow chubby.

What, exactly, is inherited by people who are prone to obesity? One obvious hypothesis is that some people inherit a sluggish metabolism. Your **basal metabolic rate is your body's rate of energy output at rest after a 12-hour fast.** Although metabolic rate can be increased by exercise, basal metabolic processes generally account for about two-thirds of our energy output. People vary in their basal metabolic rate: some of us burn off calories faster than others. Calories that are burned off won't be stored as fat.

Thus it's plausible that hereditary factors lead obese people to have relatively low metabolic rates. However, investigators who have compared the average metabolic rates of obese and lean subects have *not* found slower metabolism in the obese group (Garrow, 1986). So the physiological bases for inherited differences in the tendency to gain weight remain obscure. Some theorists believe that obese people are

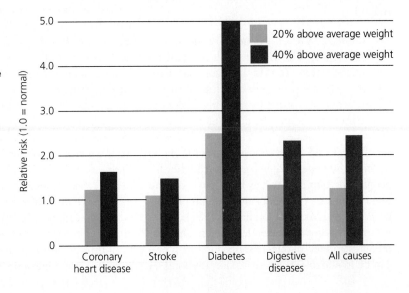

FIGURE 14.8
Obesity and mortality
This graph shows the increased mortality risks for men who are either 20% or 40% above average weight for their age and height. Clearly obesity is a significant health risk. (Data from Van Itallie, 1979.)

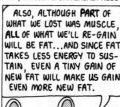

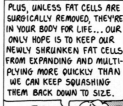

genetically programmed to develop an excessive number of fat cells (Grinker, 1982). This hypothesis remains unproved, but it brings us to set-point theory, which concerns how our bodies may regulate fat deposits.

People who lose weight on a diet have a rather strong (and depressing) tendency to gain back the weight they lose. The reverse is also true. People who have to work to put weight on often have trouble keeping it on. According to Richard Nisbett (1972), these observations suggest that your body may have a **set point, which represents its natural point of stability in body weight.** According to set-point theory, our bodies monitor fat-cell levels to keep them fairly stable (Keesey & Powley, 1975, 1986). When fat stores slip below a crucial set point, our bodies supposedly try to compensate for this change by increasing our hunger and slowing our metabolism. The processes hypothesized by set-point theory function to keep one's weight within a limited range (not at one precise weight, as the theory's name suggests).

What determines your set point? Advocates of set-point theory note that gains or reductions in weight generally do *not* lead to increases or decreases in the *number* of fat cells. Instead, fat cells increase or decrease in average *size* (Hirsch, Fried, Edens, & Leibel, 1989). Although the number of fat cells in the body can be increased at any age (through persistent overeating), the count typically stabilizes in early childhood (Knittle et al., 1981). This curious stability suggests that the number of fat cells has something to do with one's set point. It also suggests that childhood eating habits may exert considerable influence over one's set point, and one's vulnerability to obesity (Brownell, 1986).

Can your set point be changed? The evidence on this issue is not very encouraging. Studies suggest that long-term excessive eating can gradually increase one's set point, but decreasing it seems to be very difficult (Keesey, 1986). This finding does *not* mean that all obese people are doomed to remain obese forever, but it does suggest that most overweight people must be prepared to make *permanent* changes in their eating and exercise habits if they expect to keep their weight down (Keesey, 1988).

While a variety of physiological factors may influence vulnerability to obesity, chronic overeating undeniably plays a prominent role in it. Why is overeating such a routine habit for so many people? Stanley Schachter (1971) advanced the hypothesis that obese people are *overly sensitive to external cues* that affect their hunger and *relatively insensitive to internal physiological cues* that signal the true need for food. According to this notion, overweight people pay little attention to messages from their bodies but respond readily to external cues such as the availability of food, the attractiveness of the food, and the time of day. This formulation suggested that people overeat because they cannot ignore environmental cues that trigger hunger. For example, people who are not really hungry may be stimulated to pursue food simply by seeing a delectable commercial on TV.

Schachter's theory proved to be an incomplete explanation of obesity because it ignored the importance of the various physiological factors that we have discussed (Rodin, 1981). Furthermore, studies have raised doubts about whether obese people really eat all that much more than people of normal weight (Rodin et al., 1989). Nonetheless, Schachter deserves credit for showing how external food cues can contribute to overeating.

Losing Weight

Whether out of concern about their health or just old-fashioned vanity, an ever-increasing number of people are trying to lose weight. One recent survey of over 4600 subjects found that 47% of the men and 75% of the women had dieted to lose weight at one time or another (Jeffery, Adlis, & Forster, 1991). Unfortunately, our obsession with weight loss can sometimes become dangerous. According to medical and nutritional experts, many of the popular fad

diets that promise large, rapid weight reductions can be hazardous to one's health (Atkinson, 1989). An article in the *Journal of the American Medical Association* (Wadden, Stunkard, Brownell, & Van Itallie, 1983) revealed that by the end of 1982 the U.S. Food and Drug Administration had received 138 complaints of illness (including six deaths) from people who went on the Cambridge diet. It also mentioned that liquid-protein diets were thought to be associated with some 58 deaths before they faded from view. It is important to understand that faddish, extreme nutritional programs are moneymaking ventures for their developers. They usually have little genuine merit and may even be dangerous. What, by the way, do these researchers (1983) recommend to achieve safe, durable weight loss? They advocate "behavior modification, nutrition counseling and exercise" (p. 2834).

While obesity may have a variety of causes, there is only one way to lose weight. You must change the ratio of your energy intake (from food consumption) to your energy output (from physical activities). To lose one pound you need to burn up 3500 more calories than you consume. You have three options: (1) You can sharply reduce your food consumption. (2) You can sharply increase your exercise output. (3) You can simultaneously decrease your food intake and step up your exercise output more moderately. Most experts recommend the third option, with an emphasis on reducing food intake. Although exercise clearly can contribute to weight loss, its effects are limited (Segal & Pi-Sunyer, 1989). Even a vigorous hour-long workout will burn off only an extra 200 to 300 calories—a drop in the bucket in comparison with what most people could achieve by eating less (exercise does help, though, and it can yield many other benefits, which we will discuss shortly).

Although popular diet regimens promise rapid weight loss, experts agree that slow, grad-

ual reductions in weight are more likely to be maintained (Brownell, 1989). Self-modification techniques (see Chapter 4) can be very helpful in achieving gradual weight loss. It is important to avoid yo-yo dieting, the syndrome in which the same weight is lost and regained over and over (Brownell, 1988). Yo-yo dieting appears to alter metabolism in ways that gradually make it harder and harder to lose weight.

Can medication be helpful in efforts to lose weight? Perhaps a little, although "diet pills" remain controversial because they have problematic side effects and some potential for abuse and drug dependence. A variety of prescription drugs can decrease hunger (Weintraub & Bray, 1989), but the appetite-suppressant effects of these drugs are modest and temporary, so they don't work miracles and they aren't a substitute for permanent alterations in eating habits. Nonetheless, appetite suppressants may have some legitimate value when they are used in conjunction with other interventions that strive to produce enduring changes in patterns of eating.

Recent evidence suggests that dieters should monitor the *kinds* of calories they consume as well as the *number* of calories. Foods with a high fat content are converted into body fat more readily than foods high in carbohydrates or protein (Gurin, 1989). Thus people who want to shape up should consume low-fat diets.

Nutrition

Nutrition **is a collection of processes (mainly food consumption) through which an organism uses the materials (nutrients) required for survival and growth.** The term also refers to the *study* of these processes. Unfortunately, most of us don't study nutrition very much. Moreover, the cunning mass marketing of nutritionally worthless foods makes it more and more difficult to maintain sound nutritional habits.

Nutrition and Health

Evidence is accumulating that patterns of nutrition influence susceptibility to a variety of diseases and health problems. In addition to the problems associated with obesity, which we have already discussed, other possible connections between eating patterns and health include the following.

1. Heavy consumption of foods that elevate the serum cholesterol level (eggs, cheeses, butter, shellfish, sausage, and the like) appears to increase the risk of heart disease (Hegsted, 1984). Eating habits are only one of several factors that influence serum cholesterol level, but they do make an important contribution.

2. High salt intake is thought to contribute to the development of hypertension (Kaplan, 1986), although there is still some debate about its exact role.

3. High caffeine consumption may elevate one's risk for hypertension (France & Ditto, 1988) and for coronary disease (LaCroix et al., 1986). The findings are inconsistent, however, and a recent large-scale study of over 45,000 subjects found no association between caffeine consumption and cardiovascular risk (Grobbee et al., 1990).

4. A high-fat diet has been implicated as a possible contributor to some forms of cancer, especially cancer of the colon, prostate, and breast (Levy, 1985). Some studies also suggest that a high-fiber diet may reduce one's risk for colon and rectal cancer (Rosen, Nystrom, & Wall, 1988), but the evidence is far from conclusive.

5. Certain patterns of sugar consumption may hasten the onset of diabetes (Mayer, 1980). Moreover, once diabetes has emerged, patterns of food consumption are critical in the management of the disease. Diabetics need to balance their caloric intake against their insulin intake. They also are advised to consume a diet low in fat and simple sugars, but high in fiber and complex carbohydrates (Wing, Epstein, & Nowalk, 1984).

6. Severe vitamin deficiencies can lead to a variety of diseases. Vitamin C deficiency can cause scurvy (which results in a degeneration of bones, teeth, and gums), and vitamin D deficiency can cause rickets (which produces bone deformities) in children. Deficiencies severe enough to cause these illnesses are seen only rarely in North America but are common in some Third World countries (Hui, 1985).

7. Vulnerability to osteoporosis, an abnormal loss of bone mass observed most commonly in postmenopausal women, appears to be elevated by a lifelong pattern of inadequate calcium intake (Fahey & Gallagher-Allred, 1990).

8. In some people, high caffeine consumption can lead to chronic headaches (Shirlow & Mathers, 1985). Many people also report that they get headaches when they eat chocolate, but this connection has proved difficult to document in controlled studies (Moffett, Swash, & Scott, 1974).

9. Nutritional patterns play a role in the course and management of a host of diseases, prominent among them gallstones, kidney stones, gout, peptic ulcers, and rheumatoid arthritis (Werbach, 1988). Eating habits may also contribute to the causation of some of these diseases, although the evidence is less compelling on this point.

Of course, nutritional habits interact with other factor—genetics, exercise, environment, and so on—to determine whether one develops a particular disease. Nonetheless, our eating habits clearly *can* influence our physical health.

Many popular books and articles suggest that the link between nutrition and health can be taken one step further and that large doses of vitamins or heavy reliance on particular foods can raise resistance to exceptionally high levels. A prime example of this line of thought is the assertion that vitamin C can prevent cancer. Rather extravagant claims have also been made for the benefits of vitamin E, the B vitamins, high-fiber diets, and some minerals and vegetables. The last couple of decades have seen the emergence of a number of nutritional fads based on such claims.

What is the current thinking of nutritional experts on this issue? Can nutritional extremes provide superresistance to disease? According to Whitney and Cataldo (1987), probably not. They conclude that the research findings contradict most of these claims and are inconclusive at best. Thus there is little evidence that highly touted nutritional extremes can prevent disease. However, there is clear consensus that inadequate nutrition can have negative effects on health, so that adequate nutrition is a key part of a healthy lifestyle.

The Basis for Poor Nutrition

Nutritional deficiencies are more widespread in the United States than most people realize. One recent study found that 70% of men and 80% of women consumed a diet that was deficient in at least one of 15 essential nutrients

FIGURE 14.9
The four basic food groups
The four key categories of food are described here, along with dietary recommendations.

Four Basic Food Groups		
Food group	Amount suggested and foods included	Nutrients provided
1 Milk or milk products	CHILDREN: 3 or more glasses; smaller glasses for children under 9; TEENAGERS: 4 or more glasses (low-fat); ADULTS: 2 or more glasses (low-fat) 1 cup milk = 1 cup yogurt = 1 1/3 oz processed cheddar cheese = 1 1/2 cups cottage cheese = 2 cups ice cream	Protein, fat, carbohydrate Minerals: calcium, phosphorus, magnesium Vitamins: riboflavin, pyridoxine, D, and A (if fortified)
2 Meats or other protein sources	2 or more servings (1 serving = 2 to 3 oz cooked lean meat) Meat, poultry, fish, legumes	Protein, fat Minerals: iron, magnesium, phosphorus, zinc Vitamins: B vitamins (cobalamin, folic acid, niacin, pyridoxine, thiamine)
3 Fruits and vegetables	4 or more servings (1 serving = 1/2 cup raw or cooked) All fruits and vegetables (include one citrus fruit for vitamin C and one dark green or yellow vegetable for carotene)	Carbohydrate Minerals: calcium and iron (some greens) Vitamins: A (as carotene), B vitamins (folic acid, thiamine), C, E, K
4 Breads and cereals*	4 or more servings (1 serving = 1 slice fortified or whole grain bread = 1 oz fortified or whole grain dry cereal = 1 corn tortilla = 1/2–3/4 cup cooked fortified or whole grain cereal, rice, grits, macaroni, etc.)	Carbohydrate, protein Minerals: iron, magnesium, phosphorus, zinc Vitamins: B vitamins (niacin, pyridoxine, thiamine), E

*Bran, whole grain breads and cereals, and, to a lesser degree, raw and dried fruits and raw vegetables will increase the amount of unabsorbable fiber in the diet.

(Murphy, Rose, Hudes, & Viteri, 1992). For the most part, these deficiencies are not due to inability to afford appropriate foods. Instead, most malnutrition in America is attributable to lack of knowledge about nutrition and lack of effort to ensure good nutrition (Quillin, 1987).

In other words, our nutritional shortcomings are due to ignorance and poor motivation. Collectively, we are remarkably naive about the basic principles of nutrition. Our schools tend to provide very little education in this area. Most of us are not highly motivated to make sure our food consumption is nutritionally sound. Instead, we approach our eating very casually, guided not by nutritional needs but by convenience, palatability, and clever advertising.

For most people, then, the first steps toward improved nutrition involve changing attitudes and acquiring information. First and foremost, people need to recognize the importance of nutrition and commit themselves to making a real effort to regulate their eating patterns. Second, people should try to acquire a basic education in regard to nutritional principles.

Nutritional Goals

The evidence indicates that the most healthful approach to nutrition is to follow well-moderated patterns of food consumption that ensure nutritional adequacy while limiting the intake of certain substances that can be counterproductive. Here are some general guidelines for achieving these goals:

1. *Consume a balanced variety of foods.* Food is made up of a variety of components, six of which are essential to your physical well-being: proteins, fats, and carbohydrates, which supply the body with its energy; vitamins and minerals, which help to release that energy and serve other important functions as well; and fiber, which provides roughage that facilitates digestion. It is probably a bit unrealistic to expect most people to keep track of which nutrients are found in which foods, but it is fairly easy to promote adequate intake of all essential nutrients. All you have to do is to consume a balanced diet in terms of the *four basic food groups:* (1) milk and milk products, (2) meats or other protein sources, (3) fruits and vegetables, and (4) breads and cereals. Figure 14.9 includes some recommendations for balanced consumption of these four basic food groups.

2. *Avoid excessive consumption of fats, cholesterol, sugar, and salt.* All of these commodities are overrepresented in the typical American diet. They are not inherently bad, but they can become problematic when they are consumed to excess. It is particularly prudent to limit the intake of saturated fats by eating less beef, pork, ham, hot dogs, sausage, lunch meats, nonskim milk, and fried foods. Consumption of many of the same foods also should be limited to reduce cholesterol intake, which influences vulnerability to heart disease. Beef, pork, lamb, sausage, cheese, butter, and eggs are high in cholesterol. Refined (processed) sugar is believed to be grossly overconsumed. Hence, people should limit their dependence on soft drinks, chocolate, candies, pies, cakes, and jams. Finally, many people should cut down on their salt intake. Doing so may require more than ignor-

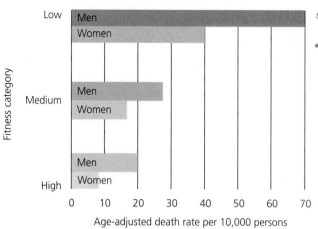

Participants were divided into five categories based on their fitness, ranging from least fit (group 1) to most fit (group 5).

Low fitness: Group 1

Medium fitness: Groups 2 and 3

High fitness: Groups 4 and 5

Age-adjusted death rate per 10,000 persons

FIGURE 14.10
Physical fitness and mortality
Blair et al. (1989) studied death rates among men and women who exhibited low, medium, and high fitness. As you can see, even medium fitness was associated with lower mortality rates in both sexes. The investigators note that one could achieve this level of fitness by taking a brisk half-hour walk each day.

ing your salt shaker, as many prepackaged foods are loaded with salt.

3. *Increase consumption of complex carbohydrates, polyunsaturated fats, natural sugars, and foods with fiber*. If you're thinking that you have to avoid all the foods mentioned in item 2, you may be wondering what's left to eat. Please note, however, that the experts suggest only that you reduce *excessive consumption* of those foods while increasing consumption in other areas. Fruits, vegetables, and whole grains contain complex carbohydrates, natural sugars, and ample fiber. In order to substitute polyunsaturated fats for saturated ones, you can eat more fish, chicken, turkey, and veal. You can also trim meats of fat more thoroughly, use skim (nonfat) milk, and switch to vegetable oils that are high in polyunsaturated fats.

Exercise

In 1984 James Fixx, the noted author of several books touting the benefits of running, died of a heart attack while out jogging. All over the country, people who rarely exercise nodded their heads knowingly and made comments about the little real value of exercise. All the same, there is considerable evidence of a link between exercise and health. Research indicates that regular exercise is associated with increased longevity (Paffenbarger, Hyde, & Wing, 1990). One recent study showed that you don't have to be a dedicated athlete to benefit from exercise (Blair et al., 1989). Even a moderate level of fitness—a level that you could achieve by taking a brisk half-hour walk each day—was associated with lower mortality rates (see Figure 14.10).

Benefits and Risks of Exercise

Why is exercise correlated with longevity? Because physical fitness promotes a diverse array of specific benefits, including the following. First, an appropriate exercise program can enhance cardiovascular fitness and thereby reduce your susceptibility to deadly cardiovascular problems. Fitness is associated with both coronary disease and hypertension (Froelicher, 1990; Hagberg, 1990). Second, regular physical activity can help you avoid obesity (Bray, 1990), so it may indirectly reduce your risk for diabetes, respiratory difficulties, arthritis, and back pain. Third, recent studies suggest that physical fitness is also associated with a decreased risk for colon cancer in men and for breast and reproductive cancer in women (Calabrese, 1990). Scientists are now scrambling to figure out the physiological mechanisms underlying the association between exercise and reduced cancer risk. Fourth, exercise

One doesn't have to be a great athlete to benefit from exercise.

How Beneficial Is Your Favorite Sport?

Physical fitness	Jogging	Bicycling	Swimming	Skating (ice or roller)	Handball/ Squash	Skiing— Nordic	Skiing— Alpine	Basketball	Tennis	Calisthenics	Walking	Golf	Softball	Bowling
Cardiorespiratory endurance (stamina)	21	19	21	18	19	19	16	19	16	10	13	8	6	5
Muscular endurance	20	18	20	17	18	19	18	17	16	13	14	8	8	5
Muscular strength	17	16	14	15	15	15	15	15	14	16	11	9	7	5
Flexibility	9	9	15	13	16	14	14	13	14	19	7	9	9	7
Balance	17	18	12	20	17	16	21	16	16	15	8	8	7	6
General well-being														
Weight control	21	20	15	17	19	17	15	19	16	12	13	6	7	5
Muscle definition	14	15	14	14	11	12	14	13	13	18	11	6	5	5
Digestion	13	12	13	11	13	12	9	10	12	11	11	7	8	7
Sleep	16	15	16	15	12	15	12	12	11	12	14	6	7	6
Total	148	142	140	140	140	139	134	134	128	126	102	67	64	51

**FIGURE 14.11
A scorecard on the benefits of 14 sports and exercises** Here is a summary of seven experts' ratings of the value of 14 sporting activities (the highest rating possible on any one item was 21). The ratings were based on vigorous participation four times a week.

can reduce the potentially damaging physical effects of stress (Brown, 1991; Brown & Siegel, 1988). Perhaps people high in fitness show less physiological reactivity to stress than those who are less fit. Fifth, an exercise program can produce desirable personality changes that may promote physical wellness. Research suggests that fitness training can improve one's mood, self-concept, and work efficiency (Folkins & Sime, 1981) and reduce tension, anxiety, and depression (Brown, 1990).

Note, however, that exercise programs have their own hazards. Jogging clearly elevates one's risk of muscular and skeletal injuries (it's especially hard on the knees) and can bring on heat stroke and possibly even a heart attack (Siscovick, 1990). The fact that exercise can both improve cardiovascular health and cause a heart attack may seem paradoxical, but this contradiction was explained in a study by Siscovick, Weiss, Fletcher, and Lasky (1984). They found that men who participated in *regular* exercise lowered their cardiac risk. Vigorous exercise does temporarily (during the exercise) increase cardiac risk—but almost exclusively among those who do not exercise regularly. Although James Fixx's death seems to be inconsistent with the assertion that exercise decreases cardiac risk, Fixx took up jogging because he knew his family had a history of heart problems. In other words, he carried a hereditary vulnerability to heart attack that might have killed him 20 years earlier if it hadn't been for his regular

exercise (his father had his first heart attack at age 35). In any case, an exercise program should be planned carefully to minimize the risks and maximize the benefits.

Devising an Exercise Program

Putting together a good exercise program is difficult for many people. Exercise is time-consuming, and if you're out of shape, your initial attempts may be painful, aversive, and discouraging. To circumvent these problems, it is wise to heed the following advice (Greenberg, 1990; Mirkin & Hoffman, 1978).

1. *Look for an activity that you will find enjoyable.* There are a great many physical activities to choose from (see Figure 14.11). Shop around for one that you enjoy. Your pleasure in the activity will make it much easier for you to engage in it regularly.

2. *Increase your participation gradually.* Don't try to do too much too quickly. An overzealous approach can lead to frustration, not to mention injury. An exercise regimen should be built up gradually. If you do experience injuries, avoid the common tendency to ignore them. Consult your physician to see whether continuing your exercise program is advisable.

3. *Exercise regularly without overdoing it.* Sporadic exercise will not improve your fitness. A widely cited rule of thumb is that you should plan on exercising vigorously for a minimum of

30 minutes three times a week, or you will gain little from your efforts. At the other extreme, don't try to become fit overnight by working out too vigorously and too frequently. Even highly trained athletes schedule days off. Off days are necessary to allow muscles to recover from their hard work.

4. *Reinforce yourself for your participation.* To offset the inconvenience or pain that may be associated with exercise, it is a good idea to reinforce yourself for your participation. The behavior modification procedures discussed in Chapter 4 can be very helpful in shaping up a viable exercise program.

5. *Avoid the competition trap.* If you choose a competitive sport for your physical activity (for example, baseball, basketball, tennis), try to avoid becoming obsessed with victory. It is easy to get overly concerned with winning at games. When this happens, you put yourself under pressure. This is obviously self-defeating, in that it adds another source of stress in your life.

Lifestyle and AIDS

Some of the most problematic links between lifestyle and health may be those related to AIDS. AIDS stands for **acquired immune deficiency syndrome, a disorder in which the immune system is gradually weakened and eventually disabled by the human immunodeficiency virus (HIV).** Being infected with the HIV virus is *not* equivalent to having AIDS. AIDS is the final stage of the HIV infection process, typically manifested about seven years

after the original infection, during which a person is left virtually defenseless against a host of opportunistic infectious agents (Lui, Darrow, & Rutherford, 1988). AIDS inflicts its harm indirectly by opening the door to other diseases. The symptoms of AIDS depend on the specific constellation of diseases that one develops. Ultimately, AIDS is a fatal disorder, and there is no cure on the horizon. Although the average length of survival for AIDS patients has increased slightly, the typical patient dies 18 to 24 months after the AIDS syndrome is manifested (Libman, 1992). Unfortunately, the prevalence of this deadly disease continues to increase at an alarming rate, as Figure 14.12 shows.

Transmission

The HIV virus is transmitted through person-to-person contact involving the exchange of body fluids, primarily semen and blood. To date the two principal modes of transmission have been sexual contact among homosexual and bisexual men and the sharing of needles by intravenous (IV) drug users. These two modes of transmission have accounted for about 88% of all AIDS cases (see Figure 14.13) The HIV virus can be found in the tears and saliva of infected individuals, but the concentrations are low and there is no evidence that the infection can be spread through casual contact (Friedland et al., 1986). Even most forms of noncasual contact, including kissing, hugging, and sharing food with infected individuals, appear safe.

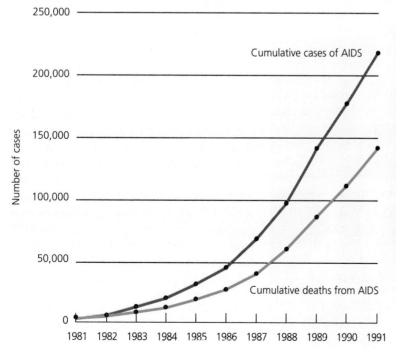

**FIGURE 14.12
The grim statistics on AIDS**
Cases of AIDS are increasing at a rapid rate, and no plateau is yet in sight. After the discovery of AIDS in 1981, it took about eight years to accumulate the first 100,000 cases, but it took less than three years to accumulate the next 100,000 cases. The data shown here, from the Centers for Disease Control, refer only to diagnosed cases of AIDS. No one knows exactly how many people in the United States are infected with the HIV virus, but the number is surely much higher. Seage et al. (1990) estimated that there were 1.5 million HIV carriers in the United States in 1990.

FIGURE 14.13
Distribution of AIDS cases among adolescents and adults
As of late 1990, 88% of known AIDS cases had been found in homosexual/bisexual males and IV (intravenous) drug abusers. Another 3% of cases involved hemophiliacs or others who received contaminated blood before blood banks began to screen for the HIV virus in 1985. About 5% of AIDS cases have been attributed to heterosexual contacts, but this percentage is likely to increase, perhaps sharply. The remaining 4% of cases in the other/undetermined category consist mostly of patients still being investigated or patients for whom risk information could not be obtained. (Data from Centers for Disease Control, 1991.)

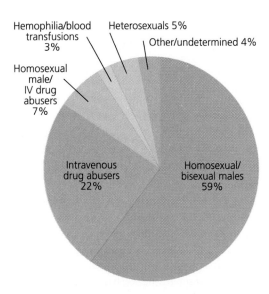

Hemophilia/blood transfusions 3%
Heterosexuals 5%
Other/undetermined 4%
Homosexual male/ IV drug abusers 7%
Intravenous drug abusers 22%
Homosexual/ bisexual males 59%

However, the virus *can* be transmitted through heterosexual relations with an affected individual. Male-to-female transmission occurs more readily than female-to-male transmission, but the virus can be transmitted from women to men (Langone, 1988). Thus the disease is slowly spreading into the population at large, and it is *not* just a "homosexual problem." Among urban blacks, who have a higher rate of intravenous drug use than other groups, over half of AIDS cases are among heterosexuals (Bakeman, Lumb, Jackson, & Smith, 1986).

Misconceptions

After investigating attitudes toward AIDS, Temoshok, Sweet, and Zich (1987) commented that "perhaps no medical phenomenon has

Magic Johnson's revelation that he had tested HIV-positive did a lot to focus Americans' attention on the problem of AIDS.

been so feared or so misunderstood by the public." Misconceptions about AIDS are widespread. Ironically, the people who hold these misconceptions fall into two polarized camps. On the one hand, a great many people have unrealistic fears that AIDS can be readily transmitted through casual contact with infected individuals. These people worry unnecessarily about contracting AIDS from a handshake, a sneeze, or an eating utensil. They tend to be paranoid about interacting with homosexuals, thus fueling discrimination against gays in regard to housing, employment, and so forth. Some people also believe that it is dangerous to donate blood, when in fact blood donors are at no risk whatsoever.

On the other hand, many young heterosexuals who are sexually active with a variety of partners foolishly downplay their risk for HIV, naively assuming that they are safe as long as they avoid IV drug use and sexual relations with gay or bisexual men (Friedman & Goodman, 1992). They greatly underestimate the probability that their sex partners previously may have (a) used IV drugs, (b) had relations with gay or bisexual men, (c) patronized prostitutes (who are at high risk for AIDS), or (d) had sex with another partner who had sex with someone in a high-risk group (IV drug users, gay and bisexual men, and prostitutes). Also, because AIDS is usually accompanied by discernible symptoms, many young people believe that prospective sex partners who carry the HIV virus will exhibit telltale signs of illness. As we have noted, however, having AIDS and being infected with HIV are not the same thing, and HIV carriers often remain healthy and symptom-free for years after they are infected.

In sum, many myths about AIDS persist, despite extensive efforts to educate the public about this complex and controversial disease. Figure 14.14 contains a short quiz to test your knowledge of the facts about AIDS.

Prevention

The lifestyle changes that minimize the risk of developing AIDS are fairly straightforward, although making the changes is often much easier said than done. In all groups, the more sex partners a person has, the higher the risk that one will be exposed to the HIV virus. Thus people can reduce their risk by having sexual contacts with fewer partners and by using condoms to control the exchange of semen. It is also important to avoid anal sex, which increases the probability that semen may mix with the blood. Intravenous drug users can greatly reduce their risk by abandoning their drug use, but since most are physically dependent on the drugs, the alternative is to make sure their needles are sterile and avoid sharing them with other users.

Efforts to alter behaviors that contribute to the spread of AIDS have met with considerable success in the gay community, although there is still room for much more improvement (Stall, Coates, & Hoff, 1988). Unfortunately, relatively little progress has been made among IV drug users (Friedman, de Jong, & Des Jarlais, 1988). Experts are also disappointed to find that heterosexuals have not modified their sexual practices much in response to the threat of AIDS (Catania et al., 1992).

Reactions to Illness

So far we have emphasized the psychosocial aspects of maintaining health and minimizing the risk of illness. Our health is also affected by the way we *respond* to physical symptoms and illnesses. Some people engage in denial and ignore early warning signs of developing diseases. Others engage in active coping efforts to conquer their diseases. In this section, we discuss the perception of pain, the decision to seek medical treatment, the sick role, and compliance with medical advice.

The Perception of Pain

Medical patients complain about pain more than anything else. Pain signals are transmitted to the brain by two pathways (Willis, 1985). A *fast pathway* registers localized pain and relays it directly to the cortex in a fraction of a second.

A Quiz on AIDS

Answer the following "true" or "false"

T F 1. AIDS is caused by a virus.

T F 2. AIDS is caused by inheriting a bad gene or genes.

T F 3. AIDS is caused by a kind of bacteria.

T F 4. A person can "carry" and pass on whatever causes AIDS without necessarily having AIDS or looking sick.

T F 5. Whatever causes AIDS can be passed on through semen.

T F 6. Whatever causes AIDS can be passed on through blood or blood products.

T F 7. You can catch AIDS like you catch a cold because whatever causes AIDS can be carried in the air.

T F 8. You can catch AIDS by being in the same room as someone with AIDS.

T F 9. You can catch AIDS by shaking hands with someone who has AIDS.

T F 10. Having a monogamous relationship decreases the risk of getting AIDS.

T F 11. Using condoms reduces the risk of getting AIDS.

T F 12. A vaccine for AIDS will be available within a year.

ANSWERS: 1.T 2.F 3.F 4.T 5.T 6.T 7.F 8.F 9.F 10.T 11.T 12.F

FIGURE 14.14
A quiz on knowledge of AIDS
Misconceptions about AIDS abound, so it may be wise to take this brief quiz to test your knowledge of AIDS. (Adapted from Temoshok et al., 1987.)

This is the system that hits you with sharp pain when you first cut your finger. A *slow pathway* routs pain signals through lower brain centers. Signals on this pathway lag a second or two behind those in the fast system. This system conveys the less localized, longer-lasting, aching pain that comes after the initial injury.

We tend to think of pain as a purely organic sensation resulting from some sort of tissue damage. Research has made it clear that the organic model of pain is much too simple. It fails to account for the host of psychological variables that can affect the experience of pain (Melzack, 1973; Steger & Fordyce, 1982). These variables include the individual's expectations, anxiety or tension level, personality, and previous conditioning.

The highly subjective nature of pain is easy to recognize. Let's say you're working in your basement at home and you hit your thumb with a hammer. An hour later your thumb is still throbbing when a family member screams from the kitchen that there's a fire in the oven. As you race to provide assistance with this emergency, the pain in your thumb will almost certainly dwindle dramatically. Your experience of pain will have been altered substantially, even though the organic basis for the pain has remained constant. If you still doubt the subjective basis of pain, just ask a nurse who routinely gives shots to many patients. You will surely be told that patients display an exceptionally wide range of pain reactions to essentially the same stimulus. In both cases we're talking about *acute* pain from specific damage to tissues. The evidence indicates that *chronic*, long-lasting pain of unclear origin (such as lower back pain) is even more strongly affected by psychological considerations.

The subjective nature of pain is also seen in the *placebo effect*. **A *placebo* is a substance that resembles a drug but has no actual pharmacological effect.** Many people suffering from pain report analgesic effects when a placebo is presented to them as if it were a painkilling drug (Agras, 1984).

Tissue damage that sends pain impulses on their way to the brain, then, doesn't necessarily result in the experience of pain. Cognitive and emotional processes that unfold in higher brain centers can somehow block pain signals from peripheral receptors. How does the central nervous system block incoming pain signals? In an influential effort to answer this question, Ronald Melzack and Patrick Wall (1965) devised the gate-control theory of pain. ***Gate-control theory* holds that incoming pain sensations must pass through a "gate" in the spinal cord that can be closed, thus blocking ascending pain signals.** The gate in this model is not an anatomical structure but a pattern of neural activity that inhibits incoming pain signals. Melzack and Wall suggested that this imaginary gate could somehow be closed by the brain, thus explaining how such factors as attention and expectations can shut off pain. As a whole, research suggests that the concept of a gating mechanism for pain appears to have merit, yet relatively little support has been found for the neural circuitry hypothesized by Melzack and Wall. Other neural mechanisms, discovered after gate-control theory was proposed, appear to be responsible for blocking the perception of pain.

One of these discoveries was the identification of endorphins. ***Endorphins* are chemicals in the central nervous system that resemble morphine in structure and effects.** They are the body's own natural painkillers. Studies suggest that the release of endorphins underlies the pain-relieving effects of placebo drugs (Fields & Levine, 1984). The analgesic effects that can be achieved through the ancient Chinese art of acupuncture may likewise involve endorphins (Watkins & Mayer, 1982). The increased tolerance of pain seen among women during their last two weeks of pregnancy may also be due to increased secretion of endorphins (Gintzler, 1980). Endorphins are widely distributed in the central nervous system. Scientists are still working out the details of how they suppress pain.

The highly psychological nature of many chronic pain problems helps to account for the very modest success of medical treatment of chronic pain. Improvement rates for organic treatments typically range from 30% to 60% (Gatchel & Baum, 1988). The increasing recognition of the psychological basis of pain has led to the development of behavioral treatment programs for pain management. These new treatment regimens involve a variety of intervention procedures, including relaxation training, behavior modification, cognitive restructuring, hypnosis, and biofeedback.

The Decision to Seek Treatment

Have you ever experienced nausea, diarrhea, stiffness, headaches, cramps, chest pains, or sinus problems? Of course you have; we all experience some of these problems periodically. However, whether we view these sensations as

When physicians carefully explain their instructions, patients are more likely to comply with medical advice.

symptoms is a matter of individual interpretation. When two persons experience the same unpleasant sensations, one may shrug them off as a nuisance while the other may rush to a physician. Studies suggest that people who are relatively high in anxiety and low in self-esteem tend to report more symptoms of illness than others (Pennebaker, 1982). Those who are extremely attentive to bodily sensations and health concerns also report more symptoms than the average person (Barsky, 1988).

Variations in the perception of symptoms help to explain why people differ so greatly in their readiness to seek medical treatment. In general, people are more likely so seek medical care when their symptoms are unfamiliar or frightening, or when they disrupt their work or social activities (Zola, 1973). Another key consideration is how friends and family react to the symptoms. Medical consultation is much more likely when friends and family view symptoms as serious and encourage the person to seek medical care (Sanders, 1982).

The biggest problem in regard to treatment seeking is many people's tendency to delay seeing a doctor. Professional consultation is important because early diagnosis and quick intervention can facilitate more effective treatment of many health problems. Unfortunately, procrastination is the norm even when people are faced with a medical emergency, such as a heart attack (Gentry, 1979). Why do people dawdle in the midst of a crisis? Robin DiMatteo (1991) mentions several reasons. People delay because they often (a) misinterpret and downplay the significance of their symptoms, (b) fret about looking silly if the problem turns out to be nothing, (c) worry about "bothering" their physician, (d) are reluctant to disrupt their plans (to go out to dinner, see a movie, and so forth), and (e) waste time on trivial matters (such as taking a shower, gathering personal items, or packing clothes) before going to a hospital emergency room.

Gender is one factor associated with delay in seeking professional help. Men are more prone than women to put off seeking treatment (Mechanic, 1972). Lower education and socioeconomic status is weakly associated with delay (Rosenstock & Kirscht, 1979). Medical care is more costly for poor people, as they often have less insurance, fewer sick days, and so forth. Understandably, people who are fearful of doctors and hospitals often delay seeking treatment. People who believe strongly in self-care also tend to wait before obtaining professional care (Krantz, Baum, & Wideman, 1980).

RECOMMENDED READING

Be Sick Well: A Healthy Approach to Chronic Illness

by Jeff Kane (New Harbinger, 1991)

Although this book was written for people adjusting to chronic illness, virtually anyone could benefit from Kane's advice on how to deal with illness and how to extract better and more humane care from our modern medical system. Kane discusses how people react to being ill and how they respond to the patient role. He explains the importance of a positive attitude in ways that go beyond the usual platitudes. The discussion of how to choose physicians or other types of health professionals is particularly insightful. Kane makes a distinction between disease, which is a measurable, physical condition, and illness, which is a highly subjective psychological experience. Throughout the book he shows how people can reshape their illness experience to make it less aversive, while growing emotionally and spiritually. The book is saturated with interesting anecdotes and practical exercises.

> If this were a book about disease—the physical manifestation of sickness—I'd simply direct you to the physician best qualified to treat disease. I'd recommend that you make sure the doctor is recognized as an expert in his or her specialty, or what's called in medicine "board-certified." I'd recommend that you learn if he or she has a teaching position in a medical training institution. I'd recommend that you ask other doctors how often they ask the doctor in question to consult on their own patients.
>
> But this is a book about illness—your personal experience—so the requirements are more comprehensive. You're looking for a doctor with technical and human qualities, someone who can approach your disease as disordered physiology and at the same time recognize and seek to alleviate your suffering. This breadth, as a matter of fact, distinguishes an authentic healer from a merely competent technician. When you find such people, treasure them. [p. 76]

The Sick Role

Although many people tend to delay medical consultations, some people are positively eager to seek medical care. These people have learned that the "sick role" provides potential benefits (Lubkin, 1990; Parsons, 1979). For instance, fewer demands are placed on sick people, and they often can decide which demands to ignore. Illness can provide a convenient, face-saving excuse for one's failures. Sick people may also find themselves to be the center of attention from friends and relatives. This increase in attention from others can be very rewarding, especially to those who receive little attention otherwise. Moreover, much of this attention is favorable, in that the sick person is showered with affection, concern, and sympathy.

Thus some people grow to *like* the sick role, although they may not be aware of it. Such people readily seek professional care, but they tend to behave in ways that subtly prolong their illness (Kinsman, Dirks, & Jones, 1982). For example, they may only pretend to go along with medical advice, a common problem that we discuss next.

Adherence to Medical Advice

Many patients do not adhere to the medical regimens prescribed by their physicians and other health-care professionals. This problem, which is called either *nonadherence* or *noncompliance*, is not limited to people who have come to like the sick role, and it is a major problem in our medical system.

It is difficult to estimate the extent of non-adherence, since patients are not eager to admit their failure to comply with instructions. Nonetheless, studies suggest that between one-third and one-half of the patients do not comply with medical advice (DiMatteo & Friedman, 1982; Meichenbaum & Turk, 1987). The demographic variables (gender, social class, and education) that are related to variations in treatment seeking are *not* associated with variations in compliance (Davidson, 1982). Physicians tend to blame poor compliance on patients' uncooperative personalities, but studies find that personality factors also do not predict adherence to medical advice (DiMatteo & DiNicola, 1982).

Our discussion of compliance is not intended to suggest that you should passively accept all the professional advice you get from medical personnel. However, when you have doubts about a prescribed treatment, you should speak up and ask questions. Passive resistance can backfire. For instance, if a physician sees no improvement in a patient who falsely insists that he has been taking his medicine, the physician may abandon an accurate diagnosis in favor of an inaccurate one. The inaccurate diagnosis could lead to inappropriate treatments that might even be harmful to the patient.

Why don't people comply with the advice they have sought from highly regarded medical practitioners? Robin DiMatteo and Howard Friedman (1982) cite three reasons:

1. Noncompliance is frequently due to the patient's failure to understand the instructions. Highly trained professionals often forget that what seems obvious and simple to them may be obscure and complicated for many patients.

2. A key factor is the aversiveness or difficulty of the instructions. If the prescribed regimen has unpleasant side effects, compliance tends to decrease. The more the regimen interferes with the patient's routine, the less probable it is that the patient will cooperate.

3. A negative attitude toward the physician increases the probability of noncompliance. When patients are unhappy with their interactions with the doctor, they are more likely to ignore the medical advice provided.

Some health psychologists are exploring ways to increase patients' adherence to medical advice. They have found that the communication process between the practitioner and the patient is of critical importance. Courtesy, warmth, patience, and a decreased reliance on medical jargon can improve compliance (DiNicola & DiMatteo, 1984). Thus increasing attention is being paid to health-care professionals' communication skills.

Summary

The biopsychosocial model holds that physical health is influenced by a complex network of biological, psychological, and sociocultural factors. Stress is one of the psychological factors that can affect our physical health. The competitive, impatient, hostile behavior typical of the Type A personality may double one's risk of coronary heart disease. The evidence is contradictory, however, and more research is needed. The connection between stress and cancer is not well documented and appears to be very weak.

Stress plays a role in a host of diseases, perhaps because it can temporarily suppress our immune reaction. While there's little doubt that stress can contribute to the development of physical illness, the link between stress and illness is modest in strength.

People frequently display health-impairing habits and lifestyles. These habits creep up on people slowly, and their risks are easy to ignore because the dangers often lie in the distant future. Smokers have much higher mortality rates than nonsmokers because they are more vulnerable to a host of diseases. Giving up smoking is difficult in part because nicotine is addictive. Obesity elevates one's risk for a great variety of health problems. Body weight is influenced by genetic endowment, set point, and eating habits. The best way to lose weight is to decrease the number of calories one consumes while gradually increasing exercise.

Poor nutritional habits have been linked to a host of health problems, although much of the evidence is tentative. Nutritional fads do not offer protection against disease. One best maintains one's health by eating a balanced diet while limiting the intake of certain substances that can be counterproductive. Lack of exercise is associated with elevated mortality rates. Regular exercise can reduce one's risk for cardiovascular disease, cancer, and obesity-related diseases, buffer the effects of stress, and lead to desirable personality changes. Aspects of lifestyle are the key factors in one's risk of AIDS. HIV is transmitted almost exclusively by sexual contact and the sharing of needles by IV drug abusers. One can reduce one's risk for HIV infection by avoiding IV drug abuse, having fewer sex partners, using condoms, and avoiding anal intercourse.

The experience of pain is highly subjective. Research on gate-control theory and endorphins may explain some of this subjectivity. We all experience physical symptoms, but some of us tend to ignore them. Variations in treatment seeking are influenced by the severity of one's symptoms and the reactions of friends and family. The biggest problem is the tendency of many people to delay needed medical treatment. At the other extreme, a minority of people learn to like the sick role because it wins them attention and allows them to avoid stress. Noncompliance with medical advice is a major problem. Demographic and personality factors do not predict adherence. The likelihood of noncompliance increases when instructions are difficult to understand, when recommendations are difficult to follow, and when patients are unhappy with their doctor.

In the Application we take a look at a health-impairing habit that is all too common in our society: drug abuse.

APPLICATION Understanding the Effects of Drugs

Are the following statements true or false?

1.

Smoking marijuana can make men impotent and sterile.

2.

Overdoses of cocaine are relatively rare.

3.

It is well documented that LSD causes chromosome damage.

4.

The most widely abused drug is marijuana.

All the statements on the left are false. If you answered all of them correctly, you may already be well informed about drugs. If not, you *should* be. Intelligent decisions about drugs require an understanding of their effects and risks.

The use of drugs for their pleasureable effects, commonly referred to as *drug abuse or recreational drug use,* reaches into every corner of our society and is a very hazardous habit. The abuse of some drugs declined slightly during the 1980s (Johnson & Muffler, 1992), but it appears that recreational drug use is not about to disappear in the foreseeable future.

Like other controversial social problems, recreational drug use often inspires more rhetoric than reason. A former president of the American Medical Association made headlines when he declared that marijuana "makes a man of 35 sexually like a man of 70." In reality, the research findings do not support this assertion. This influential physician later retracted his statement, admitting that he had made it simply to campaign against marijuana use (Leavitt, 1982). Unfortunately, such scare tactics can backfire by undermining the credibility of drug education efforts. Recreational drug use involves personal, moral, political, and legal issues that are not matters for science to resolve. The more knowledgeable you are about drugs, however, the more informed your decisions and opinions about them will be. Accordingly, this Application is intended to provide you with nonjudgmental, realistic coverage of issues related to recreational drug use. We'll begin by reviewing key drug-related concepts. Then we'll examine the effects and risks of six types of widely abused drugs: narcotics, sedatives, stimulants, hallucinogens, cannabis and alcohol. We'll wrap up our coverage with a brief discussion of newer drugs that have become problematic in recent years.

Drug-Related Concepts

The drugs that people use recreationally are *psychoactive.* **Psychoactive drugs are chemical substances that modify a person's mental, emotional, or behavioral functioning.** Not all psychoactive drugs produce effects that lead to drug abuse. In general, people prefer drugs that elevate their mood or produce pleasant alterations in conscious-

FIGURE 14.15
Major categories of abused drugs
This table summarizes the methods of ingestion, chief medical uses, and principal effects of six major types of recreational drugs. (Based on Blum, 1984; Julien, 1991; Lowinson, Ruiz, & Millman, 1992.)

Comparison of Major Abused Drugs

Drugs	Methods of administration	Principal medical uses	Desired effects	Short-term side effects
Narcotics (opiates) Morphine Heroin	Injected, smoked, oral	Pain relief	Euphoria, relaxation, anxiety reduction, pain relief	Lethargy, drowsiness, nausea, impaired coordination, impaired mental functioning, constipation
Sedatives Barbiturates (e.g., Seconal) Nonbarbiturates (e.g., Quaalude)	Oral, injected	Sleeping pill, anticonvulsant	Euphoria, relaxation, anxiety reduction, reduced inhibitions	Lethargy, drowsiness, severely impaired coordination, impaired mental functioning, emotional swings, dejection
Stimulants Amphetamines Cocaine	Oral, sniffed, injected, freebased, smoked	Treatment of hyperactivity and narcolepsy, local anesthetic (cocaine only)	Elation, excitement, increased alertness, increased energy, reduced fatigue	Increased blood pressure and heart rate, increased talkativeness, restlessness, irritability, insomnia, reduced appetite, increased sweating and urination, anxiety, paranoia, increased aggressiveness, panic
Hallucinogens LSD Mescaline Psilocybin	Oral		Increased sensory awareness, euphoria, altered perceptions, hallucinations, insightful experiences	Dilated pupils, nausea, emotional swings, paranoia, jumbled thought processes, impaired judgment, anxiety, panic reaction
Cannabis Marijuana Hashish THC	Smoked, oral	Treatment of glaucoma; other uses under study	Mild euphoria, relaxation, altered perceptions, enhanced awareness	Bloodshot eyes, dry mouth, reduced short-term memory, sluggish motor coordination, sluggish mental functioning, anxiety
Alcohol	Drinking		Mild euphoria, relaxation, anxiety reduction, reduced inhibitions	Severely impaired coordination, impaired mental functioning, increased urination, emotional swings, depression, quarrelsomeness, hangover

NOTE: The principal omission from this table is PCP (phencyclidine hydrochloride), which does not fit neatly into any of the listed categories. PCP has stimulant, hallucinogenic, and anesthetic effects. Its short-term side effects can be very dangerous. Common side effects include agitation, paranoia, confusion, and severe mental disorientation that has been linked to accidents and suicides.

ness. The principal types of recreational drugs are described in Figure 14.15. This table lists representative drugs in each of six categories, how the drugs are taken, their principal medical uses, their desired effects, and their common side effects (based on Blum, 1984; Julien, 1991; Lowinson, Ruiz, & Millman, 1992).

Most drugs produce tolerance effects. *Tolerance* is a progressive decrease in responsiveness to a drug with continued use. Tolerance effects usually lead people to consume larger and larger doses of a drug to attain the effects they desire. Tolerance builds more rapidly to some drugs than to others. The second column in Figure 14.16 indicates whether various groups of drugs tend to produce rapid or gradual tolerance.

When we evaluate the potential problems associated with the use of various drugs, a key consideration is the likelihood of either physical or psychological dependence. Although recent evidence indicates that both forms of drug dependence have a physiological basis (Koob & Bloom, 1988; Ray & Ksir, 1990), important differences have been found between the two syndromes. *Physical dependence* exists when a person must continue to take a drug to avoid withdrawal illness (which occurs when drug use is terminated). The withdrawal symptoms vary with the drug. Withdrawal from heroin, barbiturates, and alcohol can produce fever, chills, tremors, convulsions, seizures, vomiting, cramps, diar-

rhea, and severe aches and pains. The agony of withdrawal from these drugs virtually compels addicts to continue using them. Withdrawal from stimulants leads to a somewhat milder syndrome dominated by fatigue, apathy, irritability, depression, and disorientation.

Psychological dependence exists when a person must continue to take a drug to satisfy intense mental and emotional craving for it. Psychological dependence is more subtle than physical dependence, as it is not marked by a clear withdrawal reaction. However, psychological dependence can create a powerful, overwhelming need for a drug. Both types of dependence are established gradually with repeated use of a drug. Drugs vary widely in their potential for creating either physical or psychological dependence. The third and fourth columns of Figure 14.16 show the estimated risk of each kind of dependence on the drugs we discussed.

An *overdose* is an excessive dose of a drug that can seriously threaten one's life. Any drug can be fatal if a person takes enough of it, but some drugs involve more danger of overdose than others. Column 5 of Figure 14.16 shows the estimated risk of accidentally consuming a lethal overdose of various drugs. Drugs that depress the central nervous system (CNS)—narcotics, sedatives, and alcohol—carry the greatest risk of overdose. It's important to understand that the effects of these drugs are additive. Many overdoses involve lethal *combinations* of CNS

depressants. What happens when people overdose on these drugs? Their respiratory system usually grinds to a halt, producing coma, brain damage, and death within a brief period. In contrast, fatal overdoses of CNS stimulants (cocaine and amphetamines) usually lead to a heart attack, stroke, or cortical seizure.

Now that our basic vocabulary is spelled out, we can begin to examine the effects and risks of major recreational drugs. Of course, we'll be describing the *typical* effects of each drug. Please bear in mind that the effects of any drug depend on the user's age, body weight, physiology, personality, mood, expectations, and previous experience with the drug. The dose and potency of the drug, the method of administration, and the setting in which the drug is taken also influence its effects. Our coverage is based largely on comprehensive books by Blum (1984), Julien (1991) and Lowinson et al. (1992), but we'll cite additional sources when we discuss specific studies or controversial points.

Narcotics

Narcotics (or opiates) are drugs derived from opium that are capable of relieving pain. Legal regulations use the term *narcotic* in a haphazard way to refer to a variety of drugs besides opiates. Our discussion will focus on heroin and morphine, but many of the points also apply to less potent opiates such as codeine, demerol, and methadone.

Risks Associated with Abused Drugs

Drugs	Tolerance	Risk of physical dependence	Risk of psychological dependence	Fatal overdose potential
Narcotics (opiates)	Rapid	High	High	High
Sedatives	Rapid	High	High	High
Stimulants	Rapid	Moderate	High	Moderate to high
Hallucinogens	Gradual	None	Very low	Very low
Cannabis	Gradual	None	Low to moderate	Very low
Alcohol	Gradual	Moderate	Moderate	Low to high

FIGURE 14.16
Specific risks for various categories of drugs
This table lists the estimated risk of tolerance, dependence, and overdose associated with the six major categories of recreational drugs.

Recreational drug users come from all ages and all walks of life.

Effects

The most significant narcotics problem in modern Western society is the use of heroin. Most users inject heroin intravenously with a hypodermic needle. The main effect of the drug is an overwhelming sense of euphoria. This euphoric effect has a "Who cares?" quality to it that makes the heroin high an attractive escape from reality. Common side effects include nausea, lethargy, drowsiness, constipation, and slowed respiration.

Risks

Narcotics carry a high risk for both *psychological dependence* and *physical dependence*. It is estimated that there are about a half-million heroin addicts in the United States (Jaffe, 1986). Although heroin withdrawal usually isn't life threatening, it can be so very unpleasant that junkies have a desperate need to continue their drug use. Once dependence is entrenched, people tend to develop a very *drug-centered lifestyle* that revolves around efforts to procure more heroin. The drug is very expensive (up to $200 a day) and available only through highly undependable black-market channels. Obviously it is difficult to lead a very produc-

tive life if one's existence is dominated by a desperate need to "score" heroin. The inordinate cost of heroin forces many junkies to resort to criminal activities to support their habit.

Overdose is also a very real danger with heroin (Jaffe, 1992). Part of the problem is that it is difficult to judge the purity of heroin obtained through black-market sources. The effects of opiates are added to those of other CNS depressants, and most narcotic overdoses occur when opiates are taken in combination with sedatives or alcohol. Junkies also risk *infectious diseases* because they often share hypodermic needles and tend to be sloppy about sterilizing them. The most common of these diseases used to be hepatitis. In recent years the acquired immune deficiency syndrome (AIDS) has been transmitted at an alarming rate through the population of intravenous drug users (Des Jarlais, Friedman, Woods, & Milliken, 1992).

Sedatives

Sedatives are sleep-inducing drugs that tend to decrease activation of the central nervous system and behavioral

activity. In street jargon they are often called "downers." Over the years, the most widely abused sedatives have been the barbiturates, which are compounds derived from barbituric acid. Although distinctions are made between barbiturate and nonbarbiturate sedatives, the functional differences are minimal.

Effects

People who abuse sedatives generally consume larger doses than those prescribed for medical purposes. These overly large doses have a euphoric effect similar to that produced by large amounts of alcohol (Wesson, Smith, & Seymour, 1992). Feelings of tension, anxiety, and depression are temporarily replaced by a very relaxed, pleasant state of intoxication, in which inhibitions may be loosened. Sedatives carry a truckload of problematic side effects. Motor coordination suffers badly, so that speech is slurred, and a walk becomes a stagger. Intellectual functioning also becomes sluggish and judgment is impaired. One's emotional tone may become unstable, with feelings of dejection often intruding on the intended euphoria.

Risks

Sedatives have the potential to produce both *psychological dependence* and *physical dependence*. They compete closely with narcotics as the leading cause of *overdoses* in the United States (O'Brien & Woody, 1986) because of their additive interactions with other CNS depressants (especially alcohol) and because of the degree to which they impair one's judgment. In their drug-induced haze, sedative abusers are prone to take doses that they would ordinarily recognize as dangerous. With prolonged use, the dose of barbiturates needed to feel high increases more rapidly than the dose the body can handle (see Figure 14.17). Thus the margin of safety between an intoxicating dose and a lethal dose gradually narrows. Sedative users also elevate their risk for *accidental injuries* because these drugs can have drastic effects on motor coordination. Many users trip on stairs, fall off bar stools, get into

FIGURE 14.17
Complexities in tolerance to barbiturates
Because of tolerance effects, the dose of barbiturates needed to get high increases gradually with continued use. The dose that the body can handle (the lethal dose) increases more slowly, so the difference between an intoxicating dose and a lethal dose gets smaller and smaller. (Because of individual differences among people, the doses shown are only approximate.)

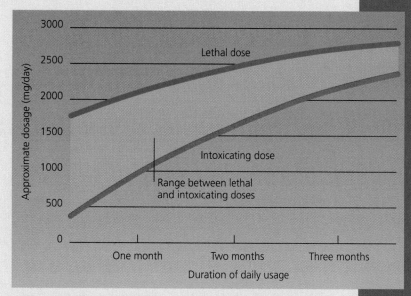

automobile accidents, and so forth.

Stimulants

Stimulants are drugs that tend to increase activation of the central nervous system and behavioral activity. They range from mild, widely available substances such as caffeine and nicotine to stronger, carefully regulated drugs, such as cocaine and amphetamines ("speed"). We'll focus on the latter two drugs. Synthesized in a pharmaceutical laboratory, amphetamines are usually consumed orally. Speed is also sold as a crystalline powder (called "crank") that may be snorted or injected intravenously. Recently a smokable form of methamphetamine (called "ice") has been developed.

Cocaine is an organic substance extracted from the coca shrub, which grows most prominently in South America. It is usually consumed as a crystalline powder that is snorted through the nasal cavities. However, an increasing number of users are "freebasing" cocaine. Freebasing is chemical treatment that is used to extract nearly pure cocaine concentrate from ordinary street cocaine. "Crack" is the most widely distributed by-product of this process, consisting of little chips of pure cocaine, which usually are smoked. Smoking crack is far more dangerous than snorting cocaine powder because of its greater purity and because smoking leads to a more rapid absorption of the drug into the bloodstream (Cregler & Mark, 1986).

Effects

Amphetamines and cocaine have almost indistinguishable effects, except that cocaine produces a very brief high (20 to 30 minutes unless more is taken), while a speed high can last many hours (Gold, Miller, & Jonas, 1992). Stimulants produce a euphoria very different from that created by narcotics or sedatives. They produce a buoyant, elated, enthusiastic, energetic, "I can conquer the world!" feeling accompanied by increased alertness. Common side effects include increased blood pressure, muscle tension, sweating, and restlessness. Some users experience unpleasant feelings of irritability, anxiety, and paranoia.

Risks

Stimulants can cause *physical dependence,* but the physical distress caused by withdrawal of stimulants is mild in comparison with that caused by withdrawal of narcotics or sedatives (Kleber & Gawin, 1986). *Psychological dependence* on stimulants is a more common problem. Cocaine can create an exceptionally powerful psychological dependence, which compels the user to pursue the drug with a fervor normally seen only in people who are physically dependent on a drug. Both cocaine and amphetamines can suppress appetite and disrupt sleep. Thus heavy use of stimulants may lead to poor eating, poor sleeping, and ultimately a *deterioration in physical health.* Use of stimulants increases one's risk for stroke, heart attack, and other forms of cardiovascular disease, and crack smoking is associated with a host of respiratory problems (Gold, 1992). Snorting cocaine through the nasal passages can produce serious nasal damage. Heavy use of stimulants occasionally leads to a severe psychological disorder called *amphetamine or cocaine psychosis* (depending on the drug involved), which is characterized by intense paranoia (King & Ellinwood, 1992). All of the risks associated with the use of stimulants increase *greatly* with the use of more potent forms of the drugs (crack and ice).

Overdoses on stimulants used to be relatively infrequent (Kalant & Kalant, 1979). However, cocaine overdoses have increased sharply in recent years as more people experiment with freebasing, smoking crack, and other more dangerous modes of ingestion (Gold, 1992). The dangers of cocaine were underscored in a study of rats that were given unlimited access to heroin or cocaine (Bozarth & Wise, 1985). The rats earned drug injections delivered through implanted tubes by pressing a lever in an experimental chamber. The health of the rats on heroin deteriorated rapidly and 36% of them died by the end of the 30-day study. The health of the rats on cocaine deteriorated even more rapidly and by the end of the study 90% of them had died. Many of the rats on cocaine experienced severe seizures, but they went right back to pressing the lever as soon as their convulsions subsided.

Hallucinogens

Hallucinogens are a diverse group of drugs that have powerful effects on mental and emotional functioning, marked most prominently by distortions in sensory and perceptual experience. The principal hallucinogens are LSD, mescaline, and psilocybin, which have similar effects, although they vary in potency. Mescaline comes from the peyote plant, psilocybin comes from a particular type of mushroom, and LSD is a synthetic drug.

Effects

Hallucinogens intensify and distort perception in ways that are difficult to describe, and they temporarily impair intellectual functioning as thought processes become meteoric and jumbled. They can produce awesome feelings of euphoria that sometimes include an almost mystical sense of oneness with the human race. This is why they have been used in religious ceremonies in various cultures. Unfortunately, they can also produce nightmarish feelings of anxiety, fear, and paranoia, commonly referred to as a "bad trip."

Risks

No potential for physical dependence is associated with hallucinogens and no deaths attributable to overdose are known to have occurred. Psychological dependence has been reported but appears to be very rare (Grinspoon & Bakalar, 1986). Research reports that LSD increases chromosome breakage were based on poor methodology (Dishotsky, Loughman, Mogar & Lipscomb, 1971). Like most drugs, however, hallucinogens may be harmful to a fetus if they are taken by a pregnant woman.

Although the dangers of hallucinogens have probably been exaggerated in the popular press, there are some significant risks. These drugs make emotion highly volatile, so that users can never be sure that they won't experience *acute panic* from a terrifying bad trip. This disorientation generally subsides within a few hours, leaving no permanent emotional scars. However, in such a severe state of disorientation, *accidents and suicide* are possible. *Flashbacks* involve vividly reliving hallucinogenic experiences months after the original experience. Repeated frightening flashbacks can become very troublesome. In a small minority of users, hallucinogens may contribute to the development of a variety of *psychological disorders* (psychoses, depressive reactions, paranoid states) that appear partially attributable to the drug (Ungerleider & Pechnick, 1992).

Marijuana

Cannabis is the hemp plant from which marijuana, hashish, and THC are derived. Marijuana is a mixture of dried leaves, flowers, stems, and seeds taken from the plant; hashish is made from the plant's resin. THC, the active chemical ingredient in cannabis, can be synthesized for research purposes (for example, to give to animals).

Effects

When smoked, cannabis has an almost immediate impact that may last several hours. The effects of the drug vary greatly, depending on the user's expectations and experience with the drug, the potency of the drug, and the amount smoked. The drug has subtle effects on emotion, perception, and cognition. Emotionally, the drug tends to create a mild, relaxed state of euphoria. Perceptually, it enhances the impact of incoming stimulation, thus making music sound better, food taste better, and so on. Cannabis tends to produce a slight impairment in cognitive functioning (especially short-term memory) and perceptual-motor coordina-

tion while the user is high. However, there are huge variations among users.

Risks

Overdose and physical dependence are not problems, but like any other drug that produces pleasant feelings, marijuana has the potential to produce *psychological dependence* (Grinspoon & Bakalar, 1992). There is no solid evidence that cannabis causes psychological disorders, but it can cause *transient problems with anxiety and depression* in some people. Some studies also suggest that cannabis may have a more *negative effect on driving* than many people believe (Moskowitz, 1985). Like tobacco, marijuana smoke carries carcinogens and impurities into the lungs, thus increasing one's chances for *respiratory and pulmonary diseases, as well as lung cancer* (Cohen, 1986; Gold, 1989a). The evidence on other widely publicized risks remains controversial. Here is a brief overview of the evidence on some of these controversies.

• *Does marijuana cause brain damage?* The handful of studies linking marijuana to brain damage have been shown to be methodologically unsound (Kuehnle, Mendelson, Davis & New, 1977). Marijuana affects brain wave activity (Heath, 1976), but there is no clear evidence that these changes are permanent or pathological (Jenike, 1987).

• *Does marijuana cause chromosome breakage?* Findings on this issue are inconsistent, but Cohen (1980) concludes that marijuana does not appear to increase chromosomal breakage. High doses of THC have been shown to cause birth defects in animals. There is no evidence it does so in humans (Blum, 1984), but the results of the animal studies are cause for concern, and pregnant women should avoid using marijuana (Roffman & George, 1988).

• *Does marijuana reduce one's immune response?* Cannabis may suppress the body's natural immune response slightly (Nahas, 1976). However, infectious diseases are no more common among marijuana smokers than among abstainers, so this effect apparently is too small to have any practical importance (Relman, 1982).

• *Does marijuana lead to impotence and sterility in men?* Cannabis does appear to have endocrine and reproductive effects that merit further investigation. Marijuana appears to produce a small, reversible decline in sperm count among male smokers and may have temporary effects on hormone levels (Bloodworth, 1987). The popular media have frequently implied that marijuana therefore makes men sterile and impotent. In reality, there is no evidence that marijuana produces any lasting effects on male smokers' fertility or sexual functioning (Grinspoon & Bakalar, 1992).

Alcohol
Alcohol encompasses a variety of beverages containing ethyl alcohol, such as beers, wines, and distilled spirits. The concentration of alcohol in these drinks varies from about 4% in most beers up to 50% in 100-proof liquor. Alcohol is the most widely used drug in our society. Because it is legal, many people use it very casually without even thinking of it as a drug.

Effects
The effects of alcohol are influenced by the user's experience, motivation, and mood, as well as the presence of food in the stomach, the proof of the beverage, and the rate of drinking. Thus, there is great variability in how alcohol affects different people on different occasions. The central effect is a "Who cares?" euphoria that temporarily boosts self-esteem as one's problems melt away. Negative emotions such as tension, worry, anxiety, and depression are dulled, and inhibitions may be loosened.

The side effects of alcohol are numerous. In substantial amounts, alcohol has a decidedly negative effect on intellectual functioning and perceptual-motor coordination. With their inhibitions released, some people become argumentative and prone to aggression. Finally, of course, there is that infamous source of regret, the hangover, which may include headache, dizziness, nausea, and vomiting.

Risks
Many people develop *psychological dependence* on alcohol. They need to drink constantly to alleviate anxiety or forget their problems. Eventually *physical dependence* may be established. Estimates suggest that roughly 10 million alcoholics in the United States are physically dependent on alcohol. It's possible to *overdose* on alcohol alone, but a much more frequent problem is overdosing on combinations of alcohol and sedatives or narcotics. *Drunk driving* is a major social problem. It's estimated that alcohol contributes to 50% of all auto accidents.

Chronic heavy consumption of alcohol is associated with an elevated risk for *a wide range of serious health problems.* Among them are liver disease, ulcers, complications of pregnancy, malnutrition, heart disease, hypertension, stroke, some types of cancer, brain damage, and neurological disorders (Goodwin, 1992). Alcoholism can also produce severe *psychotic states,* characterized by delirium, disorientation, and hallucinations.

We have focused on the personal risks of drug abuse, but the enormous social costs of alcohol should also be mentioned. Alcohol contributes to a substantial portion of drownings, fire fatalities, homicides, suicides, rapes, assaults, home accidents, and incidents of child abuse (see Figure 14.18). Alcohol-related absenteeism from work and reduced efficiency on the job cost American industry billions of dollars annually. It is hard to put a dollar value on all the social costs of drug abuse, but one study (Harwood, Napolitano, Kristiansen, & Collins, 1984) estimated that alcohol cost the U.S. economy $89.5 billion in 1980. The comparable estimate for all other types of drugs *combined* was about half as much ($46.9 billion). In summary, the social costs of alcohol are staggering. Though alcohol is legal (maybe *because* it is legal), it is far and away the most problematic and costly of the recreational drugs.

Other Drugs
Thus far we have focused on the drugs most commonly abused in our culture. Most of them have been abused for centuries, and even the newest have been around for many decades. Let's take a brief look at some newer, less widely abused drugs.

Alcohol Misuse Is Blamed in . . .	
64%	of murders in U.S.
41%	of assaults
34%	of rapes
29%	of other sex crimes
30%	of suicides
56%	of fights or assaults in the home
60%	of child abuse
50%	of all road fatalities
45%	of fire deaths
45%	of drownings
22%	of home accidents
36%	of pedestrian accidents
55%	of arrests

FIGURE 14.18 The costs of alcohol Although legal, alcohol is a very problematic drug, as the estimates shown here clearly demonstrate. All the estimates are based on U.S. statistics.

Drugs, Society, & Human Behavior
by Oakley Ray and Charles Ksir (Times Mirror/Mosby, 1990)

This is a thorough, well-documented, up-to-date introduction to the complex and controversial topic of recreational drug use. It is intended primarily for undergraduates and it is very readable. The authors emphasize the historical and social context in which drug abuse takes place. They begin by discussing the sociolegal ramifications of drug use and then move on to three concise chapters on how drugs work physiologically. The next ten chapters examine specific categories of drugs in some detail. There are chapters on nicotine, caffeine, over-the-counter drugs, and psychotherapeutic drugs, as well as on alcohol and illicit substances. The final four chapters return to general issues, such as drug education and treatment of substance abuse. One of these chapters is an interesting look at drugs and athletics.

> Given this effort and these costs, are our drug enforcement efforts effective? Do they work? Critics have pointed out that despite escalating expenditures, more agents, and an increasing variety of supply-reduction efforts, the supplies of cocaine, heroin, and marijuana have not dried up. In fact, they actually may have increased. Although there were record-breaking seizures of cocaine year after year, the price of cocaine did not change on the streets during the 1980s, and there seemed to be more suppliers than ever. The United States government made a decision in 1924 to make heroin completely unavailable to addicts in this country, and after more than 65 years we can say only that we have been consistent in our failure to accomplish that goal. . . . To some, the final irony of all these enforcement efforts is that they seem only to strengthen the drug-dealing organizations, which become more efficient and better-armed. [p. 55]

PCP

PCP (phencyclidine hydrochloride) is a perplexing drug that has gained some popularity in recent years. It is known on the street as "angel dust." PCP, which can be synthesized easily by an underground chemist, defies classification because it has stimulant, hallucinogenic, and sedative effects (Vourakis & Bennett, 1979). This combination of effects produces a unique euphoria that often includes feelings of depersonalization.

Little is known about the long-term use of PCP, but the drug clearly carries many risks (Zukin & Zukin, 1992). Because of its sedative properties, overdose through respiratory depression is a problem. Although it is a less potent hallucinogen than LSD, PCP seems to produce a higher proportion of bad trips, dominated by feelings of paranoia and agitation. PCP can produce a severe state of confusion and disorientation that has been linked to automobile accidents, drownings, and suicides. In fact, one study of 16 PCP-related deaths in the Los Angeles area (Noguchi & Nakamura, 1978) found that the majority were attributable to disordered behavior rather than to fatal doses of the drug.

Designer Drugs

Designer drugs are illicitly manufactured variations of known recreational drugs. Underground chemists typically make slight alterations in the chemical structures of opiates, amphetamines, or hallucinogens or assemble them into new combinations. Designer drugs were originally invented to circumvent legal restrictions on the drugs currently available. Reasoning that authorities couldn't restrict drugs that were not specified in any regulations, enterprising drug dealers figured that they couldn't be prosecuted successfully for selling their new compounds. Flexible regulations that outlawed these new compounds were developed eventually, but the market for designer drugs remains and they continue to be manufactured.

The best-known designer drug is MDMA, which is sold on the street as "ecstasy" (Beck & Morgan, 1986). This compound is related to amphetamines and hallucinogens. It produces a short-lived high (about 90 minutes). Users feel warm, friendly, sensual, and serene, but alert. Problematic side effects include increased blood pressure, heart arrhythmias, and transient anxiety. Fentanyl is another designer drug that has gained a following among narcotics users (Stanford, 1987). Known on the street as "China white," this synthetic opiate is much more potent than heroin. It carries a very high risk of overdose.

At present, designer drugs probably account for less than 1% of the illicit drug use in the United States (Morgan, 1992), but the emergence of these drugs is alarming for two reasons. First, designer drugs haven't been studied much yet and their long-term risks are unknown. Second, these drugs are manufactured by "kitchen chemists" whose quality control varies enormously. Potentially harmful impurities, contaminants, and toxic by-products are often found in designer drugs because of inadvertent errors in the manufacturing process.

CHAPTER 14 REVIEW

Key Terms

acquired immune deficiency syndrome (AIDS)
alcohol
atherosclerosis
basal metabolic rate
biopsychosocial model
cancer
cannabis
coronary heart disease
designer drugs
endorphins
gate-control theory
hallucinogens
health psychology
immune response

narcotics
nutrition
obesity
overdose
physical dependence
placebo
psychoactive drugs
psychological dependence
sedatives
set point
stimulants
tolerance
Type A personality
Type B personality

Key People

Robin DiMatteo
Meyer Friedman and Ray Rosenman

Janice Kiecolt-Glaser
Ronald Melzack and Patrick Wall

15 Psychological Disorders

"THE GOVERNMENT OF THE UNIted States was overthrown more than a year ago! I'm the president of the United States of America and Bob Dylan is vice president!" So said Ed, the author of a prominent book on journalism, who was speaking to a college journalism class as a guest lecturer. Ed also informed the class that he had killed both John and Robert Kennedy, as well as Charles de Gaulle, the former president of France. He went on to tell the class that all rock songs were written about him, that he was the greatest karate expert in the universe, and that he had been fighting "space wars" for 2000 years. The students in the class were mystified by Ed's bizarre, disjointed "lecture," but they assumed that he was putting on a show that would eventually lead to a sensible conclusion. Their perplexed but expectant calm was shattered when Ed pulled a hatchet from the props he had brought with him and hurled it at the class. Fortunately, the hatchet sailed over the students' heads. At that point, the class's professor realized that Ed's irrational behavior was not a pretense. The professor evacuated the class quickly while Ed continued to rant about his presidential administration, space wars, vampires, his romances with female rock stars, and his harem of 38 "chicks." [Adapted from Pearce, 1974, pp. 40–41]

Clearly Ed's behavior was abnormal. Even he recognized that when he agreed later to be admitted to a mental hospital (where he signed himself in as the "President of the United States of America"). What causes such abnormal behavior? Does Ed have a mental illness, or does he just behave strangely? What is the basis for judging behavior as normal or abnormal? Are people who have psychological disorders dangerous? How common are such disorders? Can they be cured? These are just a few of the questions that we will address as we discuss psychological disorders and their complex causes. In the Application we'll consider the troubling issue of suicide.

Abnormal Behavior: Myths, Realities, and Controversies

Misconceptions about abnormal behavior are common. Hence we need to clear up some preliminary issues before we describe the various types of disorders. In this section we will discuss (1) the medical model of abnormal behavior, (2) the criteria of abnormal behavior, (3) stereotypes regarding psychological disorders, (4) the classification of psychological disorders, and (5) how common such disorders are.

The Medical Model Applied to Abnormal Behavior

There's no question about Ed's behavior: it was abnormal. But does it make sense to view his unusual and irrational behavior as a disease? This is a very controversial question. **The medical model proposes that it is useful to think of abnormal behavior as a disease.** This point of view is the basis for many of the terms that are used to refer to abnormal behavior: mental *illness*, psychological *disorder*, psycho*pathology* (*pathology* refers to manifestations of disease). The medical model gradually became the dominant way of thinking about abnormal behavior during the 18th and 19th centuries, and its influence remains strong today.

The medical model clearly represented progress over earlier models of abnormal behavior. Before the 18th century, most conceptions of abnormal behavior were based on superstition. People who behaved strangely were thought to be possessed by demons, witches in league with the devil, or victims of God's punishment. Their disorders were "treated" with chants, rituals, exorcisms, and such. If their behavior was seen as threatening, they were candidates for chains, dungeons, torture, and death (see Figure 15.1).

The rise of the medical model brought great improvements in the treatment of people who exhibited abnormal behavior. As victims of an illness, they were viewed with sympathy rather than hatred and fear. Although living conditions in early asylums were often deplorable, there was gradual progress toward more humane care of the mentally ill. It took time, but ineffectual approaches to treatment eventually gave way to scientific investigation of the causes and cures of psychological disorders.

Problems with the Medical Model

In recent decades, however, critics have suggested that the medical model may have outlived its usefulness. A particularly vocal critic has been Thomas Szasz (1974). Szasz asserts that "strictly speaking, disease or illness can affect only the body; hence there can be no mental illness. . . . Minds can be 'sick' only in the sense that jokes are 'sick' or economies are 'sick'" (1974, p. 267). He further argues that abnormal behavior usually involves a deviation

FIGURE 15.1
**Historical conceptions
of mental illness**
Throughout most of history, psychological
disorders were thought to be caused by
demonic possession, and the mentally ill
were often victims of torture.

473
CHAPTER 15
Psychological
Disorders

from social norms rather than an illness. He contends that such deviations are "problems in living" rather than medical problems. According to Szasz, the medical model's disease analogy converts moral and social questions about what is acceptable behavior into medical questions. Under the guise of "healing the sick," this conversion allegedly allows modern society to lock up deviant people and to enforce its norms of conformity.

The medical model has been criticized on other grounds, too. Three criticisms are especially prominent.

1. *Labeling.* Some critics are troubled because medical diagnoses of abnormal behavior pin potentially derogatory labels on people (Becker, 1973; Rothblum, Solomon, & Albee, 1986). The label *psychotic, schizophrenic,* or *mentally ill* carries a social stigma that can be difficult to shake. Even after a full recovery, someone who has been labeled mentally ill may have difficulty finding a place to live, getting a job, or making friends. Deep-seated prejudice against people who have been labeled mentally ill is commonplace. The stigma of mental illness is not impossible to shed (Gove, 1975), but it undoubtedly creates additional difficulties for people who already have their share of problems. Critics of the medical model also maintain that diagnostic labels such as *alcoholic* and *neurotic* can create unfortunate self-fulfilling prophecies (Scheff, 1975). Some people who

are labeled alcoholic, for instance, seem to accept this designation as part of their identity. They proceed to live out the "alcoholic role" created for them instead of working to alter their behavior and conquer their problems.

2. *Pseudoexplanations.* Other critics of the medical model argue that the technical-sounding diagnoses that are part of the medical approach create an illusion that we understand more than we really do (Krasner & Ullmann, 1965). Let's say that a fellow arrives at a psychiatric facility exhibiting a variety of symptoms that are characteristic of schizophrenic disorders. He says that he hears voices of nonexistent people, and he displays withdrawal, flat emotions, and disorganized, incoherent thinking. He is correctly diagnosed as having a schizophrenic disorder. Later his bewildered family asks, "Doctor, why does he behave in these strange ways?" The doctor is likely to reply, "Because he is schizophrenic." That explanation may *sound* reasonable, but it's a pseudoexplanation because the reasoning is circular. Saying that someone exhibits schizophrenic behavior because he is a schizophrenic is like saying that the reason a woman has red hair is that she is a redhead. It is *not* accurate to say that a patient hears voices and is withdrawn, emotionally flat, and incoherent *because* he is schizophrenic. Quite the opposite is true. He is called schizophrenic because he hears voices and is withdrawn, emotionally flat, and incoherent. Schizophrenia and other diagnoses are

Thomas Szasz

only descriptive labels. They explain nothing.

3. *The patient role.* The medical model has also been criticized because it suggests that people with behavioral problems should adopt the passive role of medical patient (Korchin, 1976). In this passive role, mental patients are implicitly encouraged to wait for their therapists to do the work to effect a cure. Such passiveness can be problematic even when an illness is purely physical. Passiveness in the face of a psychological disorder can seriously undermine the likelihood of improvement in the person's condition. In general, people with psychological problems need to be actively involved in their recovery efforts.

Putting the Medical Model in Perspective

So what position should we take on the medical model? We take an intermediate position, neither entirely accepting the model nor entirely discarding it. There certainly are significant problems with the medical model, and the questions raised by its critics deserve serious attention. In its defense, however, we must acknowledge that the medical model *has* stimulated scientific research on abnormal behavior. Moreover, some of the problems that are blamed on the disease analogy are not unique to this conception of abnormality. People who displayed strange, irrational behavior were labeled and stigmatized long before the medical model came along. Pseudoexplanations of psychological disorders were even more common and more primitive before the advent of the medical model.

Hence we take the position that the disease analogy can be useful as long as we remember that it is only an analogy. Medical concepts such as *diagnosis, etiology,* and *prognosis* have proved useful in the treatment and study of abnormality. **Diagnosis involves distinguishing one illness from another. Etiology refers to the apparent causation and developmental history of an illness. A *prognosis* is a forecast about the probable course of an illness.** These concepts have widely shared meanings that permit clinicians, researchers, and the public to communicate more effectively in their discussions of abnormal behavior.

So, flawed though it may be, we employ the disease analogy and use terms such as *abnormal behavior, mental illness,* and *psychological disorders* interchangeably. Do keep in mind, however, that the medical model is only an analogy. Most psychological disorders are not genuine diseases. Medical labels do not explain abnor-

mal behavior, and we need to be wary of the negative stereotypes associated with these labels. Remember, too, that the passive role of medical patient is not well suited to the treatment of psychological problems.

Criteria of Abnormal Behavior

If your next-door neighbor scrubs his front porch twice every day and spends virtually all his time cleaning and recleaning his house, is he normal? If your sister-in-law goes to one physician after another to seek treatment for aches and pains that appear imaginary, is she psychologically healthy? How are we to judge what's normal and what's abnormal? More important, who is to judge?

These are complex questions. In a sense, we all make judgments about normality, in that we all express opinions about others' (and perhaps our own) mental health. Of course, formal diagnoses of psychological disorders are made by mental health professionals. In making these judgments, clinicians and nonprofessionals generally apply the same criteria, albeit with highly varied levels of knowledge. Let's examine the criteria that are most frequently used in judgments of abnormality. Although two or three criteria may apply in a particular case, people are often viewed as disordered when only one criterion is met.

• *Deviance.* As Szasz has pointed out, people often are said to have a disorder because their behavior deviates from what their society considers acceptable. Standards for normal behavior vary somewhat from one culture to another, but all cultures have them. When people ignore these norms and expectations, they may be labeled mentally ill. Consider transvestites, for instance. **Transvestism is a sexual disorder in which a man achieves sexual arousal by dressing in women's clothing.** This behavior is regarded as disordered because a man who wears a dress, brassiere, and pantyhose is deviating from our culture's norms. Transvestism illustrates the arbitrary nature of cultural standards. In our society, it is normal for women to dress in clothing considered appropriate for men, but not vice versa. Thus exactly the same overt behavior (cross-sex dressing) is acceptable for one sex but deviant for the other.

• *Maladaptive behavior.* Many people are judged to have a psychological disorder because their everyday adaptive behavior is impaired. This is the key criterion in the diagnosis of substance use (drug) disorders. By itself, the use of recreational drugs is neither unusual nor necessarily deviant. However, when the use of cocaine, for instance, begins to interfere with a person's social or occupational functioning, that person has a substance use disorder. In such cases, it is the maladaptive quality of the behavior that makes it disordered.

• *Personal distress.* The diagnosis of a psychological disorder is often based on an individual's report of great personal distress. This is usually the criterion met by people who are troubled by depression or anxiety disorders. Depressed people may or may not exhibit deviant or maladaptive behavior. Such people are usually labeled disordered when they describe their subjective pain and suffering to friends, relatives, and mental health professionals.

Normality and Abnormality as a Continuum

Antonyms such as *normal* versus *abnormal* and *mental health* versus *mental illness* imply that people can be divided neatly into two distinct groups: those who are normal and those who are not. In reality, it is often difficult to draw a line that clearly separates normality from abnormality. On occasion, we all experience personal distress. We all act in deviant ways once in a while. And we all display some maladaptive behavior. People are judged to have psychological disorders only when their behavior becomes *extremely* deviant, maladaptive, or distressing. Thus normality and abnormality form a continuum. It's a matter of degree, not an either-or proposition (see Figure 15.2).

The Cultural Bounds of Normality

Judgments of normality and abnormality are influenced by cultural norms and values. Behavior that is considered deviant or maladaptive in one society may be quite acceptable in another. For example, in modern Western society people who "hear voices" are assumed to be irrational and are routinely placed in mental hospitals. In some cultures, however, hearing voices is so commonplace that no one raises an eyebrow.

Cultural norms regarding acceptable behavior may change over time. Consider how views of homosexuality have changed in our society. Homosexuality used to be listed as a sexual disorder in the American Psychiatric Association's diagnostic system. In 1973, however, a committee appointed by the association voted to delete homosexuality from the official list of psychological disorders. It took this action for several reasons. First, attitudes

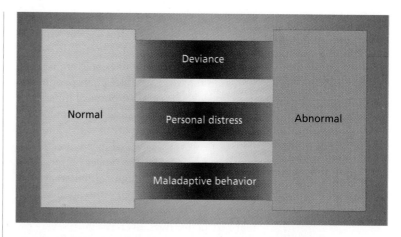

FIGURE 15.2
Normality and abnormality as a continuum
There is no sharp boundary between normal and abnormal behavior. The degree to which behavior is normal or abnormal depends on the extent to which it is deviant, personally distressing, or maladaptive.

toward homosexuality in our society had become more accepting. Second, gay rights activists campaigned vigorously for the change. Third, research showed that gays and heterosexuals did not differ overall on measures of psychological health (Rothblum et al., 1986). As you might guess, this change stimulated a great deal of debate.

Gays are not the only group that has tried to influence the psychiatric diagnostic system. In recent years women's groups have lobbied against the addition of a new diagnosis called *masochistic personality disorder,* because they see it as a sexist means to blame battered women for their partners' violence against them (Kass, Spitzer, Williams, & Widiger, 1989).

The key point is that diagnoses of psychological disorders involve *value judgments* about what represents normal and abnormal behavior. The criteria of mental illness are not nearly as value-free as the criteria of physical illness. In evaluating physical diseases, people usually can agree that a weak heart or a bad kidney is pathological, regardless of their personal values. Judgments about mental illness, however, reflect prevailing cultural values, social trends, and political forces as well as scientific knowledge.

Stereotypes of Psychological Disorders

We've seen that mental illnesses are not diseases in a strict sense and that judgments of mental health are not value-free. Still other myths about abnormal behavior need to be exposed as such. Let's examine four stereotypes about psychological disorders that are largely inaccurate.

1. *Psychological disorders are a sign of personal weakness.* Psychological disorders are often seen as manifestations of personal weakness and thus as causes for shame. In reality, psychological disorders are functions of many factors—

such as genetic predisposition, family background, and exposure to stress—over which we have little or no control. Mental illness can strike anyone. Mentally ill people are no more to blame for their troubles than people who develop leukemia or other physical illnesses.

2. *Psychological disorders are incurable.* Admittedly, treatment fails to cure some mentally ill people. However, they are greatly outnumbered by people who *do* get better, either spontaneously or through formal treatment. The vast majority of people who are diagnosed as mentally ill eventually improve and lead normal, productive lives. Even the most severe psychological disorders can be treated successfully.

3. *People with psychological disorders are often violent and dangerous.* There appears to be little or no association between mental illness and a tendency to violence (Cockerham, 1981). The disorder that is most widely believed to be linked to violent behavior is schizophrenia. A recent study in Alaska, however, found that schizophrenic patients are *not* arrested for violent crimes noticeably more than the general population (Phillips, Wolf, & Coons, 1988). This stereotype thrives because incidents of violence involving the mentally ill tend to command media attention. For example, our opening case history, which describes Ed's breakdown and the incident with the hatchet, was written up in a national newsmagazine. People such as John Hinckley, whose mental illness led him to attempt to assassinate President Reagan, receive extensive publicity. However, these individuals are not very representative of the large number of people who have struggled with psychological disorders.

4. *People with psychological disorders behave in bizarre ways and are very different from normal people.* This belief is true in only a small minority of cases, usually involving relatively severe disorders. At first glance, people with psychological disorders usually are indistinguishable from those without disorders. A study by David Rosenhan (1973) showed that even mental health professionals may have difficulty distinguishing normality from abnormality. To study diagnostic accuracy, Rosenhan arranged for several normal people to seek admission to mental hospitals. These "pseudopatients" arrived at the hospitals complaining of one false symptom—hearing voices. Except for this single symptom, they acted as they normally would and gave accurate information about their personal histories. All the pseudopatients were admitted, and the average length of their hospitalization was 19 days! Why is it so hard to distinguish normality from abnormality? The pseudopatients' observations about life on the

David Rosenhan

psychiatric wards offer a clue. They noted that the real patients acted normal most of the time and only infrequently acted in a deviant manner. As you might imagine, Rosenhan's study evoked quite a controversy about our diagnostic system for mental illness. Let's take a look at how this diagnostic system has evolved.

Psychodiagnosis: The Classification of Disorders

We can't lump all psychological disorders together without giving up hope of understanding them better. Hence a great deal of effort has been invested in devising an elaborate system for classifying psychological disorders.

A modern landmark in this classification effort was established in 1952 when the American Psychiatric Association unveiled its *Diagnostic and Statistical Manual of Mental Disorders.* Eventually known as DSM-I, this classification scheme described 60 disorders. Revisions intended to improve the system were completed in 1968 (DSM-II), 1980 (DSM-III), and 1987 (DSM-III-R). The next edition, DSM-IV, is due in 1993. More than ever before, the architects of DSM-IV are striving to base their revision on empirical research, as opposed to the consensus of experts (Widiger et al., 1991). Each revision of the DSM system has expanded the list of disorders covered. The current version describes over 200 types of psychological disorders.

The Multiaxial System

The publication of DSM-III in 1980 introduced a new *multiaxial system* of classification. The multiaxial system asks for judgments about individuals on five separate dimensions, or "axes." Figure 15.3 provides an overview of the entire system and the five axes. The diagnoses of disorders are made on Axes I and II. Clinicians record any major disorders that are apparent on Axis I. They use Axis II to list any personality or developmental disorders, which often coexist with Axis I syndromes. People may receive diagnoses on both axes.

The remaining axes are used to record supplemental information. A patient's physical disorders are listed on Axis III. On Axis IV, the clinician makes notations and ratings on the severity of stress experienced by the individual in the past year. On Axis V, estimates are made of the individual's current level of adaptive functioning (social and occupational behavior, viewed as a whole) and of the individual's highest level of functioning in the past year.

The multiaxial system, which recognizes

Axis I
Major Clinical Syndromes

1 *Disorders usually first evident in infancy, childhood, or adolescence*
This category includes disorders that arise before adolescence, such as attention deficit disorders, bulimia, anorexia, enuresis, and stuttering.

2 *Organic mental disorders*
These disorders are temporary or permanent dysfunctions of brain tissue caused by diseases or chemicals. Examples are delirium, dementia, and amnesia.

3 *Psychoactive substance-use disorders*
This category refers to the *maladaptive* use of drugs and alcohol. Mere consumption and recreational use of such substances are not disorders. This category requires an abnormal pattern of use, as with alcohol abuse and cocaine dependence.

4 *Schizophrenic disorders*
The schizophrenias are characterized by psychotic symptoms (for example, grossly disorganized behavior, delusions, and hallucinations) and by over 6 months of behavioral deterioration.

5 *Delusional disorders*
These disorders, of which paranoia is the most common, are characterized by persecutory delusions in the absence of other psychotic symptoms. In general, delusional patients are less impaired than schizophrenics.

6 *Mood disorders*
The cardinal feature is emotional disturbance. Patients may, or may not, have psychotic symptoms. These disorders include major depression, bipolar disorder, dysthymic disorder, and cyclothymic disorder.

7 *Anxiety disorders*
These disorders are characterized by physiological signs of anxiety (for example, palpitations) and subjective feelings of tension, apprehension, or fear. Anxiety may be acute and focused (panic disorder) or continual and diffuse (generalized anxiety disorder).

8 *Somatoform disorders*
These disorders are dominated by somatic symptoms that resemble physical illnesses. The symptoms cannot be accounted for by organic damage. There *must* also be strong evidence that these symptoms are produced by psychological factors or conflicts. This category includes somatization and conversion disorders and hypochondriasis.

9 *Dissociative disorders*
These disorders all feature a sudden, temporary alteration or dysfunction of memory, consciousness, identity, and behavior, as in depersonalization disorder, psychogenic amnesia, and multiple personality.

10 *Psychosexual disorders*
Psychological factors play major etiological roles in all of these disorders. There are 3 basic types: gender identity disorders (discomfort with identity as male or female), paraphilias (preference for unusual acts to achieve sexual arousal), and sexual dysfunctions (impairments in sexual functioning).

Axis II
Personality and Developmental Disorders

Personality disorders
These disorders are patterns of personality traits that are long standing, maladaptive, and inflexible and involve impaired functioning or subjective distress. Examples include borderline, schizoid, and passive-aggressive personality disorders.

Specific developmental disorders
These are disorders of specific developmental areas that are not due to another disorder. Examples include mental retardation; autism; and reading, writing, and arithmetic disorders.

Axis III
Physical Disorders and Conditions

Physical disorders or conditions are recorded on this axis. Examples include diabetes, arthritis, and hemophilia.

Axis IV
Severity of Psychosocial Stressors

Code	Term	Adult example
1	None	No relevant events
2	Mild	Starting or graduating from school
3	Moderate	Loss of job
4	Severe	Divorce
5	Extreme	Death of loved one
6	Catastrophic	Devastating natural disaster

Axis V
Global Assessment of Functioning (GAF) Scale

Code	Symptoms
90	Absent or minimal symptoms, good functioning in all areas.
80	Symptoms are transient and expectable reactions to psychosocial stressors.
70	Some mild symptoms or some difficulty in social, occupational, or school functioning, but generally functioning pretty well.
60	Moderate symptoms or difficulty in social, occupational, or school functioning.
50	Serious symptoms or impairment in social, occupational, or school functioning.
40	Some impairment in reality testing or communication, or major impairment in family relations, judgment, thinking, or mood.
30	Behavior is considerably influenced by delusions or hallucinations, serious impairment in communication or judgment, or inability to function in almost all areas.
20	Some danger of hurting self or others, occasional failure to maintain minimal personal hygiene, or gross impairment in communication.
10	Persistent danger of severely hurting self or others.

FIGURE 15.3
Overview of the DSM-III-R system
DSM-III-R is the formal classification system used in the diagnosis of psychological disorders. In this *multiaxial system*, information is recorded on the five axes described here. (Adapted with permission from the *Diagnostic and Statistical Manual of Mental Disorders* [3d ed., rev.]. Copyright © 1987, American Psychiatric Association.)

the importance of several kinds of information besides a traditional diagnostic label, has been widely lauded as a step in the right direction (Maser, Kaelber, & Weise, 1991). However, the distinction between Axis I disorders and Axis II disorders is plagued by conceptual inconsistencies (Frances et al., 1991) and it appears that clinicians make little use of Axis III (Maricle, Leung, & Bloom, 1987). Furthermore, Axes IV and V are poorly defined and there is little evidence regarding their validity (Rey et al., 1988; Williams, 1985). Additional research should lead to improvement of the supplementary axes in future editions of the DSM system.

Controversies over New Directions

You have undoubtedly heard people described as "neurotic." In the future, you will probably hear such descriptions less frequently. In a controversial move, DSM-III did away with a long-standing distinction between *neuroses* and *psychoses*, making both terms somewhat dated. Essentially, the accumulated evidence indicated that the disorders listed in each of these categories did not share enough factors to merit being grouped together. These disorders still exist, but they have been subdivided into smaller groups that have more in common.

Although neurosis and psychosis are no longer official diagnostic categories, these concepts are still used informally as broad descriptive terms. **Neurosis is applied to behavior marked by subjective distress (usually chronic anxiety) and reliance on avoidance coping.** People who are characterized as neurotic may be deeply troubled, but their contact with reality and their adaptive behavior are basically sound. In contrast, *psychosis* is applied to **behavior marked by impaired contact with**

reality and profound deterioration of adaptive functioning. In general, psychotic behavior is more obvious, more problematic for society, and more debilitating for the individual.

DSM-III also sparked controversy by adding everyday problems that are not traditionally thought of as mental illnesses to the diagnostic system. For example, DSM-III-R includes an academic underachievement disorder (not performing up to ability in school) and a nicotine dependence disorder (distress derived from quitting smoking). Critics argue that everyday problems such as these should not be listed in the diagnostic structure because this listing casts the shadow of pathology on normal behavior (McReynolds, 1979). However, critics of the old system (DSM-II) complained because it omitted many common problems that were being treated by psychologists and psychiatrists.

Shifting definitions of normality and abnormality inevitably affect estimates regarding the number of people who suffer from psychological disorders. The changes made in DSM-III stimulated a flurry of research on the prevalence of specific mental disorders. Let's examine some of this research.

The Prevalence of Psychological Disorders

How common are psychological disorders? What percentage of the population is afflicted with mental illness? Is it 10%? Perhaps 25%? Could the figure range as high as 40% or 50%?

Such questions fall within the domain of *epidemiology,* **the study of the distribution of mental or physical disorders in a population.** In epidemiology, *prevalence* refers to the percentage of people in a population who exhibit a disorder during a specified time period. In the case of psychological disorders, the most

FIGURE 15.4
Prevalence of common psychological disorders in the United States
The estimated percentage of people who have, at any time in their lives, suffered from one of four types of psychological disorders or from a disorder of any kind (top bar) is shown here. (Based on combined data from several chapters in Robins & Regier, 1991.)

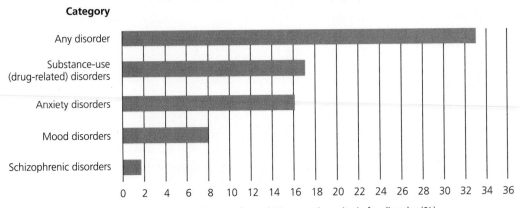

Category

Any disorder

Substance-use (drug-related) disorders

Anxiety disorders

Mood disorders

Schizophrenic disorders

0 2 4 6 8 10 12 14 16 18 20 22 24 26 28 30 32 34 36

Portion of population meeting criteria for disorder (%)

interesting data are the estimates of *lifetime prevalence*, the percentage of people who endure a specific disorder at any time in their lives.

Estimates of lifetime prevalence suggest that psychological disorders are more common than most people realize. Before the advent of DSM-III, studies suggested that about *one-fifth* of the population exhibited clear signs of mental illness (Neugebauer, Dohrenwend & Dohrenwend, 1980). The older studies did not assess drug-related disorders very effectively, however, because these disorders were vaguely described in DSM-I and DSM-II. More recent studies, employing the explicit criteria for substance use disorders in DSM-III, have found psychological disorders in roughly *one-third* of the population. This increase in mental illness is more apparent than real, as it is due mostly to more effective tabulation of drug-related disorders. As Figure 15.4 shows, the most common disorders are (1) substance (alcohol and drugs) use disorders, (2) anxiety disorders, and (3) mood disorders (Robins, Locke, & Regier, 1991).

The raw numbers are more dramatic than the prevalence rates in Figure 15.4. Estimates based on these prevalence rates suggest that the United States contains nearly 4 million people who will be troubled at some time by schizophrenic disorders. Roughly 20 million people will experience mood disorders (mostly depression). And over 40 million people will wrestle with substance use disorders or anxiety disorders. If you're thinking that these estimates add up to more than one-third of the population, you're right. Some people have more than one disorder. A substantial portion of people with substance use disorders, for instance, qualify for a second psychiatric diagnosis (Helzer, Burnam, & McEvoy, 1991). In any case, it's clear that psychological disorders are widespread. When psychologists note that mental illness can strike anyone, they mean it quite literally.

We are now ready to start examining the specific types of psychological disorders. Obviously, we cannot cover all 200 or so disorders listed in the DSM system. However, we will introduce most of the major categories of disorders to give you an overview of the many forms abnormal behavior takes. In discussing each set of disorders, we will begin with brief descriptions of the specific syndromes or subtypes that fall in the category. Then we'll focus on the *etiology* of the disorders in that category. Although there are many paths that may lead

to specific disorders, some are more common than others. We'll highlight some of the common paths to enhance your understanding of the roots of abnormal behavior.

Anxiety Disorders

e all experience anxiety from time to time. Anxiety is a natural and common reaction to many of life's difficulties. For some people, however, anxiety becomes a chronic problem. These people experience high levels of anxiety with disturbing regularity. **Anxiety disorders** are a class of

disorders marked by feelings of excessive apprehension and anxiety. There are four principal types of anxiety disorders: generalized anxiety disorders, phobic disorders, panic disorders, and obsessive-compulsive disorders. They are not mutually exclusive, as many people who exhibit one anxiety syndrome often suffer from another at some point in their lives (Weissman, 1988). People with anxiety disorders also exhibit elevated rates of depression (Klerman, 1988). Studies suggest that anxiety disorders are fairly common, occurring in roughly 17% of the population (Robins & Regier, 1991; Weissman, 1985). Most of these cases involve generalized anxiety disorder or phobic disorder (Blazer et al., 1991; Eaton, Dryman, & Weissman, 1991).

Generalized Anxiety Disorders

The *generalized anxiety disorder* is marked by a chronic high level of anxiety that is not tied to any specific threat. This anxiety is sometimes called "free-floating anxiety" because of its nonspecific nature. People with this disorder worry constantly about yesterday's mistakes and tomorrow's problems. They often dread decisions and brood over them endlessly. Their anxiety is frequently accompanied by physical symptoms, such as trembling, muscle tension, diarrhea, dizziness, faintness, sweating, and heart palpitations.

Phobic Disorders

In a phobic disorder, an individual's troublesome anxiety has a specific focus. A *phobic disorder is marked by a persistent and irrational fear of an object or situation that presents no realistic danger.* The following case provides an example of a phobic disorder.

> Hilda is 32 years of age and has a rather unusual fear. She is terrified of snow. She cannot go outside in the snow. She cannot even stand to see snow or hear about it on the weather report. Her phobia severely constricts her day-to-day behavior. Probing in therapy revealed that her phobia was caused by a traumatic experience at age 11. Playing at a ski lodge, she was buried briefly by a small avalanche of snow. She had no recollection of this experience until it was recovered in therapy. [Adapted from Laughlin, 1967, p. 227]

As Hilda's unusual snow phobia demon-

FIGURE 15.5
Common phobias
Frequently reported phobias are listed here, along with their typical age of onset and information on sex differences.

Common Phobias	Approximate percent of all phobias	Sex difference	Typical age of onset
Agoraphobias (fear of places of assembly, crowds, open spaces)	10%–50%	Large majority are women	Early adulthood
Social phobias (fear of being observed doing something humiliating)	10%	Majority are women	Adolescence
Specific phobias *Animals* Cats (ailurophobia) Dogs (cynophobia) Insects (insectophobia) Spiders (arachnophobia) Birds (avisophobia) Horses (equinophobia) Snakes (ophidiophobia) Rodents (rodentophobia)	5%–15%	Vast majority are women	Childhood
Inanimate objects Dirt (mysophobia) Storms (brontophobia) Heights (acrophobia) Darkness (nyctophobia) Closed spaces (claustrophobia)	20%	None	Any age
Illness-injury (nosophobia) Death (thanatophobia) Cancer (cancerophobia) Venereal disease (venerophobia)	15%–25%	None	Middle age

strates, people can develop phobic responses to virtually anything. Nonetheless, certain types of phobias are relatively common, including most of those listed in Figure 15.5. Particularly common are claustrophobia (fear of small, enclosed places), acrophobia (fear of heights), brontophobia (fear of storms), hydrophobia (fear of water), and various animal and social phobias (Eaton et al., 1991). Claustrophobia tends to develop before age 35, whereas animal phobias usually emerge during childhood and social phobias during adolescence (Ost, 1987). Many people troubled by phobias realize that their fears are irrational, but they still are unable to calm themselves when confronted by a phobic object.

Panic Disorders and Agoraphobia

A *panic disorder* involves recurrent attacks of overwhelming anxiety that usually occur suddenly and unexpectedly. These paralyzing attacks are accompanied by physical symptoms of anxiety. After a few anxiety attacks, victims often become very apprehensive, wondering when their next panic will occur. Their concern about exhibiting panic in public may escalate to the point where they are afraid to leave home. This development creates a condition called *agoraphobia*, which is a common complication of panic disorders.

Agoraphobia is a fear of going out to public places (its literal meaning is "fear of the marketplace"). Because of this fear, some people become prisoners confined to their homes. As its name suggests, agoraphobia was originally viewed as a phobic disorder, but studies eventually showed that it is more akin to panic disorders than to phobic disorders (Turner, McCann, Beidel, & Mezzich, 1986). Nonetheless, agoraphobia can occur independently of panic disorder, and some theorists question the wisdom of the decision to lump panic and agoraphobia together in the DSM classification scheme (Marks, 1988; Noyes, 1988). Most agoraphobics are women, and the typical age of onset for the disorder is late adolescence or early adulthood (Barlow & Waddell, 1985).

Obsessive-Compulsive Disorders

Obsessions are *thoughts* that repeatedly intrude on one's consciousness in a distressing way. Compulsions are *actions* that one feels forced to carry out. Thus an *obsessive-compulsive disorder* is marked by persistent, uncontrollable

Constant handwashing is an example of compulsive behavior.

intrusions of unwanted thoughts (obsessions) and urges to engage in senseless rituals (compulsions). To illustrate, let's examine the bizarre behavior of a man once reputed to be the wealthiest person in the world.

The famous industrialist Howard Hughes was obsessed by the possibility of being contaminated by germs. This fear led him to devise extraordinary rituals to minimize the possibility of such contamination. He would spend hours methodically cleaning a single telephone. He once wrote a three-page memo instructing assistants on exactly how to open cans of fruit for him. The following is just a small portion of the instructions that Hughes provided for a driver who delivered films to his bungalow. "Get out of the car on the traffic side. Do not at any time be on the side of the car between the car and the curb. . . . Carry only one can of film at a time. Step over the gutter opposite the place where the sidewalk dead-ends into the curb from a point as far out into the center of the road as possible. Do not ever walk on the grass at all, also do not step into the gutter at all. Walk to the bungalow keeping as near to the center of the sidewalk as possible . . ." [Adapted from Barlett & Steele, 1979, pp. 227–237]

Obsessions often center on inflicting harm on others, personal failures, suicide, or sexual acts. People troubled by obsessions may feel that they have lost control of their minds. Compulsions usually involve stereotyped rituals that temporarily relieve anxiety. Among common compulsions are constant hand washing, repetitive cleaning of things that are already clean, and endless rechecking of locks, faucets, and such. Unusual rituals intended to bring good luck are also a common form of compulsive behavior. Although many of us can be compulsive at times, full-fledged obsessive-compulsive disorders occur in roughly 2 to 4 % of the population (Karno & Golding, 1991). Most victims exhibit both obsessions and compulsions, but some experience only one or the other (Marks, 1987).

Etiology of Anxiety Disorders

Like most psychological disorders, anxiety disorders develop out of complicated interactions of a variety of factors. Conditioning processes and aspects of child rearing seem to be especially important, but biological factors may also contribute to anxiety disorders.

Biological Factors

A handful of studies suggest that there may be a weak genetic predisposition to anxiety disorders (Crowe, 1988; Noyes et al., 1987). These findings are consistent with a long-discussed theory that inherited differences in autonomic reactivity may make some people more vulnerable than others to anxiety disorders (Martin, 1971). According to this theory, people with high autonomic reactivity are especially likely to develop anxiety problems because their bodies overreact to the everyday stresses of life. Thought-provoking connections have also been found between anxiety disorders and a common heart defect, *mitral valve prolapse*. This anatomical defect, which makes people prone to heart palpitations, faintness, and chest pain, may predispose some people to problems with anxiety (Agras, 1985).

Evidence also suggests a link between anxiety disorders and neurochemical activity in the brain. **Neurotransmitters are chemicals that carry signals from one neuron to another.** Tranquilizing drugs, such as Valium, that reduce excessive anxiety appear to alter the activity of the neurotransmitter GABA. This finding and other lines of evidence suggest that disturbances in the neural circuits that are activated by GABA may play a role in anxiety disorders (Paul, Crawley, & Skolnick, 1986). Also, abnormalities in the neural circuits that are activated by another neurotransmitter (serotonin) have been implicated in obsessive-compulsive disorders (Rapoport, 1989). Thus scientists are beginning to unravel the neurochemical bases for anxiety disorders.

Conditioning

Many of our anxiety responses may be *acquired through classical conditioning* and *maintained through operant conditioning*. According to Mowrer (1947), an originally neutral stimulus (the snow in Hilda's case, for instance) may be paired with a frightening event (the avalanche) so that it becomes a conditioned stimulus eliciting anxiety (see Figure 15.6). This is classical conditioning, which we first described in Chapter 2.

Once a conditioned fear is acquired, a person may start avoiding the anxiety-producing stimulus. This avoidance response is negatively reinforced because it is followed by a reduction in unpleasant anxiety (see Figure 15.6). This is an instance of operant conditioning (also explained in Chapter 2). Thus separate conditioning processes may create and then sustain specific anxiety responses (McAllister, McAllister, Scoles, & Hampton, 1986).

Our tendency to develop irrational fears of certain types of objects and situations rather than others may be explained by Martin Seligman's (1971) concept of *preparedness*. Like many theorists, Seligman believes that classical conditioning creates most phobic responses. He theorizes, however, that *we are biologically prepared by our evolutionary history to acquire some*

**FIGURE 15.6
Conditioning as an explanation for phobias**
Many phobias appear to be acquired through classical conditioning when a neutral stimulus is paired with an anxiety-arousing stimulus. Once acquired, a phobia may be maintained through operant conditioning because avoidance of the phobic stimulus leads to a reduction in anxiety, resulting in negative reinforcement.

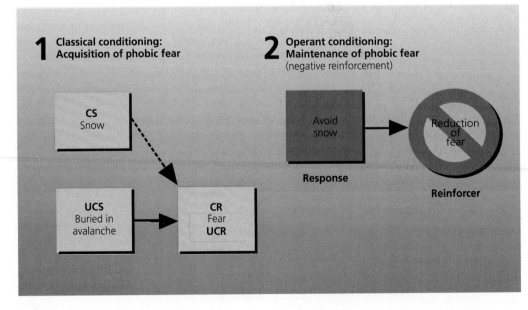

fears much more easily than others. His theory would explain why we develop phobias of ancient sources of threat (for example, snakes and spiders) much more readily than modern sources of threat (for example, electrical outlets and hot irons). Thus far, laboratory studies have provided inconsistent support for Seligman's theory of preparedness (Cook & Mineka, 1989; McNally, 1987).

The conditioning model of phobias is brought into question by evidence that many people with phobias cannot recall or identify a traumatic conditioning experience that led to their phobia (Rachman, 1990). However, these failures to recall relevant conditioning experiences could reflect poor memory of childhood trauma. Or they could be due to unconscious repression, as in Hilda's case. Although the details are still being worked out, there is ample evidence that conditioning frequently contributes to the development of anxiety disorders.

Child-Rearing Patterns

The way we are reared may affect our vulnerability to anxiety disorders. Parents may unintentionally foster anxiety in their children in a variety of ways. Some children may acquire fears and anxieties through *observational learning* (Bandura & Rosenthal, 1966). For example, if a father hides in a closet every time there's a thunderstorm, his children may acquire their father's fear of storms. Laboratory studies have shown that conditioned fears can be created in animals through observational learning (Mineka & Cook, 1986).

Associations have also been found between overprotection by parents and elevated anxiety in their children (Parker, 1988). Parents who are overprotective may make their children feel that the world is a dangerous place. This sense of threat could predispose the children to anxiety reactions later in life. Howard Hughes's mother, for instance, was extremely overprotective. She worried constantly about his health and tried to shelter him from the real world throughout his childhood (Fowler, 1986). She may have planted the seeds for Hughes's lifelong chronic anxiety.

Stress

Like many other types of psychological disorders, anxiety disorders appear to be related to stress. Studies have found an association between high stress and the onset of generalized anxiety disorders (Blazer, Hughes, & George, 1987) and of panic disorders (Faravelli & Pallanti, 1989). The evidence suggests that stress helps to precipitate anxiety disorders.

Somatoform Disorders

 hances are you have met people who always seem to be complaining about aches, pains, and physical maladies of doubtful authenticity. You may have thought to yourself, "It's all in his head" and concluded that the person exhibited a "psychosomatic" condition. As we noted in Chapter 3, however, the term *psychosomatic* is widely misused. **Psychosomatic diseases are genuine physical ailments caused in part by psychological factors, especially emotional distress.** These diseases, which include such maladies as ulcers, asthma, and high blood pressure, have a genuine organic basis and are not imagined ailments. They are recorded on the DSM axis for physical problems (Axis III). When physical illness appears *entirely* psychological in origin, we are dealing with *somatoform disorders*, which are recorded on Axis I. **Somatoform disorders are physical ailments that have no authentic organic basis but are due solely to psychological factors.** Although their symptoms are more imaginary than real, victims of somatoform disorders are *not* simply faking illness. Their subjective distress is real. Deliberate feigning of illness for personal gain is another matter altogether, called *malingering*.

People with somatoform disorders typically seek treatment from physicians practicing neurology, internal medicine, and family medicine instead of psychologists or psychiatrists. Somatoform disorders can be difficult to diagnose accurately because the causes of physical ailments are sometimes hard to identify. In some cases, a diagnosis of somatoform disorder is wrongly made when a genuine organic cause for a person's physical symptoms goes undetected in spite of extensive medical examinations and tests (Rubin, Zorumski, & Guze, 1986).

We will discuss three specific types of somatoform disorders: somatization disorders, conversion disorders, and hypochondriasis. Diagnostic difficulties make it hard to obtain sound data on the prevalence of somatoform disorders. Hypochondriasis appears to be fairly common, but somatization and conversion disorders seem to be relatively infrequent (Barsky, 1989).

Somatization Disorders

Individuals with somatization disorders are often said to "cling to ill health." *A somatization disorder is marked by a history of diverse physical complaints that appear to be psychological in origin.* Somatization disorders occur mostly in women. Victims report an endless succession of minor physical ailments. They usually have a long and complicated history of medical treatment by many doctors. The distinguishing feature of this disorder is the diversity of victims' physical complaints. Over the years they report a mixed bag of cardiovascular, gastrointestinal, pulmonary, neurological, and genitourinary symptoms. The improbability of such a smorgasbord of symptoms often alerts a physician to the possible psychological basis for the patient's problems.

Conversion Disorders

Conversion disorders involve a significant loss of physical function (with no apparent organic basis), usually in a single organ system. Common symptoms include partial or complete loss of vision, partial or complete loss of hearing, partial paralysis, severe laryngitis or mutism, and loss of feeling or function in limbs, such as that seen in the following case.

> Mildred was a rancher's daughter who lost the use of both of her legs during adolescence. Mildred was at home alone one afternoon when a male relative attempted to assault her. She screamed for help, and her legs gave way as she slipped to the floor. She was found on the floor a few minutes later when her mother returned home. She could not get up, so she was carried

to her bed. Her legs buckled when she made subsequent attempts to walk on her own. Due to her illness, she was waited on hand and foot by her family and friends. Neighbors brought her homemade things to eat or to wear. She became the center of attention in the household. [Adapted from Cameron, 1963, pp. 312–313]

People with conversion disorders are usually troubled by more severe ailments than people with somatization disorders. Some cases of conversion disorder offer telltale clues about the psychological origins of the illness because the patient's symptoms are not consistent with medical knowledge about their apparent disease. For instance, the loss of feeling in one hand—"glove anesthesia"—is inconsistent with the known facts of neurological organization (see Figure 15.7).

Hypochondriasis

Hypochondriacs constantly monitor their physical condition, looking for signs of illness. Any tiny alteration from their physical norm leads them to conclude that they have contracted a disease. *Hypochondriasis (more widely known as hypochondria) involves excessive preoccupation with health concerns and incessant worry about developing physical illnesses.* The following case illustrates the nature of hypochondria.

> Jeff is a middle-aged man who works as a clerk in a drugstore. He spends long hours describing his health problems to anyone who will listen. Jeff is an avid reader of popular magazine articles on medicine. He can tell you all about the latest medical discoveries. He takes all sorts of

EDGAR ARGO

"THE WAY HE MOANS AND GROANS WHEN HE GETS A LITTLE COLD... I CAN'T DECIDE WHETHER HE SHOULD CALL A DOCTOR OR A DRAMA CRITIC."

Reprinted by permission of Edgar Argo.

pills and vitamins to ward off possible illnesses. He's the first to try every new product on the market. Jeff is constantly afflicted by new symptoms of illness. His most recent problems are poor digestion and a heartbeat that he thinks is irregular. He frequently goes to physicians who can find nothing wrong with him physically. They tell him that he is healthy. He thinks they use "backward techniques." He suspects that his illness is too rare to be diagnosed successfully. [Adapted from Suinn, 1984, p. 236]

When hypochondriacs are assured by their physicians that they do not have any real illness, they often are skeptical and disbelieving. As in Jeff's case, they assume that the physician must be incompetent and they go shopping for another doctor. Hypochondriacs don't subjectively suffer from physical distress as much as they *overinterpret* every conceivable sign of illness. Hypochondria often appears alongside other psychological disorders, especially anxiety disorders and depression (Turner, Jacob, & Morrison, 1984). Howard Hughes's obsessive-compulsive disorder, for example, was coupled with profound hypochondria.

Etiology of Somatoform Disorders

Inherited aspects of physiological functioning may predispose people to somatoform disorders (Jacob & Turner, 1984). Available evidence suggests, however, that these disorders are largely a function of personality and learning.

Personality Factors

People with certain personality traits seem to be particularly prone to develop somatoform disorders. The prime candidates are people with *histrionic* personality characteristics (Nemiah, 1985). The histrionic personality tends to be self-centered, suggestible, excitable, highly emotional, and overly dramatic. Such people thrive on the attention they get when they become ill.

Learning: The Sick Role

As we discussed in Chapter 4, some people grow fond of the role associated with being sick (Lubkin, 1990). Their complaints of physical symptoms may be reinforced by indirect benefits derived from their illness. What benefits are commonly associated with physical illness? For one thing, becoming ill is a superb way to avoid the need to confront life's challenges. Many

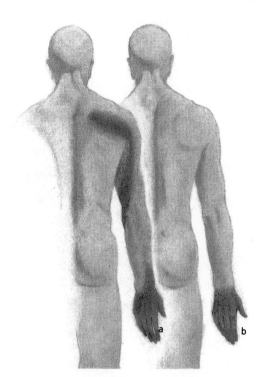

FIGURE 15.7
Glove anesthesia
The physical complaints of people with conversion disorders are sometimes inconsistent with the known facts of physiology. Such is the case in glove anesthesia, in which the patient complains of losing feeling in a hand. Given the patterns of nerve distribution in the arm (a), a loss of feeling in the hand exclusively (b) is a physical impossibility—an indication that the patient's problem is psychological in origin.

people with somatoform disorders are avoiding facing up to marital problems, career frustrations, family responsibilities, and the like. After all, when you're sick, no one can place great demands upon you.

Attention is another payoff that may reinforce complaints of physical illness. When people become ill, they command the attention of family, friends, co-workers, and doctors. The sympathy that illness often brings may strengthen a person's tendency to feel ill. This was clearly the case in Mildred's conversion disorder. Her illness paid handsome dividends in attention, consolation, and kindhearted assistance.

Dissociative Disorders

issociative disorders are among the more unusual syndromes that we'll discuss. *Dissociative disorders* **are a class of disorders characterized by loss of contact with portions of one's consciousness or memory, which results in disruptions in one's sense of identity.** We'll describe two dissociative syndromes, both of which are relatively uncommon.

Psychogenic Amnesia

Psychogenic amnesia **is a sudden loss of memory for important personal information that is too extensive to be due to normal forgetting.** Psychogenic memory losses may cover anything from a few hours to an entire lifetime, although the latter is rare. These memory losses center on one's identity or on a specific disturbing incident. When identity-related memory losses occur, people may forget their names, their families, where they live, and where they work. Yet they remember matters unrelated to their identity, such as how to drive a car or the square root of 9. When memory losses center on a traumatic incident (such as an automobile accident or a fire), the person usually has no memory of the incident itself or of the events of the next several hours to several days.

Multiple-Personality Disorders

Multiple-personality disorders involve the coexistence in one person of two or more largely complete, and usually very different, personalities. In multiple-personality disorders, the divergences in behavior go far beyond those that people normally display in adapting to different roles in life. Indeed, people with multiple personalities feel that they have more than one identity. Each personality has its own name, memories, traits, and physical mannerisms. Although rare, this "Dr. Jekyl and Mr. Hyde" syndrome is frequently portrayed in novels, movies, and television shows. In popular media portrayals, the syndrome is often mistakenly called "schizophrenia." As we shall see, schizophrenic disorders are entirely different.

In a multiple-personality disorder, the original personality often is not aware of the alternate personalities. The alternate personalities usually *are* aware of the original one, however, and have varying amounts of awareness of each other. The alternate personalities frequently display traits that are quite foreign to the original personality. A shy, inhibited person may develop a flamboyant, extraverted alternate personality. Transitions between personalities often occur suddenly.

Multiple-personality disorders were thought to be very rare until the 1980s, when there was a dramatic increase in this diagnosis (Braun, 1986; Ross, Anderson, Fleisher, & Norton, 1991). Some theorists believe that multiple-personality disorders used to be underdiagnosed; that is, they frequently went undetected (Kluft, 1987). Skeptics argue that a handful of clinicians are overdiagnosing the condition (Thigpen & Cleckley, 1984). The debate about the reason for the sudden upsurge in multiple-personality diagnoses is far from settled. It probably won't be resolved without a great deal of additional research.

Etiology of Dissociative Disorders

Psychogenic amnesia is usually attributed to excessive stress. However, relatively little is known about why this extreme reaction to stress occurs in certain people but not others. The causes of multiple-personality disorders are equally obscure. Some skeptical theorists believe that people with multiple personalities are engaging in intentional role playing to use mental illness as a face-saving excuse for their personal failings (Spanos, Weekes, & Bertrand, 1985). Indeed, there is evidence that multiple-personality disorders are faked with some regularity.

However, various lines of evidence suggest to most theorists that at least some cases are authentic (Aalpoel & Lewis, 1984). Many of these cases seem to be rooted in severe emotional trauma during childhood. A substantial portion of people with multiple-personality disorder have a history of disturbed home life, beatings and rejection by parents, and sexual abuse (Ross et al., 1990). In the final analysis, however, we know very little about the causes of multiple-personality disorders.

Mood Disorders

hat did Abraham Lincoln, Marilyn Monroe, Ernest Hemingway, Winston Churchill, Janis Joplin, and Leo Tolstoy have in common? Yes, they all achieved great prominence, albeit in different ways at different times. But, more pertinent to our interest, they all suffered from severe mood disorders. Although mood disorders can be terribly debilitating, people with mood disorders may still achieve greatness, because such disorders tend to be *episodic*. In other words, emotional disorders tend to come and go. Episodes of disturbance are interspersed among periods of normality.

Of course, we all have our ups and downs in mood. Life would be dull indeed if our emotional tone was constant. All of us experience depression occasionally, and all of us have days that we sail through on an emotional high. Such emotional fluctuations are natural, but some people are prone to extreme distortions of mood. **Mood disorders are marked by emotional disturbances that may spill over to disrupt physical, perceptual, social, and thought processes.**

There are two basic types of mood disorders: unipolar and bipolar (see Figure 15.8). People with *unipolar disorders* experience emotional extremes at just one end of the mood continuum—*depression*. People with *bipolar disorders* experience emotional extremes at both ends of the mood continuum, going through periods of both *depression and mania* (excitement and elation). The mood swings in bipolar disorders can be patterned in many ways.

Recent studies suggest that periods of emotional disturbance may follow a seasonal pattern in some people. **In a *seasonal affective (mood) disorder,* an individual's periods of depression or mania tend to occur repeatedly at about the same time each year.** A seasonal pattern may be seen in either unipolar or bipolar disorders. The most common pattern appears to be recurrent depression in the winter (Wehr & Rosenthal, 1989). Researchers suspect that seasonal patterns in mood disorders are tied to human biological rhythms (Lewy et al., 1989). These rhythms are presumably affected by exposure to daylight, which at latitudes far from the equator varies according to the time of year (Wehr, Sack, Parry, & Rosenthal, 1986). Evidence on these hypothesized relations between biological rhythms and emotional disturbances is still fragmentary.

Depressive Disorders

The line between normal and abnormal depression can be very difficult to draw. Ultimately, a subjective judgment is required. Crucial considerations are the duration of the depression and its disruptive effects. When a depression significantly impairs everyday adaptive behavior for more than a few weeks, there is reason for concern.

People with *depressive disorders* show persistent feelings of sadness and despair and a loss of interest in previous sources of pleasure. The most common symptoms of depressive disorders are summarized in Figure 15.9,

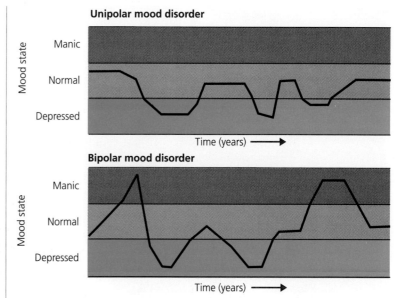

Unipolar mood disorder

Bipolar mood disorder

FIGURE 15.8
Episodic patterns in mood disorders
Episodes of emotional disturbance come and go unpredictably in people with mood disorders. People with unipolar disorders suffer from bouts of depression only, while people with bipolar disorders experience both manic and depressed episodes. The time between episodes of disturbance varies greatly.

along with the symptoms of mania. Negative emotions form the heart of the depressive syndrome, but many other symptoms may also appear. Depressed people often give up activities that they used to find enjoyable. For example, a depressed person may stop going bowling or give up a favorite hobby such as photography. Reduced appetite and insomnia are common. People with depression often lack energy. They tend to move sluggishly and talk slowly. Anxiety, irritability, and brooding are frequently observed. Self-esteem tends to sink as the depressed person begins to feel worthless. Depression plunges people into feelings of hopelessness, dejection, and boundless guilt. The severity of abnormal depression varies considerably.

How common are depressive disorders? Very common. Recent studies suggest that about 7% of the population endures a unipolar depressive disorder at some point in time (Weissman et al., 1991). The onset of unipolar disorders can occur throughout the life span and is *not* strongly related to age (Lewinsohn, Duncan, Stanton, & Hautzinger, 1986).

Comparison of Manic and Depressive Symptoms

Characteristics	Manic episode	Depressive episode
Emotional	Elated, euphoric, very sociable, impatient at any hindrance	Gloomy, hopeless, socially withdrawn, irritable
Cognitive	Characterized by racing thoughts, flight of ideas, desire for action, and impulsive behavior; talkative, self-confident; experiencing delusions of grandeur	Characterized by slowness of thought processes, obsessive worrying, inability to make decisions, negative self-image, self-blame, and delusions of guilt and disease
Motor	Hyperactive, tireless, requiring less sleep than usual, showing increased sex drive and fluctuating appetite	Less active, tired, experiencing difficulty in sleeping, showing decreased sex drive and decreased appetite

FIGURE 15.9
Common symptoms in manic and depressive episodes
The emotional, cognitive, and motor symptoms exhibited in manic and depressive illnesses are largely the opposites of each other.

Ernest Hemingway and Janis Joplin suffered from depression, a common psychological disorder that causes its victims to feel worthless and hopeless.

Bipolar Mood Disorders

Bipolar mood disorders (formerly known as manic-depressive disorders) are marked by the experience of both depressed and manic periods. The symptoms seen in manic periods generally are the opposite of those seen in depression (see Figure 15.9). In a manic episode, a person's mood becomes elevated to the point of euphoria. Self-esteem skyrockets as the person bubbles over with optimism, energy, and extravagant plans. People become hyperactive and may go for days without sleep. They talk rapidly and shift topics wildly as their minds race at breakneck speed. Judgment is often impaired. Some people in manic periods gamble impulsively, spend money frantically, or become sexually reckless. Like depressive disorders, bipolar disorders vary considerably in severity.

You may be thinking that the euphoria in manic episodes sounds appealing. If so, you are not entirely wrong. In their milder forms, manic states can seem attractive. The increases in energy, self-esteem, and optimism can be deceptively seductive. Because of the increase in energy, many bipolar patients report temporary surges of productivity and creativity (Jamison, Gerner, Hammen, & Padesky, 1980).

Although manic episodes may have some positive aspects, bipolar mood disorders ultimately prove to be very troublesome for most victims. Manic periods often have a paradoxical negative undertow of uneasiness and irritability. Moreover, mild manic episodes usually escalate to higher levels that become scary and disturbing. Impaired judgment leads many victims to do things that they greatly regret later, as in the following case.

Robert, a dentist, awoke one morning with the idea that he was the most gifted dental surgeon in his area. He decided that he should try to provide services to as many people as possible, so that more people could benefit from his talents. So he decided to remodel his two-chair dental office, installing 20 booths so that he could simultaneously attend to 20 patients. That very day he drew up plans for this arrangement, telephoned a number of remodelers, and invited bids for the work. Later that day, impatient to get going on his remodeling, he rolled up his sleeves, got himself a sledgehammer, and began to knock down the walls in his office. Annoyed when that didn't go so well, he smashed his dental tools, washbasins, and X-ray equipment. Later, Robert's wife became concerned about his behavior and summoned two of her adult daughters for assistance. The daughters responded quickly, arriving at the family home with their husbands. In the ensuing discussion, Robert—after bragging about his sexual prowess—made advances toward his daughters. He had to be subdued by their husbands. [Adapted from Kleinmuntz, 1980, p. 309]

Although bipolar disorders are not rare, they are much less common than unipolar depression. Bipolar disorders affect a little under 1% of the population (Weissman et al., 1991). The onset of bipolar disorders is age-related, with the peak of vulnerability occurring between the ages of 24 and 31 (Murphy, 1980).

Etiology of Mood Disorders

We know quite a bit about the etiology of mood disorders, although the puzzle hasn't been assembled completely. There appear to be a variety of routes into these disorders, each

involving intricate interactions between psychological and biological factors.

Genetic Vulnerability

The evidence strongly suggests that genetic factors influence the likelihood that one will develop a major depression or a bipolar mood disorder. In studies that assess the impact of heredity on psychological disorders, investigators look at *concordance rates*. **A concordance rate indicates the percentage of twin pairs or other pairs of relatives who exhibit the same disorder.** If relatives who share more genetic similarity show higher concordance rates than relatives who share less genetic overlap, this finding supports the genetic hypothesis. Twin studies, which compare identical and fraternal twins (see Chapter 2), suggest that genetic factors *are* involved in mood disorders (Gershon, Berrettini, & Goldin, 1989). Concordance rates average around 67% for identical twins but only 15% for fraternal twins, who share less genetic similarity. Thus, evidence suggests that heredity can create a *predisposition* to mood disorders. Environmental factors probably determine whether this predisposition is converted into an actual disorder.

Neurochemical Factors

Heredity may influence susceptibility to mood disorders by creating a predisposition toward certain types of neurochemical activity in the brain. Correlations have been found between mood disorders and the levels of two neurotransmitters in the brain—norepinephrine and serotonin (Hirschfeld & Goodwin, 1988; Kandel, 1990). Although the details remain elusive, it seems clear that at least some mood disorders have a neurochemical basis. A variety of drug therapies are fairly effective in the treatment of severe mood disorders. Most of these drugs are known to affect the availability (in the brain) of the neurotransmitters that have been related to mood disorders (Zis & Goodwin, 1982). Since this effect is unlikely to be a

coincidence, it bolsters the plausibility of the idea that neurochemical changes produce mood disturbances.

If alterations in neurotransmitter activity are the basis for many mood disorders, what causes the alterations in neurotransmitter activity? These neurochemical changes probably depend on our reactions to environmental events. Thus a variety of psychological factors have been implicated in the etiology of mood disorders.

Cognitive Factors

A variety of theories emphasize how cognitive factors contribute to depressive disorders (Abramson, Metalsky, & Alloy, 1988; Beck, 1976; Ellis, 1984; Seligman, 1983). In recent years, theories that focus on our patterns of *attribution* have generated a great deal of research on the cognitive roots of depression. As we noted in Chapter 5, **attributions are inferences that people draw about the causes of events, others' behavior, and their own behavior.** We routinely make attributions because we want to understand our personal fates and the events that take place around us. If your boss criticizes your work, for example, you will probably ask yourself why. Was your work really that sloppy? Was your boss just in a grouchy mood? Was the criticism a manipulative effort to motivate you to work harder? Each of these potential explanations is an attribution.

Attributions can be analyzed along several dimensions, three of which are illustrated in Figure 15.10. The most prominent dimension is the degree to which we attribute events to *internal, personal factors versus external, situational factors*. If you performed poorly on a standardized mathematics test, for instance, you might attribute your poor showing to your lack of intelligence (an internal attribution) or to the heat and humidity in the exam room (an external attribution).

Another key dimension is the degree to which we attribute events to factors that are *stable or unstable over time*. Thus you might

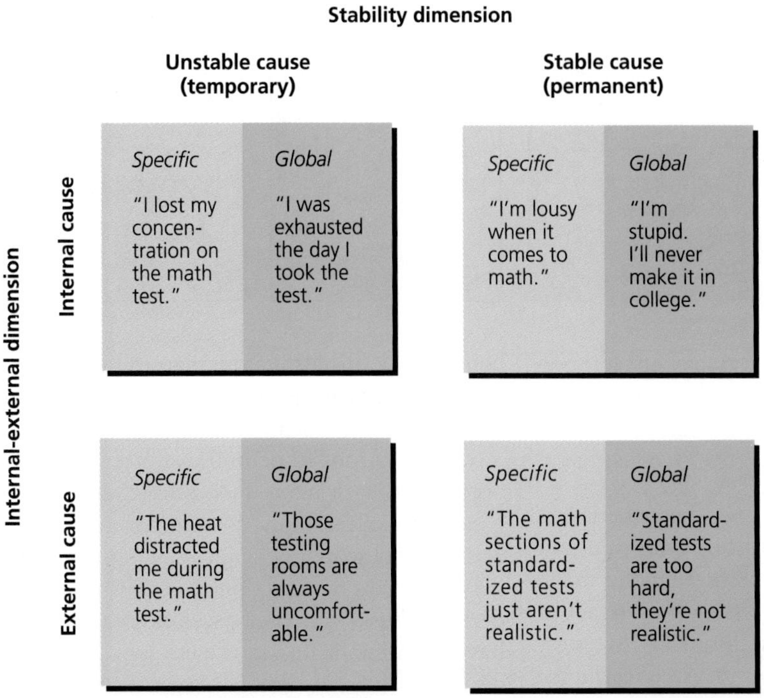

FIGURE 15.10
Attributional style and depression
Possible attributions for poor performance on a standardized math exam are shown here. Note how these explanations vary in the factors to which poor performance is attributed—internal-external, stable-unstable, or specific-global. People who consistently explain their failures with attributions that are internal, stable, and global are particularly vulnerable to depression.

Stability dimension

Internal-external dimension

Internal cause

Unstable cause (temporary)

Specific
"I lost my concentration on the math test."

Global
"I was exhausted the day I took the test."

Stable cause (permanent)

Specific
"I'm lousy when it comes to math."

Global
"I'm stupid. I'll never make it in college."

External cause

Specific
"The heat distracted me during the math test."

Global
"Those testing rooms are always uncomfortable."

Specific
"The math sections of standardized tests just aren't realistic."

Global
"Standardized tests are too hard, they're not realistic."

blame your poor test performance on exhaustion (an internal but unstable factor that could change next time) or on your low intelligence (an internal but stable factor). Some theorists are also interested in the degree to which our attributions have *global versus specific implications*. Thus you might attribute your low test score to your lack of intelligence (which has very general, global implications) or your poor math ability (the implications are specific to math). Figure 15.10 provides additional attributions that might be made to explain poor test performance.

Theorists who link attribution to depression are interested in the *attributional style* that people display, especially when they are trying to explain failures, setbacks, and other negative events. Studies show that *people who consistently tend to make internal, stable, and global attributions are more prone to depression* than people who exhibit the opposite attributional styles (Robins, 1988; Sweeney, Anderson, & Bailey, 1986). Why? Because in making internal, stable,

and global attributions, people blame their setbacks on personal inadequacies (internal) that they see as unchangeable (stable) and draw far-reaching (global) conclusions about their lack of worth as human beings. In other words, they draw depressing conclusions about themselves.

Thus cognitive models of depression maintain that it is negative thinking that makes many people feel dejected, helpless, and hopeless. The main problem with cognitive theories is their difficulty in separating cause from effect (Barnett & Gotlib, 1988). Does negative thinking cause depression? Or does depression cause negative thinking? Could both be caused by a third variable, such as neurochemical changes (see Figure 15.11)? Evidence can be mustered to support all three of these possibilities, suggesting that negative thinking, depression, and neurochemical alterations may feed off each other as a depression deepens.

In accord with this line of thinking, Susan Nolen-Hoeksema (1991) has found that depressed people who *ruminate* about their depression remain depressed longer than those who try to distract themselves. People who respond to depression with rumination repetitively focus their attention on their depressing feelings, thinking constantly about how sad, lethargic, and unmotivated they are. According to Nolen-Hoeksema, excessive rumination tends to extend and amplify individuals' episodes of depression.

Ironically, depressed individuals' negative thinking may be more *realistic* than nondepressed individuals' more positive thinking. This unexpected possibility first surfaced in a study by Lauren Alloy and Lyn Abramson (1979). Depressed and nondepressed subjects worked on a laboratory task. The experimenters controlled the degree to which the subjects' responses on the task (pressing or not pressing a button) influenced their outcomes (turning on a light, winning money). Afterward, subjects were asked to estimate how much their respons-

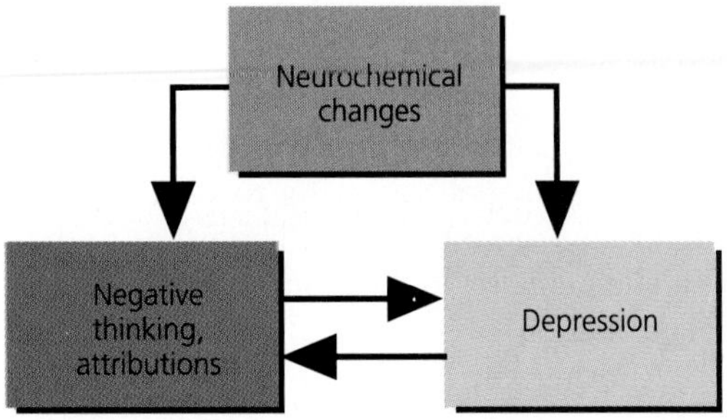

FIGURE 15.11
Interpreting the correlation between negative thinking and depression
Cognitive theories of depression assert that consistent patterns of negative thinking cause depression. Although these theories are highly plausible, depression could cause negative thoughts, or both could be caused by a third factor, such as neurochemical changes in the brain.

Neurochemical changes

Negative thinking, attributions

Depression

es influenced their outcomes. As expected, the depressed subjects estimated that they had less control than the nondepressed subjects. This difference occurred, however, because the nondepressed subjects *overestimated* their control. In comparison, the depressed subjects made fairly accurate estimates. Since then, numerous studies have shown that depressed subjects' self-evaluations, recall of feedback from others, and attributions for success and failure tend to be more realistic than those made by nondepressed subjects (Alloy & Abramson, 1988). This evidence suggests that depressed people may not be overly pessimistic so much as nondepressed people are overly optimistic. However, a recent study by Dunning and Story (1991) that asked students to predict whether certain personal events (such as making the dean's list, getting a parking ticket, or beginning a major relationship) would occur during the course of the semester failed to find greater realism among the depressed subjects, whose predictions were slightly less accurate than those of the nondepressed subjects. This finding raises the possibility that depressive realism may occur only under certain circumstances or only when subjects are asked for certain types of evaluations.

Interpersonal Roots

Behavioral approaches to depression emphasize how inadequate social skills put people on the road to depressive disorders (Lewinsohn, 1974; Lewinsohn & Arconad, 1981). According to this notion, depression-prone people lack the social finesse needed to acquire many important kinds of reinforcers, such as good friends, top jobs, and desirable spouses. This paucity of reinforcers could understandably lead to negative emotions and depression. In accord with this theory, researchers have found correlations between poor social skills and depression (Blechman, McEnroe, Carella, & Audette, 1986).

Another interpersonal consideration is that depressed people tend to be depressing. Individuals suffering from depression are often irritable and pessimistic. They complain a lot, and they aren't very enjoyable companions. As a consequence, depressed people tend to court rejection from those around them (Coyne, 1976; Coyne, Burchill, & Stiles, 1990). Depressed people thus have fewer sources of social support than nondepressed people (Billings, Cronkite, & Moos, 1983). Social rejection and lack of support may in turn aggravate and deepen a person's depression (Segrin & Dillard, 1992).

Precipitating Stress

Mood disorders sometimes appear mysteriously "out of nowhere" in people who are leading benign, nonstressful lives. For this reason, experts used to believe that mood disorders were not influenced much by stress. However, recent advances in the measurement of personal stress have altered this picture. The evidence available today suggests that there is a moderately strong link between stress and the onset of mood disorders (Ambelas, 1987; Hammen, Marks, Mayol, & deMayo, 1985). Some theorists believe that stress leads to disruptions of biological rhythms and sleep loss, which lead to neurochemical changes that cause mood disorders (Healy & Williams, 1988; Wehr, Sack, & Rosenthal, 1987).

Stress seems to act as a precipitating factor that triggers depression in some people. Of course, many people endure great stress without getting depressed. The impact of stress varies, in part because people differ in their *vulnerability* to mood disorders. Variations in vulnerability appear to depend primarily on one's biological makeup. Similar interactions between stress and vulnerability probably influence the development of many kinds of disorders, including the schizophrenic disorders.

Schizophrenic Disorders

iterally, *schizophrenia* means "split mind." When Eugen Bleuler coined the term in 1911, however, he was referring to the fragmenting of thought processes seen in the disorder, not to a "split personality." Unfortunately, writers in the popular media often assume that the split-mind notion refers to the rare syndrome in which a person manifests two or more personalities. As we know, this syndrome is actually *multiple-personality disorder*. Schizophrenia is a much more common and altogether different disorder.

***Schizophrenic disorders* are marked by disturbances in thought that spill over to affect perceptual, social, and emotional processes.** How common is schizophrenia? Prevalence estimates suggest that about 1 to 1.5% of the population may suffer from schizophrenic disorders (Keith, Regier, & Rae, 1991). That may not sound like much, but it means that 4 million

Susan Nolen-Hoeksema

people may be troubled by schizophrenic distur-bances in the United States alone.

General Symptoms

There are four distinct schizophrenic syn-dromes, but they share some general character-istics that we will examine before we look at the subtypes. Many of these characteristics are apparent in the following case history (adapted from Sheehan, 1982).

Sylvia was first diagnosed as schizophrenic at age 15. She has been in and out of psychiatric facilities since then. She has never been able to hold a job for any length of time. During severe flare-ups of her disorder her personal hygiene deteriorates. She rarely washes, wears clothes that neither fit nor match, smears makeup on heavily but randomly, and slops food all over herself. Sylvia occasionally hears voices talking to her. She tends to be argumentative, aggres-sive, and emotionally volatile. Over the years she has been involved in innumerable fights with fellow patients, psychiatric staff members, and strangers. Her thoughts can be highly irra-tional. She was a patient in a psychiatric insti-tution called Creedmoor when she offered the following observations:

> "Mick Jagger wants to marry me. If I have Mick Jagger, I don't have to covet Geraldo Rivera. Mick Jagger is St. Nicholas and the Maharishi is Santa Claus. I want to form a gospel rock group called the Thorn Oil, but Geraldo wants me to be the music critic on "Eyewitness News," so what can I do? Got to listen to my boyfriend. Teddy Kennedy cured me of my ugliness. I'm pregnant with the son of God. I'm going to marry David Berkowitz and get it over with. Creedmoor is the headquarters of the American Nazi Party. They're eating the patients here. Archie Bunker wants me to play his niece on his TV show. I work for Epic Records. I'm Joan of Arc. I'm Florence Nightingale. The door between the ward and the porch is the dividing line between New York and California. Divorce isn't a piece of paper, it's a feeling. Forget about Zip Codes. I need shock treatment. The body is run by electricity. My wiring is all faulty. A fly is a teen-age wasp. I'm marrying an accountant. I'm in the Pentecostal Church, but I'm consid-ering switching my loyalty to the Charismatic Church." [Sheehan, 1982, pp.104–105]

Sylvia's case clearly shows that schizo-phrenic thinking can be bizarre and that schiz-ophrenia can be a severe and debilitating disor-der. Although no single symptom is inevitably present, the following symptoms are commonly seen in schizophrenia.

• *Irrational thought.* Disturbed, irrational thought processes are the central feature of schizophrenic disorders. Various kinds of delu-sions are common. **Delusions are false beliefs that are maintained even though they clearly have no basis in reality.** One patient's delusion that he is a tiger (with a deformed body) has persisted for 15 years (Kulick, Pope, & Keck, 1990). More typically, affected persons believe that their private thoughts are being broadcast to other people. They may also believe that thoughts are being injected into their minds against their will. People with *delusions of grandeur* maintain that they are extremely famous or important. Sylvia expressed an end-less array of grandiose delusions: Mick Jagger wanted to marry her, she had dictated the Hobbit stories to Tolkien, she was going to win the Nobel Prize for medicine, and on and on.

As the delusions progress, the schizo-phrenic person's train of thought deteriorates. Thinking becomes chaotic rather than logical and linear. There is a "loosening of associa-tions" as the schizophrenic shifts topics in dis-jointed ways. Sylvia's monologue demonstrates a wild flight of ideas, and at one point (begin-ning with the sentence "Creedmoor is the head-quarters . . .") she rattles off ten consecutive sentences that have no apparent connection.

• *Deterioration of adaptive behavior.* Schizophrenia usually involves a noticeable deterioration in the quality of one's routine functioning in work, social relations, and per-sonal care. Friends often make such remarks as "Hal just isn't himself anymore." This deterio-ration is readily apparent in Sylvia's inability to get along with others or to function in the work world. It's also apparent in her neglect of per-sonal hygiene.

• *Distorted perception.* The person with schizophrenia is subject to a variety of percep-tual distortions, the most common being audi-tory hallucinations. **Hallucinations are senso-ry perceptions that occur in the absence of a real, external stimulus or that represent gross distortions of perceptual input.** Schizophre-nics frequently report that they hear the voices of nonexistent or absent people. Sylvia heard messages from the former Beatle Paul McCartney. These voices often provide an insulting running commentary on the person's behavior ("You're an idiot for shaking his hand"). The voices may be argumentative ("You don't need a bath"), and they may issue commands ("Prepare your home for visitors from outer space").

• *Disturbed emotion.* Normal emotional tone can be disrupted in a variety of ways. Some victims show a flattening of emotions. In other words, they show little emotional responsiveness. Others show inappropriate emotional responses that don't gibe with the situation or with what they are saying. For instance, a schizophrenic patient may cry over a Smurfs cartoon and then laugh about a news story describing the death of a child. People with schizophrenia may also become emotionally volatile. This pattern was displayed by Sylvia, who often overreacted emotionally in erratic, unpredictable ways.

• *Other features*. People with schizophrenic disorders may display a variety of less central symptoms. Many exhibit *social withdrawal*, interacting with others only very reluctantly. Some experience a *disturbed sense of self* or individuality. Also common is *poverty of speech*, which involves hesitant, uncommunicative verbal interactions. Sometimes *abnormal motor behavior* is observed. A patient may rock back and forth constantly or become immobilized for great lengths of time.

Subtypes

Four subtypes of schizophrenic disorders are recognized, including a category for people who don't fit neatly into any of the first three categories.

• *Paranoid type*. As its name implies, **paranoid schizophrenia is dominated by delusions of persecution, along with delusions of grandeur.** In this common form of schizophrenia, people come to believe that they have many enemies who want to harass and oppress them. They may become suspicious of friends and relatives, or they may attribute the persecution to mysterious unknown persons. They are convinced that they are being watched and manipulated in malicious ways. To make sense of this persecution, they often develop delusions of grandeur. They believe that they must be enormously important people, frequently seeing themselves as great inventors or as great religious or political leaders. In the case described at the beginning of the chapter, for example, Ed's belief that he was president of the United States was a delusion of grandeur.

• *Catatonic type*. **Catatonic schizophrenia is marked by striking motor disturbances, ranging from muscular rigidity to random motor activity.** Some catatonics go into an extreme form of withdrawal known as a catatonic stupor. They may remain virtually motionless and seem oblivious of the environment around them for long periods of time. Others go into a state of catatonic excitement.

They become hyperactive and incoherent. Some alternate between these dramatic extremes. The catatonic subtype is not particularly common, and its prevalence seems to be declining.

• *Disorganized type*. **People with disorganized schizophrenia experience a particularly severe deterioration of adaptive behavior.** Prominent symptoms include emotional indifference, frequent incoherence, and virtually complete social withdrawal. Aimless babbling and giggling are common. Delusions often center on body functions ("My brain is melting out my ears").

• *Undifferentiated type*. People who are clearly schizophrenic but who cannot be placed in any of the three previous categories are said to have **undifferentiated schizophrenia, which is marked by idiosyncratic mixtures of schizophrenic symptoms.** The undifferentiated subtype is fairly common.

Some theorists are beginning to doubt the value of dividing schizophrenic disorders into the four subtypes just described (Pfohl & Andreasen, 1986). Critics note that the catatonic subtype is disappearing and that undifferentiated cases aren't a subtype as much as a hodgepodge of leftovers. Critics also point out that the classic schizophrenic subtypes do not differ meaningfully in etiology, prognosis, or response to treatment. The absence of such differences casts doubt on the value of the current classification scheme.

Such problems have led Nancy Andreasen and others (Andreasen, 1982; Lewine, Fogg, & Meltzer, 1983; Pogue-Geile, 1989) to propose a new scheme that divides schizophrenic disorders into just two categories on the basis of predominantly negative or positive symptoms. *Negative symptoms* involve behavioral *deficits*, such as flattened emotions, social withdrawal, apathy, impaired attention, and poverty of speech. *Positive symptoms* involve behavioral *excesses* or peculiarities, such as hallucinations, delusions, bizarre behavior, and wild flights of ideas. Andreasen believes that researchers will find consistent differences between these two subtypes in etiology, prognosis, and response to treatment. Only time (and research) will tell whether the proposed subdivision based on positive versus negative symptoms will prove useful.

Course and Outcome

Schizophrenic disorders usually emerge during adolescence or early adulthood and only rarely after age 45 (Murphy & Helzer, 1986). The

Nancy Andreasen

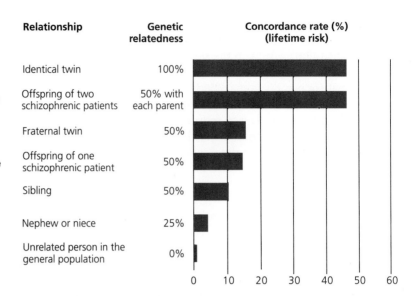

FIGURE 15.12
Genetic vulnerability to schizophrenic disorders
Relatives of schizophrenic patients have an elevated risk for schizophrenia. The closer the relationship, the greater the risk. Although environment also plays a role in the etiology of schizophrenia, the concordance rates shown here suggest that there must be a genetic vulnerability to the disorder. (Data from Nicol & Gottesman, 1983.)

Relationship	Genetic relatedness	Concordance rate (%) (lifetime risk)
Identical twin	100%	45
Offspring of two schizophrenic patients	50% with each parent	46
Fraternal twin	50%	14
Offspring of one schizophrenic patient	50%	13
Sibling	50%	10
Nephew or niece	25%	3
Unrelated person in the general population	0%	1

emergence of schizophrenia may be either very sudden or very gradual. Once it clearly emerges, its course is variable (Ciompi, 1980; Marengo, Harrow, Sands, & Galloway, 1991), but patients tend to fall into three broad groups. Some patients, presumably those with milder disorders, are treated successfully and enjoy a full recovery. In other patients, treatment produces a partial recovery so that they can return to a reasonably normal life. They experience frequent relapses, however, and are in and out of treatment facilities for much of the remainder of their lives. A third group of patients endure chronic illness that sometimes results in permanent hospitalization.

Several factors are related to the likelihood of recovery from schizophrenic disorders (Lehmann & Cancro, 1985). A patient has a relatively *favorable prognosis* when (1) the onset of the disorder has been sudden rather than gradual, (2) the onset has occurred at a later age, (3) the patient's social and work adjustment were relatively good before the onset of the disorder, and (4) the patient has a relatively healthy, supportive family situation to return to. All of these predictors are concerned with the etiology of schizophrenic illness.

Etiology of Schizophrenia

Most of us can identify, at least to some extent, with people who suffer from mood disorders, somatoform disorders, and anxiety disorders. You probably can imagine events that might leave you struggling with depression, or grappling with anxiety, or worrying about your physical health. But what could possibly have led Ed to believe that he had been fighting space wars and vampires? What could account for Sylvia's belief that she was Joan of Arc? Or

that she dictated the Hobbit novels to Tolkien? As mystifying as these delusions may seem, you'll see that the etiology of schizophrenic disorders is not so very different from the etiology of other disorders.

Genetic Vulnerability

Evidence is plentiful that hereditary factors play a role in the development of schizophrenic disorders (Loehlin, Willerman, & Horn, 1988). In twin studies, for instance, concordance rates average around 48% for identical twins but about 17% for fraternal twins (Gottesman, 1991). Studies also indicate that a child born to two schizophrenic parents has about a 46% probability of developing a schizophrenic disorder (as compared to the probability of about 1% for the population as a whole). These and other findings that demonstrate the genetic roots of schizophrenia are summarized in Figure 15.12. Overall, the picture is similar to that seen for mood disorders. Several converging lines of evidence indicate that people inherit a genetically transmitted *vulnerability* to schizophrenia.

Neurochemical Factors

Like mood disorders, schizophrenic disorders appear to be accompanied by changes in neurotransmitter activity in the brain (Karson, Kleinman, & Wyatt, 1986). Excess *dopamine* activity has been implicated as the probable cause of schizophrenia because most of the drugs that are useful in the treatment of schizophrenia are known to dampen dopamine activity in the brain (S. H. Snyder, 1986). However, the evidence linking schizophrenia to high dopamine levels has been riddled with inconsistencies, complexities, and interpretive problems

(Davidson, Losonczy, & Davis, 1986). Many of these inconsistencies may be resolved by a new theory that links schizophrenia to abnormally high dopamine activity in subcortical areas of the brain, coupled with abnormally low dopamine activity in the prefrontal cortex (Davis, Kahn, Ko, & Davidson, 1991). Thus investigators are making progress in their search for the neurochemical bases of schizophrenia.

Structural Abnormalities in the Brain

Various studies have suggested that schizophrenic individuals have difficulty in focusing their attention (Mirsky & Duncan, 1986). Some theorists believe that many bizarre aspects of schizophrenic behavior may be due mainly to an inability to filter out unimportant stimuli. This lack of selectivity supposedly leaves victims of the disorder flooded with overwhelming, confusing sensory input.

These problems with attention suggest that schizophrenic disorders may be caused by neurological defects (Lehmann, 1985). Until recently this theory was based more on speculation than on actual research. Now, however, advances in brain-imaging technology are beginning to yield some intriguing data. The findings suggest an association between enlarged brain ventricles (the hollow, fluid-filled cavities in the brain shown in Figure 15.13) and chronic schizophrenic disturbance (Andreasen, 1985; Suddath et al., 1990).

The significance of enlarged ventricles in the brain is hotly debated, however. Enlarged ventricles are not unique to schizophrenia. They are a sign of many kinds of brain pathology. Furthermore, even if the association between enlarged ventricles and schizophrenia is replicated consistently, it will be difficult to sort out whether this brain abnormality is a cause or an effect of schizophrenia.

Communication Deviance

Over the years, hundreds of investigators have tried to relate patterns of family interaction to the development of schizophrenia. Popular theories have come and gone as empirical evidence has overturned once-plausible hypotheses (Goldstein, 1988). Vigorous research and debate in this area continue today. The current emphasis is on families' communication patterns and their expression of emotions.

Various theorists assert that vulnerability to schizophrenia is increased by exposure to defective interpersonal communication during childhood. Studies have found a relationship

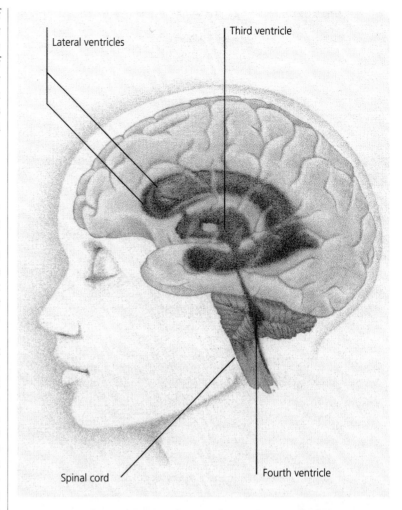

between schizophrenia and *communication deviance* (Goldstein, 1984; Singer, Wynne, & Toohey, 1978). Communication deviance includes unintelligible speech, stories with no endings, heavy use of unusual words, extensive contradictions, and poor attention to children's communication efforts. The evidence suggests that schizophrenia is more likely to develop when youngsters grow up in homes characterized by vague, muddled, fragmented communication. Researchers speculate that communication deviance gradually undermines a child's sense of reality and encourages youngsters to withdraw into their own private worlds, setting the stage for schizophrenic thinking later in life.

Expressed Emotion

Studies of expressed emotion have focused primarily on how this element of family dynamics influences the *course* of schizophrenic illness after the onset of the disorder (Leff & Vaughn, 1985). *Expressed emotion* reflects the degree to which a relative of a schizophrenic patient displays a highly critical or emotionally overinvolved attitude toward the patient. Audiotaped

FIGURE 15.13
Schizophrenia and the ventricles of the brain
Cerebrospinal fluid (CSF) circulates around the brain and the spinal cord. The hollow cavities in the brain filled with CSF are called ventricles. The four ventricles in the human brain are depicted here. Recent studies with new brain imaging techniques suggest that there is an association between enlarged ventricles in the brain and the occurrence of schizophrenic disorders.

Lateral ventricles

Third ventricle

Spinal cord

Fourth ventricle

Surviving Schizophrenia: A Family Manual

by E. Fuller Torrey (Harper & Row, 1988)

E. Fuller Torrey is a very prominent psychiatrist who has specialized in the treatment and study of schizophrenia. He has conducted basic research and written technical articles on schizophrenia, as well as this practical book intended for the lay public. This book examines schizophrenia from every angle and offers plenty of down-to-earth advice on how to deal with this debilitating mental illness.

Torrey points out that many myths surrounding schizophrenia have added to the anguish of families that have been victimized by this illness. He explains that schizophrenia is *not* caused by childhood trauma, domineering mothers, or passive fathers. He discusses how genetic vulnerability, flawed brain chemistry, and other factors contribute to the development of schizophrenic disorders.

Torrey discusses the treatment of schizophrenia at great length. He evaluates the utility of traditional psychotherapy, hospitalization, and medication. He also explains the various ways in which the disease can evolve. Some of the best material is found in chapters on what the patient needs and what the family needs.

Torrey writes with clarity, eloquence, and conviction. He's not reluctant to express strong opinions. For instance, in an appendix he lists the ten worst readings on schizophrenia (along with the ten best), and his evaluations are brutal. He characterizes one book as "absurd drivel" and dismisses another by saying, "If a prize were to be given to the book which has produced the most confusion about schizophrenia over the past twenty years, this book would win going away." Scientists and academicians are usually reluctant to express such strong opinions, and Torrey's candor is refreshing.

> Psychoanalysis is to schizophrenia as Laetrile is to cancer. Both have enjoyed surprising popularity considering the fact that they lack scientific basis, are completely ineffective, may make the patient worse if administered in toxic doses, and still attract patients who are willing to pay vast sums of money in desperation for a cure. Freud himself recognized that schizophrenic patients "are inaccessible to the influence of psychoanalysis and cannot be cured by our endeavors," but that observation has not stopped his followers from trying. [p. 220]

interviews are used to assess relatives' expressed emotions. The interviews are carefully evaluated for critical comments, resentment toward the patient, and excessive emotional involvement (overprotectiveness, overconcern).

Studies show that a family's expressed emotion is a good predictor of the course of a schizophrenic patient's illness (Leff & Vaughn, 1981). After release from a hospital, schizophrenic patients who return to a family high in expressed emotion show relapse rates three or four times that of patients who return to a family low in expressed emotion. Part of the problem for patients returning to homes high in expressed emotion is that their families probably are sources of more stress than social support. And like virtually all mental disorders, schizophrenia is influenced to some extent by life stress (Schwartz & Myers, 1977).

Precipitating Stress

Most theories of schizophrenia assume that stress plays a key role in triggering schizophrenic disorders (McGlashan, 1986; Zubin, 1986). According to this notion, various biological and psychological factors influence individuals' *vulnerability* to schizophrenia. High stress may then serve to precipitate a schizophrenic disorder in someone who is vulnerable. A recent study indicates that high stress can also trigger relapses in schizophrenic patients who have made progress toward recovery (Ventura, Neuchterlein, Lukott, & Hardesty, 1989).

Schizophrenia is the last of the major, Axis I diagnostic categories that we will consider. We'll complete our overview of different types of abnormal behavior with a brief look at the personality disorders. These disorders are recorded on Axis II in the DSM classification system.

Personality Disorders

e have seen repeatedly that it is often difficult to draw that imaginary line between healthy and disordered behavior. This is especially true in the case of personality disorders, which are relatively mild disturbances in comparison with most of the Axis I disorders. **Personality disorders are marked by extreme, inflexible personality traits that cause subjective distress or impaired social and occupational functioning.** Essentially, people with these disorders display certain personality traits to an excessive degree and in rigid ways that undermine their adjustment. Personality disorders usually emerge in late childhood or adolescence and often continue throughout adulthood. It is difficult to estimate the prevalence of these subtle disorders, but it is clear that many of them are common (Merikangas & Weissman, 1986).

DSM-III-R lists 11 personality disorders. All are described briefly in Figure 15.14. If you examine this table, you will notice that some personality disorders essentially are mild versions of more severe Axis I disorders.

Clusters of Personality Disorders

As Figure 15.14 indicates, the 11 personality disorders are grouped into three related clusters. The four disorders in the *anxious/fearful cluster* are marked by maladaptive efforts to control anxiety and fear of social rejection. People with the three disorders in the *odd/eccentric cluster* are distrustful, socially aloof, and unable to "connect" with others emotionally. The four personality disorders in the *dramatic/impulsive cluster* have less in common with one another than those grouped in the first two clusters. The histrionic and narcissistic personalities share a flair for overdramatizing everything. Impulsiveness is the common ground shared by the borderline and antisocial personality disorders.

Diagnostic Problems

Since the publication of DSM-III in 1980, many critics have argued that the personality disorders overlap too much with Axis I disorders and with one another (Frances & Widiger, 1986). The extent of this problem was documented in a study by Leslie Morey (1988), who reviewed the cases of 291 patients who had received a diagnosis of a specific personality disorder to see how many of them could have met the criteria for any of the other ten personality disorders. Morey found massive overlap among the diagnoses. Among patients with a diagnosis of histrionic personality disorder, for example, 56% also qualified for a borderline disorder, 54% for a narcissistic disorder, 32% for an avoidant disorder, 30% for a dependent disorder, and 29% for a paranoid disorder.

Clearly there are fundamental problems with Axis II as a classification system, and revisions are sorely needed (Kiesler, 1986; Millon, 1986). The overlap among the personality disorders makes it virtually impossible to achieve consistent diagnoses. The inadequacy of the definitions of personality disorders also hinders research. The only personality disorder that has a long history of extensive research is the antisocial personality disorder.

Antisocial Personality Disorder

The antisocial personality disorder has a misleading name. The antisocial designation does *not* mean that people with this disorder shun social interaction. Rather than shrinking from social interaction, many are sociable, friendly,

Personality Disorders

Cluster	Disorder	Description	% male
Anxious/fearful	Avoidant personality disorder	Excessively sensitive to potential rejection, humiliation, or shame; socially withdrawn in spite of desire for acceptance from others	50
	Dependent personality disorder	Excessively lacking in self-reliance and self-esteem; passively allowing others to make all decisions; constantly subordinating own needs to others' needs	31
	Passive-aggressive personality disorder	Indirectly resistant to demands for adequate social and occupational performance; tending to procrastinate, dawdle, and "forget"	54
	Obsessive-compulsive personality disorder	Preoccupied with organization, rules, schedules, lists, trivial details; extremely conventional, serious, and formal; unable to express warm emotions	50
Odd/eccentric	Schizoid personality disorder	Defective in capacity for forming social relationships, showing absence of warm, tender feelings for others	78
	Schizotypal personality disorder	Showing social deficits and oddities of thinking, perception, and communication that resemble schizophrenia	55
	Paranoid personality disorder	Showing pervasive and unwarranted suspiciousness and mistrust of people; overly sensitive; prone to jealousy	67
Dramatic/impulsive	Histrionic personality disorder	Overly dramatic; tending to exaggerated expressions of emotion; egocentric, seeking attention	15
	Narcissistic personality disorder	Grandiosely self-important; preoccupied with success fantasies; expecting special treatment; lacking interpersonal empathy	70
	Borderline personality disorder	Unstable in self-image, mood, and interpersonal relationships; impulsive and unpredictable	38
	Antisocial personality disorder	Chronically violating the rights of others; failing to accept social norms, to form attachments to others, or to sustain consistent work behavior; exploitive and reckless	82

FIGURE 15.14
Personality disorders
DSM-III-R describes 11 personality disorders that fall into three clusters, as shown here. Some of these disorders are more common in men and some in women, as the figures at the far right indicate. (Based on Millon, 1981.)

and superficially charming. People with this disorder are antisocial in that they choose to reject widely accepted social norms regarding moral principles and behavior.

Description

The *antisocial personality disorder* is marked by impulsive, callous, manipulative, aggressive, and irresponsible behavior that reflects a failure to accept social norms. Antisocial personalities chronically violate the rights of others. They often use their social charm to cultivate others' liking or loyalty in order to exploit them. Since they haven't accepted the social norms they violate, antisocial personalities rarely feel guilty about their transgressions. Essentially, they lack an adequate conscience. The antisocial personality disorder occurs much more frequently among men than among women. Studies suggest that it is a moderately common disorder, seen in roughly 2 to 4% of the population (Robins, Tipp, & Przybeck, 1991).

Many antisocial personalities get involved in illegal activities. Hare (1983) estimates that about 40% of convicted felons meet the criteria for an antisocial personality disorder. However, many antisocial personalities keep their exploitive, amoral behavior channeled within the boundaries of the law. Such people may even enjoy high status in our society (Sutker & Allain, 1983). In other words, the concept of the antisocial personality disorder applies to cutthroat business executives, scheming politicians, unprincipled lawyers, and money-hungry evangelists as well as to con artists, drug dealers, thugs, burglars, and petty thieves.

Antisocial personalities rarely experience genuine affection for others. However, they may be skilled at faking affection so they can exploit people. Sexually they are predatory and promiscuous. They also tend to be irresponsible and impulsive. They can tolerate very little frustration, and they pursue immediate gratification. These characteristics make them unreliable employees, unfaithful spouses, inattentive parents, and undependable friends. Many antisocial personalities have a checkered history of divorce, child abuse, and job instability.

Etiology

Investigating the roots of antisocial personality disorders has proved difficult because people with these disorders generally do not voluntarily seek help from our mental health system. They usually don't see anything wrong with

themselves. Many theorists believe that biological factors contribute to the development of antisocial personality disorders. Twin studies suggest that there is a genetic predisposition toward these disorders (Crowe, 1983).

Efforts to relate psychological factors to antisocial behavior have emphasized observational learning and inadequate socialization. Meyer (1980) reports that antisocial personalities tend to come from homes where discipline is inconsistent, ineffective, or nonexistent. Antisocial personalities are also more likely to emerge from homes where one or both parents exhibit antisocial traits (Robins, 1966). These parents presumably model exploitive, amoral behavior, which their children acquire through observational learning.

Summary

he medical model assumes that it is useful to view abnormal behavior as a disease. There are serious problems with the medical model, but the disease analogy is useful if one remembers that it is only an analogy.

Three criteria are employed in deciding whether people suffer from psychological disorders: deviance, personal distress, and maladaptive behavior. It is often difficult to draw a line between normality and abnormality. Contrary to the popular stereotype, people with psychological disorders are not particularly bizarre or dangerous. Psychological disorders are not a manifestation of personal weakness, and even the most severe disorders are potentially curable.

DSM-III-R is the official psychodiagnostic classification system in the United States. This system describes over 200 disorders and asks for information about patients on five axes. It is clear that psychological disorders are more common than they are widely believed to be, affecting roughly one-third of the population.

The anxiety disorders include the generalized anxiety disorder, phobic disorder, panic disorder, and obsessive-compulsive disorder. These disorders have been linked to neurochemical abnormalities in the brain, a highly reactive autonomic nervous system, mitral valve prolapse, and child-rearing styles. Many anxiety responses, especially phobias, may be caused by classical conditioning and maintained by operant conditioning.

Somatoform disorders include somatization disorders, conversion disorders, and hypochondria. These disorders often emerge in people with highly suggestible, histrionic personalities. Somatoform disorders may be a learned avoidance strategy reinforced by attention and sympathy. Dissociative disorders include psychogenic amnesia and multiple personality. These disorders are uncommon, and their causes are not well understood.

The principal mood disorders are major (unipolar) depression and bipolar mood disorder. People vary in their genetic vulnerability to mood disorders, which are accompanied by changes in neurochemical activity in the brain. Cognitive models posit that an attributional style emphasizing internal, stable, and global attributions contributes to depression. Depression is often rooted in interpersonal inadequacies and sometimes is stress-related.

Schizophrenic disorders are characterized by deterioration of adaptive behavior, irrational thought, distorted perception, and disturbed mood. Schizophrenic disorders are classified as paranoid, catatonic, disorganized, or undifferentiated, although a new classification scheme is under study. Research has linked schizophrenia to a genetic vulnerability, changes in neurotransmitter activity, and structural abnormalities in the brain. Precipitating stress and unhealthy family dynamics, especially communication deviance and expressed emotion, may also contribute to the disorders.

Eleven personality disorders are recorded on Axis II in DSM. Personality disorders can be grouped in three clusters: anxious/fearful, odd/eccentric, and dramatic/impulsive. However, specific personality disorders are poorly defined and there is excessive overlap among them. The antisocial personality disorder involves manipulative, impulsive, exploitive, aggressive behavior. Research on the etiology of this disorder has implicated genetic vulnerability, inadequate socialization, and observational learning.

In the Application we take a look at a deadly problem: suicide. We'll describe some common myths about suicide and discuss suicide prevention.

Are the following statements true or false?

1.

People who talk about suicide usually don't kill themselves.

2.

Most people who commit suicide give little or no warning of their intentions.

3.

People who attempt suicide are fully intent on dying.

4.

People who are suicidal remain so forever.

All of the statements on the left are false. They are myths that we will dispose of shortly. First, however, let's discuss the magnitude of this tragic problem.

Prevalence of Suicide

It is estimated that about 250,000 people attempt suicide in the United States each year. Roughly one in eight of these attempts is "successful." This makes suicide the eighth leading cause of death in the United States. Worse yet, official statistics may underestimate the scope of the problem. Many suicides are disguised as accidents, either by the suicidal person or by survivors who try to cover up afterward. Experts estimate that suicides may be ten times more numerous than those officially reported (Hirschfeld & Davidson, 1988).

Who Commits Suicide?

Anyone can commit suicide. No segment of society is immune. Nonetheless, some groups are at higher risk than others (Buda & Tsuang, 1990; Cross & Hirschfeld, 1986). For instance, the prevalence of suicide varies according to *marital status*. Married people commit suicide less frequently than divorced, bereaved, or single people. In regard to *occupational status*, suicide rates are particularly high among people who are unemployed and among presti-

gious and pressured professionals, such as doctors and lawyers.

Sex and *age* have complex relations to suicide rates. On the one hand, women *attempt* suicide more often than men. On the other hand, men are more likely to actually kill themselves, so they *complete* four times as many suicides as women. Suicide attempts peak between ages 24 and 44, but completed suicides are most frequent after age 55. Age trends differ for men and women, however, as Figure 15.15 indicates.

Unfortunately, suicide rates have tripled among adolescents and young adults in the last several decades (Brent & Kolko, 1990). Among college students academic pressures and setbacks do *not* appear to be the principal cause of suicide. Interpersonal problems and loneliness seem to be more important (see Figure 15.16).

Suicide is *not* committed only by people with severe mental illness, although elevated suicide rates are found for most categories of psychological disorders (Black & Winokur, 1990). As you might predict, suicide rates are highest among people with mood disorders, especially depression. Figure 15.17 shows how mood disorders and suicide attempts overlap.

Myths about Suicide

We began with four false statements about suicide. Let's examine these myths, which are

discussed by Edwin Shneidman and his colleagues (Shneidman, 1985; Shneidman, Farberow, & Litman, 1970).

Myth 1: People who talk about suicide don't actually kill themselves. Undoubtedly many people threaten suicide without ever going through with it. Nonetheless, there is no group at higher risk for suicide than those who openly discuss the possibility. Many people who kill themselves have a history of earlier threats that they did not carry out.

Myth 2: Most people who commit suicide give little or no warning of their intentions. It is estimated that eight of ten suicide attempts are preceded by some kind of warning. These warnings may range from clear threats to vague statements. At dinner with friends the night before he committed suicide, one prominent attorney cut up his American Express card, saying, "I'm not going to need this anymore." The probability of an actual suicide attempt is greatest when a threat is clear, when it includes a detailed plan, and when the plan involves a relatively deadly method.

Myth 3: People who attempt suicide are fully intent on dying. It appears that only about 3 to 5% of people who attempt suicide definitely want to die. About 30% of those who make an attempt seem ambivalent. They arrange things so that their fate is largely a matter of chance. The remaining two-thirds of suicide attempts are

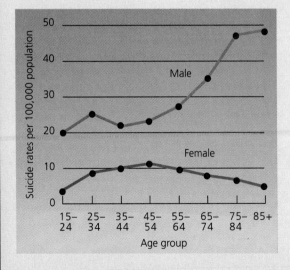

FIGURE 15.15
Suicide rates in the United States by age and sex
More men than women commit suicide at all ages, but the age patterns for the two sexes are noticeably different. The rate of male suicide peaks during the retirement years, whereas the rate of female suicide peaks in middle adulthood. (Data from Cross & Hirschfeld, 1986.)

Problem type

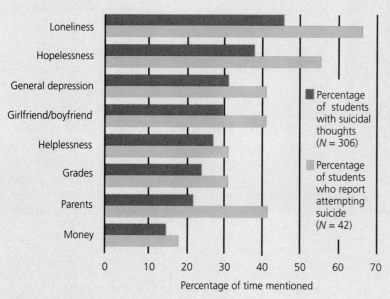

Loneliness
Hopelessness
General depression
Girlfriend/boyfriend
Helplessness
Grades
Parents
Money

■ Percentage of students with suicidal thoughts (N = 306)

■ Percentage of students who report attempting suicide (N = 42)

0 10 20 30 40 50 60 70

Percentage of time mentioned

FIGURE 15.16
Personal problems reported by suicidal students
Westefeld and Furr (1987) gathered data on the problems mentioned by students who had attempted suicide or who reported suicidal thoughts. On the whole, interpersonal problems dominate this list.

made by people who appear to have no interest in dying; they only want to send out a very dramatic distress signal. They arrange their suicide so that a rescue is quite likely. These variations in intent probably explain why only about one-eighth of suicide attempts end in death.

Myth 4: People who are suicidal remain so forever. Many people who become suicidal do so for a limited period of time. If they manage to ride through their cri-

sis period, thoughts of suicide may disappear entirely. Apparently time heals many wounds—if it is given the opportunity to do so.

Preventing Suicide

There is no simple and dependable way to prevent someone from going ahead with a threatened suicide. One expert on suicide (Wekstein, 1979) makes

the point that "perhaps nobody really knows *exactly* what to do when dealing with an imminent suicide" (p. 129). However, we will review some general advice that may be useful if you ever have to help someone through a suicidal crisis (Farberow, 1974; Rosenthal, 1988; Shneidman et al., 1970).

1. *Take suicidal talk seriously.* When people talk about suicide in vague generalities, it's easy to dis-

People with mood disorders

15% commit suicide

People who attempt suicide

10% subsequently commit suicide within 10 years

People who commit suicide

45%–70% of suicides have mood disorders

19%–24% of suicides have a prior suicide attempt

FIGURE 15.17
The relationship between suicide and mood disorders
Two groups with elevated risk of suicide are people with mood disorders and people who have made previous suicide attempts. Between them, these groups account for a high percentage of suicides. (Adapted from Avery & Winokur, 1978.)

miss it as "idle talk" and let it go. However, people who talk about suicide are a high-risk group and their veiled threats should not be ignored. According to Rosenthal (1988), the first step in suicide prevention is to ask such people directly if they're contemplating suicide.

2. *Provide empathy and social support.* It is important to show the suicidal person that you care. People often contemplate suicide because they see the world around them as indifferent and uncaring. You must demonstrate to the suicidal person that you are genuinely concerned. Even if you are thrust into a situation in which you barely know the suicidal person, you need to provide empathy. Suicide threats are often a last-ditch cry for help. It is therefore imperative that you offer to help.

3. *Identify and clarify the crucial problem.* The suicidal person is often terribly confused and feels lost in a sea of frustration and problems. It is a good idea to try to help sort through this confusion. Encourage the person to try to identify the crucial problem. Once it is isolated, the crucial

problem may not seem quite so overwhelming. It also may help to point out that the person's confusion is clouding his or her ability to judge the seriousness of the problem rationally.

4. *Suggest alternative courses of action.* People thinking about suicide often see it as the only solution to their problems. This is obviously an irrational view. Try to chip away at this premise by offering other possible solutions for the problem that has been identified as crucial. Suicidal people often are too distraught and disoriented to do this on their own. Therefore, it may help if you assist them.

5. *Capitalize on any doubts.* For most people, life is not easy to give up. They are racked by doubts about the wisdom of their decision. Many people will voice their unique reasons for doubting whether they should take the suicidal path. Zero in on these doubts. They may be your best arguments for life over death. For

instance, if a person expresses concern about how her or his suicide will affect family members, capitalize on this source of doubt.

6. *Encourage professional consultation.* Most mental health professionals have at least some experience in dealing with suicide crises. Many cities have suicide-prevention centers with 24-hour hotlines. These centers are staffed by people who have been specially trained to deal with suicide problems. It is important to try to get a suicidal person to seek professional assistance. The mere fact that you have talked a person out of attempting a threatened suicide does not mean that the crisis is over. The contemplation of suicide indicates that a person is experiencing great distress. Given this reality, professional intervention is crucial.

Key Learning Objectives

1. Describe and evaluate the medical model of abnormal behavior.
2. Explain the most commonly used criteria of abnormality and discuss two complexities in their application.
3. List four myths about psychological disorders.
4. Describe the five axes of DSM-III-R and discuss some controversial aspects of this system.
5. Discuss the prevalence of psychological disorders.
6. List four types of anxiety disorders and the symptoms of each.
7. Discuss the contributions of biological factors, conditioning, stress, and child rearing to the etiology of anxiety disorders.
8. Compare and contrast the three somatoform disorders and discuss their etiology.
9. Describe two dissociative disorders and discuss their etiology.
10. Describe the two major mood disorders: depression and bipolar mood disorder.
11. Explain how genetic and neurochemical factors may be related to the development of mood disorders.
12. Explain how cognitive factors, interpersonal factors, and stress may contribute to mood disorders.
13. Describe the general symptoms of schizophrenia.
14. Describe the subtypes of schizophrenia and discuss the course of the disorder.
15. Summarize how genetic vulnerability, neurochemical factors, and structural abnormalities in the brain may contribute to the etiology of schizophrenia.
16. Summarize evidence on how communication deviance, expressed emotion, and stress may contribute to schizophrenia.
17. Describe three broad clusters of personality disorders and diagnostic problems with these disorders.
18. Describe the antisocial personality disorder and discuss its etiology.
19. Summarize how age, sex, marital status, and occupation are related to the prevalence of suicide.
20. List four myths about suicidal behavior and summarize advice on preventing a suicide.

Key Terms

agoraphobia
antisocial personality disorder
anxiety disorders
attributions
bipolar mood disorder
catatonic schizophrenia
concordance rate
conversion disorders
delusions
depressive disorders
diagnosis
disorganized schizophrenia
dissociative disorders
epidemiology
etiology
generalized anxiety disorder
hallucinations
hypochondriasis
medical model
mood disorders
multiple-personality disorders
neurosis
neurotransmitters
obsessive-compulsive disorder
panic disorder
paranoid schizophrenia
personality disorders
phobic disorders
prevalence
prognosis
psychogenic amnesia
psychosis
psychosomatic diseases
schizophrenic disorders
seasonal affective disorder
somatization disorder
somatoform disorders
transvestism
undifferentiated schizophrenia

Key People

Lauren Alloy and Lyn Abramson
Nancy Andreasen
Susan Nolen-Hoeksema

David Rosenhan
Martin Seligman
Thomas Szasz

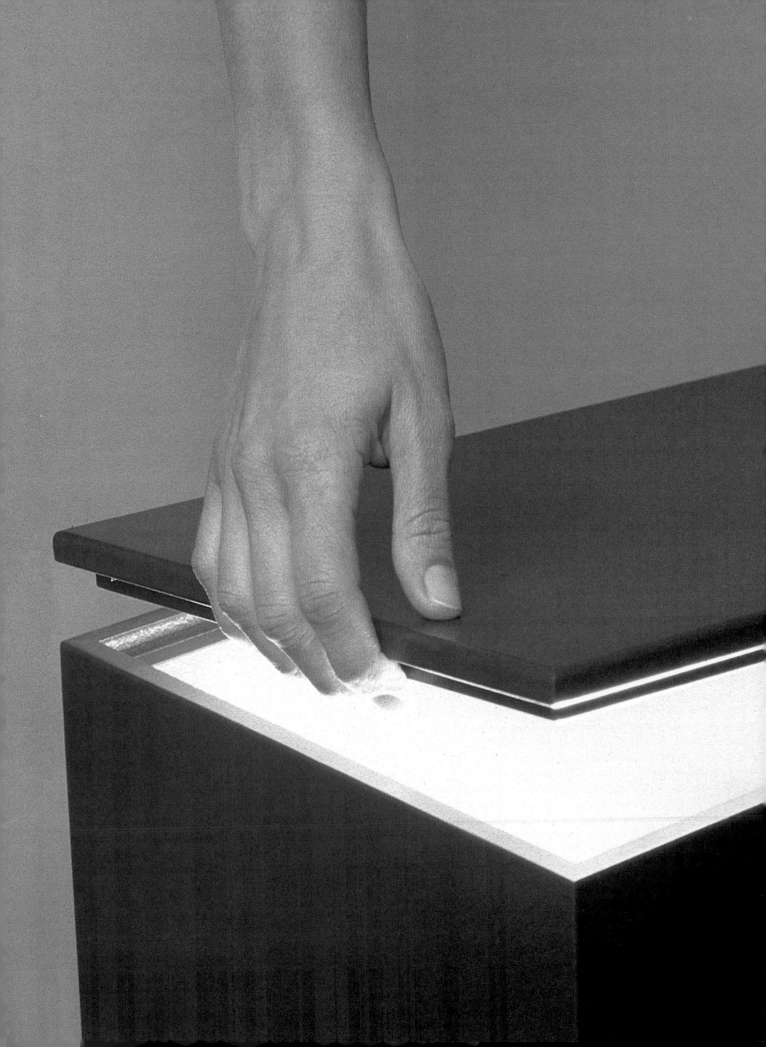

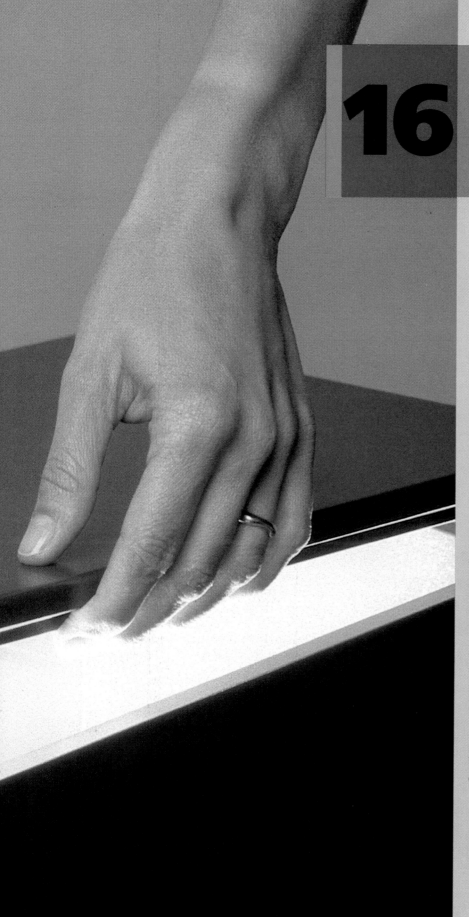

16 Psychotherapy

WHAT DO YOU PICTURE WHEN you hear the term *psychotherapy*? If you're like most people, you probably picture a troubled patient lying on a couch in a therapist's office, with the therapist asking penetrating questions and providing sage advice. Typically, people believe that psychotherapy is only for those who are "sick" and that therapists have special powers that allow them to "see through" their clients. It is also widely believed that therapy requires years of deep probing into a client's innermost secrets. Many people further assume that therapists routinely tell their patients how to lead their lives. Like most stereotypes, this picture of psychotherapy is a mixture of fact and fiction.

In this chapter we'll take a down-to-earth look at the complex process of psychotherapy. We'll start by discussing some general questions about the provision of therapy. Who seeks therapy? What kinds of professionals provide therapy? How many different types of therapy are there? After we've considered these general issues, we'll examine some of the more widely used approaches to psychotherapy, analyzing their goals, techniques, and effectiveness. In the Application we focus on practical issues in case you ever have to advise someone about seeking help.

The Elements of Psychotherapy: Treatments, Clients, and Therapists

Sigmund Freud, whom we discussed in Chapter 2, is widely credited with launching modern psychotherapy. Ironically, the landmark case that inspired Freud was actually treated by one of his colleagues, Josef Breuer. Around 1880 Breuer began to treat a young woman he called Anna O. (a pseudonym). Anna exhibited a variety of physical maladies, including headaches, coughing, and a loss of feeling and movement in her right arm. Much to his surprise, Breuer discovered that Anna's physical symptoms cleared up when he encouraged her to talk about emotionally charged experiences in her past.

Breuer and Freud discussed the case, and they speculated that talking things through enabled Anna to drain off bottled-up emotions that had caused her symptoms. Breuer found the intense emotional exchange in this treatment

not to his liking, so he didn't follow through on his discovery. However, Freud applied Breuer's insight to other patients, and his successes led him to develop a systematic treatment procedure, which he called *psychoanalysis*. Anna O. called her treatment "the talking cure." As you'll see, however, psychotherapy isn't always curative, and many modern therapies place little emphasis on talking.

Freud's breakthrough ushered in a century of progress for psychotherapy. Psychoanalysis spawned many offspring as Freud's followers developed their own systems of treatment. Since then, approaches to psychotherapy have steadily grown more numerous, more diverse, and more effective. Today people can choose from a bewildering array of therapies.

The immense diversity of therapeutic treatments makes it difficult to define the concept of *psychotherapy*. After organizing an unprecedented conference that brought together many of the world's leading authorities on psychotherapy, Jeffrey Zeig commented, "I do not believe there is any capsule definition of psychotherapy on which the 26 presenters could agree" (Zeig, 1987, p. xix). In lieu of a definition, we can identify a few basic elements that the various approaches to therapy have in common. All psychotherapies involve a helping relationship (the treatment) between a professional with special training (the therapist) and another person in need of help (the client). As we look at each of these elements—the treatment, the therapist, and the client—you'll see the diverse nature of modern psychotherapy.

Treatments: How Many Types Are There?

In their efforts to help people, psychotherapists employ a wide variety of methods. Among them are discussion, emotional support, persuasion, conditioning procedures, relaxation training, role playing, prescription of drugs, biofeedback, and group therapy. Some therapists also use less conventional procedures, such as rebirthing, poetry therapy, and primal therapy. No one knows exactly how many approaches to treatment there are. One handbook (Herink, 1980) lists over 250 distinct types of psychotherapy.

Fortunately, we can impose some order on this chaos. As varied as therapists' procedures are, approaches to treatment can be classified in three major categories.

1. *Insight therapies.* Insight therapy is "talk therapy" in the tradition of Freud's psycho-

analysis. This is probably the approach to treatment that you envision when you think of psychotherapy. Clients who receive insight therapies engage in complex, often lengthy verbal interactions with their therapists. The goal of these discussions is insight into the nature of the client's difficulties so that solutions can be found. Insight therapy can be conducted with an individual or with a group.

2. *Behavior therapies.* Behavior therapies are based on the principles of learning and conditioning, which were introduced in Chapter 2. Instead of emphasizing personal insights, behavior therapists make direct efforts to alter problematic responses (phobic behaviors, for instance) and maladaptive habits (such as drug use). Behavior therapists work on changing clients' overt behaviors. The procedures they employ vary with the problems. Most of their procedures involve either classical conditioning or operant conditioning.

3. *Biomedical therapies.* Biomedical approaches to therapy involve interventions into a person's biological functioning. The most widely used procedures are the prescription of drugs and electroconvulsive (shock) therapy. As the term *biomedical* suggests, these treatments have traditionally been provided only by physicians with a medical degree (usually psychiatrists). This situation may change, however, as psychologists have begun to campaign for limited prescription privileges and the federal government has funded a pilot study to assess the feasibility of this proposal (VandenBos, Cummings, & DeLeon, 1992).

We will examine approaches to therapy that fall into each of these three categories. Although we'll find very different methods in each category, the three major classes of treatment are not entirely incompatible. For example, a client might be seen in insight therapy and be given medication at the same time.

Clients: Who Seeks Therapy?

In the therapeutic triad (treatments, therapists, clients), the greatest diversity of all is seen among the clients. They bring to therapy the full range of human problems: anxiety, depression, unsatisfactory interpersonal relations, troublesome habits, poor self-control, low self-esteem, marital conflicts, self-doubt, a sense of emptiness, and feelings of personal stagnation. Therapy is sought by people who feel troubled, but the nature and severity of the trouble varies greatly from one person to another. The two most common presenting problems are exces-

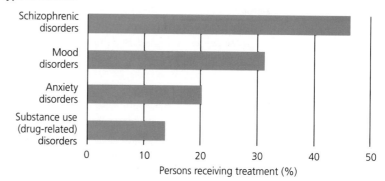

Type of disorder

Persons receiving treatment (%)

sive anxiety and depression (Lichtenstein, 1980).

A client in treatment does *not* necessarily have an identifiable psychological disorder. Some people seek professional help for everyday problems (career decisions, for instance) or vague feelings of discontent. Thus therapy includes efforts to foster clients' personal growth as well as professional interventions for mental disorders.

People vary considerably in their willingness to seek psychotherapy. Men are less likely than women to enter therapy, and people of the lower socioeconomic classes are more reluctant to seek therapy than those of the upper classes (Lichtenstein, 1980). *Unfortunately, it appears that many people who need therapy don't receive it.* As Figure 16.1 shows, only a minority of people with actual disorders receive treatment (Robins, Locke, & Regier, 1991). People who could benefit from therapy do not seek it for a variety of reasons. Some are unaware of its availability, and some believe that it is always expensive. The biggest roadblock is that many people equate being in therapy with admitting personal weakness.

A small portion of clients are essentially forced into psychotherapy. In most cases, coercion takes the form of pressure from a spouse, parent, friend, or employer. Sometimes, however, people are ordered into treatment by the courts, as in cases of involuntary commitment to a mental hospital.

Therapists: Who Provides Professional Treatment?

Friends and relatives may provide us with excellent advice about our personal problems, but their assistance does not qualify as therapy. *Psychotherapy* refers to professional treatment by someone with special training. A common source of confusion about psychotherapy is the variety of "helping professions" involved. Psychology and psychiatry are the principal

FIGURE 16.1 Patterns of seeking treatment Not everyone who has a psychological disorder receives professional treatment. This graph shows the percentage of people with specific disorders who obtained mental health treatment during a six-month period. Research suggests that only a minority of people with disorders receive treatment. (Data based on Shapiro et al., 1984.)

professions involved in the provision of psychotherapy, but therapy is also provided by psychiatric social workers, psychiatric nurses, and counselors, as Figure 16.2 indicates. Let's look at these mental health professions.

Psychologists

Two types of psychologists may provide therapy, although the distinction between them is more theoretical than real. *Clinical psychologists* and *counseling psychologists* specialize in the diagnosis and treatment of psychological disorders and everyday behavioral problems. In theory, the training of clinical psychologists emphasizes treatment of full-fledged disorders, whereas the training of counseling psychologists is slanted toward treatment of everyday adjustment problems in normal people. In practice, however, there is great overlap between clinical and counseling psychologists in training, in skills, and in the clienteles they serve, so that they are virtually interchangeable.

Both types of psychologists must earn a doctoral degree (Ph.D., Psy.D., or Ed.D.). A doctorate in psychology requires five to seven years of training beyond a bachelor's degree. The process of gaining admission to a Ph.D. program in clinical psychology is highly competitive (about as competitive as for medical school). Psychologists receive most of their training on university campuses, although they serve a one- to two-year internship in a clinical setting, such as a hospital.

In providing therapy, psychologists use either insight or behavioral approaches. They are more likely than psychiatrists to use behavioral techniques and less likely to use psychoanalytic methods. Clinical and counseling psychologists do psychological testing as well as psychotherapy, and many also conduct research.

Psychiatrists

Psychiatrists are physicians who specialize in the treatment of psychological disorders. Many psychiatrists also treat everyday behavioral problems. In comparison with psychologists, however, psychiatrists devote more time to relatively severe disorders (schizophrenia, mood disorders) and less time to everyday marital, family, job, and school problems. Psychiatrists have an M.D. degree. Their graduate training requires four years of coursework in medical school and a four-year apprenticeship in a residency at an approved hospital. They receive their psychotherapy training during their residency, since the required coursework in medical school is essentially the same for all students, whether they are going into surgery, pediatrics, or psychiatry.

In their provision of therapy, psychiatrists tend to emphasize biomedical treatments, which historically have been their exclusive province (drug therapy, for instance). Psychiatrists employ a variety of insight therapies, but psychoanalysis retains its influence through its descendants. Psychiatrists are less likely than psychologists to use group therapies or behavior therapies.

FIGURE 16.2
The principal mental health professions
The majority of therapeutic services are provided by people trained in the five professions described here.

Different Types of Therapists

Title	Degree*	Years beyond bachelor's degree	Typical roles and activities
Clinical or counseling psychologist	Ph.D. Psy.D. Ed.D.	5–7	Diagnosis, psychological testing, insight and behavior therapy
Psychiatrist	M.D.	8	Diagnosis; insight, behavior, and biomedical therapy
Social worker	M.S.W.	2	Insight and behavior therapy, family therapy, helping patients return to the community
Psychiatric nurse	B.S., B.A., M.A.	0–2	Inpatient care, insight and behavior therapy
Counselor	M.A. M.S.	2	Insight and behavior therapy, working primarily with everyday adjustment problems and marital and career issues

*Ph.D = Doctor of Philosophy; Psy.D. = Doctor of Psychology; Ed.D. = Doctor of Education; M.D. = Doctor of Medicine; M.S.W. = Master of Social Work; B.S. = Bachelor of Science; B.A. = Bachelor of Arts; M.A. = Master of Arts; M.S. = Master of Science

Other Mental Health Professionals

Several other mental health professions provide psychotherapy services. In hospitals and other institutions, *psychiatric social workers* and *psychiatric nurses* often work as part of a treatment team with a psychologist or psychiatrist. Psychiatric nurses, who may have a bachelor's or master's degree in their field, play a large role in hospital inpatient treatment. Psychiatric social workers generally have a master's degree and typically work with patients and their families to ease the patient's integration back into the community. Although social workers have traditionally worked in hospitals and social service agencies, they are now licensed in all states as independent, private practitioners who provide a wide range of therapeutic services.

Many kinds of *counselors* also provide therapeutic services. Counselors are usually found working in schools, colleges, and human service agencies (youth centers, geriatric centers, family planning centers, and so forth). Counselors typically have a master's degree. They often specialize in particular types of problems, such as vocational counseling, marital counseling, rehabilitation counseling, and drug counseling.

Although there are clear differences among helping professionals in education and training, their roles in the treatment process overlap considerably. We will refer to psychologists or psychiatrists as appropriate, but otherwise we'll use the terms *clinician*, *therapist*, and *mental health professional* to refer to psychotherapists of all kinds, regardless of their professional degree.

Now that we have discussed the basic elements in psychotherapy, we can examine specific approaches to treatment in terms of their goals, procedures, and effectiveness. We'll begin with a few representative insight therapies.

Insight Therapies

There are many schools of thought about how to do insight therapy. Therapists with different theoretical orientations use different methods to pursue different kinds of insights. What these varied approaches have in common is that **insight therapies involve verbal interactions intended to enhance clients' self-knowledge and thus promote healthful changes in personality and behavior.** There probably are around 200 different insight therapies, but the leading eight or ten approaches appear to account for the lion's share of treat-

ment. In this section we'll delve into psychoanalysis, related psychodynamic approaches, client-centered therapy, and cognitive therapy. We'll also discuss how insight therapy can be done with groups as well as individuals.

Psychoanalysis

After the case of Anna O., Sigmund Freud worked as a psychotherapist for almost 50 years in Vienna. Through a painstaking process of trial and error, he developed innovative techniques for the treatment of psychological disorders and distress. His system of *psychoanalysis* came to dominate psychiatry for many decades. Although the dominance of psychoanalysis has eroded in recent decades (Reiser, 1989), a diverse array of psychoanalytic approaches to therapy continue to evolve and continue to remain influential today (Eagle & Wolitzky, 1992).

Psychoanalysis is an insight therapy that emphasizes the recovery of unconscious conflicts, motives, and defenses through techniques such as free association, dream analysis, and transference. To appreciate the logic of psychoanalysis, we have to look at Freud's thinking about the roots of mental disorders. Freud treated mostly anxiety-dominated disturbances, such as obsessive-compulsive, phobic, panic, and conversion disorders, which were then called *neuroses*. He believed that neurotic problems were caused by unconscious conflicts left over from early childhood. As we saw in Chapter 2, he thought that these inner conflicts involved battles among the id, ego, and superego, usually over sexual and aggressive impulses. Freud theorized that people depend on defense mechanisms to avoid confronting these conflicts, which remain hidden in the depths of the unconscious. He noted, however, that defensive maneuvers often lead to self-defeating behavior. Furthermore, he asserted that defenses usually are only partially successful in alleviating anxiety, guilt, and other distressing emotions. With this model in mind, let's take a look at the therapeutic procedures employed in psychoanalysis.

Probing the Unconscious

Given Freud's assumptions, we can see that the logic of psychoanalysis is very simple. The analyst attempts to probe the murky depths of the unconscious to discover the unresolved conflicts causing the client's neurotic behavior. In a sense, the analyst functions as a psychological detective. In this effort to explore the unconscious, the therapist relies on two techniques: free association and dream analysis.

In *free association,* **clients spontaneously express their thoughts and feelings exactly as they occur, with as little censorship as possible.** Clients lie on a couch so they will be better able to let their minds drift freely. In free associating, clients expound on anything that comes to mind, regardless of how trivial, silly, or embarrassing it might be. Gradually, most clients begin to let everything pour out without conscious censorship. The analyst studies these free associations for clues about what is going on in the unconscious.

In *dream analysis,* **the therapist interprets the symbolic meaning of the client's dreams.** For Freud, dreams were the "royal road to the unconscious," the most direct means of access to patients' innermost conflicts, wishes, and impulses. Clients are encouraged and trained to remember their dreams, which they describe in therapy. The therapist then analyzes the symbolism in these dreams to interpret their meaning.

Let's look at an actual case treated through psychoanalysis (adapted from Greenson, 1967, pp. 40–41). Mr. N. was troubled by an unsatisfactory marriage. He claimed to love his wife, but he preferred sexual relations with prostitutes. Mr. N. reported that his parents also endured lifelong marital difficulties. His childhood conflicts about their relationship appeared to be related to his problems. Both dream analysis and free association can be seen in the following description of a session in Mr. N.'s treatment.

> Mr. N. reports a fragment of a dream. All that he can remember is that he is waiting for a red traffic light to change when he feels that someone has bumped into him from behind. . . . The associations led to Mr. N.'s love of cars, especially sports cars. He loved the sensation, in particular, of whizzing by those fat, old, expensive cars. . . . His father always hinted that he had been a great athlete, but he never substantiated it. . . . Mr. N. doubted whether his father could really perform. His father would flirt with a waitress in a café or make sexual remarks about women passing by, but he seemed to be showing off. If he were really sexual, he wouldn't resort to that.

As is characteristic of free association, Mr. N.'s train of thought meanders about with little direction. Nonetheless, clues about his unconscious conflicts are apparent. What did Mr. N.'s therapist extract from this session? The therapist saw sexual overtones in the dream fragment, where Mr. N. was bumped from behind. From Mr. N's free association about whizzing by "fat, old, expensive cars" the therapist also inferred that he had a competitive orientation toward his father. As you can see, analysts must *interpret* their clients' dreams and free associations. This is a critical process throughout psychoanalysis.

Interpretation

Interpretation **involves the therapist's attempts to explain the inner significance of the client's thoughts, feelings, memories, and behaviors.** Contrary to popular belief, analysts do not interpret everything, and they generally don't try to dazzle clients with startling revelations. Instead, analysts move forward inch by inch, offering interpretations that should be just out of the client's own reach. Mr. N.'s therapist eventually offered the following interpretations to his client.

> I said to Mr. N. near the end of the hour that I felt he was struggling with his feelings about his father's sexual life. He seemed to be saying that his father was sexually not a very potent man . . . . He also recalls that he once found a packet of condoms under his father's pillow when he was an adolescent and he thought "My father must be going to prostitutes." I then intervened and pointed out that the condoms under his father's pillow seemed to indicate more obviously that his father used the condoms with his mother, who slept in the same bed. However, Mr. N. wanted to believe his wish-fulfilling fantasy: mother doesn't want sex with father and father is not very potent. The patient was silent and the hour ended.

As you may already have guessed, the therapist has concluded that Mr. N.'s difficulties are rooted in the Oedipus complex (see Chapter 2). Mr. N. has unresolved sexual feelings toward his mother and hostile feelings about his father. These unconscious conflicts, which are rooted in his childhood, are distorting his intimate relations as an adult.

Resistance

How would you expect Mr. N. to respond to his therapist's suggestion that he was in competition with his father for the sexual attention of his mother? Obviously, most clients would have great difficulty accepting such an interpretation. Freud fully expected clients to display some resistance to therapeutic efforts. *Resis-* *tance* **involves largely unconscious defensive maneuvers intended to hinder the progress of therapy.** Why do clients try to resist the helping process? Because they don't want to face up to the painful, disturbing conflicts that they have buried in their unconscious. Although they have sought help, they are reluctant to confront their real problems.

Resistance may take many forms. Patients may show up late for their sessions, merely pretend to engage in free association, or express hostility toward the therapist. For instance, Mr. N.'s therapist noted that after the session just described, "the next day he began by telling me that he was furious with me." Analysts use a variety of strategies to deal with their clients' resistance. Often a key consideration is the handling of transference.

Transference

Transference **occurs when clients start relating to their therapists in ways that mimic significant relationships in their lives.** Thus a client might start relating to a therapist as if the therapist were an overprotective mother, rejecting brother, or passive spouse. In a sense, the client *transfers* conflicting feelings about important people onto the therapist. Mr. N., for instance, in his treatment, transferred some of the competitive hostility he felt toward his father onto his analyst.

Sigmund Freud

Psychoanalysts often encourage transference so that clients begin to reenact relations with crucial people in the context of therapy. These reenactments can help bring repressed feelings and conflicts to the surface, allowing the client to work through them. The therapist's handling of transference is complicated and difficult because transference may arouse confusing, highly charged emotions in the client.

Undergoing psychoanalysis is not easy. It can be a slow, painful process of self-examination that routinely requires three to five years of hard work. Ultimately, if resistance and transference can be handled effectively, the therapist's interpretations should lead the client to profound insights. For instance, Mr. N. eventually admitted, "The old boy is probably right, it does tickle me to imagine that my mother preferred me and I could beat out my father. Later, I wondered whether this had something to do with my own screwed-up sex life with my wife." According to Freud, once clients recognize the unconscious sources of their conflicts, they can resolve these conflicts and discard their neurotic defenses.

Modern Psychodynamic Therapies

Though still available, the kind of classical psychoanalysis Freud offered is not widely practiced anymore. Freud's psychoanalytic method was geared to a particular kind of clientele in Vienna many years ago. As his followers fanned out across Europe and America, many found that it was necessary to adapt psychoanalysis to different cultures, changing times, and new kinds of patients. Thus many variations on Freud's original approach to psychoanalysis have developed over the years. These descendants of psychoanalysis are collectively known as *psychodynamic approaches* to therapy.

Some of these adaptations, such as those developed by Carl Jung (1917) and Alfred Adler (1927), were sweeping revisions based on fundamental differences in theory. Other variations, such as those devised by Melanie Klein (1948) and Heinz Kohut (1971), involved more subtle changes in theory. Still other revisions (Alexander, 1954; Stekel, 1950) simply involved efforts to modernize and streamline psychoanalytic techniques (rather than theory), as outlined in Figure 16.3. Today we have a rich diversity of psychodynamic approaches to therapy. Although these many variations are beyond the scope of our review, we will examine a few key trends seen in modern psychodynamic therapies, as highlighted by Kutash (1976) and Baker (1985).

First, many new approaches have tried to speed up the pace of psychodynamic therapy. Modern approaches are less likely to assume that it will take three to five years to make therapeutic gains.

Second, the goals of modern psychodynamic therapies usually go beyond the discovery of repressed conflicts and defenses. Modern analysts devote less attention to the workings of the unconscious than to conscious processes.

Third, client-therapist interactions have become more direct. Modern analysts depend less on the gradual, rambling process of free association. Many analysts have abandoned the couch and free association in favor of face-to-face interaction that emphasizes candid communication.

Fourth, modern psychodynamic therapies no longer assume that neuroses grow out of conflicts centering on sex and aggression. Today analysts put less emphasis on probing into these areas, especially clients' sexuality.

Fifth, there also is less emphasis on delving into a client's distant past to reconstruct early childhood experiences. Instead, there is increased interest in understanding the client's present problems and current social relations.

Psychodynamic therapies have continued to evolve since Freud's era. In recent decades, though, most of the major innovations in insight therapy have emerged out of the humanistic tradition born in the 1950s. The most widely practiced humanistic therapy is Carl Rogers's client-centered therapy.

Client-Centered Therapy

You may have heard of people going into therapy to "find themselves" or to "get in touch with their real feelings." These now-familiar phrases emerged out of the human potential movement, which was stimulated in part by Carl Rogers's work (Rogers, 1951, 1986). Employing a humanistic perspective, Rogers devised *client-centered therapy* (also known as *person-centered therapy*) in the 1940s and 1950s.

Client-centered therapy is an insight therapy that emphasizes providing a supportive emotional climate for clients, who play a major role in determining the pace and direction of their therapy. You may wonder why the troubled, untrained client is put in charge of the pace and direction of the therapy. Rogers (1961) provided a compelling justification:

> It is the client who knows what hurts, what directions to go, what problems are crucial,

**FIGURE 16.3
Comparing classical and modern psychoanalysis**
Contemporary psychoanalytic therapists continue to practice in the tradition established by Freud, but differences have emerged. Baker (1985) divides contemporary psychodynamic therapies into three subgroups. "Modern psychoanalysis," profiled at the right, refers to the group that has remained most loyal to Freud's ideas while modifying clinical techniques. (Adapted from Baker, 1985.)

Some Differences between Classical and Modern Psychoanalysis	
Classical psychoanalysis	Modern psychoanalysis
Frequency of treatment is usually four to five times per week.	Frequency of treatment is typically one to two times per week.
Patient is treated "on the couch."	Patient is typically seen "face to face."
Treatment goals emphasize character reconstruction.	Treatment emphasizes problem resolution, enhanced adaptation, and support of ego functions with limited character change.
Treatment approach emphasizes the neutrality and nonintrusion of the analyst.	Therapist assumes an active and direct stance.
Technique emphasizes "free association," uncovering, interpretation, and analysis of the transference and resistance.	A wide range of interventions are used, including interpretive, supportive, and educative techniques. Transference is typically kept less intense.

what experiences have been deeply buried. It began to occur to me that unless I had a need to demonstrate my own cleverness and learning, I would do better to rely upon the client for the direction of movement in the process. [pp. 11–12]

Rogers's theory about the principal causes of neurotic anxieties is quite different from the Freudian explanation. As we saw in Chapter 2, Rogers maintained that most personal distress is caused by inconsistency, or "incongruence," between a person's self-concept and reality. According to his theory, incongruence makes people prone to feel threatened by realistic feedback about themselves from others. If you inaccurately viewed yourself as a hardworking, dependable person, for example, you would feel threatened by contradictory feedback from friends or co-workers. According to Rogers, anxiety about such feedback often leads to reliance on defense mechanisms, distortions of reality, and stifled personal growth. Excessive incongruence is thought to be rooted in clients' overdependence on others for approval and acceptance.

Given Rogers's theory, client-centered therapists stalk insights that are quite different from the repressed conflicts that psychoanalysts try to track down. Client-centered therapists help clients to realize that they do not have to worry constantly about pleasing others and winning acceptance. They encourage clients to respect their own feelings and values. They help people to restructure their self-concept to correspond better to reality. Ultimately, they try to foster self-acceptance and personal growth.

Therapeutic Climate

The process of client-centered therapy is not so important as the emotional *climate* in which the therapy takes place. According to Rogers, it is critical for the therapist to provide a warm, supportive, accepting climate. In this safe environment clients can confront their shortcomings without feeling threatened. The lack of threat should reduce clients' defensive tendencies and thus help them to open up. To create this atmosphere of emotional support, Rogers believed, client-centered therapists must provide three conditions.

1. *Genuineness.* The therapist must be genuine with the client, communicating in an honest and spontaneous manner. The therapist should not be phony or defensive.

2. *Unconditional positive regard.* The thera-

Modern therapy sessions tend to be face-to-face conversations between therapist and client.

pist must show complete, nonjudgmental acceptance of the client as a person. The therapist should provide warmth and caring for the client with no strings attached. This does not mean that the therapist must approve of everything that the client says or does. A therapist can disapprove of a particular behavior while continuing to value the client as a human being.

3. *Empathy.* Finally, the therapist must provide accurate empathy for the client. To do so the therapist must understand the client's world from the client's point of view, and must be articulate enough to communicate this understanding to the client.

Rogers firmly believed that a supportive emotional climate was the major force promoting healthy changes in therapy. In recent years, however, some client-centered therapists have begun to place more emphasis on the therapeutic process (Rice & Greenberg, 1992).

Therapeutic Process

In client-centered therapy, the client and therapist work together as equals. The therapist provides relatively little guidance and keeps interpretation and advice to a minimum. So just what does the client-centered therapist do, besides creating a supportive climate? Primarily, the therapist provides feedback to help clients sort out their feelings. The therapist's key task is *clarification.* Client-centered therapists try to function like a human mirror, reflecting statements back to their clients, but with enhanced clarity. They help clients to become more aware of their true feelings by highlighting themes that may be obscure in the clients' rambling discourse. The reflective nature of client-centered therapy can be seen in the following exchange between a client and therapist.

CLIENT: I really feel bad today . . . just terrible.

THERAPIST: You're feeling pretty bad.

CLIENT: Yeah, I'm angry and that's made me feel bad, especially when I can't do anything about it. I just have to live with it and shut up.

THERAPIST: You're very angry and feel like there's nothing you can safely do with your feelings.

CLIENT: Uh-huh. I mean . . . if I yell at my wife she gets hurt. If I don't say anything to her I feel tense.

THERAPIST: You're between a rock and a hard place—no matter what you do, you'll wind up feeling bad.

CLIENT: I mean she chews ice all day and all night. I feel stupid saying this. It's petty, I know. But when I sit there and try to concentrate, I hear all these slurping and crunching noises. I can't stand it . . . and I yell. She feels hurt—I feel bad—like I shouldn't have said anything.

THERAPIST: So when you finally say something you feel bad afterward.

CLIENT: Yeah, I can't say anything to her without getting mad and saying more than I should. And then I cause more trouble than it's worth. [Duke & Nowicki, 1979, p. 565]

By working with clients to clarify their feelings, client-centered therapists hope to build gradually toward more far-reaching insights. In particular, they try to help clients to become more aware of and comfortable about their genuine selves. Obviously, these are very ambitious goals. Client-centered therapy resembles psychoanalysis in that both seek to achieve a major reconstruction of a client's personality. We'll see more limited and specific goals in cognitive therapy, which we consider next.

Cognitive Therapy

In Chapter 3 we saw that our cognitive interpretations of events make all the difference in the world as to how well we handle stress. In Chapter 15 we learned that cognitive factors play a key role in the development of depressive disorders. Citing the importance of findings such as these, two former psychoanalysts—Aaron Beck (1976, 1987) and Albert Ellis (1973, 1989)—independently devised cognitive-oriented therapies that became highly influential (Arnkoff & Glass, 1992). Since we covered the main ideas underlying Ellis's *rational-emotive therapy* in our discussion of coping strategies in Chapter 4, we'll focus on Beck's system of *cognitive therapy* here. **Cognitive therapy is an insight therapy that emphasizes recognizing and changing negative thoughts and maladaptive beliefs.**

In recent years cognitive therapy has been applied fruitfully to a wide range of disorders (Beck, 1991), but it was originally devised as a treatment for depression. According to Beck, depression is caused by "errors" in thinking. He asserts that depression-prone people tend to do the following: (1) They blame their setbacks on personal inadequacies without considering circumstantial explanations. (2) They focus selectively on negative events while ignoring positive events. (3) They make unduly pessimistic projections about the future. (4) They draw negative conclusions about their worth as persons on the basis of insignificant events. Imagine that you and someone you've been dating for six weeks have just had your first disagreement. If you made the kind of errors in thinking just described, you might dismiss the fact that both of you had had highly stressful weeks, decide that you have nothing in common, hysterically predict that the relationship is over, and conclude that you will live out the rest of your days alone, in abject loneliness.

Goals and Techniques

The goal of cognitive therapy is to change the way clients think. To begin, clients are taught to detect their automatic negative thoughts. These are self-defeating statements that people are prone to make when they analyze problems: "I'm just not smart enough"; "No one really likes me"; and "It's all my fault." Clients are then trained to subject these automatic thoughts to reality testing. The therapist helps them to see how unrealistically negative the thoughts are.

The therapist's goal is not to promote unwarranted optimism but to help the client to employ more reasonable standards of evaluation. For example, a cognitive therapist might point out that a client's failure to get a desired promotion at work may be attributable to many factors and that this setback doesn't mean that the client is incompetent. Gradually the therapist digs deeper, looking for the unrealistic assumptions that underlie the client's constant negative thinking. These, too, have to be changed.

Unlike client-centered therapists, cognitive therapists are actively involved in determining the pace and direction of treatment. They usually talk extensively in the therapy sessions. They may argue openly with clients as

Carl Rogers

they try to persuade them to alter their patterns of thinking. The assertive nature of cognitive therapy is apparent in the following exchange between a patient and a therapist.

THERAPIST: What has your marriage been like?

PATIENT: It has been miserable from the very beginning . . . Raymond has always been unfaithful . . . I have hardly seen him in the past five years.

THERAPIST: You say you can't be happy without Raymond . . . Have you found yourself happy when you are with Raymond?

PATIENT: No, we fight all the time and I feel worse.

THERAPIST: Then why do you feel that Raymond is essential for your living?

PATIENT: I guess it's because without Raymond I am nothing.

THERAPIST: Would you please repeat that?

PATIENT: Without Raymond I am nothing.

THERAPIST: What do you think of that idea?

PATIENT: . . . Well, now that I think about it, I guess it's not completely true.

THERAPIST: You said you are "nothing" without Raymond. Before you met Raymond, did you feel you were "nothing"?

PATIENT: No, I felt I was somebody.

THERAPIST: Are you saying then that it's possible to be something without Raymond?

PATIENT: I guess that's true. I can be something without Raymond.

THERAPIST: If you were somebody before you knew Raymond, why do you need him to be somebody now?

PATIENT: (puzzled) Hmmm . . . Well, I just don't think that I can find anybody else like him.

THERAPIST: Did you have male friends before you knew Raymond?

PATIENT: I was pretty popular then.

THERAPIST: If I understand you correctly then, you were able to fall in love before with other men and other men have fallen in love with you.

PATIENT: Uh huh.

THERAPIST: Why do you think you will be unpopular without Raymond now?

PATIENT: Because I will not be able to attract any other man.

THERAPIST: Have any men shown an interest in you since you have been married?

PATIENT: A lot of men have made passes at me but I ignore them.

THERAPIST: If you were free of the marriage, do you think that men might be interested in you—knowing that you were available?

PATIENT: I guess that maybe they would be. [Beck, Rush, Shaw, & Emery, 1979, pp. 217–219]

Kinship with Behavior Therapy

Cognitive therapy borrows heavily from behavioral approaches to treatment, which we will discuss shortly. Specifically, cognitive thera-

pists often use "homework assignments" that focus on changing clients' overt behaviors. Clients may be instructed to engage in overt responses on their own, outside of the clinician's office. One shy, insecure young man in cognitive therapy was told to go to a singles bar and engage three women in conversations for up to five minutes each (Rush, 1984). He was instructed to record his thoughts before and after each of the conversations. This assignment elicited various maladaptive patterns of thought that gave the young man and his therapist plenty to talk about in subsequent sessions. As this example demonstrates, cognitive therapy is a creative blend of talk therapy and behavior therapy, although it is primarily an insight therapy.

Cognitive therapy was originally designed as a treatment for individuals, but it has recently been adapted for use with groups (Covi & Primakoff, 1988). Many insight therapies can be conducted on either an individual or a group basis.

Aaron Beck

Group Therapy

Although it dates back to the early part of the 20th century (Rosenbaum, Lakin, & Roback, 1992), group therapy came of age during the 1950s and 1960s. During this period, the expanding demand for therapeutic services forced clinicians to use group techniques. *Group therapy* **is the simultaneous treatment of several clients in a group.** Most major insight therapies have been adapted for use with groups. In fact, the ideas underlying Rogers's client-centered therapy spawned the much-publicized encounter group movement. Although group therapy can be conducted in a variety of ways, we can provide a general overview of the process as it usually unfolds (see Fuchs, 1984; Vinogradov & Yalom, 1988).

Participants' Roles

A therapy group typically consists of about five to ten participants. The therapist usually screens the participants, and most therapists exclude persons who seem likely to be disruptive. There is some debate about whether or not it is best to have a homogeneous group (people who are similar in age, sex, and presenting problem). Practical necessities usually dictate that groups are at least somewhat diversified.

The therapist plays a subtle role in group therapy. Therapists often stay in the background and focus mainly on promoting group cohesiveness. They model supportive behaviors for the participants and try to promote a healthy climate. The therapist always retains a special status, but the therapist and clients are on much more equal footing in group therapy than in individual therapy. The group leader expresses emotions, shares feelings, and copes with challenges from group members. In other words, group therapists participate in the group's exchanges and bare their own souls to some extent.

The group members essentially function as therapists for one another. They describe their problems, trade views, share experiences, and discuss coping strategies. Most important, they provide acceptance and emotional support for one another. In this supportive atmosphere, group members work at peeling away the social masks that cover their insecurities. Once their problems are exposed, members work at correcting them. As members come to value one another's opinions, they work hard to display healthy changes to win the group's approval.

Hans Eysenck

Advantages of the Group Experience

Group therapies obviously save time and money, which can be critical in understaffed mental hospitals and other institutional settings. Therapists in private practice usually charge less for group than individual therapy, making therapy affordable for more people. However, group therapy is *not* just a less costly substitute for individual therapy. Group therapy has unique strengths of its own. Irwin Yalom (1975), who has studied group therapy extensively, has described some of these advantages.

1. *Participants in group therapy often come to realize that their misery is not unique.* Clients often enter therapy feeling very sorry for themselves. They think that they alone have a terribly burdensome cross to bear. In the group situation, they quickly see that they are not unique. They are reassured to learn that many other people have similar or even worse problems.

2. *Group therapy provides an opportunity for participants to work on their social skills in a safe environment.* Many personal problems essentially involve difficulties in relating effectively to people. Group therapy can provide a workshop for improving interpersonal skills that cannot be matched by individual therapy.

3. *Certain kinds of problems are especially well suited to group treatment.* Specific types of problems and clients respond especially well to the social support that group therapy can provide. In peer self-help groups, people who have a common problem get together regularly to help one another out. The original peer self-help group was Alcoholics Anonymous. Today there are similar groups made up of former psychiatric patients, single parents, drug addicts, and so forth.

Whether therapy is conducted on a group basis or an individual basis, clients usually invest considerable time, effort, and money in insight therapies. Are they worth the investment? Let's examine the evidence.

Evaluating Insight Therapies

In 1952 Hans Eysenck shocked mental health professionals by reporting that there was no sound evidence that insight therapy actually helped people. What was the basis for this startling claim? Eysenck (1952) reviewed numerous studies of therapeutic outcomes for clients suffering from neurotic problems. He found that about two-thirds of the clients recovered. A two-thirds recovery rate sounds reasonable, except that Eysenck found a similar recovery rate among *untreated* neurotics. As we noted in Chapter 15, psychological disorders sometimes clear up on their own. **A *spontaneous remission* is a recovery from a disorder that occurs without formal treatment.** His estimate of the spontaneous remission rate for neurotic disorders lead Eysenck (1952) to conclude that the therapeutic effects of insight psychotherapy are small or nonexistent.

In the ensuing years, critics searched for flaws in Eysenck's article. They found a variety of shortcomings in his data. For instance, Eysenck used different time frames in comparing the recovery rates of treated and untreated neurotics. The two-thirds recovery rate in the untreated groups was based on a *two-year* time period, whereas the two-thirds recovery rate for the treated groups occurred in a *two-month* time frame (Strupp & Howard, 1992). Moreover, the treated and untreated groups were not matched in terms of the severity of their disorders, their attitudes and expectations in regard to therapy, or any other relevant variables that might influence therapeutic outcomes. Eysenck also made many arbitrary judgments about "recoveries" that were consistently favorable to the untreated groups. After taking a close look at Eysenck's data, Bergin (1971) argued that the data really suggested that the spontaneous remission rate for neurotic disorders was in the vicinity of 30 to 40%. Although Eysenck's conclusions were unduly pessimistic, he made an important contribution to the mental health field by sparking debate and research on the effectiveness of insight therapy.

Evaluating the effectiveness of any approach to psychotherapy is a complicated matter (Garfield, 1992). If you were to undergo insight therapy, how would you judge its effectiveness? By how you felt? By looking at your behavior? By asking your therapist? By consulting your friends and family? What would you be looking for? People enter therapy with different problems and needs. Different schools of thought seek to realize entirely different goals. Thus measures of therapeutic outcome are inevitably subjective.

A key problem is that both therapists and clients are biased strongly in the direction of evaluating therapy favorably (Rachman & Wilson, 1980). Therapists want to see improvement because it reflects on their professional competence. Obviously, they hope to see clients getting better as a result of their work. Clients are slanted toward a favorable evaluation because they want to justify their effort, their heartache, their expense, and their time.

In spite of these difficulties, hundreds of therapy outcome studies have been conducted since Eysenck prodded researchers into action. These studies consistently indicate that insight therapy *is* superior to no treatment (Lambert & Bergin, 1992). Two major reviews of the literature (Luborsky, Singer, & Luborsky, 1975; Meltzoff & Kornreich, 1970) both conclude that therapy outshines no treatment in about 80% of the studies. In a comprehensive review, Smith, Glass, and Miller (1980) examined 475 studies and estimated that the average therapy client ends up better off than 80% of comparable untreated controls.

Admittedly, this outcome research does not indicate that insight therapy leads to miraculous results. The superiority of therapy over no treatment is usually characterized as modest. In light of the price of therapy, there is room for debate about its cost-effectiveness. Overall, about 70 to 80% of clients appear to benefit from insight therapy, while 20 to 30% fail to show any clear improvement.

Some investigators have tried to figure out which clients are most likely to benefit from insight therapy. Schofield (1964) concluded that "YAVIS" clients are the best candidates for insight therapy. The letters are an abbreviation for young, attractive, verbal, intelligent, and successful. However, a recent review of hundreds of studies on the prediction of therapeutic outcomes found little support for the first three of these factors (Luborsky, Crits-Christoph, Mintz, & Auerbach, 1988). This review *did* identify some other factors—besides intelligence and success—that are important.

People who benefit most from insight therapy are those who expect it to help them, who are motivated to make it work, and who do not suffer from severe psychological disorders.

Luborsky and his colleagues found that insight therapy works out better for patients who are highly motivated and who have positive attitudes toward therapy. They also found that less severely disturbed patients are more likely to benefit from insight therapy than patients with severe pathology.

Clients' personal characteristics tend to be considerably less important when behavioral treatments are employed. Behavior therapies can be useful with a wide range of clients and disorders.

Behavior Therapies

Behavior therapy differs from insight therapy in that behavior therapists make no attempt to help clients achieve grand insights about themselves. Why not? Because behavior therapists believe that such insights aren't necessary to produce constructive change. Consider a client troubled by compulsive gambling. The behavior therapist doesn't care whether this behavior is rooted in unconscious conflicts or parental rejection. What the client needs is to get rid of the maladaptive behavior. Consequently, the therapist simply designs a program to eliminate the compulsive gambling. Actually, behavior therapists may work with clients to attain very limited insights about how environmental factors evoke troublesome behaviors (Franks & Barbrack, 1983). This information can then be helpful in the design of a behavioral therapy program.

The crux of the difference between insight therapy and behavior therapy lies in their views of symptoms. Insight therapists treat pathological symptoms as signs of an underlying problem. Behavior therapists think that the symptoms *are* the problem. Thus **behavior therapies apply the principles of learning to direct efforts to change clients' maladaptive behaviors.**

Behaviorism has been an influential school of thought in psychology since the 1920s. But behaviorists devoted little attention to clinical issues until the 1950s, when behavior therapy emerged out of three independent lines of research fostered by B. F. Skinner and his colleagues (Skinner, Solomon, & Lindsley, 1953) in the United States, Hans Eysenck (1959) and his colleagues in Britain, and Joseph Wolpe (1958) and his colleagues in South Africa (Glass & Arnkoff, 1992). Since then, there has been an explosion of interest in behavioral approaches to psychotherapy. Today more and more psychologists are using behavioral approaches, especially those who work with children (O'Leary, 1984).

FIGURE 16.4
A sample anxiety hierarchy
Systematic desensitization requires the construction of an anxiety hierarchy like the one shown here, which was developed for a woman with a fear of heights who had a penchant for hiking in the mountains.

An Anxiety Hierarchy for Systematic Desensitization	
Degree of fear	Anxiety-arousing stimulus situations
5	I'm standing on the balcony on the top floor of an apartment tower.
10	I'm standing on a stepladder in the kitchen to change a light bulb.
15	I'm walking on a ridge. The edge is hidden by shrubs and treetops.
20	I'm sitting on the slope of a mountain, looking out over the horizon.
25	I'm crossing a bridge 6 feet above a creek. The bridge consists of an 18-inch-wide board with a handrail on one side.
30	I'm riding a ski lift 8 feet above the ground.
35	I'm crossing a shallow, wide creek on an 18-inch-wide board, 3 feet above water level.
40	I'm climbing a ladder outside the house to reach a second-story window.
45	I'm pulling myself up a 30-degree wet, slippery slope on a steel cable.
50	I'm scrambling up a rock, 8 feet high.
55	I'm walking 10 feet on a resilient, 18-inch-wide board, which spans an 8-foot-deep gulch.
60	I'm walking on a wide plateau, 2 feet from the edge of a cliff.
65	I'm skiing an intermediate hill. The snow is packed.
70	I'm walking over a railway trestle.
75	I'm walking on the side of an embankment. The path slopes to the outside.
80	I'm riding a chairlift 15 feet above the ground.
85	I'm walking up a long, steep slope.
90	I'm walking up (or down) a 15-degree slope on a 3-foot-wide trail. On one side of the trail the terrain drops down sharply; on the other side is a steep upward slope.
95	I'm walking on a 3-foot-wide ridge. The slopes on both sides are long and more than 25 degrees steep.
100	I'm walking on a 3-foot-wide ridge. The trail slopes on one side. The drop on either side of the trail is more than 25 degrees.

General Principles

Behavior therapies are based on certain assumptions (Agras & Berkowitz, 1988). *First, it is assumed that behavior is a product of learning.* No matter how self-defeating or pathological a client's behavior may be, the behaviorist believes that it is the result of past conditioning. *Second, it is assumed that what has been learned can be unlearned.* The same learning principles that explain how the maladaptive behavior was acquired can be used to get rid of it. Thus behavior therapists attempt to change clients' behavior by applying the principles of classical conditioning, operant conditioning, and observational learning.

Behavior therapies are close cousins of the self-modification procedures described in the Chapter 4 Application. Both employ the same principles of learning to alter behavior directly. In discussing *self-modification,* we examined some relatively simple procedures that people can apply to themselves to improve everyday self-control. In our discussion of *behavior therapy* we will examine more complex procedures used by mental health professionals in the treatment of more severe problems.

Like self-modification, behavior therapy requires clients to translate their vague complaints ("My life is filled with frustration") into specific, concrete behavioral goals ("I need to increase my use of assertive responses in dealing with colleagues"). Once the troublesome behaviors have been targeted, the therapist designs a program to alter them. The nature of the therapeutic program depends on the types of problems identified. Specific procedures are designed for specific types of problems, as you'll see in the following discussion of systematic desensitization.

Systematic Desensitization

Systematic desensitization, devised by Joseph Wolpe (1958, 1987), revolutionized the treatment of phobic disorders. **Systematic desensitization is a behavior therapy used to reduce clients' anxiety responses through counterconditioning.** The treatment assumes that most anxiety responses are acquired through classical conditioning (as we discussed in Chapter 15). According to this model, a harmless stimulus (for instance, a bridge) may be paired with a frightening event (lightning strikes it) so that it becomes a conditioned stimulus eliciting anxiety. The goal of systematic desensitization is to weaken the association between the conditioned stimulus (the bridge) and the condi-

"Leave us alone! I am a behavior therapist! I am helping my patient overcome a fear of heights."

tioned response of anxiety. Systematic desensitization involves three steps.

First, the therapist helps the client to build an anxiety hierarchy. The hierarchy is a list of anxiety-arousing stimuli centering on the specific source of anxiety, such as flying, academic tests, or snakes. The client ranks the stimuli from the least anxiety-arousing to the most anxiety-arousing. This ordered list of related, anxiety-provoking stimuli is the anxiety hierarchy. The anxiety hierarchy of one woman who was afraid of heights is shown in Figure 16.4.

The second step is to train the client in deep muscle relaxation. This second phase may begin during early sessions while the therapist and client are still constructing the anxiety hierarchy. Different therapists use different relaxation training procedures. Whatever procedures are employed, the client must learn to engage in deep and thorough relaxation at the therapist's command.

In the third step, the client tries to work through the hierarchy, learning to remain relaxed while imagining each stimulus. Starting with the least anxiety-arousing stimulus, the client imagines the situation as vividly as possible while relaxing. If clients experience strong anxiety, they drop the imaginary scene and concentrate on relaxation. The clients keep repeating this process until they can imagine a scene with little or no anxiety. Once a particular scene is conquered, a client moves on to the next stimulus situation in the anxiety hierarchy. Gradually, over a number of therapy sessions, clients progress through the hierarchy, unlearning troublesome anxiety responses.

As clients conquer *imagined* phobic stimuli, they may be encouraged to confront the *real* stimuli, a process called *exposure*. Desensitiza-

tion to imagined stimuli *can* be effective by itself (Leitenberg, 1976). However, many behavior therapists advocate following it up with planned exposures to the real anxiety-arousing stimuli (Lazarus & Wilson, 1976). The desensitization to imagined stimuli should reduce anxiety enough so that clients will be able to confront situations they used to avoid at all costs. Usually these real-life confrontations prove harmless, and the person's anxiety response declines further. Although exposure is often used in conjunction with systematic desensitization, guided exposure techniques can also be used effectively by themselves in the treatment of phobic anxiety (Emmelkamp, 1986).

Aversion Therapy

Aversion therapy is far and away the most controversial of the behavior therapies. It's not something that you would sign up for unless you were pretty desperate. Psychologists usually suggest it only as a treatment of last resort, after other interventions have failed. What's so terrible about aversion therapy? The client has to endure decidedly unpleasant stimuli, such as shock or drug-induced nausea.

Aversion therapy is a behavior therapy in which an aversive stimulus is paired with a stimulus that elicits an undesirable response. For example, alcoholics have had drug-induced nausea paired with their favorite drinks during therapy sessions (Cannon, Baker, & Wehl, 1981). By pairing an *emetic drug* (one that causes vomiting) with alcohol, the therapist hopes to create a conditioned aversion to alcohol (see Figure 16.5).

Aversion therapy takes advantage of the automatic nature of responses produced through classical conditioning. Admittedly, alcoholics treated with aversion therapy know that they won't be given an emetic outside of their therapy sessions. However, their reflex response to the stimulus of alcohol may be changed so that they respond to it with nausea and distaste. Obviously, this response should make it much easier to resist the urge to drink.

Troublesome behaviors treated successfully with aversion therapy include drug abuse, sexual deviance, gambling, shoplifting, stuttering,

Joseph Wolpe

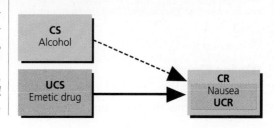

**FIGURE 16.5
Aversion therapy**
Aversion therapy uses classical conditioning to create an aversion to a stimulus that has elicited problematic behavior. In the treatment of drinking problems, for example, alcohol may be paired with a nausea-inducing drug to condition an aversion to alcohol.

cigarette smoking, and overeating (Lazarus & Wilson, 1976; Sandler, 1975). Aversion therapy is typically only one element in a larger treatment program. Of course, this procedure should be used only with willing clients when other options have failed (Rimm & Cunningham, 1985).

Social Skills Training

Many psychological problems grow out of interpersonal difficulties. Behavior therapists point out that we are not born with social finesse. We acquire our social skills through learning. Unfortunately, some people have not learned how to be friendly, how to make conversation, how to express anger appropriately, and so forth. Social ineptitude can contribute to anxiety, feelings of inferiority, and various kinds of disorders. In light of these findings, therapists are increasingly using social skills training in efforts to improve clients' social abilities (Liberman, Mueser, & DeRisi, 1989). This approach to therapy has yielded promising results in the treatment of depression, shyness, social anxiety, and even schizophrenia (Becker, 1990; Wixted, Bellack, & Hersen, 1990).

Social skills training **is a behavior therapy designed to improve interpersonal skills that emphasizes shaping, modeling, and behavioral rehearsal.** This type of behavior therapy can be conducted with individual clients or in groups. Social skills training depends on the principles of operant conditioning and observational learning. The therapist makes use of *modeling* by encouraging clients to watch socially skilled friends and colleagues, so that responses (eye contact, active listening, and so on) can be acquired through observation.

In *behavioral rehearsal*, the client tries to practice social techniques in structured role-playing exercises. The therapist provides corrective feedback and uses approval to reinforce progress. Eventually clients try their newly acquired skills in real-world interactions. Usually they are given specific homework assignments. *Shaping* is employed in that clients are gradually asked to handle more complicated and delicate social situations. For example, a nonassertive client may begin by working on making requests of friends. Only much later will the client be asked to tackle standing up to his or her boss.

Biofeedback

Biofeedback is another widely used therapy that has emerged from the behavioral tradition. In

biofeedback **a body function (such as heart rate) is monitored, and information about it is fed back to a person to facilitate improved control of the physiological process.** Armed with precise information about internal body functions, people are able to exert far more control over some of them than they had thought possible. For example, many anxious people develop problematic high blood pressure. Obviously, it would be nice if these people could learn to control their blood pressure without depending on drugs, which may have side effects. Evidence suggests that biofeedback *can* be used to train people to control their blood pressure (Shapiro, Schwartz, & Tursky, 1972).

To see how biofeedback works, let's look at *electromyograph* (EMG) feedback intended to enhance relaxation. An EMG is a device used to measure skeletal-muscular tension in the body. In a typical training session, a client is hooked up to an EMG, and its recordings are transformed into an auditory signal. Usually the signal is a tone that increases and decreases in volume. The therapist explains that changes in the tone will reflect changes in the client's level of muscular tension. The client is instructed to raise or lower the tone.

Although people often have difficulty describing how they do it, most can learn to exert better control over their level of muscular tension. Essentially, EMG feedback helps them to improve their ability to engage in deep muscle relaxation. Promising results have been obtained with EMG feedback in the treatment of anxiety (Raskin, Bali, & Peeke, 1981), tension headaches (Schwartz, 1987), and high blood pressure (Olson & Kroon, 1987).

In some respects, biofeedback is a *biological* intervention, and it could be classified as a biomedical therapy. However, it is usually grouped with the behavior therapies because its use is not limited to physicians and the strategy emerged out of behavioral research. Studies have revealed that biofeedback can help people exert some control over brain wave activity, skin temperature, blood pressure, heart rate, and muscle tension (Adler & Adler, 1984). Early proponents of biofeedback may have gotten carried away in making extravagant claims about its benefits. Nonetheless, this unique intervention appears to have potential for treating many stress-related problems.

Evaluating Behavior Therapies

Behavior therapists have historically placed more emphasis than insight therapists have on the importance of measuring therapeutic outcomes. As a result, there is ample evidence regarding the effectiveness of behavior therapy (Rachman & Wilson, 1980; Smith et al., 1980). How does the effectiveness of behavior therapy compare with that of insight therapy? In direct comparisons, the differences between the therapies are usually small (Smith et al., 1980). These modest differences, however, tend to favor behavioral approaches for certain types of disorders (Kazdin & Wilson, 1978; Lambert & Bergin, 1992). Of course, behavior therapies are not well suited to the treatment of some types of problems (vague feelings of discontent, for instance). Furthermore, it's misleading to make global statements about the effectiveness of behavior therapies because they include many different procedures designed for different purposes. The value of systematic desensitization for phobias, for example, has no bearing on the value of aversion therapy for sexual deviance.

For our purposes, it is sufficient to note that evidence on the efficacy of most of the widely used behavioral interventions is favorable (Wixted et al., 1990). Behavior therapies seem to be particularly effective in the treatment of anxiety problems, phobias, obsessive-compulsive disorders, sexual dysfunction, sexual deviance, drug-related problems, and obesity (Rachman & Wilson, 1980). Only a few of these problems would be amenable to treatment with the biomedical therapies.

Biomedical Therapies

In the 1950s a French surgeon was looking for a drug that would reduce patients' autonomic response to surgical stress. The surgeon noticed that chlorpromazine produced a mild sedation. This observation led Delay and Deniker (1952) to give chlorpromazine to hospitalized schizophrenic patients to see whether it would calm them. Their experiment was a dramatic success. Chlorpromazine became the first effective antipsychotic drug—and a revolution in psychiatry was begun. Hundreds of thousands of severely disturbed patients—patients who had appeared doomed to lead the remainder of their lives in mental hospitals—were gradually sent home, thanks to the therapeutic effects of antipsychotic drugs (see Figure 16.6). Today biomedical therapies, such as drug treatment, lie at the core of psychiatric practice.

Biomedical therapies involve physiological interventions intended to reduce symptoms associated with psychological disorders.

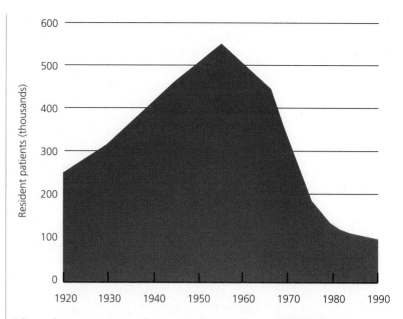

FIGURE 16.6
The declining inpatient population in mental hospitals
The number of inpatients in public mental hospitals has declined dramatically since the late 1950s. This "deinstitutionalization," encouraged by the belief that outpatient care can be as therapeutic as inpatient care and is far more economical, was made possible by the development of effective antipsychotic medications.

These therapies assume that psychological disorders are caused, at least in part, by biological malfunctions. As we saw in Chapter 15, this assumption clearly has merit so far as many disorders are concerned, especially the more severe ones. We will discuss two biomedical approaches to psychotherapy: drug therapy and electroconvulsive (shock) therapy.

Treatment with Drugs

Psychopharmacotherapy involves the treatment of mental disorders with medication. We will refer to this kind of treatment more simply as *drug therapy.* Therapeutic drugs for psychological problems fall into three major groups: (1) antianxiety drugs, (2) antipsychotic drugs, and (3) antidepressant drugs. Another important drug that does not fit neatly into any of these categories is lithium, which is used in the treatment of bipolar mood disorders. Of these drugs, the antianxiety agents are the most widely prescribed (Zorc, Larson, Lyons, & Beardsley, 1991). Surprisingly, only about 17% of the prescriptions for drugs used in the treatment of psychological problems are written by psychiatrists (Beardsley, Gardocki, Larson, & Hidalgo, 1988). The vast majority of these prescriptions are written by primary-care physicians.

Antianxiety Drugs

Most of us know someone who pops pills to relieve anxiety. The drugs involved in this common coping strategy are **antianxiety drugs, which relieve tension, apprehension, and nervousness.** The most popular of these drugs are Valium and Xanax. These are the trade names (the proprietary names that pharmaceutical companies use in marketing drugs) for diazepam and alprazolam, respectively.

Valium, Xanax, and other drugs in the benzodiazepine family, often called *tranquilizers*, are routinely prescribed for people with anxiety disorders. They are also given to millions of people who simply suffer from chronic nervous tension. In the mid-1970s pharmacists in the United States were filling nearly *100 million* prescriptions each year for Valium and similar antianxiety drugs. Many critics characterized this level of use as excessive (Lickey & Gordon, 1991).

Antianxiety drugs exert their effects almost immediately. They can be fairly effective in alleviating feelings of anxiety (Lader, 1984), but their effects are measured in hours, so their impact is relatively short-lived. Common side effects of antianxiety drugs are drowsiness, depression, nausea, and confusion (Evans, 1981). There is some potential for abuse, dependency, and overdose problems with these drugs (Salzman, 1989). These problems led to a moderate decline in the prescription of Valium and similar drugs in the 1980s. Currently researchers are studying the effects of a new antianxiety drug called Buspar (buspirone), which has less potential for abuse (Gorman & Davis, 1989). Unlike Valium, Buspar is slow-acting, exerting its effects in seven to ten days, but with fewer sedative side effects (Newton, Marunycz, Alderdice, & Napoliello, 1986).

Antipsychotic Drugs

Antipsychotic drugs are used primarily in the treatment of schizophrenia. They also are given to people with severe mood disorders who become delusional. The trade names (and generic names) of some prominent drugs in this category are Thorazine (chlorpromazine), Mellaril (thioridazine), and Haldol (haloperidol). *Antipsychotic drugs are used to gradually reduce psychotic symptoms, including hyperactivity, mental confusion, hallucinations, and delusions.*

Studies suggest that about 90% of psychotic patients respond favorably (albeit in varied degrees) to antipsychotic medication (Davis, Barter, & Kane, 1989). When antipsychotic drugs are effective, they work their magic gradually, as Figure 16.7 shows. Patients usually begin to respond within two days to a week. Improvement may continue for several months. Many schizophrenic patients are placed on antipsychotics indefinitely because these drugs can reduce the likelihood of a relapse into an active schizophrenic episode.

Antipsychotic drugs undeniably make a major contribution to the treatment of severe mental disorders, but they are not without problems. They have many unpleasant side effects (Lader & Herrington, 1990). Drowsiness, constipation, and "cotton mouth" are common. Patients may also experience tremors, muscular rigidity, and impaired coordination. After being released from a hospital, many schizophrenic patients, supposedly placed on antipsychotics indefinitely, discontinue their drug regimen because of the disagreeable side effects. Unfortunately, patients often relapse into another schizophrenic episode within three to nine months after they stop taking antipsychotic medication (J. M. Davis, 1985).

More troublesome than these minor side effects of antipsychotics is a severe and lasting problem called *tardive dyskinesia*. *Tardive dyskinesia is a neurological disorder marked by chronic tremors and involuntary spastic movements.* This debilitating syndrome resembles Parkinson's disease, and there is no cure. There has been a heated debate about how often this serious disorder is brought on by antipsychotic drug therapy (Brown & Funk, 1986). Recent evidence suggests that it develops in a little less than 20% of patients who take antipsychotics over a prolonged period (Khot & Wyatt, 1991). As the prevalence of this problem has come to be recognized, experts have urged psychiatrists to be more conservative in their prescription of antipsychotics on a long-term basis.

Psychiatrists are currently experimenting with a new antipsychotic drug called Clozaril (clozapine). Although it's not risk-free, this drug seems to produce fewer side effects than traditional antipsychotics (Davis et al., 1989).

The advent of antipsychotic drugs in the 1960s allowed mental hospitals to adopt a policy of "deinstitutionalization," which involved releasing many schizophrenic patients who used to be hospitalized indefinitely. However, many of these individuals have experienced difficulty caring for themselves, and deinstitutionalization has contributed to increased homelessness in our society.

Moreover, Clozaril appears to help a significant portion of the 10% of patients who do not respond to other antipsychotic medications (Perry, Miller, Arndt, & Cadoret, 1991). Unfortunately, at present Clozaril therapy is prohibitively expensive.

Antidepressant Drugs

As their name suggests, **antidepressant drugs gradually elevate mood and help to bring people out of a depression.** There are two principal classes of antidepressants: *tricyclics* (such as Elavil) and *MAO inhibitors* (such as Nardil). These two sets of drugs appear to affect neurochemical activity in different ways and tend to work with different patients. The tricyclics are effective for a larger percentage (60 to 80%) of depressed patients (Davis & Glassman, 1989). They also have fewer problematic side effects than the MAO inhibitors (Glenn & Taska, 1984). Like antipsychotic drugs, antidepressants exert their effects gradually over a period of weeks.

Psychiatrists are currently enthusiastic about a new antidepressant, Prozac (fluoxetine), which yields rapid therapeutic gains in the treatment of depression (Cole, 1988). Moreover, Prozac and another antidepressant (clomipramine) appear to have value in the treatment of obsessive-compulsive disorders (Jenike, Baer, & Greist, 1990). However, Prozac is not the miracle drug that some popular magazines have suggested. A minority of patients on Prozac have developed serious unexpected side effects, such as intense preoccupation with suicide (Teicher, Glod, & Cole, 1990). Like all drugs for psychological disorders, Prozac has risks that must be carefully weighed against its benefits.

Lithium

Lithium is a chemical used to control mood swings in patients with bipolar mood disorders. Lithium has excellent value in preventing *future* episodes of both mania and depression in patients with bipolar illness (Jefferson & Greist, 1989). Lithium can also be used in efforts to bring patients with bipolar illness out of *current* manic or depressive episodes. However, antipsychotics and antidepressants are more frequently used for these purposes. On the negative side of the ledger, lithium does have some dangerous side effects if its use isn't managed skillfully (Georgotas, 1985). Lithium levels in the patient's blood must be monitored carefully because high concentrations of it can

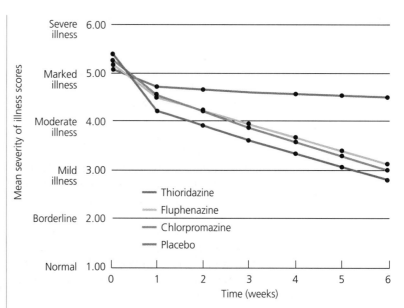

be highly toxic and even fatal. Impaired functioning of the kidneys and of the thyroid gland are the major problems associated with lithium therapy (Post, 1989).

Evaluating Drug Therapies

Drug therapies can produce clear therapeutic gains for many patients. What's especially impressive is that they can be effective in severe disorders that otherwise defy therapeutic endeavors. Nonetheless, drug therapies are controversial. As Lickey and Gordon (1991) note, critics of drug therapy have raised a variety of issues. First, some critics argue that drug therapies often produce superficial curative effects. For example, Valium does not really solve problems with anxiety. It merely provides temporary relief from an unpleasant symptom. Moreover, this temporary relief may lull patients into complacency about their problem and prevent them from working toward a more lasting solution. Second, critics charge that many drugs are overprescribed and many patients overmedicated. According to these critics, many physicians habitually hand out prescriptions without giving adequate consideration to more complicated and difficult interventions. This problem is compounded by the fact that drugs calm patients and make it easier for hospital staffs to run their wards. Thus critics argue that some institutions tend to overmedicate patients to minimize disruptive behavior. Third, some critics charge that the side effects of therapeutic drugs are worse than the illnesses that the drugs are supposed to cure. Citing problems such as tardive dyskinesia, lithium toxicity, and addiction to antianxiety agents, these critics argue

FIGURE 16.7
The effects of antipsychotic drugs over time
Antipsychotic drugs reduce psychotic symptoms gradually, over a span of weeks. Patients given placebo pills show little improvement over the same period. (Data from Cole, Goldberg, & Davis, 1966; J. M. Davis, 1985.)

that the risks of therapeutic drugs aren't worth the benefits.

Lickey and Gordon (1991) acknowledge that the issues raised by the critics of drug therapy are legitimate causes of concern, but after reviewing the evidence they defend the use of therapeutic drugs. They argue that drug therapies were never touted as *cures* and that "the relief of symptoms is a genuine benefit that must not be dismissed as trivial" (p. 358). They agree that some drugs are overprescribed and that most drugs have potentially serious side effects, but they conclude that, overall, the benefits of drug therapy far exceed any harm done.

Obviously, drug therapies have stirred up some debate. However, this controversy pales in comparison with the furious debates inspired by electroconvulsive (shock) therapy (ECT). ECT is so controversial that the residents of Berkeley, California, voted to outlaw it in their city. In subsequent lawsuits, however, the courts ruled that scientific questions cannot be settled by a vote, and they overturned the law. What makes ECT so controversial? You'll see in the next section.

Electroconvulsive Therapy (ECT)

In the 1930s a Hungarian psychiatrist named Ladislas Meduna hypothesized that epilepsy and schizophrenia could not coexist in the

This patient is being prepared for electroconvulsive therapy. The band around the forehead contains electrodes. The mouthpiece keeps the patient from biting his tongue during the electrically induced seizures.

same body. On the basis of this observation, which turned out to be inaccurate, Meduna theorized that it might be useful to induce epileptic-like seizures in schizophrenic patients. At first he used a drug to trigger these seizures. By 1938, however, a pair of Italian psychiatrists demonstrated that it was safer to elicit the seizures with electric shock. Thus modern electroconvulsive therapy was born, creating a peculiar tribute to the old advertising slogan "Better living through electricity."

Electroconvulsive therapy (ECT) **is a biomedical treatment in which electric shock is used to produce a cortical seizure accompanied by convulsions.** Electrodes are attached to the skull over the temporal lobes of the brain (see the photo on this page). A light anesthesia is induced, and the patient is given a variety of drugs to minimize the likelihood of complications, such as spinal fractures. Then an electric current is applied for about a second. The current should trigger a brief (5–20 seconds) convulsive seizure, during which the patient usually loses consciousness. Patients normally awaken in an hour or two. People typically receive between six and 20 treatments as inpatients at a hospital.

The clinical use of ECT peaked in the 1940s and 1950s, before effective drug therapies were widely available. ECT has long been controversial, and its use declined in the 1960s and 1970s. Nonetheless, ECT is *not* a rare form of therapy (Sackeim, 1985). Estimates suggest that about 60,000 to 100,000 people receive ECT treatments yearly in the United States, mainly for depression.

Controversy about ECT is fueled by patients' reports that the treatment is painful, dehumanizing, and terrifying. Concerns have also been raised by reports that staff members at some hospitals use the threat of ECT to keep patients in line (Breggin, 1979). The use of ECT for disciplinary purposes is unethical, but the essay in Figure 16.8 suggests that the practice is condoned in some institutions. This essay also provides a moving description of how aversive ECT can be for some patients.

Effectiveness of ECT

The effectiveness of ECT is hotly debated. Ardent proponents maintain that it is a remarkably effective treatment (Fink, 1988). Equally ardent opponents argue that it is no more effective than a placebo (Friedberg, 1976). Reported improvement rates for ECT treatment range from negligible to very high (Small, Small, &

Milstein, 1986). These inconsistent findings are due in part to methodological weaknesses that are often found in ECT studies. Barton (1977) could find only *six* studies among hundreds on ECT that used appropriate control groups to assess therapeutic effects. Why are ECT studies so flawed? Probably because most investigators feel very strongly (pro or con) about ECT and their biases affect their research, both intentionally and inadvertently.

In light of these problems, conclusions about the value of ECT must be tentative. Although ECT was once considered appropriate for a wide range of disorders, even most proponents now recommend it only for mood disorders (especially depression). Overall, there seems to be enough favorable evidence to justify *conservative* use of ECT in treating severe mood disorders (Weiner & Coffey, 1988).

Curiously, insofar as ECT may be effective, no one is sure why. The discarded theories about how ECT works could fill several books. Until recently it was widely accepted that the occurrence of a cortical seizure was critical to the treatment. Now many theorists are questioning this once-firm conclusion (Sackeim, 1988). Many ECT advocates theorize that the treatment must affect neurotransmitter activity in the brain, but the evidence supporting this theory is fragmentary and inconclusive (Frankel, 1984). ECT opponents have a radically different, albeit equally unproved, explanation for ECT's apparent effectiveness. They maintain that some patients find ECT so terrifying that they muster all their willpower to climb out of their depression to avoid further ECT treatments.

The debate about whether ECT works and how it works does not make ECT unique among approaches to psychotherapy. There are controversies regarding the effectiveness of many psychotherapies. Controversy is especially problematic in the case of ECT, however, because the treatment may carry substantial risks.

Risks of ECT

Even ECT proponents acknowledge that memory loss, impaired attention, and other cognitive deficits are common short-term side effects of electroconvulsive therapy. Proponents assert, however, that these deficits are mild and usually last less than a month (Weeks, Freeman, & Kendell, 1981). Critics maintain that these cognitive losses are significant and often permanent (Breggin, 1979). To complicate the issue, studies that use objective measures of

A Personal Experience with ECT

I'm not saying this is what shock is all about, or that it happens this way everywhere. I am saying that this is what happened to me in this particular institution.

Slang for shock in that institution was know as "gettin' Kentucky fried," and being taken into shock was known as "a visit to the Colonel." I was going for a visit.

Along the way, I always started making deals with God: "If you get me out of this one . . ." They never worked out. When the deals fell through, I started making every promise I knew I could keep, and just to be safe, a few I knew I couldn't. Looking back, it all seems kind of funny. At the time, I was sure they were trying to kill me.

The room where it was done was in the very center of the ward. This was not surprising. Almost all of our shock was done as a disciplinary measure, our very lives revolved around staff's ability to enforce discipline and order upon us. So to me, it was not too surprising that the Colonel set up shop where he did.

When the door opened, the intense whiteness of the fluorescent lights blinded me. Staff took advantage of this by leading me to the gurney where I was to lie down. By the time my eyes adjusted, I was on my back with several pairs of hands holding me down.

A mouthpiece was crammed rather indelicately into place, and the conductant was smeared on my temples. There was some technical talk and someone said "Now" (I wanted desperately to say wait a moment). And then there it was—one of the most excruciating pains I have ever felt. My back ached in an attempt to jump off the gurney, all the air squeezed out of my lungs, my legs flexed until they felt as if they would break, my head felt as if it would pop off. I was out of control: it was not me anymore.

I don't know how long it took but finally I passed out. When I opened my eyes again, I had the headache of headaches. I was confused, I couldn't connect two thoughts.

The next two or three days were a nightmare of confusion and awkward movements, always feeling like a thought was there, on the tip of your tongue, but not able to grab it. The more you grabbed at it, the more elusive it became, and the more frustrated you became.

Eventually, I returned to normal, but before that happened, I would go through a deep dark depression. I could fight the system, I could fight Staff, I could fight the drugs, the aides, and the other patients.

I could not fight this. I was beaten. My thoughts were exactly that, mine. Before shock they were untouched, now they had been reached and, worse still, disorganized externally. The depression then seemed to come from a sense of defeat, of being violated, and of being mentally raped.

How can I make you feel that?

patients' memory performance show that former ECT patients tend to overestimate their memory deficits (Sachs & Gelenberg, 1988).

So what can we conclude about ECT and cognitive deficits? The truth probably lies somewhere between the positions staked out by the proponents and opponents of ECT. In an unusually dispassionate review of the ECT controversy, Small and his colleagues (1986) assert that "there is little doubt that ECT produces both short- and long-term intellectual impairment." They conclude that this impairment is not inevitable, however, and that it is temporary in the vast majority of cases.

Most of the other risks once associated with ECT have been minimized by modern improvements in the procedure. Fractures and dislocations used to be a problem, but medica-

FIGURE 16.8
One patient's experience with electroconvulsive therapy
Although some patients treated with electroconvulsive therapy (ECT) have much more favorable experiences, this moving memoir paints a very unpleasant picture of ECT treatment. (Quoted by permission from a former student.)

tions administered before the treatment have virtually eliminated these complications (Kramer, 1985). In competent hands, ECT is a reasonably safe procedure with a mortality rate well under 1 in a 1000 (Weiner, 1985). The occasional deaths that occur are usually due to cardiac complications.

Blending Approaches to Psychotherapy

 e have reviewed many different approaches to therapy, which are summarized and compared in Figure 16.9. However, there is no law that a client must be treated with just one approach. A clinician is quite likely to use a variety of approaches in working with a client. A depressed person may receive cognitive therapy (an insight therapy), social skills training (a behavior therapy), and antidepressant medication (a biomedical therapy). Multiple approaches are particularly likely when a treatment *team* provides therapy.

Studies suggest that there is merit in combining multiple approaches to treatment (Klerman, 1978; Luborsky et al., 1975). One representative study compared the value of insight therapy alone, drug therapy alone, and a combination of insight and drug therapy for depression (Weissman et al., 1979). The subjects suffered from unipolar depression and were treated on an outpatient basis. The groups treated only with antidepressant medication or only with interpersonal therapy both responded

well, but the greatest improvement was found in the group treated with both. The two treatments complemented each other nicely. The drug therapy was particularly effective in relieving some symptoms, and the insight therapy was especially effective in relieving others. Thus there is much to be said for combining approaches to treatment.

The value of multiple approaches may explain why a significant trend seems to have emerged in the field of psychotherapy. There is a movement away from strong loyalty to individual schools of thought and a corresponding move toward integrating different approaches to therapy (Arkowitz, 1992; Beitman, Goldfried, & Norcross, 1989). Most clinicians used to depend exclusively on one system of therapy and rejecting the utility of all others. This era of fragmentation may be drawing to a close. In two surveys of psychologists' theoretical orientations conducted in the 1980s (Norcross & Prochaska, 1982; Smith, 1982), researchers were surprised to find that the greatest proportion of respondents described their approach as *eclectic* (see Figure 16.10). **Eclecticism involves selecting what appears to be best from a variety of theories or systems of therapy,** instead of committing oneself to just one theoretical orientation. Eclectic therapists use ideas, insights, and techniques from a variety of sources. They adjust their strategy to the unique needs of each client. Eclecticism leads to a creative blending of approaches to therapy. Some therapists, such as Arnold Lazarus (1989), have even developed systematic approaches to eclecticism.

FIGURE 16.9
The five major types of psychotherapy This overview of the behavior therapies, biomedical therapies, and three leading approaches to insight therapy permits a comparison of their attributes, goals, and techniques.

Major Approaches to Psychotherapy

Type of psychotherapy	Primary founders	Origin of disorder	Therapeutic goals	Therapeutic techniques
Psychoanalysis	Freud	Unconscious conflicts resulting from fixations in earlier development	Insights regarding unconscious conflicts and motives; personality reconstruction	Free association, dream analysis, interpretation, catharsis, transference
Client-centered therapy	Rogers	Incongruence between self-concept and actual experience; dependence on acceptance from others	Congruence between self-concept and experience; acceptance of genuine self; self-determination, personal growth	Genuineness, empathy, unconditional positive regard, clarification, reflecting back to client
Cognitive therapy	Beck Ellis	Irrational assumptions and negative, self-defeating thinking about events related to self	Detection of negative thinking; substitution of more realistic thinking	Thought stopping, recording automatic thoughts, refuting negative thinking, reattribution, homework assignments
Behavior therapies	Wolpe Skinner Eysenck	Maladaptive patterns of behavior acquired through learning	Elimination of symptomatic, maladaptive behaviors; acquisition of more adaptive responses	Classical and operant conditioning, reinforcement, punishment, extinction, shaping, aversive conditioning, systematic desensitization, social skills training, biofeedback
Biomedical therapies		Physiological malfunction, primarily abnormal neurotransmitter activity	Elimination of symptoms; prevention of relapse	Antipsychotic, antianxiety, and antidepressant drugs; lithium; electroconvulsive therapy (ECT)

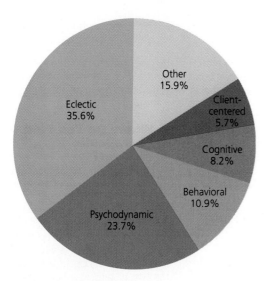

FIGURE 16.10
The leading approaches to therapy taken by psychologists
The pooled data from a survey of 415 clinical and counseling psychologists (Smith, 1982) and another survey of 479 clinical psychologists (Norcross & Prochaska, 1982) indicate that the therapies most widely employed are (in order) the eclectic, psychodynamic, behavioral, cognitive, and client-centered approaches.

Summary

Psychotherapy involves three elements: treatment, clients, and therapists. Approaches to treatment are diverse, but they can be grouped into three categories: insight therapies, behavior therapies, and biomedical therapies.

Insight therapies involve verbal interactions intended to enhance self-knowledge. In psychoanalysis, free association and dream analysis are used to explore the unconscious. When an analyst's probing hits sensitive areas, resistance can be expected. The transference relationship may be used to overcome this resistance. Classical psychoanalysis is not widely practiced anymore, but Freud's legacy lives on in a rich diversity of modern psychodynamic therapies.

The client-centered therapist tries to provide a supportive climate in which clients can restructure their self-concepts. The process of therapy emphasizes clarification of the client's feelings and self-acceptance. Cognitive therapy concentrates on changing the way clients think about events in their lives. Most theoretical approaches to insight therapy have been adapted for use with groups. Group therapy has unique advantages over individual therapy. Eysenck's work in the 1950s raised doubts about the effectiveness of insight therapy and stimulated research on its efficacy. The weight of the evidence suggests that insight therapies can be effective.

Behavior therapies use the principles of learning in direct efforts to change specific aspects of behavior. Systematic desensitization is a treatment for phobias. It involves the construction of an anxiety hierarchy, relaxation training, and step-by-step movement through the hierarchy. In aversion therapy, a stimulus associated with an unwanted response is paired with an unpleasant stimulus in an effort to eliminate the maladaptive response. Social skills training can improve clients' interpersonal skills through shaping, modeling, and behavioral rehearsal. Biofeedback provides information about body functions so that the client can attempt to exert some control over those physiological processes. There is ample evidence that behavior therapies are effective.

Biomedical therapies involve physiological interventions for psychological problems. Two biomedical treatments are drug therapy and electroconvulsive therapy. A great variety of disorders are treated with drugs. The principal types of therapeutic drugs are antianxiety drugs, antipsychotic drugs, antidepressant drugs, and lithium. Drug therapies can be very effective, but they have their pitfalls. Many drugs produce problematic side effects and some are overprescribed. Electroconvulsive therapy triggers a cortical seizure that is believed to have therapeutic value for mood disorders, especially depression. Evidence about the effectiveness of ECT is contradictory and the risks associated with its use have provoked heated debate.

Eclectic combinations of insight, behavioral, and biomedical therapies are often used fruitfully in the treatment of psychological disorders. In the Application we'll sort through a number of practical issues involved in selecting a therapist.

APPLICATION Looking for a Therapist

Are the following statements true or false?

1.

Psychotherapy is an art as well as a science.

2.

The type of professional degree that a therapist holds is relatively unimportant.

3.

Psychotherapy can be harmful or damaging to a client.

4.

Psychotherapy does not have to be expensive.

5.

It is a good idea to shop around before choosing a therapist.

All of the statements on the left are true. Do any of them surprise you? If so, you're in good company. Many people know relatively little about the practicalities of selecting a therapist.

The task of finding an appropriate therapist is no less complex than shopping for any other major service. Should you see a psychologist or a psychiatrist? Should you opt for individual therapy or group therapy? Should you see a client-centered therapist or a behavior therapist? An unfortunate complication is that people seeking psychotherapy often feel overwhelmed by their personal problems. The last thing they need is to be confronted by yet another complex problem.

Nonetheless, the importance of finding a good therapist cannot be overestimated. Therapy can sometimes have harmful rather than helpful effects. We have already discussed how drug therapies and ECT can sometimes be damaging, but problems are not limited to these interventions. Talking about your problems with a therapist may sound harmless, but studies indicate that insight therapies can also backfire (Mays & Franks, 1985; Strupp, Hadley, & Gomes-Schwartz, 1977).

Although a great many talented therapists are available, psy-

FIGURE 16.11
Sources of therapeutic services
Therapists work in a variety of organizational settings. Foremost among them are the five described here.

chotherapy, like any other profession, has incompetent practitioners as well. Therefore, you should shop for a skilled therapist, just as you would for a good attorney or a good mechanic. In this Application we'll go over some information that should be helpful if you ever have to look for a therapist for yourself or for a friend or family member (based on Amada, 1985; Bruckner-Gordon, Gangi, & Wallman, 1988; Ehrenberg & Ehrenberg, 1986).

When Should You Seek Professional Treatment?

This question has no simple answer. Obviously, people usually consider the possibility of professional treatment when they are psychologically distressed. However, there are other options besides psychotherapy. There is much to be said for seeking advice from family, friends, the clergy, and so forth. Insights about personal problems do not belong exclusively to people with professional degrees.

So when should you turn to professionals for help? You should begin to think seriously about therapy (1) when you have no one to lean on, (2) when the people you lean on indicate that they're getting tired of being leaned on, (3) when you feel helpless and overwhelmed, or (4) when your life is seriously disrupted by your problems. Of course, you do not have to be falling apart to justify

therapy. You may want to seek professional advice simply because you want to get more out of life.

Where Do You Find Therapeutic Services?

Psychotherapy can be found in a variety of settings. Contrary to general belief, most therapists are not in private practice. Many work in institutional settings such as community mental health centers, hospitals, and human service agencies. The principal sources of therapeutic services are described in Figure 16.11. The exact configuration of therapeutic services available varies from one community to another. To find out what your community has to offer, you can consult your friends, the phone book, or a community or campus mental health center.

Is the Therapist's Profession Important?

Psychotherapists may be trained in psychology, psychiatry, social work, psychiatric nursing, or counseling. Many talented therapists can be found in all of these professions. Thus the kind of degree that a therapist holds doesn't need to be a crucial consideration in your selection process. It *is* true that only a psychiatrist can prescribe drugs for disorders that merit drug therapy (this situation may change, as psychologists are seeking prescription privileges). Some critics argue, however, that drugs are overused in the treatment of psychological problems (Lickey & Gordon, 1991). In any case, other types of therapists can refer you to a psychiatrist if they think that drug therapy would be helpful. If you have a health insurance policy that covers psychotherapy, you may want to check it to see whether its coverage is restricted to therapy provided by members of only some professions.

Is the Therapist's Sex Important?

The importance of the therapist's sex depends on your attitude. If *you* feel it is important,

Principal Sources of Therapeutic Services

Source	Comments
Private practitioners	Self-employed therapists are listed in the Yellow Pages under their professional category, such as psychologists or psychiatrists. Private practitioners tend to be relatively expensive, but they also tend to be highly experienced therapists.
Community mental health centers	Community mental health centers have salaried psychologists, psychiatrists, and social workers on staff. The centers provide a variety of services and often have staff available on weekends and at night to deal with emergencies.
Hospitals	Several kinds of hospitals provide therapeutic services. There are both public and private mental hospitals that specialize in the care of people with psychological disorders. Many general hospitals have a psychiatric ward, and those that do not will usually have psychiatrists and psychologists on staff and on call. Although hospitals tend to concentrate on inpatient treatment, many provide outpatient therapy as well.
Human service agencies	Various social service agencies employ therapists to provide short-term counseling. Depending on your community, you may find agencies that deal with family problems, juvenile problems, drug problems, and so forth.
Schools and workplaces	Most high schools and colleges have counseling centers where students can get help with personal problems. Similarly, some large businesses offer in-house counseling to their employees.

then for you it is. The therapeutic relationship must be characterized by trust and rapport. If you won't feel comfortable with a therapist of one sex or the other, your discomfort could inhibit the therapeutic process. You should feel free to look for a male or female therapist if you prefer to do so. This point is probably most relevant to female clients, whose troubles may be related to the extensive sexism in our society. It is entirely reasonable for such women to seek a therapist with a feminist perspective.

Speaking of sex, you should be aware that sexual exploitation is an occasional problem in the context of therapy. Studies indicate that a small minority of therapists take advantage of their clients sexually (Pope, Keith-Spiegel, & Tabachnick, 1986). These incidents almost always involve a male therapist who makes advances to a female client. Available evidence indicates that these sexual liaisons are harmful to the clients (Williams, 1992). There are absolutely no situations in which therapist-client sexual relations are an ethical therapeutic practice. If a therapist makes sexual advances, a client should terminate treatment.

Is Therapy Always Expensive?

Psychotherapy does not have to be prohibitively expensive. Private practitioners tend to be the most expensive, charging between $25 and $100 per (50-minute) hour. These fees may seem high, but they are in line

with those of similar professionals, such as dentists and attorneys. Community mental health centers and social service agencies are usually supported by tax dollars, so they can charge lower fees than most therapists in private practice. Many of these organizations employ a sliding scale, so that clients are charged what they can afford to pay. Thus most communities provide opportunities for inexpensive psychotherapy. Moreover, many health insurance plans provide at least partial reimbursement for the cost of psychotherapy.

Is the Therapist's Theoretical Approach Important?

Logically, you might expect that the various approaches to therapy ought to vary in effectiveness. For the most part, however, this is *not* what researchers find. After reviewing the evidence, Luborsky and his colleagues (1975) quote the dodo bird who has just judged a race in *Alice in Wonderland:* "Everyone has won and all must have prizes." The

improvement rates achieved by the various theoretical orientations usually coincide pretty closely in most studies (Stiles, Shapiro, & Elliott, 1986), as the data in Figure 16.12 show.

These findings do not necessarily mean that *all* therapists are created equal. In all likelihood, some therapists are far more effective than others. These variations in effectiveness probably depend on therapists' personal skills rather than on their theoretical orientations. Good, bad, and mediocre therapists are found within each school of thought.

Effective therapy requires skill and creativity. Arnold Lazarus, who devised multimodal therapy (a form of eclectic therapy), emphasizes that therapists "straddle the fence between science and art." Therapy is scientific in that interventions are based on extensive theory and empirical research (Forsyth & Strong, 1986). Ultimately, though, each client is a unique human being, and the therapist has to creatively fashion a treatment program that will help that individual.

Type of therapy

Psychodynamic
Client-centered
Rational-emotive
Systematic desensitization
Behavior modification (operant)
Eclectic

0 10 20 30 40 50 60 70 80 90 100
Percentile rank

FIGURE 16.12
Efficacy of six approaches to therapy Smith and Glass (1977) reviewed nearly 400 studies in which clients who were treated with a specific type of therapy were compared with a control group made up of people with similar problems who went untreated. The bars indicate the percentile rank (on outcome measures) attained by the average client treated with each type of therapy in comparison with control subjects. The higher the percentile, the more effective the therapy. As you can see, the six approaches were fairly close in their apparent effectiveness.

Inside Woody Allen by Stuart Hample. Reprinted by permission.

RECOMMENDED READING
Making Therapy Work: Your Guide to Choosing, Using, and Ending Therapy

by Fredda Bruckner-Gordon, Barbara K. Gangi, and Geraldine U. Wallman (HarperCollins, 1988)

This book, written by three New York City therapists, follows in the highly practical tradition of the book by the Ehrenbergs that we recommended earlier. The two books have different strengths, however, and both are worth reading for anyone who is in therapy or is considering therapy. A key strength of this book is its step-by-step approach to finding a therapist and making therapy work. The authors lead the uninitiated through a logical progression in which they discuss how to learn about therapy options, how to interview prospective therapists, how to establish an effective therapeutic alliance, how to analyze one's reactions to therapy, and so forth. Another strength is the book's many self-analysis exercises to help readers probe their attitudes, feelings, and knowledge about therapy.

Talk about your thoughts, feelings and behavior as openly as possible. There is no magic in therapy, and no one can read your mind. Your therapist can know for sure only what you describe and demonstrate about yourself. Letting yourself be known can yield the good feelings attached to being understood and the likelihood that your therapist will be more engaged and better equipped to help you. . . .

You may be concerned about your therapist's reactions; perhaps you fear disapproval. There's no reason for you to trust automatically, but nothing will convince you like testing his or her responses. If you are having trouble revealing your thoughts and feelings, talk about this difficulty. [p. 83]

What Should You Look For in a Prospective Therapist?

Some clients are timid about asking prospective therapists about their training, approach, fees, and so forth. These are reasonable questions, however, and the vast majority of therapists are most accommodating. Usually you may ask your preliminary questions over the phone. If things seem promising, you may decide to make an appointment for an interview (you probably will have to pay for the interview). In the course of the interview the therapist will gather more information to determine the likelihood of helping you, given the therapist's training and approach to treatment. At the same time, you should be making a similar judgment about whether *you* believe the therapist could help you with your problems.

What should you look for? First, you should look for personal warmth and sincere concern. Try to judge whether you will be able to talk to this person in a candid, nondefensive way. Second, look for empathy and understanding. Is the person capable of appreciating your point of view? Third, look for self-confidence. Self-assured therapists communicate a sense of competence without trying to intimidate you with jargon or boasting about what they can do for you. When all is said and done, you should *like* your therapist.

Otherwise, it will be difficult to establish the needed rapport.

What if There Isn't Any Progress?

If you feel that your therapy isn't going anywhere, you should probably discuss these feelings with your therapist. Don't be surprised, however, if the therapist suggests that it may be your own fault. Freud's concept of resistance has some validity. Some clients *do* have difficulty facing up to their problems. So if your therapy isn't progressing, you may need to *consider* whether your resistance may be slowing progress. This self-examination isn't easy, as you are not an un-biased observer. Some common signs of resistance identified by Ehrenberg and Ehrenberg (1986) are listed in Figure 16.13.

Given the very real possibility that poor progress may be due to resistance, you should not be too quick to leave therapy when you are dissatisfied. However, it *is* possible that your therapist isn't sufficiently skilled or that the two of you are incompatible. After careful and deliberate consideration, you should feel free to terminate your therapy.

What Is Therapy Like?

It is important to have realistic expectations about therapy, or you may be unnecessarily disappointed. Some people expect miracles. They expect to turn their lives around quickly with little effort. Others expect their therapists to run their lives for them. These expectations are unrealistic.

Therapy usually is a slow process. Your problems are not likely to melt away quickly. Moreover, therapy is hard work, and your therapist is only a facilitator. Ultimately *you* have to confront the challenge of changing your behavior, your feelings, or your personality. This process may not be pleasant. You may have to face up to some painful truths about yourself. As Ehrenberg and Ehrenberg (1986) point out, "Psychotherapy takes time, effort and courage."

FIGURE 16.13
Signs of resistance
Resistance in therapy may be subtle, but Ehrenberg and Ehrenberg (1986) have identified some telltale signs to look for.

Signs of Resistance in Therapy

If you're dissatisfied with your progress in therapy, resistance may be the problem when:

1 You have nothing specific or concrete to complain about.

2 Your attitude about therapy changes suddenly just as you reach the truly sensitive issues.

3 You've had the same problem with other therapists in the past.

4 Your conflicts with the therapist resemble those that you have with other people.

5 You start hiding things from your therapist.

Key Learning Objectives

1. Identify the three major categories of therapy and discuss why people do or do not seek psychotherapy.

2. Describe the various types of mental health professionals who provide therapy.

3. Explain the logic of psychoanalysis and describe the techniques used to probe the unconscious.

4. Discuss interpretation, resistance, and transference in psychoanalysis.

5. Summarize trends in modern psychodynamic approaches to therapy.

6. Describe the therapeutic climate and process in client-centered therapy.

7. Discuss the logic, goals, and techniques of cognitive therapy.

8. Describe how group therapy is generally conducted and identify some of its advantages.

9. Summarize evidence on the efficacy of insight therapies.

10. Summarize the general approach and principles of behavior therapies.

11. Describe systematic desensitization and aversion therapy.

12. Describe the use of social skills training and biofeedback.

13. Summarize evidence on the efficacy of behavior therapies.

14. Describe the principal drug therapies used in the treatment of psychological disorders.

15. Summarize evidence on the efficacy and problems of drug therapies.

16. Describe ECT and discuss its efficacy and its risks.

17. Discuss the merits of blending approaches to therapy.

18. Discuss when and where to seek therapy, and the potential importance of a therapist's sex, theoretical approach, and professional background.

19. Summarize what one should look for in a prospective therapist and what one should expect from therapy.

Key Terms

antianxiety drugs
antidepressant drugs
antipsychotic drugs
aversion therapy
behavior therapies
biofeedback
biomedical therapies
client-centered therapy
clinical psychologists
cognitive therapy
counseling psychologists
dream analysis
eclecticism
electroconvulsive therapy (ECT)

free association
group therapy
insight therapies
interpretation
lithium
psychiatrists
psychoanalysis
psychopharmacotherapy
resistance
social skills training
spontaneous remission
systematic desensitization
tardive dyskinesia
transference

Key People

Aaron Beck
Hans Eysenck
Sigmund Freud

Carl Rogers
Joseph Wolpe

acquaintance rape Forced and unwanted sexual intercourse with someone known to the victim.

acquired immune deficiency syndrome (AIDS) A disorder in which the immune system is gradually weakened and eventually disabled by the human immunodeficiency virus (HIV).

adjustment The psychological processes through which people manage or cope with the demands and challenges of everyday life.

age cohort A group of people born in the same time period who develop in the same historical context.

ageism Discrimination against people on the basis of their age.

age roles Expectations about appropriate behavior that are based on one's chronological age.

aggression Any behavior intended to hurt someone, either physically or verbally.

aging The biological process of growing older.

agoraphobia A fear of going out to public places.

ambient stress Chronic environmental conditions that, although not urgent, are negatively valued and place adaptive demands on people.

alcohol Beverages containing ethyl alcohol.

anal intercourse The insertion of the penis into a partner's anus and rectum.

androgens The principal class of male sex hormones.

androgyny The coexistence of both masculine and feminine personality traits in an individual.

antecedents In behavior modification, events that typically precede a target behavior.

antianxiety drugs Drugs that relieve tension, apprehension, and nervousness.

antidepressant drugs Drugs that gradually elevate mood and help to bring people out of a depression.

antipsychotic drugs Drugs used to gradually reduce psychotic symptoms, including hyperactivity, mental confusion, hallucinations, and delusions.

antisocial personality disorder A type of personality disorder marked by impulsive, callous, manipulative, aggressive, and irresponsible behavior that reflects a failure to accept social norms.

anxiety disorders A class of psychological disorders marked by feelings of excessive apprehension and anxiety.

approach-approach conflict A motivational conflict in which a choice must be made between two attractive goals.

approach-avoidance conflict A motivational conflict in which a choice must be made about whether to pursue a single goal that has both attractive and unattractive aspects.

atherosclerosis A disease characterized by gradual narrowing of the coronary arteries.

attitudes Beliefs and feelings about people, objects, and ideas.

attributional style The tendency to use similar causal explanations for a wide variety of events in one's life.

attributions Inferences that people draw about the causes of events, others' behavior, and their own behavior.

autonomic nervous system (ANS) That portion of the peripheral nervous system made up of the nerves that connect to the heart, blood vessels, smooth muscles, and glands.

aversion therapy A behavior therapy in which an aversive stimulus is paired with a stimulus that elicits an undesirable response.

avoidance-avoidance conflict A motivational conflict in which a choice must be made between two unattractive goals.

basal metabolic rate The body's rate of energy output at rest, after a 12-hour fast.

baseline period A span of time before beginning a behavior modification program, during which one systematically observes one's target behavior.

battered woman A woman who is subjected to serious psychological or physical abuse by her partner.

behavior Any overt (observable) response or activity by an organism.

behavioral contract A written agreement outlining a promise to adhere to the contingencies of a behavior modification program.

behaviorism A theoretical orientation based on the premise that scientific psychology should study observable behavior.

behavior modification A systematic approach to changing behavior through the application of the principles of conditioning.

behavior therapies The application of the principles of learning to direct efforts to change clients' maladaptive behaviors.

biomedical therapies Physiological interventions intended to reduce symptoms associated with psychological disorders.

biopsychosocial model The idea that physical illness is caused by a complex interaction of biological, psychological, and sociocultural factors.

bipolar mood disorders Psychological disorders marked by the experience of both depressed and manic periods.

bisexuals People who seek emotional-sexual relationships with members of both sexes.

brainstorming Generating as many ideas as possible while withholding criticism and evaluation.

burnout Physical, mental, and emotional exhaustion that is attributable to work-related stress.

bystander effect The social phenomenon in which individuals are less likely to provide needed help when others are present than when they are alone.

cancer Malignant cell growth, which may occur in many organ systems in the body.

cannabis The hemp plant from which marijuana, hashish, and THC are derived.

cardinal trait A dominant personality trait that permeates nearly all of a person's behavior.

case study An in-depth investigation of an individual subject.

catastrophic thinking Unrealistic appraisals of stress that exaggerate the magnitude of one's problems.

catatonic schizophrenia A type of schizophrenia marked by striking motor disturbances, ranging from muscular rigidity to random motor activity.

catharsis The release of emotional tension.

central traits The prominent, general personality dispositions found in anyone.

cerebral hemispheres The right and left halves of the cerebrum, which is the convoluted outer layer of the brain.

channel The medium through which a message reaches the receiver.

classical conditioning A type of learning in which a neutral stimulus acquires the capacity to evoke a response that was originally evoked by another stimulus.

client-centered therapy An insight therapy that emphasizes providing a supportive emotional climate for clients, who play a major role in determining the pace and direction of their therapy.

clinical psychologists Psychologists who specialize in the diagnosis and treatment of psychological disorders and everyday behavioral problems.

clinical psychology The branch of psychology concerned with the diagnosis and treatment of psychological problems and disorders.

close relationship A relatively long-lasting relationship in which there are frequent interactions in a variety of settings and in which the impact of the interactions is strong.

cognition The thought processes involved in acquiring knowledge.

cognitive development Age-related transitions in patterns of thinking, including reasoning, remembering, and problem solving.

cognitive dissonance The psychological discomfort that occurs when related cognitions are inconsistent—that is, when they contradict each other.

cognitive therapy An insight therapy that emphasizes recognizing and changing negative thoughts and maladaptive beliefs.

cohabitation Living together in a sexually intimate relationship without the legal bonds of marriage.

coitus The insertion of the penis into the vagina and (typically) pelvic thrusting.

collusion The situation that occurs when two people have an unspoken agreement to deny some problematic aspect of reality in order to sustain their relationship.

commitment The decision and intent to maintain a relationship in spite of the difficulties and costs it may entail.

communication apprehension The anxiety caused by having to talk with others.

communication barrier Anything in the communication process that inhibits or blocks the accurate transmission and reception of messages.

comparison level One's standard of what constitutes an acceptable balance of rewards and costs in a relationship.

compensation A defense mechanism characterized by efforts to overcome imagined or real inferiorities by developing one's abilities.

complementary transaction A transaction in which the receiver responds from the same ego state that was addressed by the source.

compliance Yielding to social pressure in one's public behavior, even though one's private beliefs have not changed.

concordance rate A statistic indicating the percentage of twin pairs or other pairs of relatives that exhibit the same disorder.

conditioned response (CR) A learned reaction to a conditioned stimulus that occurs because of previous conditioning.

conditioned stimulus (CS) A previously neutral stimulus that has acquired the capacity to evoke a conditioned response through conditioning.

conflict The struggle that occurs when two or more incompatible motivations or behavioral impulses compete for expression.

conformity Yielding to real or imagined social pressure.

conscious According to Freud, whatever one is aware of at a particular point in time.

conservation The awareness that physical quantities remain constant despite changes in their shape or appearance.

consideration A dimension of leadership that reflects the degree to which a leader is warm, trusting, and supportive in interactions with group members.

constructive coping Efforts to deal with stressful events that are judged to be relatively healthy.

control group Subjects in an experiment who do not receive the special treatment given to the experimental group.

conversion disorders Psychological disorders characterized by a significant loss of physical function (with no apparent organic basis), usually in a single organ system.

coping Active efforts to master, reduce, or tolerate the demands created by stress.

coronary heart disease A chronic disease characterized by a reduction in blood flow from the coronary arteries, which supply the heart with blood.

correlation The extent to which two variables are related to each other.

correlation coefficient A numerical index of the degree of relationship that exists between two variables.

counseling psychologists Psychologists who specialize in the treatment of everyday behavioral problems.

crossed transaction A transaction in which the receiver does not respond from the ego state addressed by the source.

date rape Forced and unwanted intercourse with someone in the context of dating.

cunnilingus The oral stimulation of the female genitals.

death system The collection of rituals and procedures a society devises to handle death.

defense mechanisms Largely unconscious reactions that protect a person from unpleasant emotions such as anxiety and guilt.

defensive attribution A tendency to blame victims for their misfortune, so that we feel less likely to be victimized in a similar way.

deindividuation The loss of self-awareness and evaluation apprehension that occur when individuals believe they are anonymous.

delusions False beliefs that are maintained even though they clearly have no basis in reality.

denial Refusing to perceive or face unpleasant realities.

dependent variable In an experiment, the variable that is thought to be affected by manipulations of the independent variable.

depressive disorders Psychological disorders characterized by persistent feelings of sadness and despair and a loss of interest in previous sources of pleasure.

designer drugs Illicitly manufactured variations of known recreational drugs.

development The sequence of age-related changes that occur as a person progresses from conception to death.

diagnosis Distinguishing one illness from another.

diffusion of responsibility The expectation that others who are present will take responsibility for action.

discrimination Behaving differently, usually unfairly, toward members of a group.

discriminative stimuli Cues that influence operant behavior by indicating the probable consequences of a response.

disorganized schizophrenia A type of schizophrenia characterized by a particularly severe deterioration of adaptive behavior.

displacement Diverting emotional feelings (usually anger) from their original source to a substitute target.

display rules Norms that govern the appropriate display of emotions.

dissociative disorders A class of psychological disorders characterized by loss of contact with portions of one's consciousness or memory, resulting in disruptions in one's sense of identity.

door-in-the-face technique Making a very large request that is likely to be turned down to increase the chance that people will agree to a smaller request later.

downward social comparison The defensive tendency to compare ourselves with someone whose troubles are more serious than our own.

dream analysis A psychotherapeutic technique in which the therapist interprets the symbolic meaning of the client's dreams.

eclecticism Selecting what appears to be best from a variety of theories or systems of therapy.

ego According to Freud, the decision-making component of personality that operates according to the reality principle.

ego state A personality structure consisting of a coherent system of internal feelings.

egocentrism The tendency to let idiosyncratic perceptions color one's view of reality.

electroconvulsive therapy (ECT) A biomedical treatment in which electric shock is used to produce a cortical seizure accompanied by convulsions.

emotions Powerful, largely uncontrollable feelings, accompanied by physiological changes.

empathy Adopting another's frame of reference to understand her or his point of view.

empiricism The premise that knowledge should be acquired through observation.

endocrine system Glands that secrete chemicals called hormones into the bloodstream.

endogamy The tendency of people to marry within their own social group.

endorphins Chemicals in the central nervous system that resemble morphine in structure and effects.

epidemiology The study of the distribution of mental or physical disorders in a population.

erectile difficulties The male sexual dysfunction characterized by the persistent inability to achieve or maintain an erection adequate for intercourse.

erogenous zones Areas of the body that are sexually sensitive or responsive.

erotophiles People who have very favorable attitudes about sex.

erotophobes People who have very negative attitudes about sex.

estrogens The principal class of female sex hormones.

etiology The apparent causation and developmental history of an illness.

experiment A research method in which the investigator manipulates an (independent) variable under carefully controlled conditions and observes whether there are changes in a second (dependent) variable as a result.

experimental group The subjects in an experiment who receive some special treatment in regard to the independent variable.

expressive style A style of communication characterized by the ability to express tender emotions easily and to be sensitive to the feelings of others.

external attributions Ascribing the causes of behavior to situational demands and environmental constraints.

extinction The gradual weakening and disappearance of a conditioned response tendency.

extravert A person who tends to be interested in the external world of things and people.

evaluation apprehension The concern that others may evaluate us negatively.

false consensus effect The tendency to overestimate the degree to which others think and behave as we do.

false uniqueness effect The tendency to underestimate the likelihood that others possess our admirable qualities.

family life cycle An orderly sequence of developmental stages that families tend to progress through.

fantasy Gratifying frustrated desires by thinking about imaginary achievements and satisfactions.

fellatio The oral stimulation of the penis.

fight-or-flight response A physiological reaction to threat that mobilizes an organism for attacking (fight) or fleeing (flight) an enemy.

fixation In Freud's theory, a failure to move forward from one stage to another as expected.

foot-in-the-door technique Getting people to agree to a small request to increase the chances that they will agree to a larger request later.

free association A psychotherapeutic technique in which clients spontaneously express their thoughts and feelings exactly as they occur, with as little censorship as possible.

frustration The feelings that occur in any situation in which the pursuit of some goal is thwarted.

fundamental attribution error The tendency of observers to over-attribute others' behavior to internal factors.

games Manipulative interactions progressing toward a predictable outcome, in which people conceal their real motivations.

gate control theory The theory that incoming pain sensations must pass through a "gate" in the spinal cord that can be closed, thus blocking ascending pain signals.

gay See homosexuals.

gender Culturally constructed distinctions between masculinity and femininity.

gender identity The ability to correctly classify oneself as male or female.

gender-role identity A person's identification with the traits regarded as masculine or feminine.

gender roles Cultural expectations about what is appropriate behavior for each sex.

gender stereotypes Widely shared beliefs about males' and females' abilities, personality traits, and social behavior.

general adaptation syndrome A model of the body's stress response, consisting of three stages: alarm, resistance, and exhaustion.

generalized anxiety disorder A psychological disorder marked by a chronic high level of anxiety that is not tied to any specific threat.

gerontology A multidisciplinary field concerned with the study of the elderly.

gonads The sex glands.

group Two or more individuals who interact and are interdependent.

group cohesiveness The strength of the bonds that link group members to one another and to the group itself.

group norms Rules regarding appropriate behavior in a group.

group polarization The phenomenon that occurs when discussion strengthens a group's dominant point of view and produces a shift toward a more extreme decision in that direction.

group therapy The simultaneous treatment of several clients in a group.

groupthink The phenomenon that occurs when members of a cohesive group emphasize concurrence at the expense of critical thinking in arriving at a decision.

hallucinations Sensory perceptions that occur in the absence of a real, external stimulus or that represent gross distortions of perceptual input.

hallucinogens A diverse group of drugs that have powerful effects on mental and emotional functioning, marked most prominently by distortions in sensory and perceptual experience.

hardiness A personality syndrome marked by commitment, challenge, and control that is purportedly associated with strong resistance to stress.

health psychology The subfield of psychology concerned with how psychosocial factors relate to the promotion and maintenance of health, and with the causation, prevention, and treatment of illness.

heterosexism The assumption that all individuals and relationships are heterosexual.

heterosexuals People whose sexual desires and erotic behaviors are directed toward the other sex.

hierarchy of needs A systematic arrangement of needs, according to priority, in which basic needs must be met before less basic needs are aroused.

homogamy The tendency of people to marry others who have personal characteristics similar to their own.

homophobia The intense fear and intolerance of homosexuality.

homosexuals People who seek emotional-sexual relationships with members of the same sex.

hormones Chemical substances released into the bloodstream by the endocrine glands.

humanism A theoretical orientation that emphasizes the unique qualities of humans, especially their free will and their potential for personal growth.

hypochondriasis (hypochondria) Excessive preoccupation with health concerns and incessant worry about developing physical illnesses.

hypothetico-deductive reasoning The ability to formulate specific hypotheses and test them systematically.

id In Freud's theory, the primitive, instinctive component of personality that operates according to the pleasure principle.

identification Bolstering self-esteem by forming an imaginary or real alliance with some person or group.

identity A relatively clear and stable sense of who one is and what one stands for.

immune response The body's defensive reaction to invasion by bacteria, viral agents, or other foreign substances.

impression management Usually conscious efforts to influence the way others think of us.

incongruence The disparity between one's self-concept and one's actual experience.

independent variable In an experiment, a condition or event that is varied in order to see its impact on another variable.

infant attachment The strong emotional bond that infants usually develop with their caregivers during the first year of their lives.

initiating structure A dimension of leadership that reflects the degree to which a leader organizes, directs, and regulates a group's activities.

insight therapies A group of psychotherapies in which verbal interactions are intended to enhance clients' self-knowledge and thus promote healthful changes in personality and behavior.

instrumental style A style of communication that focuses on reaching practical goals and finding solutions to problems.

intellectualization Suppressing unpleasant emotions while engaging in detached analyses of threatening problems.

interference Forgetting information because of competition from other learned material.

internal attributions Ascribing the causes of behavior to personal dispositions, traits, abilities, and feelings rather than to external events.

interpersonal attraction Positive feelings toward another person.

interpersonal communication An interactional process whereby one person sends a message to another.

interpersonal conflict Disagreement among two or more people.

interpretation A therapist's attempts to explain the inner significance of the client's thoughts, feelings, memories, and behaviors.

intimacy Warmth, closeness, and sharing in a relationship.

introvert A person who tends to be preoccupied with the internal world of his or her own thoughts, feelings, and experiences.

job satisfaction The favorability or unfavorability of people's attitudes toward their jobs.

kinesics The study of communication through body movements.

labor force All people who are employed, plus those who are currently unemployed but are looking for work.

leadership A reciprocal process in which certain people are permitted to motivate and influence others to facilitate the pursuit of group goals.

learned helplessness Passive behavior produced by exposure to unavoidable aversive events.

leisure Unpaid activities people choose to engage in because they are personally meaningful.

life changes Any noticeable alterations in one's living circumstances that require readjustment.

life structure The stucture that encompasses the basic pattern or design of a person's life at a particular time.

lithium A chemical used to control mood swings in patients with bipolar mood disorders.

locus of control The personality dimension centering on whether people believe that their successes and failures are governed by their own actions.

loneliness The emotional state that occurs when a person has fewer interpersonal relationships than desired or when these relationships are not as satisfying as desired.

lowball technique Getting people to commit themselves to an attractive proposition before its hidden costs are revealed.

marriage The legally and socially sanctioned union of sexually intimate adults.

matching hypothesis The idea that people of similar levels of physical attractiveness gravitate toward each other.

meditation A family of mental exercises in which a conscious attempt is made to focus attention in a nonanalytical way.

medical model The idea that it is useful to think of abnormal behavior as a disease.

menarche The first occurrence of menstruation.

menopause The cessation of menstruation.

message The information or meaning that is transmitted from one person to another.

meta-analysis The statistical technique that evaluates the results of many studies on the same question.

mnemonic devices Strategies for enhancing memory.

mood disorders A class of disorders marked by emotional disturbances that may spill over to disrupt physical, perceptual, social, and thought processes.

multiple-personality disorders Dissociative disorders involving the coexistence in one person of two or more largely complete, and usually very different, personalities.

narcotics (opiates) Drugs derived from opium that are capable of relieving pain.

naturalistic observation An approach to research in which the researcher engages in careful observation of behavior without intervening directly with the subjects.

need for self-actualization The need to fulfill one's potential.

negative reinforcement The strengthening of a response because it is followed by the removal of an unpleasant stimulus.

neurons Individual cells that receive, integrate, and transmit information.

neurosis Broad term applied to behavior marked by subjective distress (usually chronic anxiety) and reliance on avoidance coping.

neuroticism A broad personality trait associated with chronic anxiety, insecurity, and self-consciousness.

neurotransmitters Chemicals that carry signals from one neuron to another.

nonverbal communication The transmission of meaning from one person to another through means or symbols other than words.

nurturance The provision of help, physical care, and emotional support to others.

nutrition A collection of processes (mainly food consumption) through which an organism uses the materials (nutrients) required for survival and growth.

obedience A form of compliance that occurs when people follow direct commands, usually from someone in a position of authority.

obesity The condition of being overweight.

object permanence A child's recognition that objects continue to exist even when they are no longer visible.

observational learning Learning that occurs when an organism's responding is influenced by the observation of others, who are called models.

obsessive-compulsive disorder A psychological disorder marked by persistent uncontrollable intrusions of unwanted thoughts (obsessions) and by urges to engage in senseless rituals (compulsions).

occupational interest inventories Tests that measure one's interests as they relate to various jobs or careers.

Oedipus complex According to Freud, a child's erotically tinged desires for the other-sex parent, accompanied by feelings of hostility toward the same-sex parent.

operant conditioning A form of learning in which voluntary responses come to be controlled by their consequences.

optimism A general tendency to expect good outcomes.

orgasm The release that occurs when sexual arousal reaches its peak intensity and is discharged in a series of muscular

contractions that pulsate through the pelvic area.

orgasmic difficulties Sexual disorders characterized by an ability to experience sexual arousal but persistent problems in achieving orgasm.

overcompensation Making up for frustration in one area by seeking overgratification in another area.

overdose An excessive dose of a drug that can seriously threaten one's life.

overlearning The continued rehearsal of material after one first appears to have mastered it.

panic disorder Recurrent attacks of overwhelming anxiety that usually occur suddenly and unexpectedly.

paralanguage All vocal cues other than the content of the verbal message itself.

paranoid schizophrenia A type of schizophrenia dominated by delusions of persecution, along with delusions of grandeur.

passion The intense feelings (both positive and negative) experienced in love relationships, including sexual desire.

personality An individual's unique constellation of consistent behavioral traits.

personality disorders A class of disorders marked by extreme, inflexible personality traits that cause subjective distress or impaired social and occupational functioning.

personality trait A durable disposition to behave in a particular way in a variety of situations.

personal space A zone of space surrounding a person that is felt to "belong" to that person.

perspective taking A component of empathy that involves the tendency to put oneself in another person's place.

persuasion The communication of arguments and information intended to change another person's attitudes.

phobic disorders Anxiety disorders marked by a persistent and irrational fear of an object or situation that presents no realistic danger.

physical dependence The need to continue to take a drug to avoid withdrawal illness.

placebo A substance that resembles a drug but has no actual pharmacological effect.

placebo effects Experiencing some change after an empty, fake, or ineffectual treatment because of one's positive expectations about the treatment.

pleasure principle According to Freud, the principle according to which the id operates, demanding immediate gratification of its urges.

positive reinforcement The strengthening of a response because it is followed by the arrival of a pleasant stimulus.

posttraumatic stress disorder Disturbed behavior, attributed to a major stressful event, that emerges after the stress is over.

power The potential to influence a group's decisions and individual members' behavior.

preconscious According to Freud, material just beneath the surface of awareness that can be easily retrieved.

prejudice A negative attitude toward members of a group.

premature ejaculation Impaired sexual relations because a man consistently reaches orgasm too quickly.

premenstrual syndrome A negative shift in mood, thought to occur in the days preceding a female's menstrual period.

pressure Expectations or demands that one behave in a certain way.

prevalence The percentage of a population that exhibits a disorder during a specified time period.

primacy effect The fact that initial information tends to carry more weight than subsequent information.

primary appraisal An initial evaluation of whether an event is (1) irrelevant to one, (2) relevant, but not threatening, or (3) stressful.

primary sex characteristics The structures necessary for reproduction.

process-oriented approach The view that human development unfolds in a continuous fashion, often even regressing temporarily to earlier levels of functioning.

prognosis A forecast about the probable course of an illness.

projection Attributing one's own thoughts, feelings, or motives to another person.

proxemics The study of people's use of interpersonal space.

proximity Geographic, residential, and other forms of spatial closeness.

psychiatrists Physicians who specialize in the treatment of psychological disorders.

psychoactive drugs Chemical substances that modify a person's mental, emotional, or behavioral functioning.

psychoanalysis An insight therapy that emphasizes the recovery of unconscious conflicts, motives, and defenses through techniques such as free association, dream analysis, and transference.

psychodynamic theories All the diverse theories descended from the work of Sigmund Freud that focus on unconscious mental forces.

psychogenic amnesia A sudden loss of memory for important personal information that is too extensive to be due to normal forgetting.

psychological dependence The need to continue to take a drug to satisfy intense mental and emotional craving for it.

psychological test A standardized measure of a sample of a person's behavior.

psychology The science that studies behavior and the physiological and mental processes that underlie it and the profession that applies the accumulated knowledge of this science to practical problems.

psychopharmacotherapy The treatment of mental disorders with medication.

psychosexual stages In Freud's theory, developmental periods with a characteristic sexual focus that leave their mark on adult personality.

psychosomatic diseases Genuine physical ailments caused in part by psychological factors, especially emotional distress.

psychosis Broad term applied to behavior marked by impaired contact with reality and profound deterioration of adaptive functioning.

puberty The stage that marks the beginning of adolescence, in which sexual functions reach maturity.

pubescence The two-year span preceding puberty during which the changes leading to physical and sexual maturity take place.

public self An image or façade presented to others in social interactions.

punishment The weakening (decrease in frequency) of a response because it is followed by the arrival of a (presumably) unpleasant stimulus.

rape Forced sexual intercourse without consent.

rational-emotive therapy An approach to therapy that focuses on altering clients' patterns of irrational thinking to reduce maladaptive emotions and behavior.

rationalization Creating false but plausible excuses to justify unacceptable behavior.

reactance The response that occurs when a person's freedom to behave in a certain way is impeded, and the person then attempts to restore the threatened freedom.

reaction formation Behaving in a way that is exactly the opposite of one's true feelings.

reality principle According to Freud, the principle by which the ego seeks to delay gratification of the id's urges until appropriate outlets and situations can be found.

receiver The person to whom a message is targeted.

reciprocity norm The rule that we should pay back in kind what we receive from others.

reference group A set of people against whom one compares oneself.

refractory period A time after male orgasm during which males are largely unresponsive to further stimulation.

regression A reversion to immature patterns of behavior.

reliability The consistency of a test's measurements.

repression Keeping distressing thoughts and feelings buried in the unconscious.

resistance Largely unconscious defensive maneuvers intended to hinder the progress of therapy.

role A pattern of behavior expected of a person who has a certain position in a group.

romantic jealousy A complex of thoughts, emotions, and behaviors that result from the perception of a threat to one's intimate relationship.

schizophrenic disorders A class of disorders marked by disturbances in thought that spill over to affect perceptual, social, and emotional processes.

seasonal affective (mood) disorder A disorder in which an individual's periods of depression or mania tend to occur repeatedly at about the same time each year.

secondary appraisal An evaluation of one's coping resources and options for dealing with stress.

secondary sex characteristics The physical features that distinguish one sex from the other but are not essential for reproduction.

secondary traits Personality traits that surface in some situations but not others.

sedatives Sleep-inducing drugs that tend to decrease activation of the central nervous system and behavioral activity.

self-actualization *See* need for self-actualization.

self-centered bias The tendency to take more than one's share of responsibility for a joint venture.

self-concept A collection of beliefs about one's basic nature, unique qualities, and typical behavior.

self-disclosure The voluntary act of verbally communicating private information about oneself to another person.

self-efficacy One's belief about one's ability to perform behaviors that should lead to expected outcomes.

self-enhancement The tendency to use various strategies to maintain positive views of oneself.

self-esteem One's overall assessment of one's worth as a person.

self-monitoring The degree to which people attend to and control the impressions they make on others.

self-perception theory The idea that when people are unsure of their beliefs, they try to understand themselves by inferring their attitudes from their behavior.

self-serving bias The tendency to take credit for one's successes and deny responsibility for one's failures.

senile dementia An abnormal and progressive decline in general cognitive functioning that is observed in the elderly.

sensate focus A sex-therapy exercise in which partners take turns pleasuring each other with guided verbal feedback while certain kinds of stimulation are temporarily forbidden.

sensation seeking A generalized preference for high or low levels of sensory stimulation.

set point A natural point of stability in body weight, thought to involve the monitoring of fat-cell levels.

sex The biologically based categories of male and female.

sexism Discrimination against people on the basis of their sex.

sex therapy The professional treatment of sexual dysfunctions.

sexual dysfunctions Impairments in sexual functioning that cause subjective distress.

sexual harassment The subjection of individuals to unwelcome sexually oriented behavior.

sexual identity The complex of personal qualities, self-perceptions, attitudes, values, and preferences that guide one's sexual behavior.

sexually transmitted disease (STD) An illness that is transmitted primarily through sexual contact.

sexual orientation A person's preference for emotional and sexual relationships with individuals of the same sex, the other sex, or either sex.

shaping Modifying behavior by reinforcing closer and closer approximations of a desired response.

shyness Discomfort, inhibition, and excessive caution in interpersonal relations.

social clock A person's notion of a developmental schedule that specifies what the person should have accomplished by certain points in life.

social comparison theory The idea that people need to compare themselves with others in order to gain insight into their own behavior.

social facilitation The tendency to perform dominant responses when others are present.

socialization The process by which individuals acquire the norms and roles expected of people in a particular society or segment of a society.

social loafing A reduction in effort by individuals when they work in groups as compared to when they work by themselves.

social penetration theory The theory that focuses on how relationships develop and sometimes dissolve.

social scripts Culturally programmed sets of expectations about the way various social transactions should evolve.

social skills training A behavior therapy designed to improve interpersonal skills that emphasizes shaping, modeling, and behavioral rehearsal.

social support Aid and succor provided by members of one's social networks.

socioemotional roles Roles within a group that focus on keeping interactions in the group friendly and supportive.

sociology The scientific study of human society and its institutions.

somatization disorder A psychological disorder marked by a history of diverse physical complaints that appear to be psychological in origin.

somatoform disorders A class of psychological disorders involving physical ailments that have no authentic organic basis but are due solely to psychological factors.

source The person who initiates, or sends, a message.

spontaneous remission A recovery from a disorder that occurs without formal treatment.

SQ3R A study system that consists of five steps—survey, question, read, recite, and review—designed to promote effective reading.

stage A developmental period during which a person exhibits certain characteristic patterns of behavior and acquires specific capacities.

standardization The uniform procedures used to administer and score a test.

stereotypes Widely held beliefs that people have certain characteristics simply because of their membership in a particular group.

stimulants Drugs that tend to increase activation of the central nervous system and behavioral activity.

stress Any circumstances that threaten or are perceived to threaten our well-being and thereby tax our coping abilities.

subjects The persons or animals whose behavior is systematically observed in a study.

superego According to Freud, the moral component of personality that incorporates social standards about what represents right and wrong.

surveys Structured questionnaires designed to solicit information about specific aspects of subjects' behavior.

systematic desensitization A behavior therapy used to reduce clients' anxiety responses through counterconditioning.

tardive dyskinesia A neurological disorder marked by chronic tremors and involuntary spastic movements.

task-related roles Roles within a group that focus on moving the group toward completion of its mission.

territoriality The marking off and defending of certain areas as one's own.

test norms Statistics that provide information about where a score on a psychological test ranks in relation to other scores on that test.

testwiseness The ability to use the characteristics and formats of an exam to maximize one's score.

token A symbol of all the members of a group.

token economy A system for doling out symbolic reinforcers that are exchanged later for a variety of genuine reinforcers.

tolerance A progressive decrease in responsiveness to a drug with continued use.

transaction An initial statement by a communicating source and a response by the receiver.

Transactional Analysis A broad theory of personality and interpersonal relations that emphasizes patterns of communication.

transference A phenomenon that occurs when clients start relating to their therapists in ways that mimic critical relationships in their lives.

transvestism A sexual disorder in which a man achieves sexual arousal by dressing in women's clothing.

twin studies Studies in which researchers assess hereditary influence by comparing the resemblance of identical twins and fraternal twins on a trait.

Type A personality A personality style marked by competitive, aggressive, impatient, hostile behavior.

Type B personality A personality style marked by relatively relaxed, patient, easygoing, amicable behavior.

ulterior transaction A special type of complementary transaction that includes hidden messages intended to serve ulterior motives.

unconditioned response (UCR) An unlearned reaction to an unconditioned stimulus that occurs without previous conditioning.

unconditioned stimulus (UCS) A stimulus that evokes an unconditioned response without previous conditioning.

unconscious According to Freud, thoughts, memories, and desires that are well below the surface of conscious awareness but that nonetheless exert great influence on our behavior.

underemployment Settling for a job that does not make full use of one's skills, abilities, and training.

undifferentiated schizophrenia A type of schizophrenia marked by idiosyncratic mixtures of schizophrenic symptoms.

undoing Rituals intended to atone for unacceptable desires or behaviors.

validity The ability of a test to measure what it was designed to measure.

variables Any measurable conditions, events, characteristics, or behaviors that are controlled or observed in a study.

vasocongestion Engorgement of blood vessels.

verbal communication The sending and receiving of messages through written or spoken words.

work An activity that produces something of value for others.

REFERENCES

Aalpoel, P. J., & Lewis, D. J. (1984). Dissociative disorders. In H. E. Adams & P. B. Sutker (Eds.), *Comprehensive handbook of psychopathology*. New York: Plenum.

Abramson, L. Y., Metalsky, G. I., & Alloy, L. B. (1988). The hopelessness theory of depression: Does the research test the theory? In L. Y. Abramson (Ed.), *Social cognition and clinical psychology: A synthesis*. New York: Guilford Press.

Abramson, L. Y., Seligman, M. E. P., & Teasdale, J. D. (1978). Learned helplessness in humans: Critique and reformulation. *Journal of Abnormal Psychology, 87,* 49–74.

Adams, G. R. (1992, Fall). Identity and intimacy: Some observations after a decade of investigations. *Society for Research on Adolescence Newsletter,* pp. 4–5.

Ader, R., & Cohen, N. (1984). Behavior and the immune system. In W. D. Gentry (Ed.), *Handbook of behavioral medicine*. New York: Guilford Press.

Adler, A. (1917). *Study of organ inferiority and its psychical compensation*. New York: Nervous and Mental Diseases Publishing Co.

Adler, A. (1927). *Practice and theory of individual psychology*. New York: Harcourt, Brace & World.

Adler, A. (1964). *Superiority and social interest: A collection of later writings* (Edited by H. L. Ansbacher & R. Ansbacher). New York: Viking Press.

Adler, C. S., & Adler, S. M. (1984). Biofeedback. In T. B. Karasu (Ed.), *The psychiatric therapies*. Washington, DC: American Psychiatric Association.

Adler, R., & Towne, N. (1987). *Looking out/looking in*. New York: Holt, Rinehart & Winston.

Adler, S., & Aranya, N. (1984). A comparison of the work needs, attitudes, and preferences of professional accountants at different career stages. *Journal of Vocational Behavior, 25,* 45–57.

Agras, W. S. (1984). The behavioral treatment of somatic disorders. In W. D. Gentry (Ed.), *Handbook of behavioral medicine*. New York: Guilford Press.

Agras, W. S. (1985). Stress, panic and the cardiovascular system. In A. H. Tuma & J. Maser (Eds.), *Anxiety and the anxiety disorders*. Hillsdale, NJ: Erlbaum.

Agras, W. S., & Berkowitz, R. (1988). Behavior therapy. In J. A. Talbott, R. E. Hales, & S. C. Yudofsky (Eds.), *The American Psychiatric Press textbook of psychiatry*. Washington, DC: American Psychiatric Press.

Ainsworth, M. D. S., Blehar, M. C., Waters, E., & Wall, S. (1978). *Patterns of attachment: A psychological study of the strange situation*. Hillsdale, NJ: Erlbaum.

Alberti, R. E., & Emmons, M. L. (1990). *Your perfect right: A guide to assertive living* (6th ed.). San Luis Obispo, CA: Impact.

Alexander, C. N., & Knight, G. W. (1971). Situated identities and social psychological experimentation. *Sociometry, 34,* 65–82.

Alexander, F. (1954). Psychoanalysis and psychotherapy. *Journal of the American Psychoanalytic Association, 2,* 722–733.

Alicke, M. D., Smith, R. H., & Klotz, J. L. (1986). Judgments of personal attractiveness: The role of faces and bodies. *Personality and Social Psychology Bulletin, 12,* 381–389.

Al-Issa, I. (1982). Sex-differences in psychopathology. In I. Al-Issa (Ed.), *Culture and psychopathology*. Baltimore: University Park Press.

Allen, K. M., Blascovich, J., Tomaka, J., & Kelsey, R. M. (1991). Presence of human friends and pet dogs as moderators of autonomic responses to stress in women. *Journal of Personality and Social Psychology, 61*(4), 582–589.

Alloy, L. B., & Abramson, L. Y. (1979). Judgment of contingency in depressed and nondepressed students: Sadder but wiser. *Journal of Experimental Psychology: General, 108,* 441–485.

Alloy, L. B., & Abramson, L. Y. (1988). Depressive realism: Four theoretical perspectives. In L. B. Alloy (Ed.), *Cognitive processes in depression*. New York: Guilford Press.

Alloy, L. B., Clements, C., & Kolden, G. (1985). The cognitive diathesis-stress theories of depression: Therapeutic implications. In S. Reiss & R. R. Bootzin (Eds.), *Theoretical issues in behavior therapy*. Orlando, FL: Academic Press.

Allport, G. W. (1937). *Personality: A psychological interpretation*. New York: Holt.

Allport, G. W. (1961). *Pattern and growth in personality*. New York: Holt, Rinehart & Winston.

Almquist, E. M., & Angrist, S. S. (1971). Role model influences on college women's career aspirations. *Merrill-Palmer Quarterly, 17,* 263–279.

Alpert, D., & Culbertson, A. (1987). Daily hassles and coping strategies of dual-earner and nondual-earner women. *Psychology of Women Quarterly, 11,* 359–366.

Altman, I., & Haythorn, W. W. (1965). Interpersonal exchange in socialization. *Sociometry, 23,* 411–426.

Altman, I., & Taylor, D. A. (1983). *Social penetration: The development of interpersonal relationships*. New York: Irvington.

Altman, I., Vinsel, A., & Brown, B. A. (1981). Dialectic conceptions in social psychology: An application to social penetration and privacy regulation. In L. Berkowitz (Ed.), *Advances in experimental social psychology* (Vol. 14). New York: Academic Press.

Amada, G. (1985). *A guide to psychotherapy*. Lanham, MD: Madison Books.

Amaro, H., Russo, N. F., & Johnson, J. (1987). Family and work predictors of psychological well-being among Hispanic women professionals. *Psychology of Women Quarterly, 11,* 523–532.

Amatea, E. S., & Fong, M. L. (1991). The impact of role stressors and personal resources on the stress experience of professional women. *Psychology of Women Quarterly, 15*(3), 419–430.

Amato, P. R., & Keith, B. (1991). Parental divorce and adult well-being: A meta-analysis. *Journal of Marriage and the Family, 53,* 43–58.

Ambelas, A. (1987). Life events and mania: A special relationship? *British Journal of Psychiatry, 150,* 235–240.

Amberson, J. I., & Hoon, P. W. (1985). Hemodynamics of sequential orgasm. *Archives of Sexual Behavior, 14*(4), 351–360.

American Psychiatric Association. (1952). *Diagnostic and statistical manual of mental disorders* (1st ed.). Washington, DC: Author.

American Psychiatric Association. (1968). *Diagnostic and statistical manual of mental disorders* (2nd ed.). Washington, DC: Author.

American Psychiatric Association. (1980). *Diagnostic and statistical manual of mental disorders* (3rd ed.). Washington, DC: Author.

American Psychiatric Association. (1987). *Diagnostic and statistical manual of mental disorders* (3rd ed. rev.). Washington, DC: Author.

Anderson, C. A., & Harvey, R. J. (1988). Discriminating between problems in living: An examination of depression, loneliness, shyness, and social anxiety. *Journal of Social and Clinical Psychology, 6,* 482–491.

Anderson, C. A., Horowitz, L. M., & French, R. D. (1983). Attributional style of lonely and depressed people. *Journal of Personality and Social Psychology, 45*(1), 127–136.

Anderson, J. R. (1980). *Cognitive psychology and its implications*. New York: W. H. Freeman.

Anderson, K. J. (1990). Arousal and the inverted-U hypothesis: A critique of Neiss's "reconceptualizing arousal." *Psychological Bulletin, 107*(1), 96–100.

Anderson, N. H. (1968). Likableness ratings of 555 personality trait words. *Journal of Personality and Social Psychology, 9,* 272–279.

Andre, R. (1991). *Positive solitude: A practical program for mastering loneliness and achieving self-fulfillment*. New York: HarperCollins.

Andreasen, N. C. (1982). Negative versus positive schizophrenia: Definition and validation. *Archives of General Psychiatry, 39,* 789–794.

Andreasen, N. C. (1985). Structural brain abnormalities in schizophrenia. In M. N. Menuck & M. V. Seeman (Eds.), *New perspectives in schizophrenia*. New York: Macmillan.

Antill, J. K., & Cotton, S. (1988). Factors affecting the division of labor in households. *Sex Roles, 18,* 531–553.

Aquilino, W. S. (1990). The likelihood of parent-adult child coresidence: Effects of family structure and parental characteristics. *Journal of Marriage and the Family, 52,* 405–419.

Arbeiter, S. (1979). Mid-life career change. *AAHE Bulletin (American Association for Higher Education), 32*(2), 1, 11–12.

Arbeiter, S., Aslanian, C. B., Schmerbeck, F. A., & Brickell, H. M. (1978). *40 million Americans in career transition*. New York: College Entrance Examination Board.

Archer, J. (1984). Gender roles as developmental pathways. *British Journal of Social Psychology, 23,* 245–256.

Archer, R. L. (1979). Role of personality and the social situation. In G. J. Chelune & associates (Eds.), *Self-disclosure: Origins, patterns, and implications of openness in inter-*

personal relationships. San Francisco: Jossey-Bass.

Archer, R. L. (1980). Self-disclosure. In D. M. Wegner & R. R. Vallacher (Eds.), *The self in social psychology.* New York: Oxford University Press.

Archer, S. L. (1982). The lower age boundaries of identity development. *Child Development, 53,* 1551–1556.

Arentewicz, G., & Schmidt, G. (Eds.). (1983). *The treatment of sexual disorders.* New York: Basic Books.

Argyle, M. (1969). *Social interaction.* New York: Aldine-Atherton.

Argyle, M. (1987). *The psychology of happiness.* London: Metheun.

Argyle, M., & Dean, J. (1965). Eye-contact, distance, and affiliation. *Sociometry, 28,* 289–304.

Argyle, M., & Henderson, M. (1984). The rules of friendship. *Journal of Social and Personal Relationships, 1,* 211–237.

Argyle, M., & McHenry, R. (1971). Do spectacles really affect judgments of intelligence? *British Journal of Social and Clinical Psychology, 10,* 27–29.

Arkowitz, H. (1992). Integrative theories of therapy. In D. K. Freedheim (Ed.), *History of psychotherapy: A century of change.* Washington, DC: American Psychological Association.

Arlin, P. K. (1975). Cognitive development in adulthood: A fifth stage? *Developmental Psychology, 11,* 602–606.

Arnkoff, D. B., & Glass, C. R. (1992). Cognitive therapy and psychotherapy. In D. K. Freedheim (Ed.), *History of psychotherapy: A century of change.* Washington, DC: American Psychological Association.

Aron, A. (1988). The matching hypothesis reconsidered again: Comment on Kalick and Hamilton. *Journal of Personality and Social Psychology, 54*(3), 441–446.

Aronson, E., & Mills, J. (1959). The effect of severity of initiation on liking for a group. *Journal of Abnormal and Social Psychology, 59,* 177–181.

Aronson, E., Willerman, B., & Floyd, J. (1966). The effect of a pratfall on increasing interpersonal attractiveness. *Psychonomic Science, 4,* 157–158.

Asch, S. E. (1946). Forming impressions of personality. *Journal of Abnormal and Social Psychology, 41,* 258–290.

Asch, S. E. (1951). Effects of group pressure on the modification and distortion of judgments. In H. Guetzkow (Ed.), *Groups, leadership and men.* Pittsburgh: Carnegie Press.

Asch, S. E. (1955). Opinions and social pressures. *Scientific American, 193*(5), 31–35.

Asch, S. E. (1956). Studies of independence and conformity: A minority of one against a unanimous majority. *Psychological Monographs, 70*(9, Whole No. 416).

Asendorpf, J. B. (1986). Shyness in middle and late childhood. In W. H. Jones, J. M. Cheek, & S. R. Briggs (Eds.), *Shyness: Perspectives on research and treatment.* New York: Plenum.

Asendorpf, J. B. (1989). Shyness as a final common pathway for two different kinds of inhibition. *Journal of Personality and Social Psychology, 57*(3), 481–492.

Ashour, A. S. (1973). The contingency model of leadership effectiveness: An evaluation.

Organizational Behavior and Human Performance, 9, 339–355.

Asterita, M. F. (1985). *The physiology of stress.* New York: Human Sciences Press.

Athanasiou, R., Shaver, P., & Tavris, C. (1970, July). Sex. *Psychology Today,* pp. 39–52.

Atkins, A., Deaux, K., & Bieri, J. (1967). Latitude of acceptance and attitude change: Empirical evidence for a reformulation. *Journal of Personality and Social Psychology, 6,* 47–54.

Atkinson, R. L. (1989). Low and very low calorie diets. *Medical Clinics of North America, 73*(1), 203–215.

Atwater, L. (1982). *The extramarital connection: Sex, intimacy, and identity.* New York: Irvington.

Atwood, J. D., & Gagnon, J. H. (1987). Masturbatory behavior in college youth. *Journal of Sex Education and Therapy, 13*(2), 35–42.

Averill, J. R. (1982). *Anger and aggression: An essay on aggression.* New York: Springer–Verlag.

Avery, D., & Winokur, G. (1978). Suicide, attempted suicide, and relapse rates in depression. *Archives of General Psychiatry, 35,* 749–753.

Axelrod, S., & Apsche, J. (1983). *The effects of punishment on human behavior.* New York: Academic Press.

Baber, K. M., & Monaghan, P. (1988). College women's career and motherhood expectations: New options, old dilemmas. *Sex Roles, 19*(3/4), 189–203.

Baenninger, M., & Newcombe, N. (1989). The role of experience in spatial test performance: A meta-analysis. *Sex Roles, 20,* 327–344.

Bailey, J. M, & Benishay, D. S. (1993). Familial aggregation of female sexual orientation. *American Journal of Psychiatry, 150,* 272–277.

Bakeman, R., Lumb, J. R., Jackson, R. E., & Smith, D. W. (1986). AIDS-risk group profiles in whites and members of minority groups. *New England Journal of Medicine, 315,* 191–192.

Baker, E. L. (1985). Psychoanalysis and psychoanalytic therapy. In S. J. Lynn & J. P. Garske (Eds.), *Contemporary psychotherapies: Models and methods.* Columbus, OH: Charles E. Merrill.

Baker, G. H. B. (1982). Life events before the onset of rheumatoid arthritis. *Psychotherapy and Psychosomatics, 38,* 173–177.

Bales, R. F. (1958). Task roles and social roles in problem-solving groups. In E. E. Maccoby, T. M. Newcomb, & E. L. Hartley (Eds.), *Readings in social psychology.* New York: Holt, Rinehart & Winston.

Balswick, J., & Avertt, C. P. (1977). Differences in expressiveness: Gender, interpersonal orientation, and perceived expressiveness as contributing factors. *Journal of Marriage and the Family, 39,* 121–127.

Bandura, A. (1973). *Aggression: A social learning analysis.* Englewood Cliffs, NJ: Prentice-Hall.

Bandura, A. (1977). *Social learning theory.* Englewood Cliffs, NJ: Prentice-Hall.

Bandura, A. (1986). *Social foundations of thought and action: A social-cognitive theory.* Englewood Cliffs, NJ: Prentice-Hall.

Bandura, A., & Rosenthal, T. L. (1966). Vicarious classical conditioning as a function of arousal level. *Journal of Personality and Social Psychology, 3,* 54–62.

Bandura, A., Ross, D., & Ross, S. (1963). Vicarious reinforcement and imitative learning. *Journal of Abnormal and Social Psychology, 67*(6), 601–607.

Banks, M. H., & Jackson, P. R. (1982). Unemployment and the risk of minor psychiatric disorder in young people: Cross-sectional and longitudinal evidence. *Psychological Medicine, 12,* 789–798.

Banmen, J., & Vogel, N. A. (1985). The relationship between marital quality and interpersonal sexual communication. *Family Therapy, 12*(1), 45–58.

Barbach, L. G. (1982). *For each other: Sharing sexual intimacy.* Garden City, NY: Anchor.

Bardwick, J. M. (1973, May). Women's liberation: Nice idea, but it won't be easy. *Psychology Today,* pp. 26–33, 110–111.

Barfield, A. (1976). Biological influences on sex differences in behavior. In M. S. Teitelbaum (Ed.), *Sex differences: Social and biological perspectives.* New York: Anchor.

Barlett, D. L., & Steele, J. B. (1979). *Empire: The life, legend and madness of Howard Hughes.* New York: Norton.

Barlow, D. H., & Waddell, M. T. (1985). Agoraphobia. In D. H. Barlow (Ed.), *Clinical handbook of psychological disorders.* New York: Guilford Press.

Barnes, M. L., & Buss, D. M. (1985). Sex differences in the interpersonal behavior of married couples. *Journal of Personality and Social Psychology, 48,* 654–661.

Barnett, P. A., & Gotlib, I. H. (1988). Psychosocial functioning and depression: Distinguishing among antecedents, concomitants, and consequences. *Psychological Bulletin, 104*(1), 97–126.

Barofsky, I. (1981). Issues and approaches to the assessment of the cancer patient. In C. K. Prokop & L. A. Bradley (Eds.), *Medical psychology: Contributions to behavioral medicine.* New York: Academic Press.

Baron, P. H. (1974). Self-esteem, ingratiation, and evaluation of unknown others. *Journal of Personality and Social Psychology, 30,* 104–109.

Baron, R. A., & Greenberg, J. (1990). *Behavior in organizations: Understanding and managing the human side of work.* Boston: Allyn & Bacon.

Baron, R. S., Cutrona, C. E., Hicklin, D., Russell, D. W., & Lubaroff, D. M. (1990). Social support and immune function among spouses of cancer patients. *Journal of Personality and Social Psychology, 59*(2), 344–352.

Barrett, J. E., Rose, R. M., & Klerman, G. L. (Eds.). (1979). *Stress and mental disorder.* New York: Raven.

Barsky, A. J. (1988). The paradox of health. *New England Journal of Medicine, 318,* 414–418.

Barsky, A. J. (1989). Somatoform disorders. In H. I. Kaplan & B. J. Sadock (Eds.), *Comprehensive textbook of psychiatry/V.* Baltimore: Williams & Wilkins.

Barton, J. L. (1977). ECT in depression: The evidence of controlled studies. *Biological Psychiatry, 12,* 687–695.

Baruch, G. K. (1984). The psychological well-being of women in the middle years. In G.

Baruch & J. Brooks-Gunn (Eds.), *Women in midlife*. New York: Plenum.

Baruch, G. K., Barnett, R., & Rivers, C. (1983). *Lifeprints: New patterns of love and work for today's women*. New York: New American Library.

Baruch, G. K., Biener, L., & Barnett, R. C. (1987). Women and gender in research on stress. *American Psychologist, 42*, 130–136.

Basow, S. A. (1986). *Gender stereotypes: Traditions and alternatives*. Pacific Grove, CA: Brooks/Cole.

Bass, B. M. (1985). *Leadership and performance beyond expectations*. New York: Free Press.

Bass, B. M. (1990). *Bass and Stogdill's handbook of leadership: Theory, research, and managerial applications*. New York: Free Press.

Bass, E., & Davis, L. (1988). *The courage to heal: A guide for women survivors of child sexual abuse*. New York: HarperCollins.

Basseches, M. (1984). *Dialectical thinking and adult development*. Norwood, NJ: Ablex.

Baum, A. (1990). Stress, intrusive imagery, and chronic distress. *Health Psychology, 9*(6), 653–675.

Baumeister, R. F. (1982). A self-presentational view of social phenomena. *Psychological Bulletin, 91*, 3–26.

Baumeister, R. F. (1984). Choking under pressure: Self-consciousness and paradoxical effects of incentives on skillful performance. *Journal of Personality and Social Psychology, 46*(3), 610–620.

Baumeister, R. F. (1989). The optimal margin of illusion. *Journal of Social and Clinical Psychology, 8*(2), 176–189.

Baumeister, R. F., & Scher, S. J. (1988). Self-defeating behavior patterns among normal individuals: Review and analysis of common self-destructive tendencies. *Psychological Bulletin, 104*(1), 3–22.

Baumeister, R. F., & Steinhilber, A. (1984). Paradoxical effects of supportive audiences on performance under pressure: The home field disadvantage in sports championships. *Journal of Personality and Social Psychology, 47*(1), 85–93.

Baumeister, R. F., Tice, D. M., & Hutton, D. G. (1989). Self-presentational motivations and personality differences in self-esteem. *Journal of Personality, 57*, 547–579.

Baumrind, D. (1964). Some thoughts on the ethics of reading Milgram's "Behavioral study of obedience." *American Psychologist, 19*, 421–423.

Baumrind, D. (1967). Child care practices anteceding three patterns of preschool behavior. *Genetic Psychology Monographs, 75*, 43–88.

Baumrind, D. (1971). Current patterns of parental authority. *Developmental Psychology Monographs, 4*(1, Pt. 2).

Baumrind, D. (1978). Parental disciplinary patterns and social competence in children. *Youth and Society, 9*(3), 239–276.

Baumrind, D. (1989). Rearing competent children. In W. Damon (Ed.), *Child development today and tomorrow*. San Francisco: Jossey-Bass.

Baumrind, D. (1991). Effective parenting during the early adolescent transition. In P. A. Cowan & M. Hetherington (Eds.), *Family transitions*. Hillsdale, NJ: Erlbaum.

Baxter, L. A. (1988). A dialectical perspective on communication strategies in relation-ship development. In S. Duck (Ed.), *Handbook of personal relationships*. New York: Wiley.

Baxter, L. A., & Wilmot, W. W. (1985). Taboo topics in close relationships. *Journal of Social and Personal Relationships, 2*, 253–269.

Beardsley, R. S., Gardocki, G. J., Larson, D. B., & Hidalgo, J. (1988). Prescribing of psychotropic medication by primary care physicians and psychiatrists. *Archives of General Psychiatry, 45*, 1117–1119.

Beattie, M. (1987). *Co-dependent no more*. New York: HarperCollins.

Beattie, M. (1989). *Beyond codependency: And getting better all the time*. New York: HarperCollins.

Beck, A. T. (1976). *Cognitive therapy and the emotional disorders*. New York: International Universities Press.

Beck, A. T. (1987). Cognitive therapy. In J. K. Zeig (Ed.), *The evolution of psychotherapy*. New York: Brunner/Mazel.

Beck, A. T. (1988). *Love is never enough*. New York: HarperCollins.

Beck, A. T. (1991). Cognitive therapy: A 30-year retrospective. *American Psychologist, 46*(4), 368–375.

Beck, A. T., Rush, A. J., Shaw, B. F., & Emery, G. (1979). *Cognitive therapy of depression*. New York: Guilford Press.

Beck, D. F., & Jones, M. A. (1973). *Progress on family problems: A nationwide study of clients' and counselors' views on family agency services*. New York: Family Service Association of America.

Beck, J., & Morgan, P. A. (1986). Designer drug confusion: A focus on MDMA. *Journal of Drug Education, 16*(3), 287–302.

Becker, H. S. (1973). *Outsiders: Studies in the sociology of deviance*. New York: Free Press.

Becker, R. E. (1990). Social skills training. In A. S. Bellack & M. Hersen (Eds.), *Handbook of comparative treatments for adult disorders*. New York: Wiley.

Behar, R. (1991, May 6). The thriving cult of greed and power. *Time, 137*, pp. 50–57.

Beitman, B. D., Goldfried, M. R., & Norcross, J. C. (1989). The movement toward integrating the psychotherapies: An overview. *American Journal of Psychiatry, 146*, 138–147.

Bell, A. P., & Weinberg, M. S. (1978). *Homosexualities: A study of diversity among men and women*. New York: Simon & Schuster.

Bell, A. P., Weinberg, M. S., & Hammersmith, K. S. (1981). *Sexual preference—Its development in men and women*. Bloomington, IN: Indiana University Press.

Bell, I. P. (1989). The double standard: Age. In J. Freeman (Ed.), *Women: A feminist perspective* (4th ed.). Mountain View, CA: Mayfield.

Bell, R. (1988). *Changing bodies, changing lives*. New York: Vintage Books.

Bell, R. R. (1981). *Worlds of friendship*. Newbury Park, CA: Sage Publications.

Bell, R. R., Turner, S., & Rosen, L. (1975). A multivariate analysis of female extramarital coitus. *Journal of Marriage and the Family, 37*, 375–383.

Belsky, J. (1985). Exploring differences in marital change across the transition to parenthood: The role of violated expectations.

Journal of Marriage and the Family, 47, 1037–1044.

Belsky, J. (1990). Children and marriage. In F. D. Fincham & T. N. Bradbury (Eds.), *The psychology of marriage: Basic issues and applications*. New York: Guilford Press.

Bem, D. J. (1972). Self-perception theory. In L. Berkowitz (Ed.), *Advances in experimental social psychology* (Vol. 6). New York: Academic Press.

Bem, S. L. (1975, September). Androgyny vs. the tight little lives of fluffy women and chesty men. *Psychology Today*, pp. 58–62.

Bem, S. L. (1981). Gender schema theory: A cognitive account of sex typing. *Psychological Review, 88*, 354–364.

Bem, S. L. (1983). Gender schema theory and its implications for child development: Raising gender-aschematic children in a gender-schematic society. *Signs, 8*, 598–616.

Bem, S. L. (1985). Androgyny and gender schema theory: A conceptual and empirical integration. In T. B. Sonderegger (Ed.), *Nebraska symposium on motivation 1984: Psychology and gender* (Vol. 32). Lincoln, NE: University of Nebraska Press.

Beneke, W. M., & Harris, M. B. (1972). Teaching self-control of study behavior. *Behavior Research and Therapy, 10*, 35–41.

Benjamin, L. T., Jr., Cavell, T. A., & Shallenberger, W. R., III. (1984). Staying with initial answers on objective tests: Is it a myth? *Teaching of Psychology, 11*(3), 133–141.

Benson, H. (1975). *The relaxation response* (1st ed.). New York: Morrow.

Benson, H., & Klipper, M. Z. (1988). *The relaxation response* (2nd ed.). New York: Avon.

Berardo, D. H., Shehan, C. L., & Leslie, G. R. (1987). A residue of tradition: Jobs, careers, and spouses' time in housework. *Journal of Marriage and the Family, 49*, 381–390.

Berg, J. H., & Clark, M. S. (1986). Differences in social exchange between intimate and other relationships: Gradually evolving or quickly apparent? In V. J. Derlega & B. A. Winstead (Eds.), *Friendship and social interaction*. New York: Springer-Verlag.

Berg, J. H., & McQuinn, R. D. (1986). Attraction and exchange in continuing and noncontinuing dating relationships. *Journal of Personality and Social Psychology, 50*, 942–952.

Berg, S. (1987). Intelligence and terminal decline. In G. L. Maddox & E. W. Busse (Eds.), *Aging: The universal human experience*. New York: Springer.

Bergin, A. E. (1971). The evaluation of therapeutic outcomes. In A. E. Bergin & S. L. Garfield (Eds.), *Handbook of psychotherapy and behavior change: An empirical analysis*. New York: Wiley.

Berkowitz, L. (1969). The frustration-aggression hypothesis revisited. In L. Berkowitz (Ed.), *Roots of aggression: A reexamination of the frustration-aggression hypothesis*. New York: Atherton.

Berlo, D. K. (1960). *The process of communication: An introduction to theory and practice*. New York: Holt, Rinehart & Winston.

Berman, P. W. (1976). Social context as a

determinant of sex differences in adults' attraction to infants. *Developmental Psychology, 12,* 365–366.

Berman, P. W. (1980). Are women more responsive than men to the young? A review of developmental and situational variables. *Psychological Bulletin, 88,* 668–695.

Berne, E. (1961). *Transactional analysis in psychotherapy.* New York: Ballantine.

Berne, E. (1964). *Games people play.* New York: Grove Press.

Berne, E. (1972). *What do you say after hello?* New York: Grove Press.

Berscheid, E. (1966). Opinion change and communicator-comunicatee similarity and dissimilarity. *Journal of Personality and Social Psychology, 4,* 670–680.

Berscheid, E. (1985). Interpersonal attraction. In G. Lindzey & E. Aronson (Eds.), *The handbook of social psychology: Vol. 2. Special fields and applications.* New York: Random House.

Berscheid, E. (1988). Some comments on love's anatomy: Or, whatever happened to old-fashioned lust. In R. J. Sternberg & M. L. Barnes (Eds.), *The psychology of love.* New Haven, CT: Yale University Press.

Berscheid, E., Dion, K., Walster, E., & Walster, G. W. (1971). Physical attractiveness and dating choice: A test of the matching hypothesis. *Journal of Experimental Social Psychology, 7,* 173–189.

Berscheid, E., Snyder, M., & Omoto, A. M. (1989). The relationship closeness inventory: Assessing the closeness of interpersonal relationships. *Journal of Personality and Social Psychology, 57,* 792–807.

Berscheid, E., & Walster, E. (1978). *Interpersonal attraction.* Reading, MA: Addison-Wesley.

Berscheid, E., Walster, E., & Bohrnstedt, G. (1973, November). The happy American body, a survey report. *Psychology Today,* pp. 119–131.

Bettelheim, B. (1943). Individual and mass behavior in extreme situations. *Journal of Abnormal and Social Psychology, 38,* 417–452.

Betz, N. E., & Fitzgerald, L. E. (1987). *The career psychology of women.* New York: Academic Press.

Betz, N. E., & Hackett, G. (1986). Applications of self-efficacy theory to understanding career choice behavior. *Journal of Social and Clinical Psychology, 4*(3), 279–289.

Bickman, L. (1971). The effect of social status on the honesty of others. *Journal of Social Psychology, 85,* 87–92.

Biegel, D. E., Sales, E., & Schulz, R. (1991). *Family caregiving in chronic illness.* Newbury Park, CA: Sage Publications.

Biener, L., & Abrams, D. B. (1991). The contemplation ladder: Validation of a measure of readiness to consider smoking cessation. *Health Psychology, 10*(5), 360–365.

Billings, A. (1979). Conflict in distressed and nondistressed married couples. *Journal of Consulting and Clinical Psychology, 47,* 368–376.

Billings, A. G., Cronkite, R. C., & Moos, R. H. (1983). Social-environment factors in unipolar depression. *Journal of Abnormal Psychology, 92,* 119–133.

Binet, A., & Simon, T. (1905). Methodes nouvelles pour le diagnostic du niveau intellectuel des anormaux. *L'Annee Psychologique, 11,* 191–244.

Birchler, G. R., & Webb, L. J. (1977). Discriminating interaction behavior in happy and unhappy marriages. *Journal of Consulting and Clinical Psychology, 45,* 494–495.

Birchler, G. R., Weiss, R. L., & Vincent, J. P. (1975). Multimethod analysis of social reinforcement exchange between maritally distressed and nondistressed spouse and stranger dyads. *Journal of Personality and Social Psychology, 31,* 349–360.

Birren, J. E. (1983). Aging in America: Roles for psychology. *American Psychologist, 38,* 298–299.

Birren, J. E., Woods, A. M., & Williams, M. V. (1980). Behavioral slowing with age: Causes, organization, and consequences. In L. W. Poon (Ed.), *Aging in the 1980s: Psychological issues.* Washington, DC: American Psychological Association.

Bitter, R. G. (1986). Late marriage and marital instability: The effects of heterogeneity and inflexibility. *Journal of Marriage and the Family, 48,* 631–640.

Black, D. W., & Winokur, G. (1990). Suicide and psychiatric diagnosis. In S. J. Blumenthal & D. J. Kupfer (Eds.), *Suicide over the life cycle: Risk factors, assessment, and treatment of suicidal patients.* Washington, DC: American Psychiatric Press.

Blair, S. L., & Johnson, M. P. (1992). Wives' perceptions of the fairness of the division of household labor: The intersection of housework and ideology. *Journal of Marriage and the Family, 54,* 570–581.

Blair, S. N., Kohl, H. W., Paffenbarger, R. S., Clark, D. G., Cooper, K. H., & Gibbons, L. W. (1989). Physical fitness and all-cause mortality: A prospective study of healthy men and women. *Journal of the American Medical Association, 262,* 2395–2401.

Blake, R. R., & Mouton, J. S. (1964). *The managerial grid.* Houston: Gulf Publishing.

Blank, A. S., Jr. (1982). Stresses of war: The example of Viet Nam. In L. Goldberger & S. Breznitz (Eds.), *Handbook of stress: Theoretical and clinical aspects.* New York: Free Press.

Blank, T. O. (1982). *A social psychology of developing adults.* New York: Wiley.

Blasband, D., & Peplau, L. A. (1985). Sexual exclusivity versus openness in gay male couples. *Archives of Sexual Behavior, 14,* 395–412.

Blau, G. (1981). An empirical investigation of job stress, social support, service length, and job strain. *Organizational Behavior and Human Performance, 27,* 279–302.

Blau, Z. S. (1971). *Old age in a changing society.* New York: Van Nostrand.

Blazer, D. G., Hughes, D., & George, L. K. (1987). Stressful life events and the onset of generalized anxiety syndrome. *American Journal of Psychiatry, 144,* 1178–1183.

Blazer, D. G., Hughes, D., George, L. K., Swartz, M., & Boyer, R. (1991). Generalized anxiety disorder. In L. N. Robins & D. A. Regier (Eds.), *Psychiatric disorders in America: The epidemiologic catchment area study.* New York: Free Press.

Blechman, E. A., McEnroe, M. J., Carella, E. T., & Audette, D. P. (1986). Childhood competence and depression. *Journal of Abnormal Psychology, 95*(3), 223–227.

Bleier, R. (1984). *Science and gender: A critique of biology and its theories on women.* New York: Pergamon Press.

Block, J. D. (1980). *Friendship: How to give it; how to get it.* New York: Macmillan.

Block, J. H. (1973). Conceptions of sex role: Some cross-cultural and longitudinal perspectives. *American Psychologist, 28,* 512–526.

Block, J. H. (1976). Issues, problems, and pitfalls in assessing sex differences: A critical review of *The psychology of sex differences. Merrill-Palmer Quarterly, 22,* 283–308.

Bloodworth, R. C. (1987). Major problems associated with marijuana abuse. *Psychiatric Medicine, 3*(3), 173–184.

Bloomfield, H. H., & Kory, R. B. (1976). *Happiness: The TM program, psychiatry, and enlightenment.* New York: Simon & Schuster.

Blum, K. (1984). *Handbook of abusable drugs.* New York: Gardner Press.

Blumstein, P., & Schwartz, P. (1983). *American couples: Money, work, sex.* New York: Morrow.

Blumstein, P., & Schwartz, P. (1989). Intimate relationships and the creation of sexuality. In B. Risman & P. Schwartz (Eds.), *Gender in intimate relationships: A microstructural approach.* Belmont, CA: Wadsworth.

Blumstein, P., & Schwartz, P. (1990). Intimate relationships and the creation of sexuality. In D. P. McWhirter, S. A. Sanders, & J. M. Reinisch (Eds.), *Homosexuality/heterosexuality: Concepts of sexual orientation.* New York: Oxford University Press.

Bograd, M. (1982). Battered women, cultural myths and clinical interventions: A feminist analysis. *Women and therapy, 1,* 69–77.

Bolger, N. (1990). Coping as a personality process: A prospective study. *Journal of Personality and Social Psychology, 59*(3), 525–537.

Bolger, N., DeLongis, A., Kessler, R. C., & Schilling, E. A. (1989). Effects of daily stress on negative mood. *Journal of Personality and Social Psychology, 57*(5), 808–818.

Bolles, R. N. (1987). *What color is your parachute? A practical manual for job-hunters and career-changers.* Berkeley, CA: Ten Speed Press.

Bolles, R. N. (1990). *What color is your parachute? A practical manual for job-hunters and career-changers.* Berkeley, CA: Ten Speed Press.

Bolles, R. N. (1991). *What color is your parachute? A practical manual for job-hunters and career-changers.* Berkeley, CA: Ten Speed Press.

Boor, M. (1980). Relationships between unemployment rates and suicide rates in eight countries, 1962–1976. *Psychological Reports, 60,* 562–564.

Booth-Kewley, S., & Friedman, H. S. (1987). Psychological predictors of heart disease: A quantitative review. *Psychological Bulletin, 101*(3), 343–362.

Bordelon, K. W. (1985). Sexism in reading materials. *Reading Teacher, 38,* 792–797.

Boshier, R. (1975). A video-tape study on the relationship between wearing spectacles and judgments of intelligence. *Perceptual and Motor Skills, 40,* 69–70.

Boskind-Lodahl, M. (1976). Cinderella's stepsisters: A feminist perspective on anorexia nervosa and bulimia. *Signs, 2,* 120–146.

Boston Women's Health Book Collective. (1992). *The new our bodies ourselves: A book by and for women.* New York: Simon & Schuster.

Bowen, D. D. (1985). Were men meant to mentor women? *Training and Development Journal, 39*(2), 31–34.

Bower, G. H. (1970). Organizational factors in memory. *Cognitive Psychology, 1,* 18–46.

Bower, G. H., & Clark, M. C. (1969). Narrative stories as mediators of serial learning. *Psychonomic Science, 14,* 181–182.

Bower, S. A., & Bower, G. H. (1991). *Asserting yourself: A practical guide for positive change* (2nd ed.). Reading, MA: Addison-Wesley.

Bowers, J. W., Metts, S. M., & Duncanson, W. T. (1985). Emotion and interpersonal communication. In M. L. Knapp & G. R. Miller (Eds.), *Handbook of interpersonal communication.* Newbury Park, CA: Sage Publications.

Bozarth, M. A., & Wise, R. A. (1985). Toxicity associated with long-term intravenous heroin and cocaine self-administration in the rat. *Journal of the American Medical Association, 254*(1), 81–83.

Bradburn, N., & Sudman, S. (1979). *Improving interview method and questionnaire design.* Washington, DC: Jossey-Bass.

Bradbury, T. N., & Fincham, F. D. (1988). Individual difference variables in close relationships: A contextual model of marriage as an integrative framework. *Journal of Personality and Social Psychology, 54*(4), 713–721.

Bradford, J., & Ryan, C. (1987). *National lesbian health care survey: Mental health implications.* Washington, DC: National Lesbian and Gay Health Foundation.

Bradley, C. (1979). Life events and the control of diabetes mellitus. *Journal of Psychosomatic Research, 23,* 159–162.

Bradley, P. H. (1981). The folk-linguistics of women's speech: An empirical examination. *Communications Monographs, 48,* 73–90.

Bradshaw, J. (1988). *Healing the shame that binds you.* Pompano Beach, FL: Health Communications.

Braiker, H. B., & Kelley, H. H. (1979). Conflict in the development of close relationships. In R. L. Burgess & T. L. Huston (Eds.), *Social exchange in developing relationships.* New York: Academic Press.

Bram, S. (1985). Childlessness revisited: A longitudinal study of voluntarily childless couples, delayed parents, and parents. *Lifestyles: A Journal of Changing Patterns, 8*(1), 46–66.

Brannon, R. (1976). The male sex role: Our culture's blueprint of manhood, and what it's done for us lately. In D. David & R. Brannon (Eds.), *The forty-nine percent majority.* Reading, MA: Addison-Wesley.

Braun, B. G. (1986). Issues in the psychotherapy of multiple personality disorder. In B.

G. Braun (Ed.), *Treatment of multiple personality disorder.* Washington, DC: American Psychiatric Press.

Bray, G. A. (1990). Exercise and obesity. In C. Bouchard, R. J. Shephard, T. Stephens, J. R. Sutton, & B. D. McPherson (Eds.), *Exercise, fitness and health: A consensus of current knowledge.* Champaign, IL: Human Kinetics Books.

Brecher, E. M. (1984). *Love, sex, and aging.* Boston: Little, Brown.

Breckler, S. J., & Greenwald, A. J. (1986). Motivational facets of the self. In R. M. Sorrentino & E. T. Higgins (Eds.), *Handbook of motivation and cognition: Foundations of social behavior.* New York: Guilford Press.

Breggin, P. R. (1979). *Electroshock: Its brain disabling effects.* New York: Springer.

Brehm, J. W. (1966). *A theory of psychological reactance.* New York: Academic Press.

Brehm, S. S. (1992). *Intimate relationships* (2nd ed.). New York: McGraw-Hill.

Brehm, S. S., & Kassin, S. M. (1993). *Social psychology.* Boston: Houghton Mifflin.

Breier, A., Albus, M., Pickar, D., Zahn, T. P., Wolkowitz, O. M., & Paul, S. M. (1987). Controllable and uncontrollable stress in humans: Alterations in mood and neuroendocrine and psychophysiological function. *American Journal of Psychiatry, 144*(11), 1419–1425.

Brent, D. A., & Kolko, D. J. (1990). The assessment and treatment of children and adolescents at risk for suicide. In S. J. Blumenthal & D. J. Kupfer (Eds.), *Suicide over the life cycle: Risk factors, assessment, and treatment of suicidal patients.* Washington, DC: American Psychiatric Press.

Bretherton, I. (1985). Attachment theory: Retrospect and prospect. In I. Bretherton & E. Waters (Eds.), *Growing points of attachment theory and research: Monographs of the Society for Research in Child Development* (Vol. 50).

Bretl, D. J., & Cantor, J. (1988). The portrayal of men and women in U. S. television commercials: A recent content analysis and trends over 15 years. *Sex Roles, 18,* 595–609.

Bretschneider, J. G., & McCoy, N. L. (1988). Sexual interest and behavior in healthy 80- to 102-year-olds. *Archives of Sexual Behavior, 17,* 109–130.

Brett, J. F., Brief, A. P., Burke, M. J., George, J. M., & Webster, J. (1990). Negative affectivity and the reporting of stressful life events. *Health Psychology, 9*(1), 57–68.

Brett, J. M. (1980). The effect of job transfer on employees and their families. In C. L. Cooper & R. Payne (Eds.), *Current concerns in occupational stress.* New York: Wiley.

Brewer, M. (1975, August). Erhard Seminars Training: "We're gonna tear you down and put you back together." *Psychology Today,* pp. 35–40, 82, 88–89.

Brim, O. G., Jr., & Kagan, J. (1980). Constancy and change: A view of the issues. In O. G. Brim, Jr., & J. Kagan (Eds.), *Constancy and change in human development.* Cambridge, MA: Harvard University Press.

Brod, C. (1988). *Technostress: Human cost of the computer revolution.* Reading, MA: Addison-Wesley.

Bromage, B. K., & Mayer, R. E. (1986). Quantitative and qualitative effects of repetition on learning from technical text. *Journal of Educational Psychology, 78*(4), 271–278.

Bronfenbrenner, U., & Crouter, A. C. (1982). Work and family through time and space. In S. B. Kamerman & C. D. Hayes (Eds.), *Families that work: Children in a changing world.* Washington, DC: National Academy Press.

Brooks-Gunn, J. (1986). The relationship of maternal beliefs about sex typing to maternal and young children's behavior. *Sex Roles, 14,* 21–35.

Brooks-Gunn, J., & Petersen, A. C. (1983). *Girls at puberty: Biological and psychosocial perspectives.* New York: Plenum.

Broverman, I. K., Vogel, S. R., Broverman, D. M., Clarkson, F. E., & Rosenkrantz, P. S. (1972). Sex roles stereotypes: A current appraisal. *Journal of Social Issues, 28,* 59–78.

Brown, D. G. (1972). Stress as a precipitant of eczema. *Journal of Psychosomatic Research, 16,* 321–327.

Brown, D. R. (1990). Exercise, fitness, and mental health. In C. Bouchard, R. J. Shephard, T. Stephens, J. R. Sutton, & B. D. McPherson (Eds.), *Exercise, fitness, and health: A consensus of current knowledge.* Champaign, IL: Human Kinetics Books.

Brown, J. D. (1991). Staying fit and staying well: Physical fitness as a moderator of life stress. *Journal of Personality and Social Psychology, 60*(4), 555–561.

Brown, J. D., & McGill, K. L. (1989). The cost of good fortune: When positive life events produce negative health consequences. *Journal of Personality and Social Psychology, 57*(6), 1103–1110.

Brown, J. D., & Siegel, J. M. (1988). Exercise as a buffer of life stress: A prospective study of adolescent health. *Health Psychology, 7*(4), 341–353.

Brown, P., & Funk, S. C. (1986). Tardive dyskinesia: Barriers to the professional recognition of an iatrogenic disease. *Journal of Health and Social Behavior, 27,* 116–132.

Brownell, K. D. (1986). Social and behavioral aspects of obesity in children. In N. A. Krasnegor, J. D. Arasteh, & M. F. Cataldo (Eds.), *Child health behavior: A behavioral pediatrics perspective.* New York: Wiley.

Brownell, K. D. (1988, January). Yo-yo dieting. *Psychology Today,* pp. 20–23.

Brownell, K. D. (1989, June). When and how to diet. *Psychology Today,* pp. 40–46.

Brubaker, T. (1990). Families in later life: A burgeoning research area. *Journal of Marriage and the Family, 52,* 959–982.

Bruckner-Gordon, F., Gangi, B. K., & Wallman, G. U. (1988). *Making therapy work: Your guide to choosing, using, and ending therapy.* New York: HarperCollins.

Bry, A. (1976). *EST.* New York: Avon.

Bryan, J. H., & Test, M. A. (1967). Models and helping: Naturalistic studies in aiding behavior. *Journal of Personality and Social Psychology, 6,* 400–407.

Bryer, K. B. (1979). The Amish way of death: A study of family support systems. *American Psychologist, 34,* 255–261.

Buckhout, R. (1980). Nearly 2,000 witnesses can be wrong. *Bulletin of the Psychonomic Society, 16,* 307–310.

Buda, M., & Tsuang, M. T. (1990). The epidemiology of suicide: Implications for clinical practice. In S. J. Blumenthal & D. J. Kupfer (Eds.), *Suicide over the life cycle: Risk factors, assessment, and treatment of suicidal patients*. Washington, DC: American Psychiatric Press.

Buehler, C., & Langenbrunner, M. (1987). Divorce-related stressors: Occurrence, disruptiveness, and area of life change. *Journal of Divorce, 11*(1), 25–50.

Buehlman, K. T., Gottman, J. M., & Katz, L. F. (1992). How a couple views their past predicts their future: Predicting divorce from an oral history interview. *Journal of Family Psychology, 5*(3 & 4), 295–318.

Buffum, J., Pharm, D., Smith, D. E., Moser, C., Apter, M., Buxton, M., & Davison, J. (1981). Drugs and sexual function. In H. I. Lief (Ed.), *Sexual problems in medical practice*. Chicago: American Medical Association.

Bumiller, E. (1989). First comes marriage— Then, maybe, love. In J. M. Henslin (Ed.), *Marriage and family in a changing society* (3rd ed.). New York: Free Press.

Bumpass, L. L., & Sweet, J. A. (1989). National estimates of cohabitation: Cohort levels and union stability. *Demography, 25*, 615–625.

Bumpass, L. L., Sweet, J. A., & Cherlin, A. (1991). The role of cohabitation in declining rates of marriage. *Journal of Marriage and the Family, 53*, 913–927.

Bumpass, L. L., Sweet, J. A., & Martin, T. C. (1990). Changing patterns of remarriage. *Journal of Marriage and the Family, 52*, 747–756.

Burg, B. (1974, November). Est: 60 hours to happiness. *Human Behavior*, pp. 16–23.

Burger, J. M. (1989). Negative reactions to increases in perceived personal control. *Journal of Personality and Social Psychology, 56*(2), 246–256.

Burger, J. M., & Petty, R. E. (1981). The low-ball compliance technique: Task or person commitment? *Journal of Personality and Social Psychology, 40*, 492–500.

Burgess, E., & Wallin, P. (1953). *Engagement and marriage*. Philadelphia: Lippincott.

Burks, N., & Martin, B. (1985). Everyday problems and life change events: Ongoing versus acute sources of stress. *Journal of Human Stress, 11*(1), 27–35.

Burleson, B. R. (1982). The development of comforting communication skills in childhood and adolescence. *Child Development, 53*, 1578–1588.

Burman, B., & de Anda, D. (1986). Parenthood or nonparenthood: A comparison of intentional families. *Lifestyles: A Journal of Changing Patterns, 8*(2), 69–84.

Burns, D. D. (1980). *Feeling good: The new mood therapy*. New York: Morrow.

Burt, M. R. (1980). Cultural myths and supports for rape. *Journal of Personality and Social Psychology, 38*, 217–230.

Buscaglia, L. (1982). *Living, loving & learning*. Thorofare, NJ: Charles B. Slack.

Busch-Rossnagel, N. A., & Vance, A. K. (1982). The impact of the schools on social and emotional development. In B. B. Wolman (Ed.), *Handbook of developmental psychology*. Englewood Cliffs, NJ: Prentice-Hall.

Buss, D. M. (1985). Human mate selection. *American Scientist, 73*, 47–51.

Buss, D. M. (1988). The evolution of human intrasexual competition: Tactics of mate attraction. *Journal of Personality and Social Psychology, 54*, 616–628.

Buss, D. M. (1989). Sex differences in human mate preferences: Evolutionary hypotheses tested in 37 cultures. *Behavioral and Brain Sciences, 12*, 1–14.

Buss, D. M., & Barnes, M. (1986). Preferences in human mate selection. *Journal of Personality and Social Psychology, 50*, 559–570.

Bussey, K., & Bandura, A. (1984). Influence of gender constancy and social power on sex-linked modeling. *Journal of Personality and Social Psychology, 47*, 1292–1302.

Buunk, B. (1980). Extramarital sex in the Netherlands: Motivations in social and marital context. *Alternative Lifestyles, 3*(1), 11–39.

Buunk, B., & Bringle, R. G. (1987). Jealousy in love relationships. In D. Perlman & S. W. Duck (Eds.), *Intimate relationships: Development, dynamics, and deterioration*. Newbury Park, CA: Sage Publications.

Buxton, M. N., Arkel, Y., Lagos, J., Deposito, F., Lowenthal, H., & Simring, S. (1981). Stress and platelet aggregation in hemophiliac children and their family members. *Research Communications in Psychology, Psychiatry and Behavior, 6*(1), 21–48.

Byers, E. S., & Heinlein, L. (1989). Predicting initiations and refusals of sexual activities in married and cohabiting heterosexual couples. *The Journal of Sex Research, 26*(2), 210–231.

Byrd, J. C. (1992). Environmental tobacco smoke: Medical and legal issues. *Medical Clinics of North America, 76*(2), 377–398.

Byrne, D. (1971). *The attraction paradigm*. New York: Academic Press.

Byrne, D., Clore, G. L., & Smeaton, G. (1986). The attraction hypothesis: Do similar attitudes affect anything? *Journal of Personality and Social Psychology, 51*(6), 1167–1170.

Byrne, D., & Murnen, S. K. (1988). Maintaining loving relationships. In R. J. Sternberg & M. L. Barnes (Eds.), *The psychology of love*. New Haven, CT: Yale University Press.

Byrne, D. G., & Rosenman, R. H. (1986). The type A behavior pattern as a precursor to stressful life-events: A confluence of coronary risks. *British Journal of Medical Psychology, 59*, 75–82.

Byrne, J. D. (1975, February). Mobility rate of employed persons in new occupations. *Monthly Labor Review*, pp. 53–59.

Calabrese, L. H. (1990). Exercise, immunity, cancer, and infection. In C. Bouchard, R. J. Shephard, T. Stephens, J. R. Sutton, & B. D. McPherson (Eds.), *Exercise, fitness, and health: A consensus of knowledge*. Champaign, IL: Human Kinetics Books.

Calderone, M. S., & Johnson, E. W. (1989). *The family book about sexuality*. New York: Harper & Row.

Calderone, M. S., & Ramey, J. (1982). *Talking with your child about sex*. New York: Random House.

Caldwell, M. A., & Peplau, L. A. (1982). Sex differences in same-sex friendship. *Sex Roles, 8*(7), 721–732.

Calhoun, L. G., & Selby, J. W. (1980). Voluntary childlessness, involuntary childlessness, and having children: A study of social perceptions. *Family Relations, 29*, 181–183.

Cameron, N. (1963). *Personality development and psychopathology*. Boston: Houghton Mifflin.

Cannon, D. S., Baker, T. B., & Wehl, C. K. (1981). Emetic and electric shock alcohol aversion therapy: Six- and twelve-month follow-up. *Journal of Consulting and Clinical Psychology, 49*(3), 360–368.

Cannon, W. B. (1932). *The wisdom of the body*. New York: Norton.

Cargan, L., & Melko, M. (1982). *Singles: Myths and realities*. Newbury Park, CA: Sage Publications.

Carlson, V., Cicchetti, D., Barnett, D., & Braunwald, K. (1989). Disorganized/disoriented attachment relationships in maltreated infants. *Developmental Psychology, 25*, 525–531.

Carnegie, D. (1936). *How to win friends and influence people*. New York: Simon & Schuster.

Carney, C. G., & Wells, C. F. (1991). *Discover the career within you* (3rd ed.). Pacific Grove, CA: Brooks/Cole.

Carrington, P. (1987). Managing meditation in clinical practice. In M. A. West (Ed.), *The psychology of meditation*. Oxford: Clarendon Press.

Carroll, J. L., Volk, K. D., & Hyde, J. S. (1985). Differences between males and females in motives for engaging in sexual intercourse. *Archives of Sexual Behavior, 14*, 131–139.

Carroll, L. (1988). Concern with AIDS and the sexual behavior of college students. *Journal of Marriage and the Family, 50*, 405–411.

Carter, E. A., & McGoldrick, M. (1988). Overview: The changing family life cycle— A framework for family therapy. In E. A. Carter & M. McGoldrick (Eds.), *The changing family life cycle: A framework for family therapy* (2nd ed.). New York: Gardner Press.

Carter, R. J., & Myerowitz, B. E. (1984). Sex-role stereotypes: Self-reports of behavior. *Sex Roles, 10*, 293–306.

Cartwright, D. (1968). The nature of group cohesiveness. In D. Cartwright & A. Zander (Eds.), *Group dynamics: Research and theory* (3rd ed.). New York: Harper & Row.

Carver, C. S., Diamond, E. L., & Humphries, C. (1985). Coronary prone behavior. In N. Schneiderman & J. T. Tapp (Eds.), *Behavioral medicine: The biopsychosocial approach*. Hillsdale, NJ: Erlbaum.

Carver, C. S., Scheier, M. F., & Weintraub, J. K. (1989). Assessing coping strategies: A theoretically based approach. *Journal of Personality and Social Psychology, 56*(2), 267–283.

Caspi, A., Bolger, N., & Eckenrode, J. (1987). Linking person and context in the daily stress process. *Journal of Personality and Social Psychology, 52*(1), 184–195.

Castro, K. G., Newcomb, M. D., McCreary, C., & Baezconde-Garbanati, L. (1989). Cigarette smokers do more than just smoke cigarettes. *Health Psychology, 8*(1), 107–129.

Catania, J. A., Coates, T. J., Stall, R., Turner, H., Peterson, J., Hearst, N., Dolcini, M. M., Hudes, E., Gagnon, J., Wiley, J., & Groves, R. (1992). Prevalence of AIDS-related risk factors and condom use in the United States. *Science, 258,* 1101–1106.

Catania, J. A., McDermott, L. J., & Pollack, L. M. (1986). Questionnaire response bias and face-to-face interview sample bias in sexuality research. *Journal of Sex Research, 22*(1), 52–72.

Cate, R. M., Huston, T. L., & Nesselroade, J. R. (1986). Premarital relationships: Toward the identification of alternative pathways to marriage. *Journal of Social and Clinical Psychology, 4,* 3–22.

Cattell, R. B. (1950). *Personality: A systematic, theoretical and factual study.* New York: McGraw-Hill.

Cattell, R. B. (1966). *The scientific analysis of personality.* Chicago: Aldine.

Cattell, R. B. (1990). Advances in Cattellian personality theory. In L. A. Pervin (Ed.), *Handbook of personality: Theory and research.* New York: Guilford Press.

Cattell, R. B., Eber, H. W., & Tatsuoka, M. M. (1970). *Handbook of the Sixteen Personality Factor Questionnaire (16PF).* Champaign, IL: Institute for Personality and Ability Testing.

Cattell, R. B., Kawash, G. F., & DeYoung, G. E. (1972). Validation of objective measures of ergic tension: Response of the sex erg to visual stimulation. *Journal of Experimental Research in Personality, 6,* 76–83.

Cermak, T. L. (1986). Diagnostic criteria for codependency. *Journal of Psychoactive Drugs, 18*(1), 15–20.

Cernovsky, Z. Z. (1989). Life stress measures and reported frequency of sleep disorders. In T. W. Miller (Ed.), *Stressful life events.* Madison, CT: International Universities Press.

Chaiken, S. (1979). Communicator's physical attractiveness and persuasion. *Journal of Personality and Social Psychology, 37,* 1387–1397.

Chaiken, S., & Baldwin, M. W. (1981). Affective-cognitive consistency and the effect of salient behavioral information on self-perception of attitudes. *Journal of Personality and Social Psychology, 41,* 1–12.

Chapman, B. E., & Brannock, J. C. (1987). A proposed model of lesbian identity development: An empirical investigation. *Journal of Homosexuality, 14*(3–4), 69–80.

Charlesworth, W. R., & Dzur, C. (1987). Gender comparisons of preschoolers' behavior and resource utilization in group problem-solving. *Child Development, 58,* 191–200.

Charness, N. (1985). Aging and problem-solving performance. In N. Charness (Ed.), *Aging and human performance.* Chichester, England: Wiley.

Chase-Lansdale, P. L. (1981). Maternal employment and quality of infant-mother and infant-father attachment (Doctoral dissertation, University of Michigan, 1981). *Dissertation Abstracts International, 42,* 2562B.

Chassin, L., Presson, C. C., Sherman, S. J., & Edwards, D. A. (1990). The natural history of cigarette smoking: Predicting young-adult smoking outcomes from adolescent smoking patterns. *Health Psychology, 9*(6), 701–716.

Check, J. V. P., Perlman, D., & Malamuth, N. M. (1985). Loneliness and aggressive behavior. *Journal of Social and Personal Relationships, 2,* 243–252.

Cheek, J. M., & Busch, C. M. (1981). The influence of shyness on loneliness in a new situation. *Personality and Social Psychology Bulletin, 7*(4), 572–577.

Cheek, J. M., & Buss, A. H. (1981). Shyness and sociability. *Journal of Personality and Social Psychology, 41,* 330–337.

Chelune, G. J. (1979). Measuring openness in interpersonal communication. In G. J. Chelune & associates (Eds.), *Self-disclosure: Origins, patterns, and implications of openness in interpersonal relationships.* San Francisco: Jossey-Bass.

Chelune, G. J. (1987). A neuropsychological perpective of interpersonal communication. In V. J. Derlega & J. H. Berg (Eds.), *Self-disclosure: Theory, research, and therapy.* New York: Plenum.

Cherlin, A. J. (1981). *Marriage, divorce, remarriage.* Cambridge, MA: Harvard University Press.

Cherry, F., & Deaux, K. (1978). Fear of success versus fear of gender-inappropriate behavior. *Sex Roles, 4,* 97–102.

Children's Safety Network. (1991). *A data book of child and adolescent injury.* Washington, DC: National Center for Education in Maternal and Child Health.

Chodorow, N. (1978). *The reproduction of mothering.* Berkeley, CA: University of California Press.

Christensen, A., & Heavey, C. L. (1990). Gender and social structure in the demand/withdraw pattern of marital conflict. *Journal of Personality and Social Psychology, 59,* 73–81.

Chumlea, W. C. (1982). Physical growth in adolescence. In B. B. Wolman (Ed.), *Handbook of developmental psychology.* Englewood Cliffs, NJ: Prentice–Hall.

Cialdini, R. B. (1993). *Influence: Science and practice* (3rd ed.). Glenview, IL: HarperCollins.

Cialdini, R. B., Vincent, J. E., Lewis, S. K., Catalan, J., Wheeler, D., & Darby, B. L. (1975). Reciprocal concessions procedure for inducing compliance: The door-in-the-face technique. *Journal of Personality and Social Psychology, 31,* 206–215.

Ciompi, L. (1980). Catamnestic long-term study on the course of life and aging in schizophrenics. *Schizophrenia Bulletin, 6,* 607–618.

Clanton, G. (1973). The contemporary experience of adultery: Bob and Carol and Updike and Rimmer. In R. W. Libby & R. N. Whitehurst (Eds.), *Renovating marriage.* Danville, CA: Consensus.

Clark, H. H. (1985). Language use and language users. In G. Lindzey & E. Aronson (Eds.), *The handbook of social psychology: Vol. 2. Special fields and applications.* New York: Random House.

Clark, L. A., & Watson, D. (1988). Mood and the mundane: Relations between daily life events and self-reported mood. *Journal of Personality and Social Psychology, 54*(2), 296–308.

Clark, M. S. (1984). Record-keeping in two types of relationships. *Journal of Personality and Social Psychology, 47,* 549–557.

Clark, M. S., & Mills, J. (1979). Interpersonal attraction in exchange and communal relationships. *Journal of Personality and Social Psychology, 37,* 12–24.

Clark, M. S., Mills, J., & Powell, M. C. (1986). Keeping track of needs in communal and exchange relationships. *Journal of Personality and Social Psychology, 51*(2), 333–338.

Clarke-Stewart, K. A., & Bailey, B. L. (1989). Adjusting to divorce: Why do men have it easier? *Journal of Divorce, 13*(2), 75–94.

Cleary, P. J. (1980). A checklist for life event research. *Journal of Psychosomatic Research, 24,* 199–207.

Cleek, M., & Pearson, T. (1985). Perceived causes of divorce: An analysis of interrelationships. *Journal of Marriage and the Family, 47,* 179–183.

Cobb, S., & Rose, R. M. (1973). Hypertension, peptic ulcer, and diabetes in air traffic controllers. *Journal of the American Medical Association, 224,* 489–492.

Cockerham, W. C. (1981). *Sociology of mental disorder.* Englewood Cliffs, NJ: Prentice-Hall.

Cocks, J. (1991, July 1). A nasty jolt for the top pops. *Time,* pp. 78–79.

Cocores, J. (1987). Co-addiction: A silent epidemic. *Psychiatry Letter, 5,* 5–8.

Cohen, F. (1979). Personality, stress and the development of physical illness. In G. C. Stone, F. Cohen, N. E. Adler, & associates (Eds.), *Health psychology—A handbook.* San Francisco: Jossey-Bass.

Cohen, S. (1980). *The substance abuse problem.* New York: Haworth Press.

Cohen, S. (1986). Marijuana. In A. J. Frances & R. E. Hales (Eds.), *Psychiatry Update: Annual Review* (Vol. 5). Washington, DC: American Psychiatric Press.

Cohen, S. (1988). Psychosocial models of the role of social support in the etiology of physical disease. *Health Psychology, 7*(3), 269–297.

Cohen, S., & Edwards, J. R. (1989). Personality characteristics as moderators of the relationship between stress and disorder. In R. W. J. Neufeld (Ed.), *Advances in the investigation of psychological stress.* New York: Wiley.

Cohen, S., Evans, G. W., Krantz, D. S., & Stokols, D. (1980). Physiological, motivational, and cognitive effects of aircraft noise on children: Moving from the laboratory to the field. *American Psychologist, 35,* 231–243.

Cohen, S., Glass, D. C., & Phillips, S. (1977). Environment and health. In H. E. Freeman, S. Levine, & L. G. Reeder (Eds.), *Handbook of medical sociology.* Englewood Cliffs, NJ: Prentice-Hall.

Cohen, S., Kamarck, T., & Mermelstein, R. (1983). A global measure of perceived stress. *Journal of Health and Social Behavior, 24,* 385–396.

Cohen, S., & Lichtenstein, E. (1990). Perceived stress, quitting smoking, and smoking relapse. *Health Psychology, 9*(4), 466–478.

Cohen, S., Lichtenstein, E., Prochaska, J. O., Rossi, J. S., Gritz, E. R., Carr, C. R.,

Orleans, C. T., Schoenbach, V. J., Biener, L., Abrams, D., DiClemente, C., Curry, S., Marlatt, G. A., Cummings, K. M., Emont, S. L., Giovino, A., & Ossip-Klein, D. (1989). Debunking myths about self-quitting: Evidence from 10 prospective studies of persons who attempt to quit smoking by themselves. *American Psychologist, 44*(11), 1355–1365.

Cohen, S., Sherrod, D., & Clark, M. (1986). Social skills and the stress-protective role of social support. *Journal of Personality and Social Psychology, 50*, 963–973.

Cohen, S., & Syme, S. L. (Eds.). (1985). *Social support and health.* New York: Academic Press.

Cohen, S., Tyrrell, D. A., & Smith, A. P. (1991). Psychological stress and susceptibility to the common cold. *New England Journal of Medicine, 325*(9), 606–612.

Cohen, S., & Wills, T. A. (1985). Stress, social support, and the buffering hypothesis. *Psychological Bulletin, 98*, 310–357.

Cohen, S. I., & Hajioff, J. (1972). Life events and the onset of acute closed-angle glaucoma. *Journal of Psychosomatic Research, 16*, 335–341.

Cohn, L. D., & Adler, N. E. (1992). Female and male perceptions of ideal body shapes: Distorted views among caucasian college students. *Psychology of Women Quarterly, 16*, 69–79.

Cohn, N. B., & Strassberg, D. S. (1983). Self-disclosure reciprocity among preadolescents. *Personality and Social Psychology Bulletin, 9*, 97–102.

Cole, J. O. (1988). The drug treatment of anxiety and depression. *Medical Clinics of North America, 72*(4), 815–830.

Cole, J. O., Goldberg, S. C., & Davis, J. M. (1966). Drugs in the treatment of psychosis. In P. Solomon (Ed.), *Psychiatric Drugs.* New York: Grune & Stratton.

Coleman, J. C. (1978). Current contradictions in adolescent theory. *Journal of Youth and Adolescence, 7*, 1–12.

Coleman, L. M., & Antonucci, T. C. (1983). Impact of work on women at midlife. *Developmental Psychology, 19*(2), 290–294.

Colgrove, M., Bloomfield, H., & McWilliams, P. (1984). *How to survive the loss of a love.* New York: Bantam Books.

Collins, N. L., & Read, S. J. (1990). Adult attachment, working models, and relationship quality in dating couples. *Journal of Personality and Social Psychology, 58*(4), 644–663.

Coltrane, S., & Ishii-Kuntz, M. (1992). Men's housework: A life course perspective. *Journal of Marriage and the Family, 54*, 43–57.

Commons, M. L., Richards, F. A., & Kuhn, D. (1982). Systematic and metasystematic reasoning: A case for levels of reasoning beyond Piaget's stage of formal operations. *Child Development, 53*, 1058–1069.

Condry, J. C., & Condry, S. (1976). Sex differences: A study of the eye of the beholder. *Child Development, 47*, 812–819.

Conger, R., Elder, G., Lorenz, F., Conger, K., Simons, R., Whitbeck, L., Huck, S., & Melby, J. (1990). Linking economic hardship to marital quality and instability. *Journal of Marriage and the Family, 52*, 643–656.

Conley, J. J. (1985). Longitudinal stability of personality traits: A multitrait-multi-method-multioccasion analysis. *Journal of Personality and Social Psychology, 49*(5), 1266–1282.

Cook, E. P. (1985). *Psychological androgyny.* New York: Pergamon Press.

Cook, M., & Mineka, S. (1989). Observational conditioning of fear to fear-relevant versus fear-irrelevant stimuli in Rhesus monkeys. *Journal of Abnormal Psychology, 98*(4), 448–459.

Cooper, C. L. (1984). The social-psychological precursors to cancer. *Journal of Human Stress, 10*(1), 4–11.

Cooper, H. M. (1979). Statistically combining independent studies: A meta-analysis of sex differences in conformity research. *Journal of Personality and Social Psychology, 37*, 131–146.

Coopersmith, S. (1967). *The antecedents of self-esteem.* San Francisco: W. H. Freeman.

Coopersmith, S. (1975). Studies in self-esteem. In R. C. Atkinson (Ed.), *Psychology in progress: Readings from Scientific American.* San Francisco: W. H. Freeman.

Costa, P. T., & McCrae, R. R. (1986). Personality stability and its implications for clinical psychology. *Clinical Psychology Review, 6*, 407–423.

Cottrell, N. B. (1972). Social facilitation. In C. G. McClintock (Ed.), *Experimental social psychology.* New York: Holt, Rinehart & Winston.

Cottrell, N. B., Wack, K. L., Sekerak, G. J., & Rittle, R. (1968). Social facilitation of dominant responses by the presence of an audience and the mere presence of others. *Journal of Personality and Social Psychology, 9*, 245–250.

Covi, L., & Primakoff, L. (1988). Cognitive group therapy. In A. J. Frances & R. E. Hales (Eds.), *Review of psychiatry* (Vol. 7). Washington, DC: American Psychiatric Association.

Cowan, C., & Kinder, M. (1987). *Women men love—women men leave.* New York: New American Library.

Cox, F. D. (1979). *Human intimacy: Marriage, the family, and its meaning.* St. Paul, MN: West.

Cox, T., & Mackay, C. (1982). Psychosocial factors and psychophysiological mechanisms in the etiology and development of cancer. *Social Science and Medicine, 16*, 381–396.

Coyle, J. T., Price, D. L., & DeLong, M. R. (1983). Alzheimer's disease: A disorder of cortical cholinergic innervation. *Science, 219*, 1184–1190.

Coyne, J. C. (1976). Depression and the response of others. *Journal of Abnormal Psychology, 85*, 186–193.

Coyne, J. C., Burchill, S. A. L., & Stiles, W. B. (1990). An interactional perspective on depression. In C. R. Snyder & D. R. Forsyth (Eds.), *Handbook of social and clinical psychology: The health perspective.* New York: Pergamon Press.

Cozby, P. C. (1973). Self-disclosure: A literature review. *Psychological Bulletin, 79*, 73–91.

Crane, P. T. (1985). Voluntary childlessness: Some notes on the decision-making process. In D. B. Gutknecht & E. W. Butler (Eds.), *Family, self, and society: Emerging issues, alternatives, and interventions* (2nd ed.). New York: UPA.

Creed, F. (1989). Appendectomy. In G. W. Brown & T. O. Harris (Eds.), *Life events and illness.* New York: Guilford Press.

Cregler, L. L., & Mark, H. (1986). Medical complications of cocaine abuse. *New England Journal of Medicine, 315*(23), 1495–1500.

Crites, J. O. (1980). Career development. In J. F. Adams (Ed.), *Understanding adolescence: Current developments in adolescent psychology* (4th ed.). Boston: Allyn & Bacon.

Crook, R. H., Healy, C. C., & O'Shay, D. W. (1984). The linkage of work achievement to self-esteem, career maturity, and college achievement. *Journal of Vocational Behavior, 25*, 70–79.

Crooks, R., & Baur, K. (1983). *Our sexuality* (2nd ed.). Menlo Park, CA: Benjamin/ Cummings.

Crooks, R., & Baur, K. (1990). *Our sexuality* (4th ed.). Menlo Park, CA: Benjamin/Cummings.

Crosby, P. (1980). A critique of divorce statistics and their interpretation. *Family Relations, 29*, 51–58.

Cross, C. K., & Hirschfeld, R. M. A. (1986). Epidemiology of disorders in adulthood: Suicide. In G. L. Klerman, M. M. Weissman, P. S. Appelbaum, & L. H. Roth (Eds.), *Psychiatry: Vol. 5. Social, epidemiologic, and legal psychiatry.* New York: Basic Books.

Crovitz, H. F. (1971). The capacity of memory loci in artificial memory. *Psychonomic Science, 24*, 187–188.

Crowe, R. (1983). Antisocial personality disorder. In R. Tarter (Ed.), *The child at psychiatric risk.* New York: Oxford University Press.

Crowe, R. R. (1988). Family and twin studies of panic disorders and agoraphobia. In M. Roth, R. Noyes, & G. D. Burrows (Eds.), *Handbook of anxiety: Biological, clinical, and cultural perspectives.* (Vol. 1). Amsterdam: Elsevier.

Crozier, W. R. (1981). Shyness and self-esteem. *British Journal of Social Psychology, 20*, 220–222.

Crull, P. (1979). *The impact of sexual harassment on the job: A profile of the experiences of 92 women.* Working Women's Research Series, Report No. 3.

Csikszentmihalyi, M., & Kleiber, D. A. (1991). Leisure and self-actualization. In B. C. Drirer, P. J. Brown, & G. L. Peterson (Eds.), *Benefits of leisure.* State College, PA: Venture.

Csikszentmihalyi, M., & Kubey, R. (1981). Television and the rest of life. *Public Opinion Quarterly, 45*, 317–328.

Culp, R. E., Cook, A. S., & Housley, P. C. (1983). A comparison of observed and reported adult-infant interactions: Effects of perceived sex. *Sex Roles, 9*, 475–479.

Cumming, E. (1963). Further thoughts on the theory of disengagement. *International Social Science Journal, 15*, 377–393.

Cumming, E. (1975). Engagement with an old theory. *International Journal of Aging and Human Development, 15*, 187–191.

Cumming, E., & Henry, W. (1961). *Growing old: The process of disengagement.* New York: Basic Books.

Cunningham, J. A., Strassberg, D. S., & Haan, B. (1986). Effects of intimacy and sex-role congruency on self-disclosure. *Journal of Social and Clinical Psychology, 4,* 393–401.

Cunningham, J. D. (1981). Self-disclosure intimacy: Sex, sex of target, cross-national, and "generational" differences. *Personality and Social Psychology Bulletin, 7*(2), 314–319.

Curran, D. K. (1987). *Adolescent suicidal behavior.* Washington, DC: Hemisphere.

Cutrona, C. E. (1982). Transition to college: Loneliness and the process of social adjustment. In L. A. Peplau & D. Perlman (Eds.), *Loneliness: A sourcebook of current theory, research, and therapy.* New York: Wiley.

Cutrona, C. E. (1990). Stress and social support—In search of optimal matching. *Journal of Social and Clinical Psychology, 9*(1), 3–14.

Cvetkovich, G., Grote, B., Bjorseth, A., & Sarkissian, J. (1975). On the psychology of adolescent use of contraception. *Journal of Sex Research, 11,* 256–270.

D'Andrade, R. G. (1966). Sex differences and cultural institutions. In E. Maccoby (Ed.), *The development of sex differences.* Stanford, CA: Stanford University Press.

Dambrot, F. H., Papp, M. E., & Whitmore, C. (1984). The sex-role attitudes of three generations of women. *Personality and Social Psychology Bulletin, 10*(3), 469–473.

Dan, A. J. (1976). Patterns of behavioral and mood variation in men and women: Variability and the menstrual cycle. *Dissertation Abstracts International, 37*(6–B), 3145–3146.

Daniels, D., & Plomin, R. (1985). Origins of individual differences in infant shyness. *Developmental Psychology, 21,* 118–121.

Danziger, N. (1983). Sex-related differences in the aspirations of high school students. *Sex Roles, 9,* 683–695.

Darley, J. M., & Gross, P. H. (1983). A hypothesis-confirming bias in labeling effects. *Journal of Personality and Social Psychology, 44,* 20–33.

Darley, J. M., & Latané, B. (1968). Bystander intervention in emergencies: Diffusion of responsibility. *Journal of Personality and Social Psychology, 8,* 377–383.

Datan, N., Rodeheaver, D., & Hughes, F. (1987). Adult development and aging. *Annual Review of Psychology, 38,* 153–180.

Datan, N., & Thomas, J. (1984). Late adulthood: Love, work, and the normal transitions. In D. Offer & M. Sabshin (Eds.), *Normality and the life cycle.* New York: Basic Books.

Dattore, P. J., Shontz, F. C., & Coyne, L. (1980). Premorbid personality differentiation of cancer and noncancer groups: A list of the hypotheses of cancer proneness. *Journal of Consulting and Clinical Psychology, 48,* 388–394.

Davenport, W. (1977). Sex in cross-cultural perspective. In F. A. Beach (Ed.), *Human sexuality in four perspectives.* Baltimore: Johns Hopkins University Press.

Davidson, J. (1976). Physiology of meditation and mystical states of consciousness. *Perspectives in Biology and Medicine, 19,* 345–380.

Davidson, J. (1985). The utilization of sexual fantasies by sexually experienced university students. *Journal of American College Health, 34*(1), 24–32.

Davidson, J. (1988). *The agony of it all.* Los Angeles: J. P. Tarcher.

Davidson, L. R., & Duberman, L. (1982). Friendship: Communication and interactional patterns in same-sex dyads. *Sex Roles, 8,* 809–822.

Davidson, M., Losonczy, M. F., & Davis, K. L. (1986). Biological hypotheses of schizophrenia. In P. A. Berger & H. K. H. Brodie (Eds.), *American handbook of psychiatry: Vol. 8. Biological psychiatry* (2nd ed.). New York: Basic Books.

Davidson, P. O. (1982). Issues in patient compliance. In T. Millon, G. Green, & R. Meagher (Eds.), *Handbook of clinical health psychology.* New York: Plenum.

Davis, J. A. (1966). The campus as a frog pond. *American Journal of Sociology, 72,* 17–31.

Davis, J. M. (1985). Antipsychotic drugs. In H. I. Kaplan & B. J. Sadock (Eds.), *Comprehensive textbook of psychiatry/IV.* Baltimore: Williams & Wilkins.

Davis, J. M., & Glassman, A. H. (1989). Antidepressant drugs. In H. I. Kaplan & B. J. Sadock (Eds.), *Comprehensive textbook of psychiatry/V.* Baltimore: Williams & Wilkins.

Davis, J. M., Barter, J. T., & Kane, J. M. (1989). Antipsychotic drugs. In H. I. Kaplan & B. J. Sadock (Eds.), *Comprehensive textbook of psychiatry/V.* Baltimore: Williams & Wilkins.

Davis, K. E. (1985, February). Near and dear: Friendship and love compared. *Psychology Today,* pp. 22–30.

Davis, K. L., Kahn, R. S., Ko, G., & Davidson, M. (1991). Dopamine in schizophrenia: A review and reconceptualization. *American Journal of Psychiatry, 148,* 1474–1486.

Davis, L. (1990) *The courage to heal workbook for women and men survivors of child sexual abuse.* New York: HarperCollins.

Davis, M. H., & Franzoi, S. L. (1986). Adolescent loneliness, self-disclosure, and private self-consciousness: A longitudinal investigation. *Journal of Personality and Social Psychology, 51,* 595–608.

Deaux, K. (1972). To err is humanizing: But sex makes a difference. *Representative Research in Social Psychology, 3,* 20–28.

Deaux, K. (1976). *The behavior of women and men.* Pacific Grove, CA: Brooks/Cole.

Deaux, K., & Hanna, R. (1984). Courtship in the personals column: The influence of gender and sexual orientation. *Sex Roles, 11,* 363–375.

DeBuono, B. A., Zinner, S. H., Daamen, M., & McCormack, W. M. (1990). Sexual behavior of college women in 1975, 1986, and 1989. *New England Journal of Medicine, 322,* 821–825.

DeJong, W. (1979). An examination of self-perception mediation in the foot-in-the-door effect. *Journal of Personality and Social Psychology, 37,* 2221–2239.

DeLamater, J. (1987). A sociological perspective. In J. H. Geer & W. T. O'Donohue (Eds.), *Theories of human sexuality.* New York: Plenum.

Delay, J., & Deniker, P. (1952). *Trente-huit cas de psychoses traitées par la cure prolongée et continué de 4560 RP.* Paris: Masson et Cie.

DeLongis, A., Folkman, S., & Lazarus, R. S. (1988). The impact of daily stress on health and mood: Psychological and social resources as mediators. *Journal of Personality and Social Psychology, 54*(3), 486–495.

Demo, D. H. (1992). Parent-child relations: Assessing recent changes. *Journal of Marriage and the Family, 54,* 104–117.

Demo, D. H., & Acock, A. C. (1988). The impact of divorce on children. *Journal of Marriage and the Family, 50,* 619–648.

Dennis, W. (1966). Creative productivity between the ages of 20 and 80 years. *Journal of Gerontology, 21,* 1–8.

Denny, N., Field, J., & Quadagno, D. (1984). Sex differences in sexual needs and desires. *Archives of Sexual Behavior, 13,* 233–245.

DePaulo, B. M., Lanier, K., & Davis, T. (1983). Detecting the deceit of the motivated liar. *Journal of Personality and Social Psychology, 45*(5), 1096–1103.

DePaulo, B. M., LeMay, C. S., & Epstein, J. A. (1991). Effects of importance of success and expectations for success on effectiveness at deceiving. *Personality and Social Psychology Bulletin, 17*(1), 14–24.

DePaulo, B. M., Stone, J., & Lassiter, G. D. (1985). Deceiving and detecting deceit. In B. R. Schlenker (Ed.), *The self and social life.* New York: McGraw-Hill.

Derlega, V. J., & Chaikin, A. L. (1975). *Sharing intimacy: What we reveal to others and why.* Englewood Cliffs, NJ: Prentice-Hall.

Derlega, V. J., & Grezlak, J. (1979). Appropriateness of self-disclosure. In G. J. Chelune & associates (Eds.), *Self-disclosure: Origins, patterns, and implications of openness in interpersonal relationships.* San Francisco: Jossey-Bass.

Derlega, V. J., Wilson, M., & Chaikin, A. L. (1976). Friendship and disclosure reciprocity. *Journal of Personality and Social Psychology, 34,* 578–587.

Derlega, V. J., Winstead, B. A., Wong, P. T. P., & Greenspan, M. (1987). Self-disclosure and relationship development: An attributional analysis. In M. E. Roloff & G. R. Miller (Eds.), *Interpersonal processes: New directions in communication research.* Newbury Park, CA: Sage Publications.

Derlega, V. J., Winstead, B. A., Wong, P. T. P., & Hunter, S. (1985). Gender effects in an initial encounter: A case where men exceed women in disclosure. *Journal of Social and Personal Relationships, 2,* 25–44.

Derogatis, L. R. (1982). Self-report measures of stress. In L. Goldberger & S. Breznitz (Eds.), *Handbook of stress: Theoretical and clinical aspects.* New York: Free Press.

Derogatis, L. R. (1987). The Derogatis Stress Profile (DSP): Quantification of psychological stress. *Advances in Psychosomatic Medicine, 17,* 30–54.

Des Jarlais, D. C., Friedman, S. R., Woods, J., & Milliken, J. (1992). HIV infection among intravenous drug users: Epidemiology and emerging public health perspectives. In J. H. Lowinson, P. Ruiz, & R. B. Millman (Eds.), *Substance abuse: A comprehensive textbook* (2nd ed.). Baltimore: Williams & Wilkins.

Deutsch, M., & Gerard, H. B. (1955). A study of normative and informational social influences upon individual judgment. *Journal of Abnormal and Social Psychology, 51,* 629–636.

Diamond, E. E. (1979). Sex equality and measurement practices. *New Directions for Testing and Measurement, 3,* 61–78.

Diamond, M., & Karlen, A. (1981). The sexual response cycle. In H. I. Lief (Ed.), *Sexual problems in medical practice.* Chicago: American Medical Association.

Dickens, W. J., & Perlman, D. (1981). Friendship over the life-cycle. In S. Duck & R. Gilmour (Eds.), *Personal relationships* (Vol. 2). New York: Academic Press.

Diedrick, P. (1991). Gender differences in divorce adjustment. *Journal of Divorce and Remarriage, 14,* 33–45.

Diener, E. (1984). Subjective well-being. *Psychological Bulletin, 93,* 542–575.

Diener, F. (1980). Deindividuation: The absence of self-awareness and self-regulation in group members. In P. B. Paulus (Ed.), *Psychology of group influence.* Hillsdale, NJ: Erlbaum.

Di Leonardo, M. (1987). The female world of cards and holidays: Women, families, and the work of kinship. *Signs, 12,* 440–453.

Dillard, J. P. (1991). The current status of research on sequential-request compliance techniques. *Personality and Social Psychology Bulletin, 17*(3), 283–288.

DiMatteo, M. R. (1991). *The psychology of health, illness, and medical care: An individual perspective.* Pacific Grove, CA: Brooks/Cole.

DiMatteo, M. R., & DiNicola, D. D. (1982). *Achieving patient compliance: The psychology of the medical practitioner's role.* New York: Pergamon Press.

DiMatteo, M. R., & Friedman, H. S. (1982). *Social psychology and medicine.* Cambridge, MA: Oelgeschlager, Gunn & Hain.

Dimsdale, J. E. (1988). A perspective on Type A behavior and coronary disease. *New England Journal of Medicine, 318*(2), 110–112.

Dindia, K., & Fitzpatrick, M. A. (1985). Marital communication: Three approaches compared. In S. Duck & D. Perlman (Eds.), *Understanding personal relationships: An interdisciplinary approach.* London: Sage Publications.

DiNicola, D. D., & DiMatteo, M. R. (1984). Practitioners, patients, and compliance with medical regimens: A social psychological perspective. In A. Baum, S. E. Taylor, & J. E. Singer (Eds.), *Handbook of psychology and health: Vol. 4. Social psychological aspects of health.* Hillsdale, NJ: Erlbaum.

Dion, K. K. (1986). Stereotyping based on physical attractiveness: Issues and conceptual perspectives. In C. P. Herman, M. P. Zanna, & E. T. Higgins (Eds.), *Appearance, stigma and social behavior: The Ontario symposium on personality and social psychology* (Vol. 3). Hillsdale, NJ: Erlbaum.

Dion, K. K., Berscheid, E., & Walster, E. (1972). What is beautiful is good. *Journal of Personality and Social Psychology, 24,* 285–290.

Dion, K. L., & Dion, K. K. (1988). Romantic love: Individual and cultural perspectives. In R. J. Sternberg & M. L. Barnes (Eds.), *The psychology of love.* New Haven, CT: Yale University Press.

Dishotsky, N. I., Loughman, W. D., Mogar, R. E., & Lipscomb, W. R. (1971). LSD and genetic damage: Is LSD chromosome damaging, carcinogenic, mutagenic, or teratogenic. *Science, 172,* 431–440.

Dixon, N. F. (1980). Humor: A cognitive alternative to stress? In I. G. Sarason & C. D. Spielberger (Eds.), *Stress and anxiety* (Vol. 7). Washington, DC: Hemisphere.

Dobbins, G. H., Cardy, R. L., & Truxillo, D. M. (1986). Effects of ratee sex and purpose of appraisal on the accuracy of performance evaluations. *Basic and Applied Social Psychology, 7,* 225–241.

Dobbins, G. H., Cardy, R. L., & Truxillo, D. M. (1988). The effects of purpose of appraisal and individual differences in stereotypes of women on sex differences in performance ratings: A laboratory and field study. *Journal of Applied Psychology, 73,* 551–558.

Doerr, P., Pirke, K. M., Kockott, G., & Dittmor, F. (1976). Further studies on sex hormones in male homosexuals. *Archives of General Psychiatry, 33,* 611–614.

Dohrenwend, B. S., & Dohrenwend, B. P. (1981). Life stress and illness: Formulation of the issues. In B. S. Dohrenwend & B. P. Dohrenwend (Eds.), *Stressful life events and their contexts.* New York: Prodist.

Dohrenwend, B. S., Krasnoff, L., Askenasy, A. R., & Dohrenwend, B. P. (1978). Exemplification of a method for scaling life events: The PERI life events scale. *Journal of Health and Social Behavior, 19,* 205–229.

Dollard, J., Doob, L. W., Miller, N. E., Mowrer, O. H., & Sears, R. R. (1939). *Frustration and aggression.* New Haven, CT: Yale University Press.

Dollard, J., & Miller, N. E. (1950). *Personality and psychotherapy: An analysis in terms of learning, thinking and culture.* New York: McGraw-Hill.

Donnerstein, E., & Linz, D. (1984, January). Sexual violence in the media: A warning. *Psychology Today,* pp. 14–15.

Donovan, R. L., & Jackson, B. L. (1990). Deciding to divorce: A process guided by social exchange, attachment and cognitive dissonance theories. *Journal of Divorce, 13*(4), 23–35.

Dorner, G. (1988). Neuroendocrine response to estrogen and brain differentiation in heterosexuals, homosexuals, and transsexuals. *Archives of Sexual Behavior, 17*(1), 57–75.

Dosser, D. A., Jr., Balswick, J. O., & Halverson, C. F., Jr. (1986). Male inexpressiveness and relationships. *Journal of Social and Personal Relationships, 3,* 241–258.

Douthitt, R. A. (1989). The division of labor within the home: Have gender roles changed? *Sex Roles, 20,* 693–704.

Douvan, E., & Adelson, J. (1966). *The adolescent experience.* New York: Wiley.

Dovidio, J. F., & Gaertner, S. L. (Eds.). (1986). *Prejudice, discrimination, and racism.* New York: Academic Press.

Doyle, J. A. (1989). *The male experience.* Dubuque, IA: William C. Brown.

Doyle, J. A., & Paludi, M. A. (1991). *Sex and gender.* Dubuque, IA: William C. Brown.

Drachman, D. A. (1986). Memory and cognitive function in normal aging. *Developmental Neuropsychology, 2,* 277–285.

Dreyer, P. H. (1982). Sexuality during adolescence. In B. B. Wolman (Ed.), *Handbook of developmental psychology.* Englewood Cliffs, NJ: Prentice-Hall.

Duck, S. (1983). *Friends for life: The psychology of close relationships.* New York: St. Martin's Press.

Duffy, S. M., & Rusbult, C. E. (1985/1986). Satisfaction and commitment in homosexual and heterosexual relationships. *Journal of Homosexuality, 12*(2), 1–23.

Duke, M., & Nowicki, S., Jr. (1979). *Abnormal psychology: Perspectives on being different.* Pacific Grove, CA: Brooks/Cole.

Duncan, B. L. (1976). Differential social perception and attribution of intergroup violence: Testing the lower limits of stereotyping of blacks. *Journal of Personality and Social Psychology, 34,* 590–598.

Dunn, M. E., & Trost, J. E. (1989). Male multiple orgasms: A descriptive study. *Archives of Sexual Behavior, 18*(5), 377–387.

Dunning, D., & Story, A. L. (1991). Depression, realism, and the overconfidence effect: Are the sadder wiser when predicting future actions and events? *Journal of Personality and Social Psychology, 61*(4), 521–532.

Dusek, J. B., & Flaherty, J. F. (1981). The development of the self-concept during the adolescent years. *Monographs of the Society for Research in Child Development, 46*(4, Serial No. 191).

Dutton, D. G., & Aron, A. P. (1974). Some evidence for heightened sexual attraction under conditions of high anxiety. *Journal of Personality and Social Psychology, 30*(4), 510–517.

Duxbury, L. E., & Higgins, C. A. (1991). Gender differences in work-family conflict. *Journal of Applied Psychology, 76*(1), 60–74.

Dweck, C. S., Davidson, W., Nelson, S., & Enna, B. (1978). Sex differences in learned helplessness: II. The contingencies of evaluative feedback in the classroom, and III. An experimental analysis. *Developmental Psychology, 14,* 268–276.

Dyer, W. W. (1976). *Your erroneous zones.* New York: Thomas Y. Crowell.

Dziech, B. W., & Weiner, L. (1990). *The lecherous professor: Sexual harassment on campus.* Urbana, IL: University of Illinois Press.

D'Zurilla, T. J., & Sheedy, C. F. (1991). Relation between social problem-solving ability and subsequent level of psychological stress in college students. *Journal of Personality and Social Psychology, 61*(5), 841–846.

Eagle, M. N., & Wolitzky, D. L. (1992). Psychoanalytic theories of psychotherapy. In D. K. Freedheim (Ed.), *History of psychotherapy: A century of change.* Washington, DC: American Psychological Association.

Eagly, A. H. (1978). Sex differences in influenceability. *Psychological Bulletin, 85,* 86–116.

Eagly, A. H. (1983). Gender and social influence: A social-psychological analysis. *American Psychologist, 38,* 971–981.

Eagly, A. H. (1987). *Sex differences in social behavior: A social-role interpretation.* Hillsdale, NJ: Erlbaum.

Eagly, A. H., Ashmore, R. D., Makhijani, M. G., & Longo, L. C. (1991). What is beautiful is good, but . . . : A meta-analytic review of research on the physical attractiveness stereotype. *Psychology Bulletin, 110,* 107–128.

Eagly, A. H., & Carli, L. L. (1981). Sex of researchers and sex-typed communications as determinants of sex differences in influenceability: A meta-analysis of social influence studies. *Psychological Bulletin, 90,* 1–20.

Eagly, A. H., & Johnson, B. T. (1990). Gender and leadership style: A meta-analysis. *Psychological Bulletin, 108*(2), 233–256.

Eagly, A. H., & Whitehead, G. I. (1972). Effect of choice on receptivity to favorable and unfavorable evaluations of one's self. *Journal of Personality and Social Psychology, 22,* 223–230.

Eagly, A. H., & Wood, W. (1982). Inferred sex differences in status as a determinant of gender stereotypes about social influence. *Journal of Personality and Social Psychology, 43,* 915–928.

Eagly, A. H., & Wood, W. (1985). Gender and influenceability: Stereotype versus behavior. In V. O'Leary, R. Unger, & B. Wallston (Eds.), *Women, gender and social psychology.* Hillsdale, NJ: Erlbaum.

Eagly, A. H., & Wood, W. (1991). Explaining sex differences in social behavior: A meta-analytic perspective. *Personality and Social Psychology Bulletin, 17*(3), 306–315.

Eagly, A. H., Wood, W., & Chaiken, S. (1978). Causal inferences about communicators and their effect on opinion change. *Journal of Personality and Social Psychology, 36,* 424–435.

Earle, J. R., & Perricone, P. J. (1986). Premarital sexuality: A ten-year study of attitudes and behavior on a small university campus. *Journal of Sex Research, 22*(3), 304–310.

Easterbrooks, M. A., & Goldberg, W. A. (1985). Effects of early maternal employment on toddlers, mothers, and fathers. *Developmental Psychology, 21,* 774–783.

Eaton, W. W., Dryman, A., & Weissman, M. M. (1991). Panic and phobia. In L. N. Robins & D. A. Regier (Eds.), *Psychiatric disorders in America: The epidemiologic catchment area study.* New York: Free Press.

Ebbinghaus, H. (1885/1964). Memory: A contribution to experimental psychology. In H. A. Ruger & E. R. Bussemius (Trans.), New York: Dover. (Original work published, 1885).

Eccles, J. S. (1989). Bringing young women to math and science. In M. Crawford & M. Gentry (Eds.), *Gender and thought.* New York: Springer-Verlag.

Edelman, R. J., & Hampson, S. E. (1981). Embarrassment in dyadic interaction. *Social Behavior and Personality, 9,* 171–177.

Efran, J. S., Lukens, M. D., & Lukens, R. J. (1986). It's all done with mirrors. *Family Therapy Networker, 10*(2), 41–49.

Egan, G. (1990). *The skilled helper: A systematic approach to effective helping.* Pacific Grove, CA: Brooks/Cole.

Egan, K. J., Kogan, H. N., Garber, A., & Jarrett, M. (1983). The impact of psychological distress on the control of hypertension. *Journal of Human Stress, 9*(4), 4–10.

Ehrenberg, O., & Ehrenberg, M. (1986). *The psychotherapy maze.* Northvale, NJ: Aronson.

Ehrhart, J. K., & Sandler, B. R. (1985). *Campus gang rape: Party games?* Washington, DC: Association of American Colleges.

Eichhorst, B. C. (1988). Contraception. *Primary Care, 15*(3), 437–459.

Eisen, M., & Zellman, G. L. (1987). Changes in incidence of sexual intercourse of unmarried teenagers following a community-based sex education program. *Journal of Sex Research, 23*(4), 527–544.

Ekman, P. (1975, September). The universal smile: Face muscles talk every language. *Psychology Today,* pp. 35–39.

Ekman, P. (1992). Facial expressions of emotion: New findings, new questions. *Psychological Science, 3*(1), 34–38.

Ekman, P., & Friesen, W. V. (1984). *Unmasking the face.* Palo Alto, CA: Consulting Psychologists Press.

Ekman, P., & Friesen, W. V. (1986). A new pan-cultural facial expression of emotion. *Motivation and Emotion, 10*(2), 159–168.

Ekman, P., Friesen, W. V., & Ellsworth, P. (1982). What emotion categories or dimensions can observers judge from facial behavior? In P. Ekman (Ed.), *Emotion in the human face* (2nd ed.). Cambridge, MA: Cambridge University Press.

Ekman, P., Friesen, W. V., O'Sullivan, M., Chan, A., Diacoyanni-Tarlatzis, I., Heider, K., Krause, R., LeCompte, W. A., Pitcairn, T., Ricci-Bitti, P. E., Scherer, K. R., Tomita, M., & Tzavaras, A. (1987). Universals and cultural differences in the judgments of facial expressions of emotion. *Journal of Personality and Social Psychology, 53,* 712–717.

Eliot, R. S., & Breo, D. L. (1984). *Is it worth dying for?* New York: Bantam Books.

Eliot, R. S., & Breo, D. L. (1989). *Is it worth dying for?* New York: Bantam Books.

Elkind, D. (1967). Egocentrism in adolescence. *Child Development, 38,* 1025–1034.

Elkind, D. (1988). *The hurried child: Growing up too fast, too soon.* Reading, MA: Addison-Wesley.

Elliott, G. R., & Eisdorfer, C. (Eds.). (1982). *Stress and human health: Analysis and implications of research.* New York: Springer.

Ellis, A. (1973). *Humanistic psychotherapy: The rational-emotive approach.* New York: Julian Press.

Ellis, A. (1977). *Reason and emotion in psychotherapy.* Seacaucus, NJ: Lyle Stuart.

Ellis, A. (1984). *Reason and emotion in psychotherapy.* Seacaucus, NJ: Lyle Stuart.

Ellis, A. (1985). *How to live with and without anger.* New York: Citadel Press.

Ellis, A. (1987). The evolution of rational-emotive therapy (RET) and cognitive behavior therapy (CBT). In J. K. Zeig (Ed.), *The evolution of psychotherapy.* New York: Brunner/Mazel.

Ellis, A. (1988). *How to stubbornly refuse to make yourself miserable about anything—yes, anything!* Seacaucus, NJ: Lyle Stuart.

Ellis, A. (1989). Rational-emotive therapy. In R. J. Corsini & D. Wedding (Eds.), *Current Psychotherapies.* Itasca, IL: F. E. Peacock.

Ellis, L. (1987). Relationships of criminality and psychopathy with eight other apparent behavioral manifestations of sub-optimal arousal. *Personality and Individual Differences, 8*(6), 905–925.

Ellsworth, P. C., Carlsmith, J. M., & Henson, A. (1972). The stare as a stimulus to flight in human subjects: A series of field experiments. *Journal of Personality and Social Psychology, 21,* 302–311.

Emanuel, H. M. (1987). Put time on your side. In A. D. Timpe (Ed.), *The management of time.* New York: Facts On File.

Emerson, G. (1985). *Some American men.* New York: Simon & Schuster.

Emmelkamp, P. M. (1986). Behavior therapy with adults. In S. L. Garfield & A. E. Bergin (Eds.), *Handbook of psychotherapy and behavior change.* New York: Wiley.

Emmons, R. A., & King, L. A. (1988). Conflict among personal strivings: Immediate and long-term implications for psychological and physical well-being. *Journal of Personality and Social Psychology, 54*(6), 1040–1048.

Engel, J. W., & Saracino, M. (1986). Love preferences and ideals: A comparison of homosexual, bisexual, and heterosexual groups. *Contemporary Family Therapy, 8*(3), 241–250.

Enright, R. D., Shukla, D. G., & Lapsley, D. K. (1980). Adolescent egocentrism, sociocentrism and self-consciousness. *Journal of Youth and Adolescence, 9*(2), 101–116.

Epstein, S. P. (1982). Conflict and stress. In L. Goldberger & S. Breznitz (Eds.), *Handbook of stress: Theoretical and clinical aspects.* New York: Free Press.

Epstein, S. P. (1983). Natural healing processes of the mind: Graded stress inoculation as an inherent coping mechanism. In D. H. Meichenbaum & M. E. Jaremko (Eds.), *Stress reduction and prevention.* New York: Plenum.

Epstein, S. P. (1990). Cognitive-experiential self-theory. In L. A. Pervin (Ed.), *Handbook of personality: Theory and research.* New York: Guilford Press.

Epstein, S. P., & Katz, L. (1992). Coping ability, stress, productive load, and symptoms. *Journal of Personality and Social Psychology, 62*(5), 813–825.

Epstein, S. P., & Meier, P. (1989). Constructive thinking: A broad coping variable with specific components. *Journal of Personality and Social Psychology, 57*(2), 332–350.

Erdwins, C. J., & Mellinger, J. C. (1984). Mid-life women: Relation of age and role to personality. *Journal of Personality and Social Psychology, 47,* 390–395.

Erikson, E. H. (1963). *Childhood and society.* New York: Norton.

Erikson, E. H. (1968). *Identity: Youth and crisis.* New York: Norton.

Ernst, C., & Angst, J. (1983). Birth order: Its influence on personality. *Behavioral and Brain Sciences, 10*(1), 55.

Etaugh, C. F., & Harlow, H. (1975). Behaviors of male and female teachers as related to behaviors and attitudes of elementary school children. *Journal of Genetic Psychology, 127,* 163–170.

Evans, R. L. (1981). New drug evaluations: Alprazolam. *Drug Intelligence and Clinical Pharmacy, 15,* 633–637.

Exline, R. V. (1963). Explorations in the process of person perception: Visual interaction in relation to competition, sex, and the need for affiliation. *Journal of Personality, 31,* 1–20.

Eysenck, H. J. (1952). The effects of psychotherapy: An evaluation. *Journal of Consulting Psychology, 16,* 319–324.

Eysenck, H. J. (1959). Learning theory and behaviour therapy. *Journal of Mental Science, 195,* 61–75.

Eysenck, H. J. (1967). *The biological basis of personality*. Springfield, IL: Charles C. Thomas.

Eysenck, H. J. (1976). *Sex and personality*. London: Open Books.

Eysenck, H. J. (1982). *Personality, genetics and behavior: Selected papers*. New York: Praeger.

Eysenck, H. J. (1988, December). Health's character. *Psychology Today*, pp. 28–35.

Eysenck, H. J. (1990). Biological dimensions of personality. In L. A. Pervin (Ed.), *Handbook of personality: Theory and research*. New York: Guilford Press.

Eysenck, H. J., & Eysenck, S. B. G. (1969). *Personality structure and measurement*. San Diego, CA: EDITS.

Eysenck, H. J., & Levey, A. (1972). Conditioning, introversion-extraversion and the strength of the nervous system. In V. D. Nebylitsyn & J. A. Gray (Eds.), *Biological bases of individual behavior*. New York: Academic Press.

Fagley, N. S. (1987). Positional response bias in multiple-choice tests of learning: Its relation to testwiseness and guessing strategy. *Journal of Educational Psychology, 79*(1), 95–97.

Fagot, B. I. (1978). The influence of sex of child on parental reactions to toddler children. *Child Development, 49*, 459–465.

Fagot, B. I. (1981). Stereotypes versus behavioral judgments of sex differences in young children. *Sex Roles, 7*, 1093–1096.

Fagot, B. I. (1985). Changes in thinking about early sex role development. *Developmental Review, 5*, 83–98.

Fagot, B. I., & Hagan, H. (1985). Aggression in toddlers: Responses to the assertive acts of boys and girls. *Sex Roles, 12*, 341–351.

Fahey, P. J., & Gallagher-Allred, C. (1990). Nutrition. In R. E. Rakel (Ed.), *Textbook of family practice* (4th ed.). Philadelphia: W. B. Saunders.

Fain, T. C., & Anderton, D. L. (1987). Sexual harassment: Organizational context and diffuse status. *Sex Roles, 17*, 291–311.

Fancher, R. E. (1979). *Pioneers of psychology*. New York: Norton.

Faravelli, C., & Pallanti, S. (1989). Recent life events and panic disorders. *American Journal of Psychiatry, 146*, 622–626.

Farberow, N. L. (1974). *Suicide*. Morristown, NJ: General Learning Press.

Farina, A., Burns, G. L., Austad, C., Bugglin, C., & Fischer, E. H. (1986). The role of physical attractiveness in the readjustment of discharged psychiatric patients. *Journal of Abnormal Psychology, 95*(2), 139–143.

Farley, J. (1980). Worklife problems for both women and men. In D. A. Neugarten & J. M. Shafritz (Eds.), *Sexuality in occupations: Romantic and coercive behavior at work*. Oak Park, IL: Moore.

Farrell, M. P., & Rosenberg, S. D. (1981). *Men at midlife*. Boston: Auburn House.

Fasteau, M. F. (1974). *The male machine*. New York: McGraw-Hill.

Fausto-Sterling, A. (1985). *Myths of gender: Biological theories about women and men*. New York: Basic Books.

Featherstone, H. J., & Beitman, (1984). Marital migraine: A refractory daily headache. *Psychosomatics, 25*(1), 30–38.

Feder, H. H. (1984). Hormones and sexual behavior. In M. R. Rosenzweig & L. W. Porter (Eds.), *Annual review of psychology: 1984* (Vol. 35). Palo Alto, CA: Annual Reviews.

Federal Bureau of Investigation. (1985). *Uniform crime reports: Crime in the United States*. Washington, DC: U. S. Government Printing Office.

Feeney, J. A., & Noller, P. (1990). Attachment style as a predictor of adult romantic relationships. *Journal of Personality and Social Psychology, 58*(2), 281–291.

Feingold, A. (1988). Matching for attractiveness in romantic partners and same-sex friends: A meta-analysis and theoretical critique. *Psychological Bulletin, 104*(2), 226–235.

Feingold, A. (1990). Gender differences in effects of physical attractiveness on romantic attraction: A comparison across five research paradigms. *Journal of Personality and Social Psychology, 59*, 981–993.

Feingold, A. (1992). Good-looking people are not what we think. *Psychological Bulletin, 111*, 304–341.

Feiring, C., & Lewis, M. (1987). The child's social network: Sex differences from three to six years. *Sex Roles, 17*, 621–636.

Fenwick, P. (1987). Meditation and the EEG. In M. A. West (Ed.), *The psychology of meditation*. Oxford: Clarendon Press.

Fenz, W. D., & Epstein, S. (1967). Gradients of physiological arousal, skin conductance, heart rate, and respiration rate as a function of experience. *Psychosomatic Medicine, 29*, 33–51.

Ferree, M. M. (1976, September). The confused American housewife. *Psychology Today*, pp. 76–80.

Festinger, L. (1954). A theory of social comparison processes. *Human Relations, 7*, 117–140.

Festinger, L. (1957). *A theory of cognitive dissonance*. Stanford, CA: Stanford University Press.

Festinger, L., Schachter, S., & Back, K. (1950). *Social pressures in informal groups: A study of human factors in housing*. Stanford, CA: Stanford University Press.

Fidell, L. S. (1970). Empirical verification of sex discrimination in hiring practices in psychology. *American Psychologist, 25*, 1094–1098.

Fiedler, F. E. (1967). *A theory of leadership effectiveness*. New York: McGraw-Hill.

Fiedler, F. E. (1978). Recent developments in research on the contingency model. In L. Berkowitz (Ed.), *Group processes*. New York: Academic Press.

Fiedler, F. E., & Chemers, M. M. (1984). *Improving leadership effectiveness: The Leader Match Concept*. New York: Wiley.

Fiedler, F. E., & Garcia, J. E. (1987). *Leadership: Cognitive resources and performance*. New York: Wiley.

Field, D., Schaie, K. W., & Leino, E. V. (1988). Continuity in intellectual functioning: The role of self-reported health. *Psychology and Aging, 3*, 385–392.

Fielding, J. E. (1985). Smoking: Health effects and control. *New England Journal of Medicine, 313*, 491–498, 555–561.

Fields, H. L., & Levine, J. D. (1984). Placebo analgesia: A role for endorphins. *Trends in Neuroscience, 7*, 271–273.

Fincham, F. D., Beach, S. R., & Baucom, D. H. (1987). Attribution processes in distressed and nondistressed couples: 4. Self-partner attribution differences. *Journal of Personality and Social Psychology, 52*(4), 739–748.

Fincham, F. D., & Bradbury, T. N. (1992). Assessing attributions in marriage: The relationship attribution measure. *Journal of Personality and Social Psychology, 62*(3), 457–468.

Fine, M. (1988). Sexuality, schooling, and adolescent females: The missing discourse of desire. *Harvard Educational Review, 58*, 29–53.

Fine, M. A. (1992). Families in the United States: Their current status and future prospects. *Family Relations, 41*, 430–435.

Fink, M. (1988). Convulsive therapy: A manual of practice. In A. J. Frances & R. E. Hales (Eds.), *Review of psychiatry* (Vol. 7). Washington, DC: American Psychiatric Press.

Finn, S. E. (1986). Stability of personality self-ratings over 30 years: Evidence for an age/cohort interaction. *Journal of Personality and Social Psychology, 50*, 813–818.

Fiore, M. C. (1992). Trends in cigarette smoking in the United States: The epidemiology of tobacco use. *Medical Clinics of North America, 76*(2), 289–303.

Fischer, J. L., Spann, L., & Crawford, D. W. (1991). Measuring codependency. *Alcoholism Treatment Quarterly, 8*(1), 87–100.

Fischer, L. R. (1983). Mothers and mothers-in-law. *Journal of Marriage and the Family, 45*, 187–192.

Fisher, J. D., Bell, P. A., & Baum, A. S. (1984). *Environmental psychology*. New York: Holt, Rinehart & Winston.

Fisher, T. D. (1988). The relationship between parent-child communication about sexuality and college students' sexual behavior and attitudes as a function of parental proximity. *Journal of Sex Research, 24*, 305–311.

Fisher, W. A., Byrne, D., White, L. A., & Kelley, K. (1988). Erotophobia-erotophilia as a dimension of personality. *Journal of Sex Research, 25*(1), 123–151.

Fiske, S. T., & Taylor, S. E. (1991). *Social cognition*. New York: McGraw-Hill.

Fitch, S. A., & Adams, G. R. (1983). Ego identity and intimacy status: Replication and extension. *Developmental Psychology, 19*(6), 839–845.

Fitts, W. (1972). *The self-concept and psychopathology*. Nashville, TN: Counselor Recording and Tests.

Fitzgerald, L. F., & Betz, N. E. (1983). Issues in the vocational psychology of women. In W. B. Walsh & S. H. Osipow (Eds.), *Handbook of vocational psychology: Vol. 1. Foundations*. Hillsdale, NJ: Erlbaum.

Fitzgerald, L. F., & Crites, J. O. (1980). Toward a career psychology of women: What do we know? What do we need to know? *Journal of Counseling Psychology, 27*, 44–62.

Fitzgerald, L. F., Weitzman, L. M., Gold, Y., & Ormerod, M. (1988). Academic harassment: Sex and denial in scholarly garb. *Psychology of Women Quarterly, 12*, 329–340.

Fitzpatrick, M. A. (1987). Marriage and verbal intimacy. In V. J. Derlega & J. H. Berg (Eds.), *Self-disclosure: Theory, research, and therapy*. New York: Plenum.

Flanders, J. P. (1982). A general systems approach to loneliness. In L. A. Peplau & D. Perlman (Eds.), *Loneliness: A sourcebook of current theory, research and therapy*. New York: Wiley.

Fleming, T. C. (1986). Alcohol and other mood-changing drugs. In S. Wolf & A. J. Finestone (Eds.), *Occupational stress: Health and performance at work*. Littleton, MA: PSG Publishing.

Fletcher, G. J. O., & Fitness, J. (1990). Occurrent social cognition in close relationship interaction: The role of proximal and distal variables. *Journal of Personality and Social Psychology, 59*, 464–474.

Folbre, N. (1987). *A field guide to the U.S. economy*. New York: Pantheon.

Folkes, V. S. (1982). Forming relationships and the matching hypothesis. *Personality and Social Psychology Bulletin, 8*, 631–636.

Folkes, V. S., & Sears, D. O. (1977). Does everybody like a liker? *Journal of Experimental Social Psychology, 13*(6), 505–519.

Folkins, C. H., & Sime, W. (1981). Physical fitness training and mental health. *American Psychologist, 36*, 373–389.

Folkman, S. (1984). Personal control and stress and coping processes: A theoretical analysis. *Journal of Personality and Social Psychology, 46*(4), 839–852.

Folkman, S., Lazarus, R. S., Dunkel-Schetter, C., DeLongis, A., & Gruen, R. J. (1986). Dynamics of a stressful encounter: Cognitive appraisal, coping, and encounter outcomes. *Journal of Personality and Social Psychology, 50*(5), 992–1003.

Folkman, S., Lazarus, R. S., Gruen, R. J., & DeLongis, A. (1986). Appraisal, coping, health status, and psychological symptoms. *Journal of Personality and Social Psychology, 50*(3), 571–579.

Forsyth, D. R. (1983). *An introduction to group dynamics*. Pacific Grove, CA: Brooks/Cole.

Forsyth, D. R., & McMillan, J. H. (1981). Attributions, affect, and expectations: A test of Weiner's three-dimensional model. *Journal of Educational Psychology, 73*, 393–403.

Forsyth, D. R., & Strong, S. R. (1986). The scientific study of counseling and psychotherapy: A unificationist view. *American Psychologist, 41*(2), 113–119.

Foss, R. D., & Dempsey, C. B. (1979). Blood donation and the foot-in-the-door technique. *Journal of Personality and Social Psychology, 37*, 580–590.

Fowers, B. J., & Olson, D. H. (1989). ENRICH Marital Inventory: A discriminant validity and cross-validation assessment. *Journal of Marital and Family Therapy, 15*(1), 65–79.

Fowler, R. D. (1986, May). Howard Hughes: A psychological autopsy. *Psychology Today*, pp. 22–33.

Fracher, J. C., & Kimmel, M. S. (1987). Hard issues and soft spots: Counseling men about sexuality. In M. Scher, M. Stevens, G. Good, & G. A. Eichenfield (Eds.), *Handbook of counseling and psychotherapy with men*. Newbury Park, CA: Sage Publications.

France, C., & Ditto, B. (1988). Caffeine effects on several indices of cardiovascular activity at rest and during stress. *Journal of Behavioral Medicine, 11*, 473–482.

Frances, A. J., First, M. B., Widiger, T. A., Miele, G. M., Tilly, S. M., Davis, W. W., & Pincus, H. A. (1991). An A to Z guide to DSM-IV conundrums. *Journal of Abnormal Psychology, 100*(3), 407–412.

Frances, A. J., & Widiger, T. A. (1986). The classification of personality disorders: An overview of problems and solutions. In A. J. Frances & R. E. Hales (Eds.), *Psychiatry Update: Annual Review* (Vol. 5). Washington, DC: American Psychiatric Press.

Francoeur, R. T. (1982). *Becoming a sexual person*. New York: Wiley.

Frank, E., Anderson, C., & Rubinstein, D. (1978). Frequency of sexual dysfunction in "normal" couples. *New England Journal of Medicine, 299*, 111–115.

Frank, H. B. (1985). Gender differences in postmarital adjustment. In D. C. Goldberg (Ed.), *Contemporary marriage: Special issues in couples therapy*. Homewood, IL: Dorsey Press.

Franken, R. E., Gibson, K. J., & Rowland, G. L. (1992). Sensation seeking and the tendency to view the world as threatening. *Personality and Individual Differences, 13*(1), 31–38.

Franks, C. M., & Barbrack, C. R. (1983). Behavior therapy with adults: An integrative perspective. In M. Hersen, A. E. Kazdin, & A. S. Bellack (Eds.), *The clinical psychology handbook*. New York: Pergamon Press.

Franzoi, S. L., & Herzog, M. E. (1987). Judging personal attractiveness: What body aspects do we use? *Personality and Social Psychology Bulletin, 13*, 19–33.

Frasher, J. M., Frasher, R. S., & Wims, F. B. (1982). Sex-role stereotyping in school superintendents' personnel decisions. *Sex Roles, 8*, 261–268.

Freedman, J. (1978). *Happy people*. New York: Harcourt Brace Jovanovich.

Freedman, J. L., & Fraser, S. C. (1966). Compliance without pressure: The foot-in-the-door technique. *Journal of Personality and Social Psychology, 4*, 195–202.

Freeman, R. B. (1976). *The over-educated American*. New York: Academic Press.

French, J. R. P., Jr., Caplan, R. D., & Van Harrison, R. (1982). *The mechanisms of job stress and strain*. New York: Wiley.

French, J. R. P., Jr., & Raven, B. (1959). The bases of social power. In D. Cartwright (Ed.), *Studies in social power*. Ann Arbor, MI: Institute for Social Research.

Freud, S. (1923). *The ego and the id. Standard edition*, Vol. 19. London: Hogarth.

Freud, S. (1920/1924). *A general introduction to psychoanalysis*. New York: Boni and Liveright. (Original work published 1920).

Freud, S. (1901/1960). *The psychopathology of everyday life. Standard edition*, Vol. 6. London: Hogarth. (Original work published 1901).

Friedan, B. (1964). *The feminine mystique*. New York: Dell.

Friedberg, J. (1976). *Shock treatment is not good for your brain*. San Francisco: Glide Publications.

Friedland, G. H., Saltzman, B. R., Rogers, M. F., Kahl, P. A., Lesser, M. L., Mayers, M.

M., & Kelin, R. S. (1986). Lack of transmission of HTLV-III/LAV infection to household contacts of patients with AIDS or AIDS-related complex with oral candidiasis. *New England Journal of Medicine, 314*, 344–349.

Friedman, A. (1987). Getting powerful with age: Changes in women over the life cycle. *Israel Social Science Research, 5*, 76–86.

Friedman, D. E. (1987). Work vs. family: War of the worlds. *Personnel Administrator, 32*(8), 36–39.

Friedman, H. S. (1983). Social perception and face-to-face interaction. In D. Perlman & D. C. Cozby (Eds.), *Social psychology*. New York: Holt, Rinehart & Winston.

Friedman, H. S., & Booth-Kewley, S. (1987). The "disease-prone personality": A meta-analytic view of the construct. *American Psychologist, 42*(6), 539–555.

Friedman, H. S., & Booth-Kewley, S. (1988). Validity of the Type A construct: A reprise. *Psychological Bulletin, 104*(3), 381–384.

Friedman, H. S., Prince, L. M., Riggio, R. E., & DiMatteo, M. R. (1980). Understanding and assessing nonverbal expressiveness: The affective communication test. *Journal of Personality and Social Psychology, 39*(2), 333–351.

Friedman, J. (1989). The impact of homophobia on male sexual development. *Siecus Report, 17*(5), 8–9.

Friedman, L. S., & Goodman, E. (1992). Adolescents at risk for HIV infection. *Primary Care, 19*(1), 171–190.

Friedman, M., & Rosenman, R. F. (1974). *Type A behavior and your heart*. New York: Knopf.

Friedman, S. R., de Jong, W. M., & Des Jarlais, D. C. (1988). Problems and dynamics of organizing intravenous drug users for AIDS prevention. *Health Education Research, 3*, 49–57.

Fries, H., Nillius, J., & Petersson, F. (1974). Epidemiology of secondary amenorrhea. *American Journal of Obstetrics and Gynecology, 118*, 473–479.

Frieze, I. H., & Ramsey, S. J. (1976). Nonverbal maintenance of traditional sex roles. *Journal of Social Issues, 32*(3), 133–141.

Froelicher, V. F. (1990). Exercise, fitness, and coronary heart disease. In C. Bouchard, R. J. Shephard, T. Stephens, J. R. Sutton, & B. D. McPherson (Eds.), *Exercise, fitness, and health: A consensus of current knowledge*. Champaign, IL: Human Kinetics Books.

Fromm, E. (1963). *Escape from freedom*. New York: Holt.

Fuchs, R. M. (1984). Group therapy. In T. B. Karasu (Ed.), *The psychiatric therapies*. Washington, DC: American Psychiatric Association.

Fuller, R. G. C., & Sheehy-Skeffington, A. (1974). Effects of group laughter on responses to humorous materials: A replication and extension. *Psychological Reports, 35*, 531–534.

Funk, S. C., & Houston, B. K. (1987). A critical analysis of the Hardiness Scale's validity and utility. *Journal of Personality and Social Psychology, 53*(3), 572–578.

Furstenberg, F. F., Jr. (1988). Good dads, bad dads: Two faces of fatherhood. In A. J. Cherlin (Ed.), *The changing American family* and public policy. Washington, DC: Urban Institute Press.

Furstenberg, F. F., Jr., & Spanier, G. B. (1984). *Recycling the family: Remarriage after divorce.* Newbury Park, CA: Sage Publications.

Gadpaille, W. J. (1975). *The cycles of sex.* New York: Scribner's.

Gagnon, J. H. (1985). Attitudes and responses of parents to pre-adolescent masturbation. *Archives of Sexual Behavior, 14*(5), 451–466.

Gagnon, J. H., & Simon, J. (1973). *Sexual conduct: The social origins of human sexuality.* Chicago: Aldine.

Gagnon, J. H., & Simon, W. (1987). The sexual scripting of oral genital contacts. *Archives of Sexual Behavior, 16*(1), 1–25.

Galanter, H. (1989). *Cults: Faith, healing, and coercion.* New York: Oxford University Press.

Gale, A. (1983). Electroencephalographic studies of extraversion-introversion: A case study in the psychophysiology of individual differences. *Personality and Individual Differences, 4,* 371–380.

Gantt, W. H. (1975, April 25). Unpublished lecture, Ohio State University. Cited in D. Hothersall (1984), *History of psychology.* New York: Random House.

Gardner, J. N., & Jewler, A. J. (Eds.). (1989). *College is only the beginning: A student guide to higher education.* Belmont, CA: Wadsworth.

Gardner, R. A. (1971). *The boys and girls book about divorce.* New York: Bantam Books.

Garfield, S. L. (1992). Major issues in psychotherapy research. In D. K. Freedheim (Ed.), *History of psychotherapy: A century of change.* Washington, DC: American Psychological Association.

Garner, D., Garfinkel, P., Schwartz, D., & Thompson, M. (1980). Cultural expectations of thinness in women. *Psychological Reports, 47,* 483–491.

Garnets, L., & Kimmel, D. (1991). Lesbian and gay male dimensions in the psychological study of human diversity. In J. D. Goodchilds (Ed.), *Psychological perspectives on human diversity in America.* Washington, DC: American Psychological Association.

Garrow, J. S. (1986). Physiological aspects of obesity. In K. D. Brownell & J. P. Foreyt (Eds.), *Handbook of eating disorders: Physiology, psychology, and treatment of obesity, anorexia and bulimia.* New York: Basic Books.

Gatchel, R. J., & Baum, A. (1988). *An introduction to health psychology.* New York: Random House.

Gebhard, P. H. (1966). Factors in marital orgasm. *Journal of Social Issues, 22,* 88–95.

Gebhardt, D. L., & Crump, C. E. (1990). Employee fitness and wellness programs in the workplace. *American Psychologist, 45*(2), 262–272.

Gecas, V., & Seff, M. A. (1990). Families and adolescents: A review of the 1980s. *Journal of Marriage and the Family, 52,* 941–958.

Geis, B. D., & Gerrard, M. (1984). Predicting male and female contraceptive behavior: A discriminant analysis of groups high, moderate, and low in contraceptive effectiveness. *Journal of Personality and Social Psychology, 46,* 669–680.

Geiser, R. L., Rarick, D. L., & Soldow, G. F. (1977). Deception and judgment accuracy: A study in person perception. *Personality and Social Psychology Bulletin, 3,* 446–449.

Gentry, W. D. (1979). Preadmission behavior. In W. D. Gentry & R. B. Williams (Eds.), *Psychological aspects of myocardial infarction and coronary care* (2nd ed.). St. Louis: C. V. Mosby.

Georgas, J., Giakoumaki, E., Georgoulias, N., Koumandakis, E., & Kaskarelis, D. (1984). Psychosocial stress and its relation to obstetrical complications. *Psychotherapy and Psychosomatics. 41,* 200–206.

George, L. K., Fillenbaum, G. G. , & Palmore, E. (1984). Sex differences in the antecedents and consequences of retirement. *Journal of Gerontology, 39,* 364–371.

George, L. K., & Weiler, J. J. (1981). Sexuality in middle and later life. *Archives of General Psychiatry, 38,* 919–923.

Georgotas, A. (1985). Affective disorders: Pharmacotherapy. In H. I. Kaplan & B. J. Sadock (Eds.), *Comprehensive textbook of psychiatry/IV.* Baltimore: Williams & Wilkins.

Gerdes, E., Gehling, J., & Rapp, J. (1981). The effects of sex and sex-role concept on self-disclosure. *Sex Roles, 7,* 989–998.

Gerrard, M. (1987). Emotional and cognitive barriers to effective contraception: Are males and females really different? In K. Kelley (Ed.), *Females, males, and sexuality: Theories and research.* Albany: State University of New York Press.

Gershon, E. S., Berrettini, W. H., & Goldin, L. R. (1989). Mood disorders: Genetic aspects. In H. I. Kaplan & B. J. Sadock (Eds.), *Comprehensive textbook of psychiatry/V.* Baltimore: Williams & Wilkins.

Gerstel, N. (1988). Divorce, gender, and social integration. *Gender and Society, 2,* 343–367.

Gerstel, N., Reissman, C. K., & Rosenfield, S. (1985). Explaining the symptomatology of separated and divorced women and men: The role of material conditions and social network. *Social Forces, 64*(1), 84–101.

Gibb, J. R. (1973). Defensive communication. In W. G. Bennis, D. E. Berlew, E. H. Schein, & F. I. Steele (Eds.), *Interpersonal dynamics.* Homewood, IL: Dorsey Press.

Gibbs, N. (1989, July 31). Sick and tired. *Time,* pp. 48–53.

Gibbs, N. (1991, October 21). Office crimes. *Time,* pp. 52–54, 63–64.

Gierymski, T., & Williams, T. (1986). Codependency. *Journal of Psychoactive Drugs, 18,* 7–13.

Gilder, G. F. (1986). *Men and marriage.* New York: Pelican.

Giles, H., & Street, R. L., Jr. (1985). Communicator characteristics and behavior. In M. L. Knapp & G. R. Miller (Eds.), *Handbook of interpersonal communication.* Newbury Park, CA: Sage Publications.

Gilligan, C. (1982). *In a different voice.* Cambridge, MA: Harvard University Press.

Gilmer, B. V. H. (1975). *Applied psychology: Adjustments in living and work.* New York: McGraw-Hill.

Ginott, H. G. (1976). *Between parent and child.* New York: Avon.

Gintzler, A. R. (1980). Endorphin-mediated increases in pain threshold during pregnancy. *Science, 210,* 193–195.

Ginzberg, E. (1952). Toward a theory of occupational choice. *Occupations, 30,* 491–494.

Ginzberg, E. (1972). Toward a theory of occupational choice: A restatement. *Vocational Guidance Quarterly, 20,* 169–176.

Gladue, B. A. (1987). Psychobiological contributions. In L. Diamant (Ed.), *Male and female homosexuality: Psychological approaches.* Washington, DC: Hemisphere.

Glantz, S. A., & Parmley, W. W. (1991). Passive smoking and heart disease: Epidemiology, physiology, and biochemistry. *Circulation, 83*(1), 1–12.

Glaser, R., Kiecolt-Glaser, J. K., Speicher, C. E., & Holliday, J. E. (1985). Stress, loneliness, and changes in herpesvirus latency. *Journal of Behavioral Medicine, 8,* 249–260.

Glasgow, R. E., Klesges, R. C., Mizes, J. S., & Pechacek, T. F. (1985). Quitting smoking: Strategies used and variables associated with success in a stop-smoking contest. *Journal of Consulting and Clinical Psychology, 53,* 905–912.

Glass, C. R., & Arnkoff, D. B. (1992). Behavior therapy. In D. K. Freedheim (Ed.), *History of psychotherapy: A century of change.* Washington, DC: American Psychological Association.

Glass, S. P., & Wright, T. L. (1985). Sex differences in type of extramarital involvement and marital dissatisfaction. *Sex Roles, 12,* 1101–1120.

Glasser, W. (1975). *Schools without failure.* New York: Harper & Row.

Glenn, M., & Taska, R. J. (1984). Antidepressants and lithium. In T. B. Karasu (Ed.), *The psychiatric therapies.* Washington, DC: American Psychiatric Association.

Glenn, N. D. (1990). Quantitative research on marital quality in the 1980s: A critical review. *Journal of Marriage and the Family, 52,* 818–831.

Glenn, N. D., & McLanahan, S. (1982). Children and marital happiness: A further specification of the relationship. *Journal of Marriage and the Family, 44,* 63–72.

Glenn, N. D., & Weaver, C. N. (1988). The changing relationship of marital status to reported happiness. *Journal of Marriage and the Family, 50,* 317–324.

Glick, P., Zion, C., & Nelson, C. (1988). What mediates sex discrimination in hiring decisions? *Journal of Personality and Social Psychology, 55,* 178–186.

Glick, P. C. (1984). Marriage, divorce, and living arrangements: Prospective changes. *Journal of Family Issues, 5,* 7–26.

Glick, P. C., & Lin, S. (1986). More young adults are living with their parents: Who are they? *Journal of Marriage and the Family, 48,* 107–112.

Godbey, G. (1990). *Leisure in your life: An exploration* (3rd ed.). State College, PA: Venture.

Goethals, G. R., & Darley, J. M. (1977). Social comparison theory: An attributional approach. In J. M. Suls & R. L. Miller (Eds.), *Social comparison processes: Theoretical and empirical perspectives.* Washington, DC: Hemisphere/Halsted.

Goetting, A. (1986). Parental satisfaction: A review of research. *Journal of Family Issues, 7*(1), 83–109.

Goffman, E. (1956). The nature of deference and demeanor. *American Anthropologist, 58,* 473–502.

Goffman, E. (1959). *The presentation of self in everyday life*. Garden City, NY: Doubleday/ Anchor.

Goffman, E. (1971). *Relations in public*. New York: Basic Books.

Gold, M. S. (1989a). *Marijuana*. New York: Plenum.

Gold, M. S. (1989b). *The good news about panic, anxiety and phobias*. New York: Willard.

Gold, M. S. (1992). Cocaine (and crack): Clinical aspects. In J. H. Lowinson, P. Ruiz, & R. B. Millman (Eds.), *Substance abuse: A comprehensive textbook* (2nd ed.). Baltimore: Williams & Wilkins.

Gold, M. S., Miller, N. S., & Jonas, J. M. (1992). Cocaine (and crack): Neurobiology. In J. H. Lowinson, P. Ruiz, & R. B. Millman (Eds.), *Substance abuse: A comprehensive textbook* (2nd ed.). Baltimore: Williams & Wilkins.

Goldberg, H. (1976). *The hazards of being male: Surviving the myth of masculine privilege*. New York: Nash.

Goldberg, H. (1979). *The new male*. New York: Signet.

Goldberg, M. (1985). Remarriage: Repetition versus new beginnings. In D. C. Goldberg (Ed.), *Contemporary marriage: Special issues in couples therapy*. Homewood, IL: Dorsey Press.

Goldstein, M. A., Kilroy, M. C., & Van de Voort, D. (1976). Gaze as a function of conversation and degree of love. *Journal of Psychology, 92*, 227–234.

Goldstein, M. J. (1984). *Family factors that antedate the onset of schizophrenia and related disorders: The results of a fifteen-year prospective longitudinal study*. Paper presented at the Regional Symposium of the World Psychiatric Association Meeting, Helsinki, Finland.

Goldstein, M. J. (1988). The family and psychopathology. *Annual Review of Psychology, 39*, 283–300.

Goleman, D. (1978, November). Special abilities of the sexes: Do they begin in the brain? *Psychology Today*, pp. 48–59, 120.

Goleman, D. (1979, November). [Interview with Richard S. Lazarus, Positive denial: The case for not facing reality]. *Psychology Today*, pp. 44–60.

Golub, S., & Harrington, D. M. (1981). Premenstrual and menstrual mood changes in adolescent women. *Journal of Personality and Social Psychology, 41*, 961–965.

Gomberg, E. L. (1989). On terms used and abused: The concept of "codependency". *Drug and Society, 3*, 113–122.

Gonsiorek, J. C., & Weinrich, J. D. (1991). The definition and scope of sexual orientation. In J. C. Gonsiorek & J. D. Weinrich (Eds.), *Homosexuality: Research implications for public policy*. Newbury Park, CA: Sage Publications.

Gonzales, M. H., Davis, J. M., Loney, G. L., Lukens, C. K., & Junghans, C. H. (1983). Interactional approach to interpersonal attraction. *Journal of Personality and Social Psychology, 44*, 1192–1197.

Good, P. R., & Smith, B. D. (1980). Menstrual distress and sex-role attributes. *Psychology of Women Quarterly, 4*, 482–491.

Good, T. L., Sikes, J. N., & Brophy, J. E. (1973). Effects of teacher sex and student sex on classroom interaction. *Journal of Educational Psychology, 65*, 74–87.

Goodall, K. (1972, November). Field report: Shapers at work. *Psychology Today*, pp. 53–63, 132–138.

Goodwin, D. W. (1992). Alcohol: Clinical aspects. In J. H. Lowinson, P. Ruiz, & R. B. Millman (Eds.), *Substance abuse: A comprehensive textbook* (2nd ed.). Baltimore: Williams & Wilkins.

Goodwin, R. (1990). Sex differences among partner preferences: Are the sexes really very similar? *Sex Roles, 23*(9–10), 501–513.

Gordon, S., & Snyder, C. W. (1989). *Personal issues in human sexuality: A guidebook for better sexual health*. Boston: Allyn & Bacon.

Gordon, T. (1970). *Parent effectiveness training*. New York: McKay.

Gore, S. (1978). The effect of social support in moderating the health consequences of unemployment. *Journal of Health and Social Behavior, 19*, 157–165.

Gorman, J. M., & Davis, J. M. (1989). Antianxiety drugs. In H. I. Kaplan & B. J. Sadock (Eds.), *Comprehensive textbook of psychiatry/V*. Baltimore: Williams & Wilkins.

Gotlib, I. H., & McCabe, S. B. (1990). Marriage and psychopathology. In F. D. Fincham & T. N. Bradbury (Eds.), *The psychology of marriage: Basic issues and applications*. New York: Guilford Press.

Gottesman, I. I. (1991). *Schizophrenia genesis: The origins of madness*. New York: W. H. Freeman.

Gottfredson, G. D. (1977). Career stability and redirection in adulthood. *Journal of Applied Psychology, 62*, 436–445.

Gottman, J. M. (1979). *Marital interaction*. New York: Academic Press.

Gottman, J. M., & Levenson, R. S. (1988). The social psychophysiology of marriage. In P. Noller & M. A. Fitzpatrick (Eds.), *Perspectives on marital interaction*. Clevedon, England, and Philadelphia: Multilingual Matters.

Gould, R. L. (1972). The phases of adult life: A study in developmental psychology. *American Journal of Psychiatry, 129*, 521–531.

Gould, R. L. (1978). *Transformations: Growth and change in adult life*. New York: Simon & Schuster.

Gove, W. R. (1975). Labeling and mental illness: A critique. In W. R. Gove (Ed.), *The labeling of deviance: Evaluating a perspective*. New York: Halsted.

Grant, I., McDonald, W. I., Patterson, T., & Trimble, M. R. (1989). Multiple sclerosis. In G. W. Brown & T. O. Harris (Eds.), *Life events and illness*. New York: Guilford Press.

Gray, J. D. (1983). The married professional woman: An examination of her role conflicts and coping strategies. *Psychology of Women Quarterly, 7*, 235–243.

Green, L. W., Tryon, W. W., Marks, B., & Huryn, J. (1986). Periodontal disease as a function of life events stress. *Journal of Human Stress, 12*(1), 32–36.

Green, S. K., Buchanan, D. R., & Heuer, S. K. (1984). Winners, losers, and choosers: A field investigation of dating initiation. *Personality and Social Psychology Bulletin, 10*, 502–511.

Greenberg, J., Pyszczynski, T., & Solomon, S. (1982). The self-serving attributional bias: Beyond self-presentation. *Journal of Experimental Social Psychology, 8*, 99–111.

Greenberg, J. S. (1990). *Comprehensive stress management*. Dubuque, IA: William C. Brown.

Greenberg, J. S. (1992). *Comprehensive stress management*. Dubuque, IA: William C. Brown.

Greenberger, E., & Goldberg, W. A. (1989). Work, parenting, and the socialization of children. *Developmental Psychology, 25*, 22–35.

Greenberger, E., Goldberg, W. A., Crawford, T., & Granger, J. (1988). Beliefs about the consequences of maternal employment for children. *Psychology of Women Quarterly, 12*, 35–59.

Greenblat, C. S. (1983). The salience of sexuality in the early years of marriage. *Journal of Marriage and the Family, 45*(2), 289–299.

Greene, W. A., & Swisher, S. N. (1969). Psychological and somatic variables associated with the development and course of monozygotic twins discordant for leukemia. *Annals of the New York Academy of Sciences, 164*, 394–408.

Greenhaus, J. H., Bedeian, A. G., & Mossholder, K. W. (1987). Work experiences, job performance, and feelings of personal and family well-being. *Journal of Vocational Behavior, 31*, 200–215.

Greenson, R. R. (1967). *The technique and practice of psychoanalysis* (Vol. 1). New York: International Universities Press.

Greenwald, J. (1982). *Be the person you were meant to be*. New York: Dell.

Greenwald, P., & Sondik, E. J. (1986). *Cancer control objectives for the nation: 1985–2000*. Bethesda, MD: National Cancer Institute.

Griffin, R. W. (1988). Consequences of quality circles in an industrial setting: A longitudinal assessment. *Academy of Management Journal, 31*, 338–358.

Griggs, L. (1990, July 2). A losing battle with AIDS. *Time*, pp. 41–43.

Grinker, J. A. (1982). Physiological and behavioral basis for human obesity. In D. W. Pfaff (Ed.), *The physiological mechanisms of motivation*. New York: Springer-Verlag.

Grinspoon, L., & Bakalar, J. B. (1986). Psychedelics and arylcyclohexylamines. In A. J. Frances & R. E. Hales (Eds.), *Psychiatric Update: Annual Review* (Vol. 5). Washington, DC: American Psychiatric Press.

Grinspoon, L., & Bakalar, J. B. (1992). Marihuana. In J. H. Lowinson, P. Ruiz, & R. B. Millman (Eds.), *Substance abuse: A comprehensive textbook* (2nd ed.). Baltimore: Williams & Wilkins.

Grob, G. N. (1983). Disease and environment in American history. In D. Mechanic (Ed.), *Handbook of health, health care, and the health professions*. New York: Free Press.

Grobbee, D. E., Rimm, E. B., Giovannucci, E., Colditz, G., Stampfer, M., & Willett, W. (1990). Coffee, caffeine, and cardiovascular disease in men. *New England Journal of Medicine, 323*, 1026–1032.

Grover, K. J., Russell, C. S., Schumm, W. R., & Paff-Bergen, L. A. (1985). Mate selection processes and marital satisfaction. *Family Relations, 34*, 383–386.

Grunberg, N. E., Bowen, D. J., & Winders, S. E. (1986). Effects of nicotine on body weight and food consumption in female rats. *Psychopharmacology, 90*, 101–105.

Gruneberg, M. M. (1979). *Understanding job satisfaction*. New York: Wiley.

Guidubaldi, J., Perry, J. D., & Nastasi, B. K. (1987). Growing up in a divorced family: Initial and long–term perspectives on children's adjustment. In S. Oskamp (Ed.), *Family processes and problems: Social psychological aspects* (Vol. 7, *Applied Social Psychology Annual*). Newbury Park, CA: Sage Publications.

Gunter, N. C., & Gunter, B. G. (1990). Domestic division of labor among working couples: Does androgyny make a difference? *Psychology of Women Quarterly, 14*, 355–370.

Gurin, J. (1989, June). Leaner, not lighter. *Psychology Today*, pp. 32–36.

Gutek, B. A. (1985). *Sex and the workplace.* San Francisco: Jossey-Bass.

Haaken, J. (1990). A critical analysis of the co–dependence construct. *Psychiatry, 53*, 396–406.

Haan, N., Millsap, R., & Hartka, E. (1986). As time goes by: Change and stability in personality over 50 years. *Psychology and Aging, 1*, 220–232.

Haas, A., & Haas, K. (1990). *Understanding sexuality.* St. Louis: Times Mirror/Mosby.

Hackman, J. R., Brousseau, K. R., & Weiss, J. A. (1976). The interaction of task design and group performance strategies in determining group effectiveness. *Organizational Behavior and Human Performance, 16*, 350–365.

Hagberg, J. M. (1990). Exercise, fitness, and hypertension. In C. Bouchard, R. J. Shephard, T. Stephens, J. R. Sutton, & B. D. McPherson (Eds.), *Exercise, fitness, and health: A consensus of current knowledge.* Champaign, IL: Human Kinetics Books.

Hall, D. T. (1986). An overview of current career development theory, research, and practice. In D. Hall & associates (Eds.), *Career development in organizations.* San Francisco: Jossey-Bass.

Hall, E. R., Howard, J. A., & Boezio, S. L. (1986). Tolerance of rape: A sexist or antisocial attitude? *Psychology of Women Quarterly, 10*, 101–118.

Hall, E. T. (1973). *The silent language.* Garden City, NY: Doubleday.

Hall, E. T. (1990). *The hidden dimension.* Garden City, NY: Doubleday.

Hall, G. S. (1904). *Adolescence.* New York: Appleton.

Hall, J. A. (1984). *Nonverbal sex differences: Communication accuracy and expressive style.* Baltimore: Johns Hopkins University Press.

Hall, J. A. (1990). *Nonverbal sex differences: Communication accuracy and expressive style.* Baltimore: Johns Hopkins University Press.

Hall, K., & Savery, L. K. (1986, January–February). Tight rein, more stress. *Harvard Business Review*, pp. 160–164.

Hall, R. M., & Sandler, B. R. (1982). *The classroom climate: A chilly one for women?* Washington, DC: Association of American Colleges.

Hallie, P. P. (1971). Justification and rebellion. In N. Sanford & C. Comstock (Eds.), *Sanctions for evil.* San Francisco: Jossey-Bass.

Halpin, A. W., & Winer, B. J. (1952). *The leadership behavior of the airplane commander.* Columbus: Ohio State University Research Foundation.

Hamachek, D. E. (1992). *Encounters with the self.* Fort Worth: Harcourt Brace Jovanovich.

Hamburger, A. C. (1988, May). Beauty quest. *Psychology Today*, pp. 28–32.

Hamer, D. H., Hu, S., Magnuson, V. L., Hu, N., & Pattatucci, A. M. L. (1993). A linkage between DNA markers on the X chromosome and male sexual orientation. *Science, 261*, 321–327.

Hamilton, M. H. (1988, July 10). Employing new tools to recruit workers. *Washington Post*, pp. H1, H3.

Hammen, C., Marks, T., Mayol, A., & deMayo, R. (1985). Depressive self-schemas, life stress, and vulnerability to depression. *Journal of Abnormal Psychology, 94*(3), 308–319.

Hammen, C., Mayol, A., deMayo, R., & Marks, T. (1986). Initial symptom levels and the life-event-depression relationship. *Journal of Abnormal Psychology, 95*(2), 114–122.

Hammond, E. C., & Horn, D. (1984). Smoking and death rates—Report on 44 months of followup of 187,783 men. *Journal of the American Medical Association, 251*(21), 2840–2853.

Hansen, C. H., & Hansen, R. D. (1988). How rock music videos can change what is seen when boy meets girl: Priming stereotypic appraisal of social interactions. *Sex Roles, 19*(5–6), 287–316.

Hansen, J. C., & Campbell, D. P. (1985). *Manual for the SVIB-SCII* (4th ed.). Stanford, CA: Stanford University Press.

Hansen, J. E., & Schuldt, W. J. (1984). Marital self-disclosure and marital satisfaction. *Journal of Marriage and the Family, 46*, 923–926.

Hansen, W. B., Graham, J. W., Sobel, J. L., Shelton, D. R., Flay, B. R., & Johnson, C. A. (1987). The consistency of peer and parent influences on tobacco use among young adolescents. *Journal of Behavioral Medicine, 10*, 559–579.

Hanson, R. O., Jones, W. H., & Carpenter, B. N. (1984). Relational competence and social support. In P. Shaver (Ed.), *Review of personality and social psychology* (Vol. 5). Newbury Park, CA: Sage Publications.

Hardy, J. H., & Smith, T. W. (1988). Cynical hostility and vulnerability to disease: Social support, life stress, and physiological responses to conflict. *Health Psychology, 7*, 447–459.

Hare, R. D. (1983). Diagnosis of antisocial personality disorder in criminals. *American Journal of Psychiatry, 140*, 887–890.

Harkins, S. G., & Szymanski, K. (1989). Social loafing and group evaluation. *Journal of Personality and Social Psychology, 56*(6), 934–941.

Harper, J., & Capdevila, C. (1990). Codependency: A critique. *Journal of Psychoactive Drugs, 22*(3), 285–292.

Harper, N. L., & Askling, L. R. (1980). Group communication and quality of task solution in a media production organization. *Communication Monographs, 47*, 77–100.

Harriman, L. C. (1986). Marital adjustment as related to personal and marital changes accompanying parenthood. *Family Relations, 35*, 233–239.

Harris, L. (1987). *Inside America.* New York: Vintage Books.

Harris, L., & Associates. (1986). *American teens speak: Sex, myths, TV and birth control.* New York: Planned Parenthood.

Harris, L. J. (1980). Lateralized sex differences: Substrates and significance. *Behavioral and Brain Sciences, 3*, 236–237.

Harris, M. B., Harris, R. J., & Bochner, S. (1982). Fat, four-eyed, and female: Stereotypes of obesity, glasses, and gender. *Journal of Applied Social Psychology, 12*, 503–516.

Harris, T. (1967). *I'm OK—you're OK.* New York: HarperCollins.

Harrison, A. A., & Saeed, I. (1977). Let's make a deal: An analysis of revelations and stipulations in lonely heart advertisements. *Journal of Personality and Social Psychology, 35*, 257–264.

Harry, J. (1983). Gay male and lesbian relationships. In E. D. Macklin & R. H. Rubin (Eds.), *Contemporary families and alternative lifestyles: Handbook on research and theory.* Newbury Park, CA: Sage Publications.

Hart, D. H., Rayner, F., & Christensen, E. R. (1971). Planning, preparation, and chance in occupational entry. *Journal of Vocational Behavior, 1*, 279–285.

Hartley, R. L. (1959). Sex-role pressures in the socialization of the male child. *Psychological Reports, 5*, 459–468.

Hartman, W. E., & Fithian, M. A. (1974). *Treatment of sexual dysfunction: A biopsycho-social approach.* New York: Aronson.

Hartmann, E. L. (1985). Sleep disorders. In H. I. Kaplan & B. J. Sadock (Eds.), *Comprehensive textbook of psychiatry* (4th ed.). Baltimore: Williams & Wilkins.

Harvey, J. H., Town, J. P., & Yarkin, K. L. (1981). How fundamental is "the fundamental attribution error"? *Journal of Personality and Social Psychology, 40*(2), 346–349.

Harvey, S. M. (1987). Female sexual behavior: Fluctuations during the menstrual cycle. *Journal of Psychosomatic Research, 31*(1), 101–110.

Harwood, H., Napolitano, D., Kristiansen, P., & Collins, J. (1984). *Economic costs to society of alcohol and drug abuse and mental illness: 1980.* Research Triangle Park, NC: Research Triangle Institute.

Hass, R. G. (1981). Effects of source characteristics on cognitive responses and persuasion. In R. E. Petty, T. M. Ostrom, & T. C. Brock (Eds.), *Cognitive responses in persuasion.* Hillsdale, NJ: Erlbaum.

Hatcher, R. A., Stewart, F., Trussell, J., Kowal, D., Guest, F., Stewart, G. K., & Cates, W. (1990). *Contraceptive technology: 1990–1992.* New York: Irvington.

Hatfield, E. (1988). Passionate and companionate love. In R. J. Sternberg & M. L. Barnes (Eds.), *The psychology of love.* New Haven, CT: Yale University Press.

Hatfield, E., & Walster, G. W. (1985). *A new look at love.* Lanham, MD: UPA.

Hatfield, M. O. (1990). Stress and the American worker. *American Psychologist, 45*(10), 1162–1164.

Havighurst, R. J., Neugarten, B., & Tobin, S. (1968). Disengagement and patterns of aging. In B. Neugarten (Ed.), *Middle age and aging.* Chicago: University of Chicago Press.

Haviland, J. J., & Malatesta, C. Z. (1982). The development of sex differences in nonverbal signals. In C. Mayo & N. Henley (Eds.), *Gender and nonverbal behavior.* New York: Springer-Verlag.

Haynes, S. G., Feinleib, M., & Eaker, E. D. (1983). Type A behavior and the ten-year incidence of coronary heart disease in the Framingham heart study. In R. H. Rosenman (Ed.), *Psychosomatic risk factors and coronary heart disease.* Bern, Switzerland: Huber.

Hays, R. B. (1985). A longitudinal study of friendship development. *Journal of Personality and Social Psychology, 48,* 909–924.

Hazan, C., & Shaver, P. (1986). *Parental caregiving style questionnaire.* Unpublished questionnaire.

Hazan, C., & Shaver, P. (1987). Romantic love conceptualized as an attachment process. *Journal of Personality and Social Psychology, 52,* 511–524.

Healy, D., & Williams, J. M. G. (1988). Dysrhythmia, dysphoria, and depression: The interaction of learned helplessness and circadian dysrhythmia in the pathogenesis of depression. *Psychological Bulletin, 103*(2), 163–178.

Heath, R. G. (1976). Cannabis sativa derivatives: Effects on brain function of monkeys. In G.G. Nahas (Ed.), *Marijuana: Chemistry, biochemistry and cellular effects.* New York: Springer.

Hegsted, D. M. (1984). What is a healthful diet? In J. D. Matarazzo, S. M. Weiss, J. A. Herd, N. E. Miller, & S. M. Weiss (Eds.), *Behavioral health: A handbook of health enhancement and disease prevention.* New York: Wiley.

Heider, F. (1958). *The psychology of interpersonal relations.* New York: Wiley.

Heiman, J. R. (1977). A psychophysiological exploration of sexual arousal patterns in females and males. *Psychophysiology, 14,* 266–274.

Helson, H., Blake, R. R., & Mouton, J. S. (1958). Petition-signing as adjustment to situational and personal factors. *Journal of Social Psychology, 48,* 3–10.

Helson, R., Mitchell, V., & Moane, G. (1984). Personality and patterns of adherence and nonadherence to the social clock. *Journal of Personality and Social Psychology, 46,* 1079–1096.

Helson, R., & Moane, G. (1987). Personality change in women from college to midlife. *Journal of Personality and Social Psychology, 53,* 176–186.

Helzer, J. E., Burnam, A., & McEvoy, L. T. (1991). Alcohol abuse and dependence. In L. N. Robins & D. A. Regier (Eds.), *Psychiatric disorders in America: The epidemiologic catchment area study.* New York: Free Press.

Helzer, J. E., Robins, L. N., & McEvoy, L. (1987). Post-traumatic stress disorder in the general population: Findings of the epidemiologic catchment area survey. *The New England Journal of Medicine, 317*(26), 1630–1634.

Hemphill, J. K. (1961). Why people attempt to lead. In L. Petrullo & B. M. Bass (Eds.), *Leadership and interpersonal behavior.* New York: Holt, Rinehart & Winston.

Hemsley, G. D., & Doob, A. N. (1978). The effect of looking behavior on perceptions of a communicator's credibility. *Journal of Applied Social Psychology, 8,* 136–144.

Hencken, J. (1984). Conceptualizations of homosexual behavior which preclude homosexual self-labeling. *Journal of Homosexuality, 9*(4), 53–63.

Hendrick, C., & Hendrick, S. S. (1983). *Liking, loving and relating.* Pacific Grove, CA: Brooks/Cole.

Hendrick, C., & Hendrick, S. S. (1989). Research on love: Does it measure up? *Journal of Personality and Social Psychology, 56,* 784–794.

Hendrick, S. S. (1981). Self-disclosure and marital satisfaction. *Journal of Personality and Social Psychology, 40,* 1150–1159.

Hendrick, S. S., Hendrick, C., & Adler, N. L. (1988). Romantic relationships: Love, satisfaction, and staying together. *Journal of Personality and Social Psychology, 54*(6), 980–988.

Henley, N. M. (1977). *Body politics: Power, sex and non-verbal communication.* Englewood Cliffs, NJ: Prentice–Hall.

Henley, N. M. (1986). *Body politics: Power, sex, and nonverbal communication* (2nd ed.). New York: Simon & Schuster.

Henley, N. M., & Freeman, J. (1981). The sexual politics of interpersonal behavior. In S. Cox (Ed.), *Female psychology: The emerging self.* New York: St. Martin's Press.

Herek, G. M. (1986). On heterosexual masculinity: Some psychical consequences of the social construction of gender and sexuality. *American Behavioral Scientist, 29,* 563–577.

Herek, G. M. (1988). Heterosexuals' attitudes toward lesbians and gay men: Correlates and gender differences. *Journal of Sex Research, 25,* 451–477.

Herek, G. M. (1991). Stigma, prejudice, and violence against lesbians and gay men. In J. C. Gonsiorek & J. D. Weinrich (Eds.), *Homosexuality: Research implications for public policy.* Newbury Park, CA: Sage Publications.

Herink, R. (Ed.). (1980). *The psychotherapy handbook.* New York: New American Library.

Hertzog, C., & Schaie, K. W. (1988). Stability and changes in adult intelligence: 2. Simultaneous analysis of longitudinal means and covariance structures. *Psychology and Aging, 3,* 122–130.

Herzberg, F. (1968). *Work and the nature of man.* London: Staples.

Hetherington, E. M. (1991). The role of individual differences and family relationships in children's coping with divorce and remarriage. In P. A. Cowan & M. Hetherington (Eds.), *Family transitions.* Hillsdale, NJ: Erlbaum.

Heun, L. R., & Heun, R. E. (1978). *Developing skills for human interactions.* Columbus, OH: Charles E. Merrill.

Hilgard, E. R. (1987). *Psychology in America: A historical survey.* San Diego: Harcourt Brace Jovanovich.

Hill, C. T., Rubin, Z., & Peplau, L. A. (1976). Breakups before marriage: The end of 103 affairs. *Journal of Social Issues, 32,* 147–168.

Hill, C. T., & Stull, D. E. (1987). Gender and self-disclosure: Strategies for exploring the issues. In V. J. Derlega & J. H. Berg (Eds.), *Self-disclosure: Theory, research, and therapy.* New York: Plenum.

Hill, J. P. (1987). Research on adolescents and their families: Past and prospect. In C. E. Irwin (Ed.), *Adolescent social behavior and health.* San Francisco: Jossey-Bass.

Hill, J. P., & Lynch, M. E. (1983). The intensification of gender-related role expectations during early adolescence. In J. Brooks-Gunn & A. C. Petersen (Eds.), *Girls at puberty.* New York: Plenum.

Hirokawa, R. Y. (1980). A comparative analysis of communication patterns within effective and ineffective decision-making groups. *Communication Monographs, 47,* 312–321.

Hiroto, D. S., & Seligman, M. E. P. (1975). Generality of learned helplessness in man. *Journal of Personality and Social Psychology, 31,* 311–327.

Hirsch, J., Fried, S. K., Edens, N. K., & Leibel, R. L. (1989). The fat cell. *Medical Clinics of North America, 73*(1), 83–96.

Hirschfeld, R. M. A., & Davidson, L. (1988). Risk factors for suicide. In A. J. Frances & R. E. Hales (Eds.), *Review of psychiatry* (Vol. 7). Washington, DC: American Psychiatric Press.

Hirschfeld, R. M. A., & Goodwin, F. K. (1988). Mood disorders. In J. A. Talbott, R. E. Hales, & S. C. Yudofsky (Eds.), *The American Psychiatric Press textbook of psychiatry.* Washington, DC: American Psychiatric Press.

Hite, S. (1976). *The Hite report.* New York: Macmillan.

Hobfoll, S. E. (1989). Conservation of resources: A new attempt at conceptualizing stress. *American Psychologist, 44,* 513–524.

Hochschild, A. (1989). *The second shift: Working parents and the revolution at home.* New York: Viking Penguin.

Hodges, B. H. (1974). Effects of valence on relative weighting in impression formation. *Journal of Personality and Social Psychology, 30,* 378–381.

Hodgson, J. W., & Fischer, J. L. (1981). Pathways of identity development in college women. *Sex Roles, 7,* 681–690.

Hofferth, S. L., & Phillips, D. A. (1987). Child care in the United States: 1970–1995. *Journal of Marriage and the Family, 49,* 559–571.

Hoffman, L. (1987). The effects on children of maternal and paternal employment. In N. Gerstel & H. Gross (Eds.), *Families and work.* Philadelphia: Temple University Press.

Hogan, D. P. (1978). The variable order of events in the life course. *American Sociological Review, 43,* 573–586.

Hogan, R., Raskin, R., & Fazzini, D. (1990). The dark side of charisma. In K. E. Clark & M. B. Clark (Eds.), *Measures of leadership.* West Orange, NJ: Leadership Library of America.

Hokanson, J. E., & Burgess, M. (1962). The effects of three types of aggression on vascular processes. *Journal of Abnormal and Social Psychology, 65,* 446–449.

Holahan, C. J. (1986). Environmental Psychology. *Annual Review of Psychology, 37,* 381–407.

Holahan, C. J., & Moos, R. H. (1985). Life stress and health: Personality, coping, and family support in stress resistance. *Journal of Personality and Social Psychology, 49*(3), 739–747.

Holahan, C. J., & Moos, R. H. (1990). Life stressors, resistance factors, and improved psychological functioning: An extension of the stress resistance paradigm. *Journal of Personality and Social Psychology, 58*(5), 909–917.

Holland, D. C., & Eisenhart, M. A. (1990). *Educated in romance: Women, achievement, and college culture.* Chicago: University of Chicago Press.

Holland, J. L. (1973). *Making vocational choices: A theory of careers.* Englewood Cliffs, NJ: Prentice-Hall.

Holland, J. L. (1985). *Making vocational choices: A theory of vocational personalities and work environments.* Englewood Cliffs, NJ: Prentice-Hall.

Hollander, E. P. (1985). Leadership and power. In G. Lindzey & E. Aronson (Eds.), *Handbook of social psychology* (3rd ed.). New York: Random House.

Hollander, E. P. (1992). The essential interdependence of leadership and followership. *Current Directions in Psychological Science, 1*(2), 71–75.

Holman, T. B., & Jacquart, M. (1988). Leisure-activity patterns and marital satisfaction: A further test. *Journal of Marriage and the Family, 50,* 69–77.

Holmes, D. S. (1984). Meditation and somatic arousal reduction: A review of the experimental evidence. *American Psychologist, 39*(1), 1–10.

Holmes, T. H. (1979). Development and application of a quantitative measure of life change magnitude. In J. E. Barrett, R. M. Rose, & G. L. Klerman (Eds.), *Stress and mental disorder.* New York: Raven.

Holmes, T. H., & Masuda, M. (1974). Life change and illness susceptibility. In B. S. Dohrenwend & B. P. Dohrenwend (Eds.), *Stressful life events: Their nature and effects.* New York: Wiley.

Holmes, T. H., & Rahe, R. H. (1967). The Social Readjustment Rating Scale. *Journal of Psychosomatic Research, 11,* 213–218.

Holt, R. R. (1982). Occupational stress. In L. Goldberger & S. Breznitz (Eds.), *Handbook of stress: Theoretical and clinical aspects.* New York: Free Press.

Holter, H. (1975). Sex roles and social change. In M. T. S. Mednick, S. S. Tangri, & L. W. Hoffman (Eds.), *Women and achievement: Social and motivational analyses.* Washington, DC: Hemisphere.

Honeycutt, J. M. (1986). A model of marital functioning based on an attraction paradigm and social-penetration dimensions. *Journal of Marriage and the Family, 48,* 651–667.

Hopkins, A. H. (1983). *Work and satisfaction in the public sector.* Totowa, NJ: Rowman & Allanheld.

Horner, M. J. (1972). Toward an understanding of achievement related conflicts in women. *Journal of Social Issues, 28,* 157–176.

Horowitz, F. D., & O'Brien, M. (1989). In the interest of the nation: A reflective essay on the state of our knowledge and the challenges before us. *American Psychologist, 44,* 441–445.

Horowitz, M. J. (1979). Psychological response to serious life events. In V. Hamilton & D. M. Warburton (Eds.), *Human stress and cognition: An information processing approach.* New York: Wiley.

House, J. S. (1981). *Work stress and social support.* Reading, MA: Addison-Wesley.

House, J. S., Landis, K. R., & Umberson, D. (1988). Social relationships and health. *Science, 241,* 540–545.

House, R. J., & Singh, J. V. (1987). Organizational behavior: Some new directions for I/O psychology. *Annual Review of Psychology, 38,* 669–718.

Houston, B. K., & Kelly, K. E. (1989). Hostility in employed women: Relation to work and marital experiences, social support, stress, and anger expression. *Personality and Social Psychology Bulletin, 15,* 175–182.

Howe, M. L., & Hunter, M. A. (1986). Long-term memory in adulthood: An examination of the development of storage and retrieval processes at acquisition and retention. *Developmental Review, 6,* 334–364.

Howell, J. M., & Frost, P. J. (1989). A laboratory study of charismatic leadership. *Organizational Behavior and Human Decision Processes, 43,* 243–269.

Hubbard, L. R. (1989). *Scientology: The fundamentals of thought.* Los Angeles: Bridge.

Huesmann, L. R., & Morikawa, S. (1985). Learned helplessness and depression: Cognitive factors in treatment and inoculation. In S. Reiss & R. R. Bootzin (Eds.), *Theoretical issues in behavior therapy.* Orlando, FL: Academic Press.

Hui, Y. H. (1985). *Principles and issues in nutrition.* Monterey, CA: Wadsworth Health Sciences.

Hull, J. G., Van Treuren, R. R., & Virnelli, S. (1987). Hardiness and health: A critique and alternative approach. *Journal of Personality and Social Psychology, 53*(3), 518–530.

Hultsch, D. F., & Dixon, R. A. (1990). Learning and memory in aging. In J. E. Birren & K. W. Schaie (Eds.), *Handbook of the psychology of aging* (3rd ed.). San Diego: Academic Press.

Humphreys, M. S., & Revelle, W. (1984). Personality, motivation, and performance: A theory of the relationship between individual differences and information processing. *Psychological Review, 91,* 153–184.

Hunt, M. (1974). *Sexual behavior in the 1970s.* Chicago: Playboy Press.

Hunt, W. A., & Matarazzo, J. D. (1982). Changing smoking behavior: A critique. In R. J. Gatchel, A. Baum, & J. E. Singer (Eds.), *Handbook of psychology and health: Vol. 1. Clinical psychology and behavioral medicine, overlapping disciplines.* Hillsdale, NJ: Erlbaum.

Huseman, R. C., Lahiff, J. M., & Hatfield, J. D. (1976). *Interpersonal communication in organizations.* Boston: Holbrook Press.

Huston, A. C. (1983). Sex-typing. In P. H. Mussen (Ed.), *Handbook of child psychology* (Vol. 4, 4th ed.). New York: Wiley.

Huston, A. C., Wright, J. C., Rice, M. L., Kerkman, D., & St. Peters, M. (1990). Development of television viewing patterns in early childhood: A longitudinal investigation. *Developmental Psychology, 26,* 409–420.

Huston-Stein, A., & Bailey, M. (1973). The socialization of achievement motivation in females. *Psychological Bulletin, 80*(5), 345–366.

Huyck, M. H., & Hoyer, W. J. (1982). *Adult development and aging.* Belmont, CA: Wadsworth.

Hyde, J. S. (1981). How large are cognitive gender differences? *American Psychologist, 36,* 892–901.

Hyde, J. S. (1984). How large are gender differences in aggression? A developmental meta-analysis. *Developmental Psychology, 20,* 722–736.

Hyde, J. S. (1990). *Understanding human sexuality* (4th ed.). New York: McGraw-Hill.

Hyde, J. S. (1991). *Half the human experience: The psychology of women.* Lexington, MA: D. C. Heath.

Hyde, J. S., Fennema, E., & Lamon, S. J. (1990). Gender differences in mathematics performance: A meta-analysis. *Psychological Bulletin, 107,* 139–155.

Hyde, J. S., & Linn, M. C. (1988). Gender differences in verbal ability: A meta-analysis. *Psychological Bulletin, 104,* 53–69.

Hyman, B. T., Van Hoesen, G. W., Damasio, A. R., & Barnes, C. L. (1984). Alzheimer's disease: Cell-specific pathology isolates the hippocampal formation. *Science, 225,* 1168–1170.

Ineichen, B. (1979). The social geography of marriage. In M. Cook & G. Wilson (Eds.), *Love and attraction.* New York: Pergamon Press.

Inhelder, B., & Piaget, J. (1958). *The growth of logical thinking from childhood to adolescence.* New York: Basic Books.

Irwin, M., Daniels, M., Smith, T. L., Bloom, E., & Weiner, H. (1987). Impaired natural killer cell activity during bereavement. *Brain, Behavior, and Immunity, 1,* 98–104.

Isherwood, J., Adam, K. S., & Hornblow, A. R. (1982). Readjustment, desirability, expectedness, mastery and outcome dimensions of life stress suicide attempt and auto-accident. *Journal of Human Stress, 8*(1), 11–18.

Ivancevich, J. M., Matteson, M. T., Freedman, S. M., & Phillips, J. S. (1990). Worksite stress management interventions. *American Psychologist, 45*(2), 252–261.

Jackman, M. R., & Senter, M. S. (1981). Beliefs about race, gender, and social class: Different, therefore unequal. In D. J. Treiman & R. V. Robinson (Eds.), *Research in stratification and mobility* (Vol. 2). Greenwich, CT: JAI.

Jackson, S., & Schuler, R. (1985). A meta-analysis and conceptual critique of research on role ambiguity and role conflict in work settings. *Organizational Behavior and Human Decision Processes, 36,* 16–78.

Jacob, R. G., & Turner, S. M. (1984). Somatoform disorders. In S. M. Turner & M. Hersen (Eds.), *Adult psychopathology and diagnosis.* New York: Wiley.

Jacobs, J. (1971). *Adolescent suicide.* New York: Wiley-Interscience.

Jacobs, T. J., & Charles, E. (1980). Life events and the occurrence of cancer in children. *Psychosomatic Medicine, 42*(1), 11–24.

Jacobson, E. (1938). *Progressive relaxation.* Chicago: University of Chicago Press.

Jacobson, E. (1970). *You must relax.* New York: McGraw-Hill.

Jaffe, J. H. (1986). Opioids. In A. J. Frances & R. E. Hales (Eds.), *Psychiatric Update: Annual Review* (Vol. 5). Washington, DC: American Psychiatric Press.

Jaffe, J. H. (1992). Opiates: Clinical aspects. In J. H. Lowinson, P. Ruiz, & R. B. Millman (Eds.), *Substance abuse: A compre-*

hensive textbook (2nd ed.). Baltimore: Williams & Wilkins.

Jahoda, M. (1958). *Current concepts of positive mental health.* New York: Basic Books.

Jamison, K. R., Gerner, R. H., Hammen, C., & Padesky, C. (1980). Clouds and silver linings: Positive experiences associated with the primary affective disorders. *American Journal of Psychiatry, 137*(2), 198–202.

Jangid, R. K., Vyas, J. N., & Shukla, T. R. (1988). The effect of the Transcendental Meditation Programme on the normal individual. *Journal of Personality & Clinical Studies, 4*(1), 145–149.

Janis, I. L. (1958). *Psychological stress.* New York: Wiley.

Janis, I. L. (1972). *Victims of groupthink.* Boston: Houghton Mifflin.

Janis, I. L. (1973, January). Groupthink. *Yale Alumni Magazine,* pp. 16–19.

Janis, I. L. (1982). *Groupthink: Psychological studies of policy decisions and fiascoes.* Boston: Houghton Mifflin.

Janis, I. L. (1983). Stress inoculation in health care. In D. H. Meichenbaum & M. E. Jaremko (Eds.), *Stress reduction and prevention.* New York: Plenum.

Jarvik, M. E., & Schneider, N. G. (1992). Nicotine. In J. H. Lowinson, P. Ruiz, & R. B. Millman (Eds.), *Substance abuse: A comprehensive textbook* (2nd ed.). Baltimore: Williams & Wilkins.

Jay, K., & Young, A. (1979). *The gay report.* New York: Summit Books.

Jefferson, J. W., & Greist, J. H. (1989). Lithium therapy. In H. I. Kaplan & B. J. Sadock (Eds.), *Comprehensive textbook of psychiatry/V.* Baltimore: Williams & Wilkins.

Jeffery, R. W., Adlis, S. A., & Forster, J. L. (1991). Prevalence of dieting among working men and women: The healthy worker project. *Health Psychology, 10*(4), 274–281.

Jeffrey, D. B., & Lemnitzer, N. (1981). Diet, exercise, obesity and related health problems: A macroenvironmental analysis. In J. M. Ferguson & C. B. Taylor (Eds.), *The comprehensive handbook of behavioral medicine: Vol. 2. Syndromes and special areas.* Jamaica, NY: Spectrum.

Jemmott, J. B., III, & Magloire, K. (1988). Academic stress, social support, and secretory Immunoglobin A. *Journal of Personality and Social Psychology, 55*(5), 803–810.

Jenike, M. A. (1987). Drug abuse. In E. Rubenstein & D. D. Federman (Eds.), *Scientific American medicine.* New York: Scientific American Press.

Jenike, M. A., Baer, L., & Greist, J. H. (1990). Clomipramine versus fluoxetine in obsessive-compulsive disorder: A retrospective comparison of side effects and efficacy. *Journal of Clinical Psychopharmacology, 10*(2), 122–124.

Jepson, C., & Chaiken, S. (1986). *The effect of anxiety on the systematic processing of persuasive communications.* Washington, DC: Paper presented at the annual meeting of the American Psychological Association.

John, O. P. (1990). The "big five" factor taxonomy: Dimensions of personality in the natural language and in questionnaires. In L. A. Pervin (Ed.), *Handbook of personality: Theory and research.* New York: Guilford Press.

Johnson, B. D., & Muffler, J. (1992). Sociocultural aspects of drug use and abuse in the 1990s. In J. H. Lowinson, P. Ruiz, & R. B. Millman (Eds.), *Substance abuse: A comprehensive textbook* (2nd ed.). Baltimore: Williams & Wilkins.

Johnson, D. R., White, L. K., Edwards, J. N., & Booth, A. (1986). Dimensions of marital quality: Toward methodological and conceptual refinement. *Journal of Family Issues, 7,* 31–49.

Johnson, D. W. (1981). *Reaching out: Interpersonal effectiveness and self-actualization.* Englewood Cliffs, NJ: Prentice-Hall.

Johnson, D. W., & Johnson, F. (1991). *Joining together* (4th ed.). Englewood Cliffs, NJ: Prentice-Hall.

Johnson, J. G., & Bornstein, R. F. (1991). Does daily stress independently predict psychopathology? *Journal of Social and Clinical Psychology, 10*(1), 58–74.

Johnston, W. B., & Packer, A. H. (1987). *Workforce 2000: Work and workers for the twenty-first century.* Indianapolis, IN: Hudson Institute.

Jones, E. E. (1964). *Ingratiation.* New York: Appleton-Century-Crofts.

Jones, E. E., & Davis, K. (1965). From acts to dispositions: The attribution process in person perception. In L. Berkowitz (Ed.), *Advances in experimental social psychology* (Vol. 2). New York: Academic Press.

Jones, E. E., & Nisbett, R. E. (1971). *The actor and the observer: Divergent perceptions of the causes of behavior.* Morristown, NJ: General Learning Press.

Jones, E. E., & Pittman, T. S. (1982). Toward a general theory of strategic self-presentation. In J. Suls (Ed.), *Psychological perspectives on the self.* Hillsdale, NJ: Erlbaum.

Jones, E. E., Rhodewalt, F., Berglas, S., & Skelton, J. A. (1981). Effects of strategic self-presentation on subsequent self-esteem. *Journal of Personality and Social Psychology, 41,* 407–421.

Jones, J. (1990, October). Directorate focuses efforts on problem of violence in U. S. *APA Monitor,* p. 22.

Jones, M. C. (1965). Psychological correlates of somatic development. *Child Development, 36,* 899–911.

Jones, R. A., & Brehm, J. W. (1970). Persuasiveness of one- and two-sided communications as a function of awareness there are two sides. *Journal of Experimental Social Psychology, 6,* 47–56.

Jones, S. C. (1973). Self- and interpersonal evaluations: Esteem theories versus consistency theories. *Psychological Bulletin, 79*(3), 185–199.

Jones, W. H., Briggs, S. R., & Smith, T. G. (1986). Shyness: Conceptualization and measurement. *Journal of Personality and Social Psychology, 51,* 629–639.

Jones, W. H., & Carpenter, B. N. (1986). Shyness, social behavior, and relationships. In W. H. Jones, J. M. Cheek, & S. R. Briggs (Eds.), *Shyness: Perspectives on research and treatment.* New York: Plenum.

Jones, W. H., Freeman, J. A., & Goswick, R. A. (1981). The persistence of loneliness: Self and other determinants. *Journal of Personality, 49,* 27–48.

Jones, W. H., Hobbs, S. A., & Hockenbury, D. (1982). Loneliness and social skill deficits. *Journal of Personality and Social Psychology, 42*(4), 682–689.

Jones, W. H., Sansome, C., & Helm, B. (1983). Loneliness and interpersonal judgments. *Personality and Social Psychology Bulletin, 9,* 437–442.

Josselson, R. (1987). *Finding herself: Pathways to identity development in women.* San Francisco: Jossey-Bass.

Jourard, S. M. (1971). *The transparent self.* New York: Van Nostrand Reinhold.

Jourard, S. M., & Landsman, T. (1980). *Healthy personality: An approach from the viewpoint of humanistic psychology.* New York: Macmillan.

Julien, R. M. (1991). *A primer of drug action* (6th ed.). New York: W. H. Freeman.

Jung, C. G. (1917). On the psychology of the unconscious. In *Collected Works* (Vol. 7). Princeton, NJ: Princeton University Press.

Kabanoff, B. (1980). Work and nonwork: A review of models, methods, and findings. *Psychological Bulletin, 88,* 60–77.

Kacerguis, M. A., & Adams, G. R. (1980). Erikson stage resolution: The relationship between identity and intimacy. *Journal of Youth and Adolescence, 9,* 117–126.

Kahle, L. R., & Homer, P. M. (1985). Physical attractiveness of the celebrity endorser: A social adaptation perspective. *Journal of Consumer Research, 11,* 954–961.

Kahn, S., Zimmerman, G., Csikszentmihalyi, M., & Getzels, J. W. (1985). Relations between identity in young adulthood and intimacy at midlife. *Journal of Personality and Social Psychology, 49,* 1316–1322.

Kalant, H., & Kalant, O. J. (1979). Death in amphetamine users: Causes and rates. In D. E. Smith (Ed.), *Amphetamine use, misuse and abuse.* Boston: G. K. Hall.

Kalick, S. M., & Hamilton, T. E., III. (1986). The matching hypothesis reexamined. *Journal of Personality and Social Psychology, 51*(4), 673–682.

Kalmuss, D., Davidson, A., & Cushman, L. (1992). Parenting expectations, experiences, and adjustment to parenthood: A test of the violated expectations framework. *Journal of Marriage and the Family, 52,* 516–526.

Kaminer, W. (1992). *I'm dysfunctional, you're dysfunctional.* Reading, MA: Addison-Wesley.

Kandel, D. B. (1978). Similarity in real-life adolescent friendship pairs. *Journal of Personality and Social Psychology, 36,* 306–312.

Kandel, E. R. (1990). Disorders of mood: Depression, mania, and anxiety disorders. In E. R. Kandel, J. H. Schwartz, & T. M. Jessell (Eds.), *Principles of neural science* (3rd ed.). New York: Elsevier.

Kane, J. (1991). *Be sick well: A healthy approach to chronic illness.* Oakland, CA: New Harbinger.

Kanin, E. J., Davidson, K. R., & Scheck, S. R. (1970). A research note on male-female differentials in the experience of heterosexual love. *Journal of Sex Research, 6,* 64–72.

Kannel, W. B., & Cupples, L. A. (1989). Cardiovascular and noncardiovascular consequences of obesity. In A. J. Stunkard & A. Baum (Eds.), *Perspectives in behavioral medicine: Eating, sleeping, and sex.* Hillsdale, NJ: Erlbaum.

Kanner, A. D., Coyne, J. C., Schaefer, C., & Lazarus, R. S. (1981). Comparison of two modes of stress measurement: Daily hassles and uplifts versus major life events. *Journal of Behavioral Medicine, 4,* 1–39.

Kanter, R. M. (1977). *Men and women of the corporation.* New York: Basic Books.

Kaplan, H. I. (1985). History of psychosomatic medicine. In H. I. Kaplan & B. J. Sadock (Eds.), *Comprehensive textbook of psychiatry/IV.* Baltimore: Williams & Wilkins.

Kaplan, H. S. (1974). *The new sex therapy.* New York: Brunner/Mazel.

Kaplan, H. S. (1979). *Disorders of sexual desire and other new concepts and techniques in sex therapy.* New York: Simon & Schuster.

Kaplan, H. S. (1983). *The evaluation of sexual disorders: Psychological and medical aspects.* New York: Brunner/Mazel.

Kaplan, M. (1983). A woman's view of DSM-III. *American Psychologist, 38,* 786–792.

Kaplan, M. F., & Anderson, N. H. (1973). Information integration theory and reinforcement theory as approaches to interpersonal attraction. *Journal of Personality and Social Psychology, 28,* 301–312.

Kaplan, N. M. (1986). Dietary aspects of the treatment of hypertension. In L. Breslow, J. E. Fielding, & L. B. Lave (Eds.), *Annual review of public health* (Vol. 7). Palo Alto, CA: Annual Reviews.

Karasek, R. A., Jr. (1979). Job demands, job decision latitude, and mental strain: Implications for job redesign. *Administrative Science Quarterly, 24,* 285–308.

Karasek, R. A., Jr., Baker, D., Marxer, F., Ahlbom, A., & Theorell, T. (1981). Job decision latitude, job demands, and cardiovascular disease: A prospective study of Swedish men. *American Journal of Public Health, 71,* 694–705.

Karasek, R. A., Jr., & Theorell, T. (1990). *Healthy work: Stress, productivity, and the reconstruction of working life.* New York: Basic Books.

Karlen, A. (1971). *Sexuality and homosexuality.* New York: Norton.

Karno, M., & Golding, J. M. (1991). Obsessive compulsive disorder. In L. N. Robins & D. A. Regier (Eds.), *Psychiatric disorders in America: The epidemiologic catchment area study.* New York: Free Press.

Karson, C. N., Kleinman, J. E., & Wyatt, R. J. (1986). Biochemical concepts of schizophrenia. In T. Millon & G. L. Klerman (Eds.), *Contemporary directions in psychopathology.* New York: Guilford Press.

Kass, F., Spitzer, R. L., Williams, J. B. W., & Widiger, T. (1989). Self-defeating personality disorder and DSM-III-R: Development of the diagnostic criteria. *American Journal of Psychiatry, 146,* 1022–1026.

Kastenbaum, R. (1985). Dying and death: A life–span approach. In J. E. Birren & K. W. Schaie (Eds.), *Handbook of the psychology of aging* (2nd ed.). New York: Van Nostrand Reinhold.

Kastenbaum, R. (1986). *Death, dying, and human experience.* Columbus, OH: Charles E. Merrill.

Katz, B. L. (1991). The psychological impact of stranger versus nonstranger rape on victims' recovery. In A. Parrot & L. Bechhofer (Eds.), *Acquaintance rape: The hidden crime.* New York: Wiley.

Katz, L., & Epstein, S. (1991). Constructive thinking and coping with laboratory-induced stress. *Journal of Personality and Social Psychology, 61*(5), 789–800.

Katz, S., & Mazur, M. A. (1979). *Understanding the rape victim.* New York: Wiley.

Kauffman, D. R., & Steiner, I. D. (1968). Conformity as an ingratiation technique. *Journal of Experimental Social Psychology, 4,* 404–414.

Kausler, D. H. (1985). Episodic memory: Memorizing performance. In N. Charness (Ed.), *Aging and human performance.* Chichester, England: Wiley.

Kavesh, L., & Lavin, C. (1988). *Tales from the front.* New York: Doubleday.

Kazdin, A. E. (1982). History of behavior modification. In A.S. Bellack, M. Hersen, & A.E. Kazdin (Eds.), *International handbook of behavior modification and behavior therapy.* New York: Plenum.

Kazdin, A. E., & Wilson, G. T. (1978). *Evaluation of behavior therapy: Issues, evidence and research strategies.* Cambridge, MA: Ballinger.

Keen, S. (1991). *Fire in the belly: On being a man.* New York: Bantam Books.

Keesey, R. E. (1986). A set-point theory of obesity. In K. D. Brownell & J. P. Foreyt (Eds.), *Handbook of eating disorders: Physiology, psychology, and treatment of obesity, anorexia, and bulimia.* New York: Basic Books.

Keesey, R. E. (1988). The body-weight set point. *Postgraduate Medicine, 83,* 114–127.

Keesey, R. E., & Powley, T. L. (1975). Hypothalamic regulation of body weight. *American Scientist, 63,* 558–565.

Keesey, R. E., & Powley, T. L. (1986). The regulation of body weight. *Annual Review of Psychology, 37,* 109–133.

Keinan, G. (1987). Decision making under stress: Scanning of alternatives under controllable and uncontrollable threats. *Journal of Personality and Social Psychology, 52*(3), 639–644.

Keith, P. M. (1986). The social context and resources of the unmarried in old age. *International Journal of Aging and Human Development, 23*(2), 81–96.

Keith, S. J., Regier, D. A., & Rae, D. S. (1991). Schizophrenic disorders. In L. N. Robins & D. A. Regier (Eds.), *Psychiatric disorders in America: The epidemiologic catchment area study.* New York: Free Press.

Kelley, H. H. (1950). The warm-cold dimension in first impressions of persons. *Journal of Personality, 18,* 431–439.

Kelley, H. H. (1967). Attribution theory in social psychology. In D. Levine (Ed.), *Nebraska Symposium on Motivation* (Vol. 15). Lincoln: University of Nebraska Press.

Kelley, H. H., & Thibaut, J. W. (1978). *Interpersonal relations: A theory of interdependence.* New York: Wiley-Interscience.

Kelley, K., Byrne, D., Przybyla, D. P. J., Eberly, C., Eberly, B., Greendlinger, V., Wan, C. K., & Gorsky, J. (1985). Chronic self-destructiveness: Conceptualization, measurement and initial validation of the construct. *Motivation and Emotion, 9*(2), 135–151.

Kennedy, J. L., & Laramore, D. (1988). *Joyce Lain Kennedy's career book* (1st ed.). Lincolnwood, IL: VGM Career Horizons.

Kennedy, J. L., & Laramore, D. (1993). *Joyce Lain Kennedy's career book* (2nd ed.). Lincolnwood, IL: VGM Career Horizons.

Kenrick, D. T. (1987). Gender, genes, and the social environment. In P. C. Shaver & C. Hendrick (Eds.), *Review of Personality and Social Psychology* (Vol. 8). Newbury Park, CA: Sage Publications.

Kessler-Harris, A. (1982). *Out to work: A history of wage-earning women in the United States.* New York: Oxford University Press.

Keyes, R. (1980). We, the lonely people. In J. Hartog, J. R. Audy, & Y. A. Cohen (Eds.), *The anatomy of loneliness.* New York: International Universities Press.

Keyes, R. (1991). *Timelock: How life got so hectic and what you can do about it.* New York: HarperCollins.

Khot, V., & Wyatt, R. J. (1991). Not all that moves is tardive dyskinesia. *American Journal of Psychiatry, 148*(5), 661–666.

Kiecolt-Glaser, J. K., Garner, W., Speicher, C., Penn, G. M., Holliday, J., & Glaser, R. (1984). Psychosocial modifiers of immunocompetence in medical students. *Psychosomatic Medicine, 46*(1), 7–14.

Kiecolt-Glaser, J. K., Glaser, R., Williger, D., Stout, J., Messick, G., Sheppard, S., Ricker, D., Romisher, S. C., Briner, W., Bonnell, G., & Donnerberg, R. (1985). Psychosocial enhancement of immunocompetence in a geriatric population. *Health Psychology, 4*(1), 25–42.

Kiecolt-Glaser, J. K., Kennedy, S., Malkoff, S., Fisher, L., Speicher, C. E., & Glaser, R. (1988). Marital discord and immunity in males. *Psychosomatic Medicine, 50,* 213–229.

Kiesler, D. J. (1986). The 1982 interpersonal circle: An analysis of DSM-III personality disorders. In T. Millon & G. L. Klerman (Eds.), *Contemporary directions in psychopathology: Toward the DSM-IV.* New York: Guilford Press.

Kiesler, S. B., & Baral, R. L. (1970). The search for a romantic partner: The effects of self-esteem and physical attractiveness on romantic behavior. In K. J. Gergen & D. Marlowe (Eds.), *Personality and social behavior.* Reading, MA: Addison-Wesley.

Kimball, M. M. (1989). A new perspective on women's math achievement. *Psychological Bulletin, 105,* 198–214.

King, G. R., & Ellinwood, E. H. (1992). Amphetamines and other stimulants. In J. H. Lowinson, P. Ruiz, & R. B. Millman (Eds.), *Substance abuse: A comprehensive textbook* (2nd ed.). Baltimore: Williams & Wilkins.

Kinsbourne, M. (1980). If sex differences in brain lateralization exist, they have yet to be discovered. *Behavioral and Brain Sciences, 3,* 241–242.

Kinsey, A. C., Pomeroy, W. B., & Martin, C. E. (1948). *Sexual behavior in the human male.* Philadelphia: Saunders.

Kinsey, A. C., Pomeroy, W. B., Martin, C. E., & Gebhard, P. H. (1953). *Sexual behavior in the human female.* Philadelphia: Saunders.

Kinsman, R. A., Dirks, J. F., & Jones, N. F. (1982). Psychomaintenance of chronic physical illness: Clinical assessment of personal styles affecting medical management. In T. Millon, C. Green, & R. Meagher (Eds.), *Handbook of clinical health psychology.* New York: Plenum.

Kirby, D. F., & Julian, N. B. (1981). Treatment of women in high school history textbooks. *Social Studies, 72*, 203–207.

Kissebah, A. H., Freedman, D. S., & Peiris, A. N. (1989). Health risks of obesity. *Medical Clinics of North America, 73*(1), 111–138.

Kite, M. E. (1984). Sex differences in attitudes towards homosexuals: A meta-analytic review. *Journal of Homosexuality, 10*(1–2), 69–81.

Kitson, G. C., & Morgan, L. A. (1990). The multiple consequences of divorce: A decade review. *Journal of Marriage and the Family, 52*, 913–924.

Kitson, G. C., & Sussman, M. B. (1982). Marital complaints, demographic characteristics, and symptoms of mental distress in divorce. *Journal of Marriage and the Family, 44*, 87–101.

Klassen, M. (1987). How to get the most out of your time. In A. D. Timpe (Ed.), *The management of time*. New York: Facts On File.

Kleber, H. D., & Gawin, F. H. (1986). Cocaine. In A. J. Frances & R. E. Hales (Eds.), *Psychiatric Update: Annual Review* (Vol. 5). Washington, DC: American Psychiatric Press.

Klein, D. N., & Rubovits, D. R. (1987). The reliability of subjects' reports of life events inventories: A longitudinal study. *Journal of Behavioral Medicine, 10*, 501–512.

Klein, M. (1948). *Contributions to psychoanalysis*. London: Hogarth.

Kleinginna, P. R., & Kleinginna, A. M. (1988). Current trends toward convergence of the behavioristic, functional, and cognitive perspectives in experimental psychology. *The Psychological Record, 38*, 369–392.

Kleinke, C. L. (1986). Gaze and eye contact: A research review. *Psychological Bulletin, 100*, 78–100.

Kleinke, C. L. (1991). *Coping with life challenges*. Pacific Grove, CA: Brooks/Cole.

Kleinke, C. L., & Staneski, R. A. (1980). First impressions of female bust size. *Journal of Social Psychology, 110*, 123–134.

Kleinmuntz, B. (1980). *Essentials of abnormal psychology*. San Francisco: Harper & Row.

Klerman, G. L. (1978). Long-term treatment of affective disorders. In M. A. Lipton, A. DiMascio, & K. F. Killam (Eds.), *Psychopharmacology: A generation of progress*. New York: Raven.

Klerman, G. L. (1988). Relationship between anxiety and depression. In M. Roth, R. Noyes, & G. D. Burrows (Eds.), *Handbook of anxiety: Biological, clinical, and cultural perspectives* (Vol. 1). Amsterdam: Elsevier.

Kluft, R. P. (1987). Making the diagnosis of multiple personality disorder. In F. Flach (Ed.), *Diagnostics and psychopathology*. New York: Norton.

Knittle, J. L., Merritt, R. J., Dixon-Shanies, D., Ginsberg-Fellner, F., Timmers, K. I., & Katz, D. P. (1981). Childhood obesity. In R. M. Suskind (Ed.), *Textbook of pediatric nutrition*. New York: Raven Press.

Knoth, R., Boyd, K., & Singer, B. (1988). Empirical tests of sexual selection theory: Predictions of sex differences in onset, intensity, and time course of sexual arousal. *Journal of Sex Research, 24*, 73–89.

Knox, D., & Wilson, K. (1981). Dating behaviors of university students. *Family Relations, 30*, 255–258.

Knussman, R., Christiansen, K., & Couwenbergs, C. (1986). Relations between sex hormone levels and sexual behavior in men. *Archives of Sexual Behavior, 15*(5), 429–445.

Kobak, R. R., & Sceery, A. (1988). Attachment in late adolescence: Working models, affect regulation, and representations of self and others. *Child Development, 59*, 135–146.

Kobasa, S. C. (1979). Stressful life events, personality, and health: An inquiry into hardiness. *Journal of Personality and Social Psychology, 37*, pp. 1–11.

Kobasa, S. C. (1984, September). How much stress can you survive? *American Health*, pp. 64–77.

Kobasa, S. C., Maddi, S. R., & Kahn, S. (1982). Hardiness and health: A prospective study. *Journal of Personality and Social Psychology, 42*(1), 168–177.

Kogan, N., & Wallach, M. (1964). *Risk taking: A study in cognition and personality*. New York: Holt, Rinehart & Winston.

Kohlberg, L. (1966). A cognitive-developmental analysis of children's sex-role concepts and attitudes. In E. E. Maccoby (Ed.), *The development of sex differences*. Stanford, CA: Stanford University Press.

Kohn, P. M., Lafreniere, K., & Gurevich, M. (1991). Hassles, health, and personality. *Journal of Personality and Social Psychology, 61*(3), 478–482.

Kohut, H. (1971). *Analysis of the self*. New York: International Universities Press.

Komarovsky, M. (1976). *Dilemmas of masculinity*. New York: Norton.

Koob, G. F., & Bloom, F. E. (1988). Cellular and molecular mechanisms of drug dependence. *Science, 242*, 715–723.

Koocher, G. P. (1971). Swimming, social competence, and personality change. *Journal of Personality and Social Psychology, 18*, 275–278.

Korchin, S. J. (1976). *Modern clinical psychology: Principles of intervention in the clinic and community*. New York: Basic Books.

Koren, P., Carlton, K., & Shaw, D. (1980). Marital conflict: Relations among behaviors, outcomes, and distress. *Journal of Consulting and Clinical Psychology, 48*, 460–468.

Koss, M. P. (1985). The hidden rape victim: Personality, attitudinal, and situational characteristics. *Psychology of Women Quarterly, 9*, 193–212.

Koss, M. P., Gidycz, C. A., & Wisniewski, N. (1987). The scope of rape: Incidence and prevalence of sexual aggression and victimization in a national sample of higher education students. *Journal of Consulting and Clinical Psychology, 55*, 162–170.

Kotkin, M. (1985). To marry or live together? *Lifestyles: A Journal of Changing Patterns, 7*(3), 156–170.

Kraemer, D. L., & Hastrup, J. L. (1988). Crying in adults: Self-control and autonomic correlates. *Journal of Social and Clinical Psychology, 6*(1), 53–68.

Kramer, B. A. (1985). Use of ECT in California, 1977–1983. *American Journal of Psychiatry, 142*(10), 1190–1192.

Kramer, M. A., Aral, S. O., & Curran, J. W. (1980). Self-reported behavior pattern of patients attending a sexually transmitted disease clinic. *American Journal of Public Health, 70*, 997–1000.

Krantz, D. S., Baum, A., & Wideman, M. V. (1980). Assessment of preferences for self-treatment and information in health care. *Journal of Personality and Social Psychology, 39*, 977–990.

Krantz, D. S., Glass, D. C., Contrada, R., & Miller, N. E. (1981). *Behavior and health: National Science Foundation's second five-year outlook on science and technology*. Washington, DC: U. S. Government Printing Office.

Krantz, D. S., & Manuck, S. B. (1984). Acute psychophysiologic reactivity and risk of cardiovascular disease: A review and methodological critique. *Psychological Bulletin, 96*, 435–464.

Krasner, L., & Ullmann, L. P. (Eds.). (1965). *Research in behavior modification*. New York: Holt, Rinehart & Winston.

Kravitz, D. A., & Martin, B. (1986). Ringelmann rediscovered: The original article. *Journal of Personality and Social Psychology, 50*, 936–941.

Krilov, L. R. (1988, March). Sexually transmitted diseases in adolescents. *Medical Aspects of Human Sexuality*, 67–77.

Krueger, D. W. (1981). Stressful life events and the return to heroin use. *Journal of Human Stress, 7*(2), 3–8.

Krueger, W. C. F. (1929). The effect of overlearning on retention. *Journal of Experimental Psychology, 12*, 71–78.

Kubey, R., & Csikszentmihalyi, M. (1990). *Leisure and the benefits of television*. Hillsdale, NJ: Erlbaum.

Kübler-Ross, E. (1969). *On death and dying*. New York: Macmillan.

Kübler-Ross, E. (1970). The dying patient's point of view. In O. G. Brim, Jr., H. E. Freeman, S. Levine, & N. A. Scotch (Eds.), *The dying patient*. New York: Russell Sage Foundation.

Kuehnle, J., Mendelson, J. H., Davis, K. R., & New, P. F. J. (1977). Computerized tomographic examination of heavy marijuana smokers. *Journal of the American Medical Association, 237*, 1231–1232.

Kulick, A. R., Pope, H. G., & Keck, P. E. (1990). Lycanthropy and self-identification. *Journal of Nervous and Mental Disease, 178*(2), 134–137.

Kurdek, L. A. (1988). Perceived social support in gays and lesbians in cohabitating relationships. *Journal of Personality and Social Psychology, 54*, 504–509.

Kurdek, L. A., & Schmitt, J. P. (1986a). Relationship quality of gay men in closed or open relationships. *Journal of Homosexuality, 12*(2), 85–99.

Kurdek, L. A., & Schmitt, J. P. (1986b). Relationship quality of partners in heterosexual married, heterosexual cohabitating, and gay and lesbian relationships. *Journal of Personality and Social Psychology, 51*, 711–720.

Kurdek, L. A., & Schmitt, J. P. (1988). Relationship quality of gay men in closed or open relationships. In J. P. De Cecco (Ed.), *Gay relationships*. New York: Harrington Park Press.

Kutash, S. B. (1976). Modified psychoanalytic therapies. In B. B. Wolman (Ed.), *The therapist's handbook: Treatment methods of mental disorders*. New York: Van Nostrand Reinhold.

Kyle, G. R. (1989). Philosophos: AIDS and the new sexual order. *The Journal of Sex Research, 26*, 276–278.

Lachman, M. E. (1983). Perceptions of intellectual aging: Antecedent or consequence of intellectual functioning? *Developmental Psychology, 19,* 482–498.

Lachman, M. E. (1985). Personal efficacy in middle and old age: Differential and normative patterns of change. In G. H. Elder, Jr. (Ed.), *Life-course dynamics: Trajectories and transitions, 1968–1980.* Ithaca, NY: Cornell University Press.

Lachman, M. E. (1986). Locus of control in aging research: A case for multidimensional and domain-specific assessment. *Journal of Psychology and Aging, 1,* 34–40.

Lachman, M. E., & Leff, R. (1989). Perceived control and intellectual functioning in the elderly: A 5-year longitudinal study. *Developmental Psychology, 25,* 722–728.

LaCroix, A. Z., Mead, L. A., Liang, K. Y., Thomas, C. B., & Pearson, T. A. (1986). Coffee consumption and the incidence of coronary heart disease. *New England Journal of Medicine, 315,* 977–982.

Lader, M., & Herrington, R. (1990). *Biological treatments in psychiatry.* New York: Oxford University Press.

Lader, M. H. (1984). Antianxiety drugs. In T. B. Karasu (Ed.), *The psychiatric therapies.* Washington, DC: American Psychiatric Association.

Lafontaine, E., & Tredeau, L. (1986). The frequency, sources, and correlates of sexual harassment among women in traditional male occupations. *Sex Roles, 15,* 433–442.

La France, M., & Mayo, C. (1976). Racial differences in gaze behavior during conversations: Two systemic observational studies. *Journal of Personality and Social Psychology, 33,* 547–552.

Lakein, A. (1973). *How to get control of your time and your life.* New York: Peter H. Wyden.

Lakoff, R. (1973). Language and woman's place. *Language and Society, 2,* 45–79.

Lal, N., Ahuja, R. C., & Madhukar. (1982). Life events in hypertensive patients. *Journal of Psychosomatic Research, 26*(4), 441–445.

Lambert, M. J., & Bergin, A. E. (1992). Achievements and limitations of psychotherapy research. In D. K. Freedheim (Ed.), *History of psychotherapy: A century of change.* Washington, DC: American Psychological Association.

Landau, E. (1988). *Teenagers talk about school.* Englewood Cliffs, NJ: Julian Messner.

Landers, A. D. (1977). The menstrual experience. In E. Donelson & J. Gullahorn (Eds.), *Women: A psychological perspective.* New York: Wiley.

Landy, F. J. (1989). *Psychology of work behavior.* Pacific Grove, CA: Brooks/Cole.

Laner, M. R. (1988). Permanent partner priorities: Gay and straight. In J. P. De Cecco (Ed.), *Gay relationships.* New York: Harrington Park Press.

Langlois, J. H., & Downs, A. C. (1980). Mothers, fathers, and peers as socialization agents of sex-typed play behaviors in young children. *Child Development, 51,* 1237–1247.

Langone, J. (1988). *AIDS: The facts.* Boston: Little, Brown.

Lareau, W. (1985). *Inside track: A successful job search strategy.* Piscataway, NJ: New Century.

Larwood, L., & Gutek, B. A. (1984). Women at work in the USA. In M. J. Davidson & C. L. Cooper (Eds.), *Women at work.* Chichester, England: Wiley.

Latané, B. (1981). The psychology of social impact. *American Psychologist, 36,* 343–356.

Latané, B., & Nida, S. A. (1981). Ten years of research on group size and helping. *Psychological Bulletin, 89,* 308–324.

Latané, B., Williams, K., & Harkins, S. (1979). Many hands make light the work: The causes and consequences of social loafing. *Journal of Personality and Social Psychology, 37,* 822–832.

Latham, G., & Yukl, G. (1975). Assigned vs. participative goal setting with educated and uneducated woods workers. *Journal of Applied Psychology, 60,* 299–302.

Lau, S., & Gruen, G. E. (1992). The social stigma of loneliness: Effect of target person's and perceiver's sex. *Personality and Social Psychology Bulletin, 18*(2), 182–189.

Lauer, J., & Lauer, R. (1985, June). Marriages made to last. *Psychology Today,* pp. 22–26.

Laughlin, H. (1967). *The neuroses.* Washington, DC: Butterworth.

Laughlin, H. (1979). *The ego and its defenses.* New York: Aronson.

Lavine, L. O., & Lombardo, J. P. (1984). Self-disclosure: Intimate and non-intimate disclosures to parents and best friends as a function of Bem sex-role category. *Sex Roles, 11,* 735–744.

Lavrakas, P. J. (1975). Female preferences for male physiques. *Journal of Research in Personality, 9,* 324–334.

Lawler, K. A. (1980). Cardiovascular and electrodermal response patterns in heart rate reactive individuals during psychological stress. *Psychophysiology, 17*(5), 464–470.

Lawson, E. D. (1971). Hair color, personality, and the observer. *Psychological Reports, 28,* 311–322.

Lazarus, A. A. (1989). Multimodal therapy. In R. J. Corsini & D. Wedding (Eds.), *Current Psychotherapies.* Itasca, IL: F. E. Peacock.

Lazarus, A. A., & Wilson, G. T. (1976). Behavior modification: Clinical and experimental perspectives. In B. B. Wolman (Ed.), *The therapist's handbook: Treatment methods of mental disorders.* New York: Van Nostrand Reinhold.

Lazarus, R. S. (1990). Theory-based stress measurement and commentaries. *Psychological Inquiry, 1,* 3–51.

Lazarus, R. S., & Folkman, S. (1984). *Stress, appraisal and coping.* New York: Springer.

Leary, M. R., & Atherton, S. C. (1986). Self-efficacy, social anxiety, and inhibition in interpersonal encounters. *Journal of Social and Clinical Psychology, 4*(3), 256–267.

Leavitt, F. (1982). *Drugs and behavior.* New York: Wiley.

Leavy, R. L. (1983). Social support and psychological disorder: A review. *Journal of Community Psychology, 11,* 3–21.

LeBoeuf, M. (1980, February). Managing time means managing yourself. *Business Horizons,* pp. 41–46.

Lebov, M. (1980). *Practical tools & techniques for managing time.* Englewood Cliffs, NJ: Prentice-Hall.

Lee, G. R. (1988). Marital satisfaction in later life: The effects of nonmarital roles. *Journal of Marriage and the Family, 50,* 775–783.

Lee, G. R., Seccombe, K., & Shehan, C. L. (1991). Marital status and personal happiness: An analysis of trend data. *Journal of Marriage and the Family, 53,* 839–844.

Leff, J., & Vaughn, C. (1981). The role of maintenance therapy and relatives' expressed emotion in relapse of schizophrenia: A two-year follow-up. *British Journal of Psychiatry, 139,* 102–104.

Leff, J., & Vaughn, C. (1985). *Expressed emotion in families.* New York: Guilford Press.

LeFrancois, G. R. (1983). *Psychology.* Belmont, CA: Wadsworth.

Lehmann, H. E. (1985). Current perspectives on the biology of schizophrenia. In M. N. Menuck & M. V. Seeman (Eds.), *New perspectives in schizophrenia.* New York: Macmillan.

Lehmann, H. E., & Cancro, R. (1985). Schizophrenia: Clinical features. In H. I. Kaplan & B. J. Sadock (Eds.), *Comprehensive textbook of psychiatry/IV.* Baltimore: Williams & Wilkins.

Lehrer, P. M., & Woolfolk, R. L. (1984). Are stress reduction techniques interchangeable, or do they have specific effects? A review of the comparative empirical literature. In R. L. Woolfolk & P. M. Lehrer (Eds.), *Principles and practice of stress management.* New York: Guilford Press.

Leigh, B. C. (1989). Reasons for having and avoiding sex: Gender, sexual orientation, and relationship to sexual behavior. *Journal of Sex Research, 26*(2), 299–209.

Leigh, G. K., Holman, T. B., & Burr, W. R. (1984). An empirical test of sequence in Murstein's SVR Theory of mate selection. *Family Relations, 33,* 225–231.

Leigh, G. K., Holman, T. B., & Burr, W. R. (1987). Some confusions and exclusions of the SVR theory of dyadic pairing: A response to Murstein. *Journal of Marriage and the Family, 49,* 933–937.

Leiker, M., & Hailey, B. J. (1988). A link between hostility and disease: Poor health habits. *Behavioral Medicine, 14,* 129–133.

Leitenberg, H. (1976). Behavioral approaches to the treatment of neuroses. In H. Leitenberg (Ed.), *Handbook of behavior modification and behavior therapy.* Englewood Cliffs, NJ: Prentice-Hall.

Lemon, B. W., Bengston, V. L., & Peterson, J. A. (1972). An exploration of the activity theory of aging: Activity and life satisfaction among inmovers to a retirement community. *Journal of Gerontology, 27,* 511–523.

Lenney, E. (1977). Women's self-confidence in achievement settings. *Psychological Bulletin, 84,* 1–13.

Lenney, E. (1981). What's fine for the gander isn't always good for the goose: Sex differences in self-confidence as a function of ability area and comparison with others. *Sex Roles, 7,* 905–924.

Leo, J. (1987, January 12). Exploring the traits of twins. *Time,* p. 63.

Lerner, M. J., & Miller, D. T. (1976). Deserving and the emergence of forms of justice. In L. Berkowitz (Ed.), *Advances in experimental social psychology* (Vol. 9). New York: Academic Press.

LeShan, L. (1966). An emotional life-history pattern associated with neoplastic disease. *Annals of the New York Academy of Sciences, 125,* 780–793.

Levay, A. N., Weissberg, J. H., & Woods, S. M. (1981). Intrapsychic factors in sexual dysfunctions. In H. I. Lief (Ed.), *Sexual problems in medical practice*. Chicago: American Medical Association.

LeVay, S. (1991). A difference in hypothalamic structure between heterosexual and homosexual men. *Science, 253*, 1034–1037.

Levenkron, S. (1982). *Treating and overcoming anorexia nervosa*. New York: Scribner's.

Levenson, H., Hirschfeld, M. L., Hirschfeld, A., & Dzubay, B. (1983). Recent life events and accidents: The role of sex differences. *Journal of Human Stress, 9*(1), 4–11.

Leventhal, H. (1970). Findings and theory in the study of fear communications. In L. Berkowitz (Ed.), *Advances in experimental social psychology* (Vol. 5). New York: Academic Press.

Leventhal, H., & Cleary, P. D. (1980). The smoking problem: A review of research and theory in behavioral risk modification. *Psychological Bulletin, 88*, 370–405.

Levering, R. (1988). *A great place to work*. New York: Random House.

Levi, L. (1990). Occupational stress: Spice of life or kiss of death? *American Psychologist, 45*(10), 1142–1145.

Levin, R. J., & Levin, A. (1975, September). Sexual pleasure: The surprising preferences of 100,000 women. *Redbook, 145*, pp. 51ff.

LeVine, R. A., & White, M. (1987). Parenthood in social transformation. In J. B. Lancaster, J. Altmann, A. S. Rossi, & L. R. Sherrod (Eds.), *Parenting across the life span: Biosocial dimensions*. New York: Aldine de Gruyter.

Levinger, G. (1970). Husbands' and wives' estimates of coital frequency. *Medical Aspects of Human Sexuality, 4*, 42–57.

Levinger, G. (1980). Toward the analysis of close relationships. *Journal of Experimental Social Psychology, 16*, 510–544.

Levinson, D. J. (1985). The life cycle. In H. I. Kaplan & B. J. Sadock (Eds.), *Comprehensive textbook of psychiatry/IV*. Baltimore: Williams & Wilkins.

Levinson, D. J. (1986). A conception of adult development. *American Psychologist, 41*, 3–13.

Levinson, D. J., Darrow, C. M., Klein, E. G., Levinson, M. H., & McKee, B. (1974). The psychosocial development of men in early adulthood and the midlife transition. In D. F. Ricks, A. Thomas, & M. Roff (Eds.), *Life history research in psychopathology* (Vol. 3). Minneapolis: University of Minnesota Press.

Levinson, D. J., Darrow, C. M., Klein, E. G., Levinson, M. H., & McKee, B. (1978). *The seasons of a man's life*. New York: Knopf.

Levitin, T., Quinn, R. P., & Staines, G. L. (1971). Sex discrimination against the American working woman. *American Behavioral Scientist, 15*, 237–254.

Levy, M. B., & Davis, K. E. (1988). Love-styles and attachment styles compared: Their relations to each other and to various relationship characteristics. *Journal of Social and Personal Relationships, 5*, 439–471.

Levy, S. M. (1985). *Behavior and cancer*. San Francisco: Jossey-Bass.

Levy, S. M., Herberman, R. B., Simons, A., Whiteside, T., Lee, J., McDonald, R., &

Beadle, M. (1989). Persistently low natural killer cell activity in normal adults: Immunological, hormonal and mood correlates. *Natural Immune Cell Growth Regulation, 8*, 173–186.

Lewin, K. (1935). *A dynamic theory of personality*. New York: McGraw-Hill.

Lewine, R. J., Fogg, L., & Meltzer, H. Y. (1983). Assessment of negative and positive symptoms in schizophrenia. *Schizophrenia Bulletin, 9*, 968–976.

Lewinsohn, P. M. (1974). A behavioral approach to depression. In R. J. Friedman & M. M. Katz (Eds.), *The psychology of depression: Contemporary theory and research*. New York: Halsted.

Lewinsohn, P. M., & Arconad, M. (1981). Behavioral treatment of depression: A social learning approach. In J. F. Clarkin & H. I. Glazer (Eds.), *Depression: Behavioral and directive intervention strategies*. New York: Garland STPM.

Lewinsohn, P. M., Duncan, E. M., Stanton, A. K., & Hautzinger, M. (1986). Age at first onset for nonbipolar depression. *Journal of Abnormal Psychology, 95*(4), 378–383.

Lewis, J. M. (1988). The transition to parenthood: II. Stability and change in marital structure. *Family Process, 27*, 273–283.

Lewis, J. M., Owen, M. T., & Cox, M. J. (1988). The transition to parenthood: III. Incorporation of the child into the family. *Family Process, 27*, 411–421.

Lewis, R. A. (1986). Men's changing roles in marriage and the family. *Marriage and Family Review, 9*(3/4), 1–10.

Lewis, R. J., & Janda, L. H. (1988). The relationship between adult sexual adjustment and childhood experiences regarding exposure to nudity, sleeping in the parental bed, and parental attitudes toward sexuality. *Archives of Sexual Behavior, 17*(4), 349–362.

Lewy, A. J., Sack, R. L., Singer, C. M., White, D. M., & Hoban, T. M. (1989). Winter depression and the phase-shift hypothesis for bright light's therapeutic effects: History, theory and experimental evidence. In N. E. Rosenthal & M. C. Blehar (Eds.), *Seasonal affective disorders and phototherapy*. New York: Guilford Press.

Liberman, R. P., Mueser, K. T., & DeRisi, W. J. (1989). *Social skills training for psychiatric patients*. New York: Pergamon Press.

Libman, H. (1992). Pathogenesis, natural history, and classification of HIV infection. *Primary Care, 19*(1), 1–17.

Lichtenstein, E. (1980). *Psychotherapy: Approaches and applications*. Pacific Grove, CA: Brooks/Cole.

Lickey, M. E., & Gordon, B. (1991). *Medicine and mental illness: The use of drugs in psychiatry*. New York: W. H. Freeman.

Liebert, R. M., & Sprafkin, J. N. (1988). *The early window: Effects of television on children and youth*. New York: Pergamon Press.

Liem, R., & Rayman, P. (1982). Health and social costs of unemployment. *American Psychologist, 37*, 1116–1123.

Lindgren, H. C. (1969). *The psychology of college success: A dynamic approach*. New York: Wiley.

Linn, M. C., & Hyde, J. S. (1989). Gender, mathematics, and science. *Educational Researcher, 18*(8), 17–19, 22–27.

Linn, M. C., & Petersen, A. C. (1986). A meta-analysis of gender differences in spatial ability: Implications for mathematics and science achievement. In J. S. Hyde & M. C. Linn (Eds.), *The psychology of gender: Advances through meta-analysis*. Baltimore: Johns Hopkins University Press.

Lipman, B. E. (1983). *The personal job search program: How to market yourself*. New York: Wiley.

Lips, H. M. (1993). *Sex and gender: An introduction*. Mountain View, CA: Mayfield.

Litwack, M., & Resnick, M. R. (1984). *The art of self-fulfillment*. New York: Simon & Schuster.

Lloyd, C., Alexander, A. A., Rice, D. G., & Greenfield, N. S. (1980). Life events as predictors of academic performance. *Journal of Human Stress, 6*(3), 15–26.

Lloyd, M. A. (1985). *Adolescence*. New York: HarperCollins.

Lobel, K. (1986). *Naming the violence*. Seattle: Seal Press.

Lock, R. D. (1988). *Taking charge of your career direction: Career planning guide, Book I*. Pacific Grove, CA: Brooks/Cole.

Locke, E. A. (1983). The nature and causes of job satisfaction. In M. D. Dunnette (Ed.), *Handbook of industrial and organizational psychology*. New York: Wiley.

Locksley, A., & Colten, M. E. (1979). Psychological androgyny: A case of mistaken identity? *Journal of Personality and Social Psychology, 37*, 1017–1031.

Loehlin, J. C., Willerman, L., & Horn, J. M. (1988). Human behavior genetics. *Annual Review of Psychology, 39*, 101–134.

Lombardo, J., & Lavine, L. (1981). Sex-role stereotyping and patterns of self-disclosure. *Sex Roles, 7*, 403–411.

London, K. A., & Wilson, B. F. (1988). Divorce. *American Demographics, 10*(10), 22–26.

London, M., Crandall, R., & Seals, G. W. (1977). The contribution of job and leisure satisfaction to the quality of life. *Journal of Applied Psychology, 62*, 328–334.

London, M., & Strumpf, S. A. (1986). Individual and organizational career development in changing times. In D. T. Hall & associates (Eds.), *Career development in organizations*. San Francisco: Jossey-Bass.

Long, E. C. J., & Andrews, D. W. (1990). Perspective taking as a predictor of marital adjustment. *Journal of Personality and Social Psychology, 59*(1), 126–131.

Longley, J., & Pruitt, D. G. (1980). Groupthink: A critique of Janis' theory. *Review of Personality and Social Psychology, 1*, 74–93.

Longman, D. G., & Atkinson, R. H. (1988). *College learning and study skills*. St. Paul, MN: West.

Longman, D. G., & Atkinson, R. H. (1991). *College learning and study skills*. St. Paul, MN: West.

LoPiccolo, J., & Daiss, S. (1987). Assessment of sexual dysfunction. In K. D. O'Leary (Ed.), *Assessment of marital discord: An integration for research and clinical practice*. Hillsdale, NJ: Erlbaum.

LoPiccolo, J., & Lobitz, C. (1972). The role of masturbation in the treatment of sexual dysfunction. *Archives of Sex Research, 2*, 163–171.

Lott, B. (1981). A feminist critique of androgyny: Toward the elimination of gender attributions for learned behavior. In C. Mayo & N. M. Henley (Eds.), *Gender and nonverbal behavior*. New York: Springer-Verlag.

Lott, B. (1987). *Women's lives: Themes and variations in gender learning*. Pacific Grove, CA: Brooks/Cole.

Loughead, T. A. (1991). Addictions as a process: Commonalities or codependence. *Contemporary Family Therapy: An International Journal, 13*(5), 455–470.

Lowe, C. A., & Goldstein, J. W. (1970). Reciprocal liking and attributions of ability: Mediating effects of perceived intent and personal involvement. *Journal of Personality and Social Psychology, 16*, 291–297.

Lowenthal, M. F. (1975). *Four stages of life: A comparative study of women and men facing transitions*. San Francisco: Jossey-Bass.

Lowinson, J. H., Ruiz, P., & Millman, R. B. (Eds.). (1992). *Substance abuse: A comprehensive textbook* (2nd ed.). Baltimore: Williams & Wilkins.

Lowry, D. T., & Towles, D. E. (1989). Soap opera portrayals of sex, contraception, and sexually transmitted diseases. *Journal of Communication, 39*(2), 76–83.

Lubkin, I. M. (1990). Illness roles. In I. M. Lubkin (Ed.), *Chronic Illness: Impact and interventions* (2nd ed.). Boston: Jones and Bartlett.

Luborsky, L., Crits-Christoph, P., Mintz, J., & Auerbach, A. (1988). *Who will benefit from psychotherapy?* New York: Basic Books.

Luborsky, L., Singer, B., & Luborsky, L. (1975). Comparative studies of psychotherapies: Is it true that everyone has won and all must have prizes? *Archives of General Psychiatry, 32*, 995–1008.

Lui, K. J., Darrow, W. W., & Rutherford, G. W. (1988). A model-based estimate of the mean incubation period for AIDS in homosexual men. *Science, 240*, 1333–1335.

Luker, K. C. (1975). *Taking chances: Abortion and the decision not to contracept*. Berkeley, CA: University of California Press.

Lumsdaine, A., & Janis, I. (1953). Resistance to counterpropaganda presentation. *Public Opinion Quarterly, 17*, 311–318.

Lundberg, U., & Theorell, T. (1976). Scaling of life changes: Differences between three diagnostic groups and between recently experienced and non-experienced events. *Journal of Human Stress, 2*, 7–17.

Luria, Z. (1974). Recent women college graduates: A study of rising expectations. *American Journal of Orthopsychiatry, 44*, 312–326.

Luthe, W. (1962). Method, research and application of autogenic training. *American Journal of Clinical Hypnosis, 5*, 17–23.

Lyman, B., Hatlelid, D., & Macurdy, C. (1981). Stimulus-person cues in first-impression attraction. *Perceptual and Motor Skills, 52*, 59–66.

Lynn, D. B. (1959). A note on sex differences in the development of masculine and feminine identification. *Psychological Review, 66*(2), 126–135.

Lyon, D., & Greenberg, J. (1991). Evidence of codependency in women with an alcoholic parent: Helping out Mr. Wrong. *Journal of Personality and Social Psychology, 61*(3), 435–439.

Maccoby, E. E. (1988). Gender as a social category. *Developmental Psychology, 24*, 755–765.

Maccoby, E. E. (1990). Gender and relationships: A developmental account. *American Psychologist, 45*, 513–520.

Maccoby, E. E., & Jacklin, C. N. (1974). *The psychology of sex differences*. Stanford, CA: Stanford University Press.

Maccoby, E. E., & Jacklin, C. N. (1987). Gender segregation in childhood. In E. H. Reese (Ed.), *Advances in child development*. New York: Academic Press.

Maccoby, E. E., & Martin, J. A. (1983). Socialization in the context of the family: Parent-child interaction. In P. H. Mussen (Series Ed.) & E. M. Hetherington (Vol. Ed.), *Handbook of child psychology: Vol. 4. Socialization, personality, and social development*. New York: Wiley.

Machlowitz, M. M. (1980). *Workaholics: Living with them, working with them*. Reading, MA: Addison-Wesley.

Machung, A. (1989). Talking career, thinking job: Gender differences in career and family expectations of Berkeley seniors. *Family Studies, 15*, 35–58.

Macke, A. S., Richardson, L. W., & Cook, J. (1980). *Sex-typed teaching styles of university professors and student reactions*. Columbus, OH: Ohio State University Research Foundation.

Mackenzie, R. A. (1972). *The time trap*. New York: Amacom.

Macklin, E. D. (1983). Nonmarital heterosexual cohabitation: An overview. In E. D. Macklin & R. H. Rubin (Eds.), *Contemporary families and alternative lifestyles: Handbook on research and theory*. Newbury Park, CA: Sage Publications.

Macklin, E. D. (1987). Nontraditional family forms. In M. B. Sussman & S. K. Steinmetz (Eds.), *Handbook of marriage and the family*. New York: Plenum.

Maddock, J. W. (1989). Healthy family sexuality: Positive principles for educators and clinicians. *Family Relations, 38*, 130–136.

Mahoney, E. R., Shively, M. D., & Traw, M. (1986). Sexual coercion and assault: Male socialization and female risk. *Sexual Coercion and Assault, 1*, 2–8.

Mahoney, M. J. (1979). *Self-change: Strategies for solving personal problems*. New York: Norton.

Main, M., & Solomon, J. (1990). Procedures for identifying infants as disorganized/disoriented during the Ainsworth Strange Situation. In M. T. Greenberg, D. Cicchetti, & E. M. Cummings (Eds.), *Attachment in the preschool years: Theory, research, and intervention*. Chicago: University of Chicago Press.

Major, B. (1981). Gender patterns in touching behavior. In C. Mayo & N. M. Henley (Eds.), *Gender and nonverbal behavior*. New York: Springer-Verlag.

Major, B., Schmidlin, A. M., & Williams, L. (1990). Gender patterns in social touch: The impact of setting and age. *Journal of Personality and Social Psychology, 58*(4), 634–643.

Malamuth, N. M. (1984). Violence against women: Cultural and individual cases. In N. M. Malamuth & E. Donnerstein *Pornography and sexual aggression*. New York: Academic Press.

Malamuth, N. M. (1986). Predictors of naturalistic sexual aggression. *Journal of Personality and Social Psychology, 50*, 953–962.

Malamuth, N. M., & Check, J. V. P. (1981). The effects of mass media exposure on acceptance of violence against women: A field experiment. *Journal of Research in Personality, 15*, 436–446.

Malamuth, N., & Donnerstein, E. (1982). The effects of aggressive-pornographic mass media stimuli. In L. Berkowitz (Ed.), *Advances in Experimental Social Psychology* (Vol. 15). New York: Academic Press.

Malatesta, V. J., & Adams, H. E. (1984). The sexual dysfunctions. In H. E. Adams & P. B. Sutker (Eds.), *Comprehensive handbook of psychopathology*. New York: Plenum.

Maltz, D. N., & Borker, R. A. (1983). A cultural approach to male-female miscommunication. In J. A. Gumperz (Ed.), *Language and social identity*. New York: Cambridge University Press.

Mandler, G. (1982). Stress and thought processes. In L. Goldberger & S. Breznitz (Eds.), *Handbook of stress: Theoretical and clinical aspects*. New York: Free Press.

Mansfield, R., & Evans, M. G. (1975). Work and non-work in two occupational groups. *Industrial Relations, 6*, 48–54.

Manuck, S. B., & Garland, F. N. (1980). Stability of individual differences in cardiovascular reactivity. *Physiology and Behavior, 24*(3), 621–624.

Manuck, S. B., & Krantz, D. S. (1986). Psychophysiological reactivity in coronary heart disease and essential hypertension. In K. A. Mathews, S. M. Weiss, T. Detre, T. M. Dembroski, B. Falkner, S. B. Manuck, & R. B. Williams, Jr. (Eds.), *Handbook of stress, reactivity, and cardiovascular disease*. New York: Wiley.

Marcia, J. E. (1976). Identity six years after: A follow-up study. *Journal of Youth and Adolescence, 5*, 145–160.

Marcia, J. E. (1980). Identity in adolescence. In J. Adelson (Ed.), *Handbook of adolescent psychology*. New York: Wiley.

Marecek, J., Finn, S. E., & Cardell, M. (1988). Gender roles in the relationships of lesbians and gay men. In J. P. De Cecco (Ed.), *Gay relationships*. New York: Harrington Park Press.

Marengo, J., Harrow, M., Sands, J., & Galloway, C. (1991). European versus U. S. data on the course of schizophrenia. *American Journal of Psychiatry, 148*, 606–611.

Margolin, G., & Wampold, B. E. (1981). A sequential analysis of conflict and accord in distressed and nondistressed marital partners. *Journal of Consulting and Clinical Psychology, 49*, 554–567.

Maricle, R., Leung, P., & Bloom, J. D. (1987). The use of DSM-III axis III in recording physical illness in psychiatric patients. *American Journal of Psychiatry, 144*(11), 1484–1486.

Marini, M. M. (1978). Sex differences in the determination of adolescent aspirations: A review of research. *Sex Roles, 4*, 723–753.

Markman, H. J. (1981). Prediction of marital distress: A 5-year follow-up. *Journal of Consulting and Clinical Psychology, 49*, 760–762.

Marks, G. (1984). Thinking one's abilities are unique and one's opinions are common. *Personality and Social Psychology Bulletin, 10*(2), 203–208.

Marks, G., & Miller, N. (1987). Ten years of research on the false-consensus effect: An empirical and theoretical view. *Psychological Bulletin, 102*, 72–90.

Marks, I. M. (1987). *Fears, phobias, and rituals: Panic, anxiety, and their disorders.* New York: Oxford University Press.

Marks, I. M. (1988). Classification of phobic disorders. In R. Noyes, M. Roth, & G. D. Burrows (Eds.), *Handbook of anxiety: Classification, etiological factors and associated disturbances* (Vol. 2). Amsterdam: Elsevier.

Marks, M. L. (1986, March). The question of quality circles. *Psychology Today*, pp. 36–38, 42, 44, 46.

Markus, H. (1981). The drive for integration: Some comments. *Journal of Experimental Social Psychology, 17*, 257–261.

Markus, H., & Nurius, P. (1986). Possible selves. *American Psychologist, 41*, 954–969.

Markus, H., & Ruvolo, A. (1989). Possible selves: Personalized representations of goals. In L. A. Pervin (Ed.), *Goal concepts in personality and social psychology.* Hillsdale, NJ: Erlbaum.

Marlatt, G. A., & Rose, F. (1980). Addictive disorders. In A. E. Kazdin, A. S. Bellack, & M. Hersen (Eds.), *New perspectives in abnormal psychology.* New York: Oxford University Press.

Marotz-Baden, R., & Cowan, D. (1987). Mothers-in-law and daughters-in-law: The effects of proximity on conflict and stress. *Family Relations, 36*, 385–390.

Marsh, H. W., & Parker, J. W. (1984). Determinants of student self-concept: Is it better to be a relatively large fish in a small pond even if you don't learn to swim well? *Journal of Personality and Social Psychology, 47*(1), 213–231.

Marsh, P. (Ed.). (1988). *Eye to eye: How people interact.* Topsfield, MA: Salem House.

Marshall, J., & Cooper, C. L. (1981). The causes of managerial stress: A research note on methods and initial findings. In E. N. Corlett & J. Richardson (Eds.), *Stress, work, design, and productivity.* Chichester, England: Wiley.

Martin, B. (1971). *Anxiety and neurotic disorders.* New York: Wiley.

Martin, C. A., Warfield, M. C., & Braen, G. R. (1983). Physicians' management of the psychological aspects of rape. *Journal of the American Medical Association, 249*, 501–503.

Martin, C. L. (1987). A ratio measure of sex stereotyping. *Journal of Personality and Social Psychology, 52*, 489–499.

Martin, C. L., & Halverson, C. F., Jr. (1981). A schematic processing model of sex typing and stereotyping in children. *Child Development, 52*, 1119–1134.

Martin, R. A., & Lefcourt, H. M. (1983). Sense of humor as a moderator of the relation between stressors and moods. *Journal of Personality and Social Psychology, 45*(6), 1313–1324.

Martin, T. C., & Bumpass, L. L. (1989). Recent trends in marital disruption. *Demography, 26*(1), 37–51.

Martinson, F. M. (1980). Childhood sexuality. In B. B. Wolman & J. Money (Eds.), *Handbook of human sexuality.* Englewood Cliffs, NJ: Prentice-Hall.

Maser, J. D., Kaelber, C., & Weise, R. E. (1991). International use and attitudes toward DSM-III and DSM-III-R: Growing consensus in psychiatric classification. *Journal of Abnormal Psychology, 100*(3), 271–279.

Maslach, C. (1982). Understanding burnout: Definitional issues in analyzing a complex phenomenon. In W. S. Paine (Ed.), *Job stress and burnout: Research, theory and intervention perspectives.* Newbury Park, CA: Sage Publications.

Maslow, A. (1968). *Toward a psychology of being.* New York: Van Nostrand.

Maslow, A. (1970). *Motivation and personality.* New York: Harper & Row.

Masters, W. H., & Johnson, V. E. (1966). *Human sexual response.* Boston: Little, Brown.

Masters, W. H., & Johnson, V. E. (1970). *Human sexual inadequacy* (1st ed.). Boston: Little, Brown.

Masters, W. H., & Johnson, V. E. (1979). *Homosexuality in perspective.* Boston: Little, Brown.

Masters, W. H., & Johnson, V. E. (1980). *Human sexual inadequacy* (2nd ed.). New York: Bantam Books.

Masters, W. H., Johnson, V. E., & Kolodny, R. C. (1988). *Human sexuality.* Glenview, IL: Scott, Foresman.

Mathes, E. (1975). The effects of physical attractiveness and anxiety on heterosexual attraction over a series of five encounters. *Journal of Marriage and the Family, 37*, 769–774.

Mathes, E. W., Brennan, S. M., Haugen, P. M., & Rice, H. B. (1985). Ratings of physical attractiveness as a function of age. *Journal of Social Psychology, 125*(2), 157–168.

Matteson, M. T., & Ivancevich, J. M. (1987). *Controlling work stress: Effective human resource and management strategies.* San Francisco: Jossey-Bass.

Mattessich, P., & Hill, R. (1987). Life cycle and family development. In M. B. Sussman & S. K. Steinmetz (Eds.), *Handbook of marriage and the family.* New York: Plenum.

Matthews, K. A. (1982). Psychological perspectives on the Type-A behavior pattern. *Psychological Bulletin, 91*, 293–323.

Matthews, K. A., & Rodin, J. (1989). Women's changing work roles: Impact on health, family, and public policy. *American Psychologist, 44*(11), 1389–1393.

Matthews, K. A., Scheier, M. F., Brunson, B. I., & Carducci, B. (1989). Why do unpredictable events lead to reports of physical symptoms? In T. W. Miller (Ed.), *Stressful life events.* Madison, CT: International Universities Press.

Mayer, J. (1980). The bitter truth about sugar. In C. Borg (Ed.), *Annual editions: Readings in health.* Guilford, CT: Dushkin.

Mayo, C., & Henley, N. (1981). *Gender and nonverbal behavior.* New York: Springer-Verlag.

Mays, D. T., & Franks, C. M. (1985). *Negative outcome in psychotherapy and what to do about it.* New York: Springer.

McAdams, D. P. (1982). Intimacy motivation. In A. J. Stewart (Ed.), *Motivation and society.* San Francisco: Jossey-Bass.

McAdams, D. P., & Bryant, F. B. (1987). Intimacy motivation and subjective mental health in a nationwide sample. *Journal of Personality, 55*, 395–414.

McAdams, D. P., Healy, S., & Krause, S. (1984). Social motives and friendship patterns. *Journal of Personality and Social Psychology, 47*, 828–838.

McAllister, W. R., McAllister, D. E., Scoles, M. T., & Hampton, S. R. (1986). Persistence of fear-reducing behavior: Relevance for the conditioning theory of neurosis. *Journal of Abnormal Psychology, 95*(4), 365–372.

McBride, P. E. (1992). The health consequences of smoking: Cardiovascular diseases. *Medical Clinics of North America, 76*(2), 333–353.

McCann, C. D., & Hancock, R. D. (1983). Self-monitoring in communicative interactions: Social cognitive consequences of goal-directed message modification. *Journal of Experimental Social Psychology, 19*, 109–121.

McCary, J. L. (1971). *Sexual myths and fallacies.* New York: Schocken Books.

McCrae, R. R. (1984). Situational determinants of coping responses: Loss, threat and challenge. *Journal of Personality and Social Psychology, 46*(4), 919–928.

McCrae, R. R., & Costa, P. T., Jr. (1984). *Emerging lives, enduring dispositions: Personality in adulthood.* Boston: Little, Brown.

McCrae, R. R., & Costa, P. T., Jr. (1985). Updating Norman's "adequate taxonomy": Intelligence and personality dimensions in natural language and in questionnaires. *Journal of Personality and Social Psychology, 49*, 710–721.

McCrae, R. R., & Costa, P. T., Jr. (1987). Validation of the five-factor model of personality across instruments and observers. *Journal of Personality and Social Psychology, 52*(1), 81–90.

McCrae, R. R., & Costa, P. T., Jr. (1990). *Personality in adulthood.* New York: Guilford Press.

McCroskey, J. C., & Beatty, M. J. (1986). Oral communication apprehension. In W. H. Jones, J. M. Cheek, & S. R. Briggs (Eds.), *Shyness: Perspectives on research and treatment.* New York: Plenum.

McDaniel, M. A., & Einstein, G. O. (1986). Bizarre imagery as an effective memory aid: The importance of distinctiveness. *Journal of Experimental Psychology: Learning, Memory & Cognition, 12*, 54–65.

McDonald, G. J. (1982). Individual differences in the coming out process of gay men: Implications for theoretical models. *Journal of Homosexuality, 8*(1), 47–60.

McDougle, L. G. (1987). Time management: Making every minute count. In A. D. Timpe (Ed.), *The management of time.* New York: Facts On File.

McGhee, P. E., & Frueh, T. (1980). Television viewing and the learning of sex-role stereotypes. *Sex Roles, 6*, 179–188.

McGinnies, E., & Ward, C. D. (1980). Better liked than right: Trustworthiness and expertise as factors in credibility. *Personality and Social Psychology Bulletin, 6*, 467–472.

McGinnis, J. M., Shopland, D., & Brown, C. (1987). Tobacco and health: Trends in smoking and smokeless tobacco consumption in the United States. In L. Breslow, J. E. Fielding, & L. B. Lave (Eds.), *Annual review of public health* (Vol. 8). Palo Alto, CA: Annual Reviews.

McGlashan, T. H. (1986). Schizophrenia: Psychosocial treatments and the role of psychosocial factors in its etiology and pathogenesis. In A. J. Frances & R. E. Hales (Eds.), *Psychiatry update: Annual review* (Vol. 5). Washington, DC: American Psychiatric Press.

McGlone, J. (1980). Sex differences in human brain asymmetry: A critical review. *Behavioral and Brain Sciences, 3,* 215–263.

McGoldrick, M., & Carter, E. A. (1989). The family life cycle—Its stages and dislocations. In J. M. Henslin (Ed.), *Marriage and family in a changing society.* New York: Free Press.

McGowan, A. S. (1977). Vocational maturity and anxiety among vocationally undecided and indecisive students. *Journal of Vocational Behavior, 10,* 196–204.

McGrath, J. E. (1977). Settings, measures and themes: An integrative review of some research on social-psychological factors in stress. In A. Monat & R. S. Lazarus (Eds.), *Stress and coping: An anthology.* New York: Columbia University Press.

McGrath, J. E. (1984). *Groups: Interaction and performance.* Englewood Cliffs, NJ: Prentice-Hall.

McGregor, D. (1960). *The human side of enterprise.* New York: McGraw-Hill.

McGuire, J. (1988). Gender stereotypes of parents with two-year-olds and beliefs about gender differences in behavior. *Sex Roles, 19,* 233–240.

McGuire, W. J. (1964). Inducing resistance to persuasion. In L. Berkowitz (Ed.), *Advances in Experimental Psychology* (Vol. 1). New York: Academic Press.

McHale, S. M., & Crouter, A. C. (1992). You can't always get what you want: Incongruence between sex-role attitudes and family work roles and its implications for marriage. *Journal of Marriage and the Family, 54,* 537–547.

McKay, M., Davis, M., & Fanning, P. (1983). *Messages: The communication book.* Oakland, CA: New Harbinger.

McKay, M., & Fanning, P. (1987). *Self-esteem.* Oakland, CA: New Harbinger.

McKeon, J., Roa, B., & Mann, A. (1989). Life events and personality traits in obsessive-compulsive neurosis. In T. W. Miller (Ed.), *Stressful life events.* Madison, CT: International Universities Press.

McKillip, J., & Riedel, S. L. (1983). External validity of matching on physical attractiveness for same and opposite sex couples. *Journal of Applied Social Psychology, 13,* 328–337.

McKinlay, J. B., McKinlay, S. M., & Brambilla, D. (1987). The relative contributions of endocrine changes and social circumstances to depression in mid-aged women. *Journal of Health and Social Behavior, 28*(4), 345–363.

McLoyd, V. C. (1989). Socialization and development in a changing economy. *American Psychologist, 44,* 293–302.

McMahan, I. D. (1982). Expectancy of success on sex-linked tasks. *Sex Roles, 8,* 949–958.

McMillan, J. R., Clifton, A. K., McGrath, D., & Gale, W. S. (1977). Women's language: Uncertainty or interpersonal sensitivity and emotionality? *Sex Roles, 3,* 545–560.

McNally, R. J. (1987). Preparedness and phobias: A review. *Psychological Bulletin, 101*(2), 283–303.

McReynolds, W. T. (1979). DSM-III and the future of applied social science. *Professional Psychology, 10,* 123–132.

Mead, M. (1950). *Sex and temperament in three primitive societies.* New York: Mentor Books.

Mechanic, D. (1972). Social psychologic factors affecting the presentation of bodily complaints. *New England Journal of Medicine, 286,* 1132–1139.

Mehrabian, A. (1971). *Silent messages.* Belmont, CA: Wadsworth.

Mehrabian, A. (1972). *Nonverbal communication.* Chicago: Aldine-Atherton.

Meichenbaum, D., & Turk, D. C. (1987). *Facilitating treatment adherence: A practitioner's guidebook.* New York: Plenum.

Meilman, P. W. (1979). Cross-sectional age changes in ego identity status during adolescence. *Developmental Psychology, 15*(2), 230–232.

Melman, A., & Leiter, E. (1983). The urologic evaluation of impotence (male excitement phase disorder). In H. S. Kaplan (Ed.), *The evaluation of sexual disorders: Psychological and medical aspects.* New York: Brunner/Mazel.

Meltzoff, J., & Kornreich, M. (1970). *Research in psychotherapy.* New York: Atherton.

Melzack, R. (1973). *The puzzle of pain.* New York: Basic Books.

Melzack, R., & Wall, P. D. (1965). Pain mechanisms: A new theory. *Science, 150,* 971–979.

Menaghan, E. G., & Parcel, T. L. (1990). Parental employment and family life: Research in the 1980s. *Journal of Marriage and the Family, 52,* 1079–1098.

Mendenhall, W. (1989). Co-dependency definitions and dynamics. *Alcoholism Treatment Quarterly, 6*(1), 3–17.

Mentzer, R. L. (1982). Response biases in multiple-choice test item files. *Educational and Psychological Measurement, 42,* 437–448.

Merikangas, K. R., & Weissman, M. M. (1986). Epidemiology of DSM-III axis II personality disorders. In A. J. Frances & R. E. Hales (Eds.), *Psychiatry update: Annual Review* (Vol. 5). Washington, DC: American Psychiatric Press.

Meyer, R. (1980). The antisocial personality. In R. Woody (Ed.), *The encyclopedia of mental assessment.* San Francisco: Jossey-Bass.

Meyerhoff, J. L., Oleshansky, M. A., & Mougey, M. S. (1988). Psychologic stress increases plasma levels of prolactin, cortisol, and POMC-derived peptides in man. *Psychosomatic Medicine, 50,* 295–303.

Michela, J. L., Peplau, L. A., & Weeks, D. G. (1982). Perceived dimensions of attributions for loneliness. *Journal of Personality and Social Psychology, 43,* 929–936.

Michelozzi, B. N. (1988). *Coming alive from nine to five: The career search handbook.* Palo Alto, CA: Mayfield.

Mikulincer, M., & Nachshon, O. (1991). Attachment styles and patterns of self-disclosure. *Journal of Personality and Social Psychology, 61*(2), 321–331.

Milgram, S. (1963). Behavioral study of obedience. *Journal of Abnormal and Social Psychology, 67,* 371–378.

Milgram, S. (1964). Issues in the study of obedience. *American Psychologist, 19,* 848–852.

Milgram, S. (1968). Reply to the critics. *International Journal of Psychiatry, 6,* 294–295.

Milgram, S. (1974). *Obedience to authority.* New York: Harper & Row.

Miller, A. G. (1986). *The obedience experiments: A case study of controversy in social science.* New York: Praeger.

Miller, B. C., & Sollie, D. L. (1986). Normal stresses during the transition to parenthood. In R. H. Moos (Ed.), *Coping with life crises: An integrated approach.* New York: Plenum.

Miller, C. T., Byrne, D., & Fisher, J. D. (1980). Order effects on sexual and affective responses to erotic stimuli by males and females. *Journal of Sex Research, 16,* 131–147.

Miller, D. T., & Ross, M. (1975). Self-serving biases in the attribution of causality: Fact or fiction? *Psychological Bulletin, 82,* 213–225.

Miller, G. P. (1978). *Life choices: How to make the critical decisions—about your education, career, marriage, family, life style.* New York: Thomas Y. Crowell.

Miller, G. T., Jr. (1985). *Living in the environment: An introduction to environmental science.* Belmont, CA: Wadsworth.

Miller, K. (1989). *Retraining the American workforce.* Reading, MA: Addison-Wesley.

Miller, L. C. (1990). Intimacy and liking: Mutual influence and the role of unique relationships. *Journal of Personality and Social Psychology, 59,* 50–60.

Miller, L. C., Berg, J. H., & Archer, R. L. (1983). Openers: Individuals who elicit intimate self-disclosure. *Journal of Personality and Social Psychology, 44*(6), 1234–1244.

Miller, N. E. (1944). Experimental studies of conflict. In J. McV. Hunt (Ed.), *Personality and the behavior disorders* (Vol. 1). New York: Ronald.

Miller, N. E. (1959). Liberalization of basic S-R concepts: Extension to conflict behavior, motivation, and social learning. In S. Koch (Ed.), *Psychology: A study of a science* (Vol. 2). New York: McGraw-Hill.

Miller, N. E. (1983). Behavioral medicine: Symbiosis between laboratory and clinic. *Annual Review of Psychology, 34,* 1–31.

Miller, P. Y., & Simon, W. (1974). Adolescent sexual behavior: Context and change. *Social Problems, 22,* 58–76.

Miller, P. Y., & Simon, W. (1980). The development of sexuality in adolescence. In J. Adelson (Ed.), *Handbook of adolescent psychology.* New York: Wiley.

Miller, T. Q., Turner, C. W., Tindale, R. S., Posavac, E. J., & Dugoni, B. L. (1991). Reasons for the trend toward null findings in research on Type A behavior. *Psychological Bulletin, 110*(3), 469–485.

Miller, T. W. (Ed.). (1989). *Stressful life events.* Madison, CT: International Universities Press.

Millett, K. (1970). *Sexual politics.* Garden City, NY: Doubleday.

Millman, J., Bishop, C. H., & Ebel, R. (1965). An analysis of test-wiseness. *Educational and Psychological Measurement, 25*, 707–726.

Millon, T. (1981). *Disorders of personality: DSM-III, Axis II.* New York: Wiley.

Millon, T. (1986). A theoretical derivation of pathological personalities. In T. Millon & G. L. Klerman (Eds.), *Contemporary directions in psychopathology: Toward the DSM-IV.* New York: Guilford Press.

Mindel, C. H., & Vaughan, C. E. (1978). A multidimensional approach to religiosity and disengagement. *Journal of Gerontology, 23*, 103–108.

Mineka, S., & Cook, M. (1986). Immunization against the observational conditioning of snake fear in rhesus monkeys. *Journal of Abnormal Psychology, 95*(4), 307–318.

Mirkin, G., & Hoffman, M. (1978). *The sports medicine book.* Boston: Little, Brown.

Mirsky, A. F., & Duncan, C. C. (1986). Etiology and expression of schizophrenia: Neurobiological and psychosocial factors. *Annual Review of Psychology, 37*, 291–320.

Mischel, W. (1970). Sex-typing and socialization. In P. H. Mussen (Ed.), *Carmichael's manual of child psychology* (Vol. 2). New York: Wiley.

Mischel, W. (1973). Toward a cognitive social learning conceptualization of personality. *Psychological Review, 80*, 252–283.

Mischel, W. (1990). Personality dispositions revisited and revised: A view after three decades. In L. A. Pervin (Ed.), *Handbook of personality: Theory and research.* New York: Guilford Press.

Mischel, W., & Mischel, H. N. (1976). A cognitive social learning approach to morality and self-regulation. In T. Lickona (Ed.), *Moral development and behavior: Theory, research and social issues.* New York: Holt, Rinehart & Winston.

Mishell, D. R. (1986). Contraceptive use and effectiveness. In D. R. Mishell & V. Davajan (Eds.), *Infertility, contraception, and reproductive endocrinology* (2nd ed.). Oradell, NJ: Medical Economics Books.

Mitchell, V. F. (1987). Rx for improving staff effectiveness. In A. D. Timpe (Ed.), *The management of time.* New York: Facts On File.

Mobley, W. H., Horner, S. O., & Hollingsworth, A. T. (1978). An evaluation of precursors of hospital employee turnover. *Journal of Applied Psychology, 63*, 408–414.

Model, S. (1982). Housework by husbands: Determinants and implications. In J. Aldous (Ed.), *Two paychecks.* Newbury Park, CA: Sage Publications.

Moffett, A. M., Swash, M., & Scott, D. F. (1974). Effect of chocolate in migraine: A double-blind study. *Journal of Neurology, Neurosurgery, and Psychiatry, 37*(4), 445–448.

Money, J., & Ehrhardt, A. A. (1972). *Man and woman, boy and girl: Differentiation and dimorphism of gender identity.* Baltimore: Johns Hopkins University Press.

Monroe, S. M. (1982). Life events assessment: Current practices, emerging trends. *Clinical Psychology Review, 2*(4), 435–453.

Montemayor, R. (1986). Family variation in parent-adolescent storm and stress. *Journal of Adolescent Research, 1*, 15–31.

Moos, R. H., & Billings, A. G. (1982). Conceptualizing and measuring coping resources and processes. In L. Goldberger & S. Breznitz (Eds.), *Handbook of stress: Theoretical and clinical aspects.* New York: Free Press.

Morell, M. A., Twillman, R. K., & Sullaway, M. E. (1989). Would a Type A date another Type A? Influence of behavior type and personal attributes in the selection of dating partners. *Journal of Applied Social Psychology, 19*, 918–931.

Morey, L. C. (1988). Personality disorders in DSM-III and DSM-III-R: Convergence, coverage, and internal consistency. *American Journal of Psychiatry, 145*(5), 573–577.

Morgan, E., & Farber, B. A. (1982). Toward a reformulation of the Eriksonian model of identity development. *Adolescence, 17*, 199–211.

Morgan, J. P. (1992). Controlled substance analogues: Current clinical and social issues. In J. H. Lowinson, P. Ruiz, & R. B. Millman (Eds.), *Substance abuse: A comprehensive textbook* (2nd ed.). Baltimore: Williams & Wilkins.

Morgan, M. (1982). Television and adolescents' sex role stereotypes: A longitudinal study. *Journal of Personality and Social Psychology, 43*, 947–955.

Morgan, M. Y., & Scanzoni, J. (1987). Assessing variation in permanence/pragmatism orientations: Implications for marital stability. *Journal of Divorce, 11*(1), 1–24.

Morrison, A. M., & Von Glinow, M. A. (1990). Women and minorities in management. *American Psychologist, 45*(2), 200–208.

Morrow, L. (1993, March 29). The temping of America. *Time,* pp. 40–44, 46–47.

Morse, S., & Gergen, K. J. (1970). Social comparison, self-consistency, and the concept of self. *Journal of Personality and Social Psychology, 16*, 148–156.

Mortimer, J. A. (1988). The epidemiology of dementia: International comparisons. In J. A. Brody & G. L. Maddox (Eds.), *Epidemiology and aging.* New York: Springer.

Mosher, D. L. (1973). Sex differences, sex experience, sex guilt, and explicitly sexual films. *Journal of Social Issues, 29*, 95–112.

Moskowitz, H. (1985). Marijuana and driving. *Accident Analysis & Prevention, 17*, 323–345.

Mowrer, O. H. (1947). On the dual nature of learning: A reinterpretaton of "conditioning" and "problem-solving". *Harvard Educational Review, 17*, 102–150.

Muehlenhard, C. L. (1988). Misinterpreted dating behaviors and the risk of date rape. *Journal of Social and Clinical Psychology, 6*, 20–37.

Muehlenhard, C. L., & Hollabaugh, L. C. (1988). Do women sometimes say no when they mean yes? The prevalence and correlates of women's token resistance to sex. *Journal of Personality and Social Psychology, 54*(5), 872–879.

Muehlenhard, C. L., & Linton, M. A. (1987). Date rape and sexual aggression in dating situations: Incidence and risk factors. *Journal of Counseling Psychology, 34*, 186–196.

Muehlenhard, C. L., & McCoy, M. L. (1991). Double standard/double bind: The sexual double standard and women's communication about sex. *Psychology of Women Quarterly, 15*, 447–461.

Mullen, B., Atkins, J. L., Champion, D. S., Edwards, C., Hardy, D., Storey, J. E., & Vanderklok, M. (1985). The false consensus effect: A meta-analysis of 115 hypothesis tests. *Journal of Experimental Social Psychology, 21*, 262–283.

Mullen, B., & Felleman, B. (1990). Tripling in the dorms: A meta-analytic integration. *Basic and Applied Social Psychology, 11*, 33–44.

Munroe, R. L., & Munroe, R. H. (1975). *Cross-cultural human development.* Pacific Grove, CA: Brooks/Cole.

Murphy, J. M. (1980). Continuities in community-based psychiatric epidemiology. *Archives of General Psychiatry, 37*, 1215–1223.

Murphy, J. M., & Helzer, J. E. (1986). Epidemiology of schizophrenia in adulthood. In G. L. Klerman, M. M. Weissman, P. S. Appelbaum, & L. H. Roth (Eds.), *Psychiatry: Vol. 5. Social, epidemiologic, and legal psychiatry.* New York: Basic Books.

Murphy, K., & Welch, F. (1989). Wage premiums for college graduates: Recent growth and possible explanations. *Educational Researcher, 18*(4), 17–26.

Murphy, S. P., Rose, D., Hudes, M., & Viteri, F. E. (1992). Demographic and economic factors associated with dietary quality for adults in the 1987-88 nationwide food consumption theory. *Journal of the American Diet Association, 92*, 1352–1357.

Murstein, B. I. (1971). Critique of models of dyadic attraction. In B. I. Murstein (Ed.), *Theories of attraction and love.* New York: Springer.

Murstein, B. I. (1976). *Who will marry whom? Theories and research in marital choice.* New York: Springer.

Murstein, B. I. (1986). *Paths to marriage.* Newbury Park, CA: Sage Publications.

Myer, R. A., Peterson, S. E., & Stoffel-Rosales, M. (1991). Co-dependency: An examination of underlying assumptions. *Journal of Mental Health Counseling, 13*(4), 449–458.

Myers, D. G. (1980). *Inflated self: Human illusions and the biblical call to hope.* New York: Seabury Press.

Myers, D. G. (1992). *The pursuit of happiness: Who is happy—and why.* New York: Morrow.

Myers, D. G., & Lamm, H. (1976). The group polarization phenomenon. *Psychological Bulletin, 83*, 602–627.

Nadelson, C. C., Notman, M. T., Jackson, H., & Gornick, J. (1982). A follow-up study of rape victims. *American Journal of Psychiatry, 133*, 408–413.

Nahas, G. G. (1976). *Marijuana: Chemistry, biochemistry and cellular effects.* New York: Springer.

Nash, S. C., & Feldman, S. S. (1981). Sex-related differences in the relationship between sibling status and responsibility to babies. *Sex Roles, 7*, 1035–1042.

Nass, G. D., Libby, R. W., & Fisher, M. P. (1981). *Sexual choices: An introduction to human sexuality.* Monterey, CA: Wadsworth.

National Commission on Working Women. (1983). *Women's work: Undervalued, underpaid.* Washington, DC: Center for Women and Work.

National Institute for Occupational Safety and Health. (1988). *A proposed national strategy for the prevention of work-related psychological disorders.* Cincinnati, OH: Author.

Naughton, T. J. (1987). A conceptual view of workaholism and implications for career counseling and research. *Career Development Quarterly, 35,* 180–187.

Neimark, E. D. (1982). Adolescent thought: Transition to formal operations. In B. B. Wolman (Ed.), *Handbook of developmental psychology.* Englewood Cliffs, NJ: Prentice-Hall.

Nemiah, J. C. (1985). Somatoform disorders. In H. I. Kaplan & B. J. Sadock (Eds.), *Comprehensive textbook of psychiatry/IV.* Baltimore: Williams & Wilkins.

Neubeck, G. (1972). The myriad motives for sex. *Sexual Behavior, 2*(7), 51–56.

Neugarten, B. L., & Neugarten, D. A. (1986). Age in the aging society. *Daedalus, 115*(1), 31–49.

Neugebauer, R., Dohrenwend, B. P., & Dohrenwend, B. S. (1980). Formulation of hypotheses about the true prevalence of functional psychiatric disorders among adults in the United States. In B. P. Dohrenwend, B. S. Dohrenwend, M. S. Gould, B. Link, R. Neugebauer, & R. Wunsch-Hitzig (Eds.), *Mental illness in the United States: Epidemiological estimates.* New York: Praeger.

Newcomb, M. D. (1983). Relationship qualities of those who live together. *Alternative Lifestyles, 6*(2), 78–102.

Newcomb, M. D. (1990). Social support and personal characteristics: A developmental and interactional perspective. *Journal of Social and Clinical Psychology, 9*(1), 54–68.

Newcomb, P. A., & Carbone, P. P. (1992). The health consequences of smoking: Cancer. *Medical Clinics of North America, 76*(2), 305–331.

Newcomb, T. M. (1961). *The acquaintance process.* New York: Holt, Rinehart & Winston.

Newcomer, S. F., & Udry, J. R. (1985). Oral sex in an adolescent population. *Archives of Sexual Behavior, 14*(1), 41–46.

Newman, M., & Berkowitz, B. (1976). *How to be awake and alive.* Westminster, MD: Ballantine.

Newsom, C., Favell, J. E., & Rincover, A. (1983). Side effects of punishment. In S. Axelrod & J. Apsche (Eds.), *The effects of punishment on human behavior.* New York: Academic Press.

Newton, R. E., Marunycz, J. D., Alderdice, M. T., & Napoliello, M. J. (1986). Review of the side-effect profile of Buspirone. *American Journal of Medicine, 80*(Supp. 3b), 17–21.

Nezu, A. M. (1986). Efficacy of a social-problem therapy approach for unipolar depression. *Journal of Consulting and Clinical Psychology, 54,* 196–202.

Nezu, A. M., Nezu, C. M., Blissett, S. E. (1988). Sense of humor as a moderator of the relation between stressful events and psychological distress: A prospective analysis. *Journal of Personality and Social Psychology, 54*(3), 520–525.

Nichols, M. (1990). Lesbian relationships: Implications for the study of sexuality and gender. In D. P. McWhirter, S. A. Sanders, & J. M. Reinisch (Eds.), *Homosexuality/heterosexuality: Concepts of sexual orientation.* New York: Oxford University Press.

Nickerson, E. T., & Pitochelli, E. T. (1978, March). *Learned helplessness and depression in married women: Marriage as a depressing life style for women.* Paper presented at the meeting of the Eastern Psychological Association, Washington, DC.

Nicol, S. E., & Gottesman, I. I. (1983). Clues to the genetics and neurobiology of schizophrenia. *American Scientist, 71,* 398–404.

Nielsen, J. M. (1978). *Sex in society: Perspectives in stratification.* Belmont, CA: Wadsworth.

Nisbett, R. E. (1972). Hunger, obesity, and the ventromedial hypothalamus. *Psychological Review, 79,* 433–453.

Noe, R. A. (1988). Women and mentoring: A review and research agenda. *Academy of Management Review, 13,* 65–78.

Noguchi, T. T., & Nakamura, G. R. (1978). Phencyclidine-related deaths in Los Angeles County, 1976. *Journal of Forensic Science, 25*(3), 503–507.

Nolen-Hoeksema, S. (1991). Responses to depression and their effects on the duration of depressive episodes. *Journal of Abnormal Psychology, 100*(4), 569–582.

Nolen-Hoeksema, S., & Morrow, J. (1991). A prospective study of depression and post-traumatic stress symptoms after a natural disaster: The 1989 Loma Prieta earthquake. *Journal of Personality and Social Psychology, 61*(1), 115–121.

Noller, P. (1982). Channel consistency and inconsistency in the communications of married couples. *Journal of Personality and Social Psychology, 43,* 732–741.

Noller, P. (1985). Negative communications in marriage. *Journal of Social and Personal Relationships, 2,* 289–301.

Noller, P. (1987). Nonverbal communication in marriage. In D. Perlman & S. Duck (Eds.), *Intimate relationships: Development, dynamics, and deterioration.* Newbury Park, CA: Sage Publications.

Noller, P., & Fitzpatrick, M. A. (1990). Marital communication in the eighties. *Journal of Marriage and the Family, 52,* 832–843.

Noller, P., & Gallois, C. (1988). Understanding and misunderstanding in marriage: Sex and marital adjustment differences in structured and free interaction. In P. Noller & M. A. Fitzpatrick (Eds.), *Perspectives on marital interaction.* Clevedon, Avon, England: Multilingual Matters Ltd.

Norcross, J. C., & Prochaska, J. O. (1982). National survey of clinical psychologists: Affiliations and orientations. *Clinical Psychologist, 35*(3), 1, 4–6.

Novaco, R. W., Stokols, D., Campbell, J., & Stokols, J. (1979). Transportation, stress and community psychology. *American Journal of Community Psychology, 7*(4), 361–380.

Noyes, R., Jr. (1988). Revision of the DSM-III classification of anxiety disorders. In R. Noyes, M. Roth, & G. D. Burrows (Eds.), *Handbook of anxiety: Classification, etiological factors and associated disturbances* (Vol. 2). Amsterdam: Elsevier.

Noyes, R., Jr., Clarkson, C., Crowe, R. R., Yates, W. R., & McChesney, C. M. (1987). A family study of generalized anxiety disorder. *American Journal of Psychiatry, 8,* 1019–1024.

Nurnberger, J. I., & Zimmerman, J. (1970). Applied analysis of human behavior: An alternative to conventional motivational inferences and unconscious determination in therapeutic programming. *Behavior Therapy, 1,* 59–69.

Nye, R. D. (1992). *Three psychologies: Perspectives from Freud, Skinner, and Rogers.* Pacific Grove, CA: Brooks/Cole.

O'Brien, C. P., & Woody, G. E. (1986). Sedative-hypnotics and antianxiety agents. In A. J. Frances & R. E. Hales (Eds.), *Psychiatric Update: Annual Review* (Vol. 5). Washington, DC: American Psychiatric Press.

O'Brien, P. E., & Gaborit, M. (1992). Codependency: A disorder separate from chemical dependency. *Journal of Clinical Psychology, 48*(1), 129–136.

O'Leary, K. D. (1984). The image of behavior therapy: It is time to take a stand. *Behavior Therapy, 15,* 219–233.

O'Leary, V. E. (1977). *Toward understanding women.* Pacific Grove, CA: Brooks/Cole.

Offer, D., & Offer, J. (1975). *From teenage to young manhood.* New York: Basic Books.

Offer, D., Ostrov, E., Howard, K. I., & Atkinson, R. (1988). *The teenage world: Adolescents' self-image in ten countries.* New York: Plenum.

Offermann, L. R., & Gowing, M. K. (1990). Organizations of the future: Changes and challenges. *American Psychologist, 45*(2), 95–108.

Okun, L. (1986). *Woman abuse.* Albany, NY: State University of New York Press.

Olson, R. P., & Kroon, J. S. (1987). Biobehavioral treatment of essential hypertension. In M. S. Schwartz (Ed.), *Biofeedback: A practitioner's guide.* New York: Guilford Press.

Oppenheimer, V. K. (1988). A theory of marriage timing. *American Journal of Sociology, 94,* 563–591.

Orleans, C. T., Rimer, B. K., Cristinzio, S., Keintz, M. K., & Fleisher, L. (1991). A national survey of older smokers: Treatment needs of a growing population. *Health Psychology, 10*(5), 343–351.

Orlofsky, J. L., Marcia, J. E., & Lesser, I. M. (1973). Ego identity status and the intimacy versus isolation crisis of young adulthood. *Journal of Personality and Social Psychology, 27*(2), 211–219.

Orne, M. T., & Holland, C. C. (1968). On the ecological validity of laboratory deceptions. *International Journal of Psychiatry, 6,* 282–293.

Osborn, A. F. (1963). *Applied imagination: Principles and procedures for creative problem solving* (3rd ed.). New York: Scribner's.

Osipow, S. H. (1987). Counseling psychology: Theory, research, and practice in career counseling. *Annual Review of Psychology, 38,* 257–278.

Ost, L. (1987). Age of onset in different phobias. *Journal of Abnormal Psychology, 96*(3), 223–229.

Oster, G., Huse, D. M., Delea, T. E., & Colditz, G. A. (1986). Cost-effectiveness of nicotine gum as an adjunct to physician's advice against cigarette smoking. *Journal of the American Medical Association, 256,* 1315–1318.

Otto, L. B. (1988). America's youth: A changing profile. *Family Relations, 37,* 385–391.

Ouchi, W. G. (1981). *Theory Z: How American business can meet the Japanese challenge.* New York: Avon.

Packard, V. (1972). *A nation of strangers*. New York: David McKay.

Paffenbarger, R. S., Hyde, R. T., & Wing, A. L. (1990). Physical activity and physical fitness as determinants of health and longevity. In C. Bouchard, R. J. Shephard, T. Stephens, J. R. Sutton, & B. D. McPherson (Eds.), Champaign, IL: Human Kinetics Books.

Pagel, M. D., Erdly, W. W., & Becker, J. (1987). Social networks: We get by with (and in spite of) a little help from our friends. *Journal of Personality and Social Psychology, 53*(4), 793–804.

Paige, K. E. (1973, September). Women learn to sing the menstrual blues. *Psychology Today*, pp. 41–46.

Paivio, A. (1986). *Mental representations: A dual coding approach*. New York: Oxford University Press.

Palkovitz, R. J., & Lore, R. K. (1980). Note taking and note review: Why students fail questions based on lecture material. *Teaching of Psychology, 7*(3), 159–161.

Pallak, S. R. (1983). Salience of a communicator's physical attractiveness and persuasion: A heuristic versus systematic processing interpretation. *Social Cognition, 2*, 158–170.

Palmore, E. (1969). Predicting longevity: A follow-up controlling for age. *Gerontologist, 9*, 247–250.

Palmore, E. (1975). *The honorable elders*. Durham, NC: Duke University Press.

Palmore, E., Fillenbaum, G. G., & George, L. K. (1984). Consequences of retirement. *Journal of Gerontology, 39*, 109–116.

Park, C. C., & Shapiro, L. N. (1979). *You are not alone: Understanding and dealing with mental illness*. Boston: Little, Brown.

Park, C. W., & Young, S. M. (1986). Consumer response to television commercials: The impact of involvement and background music on brand attitude formation. *Journal of Marketing Research, 23*, 11–24.

Parke, R. D. (1977). Some effects of punishment on children's behavior—revisited. In In E. M. Hetherington & R. D. Parke (Eds.), *Contemporary readings in child psychology*. New York: McGraw-Hill.

Parker, G. (1988). Developmental factors in anxiety. In R. Noyes, M. Roth, & G. D. Burrows (Eds.), *Handbook of anxiety: Classification, etiological factors and associated disturbances* (Vol. 2). Amsterdam: Elsevier.

Parlee, M. B. (1973). The premenstrual syndrome. *Psychological Bulletin, 80*, 454–465.

Parlee, M. B. (1982). Changes in moods and activation levels during the menstrual cycle in experimentally naive subjects. *Psychology of Women Quarterly, 7*, 119–131.

Parlee, M. B., & the editors of *Psychology Today*. (1979, September). The friendship bond: PT's survey report on friendship in America. *Psychology Today*, pp. 43–54, 113.

Parrot, A. (1988). *Coping with date rape and acquaintance rape*. New York: Rosen Publishing Group.

Parrot, A., & Bechhofer, L. (1991). *Acquaintance rape: The hidden crime*. New York: Wiley.

Parsons, T. (1979). Definitions of health and illness in light of the American values and social structure. In E. G. Jaco (Ed.), *Patients, physicians and illness: A sourcebook in behavioral science and health*. New York: Free Press.

Passer, M. W., & Seese, M. (1983). Life stress and athletic injury: Examination of positive versus negative events and three moderator variables. *Journal of Human Stress, 9*, 11–16.

Patai, D. (1991, October 30). Minority status and the stigma of "surplus visibility". *The Chronicle of Higher Education*, p. A52.

Patterson, M. L. (1988). Functions of nonverbal behavior in close relationships. In S. Duck (Ed.), *Handbook of personal relationships: Theory, research, and interventions*. New York: Wiley.

Pauk, W. (1984). *How to study in college*. Boston: Houghton Mifflin.

Paul, S. M., Crawley, J. N., & Skolnick, P. (1986). The neurobiology of anxiety: The role of the GABA/benzodiazepine receptor complex. In P. A. Berger & H. K. H. Brodie (Eds.), *American handbook of psychiatry: Biological psychiatry* (Vol. 8, 2nd ed.). New York: Basic Books.

Paul, W., & Weinrich, J. D. (1982). Whom and what we study: Definition and scope of sexual orientation. In W. Paul, J. D. Weinrich, J. C. Gonsiorek, & M. E. Hotvedt (Eds.), *Homosexuality: Social, psychological and biological issues*. Newbury Park, CA: Sage Publications.

Pavlov, I. P. (1906). The scientific investigation of psychical faculties or processes in the higher animals. *Science, 24*, 613–619.

Paykel, E. S. (1974). Life stress and psychiatric disorder. In B. S. Dohrenwend & B. P. Dohrenwend (Eds.), *Stressful life events: Their nature and effects*. New York: Wiley.

Pearce, L. (1974). Duck! It's the new journalism. *New Times, 2*(10), 40–41.

Pedhazur, E. J., & Tetenbaum, T. J. (1979). Bem sex-role inventory: A theoretical and methodological critique. *Journal of Personality and Social Psychology, 37*, 996–1016.

Pennebaker, J. W. (1982). *The psychology of physical symptoms*. New York: Springer-Verlag.

Pennebaker, J. W. (1990). *Opening up: The healing power of confiding in others*. New York: Morrow.

Pennebaker, J. W., Colder, M., & Sharp, L. K. (1990). Accelerating the coping process. *Journal of Personality and Social Psychology, 58*(3), 528–537.

Pennebaker, J. W., Kiecolt-Glaser, J. K., & Glaser, R. (1988). Disclosure of traumas and immune function: Health implications for psychotherapy. *Journal of Consulting and Clinical Psychology, 56*, 239–245.

Pennebaker, J. W., & O'Heeron, R. C. (1984). Confiding in others and illness rate among spouses of suicide and accidental death victims. *Journal of Abnormal Psychology, 93*, 473–476.

Pennebaker, J. W., & Susman, J. R. (1988). Disclosure of traumas and psychosomatic processes. *Social Science and Medicine, 26*, 327–332.

Peplau, L. A. (1981, March). What homosexuals want. *Psychology Today*, pp. 28–38.

Peplau, L. A. (1983). Roles and gender. In H. H. Kelley, E. Berscheid, A. Christensen, J. H. Harvey, T. L. Huston, G. Levinger, E. McClintock, L. A. Peplau, & D. R. Peterson (Eds.), *Close relationships*. San Francisco: W. H. Freeman.

Peplau, L. A. (1988). Research on homosexual couples: An overview. In J. P. De Cecco (Ed.), *Gay relationships*. New York: Harrington Park Press.

Peplau, L. A. (1991). Lesbian and gay relationships. In J. C. Gonsiorek & J. D. Weinrich (Eds.), *Homosexuality: Research implications for public policy*. Newbury Park, CA: Sage Publications.

Peplau, L. A., Bikson, T. K., Rook, K. S., & Goodchilds, J. D. (1982). Being old and living alone. In L. A. Peplau & D. Perlman (Eds.), *Loneliness: A sourcebook of current theory, research, and therapy*. New York: Wiley-Interscience.

Peplau, L. A., & Cochran, S. D. (1990). A relational perspective on homosexuality. In D. P. McWhirter, S. A. Sanders, & J. M. Reinisch (Eds.), *Homosexuality/heterosexuality: Concepts of sexual orientation*. New York: Oxford University Press.

Peplau, L. A., & Gordon, S. L. (1983). The intimate relationships of lesbians and gay men. In E. R. Allgeier & N. B. McCormick (Eds.), *The changing boundaries: Gender roles and sexual behavior*. Palo Alto, CA: Mayfield.

Peplau, L. A., Rubin, Z., & Hill, C. T. (1977). Sexual intimacy in dating relationships. *Journal of Social Issues, 33*, 86–109.

Perkins, D. V. (1982). The assessment of stress using life events scales. In L. Goldberger & S. Breznitz (Eds.), *Handbook of stress: Theoretical and clinical aspects*. New York: Free Press.

Perls, F. S. (1969). *Gestalt therapy verbatim*. Lafayette, CA: Real People Press.

Perry, D. G., & Bussey, K. (1979). The social learning theory of sex differences: Imitation is alive and well. *Journal of Personality and Social Psychology, 37*, 1699–1712.

Perry, P. J., Miller, D. D., Arndt, S. V., & Cadoret, R. J. (1991). Clozapine and norclozapine plasma concentrations and clinical response of treatment-refractory schizophrenic patients. *American Journal of Psychiatry, 148*(2), 231–235.

Persky, H. (1983). Psychosexual effects of hormones. *Medical Aspects of Human Sexuality, 17*(9), 74–101.

Persky, H., Lief, H. I., Straus, D., Miller, W. R., & O'Brien, C. P. (1978). Plasma testosterone level and sexual behavior of couples. *Archives of Sexual Behavior, 7*, 157–173.

Peterman, T. A., & Curran, J. W. (1986). Sexual transmission of human immunodeficiency virus. *Journal of the American Medical Association, 256*, 2222–2226.

Petersen, A. C. (1987, September). Those gangly years. *Psychology Today*, pp. 28–34.

Petersen, A. C. (1988). Adolescent development. *Annual Review of Psychology, 39*, 583–607.

Petersen, A. C., Crockett, L., & Tobin-Richards, M. H. (1982). Sex differences. In H. E. Mitzel (Ed.), *Encyclopedia of education research* (5th ed.). New York: Free Press.

Petersen, J. R., Kretchmer, A., Nellis, B., Lever, J., & Hertz, R. (1983, January and March). The Playboy readers' sex survey (Parts 1 and 2). *Playboy*, pp. 108, 90.

Peterson, C., & Seligman, M. E. P. (1984). Causal explanations as a risk factor for depression: Theory and evidence. *Psychological Review, 91*, 347–374.

Peterson, C., & Seligman, M. E. P. (1987). Explanatory style and illness. *Journal of Personality, 55*, 237–265.

Peterson, C., Seligman, M. E. P., & Vaillant, G. E. (1988). Pessimistic explanatory style is a risk factor for physical illness: A thirty-five-year longitudinal study. *Journal of Personality and Social Psychology, 55*(1), 23–27.

Pettigrew, T. F. (1979). The ultimate attribution error: Extending Allport's cognitive analysis of prejudice. *Personality and Social Psychology Bulletin, 5*, 461–476.

Pettigrew, T. F., & Martin, J. (1987). Shaping the organizational context for Black American inclusion. *Journal of Social Issues, 43*, 41–78.

Petty, R. E., & Cacioppo, J. T. (1979). Effects of forewarning of persuasive intent and involvement on cognitive responses and persuasion. *Personality and Social Psychology Bulletin, 5*, 173–176.

Pfeiffer, S. M., & Wong, P. T. P. (1989). Multidimensional jealousy. *Journal of Social and Personal Relationships, 6*, 181–196.

Pfohl, B., & Andreasen, N. C. (1986). Schizophrenia: Diagnosis and classification. In A. J. Frances & R. E. Hales (Eds.), *Psychiatry update: Annual review* (Vol. 5). Washington, DC: American Psychiatric Press.

Phelps, S., & Austin, N. (1987). *The assertive woman.* San Luis Obispo, CA: Impact.

Phillips, M. R., Wolf, A. S., & Coons, D. J. (1988). Psychiatry and the criminal justice system: Testing the myths. *American Journal of Psychiatry, 145*, 605–610.

Philpott, J. S. (1983). *The relative contribution to meaning of verbal and nonverbal channels of communication: A meta-analysis.* Unpublished master's thesis, University of Nebraska, Omaha.

Piaget, J. (1929). *The child's conception of the world.* New York: Harcourt Brace.

Piaget, J. (1952). *The origins of intelligence in children.* New York: International Universities Press.

Piaget, J. (1972). Intellectual evolution from adolescence to adulthood. *Human Development, 15*, 1–12.

Piaget, J. (1983). Piaget's theory. In P. H. Mussen (Ed.), *Handbook of child psychology* (Vol. 1). New York: Wiley.

Pines, A. M., & Aronson, E. (1983). Antecedents, correlates, and consequences of sexual jealousy. *Journal of Personality, 51*, 108–136.

Pines, A. M., & Aronson, E. (1988). *Career burnout: Causes and cures.* New York: Free Press.

Pines, A. M., Aronson, E., & Kafry, D. (1981). *Burnout: From tedium to personal growth.* New York: Free Press.

Piotrkowski, C. S., Rapoport, R. N., & Rapoport, R. (1987). Families and work. In M. B. Sussman & S. K. Steinmetz (Eds.), *Handbook of marriage and the family.* New York: Plenum.

Pittman, J. F., & Lloyd, S. A. (1988). Quality of family life, social support, and stress. *Journal of Marriage and the Family, 50*, 53–67.

Pleck, J. H. (1976). The male sex role: Definitions, problems, and sources of change. *Journal of Social Issues, 32*(3), 155–164.

Pleck, J. H. (1977). The work-family role system. *Social Problems, 24*, 417–427.

Pleck, J. H. (1981a). *The myth of masculinity.* Cambridge, MA: MIT Press.

Pleck, J. H. (1981b). The work-family problem: Overloading the system. In B. Forisha & B. Goldman (Eds.), *Outsiders on the inside: Women in organizations.* Englewood Cliffs, NJ: Prentice-Hall.

Plomin, R. (1990). *Nature and nurture: An introduction to human behavioral genetics.* Pacific Grove, CA: Brooks/Cole.

Plomin, R., & Daniels, D. (1987). Why are children in the same family so different from each other? *Behavioral and Brain Sciences, 10*, 1–16.

Plomin, R., Chipuer, H. M., & Loehlin, J. C. (1990). Behavioral genetics and personality. In L. A. Pervin (Ed.), *Handbook of personality: Theory and research.* New York: Guilford Press.

Plude, D. J., & Hoyer, W. J. (1985). Attention and performance: Identifying and localizing age deficits. In N. Charness (Ed.), *Aging and human performance.* Chichester, England: Wiley.

Plutchik, R. (1980, February). A language for the emotions. *Psychology Today*, pp. 68–78.

Plutchik, R., Williams, M. H., Jerrett, I., Karasu, T. B., & Kane, C. (1978). Emotions, personality, and life stresses in asthma. *Journal of Psychosomatic Research, 22*, 425–431.

Pocs, O., & Godow, A. G. (1977). Can students view parents as sexual beings? *Family Coordinator, 26*, 31–36.

Pogue-Geile, M. F. (1989). The prognostic significance of negative symptoms in schizophrenia. *British Journal of Psychiatry, 155*, 123–127.

Polivy, J., & Thomsen, L. (1988). Dieting and other eating disorders. In E. A. Blechman & K. D. Brownell (Eds.), *Handbook of behavioral medicine for women.* New York: Pergamon.

Pomerleau, O. F., & Pomerleau, C. S. (Eds.). (1988). *Nicotine replacement: A critical evaluation.* New York: Liss.

Pope, K. S., Keith-Spiegel, P., & Tabachnick, B. G. (1986). Sexual attraction to clients. *American Psychologist, 41*(2), 147–158.

Pope, M. K., & Smith, T. W. (1991). Cortisol excretion in high and low cynically hostile men. *Psychosomatic Medicine, 53*(4), 386–392.

Porter, S. A. (1985, August 23). What's a housewife worth? More than numbers show. *Providence Evening Bulletin.*

Post, R. M. (1989). Mood disorders: Somatic treatment. In H. I. Kaplan & B. J. Sadock (Eds.), *Comprehensive textbook of psychiatry/V* (Vol. 2). Baltimore: Williams & Wilkins.

Powell, J. (1969). *Why am I afraid to tell you who I am?* Niles, IL: Argus Communications.

Powell, J. (1990). *Why am I afraid to tell you who I am?* Allen, TX: Tabor.

Powell, L. H., Friedman, M., Thoresen, C. E., Gill, J. J., & Ulmer, D. K. (1984). Can the Type A behavior pattern be altered after myocardial infarction? A second year report from the recurrent coronary prevention unit. *Psychosomatic Medicine, 46*(4), 293–313.

Powell, M. (1973). Age and occupational change among coal-miners. *Occupational Psychology, 47*, 37–49.

Powers, S. I., Hauser, S. T., & Kilner, L. A. (1989). Adolescent mental health. *American Psychologist, 44*, 200–208.

Pratkanis, A. R., & Aronson, E. (1992). *Age of propaganda: The everyday use and abuse of persuasion.* New York: W. H. Freeman.

Price, S. J., & McKenry, P. C. (1988). *Divorce.* Newbury Park, CA: Sage Publications.

Prochaska, J. O., Velicer, W. F., DiClemente, C. C., & Fava, J. (1988). Measuring processes of change: Applications to the cessation of smoking. *Journal of Consulting and Clinical Psychology, 56*, 520–528.

Pruitt, D. G. (1971). Choice shifts in group discussion: An introductory review. *Journal of Personality and Social Psychology, 20*, 339–360.

Pursell, S. A., & Banikiotes, P. G. (1978). Androgyny and initial interpersonal attraction. *Personality and Social Psychology Bulletin, 4*, 235–243.

Pyke, S. W., & Kahill, S. P. (1983). Sex differences in characteristics presumed relevant to professional productivity. *Psychology of Women Quarterly, 8*, 189–192.

Quillin, P. (1987). *Healing nutrients.* New York: Random House.

Quina, K., & Carlson, N. L. (1989). *Rape, incest, and sexual harassment: A guide for helping survivors.* New York: Praeger.

Rabbitt, P., & McGinnis, L. (1988). Do clever old people have earlier and richer first memories? *Psychology and Aging, 3*, 338–341.

Rabkin, J. G., & Streuning E. L. (1976). Life events, stress and illness. *Science, 194*, 1013–1020.

Rachman, S. J. (1990). *Fear and courage.* New York: W. H. Freeman.

Rachman, S. J., & Wilson, G. T. (1980). *The effects of psychological therapy.* New York: Pergamon Press.

Radecki-Bush, C., Bush, J. P., & Jennings, J. (1988). Effects of jealousy threats on relationship perceptions and emotions. *Journal of Social and Personal Relationships, 5*, 285–303.

Ragland, D. R., & Brand, R. J. (1988). Type A behavior and mortality from coronary heart disease. *New England Journal of Medicine, 318*(2), 65–69.

Rahe, R. H., & Arthur, R. H. (1978). Life change and illness studies. *Journal of Human Stress, 4*(1), 3–15.

Rahe, R. H., & Holmes, T. H. (1965). Social, psychologic and psychophysiologic aspects of inguinal hernia. *Journal of Psychosomatic Research, 8*, 487–491.

Raley, P. E. (1976). *Making love: How to be your own sex therapist.* New York: Dial Press.

Raley, P. E. (1980). *Making love: How to be your own sex therapist.* New York: Avon. (Paperback edition).

Rapaport, K., & Burkhart, B. R. (1984). Personality and attitudinal characteristics of sexually coercive college males. *Journal of Abnormal Psychology, 93*(2), 216–221.

Raphael, K. G., Cloitre, M., & Dohrenwend, B. P. (1991). Problems of recall and misclassification with checklist methods of measuring stressful life events. *Health Psychology, 10*(1), 62–74.

Rapoport, J. L. (1989). The biology of obsessions and compulsions. *Scientific American, 260*, 82–89.

Raschke, H. J. (1987). Divorce. In M. B. Sussman & S. K. Steinmetz (Eds.), *Handbook of marriage and the family.* New York: Plenum.

Raskin, R., Bali, L. R., & Peeke, H. V. (1981). Muscle biofeedback and transcendental meditation: A controlled evaluation of efficacy in the treatment of chronic anxiety. In D. Shapiro, Jr., J. Stoyva, J. Kamiya, T. X. Barber, N. E. Miller, & G. E. Schwartz (Eds.), *Biofeedback and behavioral medicine 1979/80: Therapeutic applications and experimental foundations.* Chicago: Aldine.

Raugh, M. R., & Atkinson, R. C. (1975). A mnemonic method for learning a second-language vocabulary. *Journal of Educational Psychology, 67*, 1–16.

Raush, H. L., Barry, W. A., Hertel, R. K., & Swain, M. A. (1974). *Communication, conflict and marriage.* San Francisco: Jossey-Bass.

Ray, L., Soares, E. J., & Tolchinsky, B. (1988). Explicit lyrics: A content analysis of top 100 songs from the 50's to the 80's. *The Speech Communication Annual, 2,* 43–56.

Ray, O., & Ksir, C. (1990). *Drugs, society & human behavior.* St. Louis: Times Mirror/Mosby.

Reese, H. W., & Rodeheaver, D. (1985). Problem solving and complex decision making. In J. E. Birren & K. W. Schaie (Eds.), *Handbook of the psychology of aging* (2nd ed.). New York: Van Nostrand Reinhold.

Reinisch, J. M. (1990). *The Kinsey Institute new report on sex: What you must know to be sexually literate.* New York: St. Martin's Press.

Reinke, B. J., Ellicott, A. M., Harris, R. L., & Hancock, E. (1985). Timing of psychosocial changes in women's lives. *Human Development, 28,* 259–280.

Reis, H. T., Senchak, M., & Solomon, B. (1985). Sex differences in the intimacy of social interaction: Further examination of potential explanation. *Journal of Personality and Social Psychology, 48,* 1204–1217.

Reiser, M. F. (1989). The future of psychoanalysis in academic psychiatry: Plain talk. *Psychoanalytic Quarterly, 58*(2), 185–209.

Reiss, I. L. (1967). *The social context of premarital sexual permissiveness.* New York: Holt, Rinehart & Winston.

Reiss, I. L. (1980). *Family systems in America.* New York: Holt, Rinehart & Winston.

Reiss, I. L., Anderson, R. E., & Sponaugle, G. C. (1980). A multivariate model of the determinants of extramarital sexual permissiveness. *Journal of Marriage and the Family, 42,* 395–411.

Reiss, I. L., & Furstenberg, F. F., Jr. (1981). Sociology and human sexuality. In H. I. Lief (Ed.), *Sexual problems in medical practice.* Chicago: American Medical Association.

Reiss, M., Rosenfeld, P., Melburg, V., & Tedeschi, J. T. (1981). Self-serving attributions: Biased private perceptions and distorted public descriptions. *Journal of Personality and Social Psychology, 41,* 224–231.

Relman, A. (1982). Marijuana and health. *New England Journal of Medicine, 306*(10), 603–604.

Renwick, P. A., & Lawler, E. E. (1978, May). What do you really want from your job? *Psychology Today,* pp. 53–65.

Repetti, R. L. (1984). Determinants of children's sex-stereotyping: Parental sex-role traits and television viewing. *Personality and Social Psychology Bulletin, 10*(3), 457–468.

Revenson, T. A., & Felton, B. J. (1989). Disability and coping as predictors of psychological adjustment to rheumatoid arthritis. *Journal of Consulting and Clinical Psychology, 57,* 344–348.

Rey, J. M., Stewart, G. W., Plapp, J. M., Bashir, M. R., & Richards, I. N. (1988). DSM-III axis IV revisited. *American Journal of Psychiatry, 145,* 286–292.

Rhodewalt, F., & Agustsdottir, S. (1986). Effects of self-presentation on the phenomenal self. *Journal of Personality and Social Psychology, 50,* 47–55.

Rhodewalt, F., & Zone, J. B. (1989). Appraisal of life change, depression, and illness in hardy and nonhardy women. *Journal of Personality and Social Psychology, 56*(1), 81–88.

Rice, F. P. (1989). *Human sexuality.* Dubuque, IA: William C. Brown.

Rice, L. N., & Greenberg, L. S. (1992). Humanistic approaches to psychotherapy. In D. K. Freedheim (Ed.), *History of psychotherapy: A century of change.* Washington, DC: American Psychological Association.

Richardson, J. G., & Simpson, C. H. (1982). Children, gender and social structure: An analysis of the contents of letters to Santa Claus. *Child Development, 53,* 429–436.

Ricketts, W. (1984). Biological research on homosexuality: Ansell's cow or Occam's razor? *Journal of Homosexuality, 10,* 65–93.

Ridgeway, C. L. (1983). *The dynamics of small groups.* New York: St. Martin's Press.

Ries, P., & Stone, A. J. (1992). *The American woman 1992–93: A status report.* New York: Norton.

Rifkin, J. (1987). *Time wars: The primary conflict in human history.* New York: Simon & Schuster.

Rimer, B. K., Orleans, C. T., Keintz, M. K., Cristinzio, S., & Fleisher, L. (1990). The older smoker: Status, challenges and opportunities for intervention. *Chest, 97,* 547–553.

Rimm, D. C., & Cunningham, H. M. (1985). Behavior therapies. In S. J. Lynn & J. P. Garske (Eds.), *Contemporary psychotherapies: Models and methods.* Columbus, OH: Charles E. Merrill.

Ringer, R. J. (1978). *Winning through intimidation.* New York: Fawcett.

Rivera, R. R. (1991). Sexual orientation and the law. In J. C. Gonsiorek & J. D. Weinrich (Eds.), *Homosexuality: Research implications for public policy.* Newbury Park, CA: Sage Publications.

Robbins, A. (1991). *Awaken the giant within: How to take immediate control of your mental, emotional, physical, and financial destiny.* New York: Simon & Schuster (Summit Books).

Roberts, J. V., & Herman, C. P. (1986). The psychology of height: An empirical review. In C. P. Herman, M. P. Zanna, & E. T. Higgins (Eds.), *Physical appearance, stigma,* *and social behavior: The Ontario symposium* (Vol. 3). Hillsdale, NJ: Erlbaum.

Roberts, L. J., & Krokoff, L. L. (1990). A time-series analysis of withdrawal, hostility, and displeasure in satisfied and dissatisfied marriages. *Journal of Marriage and the Family, 52,* 95–105.

Roberts, P., & Newton, P. M. (1987). Levinsonian studies of women's adult development. *Psychology and Aging, 2*(2), 154–163.

Robins, C. J. (1988). Attributions and depression: Why is the literature so inconsistent? *Journal of Personality and Social Psychology, 54*(5), 880–889.

Robins, E. (1990). The study of interdependence in marriage. In F. D. Fincham & T. N. Bradbury (Eds.), *The psychology of marriage: Basic issues and applications.* New York: Guilford Press.

Robins, L. N. (1966). *Deviant children grow up.* Baltimore: Williams & Wilkins.

Robins, L. N., Helzer, J. E., Weissman, M. M., Orvaschel, H., Gruenberg, E., Burke, J. D., & Regier, D. A. (1984). Lifetime prevalence of specific psychiatric disorders in three sites. *Archives of General Psychiatry, 41,* 949–958.

Robins, L. N., Locke, B. Z., & Regier, D. A. (1991). An overview of psychiatric disorders in America. In L. N. Robins & D. A. Regier (Eds.), *Psychiatric disorders in America: The epidemiologic catchment area study.* New York: Free Press.

Robins, L. N., & Regier, D. A. (Eds.). (1991). *Psychiatric disorders in America: The epidemiologic catchment area study.* New York: Free Press.

Robins, L. N., Tipp, J., & Przybeck, T. (1991). Antisocial personality. In L. N. Robins & D. A. Regier (Eds.), *Psychiatric disorders in America: The epidemiologic catchment area study.* New York: Free Press.

Robinson, F. P. (1970). *Effective study* (4th ed.). New York: HarperCollins.

Robinson, I. E., & Jedlicka, D. (1982). Change in sexual attitudes and behavior of college students from 1965 to 1980: A research note. *Journal of Marriage and the Family, 44*(1), 237–240.

Robinson, J. (1980). Housework technology and household work. In S. Berk (Ed.), *Women and household labor.* Newbury Park, CA: Sage Publications.

Roche, A. F. (1979). Secular trends in stature, weight, and maturation. *Monographs of the Society for Research on Child Development, 44* (4, Serial No. 179).

Rodin, J. (1981). Current status of the internal-external hypothesis for obesity: What went wrong? *American Psychologist, 36*(4), 361–372.

Rodin, J., Schank, D., & Striegel-Moore, R. H. (1989). Psychological features of obesity. *Medical Clinics of North America, 73*(1), 47–66.

Rodin, J., Silberstein, L., & Striegel-Moore, R. H. (1985). Women and weight: A normative discontent. In T. B. Sonderegger (Ed.), *Nebraska symposium on motivation 1984: Psychology and gender* (Vol. 32). Lincoln: University of Nebraska Press.

Rodman, H., & Sidden, J. (1992). A critique of pessimistic views about U. S. families. *Family Relations, 41,* 436–439.

Roe, A. (1977). *The psychology of occupations.* New York: Wiley.

Roffman, R. A., & George, W. H. (1988). Cannabis abuse. In D. M. Donovan & G. A. Marlatt (Eds.), *Assessment of addictive behaviors.* New York: Guilford Press.

Rogers, C. R. (1951). *Client-centered therapy: Its current practice, implications, and theory.* Boston: Houghton Mifflin.

Rogers, C. R. (1959). A theory of therapy, personality, and interpersonal relationships, as developed in the client-centered framework. In S. Koch (Ed.), *Psychology: A study of a science* (Vol. 3). New York: McGraw-Hill.

Rogers, C. R. (1961). *On becoming a person: A therapist's view of psychotherapy.* Boston: Houghton Mifflin.

Rogers, C. R. (1977). *Carl Rogers on personal power.* New York: Delacorte.

Rogers, C. R. (1980). *A way of being.* Boston: Houghton Mifflin.

Rogers, C. R. (1986). Client-centered therapy. In I. L. Kutash & A. Wolf (Eds.), *Psychotherapist's casebook.* San Francisco: Jossey-Bass.

Rogers, R. W. (1975). A protection motivation theory of fear appeals and attitude change. *Journal of Psychology, 91,* 93–114.

Rollins, B., & Feldman, H. (1970). Marital satisfaction over the family life cycle. *Journal of Marriage and the Family, 32,* 20–28.

Rook, K. S. (1984). Research on social support, loneliness, and social isolation: Toward an integration. In P. Shaver (Ed.), *Review of personality and social psychology* (Vol. 5). Newbury Park, CA: Sage Publications.

Rook, K. S. (1990). Parallels in the study of social support and social strain. *Journal of Social and Clinical Psychology, 9*(1), 118–132.

Rook, K. S., Dooley, D., & Catalano, R. (1991). Stress transmission: The effects of husbands' job stressors on the emotional health of their wives. *Journal of Marriage and the Family, 53,* 165–177.

Roosa, M. W. (1988). The effect of age in the transition to parenthood: Are delayed childbearers a unique group? *Family Relations, 37,* 322–327.

Rosch, P. J., & Pelletier, K. R. (1987). Designing worksite stress management programs. In L. R. Murphy & T. F. Schoenborn (Eds.), *Stress management in work settings.* Washington, DC: National Institute for Occupational Safety and Health.

Rosen, G. M. (1987). Self-help treatment books and the commercialization of psychotherapy. *American Psychologist, 42*(1), 46–51.

Rosen, M., Nystrom, L., & Wall, S. (1988). Diet and cancer mortality in the counties of Sweden. *American Journal of Epidemiology, 127,* 42–49.

Rosen, R. D. (1977). *Psychobabble.* New York: Atheneum.

Rosenbaum, M., Lakin, M., & Roback, H. B. (1992). Psychotherapy in groups. In D. K. Freedheim (Ed.), *History of psychotherapy: A century of change.* Washington, DC: American Psychological Association.

Rosenbaum, M. E. (1986). The repulsion hypothesis: On the nondevelopment of relationships. *Journal of Personality and Social Psychology, 51*(6), 1156–1166.

Rosenberg, M. (1979). *Conceiving the self.* New York: Basic Books.

Rosenberg, M. (1985). Self-concept and psychological well-being in adolescence. In R. L. Leahy (Ed.), *The development of the self.* Orlando, FL: Academic Press.

Rosenfeld, L. B., Civikly, J. M., & Herron, J. R. (1979). Anatomical and psychological sex differences. In G. J. Chelune & associates (Eds.), *Self-disclosure: Origins, patterns, and implications of openness in interpersonal relationships.* San Francisco: Jossey-Bass.

Rosenhan, D. L. (1973). On being sane in insane places. *Science, 179,* 250–258.

Rosenheim, E., & Muchnik, B. (1984/1985). Death concerns in differential levels of consciousness as functions of defense strategy and religious beliefs. *Omega, Journal of Death and Dying, 155,* 15–24.

Rosenman, R. H. (1991). Type A behavior pattern and coronary heart disease: The hostility factor? *Stress Medicine, 7*(4), 245–253.

Rosenman, R. H., & Chesney, M. A. (1982). Stress, Type A behavior, and coronary disease. In L. Goldberger & S. Breznitz (Eds.), *Handbook of stress: Theoretical and clinical aspects.* New York: Free Press.

Rosenstock, I. M., & Kirscht, J. P. (1979). Why people seek health care. In G. C. Stone, F. Cohen, N. E. Adler, & associates (Eds.), *Health psychology—A handbook.* San Francisco: Jossey-Bass.

Rosenthal, H. (1988). *Not with my life I don't: Preventing your suicide and that of others.* Muncie, IN: Accelerated Development.

Ross, C. A., Anderson, G., Fleisher, W. P., & Norton, G. R. (1991). The frequency of multiple personality disorder among psychiatric inpatients. *American Journal of Psychiatry, 148,* 1717–1720.

Ross, C. A., Miller, S. D., Reagor, P., Bjornson, L., Fraser, G. A., & Anderson, G. (1990). Structured interview data on 102 cases of multiple personality disorder from four centers. *American Journal of Psychiatry, 147,* 596–601.

Ross, L. (1977). The intuitive psychologist and his shortcomings: Distortions in the attribution process. In L. Berkowitz (Ed.), *Advances in experimental social psychology* (Vol. 10). New York: Academic Press.

Ross, L. D. (1988). The obedience experiments: A case study of controversy. *Contemporary Psychology, 33*(2), 101–104.

Ross, L. D., Greene, D., & House, P. (1977). The "false consensus effect": An egocentric bias in social perception and attribution processes. *Journal of Experimental Social Psychology, 13,* 279–301.

Ross, M., & Sicoly, F. (1979). Egocentric biases in availability and attribution. *Journal of Personality and Social Psychology, 37,* 322–337.

Rothbart, M., & Park, B. (1986). On the confirmability and disconfirmability of trait concepts. *Journal of Personality and Social Psychology, 50,* 131–142.

Rothblum, E. D., Solomon, L. J., & Albee, G. W. (1986). A sociopolitical perspective of DSM-III. In T. Millon & G. L. Klerman (Eds.), *Contemporary directions in psychopathology: Toward the DSM-IV.* New York: Guilford Press.

Rotter, J. B. (1966). Generalized expectancies for internal versus external control of reinforcement. *Psychological Monographs,* (Whole No. 609).

Rotter, J. B. (1975). Some problems and misconceptions related to the construct of internal versus external control of reinforcement. *Journal of Consulting and Clinical Psychology, 43,* 56–67.

Rotter, J. B. (1982). *The development and application of social learning theory.* New York: Praeger.

Rotter, J. B. (1990). Internal versus external control of reinforcement: A case history of a variable. *American Psychologist, 45*(4), 489–493.

Rotton, J., & Frey, J. (1984). Psychological costs of air pollution: Atmospheric conditions, seasonal trends, and psychiatric emergencies. *Population and Environmental Behavior and Social Issues, 7,* 3–16.

Rowlison, R. T., & Felner, R. D. (1988). Major life events, hassles, and adaptation in adolescence: Confounding in the conceptualization and measurement of life stress and adjustment revisited. *Journal of Personality and Social Psychology, 55*(3), 432–444.

Roy, M. (Ed.). (1977). *Battered women.* New York: Van Nostrand.

Rozee, P. D., Bateman, P., & Gilmore, T. (1991). The personal perspective of acquaintance rape prevention: A three-tier approach. In A. Parrot & L. Bechhofer (Eds.), *Acquaintance rape: The hidden crime.* New York: Wiley.

Rubenstein, C. M., & Shaver, P. (1980). Loneliness in two northeastern cities. In J. Hartog, J. R. Audy, & Y. A. Cohen (Eds.), *The anatomy of loneliness.* New York: International Universities Press.

Rubenstein, C. M., & Shaver, P. (1982). The experience of loneliness. In L. A. Peplau & D. Perlman (Eds.), *Loneliness: A sourcebook of current theory, research and therapy.* New York: Wiley.

Rubin, E. H., Zorumski, C. F., & Guze, S. B. (1986). Somatoform disorders. In T. Millon & G. L. Klerman (Eds.), *Contemporary directions in psychopathology: Toward the DSM-IV.* New York: Guilford Press.

Rubin, L. (1985). *Just friends: The role of friendship in our lives.* New York: HarperCollins.

Rubin, Z. (1970). Measurement of romantic love. *Journal of Personality and Social Psychology, 16,* 265–273.

Rubin, Z. (1973). *Liking and loving: An introduction to social psychology.* New York: Holt, Rinehart & Winston.

Rubin, Z. (1974). Lovers and other strangers: The development of intimacy in encounters and relationships. *American Scientist, 62,* 182–190.

Rubin, Z. (1983). *Intimate strangers: Men and women together.* New York: Harper & Row.

Rubin, Z., Hill, C. T., Peplau, L. A., & Dunkel-Schetter, C. (1980). Self-disclosure in dating couples: Sex roles and the ethic of openness. *Journal of Marriage and the Family, 42,* 305–317.

Rubin, Z., Peplau, L. A., & Hill, C. T. (1981). Loving and leaving: Sex differences in romantic attachments. *Sex Roles, 7*(8), 821–835.

Ruble, D. N., Fleming, A. S., Hackel, L. S., & Stangor, C. (1988). Changes in the marital relationship during the transition to first time motherhood: Effects of violated expectations concerning division of household labor. *Journal of Personality and Social Psychology, 55,* 78–87.

Ruble, T. L. (1983). Sex stereotypes: Issues of change in the 1970s. *Sex Roles, 9,* 397–402.

Ruble, T. L., Cohen, R., & Ruble, D. N. (1984). Sex stereotypes: Occupational barriers for women. *American Behavioral Scientist, 27,* 339–356.

Rubonis, A. V., & Bickman, L. (1991). Psychological impairment in the wake of disaster: The disaster-psychopathology relationship. *Psychological Bulletin, 109,* 384–399.

Rukeyser, L., Cooney, J., & Winslow, W. (1988). *Louis Rukeyser's business almanac.* New York: Simon & Schuster.

Rule, B. G., Bisanz, G. L., & Kohn, M. (1985). Anatomy of a persuasion schema: Targets, goals, and strategies. *Journal of Personality and Social Psychology, 48,* 1127–1140.

Rush, A. J. (1984). Cognitive therapy. In T. B. Karasu (Ed.), *The psychiatric therapies.* Washington, DC: American Psychiatric Association.

Rushton, J. P., Fulker, D. W., Neale, M. C., Nias, D. K. B., & Eysenck, H. J. (1986). Altruism and aggression: The heritability of individual differences. *Journal of Personality and Social Psychology, 50*(6), 1192–1198.

Russek, H. I., & Russek, L. G. (1976). Is emotional stress an etiological factor in coronary heart disease? *Psychosomatics, 17,* 63.

Russo, N. F. (1979). Overview: Sex roles, fertility, and the motherhood mandate. *Psychology of Women Quarterly, 4,* 7–15.

Russo, N. F., & Sobel, S. B. (1981). Sex differences in the utilization of mental health facilities. *Professional Psychology, 12,* 7–19.

Sabatelli, R. M. (1988). Exploring relationship satisfaction: A social exchange perspective on the interdependence between theory, research, and practice. *Family Relations, 37,* 217–222.

Sabini, J. (1992). *Social psychology.* New York: Norton.

Sachs, G. S., & Gelenberg, A. J. (1988). Adverse effects of electroconvulsive therapy. In A. J. Frances & R. E. Hales (Eds.), *Review of psychiatry* (Vol. 7). Washington, DC: American Psychiatric Press.

Sackeim, H. A. (1985, June). The case for ECT. *Psychology Today,* pp. 35–40.

Sackeim, H. A. (1988). Mechanisms of action of electroconvulsive therapy. In A. J. Frances & R. E. Hales (Eds.), *Annual review of psychiatry* (Vol. 7). Washington, DC: American Psychiatric Press.

Sadker, M., & Sadker, D. (1985, March). Sexism in the schoolroom of the '80s. *Psychology Today,* pp. 54–57.

Safilios-Rothschild, C. (1977). *Love, sex, and sex roles.* Englewood Cliffs, NJ: Prentice-Hall.

Saghir, M. T., & Robins, E. R. (1973). *Male and female homosexuality: A comprehensive investigation.* Baltimore: Williams & Wilkins.

Salovey, P., & Rodin, J. (1986). The differentiation of social-comparison jealousy and romantic jealousy. *Journal of Personality and Social Psychology, 50,* 1100–1112.

Salzman, C. (1989). Treatment with antianxiety agents. In *Treatment of psychiatric disorders* (Vol. 3). Washington, DC: American Psychiatric Association.

Samet, J. M. (1992). The health benefits of smoking cessation. *Medical Clinics of North America, 76*(2), 399–414.

Sandberg, G., Jackson, T. L., & Petretic-Jackson, P. (1987). College students' attitudes regarding sexual coercion and aggression: Developing educational and preventive strategies. *Journal of College Student Personnel, 28*(4), 302–311.

Sanders, G. S. (1982). Social comparison and perceptions of health and illness. In G. S. Sanders & J. Suls (Eds.), *Social psychology of health and illness.* Hillsdale, NJ: Erlbaum.

Sandler, J. (1975). Aversion methods. In F. H. Kanfer & A. P. Goldstein (Eds.), *Helping people change: A textbook of methods.* New York: Pergamon Press.

Santrock, J. W., & Sitterle, K. (1985). The developmental world of children in divorced families: Research findings and clinical implications. In D. C. Goldberg (Ed.), *Contemporary marriage: Special issues in couples therapy.* Homewood, IL: Dorsey Press.

Sarason, I. G. (1984). Stress, anxiety and cognitive interference: Reactions to stress. *Journal of Personality and Social Psychology, 46*(4), 929–938.

Sarason, I. G., Johnson, J. H., & Siegel, J. M. (1978). Assessing the impact of life changes: Development of the Life Experiences Survey. *Journal of Consulting and Clinical Psychology, 46,* 932–946.

Sarason, I. G., Levine, H. M., & Sarason, B. R. (1982). Assessing the impact of life changes. In T. Millon, C. Green, & R. Meagher (Eds.), *Handbook of clinical health psychology.* New York: Plenum.

Sarnacki, R. E. (1979). An examination of test-wiseness in the cognitive domain. *Review of Educational Research, 49,* 252–279.

Scarf, M. (1987). *Intimate partners: Patterns in love and marriage.* New York: Random House.

Schachter, S. (1959). *The psychology of affiliation.* Stanford, CA: Stanford University Press.

Schachter, S. (1964). The interaction of cognitive and physiological determinants of emotional state. In L. Berkowitz (Ed.), *Advances in experimental social psychology* (Vol. 1). New York: Academic Press.

Schachter, S. (1971). *Emotion, obesity and crime.* New York: Academic Press.

Schaef, A. W. (1986). *Codependence misdiagnosed-mistreated.* Minneapolis: Winston Press.

Schaefer, E. S., & Burnett, C. K. (1987). Stability and predictability of quality of women's marital relationships and demoralization. *Journal of Personality and Social Psychology, 53,* 1129–1136.

Schaffer, H. R., & Emerson, P. E. (1964). The development of social attachment in infancy. *Monographs of the Society for Research in Child Development, 29*(3, Serial No. 94).

Schaie, K. W. (1983). Age changes in adult intelligence. In D. S. Woodruff & J. E. Birren (Eds.), *Aging: Scientific perspectives and social issues.* Pacific Grove, CA: Brooks/Cole.

Schaie, K. W. (1990). Intellectual development in adulthood. In J. E. Birren & K. W. Schaie (Eds.), *Handbook of the psychology of aging* (3rd ed.). San Diego: Academic Press.

Schaninger, C. M., & Buss, W. C. (1986). A longitudinal comparison of consumption and finance handling between happily married and divorced couples. *Journal of Marriage and the Family, 48,* 129–136.

Schechter, S., & Gary, L. T. (1988). A framework for understanding and empowering battered women. In M. B. Straus (Ed.), *Abuse and victimization across the life span.* Baltimore: Johns Hopkins University Press.

Scheff, T. (1975). *Labeling madness.* Englewood Cliffs, NJ: Prentice-Hall.

Scheflen, A. E., & Scheflen, A. (1972). *Body langauge and social order: Communication as behavioral control.* Englewood Cliffs, NJ: Prentice-Hall.

Scheier, M. F., & Carver, C. S. (1985). Optimism, coping and health: Assessment and implications of generalized expectancies. *Health Psychology, 4,* 219–247.

Scheier, M. F., & Carver, C. S. (1992). Effects of optimism on psychological and physical well-being: Theoretical overview and empirical update. *Cognitive Theory and Research, 16*(2), 201–228.

Scheier, M. F., Matthews, K. A., Owens, J. F., Magovern, G. J., Sr., Lefebvre, R. C., Abbott, R. A., & Carver, C. S. (1989). Dispositional optimism and recovery from coronary artery bypass surgery: The beneficial effects on physical and psychological well-being. *Journal of Personality and Social Psychology, 57*(6), 1024–1040.

Scheier, M. F., Weintraub, J. K., & Carver, C. S. (1986). Coping with stress: Divergent strategies of optimists and pessimists. *Journal of Personality and Social Psychology, 51*(6), 1257–1264.

Schein, E. H. (1980). *Organizational Psychology.* Englewood Cliffs, NJ: Prentice-Hall.

Schein, E. H. (1981). Increasing organizational effectiveness through better human resource planning and development. In D. E. Klinger (Ed.), *Public personnel management: Reading its contexts and strategies.* Palo Alto, CA: Mayfield.

Schein, M., Zyzanski, S. J., Levine, S., & Medalie, J. H. (1988). The frequency of sexual problems among family practice patients. *Family Practice Research Journal, 7*(3), 122–134.

Scherg, H. (1987). Psychosocial factors and disease bias in breast cancer patients. *Psychosomatic Medicine, 49,* 302–312.

Schilit, W. K. (1987). Thinking about managing your time. In A. D. Timpe (Ed.), *The management of time.* New York: Facts On File.

Schlenker, B. R., Weigold, M. F., & Hallam, J. R. (1990). Self-serving attributions in social context: Effects of self-esteem and social pressure. *Journal of Personality and Social Psychology, 58,* 855–863.

Schmidt, G., & Weiner, B. (1988). An attribution-affect-action theory of behavior: Replications of judgments of help-giving. *Personality and Social Psychology Bulletin, 14,* 610–621.

Schmidt, N., & Sermat, V. (1983). Measuring loneliness in different relationships. *Journal of Personality and Social Psychology, 44*(5), 1038–1047.

Schoen, R. (1992). First unions and the stability of first marriages. *Journal of Marriage and the Family, 54*, 281–284.

Schoen, R., & Wooldredge, J. (1989). Marriage choices in North Carolina and Virginia, 1969–71 and 1979–81. *Journal of Marriage and the Family, 51*, 465–481.

Schofield, W. (1964). *Psychotherapy: The purchase of friendship.* Englewood Cliffs, NJ: Prentice-Hall.

Schroeder, D. H., & Costa, P. T., Jr. (1984). Influence of life events stress on physical illness: Substantive effects or methodological flaws? *Journal of Personality and Social Psychology, 46*(4), 853–863.

Schroth, M. L. (1991). Dyadic adjustment and sensation seeking compatibility. *Personality and Individual Differences, 12*(5), 467–471.

Schultz, N. R., Jr., & Moore, D. (1984). Loneliness: Correlates, attributions, and coping among older adults. *Personality and Social Psychology Bulletin, 10*(1), 67–77.

Schwartz, C. C., & Myers, J. K. (1977). Life events and schizophrenia: I. Comparison of schizophrenics with a community sample. *Archives of General Psychiatry, 34*, 1238–1241.

Schwartz, G. E. (1974, April). The facts on transcendental meditation, part II: TM relaxes some people and makes them feel better. *Psychology Today*, pp. 39–44.

Schwartz, H. S. (1982). Job involvement as obsession. *Academy of Management Review, 7*, 429–432.

Schwartz, M. S. (1987). Headache: Selected issues and considerations in biofeedback evaluations and therapies. In M. S. Schwartz (Ed.), *Biofeedback: A practitioner's guide.* New York: Guilford Press.

Seage, G. R., Landers, S., Lamb, G. A., & Epstein, A. M. (1990). Effect of changing patterns of care and duration of survival on the cost of treating the acquired immunodeficiency syndrome (AIDS). *American Journal of Public Health, 80*, 835–839.

Seashore, S. E., & Barnowe, J. T. (1972, August). Collar color doesn't count. *Psychology Today*, pp. 53–54, 80–82.

Sebald, H. (1981). Adolescents' concept of popularity and unpopularity, comparing 1960 with 1976. *Adolescence, 16*(61), 187–193.

Seccombe, K. (1991). Assessing the costs and benefits of children: Gender comparisons among childfree husbands and wives. *Journal of Marriage and the Family, 53*, 191–202.

Seeman, M. (1971). The urban alienations: From Marx to Marcuse. *Journal of Personality and Social Psychology, 19*, 135–143.

Segal, K. R., & Pi-Sunyer, F. X. (1989). Exercise and obesity. *Medical Clinics of North America, 73*(1), 217–236.

Segal, M. W. (1974). Alphabet and attraction: An unobtrusive measure of the effect of propinquity in a field setting. *Journal of Personality and Social Psychology, 30*, 654–657.

Segrin, C., & Dillard, J. P. (1992). The interactional theory of depression: A meta-analysis of the research literature. *Journal of Social and Clinical Psychology, 11*(1), 43–70.

Seligman, M. E. P. (1971). Phobias and preparedness. *Behavior Therapy, 2*, 307–321.

Seligman, M. E. P. (1974). Depression and learned helplessness. In R. J. Friedman & M. M. Katz (Eds.), *The psychology of depression: Contemporary theory and research.* New York: Wiley.

Seligman, M. E. P. (1983). Learned helplessness. In E. Levitt, B. Rubin, & J. Brooks (Eds.), *Depression: Concepts, controversies and some new facts.* Hillsdale, NJ: Erlbaum.

Seligman, M. E. P. (1990). *Learned optimism: How to change your mind and your life.* New York: Pocket Books.

Selye, H. (1936). A syndrome produced by diverse nocuous agents. *Nature, 138*, 32.

Selye, H. (1956). *The stress of life* (1st ed.). New York: McGraw-Hill.

Selye, H. (1974). *Stress without distress.* New York: Lippincott.

Selye, H. (1976). *The stress of life* (2nd ed.). New York: McGraw-Hill.

Selye, H. (1982). History and present status of the stress concept. In L. Goldberger & S. Breznitz (Eds.), *Handbook of stress: Theoretical and clinical aspects.* New York: Free Press.

Serbin, L. A., Connor, J. M., & Citron, C. C. (1978). Environmental control of independent and dependent behaviors in preschool girls and boys: A model for early independence training. *Sex Roles, 4*, 867–875.

Seta, J. J., Seta, C. E., & Wang, M. A. (1991). Feelings of negativity and stress: An averaging-summation analysis of impressions of negative life experiences. *Personality and Social Psychology Bulletin, 17*(4), 376–384.

Sewell, W. H., Hauser, R. M., & Wolf, W. C. (1980). Sex, schooling, and occupational success. *American Journal of Sociology, 86*, 551–583.

Shaffer, D. R. (1989). *Developmental psychology: Childhood and adolescence.* Pacific Grove, CA: Brooks/Cole.

Shapiro, D. H., Jr. (1984). Overview: Clinical and physiological comparison of meditation with other self-control strategies. In D. H. Shapiro, Jr., & R. N. Walsh (Eds.), *Meditation: Classic and contemporary perspectives.* New York: Aldine.

Shapiro, D. H., Jr. (1987). Implications of psychotherapy research for the study of meditation. In M. A. West (Ed.), *The psychology of meditation.* Oxford: Clarendon Press.

Shapiro, D. H., Jr., Schwartz, G. E., & Tursky, B. (1972). Control of diastolic blood pressure in man by feedback and reinforcement. *Psychophysiology, 9*, 296–304.

Shapiro, S., Skinner, E. A., Kessler, L. G., Von Korff, M., German, P. S., Tischler, G. L., Leaf, P. J., Benham, L., Cottler, L., & Regier, D. A. (1984). Utilization of health and mental health services. *Archives of General Psychiatry, 41*, 971–978.

Shatan, C. F. (1978). Stress disorders among Viet Nam veterans: The emotional content of combat continues. In C. R. Figley (Ed.), *Stress disorders among Viet Nam veterans: Theory, research and treatment.* New York: Brunner/Mazel.

Shavelson, R. J., Hubner, J. J., & Stanton, G. C. (1976). Self-concept: Validation of construct interpretations. *Review of Educational Research, 46*, 407–411.

Shaver, P. R., & Brennan, K. A. (1992). Attachment styles and the "big five" personality traits: Their connections with each other and with romantic relationship outcomes. *Personality and Social Psychology Bulletin, 18*(5), 536–545.

Shaver, P. R., & Hazan, C. (1992). Adult romantic attachment: Theory and evidence. In D. Perlman & W. Jones (Eds.), *Advances in personal relationships* (Vol. 4). Bristol, PA: Taylor & Francis.

Shaver, P. R., & Rubenstein, C. (1980). Childhood attachment experience and adult loneliness. In L. Wheeler (Ed.), *Review of personality and social psychology* (Vol. 1). Newbury Park, CA: Sage Publications.

Shaw, M. E. (1981). *Group dynamics: The psychology of small group behavior.* New York: McGraw-Hill.

Sheehan, S. (1982). *Is there no place on earth for me?* Boston: Houghton Mifflin.

Sheehy, G. (1976). *Passages.* Toronto: Bantam Books.

Sheehy, G. (1981). *Pathfinders.* New York: Morrow.

Sheehy, G. (1984). *Passages.* Toronto: Bantam Books.

Shekelle, R. B., Hulley, S. B., Neaton, J. D., Billings, J. H., Borhani, N. O., Gerace, T. A., Jacobs, D. R., Lasser, N. L., Mittlemark, M. B., & Stamler, J. (1985). The MRFIT behavior pattern study: II. Type A behavior and incidence of coronary heart disease. *American Journal of Epidemiology, 122*, 559–570.

Shephard, R. J. (1986). Passive smoking: Attitudes, health, and performance. In T. Ney & A. Gale (Eds.), *Smoking and human behavior.* Chichester: Wiley.

Sheras, P. L. (1983). Suicide in adolescence. In C. E. Walker & M. C. Roberts (Eds.), *Handbook of clinical child psychology.* New York: Wiley.

Sherer, M., Maddox, J. E., Mercandante, B., Prentice-Dunn, S., Jacobs, B., & Rogers, R. W. (1982). The self-efficacy scale: Construction and validation. *Psychological Reports, 51*, 663–671.

Sherif, M., & Hovland, C. I. (1961). *Social judgment: Assimilation and contrast effects in communication and attitude change.* New Haven, CT: Yale University Press.

Sherman, B. L., & Dominick, J. R. (1986). Violence and sex in music videos: TV and rock'n'roll. *Journal of Communication, 36*(1), 79–93.

Sherman, C. B. (1992). The health consequences of cigarette smoking: Pulmonary diseases. *Medical Clinics of North America, 76*(2), 355–375.

Sherrod, D. (1989). The influence of gender on same-sex friendships. In C. Hendrick (Ed.), *Review of personality and social psychology: Vol. 10. Close relationships.* Newbury Park, CA: Sage Publications.

Shertzer, B. (1985). *Career planning: Freedom to choose.* Boston: Houghton Mifflin.

Shields, S. A. (1975). Functionalism, Darwinism, and the psychology of women: A study in social myth. *American Psychologist, 30*, 739–754.

Shirlow, M. J., & Mathers, C. D. (1985). A study of caffeine comsumption and symptoms: Indigestion, palpitations, tremor, headache, and insomnia. *International Journal of Epidemiology, 14*(2), 239–248.

Shneidman, E. S. (1985). *At the point of no return.* New York: Wiley.

Shneideman, E. S., Farberow, N. L., & Litman, R. E. (Eds.). (1970). *The psychology of suicide.* New York: Science House.

Shostak, A. (1987). Singlehood. In M. B. Sussman & S. K. Steinmetz (Eds.), *Handbook of marriage and the family.* New York: Plenum.

Shostak, A. B. (1980). *Blue-collar stress.* Reading, MA: Addison-Wesley.

Shotland, R. L. (1989). A model of the causes of date rape in developing and close relationships. In C. Hendrick (Ed.), *Review of personality and social psychology: Vol. 10. Close relationships.* Newbury Park, CA: Sage Publications.

Shrauger, J. S. (1975). Responses to evaluation as a function of initial self-perception. *Psychological Bulletin, 82*(4), 581–596.

Siegel, J. M. (1990). Stressful life events and use of physician services among the elderly. *Journal of Personality and Social Psychology, 58,* 1081–1086.

Siegel, J. M., Johnson, J. H., & Sarason, I. G. (1979). Life changes and menstrual discomfort. *Journal of Human Stress, 5,* 41–46.

Siegel, O. (1982). Personality development in adolescence. In B. B. Wolman (Ed.), *Handbook of developmental psychology.* Englewood Cliffs, NJ: Prentice-Hall.

Siegler, I. C., & Gatz, M. (1985). Age patterns in locus of control. In E. Palmore, E. Busse, G. Maddox, J. Nowlin, & I. E. Siegler (Eds.), *Normal aging III.* Durham, NC: Duke University Press.

Siegler, I. C., Nowlin, J. B., & Blumenthal, J. A. (1980). Health and behavior: Methodological considerations for adult development and aging. In L. W. Poon (Ed.), *Aging in the 1980s: Psychological issues.* Washington, DC: American Psychological Association.

Siegler, R. S. (1986). *Children's thinking.* Englewood Cliffs, NJ: Prentice-Hall.

Sigler, R. T. (1989). *Domestic violence in context.* Lexington, MA: Lexington Books.

Silva, J., & Miele, P. (1977). *The Silva mind control method.* New York: Simon & Schuster.

Silverstein, B., Perdue, L., Peterson, B., & Kelly, E. (1986). The role of the mass media in promoting a thin standard of bodily attractiveness for women. *Sex Roles, 14,* 519–532.

Simmons, R. G., & Blyth, D. A. (1987). *Moving into adolescence: The impact of pubertal change and school context.* New York: Aldine de Gruyter.

Simon, B. L. (1987). *Never-married women.* Philadelphia: Temple University Press.

Simon, W., & Gagnon, J. (1977). Psychosexual development. In D. Byrne & L. A. Byrne (Eds.), *Exploring human sexuality.* New York: Thomas Y. Crowell.

Simon, W., & Gagnon, J. (1986). Sexual scripts: Permanence and change. *Archives of Sexual Behavior, 15*(2), 97–120.

Simonton, D. K. (1988). Age and outstanding achievement: What do we know after a century of research? *Psychological Bulletin, 104,* 251–267.

Simpson, J. A. (1990). Influence of attachment styles on romantic relationships. *Journal of Personality and Social Psychology, 59*(5), 971–980.

Singer, M. T., Wynne, L. C., & Toohey, M. L. (1978). Communication disorders and the families of schizophrenics. In L. C.

Wynne, R. L. Cromwell, & S. Matthysse (Eds.), *The nature of schizophrenia: New approaches to research and treatment.* New York: Wiley Medical.

Siscovick, D. S. (1990). Risks of exercising: Sudden cardiac death and injuries. In C. Bouchard, R. J. Shephard, T. Stephens, J. R. Sutton, & B. D. McPherson (Eds.), *Exercise, fitness, and health: A consensus of current knowledge.* Champaign, IL: Human Kinetics Books.

Siscovick, D. S., Weiss, N. S., Fletcher, R. H., & Lasky, T. (1984). The incidence of primary cardiac arrest during vigorous exercise. *New England Journal of Medicine, 311*(14), 874–877.

Skinner, B. F. (1953). *Science and human behavior.* New York: Macmillan.

Skinner, B. F. (1974). *About behaviorism.* New York: Knopf.

Skinner, B. F. (1987). Whatever happened to psychology as the science of behavior? *American Psychologist, 42*(8), 780–786.

Skinner, B. F. (1990). Can psychology be a science of mind? *American Psychologist, 45*(11), 1206–1210.

Skinner, B. F., Solomon, H. C., & Lindsley, O. R. (1953). *Studies in behavior therapy: Status report I.* Waltham, MA: Unpublished report, Metropolitan State Hospital.

Sklar, L. S., & Anisman, H. (1981). Contributions of stress and coping to cancer development and growth. In K. Bammer & B. H. Newberry (Eds.), *Stress and cancer.* Toronto: C. J. Hogrefe.

Slater, E. J., & Haber, J. D. (1984). Adolescent adjustment following divorce as a function of familial conflict. *Journal of Consulting and Clinical Psychology, 52,* 920–921.

Sloan, W. W., Jr., & Solano, C. H. (1984). The conversational style of lonely males with strangers and roommates. *Personality and Social Psychology Bulletin, 10*(2), 293–301.

Slobin, D. I., Miller, S. H., & Porter, L. W. (1968). Forms of address and social relations in a business organization. *Journal of Personality and Social Psychology, 8,* 289–293.

Slochower, J. (1976). Emotional labelling of overeating in obese and normal weight individuals. *Psychosomatic Medicine, 38,* 131–139.

Small, I. F., Small, J. G., & Milstein, V. (1986). Electroconvulsive therapy. In P. A. Berger & H. K. H. Brodie (Eds.), *American handbook of psychiatry: Biological psychiatry* (Vol. 8, 2nd ed.). New York: Basic Books.

Small, S. A., & Riley, D. (1990). Toward a multidimensional assessment of work spillover into family life. *Journal of Marriage and the Family, 52,* 51–61.

Smeaton, G., Byrne, D., & Murnen, S. K. (1989). The repulsion hypothesis revisited: Similarity irrelevance or dissimilarity bias. *Journal of Personality and Social Psychology, 56*(1), 54–59.

Smith, D. (1982). Trends in counseling and psychotherapy. *American Psychologist, 37*(3), 802–809.

Smith, G. T., Snyder, D. K., Trull, T. J., & Monsma, B. R. (1988). Predicting relationship satisfaction from couples' use of leisure time. *American Journal of Family Therapy, 16,* 3–13.

Smith, M. (1985). *When I say no I feel guilty.* New York: Bantam Books.

Smith, M. L., & Glass, G. V. (1977). Meta-analysis of psychotherapy outcome studies. *American Psychologist, 32,* 752–760.

Smith, M. L., Glass, G. V., & Miller, R. L. (1980). *The benefits of psychotherapy.* Baltimore: Johns Hopkins University Press.

Smith, P. A., & Midlarsky, E. (1985). Empirically derived conceptions of femaleness and maleness: A current view. *Sex Roles, 12,* 313–328.

Smith, R. E., Smoll, F. L., & Ptacek, J. T. (1990). Conjunctive moderator variables in vulnerability and resiliency research: Life stress, social support and coping skills, and adolescent sport injuries. *Journal of Personality and Social Psychology, 58*(2), 360–370.

Smith, T. W., & Brown, P. C. (1991). Cynical hostility, attempts to exert social control, and cardiovascular reactivity in married couples. *Journal of Behavioral Medicine, 14*(6), 581–592.

Smith, T. W., & Pope, M. K. (1990). Cynical hostility as a health risk: Current status and future directions. *Journal of Social Behavior and Personality, 5,* 77–88.

Smith, T. W., Pope, M. K., Sanders, J. D., Allred, K. D., & O'Keefe, J. L. (1988). Cynical hostility at home and work: Psychosocial vulnerability across domains. *Journal of Research in Personality, 22,* 525–548.

Smith, T. W., Turner, C. W., Ford, M. H., Hunt, S. C., Barlow, G. K., Stults, B. M., & Williams, R. R. (1987). Blood pressure reactivity in adult male twins. *Health Psychology, 6*(3), 209–220.

Smollar, J., & Youniss, J. (1985). Adolescent self-concept development. In R. L. Leahy (Ed.), *The development of the self.* Orlando, FL: Academic Press.

Smolowe, J. (1992, July 27). Don't call them pixies. *Time,* pp. 56–59.

Smyth, M. M., & Fuller, R. G. C. (1972). Effects of group laughter on responses to humorous materials. *Psychological Reports, 30,* 132–134.

Snelling, R. O., & Snelling, A. M. (1985). *Jobs! What they are . . . Where they are . . . What they pay!* New York: Simon & Schuster.

Snyder, M. (1979). Self-monitoring processes. In L. Berkowitz (Ed.), *Advances in experimental social psychology* (Vol. 12). New York: Academic Press.

Snyder, M. (1986). *Public appearances/Private realities: The psychology of self-monitoring.* New York: W. H. Freeman.

Snyder, M., & Campbell, B. (1982). Self-monitoring: The self in action. In J. Suls (Ed.), *Psychological perspectives on the self.* Hillsdale, NJ: Erlbaum.

Snyder, M., Simpson, J. A., & Gangestad, S. (1986). Personality and sexual relations. *Journal of Personality and Social Psychology, 51,* 181–190.

Snyder, M., Tanke, E. D., & Berscheid, E. (1977). Social perception and interpersonal behavior: On the self-fulfilling nature of social stereotypes. *Journal of Personality and Social Psychology, 35,* 655–666.

Snyder, S. H. (1986). *Drugs and the brain.* New York: Scientific American Books.

Soares, L. M., & Soares, A. T. (1971). Comparative differences in the self-perceptions of disadvantaged and advantaged students. *Journal of School Psychology*, 9, 424–429.

Solano, C. H., Batten, P. G., & Parish, E. A. (1982). Loneliness and patterns of self-disclosure. *Journal of Personality and Social Psychology*, 43(3), 524–531.

Solano, C. H., & Koester, N. H. (1989). Loneliness and communication problems: Subjective anxiety or objective skills? *Personality and Social Psychology Bulletin*, 15(1), 126–133.

Solomon, G. F., Amkraut, A., & Rubin, R. T. (1985). Stress, hormones, neuroregulation and immunity. In S. R. Burchfield (Ed.), *Stress: Psychological and physiological interactions*. New York: Hemisphere.

Sontag, S. (1972, October). The double standard of aging. *Saturday Review*, pp. 29–38.

Sorenson, R. C. (1973). *Adolescent sexuality in contemporary America*. New York: World.

Sotiriou, P. E. (1989). *Integrating college study skills: Reasoning in reading, listening and writing*. Belmont, CA: Wadsworth.

South, S. J. (1991). Sociodemographic differentials in mate selection preferences. *Journal of Marriage and the Family*, 53, 928–940.

Spain, J. (1985). Counseling adolescents for contraceptive and sexual decisions. In P. B. Smith & D. M. Mumford (Eds.), *Adolescent reproductive health: Handbook for the health professional*. New York: Gardner Press.

Spanier, G. B. (1977). Sources of sex information and premarital sexual behavior. *Journal of Sex Research*, 13(2), 73–88.

Spanier, G. B., & Furstenberg, F. F., Jr. (1982). Remarriage after divorce: A longitudinal analysis of well-being. *Journal of Marriage and the Family*, 44, 709–720.

Spanos, N. P., Weekes, J. R., & Bertrand, L. D. (1985). Multiple personality: A social psychological perspective. *Journal of Abnormal Psychology*, 94(3), 362–376.

Spence, J. T. (1983). Comment on Lubinski, Tellegen, and Butcher's "Masculinity, femininity, and androgyny viewed and assessed as distinct concepts." *Journal of Personality and Social Psychology*, 44, 440–446.

Sperry, R. W. (1982). Some effects of disconnecting the cerebral hemispheres. *Science*, 217, 1223–1226, 1250.

Spielberger, C. D., Johnson, E. H., Russell, S. F., Crane, R. J., Jacobs, G. A., & Worden, T. J. (1985). The experience and expression of anger. In M. A. Chesney, S. E. Goldston, & R. H. Rosenman (Eds.), *Anger and hostility in behavioral medicine*. New York: McGraw-Hill.

Spitze, G. (1988). Women's employment and family relations: A review. *Journal of Marriage and the Family*, 50, 595–618.

Sporakowski, M. J. (1988). A therapist's views on the consequences of change for the contemporary family. *Family Relations*, 37, 373–378.

Sprecher, S. (1989). Premarital sexual standards for different categories of individuals. *The Journal of Sex Research*, 26(2), 232–248.

Spring, B. (1989). Stress and schizophrenia: Some definitional issues. In T. W. Miller (Ed.), *Stressful life events*. Madison, CT: International Universities Press.

Springer, S. P., & Deutsch, G. (1984). *Left brain, right brain*. New York: W. H. Freeman.

Stake, J., & Katz, J. F. (1982). Teacher-pupil relationships in the elementary school classroom: Teacher-gender and pupil-gender differences. *American Educational Research Journal*, 19, 465–471.

Stall, R. D., Coates, T. J., & Hoff, C. (1988). Behavioral risk reduction for HIV infection among gay and bisexual men: A review of results from the United States. *American Psychologist*, 43, 878–885.

Stanford, M. W. (1987). Designer drugs: Medical aspects and clinical management. *Alcoholism Treatment Quarterly*, 4(4), 97–125.

Stanislaw, H., & Rice, F. J. (1988). Correlation between sexual desire and menstrual cycle characteristics. *Archives of Sexual Behavior*, 17(6), 499–508.

Stankov, L. (1988). Aging, attention, and intelligence. *Psychology and Aging*, 3, 59–74.

Stark, E. (1989, June). Rx: 2 self-help books and call me in the morning. *Psychology Today*, p. 26.

Staw, B. M., & Ross, J. (1985). Stability in the midst of change: A dispositional approach to job attitudes. *Journal of Applied Psychology*, 70(3), 469–480.

Steele, C. M. (1975). Name-calling and compliance. *Journal of Personality and Social Psychology*, 31, 361–369.

Steger, J., & Fordyce, W. (1982). Behavioral health care in the management of chronic pain. In T. Millon, C. Green, & R. Meagher (Eds.), *Handbook of clinical health psychology*. New York: Plenum.

Steil, J. M., & Turetsky, B. A. (1987). Is equal better? The relationship between marital equality and psychological symptomatology. In S. Oskamp (Ed.), *Family processes and problems: Social psychological aspects*. Newbury Park, CA: Sage Publications.

Stein, P. J. (1975). Singlehood: An alternative to marriage. *Family Coordinator*, 24, 489–503.

Stein, P. J. (1976). *Single*. Englewood Cliffs, NJ: Prentice-Hall.

Stein, P. J. (1989). The diverse world of single adults. In J. M. Henslin (Ed.), *Marriage and family in a changing society* (3rd ed.). New York: Free Press.

Steinberg, L., & Silverberg, S. B. (1987). Influences on marital satisfaction during the middle stages of the family life cycle. *Journal of Marriage and the Family*, 49, 751–760.

Steiner, I. D. (1976). Task-performing groups. In J. W. Thibaut, J. T. Spence, & R. C. Carson (Eds.), *Contemporary topics in social psychology*. Morristown, NJ: General Learning Press.

Stekel, W. (1950). *Techniques of analytical psychotherapy*. New York: Liveright.

Stephan, F. F., & Mishler, E. G. (1952). The distribution of participation in small groups: An exponential approximation. *American Sociological Review*, 17, 598–608.

Stephen, T. D. (1985). Fixed-sequence and circular-causal models of relationship development: Divergent views on the role of communication in intimacy. *Journal of Marriage and the Family*, 47, 955–963.

Stern, G. S., McCants, T. R., & Pettine, P. W. (1982). Stress and illness: Controllable and uncontrollable events' relative contributions. *Personality and Social Psychology Bulletin*, 8(1), 140–145.

Sternberg, R. J. (1986). A triangular theory of love. *Psychological Review*, 93, 119–135.

Sternberg, R. J. (1988). Triangulating love. In R. J. Sternberg & M. L. Barnes (Eds.), *The psychology of love*. New Haven, CT: Yale University Press.

Sternberg, R. J., & Grajek, S. (1984). The nature of love. *Journal of Personality and Social Psychology*, 47, 312–329.

Sternberg, R. J., & Soriano, L. J. (1984). Styles of conflict resolution. *Journal of Personality and Social Psychology*, 47(1), 115–126.

Stets, J. E., & Straus, M. A. (1989). The marriage license as a hitting license: A comparison of assaults in dating, cohabitating, and married couples. In M. A. Pirog-Good & J. E. Stets (Eds.), *Violence in dating relationships*. New York: Praeger.

Stevens, D. P., & Truss, C. V. (1985). Stability and change in adult personality over 12 and 20 years. *Developmental Psychology*, 21, 568–584.

Stevens, J. H., Turner, C. W., Rodewalt, F., & Talbot, S. (1984). The Type A behavior pattern and carotid artery atherosclerosis. *Psychosomatic Medicine*, 46(2), 105–113.

Stiles, D. A., Gibbons, J. L., Hardardottir, S., & Schnellmann, J. (1987). The ideal man or woman as described by young adolescents in Iceland and the United States. *Sex Roles*, 17, 313–320.

Stiles, W. B., Shapiro, D. A., & Elliott, R. (1986). "Are all psychotherapies equivalent?" *American Psychologist*, 41(2), 165–180.

Stoffer, G. R., Davis, K. E., & Brown, J. B., Jr. (1977). The consequences of changing initial answers on objective tests: A stable effect and a stable misconception. *Journal of Educational Research*, 70, 272–277.

Stogdill, R. M. (1963). *Manual for the Leader Behavior Description Questionnaire-Form XII*. Columbus, OH: Bureau of Business Research, Ohio State University.

Stokes, J., Childs, L., & Fuehrer, A. (1981). Gender and sex roles as predictors of self-disclosure. *Journal of Counseling Psychology*, 28(6), 510–514.

Stolberg, A. L., Camplair, C., Currier, K., & Wells, M. J. (1987). Individual, familial and environmental determinants of children's post-divorce adjustment and maladjustment. *Journal of Divorce*, 11, 51–70.

Stone, A. A., & Neale, J. M. (1984). New measure of daily coping: Development and preliminary results. *Journal of Personality and Social Psychology*, 46(4), 892–906.

Stoner, J. A. F. (1961). *A comparison of individual and group decisions involving risk*. Unpublished master's thesis, Massachusetts Institute of Technology.

Straus, M. A., Gelles, R. J., & Steinmetz, S. K. (1980). *Behind closed doors: Violence in the American family*. Garden City, NY: Anchor Press/Doubleday.

Strober, M. (1989). Stressful life events associated with bulimia in anorexia nervosa: Empirical findings and theoretical speculations. In T. W. Miller (Ed.), *Stressful life events*. Madison, CT: International Universities Press.

Strouse, J., & Fabes, R. A. (1985). Formal vs. informal sources of sex education: Competing forces in the sexual socialization of adolescents. *Adolescence, 78,* 251–263.

Strube, M. J., & Garcia, J. E. (1981). A meta-analytic investigation of Fiedler's contingency model of leadership effectiveness. *Psychological Bulletin, 90,* 307–321.

Strupp, H. H., Hadley, S. W., & Gomes-Schwartz, B. (1977). *Psychotherapy for better or worse: The problem of negative effects.* New York: Aronson.

Strupp, H. H., & Howard, K. I. (1992). A brief history of psychotherapy research. In D. K. Freedheim (Ed.), *History of psychotherapy: A century of change.* Washington, DC: American Psychological Association.

Stunkard, A. J., Harris, J. R., Pederson, N. L., & McClearn, G. E. (1990). The body-mass index of twins who have been reared apart. *New England Journal of Medicine, 322,* 1483–1487.

Stunkard, A. J., Sorensen, T., Hanis, C., Teasdale, T. W., Chakraborty, R., Schull, W. J., & Schulsinger, F. (1986). An adoption study of human obesity. *New England Journal of Medicine, 314,* 193–198.

Suddath, R. L., Christison, G. W., Torrey, E. F., Casanova, M. F., & Weinberger, D. L. (1990). Anatomical abnormalities in the brains of monozygotic twins discordant for schizophrenia. *The New England Journal of Medicine, 322*(12), 789–794.

Sue, D. (1979). Erotic fantasies of college students during coitus. *Journal of Sex Research, 15,* 299–305.

Suedfeld, P. (1979). Stressful levels of environmental stimulation. In I. G. Sarason & C. D. Spielberger (Eds.), *Stress and anxiety* (Vol. 6). Washington, DC: Hemisphere.

Suinn, R. M. (1984). *Fundamentals of abnormal psychology.* Chicago: Nelson-Hall.

Sulloway, F. J. (1991). Reassessing Freud's case histories: The social construction of psychoanalysis. *ISIS, 82,* 245–275.

Suls, J., & Marco, C. A. (1990). Relationship between JAS- and FTAS-Type A behavior and Non-CHD illness: A prospective study controlling for negative affectivity. *Health Psychology, 9*(4), 479–492.

Sundstrom, E. (1978). Crowding as a sequential process: Review of research on the effects of population density on humans. In A. Baum & Y. M. Epstein (Eds.), *Human response to crowding.* Hillsdale, NJ: Erlbaum.

Super, D. E. (1957). *The psychology of careers.* New York: HarperCollins.

Super, D. E. (1985). Career and life development. In D. Brown & L. Brooks (Eds.), *Career choice and development.* San Francisco: Jossey-Bass.

Super, D. E. (1988). Vocational adjustment: Implementing a self-concept. *The Career Development Quarterly, 36,* 351–357.

Surra, C. A. (1990). Research and theory on mate selection and premarital relationships in the 1980s. *Journal of Marriage and the Family, 52,* 844–865.

Sutker, P. B., & Allain, A. N. (1983). Behavior and personality assessment in men labeled adaptive sociopaths. *Journal of Behavioral Assessment, 5,* 65–79.

Swacker, M. (1975). The sex of the speaker as a sociolinguistic variable. In B. Thorne & N. Henley (Eds.), *Language and sex: Difference and dominance.* Rowley, MA: Newbury House.

Swaney, K., & Prediger, D. (1985). The relationship between interest–occupation congruence and job satisfaction. *Journal of Vocational Behavior, 26,* 13–24.

Swann, W. B., Jr., Griffin, J. J., Predmore, S. C., & Gaines, B. (1987). The cognitive affective crossfire: When self-consistency confronts self-enhancement. *Journal of Personality and Social Psychology, 52,* 881–889.

Sweeney, P. D., Anderson, K., & Bailey, S. (1986). Attributional style in depression: A meta-analytic review. *Journal of Personality and Social Psychology, 50,* 974–991.

Swenson, C. H., Jr. (1973). *Introduction to interpersonal relations.* Glenview, IL: Scott, Foresman.

Szasz, T. S. (1974). *The myth of mental illness.* New York: HarperCollins.

Tajfel, H., Billig, M., Bundy, R. P., & Flament, C. (1971). Social categorization and intergroup behavior. *European Journal of Social Psychology, 1,* 149–177.

Takanishi, R. (1993). The opportunities of adolescence—Research, interventions, and policy. *American Psychologist, 48*(2), 85–87.

Tanfer, K. (1987). Patterns of premarital cohabitation among never-married women in the United States. *Journal of Marriage and the Family, 49,* 483–497.

Tanfer, K., & Horn, M. C. (1985). *Family planning: Family planning perspectives.* New York: Alan Guttmacher Institute.

Tannen, D. (1990). *You just don't understand: Women and men in conversation.* New York: Ballantine.

Tanner, J. M. (1971). Sequence, tempo, and individual variation in the growth and development of boys and girls aged twelve to sixteen. *Daedalus, 100,* 907–930.

Tanner, J. M. (1978). *Fetus into man: Physical growth from conception to maturity.* Cambridge, MA: Harvard University Press.

Tavris, C. (1977, January). Men and women report their views on masculinity. *Psychology Today,* pp. 34–42, 82.

Tavris, C. (1982). *Anger: The misunderstood emotion.* New York: Simon & Schuster.

Tavris, C. (1989). *Anger: The misunderstood emotion* (2nd ed.). New York: Simon & Schuster.

Tavris, C. (1991). The mismeasure of woman: Paradoxes and perspectives in the study of gender. In J. D. Goodchilds (Ed.), *Psychological perspectives on human diversity in America.* Washington, DC: American Psychological Association.

Tavris, C. (1992). *The mismeasure of woman.* New York: Simon & Schuster.

Tavris, C. (1993, January 3). Beware the incest-survivor machine. *New York Times Book Review,* pp. 1, 16–17.

Tavris, C., & Sadd, S. (1977). *The Redbook report on female sexuality.* New York: Delacorte.

Tavris, C., & Wade, C. (1984). *The longest war: Sex differences in perspective.* New York: Harcourt Brace Jovanovich.

Taylor, D. A., & Altman, I. (1987). Communication in interpersonal relationships: Social penetration processes. In M. E. Roloff & G. R. Miller (Eds.), *Interpersonal processes: New directions in communication research.* Newbury Park, CA: Sage Publications.

Taylor, J. A. (1953). A personality scale of manifest anxiety. *Journal of Abnormal and Social Psychology, 48,* 285–290.

Taylor, M. C., & Hall, J. A. (1982). Psychological androgyny: Theories, methods, and conclusions. *Psychological Bulletin, 92,* 347–366.

Taylor, S. E., & Brown, J. D. (1988). Illusion and well-being: A social psychological perspective on mental health. *Psychological Bulletin, 103*(2), 193–210.

Teachman, J. D., Polonko, K. A., & Scanzoni, J. (1987). Demography of the family. In M. B. Sussman & S. K. Steinmetz (Eds.), *Handbook of marriage and the family.* New York: Plenum.

Teicher, M. H., Glod, C., & Cole, J. O. (1990). Emergence of intense suicidal preoccupation during fluoxetine treatment. *American Journal of Psychiatry, 147*(2), 207–210.

Tellegen, A., Lykken, D. T., Bouchard, T. J., Jr., Wilcox, K. J., Segal, N. L., & Rich, S. (1988). Personality similarity in twins reared apart and together. *Journal of Personality and Social Psychology, 54*(6), 1031–1039.

Temoshok, L. (1987). Personality, coping style, emotion and cancer: Towards an integrative model. *Cancer Surveys, 6,* 545–567.

Temoshok, L., Sweet, D. M., & Zich, J. (1987). A three city comparison of the public's knowledge and attitudes about AIDS. *Psychology & Health, 1*(1), 43–60.

Tenenbaum, G., & Furst, D. M. (1986). Consistency of attributional responses by individuals and groups differing in gender, perceived ability and expectations for success. *British Journal of Social Psychology, 25,* 315–321.

Terkel, S. (1974). *Working: People talk about what they do all day and how they feel about what they do.* New York: Pantheon.

Terpstra, D. E., & Baker, D. D. (1989). The identification and classification of reactions to sexual harassment. *Journal of Organizational Behavior, 10,* 1–14.

Terry, R. L., & Kroger, D. L. (1976). Effects of eye correctives on ratings of attractiveness. *Perceptual and Motor Skills, 42,* 562.

Tetlock, P. E., & Manstead, A. S. R. (1985). Impression management versus intrapsychic explanations in social psychology: A useful dichotomy? *Psychological Review, 92,* 59–77.

Tetlock, P. E., Peterson, R. S., McGuire, C., Chang, S., & Feld, P. (1992). Assessing political group dynamics: A test of the groupthink model. *Journal of Personality and Social Psychology, 63*(3), 403–425.

Thibaut, J. W., & Kelley, H. H. (1959). *The social psychology of groups.* New York: Wiley.

Thigpen, C. H., & Cleckley, H. M. (1984). On the incidence of multiple personality disorder: A brief communication. *International Journal of Clinical and Experimental Hypnosis, 32,* 63–66.

Thomas, K. (1976). Conflict and conflict management. In M. D. Dunnette (Ed.), *Handbook of industrial and organizational psychology.* Chicago: Rand McNally.

Thompson, A. P. (1983). Extramarital sex: A review of the research literature. *Journal of Sex Research, 19*(1), 1–22.

Thompson, A. P. (1984). Emotional and sexual components of extramarital relations. *Journal of Marriage and the Family, 46,* 35–42.

Thompson, E. H., & Pleck, J. H. (1986). The structure of male role norms. *American Behavioral Scientist, 29*, 531–543.

Thomson, E., & Colella, U. (1992). Cohabitation and marital stability: Quality or commitment? *Journal of Marriage and the Family, 54*, 259–267.

Thorndyke, P. W., & Hayes-Roth, B. (1979). The use of schemata in the acquisition and transfer of knowledge. *Cognitive Psychology, 11*, 83–106.

Thorne, B., & Luria, Z. (1986). Sexuality and gender in children's daily worlds. *Social Problems, 33*, 176–190.

Thornton, A. (1989). Changing attitudes toward family issues in the United States. *Journal of Marriage and the Family, 51*, 873–893.

Thornton, B. (1984). Defensive attribution of responsibility: Evidence for an arousal-based motivational bias. *Journal of Personality and Social Psychology, 46*(4), 721–734.

Tolstedt, B. E., & Stokes, J. P. (1984). Self-disclosure, intimacy, and the depenetration process. *Journal of Personality and Social Psychology, 46*, 84–90.

Tomkins, S. S. (1966). Psychological model for smoking behavior. *American Journal of Public Health, 56*, 17–20.

Tonnesen, P., Norregaard, J., Simonsen, K., & Sawe, U. (1991). A double-blind trial of a 16-hour transdermal nicotine patch in smoking cessation. *New England Journal of Medicine, 325*(5), 311–315.

Torrey, E. F. (1988). *Surviving schizophrenia: A family manual.* New York: Harper & Row.

Totman, R., Kiff, J., Reed, S. E., & Craig, J. W. (1980). Predicting experimental colds in volunteers from different measures of recent life stress. *Journal of Psychosomatic Research, 24*, 155–163.

Tourney, G. (1980). Hormones and homosexuality. In J. Marmor (Ed.), *Homosexual behavior.* New York: Basic Books.

Treas, J. (1983). Aging and the family. In D. S. Woodruff & J. E. Birren (Eds.), *Aging: Scientific perspectives and social issues.* Pacific Grove, CA: Brooks/Cole.

Tresemer, D. (1974, March). Fear of success: Popular, but unproven. *Psychology Today*, pp. 82–85.

Tripp, C. A. (1987). *The homosexual matrix.* New York: Meridian.

Troll, L. E. (1982). *Continuations: Adult development and aging.* Pacific Grove, CA: Brooks/Cole.

Troll, L. E. (1985). *Early and middle adulthood: The best is yet to be.* Pacific Grove, CA: Brooks/Cole.

Trovato, F., & Lauris, G. (1989). Marital status and mortality in Canada: 1951–1981. *Journal of Marriage and the Family, 51*, 907–922.

Trussell, J., & Westoff, C. F. (1980). Contraceptive practice and trends in coital frequency. *Family Planning Perspectives, 12*, 246–249.

Tschann, J. M., Johnston, J. R., Kline, M., & Wallerstein, J. S. (1989). Family process and children's functioning during divorce. *Journal of Marriage and the Family, 51*, 431–444.

Tschann, J. M., Johnston, J. R., Kline, M., & Wallerstein, J. S. (1990). Conflict, loss, change and parent-child relationships: Predicting children's adjustment during divorce. *Journal of Divorce, 13*(4), 1–22.

Turnage, J. J. (1990). The challenge of new workplace technology for psychology. *American Psychologist, 45*(2), 171–178.

Turner, B. F., & Adams, C. G. (1988). Reported change in preferred sexual activity over the adult years. *Journal of Sex Research, 25*, 289–303.

Turner, S. M., Jacob, R. G., & Morrison, R. (1984). Somatoform and factitious disorders. In H. E. Adams & P. B. Sutker (Eds.), *Comprehensive handbook of psychopathology.* New York: Plenum.

Turner, S. M., McCann, B. S., Beidel, D. C., & Mezzich, J. E. (1986). DSM-III classification of the anxiety disorders: A psychometric study. *Journal of Abnormal Psychology, 95*(2), 168–172.

U.S. Bureau of Labor Statistics. (1991, January). *Employment and earnings.* Washington, DC: U. S. Government Printing Office.

U.S. Bureau of the Census. (1991). *Statistical Abstract of the United States: 1991* (111th ed.). Washington, DC: U. S. Government Printing Office.

U.S. Department of Health and Human Services. (1989). *Reducing the health consequences of smoking: 25 years of progress.* Rockville, MD: U. S. Government Printing Office.

U.S. Department of Health and Human Services. (1990). *The health benefits of smoking cessation: A report of the surgeon general.* Washington, DC: U. S. Government Printing Office.

U.S. Department of Health and Human Services. (1991). *HIV/AIDS surveillance report.* Washington, DC: Center for Disease Control.

U.S. Department of Labor Statistics. (1990, September). *Twenty facts on women workers.* Washington, DC: U. S. Government Printing Office.

Unger, R. K. (1981). Sex as a social reality: Field and laboratory research. *Psychology of Women Quarterly, 5*, 645–653.

Unger, R. K., & Crawford, M. (1992). *Women and gender: A feminist psychology.* New York: McGraw-Hill.

Ungerleider, J. T., & Pechnick, R. (1992). Hallucinogens. In J. H. Lowinson, P. Ruiz, & R. B. Millman (Eds.), *Substance abuse: A comprehensive textbook* (2nd ed.). Baltimore: Williams & Wilkins.

Upshaw, H. S. (1969). The personal reference scale: An approach to social judgment. In L. Berkowitz (Ed.), *Advances in experimental social psychology* (Vol. 4). New York: Academic Press.

Vaillant, G. E. (1977). *Adaptation to life.* Boston: Little, Brown.

Valins, S. (1966). Cognitive effects of false heart-rate feedback. *Journal of Personality and Social Psychology, 4*, 400–408.

Van Houten, R. (1983). Punishment: From the animal laboratory to the applied setting. In S. Axelrod & J. Apsche (Eds.), *The effects of punishment on human behavior.* New York: Academic Press.

Van Wormer, K. (1989). Co-dependency: Implictions for women and therapy. *Women and Therapy, 8*(4), 51–63.

Van Wyk, P. H., & Geist, C. S. (1984). Psychosocial development of heterosexual, bisexual, and homosexual behavior. *Archives of Sexual Behavior, 13*(6), 505–544.

Vance, B. K., & Green, V. (1984). Lesbian identities: An examination of sexual behavior and sex role acquisition as related to age of initial same-sex encounter. *Psychology of Women Quarterly, 8*, 293–307.

Vance, E. B., & Wagner, N. N. (1976). Written descriptions of orgasm: A study of sex differences. *Archives of Sexual Behavior, 5*, 87–98.

VandenBos, G. R., Cummings, N. A., & DeLeon, P. H. (1992). A century of psychotherapy: Economic and environmental influences. In D. K. Freedheim (Eds.), *History of psychotherapy: A century of change.* Washington, DC: American Psychological Association.

VanderPlate, C., Aral, S. O., & Magder, L. (1988). The relationship among genital herpes simplex virus, stress, and social support. *Health Psychology, 7*(2), 159–168.

VanItallie, T. B. (1979). Obesity: Adverse effects on health and longevity. *American Journal of Clinical Nutrition, 32*, 2727.

Vaux, A. (1988). Social and personal factors in loneliness. *Journal of Social and Clinical Psychology, 6*, 462–471.

Vemer, E., Coleman, M., Ganong, L. H., & Cooper, H. (1989). Marital satisfaction in remarriage: A meta-analysis. *Journal of Marriage and the Family, 51*, 713–725.

Ventura, J., Nuechterlein, K. H., Lukoff, D., & Hardesty, J. P. (1989). A prospective study of stressful life events and schizophrenic relapse. *Journal of Abnormal Psychology, 98*(4), 407–411.

Verderber, K. S., & Verderber, R. F. (1989). *Inter-act: Using interpersonal communication skills* (2nd ed.). Belmont, CA: Wadsworth.

Verinis, J., & Roll, S. (1970). Primary and secondary male characteristics. *Psychological Reports, 26*, 123–126.

Vinogradov, S., & Yalom, I. D. (1988). Group therapy. In J. A. Talbott, R. E. Hales, & S. C. Yudofsky, (Eds.), *The American Psychiatric Press textbook of psychiatry.* Washington, DC: American Psychiatric Press.

Vitaliano, P. P., Katon, W., Maiuro, R. D., & Russo, J. (1989). Coping in chest pain patients with and without psychiatric disorders. *Journal of Consulting and Clinical Psychology, 57*, 338–343.

von Baeyer, C. L., Sherk, D. L., & Zanna, M. P. (1981). Impression management in the job interview: When the female applicant meets the male (chauvinist) interviewer. *Personality and Social Psychology Bulletin, 7*(1), 45–51.

Vourakis, C., & Bennett, G. (1979). Angel dust: Not heaven sent. *American Journal of Nursing, 79*, 649–653.

Voydanoff, P. (1990). Economic distress and family relations: A review of the eighties. *Journal of Marriage and the Family, 52*, 1099–1115.

Wachtel, P. L. (1989). *The poverty of affluence: A psychological portrait of the American way of life.* Philadelphia: New Society.

Wadden, T. A., Stunkard, A. J., Brownell, K. D., & VanItallie, T. B. (1983). The Cambridge diet. *Journal of the American Medical Association, 250*(20), 2833–2834.

Wade, C., & Tavris, C. (1990). *Learning to think critically: A handbook to accompany psychology.* New York: HarperCollins.

Walker, L. E. (1980). Battered women. In A. M. Brodsky & R. T. Hare-Mustin (Eds.), *Women and psychotherapy.* New York: Guilford Press.

Walker, L. E. (1984). *The battered woman syndrome.* New York: Springer.

Walker, L. E. (1989). Psychology and violence against women. *American Psychologist, 44,* 695–702.

Walker, L. O., & Best, M. A. (1991). Well-being of mothers with infant children: A preliminary comparison of employed women and homemakers. *Women and Health, 17*(1), 71–89.

Wallace, R. K., & Benson, H. (1972). The physiology of meditation. *Scientific American, 226,* 84–90.

Wallerstein, J. S., & Blakeslee, S. (1990). *Second chances: Men, women and children a decade after divorce.* New York: Ticknor & Fields.

Walster, E., & Berscheid, E. (1974). A little bit about love: A minor essay on a major topic. In T. L. Huston (Ed.), *Foundations of interpersonal attraction.* New York: Academic Press.

Walster, E., Aronson, E., Abrahams, D., & Rottman, L. (1966). Importance of physical attractiveness in dating behavior. *Journal of Personality and Social Psychology, 4,* 508–516.

Walster, E., Walster, G. W., Piliavin, J., & Schmidt, L. (1973). Playing hard-to-get: Understanding an elusive phenomenon. *Journal of Personality and Social Psychology, 26,* 113–121.

Walters, C. C., & Grusec, J. E. (1977). *Punishment.* San Francisco: W. H. Freeman.

Ward, S. E., Leventhal, H., & Love, R. (1988). Repression revisited: Tactics used in coping with a severe health threat. *Personality and Social Psychology Bulletin, 14*(4), 735–746.

Warr, P. B. (1987). *Work, unemployment, and mental health.* Oxford: Clarendon.

Watkins, L. R., & Mayer, D. J. (1982). Organization of the endogenous opiate and nonopiate pain control systems. *Science, 216,* 1185–1193.

Watson, A., & Boundy, D. (1989). *Willpower's not enough.* New York: Harper & Row.

Watson, D., & Pennebaker, J. W. (1989). Health complaints, stress, and distress: Exploring the central role of negative affectivity. *Psychological Review, 96*(2), 234–254.

Watson, D. L., & Tharp, R. G. (1989). *Self-directed behavior: Self-modification for personal adjustment* (5th ed.). Pacific Grove, CA: Brooks/Cole.

Watson, D. L., & Tharp, R. G. (1993). *Self-directed behavior: Self-modification for personal adjustment* (6th ed.). Pacific Grove, CA: Brooks/Cole.

Watson, J. B. (1913). Psychology as the behaviorist views it. *Psychological Review, 20,* 158–177.

Wattenberg, W. W., & Clifford, C. (1964). Relation of self-concept to beginning achievement in reading. *Child Development, 35,* 461–467.

Weaver, R. C., & Rodnick, J. E. (1986). Type-A behavior: Clinical significance, evaluation, and management. *Journal of Family Practice, 23*(3), 255–261.

Webb, S. L. (1991). *Step forward: Sexual harassment in the workplace—What you need to know!* New York: Mastermedia.

Wechsler, D. (1958). *The measurement of adult intelligence.* Baltimore: Williams & Wilkins.

Weeks, D., Freeman, C. P. L., & Kendell, R. E. (1981). Does ECT produce enduring cognitive deficits? In R. L. Palmer (Ed.), *Electroconvulsive therapy: An appraisal.* New York: Oxford University Press.

Weeks, M. O., & Gage, B. A. (1984). A comparison of the marriage-role expectations of college women enrolled in a functional marriage course in 1961, 1972, and 1978. *Sex Roles, 11,* 377–388.

Wehr, T. A., & Rosenthal, N. E. (1989). Seasonality and affective illness. *American Journal of Psychiatry, 146,* 829–839.

Wehr, T. A., Sack, D. A., Parry, B. L., & Rosenthal, N. E. (1986). The role of biological rhythms in the biology and treatment of insomnia and depression. In P. A. Berger & H. K. H. Brodie (Eds.), *American handbook of psychiatry: Biological psychiatry* (Vol. 8, 2nd ed.). New York: Basic Books.

Wehr, T. A., Sack, D. A., & Rosenthal, N. E. (1987). Sleep reduction as a final common pathway in the genesis of mania. *American Journal of Psychiatry, 144,* 201–204.

Weinberg, C. (1979). *Self creation.* New York: Avon.

Weiner, B. (Ed.). (1974). *Achievement motivation and attribution theory.* Morristown, NJ: General Learning Press.

Weiner, B. (1986). *An attribution theory of emotion and motivation.* New York: Springer-Verlag.

Weiner, B. (1988). An attributional analysis of changing reactions to persons with AIDS. In R. A. Berk (Ed.), *The social impact of AIDS in the U. S.* Cambridge, MA: Abt Books.

Weiner, B., Frieze, I., Kukla, A., Reed, L., Rest, S., & Rosenbaum, R. M. (1972). Perceiving the causes of success and failure. In E. E. Jones, D. E. Kanouse, H. H. Kelley, R. E. Nisbett, S. Valins, & B. Weiner (Eds.), *Perceiving the causes of behavior.* Morristown, NJ: General Learning Press.

Weiner, H. (1977). *Psychobiology and human disease.* New York: Elsevier.

Weiner, H. (1978). Emotional factors. In S. C. Werner & S. H. Ingbar (Eds.), *The thyroid.* New York: HarperCollins.

Weiner, I. B. (1980). Psychopathology in adolescence. In J. Adelson (Ed.), *Handbook of adolescent psychology.* New York: Wiley.

Weiner, R. D. (1985). Convulsive therapies. In H. I. Kaplan & B. J. Sadock (Eds.), *Comprehensive textbook of psychiatry/IV.* Baltimore: Williams & Wilkins.

Weiner, R. D., & Coffey, C. E. (1988). Indications for use of electroconvulsive therapy. In A. J. Frances & R. E. Hales (Eds.), *Review of psychiatry* (Vol. 7). Washington, DC: American Psychiatric Press.

Weinrach, S. G. (1979). *Career counseling: Theoretical and practical perspectives.* New York: McGraw-Hill.

Weinstein, N. D. (1984). Why it won't happen to me: Perceptions of risk factors and susceptibility. *Health Psychology, 3*(5), 431–458.

Weintraub, M., & Bray, G. A. (1989). Drug treatment of obesity. *Medical Clinics of North America, 73*(1), 237–249.

Weis, D. L. (1983). Affective reactions of women to their initial experience of coitus. *Journal of Sex Research, 19,* 209–237.

Weiss, R. S. (1975). *Marital separation.* New York: Basic Books.

Weissenberg, P., & Kavanagh, M. H. (1972). The independence of initiating structure and consideration: A review of the evidence. *Personnel Psychology, 25,* 119–130.

Weissman, M. M. (1985). The epidemiology of anxiety disorders: Rates, risks and familial patterns. In A. H. Tuma & J. Maser (Eds.), *Anxiety and the anxiety disorders.* Hillsdale, NJ: Erlbaum.

Weissman, M. M. (1988). Anxiety disorders: An epidemiologic perspective. In M. Roth, R. Noyes, & G. D. Burrows (Eds.), *Handbook of anxiety: Biological, clinical, and cultural perspectives* (Vol. 1). Amsterdam: Elsevier.

Weissman, M. M., Bruce, M. L., Leaf, P. J., Florio, L. P., & Holzer, C., III. (1991). Affective disorders. In L. N. Robins & D. A. Regier (Eds.), *Psychiatric disorders in America: The epidemiologic catchment area study.* New York: Free Press.

Weissman, M. M., Prusoff, B. A., DiMascio, A., Neu, C., Goklaney, M., & Klerman, G. L. (1979). The efficacy of drugs and psychotherapy in the treatment of acute depressive episodes. *American Journal of Psychiatry, 136,* 555–558.

Weiten, W. (1984). Violation of selected item-construction principles in educational measurement. *Journal of Experimental Education, 51,* 46–50.

Weiten, W. (1988). Pressure as a form of stress and its relationship to psychological symptomatology. *Journal of Social and Clinical Psychology, 6*(1), 127–139.

Weiten, W., & Dixon, J. (1984, August). *Measurement of pressure as a form of stress.* Paper presented at the meeting of the American Psychological Association, Toronto, Ontario.

Weitzman, L. J. (1989). The divorce revolution and the feminization of poverty. In J. M. Henslin (Ed.), *Marriage and the family in a changing society* (3rd ed.). New York: Free Press.

Weizman, R., & Hart, J. (1987). Sexual behavior in healthy married elderly men. *Archives of Sexual Behavior, 16*(1), 39–44.

Wekstein, L. (1979). *Handbook of suicidology.* New York: Brunner/Mazel.

Weldon, E., & Gargano, G. M. (1988). Cognitive loafing: The effects of accountability and shared responsibility on cognitive effort. *Personality and Social Psychology Bulletin, 14*(1), 159–171.

Wellesley College Center for Research on Women. (1992). *How schools shortchange girls.* Washington, DC: American Association of University Women Educational Foundation.

Wells, L. E., & Marwell, G. (1976). *Self-esteem: Its conceptualization and measurement.* Newbury Park, CA: Sage Publications.

Werbach, M. R. (1988). *Nutritional influences on illness: A sourcebook of clinical research.* Tarzana, CA: Third Line Press.

Wesson, D. R., Smith, D. E., & Seymour, R. B. (1992). Sedative-hypnotics and tricyclics. In J. H. Lowinson, P. Ruiz, & R. B. Millman (Eds.), *Substance abuse: A comprehensive textbook* (2nd ed.). Baltimore: Williams & Wilkins.

Westefeld, J. S., & Furr, S. R. (1987). Suicide and depression among college students. *Professional Psychology: Research and Practice, 18,* 119–123.

Westen, D. (1990). Psychoanalytic approaches to personality. In L. A. Pervin (Ed.), *Handbook of personality: Theory and research.* New York: Guilford Press.

Westoff, C. (1974). Coital frequency and contraception. *Family Planning Perspectives, 6,* 136–141.

Whitbourne, S. K. (1985). *The aging body: Physiological changes and psychological consequences.* New York: Springer-Verlag.

Whitbourne, S. K., Zuschlag, M. K., Elliot, L. B., & Waterman, A. S. (1992). Psychosocial development in adulthood: A 22-year sequential study. *Journal of Personality and Social Psychology, 63*(2), 260–271.

White, G. L. (1981). Some correlates of romantic jealousy. *Journal of Personality and Social Psychology, 49,* 129–147.

White, J. M. (1987). Premarital cohabitation and marital stability in Canada. *Journal of Marriage and the Family, 49,* 641–647.

White, L. K. (1990). Determinants of divorce: A review of research in the eighties. *Journal of Marriage and the Family, 32,* 904–912.

White, L. K., & Booth, A. (1985). Stepchildren in remarriages. *American Sociological Review, 50,* 689–698.

White, M. J., Kruczek, T. A., Brown, M. T., & White, G. B. (1989, May). *Occupational sex stereotypes among college students.* Paper presented at the meeting of the Midwestern Psychological Association, Chicago, Illinois.

Whitfield, C. L. (1987). *Healing the child within: Discovery and recovery for adult children of dysfunctional families.* Deerfield Beach, FL: Health Communications.

Whitfield, C. L. (1991). *Co-dependence: Healing the human condition.* Deerfield Beach, FL: Health Communications.

Whitley, B. E., Jr. (1988a). *College students' reasons for sexual intercourse: A sex role perspective.* Paper presented at the 96th Annual Meeting of the American Psychological Association, Atlanta, Georgia.

Whitley, B. E., Jr. (1988b). The relation of gender-role orientation to sexual experience among college students. *Sex Roles, 19,* 619–638.

Whitley, B. E., Jr., & Frieze, I. H. (1983). *Expectancy confirmation and egotism as determinants of causal attributions: Two meta-analyses.* Manuscript submitted for publication.

Whitley, B. E., Jr., & Frieze, I. H. (1985). Children's causal attributions for success and failure in achievement settings: A meta-analysis. *Journal of Educational Psychology, 77*(5), 608–616.

Whitley, B. E., Jr., & Hern, A. L. (1991). Perceptions of vulnerability to pregnancy and the use of effective contraception. *Personality and Social Psychology Bulletin, 17*(1), 104–110.

Whitley, B. E., Jr., & Schofield, J. W. (1986). A meta-analysis of research on adolescent contraceptive use. *Population and Environment, 8,* 173–203.

Whitney, E. N., & Cataldo, C. B. (1987). *Understanding normal and clinical nutrition.* St. Paul, MN: West.

Widiger, T. A., Frances, A. J., Pincus, H. A., Davis, W. W., & First, M. B. (1991). Toward an empirical classification for the DSM-IV. *Journal of Abnormal Psychology, 100*(3), 280–288.

Wiebe, D. J. (1991). Hardiness and stress moderation: A test of proposed mechanisms. *Journal of Personality and Social Psychology, 60*(1), 89–99.

Wiest, W. (1977). Semantic differential profiles of orgasm and other experiences among men and women. *Sex Roles, 3,* 399–403.

Wiggins, J. D., Lederer, D. A., Salkowe, A., & Rys, G. S. (1983). Job satisfaction related to tested congruence and differentiation. *Journal of Vocational Behavior, 23,* 112–121.

Wilder, C. S. (1971). Chronic conditions and limitations of activity and mobility: United States, July 1965 to June 1967. *U. S. Vital and Health Statistics, 10*(6), 334.

Williams, J. B. W. (1985). The multiaxial system of DSM-III, where did it come from and where should it go? II: Empirical studies, innovations, and recommendations. *Archives of General Psychiatry, 42,* 181–186.

Williams, J. C., & Solano, C. H. (1983). The social reality of feeling lonely: Friendship and reciprocation. *Personality and Social Psychology Bulletin, 9,* 237–242.

Williams, J. E., & Best, D. L. (1982). *Measuring sex stereotypes: A thirty-nation study.* Newbury Park, CA: Sage Publications.

Williams, M. H. (1992). Exploitation and inference: Mapping the damage from therapist-patient sexual involvement. *American Psychologist, 47*(3), 412–421.

Williams, N. A., & Deffenbacher, J. L. (1983). Life stress and chronic yeast infections. *Journal of Human Stress, 9*(1), 26–31.

Williams, R. B., & Barefoot, J. C. (1988). Coronary-prone behavior: The emerging role of the hostility complex. In B. K. Houston & C. R. Snyder (Eds.), *Type A behavior pattern: Research, theory, and intervention.* New York: Wiley.

Willis, W. D. (1985). *The pain system. The neural basis of nococeptive transmission in the mammalian nervous system.* Basel, Switzerland: Karger.

Wills, T. A. (1981). Downward comparison principles in social psychology. *Psychological Bulletin, 90,* 245–271.

Wilson, G. (1990). Personality, time of day and arousal. *Personality and Individual Differences, 11,* 153–168.

Wilson, W. C. (1975). The distribution of selected sexual attitudes and behaviors among the adult population of the United States. *Journal of Sex Research, 11,* 46–64.

Windshuttle, K. (1980). *Unemployed.* Melbourne, Australia: Penguin.

Windsor, R. A., Cutter, G., Morris, J., Reese, Y., Manzella, B., Bartlett, E. E., Samuelson, C., & Spanos, D. (1985). The effectiveness of smoking cessation methods for smokers in public health maternity clinics: A randomized trial. *American Journal of Public Health, 75,* 1389–1392.

Wine, J. D. (1982). Evaluation anxiety: A cognitive-attentional construct. In H. W. Krohne & L. Laux (Eds.), *Achievement, stress and anxiety.* New York: Hemisphere.

Wing, R. R., Epstein, L. H., & Nowalk, M. P. (1984). Dietary adherence in patients with diabetes. *Behavioral Medicine Update, 6,* 17–21.

Wisensale, S. K. (1992). Toward the 21st century: Family change and public policy. *Family Relations, 41,* 417–422.

Wittenberg, M. T., & Reis, H. T. (1986). Loneliness, social skills, and social perception. *Personality and Social Psychology Bulletin, 12,* 121–130.

Wixted, J. T., Bellack, A. S., & Hersen, M. (1990). Behavior therapy. In A. S. Bellack & M. Hersen (Eds.), *Handbook of comparative treatments for adult disorders.* New York: Wiley.

Wolchik, S. A., Braver, S. L., & Jensen, K. (1985). Volunteer bias in erotica research: Effects of intrusiveness of measure and sexual background. *Archives of Sexual Behavior, 14*(2), 93–107.

Wolf, S. (1986). Common and grave disorders identified with occupational stress. In S. Wolf & A. J. Finestone (Eds.), *Occupational stress: Health and performance at work.* Littleton, MA: PSG Publishing.

Wolf, S., & Goodell, H. (1968). *Stress and disease.* Springfield, IL: Charles C. Thomas.

Wolfe, L. (1981). *The Cosmo report.* New York: Arbor House.

Woll, S. (1986). So many to choose from: Decision strategies in videodating. *Journal of Social and Personal Relationships, 3*(1), 43–52.

Wolpe, J. (1958). *Psychotherapy by reciprocal inhibition.* Stanford, CA: Stanford University Press.

Wolpe, J. (1987). The promotion of scientific therapy: A long voyage. In J. K. Zeig (Ed.), *The evolution of psychotherapy.* New York: Brunner/Mazel.

Women on Words and Images. (1972). *Dick and Jane as victims: Sex stereotyping in children's readers.* Princeton, NJ: Author.

Wood, J. V. (1989). Theory and research concerning social comparisons of personal attributes. *Psychological Bulletin, 106,* 231–248.

Wood, W. (1987). Meta-analytic review of sex differences in group performance. *Psychological Bulletin, 102,* 53–71.

Wood, W., & Kallgren, C. A. (1988). Communicator attributes and persuasion: Recipients' access to attitude-relevant information in memory. *Personality and Social Psychology Bulletin, 14,* 172–182.

Wood, W., Polek, D., & Aiken, C. (1985). Sex differences in group task performance. *Journal of Personality and Social Psychology, 48,* 63–71.

Woolfolk, R. L. (1975). Psychophysiological correlates of meditation. *Archives of General Psychiatry, 32,* 1326–1333.

Woolfolk, R. L., & Richardson, F. C. (1978). *Stress, sanity and survival.* New York: Sovereign/Monarch.

Wright, P. H. (1982). Men's friendships, women's friendships, and the alleged inferiority of the latter. *Sex Roles, 8,* 1–20.

Wright, P. H., & Wright, K. D. (1991). Codependency: Addictive love, adjustive relating, or both? *Contemporary Family*

Therapy: An International Journal, 13(5), 435–454.

Wurman, R. S. (1989). *Information anxiety.* New York: Doubleday.

Wurtele, S. K. (1986). Self-efficacy and athletic performance: A review. *Journal of Social and Clinical Psychology, 4*(3), 290–301.

Wyatt, G. E., Peters, S. D., & Guthrie, D. (1988). Kinsey revisited, Part I: Comparison of the sexual socialization and sexual behavior of white women over 33 years. *Archives of Sexual Behavior, 17*(3), 201–239.

Wyler, A. R., Masuda, M., & Holmes, T. H. (1971). Magnitude of life events and seriousness of illness. *Psychosomatic Medicine, 33*(2), 115–122.

Wylie, R. C. (1979). *The self-concept: Theory and research on selected topics.* Lincoln, NE: University of Nebraska Press.

Yalom, I. D. (1975). *The theory and practice of group psychotherapy.* New York: Basic Books.

Yoder, J. D., Adams, J., Grove, S., & Priest, R. F. (1985). To teach is to learn: Overcoming tokenism with mentors. *Psychology of Women Quarterly, 9,* 119–132.

Young, J. E. (1982). Loneliness, depression and cognitive therapy: Theory and application. In L. A. Peplau & D. Perlman (Eds.), *Loneliness: A sourcebook of current theory, research and therapy.* New York: Wiley.

Young, T. J. (1990, June). Sensation seeking and self-reported criminality among student-athletes. *Perceptual and Motor Skills, 70*(3, Pt. 1), 959–962.

Zaccaro, S. J. (1984). Social loafing: The role of task attractiveness. *Personality and Social Psychology Bulletin, 10,* 99–106.

Zacks, E., Green, R. J., & Marrow, J. (1988). Comparing lesbian and heterosexual couples on the Circumplex Model: An initial investigation. *Family Process, 27,* 471–484.

Zajonc, R. B. (1965). Social facilitation. *Science, 149,* 269–274.

Zajonc, R. B. (1980). Compresence. In P. B. Paulus (Ed.), *Psychology of group influence.* Hillsdale, NJ: Erlbaum.

Zanna, M., Goethals, G. R., & Hill, J. (1975). Evaluating a sex-rated ability: Social comparison with similar others and standard setters. *Journal of Experimental Social Psychology, 11,* 86–93.

Zanna, M. P., & Olson, J. M. (1982). Individual differences in attitudinal relations. In M. P. Zanna, E. T. Higgins, & C. P. Herman (Eds.), *Consistency in social behavior: The Ontario symposium, Vol. 2.* Hillsdale, NJ: Erlbaum.

Zautra, A. J., Okun, M. A., Robinson, S. E., Lee, D., Roth, S. H., & Emmanual, J. (1989). Life stress and lymphocyte alterations among patients with rheumatoid arthritis. *Health Psychology, 8,* 1–14.

Zechmeister, E. B., & Nyberg, S. E. (1982). *Human memory: An introduction to research and theory.* Pacific Grove, CA: Brooks/Cole.

Zedeck, S., & Mosier, K. L. (1990). Work in the family and employing organization. *American Psychologist, 45*(2), 240–251.

Zeig, J. K. (1987). Introduction: The evolution of psychotherapy—Fundamental issues. In J. K. Zeig (Ed.), *The evolution of psychotherapy.* New York: Brunner/Mazel.

Zeiss, A. M. (1980). Aversiveness versus change in the assessment of life stress. *Journal of Psychosomatic Stress, 24,* 15–19.

Zelnick, M., & Kantner, J. F. (1977). Sexual and contraceptive experience of young unmarried women in the United States, 1976 and 1971. *Family Planning Perspectives, 9,* 55–71.

Zener, T. B., & Schnuelle, L. (1976). Effects of the Self-Directed Search on high school students. *Journal of Counseling Psychology, 23,* 353–359.

Zilbergeld, B., & Evans, M. (1980, August). The inadequacy of Masters and Johnson. *Psychology Today,* pp. 28–34, 37–43.

Zillmann, D., & Bryant, J. (1984). Effects of massive exposure to pornography. In N. M. Malamuth & E. Donnerstein (Eds.), *Pornography and sexual aggression.* New York: Academic Press.

Zimbardo, P. G. (1970). The human choice: Individuation, reason, and order versus deindividuation, impulse, and chaos. In W. J. Arnold & D. Levine (Eds.), *Nebraska symposium on motivation: 1969* (Vol. 17). Lincoln, NB: University of Nebraska Press.

Zimbardo, P. G. (1977). *Shyness: What it is, what to do about it.* Reading, MA: Addison-Wesley.

Zimbardo, P. G. (1987). *Shyness.* New York: Jove.

Zimbardo, P. G. (1990). *Shyness.* Reading, MA: Addison-Wesley.

Zimbardo, P. G., & Leippe, M. R. (1991). *The psychology of attitude change and social influence.* New York: McGraw-Hill.

Zimmer, D. (1983). Interaction patterns and communication skills in sexually distressed and normal couples: Two experimental studies. *Journal of Sex and Marital Therapy, 9,* 251–265.

Zis, A. P., & Goodwin, F. K. (1982). The amine hypothesis. In E. S. Paykel (Ed.), *Handbook of affective disorders.* New York: Guilford Press.

Zola, I. K. (1973). Pathways to the doctor—from person to patient. *Social Science and Medicine, 7,* 677–689.

Zorc, J. J., Larson, D. B., Lyons, J. S., & Beardsley, R. S. (1991). Expenditures for psychotropic medications in the United States in 1985. *American Journal of Psychiatry, 148*(5), 644–647.

Zubin, J. (1986). Implications of the vulnerability model for DSM-IV with special reference to schizophrenia. In T. Millon & G. L. Klerman (Eds.), *Contemporary directions in psychopathology: Toward the DSM-IV.* New York: Guilford Press.

Zuckerman, M. (1971). Dimensions of sensation seeking. *Journal of Consulting and Clinical Psychology, 36,* 45–52.

Zuckerman, M. (1979). *Sensation seeking: Beyond the optimal level of arousal.* Hillsdale, NJ: Erlbaum.

Zuckerman, M. (1990). The psychophysiology of sensation seeking. *Journal of Personality, 58*(1), 313–345.

Zuckerman, M., Lazzaro, M. M., & Waldgeir, D. (1979). Undermining effects of the foot-in-the-door technique with extrinsic rewards. *Journal of Applied Social Psychology, 9,* 292–296.

Zukin, S. R., & Zukin, R. S. (1992). Phencyclidine. In J. H. Lowinson, P. Ruiz, & R. B. Millman (Eds.), *Substance abuse: A comprehensive textbook* (2nd ed.). Baltimore: Williams & Wilkins.

Zunin, L., & Zunin, N. (1988). *Contact: The first four minutes.* New York: Ballantine.

SUBJECT INDEX

A

abandonment, 252
ability-achievement gap, 316
abnormal behavior. *See* mental illness absenteeism
abstinence, 428
abstractions, 338
abuse. *See* child abuse; physical abuse; psychological abuse
academic performance, 86, 144
  gender bias, 311
  improving, 26–32
  underachievement, 478
acceptance
  of death, 356
  latitude of, 199
  parental, 358
accidents
  alcohol and, 467
  stress and, 444
accommodation, 187–188
achievement, 144
  identity, 147, 313, 340, 344
achievement-ability gap, 316
achievement behavior, 137
achievement ethic, 417
acquaintance rape, 180, 181
acquired immune deficiency syndrome. *See* AIDS
acronyms, 30
acrostics, 30
ACTH (adrenocorticotropic hormone), 82
action in problem solving, 116
activity theory, 350
actor-observer differences, 137–138
acupuncture, 458
adaptation, diseases of, 81
adaptational outcomes, 83
addiction models, 446–447
addictions, work, 371
additive tasks, 213
adjustment, 14–15, 68
  personal, 137
  personality and, 36
adolescent growth spurt, 341
adolescents
  cognitive changes, 343–344
  cognitive development theories, 338
  contraception and, 424
  development, 341–346
  early or late maturing, 343
  emotions, 344–345
  gender-role socialization, 313
  identity development, 146–147
  identity search, 344
  loneliness, 256
  parenting of, 360–361
  parents, 274–275
  physical changes, 341–343
  psychosocial development theory, 339–340
  self-concepts, 142
  sexual development, 404
  sexual identity development, 405
  sexual socialization, 406–407
  similarity effects, 243
  smoking and, 446
  STDs and, 426
  suicide among, 345–346
  television watching average, 311
adrenal cortex, 82
adrenal medulla, 82
adrenocorticotropic hormone (ACTH), 82

Adult ego state, 292
adultery. *See* infidelity
adults
  care of parents by, 274–275
  cognitive development theories, 339
  development theories, 346–350, 347–349
  love relationship categories, 252–253
  psychosocial development theory, 339, 340–341
  secure, 252, 253
  See also young adults
adult survivors of child abuse, 321, 412
affection, 117, 409
  conditional, 244
affect regulation models, 446
affiliation needs, 16–18, 241, 250
African-Americans
  AIDS, 456
  death rates, 345
  job access for women, 318
age cohorts, 335
age factors
  happiness, 21
  homogamy, 269
  interpersonal attraction, 237
  loneliness, 256
  marital success, 271
  mathematical ability, 300–301
  remarriage, 286
  sexual activity, 421–422
  suicide, 500
  See also development
age groups. *See* adolescents; adults; children; elderly; infants; young adults
ageism, 336
Age of Propaganda (Pratkanis and Aronson), 197
age roles, 336–337
aggression, 104–105
  gender differences, 302, 304
  indirect, 178
  male gender role, 313
  military men, 321
  modeled, 51
  negative reinforcement, 311
  physical punishment and, 361–362
  psychoanalytic theory, 40
  stares and, 169
  toward females, 318, 319–321
  unemployed men, 321
  See also violence
aggression-frustration hypothesis, 104
aggressive behavior, 190
aggressive communication, 178
aggressive pornography, 182, 406
aging, 335, 350–355
agoraphobia, 480, 481
agreeableness, 37
AIDS (acquired immune deficiency syndrome), 137, 156, 248, 290, 426
  anal intercourse, 418
  condoms and, 426
  cumulative cases/cumulative deaths, 455
  lifestyle, 455–457
  oral sex, 418
  transmission and symptoms, 427
air pollution, 70, 381
alarm reaction, 81
Alcoholics Anonymous (AA), 8, 516
alcohol use/abuse, 106, 180, 462, 463, 467
  abusive men, 321
  aggression and, 182

codependency and, 7
  prevalence, 303
  sex and, 424
  transition to adulthood, 345
alprazolam (Xanax), 521–522
Alzheimer's disease, 351–352
ambient stress, 70
American Psychiatric Association (APA) diagnoses, 475, 476–478
Amish, 355
amnesia, psychogenic, 485–486
amphetamines, 462, 463, 465
anal intercourse, 418, 428, 457
anal stage, 42
androcentric bias, 299
  in brain size, 305
  in communication styles, 329
  in the workplace, 300
androgenized females, 306
androgens, 306, 404
androgyny, 323
anesthesia, glove, 484, 485
A New Look at Love (Hatfield and Walster), 24
angel dust, 468
anger, 78, 105, 108, 121, 167–168
  dying and, 356
  gender differences, 301
  in love, 248
Anger (Tavris), 105
angina pectoris, 439
animal research, 14, 52
annoyance, 78
anonymity, 207–208
ANS (autonomic nervous system), 80
antecedents, 127, 130
antianxiety drugs, 521–522
antidepressant drugs, 523
antipsychotic drugs, 522–523
antisocial behavior, 303
antisocial personality disorder, 497–498
anxiety, 86
  about social skills, 257
  classical conditioning, 47
  coping patterns, 102, 103
  defense mechanisms, 108
  drug therapy, 521–522
  experimental research, 16–18
  gender role, 322
  learned helplessness, 104
  marital satisfaction, 284
  paralanguage, 171
  person-centered theory, 54
  problem solving, 114
  psychoanalytic theory, 40
  self-efficacy, 52
  sexual performance, 432, 433
  stress-elicited, 78
  symptom reporting, 459
  test, 79
  treatments, 520, 521
anxiety disorders, 477, 479–483
  etiology, 482–483
  gender differences, 303
  generalized, 480
  genetic factors, 482
  prevalence, 478, 479
anxiety hierarchy, 518, 519
anxious-ambivalent attachment, 252, 253, 358
anxious/fearful cluster, 496, 497
APA (American Psychiatric Association) diagnoses, 475, 476–478
apathy, 103–104

appendicitis, 443
appraisal-focused coping, 110–114
appraisal support, 88–89, 117
apprehension, 78
    communication, 206–207
    evaluation, 205, 207, 214, 261
approach-approach conflict, 72
approach-avoidance conflict, 72–73, 260–261
approval-seeking behavior, 56
arguments, 78, 198
arousal levels, 57–58
    optimal, 79
    See also emotional arousal; physiological arousal
arteriosclerosis, 445
arthritis, 86, 443, 448, 451, 453
artificial insemination, 322
aspirations, diminished, 316–317
Asserting Yourself (Bower and Bower), 191
assertive communications, 185, 190–192
assessment, personality, 62
assumptions, irrational, 111–113
asthma, 86, 438, 443, 446, 483
atherosclerosis, 439
athletes, 180
attachment theories, 252–253
attention, 485
    selective, 179
attitudes, 197
    similarity, 243
    toward sex, 411
attraction. See interpersonal attraction
attractiveness. See physical attractiveness
attributional style, 149–150, 490
attributions, 136–138
    children's failures, 311
    defensive, 153–154, 156
    depression, 489–491
    fundamental error in, 153
    gender roles, 309
    global, 490
    loneliness, 257
    marital miscommunication, 280–281
    rape, 182
audience, imaginary, 343
authentic self, 147–148
authoritarian parenting style, 359–360
authoritative parenting style, 359–360
authority figures, 5, 196, 200, 203, 204
autocratic leadership style, 220, 222
autoeroticism. See self-stimulation
autogenic training, 124
automobile accidents, 466, 467
autonomic nervous system (ANS), 80
autonomic reactivity, 87, 92
autonomy, 378–379
aversion therapy, 519–520
avoidance, 127, 187
    communication, 206
    See also defense mechanisms
avoidance-avoidance conflict, 72, 183
avoidant adults, 253
avoidant attachment, 252, 253, 358
avoidant personality disorder, 497

B

baby boomers, 378
back pain, 438, 443, 448, 453
bacterial vaginosis, 427
barbiturates, 462, 463, 464–465
barriers, communication, 178
basal metabolic rate, 448
baseline period, 126
battered women, 320–321, 475
Bay of Pigs, 215–216

beautiful-is-good stereotype, 152
behavior
    attributions regarding, 136–138
    defined, 14
    distinguishing between people and, 184
    maladaptive, 474–475
    studying, 15–21
behavioral contract, 131–132
behavioral disengagement, 104
behavioral responses
    to illness, 439
    to stress, 77, 83
behaviorism, 45–52, 60
behavior modification, 121, 126–132, 458
    effectiveness, 529
    study tips and, 27
behavior therapies, 507, 517–521, 526
beliefs, 146, 201
belongingness, 209
benzodiazepines, 522
bereavement, 444
Be Sick Well (Kane), 459
Be the Person You Were Meant to Be
        (Greenwald), 147
biases
    against single people, 287
    gender, 303–304
    in groupthink, 216
    self-centered, 149
    self-concept, 14
    self-reporting, 143
    self-serving, 148–149
    test, 311
    See also androcentric bias; gender bias
bicycling, 454
biofeedback, 458, 520
biological perspectives, 57–60
biological rhythms, 487, 491
biomedical therapies, 507, 521–526, 526
biopsychosocial factors, 444–445
biopsychosocial model of illness, 439
bipolar mood disorders, 487, 488, 523
birth control. See contraception
birth order, 43–44
bisexuals, 249, 298, 402, 403
    See also sexual identity
blacks. See African-Americans
blaming others, 178, 255
blaming victims, 154
    of battering, 321
    defensive attributions, 156
    of rape, 181, 320
blaming yourself. See self-blame
blood pressure. See high blood pressure
body build, 238
body image, 403
body language, 169–170, 186
body mass index, 448
boom-and-bust encounters, 175–176
borderline personality disorder, 497
Boxer, Barbara, 220
brain
    organization, 305–306
    schizophrenia and, 495
    size, 305
brain abnormalities, 495
brain-body pathways, 81–82
brain damage, 467
brainstorming, 115, 214
Braun, Carol Mosley, 220
bronchitis, 445
bureaucrats, 204
burnout, 85, 372
buspirone (Buspar), 522
bystander effect, 207

C

caffeine, 451, 465
calcium, 451
Cambridge diet, 449
cancer, 86, 88, 109, 438, 442
    alcohol and, 467
    cannabis and, 466
    contraceptive methods and, 426
    exercise and, 453–454
    nutrition and, 451
    overeating and, 448
    smoker–nonsmoker deaths, 445
    stress and, 442–443
cancer-prone personality, 442
candidiasis, 427
cannabis, 462, 463, 466–467
cardinal traits, 36
cardiovascular reactivity, 92
careers, 366
    choosing, 390–395
    developing, 386–390
    development theories, 339–340
    gender-role socialization, 314, 316–317
    identity and, 146
    sensation seeking and, 91
Carnegie, D., 244
case studies, 20, 44–45, 56
catastrophic thinking, 106–107, 111–113
catatonic schizophrenia, 493
catecholamines, 82
categorizing, 150–151, 155
catharsis, 105, 121
cause and effect
    correlational research and, 20–21
    negative thinking/depression, 490
    self-esteem, 143
    See also attributions
centralized networks, 211
central nervous system (CNS), 463
central traits, 36–37
cerebral hemispheres, 305
cerebrum, 305
cervical cap, 425
challenges, 89, 378
chance, 89
change, 71, 73–75, 78, 89, 115
Changing Bodies, Changing Lives (Bell), 407
channels (communications), 164–165, 197
charisma, 172
charismatic leaders, 220, 221
child abuse
    alcohol and, 467
    multiple-personality disorders and, 486
    See also adult survivors
child care, 317, 367, 368, 372
Child ego state, 292
childhood
    anxiety disorders, 483
    eating habits during, 449
    individual psychology, 43–44
    person-centered theory, 53–54
    psychoanalytic theory, 38, 40
childlessness, 267, 273
child rearing, 358–362
    anxiety disorders and, 483
    See also parenting
children
    cognitive development theories, 337–339
    divorce and, 284–285
    gender-role socialization, 307–313, 312–313
    marital satisfaction and, 273
    psychosocial development theory, 339
    self-esteem development, 143–144
    self-observation, 140
    sexual information sources, 405

endogamy, 269
endorphins, 82, 458
energy resources, 373
engrams, 6
enhancement hypothesis, 373
environmental stress, 70, 71–72
epidemiology, 478
episodic disorders, 486
equality, 184
 views on, 276–277
equity in self–disclosure, 176
erectile difficulties, 431–432, 433
Erhard, W., 6, 7
erogenous zones, 416
erotic materials, 406
erotic preferences, 403
erotophiles, 411
erotophobes, 411
Escape from Freedom (Fromm), 4
ESP (extrasensory perception), 6
est, 6
estrogens, 404
ethical issues
 ECT, 524
 Milgrams's study, 204
 self-help books, 11
 therapist-client sex, 529
ethnic factors
 eye contact, 16
 interpersonal attraction, 243
ethnic stereotypes, 151
etiology, 474
eustress, 69
evaluation apprehension, 205, 207, 214
 shyness and, 261
excessive communication, 206
excessive frustration, 41
excessive gratification, 41
exchange relationships, 236
exchange theory. *See* social exchange theory
excitement phase, 413
executives, 89
exercise, 4, 129, 130, 375, 384, 450, 453–455
exhaustion stage, 81
expectations, 139, 152
 housework, 277
 marriage, 276–278
 mothers, 274
 of pain, 457, 458
 pressures to conform, 75
 scripts and, 410
 sexual relationships, 407
 of success, 301
 of therapy, 530
 See also comparison level
experience, openness to, 37
experimental groups, 17
experimental research methods, 16–18
experiments, 16–17
expertise, 197, 262
expert power, 211– 212
explanations, pseudo-, 473
exposure, 519
expressed emotion, 495–496
expressions, facial, 165, 167–168
expressive style of communication, 326–327
external attributions, 136
extinction
 classical conditioning, 47–48
 operant conditioning, 48, 49
extramarital sex. *See* infidelity
extrasensory perception (ESP), 6
extraversion, 24, 37, 57–58
eye contact, 165, 168–169, 186
eyeglasses, 153

Eysenck's biological theory, 57–58, 60

F
fables, personal, 343–344
facial expressions, 165, 167–168
facial hair, 153
failure rates of contraception, 425
failures, 71, 116
 attributional style, 149–150
 attribution process, 137, 138
 self-esteem and, 144
 self-serving bias, 148
false consensus effect, 154
false uniqueness effect, 154
familiarity, 76
family, 4–5
 antisocial personality disorder, 498
 decline in nuclear, 267–268
 deficits in relationships, 255
 effects of environment on personality, 58–59
 mental illness in, 495, 496
 persuasion from, 196
 schizophrenia and communication in, 495
 sexual identity and, 404–405
 as system, 8
Family and Medical Leave Act of 1993, 384
family life cycle, 271–275
fantasy, 107, 109
 See also sexual fantasies
fast pathway pain, 457
fat cells, 449
fate, 89
fathers, children's development and, 279
fats, 452
fatuous love, 250, 251
faultfinding, 159–160, 178, 214
favors, 145
fears, 78, 167–168
 classical conditioning, 47
 of death, 355
 persuasive messages, 198
 public speaking and, 206
 shyness and, 261
 See also phobias; phobic disorders
feedback, 142, 158
 negative, 241
feelings, attributions and, 136
feigned scarcity technique, 226
Feingold, Russ, 220
fellatio, 418
felons, 498
female role, 315–318
femininity, 323–324
 See also gender roles
fentanyl, 468
fight-or-flight responses, 80, 206
financial concerns. *See* economic factors
first impressions, 154, 155
fitness. *See* exercise
five-factor model of personality, 37
fixation, 41–42
Fixx, James, 453, 454
flattery, 244
flexibility, 116
fluoxetine (Prozac), 523
foot-in-the-door technique, 224
foreclosure, identity, 146–147, 344
foreplay, 415
forewarning, 198–199
formal operations period, 338, 339, 340
The Forum (Erhard), 6, 7, 11
frame of reference, 179, 184, 185
fraternities, 180, 210, 227
free association, 510, 512
freedom, personal, 4–5

Freudian theory. *See* psychoanalysis
Friends for Life (Duck), 235
friendships, 87, 142, 244–247
 committed romantic relationships and, 246–247
 cross-sex, 246
 deficits, 255
 matching hypothesis, 239
 persuasion in, 196
 self-esteem and, 143
 single people and, 287
 work, 379
 See also social support
frigidity. *See* orgasmic difficulties
frustration, 71–72, 74, 78, 115
 aggression and, 104
 excessive, 41
 gender differences, 301
frustration-aggression hypothesis, 104
fundamental attribution errors, 153, 156
future
 identity and, 146
 visions of, 347

G
GABA (gamma-aminobutyric acid), 482
GAF (Global Assessment of Functioning) Scale, 477
gall bladder disease, 448
gambling, 520
game playing, 179, 183
 by couples, 292–294
games, 375
 childrens' preferences, 312, 326
Games People Play (Berne), 294
gang rape, 180
gate-control theory of pain, 458
gay men, 249
 intimate relationships, 408–409
 sexual activities, 419, 422
 See also homosexuals
gazing, 168–169
gender, 298
 in psychodynamic theories, 45
gender bias
 children's books, 311
 diagnosis of mental disorders, 303–304
 occupational interest inventories, 392–393
 television, 310
 textbooks, 311
gender differences, 298
 behavioral perspective, 304–305
 in being single, 287
 biological origins, 305–307
 body movement, 170
 in codependency, 8
 cognitive abilities, 300–301
 desire for children, 273
 divorce adjustment, 246
 divorced men and women, 285
 environmental origins, 307–313
 eye contact, 169
 first sexual experience, 420
 friendships, 245–246
 groups, 210
 happiness, 21–22
 hardiness, 89–90
 help-seeking behavior, 459
 hormonal influences, 306–307
 identity status and marriage, 340
 importance of physical attractiveness, 237–239
 infidelity motivations, 423
 interrupting, 302–303
 leadership, 220, 221–222

phallic state, 42–43
phencyclidine hydrochloride (PCP), 462, 486
philosophy of life, 5
phobias, 47, 52
phobic disorders, 480–481
    classical conditioning, 482
physical abuse, 320–321
physical appearance, 152–153, 197
    See also body image
physical attractiveness
    aging and, 351
    gender bias on television, 310
    interpersonal attraction and, 237–239
    persuasion and, 197–198
    of psychiatric patients, 20
    social status, 241
physical dependence on drugs, 463
physical development, 341–343
    age-related changes, 351–352
physical health
    age-related changes, 352, 353
    constructive thinking, 110
    coping and, 102
    exercise, 453–455
    happiness, 22
    loneliness, 256
    nutrition, 450–453
    optimism, 90
    psychological factors, 439
    self–esteem, 143
    singlehood, 287
    social support, 88
    writing and, 122
physical illness
    alcohol, 467
    job stress, 377, 383
    overeating, 448
    patterns, 438–439
    positive life changes, 75
    reactions to, 439, 457–460
    smoking, 445–446
    stress, 74
    stress and, 81, 86, 439–445
    See also somatoform disorders
physical inactivity, 439
physical pain, 79
physicians, consulting, 459
physiological arousal, 57–58, 68
    communication apprehension, 206
    controllability, 76, 77
    during sex, 413–414
    emotional arousal and, 241–242
    familiarity and, 76
    response, 80–82
    shyness, 260
    stress, 77
    suppressed, 123
    Type A personality, 440, 441
physiological processes, 14
pituitary gland, 82, 341
placebo effects, 7, 25, 458
planning, 120
plateau phase, 413–414
play, 311–312, 326
playing hard to get, 244
pleasure principle, 38
PMS (premenstrual syndrome), 306
polarization, 214–215
pollution, air, 70, 381
pornography, 182, 406
positive, accentuating, 254–255
positive events, 74, 75
positive feelings, generating, 198
positive reinforcement, 48–49
positive reinterpretation, 113–114

positive self–talk, 257
possible selves, 140
post-traumatic stress disorder, 85
poverty
    divorce and, 271
    happiness and, 21
    marital adjustment and, 279–280
power, 211–212
power issues
    communication styles, 327
    interrupting, 303
    personal space, 167
    self-disclosure and, 174
    status issues and, 211
    See also status issues
power structure, group, 210, 211–212
practicing, 30
preconscious, 38–39
predictability, 76–77
predispositions, 489
pre-ejaculatatory fluid, 413
pregnancy, 344, 407, 443, 458, 467
preintimate status of intimacy, 233, 340
prejudice, 155–156
premarital sex, 411, 419–420
premature ejaculation, 432, 433
premenstrual syndrome (PMS), 306
prenatal development, 306, 404
preoperational period, 338
preparatory grief, 356
preparedness theory, 482–483
presence of others, 204–208
pressure (general), 71, 75, 115
Pressure Inventory (PI), 75
pressure to conform, 75, 78, 214
    See also peer pressure; social pressure
pressure to perform, 75, 76, 83–84, 370
    See also performance
prevalence, 478–479
primacy effects, 154, 155
primary appraisal of stress, 69
primary process thinking, 38
primary sex characteristics, 342
priorities, 117, 120
prisoners, 103, 498
privacy, self-disclosure and, 177
private information, 174
problem finders, 339
problem-focused coping, 110, 114–121, 122
problem orientation, 114
problem solving, 353–354
    skills, 114, 300–301
    systematic, 114–116
process-oriented approaches
    dying, 356
    gays' sexual identity development, 408–409
process-oriented theories of development, 336
process planning, 214
productivity in groups, 212–214
progestin (minipill), 425
prognosis, 474
progress, paradox of, 2–5
progressive relaxation, 124
projection, 40, 41
promiscuity, 420
propaganda, 197
proxemics, 166–167
proximity, 242–243
Proxmire, William, 232
Prozac (fluoxetine), 523
pseudoexplanations, 473
pseudointimate status of intimacy, 233, 340
psilocybin, 462, 466
psychiatric nurses, 508, 509
psychiatric patient readjustment study, 20

psychiatric social workers, 509
psychiatrists, 508
psychoactive drugs, 462–463
psychoactive substance-use disorders, 477
psychoanalysis, 38, 506, 509–511
    classical vs. modern, 512
    Freud's theories, 37–43, 60
    overview, 526
psychobabble, 11
psychodiagnosis, 476–478
psychodynamic theories, 37–45
psychodynamic therapies, 512, 529
psychogenic amnesia, 485–486
psychological abuse, 320, 321
psychological dependence, 463
psychological disorders. *See* mental illness
psychological health. *See* mental health
psychological tests, 62
psychologists, 508
psychology, defined, 14, 15
psychopharmacotherapy, 521–524
psychosexual disorders, 477
psychosexual stages, 41–43
psychosis, 465, 478
psychosocial development theory (Erikson),
    339–341
psychosocial factors, 438
    health psychology and, 439
    See also stress
psychosomatic diseases, 86, 483
psychotherapy, 506–530
    gender differences, 303
The Psychotherapy Maze (Ehrenberg and
    Ehrenberg), 509
puberty, 340, 341, 342–343
pubescence, 341–342
pubic lice, 427
public selves, 144, 147–148
public speaking, 206–207
punishment, 130–131, 361–362
    gender role socialization, 307–308
    operant conditioning, 48, 49–50
purpose, sense of, 23

Q

quality circles, 379
quality of life, 375
Quality of Work Life programs, 378–379
questions, tag, 303
quiet time, 120

R

racial stereotypes, 151, 155
rage, 78
rape, 86, 318, 320
    acquaintance, 180
    alcohol and, 467
    arrests by sex, 302
    characteristics of rapists, 183
    date, 180–184
    gang, 180
    incidence, 180–181
rape survivors, 412
    stages of recovery, 181–182
rapid speech, 171
rapport talk, 328
rational-emotive therapy, 110–113, 529
rationalization, 40, 41
rational outness, 409
reactance technique, 226
reaction formation, 40–41
reactivity
    autonomic, 87, 92
    cardiovascular, 92
Reagan, Ronald, 476

reality
  depressed/nondepressed people's views on, 491
  distorting, 108–109, 141–142
  incongruence with self-concept, 513
reality principle, 38
rebounding, 286
receivers (communications), 165, 197, 198–199
reciprocity, 176–177, 244
reciprocity norm, 225–226
recognition, 379
recovery groups, 7, 8–9, 516
  See also twelve-step programs
recreation, 373–375
reference, frame of, 179, 184, 185
reference groups, 141, 144, 156
referencing gesture, 170
referent power, 212
reflex, conditioned, 47
refractory period, 414, 422
refusal to speak, 320
regression, 41
reinforcement, 48–49, 127–129, 130, 234
  gender role socialization, 307–308
reinforcement contingencies, 128
rejection, 160
relapse rates, 446–447
relational work, 367
relationship-oriented leaders, 219, 220
relationships, 232, 232–236
  alternative, 254
  communal, 236
  communication apprehension and, 207
  deficits in romantic, 255
  developing, 233–23
  development theories and, 340
  exchange, 236
  games in, 292–294
  interpersonal, 232–262
  priorities, 290
  self-disclosure and, 174, 175, 176–177
  sex in, 420–422
  at work, 379
relaxation, 123–124, 384, 458
  deep muscle, 519, 520
  progressive, 124
releasing pent-up emotions, 121–122
reliability, 62
religion, 4, 5, 23, 355
relocation, 384, 390
remarriage, 286
remission, spontaneous, 516
report talk, 328
repression, 40, 41, 109
reproductive problems, 443
repulsion hypothesis, 244
research methodology, 16–21
resentment, 286
resistance, 511, 530
resistance stage, 81
resolution phase, 414
respiratory difficulties, 448, 453
respondent conditioning. *See* classical conditioning
responses
  conditioned, 46
  dominant, 204–205
  elicited, 47
  fight-or-flight, 80, 206
  target, 127
  unconditioned, 46
responsibility, diffusion of, 207, 208, 213
restructuring, cognitive, 207, 458
résumés, 397–398
retirement, 389

rewardingness, 220
reward power, 211–212
rewards, 127, 234–236
rheumatoid arthritis, 443, 451
rhyming, 31
rhythm method, 425
rhythms, biological, 487, 491
ridiculing, 178
risky shift phenomenon, 215
rock music, 405–406
rock videos, 406
Roger's person-centered theory. *See* person-centered theory
role conflicts, 373
role models, 140
  gender, 308
  male, 285
  minority group, 156
  other-sex, 308
  overcoming shyness and, 261–262
  smoking, 446
  See also mentors; models
roles, 307, 336
  group, 210
  potential mates, 270
romantic jealousy, 282
romantic love, 246–255, 407
  as attachment, 252–253
  maintaining, 254–255
  Sternberg's theory, 250, 251
  See also love
Romeo and Juliet effect, 270
Roosevelt, Franklin Delano, 216
rumination, 490

s
sadness, 78–79, 167
  paralanguage, 171
safe sex, 428
salaries, 319, 320, 369, 370, 373, 379, 394
salt, 451, 452, 453
same-sex role models, 308
scarcity (feigned) technique, 226
scarcity hypothesis, 373
scheduling, 120
schemas, 309
schizoid personality disorder, 497
schizophrenia, 86, 476
  drug therapy, 522–523
  multiple-personality disorder vs, 486
  social skills training, 520
  vulnerability, 494, 496
schizophrenic disorders, 477, 491–496
  prevalence, 478
schizotypal personality disorder, 497
schools, gender-role socialization, 311
scientific investigations, 15–16
Scientology/Dianetics (Hubbard), 6, 7
scripts, 410
SDS (Self-Directed Search) test, 387, 392
seasonal affective disorder, 487
The Seasons of a Man's Life (Levinson), 346
secondary appraisal of stress, 69–70
secondary process thinking, 38
secondary sex characteristics, 341, 404
secondary traits, 37
Second Chances (Wallerstein and Blakeslee), 285
secondhand smoke, 446
"second shift" responsibilities, 372, 374
secure attachment, 252–253, 358
security, 379–380
sedatives, 462, 463, 464–465
seduction, 180
seeking help, 116–117

selective attention, 179
selectivity, 138–139
self
  authentic, 147–148
  possible, 140
  public, 144, 147–148
self-acceptance, 322
self-actualization theory (Maslow), 54–56
self-admiration, 343
self-affirmation, 409
self-awareness, 208
self-blame, 106–107
self-centered bias, 149
self–concept, 53, 54, 56, 139–142
  conditional affection and, 244
self-confidence, 261, 301
self-consciousness, 83–84, 206
self-control, 121, 126–132, 159
self-criticism, 106–107, 158, 343
self-deception, 108
self-defeating behavior, 71
self-destructiveness, 445
Self-Directed Behavior (Watson and Tharp), 129
Self-Directed Search (SDS) test, 387, 391
self-discipline, 121, 126–132
self-disclosure, 173–177, 232–233
  by lonely people, 257
  in romantic relationships, 253, 254
  social motives and, 241
self-efficacy, 51–52
Self-Efficacy Scale, 51, 63
self-enhancement, 148–150
self-esteem, 142–145
  attractive people, 152–153
  benefits of stress, 87
  building, 158–160
  career and, 390
  coping patterns, 102, 103
  The Forum, 6
  gender role, 322
  happiness, 24
  interpersonal attraction, 241
  jealousy, 250, 282
  learned helplessness, 104
  loneliness, 257
  men who batter, 321
  midlife women, 373
  minority groups, 156
  mood disorders, 487, 488
  negative feedback, 241
  problem solving, 114
  self-serving bias, 149
  shyness, 261
  social clocks, 337
  stress from positive events, 75
  symptom reporting, 459
  undermining of girls,' 311
  unprotected sex, 425
Self-Esteem (McKay), 159
self-evaluation, 140, 158–159
self-fulfilling prophecies, 54, 473
self-help books, 10–12, 25
self-help groups, 516
  See also recovery groups
self–improvement, 87, 159
self-indulgence, 105–106, 122
self-knowledge, 148
self-modification, 126–132, 518
self-monitoring, 145
self-perceptions, 139–148, 148
  in adolescence, 313
  gender-role socialization and, 309–310
  interpersonal attraction and, 241–242
self-perception theory (Bem), 139
self-preoccupation, 179

Valium (diazepam), 482, 521–522, 523
value judgments, 474–475
values
  comparing, 270
  cultural, 142
  personal, 146, 208
  sexual, 182, 403, 430, 432
variables, 17
variety, 378
vasocongestion, 413
venereal warts, 427
ventricles, schizophrenia and, 495
verbal communication, 165, 172–177,
    185–186, 326
  conversational skills/style, 257
  gender differences, 300, 302–303, 304
verbalization, 121–122
verbal processing, 305
victims
  bystander effect, 207
  defensive attributions and, 156
  obedience to authority and, 203
  See also adult survivors; blaming victims
Vietnam Conflict, 216
Vietnam veterans, 85
violence
  against women, 406
  alcohol, 467
  domestic, 320–321
  gender differences in crimes of, 302
  in the media, 182–183
  mental illness stereotype, 476
  stereotypes, 155
  See also aggression
viral hepatitis, 427
visibility, 156
  surplus, 151
visions of the future, 5
visual acuity, 352
visual imagery, 31
visual processing, 305
vitamin C, 451
vitamin D, 451
vitamin deficiencies, 451
vitamin E, 451
vocal emphasis, 170–171
vocal inflections, 164
vocal quality, 171

vocal tone, 165
vocational development, 386–390
vocations. *See* careers
volunteer activities, 375

W

wage gap, 394
wages. *See* salaries
walking, 454
war, 14, 216
  post-traumatic stress disorder, 86
war crimes, 202, 203
warts, genital, 427
Watergate cover–up, 216
weaning, 42
weather, stress and, 70
weight, 351
weight loss, 449–450
wellness programs, 38
What Color Is Your Parachute? (Bolles), 396,
    397
what-is-beautiful-is-good stereotype, 152
Why Am I Afraid to Tell You Who I Am?
    (Powell), 145
why don't you—yes, but (game), 294
withdrawal, communication, 206
withdrawal illness, 463
withdrawal method, 425
withdrawing, 177, 178
  after divorce, 286
  loneliness and, 257
wives
  corporate, 367
  friendships, 247
  household work, 277
  marital adjustment, 278–279
women
  career development, 390
  changing marital roles, 276
  childless, 267, 268
  codependency, 7, 9–10
  multiple roles, 373
  post-traumatic stress disorder, 86
  in psychodynamic theories, 45
  working, 267
  in the workplace, 369–371
  See also gender differences
women's movement, 314

words, 185
work, 366–398
  happiness, 23
  jobs and careers, 366–367
  job search techniques, 396–398
  marital adjustment and, 278–279
  motivations, 375–377
  paid and unpaid, 367
  trends, 367–368
  See also careers; underemployment; unem-
    ployment
workaholism, 371–372
workers
  demographics, 368–369
  education and earnings, 369
  satisfaction, 376–380
  trends, 367–368
work ethic, 375–376
workplace, androcentric bias, 300
work problems, communication apprehension
    and, 207
workweek, 373
World War II, 14
writing it out, 122

X

Xanax (alprazolam), 521–522

Y

YAVIS clients, 517
yeast infections, 426, 427, 443
yoga, 122
You Are Not Alone (Park and Shapiro), 479
You Just Don't Understand (Tannen), 327
young adults
  developmental stage, 347
  family life cycle, 272–273
  gender-role socialization, 313
  living with parents, 275
  loneliness, 256
  psychosocial development theory, 339, 340
yo-yo dieting, 450

Z

Zen, 122
Zmeskal, Kim, 205–206

CREDITS

Journal of Personality and Social Psychology, 52, 881-889.

CHAPTER 6

168: Figure 6.3: From *Unmasking the Face,* by P. Ekman & W. V. Friesens, Consulting Psychologists Press. Copyright © 1984. Courtesy of Paul Ekman; **169: Figure 6.4:** Adapted from "Explorations in the Process of Person Perception: Visual Interaction in Relation to Competition, Sex, and Need for Affiliation," by R. Exline, 1963, *Journal of Personality, 31,* p. 11. Copyright 1963 by Duke University. Reprinted by permission of the author and the American Psychological Association; **171: Figure 6.5:** Adapted from *Eye to Eye: How People Interact,* by Peter Marsh. Copyright © 1988 by Andromeda Oxford Ltd. Reprinted by permission of HarperCollins, Publishers, Inc.; **182: Figure 6.9:** Adapted from "Cultural Myths and Supports for Rape", by M. R. Burt, 1980, *Journal of Personality and Social Psychology, 38,* 217-230. Copyright © 1980 by the American Psychological Association. Adapted by permission of the author; **187: Figure 6.11:** Adapted from David W. Johnson, *Reaching Out: Interpersonal Effectiveness and Self-Actualization,* 2nd Edition, © 1981, p. 204. Reprinted by permission of Prentice-Hall, Englewood Cliffs, NJ; **192: Figure 6.12:** From *Asserting Yourself: A Practical Guide for Positive Change,* p. 68, © 1991 by Sharon Bower & Gordon Bower. Reprinted with permission of Addison-Wesley Publishing Company, Inc.

CHAPTER 7

196: Figure 7.1: Adapted from *Social Psychology,* N. Deaux & L. R. Wrightsman, 1988, p. 186, based on data from B. G. Rule, G. L. Bisanz, & M. Kohn, 1985, *Journal of Personality and Social Psychology, 48,* 1127-1140; **200: Figure 7.3:** (Adapted from illustrations by Sarah Love on p. 35, *Scientific American,* November 1955.) From "Opinion and Social Pressure," by Solomon Asch. Copyright © 1955 by Scientific American, Inc. All rights reserved. Adapted by permission; **201: Figure 7.4:** (Adapted from illustrations by Sarah Love on p. 32, *Scientific American,* November 1955.) From "Opinion and Social Pressure," by Solomon Asch. Copyright © 1955 by Scientific American, Inc. All rights reserved. Adapted by permission; **203: Figure 7.5:** Copyright 1965 by Stanley Milgram, from the film *Obedience,* distributed by the New York University Film Division and The Pennsylvania State University, PCR. By permission of the Estate of Stanley Milgram; **205: Figure 7.6:** Adapted from *Social Psychology,* by J. Sabini. Copyright © 1992 by W. W. Norton & Company, Inc.; **207: Figure 7.7:** Adapted from "Bystander Intervention in Emergencies: Diffusion of Responsiblity," by J. M. Darley & B. Latané, 1968, *Journal of Personality and Social Psychology, 8,* 377-383. Copyright © 1968 by the American Psychological Association. Adapted by permission; **211: Figure 7.8:** Adapted from "Functional Roles of Group Members," by K. D. Benne & P. Sheats, 1948, *Journal of Social Issues, 4*(2), 41-49. Adapted by permission; **212: Figure 7.9:** Adapted from "The Bases of Social Power," by J. R. P. French, Jr., & B. Raven, 1959. In D. Cartwright (Ed.), *Studies in Social Power,* Institute for Social

Research. Adapted by permission; **213: Figure 7.10:** Adapted from "Many Hands Make Light the Work: The Causes and Consequences of Social Loafing," by B. Latané, K. Williams, & S. Harkins, 1979, *Journal of Personality and Social Psychology, 37,* 822-832. Copyright © 1979 by the American Psychological Association. Adapted by permission; **216: Figure 7.12:** Reprinted with the permission of the Free Press, a Division of Macmillan, Inc. from DECISION MAKING: A Psychological Analysis of Conflict, Choice, and Commitment, by Irving L. Janis & Leon Mann. Copyright © 1977 by The Free Press; **227: Figure 7.15:** Data from "The Effects of Severity on Initiation to Liking for a Group," by E. Aronson & J. Mills, 1959, *Journal of Abnormal and Social Psychology, 59,* 177-181.

CHAPTER 8

234: Figure 8.1: Based on "Toward the Analysis of Close Relationships," by G. Levinger, 1980, *Journal of Experimental Social Psychology, 16,* 510-544. Copyright © 1980 by Academic Press, Inc. Adapted by permission; **235: Figure 8.2:** Based on S. S. Brehm and S. M. Kassin, *Social Psychology,* 2nd Edition. Copyright © 1993 by Houghton Mifflin Company. Adapted with permission; **238: Figure 8.3:** From "Sex Differences in Human Mate Preferences: Evolutionary Hypotheses Tested in 37 Cultures," by D. M. Buss, 1989, *Behavioral and Brain Sciences, 12,* 1-14. Copyright © 1989 by Cambridge University Press. Reprinted by permission; **240: Figure 8.5:** Adapted from "The Evolution of Human Intrasexual Competition: Tactics of Mate Attraction," by D. M. Buss, 1988, *Journal of Personality and Social Psychology, 54*(4), 616-628. Copyright © 1988 by the American Psychological Association. Adapted by permission of the author; **240: Figure 8.6:** From "Likableness Ratings of 555 Personality Trait Words," by N. H. Anderson, 1968, *Journal of Personality and Social Psychology, 9,* 272-279. Copyright 1968 by the American Psychological Association. Reprinted by permission; **243: Figure 8.7:** Adapted from "Interactional Approach to Interpersonal Attraction," by M. H. Gonzales, J. M. Davis, G. L. Loeny, C. K. Lukens, & C. H. Junghans, 1983, *Journal of Personality and Social Psychology, 44,* 1191-1197. Copyright 1983 by the American Psychological Association. Adapted by permission; **245: Figure 8.8:** From "The Friendship Bond," by Mary Brown Parlee and the Editors of *Psychology Today, 13*(4), 49. Reprinted with permission from Psychology Today Magazine. Copyright ©1979 (Sussex Publishers, Inc.); **245: Figure 8.9:** Adapted from "The Rules of Friendship," by M. Argyle & M. Henderson, 1984, *Journal of Social and Personal Relationships, 1,* 211-237; **250: Figure 8.10:** From "A Triangular Theory of Love," by R. J. Sternberg, 1986, *Psychological Review, 93,* 119-135. Copyright 1986 by the American Psychological Association. Reprinted by permission; **254: Figure 8.13:** Adapted from "Breakups before Marriage: The End of 103 Affairs," by C. T. Hill, Z. Rubin, & L. A. Peplau, 1976, *Journal of Social Issues, 32,* 147-168. Basic Books Publishing Co, Inc. Adapted by permission of the author. All rights reserved; **258: Figure 8.14:** From a paper presented at the annual convention of the American Psychological

Association, September 2, 1979. An expanded version of this paper appears in *New Directions in Cognitive Therapy,* edited by Emery, Hollon, & Bedrosian, Guilford Press, 1981, and in *Loneliness: A Sourcebook of Current Theory, Research and Therapy,* by L. A. Peplau and D. Perlman (Eds.). Copyright 1982 by John Wiley & Sons, Inc. Reprinted by permission of John Wiley & Sons, Inc., and Jeffrey Young; **260: Figure 8.15:** From *Shyness,* © 1977 by Philip Zimbardo. Reprinted with permission of Addison-Wesley Publishing Company, Inc.

CHAPTER 9

266: Figure 9.1: Data from U.S. Bureau of the Census, *Current Population Reports,* Series P-20, No. 412, "Households, Families, Marital Status and Living Arrangements," March 1986 (Advance Report), Washington, DC: U.S. Government Printing Office, p. 4; **267: Figure 9.2:** Data from Glick & Norton, 1979. Population Reference Bureau, Washington, DC: U.S. Bureau of the Census; **267: Figure 9.3:** Data from U.S. Bureau of Labor Statistics; **268: Figure 9.4:** Data from the National Center for Health Statistics, U.S. Bureau of the Census, 1991; **268: Figure 9.5:** Adapted from Peter J. Stein, "Singlehood: An Alternative to Marriage," *The Family Coordinator, 24*(4), 500. Copyrighted 1975 by the National Council on Family Relations, 3989 Central Ave. N. E., Suite 550, Minneapolis, MN 55421. Reprinted by permission; **273: Figure 9.8:** Based on "Marital Satisfaction over the Family Life Cycle," by Boyd C. Rollins and Harold Feldman, *Journal of Marriage and the Family, 32* (February 1970), 25. Copyrighted 1975 by the National Council on Family Relations, 3989 Central Ave., N.E., Suite 550, Minneapolis, MN 55421. Reprinted by permission; **280: Figure 9.10:** From *Progress on Family Problems: A Nationwide Study of Clients' and Counselors' Views on Family Agency Services,* by Dorothy Fahs Beck & Mary Ann Jones, by permission of the publisher. Copyright 1973 by Family Service America, New York; **287: Figure 9.12:** Data from the U.S. Bureau of the Census; **290: Figure 9.14:** From "What Homosexuals Want," by L. A. Peplau, March 1981, *Psychology Today, 3,* 28-38. Reprinted with permission from Psychology Today Magazine. Copyright © 1981 (Sussex Publishers, Inc.); **293: Figure 9.15:** From *Practical Applications of Psychology,* 2nd Edition, by Anthony F. Grasha. Copyright © 1983 by Anthony F. Grasha. Reprinted by permission of HarperCollins, Publishers, Inc.; **293: Figure 9.16:** From *Practical Applications of Psychology,* 2nd Edition, by Anthony F. Grasha. Copyright © 1983 by Anthony F. Grasha. Reprinted by permission of HarperCollins, Publishers, Inc.; **294: Figure 9.17:** From *Practical Applications of Psychology,* 2nd Edition, by Anthony F. Grasha. Copyright © 1983 by Anthony F. Grasha. Reprinted by permission of HarperCollins, Publishers, Inc.

CHAPTER 10

299: Figure 10.2: Adapted from Table 1 of "Sex Role Stereotypes: A Current Appraisal," by I. K. Broverman, S. R. Vogel, D. M. Broverman, F. E. Clarkson, & P. S. Rosenkrantz, 1972, *Journal of Social Issues, 28,* 63. By permission of SPSSI and the author; **302: Figure 10.4:** Data from U.S. Bureau of the Census, 1991; **303: Figure 10.5:** Based on table in McMillan, Clifton, McGrath, & Gale, *Sex Roles*, 1977, vol. 3, No. 6, p. 553. Reprinted by permission of Plenum Publishing; **304: Figure 10.7:** Adapted from *Social Psychology*, by John Brigham. Copyright © 1986 by John Brigham. Reprinted by permission of HarperCollins Publishers; **310: Figure 10.8:** Adapted from "Children, Gender and Social Structure: An Analysis of the Contents of Letters to Santa Claus," by J. G. Richardson & C. H. Simpson, 1982, *Child Development, 53*, 429-436. Copyright © 1982 by the Society for Research in Child Development, Inc. Adapted by permission; **311: Figure 10.9:** Data from Robert M. Liebert & Joyce Sprafkin, *The Early Window: Effects of Television on Children and Youth*, 3rd Edition. Copyright © 1988. Reprinted by permission of Allyn and Bacon; **319: Figure 10.10:** Data from U.S. Bureau of the Census, 1991; **320: Figure 10.11:** Data from U.S. Bureau of Labor Statistics, 1991; **329: Figure 10.13:** From *You Just Don't Understand: Women and Men in Conversation*, by D. Tannen. Copyright © 1990 by William Morrow & Company, Inc. Reprinted by permission of William Morrow & Company, Inc.; **330: Figure 10.14:** From *You Just Don't Understand: Women and Men in Conversation*, by D. Tannen. Copyright © 1990 by William Morrow & Company, Inc. Reprinted by permission. Reprinted by permission of William Morrow & Company, Inc.

CHAPTER 11

339: Figure 11.2: Adapted from *Childhood and Society*, 2nd Edition, by Erik H. Erikson, by permission of W. W. Norton & Company, Inc. Copyright 1950, © 1963 by W. W. Norton & Co., Inc. Copyright renewed 1978, 1991 by Erik H. Erikson; **345: Figure 11.4:** Data from *Statistical Abstract of the United States*, 1991; **349: Figure 11.6:** Adapted from *Growing Old*, by Elaine Cumming and William E. Henry. Copyright © 1961 by Basic Books Publishing Company, Inc. Copyright renewed 1989 by Elaine Cumming and William E. Henry. Reprinted by permission of Harper Collins Publishers, Inc.; **353: Figure 11.7:** Data from "Chronic Conditions and Limitations of Acitivity and Mobility: United States, July 1965 to June 1967," by C. S. Wilder. In *U.S. Vital and Health Statistics*, 1971, 10(6); **355: Figure 11.8:** Based on data from "Creative Productivity between the Ages of 20 and 80 Years," by W. Dennis, 1966. *Journal of Gerontology*, 2(1), 1-8. Copyright © 1966 the Gerontological Society of America. Adapted by permission; **359: Figure 11.9:** Table constructed from Diana Baumrind (1971). "Current Patterns of Parental Authority" (Monograph). *Developmental Psychology*, 4(1, Part 2), 1-103. Copyright © 1971 by American Psychological Association. Adapted by permission of the author; **360: Figure 11.10:** Based on data from "Socialization Determinants of Personal Agency," a paper presented at the biennial meeting of the Society for Research in Child Development, New Orleans, 1977.

CHAPTER 12

368: Figure 12.1: From *Joyce L. Kennedy's Career Book*, by J. L. Kennedy and Laramore, p. 62. Copyright © 1993 by VGM Career Horizons. Reprinted by permission; **369:**

Figure 12.2: From *The American Woman 1992-93: A Status Report*, by P. Ries & A. J. Stone. Copyright © 1992 by W. W. Norton & Company, Inc.; **370: Figure 12.3:** Adapted from K. A. Matthews and J. Rodin, 1989, *American Psychologist*, 44(11), 1391. Copyright 1989 by the American Psychological Association. Adapted by permission; **375: Figure 12.4:** From U.S. Bureau of the Census, *Statistical Abstract of the United States*, 1991, p. 226. Washington D.C., U.S. Government Printing Office; **379: Figure 12.5:** From "What You Really Want from Your Job," by P. A. Renwick & E. E. Lawler, 1978, *Psychology Today*, 11(12), 56. Reprinted with permission from Psychology Today Magazine. Copyright © 1977 (Sessex Publishers, Inc.); **382: Figure 12.7:** Adapted from *Psychology of Work Behavior*, 4th Edition, by F. J. Landy, p. 638. Copyright © 1989 by Wadsworth, Inc. Reprinted by permission of Brooks/Cole Publishing Company; **383: Figure 12.8:** Redrawn from "Job Decision Latitude, Job Demands, and Cardiovascular Disease: A Prospective Study of Swedish Men," by R. A. Karasek, D. Baker, F. Marxer, A. Ahlbom, & T. Theorell, 1981, *American Journal of Public Health*, 71, 694-705. Reprinted by permission; **384: Figure 12.9:** From "Worksite Stress Management Interventions," by J. M. Ivancevich, M. T. Matteson, S. M. Freeman, & J. S. Phillips, 1990, *American Psychologist*, 45(2), 252-261. Reprinted by permission; **385: Figure 12.10:** Data from *Statistical Abstract of the United States*, 1990; **387: Figure 12.11:** From John L. Holland, *Making Vocational Choices: A Theory of Vocational Personalities and Work Environments*, 2nd Edition. © 1985, pp. 19-23, 36-40. Adapted by permission of Prentice-Hall, Inc. Englewood Cliffs, NJ; **388: Figure 12.12:** Adapted from *Theories of Occupational Choice and Vocational Development*, by J. Zaccaria, pp. 51-52. Copyright © 1970 by Time Share Corporation, New Hampshire; **389: Figure 12.13:** Data from "Occupational Mobility of Workers," by James J. Byrne, *The Monthly Labor Review*, February 1975, and adapted from "Mid-Life Career Change," by S. Arbeiter, 1979. *AAHE Bulletin*, 32(1), 11-12; **393: Figure 12.14:** Reproduced by special permission from the *Strong Interest Inventory of the Strong Vocational Interest Blanks*, T325 of the **Strong Interest Inventory of the Strong Vocational Interest Blanks®**, Form T325. Copyright 1933, 1938, 1945, 1946, 1966, 1968, 1974, 1981, 1985 by the Board of Trustees of Leland Stanford Junior University. All rights reserved. Printed under license from Stanford University Press, Stanford, California 94305. Reproduced by special permission of the Publisher, Consulting Psychologists Press, Inc., Palo Alto, CA 94303. Further reproduction is prohibited without the Publisher's consent; **394: Figure 12.15:** From "Wage Premiums for College Graduates: Recent Growth and Possible Explanations," by K. Murphy & F. Welch, 1989, *Educational Researcher*, 18(4), 19. Copyright © 1989 by the American Educational Research Association. Reprinted by permission of the publisher; **398: Figure 12.16:** From *Job Search: Career Planning Guidebook, Book II*, by R. D. Lock. Copyright © 1988 by Wadsworth, Inc. Reprinted by permission of Brooks/Cole Publishing Company.

CHAPTER 13

405: Figure 13.2: Adapted from *The Kinsey Institute New Report on Sex*, by J. M. Reinisch, 1990, p. 21. Copyright © 1990 by The Kinsey Institute for Research in Sex, Gender, and Reproduction. From the book *The Kinsey Institute New Report on Sex* and reprinted with permission from St. Martin's Press, Inc., New York, NY; **412: Figure 13.3:** Based on *The Kinsey Institute New Report on Sex*, by J. M. Reinisch, 1990, p. 4. Copyright © 1990 by The Kinsey Institute for Research in Sex, Gender, and Reproduction. From the book *The Kinsey Institute New Report on Sex* and reprinted with permission from St. Martin's Press, Inc., New York, NY; **417: Figure 13.5:** From "The Erotic Fantasies of College Students during Coitus," by David Sue, 1979, *The Journal of Sex Research*, 15, 303. Reprinted by permission; **420: Figure 13.7:** Data from "Change in Sexual Attitudes and Behavior of College Students from 1965 to 1980: A Research Note," by I. E. Robinson & D. Jedlicka, 1982, *Journal of Marriage and the Family*, 44(1), 237-240. Copyrighted 1982 by the National Council on Family Relations, 3989 Central Ave., N. E., Suite 550, Minneapolis, MN 55421. Reprinted by permission; **421: Figure 13.8:** Reprinted with permission of PEI Books, Inc. from *Sexual Behavior in the 1970s*, by Morton Hunt. Copyright 1974 by Morton Hunt; **421: Figure 13.9:** Reproduced with the permission of The Alan Guttmacher Institute from James Trussell & Charles Westoff, "Contraceptive Practice and Trends in Coital Frequency," *Family Planning Perspectives*, Vol. 12, No. 5, September/October 1980; **430: Figure 13.12:** Adapted from "Frequency of Sexual Dysfunction in 'Normal' Couples," by E. Frank, C. Anderson, & D. Rubenstein, 1978, *The New England Journal of Medicine*, 299, 1111-1115. Copyright 1978 by the New England Journal of Medicine. Reprinted by permission; **432: Figure 13.13:** Adapted from "Frequency of Sexual Dysfunction in 'Normal' Couples," by E. Frank, C. Anderson, & D. Rubenstein, 1978, *The New England Journal of Medicine*, 299, 1111-1115. Copyright 1978 by the New England Journal of Medicine. Reprinted by permission; **433: Figure 13.14:** Adapted from *Human Sexuality*, by W. H. Masters et al. Copyright © 1988 by William H. Masters, Virginia E. Johnson, & Robert C. Kolodny. Adapted by permission of HarperCollins Publishers.

CHAPTER 14

447: Figure 14.7: Adapted from "Associative Learning, Habit and Health Behavior," by W. A. Hunt, J. D. Matarazzo, S. M. Weiss, & W. D. Gentry, 1979, *Journal of Behavioral Medicine*, 2(2), 113. Copyright © 1979 by the Plenum Publishing Corporation. Adapted by permission; **448: Figure 14.8:** Data from "Obesity: Adverse Effects on Health and Longevity," by T. B. Van Italie, 1979, *American Journal of Clinical Nutrition*, 32, 2727; **453: Figure 14.10:** Based on data taken from "Physical Fitness and All-Cause Mortality," by S. N. Blair, H. W. Kohl, R. S. Paffenbarger, D. G. Clark, K. H. Cooper, & L. W. Gibbons, 1989, *Journal of American Medical Association*, 262, 2395-2401; **454: Figure 14.11:** Adapted from "How Different Sports Rate in Promoting Physical Fitness," by C. C. Conrad, *Medical Times*, May

1976, 4-5. Copyright 1976 by Romaine Pierson Publishers. Reprinted by permission; **455: Figure 14.12:** Data from Centers for Disease Control; **456: Figure 14.13:** Data from Centers for Disease Control, 1991; **457: Figure 14.14:** Adapted from "A Three-City Comparison of the Public's Knowledge and Attitudes about AIDS," by L. Temoshok, D. M. Sweet, & J. Zich, 1987, *Psychology & Health,* *1*(1), 43-60. Copyright © 1987 by Harwood Academic Publishers GmbH. Adapted by permission; **465: Figure 14.17:** From *Barbiturates: Their Use, Misuse and Abuse,* by D. R. Wesson & D. E. Smith, 1977. Copyright 1977 by Human Sciences Press. Reprinted by permission.

CHAPTER 15

477: Figure 15.3: Adapted and reprinted with permission from the American Psychiatric Association: *Diagnostic and Statistical Manual of Mental Disorders,* 3rd Edition, Revised, Washington, DC, American Psychiatric Association, 1987; **480: Figure 15.5:** From *Fears & Phobias,* by I. M. Marks, 1969, Academic Press. Copyright 1969 by Isaac Marks. Reprinted by permission; **487: Figure 15.9:** From Sarason/Sarason, *Abnormal Psychology: The Problem of Maladaptive Behavior,* 5th Edition, © 1987, p. 283. Reprinted by permission of Prentice-Hall, Inc., Englewood Cliffs, NJ; **494: Figure 15.12:** Adapted from "Clue to the Genetics and Neurobiology of Schizophrenia," by S. E. Nichol & I. I. Gottesman, 1983, *American Scientist,* 71, 398-404. Copyright © 1983 by Sigma Xi. Adapted by permission; **500: Figure 15.15:** Adapted from "Epidemiology of Disorders in Adulthood: Suicide," by C. K. Cross & R. M. A. Hirschfeld. In G. L. Klerman, M. M. Weissman, P. S. Appelbaum, & L. H. Roth (Eds.), *Psychiatry,* *Vol. 5, Social Epidemiologic and Legal Psychiatry,* 245-260, 1986, Basic Books. Adapted by permission of J. B. Lippincott Company, New York; **501: Figure 15.16:** Adapted from "Suicide and Depression among College Students," by J. S. Westefeld & S. R. Furr, 1987, *Professional Psychology: Research and Practice,* 18, 119-123. Copyright 1987 by the American Psychological Association. Adapted by permission; **501: Figure 15.17:** Adapted from "Suicide, Attempted Suicide and Relapse Rates in Depression," by D. Avery & G. Winokur, 1978, *Archives of General Psychiatry* (June), 35, 749-753. Copyright 1978 by the American Medical Association. Adapted by permission.

CHAPTER 16

512: Figure 16.3: Adapted from "Psychoanalysis and Psychoanalytic Therapy," by E. L. Baker. In S. J. Lynn and J. P. Garske (Eds.), *Contemporary Psychotherapies: Models and Methods,* p. 52. Reprinted by permission of the authors; **518: Figure 16.4:** From *Methods of Self-Change: An ABC Primer,* by K. E. Rudestam, pp. 42-43, 1980. Copyright © 1980 by Wadsworth, Inc. Reprinted by permission of Brooks/Cole Publishing Company; **523: Figure 16.7:** From data in NIMH-PSC Collaborative Study I and reported in "Drugs in the Treatment of Psychosis," by J. O. Cole, S. C. Goldberg, & J. M. Davis, 1966. In P. Solomon (Ed.), *Psychiatric Drugs,* Grune & Stratton. By permission of the author; **529: Figure 16.12:**

Adapted from "Meta Analysis of Psychotherapy Outcome Series," by M. L. Smith & G. V. Glass, 1977, *American Psychologist, 32* (September), 752-760. Copyright © 1977 by the American Psychological Association. Adapted by permission.

PHOTOGRAPHS

CHAPTER 1

4: David Kennedy/TexaStock; **7:** Stacy Pick/Stock, Boston; **11:** Gene Fitzer; **22:** Christopher Brown/Stock, Boston; **26:** SuperStock

CHAPTER 2

38: Granger Collection; **42:** D.E.K./TexaStock; **47:** National Library of Medicine; **48:** Harvard University News Office; **49:** Courtesy, B.F. Skinner Foundation; **54:** Carl Rogers Memorial Library; **57:** Mark Gerson/Courtesy, Dr. H. J. Eysenck

CHAPTER 3

68: Courtesy, Richard Lazarus; **69:** John Coletti/Stock, Boston; **72:** Courtesy, Dr. Neal E. Miller; **73:** Bob Daemmrich/The Image Works; **78:** Superstock; **81:** The Bettmann Archives; **84:** The Bettmann Archives; **85:** Christopher Brown/Stock, Boston; **89:** Courtesy, Suzanne C. Ouelette; **90:** SuperStock; **94:** Courtesy of Eleanor Holmes Williams; **95:** J. Mahoney/The Image Works

CHAPTER 4

104: (top) Courtesy, Dr. Martin Seligman; (bottom) The Bettmann Archives; **106:** SuperStock; **110:** Courtesy, Albert Ellis; **116:** Aneal Vohra/Unicorn Stock Photos; **120:** Carini/The Image Works; **123:** SuperStock; **124:** Courtesy, Herbert Benson, M.D./Michael Lutch Photo; **130:** SuperStock

CHAPTER 5

138: © 1982 Karen Zebulon; **141:** Brooks/Cole Photos; **144:** AP/Wide World Photos; **145:** Courtesy, Mark Snyder; **146:** Gene Fitzer; **151:** (both) The Bettmann Archives; **152:** Craig McClain Photography; **154:** Superstock; **156:** Doug Menuez/Stock, Boston

CHAPTER 6

168: (both) SuperStock; **169:** Abe Rezny/The Image Works; **170:** The Bettmann Archives; **175:** Courtesy, Irwin Altman; **180:** Courtesy, Mary P. Coss, Ph.D.; **183:** (both) The Bettmann Archives

CHAPTER 7

202: (top) Jeff Greenberg/Unicorn Stock Photos; (bottom) Eric Kroll; **203:** ©1965 by Dr. Stanley Milgram, from the film *Obedience;* **208:** (top) photo supplied by Professor Philip Zimbardo; (bottom) Bob Daemmrich/Imageworks; **209:** (left) Richard Pasley/Stock, Boston; (right) Bob Daemmrich/Imageworks; **215:** Yale University, Manuscripts & Archives Library; **221:** (top left, top right, bottom right) The Bettmann Archives; (bottom left) Associated Press; **222:** Alice Eagly

CHAPTER 8

232: Ellen Berscheid ; **238:** Charles Gupton/Stock, Boston; **242:** Spencer Grant/Stock, Boston; **246:** Louie Bunde/Unicorn Stock Photos; **248:** Dr. Elaine Hatfield; **249:** Bob Daemmrich/Image Works; **251:** Steve Bourgeoise/Unicorn Stock Photos; **252:** Photo by Bill Warren/*The Ithaca Journal;* **253:** Photo supplied by Phil Shaver; **261:** Courtesy, Professor Philip Zimbardo

CHAPTER 9

269: The Bettmann Archive; **270:** SuperStock; **274:** SuperStock; **275:** Macduff Everton/The Image Works; **282:** AP/Wide World Photos; **284:** Matthew McVay/SABA; **289:** FJ Dean/The Image Works

CHAPTER 10

301: Courtesy, Janet Shibley Hyde ; **305:** Dr. C. Chumbley/Photo Researchers; **308:** (left) Wayne Floyd/Unicorn Stock Photos; (right) Tom McCarthy/Unicorn Stock Photos; **309:** Brooks/Cole Photo; **312:** Bob Daemmrich/Stock, Boston; **314:** Aneal Vohra/Unicorn Stock Photos; **322:** SuperStock

CHAPTER 11

334: (all four) Stock, Boston; **335:** Joel Dexter/Unicorn Stock Photos; **337:** Brooks/Cole Photo; **340:** The Bettmann Archive; **343:** (left) Mark Antman/The Image Works; (right) SuperStock; **348:** Edmond van Hoorick/Farbdia-Archiv; **351:** (left) Bob Daemmrich/Stock, Boston; (right) The Bettmann Archives; **356:** AP/Wide World Photos; **362:** Mark Antman/The Image Works

CHAPTER 12

368: Rob Crandall/Stock, Boston; **371:** W. Hill/The Image Works; **374:** (both) SuperStock; **384:** Pedrick/The Image Works; **398:** Bob Daemmrich/The Image Works

CHAPTER 13

406: The Bettmann Archives; **408:** Jeffry W. Meyers/Stock, Boston; **409:** Barbara Alper/Stock, Boston; **414:** (top) George Malave/Stock, Boston; (bottom) Rob Fraser; **419:** AP/Wide World Photos

CHAPTER 14

440: The Bettmann Archives; **453:** FourByFive, Inc.; **456:** The Bettmann Archives; **458:** FourByFive, Inc.; **464:** Jon Feingersh/Stock, Boston

CHAPTER 15

476: Courtesy, David Rosenhan; **481:** Deneve Feigh Bunde/Unicorn Stock Photos; **488:** (both) The Bettmann Archive; **491:** Courtesy, Susan Nolen-Hoeksema; **493:** Nancy Andreasen; **502:** (left) Vicki Lawrence/Stock, Boston; (middle) The Bettmann Archives; (right) AP/Wide World Photos

CHAPTER 16

510: SuperStock; **511:** The Granger Collection; **513:** Stephen Frisch/Stock, Boston; **514:** Carl Rogers Memorial Library; **515:** Courtesy, Aaron T. Beck; **516:** Mark Gerson/Courtesy, Dr. H. J. Eysenck; **517:** Erika Stone; **519:** Pepperdine University/Dr. Joseph Wolpe; **522:** N. R. Rowan/Stock, Boston; **524:** Photo Researchers

TO THE OWNER OF THIS BOOK

We hope that you have found *Psychology Applied to Modern Life: Adjustment in the 90s, Fourth Edition*, useful. So that this book can be improved in a future edition, would you take the time to complete this sheet and return it? Thank you.

School and address: _____

Department: _____

Instructor's name: _____

1. What I like most about this book is: _____
   _____
   _____

2. What I like least about this book is: _____
   _____
   _____

3. My general reaction to this book is: _____
   _____
   _____

4. The name of the course in which I used this book is: _____
   _____
   _____

5. Were all the chapters of the book assigned for you to read? _____

   If not, which ones weren't? _____

6. In the space below, or on a separate sheet of paper, please write specific suggestions for improving this book and anything else you'd care to share about your experience in using the book.

   _____
   _____
   _____
   _____
   _____
   _____
   _____
   _____
   _____
   _____
   _____
   _____
   _____
   _____

Optional:

Your name: _____ Date: _____

May Brooks/Cole quote you, either in promotion for *Psychology Applied to Modern Life: Adjustment in the 90s, Fourth Edition*, or in future publishing ventures?

Yes: _____   No: _____

Sincerely,

Wayne Weiten
Margaret A. Lloyd

FOLD HERE

NO POSTAGE
NECESSARY
IF MAILED
IN THE
UNITED STATES

BUSINESS REPLY MAIL
FIRST CLASS   PERMIT NO. 358   PACIFIC GROVE, CA

POSTAGE WILL BE PAID BY ADDRESSEE

ATTN: *Wayne Weiten & Margaret A. Lloyd*
Brooks/Cole Publishing Company
511 Forest Lodge Road
Pacific Grove, California 93950-9968

FOLD HERE